Lecture Notes in Computer Science 4855

Commenced Publication in 1973
Founding and Former Series Editors:
Gerhard Goos, Juris Hartmanis, and Jan van Leeuwen

T0223115

V. Arvind   Sanjiva Prasad (Eds.)

FSTTCS 2007: Foundations of Software Technology and Theoretical Computer Science

27th International Conference
New Delhi, India, December 12-14, 2007
Proceedings

 Springer

Volume Editors

V. Arvind
The Institute of Mathematical Sciences
CIT Campus, Taramani, Chennai 600 113, India
E-mail: arvind@imsc.res.in

Sanjiva Prasad
Indian Institute of Technology Delhi
Hauz Khas, New Delhi 110 016, India
E-mail: sanjiva@cse.iitd.ac.in

Library of Congress Control Number: 2007940050

CR Subject Classification (1998): F.3, D.3, F.4, F.2, F.1, G.2

LNCS Sublibrary: SL 1 – Theoretical Computer Science and General Issues

ISSN   0302-9743
ISBN-10   3-540-77049-6 Springer Berlin Heidelberg New York
ISBN-13   978-3-540-77049-7 Springer Berlin Heidelberg New York

Springer is a part of Springer Science+Business Media

springer.com

© Springer-Verlag Berlin Heidelberg 2007
Printed in Germany

Typesetting: Camera-ready by author, data conversion by Scientific Publishing Services, Chennai, India
Printed on acid-free paper   SPIN: 12198450   06/3180   5 4 3 2 1 0

Preface

This volume contains the proceedings of the 27th annual conference on the Foundations of Software Technology and Theoretical Computer Science (FSTTCS 2007) held during December 12–14, 2007 at the India International Centre in New Delhi. The conference was organized under the auspices of the Indian Association for Research in Computing Science (IARCS).

This year's conference attracted 135 submissions from 31 countries. Except for a few papers that were outside the scope of the conference, each submission was assigned to at least three Programme Committee members, who, with the assistance of external expert researchers, ensured that each paper had at least three independent reviews. Given the high quality of the submissions, the Programme Committee decided to accept 40 papers. We thank all the expert reviewers for their invaluable help. We are very grateful to the PC members who put in enormous time and work in selecting the papers. Without their untiring efforts the conference would not have been possible.

The entire process of submission, refereeing, and the subsequent electronic PC meeting for selecting the papers for the conference program was greatly facilitated by the EasyChair conference management system; we would like to thank Andrei Voronkov and his team for this wonderful software.

One of the highlights of FSTTCS is the high quality of the invited talks. This year's conference was fortunate to have five very eminent invited speakers: Maurice Herlihy, Benjamin Pierce, Thomas Reps, Salil Vadhan, and Andrew Yao. Andrew Yao delivered the keynote address at the conference titled "A Modern Theory of Trust-but-Verify." In addition, Richard Karp, who could not make it to the conference to give his invited talk, kindly agreed to send an article for inclusion in the proceedings. It gives us great pleasure to thank all the invited speakers for agreeing to talk at the conference and for contributing to this volume.

Two satellite workshops were organized in conjunction with FSTTCS this year. These workshops were hosted by the Indian Institute of Technology Delhi. The conference was preceded by a one-day workshop on Compiler Techniques on December 11, felicitating Priti Shankar on her 60th birthday. Following the conference, on December 15, there was a one-day workshop on BioInformatics and Systems Biology organized by Neelima Gupta.

We thank the Organizing Committee for making all the arrangements for the conference. We thank IARCS and the sponsors for their support. As always, Alfred Hofmann and his team at Springer were very helpful in preparing the proceedings.

December 2007

V. Arvind
Sanjiva Prasad

Conference Organization

Program Committee

Roberto Amadio *(Univ. Paris 7)*
V. Arvind *(IMSc, Chennai)*, Co-chair
Iliano Cervesato *(CMU, Qatar)*
Supratik Chakraborty *(IIT Bombay)*
Sunil Chandran *(IISc, Bangalore)*
Samir Datta *(CMI, Chennai)*
Deepak D'Souza *(IISc, Bangalore)*
Sumit Ganguly *(IIT Kanpur)*
Rajeev Goré *(ANU and NICTA)*
Aarti Gupta *(NEC Labs, Princeton)*
Vineet Gupta *(Google, Bangalore)*
Prasad Jayanti *(Dartmouth College)*
Ranjit Jhala *(UC San Diego)*
Deepak Kapur *(New Mexico, Albuquerque)*
Subhash Khot *(Georgia Tech., Atlanta)*
Johannes Köbler *(Humboldt U., Berlin)*
K. Narayan Kumar *(CMI, Chennai)*
Kim G. Larsen *(Aalborg U.)*
Satya Lokam *(Microsoft Research)*
Greg Morrissett *(Harvard U., Cambridge)*
Sanjiva Prasad *(IIT Delhi)*, Co-chair
Shaz Qadeer *(Microsoft Research)*
S. Srinivasa Rao *(ITU, Copenhagen)*
Pranab Sen *(TIFR, Mumbai)*
Helmut Seidl *(TU München)*
Aravind Srinivasan *(U. Maryland)*
C.R. Subramanian *(IMSc, Chennai)*
Denis Thérien *(McGill U., Montréal)*
Ashish Tiwari *(SRI, Palo Alto)*
Vinodchandran Variyam *(U. Nebraska)*
Heribert Vollmer *(U. Hannover)*
Hongseok Yang *(QMU, London)*

Local Organization

Amit Kumar (IIT Delhi)
Amitabha Bagchi (IIT Delhi)
S. Arun-Kumar (IIT Delhi)

S.N. Maheshwari (IIT Delhi)
Naveen Garg (IIT Delhi)
Neelima Gupta (Delhi U.)

External Reviewers

David Abraham
Bharat Adsul
Manindra Agrawal
Luca de Alfaro
Eric Allender
Rajeev Alur
Klaus Ambos-Spies
Daniel Andersson
Geneviève Arboit
Kumar Avijit
Meenakshi B.
David Mix Barrington
Surendra Baswana
Michael Bauland
Bernhard Beckert
Arnold Beckmann
Josh Berdine
Nathalie Bertrand
Dietmar Berwanger
Olaf Beyersdorff
Raghav Bhaskar
Vibhor Bhatt
Hans Bodlaender
Benedikt Bollig
Glencora Borradaile
Chris Bourke
Patricia Bouyer
Franck van Breugel
Gerth Brodal
James Brotherston
Cristiano Calcagno
Marco Carbone
Ilaria Castellani
Tanmoy Chakraborty
Sourav Chakraborty
Timothy Chan
Chris Charnes
Thomas Chatain
Krishnendu Chatterjee
Kostas Chatzikokolakis
Kaustuv Chaudhuri
Yannick Chevalier
Sherman Chow

Vincenzo Ciancia
Corina Cirstea
Sebastien Collette
D.J. Das
Anita Das
Anupam Datta
Jeremy Dawson
Arnab De
Josée Desharnais
Volker Diekert
Dino Distefano
Reza Dorrigiv
Agostino Dovier
Joydeep Dutta
Chinmoy Dutta
Yuval Emek
Marco Faella
Stephan Falke
Pierre Fraigniaud
Alan Frieze
Sibylle Froeschle
Anna Gal
Nicola Galesi
Malay Ganai
Rajiv Gandhi
Sumit Ganguly
Thomas Gawlitza
Rob van Glabbeek
Subir Ghosh
Christian Glaßer
Alexander Golynski
K.N. Gopinath
Madhu Gopinathan
Navin Goyal
Fabrizio Grandoni
Martin Grohe
Sudipto Guha
Bhargav Gulavani
Raveendra Holla
Russ Harmer
Meng He
Matthew Hennessy
Daniel Hirschkoff

Markus Holzer
Chien-Chung Huang
Gimbert Hugo
Hans Huttel
Samuel Hym
Franjo Ivancic
Purushothaman Iyer
Radha Jagadeesan
David Jansen
Alan Jeffrey
Rushikesh Joshi
Chakraborty Joy
Marcin Jurdzinski
Raghavendra K.R.
Vineet Kahlon
Aditya Kanade
Shiva Prasad Kasiviswanathan
James King
Sven Kosub
Dieter Kratsch
Steve Kremer
Neelakantan Krishnaswami
Ralf Kuesters
Oliver Kullmann
Amit Kumar
Piyush Kurur
Shankar Ram Lakshminarayanan
Klaus-Joern Lange
Stefan Langerman
Serguei Lenglet
Paul Levy
Shuhao Li
Jay Ligatti
Shanshan Liu
Kamal Lodaya
Sachin Lodha
Salvador Lucas
Carsten Lutz
Alexis Maciel
Meena Mahajan
Rupak Majumdar
Azarakhsh Malekian
Nicolas Markey
Maarten Marx
Elvira Mayordomo

Damiano Mazza
Bill McCloskey
Pierre McKenzie
Shashank Mehta
Daniel Meister
Mark Mercer
Wolfgang Merkle
Antoine Meyer
Dimitrios Michail
Maja Milicic
Sayan Mitra
Dieter Mitsche
Raj Mohan M.
David Mount
Madhavan Mukund
Anca Muscholl
Madan Musuvathi
Rahul Muthu
Kedar Namjoshi
Narayanan Narayanan
N.S. Narayanaswamy
Phuong Nguyen
Brian Nielsen
Aditya Nori
Ulrik Nyman
Peter O'Hearn
Greg O'Keefe
Jan Obdrzalek
Mitsunori Ogihara
M.V. P. Rao
Catuscia Palamidessi
Chandrasekaran Pandu Rangan
Paritosh Pandya
Matthew Parkinson
Madhusudan Parthasarathy
Mihai Patrascu
A. Pavan
Pavithra Prabhakar
Jaikumar Radhakrishnan
G. Ramalingam
Krithivasan Ramamritham
Venkatesh Raman
Revantha Ramanayake
R. Ramanujam
Jacob Illum Rasmussen

Jason Reed

Jakob Rehof

Klaus Reinhardt

Sambuddha Roy

Arnab Roy

Andrey Rybalchenko

Krishna S.

Anil Seth

Sriram Sankaranarayanan

Vijay Saraswat

Jayalal M.N. Sarma

Saket Saurabh

Alexis Saurin

Henning Schnoor

Dominik Schultes

Thomas Schwarz

Luc Segoufin

Jay Sethuraman

Priti Shankar

Naresh Sharma

Somnath Sikdar

Sunil Simon

Naveen Sivadasan

Viorica Sofronie-Stokkermans

Kannan Srinathan

Venkatesh Srinivasan

Srikanth Srinivasan

Mark-Oliver Stehr

Lutz Strassburger

Suresh S.P.

Subhash Suri

Carolyn Talcott

Till Tantau

Olivier Tardieu

Serdar Tasiran

Pascal Tesson

P.S. Thiagarajan

Alwen Tiu

Jacobo Torán

Godfried Toussaint

Rahul Tripathi

Andrea Turrini

Christian Urban

Viktor Vafeiadis

Kasturi Varadarajan

Kapil Vaswani

Jacqueline Vauzeille

Kumar Neeraj Verma

Adrian Vetta

Victor Vianu

Walter Vogler

Anil Vullikanti

Yongge Wang

Chao Wang

Bogdan Warinschi

Ian Wehrman

James Worrell

James Worthington

Henning Wunderlich

Shaofa Yang

Mihalis Yannakakis

Joseph Yukich

Chunlai Zhou

Li Zhang

Wieslaw Zielonka

Uri Zwick

Table of Contents

Invited Papers

Contributed Papers

The Multicore Revolution
The Challenges for Theory

Maurice Herlihy*

Brown University Computer Science Department

Abstract. Computer architecture is undergoing, if not another revolution, then a vigorous shaking-up. The major chip manufacturers have, for the time being, simply given up trying to make processors run faster. Instead, they have recently started shipping "multicore" architectures, in which multiple processors (cores) communicate directly through shared hardware caches, providing increased concurrency instead of increased clock speed. As a result, system designers and software engineers can no longer rely on increasing clock speed to hide software bloat. Instead, they must somehow learn to make effective use of increasing parallelism. This adaptation will not be easy. Conventional synchronization techniques based on locks and conditions are unlikely to be effective in such a demanding environment. Coarse-grained locks, which protect relatively large amounts of data, do not scale, and fine-grained locks introduce substantial software engineering problems. Transactional memory is a computational model in which threads synchronize by optimistic, lock-free transactions. This synchronization model promises to alleviate many (perhaps not all) of the problems associated with locking, and there is a growing community of researchers working on both software and hardware support for this approach. This paper surveys the area, with a focus on open research problems.

1 Introduction

The computer industry is undergoing, if not another revolution, then a vigorous shaking-up. The major chip manufacturers have, for the time being, given up trying to make processors run faster. Moore's law has not been repealed: each year, more and more transistors fit into the same space, but their clock speed cannot be increased without overheating. Instead, attention is turning toward *multicore* architectures, in which multiple computing cores are included on each processor chip. Although these changes are propelled by changes in technology, they also provide a unique opportunity for theoretical distributed computing to have a substantial impact on practice. This paper suggests some promising research directions.

These trends mean that, in the medium term, advances in technology will provide increased parallelism, but not increased single-thread performance. System designers and software engineers can no longer rely on increasing clock speed

---

* Funded by NSF 0410042 and Sun Microsystems.

V. Arvind and S. Prasad (Eds.): FSTTCS 2007, LNCS 4855, pp. 1–8, 2007.

to enable ever more ambitious applications. Instead, they must learn to make effective use of increasing parallelism.

These trends have profound implications for many branches of Computer Science. The theoretical foundations of concurrency, encompassing models, concurrent algorithms, and data structures, while an established and well-respected branch of our field, have primarily been of academic interest. There has been little pressure on the field to devise practical or realistic models because there were few opportunities to affect practice. Suddenly, however, exploiting concurrency has become a subject of compelling concern to a wider community, providing a unique opportunity for Theory to have an impact on the real world.

For software developers, adapting to an environment where concurrency is commonplace will not be easy. In today's programming practices, programmers typically rely on combinations of locks and conditions, such as monitors, to prevent concurrent access by different threads to the same shared data. While this approach allows programmers to treat sections of code as "atomic", and thus simplifies reasoning about interactions, it suffers from a number of severe shortcomings.

First, programmers must decide between *coarse-grained* locking, in which a large data structure is protected by a single lock, and *fine-grained* locking, in which a lock is associated with each component of the data structure. Coarse-grained locking is simple, but permits little or no concurrency, thereby preventing the program from exploiting multiple processing cores. By contrast, fine-grained locking is substantially more complicated because of the need to ensure that threads acquire all necessary locks (and only those, for good performance), and because of the need to avoid deadlock when acquiring multiple locks. The decision is further complicated by the fact that the best engineering solution may be platform-dependent, varying with different machine sizes, workloads, and so on, making it difficult to write code that is both scalable and portable.

Second, conventional locking provides poor support for code composition and reuse. For example, consider a lock-based hash table that provides atomic insert () and remove() methods. Ideally, it should be easy to move an element atomically from one table to another, but this kind of composition simply does not work. If the table methods synchronize internally, then there is no way to acquire and hold both locks simultaneously. If the tables export their locks, then modularity and safety are compromised.

Finally, such basic issues as the mapping from locks to data, that is, which locks protect which data, and the order in which locks must be acquired and released, are all based on convention, and violations are notoriously difficult to detect and debug. For these and other reasons, today's software practices make concurrent programs too difficult to develop, debug, understand, and maintain.

To address these problems, attention has shifted to computational models based on transactions. A *transaction* is a sequence of steps executed by a single thread. Transactions are *atomic*: each transaction either commits (it takes effect) or aborts (its effects are discarded). Transactions are linearizable [11]: they appear to take effect in a one-at-a-time order. Transactional memory supports a computational model in which each thread announces the start of a transaction, executes a sequence of operations on shared objects, and then tries to commit the transaction. If the commit succeeds, the transaction's operations take effect; otherwise, they are discarded.

Our transactions satisfy the same formal serializability and atomicity properties as database-style transactions, but they are intended to be used very differently. Unlike database transactions, our transactions are short-lived activities that access a relatively small number of objects in primary memory. The effects of database transactions are persistent, and committing a transaction involves backing up changes on a disk. Our transactions are not persistent, and involve no explicit disk I/O.

To illustrate why transactions are attractive, consider the problem of constructing a concurrent FIFO queue that permits one thread to enqueue items at the queue's tail at the same time another thread dequeues items from the queue's head. Any problem so easy to state, and that arises so naturally in practice, should have an easily-devised, understandable solution. In fact, solving this problem with locks is quite difficult. In 1996, Michael and Scott published a clever, but subtle solution [15]. It speaks poorly for fine-grained locking as a methodology that solutions to such simple problems are considered difficult enough to be publishable results.

```
class Queue {
  QNode head;
  Qnode tail ;
  public enq(Object x) {
    atomic {
      Qnode q = new Qnode(x);
      q.next = this.head;
      q.head = q;
    } catch (AbortException e)  {...}
  }
  ...
}
```

Fig. 1. Transactional queue code fragment

By contrast, it is almost trivial to solve this problem using transactions. Figure 1 shows how the queue's enqueue method might look in a language that provides direct support for transactions (for example, see Harris et al. [6]). It consists of little more than enclosing sequential code in a transaction block, and handling an exception if the transaction aborts. In practice, of course, a complete implementation would include more details (such as how often to retry a failed transaction), but even so, this concurrent queue implementation by itself is not a publishable result.

Recently the *transactional memory* programming paradigm [10] has gained momentum as an alternative to locks in concurrent programming. This approach has been investigated in hardware [1, 5, 10, 19, 18, 14], in software [3, 6, 7, 9, 12, 13, 16, 21], and in schemes that mix hardware and software [17, 20]. This area is growing at a fast pace, and a comprehensive list of citations can be found on the transactional memory web page at [22].

2   Challenges

This section describes three problem areas where the Distributed Computing community could make contributions.

2.1   Scheduling and Contention Management

Many STM systems execute transactions *speculatively*, meaning that they run until they encounter a synchronization conflict, and when they do, they either wait for the conflicting transaction to finish, or abort one of the conflicting transactions. To avoid deadlock or livelock, many STM systems employ a kind of scheduling module called a *contention manager* used to decide when one transactions should wait-for or abort one another. A contention manager is a kind of oracle: when one transaction discovers it is about to create a conflict with another, it consults the contention manager to determine whether to proceed, causing the other transaction to abort, or to pause, allowing the other transaction time to finish. At one extreme, a contention manager that always pauses can lead to deadlock, while a contention manager that always aborts can lead to livelock. There is an enormous range of possibilities between these two extremes.

Much of the work on contention managers has been experimental: testing alternative strategies against an array of benchmarks [23]. Recently, however, attention has shifted to contention managers with provable properties. For example, one way to evaluate a contention manager is by evaluating its Its *competitive ratio*: comparing it to an omniscient off-line scheduler. When presented with a collection of transactions, the *Greedy* contention manager [4] has a competitive ratio of $O(s)$, where s is the number of objects shared by transactions [2].

The Greedy manager is a start, but much more needs to be done to achieve a full understanding of the relation between contention managers and classical scheduling algorithms and lower bounds. We do not know whether the Greedy manager's competitive ratio is a good one, because we have no other contention managers whose competitive ratio is known. This ratio measures the make-span (time until last transaction commits) of a set of transactions that start at time zero. The contention manager, which does not know the transactions' read and write sets, is compared to an omniscient schedule that does. While this is a reasonable first step, in practice it is not clear that the make-span is the ideal measure, or whether a more dynamic model, where transactions arrive at random times, is more realistic. While contention manager algorithms are flourishing as an engineering topic, there is a need for more solid theoretical underpinnings.

2.2   Concurrent Data Structures and Algorithms

Transactional synchronization requires a new theory of concurrent data structures and algorithms. The conventional approach to transactional synchronization is to say that two transactions conflict of they access the same data item and one access is a write.

While read/write synchronization has the advantage that it can it can be done automatically, it can severely and unnecessarily restrict concurrency.

Here is a simple example. Consider a mutable set of integers that provides add(x), remove(x) and contains(x) methods with the obvious meanings. We could implement the set as a sorted linked list, where each list node has a value field and a reference to the next node. Nodes are sorted by value, and values are unique. The add(x) method reads along the list until it encounters the largest value less than x. If x is absent, it links a new node holding x into the list.

Recently, an alternative approach, called *transactional boosting*, has emerged that focuses on *commutativity* rather than read/write conflict as the basis for synchronization. Informally, two method invocations *commute* if applying them in either order leaves the object in the same state and returns the same response. In a Set, for example, add(x) commutes with add(y) if x and y are distinct.

Transactional boosting allows method calls to proceed in parallel as long as they commute. There are many subtleties in defining what it means for method calls to commute. Clearly, commutativity depends on the method name and arguments, but it may also depend on the method's return value and the object's current state. It is also (sometimes) necessary to provide inverses to method calls, to be applied if transactions abort. Preliminary results suggest that synchronization based on method semantics can be much more effective than synchronization based on read/write conflicts.

Nevertheless, we are still far from a complete understanding of how best to enhance concurrency in transactional data structures. While there is a well-developed theory of transactional synchronization for databases, in-memory transactions have different characteristics (for example, thread-level synchronization is much more important), and much work remains to be done to develop formal models, transaction-aware data structures, and lower bounds.

2.3   Granularity of Atomicity

Recently, Sun Microsystems announced that their next-generation processor, called *Rock* would provide hardware support for transactional memory. This welcome development opens, rather than closes, many research questions.

Nevertheless, in-cache transactions will always be limited in size and scope. There is an inherent mismatch between the fixed resources provided by an underlying architecture and the variable resources needed by software. For example, a transaction that reads too much data will overflow its cache, and be forced to abort. How much is "too much"? It makes little sense to decree a hard-and-fast bound on transaction size, because different platforms provide different cache sizes and architectures, and cache sizes are likely to change over time.

A more sensible approach is to use a hybrid technique. If the transaction is small enough to fit in the platform's cache, then run it in hardware. Otherwise, run it on a software transactional memory whose inner loop makes use of hardware transactions. If all else fails, run it completely in software. This hybrid strategy ensures that transactional applications remain portable across platforms, but will run faster on platforms that provide more resources.

While discovering the best way to mix hardware and software transactions may seem to be exclusively an engineering question, it raises the need for a broader theoretical foundation for synchronization.

Older architectures typically provided a single *compare-and-swap* (CAS) instruction that atomically reads and modifies a single memory location. While this instruction is in principle, powerful enough to construct a wait-free implementation of any object [8], such constructions are inefficient. Some concurrent objects can be implemented quite efficiently using a *double CAS*, which operates on two independent locations, and papers have studied $m - CAS$, an instruction that works on m words. An unlimited hardware transaction can be viewed as an arbitrary-size CAS, and can implement any object with a constant number of synchronization steps.

In practice, since hardware transactional memory is bounded, it is worth asking how a synchronization instruction's size (that is, the number of memory locations affected) affects the complexity of useful data structures. Clearly, CAS implements shared data structures less efficiently than 2-CAS, and so on, but little is known about characterizing the gains in synchronization efficiency when one moves from k-CAS to $(k + 1)$-CAS. If, for example, one were to discover that 16-CAS can efficiently implement a large class of data structures, then one would know what kinds of hardware support to ask for.

3   Conclusions

This paper is intended to alert the Distributed Computing community that there is a unique opportunity to apply our collective expertise in models, algorithms, and lower bounds to emerging problems of compelling practical interest. The study of concurrent algorithms and architectures has only recently caught the attention of the mainstream Systems community, but it should be familiar ground to us, the Theory community.

References

1. Ananian, S., Asanovic, K., Kuszmaul, B., Leiserson, C., Lie, S.: Unbounded transactional memory. In: Proc. 11th International Symposium on High-Performance Computer Architecture, pp. 316–327 (February 2005)

2. Attiya, H., Epstein, L., Shachnai, H., Tamir, T.: Transactional contention management as a non-clairvoyant scheduling problem. In: PODC 2006. Proceedings of the twenty-fifth annual ACM symposium on Principles of distributed computing, pp. 308–315. ACM Press, New York (2006)

3. Dice, D., Shavit, N.: What really makes transactions faster?. In: Transact: First ACM SIGPLAN Workshop on Languages, Compilers, and Hardware Support for Transactional Computing (June 2006)

4. Guerraoui, R., Herlihy, M., Pochon, B.: Toward a theory of transactional contention managers. In: Fraigniaud, P. (ed.) DISC 2005. LNCS, vol. 3724, Springer, Heidelberg (2005)

5. Hammond, L., Wong, V., Chen, M., Carlstrom, B.D., Davis, J.D., Hertzberg, B., Prabhu, M.K., Wijaya, H., Kozyrakis, C., Olukotun, K.: Transactional memory coherence and consistency. In: Proc. 31st Annual International Symposium on Computer Architecture (June 2004)

6. Harris, T., Fraser, K.: Language support for lightweight transactions. In: Proceedings of the 18th ACM SIGPLAN conference on Object-oriented programing, systems, languages, and applications, pp. 388–402. ACM Press, New York (2003)

7. Harris, T., Marlow, S., Peyton-Jones, S., Herlihy, M.: Composable memory transactions. In: PPoPP 2005. Proceedings of the 10th ACM SIGPLAN symposium on Principles and practice of parallel programming, pp. 48–60. ACM Press, New York (2005)

8. Herlihy, M.: Wait-free synchronization. ACM Transactions on Programming Languages and Systems (TOPLAS) 13(1), 124–149 (1991)

9. Herlihy, M., Luchangco, V., Moir, M., Scherer III, W.N.: Software transactional memory for dynamic-sized data structures. In: PODC 2003. Proceedings of the 22nd annual symposium on Principles of distributed computing, pp. 92–101. ACM Press, New York (2003)

10. Herlihy, M., Moss, J.E.B.: Transactional memory: architectural support for lock-free data structures. In: Proceedings of the 20th annual international symposium on Computer architecture, pp. 289–300. ACM Press, New York (1993)

11. Herlihy, M.P., Wing, J.M.: Linearizability: a correctness condition for concurrent objects. ACM Transactions on Programming Languages and Systems (TOPLAS) 12(3), 463–492 (1990)

12. Israeli, A., Rappoport, L.: Disjoint-access-parallel implementations of strong shared memory primitives. In: Proceedings of the thirteenth annual ACM symposium on Principles of distributed computing, pp. 151–160. ACM Press, New York (1994)

13. Marathe, V., Scherer, W., Scott, M.: Adaptive software transactional memory. Technical Report TR 868, Computer Science Department, University of Rochester (May 2005)

14. McDonald, A., Chung, J., Carlstrom, B., Minh, C., Chafi, H., Kozyrakis, C., Olukotun, K.: Architectural semantics for practical transactional memory (2006)

15. Michael, M.M., Scott, M.L.: Simple, fast, and practical non-blocking and blocking concurrent queue algorithms. In: Proceedings of the fifteenth annual ACM symposium on Principles of distributed computing, pp. 267–275. ACM Press, New York (1996)

16. Moir, M.: Practical implementations of non-blocking synchronization primitives. In: Proceedings of the sixteenth annual ACM symposium on Principles of distributed computing, pp. 219–228. ACM Press, New York (1997)

17. Moir, M.: Hybrid transactional memory, Unpublished manuscript (July 2005)

18. Moore, K.E., Hill, M.D., Wood, D.A.: Thread-level transactional memory. Technical Report CS-TR-2005-1524, Dept. of Computer Sciences, University of Wisconsin (March 2005)
19. Moravan, M.J., Bobba, J., Moore, K.E., Yen, L., Hill, M.D., Liblit, B., Swift, M.M., Wood, D.A.: Supporting nested transactional memory in LogTM. In: ASPLOS-XII. Proceedings of the 12th international conference on Architectural support for programming languages and operating systems, pp. 359–370. ACM Press, New York (2006)
20. Saha, B., Adl-Tabatabai, A.-R., Hudson, R., Minh, C.C., Hertzberg, B.: Mcrt-stm. In: PPoPP (2006)
21. Shavit, N., Touitou, D.: Software transactional memory. In: Proceedings of the fourteenth annual ACM symposium on Principles of distributed computing, pp. 204–213. ACM Press, New York (1995)
22. www.cs.wisc.edu/trans-memory
23. Scherer III, W.N., Scott, M.L.: Advanced contention management for dynamic software transactional memory. In: PODC 2005. Proceedings of the twenty-fourth annual ACM symposium on Principles of distributed computing, pp. 240–248. ACM Press, New York (2005)

Streaming Algorithms for Selection and Approximate Sorting

Richard M. Karp

International Computer Science Institute, Berkeley, USA
and University of California at Berkeley
karp@icsi.berkeley.edu

1   Introduction

Companies such as Google, Yahoo and Microsoft maintain extremely large data repositories within which searches are frequently conducted. In an article entitled "Data-Intensive Supercomputing: The case for DISC" Randal Bryant describes such data repositories and suggests an agenda for appying them more broadly to massive data set problems of importance to the scientific community and society in general.

Large-scale data repositories have become feasible because of the low cost of disc storage. For $10,000 one can buy a processor with 10^{12} bytes of disc storage, divided into blocks of capacity $64,000$ bytes. A typical repository (far from the largest) might contain 1000 processors, each with 10^{12} bytes of storage.

It is of interest to develop streaming algorithms for basic information processing tasks within such data repositories. In this paper we present such algorithms for selecting the elements of given ranks in a totally ordered set of n elements and for a related problem of approximate sorting. We derive bounds on the storage and time requirements of our algorithms.

Such data repositories support random access to the disc blocks. Therefore, it is reasonable to assume that the stream of input data to our sorting and selection algorithms is a random permutation of the disc blocks.

We also consider parallel algorithms in which the data arrives in several independent streams, each arriving at a single processor. Since all the processors of such a repository are co-located, we assume that interprocessor communication is not a bottleneck.

2   Streaming Algorithms

The input to a streaming algorithm is a sequence of items that arrive over time. The output of the streaming algorithm on a given sequence is specified by a function from sequences into some range. The algorithm processes each item in turn and produces an output after the last arrival. The streaming algorithm may be of three types:

V. Arvind and S. Prasad (Eds.): FSTTCS 2007, LNCS 4855, pp. 9–20, 2007.
© Springer-Verlag Berlin Heidelberg 2007

1. In a basic streaming algorithm the length of the input is specified in advance.
2. In an *anytime streaming algorithm* the input may end at any time, but an upper bound on the length of the input is given.
3. In an *everytime streaming algorithm* an upper bound on the length of the input is given, and the algorithm is required to produce a correct output for every prefix of the input.

The working storage of a streaming algorithm is a buffer of limited capacity. We are interested in the following measures of complexity: the capacity of the buffer and the time, or amortized time, to process an item.

In our case the items are keys drawn from a totally ordered set. We assume that the keys arrive in a random order, and the algorithm is required to be correct with high probability. If, more realistically, we assumed that the input consists of blocks of N keys, where the allocation of keys to blocks is arbitrary but the blocks arrive in a random order, then our results would still hold, except that the storage requirement would be multiplied by N.

We restrict attention to deterministic or randomized algorithms that gain information about the arriving keys solely by performing comparisons, and we measure time complexity by the number of comparisons.

We often make statements of the form "The algorithm is correct with high probability when provided with $O(f(n))$ units of the computational resource. (such as storage or time)." The precise meaning of such a statement is: "For every $\delta > 0$ there exist constants c and n_0 such that, for all $n > n_0$, the algorithm is correct with probability $\geq 1 - \delta$ when provided with $cf(n)$ units of the computational resource.." An algorithm is *optimal within a factor c* if, for n sufficiently large, its resource requirement is within a factor c of a lower bound that holds for every algorithm for the problem.

3 Results

The α-*quantile* of a totally ordered set of n keys is the $\lfloor \alpha n \rfloor$th smallest element. We present optimal algorithms (simultaneously for time and storage), under the random arrivals assumption, for the following problems:

1. **Selection:** Compute an α-quantile for a given α.
2. **Multiple selection:** Compute α-quantiles for many given values of α.
3. **Parallel selection:** In which the input is divided into streams, each with its own buffer, and the different streams communicate by message passing.
4. **Approximate selection:** Given α and ϵ, find a key whose rank differs from αn by at most ϵn.
5. **Approximate sorting:** Given a small positive constant ϵ, compute an ordering of the keys in which the rank assigned to each key agrees with its rank in the true ordering, within a relative error of ϵ.

The algorithm for selection is an everytime algorithm. The algorithms for multiple selection and parallel selection are anytime algorithms. The algorithm for approximate sorting requires two passes over the data.

Finally, as a byproduct of our analysis of approximate sorting, we give an elegant method for computing the expected number of comparisons for Quicksort, Quickselect and Multiple Quickselect (see [6]).

There is a large literature on streaming algorithms for sorting and selection. Our work differs from most of this literature because of the random arrivals assumption, and because we simultaneously optimize both storage and time, whereas most of the work on streaming algorithms considers only storage.

4   Selection

4.1   Previous Work on Randomized Algorithms for Selection

Among its many interesting results, the seminal paper of Munro and Paterson [5] presents a streaming algorithm with optimal storage $O(\sqrt{n})$ for the computation of the median assuming random arrival order. Their key observation, and one that we build upon, is that it is possible to maintain a buffer of $O(\sqrt{n})$ keys, such that, with high probability, at any stage in the sequence of arrivals, the median of every subsequent prefix of the entire arrival sequence of length n either lies in the buffer or has not arrived yet.

The paper [4] by Floyd and Rivest gives an algorithm for computing an α-quantile with high probability using $(1+\min(\alpha, 1-\alpha))n+o(n)$ comparisons. This result matches a simple lower bound derived as follows: let q be the α-quantile. Every key x except q must be compared with some key that is either q or lies strictly between x and q, and the first comparison involving x has probability at least $\min(\alpha, 1 - \alpha)$ of failing to fulfill this condition.

The Floyd-Rivest algorithm is not presented as a streaming algorithm but can be adapted under the random arrivals assumption to a basic streaming algorithm with the original number of comparisons that requires storage $n^{2/3} \log n$.

We present an everytime streaming algorithm for computing an α-quantile under the random arrivals assumption with optimal storage $O(\sqrt{n})$ and optimal execution time $O(m) + O(\sqrt{n} \log^2 n)$ to process the first m arrivals.

Let $q(t)$ denote the α-quantile of the prefix of length t. By straightforward random walk arguments we establish the following claims:

1. With high probability the following holds for all t and t' with $t < t'$: if key $q(t')$ lies within the prefix of length t, its rank within that prefix differs from αt by at most $O(\sqrt{n})$.
2. With high probability the cardinality of the set $\{q(t), t = 1, 2, \cdots, n\}$ is at most $\sqrt{n} \log n$; i.e., the number of distinct medians of prefixes is small.

We assume that $\frac{1-\alpha}{\alpha} = a/b$ where a and b are small integers. This assumption is not essential, but simplifies exposition.

The algorithm makes deductions based on the assumption that the input stream satisfies the above two assertions. It is divided into stages. In the first stage $(a + b)\sqrt{n} + 1$ keys arrive, and in each subsequent stage $a + b$ keys arrive. At the start of any stage, after t keys have arrived, the algorithm maintains the following information.

1. The current α-quantile $q(t)$;
2. An interval (L, U) within which every future α-quantile must lie;
3. A set HIGH of $bc\sqrt{n}$ keys greater than $q(t)$ and a set LOW of $ac\sqrt{n}$ keys smaller than $q(t)$ such that every future α-quantile that has already arrived is contained in $HIGH \cup LOW \cup \{q(t)\}$.

In the first stage $(a+b)c\sqrt{n}+1$ keys arrive. The $ac\sqrt{n}$ smallest keys are placed in LOW, the $bc\sqrt{n}$ largest keys are placed in HIGH, and the remaining key is designated $q((a + b)\sqrt{n})$. U is set to $+\infty$ and L is set to $-\infty$. Each subsequent stage has the following phases:

1. $a + b$ keys arrive. Each arriving key greater than U is reassigned the value $+\infty$ and placed in HIGH, and each arriving key less than L is reassigned the value $-\infty$. Of the remaining arriving keys, those greater than $q(t)$ are placed in HIGH and those less than $q(t)$ are placed in LOW.
2. A rebalancing process is carried out in which, depending on the number of newly arriving keys that entered $HIGH$, a new α-quantile is determined, and at most $\max(a, b)$ keys are transferred between HIGH and LOW to achieve the properties that HIGH is of cardinality $bc\sqrt{n} + b$, LOW is of cardinality $ac\sqrt{n} + a$, every key in HIGH is greater than the current α-quantile and every key in LOW is less than the current α-quantile.
3. The b largest elements of HIGH and the a smallest elements of LOW are discarded.
4. L is set to the largest value that has ever been discarded from LOW, and U is set to the smallest value that has ever been discarded from HIGH.

The algorithm uses three mechanisms to achieve efficiency:

1. It keeps a count of the number of keys greater than U and the number of keys less than L that have not yet been discarded, but does not explicitly store those elements. The computational cost of identifying and discarding each such key is $O(1)$.
2. It stores the remaining elements of the sets HIGH and LOW in min-max priority queues, implemented as lazy binomial queues, which perform the insertkey, findmin and findmax operations in amortized time $O(1)$ and the extractmin and extractmax operations in time $O(\log n)$.
3. It maintains a doubly-linked linear list containing those keys that have ever becom the α-quantile or been transferred between HIGH and LOW. Once a key has entered this list, the computation time for each subsequent transfer of the key is $O(1)$. The computation time for the first transfer of any key is $O(\log n)$, the time for an extractmin or extractmax operation.
4. The computation time to discard an element that has not been determined to lie outside $[L, U]$ is $O(\log n)$, the time for an extractmin or extractmax operation.

For all k, the conditional probability that the kth arriving key is not immediately assigned the value $+\infty$ or $-\infty$, given the sequence of previous arrivals, is at most $\frac{(a+b)c\sqrt{n}+2}{k}$. It follows that, with high probability, the total number of such arriving keys is $O(\sqrt{n}\log n)$. Hence, for all m, the time required to process the first m arrivals is $O(m) + O(\sqrt{n}\log^2 n)$.

5 Multiple Selection

In this section we present an anytime streaming algorithm for the following problem. Let $\alpha_1, \alpha_2, \cdots, \alpha_k$ be an increasing sequence of numbers in $(0, 1)$. Given a stream of n keys arriving in a random order, find the $\alpha_1, \alpha_2, \cdots, \alpha_k$-quantiles of every prefix of the stream.

Let $\alpha_0 = 0, \alpha_{k+1} = 1$ and $p_i = \alpha_{i+1} - \alpha_i$, for $i = 1, 2, ..., k + 1$. We observe that any comparison-based algorithm to determine the given quantiles must determine the relation of each of the n keys to each of the quantiles. The number of such joint relations is slightly greater than $\frac{n!}{\pi_{i=1}^{k+1}(np_i)!}$. It follows that the expected number of comparisons for any deterministic or randomized algorithm is at least the logarithm base-2 of this quantity, which, by Stirling's approximation, is $nH(p_1, p_2, \cdots, p_{k+1}) + o(n)$ where $H(p_1, p_2, \cdots, p_{k+1})$ is the entropy function $-\sum_{i=1}^{k+1} -p_i \log_2 p_i$.

Our streaming algorithm is based on a binary search tree: a rooted ordered binary tree with k internal nodes labeled in one-to-one correspondence with the α_i, such that the label of the left child of a node is less than the label of the node, and the label of the right child of the node is greater than the label of the node. If the root of the tree is labeled α then the process starts by computing the α-quantile of the set of n keys. The keys less than the α-quantile flow to the left child of the root and the keys greater than the α-quantile flow to the right child of the root. Recursively, the left subtree of the root processes the keys it receives to compute the α_i quantiles of the set of n keys for all $\alpha_i < \alpha$, and the right subtree of the root processes the keys it receives to compute the α_i-quantiles of the set of n keys. for all $\alpha_i > \alpha$. A standard construction from information theory (the Shannon-Fano code) constructs a binary search tree such that, as the keys flow down the tree, the sum of the cardinalities of the sets of keys arriving at the k internal nodes is at most $(H(p_1, p_2, \cdots, p_{k+1}) + 1)n$. A slight variant of that construction ensures that the height of the tree is $O(\log k)$ while increasing the sum of the cardinalities by an arbitrarily small factor $1 + \epsilon$. If each of the k selection problems is solved using the randomized algorithm of Floyd and Rivest the total number of comparisons will be within a factor of $1.5(1 + \epsilon)$ of the information-theoretic lower bound (with high probability).

We will convert this binary search algorithm to an anytime streaming algorithm with storage requirement $O(\sqrt{nk})$ and amortized time $O(1)$ per key (whp), on the assumption that the keys arrive in a random order. To do so, we must reconcile two conflicting requirements:

1. To ensure that the keys arrive at each node in a random order, we require that the keys flowing into each node arrive in their original order;

2. To ensure that the process terminates within time $O(n)$, we require that, as a key flows down the tree, it must dwell at each node only for $O(1)$ time steps.

At first sight, this is an unsolvable dilemma. At each node, a key must be immediately routed to the left child or right child according to whether it is less than or greater than the quantile being computed at that node; but the quantile cannot be known until all the keys have arrived at the node. To resolve the dilemma, we run our everytime streaming algorithm for selection at each node, and route each arriving key immediately to the left child if it is less than the current α-quantile (rather than the unknown eventual α-quantile of the entire input stream), and to the right child if it is greater than or equal to the current α-quantile. Since the everytime selection algorithm processes the first m arriving keys in time $O(m+\sqrt{n}\log n)$ there will be an excess delay of at most $O(\sqrt{n}\log n)$ at each node and, since our binary search tree has height at most $O(\log k)$, a total excess delay of at most $O(\sqrt{n}\log n \log k)$. However, a key will be misdirected if its relation to the current α-quantile is different from its relation to the final α-quantile. Fortunately, the keys that could potentially be misdirected are the ones that get transferred out of HIGH or out of LOW during the computation of the quantile at the node. These are precisely the keys that get placed in the doubly-linked list maintained by the algorithm, and the number of such keys is $O(\sqrt{n}\log n)$ (whp). Thus, after the computation of the final α-quantile, the selection algorithm can scan this list and send each of its children a list of all the misdirected keys. Each child can make appropriate corrections in time $O(\log n)$ per misdirected key. The correction computed at each child can affect its list of misdirected keys, and so on down the tree. The total delay incurred by the ripple effect of these misdirections is $O(\sqrt{n}\log^2 n \log^2 k)$. Thus the time required to compute all k α-quantiles is $O(n)$. The storage required at each node is proportional to the square root of the number of arriving keys; thus the total storage requirement is $O(\sqrt{nk})$.

6 Parallel Selection

In this section we consider the problem of selecting the α-quantile of a sequence of n keys, assuming that the keys arrive in k streams of length n/k to be processed in parallel by k processors. We assume that the keys arrive in a random order; $i.e.$, that all $n!$ assignments of the set of arriving keys to positions in the streams are equally likely. We give a parallel anytime algorithm based on the serial selection algorithm of Section 4. As before, we assume for convenience that $\alpha = \frac{a}{a+b}$ where a and b are small integers.

The algorithm starts by filling the buffers with arriving keys. It then goes through a series of stages, each of which (except the last) starts with all the buffers full. In each stage it is determined that the final α-quantile lies in an interval (L, U) (whp). As many keys less than L or greater than U as possible are then discarded from the buffers, subject to the requirement that the ratio between the numbers of discarded keys greater than U and less than L must be exactly b/a.The buffers are then replenished with keys from the streams. The processes of determining L and U and discarding high and low keys require communication and transfer of keys among the processors.

These processes are based on a parallel algorithm to compute an approximate β-quantile of the set of sk keys in the union of the k buffers. We begin by presenting such an algorithm for the case $\beta = 1/2$.Let 3^t be the largest power of 3 less than or equal to sk. The computation goes through t rounds of *thinning*, starting with 3^t keys from the union of the buffers. in each round the surviving keys are grouped randomly into sets of 3, and the median of each set of 3 keys survives to the next round.Analysis of this process shows that, with probability at least .96, the final surviving key is a γ-quantile, where $|\gamma - 1/2| < 2/3(11/8)^{-t}$.

During the thinning process some groups must be composed of nodes from different processors. For this purpose the processors configure themselves into a virtual linked list. Initially, each node performs the thinning process on the groups formed within its own buffer. Then, in subsequent rounds of thinning, the surviving keys are transferred to nodes whose addresses in the list are multiples of 3, then $3^2, 3^3$ etc.

For any β, the determination of an approximate β-quantile can be reduced to the determination of an approximate median by executing a special initial round of thinning. We present the details for the case $\beta < 1/2$. Let m be the greatest integer such that $(1 - \beta)^m > 1/2$. Let $p \in (0, 1)$ be such that $p(1 - \beta)^m) + (1 - p)(1 - \beta)^{m+1}) = 1/2$. Then, in the special round, the keys are grouped randomly, where the size of each group is m with probability p and $m + 1$ with probability $1 - p$, and the smallest key in each group survives. Throughout the special round and the subsequent thinning rounds, any rule for grouping the surviving keys can be used, as long as it depends on the positions of keys within the buffers, but not on their values. since the assignment of the keys to input streams, and hence the assignment of keys to positions in the buffers, is random.

The processors use the thinning algorithm to find keys L and U such that all future $\frac{a}{a+b}$-quantiles lie in the interval (L, U) (whp). This claim holds provided that L is of of rank A and U is of rank $sk - B$ in the set of sk keys contained in the buffers of the k processors, such that $A \le a((\frac{sk}{a+b} - c\sqrt{n})$ and $sk - B \le b((\frac{sk}{a+b} - c\sqrt{n})$ To achieve this, the thinning algorithm is used to find approximate β and γ-quantiles, where $\beta = (1 - \epsilon)a(\frac{sk}{a+b} - c\sqrt{n})$ and $\gamma = (1 + \epsilon)b((\frac{sk}{a+b} - c\sqrt{n})$. L is set to the approximate β-quantile and U, to the approximate γ-quantile. Here ϵ is a small positive constant, and the factors $1 - \epsilon$ and $1 + \epsilon$ are safety factors to ensure that A and B are likely to satisfy the required inequalities even though the thinning algorithm only produces approximate β and γ-quantiles.

After L and U have been determined each processor counts the number of keys less than L and the number of keys greater than U in its buffer. The processors organize themselves into a virtual rooted binary tree and, aggregate their counts by passing messages toward the root. After $O(\log k)$ parallel message-passing steps the root contains the aggregate counts A and B of the numbers of keys less than L and greater than U. In the unlikely event that A and B fail to satisfy the required inequalities the randomized thinning algorithm is invoked to recompute L and U. If A and B do satisfy the inequalities then using message passing along edges directed away from the root, the processors are directed to discard ra of the packets less than L and rb of the packets greater than U, where $r = \min(\lfloor A/a \rfloor, \lfloor B/b \rfloor)$. Each processor then receives keys from its input stream until its buffer is full.

The running time of the parallel algorithm is dominated by $O(n/k)$, the time required by each processor to read its input stream. In addition, each of the $O(n/sk)$ stages requires time $O(\log(sk))$ time for the parallel communication required in computing L, U, A and B.

7   Approximate Selection

We begin with the following problem of computing an approximate median: given an array of n keys, choose a key x such that, with probability at least $1 - \delta$, the rank of x differs from $n/2$ by at most ϵn. Vitter [7] has given the following solution: set x equal to the median of a random sample of $O(\frac{1}{\epsilon^2} \log(\frac{1}{\delta}))$ keys. If the stream of keys arrives in a random order then we can use a prefix of the stream as the sample. By applying our streaming algorithm to this prefix, we obtain an approximate median using $O(\frac{1}{\epsilon^2} \log(\frac{1}{\delta}))$ comparisons and storage $O(\frac{1}{\epsilon}\sqrt{\log(1/\delta)})$.

Here we note that an approximate median can be computed by a streaming algorithm using a slightly larger number of comparisons but only two storage locations. The algorithm considers a series of arriving keys as candidates for the ϵ-approximate median.Each candidate in turn is compared to a sequence of arriving keys, and the algorithm keeps track of the *lead* of the candidate, defined as the number of times the candidate is larger than the arriving key, minus the number of times it is smaller. If the lead remains in the interval $(-a, a)$ for s steps then the candidate is declared to be an ϵ-approximate median. Otherwise it is dismissed and the next arriving key becomes the new candidate. Here $s = O(\frac{1}{\epsilon^2} \ln(\frac{1}{\delta}))$ and $a = 0.4s\epsilon$. Using Chernoff bounds we establish the following:

1. If the rank of the candidate differs from $n/2$ by at most $\frac{\epsilon}{8}$ then, with probability at least $1 - \delta$, the candidate will be accepted.
2. If the rank of the candidate is np, where $\frac{\epsilon}{8} < |p-1/2| < \epsilon$ then the candidate may or may not be accepted, but the number of comparisons performed on it will not exceed s;
3. If the rank of the candidate is np, where $|p - 1/2| > \epsilon$, then the probability of incorrectly accepting the candidate is $O(e^{-\frac{s(|2p-1|-4\epsilon)^2}{6p}})$ and the expected number of comparisons until it is rejected is at most $\frac{4n\epsilon}{|2p-1|}$. Since $|2p - 1|$ is uniformly distributed over the interval $(2\epsilon, 1)$,we find by integrating over this interval that the expected number of comparisons performed on a candidate with $|p - 1/2| > \epsilon$ is $O(\frac{1}{\epsilon} \ln 1/\epsilon)$.
4. The number of candidates considered will be a geometric random variable with expectation $O(\frac{1}{\epsilon})$ and the number of candidates considered with $|p - 1/2| < \epsilon$ will be a geometric random variable with expectation $O(1)$.

5. The probability that the accepted candidate is not an ϵ-approximate median is bounded above by a constant times δ;
6. The number of comparisons performed by the algorithm is $O(\frac{n}{\epsilon^2} \max(\ln 1/\delta, \ln(\frac{1}{\epsilon})))$ (whp).

The computation of an approximate α-quantile can be reduced to the computation of an approximate median using the reduction based on thinning given in Section 5.

8   Approximate Sorting

In certain applications it suffices to sort a set of elements approximately rather than exactly. For example, in ranking candidates for adnmission to an academic department it may be important to rank the best candidates exactly, but an increasingly rough ranking may be adequate as we go down the list. We formulate the problem of approximate sorting in terms of a parameter $\epsilon > 0$. Our requirement is that, for all r, a candidate of rank r is assigned a rank that differs from r by at most ϵr.

Let ϵ be a positive constant. Let $x_1, x_2, \cdots, x_n$ be a linearly ordered set of keys and let π be the unique permutation of $\{1, 2, \cdots, n\}$ such that $x_{\pi(1)} < x_{\pi(2)} < \cdots < x_{\pi(n)}$. Let σ be a permutation of $\{1, 2, \cdots, n\}$. Then σ is said to ϵ-sort the keys if, whenever $\pi(i) = \sigma(j)$, $(1 - \epsilon)i \leq j \leq (1 + \epsilon)i$. In other words, σ ϵ-sorts the keys if, for all r, the key of rank r in the true ordering has rank between $(1 - \epsilon)r$ and $(1 + \epsilon)r$ in the ordering σ.

We shall derive a lower bound on the number of comparisons required to ϵ-sort a set of n keys. Call a permutation θ of $\{1, 2, \cdots, n\}$ an ϵ-permutation if, for all i, $(1 - \epsilon)i \leq \theta(i) \leq (1 + \theta)i$. If π is the true ordering of the keys, then permutation σ ϵ-sorts the keys if and only if $\sigma \circ \pi^{-1}$ is an ϵ-permutation. Let $V(n, \epsilon)$ be the number of ϵ-permutations of $\{1, 2, \cdots, n\}$ Then, if an ϵ-sorting algorithm returns the permutation σ, then there are only $V(n, \epsilon)$ possibilities for the true permutation. Since a $priori$ there are $n!$ possible true permutations, the program must be able to output at least $n!/V(n, \epsilon)$ permutations and,by a standard argument, the worst-case number of comparisons performed by any comparison algorithm for ϵ-sorting is at least the base-2 logarithm of this number of permutations. This lower bound also holds for the expected number of comparisons in a randomized algorithm when the true permutation is drawn uniformly at random from the set of all permutations.

$V(n, \epsilon)$ is the permanent of the $n \times n$ $0 - 1$-matrix A whose $i - j$ element is 1 if and only if $(1 - \epsilon)i \leq j \leq (1 + \epsilon)i$.Bregman's Theorem [1] states that if a_i is the number of 1's in the ith row of a $n \times n$ $0 - 1$-matrix then the permanent of the matrix is bounded above by $\pi_{i=1}^{n}(a_i!)^{\frac{1}{a_i}}$. For the matrix A , $a_i \leq \lceil 2\epsilon i \rceil$. A short calculation based on Stirling's Inequality yields : $\log_2 \frac{n!}{V(n, \epsilon)} \geq n \lg(\frac{\epsilon}{2\epsilon})$.

We shall give a two-pass streaming algorithm for ϵ-sorting. The first pass computes elements of all ranks of the form $\lceil \frac{n\epsilon}{(1+\epsilon)^i} \rceil$ for all positive integers i using the multiple selection algorithm of Section 5. In this case the entropy term

$H(p_1, p_2, \cdots, p_{k+1}))$ is $\lg(\frac{1}{\epsilon} + \frac{(1+\epsilon)\lg(1+\epsilon)}{\epsilon})$, which is less than $\lg(\frac{1}{\epsilon} + (1 + \epsilon)\lg e$. Thus the execution time of phase 1 is at most $1.5(1 + \lg(\frac{1}{\epsilon} + (1 + \epsilon)\lg e)n$.

In the second pass a binary search is executed on each key x to determine an i such that $r_i \leq x < r_{i+1}$, and an approximate rank is assigned to x accordingly. The number of comparisons performed in the second pass is at most $(1 + \lg(\frac{1}{\epsilon} + (1 + \epsilon)\lg e)n$.

We present an alternative algorithm for the first pass in the spirit of the well-known algorithms Quicksort and Multiple Quickselect [6]. We first describe the algorithm in a setting where the keys to be approximately sorted are presented in random order in an array. We then modify the algorithm to obtain an anytime streaming algorithm.

The array extends from address 0 to address $n + 1$. The actual keys are in locations 1 to n; location 0 contains a sentinel key equal to $-\infty$ and location $n+1$ contains a sentinel key equal to $+\infty$. At a general step the array contains a set S of *occupied locations*. Initially, locations 0 and $n + 1$ are considered occupied and the other locations are considered unoccupied. The following invariant properties hold at every step:

1. The n original keys occur in locations $1, 2, \cdots, n$ in some order;
2. If location i is occupied then the key it contains has rank i in the original set of keys, locations $1, 2, ..., \cdots, i - 1$ contain the keys of rank less than i, and locations $i + 1, \cdots, n$ contain the keys of rank greater than i.

If locations i and j are occupied, and all intervening locations are unoccupied, then the interval $[i, j]$ is considered *splittable* if $j - 1 > (1 + \epsilon)(i + 1)$. The computation terminates when no splittable intervals remain. At that point the array is ϵ-sorted.

Initially $[0, n + 1]$ is a splittable interval. At each step, a random location within a splittable interval is chosen and each of the other keys in the interval is compared with the key $x*$ in that location. Based on those comparisons, the keys within the interval are rearranged such that $x*$ is preceded by the keys less than $x*$ and precedes the keys greater than $x*$.

Next we calculate the expected number of comparisons for this algorithm. Define the length of the interval $[i, j]$ to be $j - i + 1$. Interval $[i, j]$ is *potentially splittable* if $(j - 1) > (1 + \epsilon)(i + 1)$. A potentially splittable interval becomes splittable if and only if the two end positions of the interval become occupied before any of the internal positions become occupied. If a potentially splittable interval of length t becomes splittable in the course of the algorithm then it will be split at the cost of $t - 3$ comparisons.

For each t we characterize the potentially splittable intervals of length t and the probability that they will be split. The conditions for an interval $[i, j]$ of length t to be potentially splittable are as follows:

- $t \geq 4$;
- $i \leq n + 2 - t$
- $i < \frac{t - 1 + \epsilon}{\epsilon}$

The probability of a potentially splittable interval $i, j]$ of length t becoming splittable is 1 if $i = 0$ and $j = n + 1$; $\frac{1}{t-1}$ if $i = 0$ and $j \leq n$ or $i \geq 1$ and $j = n + 1$; and $\frac{1}{\binom{t}{2}}$ if $i \geq 1$ and $j \leq n$.

Using these results we can compute the expected number of comparisons performed to split intervals of length t and, summing over t, we find that the expected number of comparisons performed by the algorithm is asymptotic to $n(\frac{2+3\epsilon}{1+\epsilon} + \ln(\frac{1+\epsilon}{\epsilon}))$.

Incidentally, by varying the definition of a potentially splittable interval, this approach also gives remarkably simple expected-time analyses of some classical randomized interval-splitting comparison algorithms such as Quicksort, Quickselect and Multiple Quickselect.

We now modify this algorithm to obtain an anytime streaming algorithm for the first phase. As the keys arrive we designate certain keys as *landmarks*; these play the same role as the keys occurring in occupied positions in the foregoing array-based algorithm. The landmarks are maintained in a self-balancing binary search tree such as a splay tree. Each arriving key is routed to a leaf of the tree (corresponding to an interval between consecutive landmarks) by comparing it with landmarks according to the usual insertion algorithm for a self-balancing binary search tree. The main difference from the array-based algorithm is that, because of storage limitations, we cannot retain all the keys that have arrived at a leaf. Instead, the algorithm counts the arriving keys, and also applies the thinning algorithm of Section 6 to compute an approximate median to be used in splitting the interval.The thinning algorithm can be implemented to run in working storage logarithmic in the number of arriving keys.

We also associate with each node (including both landmarks and leaves) an estimate of the number of keys that have arrived in the subtree rooted at that node. When a key arrives the estimate for each node along its insertion path is incremented by 1.

Let x and y be two consecutive landmarks. The interval between x and y is split when the estimate of the number of keys in that interval exceeds ϵ times the estimate of the number of keys less than or equal to x (the latter estimate is obtained from the estimates for nodes along the insertion path to x). In that case z, the approximate median computed by the thinning algorithm for the interval $[x, y]$, becomes a landmark; the leaf associated with that interval is replaced by a 2-leaf subtree rooted at z, and the estimate ascribed to each of the newly created intervals is set to half the estimate for the interval between x and y.To compensate for the inaccuracy of the approximate median provided by the thinning algorithm, the entire algorithm is run for a value of ϵ slightly smaller than the required tolerance.

With high probability,the following hold for any fixed ϵ: the number of landmarks created is $O(\log n)$, the storage requirement of the algorithm is $O(\log^2 n)$, and no interval between consecutive landmarks is splittable (*i.e.*, the actual number of keys in that interval does not exceed ϵ times the actual number of keys preceding that interval). The number of comparisons performed in the first phase is $O(n \log \frac{1}{\epsilon})$ (whp).

In the second pass each arriving key is inserted into the binary search tree created in the first pass, and a count of the exact number of keys in each interval is maintained. Then in a third pass, each key is reinserted and assigned its approximate rank according to the interval into which it falls.

References

1. Bregman, L.M.: Some properties of nonnegative matrices and their permanents. Soviet Math. Dokl 14, 945–949 (1973)
2. Bryant, R.E.: Data-intensive supercomputing: the case for DISC.Technical Report CMU-CS-07-128, Carnegie-Mellon University School of Computer Science (2007)
3. Chazelle, B.: The soft heap: an approximate priority queue with optimal error rate. Journal of the ACM 47 (2000)
4. Floyd, R.W., Rivest, R.L.: Expected time bounds for selection. Communications of the ACM 18(30), 165–172 (1975)
5. Munro, J.I., Paterson, M.S.: Selection and sorting with limited storage. Theoretical Computer Science 12, 315–323 (1980)
6. Prodinger, H.: Multiple quickselect: Hoare's find algorithm for several elements. Information Processing Letters 56, 123–129 (1995)
7. Vitter, J.S.: Random sampling with a reservoir. ACM Trans. on Math Software 11(1), 37–57 (1985)

Adventures in Bidirectional Programming

Benjamin C. Pierce

University of Pennsylvania

Most programs get used in just one direction, from input to output. But sometimes, having computed an output, we need to be able to *update* this output and then "calculate backwards" to find a correspondingly updated input. The problem of writing such *bidirectional transformations*—often called *lenses*—arises in applications across a multitude of domains and has been attacked from many perspectives [1,2,3,4,5,6,7,8,9,10,11,12, etc.]. See [13] for a detailed survey.

The Harmony project at the University of Pennsylvania is exploring a *linguistic* approach to bidirectional programming, designing domain-specific languages in which every expression simultaneously describes both parts of a lens. When read from left to right, it denotes an ordinary function that maps inputs to outputs. When read from right to left, it denotes an "update translator" that takes an input together with an updated output and produces a new input that reflects the update. These languages share some common elements with modern functional languages—in particular, they come with very expressive type systems. In other respects, they are rather novel and surprising.

We have designed, implemented, and applied bi-directional languages in three quite different domains: a language for bidirectional transformations on trees (such as XML documents), based on a collection of primitive bidirectional tree transformation operations and "bidirectionality-preserving" combining forms [13]; a language for bidirectional views of relational data, using bidirectionalized versions of the operators of relational algebra as primitives [14]; and, most recently, a language for bidirectional string transformations, with primitives based on standard notations for finite-state transduction and a type system based on regular expressions [15]. The string case is especially interesting, both in its own right and because it exposes a number of foundational issues common to all bidirectional programming languages in a simple and familiar setting.

This survey talk discusses several of these issues in depth and describes progress toward solutions.

References

1. Meertens, L.: Designing constraint maintainers for user interaction. Manuscript (1998)
2. Kennedy, A.J.: Functional pearl: Pickler combinators. Journal of Functional Programming 14(6), 727–739 (2004)
3. Benton, N.: Embedded interpreters. Journal of Functional Programming 15(4), 503–542 (2005)

V. Arvind and S. Prasad (Eds.): FSTTCS 2007, LNCS 4855, pp. 21–22, 2007.
© Springer-Verlag Berlin Heidelberg 2007

4. Ramsey, N.: Embedding an interpreted language using higher-order functions and types. In: ACM SIGPLAN Workshop on Interpreters, Virtual Machines and Emulators (IVME), San Diego, CA, pp. 6–14 (2003)
5. Hu, Z., Mu, S.C., Takeichi, M.: A programmable editor for developing structured documents based on bi-directional transformations. In: Partial Evaluation and Program Manipulation (PEPM) (2004)
6. Brabrand, C., Møller, A., Schwartzbach, M.I.: Dual syntax for XML languages. In: Bierman, G., Koch, C. (eds.) DBPL 2005. LNCS, vol. 3774, pp. 27–41. Springer, Heidelberg (2005)
7. Kawanaka, S., Hosoya, H.: Bixid: a bidirectional transformation language for XML. In: ACM SIGPLAN International Conference on Functional Programming (ICFP), Portland, Oregon, pp. 201–214 (2006)
8. Daly, M., Mandelbaum, Y., Walker, D., Fernández, M.F., Fisher, K., Gruber, R., Zheng, X.: PADS: An end-to-end system for processing ad hoc data. In: Proceedings of ACM SIGMOD International Conference on Management of Data, Chicago, IL, pp. 727–729 (2006)
9. Alimarine, A., Smetsers, S., van Weelden, A., van Eekelen, M., Plasmeijer, R.: There and back again: Arrows for invertible programming. In: ACM SIGPLAN Workshop on Haskell, pp. 86–97 (2005)
10. Stevens, P.: Bidirectional model transformations in QVT: Semantic issues and open questions. In: Engels, G., Opdyke, B., Schmidt, D.C., Weil, F. (eds.) MODELS 2007. LNCS, vol. 4735, Springer, Heidelberg (2007)
11. Bancilhon, F., Spyratos, N.: Update semantics of relational views. ACM Transactions on Database Systems 6(4), 557–575 (1981)
12. Gottlob, G., Paolini, P., Zicari, R.: Properties and update semantics of consistent views. ACM Transactions on Database Systems (TODS) 13(4), 486–524 (1988)
13. Foster, J.N., Greenwald, M.B., Moore, J.T., Pierce, B.C., Schmitt, A.: Combinators for bi-directional tree transformations: A linguistic approach to the view update problem. ACM Transactions on Programming Languages and Systems (3) (May 2007). Extended abstract in Principles of Programming Languages (POPL) (2005)
14. Bohannon, A., Vaughan, J.A., Pierce, B.C.: Relational lenses: A language for updateable views. In: Principles of Database Systems (PODS). Extended version available as University of Pennsylvania technical report MS-CIS-05-27 (2006)
15. Bohannon, A., Foster, J.N., Pierce, B.C., Pilkiewicz, A., Schmitt, A.: Boomerang: Resourceful lenses for string data. Technical report, Dept. of CIS University of Pennsylvania (July 2007), available from http://www.cis.upenn.edu/~jnfoster/boomerang-tr.pdf

Program Analysis Using Weighted Pushdown Systems*

Thomas Reps, Akash Lal, and Nick Kidd

Comp. Sci. Dept., University of Wisconsin
{reps,akash,kidd}@cs.wisc.edu

Abstract. *Pushdown systems* (PDSs) are an automata-theoretic formalism for specifying a class of infinite-state transition systems. Infiniteness comes from the fact that each configuration $\langle p, S \rangle$ in the state space consists of a (formal) "control location" p coupled with a stack S of unbounded size. PDSs can model program paths that have matching calls and returns, and automaton-based representations allow analysis algorithms to account for the infinite control state space of recursive programs.

Weighted pushdown systems (WPDSs) are a generalization of PDSs that add a general "black-box" abstraction for program data (through *weights*). WPDSs also generalize other frameworks for interprocedural analysis, such as the Sharir-Pnueli functional approach.

This paper surveys recent work in this area, and establishes a few new connections with existing work.

1 Introduction

Static analysis provides a way to obtain information about the possible states that a program reaches during execution, but without actually running the program on specific inputs. Static-analysis techniques explore the program's behavior for *all* possible inputs and account for *all* possible states that the program can reach. In this sense, static analysis is more comprehensive than traditional testing, which tests the program's behavior for a fixed (possibly randomly generated) finite set of runs of the program. For any non-trivial program, it is impossible to test explicitly all the possible behaviors within a reasonable amount of time; in contrast, static-analysis techniques use *approximations* to account for all of the actions that the program could perform [13]. To make this feasible, two techniques are used:

- The program is *run in the aggregate*. Rather than executing the program on ordinary states, the program is executed on finite-sized descriptors that represent collections of states.
- The program is *run in a non-standard fashion*. Rather than executing the program in a linear sequence, various fragments are executed (in the aggregate) so that, when stitched together, the results are guaranteed to cover all possible execution paths.

---

* Supported by ONR under grant N00014-01-1-0796 and by NSF under grants CCF-0540955 and CCF-0524051.

V. Arvind and S. Prasad (Eds.): FSTTCS 2007, LNCS 4855, pp. 23–51, 2007.

Analysis algorithms typically use the program's interprocedural control-flow graph (also known as its *ICFG*). An ICFG consists of a collection of control-flow graphs (CFGs)—one for each procedure—one of which represents the program's main procedure. The CFG for a procedure p has a unique *enter* node and a unique *exit* node. The other nodes represent the program's statements and conditions (or, alternatively, its basic blocks), except that each procedure call in the program is represented in the ICFG by two nodes, a *call* node and a *return-site* node. *Call-edges* connect call nodes to enter nodes; *return-edges* connect exit nodes to return-site nodes. A typical analysis goal is to compute, for each ICFG node n, an overapproximation (i.e., superset) of the set of states that can hold when n is reached.

The choice of which family of data descriptors that an algorithm uses impacts which behavioral properties of the program can be observed. This, in turn, affects (i) what sets of states can be represented, and (ii) which program fragments need to be explored. For example, one might use descriptors that represent only the sign of a variable's value: neg, zero, pos, and unknown. In a context in which it is known that both a and b are positive (i.e., when the memory descriptor is $\langle \mathtt{a} \mapsto \mathtt{pos}, \mathtt{b} \mapsto \mathtt{pos} \rangle$), a multiplication expression such "a*b" would be performed as "pos*pos".

Such memory descriptors generally represent a superset of the actual set of memory states that are reachable, because a descriptor such as $\langle \mathtt{a} \mapsto \mathtt{pos}, \mathtt{b} \mapsto \mathtt{pos} \rangle$ represents all states in which a and b hold positive integers (whereas, for example, only combinations with odd positive a's and even positive b's might be reachable). At a branch-point in the program, the analyzer needs to observe the possible outcomes of the branch-point's condition—as best it can, given the memory descriptors in use. This is used to determine an overapproximation of the paths along which control might flow. Thus, a more refined class of data descriptors can sometimes allow certain paths to be excluded from consideration.

On the other hand, certain paths can be excluded merely from consideration of the control-flow properties of the programming language. An important class of paths that can be excluded are those that violate the language's call/return protocol; in particular, an analysis should only consider paths in which the return from a called procedure is matched with the most recent call. Fig. 1 shows a fragment of an ICFG, and an example of a path fragment that should be excluded from consideration.

Dataflow-analysis algorithms that exclude such paths have a long history [14, 47, 26]. A natural class of dataflow-analysis problems in which this issue is reduced to a pure graph-reachability problem is also known [40]. The algorithms developed for that class of problems are useful for analyzing a family of program abstractions called Boolean programs (§2.3). (Boolean programs have become well-known due to their use in SLAM [4, 5] to represent program abstractions obtained via predicate abstraction [20].)

More recently, analysis techniques based on pushdown systems (PDSs) [6, 18, 44] have been developed. PDSs are an automata-theoretic formalism for

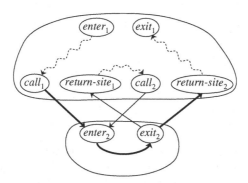

Fig. 1. An invalid-path fragment: in the path $[call_1, enter_2, exit_2, return\text{-}site_2]$, the return-edge $exit_2 \rightarrow return\text{-}site_2$ does not match with call-edge $call_1 \rightarrow enter_2$

specifying a class of infinite-state transition systems. Infiniteness comes from the fact that each configuration $\langle p, S \rangle$ in the state space consists of a (formal) "control location" p coupled with a stack S of unbounded size. Boolean programs have natural encodings as PDSs (see §2.3). Moreover, techniques developed for answering reachability queries on PDSs allow dataflow queries to be posed with respect to a *regular language of configurations*, which allows one to recover dataflow information for specific *calling contexts* (and for regular languages of calling contexts).

Subsequently, these techniques were generalized to *Weighted Pushdown Systems* (WPDSs) [7,46,41,42]. WPDSs extend PDSs by adding a general "black-box" abstraction for expressing transformations of a program's data state (through *weights*). By extending methods from PDSs that answer questions about only certain sets of paths (namely, ones that end in a specified regular language of configurations), WPDSs generalize other frameworks for interprocedural analysis, such as the Sharir-Pnueli functional approach [47], as well as the Knoop-Steffen [26] and Sagiv-Reps-Horwitz summary-based approaches [43]. In particular, conventional dataflow-analysis algorithms merge together the values for all states associated with the same program point, regardless of the states' calling context.

Because WPDSs permit dataflow queries to be posed with respect to a regular language of stack configurations,[1] one obtains several benefits from recasting an existing dataflow-analysis algorithm into the WPDS framework. First, one immediately obtains algorithms to find dataflow information for specific calling contexts and families of calling contexts, which provides information that was not previously obtainable. For instance, §3.2 and §4 discuss, respectively, how to recast Müller-Olm and Seidl's work on affine-relation analysis [34,35] and Landi and Ryder's work on may-aliasing for single-level pointer programs [32] in the

---

[1] Conventional merged dataflow information can also be obtained by issuing appropriate queries; thus, the new approach provides a strictly richer framework for interprocedural dataflow analysis than prior approaches.

WPDS framework, which makes it possible to pose stack-qualified queries about affine relations and may-alias relations. Second, the algorithms for solving path problems in WPDSs can provide a witness set of paths [42], which is useful for providing an explanation of why the answer to a dataflow query has the value reported.

Two implementations of WPDSs are publicly available [45,24], and both provide a convenient base for implementing different analyses. As a programming abstraction, these systems offer several benefits:

- An analyzer is created by means of a declarative specification: one specifies a weight domain, along with an encoding of the program's ICFG and a mapping of each ICFG edge to a weight.
- It permits the creation of libraries of reusable weight domains, which can also be used to create new weight domains by means of weight-domain-construction operations (pairing, reduced product [15], tensor product [37], etc.)
- Advances in solver technology apply to all instantiations of the framework; for instance, Lal and Reps achieved substantial speedups over previous algorithms by using more sophisticated algorithms in the WPDS solver engine [29].

WPDS++ [24] has been used to implement several of the analyses in CodeSurfer/x86 [3, 30, 1], a system for analyzing Intel x86 executables. It has also been used as a core analysis component in a system for analyzing concurrent programs [12].

Compared with other tools that support the creation of program analyzers from high-level specifications, (i) the WPDS implementations allow more sophisticated abstract domains to be used (such as the Müller-Olm/Seidl domains for affine-relation analysis [34, 35]), and also permit a broader range of dataflow-analysis queries to be posed than is possible with Banshee [27] and BDDBDDB [48]; (ii) the WPDS implementations support a broader range of dataflow-analysis queries than PAG [33].

Organization of the Paper. This paper surveys our recent work on WPDSs, and establishes a few new connections with other work. The remainder of the paper is organized into four sections: §2 provides background material on interprocedural dataflow analysis, PDSs, and Boolean programs. §3 introduces WPDSs. §4 describes how the work of Landi and Ryder [32] on single-level pointer analysis can be expressed in the WPDS framework. §5 summarizes recent work both on improving and on applying WPDS technology.

2   Background

2.1   Background on Interprocedural Dataflow Analysis

Dataflow analysis is concerned with determining an appropriate dataflow value to associate with each node n in a program, to summarize (safely) some aspect of the possible memory configurations that hold whenever control reaches n. To define an instance of a dataflow problem, one needs

- The CFG of the program.
- A meet semilattice $(V, \sqcap)$ with greatest element $\top$:
    - An element of V represents a set of possible memory configurations. Each point in the program is to be associated with some member of V.
    - The meet operator $\sqcap$ is used for combining information obtained along different paths.
- A value $v_0 \in V$ that represents the set of possible memory configurations at the beginning of the program.
- An assignment M of dataflow transfer functions (of type $V \to V$) to the edges of the CFG: $M(e) \in V \to V$.

A dataflow-analysis problem can be formulated as a *path-function problem*.

Definition 1. *A* **path** *of length j from node m to node n is a (possibly empty) sequence of j edges, denoted by $[e_1, e_2, \ldots, e_j]$, such that the source of e_1 is m, the target of e_j is n, and for all i, $1 \leq i \leq j - 1$, the target of edge e_i is the source of edge e_{i+1}.*

The path function pf_q for path $q = [e_1, e_2, \ldots, e_j]$ is the composition, in order, of q's transfer functions: $\mathrm{pf}_q = M(e_j) \circ \ldots \circ M(e_2) \circ M(e_1)$. In *intra*procedural dataflow analysis, the goal is to determine, for each node n, the "meet-over-*all-paths*" solution:

$$\mathrm{MOP}_n = \bigsqcap_{q \in \mathrm{Paths(enter}, n)} \mathrm{pf}_q(v_0),$$

where $\mathrm{Paths(enter}, n)$ denotes the set of paths in the CFG from the enter node to n [25]. MOP_n represents a summary of the possible memory configurations that can arise at n: because $v_0 \in V$ represents the set of possible memory configurations at the beginning of the program, $\mathrm{pf}_q(v_0)$ represents the contribution of path q to the memory configurations summarized at n.

The soundness of the MOP_n solution with respect to the programming language's concrete semantics is established by the methodology of *abstract interpretation* [13]:

- A Galois connection (or Galois insertion) is established to define the relationship between sets of concrete states and elements of V.
- Each dataflow transfer function $M(e)$ is shown to overapproximate the transfer function for the concrete semantics of e.

In this paper, we assume that such correctness requirements have already been taken care of; the paper concentrates on algorithms for determining dataflow values once an instance of a dataflow-analysis problem has been given.

An example ICFG is shown in Fig. 2. Let *Var* be the set of all variables in a program, and let $(\mathbb{Z}_\bot, \sqsubseteq, \sqcap)$, where $\mathbb{Z}_\bot = \mathbb{Z} \cup \{\bot\}$, be the standard constant-propagation semilattice: for all $c \in \mathbb{Z}$, $\bot \sqsubseteq c$; for all $c_1, c_2 \in \mathbb{Z}_\bot$ such that $c_1 \neq c_2$, c_1 and c_2 are incomparable; and $\sqcap$ is the greatest-lower-bound operation in this partial order. $\bot$ stands for "not-a-constant". Let $D = (Env \to Env)$ be the set

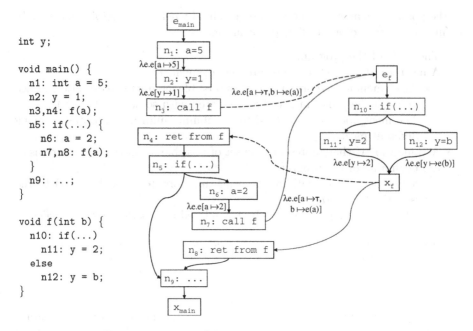

Fig. 2. A program fragment and its ICFG. For all unlabeled edges, the environment transformer is $\lambda e.e$.

of all environment transformers where an environment is a mapping for all variables: $Env = (Var \to \mathbb{Z}_\perp) \cup \{\top\}$. We use $\top$ to denote an infeasible environment. Furthermore, we restrict the set D to contain only $\top$-strict transformers, i.e., for all $d \in D$, $d(\top) = \top$. We can extend the meet operation to environments by taking meet componentwise.

$$env_1 \sqcap env_2 = \begin{cases} env_1 & \text{if } env_2 = \top \\ env_2 & \text{if } env_1 = \top \\ \lambda v.(env_1(v) \sqcap env_2(v)) & \text{otherwise} \end{cases}$$

The dataflow transformers are shown as edge labels in Fig. 2. A transformer of the form $\lambda e.e[a \mapsto 5]$ returns an environment that agrees with the argument, except that a is bound to 5. The environment $\top$ cannot be updated, and thus $(\lambda e.e[a \mapsto 5])\top$ equals $\top$.

The notion of an *(interprocedurally) valid path* captures the idea that not all paths in an ICFG represent potential execution paths. A valid path is one that respects the fact that a procedure always returns to the site of the most recent call. Let each call node in the ICFG be given a unique index from 1 to *CallSites*, where *CallSites* is the total number of call sites in the program. For each call site c_i, label the call-to-enter edge and the exit-to-return-site edge with the symbols "$(_i$" and "$)_i$", respectively. Label all other edges of the ICFG with the symbol e. Each path in the ICFG defines a word, obtained by concatenating—in order—the labels of the edges on the path. A path is a *valid path* iff the path's word is in the language $L(valid)$ generated by the context-free grammar shown below on the left; a path is a *matched path* iff the path's word is in the language $L(matched)$ of balanced-parenthesis strings (interspersed with strings of zero or more e's) generated by the context-free grammar shown below on the right. (In both grammars, i ranges from 1 to *CallSites*.)

$$
\begin{array}{ll}
valid \rightarrow matched \ \ valid & \qquad matched \rightarrow matched \ \ matched \\
\quad | \ \ (_i \ \ valid & \qquad \qquad \quad | \ \ (_i \ \ matched \ \ )_i \\
\quad | \ \ \epsilon & \qquad \qquad \quad | \ \ e \\
& \qquad \qquad \quad | \ \ \epsilon
\end{array}
$$

The language $L(valid)$ is a language of *partially* balanced parentheses: every right parenthesis ")$_i$" is balanced by a preceding left parenthesis "($_i$", but the converse need not hold.

Example 1. In the ICFG shown in Fig. 2, the path $[e_{main}, n_1, n_2, n_3, e_f, n_{10}, n_{11},$ $x_f, n_4, n_5]$ is a matched path, and hence a valid path; the path $[e_{main}, n_1, n_2, n_3,$ $e_f, n_{10}]$ is a valid path, but not a matched path, because the call-to-enter edge $n_3 \rightarrow e_f$ has no matching exit-to-return-site edge; the path $[e_{main}, n_1, n_2, n_3, e_f,$ $n_{10}, n_{11}, x_f, n_8]$ is neither a matched path nor a valid path because the exit-to-return-site edge $x_f \rightarrow n_8$ does not correspond to the preceding call-to-enter edge $n_3 \rightarrow e_f$.

In interprocedural dataflow analysis, the goal shifts from finding the meet-over-*all-paths* solution to the more precise "meet-over-*all-valid-paths*", or "context-sensitive" solution. A context-sensitive interprocedural dataflow analysis is one in which the analysis of a called procedure is "sensitive" to the context in which it is called. A context-sensitive analysis captures the fact that the results propagated back to each return site r should depend only on the memory configurations that arise at the call site that corresponds to r. More precisely, the goal of a context-sensitive analysis is to find the meet-over-all-valid-paths value for nodes of the ICFG [47, 26, 43]:

$$
\text{MOVP}_n = \prod_{q \in \text{VPaths}(e_{\text{main}}, n)} \text{pf}_q(v_0),
$$

where $\text{VPaths}(e_{\text{main}}, n)$ denotes the set of valid paths from the main procedure's enter node to n.

Although some valid paths may also be infeasible execution paths, none of the non-valid paths are feasible execution paths. By restricting attention to just the valid paths from e_{main}, we thereby exclude some of the infeasible execution paths. In general, therefore, MOVP_n characterizes the memory configurations at n more precisely than MOP_n.

2.2   Pushdown Systems

In this section, we define pushdown systems and show how they can be used to encode ICFGs.

Rule	Control flow modeled
$\langle p, u \rangle \hookrightarrow \langle p, v \rangle$	Intraprocedural edge $u \to v$
$\langle p, c \rangle \hookrightarrow \langle p, e_f \ r \rangle$	Call to f from c that returns to r
$\langle p, x_f \rangle \hookrightarrow \langle p, \varepsilon \rangle$	Return from f at exit node x_f

Fig. 3. The encoding of an ICFG's edges as PDS rules

Definition 2. *A **pushdown system** is a triple $\mathcal{P} = (P, \Gamma, \Delta)$, where P is a finite set of states (also known as "control locations"), Γ is a finite set of stack symbols, and $\Delta \subseteq P \times \Gamma \times P \times \Gamma^*$ is a finite set of rules. A **configuration** of $\mathcal{P}$ is a pair $\langle p, u \rangle$ where $p \in P$ and $u \in \Gamma^*$. A rule $r \in \Delta$ is written as $\langle p, \gamma \rangle \hookrightarrow \langle p', u \rangle$, where $p, p' \in P$, $\gamma \in \Gamma$ and $u \in \Gamma^*$. These rules define a transition relation $\Rightarrow$ on configurations of $\mathcal{P}$ as follows: If $r = \langle p, \gamma \rangle \hookrightarrow \langle p', u' \rangle$, then $\langle p, \gamma u \rangle \Rightarrow \langle p', u'u \rangle$ for all $u \in \Gamma^*$. The reflexive transitive closure of $\Rightarrow$ is denoted by $\Rightarrow^*$. For a set of configurations C, we define $pre^*(C) = \{c' \mid \exists c \in C : c' \Rightarrow^* c\}$ and $post^*(C) = \{c' \mid \exists c \in C : c \Rightarrow^* c'\}$, which are just backward and forward reachability under the transition relation $\Rightarrow$.*

Without loss of generality, we restrict the pushdown rules to have at most two stack symbols on the right-hand side [44]. A rule $r = \langle p, \gamma \rangle \hookrightarrow \langle p', u \rangle$, $u \in \Gamma^*$, is called a *pop* rule if $|u| = 0$, and a *push* rule if $|u| = 2$.

The PDS configurations model (node, stack) pairs of the program's state. Given a program P, we can use a PDS to model a limited portion of a P's behavior in the following sense: the configurations of the PDS represent a superset of P's (node, stack) pairs.

The standard approach for modeling a program's control flow with a pushdown system is as follows: P contains a single state p, Γ corresponds to the nodes of the program's ICFG, and Δ corresponds to edges of the program's ICFG (see Fig. 3). For instance, the rules that encode the ICFG shown in Fig. 2 are

$$\langle p, e_{main} \rangle \hookrightarrow \langle p, n_1 \rangle \qquad \langle p, n_5 \rangle \hookrightarrow \langle p, n_9 \rangle \qquad \langle p, e_f \rangle \hookrightarrow \langle p, n_{10} \rangle$$
$$\langle p, n_1 \rangle \hookrightarrow \langle p, n_2 \rangle \qquad \langle p, n_6 \rangle \hookrightarrow \langle p, n_7 \rangle \qquad \langle p, n_{10} \rangle \hookrightarrow \langle p, n_{11} \rangle$$
$$\langle p, n_2 \rangle \hookrightarrow \langle p, n_3 \rangle \qquad \langle p, n_7 \rangle \hookrightarrow \langle p, e_f \ n_8 \rangle \qquad \langle p, n_{11} \rangle \hookrightarrow \langle p, x_f \rangle$$
$$\langle p, n_3 \rangle \hookrightarrow \langle p, e_f \ n_4 \rangle \qquad \langle p, n_8 \rangle \hookrightarrow \langle p, n_9 \rangle \qquad \langle p, n_{10} \rangle \hookrightarrow \langle p, n_{12} \rangle$$
$$\langle p, n_4 \rangle \hookrightarrow \langle p, n_5 \rangle \qquad \langle p, n_9 \rangle \hookrightarrow \langle p, x_{main} \rangle \qquad \langle p, n_{12} \rangle \hookrightarrow \langle p, x_f \rangle$$
$$\langle p, n_5 \rangle \hookrightarrow \langle p, n_6 \rangle \qquad \langle p, x_{main} \rangle \hookrightarrow \langle p, \varepsilon \rangle \qquad \langle p, x_f \rangle \hookrightarrow \langle p, \varepsilon \rangle$$

PDSs that have only a single control location, as discussed above, are also called "context-free processes" [10]. In §2.3, we will discuss how, in addition to control flow, PDSs can also be used to encode program models that involve finite abstractions of the program's data. PDSs that have multiple control locations are used in such encodings.

The problem of interest is to find the set of all reachable configurations, starting from a given set of configurations. This can then be used, for example, for assertion checking (i.e., determining if a given assertion can ever fail) or to find the set of all data values that may arise at a program point (for dataflow analysis).

Because the number of configurations of a pushdown system is unbounded, it is useful to use finite automata to describe regular sets of configurations.

Definition 3. *If $\mathcal{P} = (P, \Gamma, \Delta)$ is a PDS then a $\mathcal{P}$-automaton is a finite automaton $(Q, \Gamma, \to, P, F)$, where $Q \supseteq P$ is a finite set of states, $\to \subseteq Q \times \Gamma \times Q$ is the transition relation, P is the set of initial states, and F is the set of final states. We say that a configuration $\langle p, u \rangle$ is accepted by a $\mathcal{P}$-automaton if the automaton can accept u when it is started in the state p (written as $p \xrightarrow{u}{}^* q$, where $q \in F$). A set of configurations is called* **regular** *if some $\mathcal{P}$-automaton accepts it. Without loss of generality, $\mathcal{P}$-automata are restricted to not have any transitions leading to an initial state.*

An important result is that for a regular set of configurations C, both $post^*(C)$ and $pre^*(C)$ (the forward and the backward reachable sets of configurations, respectively) are also regular sets of configurations [6, 9]. The algorithms for computing $post^*$ and pre^*, called *poststar* and *prestar*, respectively, take a $\mathcal{P}$-automaton $\mathcal{A}$ as input, and if C is the set of configurations accepted by $\mathcal{A}$, they produce $\mathcal{P}$-automata $\mathcal{A}_{post^*}$ and $\mathcal{A}_{pre^*}$ that accept the sets of configurations $post^*(C)$ and $pre^*(C)$, respectively [6, 17, 18]. Both *poststar* and *prestar* can be implemented as *saturation procedures*; i.e., transitions are added to $\mathcal{A}$ according to some saturation rule until no more can be added.

Algorithm *prestar*: $\mathcal{A}_{pre^*}$ can be constructed from $\mathcal{A}$ using the following saturation rule: *If $\langle p, \gamma \rangle \hookrightarrow \langle p', w \rangle$ and $p' \xrightarrow{w}{}^* q$ in the current automaton, add a transition (p, γ, q).*

Algorithm *poststar*: $\mathcal{A}_{post^*}$ can be constructed from $\mathcal{A}$ by performing Phase I and then saturating via the rules given in Phase II:

– *Phase I.* For each pair (p', γ') such that $\mathcal{P}$ contains at least one rule of the form $\langle p, \gamma \rangle \hookrightarrow \langle p', \gamma' \gamma'' \rangle$, add a new state $p'_{\gamma'}$.
– *Phase II (saturation phase).* (The symbol $\xrightarrow{\gamma}{}\rightsquigarrow$ denotes the relation $(\xrightarrow{\epsilon})^* \xrightarrow{\gamma} (\xrightarrow{\epsilon})^*$.)
  - If $\langle p, \gamma \rangle \hookrightarrow \langle p', \epsilon \rangle \in \Delta$ and $p \overset{\gamma}{\rightsquigarrow} q$ in the current automaton, add a transition (p', ϵ, q).
  - If $\langle p, \gamma \rangle \hookrightarrow \langle p', \gamma' \rangle \in \Delta$ and $p \overset{\gamma}{\rightsquigarrow} q$ in the current automaton, add a transition (p', γ', q).
  - If $\langle p, \gamma \rangle \hookrightarrow \langle p', \gamma' \gamma'' \rangle \in \Delta$ and $p \overset{\gamma}{\rightsquigarrow} q$ in the current automaton, add the transitions $(p', \gamma', p'_{\gamma'})$ and $(p'_{\gamma'}, \gamma'', q)$.

Example 2. Given the PDS that encodes the ICFG from Fig. 2 and the query automaton $\mathcal{A}$ shown in Fig. 4(a), which accepts the language $\{\langle p, e_{main} \rangle\}$, *poststar* produces the automaton $\mathcal{A}_{post^*}$ shown in Fig. 4(b).

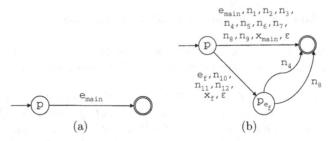

Fig. 4. (a) Automaton for the input language of configurations $\{\langle p, e_{main}\rangle\}$; (b) automaton for $post^*(\{\langle p, e_{main}\rangle\})$ (computed for the PDS that encodes the ICFG from Fig. 2)

2.3   Boolean Programs

A Boolean program can be thought of as a C program with only the Boolean datatype. It does not have any pointers or heap-allocated storage. A Boolean program consists of a finite set of procedures. It has a finite set of global variables, and a finite set of local variables for each procedure. Each variable can only hold a value from a finite domain.[2] To simplify the discussion, we assume that procedures do not have parameters (they can be passed through global variables). The variables in scope inside a procedure are the global variables and its set of local variables. Fig. 5(a) shows a Boolean program with two procedures and two global variables x and y over a finite domain $V = \{0, 1, \ldots, 7\}$.

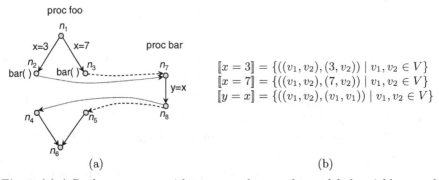

$$[\![x = 3]\!] = \{((v_1, v_2), (3, v_2)) \mid v_1, v_2 \in V\}$$
$$[\![x = 7]\!] = \{((v_1, v_2), (7, v_2)) \mid v_1, v_2 \in V\}$$
$$[\![y = x]\!] = \{((v_1, v_2), (v_1, v_1)) \mid v_1, v_2 \in V\}$$

Fig. 5. (a) A Boolean program with two procedures and two global variables x and y over a finite domain $V = \{0, 1, \ldots, 7\}$. (b) The (non-identity) transformers used in the Boolean program.

Notation. A binary relation on a set S is a subset of $S \times S$. If R_1 and R_2 are binary relations on S, then their relational composition, denoted by "$R_1; R_2$", is defined by $\{(s_1, s_3) \mid \exists s_2 \in S, (s_1, s_2) \in R_1, (s_2, s_3) \in R_2\}$. If R is a binary

---

[2] An assignment to a variable v that holds a value from a finite domain can be thought of as a collection of assignments to a *vector* of Boolean-valued variables, namely, the collection of Boolean-valued variables that holds the encoding of v's value.

relation, R^i is the relational composition of R with itself i times, and R^0 is the identity relation on S. $R^* = \cup_{i=0}^{\infty} R^i$ is the reflexive-transitive closure of R.

Let G be the set of valuations of the global variables, and let Val_i be the set of valuations of the local variables of procedure i. Let L be the set of local states of the program; each local state consists of the value of the program counter, a valuation of local variables from some Val_i, and the program stack (which, for each unfinished call to a procedure P, contains a return address and a valuation of the local variables of P).

The effect of executing an assignment or assume statement st, denoted by $[\![\mathsf{st}]\!]$, is a binary relation on $G \times \mathrm{Val}_i$ that describes how values of variables in scope can change. Fig. 5(b) shows the (non-identity) transformers used in Fig. 5(a).

To encode a Boolean program using a PDS, the state alphabet P is expanded to encode the values of global variables, and the stack alphabet is expanded to encode the values of local variables [44].

Let N_i be the set of control locations of the ith procedure. We set P to be G, and Γ to be the union of $N_i \times \mathrm{Val}_i$ over all procedures. (Note that the set of local states L equals Γ^*.) The PDS rules for the ith procedure are constructed as follows: (i) an intraprocedural ICFG edge $u \to v$ with action st is encoded via a set of rules $\langle g, (u, l) \rangle \hookrightarrow \langle g', (v, l') \rangle$, for each $((g, l), (g', l')) \in [\![\mathsf{st}]\!]$; (ii) a call edge $c \to r$ that calls procedure f, with enter node e_f, is encoded via a set of rules $\langle g, (c, l) \rangle \hookrightarrow \langle g, (e_f, l_0) (r, l) \rangle$, for each $(g, l) \in G \times \mathrm{Val}_i$ and $l_0 \in \mathrm{Val}_f$; (iii) a procedure return at node u is encoded via a set of rules $\langle g, (u, l) \rangle \hookrightarrow \langle g, \varepsilon \rangle$, for each $(g, l) \in G \times \mathrm{Val}_i$.

Under such an encoding of a Boolean program as a PDS, a configuration $\langle p, \gamma_1 \gamma_2 \cdots \gamma_n \rangle$ is an element of $G \times L$ that describes the instantaneous state of a program. The state p encodes the values of global variables; γ_1 encodes the current program location and the values of local variables in scope; and the rest of the stack encodes the list of unfinished calls with the values of local variables at the time the call was made. The PDS transition relation ($\Rightarrow$), which is essentially a transition relation on $G \times L$, represents the semantics of the Boolean program.

3   Weighted Pushdown Systems

A weighted pushdown system is obtained by augmenting a PDS with a weight domain that is a *bounded idempotent semiring* [42,7]. Such semirings are powerful enough to encode finite-state data abstractions, such as the ones required for bitvector dataflow analysis, Boolean programs, and the IFDS framework of Reps et al. [40], as well as infinite-state data abstractions, such as linear-constant propagation [43] and affine-relation analysis [34, 35]. We present some of this here; additional material about using WPDSs for interprocedural analysis can be found in [42].

Weights encode the effect that each statement (or PDS rule) has on the data state of the program. They can be thought of as abstract transformers that specify how the abstract state changes when a statement is executed.

Definition 4. *A* **bounded idempotent semiring** *(or* **weight domain***) is a tuple* $(D, \oplus, \otimes, \bar{0}, \bar{1})$*, where D is a set whose elements are called* **weights***, $\bar{0}, \bar{1} \in D$, and $\oplus$ (the combine operation) and $\otimes$ (the extend operation) are binary operators on D such that*

1. *$(D, \oplus)$ is a commutative monoid with $\bar{0}$ as its neutral element, and where $\oplus$ is idempotent. $(D, \otimes)$ is a monoid with the neutral element $\bar{1}$.*
2. *$\otimes$ distributes over $\oplus$, i.e., for all $a, b, c \in D$ we have*
   $$a \otimes (b \oplus c) = (a \otimes b) \oplus (a \otimes c) \text{ and } (a \oplus b) \otimes c = (a \otimes c) \oplus (b \otimes c).$$
3. *$\bar{0}$ is an annihilator with respect to $\otimes$, i.e., for all $a \in D$, $a \otimes \bar{0} = \bar{0} = \bar{0} \otimes a$.*
4. *In the partial order $\sqsubseteq$ defined by $\forall a, b \in D$, $a \sqsubseteq b$ iff $a \oplus b = a$, there are no infinite descending chains.*

Definition 5. *A* **weighted pushdown system** *is a triple $\mathcal{W} = (\mathcal{P}, \mathcal{S}, f)$, where $\mathcal{P} = (P, \Gamma, \Delta)$ is a PDS, $\mathcal{S} = (D, \oplus, \otimes, \bar{0}, \bar{1})$ is a bounded idempotent semiring, and $f : \Delta \to D$ is a map that assigns a weight to each rule of $\mathcal{P}$.*

WPDSs compute over the weights via the extend operation ($\otimes$). Let $\sigma \in \Delta^*$ be a sequence of rules. Using f, we can associate a value to σ; i.e., if $\sigma = [r_1, \ldots, r_k]$, we define $v(\sigma) \stackrel{\text{def}}{=} f(r_1) \otimes \ldots \otimes f(r_k)$. In program-analysis problems, weights typically represent abstract transformers that specify how the abstract state changes when a statement is executed. Thus, the extend operation is typically the reversal of function composition: $w_1 \otimes w_2 = w_2 \circ w_1$. (Computing over transformers by composing them—instead of computing on the underlying abstract states by applying transformers to abstract states—is customary in interprocedural analysis, where procedure summaries need to be calculated as compositions of abstract-state transformers [14, 26, 40].)

Reachability problems on PDSs are generalized to WPDSs as follows:

Definition 6. *Let $\mathcal{W} = (\mathcal{P}, \mathcal{S}, f)$ be a weighted pushdown system, where $\mathcal{P} = (P, \Gamma, \Delta)$. For any two configurations c and c' of $\mathcal{P}$, let $path(c, c')$ denote the set of all rule sequences that transform c into c'. Let $S, T \subseteq P \times \Gamma^*$ be regular sets of configurations. If $\sigma \in path(c, c')$, then we say $c \Rightarrow^\sigma c'$. The* **meet-over-all-valid-paths** *value $\text{MOVP}(S, T)$ is defined as $\bigoplus \{v(\sigma) \mid s \Rightarrow^\sigma t, s \in S, t \in T\}$.*

A PDS, as defined in §2.2, is simply a WPDS with the *Boolean weight domain* $(\{F, T\}, \vee, \wedge, F, T)$ and weight assignment $f(r) = T$ for all rules $r \in \Delta$. In this case, $\text{MOVP}(S, U) = T$ iff there exists a path from a configuration in S to a configuration in U, i.e., $post^*(S) \cap U$ and $S \cap pre^*(U)$ are non-empty sets.

One way of modeling a program as a WPDS is as follows: the PDS models the control flow of the program, as in Fig. 3. The weight domain models abstract transformers for an abstraction of the program's data. §3.1 and §3.2 describe several data abstractions that can be encoded using weight domains. To simplify the presentation, we only show the treatment for global variables, and do not consider local variables. Finite-state abstractions of local variables can always be encoded in the stack alphabet, as for PDSs [30, 44]. For infinite-state abstractions, local variables pose an extra complication for WPDSs [30]; their treatment is discussed in §3.4.

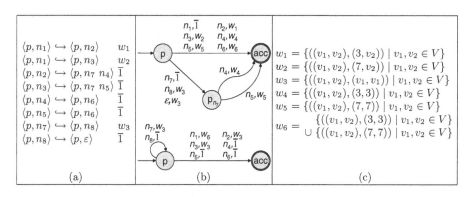

$$\langle p, n_1 \rangle \hookrightarrow \langle p, n_2 \rangle \quad w_1$$
$$\langle p, n_1 \rangle \hookrightarrow \langle p, n_3 \rangle \quad w_2$$
$$\langle p, n_2 \rangle \hookrightarrow \langle p, n_7 \, n_4 \rangle \quad \overline{1}$$
$$\langle p, n_3 \rangle \hookrightarrow \langle p, n_7 \, n_5 \rangle \quad \overline{1}$$
$$\langle p, n_4 \rangle \hookrightarrow \langle p, n_6 \rangle \quad \overline{1}$$
$$\langle p, n_5 \rangle \hookrightarrow \langle p, n_6 \rangle \quad \overline{1}$$
$$\langle p, n_7 \rangle \hookrightarrow \langle p, n_8 \rangle \quad w_3$$
$$\langle p, n_8 \rangle \hookrightarrow \langle p, \varepsilon \rangle \quad \overline{1}$$

$$w_1 = \{((v_1, v_2), (3, v_2)) \mid v_1, v_2 \in V\}$$
$$w_2 = \{((v_1, v_2), (7, v_2)) \mid v_1, v_2 \in V\}$$
$$w_3 = \{((v_1, v_2), (v_1, v_1)) \mid v_1, v_2 \in V\}$$
$$w_4 = \{((v_1, v_2), (3, 3)) \mid v_1, v_2 \in V\}$$
$$w_5 = \{((v_1, v_2), (7, 7)) \mid v_1, v_2 \in V\}$$
$$w_6 = \begin{aligned} &\{((v_1, v_2), (3, 3)) \mid v_1, v_2 \in V\} \\ &\cup \{((v_1, v_2), (7, 7)) \mid v_1, v_2 \in V\} \end{aligned}$$

(a)   (b)   (c)

Fig. 6. (a) A WPDS that encodes the Boolean program from Fig. 5(a). (b) The result of $poststar(\langle p, n_1 \rangle)$ and $prestar(\langle p, n_6 \rangle)$. The final state in each of the automata is acc. (c) Definitions of the weights used in the figure.

3.1 Finite-State Data Abstractions

An important weight domain for WPDSs is the set of all binary relations on a finite set.

Definition 7. *If G is a finite set, then the **relational weight domain** on G is defined as $(2^{G \times G}, \cup, ;, \emptyset, id)$: weights are binary relations on G, combine is union, extend is relational composition (";"), $\overline{0}$ is the empty relation, and $\overline{1}$ is the identity relation on G.*

By instantiating G to be the set of global states of a Boolean program P, we obtain a weight domain for encoding P. This approach yields a more straightforward encoding of P: the weight associated with the rule that encodes an assignment or assume statement st of P is exactly $[\![st]\!]$—i.e., its effect on the global state of P—which, as described in §2.3, is a binary relation on G. For example, the WPDS shown in Fig. 6 encodes the Boolean program from Fig. 5(a). The Boolean program has two variables that range over the set $V = \{0, 1, \ldots, 7\}$, so $G = V \times V$, where the two components represent the values of x and y, respectively.

The set of all data values that reach a node n can be calculated as follows: let S be the singleton configuration consisting of the program's enter node, and let T be the set $\{\langle p, n \, u \rangle \mid u \in \Gamma^* \}$. Let $w = \text{MOVP}(S, T)$. If $w = \overline{0}$, then the node cannot be reached. Otherwise, w captures the net transformation on the global state from when the program started. The range of w, i.e., the set $\{g \in G \mid \exists g' \in G : (g', g) \in w\}$, is the set of valuations that reach node n. For example, in Fig. 6, the MOVP weight to node n_6 is the weight w_6 shown in Fig. 6(c). Its range shows that either x = 3 and y = 3, or x = 7 and y = 7.

Because T can be any regular set, one can also answer stack-qualified queries [42]. For example, the set of values that arise at node n when its procedure is called from call site m can be found by setting $T = \{\langle p, n \, m_r \, u \rangle \mid u \in \Gamma^* \}$, where m_r is the return site for call site m.

A WPDS with a weight domain that has a finite set of weights, such as the one described above, can be encoded as a PDS. However, it is often useful to use weights because they can be symbolically encoded. Tools such as MOPED and SLAM use BDDs [8] to encode sets of data values, which allows them to scale to a large number of variables. (Using PDSs for Boolean program verification, without any symbolic encoding, is generally not a feasible approach.)

3.2   Infinite-State Data Abstractions

An infinite-state data abstraction is one in which the number of abstract states (or weights) is infinite. We begin with two simple examples of infinite weight domains, and then discuss the weight domain used for affine-relation analysis.

Finding Shortest Valid Paths

Definition 8. *The **minpath semiring** is the weight domain $\mathcal{M} = (\mathbb{N} \cup \{\infty\}, min, +, \infty, 0)$: weights are non-negative integers including "infinity", combine is minimum, and extend is addition.*

If all rules of a WPDS are given the weight 1 from this semiring (different from the semiring weight $\overline{1}$, which is the integer 0), then the MOVP weight between two configurations is the length of the shortest path (shortest rule sequence) between them.

Another infinite weight domain, which is based on the minpath semiring, is given in [28] and was shown to be useful for debugging programs.

Finding Shortest Traces. The minpath semiring can be combined with a relational weight domain, for example, to find the shortest (valid) path in a Boolean program (for finding the shortest trace that exhibits some property).

Definition 9. *A **weighted relation** on a set S, weighted with semiring $(D, \oplus, \otimes, \overline{0}, \overline{1})$, is a function from $(S \times S)$ to D. The composition of two weighted relations R_1 and R_2 is defined as $(R_1; R_2)(s_1, s_3) = \oplus\{w_1 \otimes w_2 \mid \exists s_2 \in S : w_1 = R_1(s_1, s_2), w_2 = R_2(s_2, s_3)\}$. The union of the two weighted relations is defined as $(R_1 \cup R_2)(s_1, s_2) = R_1(s_1, s_2) \oplus R_2(s_1, s_2)$. The identity relation is the function that maps each pair (s, s) to $\overline{1}$ and others to $\overline{0}$. The reflexive transitive closure is defined in terms of these operations, as before. If $\rightarrow$ is a weighted relation and $(s_1, s_2, w) \in \rightarrow$, then we write $s_1 \xrightarrow{w} s_2$.*

Definition 10. *If S is a weight domain with set of weights D and G is a finite set, then the **relational weight domain** on (G, S) is defined as $(2^{G \times G \to D}, \cup, ;, \emptyset, id)$: weights are weighted relations on G and the operations are the corresponding ones for weighted relations.*

If G is the set of global states of a Boolean program, then the relational weight domain on $(G, \mathcal{M})$ can be used for finding the shortest trace: for each rule, if

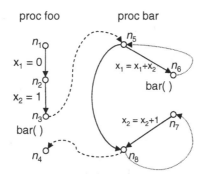

Fig. 7. An affine program that starts execution at node n_1. There are two global variables x_1 and x_2.

$R \subseteq G \times G$ is the effect of executing the rule on the global state of the Boolean program, then associate the following weight with the rule:

$$\{g_1 \xrightarrow{1} g_2 \mid (g_1, g_2) \in R\} \cup \{g_1 \xrightarrow{\infty} g_2 \mid (g_1, g_2) \notin R\}.$$

Then, if $w = \text{MOVP}(C_1, C_2)$, the length of the shortest path that starts with global state g from a configuration in C_1 and ends at global state g' in a configuration in C_2, is $w(g, g')$ (which would be ∞ if no path exists). (Moreover, if a finite-length path does exist, a witness trace [42] can be obtained to identify the elements of the path.)

Affine-Relation Analysis. An affine relation is a linear-equality constraint between integer-valued variables. Affine-relation analysis (ARA) tries to find all affine relationships that hold in the program. An example is shown in Fig. 7. For this program, ARA would, for example, infer that $x_2 = x_1 + 1$ at program node n_4.

ARA for single-procedure programs was first given by Karr [23]. ARA generalizes other analyses, including copy-constant propagation, linear-constant propagation [43], and induction-variable analysis [23]. We have used ARA on machine code to find induction-variable relationships between machine registers [2]. These help in increasing the precision of an abstract-interpretation-based pointer analysis for machine code [1].

Affine Programs. Interprocedural ARA can be performed precisely on *affine programs*, and has been the focus of several papers [34,35,21]. Affine programs are similar to Boolean programs, but with integer-valued variables. Again, we restrict our attention to global variables, and defer treatment of local variables to §3.4. If $\{x_1, x_2, \cdots, x_n\}$ is the set of global variables of the program, then all assignments have the form $x_j := a_0 + \sum_{i=1}^{n} a_i x_i$, where $a_0, \cdots, a_n$ are integer constants. An assignment can also be non-deterministic, denoted by $x_j := ?$, which may assign any integer to x_j. (This is typically used for abstracting assignments that cannot be modeled as an affine transformation of the variables.) All branch conditions in affine programs are non-deterministic.

ARA Weight Domain. We briefly describe the weight domain based on the linear-algebra formulation of ARA from [34]. An affine relation $a_0 + \sum_{i=1}^{n} a_i x_i = 0$ is represented using a column vector of size $n + 1$: $\boldsymbol{a} = (a_0, a_1, \cdots, a_n)^t$. A valuation of program variables $\overline{\mathbf{x}}$ is a map from the set of global variables to the integers. The value of x_i under this valuation is written as $\overline{\mathbf{x}}(i)$.

A valuation $\overline{\mathbf{x}}$ satisfies an affine relation $\boldsymbol{a} = (a_0, a_1, \cdots, a_n)^t$ if $a_0 + \sum_{i=1}^{n} a_i \overline{\mathbf{x}}(i) = 0$. An affine relation $\boldsymbol{a}$ represents the set of all valuations that satisfy it, written as $\text{PTS}(\boldsymbol{a})$. An affine relation $\boldsymbol{a}$ holds at a program node if the set of valuations reaching that node (in the concrete collecting semantics) is a subset of $\text{PTS}(\boldsymbol{a})$.

An important observation about affine programs is that if affine relations $\boldsymbol{a}_1$ and $\boldsymbol{a}_2$ hold at a program node, then so does any linear combination of $\boldsymbol{a}_1$ and $\boldsymbol{a}_2$. For example, one can verify that $\text{PTS}(\boldsymbol{a}_1 + \boldsymbol{a}_2) \supseteq \text{PTS}(\boldsymbol{a}_1) \cap \text{PTS}(\boldsymbol{a}_2)$, i.e., the affine relation $\boldsymbol{a}_1 + \boldsymbol{a}_2$ (componentwise addition) holds at a program node if both $\boldsymbol{a}_1$ and $\boldsymbol{a}_2$ hold at that node. The set of affine relations that hold at a program node forms a (finite-dimensional) vector space [34]. This implies that a (possibly infinite) set of affine relations can be represented by any of its bases; each such basis is always a finite set.

For reasoning about affine programs, Müller-Olm and Seidl defined an abstraction that is able to find all affine relationships in an affine program: each statement is abstracted by a set of matrices of size $(n + 1) \times (n + 1)$. This set is the weakest-precondition transformer on affine relations for that statement: if a statement is abstracted as the set $\{m_1, m_2, \cdots, m_r\}$, then the affine relation $\boldsymbol{a}$ holds after the execution of the statement if and only if the affine relations $(m_1 \boldsymbol{a}), (m_2 \boldsymbol{a}), \cdots, (m_r \boldsymbol{a})$ held before the execution of the statement.

Under such an abstraction of program statements, one can define the extend operation, which is transformer composition, as elementwise matrix multiplication, and the combine operation as set union. This is correct semantically, but it does not give an effective algorithm because the matrix sets can grow unboundedly. However, the observation that affine relations form a vector space carries over to a set of matrices as well. One can show that the transformer $\{m_1, m_2, \cdots, m_r\}$ is semantically equivalent to the transformer $\{m_1, m_2, \cdots, m_r, m\}$, where m is any linear combination of the m_i matrices. Thus, a set of matrices can be abstracted as the (infinite) set of matrices spanned by them. Once we have a vector space, we can represent it using any of its bases to get a finite and bounded representation: a vector space over matrices of size $(n + 1) \times (n + 1)$ cannot have more that $(n + 1)^2$ matrices in any basis.

If M is a set of matrices, let $\text{SPAN}(M)$ be the vector space spanned by them. Let β be the basis operation that takes a set of matrices and returns a basis of their span. We can now define the weight domain. A weight w is a vector space of matrices, which can be represented using its basis. Extend of vector spaces w_1 and w_2 is the vector space $\{(m_1 m_2) \mid m_i \in w_i\}$. Combine of w_1 and w_2 is the vector space $\{(m_1 + m_2) \mid m_i \in w_i\}$, which is the smallest vector space containing both w_1 and w_2. $\overline{0}$ is the empty set, and $\overline{1}$ is the span of the singleton set consisting of the identity matrix. The extend and combine operations, as defined above, are operations on infinite sets. They can be implemented by the corresponding operations on any basis of the weights. The following properties show that it is semantically correct to operate on the elements in the basis instead of all the elements in the vector space spanned by them:

$$\beta(w_1 \oplus w_2) = \beta(\beta(w_1) \oplus \beta(w_2))$$
$$\beta(w_1 \otimes w_2) = \beta(\beta(w_1) \otimes \beta(w_2))$$

These properties are satisfied because of the linearity of extend (matrix multiplication distributes over addition) and combine operations.

Under such a weight domain, $MOVP(S, T)$ is a weight that is the net weakest-precondition transformer between S and T. Suppose that this weight has the basis $\{m_1, \cdots, m_r\}$. The affine relation that indicates that any variable valuation might hold at S is $\mathbf{0} = (0, 0, \cdots, 0)$. Thus, $\mathbf{0}$ holds at S, and the affine relation $\boldsymbol{a}$ holds at T iff $m_1\boldsymbol{a} = m_2\boldsymbol{a} = \cdots = m_r\boldsymbol{a} = \mathbf{0}$. The set of all affine relations that hold at T can be found as the intersection of the null spaces of the matrices $m_1, m_2, \cdots, m_r$.

Extensions to ARA. ARA can also be performed for modular arithmetic [35] to precisely model machine arithmetic (which is modulo 2 to the power of the word size). The weight domain is similar to the one described above.

3.3   Solving for the MOVP Value

There are two algorithms for solving for MOVP values, called *prestar* and *poststar* (by analogy with the algorithms for PDSs). They take as input an automaton that accepts the set of initial configurations. As output, they produce a *weighted automaton*:

Definition 11. *Given a weighted pushdown system* $\mathcal{W} = (\mathcal{P}, \mathcal{S}, f)$, *a* $\mathcal{W}$-***automaton*** $\mathcal{A}$ *is a* $\mathcal{P}$-*automaton, where each transition in the automaton is labeled with a weight. The weight of a path in the automaton is obtained by taking an extend of the weights on the transitions in the path in either a forward or backward direction. The automaton is said to accept a configuration* $c = \langle p, u \rangle$ *with weight* $w = \mathcal{A}(c)$ *if* w *is the combine of weights of all accepting paths for* u *starting from state* p *in* $\mathcal{A}$. *We call the automaton a* **backward** $\mathcal{W}$-***automaton*** *if the weight of a path is read backwards, and a* **forward** $\mathcal{W}$-***automaton*** *otherwise.*

Let $\mathcal{A}$ be an unweighted automaton and $\mathcal{L}(\mathcal{A})$ be the set of configurations accepted by it. Then, *prestar*$(\mathcal{A})$ produces a forward weighted automaton $\mathcal{A}_{pre^*}$ as output, such that $\mathcal{A}_{pre^*}(c) = MOVP(\{c\}, \mathcal{L}(\mathcal{A}))$, whereas *poststar*$(\mathcal{A})$ produces a backward weighted automaton $\mathcal{A}_{post^*}$ as output, such that $\mathcal{A}_{post^*}(c) = MOVP(\mathcal{L}(\mathcal{A}), \{c\})$ [42]. Examples are shown in Fig. 6(b). One thing to note here is how the *poststar* automaton works. The procedure `bar` is analyzed independently of its calling context (i.e., without knowing the exact value of x), which generates the transitions between p and p_{n_7}. The calling context of bar, which determines the input values to bar, is represented by the transitions that leave state p_{n_7}. This is how, for instance, the automaton records that $\mathbf{x} = 3$ and $\mathbf{y} = 3$ at node n_8 when bar is called from node n_2.

Using standard automata-theoretic techniques, one can also compute $\mathcal{A}_w(C)$ for (forward or backward) weighted automaton $\mathcal{A}_w$ and a regular set of configurations C, where $\mathcal{A}_w(C) = \bigoplus\{\mathcal{A}_w(c) \mid c \in C\}$. This allows one to solve for the meet-over-all-paths value $\text{MOVP}(S, T)$ for configuration sets S and T by computing either $poststar(S)(T)$ or $prestar(T)(S)$.

We briefly describe how the *prestar* algorithm works for WPDSs. The interested reader is referred to [42] for more details (e.g., the *poststar* algorithm), as well as an efficient implementation of the algorithm. The algorithm takes an unweighted automaton $\mathcal{A}$ as input (i.e., a weighted automaton in which all weights are $\bar{1}$), and adds weighted transitions to it until no more can be added. The addition of transitions is based on the following rule: for a WPDS rule $r = \langle p, \gamma \rangle \hookrightarrow \langle q, \gamma_1 \cdots \gamma_n \rangle$ with weight $f(r)$ and transitions $(q, \gamma_1, q_1), \cdots, (q_{n-1}, \gamma_n, q_n)$ with weights $w_1, \cdots, w_n$, add the transition (p, γ, q_n) to $\mathcal{A}$ with weight $w = f(r) \otimes w_1 \otimes \cdots \otimes w_n$. If this transition already exists with weight w', change the weight to $w \oplus w'$.

This algorithm is based on the intuition that if the automaton accepts configurations c and c' with weights w and w', respectively, and rule r allows the transition $c' \Rightarrow c$, then the automaton needs to accept c' with weight $w' \oplus (f(r) \otimes w)$. Termination follows from the fact that the number of states of the automaton does not increase (hence, the number of transitions is bounded), and the fact that the weight domain satisfies the descending-chain condition (Defn. 4, item 4).

We now provide some intuition into why one needs both forwards and backwards automata. Consider the automata in Fig. 6(c). For the *poststar* automaton, when one follows a path that accepts the configuration $\langle p, n_8\ n_4 \rangle$, the transition (p, n_8, q) comes before (q, n_4, acc). However, the former transition describes the transformation inside bar, which happens *after* the transformation performed in reaching the call site at n_4 (which is stored on (q, n_4, acc)). Because the transformation for the calling context happens earlier in the program, but its transitions appear later in the automaton, the weights are read backwards. For the *prestar* automaton, the weight on (p, n_4, acc) is the transformation for going from n_4 to n_6, which occurs after the transformation inside bar. Thus, it is a forwards automaton.

The following lemma states the complexity for solving *poststar* by the algorithm of Reps et al. [42]. We will assume that the time to perform an $\otimes$ and a $\oplus$ are the same, and use the notation $O_s(.)$ to denote the time bound in terms of semiring operations. The *height* of a weight domain is defined to be the length of the longest descending chain in the domain. For ease of stating a complexity result, we will assume that there is a finite upper bound on the height. Some weight domains, such as $\mathcal{M}$ in Defn. 8, have no such finite upper bound on the height; however, WPDSs can still be used when the height is unbounded. The absence of infinite descending chains (Defn. 4, item 4) ensures that saturation-based algorithms for computing $post^*$ and pre^* will eventually terminate.

Lemma 1. *[42] Given a WPDS with PDS $\mathcal{P} = (P, \Gamma, \Delta)$, if $\mathcal{A} = (Q, \Gamma, \rightarrow, P, F)$ is a $\mathcal{P}$-automaton that accepts an input set of configurations, poststar produces a backward weighted automaton with at most $|Q| + |\Delta|$ states in time $O_s(|P||\Delta|(|Q_0| + |\Delta|)H + |P||\lambda_0|H)$, where $Q_0 = Q\backslash P$, $\lambda_0 \subseteq \rightarrow$ is the set of all transitions leading from states in Q_0, and H is the height of the weight domain.*

Approximate Analysis. Among the properties imposed by a weight domain, one important property is distributivity (Defn. 4, item 2). This is a common requirement for a precise analysis, which also arises in various *coincidence theorems* for dataflow analysis [22, 47, 26]. Sometimes this requirement is too strict and may be relaxed to monotonicity, i.e., for all $a, b, c \in D$, $a \otimes (b \oplus c) \sqsubseteq (a \otimes b) \oplus (a \otimes c)$ and $(a \oplus b) \otimes c \sqsubseteq (a \otimes c) \oplus (b \otimes c)$. In such cases, the MOVP computation may not be precise, but it will be *safe* under the partial order $\sqsubseteq$.

3.4   Local Variables and Extended Weighted Pushdown Systems

This section discusses an extension of WPDSs that permits abstractions to track the values of local variables [30].

In WPDSs, reachability problems compute the value of a rule sequence by taking an extend of the weights of each of the rules in the sequence; when WPDSs are used for dataflow analysis of a program, rule sequences represent interprocedural paths in the program. To summarize the weights of such paths, we have to maintain information about local variables of all unfinished procedures that appear on the path.

Extended WPDSs (EWPDSs) lift WPDSs to handle local variables in much the same way that Knoop and Steffen lifted conventional dataflow-analysis algorithms to handle local variables [26]: at a call site at which procedure P calls procedure Q, the local variables of P are modeled as if the current incarnations of P's locals are stored in locations that are inaccessible to Q and to procedures transitively called by Q—consequently, the contents of P's locals cannot be affected by the call to Q; we use special merging functions to combine them with the value returned by Q to create the state after Q returns.[3]

---

[3] Note that this model agrees with programming languages like Java, where it is not possible to have pointers to local variables (i.e., pointers into the stack). For languages such as C and C++, where the address-of operator (**&**) allows the address of a local variable to be obtained, if P passes such an address to Q, it is possible for Q (or a procedure transitively called from Q) to affect a local of P by making an indirect assignment through the address.

Conventional interprocedural dataflow-analysis algorithms must also worry about this issue, which is usually dealt with by (i) performing a preliminary analysis to determine which call sites might have such effects, and (ii) using the results of the preliminary analysis to create sound transformers for the primary analysis. The preliminary analysis is itself an interprocedural dataflow analysis, and (E)WPDSs can be applied to this problem as well. §4 describes how one such preliminary analysis—alias analysis for single-level pointers [32]—can be expressed as a reachability problem in an EWPDS.

For a semiring $\mathcal{S}$ on domain D, a *merging function* is defined as follows:

Definition 12. *A function $g : D \times D \to D$ is a* **merging function** *with respect to a bounded idempotent semiring $\mathcal{S} = (D, \oplus, \otimes, \bar{0}, \bar{1})$ if it satisfies the following properties.*

1. **Strictness.** *For all $a \in D$, $g(\bar{0}, a) = g(a, \bar{0}) = \bar{0}$.*
2. **Distributivity.** *The function distributes over $\oplus$. For all $a, b, c \in D$,*

$$g(a \oplus b, c) = g(a, c) \oplus g(b, c) \text{ and } g(a, b \oplus c) = g(a, b) \oplus g(a, c)$$

Definition 13. *Let $(\mathcal{P}, \mathcal{S}, f)$ be a weighted pushdown system; let $\mathcal{G}$ be the set of all merging functions on semiring $\mathcal{S}$, and let Δ_2 denote the set of push rules of $\mathcal{P}$. An* **extended weighted pushdown system** *is a quadruple $\mathcal{W}_e = (\mathcal{P}, \mathcal{S}, f, g)$ where $g : \Delta_2 \to \mathcal{G}$ assigns a merging function to each rule in Δ_2.*

Note that a push rule has both a weight and a merging function associated with it. Merging functions are used to fuse the local state of the calling procedure as it existed just before the call with the effects on the global state produced by the called procedure.

As an example, Fig. 2 shows an ICFG and the PDS that represents it. We can perform constant propagation (with uninterpreted expressions) by assigning a weight to each PDS rule. The weight semiring is $\mathcal{S} = (D, \oplus, \otimes, 0, 1)$, where $D = (Env \to Env)$ is the set of all environment transformers, and the semiring operations and constants are defined as follows:

$$\bar{0} = \lambda e. \top \qquad w_1 \oplus w_2 = \lambda e.(w_1(e) \sqcap w_2(e))$$
$$\bar{1} = \lambda e. e \qquad w_1 \otimes w_2 = w_2 \circ w_1$$

The weights for the EWPDS that models the program in Fig. 2 are shown as edge labels. The merging function for the rule $\langle p, n_3 \rangle \hookrightarrow \langle p, e_f n_4 \rangle$, which encodes the call at n_3, receives two environment transformers: one that summarizes the effect of the caller from its enter node to the call site (e_{main} to n_3) and one that summarizes the effect of the called procedure (e_f to x_f). The merging function has to produce the transformer that summarizes the effect of the caller from its enter node to the return site (e_{main} to n_4). The merging function is defined as follows:

$$g(w_1, w_2) = \textbf{if } (w_1 = \bar{0} \text{ or } w_2 = \bar{0}) \textbf{ then } \bar{0}$$
$$\textbf{else } \lambda e.e[a \mapsto w_1(e)(a), y \mapsto (w_1 \otimes w_2)(e)(y)]$$

This copies over the value of the local variable a from the call site, and gets the value of y that is returned from the called procedure. Because the merging function has access to the environment transformer just before the call, we do not have to pass the value of local variable a into procedure p. Hence the call stops tracking the value of a using the weight $\lambda e.e[a \mapsto \bot, b \mapsto e(a)]$.

The merging function for the rule $\langle p, n_7 \rangle \hookrightarrow \langle p, e_f n_8 \rangle$ is defined similarly.

Merging Functions for Boolean Programs. In this section, we assume without loss of generality that each procedure has the same number of local variables.

To encode Boolean programs that have local variables, let G be the set of valuations of the global variables and L be the set of valuations of local variables. The actions of program statements and conditions are now binary relations on $G \times L$; thus, the weight domain is a relational weight domain on the set $G \times L$, but with an extra merging function defined on weights. Because different weights can refer to local variables from different procedures, one cannot take relational composition of weights from different procedures. The *project* function is used to change the scope of a weight. It existentially quantifies out the current transformation on local variables and replaces it with an identity relation. Formally, it can be defined as follows:

$$project(w) = \{(g_1, l_1, g_2, l_1) \mid (g_1, l_1, g_2, l_2) \in w\}.$$

Once the summary of a procedure is calculated as a weight w involving local variables of the procedure, the *project* function is applied to it, and the result $project(w)$ is passed to the callers of that procedure. This makes sure that local variables of one procedure do not interfere with those of another procedure. Thus, merging functions for Boolean programs all have the form

$$g(a, b) = a \otimes project(b).$$

For encoding Boolean programs with other abstractions, such as finding the shortest trace, one can use the relational weight domain on $(G \times L, \mathcal{S})$, where $\mathcal{S}$ is a weight domain such as the minpath semiring (transparent to the presence or absence of local variables). The *project* function on weights from this domain can be defined as follows:

$$project(w) = \lambda(g_1, l_1, g_2, l_2). \text{ if } (l_1 \neq l_2) \text{ then } \overline{0}_{\mathcal{S}}$$
$$\text{else } \bigoplus_{l \in L} w(g_1, l_1, g_2, l)$$

Again, the merging functions all have the form $g(a, b) = a \otimes project(b)$.

4 Case Study: May-Aliasing for Single-Level Pointer Programs

In this section, we define an EWPDS to find variable aliasing in programs written in a C-like imperative language that is restricted to single-level pointers (i.e., one cannot have pointers to pointers).[4] This problem was defined and solved in [32], and has been chosen to illustrate the power of having merging functions in EWPDSs. We first discuss some of the results from [32], and then move on to describe an EWPDS that finds aliasing in a program. For this, we need only

---

[4] For languages in which more than one level of indirection is possible, the algorithm for single-level pointers still provides a safe solution (i.e., an overapproximation) [32].

to describe the weight domain and merging functions, because we already know how to model the control flow of a program as a PDS (Fig. 3).

We say that two access expressions a and b are aliased (written as $\langle a, b \rangle$) at a particular program point n if in *some* program execution they refer to the same memory location when execution reaches n. We limit access expressions to variables and pointer dereferences (written as $*p$ for an address-valued variable p). Given a program, we want to determine an overapproximation of all alias pairs that hold at each program point. This problem is also referred to as *may-aliasing*. In [32], this is computed in two stages. First, *conditional may-aliasing* information is computed, which answers questions of the form: "if all alias pairs in the set $\mathcal{A}$ hold at a program point n_1, does the pair $\langle a, b \rangle$ hold at point n_2?" The second stage then uses this information to build up the final may-aliasing table.

An important property that results from the fact that we only have single-level pointers is that for all program points n_1 and n_2, where n_1 is the enter node of the procedure containing n_2, if the alias pair $\langle a, b \rangle$ holds at n_2 under the assumption that the set $\mathcal{A} = \{A_1, \cdots, A_m\}$ of alias pairs holds at n_1, then either (i) we can prove that $\langle a, b \rangle$ holds at n_2, assuming that no alias pair holds at n_1; or (ii) there exists a k, $1 \leq k \leq m$, such that assuming that just A_k holds at n_1 suffices to prove that $\langle a, b \rangle$ holds at n_2. In other words, we only need to compute conditional may-alias information for each *alias pair* $A_k \in \mathcal{A}$, rather than for each *subset* of $\mathcal{A}$.

We say that the alias pair $\langle a, . \rangle$ holds at program point n if a is aliased to some access expression that is not visible (out of scope) in the procedure containing n. It is not necessary to know the particular invisible access expression to which a is aliased because a procedure will always have the same effect on all alias pairs that contain access expression a and any invisible access expression [32].

For a given program, let V denote the set of all its variables and pointer dereferences. Assume that all variables have different names (local variables can be prefixed by the name of the procedure that contains them) so that there are no name conflicts. The set $\mathcal{AP} = (V \times V) \cup (V \times \{.\}) \cup (\{.\} \times V)$ is the set of all alias pairs. Let $\mathcal{AP}_\perp = \mathcal{AP} \cup \{\perp\}$, where $\perp$ represents the absence of an alias pair.

We now construct a weight domain over the set $D = (\mathcal{AP}_\perp \to 2^{\mathcal{AP}})$ of all functions w from $\mathcal{AP}_\perp$ to the power set of $\mathcal{AP}$ with the following monotonicity restriction: for all $x \in \mathcal{AP}$, $w(\perp) \subseteq w(x)$. Operations on weights will maintain the invariant that alias relations are symmetric (i.e., if $\langle a, b \rangle$ holds, so does $\langle b, a \rangle$). Each weight $w \in D$ can be efficiently represented as a one-to-many map from $\mathcal{AP}_\perp$ to $\mathcal{AP}$.

An interprocedural path P with weight w means that if we assume $\langle a, b \rangle$ to hold at the beginning of P then all pairs in $w(\langle a, b \rangle)$ hold at the end of path P when the program execution follows P. The special element $\perp$ handles the case when no pair is assumed to hold at the beginning of the path; $w(\perp)$ is the set of all alias pairs that hold at the end of the path without assuming that any pair holds at the beginning of the path. Thus, a weight represents conditional may-aliasing information, which motivates the monotonicity condition introduced above.

For all $w_1 \neq \bar{0} \neq w_2$, the semiring operations are defined as follows. For $x \in \mathcal{AP}_\perp$,

$$(w_1 \oplus w_2)(x) = w_1(x) \cup w_2(x)$$
$$(w_1 \otimes w_2)(x) = w_2(\perp) \cup (\cup_{y \in w_1(x)} w_2(y))$$
$$\bar{1}(x) = \begin{cases} \emptyset & \text{if } x = \perp \\ \{x\} & \text{otherwise} \end{cases}$$

If path P_1 has weight w_1 and path P_2 has weight w_2, then the weight $w_1 \otimes w_2$ summarizes the conditional alias information of the path P_1 followed by P_2. In particular, $(w_1 \otimes w_2)(x)$ consists of the alias pairs that hold from w_2, regardless of the value of w_1, together with the alias pairs that hold from w_2 given $w_1(x)$. When P_1 and P_2 have the same starting and ending points, the weight $w_1 \oplus w_2$ stores conditional aliasing information when the program execution follows P_1 or P_2.

(The semiring constant $\bar{0}$ cannot be naturally described in terms of conditional aliasing, but we can add it to D as a special value that satisfies all properties of Defn. 4.)

We now consider how to associate a weight to each pushdown rule in the EWPDS that encodes the program. For a node n that contains a statement of the form $x = y$, where x and y are pointers, the weight associated with each rule of the form $\langle p, n \rangle \hookrightarrow \cdots$ is a map, where for each $x \in \mathcal{AP}_\perp$, the first applicable mapping is followed:

$$\langle *y, b \rangle \mapsto \{\langle *x, b \rangle\}$$
$$\langle a, *y \rangle \mapsto \{\langle a, *x \rangle\}$$
$$\langle *x, b \rangle \mapsto \emptyset$$
$$\langle a, *x \rangle \mapsto \emptyset$$
$$\langle a, b \rangle \mapsto \{\langle a, b \rangle\}$$
$$\perp \mapsto \{\langle a, a \rangle \mid a \in V\} \cup \{\langle *x, *y \rangle, \langle *y, *x \rangle\}$$

Roughly speaking, this generates the alias pairs $\langle *x, *y \rangle$ and $\langle *y, *x \rangle$, makes the aliases of $*y$ into aliases of $*x$, and removes the previously existing alias pairs of $*x$ (except $\langle *x, *x \rangle$). To enforce monotonicity on weights, the following closure operation is applied to the map: $cl(w) = \lambda x.(w(x) \cup w(\perp))$. The weights on other rules that represent intraprocedural edges can be defined similarly (see [32]).

For a *push* rule, the weight is determined according to the binding that occurs at the call site; the definition is presented in Fig. 8. All pop rules have the weight $\bar{1}$.

The merging functions associated with push rules reflect the way conditional aliasing information is computed for return nodes in [32]. Consider the push rule $\langle p, call_{foo} \rangle \hookrightarrow \langle p, enter_{bar} \ return_{foo} \rangle$, which is a call to procedure *bar* from *foo*, and suppose that $bind_{call}$ is the weight associated with this rule. For local access expressions l_1, l_2 of *foo* and global access expressions g_1, g_2, the following must hold.

- The alias pair $\langle l_1, l_2 \rangle$ holds at $return_{foo}$ only if the pair $\langle l_1, l_2 \rangle$ holds at the call node $call_{foo}$.
- The alias pair $\langle g_1, g_2 \rangle$ holds at $return_{foo}$ only if the pair holds at $exit_{bar}$.
- The alias pair $\langle g_1, l_1 \rangle$ holds at $return_{foo}$ only if $\langle g_1, . \rangle$ holds at $exit_{bar}$ and the invisible variable is l_1. This happens when a pair $\langle o_1, l_1 \rangle$ that held at $call_{foo}$ caused $\langle o_2, . \rangle$ to hold at $enter_{bar}$ because of the call bindings ($\langle o_2, . \rangle \in bind_{call}(\langle o_1, l_1 \rangle)$) and this pair, in turn, caused $\langle g_1, . \rangle$ to hold at $exit_{bar}$.

$$
bind_n(\bot) = \begin{pmatrix}
\{\langle *f_i, *f_j \rangle \mid [f_i, a_i], [f_j, a_j], a_i = a_j\} \\
\cup \, \{\langle *f_i, *a_i \rangle \mid [f_i, a_i], visible_p(a_i)\} \\
\cup \, \{\langle *a_i, *f_i \rangle \mid [f_i, a_i], visible_p(a_i)\} \\
\cup \, \{\langle *f_i, . \rangle \mid [f_i, a_i], \neg visible_p(a_i)\} \\
\cup \, \{\langle ., *f_i \rangle \mid [f_i, a_i], \neg visible_p(a_i)\}
\end{pmatrix}
$$

$$
bind_n(\langle a, b \rangle) = \begin{pmatrix}
bind_n(\bot) \\
\cup \, \{\langle a, b \rangle \mid visible_p(a), visible_p(b)\} \\
\cup \, \{\langle a, . \rangle \mid visible_p(a), \neg visible_p(b)\} \\
\cup \, \{\langle ., b \rangle \mid \neg visible_p(a), visible_p(b)\} \\
\cup \, \{\langle a, *f_i \rangle \mid visible_p(a), [f_i, a_i], *a_i = b\} \\
\cup \, \{\langle ., *f_i \rangle \mid \neg visible_p(a), [f_i, a_i], *a_i = b\} \\
\cup \, \{\langle *f_i, b \rangle \mid visible_p(b), [f_i, a_i], *a_i = a\} \\
\cup \, \{\langle *f_i, . \rangle \mid \neg visible_p(b), [f_i, a_i], *a_i = a\} \\
\cup \, \{\langle *f_i, *f_j \rangle \mid [f_i, a_i], [f_j, a_j], *a_i = a, *a_j = b\}
\end{pmatrix}
$$

Fig. 8. A function that models parameter binding for a call at program point n to a procedure named p. For brevity, we write $[f, a]$ to denote the fact that f is a pointer-valued formal parameter bound to actual a. Also, $visible_p(a)$ is *true* if a is visible in procedure p.

To encode these facts as weights for an algorithmic description of the merging functions, we need to define certain weights and operations on them.

- **Projection.** For a set $S \subseteq (V \cup \{.\})$, let w_S be a weight that only preserves alias pairs in $S \times S$: $w_S(\bot) = \emptyset$ and

$$
w_S(\langle a, b \rangle) = \begin{cases} \{\langle a, b \rangle\} & \text{if } a, b \in S \\ \emptyset & \text{otherwise} \end{cases}
$$

- **Restoration.** For an access expression $v \in V$, let w_S^v be a weight that changes alias pairs when v comes back in scope conditional on the set $S \subseteq (V \cup \{.\})$: $w_S^v(\bot) = \emptyset$ and

$$
w_S^v(\langle a, b \rangle) = \begin{cases} \{\langle a, v \rangle\} & \text{if } b = . \text{ and } a \in S \\ \{\langle v, b \rangle\} & \text{if } a = . \text{ and } b \in S \\ \emptyset & \text{otherwise} \end{cases}
$$

- **Conditional Extend.** For an alias pair $\langle a, b \rangle$, define $\otimes_{\langle a, b \rangle}$ to be a binary operation on weights that calculates the alias pairs that hold at the end of a path as a result of the fact that $\langle a, b \rangle$ held at a point inside the path. For $x \in \mathcal{AP}_\perp$,

$$(w_1 \otimes_{\langle a,b \rangle} w_2)(x) = \begin{cases} w_2(\langle a, b \rangle) & \text{if } \langle a, b \rangle \in w_1(x) \\ w_2(\perp) & \text{otherwise} \end{cases}$$

We can now define the merging functions. If G is the set of global access expressions of the program, then for a call from a procedure with local access expressions L and binding weight $bind_{call}$ (i.e., the weight on the push rule), the merging function is defined as follows (where L_e denotes $L \cup \{.\}$):

$$g(w_1, w_2) = \mathbf{if}(w_1 = \bar{0} \text{ or } w_2 = \bar{0}) \text{ then } \bar{0}$$
$$\mathbf{else} \begin{pmatrix} (w_1 \otimes w_{L_e}) \\ \oplus \; (w_1 \otimes bind_{call} \otimes w_2 \otimes w_G) \\ \oplus \quad \bigoplus_{\langle a,l \rangle \in V \times L_e} ((w_1 \otimes_{\langle a,l \rangle} (bind_{call} \otimes w_2)) \otimes w_G^l) \\ \oplus \quad \bigoplus_{\langle l,a \rangle \in L_e \times V} ((w_1 \otimes_{\langle l,a \rangle} (bind_{call} \otimes w_2)) \otimes w_G^l) \end{pmatrix}$$

The first term in the combine copies over from the call site the pairs for local access expressions. The second term copies over from the called procedure's exit site the pairs for global access expressions. The third and fourth terms, which are combines over all pairs in $V \times L_e$ and $L_e \times V$, respectively, account for global-local access expressions, following the strategy discussed earlier in this section.

After the EWPDS is constructed, we can run an MOVP query with respect to the configuration set $C = \{\langle p, enter_{main} \rangle\}$ (where p is the single control location of the EWPDS), and obtain the may-alias pairs as follows,

$$may\text{-}alias(n) = \text{MOVP}(C, n\Gamma^*)(\perp).$$

In addition to computing the Landi-Ryder may-alias pairs, we can also answer stack-qualified queries about may-alias relationships. For instance, we can find out the may-alias pairs that hold at n_1 when execution ends in the stack configuration $\langle p, n_1 n_2 \cdots n_k \rangle$. As discussed in §1, such queries allow us to obtain more precise information than what is obtained by merely computing a may-aliasing query for paths that end at n_1 with *any* stack configuration.

5   Recent Developments

5.1   Improvements in Solver Technology

The algorithms given in [46, 41, 42] are based on saturation (and generalize the saturation procedure used for ordinary unweighted PDSs). Lal and Reps achieved substantial speedups over previous algorithms for WPDS reachability problems by using more sophisticated algorithms in the WPDS solver engine [29].

5.2   Analysis of Concurrent Programs

Two studies have used WPDSs to perform analyses of concurrent programs.

Chaki et al. [12] considers the model-checking problem for concurrent C programs with components that communicate via synchronizing actions (where components use data drawn from large-cardinality data domains and possibly-recursive procedure calls). They model such programs using *communicating pushdown systems*, and reduce the reachability problem for this model to deciding the emptiness of the intersection of two context-free languages L_1 and L_2. Because the latter problem is undecidable, their scheme uses counterexample-guided abstraction refinement of communicating Boolean programs. The technique was implemented as an extension to MAGIC [11], using WPDS++ [24] to perform reachability queries on the models for each component. The system was able to uncover a previously unknown bug in a version of a Windows NT Bluetooth driver.

Lal et al. [31] followed an approach pioneered by Qadeer and Rehof [38], who showed that analysis of concurrent recursive programs is decidable, for a finite-state abstraction of program data, when one limits the amount of concurrency by bounding the number of *context switches*. (A context switch is defined as the transfer of control from one thread to another.)

Such an approach has proven to be useful for program analysis because many bugs can be found in a few context switches [39, 38, 36]. Note that a *context-bounded analysis* (CBA) does not impose any bound on the execution length between context switches. Thus, even with a context-switch bound, the analysis still has to consider the possibility that the next switch takes place in any one of the (possibly infinite) states that may be reached after a context switch. Because of this, CBA still considers many concurrent behaviors [36].

Qadeer and Rehof [38] showed that CBA is decidable for recursive programs under a finite-state abstraction of program data. Lal et al. use WPDSs to generalize the Qadeer-Rehof result to a family of infinite-state abstractions (and also provide a new symbolic algorithm for the finite case). The insight behind the approach is to construct a *weighted transducer* to summarize the execution of a WPDS: the WPDS can go from configuration c_1 to configuration c_2 if and only if the pair (c_1, c_2) is in the language of the transducer. These transducers are composed to solve CBA.

5.3   Polyhedral Analysis

Recently, Denis Gopan in his Ph.D. thesis [19] presented a way to perform numeric program analysis with WPDSs using the polyhedral abstract domain [16]. One of the challenges that he faced was that the polyhedral domain has infinite descending chains, and hence widening techniques are required [13].

Widening is implemented using a weight wrapper that supports the normal weight interface extended with a few extra methods. Two types of weights are used: "regular weights" and "widening weights". Regular weights behave just like ordinary weights; widening weights are placed on WPDS rules where widening must occur (e.g., rules that correspond to backedges in the ICFG). In particular, if a widening weight b is used in a combine operation by the WPDS saturation procedure, the normal operation $a \oplus b$ is replaced by $a \bigtriangledown (a \oplus b)$, (where $\bigtriangledown$ is the standard widening operator).

References

1. Balakrishnan, G.: WYSINWYX: What You See Is Not What You eXecute. PhD thesis, Comp. Sci. Dept., Univ. of Wisconsin, Madison, WI, August 2007, Tech. Rep. 1603
2. Balakrishnan, G., Reps, T.: Analyzing memory accesses in x86 executables. In: Comp. Construct., pp. 5–23 (2004)
3. Balakrishnan, G., Reps, T., Kidd, N., Lal, A., Lim, J., Melski, D., Gruian, R., Yong, S., Chen, C.-H., Teitelbaum, T.: Model checking x86 executables with CodeSurfer/x86 and WPDS++. In: Computer Aided Verif. (2005)
4. Ball, T., Rajamani, S.K.: Bebop: A symbolic model checker for Boolean programs. In: Havelund, K., Penix, J., Visser, W. (eds.) SPIN Model Checking and Software Verification. LNCS, vol. 1885, pp. 113–130. Springer, Heidelberg (2000)
5. Ball, T., Rajamani, S.K.: Bebop: A path-sensitive interprocedural dataflow engine. In: Prog. Analysis for Softw. Tools and Eng., 97–103 (June 2001)
6. Bouajjani, A., Esparza, J., Maler, O.: Reachability analysis of pushdown automata: Application to model checking. In: Mazurkiewicz, A., Winkowski, J. (eds.) CONCUR 1997. LNCS, vol. 1243, pp. 135–150. Springer, Heidelberg (1997)
7. Bouajjani, A., Esparza, J., Touili, T.: A generic approach to the static analysis of concurrent programs with procedures. In: Princ. of Prog. Lang., pp. 62–73 (2003)
8. Bryant, R.E.: Graph-based algorithms for Boolean function manipulation. IEEE Trans. on Comp. C-35(6), 677–691 (1986)
9. Büchi, J.R.: Finite Automata, their Algebras and Grammars. In: Siefkes, D. (ed.), Springer, Heidelberg (1988)
10. Burkart, O., Steffen, B.: Model checking for context-free processes. In: Cleaveland, W.R. (ed.) CONCUR 1992. LNCS, vol. 630, pp. 123–137. Springer, Heidelberg (1992)
11. Chaki, S., Clarke, E., Groce, A., Jha, S., Veith, H.: Modular verification of software components in C. In: Int. Conf. on Softw. Eng. (2003)
12. Chaki, S., Clarke, E., Kidd, N., Reps, T., Touili, T.: Verifying concurrent message-passing C programs with recursive calls. Tools and Algs. for the Construct. and Anal. of Syst. (2006)
13. Cousot, P., Cousot, R.: Abstract interpretation: A unified lattice model for static analysis of programs by construction of approximation of fixed points. In: Princ. of Prog. Lang., pp. 238–252 (1977)
14. Cousot, P., Cousot, R.: Static determination of dynamic properties of recursive procedures. In: Neuhold, E.J. (ed.) Formal Descriptions of Programming Concepts, IFIP WG 2.2, St. Andrews, Canada, August 1977, pp. 237–277. North-Holland, Amsterdam (1978)
15. Cousot, P., Cousot, R.: Systematic design of program analysis frameworks. In: Princ. of Prog. Lang., pp. 269–282 (1979)
16. Cousot, P., Halbwachs, N.: Automatic discovery of linear constraints among variables of a program. In: Princ. of Prog. Lang., pp. 84–96 (1978)

17. Esparza, J., Hansel, D., Rossmanith, P., Schwoon, S.: Efficient algorithms for model checking pushdown systems. In: Emerson, E.A., Sistla, A.P. (eds.) CAV 2000. LNCS, vol. 1855, pp. 232–247. Springer, Heidelberg (2000)
18. Finkel, A., Willems, B., Wolper, P.: A direct symbolic approach to model checking pushdown systems. Elec. Notes in Theor. Comp. Sci. 9 (1997)
19. Gopan, D.: Numeric program analysis techniques with applications to array analysis and library summarization. PhD thesis, Comp. Sci. Dept., Univ. of Wisconsin, Madison, WI, August 2007. Tech. Rep. 1602
20. Graf, S., Saïdi, H.: Construction of abstract state graphs with PVS. In: Grumberg, O. (ed.) CAV 1997. LNCS, vol. 1254, pp. 72–83. Springer, Heidelberg (1997)
21. Gulwani, S., Necula, G.C.: Precise interprocedural analysis using random interpretation. In: Princ. of Prog. Lang. (2005)
22. Kam, J.B., Ullman, J.D.: Monotone data flow analysis frameworks. Acta Inf. 7(3), 305–318 (1977)
23. Karr, M.: Affine relationship among variables of a program. Acta Inf. 6, 133–151 (1976)
24. Kidd, N., Reps, T., Melski, D., Lal, A.: WPDS++: AC++ library for weighted pushdown systems (2004), http://www.cs.wisc.edu/wpis/wpds++/
25. Kildall, G.A.: A unified approach to global program optimization. In: Princ. of Prog. Lang., pp. 194–206 (1973)
26. Knoop, J., Steffen, B.: The interprocedural coincidence theorem. In: Comp. Construct., pp. 125–140 (1992)
27. Kodumal, J., Aiken, A.: Banshee: A scalable constraint-based analysis toolkit. In: Static Analysis Symp. (2005)
28. Lal, A., Lim, J., Polishchuk, M., Liblit, B.: Path optimization in programs and its application to debugging. In: European Symp. on Programming (2006)
29. Lal, A., Reps, T.: Improving pushdown system model checking. In: Computer Aided Verif. (2006)
30. Lal, A., Reps, T., Balakrishnan, G.: Extended weighted pushdown systems. In: Computer Aided Verif. (2005)
31. Lal, A., Touili, T., Kidd, N., Reps, T.: Interprocedural analysis of concurrent programs under a context bound. Tech. Rep. TR-1598, Comp. Sci. Dept., Univ. of Wisconsin, Madison, WI (July 2007)
32. Landi, W., Ryder, B.G.: Pointer induced aliasing: A problem classification. In: Princ. of Prog. Lang., January 1991, pp. 93–103 (1991)
33. Martin, F.: PAG – An efficient program analyzer generator. Softw. Tools for Tech. Transfer (1998)
34. Müller-Olm, M., Seidl, H.: Precise interprocedural analysis through linear algebra. In: Princ. of Prog. Lang. (2004)
35. Müller-Olm, M., Seidl, H.: Analysis of modular arithmetic. In: European Symp. on Programming (2005)
36. Musuvathi, M., Qadeer, S.: Iterative context bounding for systematic testing of multithreaded programs. In: Prog. Lang. Design and Impl. (2007)
37. Nielson, F., Nielson, H.R., Hankin, C.: Principles of Program Analysis. Springer, Heidelberg (1999)
38. Qadeer, S., Rehof, J.: Context-bounded model checking of concurrent software. In: Tools and Algs. for the Construct. and Anal. of Syst. (2005)
39. Qadeer, S., Wu, D.: KISS: Keep it simple and sequential. In: Prog. Lang. Design and Impl. (2004)
40. Reps, T., Horwitz, S., Sagiv, M.: Precise interprocedural dataflow analysis via graph reachability. In: Princ. of Prog. Lang., pp. 49–61 (1995)

41. Reps, T., Schwoon, S., Jha, S.: Weighted pushdown systems and their application to interprocedural dataflow analysis. In: Static Analysis Symp., pp. 189–213 (2003)
42. Reps, T., Schwoon, S., Jha, S., Melski, D.: Weighted pushdown systems and their application to interprocedural dataflow analysis. Sci. of Comp. Prog. 58(1–2), 206–263 (2005)
43. Sagiv, M., Reps, T., Horwitz, S.: Precise interprocedural dataflow analysis with applications to constant propagation. Theor. Comp. Sci. 167, 131–170 (1996)
44. Schwoon, S.: Model-Checking Pushdown Systems. PhD thesis, Technical Univ. of Munich, Munich, Germany (July 2002)
45. Schwoon, S.: WPDS: A library for weighted pushdown systems (2003), `http://www.fmi.uni-stuttgart.de/szs/tools/wpds/`
46. Schwoon, S., Jha, S., Reps, T., Stubblebine, S.: On generalized authorization problems. In: Comp. Sec. Found. Workshop (2003)
47. Sharir, M., Pnueli, A.: Two approaches to interprocedural data flow analysis. In: Muchnick, S.S., Jones, N.D. (eds.) Program Flow Analysis: Theory and Applications, (ch. 7), pp. 189–234. Prentice-Hall, Englewood Cliffs, NJ (1981)
48. Whaley, J., Avots, D., Carbin, M., Lam, M.S.: Using Datalog with Binary Decision Diagrams for program analysis. In: Asian Symp. on Prog. Lang. and Systems (2005)

The Complexity of Zero Knowledge

Salil Vadhan*

School of Engineering and Applied Science
Harvard University
Cambridge, MA 02138
salil@eecs.harvard.edu
http://eecs.harvard.edu/~salil

Abstract. We give an informal introduction to zero-knowledge proofs, and survey their role both in the interface between complexity theory and cryptography and as objects of complexity-theoretic study in their own right.

1 Introduction

Zero-knowledge proofs are interactive protocols whereby one party, the *prover*, can convince another, the *verifier*, that some assertion is true with the remarkable property that the verifier learns nothing other than the fact that the assertion being proven is true. In the quarter-century since they were introduced by Goldwasser, Micali, and Rackoff [GMR], zero-knowledge proofs have played a central role in the design and study of cryptographic protocols. In addition, they have provided one of the most fertile grounds for interaction between complexity theory and cryptography, leading to exciting developments in each area. It is the role of zero knowledge in this interaction that is the subject of the present survey.

We begin with an informal introduction to zero-knowledge proofs in Section 2, using two classic examples. In Section 3, we survey how zero-knowledge proofs have provided an avenue for ideas and techniques to flow in both directions between cryptography and complexity theory. In Section 4, we survey the way in which zero knowledge has turned out to be interesting as a complexity-theoretic object of study on its own. We conclude in Section 5 with some directions for further research.

2 Definitions and Examples

In this section, we provide an informal introduction to zero-knowledge proofs. For a more detailed treatment, we refer the reader to [Vad1, Gol].

---

* Written while visiting U.C. Berkeley, supported by the Miller Institute for Basic Research in Science, a Guggenheim Fellowship, and NSF grant CNS-0430336.

V. Arvind and S. Prasad (Eds.): FSTTCS 2007, LNCS 4855, pp. 52–70, 2007.

Interactive Proofs and Arguments. Before discussing what it means for a proof to be "zero knowledge," we need to reconsider what we mean by a "proof." The classical mathematical notion of proof is as a static object that can be written down once and for all, and then easily verified by anyone according to fixed rules. It turns out that the power of such classical proofs can be captured by the complexity class NP. To make this precise, we consider the assertions to be proven as strings over some fixed alphabet, and consider a language L that identifies the assertions that are 'true'. For example, language SAT contains a string x iff x encodes a boolean formula ϕ such that the assertion "ϕ is satisfiable" is true. Then a *proof system* for a language L is given by a verification algorithm V with the following properties:

- (Completeness) True assertions have proofs. That is, if $x \in L$, then there exists π such that $V(x, \pi) = \texttt{accept}$.
- (Soundness) False assertions have no proofs. That is, if $x \notin L$, then for all π^*, $V(x, \pi^*) = \texttt{reject}$.
- (Efficiency) $V(x, \pi)$ runs in time poly($|x|$).

It is well-known that NP is exactly the class of languages having classical proof systems as defined above. (Indeed, NP is now often defined in this way, cf. [Sip].) Thus the P vs. NP question asks whether proofs actually help in deciding the validity of assertions, or whether deciding validity without a proof can always be done in time comparable to the time it takes to verify a proof.

Now zero-knowledge proofs are concerned with the question of how much one *learns* when verifying a proof. By definition, one learns that the assertion being proven is true. But we typically think of mathematical proofs as teaching us much more. Indeed, when given a classical NP proof, one also gains the ability to convince others that the same assertion is true, by copying the same proof. To get around this obstacle and make it possible to have proofs that leak "zero knowledge," Goldwasser, Micali, and Rackoff [GMR] added two ingredients to the classical notion of proof. The first is *randomization* — the verification of proofs can be probabilistic, and may err with a small but controllable error probability. The second ingredient is *interaction* — the static, written proof is replaced by a dynamic *prover* who exchanges messages with the verifier and tries to convince it to accept.

In more detail, we consider an interactive protocol (P, V) between a "prover" algorithm P and a "verifier" algorithm V. P and V are given a common input x, they each may privately toss coins, and then they exchange up to polynomially many messages (where the next message of each party is obtained by applying the appropriate algorithm P or V to the common input, the party's private coin tosses, and the transcript of messages exchanged so far). At the end of the interaction, the verifier accepts or rejects. We denote by $(P, V)(x)$ the interaction between P and V on input x. Analogous to classical proofs, we require the following properties:

- (Completeness) If $x \in L$, then V accepts in $(P, V)(x)$ with probability at least 2/3.
- (Soundness) If $x \notin L$, then for "all" P^*, V accepts in $(P^*, V)(x)$ with probability at most 1/3.
- (Efficiency) On common input x, V always runs in time poly($|x|$).

A consequence of the efficiency condition is that the total length of communication between the two parties is bounded by a polynomial in $|x|$. As with randomized algorithms, the constants of 2/3 and 1/3 in the completeness and soundness probabilities are arbitrary, and can be made be exponentially close to 1 and 0, respectively, by repeating the protocol many times and having the verifier rule by majority.

We think of the soundness condition as a "security" property because it protects the verifier from adversarial behavior by the prover. Like most security properties in cryptography, it has two commonly used versions:

- (Statistical Soundness) If $x \notin L$, then for all, even *computationally unbounded*, strategies P^*, V accepts in $(P^*, V)(x)$ with probability at most 1/3. This gives rise to *interactive proof systems*, the original model of [GMR].
- (Computational Soundness) If $x \notin L$, then for all (nonuniform) *polynomial-time* strategies P^*, V accepts in $(P^*, V)(x)$ with probability at most 1/3. This gives rise to *interactive argument systems*, a model proposed by Brassard, Chaum, and Crépeau [BCC].

Note that the honest prover P must have some computational advantage over the verifier to be of any use. Otherwise, the verifier could simply simulate the prover on its own, implying that the language L is decidable in probabilistic polynomial time (i.e. in the complexity class BPP). Thus, typically one either allows the honest prover P to be computationally unbounded or requires P to be polynomial time but provides it with an NP witness for the membership of x in L. The former choice is mainly of complexity-theoretic interest, and is usually made only for interactive proof systems, since they also provide security against computationally unbounded cheating provers. The latter choice, where the prover is efficient given a witness, is the one most appropriate for cryptographic applications.

Zero Knowledge. While interactive proofs and arguments are already fascinating notions on their own (cf., [LFKN, Sha, Kil, Mic]), here we are interested in when such protocols possess a "zero knowledge" property — where the verifier learns nothing other than the fact that the assertion being proven is true. Before discussing how zero-knowledge can be defined precisely, we illustrate the notion with a classic example for GRAPH NONISOMORPHISM. Here an instance is a pair of graphs (G_0, G_1), and it is a YES instance if G_0 and G_1 are nonisomorphic (written $G_0 \not\cong G_1$), and a NO instance if they are isomorphic (written $G_0 \cong G_1$).

The zero-knowledge proof is based on two observations. First, if two graphs are non-isomorphic, then their sets of isomorphic copies are disjoint. Second, if two graphs are isomorphic, then a random isomorphic copy of one graph is indistinguishable from a random isomorphic copy of the other (both have the same distribution). Thus, the proof system, given in Protocol 2.1, tests whether the (computationally unbounded) prover can distinguish between random isomorphic copies of the two graphs.

Protocol 2.1. Interactive proof (P, V) for GRAPH NONISOMORPHISM
Common Input: Graphs G_0 and G_1 on vertex set $[n]$

1. V: Select a random bit $b \in \{0, 1\}$. Select a uniformly random permutation π on $[n]$. Let H be the graph obtained by permuting the vertices of G_b according to π. Send H to P.
2. P: If $G_0 \cong H$, let $c = 0$. Else let $c = 1$. Send c to V.
3. V: If $c = b$, accept. Otherwise, reject.

We first verify that this protocol meets the definition of an interactive proof system. If G_0 and G_1 are nonisomorphic, then $G_0 \cong H$ if and only if $b = 0$. So the prover strategy specified above will make the verifier accept with probability 1. Thus completeness is satisfied. On the other hand, if G_0 and G_1 are isomorphic, then H has the same distribution when $b = 0$ as it does when $b = 1$ Thus, b is independent of H and the prover has at most probability at most $1/2$ of guessing b correctly *no matter what strategy it follows*. This shows that the protocol is sound.

For zero knowledge, observe that the only information sent from the prover to the verifier is the guess c for the verifier's coin toss b. As argued above, when the statement being proven is true (i.e. $G_0 \ncong H$), this guess is always correct. That is, the prover is sending the verifier a value that it already knows. Intuitively, this means that the verifier learns nothing from the protocol. (Note that this intuition relies on the assumption that the verifier follows the specified protocol, and actually constructs the graph H by permuting one of the two input graphs.)

The notion of zero knowledge is formalized by requiring that the verifier could have simulated everything it sees in the interaction on its own. That is, there should be a probabilistic polynomial-time, noninteractive algorithm S, called the *simulator*, that when given[1] "any" verifier strategy V^* and any instance $x \in L$, produces an output that is "indistinguishable" from the verifier's view of its interaction with the prover on input x (i.e. the transcript of the interaction together with the verifier's private coin tosses). Zero knowledge is a security property, protecting the prover from leaking unnecessary information to

---

[1] In this informal survey, we do not discuss the ways in which the simulator can be 'given' a verifier strategy. One possibility is that the simulator is given the code of the verifier, e.g. as a boolean circuit, which gives rise to the notion of *auxiliary-input zero knowledge* [GO]. Another is that the simulator is given the verifier strategy as an oracle, which gives rise to the notion of *black-box zero knowledge* [GO].

an adversarial verifier, and thus comes in both statistical and computational versions. With *statistical zero knowledge*, we require that the zero-knowledge condition hold for even computationally unbounded verifier strategies V^*, and require that the output of the simulator is statistically close (e.g. in variation distance) to the verifier's view. With *computational zero knowledge*, we only require the zero-knowledge condition to hold for (nonuniform) polynomial-time verifier strategies V^* and require that the output of the simulator "computationally indistinguishable" from the verifier's view of the interaction, which means that no (nonuniform) polynomial-time algorithm can distinguish the two distributions except with negligible probability.

For the GRAPH NONISOMORPHISM protocol above, it is easy to illustrate a simulator that produces a distribution that is *identical* to the view of "honest" verifier V, but the protocol does not appear to be zero knowledge for verifier strategies V^* that deviate from the specified protocol. Thus we refer to the protocol as being *honest-verifier* statistical zero knowledge (or even honest-verifier *perfect* zero knowledge, since the simulation produces exactly the correct distribution). Honest-verifier zero knowledge is already a very nontrivial and interesting notion, but cryptographic applications usually require the stronger and more standard notion of zero knowledge against cheating verifier strategies V^*. This stronger notion can be achieved for GRAPH NONISOMORPHISM using a more sophisticated protocol [GMW]. Thus we have:

Theorem 2.2 ([GMW]). GRAPH NONISOMORPHISM *has a statistical zero-knowledge proof system (in fact a perfect zero-knowledge proof system).*

This provides an example of the power of zero-knowledge proofs (and also of interactive proofs, since GRAPH NONISOMORPHISM is not known to be in NP). An even more striking demonstration, however, is general construction of zero-knowledge proofs for all of NP, also due to [GMW].

Zero Knowledge for NP. To achieve this, Goldreich, Micali, and Wigderson [GMW] observed that it suffices to give a zero-knowledge proof for a single NP-complete problem, such as GRAPH 3-COLORING. A *3-coloring* of a graph $G = ([n], E)$ is an assignment $C : [n] \to \{R, G, B\}$ (for "Red," "Green," and "Blue") such that no pair of adjacent vertices are assigned the same color. GRAPH 3-COLORING is the language consisting of graphs G that are 3-colorable.

The zero-knowledge proof for GRAPH 3-COLORING is based on the observation that the classical NP proof can be broken into "pieces" and randomized in such a way that (a) the entire proof is valid if and only if every piece is valid, yet (b) each piece reveals nothing on its own. For GRAPH 3-COLORING, the classical proof is a three-coloring of the graph, and the pieces are the restriction of the coloring to the individual edges: (a) An assignment of colors to vertices of the graph is a proper 3-coloring if and only if the endpoints of every edge have distinct colors, yet (b) if the three colors are randomly permuted, then the colors assigned to the endpoints of any particular edge are merely a random pair of distinct colors and hence reveal nothing.

In Protocol 2.3, we show how to use the above observations to obtain a zero-knowledge proof for GRAPH 3-COLORING which makes use of "physical" implements — namely opaque, lockable boxes. The actual proof system will obtained by replacing these boxes with a suitable cryptographic primitive.

Protocol 2.3. "Physical" Proof System (P, V) for GRAPH 3-COLORING
Common Input: A graph $G = ([n], E)$

1. P: Let C be any 3-coloring of G (either given as an auxiliary input to a polynomial-time P, or found by exhaustive search in case we allow P to be computationally unbounded). Let π be a permutation of $\{R, G, B\}$ selected uniformly at random. Let $C' = \pi \circ C$.
2. P: For every vertex $v \in [n]$, place $C'(v)$ inside a box B_v, lock the box using a key K_v, and send the box B_v to V.
3. V: Select an edge $e = (x, y) \in E$ uniformly at random and send e to P.
4. P: Receive edge $e = (x, y) \in E$, and send the keys K_x and K_y to V.
5. V: Unlock the boxes B_x and B_y, and accept if the colors inside are different.

We now explain why this protocol works. For completeness, first observe that if C is a proper 3-coloring of G then so is C'. Thus, no matter which edge $(x, y) \in E$ the verifier selects, the colors $C'(x)$ and $C'(y)$ inside boxes B_x and B_y will be different. Therefore, the verifier accepts with probability 1 when G is 3-colorable.

For soundness, consider the colors inside the boxes sent by the prover in Step 2 as assigning a color to each vertex of G. If G is not 3-colorable, then it must be the case that for some edge $(x, y) \in E$, B_x and B_y contain the same color. So the verifier will reject with probability at least $1/|E|$. By repeating the protocol $|E| + 1$ times, the probability that the verifier accepts on a non-3-colorable graph G will be reduced to $(1 - 1/|E|)^{|E|+1} < 1/3$.

To argue that Protocol 2.3 is "zero knowledge," let's consider what a verifier "sees" in an execution of the protocol (when the graph is 3-colorable). The verifier sees n boxes $\{B_v\}$, all of which are locked and opaque, except for a pair B_x, B_y corresponding to an edge in G. For that pair, the keys K_x and K_y are given and the colors $C'(x)$ and $C'(y)$ are revealed. Of all this, only $C'(x)$ and $C'(y)$ can potentially leak knowledge to the verifier. However, since the coloring is randomly permuted by π, $C'(x)$ and $C'(y)$ are simply a (uniformly) random pair of distinct colors from $\{R, G, B\}$, and clearly this is something the verifier can generate on its own.

In this intuitive argument, we have reasoned as if the verifier selects the edge (x, y) in advance, or at least independently of the permutation π. This would of course be true if the verifier follows the specified protocol and selects the edge randomly, but the definition of zero knowledge requires that we also consider cheating verifier strategies whose edge selection may depend on the messages previously received from the prover (i.e., the collection of boxes). However, the perfect opaqueness of the boxes guarantees that the verifier has no information about their contents, so we can indeed view (x, y) as being selected in advance by the verifier, prior to receiving any messages from the prover.

What is left is to describe how to implement the physical boxes algorithmically. This is done with a cryptographic primitive known as a *commitment scheme*. It is a two-stage interactive protocol between a pair of probabilistic polynomial-time parties, called the *sender* and the *receiver*. In the first stage, the sender "commits" to a string m, corresponding to locking an object in the box, as done in Step 2 of Protocol 2.3. In the second stage, the sender "reveals" m to the receiver, corresponding to opening the box, as done in Steps 4 and 5 of Protocol 2.3.

Like zero-knowledge protocols, commitment schemes have two security properties. Informally, *hiding* says that a cheating receiver should not be able to learn anything about m during the commit stage, and *binding* says that a cheating sender should not be able to reveal two different messages after the commit stage. Again, each of these properties can be statistical (holding against computationally unbounded cheating strategies, except with negligible probability) or computational (holding against polynomial-time cheating strategies, except with negligible probability). Thus we again get four flavors of commitment schemes, but it is easily seen to be impossible to simultaneously achieve statistical security for both hiding and binding. However, as long as we allow one of the security properties to be computational, it seems likely that commitment schemes exist. Indeed, commitment schemes with either statistical binding or statistical hiding can be constructed from any one-way function (a function that is easy to compute, but hard to invert even on random outputs) [HILL, Nao, NOV, HR], and the existence of one-way functions is the most basic assumption of complexity-based cryptography [DH, IL]. Thus, we conclude:

Theorem 2.4. *If one-way functions exist, then every language in NP has both a computational zero-knowledge proof system and a statistical zero-knowledge argument system.*

We note that the first construction of statistical zero-knowledge argument systems was given by Brassard, Chaum, and Crépeau [BCC], independently of [GMW], but was based on stronger cryptographic primitives than just statistically hiding commitment schemes.

3   Zero Knowledge as an Interface

In this section, we survey the way in which zero-knowledge proofs have provided an avenue for ideas and techniques to be transported between complexity theory and cryptography.

The concept of zero-knowledge proofs originated with efforts to formalize problems arising in the design of cryptographic protocols (such as [LMR]), where it is often the case that one party needs to convince another of some fact without revealing too much information. However, as evidenced even by the title of their paper "The Knowledge Complexity of Interactive Proof Systems," Goldwasser, Micali, and Rackoff [GMR] seemed to recognize the significance of the new notions for complexity theory as well. Indeed, interactive proof systems (as well as the Arthur–Merlin games independently introduced by Babai [Bab], which turned out to be equivalent in power [GS]), soon became a central concept in complexity theory. Their power was completely characterized in the remarkable works of Lund, Fortnow, Karloff, and Nisan [LFKN] and Shamir [Sha], which showed that IP, the class of languages having interactive proofs, equals PSPACE, the class of languages decidable in polynomial space. Since PSPACE is believed to be much larger than NP, this result shows that interactive proofs are much more powerful than classical written proofs.

In the other direction, we have already seen how a powerful concept from complexity theory, namely NP-completeness, was leveraged in the study zero-knowledge proofs, namely, Theorem 2.4. Traditionally, we think of NP-completeness as being used for negative purposes, to give evidence that a problem is hard, but here it has been used in a positive way — zero-knowledge proofs were obtained for an entire class by constructing them for a single complete problem. This discovery of zero-knowledge proofs for all of NP played a crucial role in striking general results of [Yao, GMW] about *secure computation*, where several parties engage in a protocol to jointly compute a function on their private inputs in such a way that no party learns anything other than the output of the protocol. These landmark results of [Yao, GMW] say that every polynomial-time computable function can be computed securely in this sense. Zero knowledge plays a crucial role, enabling the parties to convince each other that they are following the specified protocol, without revealing their private input.

In the study of secure computation, researchers realized that the use of complexity assumptions (e.g. the existence of one-way functions) could be removed by working in a model with private communication channels [CCD, BGW]. Similarly, Ben-Or, Goldwasser, Kilian, and Wigderson [BGKW] introduced the *multiprover* model for interactive proofs, where two or more noncommunicating provers try to convince the verifier of an assertion, and the verifier can interrogate with each prover on a private channel that is inaccessible to the other prover(s) (similarly to how detectives interrogate suspects). The main motivation of [BGKW] was to find a model in which zero-knowledge protocols for all of NP could be obtained without any complexity assumption (in contrast to Theorem 2.4). However, multiprover interactive proofs turned out to be even more significant for complexity theory than interactive proofs were. Following the proof that IP = PSPACE mentioned above, Babai, Fortnow, and Lund [BFL] showed that the class MIP of languages having *multiprover* interactive proofs equals NEXP, nondeterministic exponential time, a class that is provably larger than NP (by diagonalization). Multiprover interactive proofs also turned out to be equivalent in power to *probabilistically checkable proofs* (PCPs) [FRS]. PCPs are static strings, like classical NP proofs, but can be verified probabilistically by a verifier that reads only a small portion of the proof. Scaling down the proof that MIP = NEXP and incorporating a number of new ideas led to the celebrated PCP Theorem[BFLS, FGL+, AS, ALM+], showing that membership in any NP language can be proven using PCPs that can be verified by reading only a constant number of bits of the proof. The significance of the PCP Theorem was magnified by a surprising connection between PCP constructions for NP and showing that NP-complete optimization problems are hard to *approximate* [FGL+, ALM+], the latter being an open question from the early days of NP-completeness. A long line of subsequent work (beyond the scope of this survey) has optimized PCP constructions in order to get tight inapproximability results for a variety of NP-complete optimization problems.

The PCP Theorem provided returns to zero knowledge and cryptography through the work of Kilian [Kil], who used it to construct zero-knowledge *argument* systems for NP in which the verifier's computation time depends only polylogarithmically (rather than polynomially) on the length of the statement being proven. A generalization of Kilian's work, due to Micali [Mic], was used in [CGH] to obtain negative results about realizing the "random oracle model," which is an idealized model sometimes used in the design of cryptographic protocols. This technique of [CGH] was an inspiration for Barak's breakthrough work on "non-black-box simulation" zero knowledge [Bar1]. In this work, Barak showed how to exploit the actual code of the adversarial verifier's strategy to simulate a zero knowledge protocol (rather than merely treating the verifier as a black-box subroutine). Using this method, Barak obtained a zero-knowledge argument system with properties that were known to be impossible with black-box simulation [GK1]. Subsequently, non-black-box use of the adversary's code has proved to be useful in the solution of a number of other cryptographic problems, particularly ones concerned with maintaining security when several protocols are being executed concurrently [Bar2, PR1, Lin, Pas, PR2, BS].

4   Zero Knowledge as an Object of Study

We now turn zero knowledge as a complexity-theoretic object of study in itself. By this, we refer to the study of the complexity classes consisting of the languages that have zero-knowledge protocols of various types. We have already seen in the previous section that the classes IP and MIP arising from interactive proofs and their multiprover variant turned out to be very interesting and useful for complexity theory, and we might hope for the same to occur when we impose the zero knowledge constraint. From a philosophical point of view, it seems interesting to understand to what extent the requirement that we do not leak knowledge restricts the kinds of assertions we can prove. For cryptography, the complexity-theoretic study of zero knowledge can illuminate the limits of what can be achieved with zero-knowledge protocols, yield new techniques useful for other cryptographic problems, and help understand the relation of zero knowledge to other primitives in cryptography.

Recall that zero-knowledge protocols have two security conditions—soundness and zero knowledge—and these each come in both statistical and computational versions. Thus we obtain four main flavors of zero knowledge protocols, and thus four complexity classes consisting of the languages that zero-knowledge protocols of a particular type. We denote these classes SZKP, CZKP, SZKA, and CZKA, with the prefix of S or C indicating statistical or computational zero knowledge and the suffix of P or A denoting interactive proofs (statistical soundness) or arguments (computational soundness). The main goals are to characterize these classes, for example via complete problems or establishing relations with other, better-understand complexity classes; to establish properties of these classes (eg closure under various operations); and to obtain general results about zero-knowledge protocols. The first result along these lines was Theorem 2.4, which showed that the zero-knowledge classes involving computational security (namely, CZKP, SZKA, and CZKA) contain all of NP if one-way functions exist. Aside from this initial result and a follow-up that we will discuss later [IY, BGG+], much of the complexity-theoretic study of zero knowledge was developed first for SZKP.

4.1 Statistical Security: SZKP

From a security point of view, statistical zero-knowledge proofs are of course the most attractive of the four types of zero-knowledge protocols we are discussing, since their security properties hold regardless of the computational power of the adversary. So the first question is whether this high level of security is achievable for nontrivial languages (i.e. ones that cannot be decided in probabilistic polynomial time). We have already seen one candidate, GRAPH NONISOMORPHISM, and in fact SZKP is known to contain a number of other specific problems believed to be hard, such as GRAPH ISOMORPHISM [GMW], QUADRATIC RESIDUOSITY and QUADRATIC NONRESIDUOSITY [GMR], a problem equivalent to the DISCRETE LOG [GK2], approximate versions of the SHORTEST VECTOR PROBLEM and CLOSEST VECTOR PROBLEM in high-dimensional lattices [GG], and various group-theoretic problems [AD]. On the other hand, recall that the general construction of zero-knowledge protocols for NP (Theorem 2.4) does not yield SZKP protocols, because (because there do not exist commitment schemes that are simultaneously statistically hiding and statistically binding). This phenomenon was explained in the work of Fortnow, Aiello, and Håstad [For, AH], who made the first progress towards a complexity-theoretic characterization of SZKP. Specifically, they showed that SZKP is contained in AM ∩ coAM, where the complexity class AM is a randomized analogue of NP, and consequently deduced that SZKP is unlikely to contain NP-hard problems. Indeed an NP-hard problem in SZKP $\subseteq$ AM$\cap$coAM implies that AM = coAM, which seems unlikely for the same reason that NP = co-NP seems unlikely — there is no reason that a efficient provability of statements ($x \in L$) should imply efficient provability of their negations ($x \notin L$). (Like NP = co-NP, AM = coAM also implies the collapse of the polynomial-time hierarchy, which is commonly conjectured to be infinite).

The next major steps in our understanding of SZKP came in the work of Okamoto [Oka], who proved that (a) SZKP is closed under complement, and (b) every language in SZKP has a statistical zero-knowledge proof system that is *public coin*, meaning that the verifier's messages consist only of random coin tosses (a property that holds for the GRAPH 3-COLORING protocol in the previous section, but not the GRAPH NONISOMORPHISM protocol).[2] The first result, closure under complement, was particularly surprising, because as mentioned above, there is no reason to believe that the existence of proofs for certain statements should imply anything about the negations of those statements. However, it was the second result that proved most useful in subsequent work, because public-coin protocols are much easier to analyze and manipulate than general, private-coin protocol. (Indeed, the equivalence of private coins and public coins for (non-zero-knowledge) interactive proofs [GS], found numerous applications, e.g. [BM, GS, BHZ, FGM+].)

Using Okamoto's result as a starting point, SZKP was characterized exactly by two natural complete problems.[3] The first was STATISTICAL DIFFERENCE [SV], which amounts to the problem of approximating the statistical difference (i.e. variation distance) between two efficiently samplable distributions (specified by boolean circuits that sample from the distributions). The second problem, ENTROPY DIFFERENCE [GV], amounts to approximating the difference in the entropies of two efficiently samplable distributions (which is computationally equivalent to approximating the entropy of a single efficiently samplable distributions). In addition to providing a simple characterization of SZKP (as the class of problems that reduce to either of the complete problems), these complete problems show that the class SZKP is of interest beyond the study of zero-knowledge proofs. Indeed, estimating statistical properties of efficiently samplable distributions is a natural algorithmic task, and now we see that its complexity is captured by the class SZKP.

---

[2] Okamoto's results were actually proven for *honest-verifier* statistical zero knowledge, but, as mentioned below, it was subsequently shown that every honest-verifier statistical zero-knowledge proof can be transformed into one that tolerates cheating verifiers [GSV1].

[3] The complete problems for SZKP, as well as some of the other problems mentioned to be in SZKP are not actually languages, but rather *promise problems*. In a promise problem, some strings are YES instances, some strings are NO instances, and the rest are excluded (i.e. we are promised that the input is either a YES instance or a NO instance). Languages correspond to the special case where there are no excluded inputs.

Using Okamoto's results and the complete problems, other general results about statistical zero knowledge were obtained, including more closure properties [DDPY, SV], an equivalence between honest-verifier SZKP and general, cheating-verifier SZKP [DGW, GSV1], an equivalence between efficient-prover SZKP and unbounded-prover SZKP for problems in NP [MV, NV], and relations between SZKP and other models of zero-knowledge protocols [GSV2, DSY, BG2]. There have also been studies of the relation between SZKP and quantum computation, including both the question of whether every problem in SZKP has a polynomial-time quantum algorithm [Aar, AT] and a complexity-theoretic study of the quantum analogue of SZKP [Wat].

4.2 Computational Security: CZKP, SZKA, and CZKA

Perhaps one reason that the complexity theory of SZKP developed more rapidly than that of the classes involving computational security is that early results seemed to indicate the latter were completely understood. Indeed, Theorem 2.4 says that under standard complexity assumptions, all of the classes CZKP, SZKA, and CZKA are very powerful, in that they contain all of NP. Soon afterwards, this result was strengthened was extended to give zero-knowledge proofs for all of IP [IY, BGG$^+$], again under the assumption that one-way functions exist. (This result allows for the honest prover to be computationally unbounded. For efficient honest provers, IP should be replaced by MA, which is a slight generalization of NP in which the verifier is a randomized algorithm.)

In cryptography, the assumption that one-way functions exist is standard; indeed, most of modern cryptography would not be able to get off the ground without it. However, from a complexity-theoretic perspective, there is a significant difference between results that make an unproven assumption and those that are unconditional. So a natural question is whether the assumption that one-way functions is really necessary to prove Theorem 2.4 and to characterize the power of zero knowledge with computational security.

Partial converses to Theorem 2.4, suggesting that one-way functions are necessary, were given by Ostrovsky and Wigderson [OW], building on an earlier work of Ostrovsky [Ost] about SZKP. Ostrovsky and Wigderson first proved that if there is a zero-knowledge protocol (even with both security properties computational) for a "hard-on-average" language, then one-way functions exist. Thus, we get a "gap theorem" for zero knowledge: either one-way functions exist and zero knowledge is very powerful, or one-way functions do not exist, and zero knowledge is relatively weak. They also proved that if there is a zero-knowledge protocol for a language not in BPP (probabilistic polynomial time), then a "weak form" of one-way functions exist. (Note that we do not expect to deduce anything for languages in BPP, since every language in BPP has a trivial perfect zero knowledge proof, in which the prover sends nothing and the verifier decides membership on its own.)

While it was a major step in our understanding of zero knowledge, the Ostrovsky–Wigderson Theorems [OW] do not provide a complete characterization of the classes CZKA, CZKP, and SZKA. The reason is that for languages that are neither hard on average nor in BPP, we only get the "weak form" of one-way functions of their second result, which do not seem to suffice for constructing commitment schemes and hence zero-knowledge protocols. Exact characterizations were obtained more recently, using a variant of the Ostrovsky–Wigderson approach [Vad2, OV]. Instead of doing a case analysis based on whether a language is in BPP or not, we consider whether a language is in SZKP or not, and thus are able to replace the "weak form" of one-way functions with something much closer to the standard notion of one-way functions. Specifically, it was shown that every language L in CZKA can be "decomposed" into a problem[4] in SZKP together with a set I of instances from which (finite analogues of) one-way functions can be constructed. Conversely, every problem in NP having such a decomposition is in CZKA. A similar characterization is obtained for CZKP by additionally requiring that I contains only strings in L, and for SZKA by requiring that I contain only strings not in L. These results, referred to as the SZKP–OWF CHARACTERIZATIONS, reduce the study of the computational forms of zero knowledge to the study of SZKP together with the consequences of one-way functions, both of which are well-understood. Indeed, using these characterizations, a variety of unconditional general results were proven about the classes CZKP, SZKA, and CZKA, such as closure properties, the equivalence of honest-verifier zero knowledge and general, cheating-verifier zero knowledge, and the equivalence of efficient-prover and unbounded-prover zero knowledge [Vad2, NV, OV]. Moreover, ideas developed in this line of work on unconditional results, such as [NV], turned out to be helpful also for conditional results, specifically the construction of statistically hiding commitments from arbitrary one-way functions [NOV, HR], which resolved a long-standing open problem in the foundations of cryptography (previously, statistically hiding commitments were only known from stronger complexity assumptions, such as the existence of one-way *permutations* [NOVY]).

5   Future Directions

Recall that our discussion of zero knowledge as an interface between complexity and cryptography in Section 3 ended with the non-black-box zero-knowledge protocol of Barak [Bar1], which found a variety of other applications in cryptography. It seems likely that the Barak's work will also have an impact on complexity theory as well. In particular, it points to the potential power of "non-black-box reductions" between computational problems. Typically, when we say that computational problem A "reduces" to computational problem B, we mean that we can efficiently solve A given access to a black box that solves problem B. We interpret such a reduction as saying that A is no harder than B. In particular, if B can be solved efficiently, so can A. However, it is possible to establish implications of the latter form without exhibiting a (black-box) reduction in the usual sense, because it may be possible to exploit an *efficient*

---

[4] Again, the SZKP problems referred to by the SZKP–OWF CHARACTERIZATIONS are actually promise problems.

algorithm for B in ways that we cannot exploit a black-box for B (e.g. by directly using the code of the algorithm in some way). While we have had examples of "non-black-box reductions" in complexity theory for a long time (such as the collapse of the entire polynomial hierarchy to P if P = NP), Barak's work has begun to inspire complexity theorists to reexamine whether known limitations of black-box reductions (such as for worst-case/average-case connections [BT]) can be bypassed with various types of non-black-box reductions [GT].

In terms of the complexity-theoretic study of SZKP, one intriguing open problem is to find a combinatorial or number-theoretic complete problem. The known complete problems [SV, GV] can be argued to be "natural," but they still make an explicit reference to computation (since the input distributions are specified by boolean circuits). Finding a combinatorial or number-theoretic complete problem would likely further illuminate the class SZKP, and would also provide strong evidence that the particular problem is intractable. We are currently lacking in ways to provide evidence that problems are intractable short of showing them to be NP-hard. The recent sequence of results showing that NASH EQUILIBRIUM is complete for the class PPAD [DGP, CD] is one of the few exceptions. Approximate versions of lattice problems (see [GG, MV]) seem to be promising candidates for SZKP-completeness.

Another direction for further work is to carry out complexity-theoretic investigations, similar to those described in Section 4, for common variants of zero-knowledge protocols. These include noninteractive zero knowledge (for which there has been some progress [DDPY, GSV2, BG2, PS], mainly for the case of statistical security), proofs and arguments of knowledge (where the prover demonstrates that it "knows" a witness of membership), and witness-indistinguishable protocols (where the particular witness used by the prover remains hidden from the verifier, but other knowledge may be leaked). Also, we currently have a rather incomplete complexity-theoretic understanding of argument systems with sublinear communication, such as [Kil, Mic, BG1], not to mention their zero knowledge variants. The current constructions of such argument systems rely on collision-resistant hash functions, but we do not even know if one-way functions are necessary (cf., [Wee]).

References

[Aar]   Aaronson, S.: Quantum lower bound for the collision problem. In: Proceedings of the Thirty-Fourth Annual ACM Symposium on Theory of Computing, pp. 635–642. ACM, New York (2002)

[AD]   Arvind, V., Das, B.: Szk proofs for black-box group problems. In: Grigoriev, D., Harrison, J., Hirsch, E.A. (eds.) CSR 2006. LNCS, vol. 3967, pp. 6–17. Springer, Heidelberg (2006)

[AH]   Aiello, W., Håstad, J.: Statistical zero-knowledge languages can be recognized in two rounds. Journal of Computer and System Sciences 42(3), 327–345 (1991) (Preliminary version in FOCS 1987)

[ALM+]   Arora, S., Lund, C., Motwani, R., Sudan, M., Szegedy, M.: Proof verification and the hardness of approximation problems. Journal of the ACM 45(3), 501–555 (1998)

[AS]   Arora, S., Safra, S.: Probabilistic checking of proofs: a new characterization of NP. Journal of the ACM 45(1), 70–122 (1998)

[AT]   Aharonov, D., Ta-Shma, A.: Adiabatic quantum state generation. SIAM Journal on Computing 37(1), 47–82(electronic) (2007)

[Bab]   Babai, L.: Trading group theory for randomness. In: Proceedings of the 17th Annual ACM Symposium on Theory of Computing (STOC), pp. 421–429 (1985)

[Bar1]   Barak, B.: How to go beyond the black-box simulation barrier. In: Proceedings of the 42nd Annual Symposium on Foundations of Computer Science (FOCS), pp. 106–115. IEEE Computer Society, Los Alamitos (2001)

[Bar2]   Barak, B.: Constant-round coin-tossing with a man in the middle or realizing the shared random string model. In: Proceedings of the 43rd Annual Symposium on Foundations of Computer Science (FOCS), pp. 345–355 (2002)

[BCC]   Brassard, G., Chaum, D., Crépeau, C.: Minimum disclosure proofs of knowledge. Journal of Computer and System Sciences 37(2), 156–189 (1988)

[BFL]   Babai, L., Fortnow, L., Lund, C.: Nondeterministic exponential time has two-prover interactive protocols. Computational Complexity 1(1), 3–40 (1991)

[BFLS]   Babai, L., Fortnow, L., Levin, L., Szegedy, M.: Checking computations in polylogarithmic time. In: STOC, pp. 21–31. ACM, New York (1991)

[BG1]   Barak, B., Goldreich, O.: Universal arguments and their applications. In: IEEE Conference on Computational Complexity, pp. 194–203 (2002)

[BG2]   Ben-Or, M., Gutfreund, D.: Trading help for interaction in statistical zero-knowledge proofs. Journal of Cryptology 16(2), 95–116 (2003)

[BGG$^+$] Ben-Or, M., Goldreich, O., Goldwasser, S., Håstad, J., Kilian, J., Micali, S., Rogaway, P.: Everything provable is provable in zero-knowledge. In: Goldwasser, S. (ed.) CRYPTO 1988. LNCS, vol. 403, pp. 37–56. Springer, Heidelberg (1990)

[BGKW]   Ben-Or, M., Goldwasser, S., Kilian, J., Wigderson, A.: Multi-prover interactive proofs: how to remove intractability assumptions. In: Proceedings of the 20th Annual ACM Symposium on Theory of Computing (STOC), pp. 113–131. ACM Press, New York (1988)

[BGW]   Ben-Or, M., Goldwasser, S., Wigderson, A.: Completeness theorems for non-cryptographic fault-tolerant distributed computation (extended abstract). In: Proceedings of the Twentieth Annual ACM Symposium on Theory of Computing, pp. 1–10 (1988)

[BHZ]   Boppana, R.B., Håstad, J., Zachos, S.: Does co-NP have short interactive proofs? Information Processing Letters 25, 127–132 (1987)

[BM]   Babai, L., Moran, S.: Arthur-Merlin games: A randomized proof system and a hierarchy of complexity classes. Journal of Computer and System Sciences 36, 254–276 (1988)

[BS]   Barak, B., Sahai, A.: How to play almost any mental game over the net - concurrent composition via super-polynomial simulation. In: FOCS, pp. 543–552. IEEE Computer Society, Los Alamitos (2005)

[BT]   Bogdanov, A., Trevisan, L.: On worst-case to average-case reductions for NP problems. SIAM Journal on Computing 36(4), 1119–1159(electronic) (2006)

[CCD]   Chaum, D., Crépeau, C., Damgård, I.: Multiparty unconditionally secure protocols (extended abstract). In: Proceedings of the Twentieth Annual ACM Symposium on Theory of Computing, pp. 11–19 (1988)

[CD]   Chen, X., Deng, X.: Settling the complexity of two-player nash equilibrium.
          In: FOCS, pp. 261–272. IEEE Computer Society, Los Alamitos (2006)
[CGH]   Canetti, R., Goldreich, O., Halevi, S.: The random oracle methodology, re-
          visited. Journal of the ACM 51(4), 557–594(electronic) (2004)
[DDPY]   De Santis, A., Di Crescenzo, G., Persiano, G., Yung, M.: Image Density is
          complete for non-interactive-SZK. In: Automata, Languages and Program-
          ming, 25th International Colloquium, ICALP, pp. 784–795 (1998) (See also
          preliminary draft of full version, May 1999)
[DGOW]   Damgård, I., Goldreich, O., Okamoto, T., Wigderson, A.: Honest verifier
          vs. dishonest verifier in public coin zero-knowledge proofs. In: Coppersmith,
          D. (ed.) CRYPTO 1995. LNCS, vol. 963, pp. 325–338. Springer, Heidelberg
          (1995)
[DGP]   Daskalakis, C., Goldberg, P.W., Papadimitriou, C.H.: The complexity of
          computing a Nash equilibrium. In: STOC 2006. Proceedings of the 38th
          Annual ACM Symposium on Theory of Computing, pp. 71–78. ACM, New
          York (2006)
[DGW]   Damgård, I., Goldreich, O., Wigderson, A.: Hashing functions can simplify
          zero-knowledge protocol design (too). Technical Report RS-94-39, BRICS,
          November 1994. See Part 1 of [DGOW]
[DH]   Diffie, W., Hellman, M.E.: New directions in cryptography. IEEE Transac-
          tions on Information Theory 22(6), 644–654 (1976)
[DSY]   Di Crescenzo, G., Sakurai, K., Yung, M.: On zero-knowledge proofs: from
          membership to decision. In: Proceedings of the 32nd Annual ACM Sympo-
          sium on Theory of Computing (STOC), pp. 255–264. ACM Press, New York
          (2000)
[FGL+]   Feige, U., Goldwasser, S., Lovász, L., Safra, S., Szegedy, M.: Interactive proofs
          and the hardness of approximating cliques. Journal of the ACM 43(2), 268–
          292 (1996)
[FGM+]   Fürer, M., Goldreich, O., Mansour, Y., Sipser, M., Zachos, S.: On complete-
          ness and soundness in interactive proof systems. Advances in Computing
          Research 5, 429–442 (1989) (Preliminary version in FOCS 1987)
[For]   Fortnow, L.: The complexity of perfect zero-knowledge. Advances in Com-
          puting Research: Randomness and Computation 5, 327–343 (1989)
[FRS]   Fortnow, L., Rompel, J., Sipser, M.: On the power of multi-prover interactive
          protocols. Theoretical Computer Science 134(2), 545–557 (1994)
[GG]   Goldreich, O., Goldwasser, S.: On the limits of non-approximability of lattice
          problems. In: Proceedings of the 30th Annual ACM Symposium on Theory
          of Computing (STOC), pp. 1–9 (1998)
[GK1]   Goldreich, O., Krawczyk, H.: On the composition of zero-knowledge proof
          systems. SIAM Journal on Computing 25(1), 169–192 (1996) (Preliminary
          version in ICALP 1990)
[GK2]   Goldreich, O., Kushilevitz, E.: A perfect zero-knowledge proof system for
          a problem equivalent to the discrete logarithm. Journal of Cryptology 6,
          97–116 (1993)
[GMR]   Goldwasser, S., Micali, S., Rackoff, C.: The knowledge complexity of inter-
          active proof systems. SIAM Journal on Computing 18(1), 186–208 (1989)
          (Preliminary version in STOC 1985)
[GMW]   Goldreich, O., Micali, S., Wigderson, A.: Proofs that yield nothing but their
          validity or all languages in NP have zero-knowledge proof systems. Journal
          of the ACM 38(1), 691–729 (1991) (Preliminary version in FOCS 1986)

[GO]   Goldreich, O., Oren, Y.: Definitions and properties of zero-knowledge proof systems. Journal of Cryptology 7(1), 1–32 (1994)

[Gol]   Goldreich, O.: Foundations of Cryptography: Basic Tools. Cambridge University Press, Cambridge (2001)

[GS]   Goldwasser, S., Sipser, M.: Private coins versus public coins in interactive proof systems. Advances in Computing Research: Randomness and Computation 5, 73–90 (1989)

[GSV1]   Goldreich, O., Sahai, A., Vadhan, S.: Honest verifier statistical zero-knowledge equals general statistical zero-knowledge. In: Proceedings of the 30th Annual ACM Symposium on Theory of Computing (STOC), pp. 399–408 (1998)

[GSV2]   Goldreich, O., Sahai, A., Vadhan, S.: Can statistical zero-knowledge be made non-interactive? or On the relationship of SZK and NISZK. In: Wiener, M.J. (ed.) CRYPTO 1999. LNCS, vol. 1666, pp. 467–484. Springer, Heidelberg (1999)

[GT]   Gutfreund, D., Ta-Shma, A.: Worst-case to average-case reductions revisited. In: Charikar, M., Jansen, K., Reingold, O., Rolim, J.D.P. (eds.) APPROX-RANDOM. LNCS, vol. 4627, pp. 569–583. Springer, Heidelberg (2007)

[GV]   Goldreich, O., Vadhan, S.P.: Comparing entropies in statistical zero knowledge with applications to the structure of SZK. In: IEEE Conference on Computational Complexity, pp. 54–73. IEEE Computer Society, Los Alamitos (1999)

[HILL]   Håstad, J., Impagliazzo, R., Levin, L.A., Luby, M.: A pseudorandom generator from any one-way function. SIAM Journal on Computing 28(4), 1364–1396 (1999) Preliminary versions. In: STOC 1989 and STOC 1990

[HR]   Haitner, I., Reingold, O.: Statistically-hiding commitment from any one-way function. In: Proceedings of the 39th Annual ACM Symposium on Theory of Computing (STOC), 2007, New York (2007)

[IL]   Impagliazzo, R., Luby, M.: One-way functions are essential for complexity based cryptography. In: Proceedings of the 30th Annual Symposium on Foundations of Computer Science (FOCS), pp. 230–235 (1989)

[IY]   Impagliazzo, R., Yung, M.: Direct minimum-knowledge computations (extended abstract). In: Pomerance, C. (ed.) CRYPTO 1987. LNCS, vol. 293, pp. 40–51. Springer, Heidelberg (1988)

[Kil]   Kilian, J.: A note on efficient zero-knowledge proofs and arguments (extended abstract). In: Proceedings of the 24th Annual ACM Symposium on Theory of Computing (STOC), pp. 723–732 (1992)

[LFKN]   Lund, C., Fortnow, L., Karloff, H., Nisan, N.: Algebraic methods for interactive proof systems. Journal of the ACM 39(4), 859–868 (1992)

[Lin]   Lindell, Y.: Protocols for bounded-concurrent secure two-party computation in the plain model. Chicago Journal of Theoretical Computer Science, pages Article 1, 50 (2006)

[LMR]   Luby, M., Micali, S., Rackoff, C.: How to simultaneously exchange a secret bit by flipping a symmetrically-biased coin. In: FOCS, pp. 11–21. IEEE, New York (1983)

[Mic]   Micali, S.: Computationally sound proofs. SIAM Journal on Computing 30(4), 1253–1298 (2000), Preliminary version in FOCS 1994

[MV]   Micciancio, D., Vadhan, S.: Statistical zero-knowledge proofs with efficient provers: lattice problems and more. In: Boneh, D. (ed.) CRYPTO 2003. LNCS, vol. 2729, pp. 282–298. Springer, Heidelberg (2003)

[Nao]   Naor, M.: Bit commitment using pseudorandomness. Journal of Cryptology
          4(2), 151–158 (1991); Preliminary version In: Brassard, G. (ed.) CRYPTO
          1989. LNCS, vol. 435, Springer, Heidelberg (1990)
[NOV]   Nguyen, M.-H., Ong, S.J., Vadhan, S.: Statistical zero-knowledge arguments
          for NP from any one-way function. In: Proceedings of the 47th Annual Sym-
          posium on Foundations of Computer Science (FOCS), pp. 3–14. IEEE Com-
          puter Society, Los Alamitos, CA, USA (2006)
[NOVY]   Naor, M., Ostrovsky, R., Venkatesan, R., Yung, M.: Perfect zero-knowledge
          arguments for NP using any one-way permutation. Journal of Cryptology
          11(2), 87–108 (1998); Preliminary version In: Brickell, E.F. (ed.) CRYPTO
          1992. LNCS, vol. 740, Springer, Heidelberg (1993)
[NV]   Nguyen, M.-H., Vadhan, S.: Zero knowledge with efficient provers. In: Pro-
          ceedings of the 38th Annual ACM Symposium on Theory of Computing
          (STOC), pp. 287–295. ACM Press, New York (2006)
[Oka]   Okamoto, T.: On relationships between statistical zero-knowledge proofs.
          Journal of Computer and System Sciences, 60(1), 47–108 (2000), Preliminary
          version in STOC 1996
[Ost]   Ostrovsky, R.: One-way functions, hard on average problems, and statisti-
          cal zero-knowledge proofs. In: Proceedings of the 6th Annual Structure in
          Complexity Theory Conference, pp. 133–138. IEEE Computer Society, Los
          Alamitos (1991)
[OV]   Ong, S.J., Vadhan, S.: Zero knowledge and soundness are symmetric. In:
          Naor, M. (ed.) EUROCRYPT 2007. LNCS, vol. 4515, Springer, Heidelberg
          (2007)
[OW]   Ostrovsky, R., Wigderson, A.: One-way functions are essential for non-trivial
          zero-knowledge. In: Proceedings of the 2nd Israel Symposium on Theory of
          Computing Systems, pp. 3–17. IEEE Computer Society, Los Alamitos (1993)
[Pas]   Pass, R.: Bounded-concurrent secure multi-party computation with a dis-
          honest majority. In: Proceedings of the 36th Annual ACM Symposium on
          Theory of Computing, pp. 232–241. ACM, New York (2004)
[PR1]   Pass, R., Rosen, A.: Bounded-concurrent secure two-party computation in a
          constant number of rounds. In: FOCS, p. 404. IEEE Computer Society, Los
          Alamitos (2003)
[PR2]   Pass, R., Rosen, A.: New and improved constructions of non-malleable cryp-
          tographic protocols. In: STOC 2005: Proceedings of the 37th Annual ACM
          Symposium on Theory of Computing, pp. 533–542. ACM, New York (2005)
[PS]   Pass, R., Shelat, A.: Unconditional characterizations of non-interactive zero-
          knowledge. In: Shoup, V. (ed.) CRYPTO 2005. LNCS, vol. 3621, pp. 118–134.
          Springer, Heidelberg (2005)
[Sha]   Shamir, A.: IP = PSPACE. Journal of the ACM 39(4), 869–877 (1992)
[Sip]   Sipser, M.: Introduction to the Theory of Computation, 2nd edn., Boston,
          MA, USA. Thomson Course Technology (2005)
[SV]   Sahai, A., Vadhan, S.: A complete problem for statistical zero knowledge.
          Journal of the ACM, 50(2), 196–249 (2003), Preliminary version in FOCS
          1997
[Vad1]   Vadhan, S.: Probabilistic proof systems, part I — interactive & zero-
          knowledge proofs. In: Rudich, S., Wigderson, A. (eds.) Computational Com-
          plexity Theory. American Mathematical Society. IAS/Park City Mathemat-
          ics Series, vol. 10 (2004)

[Vad2]   Vadhan, S.P.: An unconditional study of computational zero knowledge. SIAM Journal on Computing, 36(4), 1160–1214 (2006). Preliminary version in FOCS 2004

[Wat]   Watrous, J.: Limits on the power of quantum statistical zero-knowledge. In: Proceedings of the 43rd Annual Symposium on Foundations of Computer Science (FOCS), pp. 459 (2002)

[Wee]   Wee, H.: Finding Pessiland. In: Halevi, S., Rabin, T. (eds.) TCC 2006. LNCS, vol. 3876, pp. 429–442. Springer, Heidelberg (2006)

[Yao]   Yao, A.C.-C.: How to generate and exchange secrets. In: Proceedings of the 27th Annual Symposium on Foundations of Computer Science (FOCS), pp. 162–167. IEEE Computer Society, Los Alamitos (1986)

The Priority k-Median Problem

Amit Kumar[1] and Yogish Sabharwal[2]

[1] Dept of Computer Science & Engg.,
Indian Institute of Technology, New Delhi - 110016, India
amitk@cse.iitd.ac.in
[2] IBM India Research Lab,
4 Block C, Institutional Area, Vasant Kunj, New Delhi - 110070, India
ysabharwal@in.ibm.com

Abstract. In this paper, we consider a generalized version of the k-median problem in metric spaces, called the priority k-median problem in which demands and facilities have priorities associated with them and a demand can only be assigned to a facility that has the same priority or better. We show that there exists a polynomial time constant factor approximation algorithm for this problem when there are two priorities. We also show that the natural integer program for the problem has an arbitrarily large integrality gap when there are four or more priorities.

1 Introduction

The problem of locating facilities to service a set of demands has been widely studied in computer science and operations research communities [15,16]. Facility location problems have applications in diverse fields, for example, locating fire stations in a city, locating base stations in wireless networks. The tradeoff involved in such problems is the following – we would like to open as few facilities as possible, but the demands should not be located too far from the nearest facility.

The k-median problem balances the two costs by fixing the number of facilities that can be opened and seeks to minimize the average distance of a demand to the nearest open facility. More concretely, an instance of the k-median problem consists of a set $\mathcal{D}$ of demand points and a set $\mathcal{F}$ of potential facility points. We are also given the distance between each demand and facility points. The k-median problem seeks to open at most k facilities in $\mathcal{F}$ so that the average distance traveled by a demand in $\mathcal{D}$ to the nearest open facility is minimized. We shall further assume that the distances between demands and facilities obey the metric property.

The k-median problem is simple to state and nicely captures the trade-offs involved in formulating facility location problems. This NP-hard problem has been intensely studied by the approximation algorithms community. Polynomial time constant factor approximation algorithms based on a variety of techniques are known for this problem [2,3,4,9].

In this paper, we consider an interesting generalization of the k-median problem. In many applications of clustering problems, we can associate a notion of

V. Arvind and S. Prasad (Eds.): FSTTCS 2007, LNCS 4855, pp. 71–83, 2007.

priority with demands and facilities. A facility can serve only those demands which have lesser or same priority. Let us see a few motivating examples.

1. There is a retail chain store and it wants to open several stores in a city. But because of various restrictions (space, regulations, etc.) there are some locations where it can open small stores, and there are locations where it can open bigger stores and hence sell more products. Now customers can be different kinds. Those having lower income may be happy with small stores, but those with more lavish lifestyle may prefer to go to bigger stores only.

2. In planning emergency evacuation plan for a city, the authorities want to build locations from which people can be evacuated. But they want to build better facilities for evacuating important people, like the mayor of the city. But only some places in the city will be well equipped to provide such facilities, e.g., a low population zone, or a port. For evacuating other people, they may have more options where to build the facilities.

There is a common theme in both the examples. The facilities that can be built are of different priorities. A high priority facility is better than a low priority facility. The demands are of different kinds as well. Some demands may be happy with any facility, but others may require facilities of a certain priority or better only. Motivated by the discussion above, we formulate the *k-median problem with priorities*, in which demands and facilities have different priorities and a demand can then only be assigned to a facility of its priority or better.

In this paper, we give a constant factor approximation algorithm for this problem when there are only two priorities. Our algorithm is based on the idea of formulating a natural linear programming relaxation for this problem and then carefully rounding it to get an integral solution. On the other hand, we show that such a linear program has high integrality gap for 4 priorities.

Related Work. As mentioned earlier, the k-median problem has been extensively studied in the past and several constant factor approximation algorithms are known for this problem. Lin and Vitter [14] gave a bicriteria constant factor approximation algorithm for this problem, even when distances do not obey triangle inequality. Assuming that distances obey triangle inequality, the first constant factor approximation algorithm was given by Charikar et al. [4]. Jain et al. [9] gave a primal-dual constant factor approximation algorithm for this problem. Several constant factor approximation algorithms based on local search techniques are known [2,3,11]. The techniques/analysis of these papers do not extend to our problem. Several polynomial time approximation schemes are known for the k-median problem in geometric settings [1,10,13].

A closely related problem is the *facility location problem*: here there is no bound on how many facilities we can open but each facility comes with an opening cost. This problem has been widely studied in computer science and operations research communities [15,16]. Several constant factor approximation algorithms are known for this problem (assuming distances obey triangle inequality) [3,6,9,18]. The variant of the *facility location* problem where the facilities and demands have priorities has already been studied before. Shmoys et al. [17] presented a 6-approximation algorithm for this problem.

Another related problem is the priority Steiner tree problem. The setting is the same as the Steiner tree problem where we have an edge-weighted graph, a source and a set of demand nodes. Further each edge and each demand has a priority assigned to it. Now a demand can use only those edges which have higher priority than itself. The goal is to find a minimum cost subset of edges so that each demand can reach the source using these edges. This problem was studied by [5] who gave a logarithmic approximation algorithm for this problem. A lower bound on the approximability of this problem was given by [7].

Our Techniques. The main result of the paper is a constant factor approximation algorithm for the priority k-median problem wherin the number of priorities is 2. Our starting step is standard : we write a natural LP relaxation for this problem. However, the rounding steps are much more involved. Our algorithm involves deeply analyzing the structure of the fractional solution and simplifying it through a sequence of carefully formulated steps. The simpler fractional solution guides us to write a simpler linear program for this problem and then we show that an optimal vertex solution to this new LP must be half-integral. We finally round the half-integral solution to an integral solution.

In Section 2 we present the natural integer program for the *priority k-median* problem and also show the integrality gap for the case of 4 priorities. In Section 3, we present the constant factor approximation algorithm for the case of 2 priorities.

2   Preliminaries

In the *priority k-median* problem, we are given a set of demands, $\mathcal{D}$ and a set of facilities $\mathcal{F}$ in a metric space. Each demand has a weight d_j associated with it, denoting the quantity of demand to be assigned to an open facility. There are m *types* of demands, with the type indicates the priority of the demand. Thus $\mathcal{D}$ is the disjoint union of $\mathcal{D}_1, \ldots, \mathcal{D}_m$, where we say that $\mathcal{D}_k$ are demands of *type k*. Similarly, there are m *types* of facilities, i.e., $\mathcal{F}$ is a disjoint union of $\mathcal{F}_1, \ldots, \mathcal{F}_m$, where we say that $\mathcal{F}_k$ are facilities of *type k*. The *type* of a facility specifies its capability in serving the demands – a facility of *type k* can serve demands of *type* at least k. Let c_{ij} denote distance between i and j where i, j can be demands or facilities. A feasible solution opens a set of facilities F, and assigns each demand to an open facility. We are given bounds k_r on the number of facilities that can be opened from $\mathcal{F}_r$. As mentioned above, a demand j can only be assigned to an open facility of its type or lower. Let $i(j)$ denote the facility that a demand j is assigned to. Then the cost of the solution is defined as $\sum_{j \in \mathcal{D}} d_j \cdot c_{ji(j)}$. The goal of the *priority k-median* problem is to obtain a solution of minimum cost. For a demand j, let $type(j) = r$ if $j \in \mathcal{D}_r$.

Fix an instance $\mathcal{I}$ of the problem as described above. We give a natural integer programming formulation for this problem.

$$\min \quad \sum_{j \in \mathcal{D}, i \in \mathcal{F}} d_j \cdot c_{ij} \cdot x_{ij} \qquad (1)$$

$$\sum_{i \in \mathcal{F}_r} y_i \leq k_r \qquad \text{for } r = 1, \ldots, m \qquad (2)$$

$$\sum_{i \in \mathcal{F}_1 \cup \ldots \cup \mathcal{F}_{type(j)}} x_{ij} = 1 \qquad \text{for all demands } j \qquad (3)$$

$$x_{ij} \leq y_i \qquad \text{for all demands } j \text{ and facilities } i \qquad (4)$$

$$x_{ij}, y_i \in \{0, 1\} \qquad \text{for all demands } j \text{ and facilities } i \qquad (5)$$

We relax the integer program to a linear program by allowing the variables x_{ij} to take arbitrary real values between 0 and 1, and y_i to take real non-negative values. We solve this linear program and let x^*, y^* be an optimal solution to the linear program. Let OPT denote the cost of this solution.

We show that the integrality gap of the above relaxation is unbounded when there are four priorities.

Theorem 1. *For the* priority k-median *problem, the LP relaxation of its natural integer programming formulation has an unbounded integrality gap (even in terms of the input number of demands/facilities) when there are four priorities.* The proof is deferred to the full version of the paper [12].

3   Two Priorities

In this section, we restrict our attention to the case of two priorities, i.e., demands $j \in \mathcal{D}_1 \cup \mathcal{D}_2$ and facilities $i \in \mathcal{F}_1 \cup \mathcal{F}_2$. A demand in $\mathcal{D}_1$ can only use facilities in $\mathcal{F}_1$ whereas a demand in $\mathcal{D}_2$ can use facilities in $\mathcal{F}_1 \cup \mathcal{F}_2$. The paper contains the statements of the Theorems and Lemmas. The proofs are deferred to the full version of the paper [12].

We start by solving the LP mentioned in the previous section. The fractional solution can be thought of as assigning a demand fractionally to several facilities. Our first step is to *consolidate demands*, i.e., we merge demands into larger demands. We do this consolidation with a constant loss in approximation ratio only. The consolidated demands can be shown to form a nice hierarchical structure called *scenarios*. The scenarios form the basic building blocks of our rounding algorithm. Each scenario has several demands and facilities associated with it (which are disjoint from those of other scenarios). This is followed by careful reassignment of the demands so that they use the facilities which are either associated with their own scenario or the scenario associated with one other demand. We then show that the assignments can be modified further so that the solution satisfies a nice property (*Structure Property*) that greatly limits the number of open facilities. We then formulate a modified LP for this nicer instance for which the modified assignments form a feasible solution. We argue that the solution to this modified LP is half-integral. Finally we show that this half-integral solution can be modified to an integral solution by suffering at most a constant factor loss in our approximation.

3.1 Consolidating Demands

For a demand j, let C_j^* denote the cost of shipping one unit of demand from j in the optimal LP solution. In other words, $C_j^* = \sum_i x_{ij}^* c_{ij}$. Note that $OPT = \sum_j d_j \cdot C_j^*$. In this step, we consolidate nearby demands. This step consists of two further substeps.

- *Substep 1:* Initially, we set $d_j' = d_j$ for all locations j. Consider the locations in ascending order of C_j^* values. When we consider a location j, we check if there is another location j' which has been considered already and which satisfies the conditions: $d_{j'}' > 0$ and $c_{jj'} \leq 32C_j^*$ and $type(j') = type(j)$. If there is such a location j', then the entire demand of j is transferred to j', i.e., set $d_{j'}'$ to $d_{j'}' + d_j'$, and d_j' to 0.
- *Substep 2:* Initially, we set $d_j'' = d_j'$ for all locations j. We consider all $type(2)$ demands. When we consider a location $j \in \mathcal{D}_2$, we check if there is another location $j' \in \mathcal{D}_1$ which satisfies the conditions: $d_{j'}'' > 0$ and $c_{jj'} \leq 32C_j^*$ and $C_{j'}^* \leq c_{jj'}$. If there is such a location j', then the entire demand of j is transferred to j', i.e., set $d_{j'}''$ to $d_{j'}'' + d_j''$, and d_j'' to 0.

Note that the condition on the type of j and j' ensures us that the demand j can use the facilities that j' is assigned to.

Let $\mathcal{I}'$ be the new instance obtained thus. Let $\mathcal{D}'$ denote the locations j for which $d_j'' > 0$. It is easy to see that x^*, y^* is still a feasible fractional solution for the modified instance. It is also easy to see that an integral solution to the original LP can be obtained from an integral solution to this modified instance with at most a constant factor loss in approximation.

Observation 1. *For two demands j, j' of the same type, $c_{jj'} > 32 \cdot max\{C_j^*, C_{j'}^*\}$. Also for two demands $j \in \mathcal{D}_2'$ and $j' \in \mathcal{D}_1'$, if $C_{j'}^* \leq c_{jj'}$, then $c_{jj'} > 32 \cdot C_j^*$.*

3.2 Scenarios

We now define a nice hierarchical structure around the demands called scenarios.

Definition 1. Ball(p,r): *For a location p, let $Ball(p, r)$ denote the set of all the locations at a distance of at most r from p.*

Definition 2. Nearest Assignable Demand, Critical Radius, Critical Ball: *With every demand $j \in \mathcal{D}'$, we associate another demand from $\mathcal{D}'$, denoted by $n(j)$ which we call its nearest assignable demand. The critical radius is denoted by r_j and is defined to be $c_{jn(j)}/16$. The critical ball, denoted by $\mathcal{B}_j$, is defined to be $Ball(j, r_j)$ The nearest assignable demand is determined as follows:*

- *If $j \in \mathcal{D}_1'$, $n(j) = argmin_{j' \in \mathcal{D}_1' \setminus \{j\}}\{c_{jj'}\}$*
- *If $j \in \mathcal{D}_2'$, $n(j) = argmin_{j' \in \mathcal{D}_1' \cup \mathcal{D}_2' \setminus \mathcal{V}}\{c_{jj'}\}$, for $\mathcal{V} = \{j' \in \mathcal{D}_1' | c_{jj'} \leq \frac{3}{2}r_j\} \cup \{j\}$.*

If there is no demand that is a candidate to be a nearest assignable demand to j, then we set $n(j) = \Gamma$ and r_j to be twice the distance to the furthest location (demand or facility). Thus, in this case, all facilities lie in $\mathcal{B}_j$.

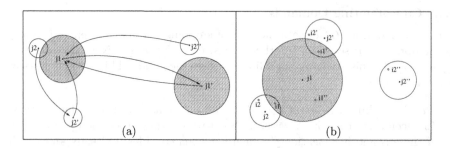

Fig. 1. (a) Nearest assignable demands, (b) Example of Level 1 and Level 2 Scenarios

Figure 1 (a) shows an example of nearest assignable demands for different demands under different situations. Let $j_1, j_1' \in \mathcal{D}_1'$ and $j_2, j_2', j_2'' \in \mathcal{D}_2'$. Note that for a $type(1)$ demand, the nearest assignable demand is always the closest $type(1)$ demand. Hence j_1 and j_1' are nearest assignable demands of each other. For the demand j_2, j_1 is not a candidate as it is not sufficiently far, i.e., $c_{j_1 j_2} \leq \frac{3}{2} r_{j_1}$, and hence the nearest assignable demand is the next closest demand, i.e., j_2'. For j_2', the closest demand is j_1 and it is sufficiently far and therefore j_1 is the nearest assignable demand for j_2'. j_2'' is again too close to j_1' and therefore its nearest assignable demand is the next closest demand j_1.

As we will see later, we can modify the solution by suffering a constant factor loss in our approximation, so that any demand j uses facilities which are either close to itself or are close to its nearest assignable demand $n(j)$.

Observation 2. *For a demand j, such that $n(j) = \Gamma$, there is only one demand of type $type(j)$, i.e., j. Also, for all $j' \in \mathcal{D}'$, $n(j') \neq j$.*

This is straightforward to see for a $type(2)$ demand. For a $type(1)$ demand, this must be the only $type(1)$ demand. The critical radius is set so large that all demands lie in the critical ball, and therefore this demand is not a candidate to be the nearest assignable demand for any $type(2)$ demand.

Lemma 1. *If there exists a demand $j \in \mathcal{D}_2'$, such that $n(j) = \Gamma$, then there is at most one $type(1)$ demand, say j_1. Moreover for this demand, $n(j_1) = \Gamma$.*

Observation 3. *For any demand j, such that $n(j) \neq \Gamma$, $type(n(j)) \leq type(j)$ and $c_{jn(j)} > \frac{3}{2} r_{n(j)}$.*

Lemma 2. *For any demand j, such that $n(j) \neq \Gamma$, $r_j + r_{n(j)} < c_{jn(j)}$. This also implies that $n(j) \neq \Gamma$, $\mathcal{B}_j \cap \mathcal{B}_{n(j)} = \phi$.*

We now show that at least a half fraction of any demand is assigned to facilities that lie within its *critical ball*.

Lemma 3. *For any demand $j \in \mathcal{D}'$, $Ball(j, 2 \cdot C_j^*) \subseteq \mathcal{B}_j$.*

We now define scenarios. For this, we construct graphs on the set of demands, which we call *intersection graphs*.

Definition 3. Intersection graphs: *The* level 1 intersection graph *is the graph* $G_1 = (V, E_1)$, *where* $V = \mathcal{D}'$ *and* $(j_1, j_2) \in E_1$ *iff* $\mathcal{B}_{j_1} \cap \mathcal{B}_{j_2} \neq \phi$ *and* $j_1, j_2 \in \mathcal{D}'_1 \cup \mathcal{D}'_2$. *We will later see that any connected component in this graph has at most one type(1) demand.*

The level 2 intersection graph *is the graph* $G_2 = (V, \phi)$, *where* $V = \mathcal{D}'$. *Therefore, there are no edges in a* level 2 intersection graph. *All connected components in this graph are isolated demands.*

Let $\mathcal{CC}_G(j)$ *denote the set of demands that are in the same connected component of the graph G as j.*

Definition 4. Scenarios: *We define a level 1* scenario *for every connected component in G_1. Let $\mathcal{J}$ be the set of demands in the connected component. Then the corresponding* level 1 scenario *is defined by the set of facilities* $\cup_{j \in \mathcal{J}}(\mathcal{B}_j \cap \mathcal{F})$.

Similarly, we define a level 2 scenario *for every connected component in G_2. Let j be a demand in G_2.*

- *If $j \in \mathcal{D}'_2$, then the* level 2 scenario *is defined by the set of facilities* $\mathcal{B}_j \cap \mathcal{F}$
- *If $j \in \mathcal{D}'_1$, then the* level 2 scenario *is defined by the set of facilities* $\{i \in \mathcal{B}_j \cap \mathcal{F} | i \notin \mathcal{B}_{j'}$ *for any* $j' \in \mathcal{CC}_{G_1}(j) \setminus \{j\}\}$.

Thus every level 1 scenario *is the union of some* level 2 scenarios. *We denote the* level k scenario *to which a demand j belongs by $\mathcal{S}_k(j)$. Also, if $k = type(j)$, then we simply denote the scenario as $\mathcal{S}(j)$, i.e. $\mathcal{S}(j) = \mathcal{S}_{type(j)}(j)$.*

Figure 1 (b) illustrates facilities in *level 1* and *level 2* scenarios. In this example, $\mathcal{S}_1(j_1) = \{i_1, i'_1, i''_1, i_2, i'_2\}$, $\mathcal{S}_2(j_2) = \{i_1, i_2\}$, $\mathcal{S}_2(j'_2) = \{i'_1, i'_2\}$ and $\mathcal{S}_2(j_1) = \{i''_1\}$. Also, $\mathcal{S}_1(j''_2) = \mathcal{S}_2(j''_2) = \{i''_2\}$

We now show that for any demand j of type k $(= 1, 2)$, the distance from the demand to any facility in $\mathcal{S}_k(j)$ cannot be more than $4 \cdot r_j$.

Lemma 4. *Let j be any demand. Let $k = type(j)$. Consider the level k intersection graph, G_k. Let $\mathcal{C}$ be the connected component in G_k spanning the demands constituting the scenario $\mathcal{S}(j)$. Then*

1. *There is only one type(k) demand in $\mathcal{C}$, i.e., j.*
2. *For any facility $i \in \mathcal{S}(j)$, $c_{ij} \leq 4 \cdot r_j$.*

3.3 Changing the Assignments

We now modify the assignments so that every demand either uses facilities in its own scenario or the scenario of its nearest assignable demand and the cost paid by a demand to any facility in the scenario of its nearest assignable demand is the same. Therefore, it does not matter which facility it uses in that scenario. We will denote the (new) distance of demand j to facilities in the scenario of its nearest assignable demand by $\bar{c}_j$.

Lemma 5. *By suffering a loss of at most a constant factor in approximation, we can modify the assignments such that for any demand j, (i) it either uses the facilities in $\mathcal{S}(j)$ or facilities in $\mathcal{S}(n(j))$; and (ii) for every facility $i \in \mathcal{S}(n(j))$, we can set $c_{ij} = \frac{11}{3}c_{jn(j)}(= \bar{c}_j)$ so that it does not matter which facility it uses in that scenario.*

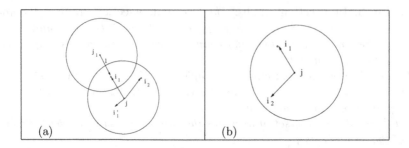

Fig. 2. Different settings for $type(2)$ demands

Therefore, we can now modify the assignments (going across to facilities that belong to the scenario of nearest assignable demands) so that a demand uses the same facilities from the nearest assignable demand that are used by the nearest assignable demand itself.

We now modify the assignments so as to reduce the number of open facilities in *level 2* scenarios. We first describe a simple structure that we desire the solution to exhibit. If a solution exhibits this structure, we say that it satisfies the *Structure Property*.

Definition 5. *A solution (x, y) to the LP defined above is said to satisfy the* Structure Property *if*

1. *For every demand $j \in \mathcal{D}'_1$,*
    (a) There is no $type(2)$ facility in $\mathcal{S}_2(j)$.
    (b) There is at most one facility of $type(1)$ in $\mathcal{S}_2(j)$.
    (c) If there is a $type(1)$ facility in $\mathcal{S}_2(j)$, then this facility is closer to j than any other $type(1)$ facility in $\mathcal{S}_1(j)$.
2. *For every demand $j \in \mathcal{D}'_2$,*
    (a) There is at most one facility of $type(2)$ in $\mathcal{S}_2(j)$.
    (b) If there is no $type(1)$ demand in $\mathcal{CC}_{G_1}(j)$, then there is at most one facility of $type(1)$ in $\mathcal{S}_2(j)$.
    (c) If $j_1 \in \mathcal{D}'_1 \cap \mathcal{CC}_{G_1}(j)$ and $r_j \leq c_{jj_1}/4$, then there is at most one facility of $type(1)$ in $\mathcal{S}_2(j)$.
    (d) If $j_1 \in \mathcal{D}'_1 \cap \mathcal{CC}_{G_1}(j)$ and $r_j > c_{jj_1}/4$, then there are at most two facilities of $type(1)$ in $\mathcal{S}_2(j)$. Moreover, If there are indeed two facilities, say i and i', then for one of these facilities, say i,
        * $x_{ij_1} = y_i = 1$,
        * $0 < x_{ij} < y_i$; and
        * i is the closest $type(1)$ facility to j_1.

Lemma 6. *We can modify the solution so that it satisfies the* Structure Property, *increasing the cost by at most a constant factor.*

Therefore a $type(2)$ demand, say j, may have one or two $type(1)$ facilities in its scenario. These settings are illustrated in Figure 2.

3.4   Modified LP

We now present an LP for this modified problem instance. Let $\mathcal{F}'(j)$ denote the set of facilities used by demand j, i.e., $\{i \in \mathcal{F}|x_{ij} > 0\}$. Let $\mathcal{F}'$ denote the set of facilities used by at least one demand. Let $\mathcal{F}'_1$ and $\mathcal{F}'_2$ denote the set of facilities in $\mathcal{F}'$ of $type(1)$ and $type(2)$ respectively.

We consider the modified LP described as follows. We replace the variables y_i's with $\bar{y}_i$'s and x_{ij}'s with $\bar{x}_{ij}$'s when solving the modified LP.

$$\min \quad \sum_{j \in \mathcal{D}', i \in \mathcal{F}'} d_j \cdot c_{ij} \cdot \bar{x}_{ij} \tag{6}$$

$$\sum_{i \in \mathcal{F}'_r} \bar{y}_i \le k_r \qquad \text{for } r = 1, \ldots, m \tag{7}$$

$$\sum_{i \in \mathcal{F}'(j)} \bar{x}_{ij} = 1 \qquad \text{for all demands } j \tag{8}$$

$$\sum_{i \in \mathcal{F}'(j) \cap \mathcal{S}(j)} \bar{x}_{ij} \ge \frac{1}{2} \qquad \text{for all demands } j \tag{9}$$

$$\bar{x}_{ij} = 1 \qquad \text{if } x_{ij} = 1 \tag{10}$$

$$\bar{y}_i = 1 \qquad \text{if } y_i = 1 \tag{11}$$

$$\bar{x}_{ij} \le \bar{y}_i \qquad \text{for all demands } j \text{ and facilities } i \in \mathcal{F}' \tag{12}$$

$$\bar{x}_{ij}, \bar{y}_i \ge 0 \qquad \text{for all demands } j \text{ and facilities } i \in \mathcal{F}' \tag{13}$$

Constraint 9 ensures that at least a half-fraction of any demand is assigned to facilities in its own scenario (and are usable by demands from other scenarios for which this demand is a nearest assignable demand). Constraints 10 and 11 ensure that facilities that were fully open remain fully open and demands that were fully assigned to a single facility remain so. These are required in order to ensure that the solution to this modified LP continues to satisfy the Structure Property (see Lemma 7 below).

Note that the modified solution obtained by changing the assignments described above is a feasible solution to this new LP. Therefore the optimal solution to this LP can only have cost at most as much as the above solution.

Lemma 7. *The assignments in the optimal solution of the modified LP, $(\bar{x}, \bar{y})$ continue to satisfy the* Structure Property.

3.5   Half-Integrality of a Vertex Solution

We now show that the solution to the modified LP is half integral.

Definition 6. Facility relocation cost : *For a* level 1 *scenario,* $\mathcal{S}_1(j)$, *let* $\mathcal{D}(\mathcal{S}_1(j)) = \mathcal{D}' \cap \mathcal{CC}_{G_1}(j)$. *For a* level 2 *scenario,* $\mathcal{S}_2(j)$, *let* $\mathcal{D}(\mathcal{S}_2(j)) = \mathcal{D}'_2 \cap \mathcal{CC}_{G_2}(j)$. *Note that for a* $type(1)$ *demand* j_1, $\mathcal{D}(\mathcal{S}_2(j_1)) = \phi$ *and for a* $type(2)$ *demand* j_2, $\mathcal{D}(\mathcal{S}_2(j_2)) = \{j_2\}$.

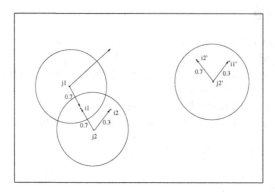

Fig. 3. Example of facility adjustments

Let $\mathcal{C}$ denote a chain of facilities $< i_1, i_2, .., i_s >$. We define $\mathcal{C} + \delta$ [$\mathcal{C} - \delta$ resp.] to be the operation where the extents to which the facilities are open are modified as follows:

- $\bar{y}_{i_t} = \bar{y}_{i_t} + \delta$, *t is odd [even resp.]*
- $\bar{y}_{i_t} = \bar{y}_{i_t} - \delta$, *t is even [odd resp.]*

Let $\Delta(\mathcal{D}(\mathcal{S}), \mathcal{C} + \delta)$ [$\Delta(\mathcal{D}(\mathcal{S}), \mathcal{C} - \delta)$ resp.] denote the change in the cost paid by the demands $\mathcal{D}(\mathcal{S})$ when the operation $\mathcal{C} + \delta$ [$\mathcal{C} + \delta$ resp.] is performed.

Our choice of the chain and the choice of δ (small enough quantity) will be such that all constraints of the modified LP will be satisfied even after the change except possibly constraint (7). Moreover, we will operate on multiple such (suitably selected) chains together so that even this constraint is not violated.

Definition 7. *Let $\mathcal{Y}_r(\mathcal{S}(j))$ denote the sum of all the type(r) facilities in the scenario $\mathcal{S}(j)$ associated with demand j, i.e., $\mathcal{Y}_r(\mathcal{S}(j)) = \sum_{i \in \mathcal{F}'_r \cap \mathcal{S}(j)} \bar{y}_i$.*
Let $\mathcal{Y}(\mathcal{S}(j))$ denote the sum of all the facilities in the scenario $\mathcal{S}(j)$ associated with demand j, i.e., $\mathcal{Y}(\mathcal{S}(j)) = \sum_{i \in \mathcal{F}' \cap \mathcal{S}(j)} \bar{y}_i = \mathcal{Y}_1(\mathcal{S}(j)) + \mathcal{Y}_2(\mathcal{S}(j))$.

The idea is to find a chain of facilities, $\mathcal{C}$, such that the cost of performing the operation $\mathcal{C} + \delta$ is equal but opposite the cost of performing the operation $\mathcal{C} - \delta$, i.e., $\Delta(\mathcal{D}', \mathcal{C} + \delta) = -\Delta(\mathcal{D}', \mathcal{C} - \delta)$. Moreover, none of these facilities should be half-integral and also the total sum of all the type(1) facilities and type(2) facilities should not be disturbed.

We show that if the solution is not half-integral, it is always possible to find such a chain. We can then essentially adjust the chain along the direction that does not increase the cost of the solution. The ability to do this implies that the solution to the LP is either not an optimal solution or is a non-vertex solution. This is a contradiction, implying that such a chain cannot exist and therefore the solution must be half integral.

We illustrate the idea by means of an example (see Figure 3). The technical details and proofs are deferred to the full version of the paper [12].

In this example $type(j_1) = 1$, $type(j_2) = type(j_2') = 2$, $type(i_1) = type(i_1') = 1$ and $type(i_2) = type(i_2') = 2$. Moreover, j_1 and j_2 use the same facility i_1. Also, $x_{i_1 j_1} = x_{i_1 j_2} = y_{i_1} = 0.7$, $x_{i_2 j_2} = y_{i_2} = 0.3$, $x_{i_1' j_1'} = y_{i_1'} = 0.3$ and $x_{i_2' j_2'} = y_{i_2'} = 0.7$. Note that $\mathcal{Y}(\mathcal{S}(j_2')) = 1$ is already integral. Therefore, decreasing only one of the facilities will cause j_2' to travel to facilities of its nearest assignable demand, which may incur a large cost. Moreover, $\mathcal{Y}(\mathcal{S}_2(j_2)) = 1$ is also integral. Therefore, decreasing only one of the facilities will cause j_2 to travel to facilities of its nearest assignable demand, which may incur a large cost. Therefore, we must include i_1 and i_2 together as well as i_1' and i_2' together in any chain that we form. Consider the chain $\mathcal{C} = \{i_1, i_2, i_2', i_1'\}$. Then, $\Delta(\mathcal{D}', \mathcal{C} + \delta) = -\Delta(\mathcal{D}', \mathcal{C} - \delta) = \delta \cdot (d_{j_1} \cdot (c_{i_1 j_1} - \bar{c}_{j_1}) + d_{j_2} \cdot (c_{i_1 j_2} - c_{i_2 j_2}) + d_{j_2'} \cdot (c_{i_2' j_2'} - c_{i_1' j_2'}))$. Therefore $\mathcal{C}$ is the required chain along which we can perform adjustments. Note that when adjusting i_1 it is important to ensure that increasing/decreasing it a small amount has equal and opposite impact on both j_1 as well as j_2 simultaneously.

We discover the chain in parts. Any *level 2* scenario for which the sum of facilities of some type is not half-integral can form a part of such a chain. For a *level 1* scenario, we concatenate chains of some *level 2* scenarios to form a longer chain. Similarly, we concatenate such chains from *level 1* scenarios to form a chain that satisfies the required properties. Note that though individual chains may violate constraint (7) of the LP, the final chain that we form by concatenating these chains will not violate this constraint.

Theorem 2. *The solution to the LP specified in Section 3.4 is half-integral.*

3.6 Rounding to an Integral Solution

Let $\bar{\mathcal{F}}_j$ denote the facilities used by demand j. Let $\bar{C}_j^* = \sum_{i \in \bar{\mathcal{F}}_j} c_{ij} \bar{x}_{ij}$.

Note that since the solution is $\frac{1}{2}$-integral, $c_{ij} \leq 2\bar{C}_j^*$ for all $i \in \bar{\mathcal{F}}_j$. Therefore, it does not matter which of the facilities in $\bar{\mathcal{F}}_j$ a demand j is assigned to in the integral solution as long as we can fully open that facility, as the cost only increases by at most a constant factor.

Lemma 8. *By loosing at most a constant factor, the $\frac{1}{2}$-integral solution to the LP obtained in the previous section can be modified to an integral solution.*

Putting together our discussions, we get the following algorithm. We solve the LP relaxation of the natural integer programming formulation specified in Section 2. We then consolidate demands in this fractional solution as specified in Section 3.1 and then modify the assignments in this fractional solution as specified in Section 3.3 to obtain a fractional solution that satisfies the Structure property. We then formulate a modified LP for this more structured instance as specified in Section 3.4. The solution to this modified LP is half-integral as shown in Theorem 2. We finally round it off to an integral solution as specified in Lemma 8. This integral solution can now be used to obtain an integral solution to the original LP by loosing at most a constant factor of approximation when separating out the demands that were consolidated together, leading to the following result.

Theorem 3. *The priority k-median problem with two priorities can be solved within a constant factor of approximation in polynomial time.*

The approximation ratio obtained using our algorithm is fairly large (in the region of a few hundreds). We have not attempted to minimize it. With more careful analysis, we believe that it can be lowered significantly.

4   Open Problems

It would be interesting to know if there is a constant factor approximation algorithm or a large integrality gap for the given LP for the prioritized k-median problem when there are exactly 3 priorities.

References

1. Arora, S., Raghavan, P., Rao, S.: Polynomial time approximation schemes for the Euclidean k-median problem. In: Proceedings of the 30th annual ACM Symposium on Theory of Computing (1998)
2. Arya, V., Garg, N., Khandekar, R., Pandit, V., Meyerson, A., Munagala, K.: Local search heuristics for k-median and facility location problems. In: Proceedings of the 33rd Annual ACM Symposium on Theory of Computing (2001)
3. Charikar, M., Guha, S.: Improved combinatorial algorithms for the facility location and k-median problems. In: Proceedings of the 40th Annual IEEE Symposium on Foundations of Computer Science (1999)
4. Charikar, M., Guha, S., Tardos, E., Shmoys, D.: A constant-factor approximation algorithm for the k-median problem. In: Proceedings of the 31st Annual ACM Symposium on Theory of Computing (1999)
5. Charikar, M., Naor, J.S., Scheiber, B.: Resource optimization in QoS multicast routing of real-time multimedia. IEEE Transactions on Networking 12(2), 340–348 (2004)
6. Chudak, F.: Improved approximation algorithms for uncapacitated facility location problem. In: Proceedings of the 6th Conference on Integer Programming and Combinatorial Optimization (1998)
7. Chuzhoy, J., Gupta, A., Naor, J., Sinha, A.: On the approximability of some network design problems. In: Proceedings of the sixteenth annual ACM-SIAM symposium on Discrete algorithms, pp. 943–951 (2005)
8. Hochbaum, D.S.: Approximation Algorithms for NP-hard Problems. PWS Publishing (1996)
9. Jain, K., Vazirani, V.: Primal-dual approximation algorithms for the metric facility location and k-median problems. In: Proceedings of the 40th Annual IEEE Symposium on Foundations of Computer Science (1999)
10. Kolliopoulos, S., Rao, S.: A nearly linear time approximation scheme for the Euclidean k-medians problem. In: Nešetřil, J. (ed.) ESA 1999. LNCS, vol. 1643, Springer, Heidelberg (1999)

11. Korupolu, M., Plaxton, C., Rajaraman, R.: Analysis of a local search heuristic for facility location problems. In: Proceedings of the 9th Annual ACM-SIAM Symposium on Discrete Algorithms (1998)
12. Kumar, A., Sabharwal, Y.: The Priority k-median Problem. Full version available, www.cse.iitd.ernet.in/~yogish
13. Kumar, A., Sabharwal, Y., Sen, S.: Linear time approximation algorithms for clustering problems in any dimensions. In: Proceedings of the 32nd International Colloquium on Automata, Languages and Programming (2005)
14. Lin, J.H., Vitter, J.S.: ε-approximations with minimum packing constraint violation. In: Proceedings of the 24th Annual ACM Symposium on Theory of Computing (1992)
15. Love, R.F., Morris, J.G., Wesolowsky, G.O.: Facilities Location: Models and Methods. North-Holland, Amsterdam (1998)
16. Mirchandani, P., Francis, R.: Discrete Location Theory. Wiley, New York (1990)
17. Shmoys, D.B., Swamy, C., Levi, R.: Facility location with service installation costs. In: Proceedings of the fifteenth annual ACM-SIAM symposium on Discrete algorithms, Philadelphia, PA, USA, pp. 1088–1097 (2004)
18. Shmoys, D., Tardos, E., Aardal, K.: Approximation algorithms for facility location problems. In: Proceedings of the 29th Annual ACM Symposium on Theory of Computing (1997)

"Rent-or-Buy" Scheduling and Cost Coloring Problems

Takuro Fukunaga[1], Magnús M. Halldórsson[2], and Hiroshi Nagamochi[1]

[1] Dept. of Applied Math. and Physics, Graduate School of Informatics,
Kyoto University, Japan
[2] School of Computer Science, Reykjavik University, Iceland

Abstract. We study several *cost coloring problems*, where we are given a graph and a cost function on the independent sets and are to find a coloring that minimizes the costs of the color classes. The "Rent-or-Buy" scheduling/coloring problem (RBC) is one that, e.g., captures job scheduling situations involving resource constraints where one can either pay a full fixed price for a color class (representing e.g., a server), or a small per-item charge for each vertex in the class (corresponding to jobs that are either not served, or are farmed out to an outside agency). We give exact and approximation algorithms for RBC and three other cost coloring problems (including the previously studied Probabilistic coloring problem), both on interval and on perfect graphs. The techniques rely heavily on the computation of maximum weight induced k-colorable subgraphs (k-MCS). We give a novel bicriteria approximation for k-MCS in perfect graphs, and extend the known exact algorithm for interval graphs to some problem extensions.

1 Introduction

Consider the following scheduling scenario. You are given a collection of jobs, some of which require exclusive access to a specialized resource, e.g., a brain scanner. The jobs have all been fixed, with known start and end times, and you must satisfy all requests. You know that the minimum number of scanners needed is exactly the largest number χ of jobs that will be in concurrent operation, so you could simply go out and buy χ scanners. However, here you also have the option to rent them at a fixed price per job. The task is then to decide for which jobs to buy a scanner and for which ones to rent a scanner.

We can formulate this more generally as a graph coloring problem, where jobs are nodes in the graph and edges corresponds to the use of a non-sharable resource. More generally, we may assume that each job i requires a quantity w_i of a given non-sharable resource (in the example above, it may correspond to the rent being a function of the length of the job). We obtain the following problem:

RENT-OR-BUY COLORING PROBLEM (RBC):
Given: Graph $G = (V, E)$, with vertex weights $w_v \in \mathbf{R}^+$.
Find: A proper vertex coloring C consisting of color classes $I_1, I_2, \ldots, I_t$.

V. Arvind and S. Prasad (Eds.): FSTTCS 2007, LNCS 4855, pp. 84–95, 2007.

Minimize: $f(C) = \sum_{i=1}^{t} f(I_i)$, where $f(I) = \min(w(I), 1)$ and $w(I) = \sum_{v \in I} w_v$.

When the weight of a color class exceeds 1, it is said to be *full*, and we are best off buying a new resource at this scaled unit price. In scheduling applications where jobs represent time intervals, the corresponding graph is an interval graph. In ordinary graph coloring, we "pay" one unit for each color that we start to use. The idea behind Rent-or-Buy coloring is that one may often be able to take care of the small independent sets cheaper, e.g., by paying some elementwise "fine".

We consider more generally *cost coloring problems*, where we have some non-negative cost function $f : 2^V \mapsto \mathbf{R}^+$ on the independent sets of the graph. We will assume anywhere in the paper that the cost of a coloring C is the sum of the costs of the color classes, i.e. $f(C) = \sum_{I \in C} f(I)$.

Intuitively, this corresponds to a scheduling scenario where the cost of a re-source is some function of the usage of the resource, when we view each color as a (copy of a) resource. This can apply to many of the innumerable applications of graph colorings. For instance, the cost of a classroom in a timetabling application is not really a unit; different classrooms may have different costs, depending on size, and depending on the amount of use. The cost of a frequency in frequency allocation may depend on time- or space-limitations of the usage. The cost of fulfilling server requests, e.g., for bandwidth allocation in networks, may depend on the willingness to deploy servers, outsource some of the traffic (at a volume-dependent cost), or to pay the indirect cost of refusing service.

The cost coloring framework is very general, which leads us to consider which types of cost functions are natural and of practical interest. First, we usually assume the function to be *monotone*, in that if you request more of a resource, it won't cost less.

Second, most reasonable cost coloring functions have the property that they depend only on the combined weight of the set, not the distribution of the weights nor on which particular vertices participate in the set. We call such functions *separable* when the costs can be represented by a single-variable function, i.e., abusing notation, when $f(I) = f(w(I))$, for any independent set I. We focus on separable functions here, with one exception.

Third, as a consumer, one normally expects there to be an incentive to buy in large quantities; i.e., that the *residual* unit cost goes down with request size. This corresponds to the cost function being concave; a separable function f is *concave* if $f(x) + f(y) \le 2f((x+y)/2)$, for any $x, y \in \mathbf{R}$. In practice, costs tend to be nearly-concave, with volume incentives following a series of thresholds.

Our objective in this paper is to address some of the most basic cost coloring problems. The very most basic one would be the ordinary Graph Coloring problem, which has the trivially monotone, concave and separable cost function $f(I) = 1$. We shall be treating, in addition to RBC, the following natural problems. Recall that the cost of a coloring is the sum of the costs of the color classes.

Two-tiered rents with opening costs (TTR): This is a generalization of RBC with two residual costs, c_1 and c_2. Once the weight of the class reaches a certain threshold, the per-item cost changes to the second cost. Additionally, we allow a fixed charge c (less than 1) for the non-zero use of any color, which can represent a cost for "opening" or initiating the use of that resource. The cost function f for each color class I is $f(I) = c + c_1 \cdot \min(w(I), T) + \max(c_2 \cdot (w(I) - T), 0)$. We are not aware of previous work on TTC or RBC.

Threshold colorings: Suppose we have two modes of servicing (independent) sets, depending on their size. E.g., we can either schedule a group by renting a taxi, at a fixed price, or by renting a bus (that will definitely fit all), at a higher fixed price. We seek as before a minimum cost schedule of everyone, taking conflicts into account. The cost function $f(w(I))$ is now constant c_1, when $w(I)$ is at most the threshold T, and a larger constant c_2, when $w(I)$ is above the threshold.

A special case is when the above-threshold cost is too high to be ever cost-effective, e.g. n-fold the below-threshold cost. We have then the *bounded-coloring* problem, which models the case of scheduling conflicting unit-size jobs with bounded number of machines. It is NP-hard on bipartite and interval graphs [2].

Probabilistic coloring: In the *Probabilistic coloring* problem [17], we are given a graph G with independent vertex probabilities $p_v \in [0, 1]$ and are to find a coloring where the cost $f(I)$ of a color class is the cumulative probability $f(I) = P(I) = 1 - \prod_{v \in I}(1 - p_v)$. This was proposed for modeling robustness in optimization, where one is presented *a priori* with a supergraph of what will be used in the future. The cost of the coloring is then the expectation of the number of colors actually used. This cost function is both concave and monotone, but not separable. Probabilistic coloring is NP-hard in bipartite graphs [17], split graphs [4], and interval graphs [11,3], but solvable in co-bipartite graphs [17], and co-interval graphs [12]. It admits a $\sqrt{\rho_{GC}n}$-approximation, where ρ_{GC} is the approximability of Graph Coloring, a 3/2-factor in bipartite graphs [17], and 2-approximation in split graphs [4].

Our Results and Techniques. We can observe that applying ordinary coloring will not give good approximations for these cost coloring problems, nor does the usual approach of repeatedly coloring maximum independent sets. Instead, we make a strong link to the problem of finding a maximum (weight) induced k-colorable subgraph (k-MCS). RBC is in fact solved exactly by finding a maximum k-MCS, for the right choice of k. For approximation, we present in Section 2 a novel bicriteria approximation for k-MCS on perfect graphs, which allows us to approximate RBC in Section 3 within a factor of 2.

In order to solve TTR, we modify the flow reduction of Arkin and Silverberg [1] for weighted k-MCS in interval graphs to give an $O(n^2 \log n)$-time algorithm to solve the following extension: given an interval graph and integers k and h, find a maximum weight k-colorable subgraph whose removal leaves a h-colorable subgraph. This allows us to solve TTR also optimally in interval graphs.

We then show in Section 4 that Probabilistic colorings are always within a factor of $e/(e - 1)$ of related RBC colorings. This gives then a complete characterization of Probabilistic coloring, within constant factors, and improved approximations for several classes of graphs.

As a third simple and natural cost function, we consider in Section 5 the approximability of Threshold colorings. These are perhaps the simplest non-concave but separable cost functions. We derive a 4.78-approximation for perfect graphs.

Related work. Entropy coloring is a problem from information theory involving the separable cost measure $f(I) = w(I) \ln(1/w(I))$. It models transmission rate with side information, and has applications in digital compression [3]. It is NP-hard on interval graphs, hard to approximate within a $\Omega(n)$-factor (its value is always at most $\log n$) [3], but polynomially solvable on co-interval graphs [12] and co-bipartite graphs [3].

Gijswijt, Jost and Queyranne [12] recently introduced a general framework for cost coloring problems that they call *value-polymatroidal*. It contains monotone problems where moving vertices from a smaller class to a bigger class does not increase the total cost, i.e., when $f(I \cup \{v\}) + f(J) \le f(I) + f(J \cup \{v\})$, for any independent sets I, J with $f(I) \ge f(J)$. This class includes all the problems treated in this paper, except Threshold coloring. It also includes the *max coloring* problem [6,18], which has the non-separable, monotone cost function $f(I) = \max_{v \in I} w_v$. They give a polynomial time algorithm for all such problems on co-interval graphs (complements of interval graphs).

In a companion paper [11], we study separable cost coloring problems, and give approximation algorithms on perfect graphs. In particular, we show that concave separable functions admit a *robust* approximation, in that there is an algorithm that given a graph, produces a coloring that *simultaneously* approximates any concave function on perfect graphs. We also show how to modify these colorings to approximate (in a function-specific way, necessarily) any monotone separable cost function. In comparison, our results here are more specialized, but the approximation factors are better (e.g., 2 for RBC on perfect graphs vs. 6 for any concave function, and 4.78 for Threshold coloring vs. 12 for any monotone separable function).

Some other types of coloring problems with weights have been considered. In the optimal chromatic cost problem (OCCP) [16], the cost of a color class is linear in its size, but each class has a different multiplier specific. The sum coloring problem [14] is a special case where the multipliers are the natural numbers. These fall outside of our framework, which assumes that all colors are equal.

Notation. Let $G = (V, E)$ be a graph given with vertex weights w_v. Let n denote the number of vertices. For a subset $S \subset V$, $G[S]$ denotes the subgraph of G induced by S. For a set S, let $w(S) = \sum_{v \in S} w_v$, and let $w(G) = w(V)$.

A coloring is a partition of V into independent sets. A k-*subgraph* is an induced k-colorable subgraph. We may overload the notation and refer to a vertex subset $S \subset V$ as a k-subgraph if $G[S]$ is k-colorable. k-*MCS* refers to the problem of finding a k-subgraph of maximum total weight, and *Graph Coloring* refers to the classical vertex coloring problem, using the minimum number $\chi(G)$ of colors.

2 Approximation of Maximum k-Subgraphs

Our approach is heavily based on finding large induced subgraphs with small chromatic number (k-subgraphs). The weighted k-MCS problem is known to be polynomially solvable on interval graphs (due to total unimodularity [20] and by a direct $O(n^2 \log n)$-time min cost flow reduction [1]), permutation graphs [19], and on chordal graphs for fixed k [20]. The unweighted version is solvable on comparability and cocomparability graphs [10] but is NP-hard on chordal graphs (for k unbounded).

The solution of the max k-subgraph problem is an important component of approximation algorithms for numerous coloring problems, e.g., sum coloring [14], sum multi-coloring, batch sum coloring [5], and co-coloring [9]. One would hope to replace the subroutine by an approximation algorithm, for graph classes where k-MCS is NP-hard. However, there are different types of approximations possible. Let W be the weight of an optimal k-subgraph.

Primal: Find a k-subgraph of weight at least cW, for c largest possible.

Dual: Find a $t \cdot k$-subgraph of weight at least W, for t smallest possible.

Complementary: Find a subgraph T such that $V \setminus T$ induces a k-subgraph, and the weight of at most s times that of a minimum such subgraph, for s smallest possible.

The primal approximation does not suffice for RBC or the abovementioned problems. For instance, suppose we are given a 3-colorable graph G with all $w_v = 0.2$. Then a $(10/9)$-approximate 3-colorable subgraph still leaves $0.1n$ vertices uncolored, for RBC cost of $0.02n = \Omega(n)$, while the optimal solution has cost 3. Instead, we need an approximation of the dual objective, which has unfortunately proved difficult.

We develop here a *bicriteria* approximation in terms of the dual and the complementary measures. We say that a vertex set S is a (t, s)-*approximation* to k-MCS if it is a tk-subgraph and $w(V \setminus S) \le s \cdot w(V \setminus S^*)$, where S^* is a maximum k-subgraph. Namely, it gives a subgraph that requires t times as many colors, and leaves behind up to s times the weight left by the optimal solution.

Theorem 1. *There is an algorithm that, given a perfect graph G and integers k and t, yields a $(t, \frac{t}{t-1})$-approximation to k-MCS.*

Proof. Let an s-clique refer to an unweighted clique, i.e. a set of s mutually adjacent vertices. Consider the following local-ratio strategy:

> Let $G' = G$ and $w'_v = w_v$ for each vertex v.
> $i \leftarrow 1$
> while there exists a $t \cdot k + 1$-clique C_i in G' do
>   Let $w_i = \min_{u \in C_i} w'_u$.
>   Let $w'_v \leftarrow w'_v - w_i$, for each $v \in C_i$.
>   Remove all vertices v with $w'_v = 0$ from G'.
> $i \leftarrow i + 1$
> od
> Output $G[S]$, where $S = V(G')$ is the remaining vertex set.

Note that since there exists no $tk+1$-clique in $G[S]$ and G is perfect, the resulting subgraph $G[S]$ is tk-colorable, establishing the first part of the claim.

The weights w' at the end of the algorithm are at most the original weights w. Thus,

$$w(G \setminus S) = w(G) - w(S) \leq w(G) - w'(S). \tag{1}$$

The weight reduced from the cliques in G' in each round are evenly spread over the $t \cdot k + 1$ vertices; thus, at most $1/t$-fraction can belong to any k-subgraph, including a maximum weight k-subgraph S^*. Hence, at least a $(t-1)/t$-fraction of the weight comes from outside S^*. Thus,

$$w(G) - w'(S) = \sum_i w_i(C_i) \leq \frac{t}{t-1}[w(G) - w(S^*)] = \frac{t}{t-1}w(G \setminus S^*).$$

Combined with (1), we have the second part of the claim.

This is a tight bound for this approach, as can be seen by adding to any k-colorable graph a collection of $t \cdot k + 1$-cliques, along with a single $t \cdot k$-clique.

A generalization of this argument can be useful in some cases. It suffices to change only the loop condition of the algorithm of the previous proof to read "while the approximation algorithm finds a $2k$-clique". In particular, we obtain a $(4, 2)$-approximation for circular arc graphs, and $(2k, 2)$-approximation of intersection graphs of k-hypergraphs (ones with maximum edge size k).

Theorem 2. *Let $\mathcal{G}$ be a hereditary class of graphs. Suppose there is an algorithm that given number s and a graph in $\mathcal{G}$ either returns a clique of size s or a coloring of size ρs. Then, there is a $(2\rho, 2)$-approximation of k-MCS in $\mathcal{G}$.*

Repeatedly finding large independent sets is a natural approach. While it does not give a constant factor approximation, it can be used to get some non-trivial bounds for hard classes of graphs. The following lemma is a slight strengthening of an argument made numerous times before (see, e.g., [13]).

Lemma 1. *Suppose the maximum independent set (MIS) problem can be approximated within a factor of ρ on a hereditary class of graphs. Then, there is a $(\rho \log n, 1)$-approximation of k-MCS. Further, if $\rho = n^{\Omega(1)}$, then there is a $(O(\rho), 1)$-approximation.*

3   Rent-or-Buy Coloring (and TTR)

It can be quickly verified that ordinary colorings can be far off the mark under the Rent-or-Buy measure. An optimal coloring can leave all colors balanced, for a unit cost per color, while by using more colors, we may only need a single large color class, with the rest in small, cheap classes.

Another approach was used for *max coloring*, where the vertex set was first partitioned into weight classes [18]. However, this would reduce to ordinary coloring in the case of uniform weights, which again would not be sufficient. Thus, a different approach is needed for RBC.

3.1 Exact Algorithms for Interval Graphs

The following result shows that RBC is closely related to a well-known optimization problem. A proof of a more general result is given in Lemma 2.

Theorem 3. *Let G be a graph, and suppose we can compute a maximum weighted k-colorable subgraph in G, for any k. Then, we can solve RBC in polynomial time.*

Corollary 1. *RBC is polynomially solvable on interval, comparability, and bipartite graphs, as well as partial k-trees.*

We now give an alternative flow formulation of k-MCS problem on interval graphs, which allows for additional constraints on the remaining subgraph. We call a vertex set $S \subset V$ a (k, h)-*subgraph* if it is a k-subgraph and $V \setminus S$ is an h-subgraph. The (k, h)-MCS problem is that of finding a maximum weight (k, h)-subgraph. Observe that a maximum weight k-subgraph is also a maximum weight (k, h)-subgraph, for some h.

Theorem 4. *Let G be an interval graph and k and h be given. Then, a maximum weight (k, h)-subgraph can be computed in time $O((k + h)n \log n)$.*

Proof. We modify the construction of [1]. Recall that an interval graph can be represented as a linearly ordered set of maximal cliques $C_1, \ldots, C_t$ of sizes $q_1, q_2, \ldots, q_t$. Let R be $k + h$. We assume that $q_i \leq R$ for every $i = 1, \ldots, t$ since otherwise G has no (k, h)-subgraph.

Construct a directed network $H = (V, E)$ with vertices $v_0, \ldots, v_t$. There is an edge (v_{i-1}, v_i) of capacity $R - q_i$ and weight 0, for each $i = 1, \ldots, t$. We call these *dummy edges*, and let E_1 denote the set of these in H. Also, for each vertex v of weight w_v that is contained in cliques $C_j, C_{j+1}, \ldots C_{j+\ell}$, add an edge to H from v_{j-1} to $v_{j+\ell}$ of capacity 1 and weight w_v. We call these edges *subgraph edges*, and let E_2 denote the set of these in H. This completes the construction. Observe that subgraph edges used by a 1-flow from v_0 to v_t in H correspond to vertices in an independent set in G. Hence a k-flow in H gives a k-subgraph of the same weight in G.

Now we show that a k-flow exists in H, and after removing the k-flow, H still has an h-flow. This implies that we can obtain a maximum weight (k, h)-subgraph of G by computing a maximum weight k-flow in H.

Let $\delta^+(v_i)$ (resp., $\delta^-(v_i)$) denote the set of edges in H leaving (resp., entering) v_i. For a set F of edges, let $c(F)$ denote the sum of capacities of those in F. In H, subgraph edges in $\delta^+(v_i)$ correspond to vertices v in G such that $v \notin C_i$ and $v \in C_{i+1}$. Similarly, subgraph edges in $\delta^-(v_i)$ correspond to vertices v in G such that $v \in C_i$ and $v \notin C_{i+1}$. Hence $c(\delta^+(v_i) \cap E_2) - c(\delta^-(v_i) \cap E_2) = q_{i+1} - q_i$ holds for each $i = 1, \ldots, t - 1$. Since $c(\delta^+(v_i) \cap E_1) = R - q_{i+1}$ and $c(\delta^-(v_i) \cap E_1) = R - q_i$, we can observe that $c(\delta^-(v_i)) = c(\delta^+(v_i))$ for each $i = 1, \ldots, t - 1$. By the construction of H, $c(\delta^+(v_0)) = c(\delta^-(v_t)) = R$ also hold. Therefore, we can observe that H has a k-flow from v_0 to v_t. After removing a

k-flow from H, $c(\delta^-(v_i)) = c(\delta^+(v_i))$ still holds for each $i = 1, \ldots, t-1$, and $c(\delta^+(v_0)) = c(\delta^-(v_t)) = R - k = h$. Hence we can still push an h-flow.

The number of vertices and edges in H is linear in n, the number vertices in G. Each flow increase can be obtained in the time required for a shortest-path computation in the residual graph [15].

Observe that in the time spent to compute the flow, we actually obtain a series of values (k_j, h_j) for each $k_j + h_j = R$. Also, observe that a maximum weight (k, h)-subgraph problem is solvable in bipartite graphs, since in this case trivially $k = 1$.

Theorem 5. *TTR is polynomially solvable on interval and bipartite graphs.*

Proof. Observe that the two-tiered rent cost of an independent set without opening costs can be viewed as the smaller value of two linear functions:

$$f(I) = c_2 w(I) + \min((c_1 - c_2) \cdot w(I), y_0),$$

where $y_0 = (c_1 - c_2)T$. Thus, the cost of the coloring C can be represented as $c_2 w(G) + \sum_{I \in C} \min((c_1 - c_2) \cdot w(I), y_0)$. Thus, it is equivalent to RBC after scaling the weights by a factor of $y_0/(c_1 - c_2)$, and adding $c_2 \cdot w(G)$ to the objective function. The addition of constant terms to the objective function does not affect the optimization of the problem.

With opening costs, we want also to minimize the number of colors used on the non-full color classes. We therefore seek a k-subgraph, with the right value of k, whose remaining graph can be colored with few colors. Hence, it suffices to try all maximum (k, h)-subgraphs, for all k and h.

3.2 Approximation of Perfect Graphs

Lemma 2. *Suppose we have a (t, t)-approximation algorithm for k-MCS. Then, we can approximate RBC within a factor of t.*

Proof. Let k' be the number of full colors in an optimal RBC coloring and S^* be the set of vertices in those colors. The cost of the optimal solution is then $k' + w(V \setminus S^*)$.

Let S be a (t, t)-approximate solution to k'-MCS. If we color S using at most $t \cdot k'$ colors, and the remaining vertices arbitrarily, we get a coloring of cost at most $t \cdot k' + w(V \setminus S) \le t(k' + w(V \setminus S^*))$. By trying all values of k, we obtain a solution as good as when using $k = k'$. Thus, we have a performance ratio of t.

By Theorem 1, we get a 2-approximation of RBC, but it applies more generally to TTR.

Corollary 2. *TTR, with non-negative costs, is 2-approximable on perfect graphs, even with opening costs.*

Proof. Recall from Theorem 5 that TTR without opening costs is equivalent to RBC after scaling. With opening costs, we want also to minimize the number of colors used on the non-full color classes. The subgraph found in Theorem 1 is trivially $\chi(G)$-colorable, and if we color the remaining graph optimally, we use at most $2\chi(G)$ colors in total. Thus, our opening costs are at most twice that of any coloring.

3.3   Hardness and Approximation of General and Split Graphs

For general graphs, we can obtain a bound using Lemma 1, that matches the best approximation factor known for the ordinary graph coloring problem [13].

Corollary 3. *Let ρ_{IS} be the best possible approximation ratio of MIS on general graphs. Then, RBC and TTC can be approximated within a factor of $O(\rho_{IS})$. In particular, they can be approximated within $O(n(\log\log n)^2/\log^3 n)$ [7].*

RBC is clearly equivalent to Graph Coloring when all $w_v = 1$. Therefore, as a more general problem, it inherits all the hardness characteristics. However, one may still ask how hard the problem is for other vertex weights. For instance, the problem is trivial when $w(G) \leq 1$, since any coloring has then the same cost. From the results of Feige and Kilian [8], that were derandomized by Zuckerman [21], we have the following.

Observation 6. *RBC is NP-hard to approximate within a $\min(n, w(G)/n^\epsilon)$-factor, and is trivially $w(G)$-approximable.*

Essentially the same reduction from X3C (exact 3-set cover) as used on related problems [4,12] shows the hardness of RBC on split graphs, a subclass of chordal graphs.

Theorem 7. *RBC is strongly NP-hard on split graphs, even in the case of uniform weights.*

Proof. Let (X,T) be an input to X3C, where $X = \{s_1, s_2, \ldots, s_{3m}\}$ is a finite set and $T = \{e_1, \ldots, e_n\}$ is a set of triples from X. Form a graph with vertex set $X \cup T$, where X is independent, T is a clique, and (s_i, e_j) is an edge iff $s_i \notin e_j$. Assign each vertex the weight $w = 1 - 1/(2n)$. Then, any coloring of cost less than n uses only n colors, with each e_i in a different class. The cost of such a coloring is $n - (n - t)/(2n)$, where t is the number of colors that contain more than one vertex. Thus, the minimum cost of an RBC coloring is $n - (n - m)/(2n)$ iff (X, T) admits a cover with m sets iff (X, T) admits an exact cover.

This is complemented with a polynomial time approximation scheme (PTAS).

Theorem 8. *RBC admits a PTAS on split graphs.*

Proof. Let (U, V, E) be a split graph with independent set U and clique V. Let $\epsilon > 0$ be given and let $k = 1/\epsilon$. Initially, assign each node in V to a different color. Try for each subset $S \subset V$ of size at most k the following: For each node $u \in N(S) = \{u \in U : \exists v \in S, (u, v) \notin E\}$, assign u to the color of some non-neighbor in S. Color the rest of U in a separate color.

Consider an optimal RBC coloring C, and let S^* be the set of nodes from U in full color classes. If $|S^*| \leq k$, then our solution is optimal when we try $S = S^*$. Otherwise, $OPT \geq |S^*| > k$. When trying $S = \emptyset$, our algorithm finds a solution with cost at most 1 for U and at most OPT for V, or at most $1 + OPT \leq OPT(1 + 1/k) = (1 + \epsilon)OPT$.

4 Probabilistic Coloring Problem

One of the useful features of Rent-or-Buy is that its colorings closely approximate Probabilistic colorings. This is helpful, since RBC is much more amenable to computation.

Theorem 9. *Let C be a coloring of a graph G with vertex weights $p_v \in (0, 1]$. Let $f_{RB}(C)$ $(f_{Pr}(C))$ be the cost of C under the Rent-or-Buy measure (the probabilistic coloring measure), respectively. Then, $f_{RB}(C) \geq f_{Pr}(C) \geq (1 - 1/e)f_{RB}(C)$.*

Proof. Let I be a color class under C. We can bound the cost $P(I)$ under the probabilistic measure from above by the weight $W(I)$ of I, since by inclusion-exclusion, $1 - P(I) = \prod_{v \in I}(1 - p_v) \geq 1 - \sum_v p_v = 1 - W(I)$. This implies the first inequality.

We can also bound $P(I)$ from below by

$$P(I) = 1 - \prod_{v \in I}(1 - p_v) \geq 1 - \prod_{v \in I} e^{-p_v} = 1 - e^{-w(I)}.$$

If $w(I) \geq 1$, then $f_{RB}(I) = 1$ and we have that $P(I) \geq 1 - e^{-1} = 1 - 1/e$. Otherwise, $f_{RB}(I) = w(I)$. Observe that the function $(1 - e^{-x})/x$ is decreasing in the interval $(0, 1]$. Hence, the ratio is maximized for $w(I) = 1$. Since the ratio holds for each color class individually, it also holds for the sum of the color classes.

These bounds are best possible. An independent set of weight 1 can consist of a single node of weight 1, or n nodes of weight $1/n$ each. In both cases, the RBC cost is the same, while the probabilistic measure results in cost of 1, in the former case, and $1 - 1/e + O(1/n)$, in the latter case.

Theorem 9 immediately implies that RBC and Probabilistic coloring have the same approximation behavior, within this factor of 1.582.

Corollary 4. *If RBC is ρ-approximable on a graph G, then Probabilistic coloring is approximable within a factor of $\rho \cdot \frac{e}{e-1} \leq 1.582\rho$ on G.*

Combining this with our bounds on RBC of Corollaries 1 and 3, and Theorem 8, we obtain the following improved bounds on Probabilistic coloring.

Theorem 10. *Probabilistic coloring is approximable within 1.582 on interval and comparability graphs, 3.164 on perfect graphs, 1.583 on split graphs, and $O(n(\log \log n)^2 / \log^3 n)$ on general graphs.*

5   Threshold Coloring

We note that neither finding an ordinary coloring nor repeatedly finding a maximum independent set leads in general to constant factor approximation. Instead, one can treat the two costs separately.

Theorem 11. *Threshold coloring can be approximated within a factor of $\rho \leq 4.78$ on perfect graphs.*

Proof. Let us denote by $R = c_2/c_1$ the ratio between the two costs. For simplicity, let us scale the costs so that $c_1 = 1$. Observe that if $R \leq 4.78$, then using an optimal graph coloring yields an R-approximation for Threshold coloring. Thus, we assume that $R \geq 4.78$.

We first find an optimal graph coloring of the subgraph induced by vertices of weight at least the threshold T. Since the optimal solution needs also to color these vertices in expensive classes, our cost is at most OPT, the cost of the optimal solution.

On the remaining graph G', we try for each value of k the following approach and retain the cheapest solution. Let $t = 3.569$. Find a $(t, t/(t-1))$-approximate k-MCS by Theorem 1, and color the $t \cdot k$-subgraph with expensive classes. Then, find an optimal graph coloring of the remaining subgraph, and divide each color into the fewest possible cheap classes.

Suppose the optimal solution used k_0 expensive classes, leaving a subgraph of size L to be covered with cheap classes. That subgraph required at least $\chi(G) - k_0$ colors, and also needed at least $\lceil L/T \rceil$ cheap classes. Hence, $OPT \geq k_0 \cdot R + \max(\chi(G) - k_0, \lceil L/T \rceil)$. For this value of $k = k_0$, our solution used $t \cdot k_0$ expensive classes, and colored a subgraph of total weight at most $t/(t-1) \cdot L$ with the inexpensive classes. At most $\chi(G)$ of those classes had weight less than $T/2$ and at most $2\lfloor t/(t-1) \cdot L/T \rfloor$ had weight more than $T/2$. Hence, the cost of the algorithm's solution is at most

$$OPT + t \cdot k_0 \cdot R + 2t/(t-1) \cdot L/T + \chi(G).$$

Rewrite this as the sum of three terms: OPT, $2t/(t-1) \cdot (k_0 \cdot R + L/T)$, and $[t - 2t/(t-1)]R \cdot k_0 + \chi(G)$. The first two terms are at most $1 + 2t/(t-1) \leq 3.78$ times OPT. We can also verify by computation that the last term is at most $(R-1) \cdot k_0 + \chi(G) \leq OPT$.

References

1. Arkin, E.M., Silverberg, E.B.: Scheduling jobs with fixed start and end times. Disc. Applied Math. 18, 1–8 (1987)
2. Bodlaender, H., Jansen, K.: Restrictions of graph partition problems. Part I. Theoretical Computer Science 148, 93–109 (1995)
3. Cardinal, J., Fiorini, S., Joret, G.: Minimum entropy coloring. In: Deng, X., Du, D.-Z. (eds.) ISAAC 2005. LNCS, vol. 3827, pp. 819–828. Springer, Heidelberg (2005)

4. Della Croce, F., Escoffier, B., Murat, C., Paschos, V.Th.: Probabilistic coloring of bipartite and split graphs. In: Gervasi, O., Gavrilova, M., Kumar, V., Laganà, A., Lee, H.P., Mun, Y., Taniar, D., Tan, C.J.K. (eds.) ICCSA 2005. LNCS, vol. 3480, pp. 202–211. Springer, Heidelberg (2005)

5. Epstein, L., Halldórsson, M.M., Levin, A., Shachnai, H.: Weighted Sum Coloring in Batch Scheduling of Conflicting Jobs. In: Díaz, J., Jansen, K., Rolim, J.D.P., Zwick, U. (eds.) APPROX 2006 and RANDOM 2006. LNCS, vol. 4110, pp. 116–127. Springer, Heidelberg (2006)

6. Escoffier, B., Monnot, J., Paschos, V.T.: Weighted Coloring: Further complexity and approximability results. Inf. Process. Lett. 97(3), 98–103 (2006)

7. Feige, U.: Approximating Maximum Clique by Removing Subgraphs. SIAM J. Discrete Math. 18(2), 219–225 (2004)

8. Feige, U., Kilian, J.: Zero knowledge and the chromatic number. JCSS 57, 187–199 (1998)

9. Fomin, F.V., Kratsch, D., Novelli, J.-C.: Approximating minimum cocolorings. Inf. Process. Lett. 84(5), 285–290 (2002)

10. Frank, A.: On chain and antichain families of a partially ordered set. Journal of Combinatorial Theory Series B 29, 176–184 (1980)

11. Fukunaga, T., Halldórsson, M.M., Nagamochi, H.: Robust cost colorings. In: SODA (2008)

12. Gijswijt, D., Jost, V., Queyranne, M.: Clique partitioning of interval graphs with submodular costs on the cliques. EGRES TR 2006-14, www.cs.elte.hu/egres

13. Halldórsson, M.M.: A still better performance guarantee for approximate graph coloring. Inform. Process. Lett. 45, 19–23 (1993)

14. Halldórsson, M.M., Kortsarz, G., Shachnai, H.: Sum coloring interval and k-claw free graphs with application to scheduling dependent jobs. Algorithmica 37, 187–209 (2003)

15. Iri, M.: Network Flow, Transportation, and Scheduling: Theory and Algorithms. Academic Press, London (1969)

16. Jansen, K.: Approximation Results for the Optimum Cost Chromatic Partition Problem. J. Algorithms 34, 54–89 (2000)

17. Murat, C., Paschos, V.Th.: On the probabilistic minimum coloring and minimum k-coloring. Disc. Appl. Math. 154, 564–586 (2006)

18. Pemmaraju, S.V., Raman, R.: Approximation Algorithms for the Max-coloring Problem. In: Caires, L., Italiano, G.F., Monteiro, L., Palamidessi, C., Yung, M. (eds.) ICALP 2005. LNCS, vol. 3580, Springer, Heidelberg (2005)

19. Saha, A., Pal, M.: Maximum weight k-independent set problem on permutation graphs. Int. J. Comput. Math. 80(12), 1477–1487 (2003)

20. Yannakakis, M., Gavril, F.: The maximum k-colorable subgraph problem for chordal graphs. Information Processing Letters 24(2), 133–137 (1987)

21. Zuckerman, D.: Linear degree extractors and the inapproximability of max clique and chromatic number. In: STOC, pp. 681–690 (2006)

Order Scheduling Models: Hardness and Algorithms

Naveen Garg[1,*], Amit Kumar[1,**], and Vinayaka Pandit[2]

[1] Indian Institute of Technology, Delhi
[2] IBM India Research Lab, Delhi

Abstract. We consider scheduling problems in which a job consists of components of different types to be processed on m machines. Each machine is capable of processing components of a single type. Different components of a job are independent and can be processed in parallel on different machines. A job is considered as completed only when all its components have been completed. We study both completion time and flowtime aspects of such problems. We show both lowerbounds and upperbounds for the completion time problem. We first show that even the unweighted completion time with single release date is MAX-SNP hard. We give an approximation algorithm based on linear programming which has an approximation ratio of 3 for weighted completion time with multiple release dates. We give online algorithms for the weighted completion time which are constant factor competitive. For the flowtime, we give only lowerbounds in both the offline and online settings. We show that it is NP-hard to approximate flowtime within $\Omega(\log m)$ in the offline setting. We show that no online algorithm for the flowtime can have a competitive ratio better than $\Omega(\sqrt{m})$.

1 Introduction

Consider the following scenario of scheduling customer orders. Each customer order consists of several components of different types. These orders are to be processed at m facilities each of which is specialized to execute components of a particular type. The order of a customer can be delivered only when all its components have been completed. In this paper, we consider scheduling problems in this setting which can be thought of as open shop scheduling with overlaps allowed between operations of a job. One may refer to the article by Chen and Hall [6] for an elaborate survey of practical applications of such a scheduling model. In their survey article, Leung et al. [11] have called this model as *Order Scheduling Model*.

We observe that order scheduling models occur in computational settings as well. Consider the following example. Large distributed computational grids are

---

* Work done as part of the "Approximation Algorithms" partner group of MPI-Informatik, Germany.
** Supported by IBM Faculty Award and a Max-Planck-Society travel award.

V. Arvind and S. Prasad (Eds.): FSTTCS 2007, LNCS 4855, pp. 96–107, 2007.

becoming very popular in solving complex scientific problems [4,12]. The Master-Worker scheme is one popular approach to solving these massive computation problems [8]. Typically, the problems are solved using a master to coordinate the exploration of the branch and bound tree with the help of a large number of worker resources [4]. There are also problems in which the computation is divided into many independent, data parallel components and executed on a grid [1,12]. Once the different independent components of the problem are mapped to specific resources, the expected running time can be estimated using the data size and the history of response times. To solve a number of these problems efficiently on the grid, the scheduler must take into account parameters like average completion time and flow time. Some of the most challenging computational problems solved on grids include genome data analysis, earthquake simulators, drug design etc.

In the three field notation for scheduling problems we use 'G' in the first field to denote this model. In this paper we consider the problem of scheduling jobs in this model under different objectives. The problem of minimizing the completion time, $G||\sum C_j$ was studied by Wagneur and Sriskandarajah [19] and they proved it to be strongly NP-Complete. However, Leung et al. [11] showed an error in their proof. Recently, Roemer [17] showed the problem to be strongly NP-complete even when $m = 2$. In this paper, we show that the problem is MAX-SNP hard even when there is a single release date (for all the jobs) and the processing time of all components is one. As for approximation algorithms, Wang and Cheng [20] gave a constant factor approximation algorithm. They considered a time-indexed linear programming formulation and a heuristic based on its solution to get an approximation ratio of 5.83. We show how to exploit a different formulation by Queyranne [14] to get an approximation ratio of 2 for the case of single release date and 3 for the case of multiple release dates. To the best of our knowledge, no non-trivial online algorithm is known for these problems. We present the first constant factor competitive online algorithms for these problems.

In Section 3 we present hardness results for both offline completion time and flowtime. We first show that the problem of minimizing the sum of completion times, $G||\sum C_j$ is MAX-SNP hard even when all components have unit processing times. This makes the problem harder than the well-studied problem of minimizing weighted completion time on parallel machines with release dates $P|r_j|\sum_j w_j C_j$ for which a PTAS[2] is known. We then show that it is NP-hard to approximate the offline flowtime within $\Omega(\log m)$. The results of Queyranne [14] and Schulz [18] yield approximation algorithms for $1|prec|\sum_j w_j C_j$ and $1|r_j, prec|\sum_j w_j C_j$ problems with approximation ratios 2 and 3 respectively. In Section 4, we show how to exploit their ideas to get approximation ratios of 2 and 3 for the $G|\sum_j w_j C_j$ and $G|r_j|\sum_j w_j C_j$ respectively.

Our online algorithm, in Section 5, uses the technique of time intervals with geometrically increasing lengths [9][5] and is 4-competitive. If we require that the computation performed by the online algorithm at each step be polynomially bounded then we obtain a 16-competitive algorithm. Hall et al.[9] gave a general technique for obtaining a 4ρ-competitive algorithm for weighted completion time with release dates provided there exists a dual ρ-approximation algorithm for the *maximum scheduled weight problem*. For our problem, we cannot show a dual ρ-approximation algorithm for any constant ρ. However, we can show a bicriterion $(2,2)$ approximation algorithm for the following problem: Given a set of jobs and a deadline D, find a schedule which minimizes the weight of jobs which are not completed by time D. We show that any (α, β) bicriterion approximation algorithm for this problem suffices to give a $4\alpha\beta$-competitive online algorithm for the problem of minimizing weighted completion time; this yields the 16-competitive algorithm mentioned above.

In section 6 we consider the problem of minimizing the total flow time in the online setting. Recall that the flowtime of a job is the difference between its completion time and release date, i.e., the amount of time it spends in the system. Here we show a family of instances where no online algorithm can achieve a competitive ratio better than $O(\sqrt{m})$ against an adaptive adversary. In this instance all job-components require unit processing time and hence the lower bound on the competitive ratio applies even if preemptions are permitted. In contrast for parallel machines, with preemptions — the problem $P|pmtn, r_j| \sum_j F_j$ — a non-migratory version of the shortest remaining processing time rule is $O(\min(\log n, P))$-competitive [3] where P is the ratio of the processing time of the longest job to the processing time of the shortest job.

The model considered in this paper is somewhat similar to open-shop scheduling with the only difference that in open-shop the operations associated with a job cannot be performed simultaneously. Some of the results known for open-shop mirror the results we obtain in this paper. In particular, it is known that $O||\sum_j C_j$ is MAX-SNP hard[10]. Queyranne and Sviridenko[15] gave a $3 + 2\sqrt{2}$-approximation for $O|r_j|\sum_j w_j C_j$ which was later improved to 5.06 by[7]. However, we are not aware of any results on $O|r_j|\sum_j w_j C_j$ in the online setting.

2   Preliminaries

We consider the problem of scheduling jobs with components on multiple machines. We have m machines and n jobs. Each job j specifies a vector P^j of processing times – we shall call this the processing time vector of job j. For each machine i, P_i^j denotes the processing requirement of job j on machine i. Define the length of a job j as the number of machines i such that $P_i^j > 0$. Each job j also has a release date r^j. In a valid schedule, each job j must be processed without interruption for P_i^j amount of time on each machine i. Further, processing of a job on any of the machines can not begin before its release date.

Given a valid schedule $\mathcal{A}$, define $C_i^j(\mathcal{A})$ as the time at which job j finishes processing on machine i. Define the completion time $C^j(\mathcal{A})$ of job j as $\max_i C_i^j(\mathcal{A})$. Define the flow time $F^j(\mathcal{A})$ of job j as $C^j(\mathcal{A}) - r^j$. Often, the schedule $\mathcal{A}$ will be clear from the context, and so we shall just use the notations C_i^j, C^j and F^j.

We also associate a weight w^j with job j. For a set S of jobs, let weight(S) denote the total weight of jobs in S. Let W be the total weight of all the jobs.

Define the weighted completion time of j in a schedule $\mathcal{A}$ as $\sum_j w^j \cdot C^j(\mathcal{A})$. The weighted flow time is defined similarly. We would like to compute schedules which minimize the weighted completion time or weighted flow time.

It is easy to observe that any algorithm that maintains a busy-schedule on each of the machines has minimum makespan even in the case of multiple release dates. As mentioned in the introduction, we focus on the weighted completion time and the total flowtime objective functions.

3 Hardness of Approximating Completion Time and Flow Time

3.1 Completion Time

We first show that the off-line problem of minimizing sum of completion times is MAX-SNP hard even when all release times are 0. We use the fact that vertex cover is MAX-SNP hard even on constant degree graphs [13]. Let C be a constant such that vertex cover is MAX-SNP hard on graphs where degrees of vertices are bounded by C.

An instance $\mathcal{I}$ of the vertex cover problem is given by a graph $G = (V, E)$ where the degree of any vertex in G is at most C. We map this to an instance $\mathcal{I}'$ of the problem of minimizing sum of completion times. $\mathcal{I}'$ has $|E|$ machines, one for each edge in G and $n = |V|$ jobs, one for each vertex in G. Corresponding to a vertex $v \in V$, we construct a job $j(v)$ such that $P_i^{j(v)}$ is 1 if edge i is incident on v, 0 otherwise. All jobs have weight 1 and release time 0.

Lemma 1. *There exists a constant K' such that it is NP-hard to get a K'-approximation algorithm for the minimum weighted completion time problem.*

Proof. Observe that all jobs in $\mathcal{I}'$ can be scheduled in two time steps as each edge job has two components corresponding to the vertices it is incident on. It is easy to see that the set of jobs completed in the first step correspond to an independent set. Hence, the set of jobs completed in the second step correspond to a vertex cover. Suppose $VC(G)$ is the size of the vertex cover of G that gets completed in second step. Then, the cost of such a solution is $(n - VC(G)) + 2VC(G) = n + VC(G)$. So the minimum completion time of $\mathcal{I}'$ has cost $CT^{OPT}(\mathcal{I}') = n + VC^{OPT}(G)$ where $VC^{OPT}(G)$ denotes the size of minimum vertex cover of G. Therefore,

$$2n \geq CT^{OPT}(\mathcal{I}') \geq (n + n/C) \tag{1}$$

As the degree of G is bounded by a constant, say C, we have

$$VC^{OPT}(G) \geq n/C \tag{2}$$

As mentioned before, there exists a constant $K > 1$ such that it is NP-hard to approximate the vertex cover of graphs whose degree is bounded by C within a factor of K. This, combined with equations 1 and 2 imply that there exists a constant $K' = \frac{1+K/C}{1+1/C}$ such that it is NP-hard to approximate the completion time of the transformed instances within a factor of K'.

3.2   Flow Time

Note that Lemma 1 implies that the problem of offline flowtime minimization is MAX-SNP hard even in the unweighted case. We now show that it is NP-hard to approximate the unweighted flowtime within $\Omega(\log m)$. We begin by explaining the intuitive ideas of our construction.

The flowtime of a given schedule can be written as the sum of the number of unfinished jobs at every time step. Given an instance of set cover, we construct an instance of the order scheduling problem such that, for any reasonable schedule, the set of unfinished jobs at a "deadline" can be interpreted as the set cover of the set system. Furthermore, we show that an α-approximation algorithm for the flowtime can be turned into an α-approximation algorithm for the set cover problem. We now proceed to the details of our construction.

We reduce the set cover problem to the problem of minimizing flowtime in our setting. We start with an instance of the set cover problem. Let $\mathcal{S}$ be the set system on the universe U. We now construct an instance of the scheduling problem. Corresponding to each element $e \in U$, we have a machine and for each set $S \in \mathcal{S}$, we have a job. We use S to denote both the set and its corresponding job, and e denotes an element and the corresponding machine. The job S has a component of length 1 on a machine e if $e \in S$. Let T, ϵ be such that $T > 2|\mathcal{S}|$ and $1/\epsilon > |\mathcal{S}|^2$. Let s_e denote the number of sets which contain e. On a machine e, we create $(T - s_e + 1)/\epsilon$ dummy jobs with just one component of length ϵ on e. All the jobs (including the dummy jobs) are released at time $t = 0$. After time T, we release "filler" jobs at regular intervals of ϵ. Each filler job has a component of length ϵ on each of the machines. The filler jobs are released for a very long time, say L. This completes the construction of the instance of order scheduling problem. Note that, as long as we keep L polynomially bounded in $|\mathcal{S}|$, our reduction can be done in polynomial time.

The volume of the jobs released on each machine at time $t = 0$ is equal to $T + 1$. So, the volume of the unfinished components on any machine at T is exactly 1. For any machine e, if all the components corresponding to the set jobs are finished by T, then, there will be $1/\epsilon$ jobs left unfinished on e. Given that $1/\epsilon > |\mathcal{S}|^2$, finishing all components belonging to set jobs would result in very high penalty from T to L. So, every schedule is forced to be left with exactly one component corresponding to a set job on each machine. Thus, for every reasonable schedule, the set of unfinished tasks at time T corresponds to a set cover. Note that the filler jobs are such that, beyond T, if a schedule tries to reduce the unfinished set jobs, it ends up accumulating too many filler jobs. So, every reasonable schedule is forced to schedule filler jobs between T and L.

Let SC_{OPT} denote the size of the optimum set cover and SC_{PACK} denote the size of the set cover left unfinished at time T by any algorithm. Let I_{OPT} and I_{PACK} be the flowtime incurred by the schedules which leave the optimum set cover and a set cover of size SC_{PACK} respectively. As argued above, beyond T, every reasonable schedule is forced to schedule only filler jobs upto L. Let F_{OPT} and F_{PACK} denote the flowtime of the set cover jobs left unfinished at time L

for the two schedules. Note that, $F_{OPT} \approx L \cdot SC_{OPT}$ and $F_{PACK} \approx L \cdot SC_{PACK}$. Let FT_{OPT} and FT_{PACK} be the total flowtimes of the two schedules. We have,

$$FT_{OPT} = L + 2 \cdot L \cdot SC_{OPT} + I_{OPT} \tag{3}$$
$$FT_{PACK} = L + 2 \cdot L \cdot SC_{PACK} + I_{PACK} \tag{4}$$

Note that, we can keep L such that, $L \gg I_{OPT}$ and $L \gg I_{PACK}$. Therefore, if $FT_{OPT}/FT_{OPT} = \alpha$, then, $SC_{PACK}/SC_{OPT} \approx \alpha$. Therefore, we can turn an $o(\log m)$ approximation algorithm for flowtime into an $o(\log m)$ approximation algorithm for set cover. As it is NP-hard to approximate set cover within $\Omega(\log m)$ [16],

Theorem 1. *It is NP-hard to approximate the flowtime of order scheduling problem within $\Omega(\log m)$ where m is the number of machines.*

4 Offline Weighted Completion Time

In this section, we show how to exploit a completion time linear programming formulation by Queyranne [14] and a scheduling heuristic based on its solution (Schulz [18]) to obtain approximation ratios of 2 and 3 for the cases of single and multiple release dates respectively. The formulation by Queyranne is called the *completion time linear program* in the literature. We adapt the completion time formulation for our problem as follows:

$$\min \sum_{j=n}^{n} w_j C_j$$
$$\text{s.t.}$$
$$C_j^m \geq r_j + p_j^m \qquad \forall j \in J, m \in M$$
$$C_j \geq C_j^m \qquad \forall j \in J, m \in M$$
$$\sum_{j \in S} p_j^m C_j^m \geq \frac{1}{2}\left[\left(\sum_{j \in S} p_j^m\right)^2 + \sum_{j \in S}(p_j^m)^2\right] \forall S \subseteq J, m \in M$$

In this formulation, M denotes the set of machines and J denotes the set of jobs. Further, the variable C_j^m indicates the completion time of job j on machine m, p_j^m is the processing time of j on machine m and C_j indicates the completion time of the job j. Queyranne showed a polynomial time separation oracle for the above set of constraints. So, the above program can be solved in polynomial time. The approximation ratios proved here are somewhat implicit and can be deduced from the work of Schulz [18]. We present an outline of the proof for the sake of completeness.

Consider the optimal solution to the above linear program. Let $\bar{C}$ denote the vector of completion times C_js and $\bar{C}^i$ denote the vector of completion times C_j^is on machine i. Let A be an algorithm which schedules the jobs independently on each of the machines. Let $\bar{D}^i$ denote the vector of completion times for the jobs it achieves on machine i. Furthermore, let D_j^i denote the completion time of job j on machine i. We claim that:

Lemma 2. *If there exists a constant K such that $D_j^i \leq K \cdot C_j^i$, then, the schedule given by $\bar{D}_i$s is an K-approximation for the $G|r_j| \sum w_j C_j$.*

Proof. Note that $C_j = \max\{C_j^i | \forall i \in \{1, \ldots, m\}\}$. The individual schedule $\bar{D}^i$ on machine i satisfies $D_j^i \leq KC_j^i$. Therefore, $D_j = \max\{D_j^i | \forall i \in \{1, \ldots, m\}\} \leq K \cdot C_j$. This implies that the schedule obtained by $\bar{D}^i$s is an K-approximation.

Schulz shows that, on a single machine, scheduling the jobs in the non-decreasing order of the completion times suggested by optimal solution to the above linear program satisfies the condition required by Lemma 2 with $K = 3$ in case of multiple release dates and $K = 2$ in case of single release date. Thus, scheduling components on a machine i in the non-decreasing order of C_j^is we get the approximation ratios stated above. At this point it is appropriate to highlight that, in the standard scheduling model, the above program and the scheduling order can be made to work even when there are precedence constraints between jobs. However, in our case, we are not able to show that the above approach can be made to work with precedence constraints.

The application of Schulz's heuristic on individual machines to get an approximation for the problem of m machines gives rise to the following question: Can algorithms for completion time minimization on single machine be used in place of Schulz? If indeed it is possible, then one could use the PTAS for $1|r_j| \sum w_j C_j$ [2] to get a PTAS for the problem and it would contradict the MAX-SNP hardness proved in Section 3. However, note that Lemma 2 is applicable to only those schedules which bound completion times of components on their corresponding machines in terms of the completion times C_j^is of the optimal solution to the above linear program. So, the heuristic by Schulz which works specifically with the output of the linear program cannot be replaced by other algorithms for completion time on single machine.

5   Online Algorithm for Minimizing Weighted Completion Time

We now consider the problem of minimizing weighted completion time in the online setting. Our approach is similar to that of Hall et al. [9] and leads to a 4-competitive algorithm for this problem.

For $k \geq 0$, let $t_k = 2^k - 1$. We divide the time line into intervals of geometrically increasing size. For $k \geq 0$, define the interval I_k as $[t_k, t_{k+1})$.

Our algorithm produces a schedule which we denote $\mathcal{A}$. It maintains the invariant that if it processes a job in an interval I_k, then the job will finish processing in this interval. More formally, let $R^{\mathcal{A}}(t_k)$ be the set of jobs released before time t_k but not scheduled before t_k in the schedule $\mathcal{A}$. Then $\mathcal{A}$ schedules only such jobs in I_k (and finishes them in I_k).

Our algorithm can be described as follows:

For $k = 0, 1, 2, \ldots$ do
    By considering all subsets of $R^{\mathcal{A}}(t_k)$, determine the maximum weight collection of jobs that can be completed in I_k.
    Schedule this set of jobs in the interval I_k so that they finish processing in this interval only.

Let $\mathcal{O}$ be the off-line schedule which minimizes the weighted completion time. Let weight$(D^{\mathcal{A}}(t_k))$ be the total weight of jobs finished by $\mathcal{A}$ by time t_k. Define weight$(D^{\mathcal{O}}(t_k))$ similarly.

Lemma 3. *weight$(D^{\mathcal{O}}(t_k))$ is at most weight$(D^{\mathcal{A}}(t_{k+1}))$.*

Proof. This is easy to see by restricting attention to the jobs in the set $R^{\mathcal{A}}(t_k)$. The jobs in $R^{\mathcal{A}}(t_k)$ which are scheduled in $\mathcal{O}$ before time t_k can also be scheduled by the online algorithm in the interval I_k (whose length is larger than t_k). □

Let W be the total weight of all jobs. Then the weighted completion time of schedule $\mathcal{O}$ is at least

$$\sum_{k \geq 1} (t_k - t_{k-1})(W - \text{weight}(D^{\mathcal{O}}(t_k))).$$

On the other hand the completion time of the schedule $\mathcal{A}$ is at most

$$\sum_{k \geq 0} (t_{k+1} - t_k)(W - \text{weight}(D^{\mathcal{A}}(t_k))).$$

Rewriting this expression we get

$$\sum_{k \geq 2} (t_{k+1} - t_k)(W - \text{weight}(D^{\mathcal{A}}(t_k))) + W + 2(W - \text{weight}(D^{\mathcal{A}}(t_1)))$$

$$\leq 3W + \sum_{k \geq 1}(t_{k+2} - t_{k+1})(W - \text{weight}(D^{\mathcal{A}}(t_{k+1})))$$

$$\leq 3W + \sum_{k \geq 1} 4(t_k - t_{k-1})(W - \text{weight}(D^{\mathcal{O}}(t_k)))$$

which implies that the weighted completion time of schedule $\mathcal{A}$ is at most 4 times the completion time of the best possible schedule plus an additive $3W$. This implies a competitive ratio of 4 for our online algorithm.

Note however, that to determine the jobs to be scheduled in an interval the online algorithm considers all possible subsets of unfinished jobs and picks the best, leading to an exponential running time. We now describe an online algorithm which takes polynomial running time. Starting from $k = 0$, we formulate a linear program to decide which jobs to schedule in the intervals I_k for all values of k (again our schedule will maintain the invariant that a job scheduled in I_k will finish in this interval only). Each job $j \in R^{\mathcal{A}}(t_k)$ has a variable x^j associated with it which is 1 if job j is scheduled in interval I_k and 0 otherwise. The linear program is as follows

$$\min \quad \sum_{j} w^j(1 - x^j) \tag{LP2}$$

$$\text{s.t.}$$

$$\sum_{j} P_i^j x^j \leq 2^k - 1 \quad \text{for all } i \tag{5}$$

$$x^j \in [0,1] \quad \text{for all } j$$

The objective function tries to minimize the total weight of jobs that cannot be finished in I_k. We will require that the total processing on each machine in this interval be no more that $2^k - 1$; note that this is equal to the total length of intervals I_0 to I_{k-1}. This is captured by the constraints (5). Since all jobs in $R^{\mathcal{A}}(t_k)$ which are scheduled before time t_k by $\mathcal{O}$ form a feasible solution to this linear program, the value of the optimum solution of this linear program is at most weight($R^{\mathcal{O}}(t_k)$).

Let $\bar{x}$ be an optimum solution to this linear program. Let J be the set of jobs for which $\bar{x}^j \geq 1/2$; our algorithm schedules all the jobs in J in I_{k+1}. On any machine i, the total processing time of jobs in J is at most $2(2^k - 1) \leq 2^{k+1}$ (which is at most the length of I_{k+1}). Further, the total weight of jobs which are not scheduled is at most twice the value of the optimum solution of the linear program.

The total weight of unfinished jobs at time t_{k+2} in $\mathcal{A}$ is at most twice the weight of unfinished jobs at time t_k in the schedule $\mathcal{O}$. The above analysis now extends to give a competitive ratio of 16 for this online algorithm.

6   Lower Bound for Minimizing Sum of Flow Times

In this section, we prove a lower bound of $\Omega(\sqrt{m})$ on the competitive ratio of any online algorithm for minimizing the sum of flowtimes. In fact this lower bound holds even when the processing times P_i^j are restricted to be either 0 or 1. Let the number of machines m be of the form k^2, where k is an integer. We first discuss the idea at a high level.

For each subset of k machines, we define a job which requires 1 unit of processing on these machines and 0 processing on other machines. Let J be the set of these jobs; note that $|J| = \binom{k^2}{k}$. All the jobs in J are released at time $t = 0$. Note that all the jobs in J can be scheduled by time $T_0 = \binom{k^2-1}{k-1}$. Let $T_1 = T_0 - k$. We show that at time T_1 in any online schedule, there is a set S of k machines such that the following condition is satisfied – there are $\Omega(k^2)$ jobs which have unscheduled components on at least one of the machines in S. Assuming this is true, we construct an adversary as follows. Let us number the machines in S from 1 to k. From time $T_1 + 1$ onwards, we release k jobs $j_1, \ldots, j_k$ of length one each. Job j_l is defined as: $P_l^{j_l} = 1$, and $P_i^{j_l} = 0$ if $i \neq l$. We then argue that with prior knowledge of these jobs, it is possible to schedule jobs such that, at time T_1, the number of jobs with unscheduled components on S is $O(k)$.

Lemma 4. *For the set of jobs J as defined above, in any schedule, at time T_1, there is a subset of k machines such that there are $\Omega(k^2)$ jobs which have unfinished components on these machines.*

Proof. Let $\mathcal{A}$ be an online schedule. Let q_j denote the number of unscheduled components of job $j \in J$ at time T_1. Note that, $0 \leq q_j \leq k$. Also note that, $\sum_{j \in J} q_j = k^3$. Consider a random subset N of k machines. Let U be the set of jobs which have unfinished components on at least one machine in N at time T_1. Consider a job j and let $\mathbf{Pr}_N^j$ denote the probability that $j \in U$. Note that

$$\mathbf{Pr}_N^j = 1 - \frac{\binom{k^2-q_j}{k}}{\binom{k^2}{k}} \geq 1 - \left(\frac{k^2-q_j}{k^2}\right)^k \geq 1 - \left(1 - \frac{q_j}{k^2}\right)^k \geq \frac{k \cdot q_j}{2k^2}$$

where the last inequality follows from the fact that for $xy \leq 1$, $(1-x)^y \leq 1-xy/2$ (note that $q_j \cdot k/k^2 \leq 1$).

The expected size of U is given by

$$\sum_{j \in J} \mathbf{Pr}_N^j \geq \sum_{j \in J} \frac{q_j k}{2k^2} \geq \frac{k^2}{2}$$

where the last inequality follows from the fact that $\sum_{j \in J} q_j = k^3$. So, there must exists a subset of k machines with the desired property.   □

Theorem 2. *There is no online algorithm for the flowtime problem with competitive ratio better than $\Omega(\sqrt{m})$.*

Proof. Let $\mathcal{A}$ be the schedule produced by an online algorithm. The theorem above implies that there is a set S of k machines such that there are $\Omega(k^2)$ jobs with unfinished components on at least one of these machines – let U be the set of such jobs. Number the machines in S from 1 to k. At each time instant from $t = T_1 + 1$, the adversary releases k jobs $j_1, \ldots, j_l$ of length 1 each such that $P_l^{j_i} = 1$ and $P_i^{j_i} = 0$ if $i \neq l$. We continue this till time $T_0 + X$. So, the schedule $\mathcal{A}$ is forced to have $\Omega(k^2)$ unfinished jobs till time $T_0 + X$. So, the weighted flowtime of $\mathcal{A}$ is at least $\sum_{j \in J-U} F^j(\mathcal{A}) + \Omega(k^2) \cdot (T_0 + X)$.

Consider some k jobs in J which require processing on all machines $1, \ldots, k-1$ in S. $\mathcal{O}$ does not schedule any component of these jobs before T_1. Further at time T_1, there are at most k jobs with unfinished components on machine k. Thus, in the schedule $\mathcal{O}$, there are at most $2 \cdot k$ jobs with unfinished components on S by time T_1 – let U' denote these jobs. Therefore, the weighted flow time of $\mathcal{O}$ is at most $\sum_{j \in J-U'} F^j(\mathcal{O}) + O(k) \cdot (T_0 + X)$. When X is very large compared to T_0, the ratio of the weighted flow time to $\mathcal{A}$ to that of $\mathcal{O}$ approaches k. This proves the theorem.   □

7   Conclusion

There are many interesting open problems in the context of order scheduling model. We highlight two of them. Firstly, we are not aware of algorithmic techniques that can handle precedence constraints between different jobs. Any non-trivial approximation of even minimum makespan would be very interesting. We were not able to use any of the standard techniques used for lower bounding the makespan in the presence precedence constraints. Secondly, it would be interesting to either get matching upperbounds or improve the lower bounds for the offline and online flowtime problem.

References

1. Abramson, D., Sosic, R., Giddy, J., Hall, B.: Nimrod: A tool for performing parameterised simulations using distributed applications. In: Proceedings of the 4th IEEE Symposium on High Performance Distributed Computing, IEEE Computer Society Press, Los Alamitos (1995)
2. Afrati, F., Bampis, E., Chekuri, C., Karger, D., Kenyon, C., Khanna, S., Milis, I., Queyranne, M., Skutella, M., Stein, C., Sviridenko, M.: Approximation schemes for minimizing average weighted completion time with release dates. In: FOCS, pp. 32–44 (1999)
3. Awerbuch, B., Azar, Y., Leonardi, S., Regev, O.: Minimizing the flow time without migration. In: ACM Symposium on Theory of Computing (STOC), pp. 198–205 (1999)
4. Brixius, N., Linderoth, J., Goux, J.: Solving large quadratic assignment problems on computational grid. Mathematical Programming, Series B 91, 563–588 (2002)
5. Chakrabarti, S., Phillips, C., Schulz, A., Shmoys, D., Stein, C., Wein, J.: Improved scheduling algorithms for minsum criteria. In: Proc. of the 23rd Int. Colloquium on Automata, Languages and Programming, pp. 646–657 (1996)
6. Chen, Z., Hall, N.: Supply chain scheduling: Assembly systems. Technical report, The Ohio State University (2000)
7. Gandhi, R., Halldorsson, M., Kortsarz, G., Shachnai, H.: Improved results for data migration and open shop scheduling. In: Proc. of the 31st Int. Colloquium on Automata, Languages, and Programming, pp. 658–669 (2004)
8. Goux, J., Kulkarni, S., Linderoth, J., Yoder, M.: Master-worker: An enabling framework for applications on the computational grids. In: Proceedings of the 9th IEEE Symposium on High Performance Distributed Computing, pp. 43–50 (2000)
9. Hall, L., Schulz, A., Shmoys, D., Wein, J.: Scheduling to minimize average completion time: offline and online algorithms. Mathematics of Operations Research 22, 513–549 (1997)
10. Hoogeveen, H., Schuurman, P., Woeginger, G.: Non-approximability results for scheduling problems with minsum criteria. In: Bixby, R.E., Boyd, E.A., Ríos-Mercado, R.Z. (eds.) Integer Programming and Combinatorial Optimization. LNCS, vol. 1412, pp. 353–362. Springer, Heidelberg (1998)
11. Leung, J., Li, H., Pindeo, M.: Multidisciplinery scheduling: Theory and Applications. chapter Order Scheduling Models: an overview, 37–56 (2005)
12. Linderoth, J., Wright, S.: Decomposition algorithms for stochastic programming on a computational grid. Computational Optimization and Applications 24, 207–250 (2003)
13. Papadimitriou, C., Yannakakis, M.: Optimization, approximation, and complexity classes. Journal of Computer and System Sciences 43, 425–440 (1991)
14. Queyranne, M.: Structure of a simple scheduling polyhedron. Mathematical Programming 58, 263–285 (1993)
15. Queyranne, M., Svirdenko, M.: New and improved algorithms for minsum shop scheduling. In: Symposium on Discrete Algorithms, pp. 871–878 (2000)
16. Raz, R., Safra, S.: A sub-constant error-probability low-degree test, and a sub-constant error-probability PCP characterization of NP. In: ACM Symposium on Theory of Computing (STOC), pp. 475–484 (1997)
17. Roemer, T.: A note on the complexity of the concurrent open shop problem. Journal of scheduling 9, 389–396 (2006)

18. Schulz, A.: Scheduling to minimize total weighted completion time: Performance guarantees of lp-based heuristics and lower bounds. In: Cunningham, W.H., Queyranne, M., McCormick, S.T. (eds.) Integer Programming and Combinatorial Optimization. LNCS, vol. 1084, pp. 301–315. Springer, Heidelberg (1996)
19. Wagneur, E., Sriskandarajah, C.: Open shops with jobs overlap. European Journal of Operations Research 71, 366–378 (1993)
20. Wang, G., Cheng, T.: Customer order scheduling to minimize total weighted completion time. Omega 35, 623–626 (2007)

On Simulatability Soundness and Mapping Soundness of Symbolic Cryptography

Michael Backes[1], Markus Dürmuth[1], and Ralf Küsters[2]

[1] Saarland University, Saarbrücken, Germany
{backes,duermuth}@cs.uni-sb.de
[2] ETH Zürich, Switzerland
ralf.kuesters@inf.ethz.ch

Abstract. The abstraction of cryptographic operations by term algebras, called Dolev-Yao models or symbolic cryptography, is essential in almost all tool-supported methods for proving security protocols. Recently significant progress was made – using two conceptually different approaches – in proving that Dolev-Yao models can be sound with respect to actual cryptographic realizations and security definitions. One such approach is grounded on the notion of simulatability, which constitutes a salient technique of Modern Cryptography with a long-standing history for a variety of different tasks. The other approach strives for the so-called mapping soundness – a more recent technique that is tailored to the soundness of specific security properties in Dolev-Yao models, and that can be established using more compact proofs. Typically, both notions of soundness for similar Dolev-Yao models are established separately in independent papers.

This paper relates the two approaches for the first time. Our main result is that simulatability soundness entails mapping soundness provided that both approaches use the same cryptographic implementation. Hence, future research may well concentrate on simulatability soundness whenever applicable, and resort to mapping soundness in those cases where simulatability soundness constitutes too strong a notion.

1 Introduction

Tool-supported verification of cryptographic protocols almost always relies on abstractions of cryptographic operations by term algebras with cancellation rules, called *symbolic cryptography* or *Dolev-Yao models* after the first authors [16]. An example term is $D_{ske}(E_{pke}(E_{pke}(N)))$, where E and D denote public-key encryption and decryption, *ske* and *pke* are corresponding private and public encryption keys, and N is a nonce (random string). The keys are written as indices for readability. Formally, E and D are binary function symbols. A typical cancellation rule is $D_{ske}(E_{pke}(t)) = t$ for all public/private key pairs (pke, ske) and terms t, thus the above term is equivalent to $E_{pke}(N)$. The proof tools handle these terms symbolically, i.e., they never evaluate them to bit strings. In other words, the tools perform abstract algebraic manipulations on trees consisting of operators and atomic messages, using only the cancellation rules, the message-construction rules of a particular protocol, and an abstract model of networks and adversaries.

It is not at all clear from the outset whether Dolev-Yao models are a sound abstraction from real cryptography with its computational security definitions, where messages are

V. Arvind and S. Prasad (Eds.): FSTTCS 2007, LNCS 4855, pp. 108–120, 2007.

bit strings and the adversary is an arbitrary probabilistic polynomial-time (ppt) Turing machine. In particular, the tools assume that *only* the modeled operations and cancellation rules are possible manipulations on terms, and that terms that cannot be constructed with these rules are completely secret. For instance, if an adversary (also called intruder) only saw the example term above and only the mentioned cancellation rule was given, then N would be considered secret. Bridging this long-standing gap between Dolev-Yao models and real cryptographic definitions has recently received considerable attention, and remarkable progress has been made using two conceptually different approaches.

One such approach, henceforth called *simulatability soundness*, is grounded on the security notion of (black-box reactive) simulatability (BRSIM), which relates a real system (also called implementation or real protocol) with an ideal system (also called ideal functionality or ideal protocol). The real system is said to be as secure as the ideal system if every attack on the real system can be turned into an "equivalent" attack on the ideal system, where "equivalent" means indistinguishable by an environment (also called honest users). This security notion essentially means that the real system can be plugged into an arbitrary protocol instead of the ideal system without any noticeable difference [20,21,10]. Basically the same notion is also called UC (universal composability) for its universal composition properties [11].[1] In terms of the semantics community, BRSIM/UC could be called an implementation or refinement relation, with a particular emphasis on retaining secrecy properties, in contrast to typical implementation relations. Now, results on simulatability soundness show that a (possibly augmented) Dolev-Yao model, specified as an ideal system, can be implemented in the sense of BRSIM/UC by a real system using standard cryptographic definitions. The first such result was presented in [8] and was extended to more cryptographic primitives in [9,7]. The use of these results in protocol proofs was illustrated in [6,3,22,2]. Simulatability soundness with more standard cryptographic assumptions and a simpler Dolev-Yao model, but a restricted class of protocols was proven in [12].

The other approach, henceforth called *mapping soundness*, is tailored to the soundness of specific security properties in standard Dolev-Yao models. Mapping soundness of a given protocol is established by showing the existence of a mapping from bit strings to terms such that applying the mapping to an arbitrary trace of the real cryptographic execution of the protocol yields a trace of an ideal, Dolev-Yao style execution of the protocol. Compared to simulatability soundness, mapping soundness can often be established by more compact proofs and sometimes more relaxed cryptographic assumptions. Unlike simulatability soundness, however, mapping soundness is restricted to specific protocol classes, and it does not entail universal composition properties. The first result on mapping soundness considered symmetric encryption under passive attacks [1]. Various later papers extended this approach to active attacks and to different cryptographic primitives and security properties [19,18,15,14,12]. In this paper, we are concerned with mapping soundness for active attacks.

---

[1] While the definitions of BRSIM and UC have not been rigorously mapped, we believe that for the results in this paper the differences do not matter, in particular if one thinks of the equivalent blackbox version of UC [11]. Similarly, we believe that the results would hold in the formalism put forward in [17].

1.1 Our Results

Our paper relates these two approaches for the first time. Our main result is that simulatability soundness entails mapping soundness provided that both approaches use the same cryptographic implementation. More precisely, we show that given an arbitrary ideal system M^{ideal} and an arbitrary real protocol M^{real}, mapping soundness of M^{real} necessarily holds provided that the following two assumptions are met: First, the traces of the ideal system constitute Dolev-Yao style traces, i.e., traces that can be constructed according to the rules of the term algebra and of the protocol under consideration; second, M^{real} is as secure as M^{ideal} in the sense of BRSIM/UC, i.e., simulatability soundness holds for the ideal and real systems under consideration. Interestingly, this result does not dependent on details of the simulator, which translates between cryptographic bit strings and their Dolev-Yao abstractions in simulatability soundness.

We note that requiring the same cryptographic implementations for both simulatability soundness and mapping soundness means that existing results on simulatability soundness do not necessarily fully supersede existing results on mapping soundness: the former results may, e.g., require stronger assumptions on the security of cryptographic primitives, specific techniques from robust protocol design such as explicit type tags, additional randomization, etc. in order to establish simulatability between the cryptographic implementation and its Dolev-Yao abstraction. However, we believe that it is now fair to say that future research may concentrate on simulatability soundness whenever applicable, and resort to mapping soundness in those cases where simulatability soundness constitutes too strong a notion.

1.2 Paper Outline

Section 2 reviews the basic terminology of symbolic cryptography, its deduction rules, and the syntax of protocols. Section 3 reviews the notion of simulatability and points out necessary requirements for a Dolev-Yao model to be sound in the sense of BR-SIM/UC. Section 4 defines executions of protocols within the reactive simulatability framework [21,10], thus preparing a common ground for comparing both notions of soundness. Section 5 finally proves that simulatability soundness implies mapping soundness.

The long version of this paper [4] contains further expositions that are omitted here for space reasons; in particular, it reviews the large body of literature substantiating the relevance of simulatability in Modern Cryptography, and the newly arising area of formulating syntactic calculi for dealing with probabilism and polynomial-time considerations directly (without relying on Dolev-Yao models).

2   Symbolic Cryptography

In this section, we review basic terminology concerning Dolev-Yao models and the corresponding deduction rules for deriving new messages from a given set of messages. In addition, we describe the syntax of protocols along the lines of works on the mapping approach [19,15,14].

2.1 Basic Terminology, Dolev-Yao Terms, and Deduction Rules

We define $\{0, 1\}^*$ to be the set of *payloads*. Payloads will typically be identifiers of protocol parties, which is why we often refer to this set by ID. By $\mathsf{ek}(A)$, $\mathsf{dk}(A)$, $\mathsf{sk}(A)$, and $\mathsf{vk}(A)$ we denote the encryption, decryption, signing, and verification key of party $A \in \mathsf{ID}$, respectively. Let Nonce be a set of nonces (random strings). Now, the set M of (Dolev-Yao) messages is defined by the following grammar:

$$\mathsf{M} ::= \mathsf{ID} \mid \langle \mathsf{M}, \mathsf{M} \rangle \mid \mathsf{Nonce} \mid \mathsf{E}_{\mathsf{ek}(\mathsf{ID})}(\mathsf{M}) \mid \mathsf{Sig}_{\mathsf{vk}(\mathsf{ID})}(\mathsf{M}) \mid \mathsf{ek}(\mathsf{ID}) \mid \mathsf{dk}(\mathsf{ID}) \mid \mathsf{sk}(\mathsf{ID}) \mid \mathsf{vk}(\mathsf{ID}).$$

Given a set φ of messages, additional messages can be derived from φ according to the following rules.

- *Initial knowledge:* $\varphi \vdash m$ for all $m \in \varphi$,
- *Pairing and unpairing:* If $\varphi \vdash m_1$ and $\varphi \vdash m_2$, then $\varphi \vdash \langle m_1, m_2 \rangle$; conversely, if $\varphi \vdash \langle m_1, m_2 \rangle$, then $\varphi \vdash m_1$ and $\varphi \vdash m_2$.
- *Encryption and decryption:* If $\varphi \vdash \mathsf{ek}(b)$ and $\varphi \vdash m$, then $\varphi \vdash \mathsf{E}_{\mathsf{ek}(b)}(m)$ for all $b \in \mathsf{ID}$; conversely, if $\varphi \vdash \mathsf{E}_{\mathsf{ek}(b)}(m)$ and $\varphi \vdash \mathsf{dk}(b)$, then $\varphi \vdash m$ for all $b \in \mathsf{ID}$.
- *Encryption-key retrieval:* If $\varphi \vdash \mathsf{E}_{\mathsf{ek}(b)}(m)$, then $\varphi \vdash \mathsf{ek}(b)$ for all $b \in \mathsf{ID}$.
- *Signature:* If $\varphi \vdash \mathsf{sk}(b)$ and $\varphi \vdash m$, then $\varphi \vdash \mathsf{Sig}_{\mathsf{vk}(b)}(m)$ for all $b \in \mathsf{ID}$.
- *Plaintext retrieval:* If $\varphi \vdash \mathsf{Sig}_{\mathsf{vk}(b)}(m)$, then $\varphi \vdash m$ for all $b \in \mathsf{ID}$.
- *Verification-key retrieval:* If $\varphi \vdash \mathsf{Sig}_{\mathsf{vk}(b)}(m)$, then $\varphi \vdash \mathsf{vk}(b)$ for all $b \in \mathsf{ID}$.

2.2 Syntax of Protocols

A k-party protocol is defined by k roles, where a role specifies the behavior of a party in a protocol run. Defining roles requires to first introduce variables. We assume disjoint sets of typed variables $\mathsf{X}.n$ for nonces and $\mathsf{X}.d$ for payloads.

The ith *role*, $i = 1, \ldots k$, is defined to be a directed, edge-labeled finite tree where the edges originating in the same node are linearly ordered. Each edge is labeled with a rule (l, r) for terms l and r, where terms are messages which may contain variables. The left-hand side l of a rule serves as a pattern for received messages; these messages are matched against the pattern and the pattern's variables are instantiated accordingly. The right-hand side r of a rule specifies the response message. We use certain distinguished variables $A_1, \ldots, A_k \in \mathsf{X}.d$ and $N_j \in \mathsf{X}.n$ for $j \geq 0$. When the ith role is instantiated with parties $a_1, \ldots, a_k$, then A_j is substituted by a_j for every $j = 1, \ldots, k$, and fresh nonces are generated for the variables N_j occurring in the role. An instance of the ith role is carried out by party a_i.

Similarly to [14], we put syntactic restrictions on the kind of terms that can occur on the left-hand side and right-hand side of rules to ensure that the corresponding role is executable, and hence, can be given a meaningful computational interpretation. For the ith role of a protocol, terms on the left-hand side of a rule are of the following form:

$$\mathsf{T}_i^l ::= \mathsf{ID} \mid \mathsf{X}.n \mid \mathsf{X}.d \mid \langle \mathsf{T}_i^l, \mathsf{T}_i^l \rangle \mid \mathsf{E}_{\mathsf{ek}(A_i)}(\mathsf{T}_i^l) \mid \mathsf{Sig}_{\mathsf{vk}(A)}(\mathsf{T}_i^l),$$

where $A \in \{A_1, \ldots, A_k\}$. Here $\mathsf{E}_{\mathsf{ek}(A_i)}(t)$ intuitively means that the party A_i (carrying out the ith role) decrypts the received message with $\mathsf{dk}(A_i)$ and then parses the plaintext according to t. Since A_i only knows its own decryption key $\mathsf{dk}(A_i)$, terms of the form $\mathsf{E}_{\mathsf{ek}(A_j)}(t)$ for $j \neq i$ are excluded since they correspond to decryptions with secret keys unknown to A_i. We, however, allow A_i to check the validity of the signatures of all other parties since their respective verification keys are considered public, i.e., A_i is assumed to know $\mathsf{vk}(A_j)$ for all j. A more comprehensive set of terms T_i^l is conceivable, e.g., by including terms that contain specific ciphertexts, variables for encryption/verification keys, or variables for ciphertexts in order to model ciphertext forwarding. While our results can be lifted to these cases, we concentrate on T_i^l as to not encumber our main ideas with details that are of only minor importance in this paper. For the ith role of a protocol, terms on the right-hand side of a rule are of the following form:

$$\mathsf{T}_i^r ::= \mathsf{ID} \mid \mathsf{X}.n \mid \mathsf{X}.d \mid \langle \mathsf{T}_i^r, \mathsf{T}_i^r \rangle \mid \mathsf{E}_{\mathsf{ek}(A)}(\mathsf{T}_i^r) \mid \mathsf{Sig}_{\mathsf{vk}(A_i)}(\mathsf{T}_i^r),$$

where $A \in \{A_1, \dots, A_k\}$. A term $\mathsf{E}_{\mathsf{ek}(A_j)}(t)$ means that party A_i computes a bit string b for t and then encrypts b with the public key of A_j; $\mathsf{Sig}_{\mathsf{vk}(A_i)}(t)$ has a similar meaning. We require that variables on the right-hand side of a rule belong to $\{A_1, \dots, A_k\} \cup \{N_j \mid j \geq 0\}$, or occur on the left-hand side of the rule, or occur on the left-hand side of a preceding rule in a role to ensure that these variables have been instantiated by the time they are used. Several extensions of T_i^l are conceivable but not considered here for reasons of clarity.

Finally, let Roles denote the set of all roles. Then, a k-party protocol is a mapping $\Pi \colon \{1, \dots, k\} \to \mathsf{Roles}$.

3   Simulatability and Requirements for Simulatability-Sound Dolev-Yao Models

In this section, we review the notion of simulatability and point out necessary requirements for a Dolev-Yao model to be sound in the sense of BRSIM/UC.

3.1   Review of Simulatability

Simulatability constitutes a general approach for comparing two systems, typically called real and ideal system. In terms of the semantics community one might speak of an implementation or refinement relation, specifically geared towards the preservation of what one might call secrecy properties compared with functional properties. We believe that all our following results are independent of the differences between the definition styles of the various recent papers on simulatability [20,21,11,10,17]. However, we have to fix a specific formalism, and we use that from [21,10].

The ideal system in [21,10] typically consists of a single machine TH, the *trusted host*, see Figure 1. In the context of simulatability soundness, TH represents a Dolev-Yao model. The real system consists of a set of machines M_u, one for every user u. In the context of simulatability soundness, the real system describes the cryptographic implementation. The ideal or real system interacts with arbitrary so-called *honest users*, collectively represented by a single machine H; this corresponds to potential protocols or human users interacting with the ideal or real system. Furthermore, the ideal or real

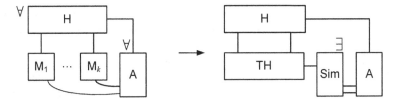

Fig. 1. Black-box reactive simulatability (BRSIM) between the real system $M_1 \| \cdots \| M_k$ and the ideal system TH, where M_u is the machine of user $u \in \{1, \ldots, k\}$

system interacts with an adversary A, who typically controls the network and can manipulate messages on the bit string level. The adversary is also granted the ability to interact with the honest users H in order to influence their behavior, e.g., to suggest which messages are to be sent. Technically, the interaction with H models known-message and chosen-message attacks.

Black-box reactive simulatability (BRSIM) states that there exists a simulator Sim such that for all A, no H can distinguish (in the sense of computational indistinguishability of families of random variables [23]) if it interacts with the real system and the real adversary, or with the ideal system and a combination of the real adversary and the simulator (which together form the ideal adversary). This is depicted in Figure 1. Indistinguishability in particular entails that the ideal and real system offer identical interfaces to the honest users to prevent trivial distinguishability. We write $M_1 \| \cdots \| M_k \leq^{BRSIM}$ TH to denote that the real system $M_1 \| \cdots \| M_k$ is *as secure as* the ideal system TH *in the sense of BRSIM/UC*.

The reader may regard the machines, i.e., the individual boxes in Figure 1, as probabilistic I/O automata, Turing machines, CSP or pi-calculus processes etc. The only requirement on the underlying system model is that the notion of an execution of a system when run together with an honest user and an adversary is well-defined. In [21,10], the machines are a type of probabilistic I/O automata which run in polynomial time.

3.2   On Simulatability-Sound Dolev-Yao Models and Their Cryptographic Implementations

We now outline necessary requirements a Dolev-Yao model M^{ideal} offering the capabilities described in Section 2 and an implementation $M^{real} = M_1^{real} \| \cdots \| M_k^{real}$ realized by actual cryptographic primitives have to fulfill for being simulatability-sound. Solely fixing minimal requirements expected from Dolev-Yao models instead of considering a specific Dolev-Yao model frees our results from specific details and idiosyncrasies of existing models.

For achieving simulatability, the Dolev-Yao model M^{ideal} and its cryptographic implementation M^{real} have to offer an identical I/O interface which the honest users connect to. We hence assume that the interaction at the I/O interface is based on handles (pointers) to objects stored in the system, i.e., the user never obtains real bit strings (nonces, ciphertexts, etc.) from the cryptographic implementation but only handles to such objects. The only exception are payloads which obviously have to be retrievable in their bit string representation in some way. Note that we do not fix any specific instantiation of these handles but we only assume that they can be operated on in the expected manner as discussed below.

The I/O interface has to permit suitable commands for constructing terms according to the Dolev-Yao style deduction rules given in Section 2, and for sending them to other principals. This in particular comprises the generation of nonces, pairs of messages (i.e., concatenations of messages), pairs of public and private keys, public-key encryption/decryption, signature generation and verification, retrieval of payloads from their handles, and sending and receiving messages to/from the network. Moreover, there have to exist commands for parsing handles, in particular for testing handles for equality (for simplicity, we assume that each user u is deterministically given the same handle again if a term is reused), and for querying the types of handles.

Concerning the network interface, $\mathsf{M}^{\mathsf{ideal}}$ and $\mathsf{M}^{\mathsf{real}}$ differ. The network interface of $\mathsf{M}^{\mathsf{ideal}}$ offers the adversary commands for constructing and parsing terms according to the Dolev-Yao style deduction rules, and for sending terms to users. The machines $\mathsf{M}^{\mathsf{real}}_u$ output bit strings to and receive bit strings from the adversary at their network interfaces.

Note that we did not describe the internal behavior of the Dolev-Yao model $\mathsf{M}^{\mathsf{ideal}}$. It turns out not to be relevant for achieving our results. We later only have to require two properties of $\mathsf{M}^{\mathsf{ideal}}$: First, $\mathsf{M}^{\mathsf{real}}$ is as secure as $\mathsf{M}^{\mathsf{ideal}}$ in the sense of BRSIM/UC; second, the behavior of $\mathsf{M}^{\mathsf{ideal}}$ in fact ensures that the adversary can only manipulate messages according to the Dolev-Yao rules presented in Section 2. More precisely, the second property requires that when $\mathsf{M}^{\mathsf{ideal}}$ is run with arbitrary honest users and an arbitrary adversary, the resulting protocol traces are so-called Dolev-Yao traces, which are formally defined in Section 4.

4   Reactive Execution of Protocols

We now describe the execution of a k-party protocol Π along with an adversary who controls the network. More precisely, we describe the *concrete* execution of Π, i.e., the execution in which actual cryptographic algorithms are used, rather than their Dolev-Yao abstractions. Our definition corresponds to the one for mapping approaches [19,15,14]. However, we present the definition in the reactive simulatability framework [21,10] using $\mathsf{M}^{\mathsf{real}}$ in order to facilitate the presentation of our main result (Section 5).

4.1   Emulating Concrete Executions Via H_Π

We use an honest user machine H_Π to emulate the execution of Π. This machine makes use of $\mathsf{M}^{\mathsf{real}}$ to carry out the necessary cryptographic operations. Recall that $\mathsf{M}^{\mathsf{real}}$ uses actual cryptographic algorithms to perform the cryptographic operations and that handles are used at its I/O interface to point to the bit strings (payloads, ciphertexts, nonces etc.) stored in $\mathsf{M}^{\mathsf{real}}$. While $\mathsf{M}^{\mathsf{real}}$ is a composition of machines $\mathsf{M}^{\mathsf{real}}_u$, $u \in \{1, \ldots, k\}$, H_Π can emulate the execution of instances of Π by only using one $\mathsf{M}^{\mathsf{real}}_u$ since within this machine key pairs for every party can be generated. This is even more general than using a separate machine for each party since it allows to model that the adversary dynamically generates new parties. We emphasize that the communication between the parties is still carried out over the network, so by using just one machine M_u^{real} we do not introduce any idealization. As usual, the network is controlled by the adversary A. The adversary can instruct H_Π to generate a new instance of a role $\Pi(i)$ of Π. Before the execution of Π starts, A can additionally corrupt parties; this corresponds to the prevalent static corruption model of Dolev-Yao models. Altogether, the run of the system $H_\Pi \parallel M^{real} \parallel A$ corresponds to a concrete execution of instances of Π. It remains to describe H_Π, i.e., the way H_Π emulates instances of Π.

States of H_Π. Similar to the definition of concrete executions in mapping approaches, the machine H_Π keeps a global state to remember which instances of Π are running and in which local state these instances are. The *global state* is a tuple (Sld, f, φ), where (i) Sld is a finite set of session IDs, (ii) φ keeps track of the knowledge of the adversary at the current point in time, and (iii) f maps every session identifier sid in Sld to the current (local) state $f(sid) = (i, \nu, p, (a_1, \ldots, a_k))$ of that session, see below, where a session is an instance of one role of the protocol. A *local state* is a tuple $(i, \nu, p, (a_1, \ldots, a_k))$ with the following components: $i \in \{1, \ldots, k\}$ is the index of the role $\Pi(i)$ that is executed in this session, ν is a substitution that maps those variables in $\Pi(i)$ that were bound in the matching processes so far to handles (pointing to bit strings stored in M^{real}), p is a node in the role $\Pi(i)$ marking the current point in the execution of $\Pi(i)$, and $(a_1, \ldots, a_k)$ are the parties participating in this session. Recall that the session is carried out by a_i with the parties a_j, $j \in \{1, \ldots, k\} \setminus \{i\}$. The *initial global state* is $(\emptyset, \emptyset, \emptyset)$. The machine H_Π additionally keeps a table in which it remembers handles to the names of honest and dishonest parties along with their encryption/decryption/signing/verification keys (in case of honest parties) and encryption/verification keys (in case of dishonest parties). It also keeps a set of known handles to payloads and nonces. The table and the set are updated in the obvious way; we will not further describe it but simply assume that H_Π knows the names and keys of all honest and dishonest parties as well as the (handles of) payloads and nonces which occurred so far in the protocol run.

Transitions of H_Π. We now describe how global states evolve in H_Π in terms of transitions. We often do not distinguish between payloads and their handles in the following, since we assumed that payloads can be efficiently retrieved from M^{real} using their handles. In particular, we do not distinguish between the name of a party (represented as payload data) and the handle to this name.

Corrupt message (from A via M_u^{real}): Following the prevalent static corruption model of Dolev-Yao models, the adversary can corrupt parties only at the beginning of a protocol execution. This is captured by the adversary sending a message (a bit string) of the form $(\text{corrupt}, a_1, \ldots, a_l, g_1, \ldots, g_l, h_1, \ldots, h_l)$ for $l \geq 0$ to M^{real} where a_i are names of parties, and g_i and h_i are their encryption and verification keys, respectively, provided by A. This corruption message is forwarded by M^{real} in terms of a handle to H_Π which then tests if all a_i are payloads (interpreted as names of parties), all g_i are handles to encryption keys and all h_i are handles to verification keys. Otherwise, the execution is aborted. Now, the knowledge of the adversary is recorded by H_Π as

$\varphi' := \{a_i, \mathsf{ek}(a_i), \mathsf{dk}(a_i), \mathsf{sk}(a_i), \mathsf{vk}(a_i) \mid 1 \leq i \leq l\}$, and H_Π changes its (initial) global state as follows:

$$(\emptyset, \emptyset, \emptyset) \xrightarrow{(\text{corrupt}, a_1, \ldots, a_l, g_1, \ldots, g_l, h_1, \ldots, h_l)} (\emptyset, \emptyset, \varphi').$$

Initiate new session (from A *via* $\mathsf{M}_u^{\text{real}}$*):* The adversary can initiate a new session at any time by sending a message of the form $(\text{new}, i, a_1, \ldots, a_k)$ where the a_j are names of parties and $i \in \{1, \ldots, k\}$. This message is forwarded by M^{real} in terms of a handle to H_Π which then tests if all a_j are payloads (interpreted as names of parties) and $i \in \{1, \ldots, k\}$, aborting at failure. Let $(\mathsf{Sld}, f, \varphi)$ denote the current global state of H_Π. Let $sid := |\mathsf{Sld}| + 1$ be the new session identifier and $\mathsf{Sld}' := \mathsf{Sld} \cup \{sid\}$. M_Π uses M^{real} to create new encryption and signature pairs $\mathsf{ek}(a_j), \mathsf{dk}(a_j), \mathsf{sk}(a_j), \mathsf{vk}(a_j)$ for all honest parties a_j that do not yet have such pairs, to create new nonces for all variables N_j occurring in $\Pi(i)$, and to create a handle to the payload sid. Let the function f' on Sld' be defined by $f'(sid') := f(sid')$ for each $sid' \in \mathsf{Sld}$, and $f'(sid) := (i, \nu, \varepsilon, (a_1, \ldots, a_k))$, where ε is the root of the role tree, and where ν maps every A_j in $\Pi(i)$ to a_j and every N_j occurring in $\Pi(i)$ to the handle of the corresponding nonce. Let $\varphi' := \varphi \cup \{sid\} \cup \{\mathsf{ek}(a_j), \mathsf{vk}(a_j) \mid j = 1, \ldots, k\}$. Then M_Π changes its global state as follows:

$$(\mathsf{Sld}, f, \varphi) \xrightarrow{(\text{new}, i, a_1, \ldots, a_k)} (\mathsf{Sld}', f', \varphi').$$

Finally, M_Π uses M^{real} to create a list containing sid and the created encryption and verification keys and to send this list to the adversary.

Send message (from A *via* $\mathsf{M}_u^{\text{real}}$*):* The adversary can at any time transmit a message m by sending a message of the form (send, sid, m). This message is forwarded by M^{real} in terms of a handle to H_Π. Let $(\mathsf{Sld}, f, \varphi)$ denote the current global state, $f(sid) = (i, \nu, p, (a_1, \ldots, a_k))$, and let $(l_1, r_1), \ldots, (l_h, r_h)$ be the labels of the outgoing edges of node p in the given order. Then H_Π parses m (see below) according to $\nu(l_j)$ starting with $\nu(l_1)$, continuing with $\nu(l_2)$, and so on, until the first parsing can be successfully completed. If the parsing fails for every $\nu(l_j)$, the local and global state remain unchanged.

The parsing of m according to $l := \nu(l_j)$ is performed by H_Π inductively on the structure of l. The parsing updates ν since variables that are not in the domain of the current ν so far may now be instantiated. The machine H_Π furthermore keeps track of new payloads and nonces created by the adversary by maintaining a set φ_{new} which at the beginning of the parsing is defined to be empty. Now, the parsing is performed by H_Π as follows: First, it checks if m and l have the same type (by querying M^{real} for the type of m and then checking if it corresponds to the one of l), aborting at failure. Otherwise H_Π continues as follows: (i) If l is a handle to a payload or a nonce, then it checks if $l = m$. (Note that the same payloads/nonces get the same handles in M^{real}. Here we use that H_Π only employs one machine $\mathsf{M}_u^{\text{real}}$ for some $u \in \{1, \ldots, k\}$. We emphasize that this is not an idealization since checking bit strings or corresponding handles for equality is equivalent.) (ii) If $l \in \{0, 1\}^*$ is a payload, then it retrieves the payload of m and checks whether it coincides with l. (iii) If $l \in \mathsf{X}.n$ ($l \in \mathsf{X}.d$), then it checks whether m is a handle to a nonce (to payload data), aborting at failure. Otherwise, it extends ν by mapping l to m. If m has not occurred before (i.e., m is a handle to a new payload or nonce that the adversary generated), then it adds m to φ_{new}. (iv) If $l \in \mathsf{X}.d$, then it checks whether m is a handle to a payload and continues as in the previous case. (v) If $l = \langle t_1, t_2 \rangle$, then it recursively parses the first component of m according to t_1 and ν, and then the second component according to t_2 and (the possibly updated) ν. (vi) If $l = \mathsf{E}_{\mathsf{ek}(a_i)}(t)$, then it decrypts m with $\mathsf{dk}(a_i)$, aborting at failure. Otherwise, it parses the resulting plaintext (given as a handle) according to t. If l is a signature, it proceeds analogously.

If the parsing of m according to l is successful, we say that m and l match and call the resulting substitution (the updated ν) the matching function. We call $\nu(l)$ the Dolev-Yao term corresponding to m. In what follows, let h be minimal such that m matches with $\nu(l_h)$ and let θ be the resulting matching function.

Next, H_Π uses $\mathsf{M}^{\mathsf{real}}$ to construct the output message according to $r := \theta(r_h)$. The result is a handle to this message in $\mathsf{M}^{\mathsf{real}}$. The construction is carried out inductively on the structure of r as follows (Note that r does not contain variables since all variables are substituted with handles by θ): (i) If r is a handle, then it returns this handle. (ii) If $r \in \{0,1\}^*$ is a payload, then it creates a handle to this payload and returns this handle. (iii) If r is a pair, then it recursively constructs messages for the two components. With the resulting handles, it retrieves a handle to the pair from $\mathsf{M}^{\mathsf{real}}$. (iv) If $r = \mathsf{E}_{\mathsf{ek}(a_j)}(t)$, then it recursively constructs a message for t. With the resulting handle and the handle to $\mathsf{ek}(a_j)$, it retrieves a handle from $\mathsf{M}^{\mathsf{real}}$ to the corresponding ciphertext and returns this handle. If $r = \mathsf{Sig}_{\mathsf{vk}(a_i)}(t)$, then it proceeds analogously, using the handle to $\mathsf{sk}(a_i)$ to produce the signature.

Let m'^{hnd} denote the handle to the output message. Let f' be defined as $f'(sid') := f(sid')$ for every $sid' \in \mathsf{SId} \setminus \{sid\}$ and $f'(sid) = (i, \theta, ph, (a_1, \ldots, a_k))$ where ph is the hth successor of p in $\Pi(i)$. Let $\varphi' = \varphi \cup \varphi_{new} \cup \{r\}$. Then H_Π changes its global state as follows:

$$(\mathsf{SId}, f, \varphi) \xrightarrow{(\mathsf{send}, sid, m)} (\mathsf{SId}, f', \varphi').$$

Finally, H_Π sends the message corresponding to m'^{hnd} to the adversary.

4.2 Dolev-Yao Traces of Π

We now define traces of Π when executed with an adversary A.

Definition 1 (Traces). *A* trace *of Π when executed with an adversary* A *is a sequence $g_0 \xrightarrow{C_1} g_1 \xrightarrow{C_2} g_2 \xrightarrow{C_3} \cdots \xrightarrow{C_n} g_n$ of transitions $g_i \xrightarrow{C_{i+1}} g_{i+1}$ as defined above for H_Π obtained by executing the system $\mathsf{H}_\Pi \parallel \mathsf{M}^{\mathsf{real}} \parallel$ A. The C_i are the corrupt, new, and send commands and $g_0 = (\emptyset, \emptyset, \emptyset)$ is the initial global state. A send transition only belongs to the trace if H_Π successfully parsed the input message.*

A trace is called a Dolev-Yao trace if it can be constructed according to the rules of the term algebra and of the protocol Π under consideration (see Section 2).

Definition 2 (Dolev-Yao Traces). *A* trace $(\mathsf{SId}_0, f_0, \varphi_0) \xrightarrow{C_1} (\mathsf{SId}_1, f_1, \varphi_1) \xrightarrow{C_2} \cdots \xrightarrow{C_r} (\mathsf{SId}_r, f_r, \varphi_r)$ *of Π when executed with an adversary* A *is called a* Dolev-Yao trace *if and only if the following holds: For all i such that C_i is of the form* (send, sid_i, m_i) *we have that $\varphi_{i-1} \cup (\varphi_{i-1})_{new} \vdash t_{m_i}$ where t_{m_i} is the Dolev-Yao term corresponding to m_i and $(\varphi_{i-1})_{new}$ contains the new constants in t_{m_i} generated by the adversary.*

5   Simulatability Soundness Implies Mapping Soundness

In this section we show that mapping soundness is implied by simulatability soundness, i.e., by results that prove cryptographic implementations as secure as Dolev-Yao style abstractions in the sense of BRSIM/UC.

Recall that mapping soundness is established in the following style: One defines *concrete protocol traces* where several instances of the protocol run along with a probabilistic polynomial-time adversary that controls the network. Messages are bit strings and the cryptographic operations are carried out by cryptographic algorithms. This corresponds to runs of the system $H_\Pi \parallel M^{real} \parallel A$. In addition, one defines *symbolic protocol traces* where messages are Dolev-Yao terms. Now one aims at constructing a mapping from bit strings to terms such that applying the mapping to an arbitrary trace of the concrete cryptographic execution yields a Dolev-Yao trace: Different payloads and nonces are mapped to different constants, encryption/decryption/verification/signing keys are represented by $ek(a)$, $dk(a)$, $vk(a)$, and $sk(a)$ where a is the constant representing the name of a party. Pairings, ciphertexts, and signatures are represented by the corresponding Dolev-Yao terms. Given such a mapping, one shows that the resulting symbolic protocol trace constitutes a Dolev-Yao trace up to a negligible probability (measured in the implicit cryptographic security parameter).

Before we can state and prove our result, let us make the following observation about $H_\Pi \parallel M^{real} \parallel A$. On the one hand, this system describes concrete protocol executions: The different instances of the protocol exchange cryptographic bit strings over the network, which is fully controlled by the probabilistic polynomial-time adversary. On the other hand, M^{real} provides an abstract interface to H_Π in the sense that H_Π does not obtain bit strings from M^{real} (except for payloads), but only abstract representations (handles) to the bit strings stored in M^{real}. Hence, M^{real} already realizes the desired mapping from bit strings to handles, and these handles one-to-one correspond to Dolev-Yao terms in the natural manner. (A handle to a payload/nonce corresponds to a constant representing this payload/nonce; a handle to an encryption/decryption/verification/signing key of a party a corresponds to the ground term $ek(a)$, $dk(a)$, $vk(a)$, and $sk(a)$, respectively; handles to pairs, ciphertexts, and signatures correspond to Dolev-Yao terms representing these objects.) Since all handles are maintained in one machine M^{real}_u for some $u \in \{1, \ldots, k\}$, different payloads/nonces/etc. are referred to by different handles. Hence, the mapping from bit strings to Dolev-Yao terms—and consequently the translation of concrete protocol traces to symbolic traces—is implicitly already performed by M^{real}, which frees us from explicitly defining it. This might be surprising since a natural intuition suggests that this translation is encompassed by the simulator.

While M^{real} implicitly provides a mapping from concrete traces to symbolic traces, this does not necessarily entail that the latter trace is a Dolev-Yao trace. Our main result now states that simulatability soundness implies that the symbolic trace derived from this mapping constitutes a Dolev-Yao trace up to a negligible probability, which is exactly what mapping soundness intends to establish. More precisely, the result relies on two assumptions: First, we have that $M^{real} \leq^{BRSIM} M^{ideal}$, i.e., the cryptographic implementation is as secure as the Dolev-Yao abstraction in the sense of BRSIM/UC. Second, if protocols are executed based on M^{ideal} instead of M^{real}, then the resulting traces are Dolev-Yao traces, i.e., for every ideal adversary A' (which may be a composition of a simulator and a real adversary) all traces of $H_\Pi \parallel M^{ideal} \parallel A'$ are Dolev-Yao traces. This exactly reflects the intuition and purpose behind the Dolev-Yao abstraction M^{ideal}.

Theorem 1 (Simulatability Soundness implies Mapping Soundness). *Let Π be a protocol. Assume the following two properties about M^{real} and M^{ideal}:*

1. $M^{real} \leq^{BRSIM} M^{ideal}$.
2. For every ideal adversary A', all traces of $H_\Pi \parallel M^{ideal} \parallel A'$ are Dolev-Yao traces.

Then, for all (real) adversaries A, the probability that a trace of $H_\Pi \parallel M^{real} \parallel A$ is not a Dolev-Yao trace is negligible.

Proof (Sketch). We define H'_Π to behave exactly as H_Π except that it checks whether each received message can be deduced by the current intruder knowledge plus the new handles (corresponding to payloads and nonces generated by the adversary) in the received message. If this is not the case, then H'_Π outputs failure. Since $\vdash$ can be decided in polynomial time (see, e.g., [13]), H'_Π runs in polynomial time. Furthermore, the definition of Dolev-Yao traces implies that the probability that a trace of $H_\Pi \parallel M^{real} \parallel A$ is not a Dolev-Yao trace is exactly the probability that H'_Π outputs failure in a run of $H'_\Pi \parallel M^{real} \parallel A$.

By the first assumption in the theorem there exists a simulator S such that for every A the view of H'_Π in $H'_\Pi \parallel M^{real} \parallel A$ and $H'_\Pi \parallel M^{ideal} \parallel S \parallel A$ is indistinguishable. We consider the ideal adversary $A' = S \parallel A$. By the second assumption in the theorem we can conclude that H'_Π never outputs failure in a run of $H'_\Pi \parallel M^{ideal} \parallel A'$. Finally, it follows that the probability that H'_Π outputs failure in a run $H'_\Pi \parallel M^{real} \parallel A$ is negligible as otherwise the views of H'_Π in $H'_\Pi \parallel M^{real} \parallel A$ and $H'_\Pi \parallel M^{ideal} \parallel A'$ could be distinguished. □

A more detailed proof can be found in the long version of this paper. We emphasize that the argument is quite generic: The proof only exploits that H_Π can be extended so that it is able to efficiently recognize Dolev-Yao traces. Moreover, only the definition of H_Π and the extension of H_Π depend on the specific cryptographic primitives and the class of protocols under consideration. The rest of the argument is independent of these details, and it resembles property preservation theorems for simulatability [5]. Therefore, the above theorem should also hold for larger classes of cryptographic primitives and protocols. We conclude by pointing out that the two assumptions in Theorem 1 are met by the concrete cryptographic implementation and its Dolev-Yao abstraction put forward in [8].

References

1. Abadi, M., Rogaway, P.: Reconciling two views of cryptography: The computational soundness of formal encryption. In: Watanabe, O., Hagiya, M., Ito, T., van Leeuwen, J., Mosses, P.D. (eds.) TCS 2000. LNCS, vol. 1872, pp. 3–22. Springer, Heidelberg (2000)

2. Backes, M., Cervesato, I., Jaggard, A.D., Scedrov, A., Tsay, J.-K.: Cryptographically sound security proofs for basic and public-key Kerberos. In: Gollmann, D., Meier, J., Sabelfeld, A. (eds.) ESORICS 2006. LNCS, vol. 4189, pp. 362–383. Springer, Heidelberg (2006)

3. Backes, M., Dürmuth, M.: A cryptographically sound Dolev-Yao style security proof of an electronic payment system. In: Proc. 18th IEEE CSFW, pp. 78–93 (2005)

4. Backes, M., Dürmuth, M., Küsters, R.: On simulatability soundness and mapping soundness of symbolic cryptography. IACR Cryptology ePrint Archive 2007/233 (2007)

5. Backes, M., Jacobi, C.: Cryptographically sound and machine-assisted verification of security protocols. In: Alt, H., Habib, M. (eds.) STACS 2003. LNCS, vol. 2607, pp. 675–686. Springer, Heidelberg (2003)

6. Backes, M., Pfitzmann, B.: A cryptographically sound security proof of the Needham-Schroeder-Lowe public-key protocol. IEEE Journal on Selected Areas in Communications 22(10), 2075–2086 (2004)

7. Backes, M., Pfitzmann, B.: Symmetric encryption in a simulatable Dolev-Yao style cryptographic library. In: Proc. 17th IEEE CSFW, pp. 204–218 (2004)

8. Backes, M., Pfitzmann, B., Waidner, M.: A composable cryptographic library with nested operations (extended abstract). In: Proc. 10th ACM CCS, pp. 220–230 (2003)

9. Backes, M., Pfitzmann, B., Waidner, M.: Symmetric authentication within a simulatable cryptographic library. In: Snekkenes, E., Gollmann, D. (eds.) ESORICS 2003. LNCS, vol. 2808, pp. 271–290. Springer, Heidelberg (2003)

10. Backes, M., Pfitzmann, B., Waidner, M.: The reactive simulatability framework for asynchronous systems. Information and Computation. Preprint on IACR ePrint (2004)/082 (2007)

11. Canetti, R.: Universally composable security: A new paradigm for cryptographic protocols. In: Proc. 42nd IEEE FOCS, pp. 136–145 (2001)

12. Canetti, R., Herzog, J.: Universally composable symbolic analysis of mutual authentication and key exchange protocols. In: Halevi, S., Rabin, T. (eds.) TCC 2006. LNCS, vol. 3876, pp. 380–403. Springer, Heidelberg (2006)

13. Chevalier, Y., Küsters, R., Rusinowitch, M., Turuani, M.: An NP decision procedure for protocol insecurity with XOR. In: Proc. 18th IEEE LICS, pp. 261–270 (2003)

14. Cortier, V., Kremer, S., Küsters, R., Warinschi, B.: Computationally sound symbolic secrecy in the presence of hash functions. In: Arun-Kumar, S., Garg, N. (eds.) FSTTCS 2006. LNCS, vol. 4337, pp. 176–187. Springer, Heidelberg (2006)

15. Cortier, V., Warinschi, B.: Computationally sound, automated proofs for security protocols. In: Sagiv, M. (ed.) ESOP 2005. LNCS, vol. 3444, pp. 157–171. Springer, Heidelberg (2005)

16. Dolev, D., Yao, A.C.: On the security of public key protocols. IEEE Transactions on Information Theory 29(2), 198–208 (1983)

17. Küsters, R.: Simulation-Based Security with Inexhaustible Interactive Turing Machines. In: Proc. 19th IEEE CSFW, pp. 309–320 (2006)

18. Laud, P.: Symmetric encryption in automatic analyses for confidentiality against active adversaries. In: Proc. 25th IEEE SSP, pp. 71–85 (2004)

19. Micciancio, D., Warinschi, B.: Soundness of formal encryption in the presence of active adversaries. In: Naor, M. (ed.) TCC 2004. LNCS, vol. 2951, pp. 133–151. Springer, Heidelberg (2004)

20. Pfitzmann, B., Waidner, M.: Composition and integrity preservation of secure reactive systems. In: Proc. 7th ACM CCS, pp. 245–254 (2000)

21. Pfitzmann, B., Waidner, M.: A model for asynchronous reactive systems and its application to secure message transmission. In: Proc. 22nd IEEE SSP, pp. 184–200 (2001)

22. Sprenger, C., Backes, M., Basin, D., Pfitzmann, B., Waidner, M.: Cryptographically sound theorem proving. In: Proc. 19th IEEE CSFW, pp. 153–166 (2006)

23. Yao, A.C.: Theory and applications of trapdoor functions. In: Proc. 23rd IEEE FOCS, pp. 80–91 (1982)

Key Substitution in the Symbolic Analysis of Cryptographic Protocols

Yannick Chevalier and Mounira Kourjieh

IRIT, Université de Toulouse, France
{ychevali,kourjieh}@irit.fr

Abstract. Key substitution vulnerable signature schemes are signature schemes that permit an intruder, given a public verification key and a signed message, to compute a pair of signature and verification keys such that the message appears to be signed with the new signature key. Schemes vulnerable to this attack thus permit an active intruder to claim to be the issuer of a signed message. In this paper, we investigate and solve positively the problem of the decidability of symbolic cryptographic protocol analysis when the signature schemes employed in the concrete realisation have this property.

1 Introduction

According to *West's Encyclopedia of American Law*, a *signature* is

> "A mark or sign made by an individual on an instrument or document
> to signify knowledge, approval, acceptance, or obligation... [Its purpose]
> is to authenticate a writing, or *provide notice of its source*[1]..."

We will not deal any further with legal considerations, but it is interesting to note that while digital signatures are primarily employed to authenticate a document, *i.e.* ensure that the signer endorses the content of the document, they can also be employed to prove the origin of a document, *i.e.* ensure that only one person could have signed it. Indeed, most of the cryptographic work on digital signatures has aimed at certifying that no-one could sign a document in the place of someone else.

The analysis of digital signature primitives has however focused on the former authentication property. Formally speaking, the yardstick security notion for assessing the robustness of a digital signature scheme is the existential enforceability against adaptative chosen-message attacks (UNF-CCA) [11]. This notion states that, given a signing key/verification key pair, it is infeasible for someone ignorant of the signing key to forge a message that can pass the verification with the public verification key, and this even when messages devised by the attacker are signed beforehand. The security goal provided by this property is the impossibility (within given computing bounds) to impersonate a legitimate user (*i.e.* one that does not reveal its signature key) when signing a message.

---

[1] We have emphasised.

V. Arvind and S. Prasad (Eds.): FSTTCS 2007, LNCS 4855, pp. 121–132, 2007.
© Springer-Verlag Berlin Heidelberg 2007

We note that this robustness does not address the issue of the identification of a source of a message. However, this latter concept is also pertaining to digital signatures when they are employed in a non-repudiation protocol. While one would not differentiate the two properties at first glance, they are different since the authentication property requires the existence of the participation of the signer in the creation of the message, while the latter mandates the unicity of a possible creator of a message.

The two notions of message authentication and source authentication collapse in the *single-user* setting when there exists only one pair of signature/verification keys. They may however be different in a *multi-user* setting. We believe that the first work in this direction was the discovery of a flaw on the Station-to-Station protocol by Blake-Wilson and Menezes [6], where the authors show how it is possible to confuse a participant into thinking it shares a key with another person than the actual one. The attack consisted in the creation, by the attacker, of a signature/verification key pair dependent upon messages sent in the protocol. Defining a signature scheme to have the Duplicate Signature Key Selection (DSKS) property if it permits such a construction with non-negligible probability, they showed that several standard signature schemes (including RSA, DSA, ECDSA and ElGamal) had this property, but also that a simple countermeasure (signing the public key along with the message) existed in all cases, but was rarely implemented. This DSKS property was formally defined as *Key substitution* in [16], where it is also discussed, after a review of what could be called an attack on a signature scheme in the multi-user setting. It was also later presented independently in [17] as *Conservative Exclusive Ownership*. The companion property of *Destructive Exclusive Ownership* by which an intruder may also change arbitrarily the signed message is also introduced. While the same attacks as in [16] are exhibited, the authors also demonstrate how this can be used in practice to poison a badly implemented PKI with fake CRLs (T. Pornin, personal communication).

Automated Validation of Security Protocols. Cryptographic protocols have been applied to securing communications over an insecure network for many years. While these protocols rely on the robustness of the employed security primitives, their design is error-prone. This difficulty is reflected by the repeated discovery of logical flaws in proposed protocols, even under the assumption that cryptographic primitives were perfect. As an attempt to solve the problem, there has been a sustained effort to devise formal methods for specifying and verifying the security goals of protocols. Various symbolic approaches have been proposed to represent protocols and reason about them, and to attempt to verify security properties such as confidentiality and authenticity, or to discover bugs. Such approaches include process algebra, model-checking, equational reasoning, constraint solving and resolution theorem-proving (e.g., [18,1,10,3]).

Our goal is to adapt the symbolic model of concrete cryptographic primitives in order to reflect inasmuch as possible their imperfections that could be used by an attacker to find a flaw on a protocol. The work described in this paper relies on the compositionality result obtained in [9] that permits us to abstract from other primitives and consider protocols that only involve a signature scheme having the DSKS properties.

Outline. In Section 2 we will present an attack by Baek *et al.* demonstrating how an actual intruder can use the DSKS property of a signature scheme to attack a protocol. We then describe in Section 3 the formalism in which we will analyse cryptographic protocols. In Section 4 we present how we model the possible actions of an intruder taking advantage of the DSKS property of a signature scheme. We present in Section 5 an algorithm that permits to reduce the analysis to an analysis in the empty equational theory, and give in Section 6 a decision procedure for the reachability problem in these protocols. We conclude in Section 7.

2   An Example Attack

We do not present here the original attack on the station-to-station protocol, but one that we believe to be simpler, and given by *Baek et al.* [4] on the KAP-HY (*Key Agreement protocol*, proposed by *Hirosi* and *Yoshida* in [12]).

Presentation of the KAP-HY Protocol. This protocol relies on a redundant signature scheme to provide key confirmation at the end of a key exchange. The signature of a message m by agent A is denoted $s_A(m)$. Abstracting the details of the Diffie-Hellman key construction with messages u_A and u_B, and of the signature scheme, the protocol reads as follows:

$$A \rightarrow B : u_A, A$$
$$B \rightarrow A : u_B, s_B(u_A), B$$
$$A \rightarrow B : s_A(s_B(u_A), u_B)$$

An unknown key share (UKS) attack on a key agreement protocol is an attack whereby two entities A and B participating in a key agreement protocol may end the protocol successfully, but with a wrong belief on who shares a key with who. In [4], *Baek et al.* showed that the redundant signature scheme employed in the KAP-HY protocol possesses the DSKS property, and elaborate on this to show that the KAP-HY is vulnerable to a UKS attack. In this attack, the intruder E waits that A initiates a session with him:

(1) $A \rightarrow E : u_A, A$ (2) $E \rightarrow A : u_B, s_B(u_A), E$
(1') $E \rightarrow B : u_A, A$ (3) $A \rightarrow E : s_A(s_B(u_A), u_B)$
(2') $B \rightarrow E(A) : u_B, s_B(u_A), B$ (3') $E \rightarrow B : s_A(s_B(u_A), u_B)$

In this attack, the intruder E records, but passes unchanged, the first message, and initiates a session as A with B. It then intercepts the second message, and builds from the public key of B and from the message $s_B(u_A)$ a signature/verification key pair, and registers this key pair. E then passes the signature, but this time accompanied by its identity (2'). The main point is that when A checks the signature of the incoming message, it accepts it on the ground that it seems to originate from E. At the end of this execution, A believes that the key is shared with E whereas it is actually shared with B.

The computation of the new pair of keys (P_E, S_E) proceeds as follows. At the end of flow (2), the intruder knows the signature of u_A made by Bob using his public key, then, by using DSKS property of the used signature scheme, he creates the new pair of keys (P_E, S_E). The crucial point, common to all DSKS attacks, is the construction of a new key pair from a public verification key and from a signed message. We will model this operation with appropriate deduction rules, and prove that protocol analysis remains decidable.

3   Formal Setting

3.1   Basic Notions

We consider an infinite set of free constants C and an infinite set of variables $\mathcal{X}$. For any signature $\mathcal{G}$ (*i.e.* sets of function symbols not in C with arities) we denote $\mathrm{T}(\mathcal{G})$ (resp. $\mathrm{T}(\mathcal{G}, \mathcal{X})$) the set of terms over $\mathcal{G} \cup \mathrm{C}$ (resp. $\mathcal{G} \cup \mathrm{C} \cup \mathcal{X}$). The former is called the set of ground terms over $\mathcal{G}$, while the latter is simply called the set of terms over $\mathcal{G}$. The arity of a function symbol g is denoted by $\mathrm{ar}(g)$. Variables are denoted by x, y, terms are denoted by s, t, u, v, and finite sets of terms are written $E, F, ...$, and decorations thereof, respectively. We abbreviate $E \cup F$ by E, F, the union $E \cup \{t\}$ by E, t and $E \setminus \{t\}$ by $E \setminus t$. The *subterms* of a term t are denoted $\mathrm{Sub}(t)$ and are defined recursively as follows. If t is an atom (*i.e.* $t \in \mathcal{X} \cup \mathrm{C}$) then $\mathrm{Sub}(t) = \{t\}$. If $t = g(t_1, \ldots, t_n)$ then $\mathrm{Sub}(t) = \{t\} \cup \bigcup_{i=1}^{n} \mathrm{Sub}(t_i)$. The *positions* in a term t are sequences of integers defined recursively as follows, ε being the empty sequence representing the root position in t. We write $p \leq q$ to denote that the position p is a prefix of position q. If u is a subterm of t at position p and if $u = g(u_1, \ldots, u_n)$ then u_i is at position $p \cdot i$ in t for $i \in \{1, \ldots, n\}$. We write $t_{|p}$ the subterm of t at position p. We denote $t[s]$ a term t that admits s as subterm. The size $\|t\|$ of a term t is the number of distinct subterms of t. The notation is extended as expected to a set of terms.

A substitution σ is an involutive mapping from $\mathcal{X}$ to $\mathrm{T}(\mathcal{G}, \mathcal{X})$ such that $\mathrm{Supp}(\sigma) = \{x | \sigma(x) \neq x\}$, the *support* of σ, is a finite set. The application of a substitution σ to a term t (resp. a set of terms E) is denoted $t\sigma$ (resp. $E\sigma$) and is equal to the term t (resp. E) where all variables x have been replaced by the term $\sigma(x)$. A substitution σ is *ground* w.r.t. $\mathcal{G}$ if the image of $\mathrm{Supp}(\sigma)$ is included in $\mathrm{T}(\mathcal{G})$.

An *equational presentation* $\mathcal{H} = (\mathcal{G}, \mathcal{A})$ is defined by a set $\mathcal{A}$ of equations $u = v$ with $u, v \in \mathrm{T}(\mathcal{G}, \mathcal{X})$ and u, v without free constants. For any equational presentation $\mathcal{H}$ the relation $=_{\mathcal{H}}$ denotes the equational theory *generated* by $(\mathcal{G}, \mathcal{A})$ on $\mathrm{T}(\mathcal{G}, \mathcal{X})$, that is the smallest congruence containing all instances of axioms of A. Abusively we shall not distinguish between an equational presentation $\mathcal{H}$ over a signature $\mathcal{G}$ and a set $\mathcal{A}$ of equations presenting it and we denote both by $\mathcal{H}$. If the equations of $\mathcal{A}$ can be oriented from left to right, we write the equations in $\mathcal{A}$ with an arrow, $l \rightarrow r$. The equations can then only be employed from left to right, and $\mathcal{A}$ is called a rewrite system. An equational theory can in this case be defined by a rewrite system. An equational theory $\mathcal{H}$ is said to be *consistent* if two free constants are not equal modulo $\mathcal{H}$ or, equivalently, if it has a model with more than one element modulo $\mathcal{H}$.

Let $\mathcal{A}$ be a set of rewrite rules $l \rightarrow r$. The rewriting relation $\rightarrow_{\mathcal{A}}$ between terms is defined by $t \rightarrow_{\mathcal{A}} t'$ if there exists $l \rightarrow r \in \mathcal{A}$ and a substitution σ such that $l\sigma = s$ and $r\sigma = s'$, $t = t[s]$ and $t' = t[s \leftarrow s']$. $\mathcal{A}$ is convergent if and only if it is terminating and confluent. In this case, all rewriting sequences starting from t are finite and have the same limit, and this limit is called the *normal form* of t. We denote this normal form $(t){\downarrow}_{\mathcal{A}}$, or $(t){\downarrow}$ when the considered rewriting system is clear from the context. A substitution σ is in normal form if for all $x \in \mathrm{Supp}(\sigma)$, the term $\sigma(x)$ is in normal form.

3.2   Unification Systems

In the rest of this section, we let $\mathcal{H}$ be an equational theory on $\mathrm{T}(\mathcal{G}, \mathcal{X})$ and $\mathcal{A}$ be a *convergent* rewriting system generating $\mathcal{H}$.

Definition 1 (*Unification systems*). *Let $\mathcal{H}$ be an equational theory on $\mathrm{T}(\mathcal{G}, \mathcal{X})$. A $\mathcal{H}$-unification system $\mathcal{S}$ is a finite set of pairs of terms in $\mathrm{T}(\mathcal{G}, \mathcal{X})$ denoted by $\{u_i \stackrel{?}{=}_{\mathcal{H}} v_i\}_{i \in \{1,...,n\}}$. It is satisfied by a substitution σ, and we note $\sigma \models_{\mathcal{H}} \mathcal{S}$, if for all $i \in \{1, \ldots, n\}$ we have $u_i\sigma =_{\mathcal{H}} v_i\sigma$. In this case we call σ a solution or a unifier of $\mathcal{S}$.*

When $\mathcal{H}$ is generated by $\mathcal{A}$, the confluence implies that if σ is a solution of a $\mathcal{H}$-unification system, then $(\sigma){\downarrow}$ is also a solution of the same unification system. Accordingly we will consider in this paper only solutions in normal form of unification systems. A *complete set of unifiers* of a $\mathcal{H}$-unification system $\mathcal{S}$ is a set Σ of substitutions such that, for any solution τ of $\mathcal{S}$, there exists $\sigma \in \Sigma$ and a substitution τ' such that $\tau =_{\mathcal{H}} \sigma\tau'$. The unifier τ is a *most general unifier* of $\mathcal{S}$ if the substitution τ' in the preceding equation must be a variable renaming.

In the context of unification modulo an equational theory, standard (or syntactic) unification will also be called unification in the empty theory. In this case, it is well-known that there exists a unique most general unifier of a set of equations. This unifier is denoted $mgu(\mathcal{S})$, or $mgu(s, t)$ in the case $\mathcal{S} = \left\{ s \stackrel{?}{=}_{\emptyset} t \right\}$.

Unifiability Problem

> **Input:**   A $\mathcal{H}$-unification system $\mathcal{S}$.
> **Output:**   SAT iff there exists a substitution σ such that $\sigma \models_{\mathcal{H}} \mathcal{S}$.

Let us now introduce the notion of narrowing, that informally permits to instantiate and rewrite a term in a single step.

Definition 2 (*Narrowing*). *Let s and t be two terms. We say $t \rightsquigarrow s$ iff there exists $l \rightarrow r \in \mathcal{A}$, a position p such that $t_{|p} \notin \mathcal{X}$ and $s = t\sigma[p \leftarrow r\sigma]$, where $\sigma = mgu(t_{|p}, l)$. We denote by $\rightsquigarrow$ the narrowing relation.*

Assume $t \rightsquigarrow t'$ with a rule $l \rightarrow r$ applied at a position p in t. A basic position in t' is either a non-variable position of t not under p or a position $p \cdot q$ where q is a non-variable position in r. Basic narrowing is a restricted form of narrowing where only terms at basic positions are considered to be narrowed. In the rest of this paper, we denote $t \rightsquigarrow_{\text{b.n.}} t'$ a basic narrowing step.

3.3   Intruder Deduction Systems

The notions that we give here have been defined in [9]. These definitions have since been generalised to consider a wider class of intruder deduction systems and constraint systems [8]. Although this general class encompasses all intruder deduction systems and constraint systems given in this paper, we have preferred to give the simpler definitions from [9] which are sufficient for stating our problem. We will refer, without further justifications, to the model of [8] as *extended* intruder systems and *extended* constraint systems. The latter correspond to symbolic derivations in which a most general unifier of the unification system has been applied on the input/output messages.

In the context of a security protocol (see *e.g.* [15] for a brief overview), we model messages as ground terms and intruder deduction rules as rewrite rules on sets of messages representing the knowledge of an intruder. The intruder derives new messages from a given (finite) set of messages by applying deduction rules. Since we assume some equational axioms $\mathcal{H}$ are satisfied by the function symbols in the signature, all these derivations have to be considered *modulo* the equational congruence $=_{\mathcal{H}}$ generated by these axioms. In the setting of [9] an intruder deduction rule is specified by a term t in some signature $\mathcal{G}$. Given values for the variables of t the intruder is able to generate the corresponding instance of t.

Definition 3. *An* intruder system *$\mathcal{I}$ is given by a triple $\langle \mathcal{G}, S, \mathcal{H} \rangle$ where $\mathcal{G}$ is a signature, $S \subseteq \mathrm{T}(\mathcal{G}, \mathcal{X})$ and $\mathcal{H}$ is a set of equations between terms in $\mathrm{T}(\mathcal{G}, \mathcal{X})$. To each $t \in S$ we associate a deduction rule $\mathrm{L}^t : \mathrm{Var}(t) \rightarrow t$. The set of rules $\mathrm{L}_{\mathcal{I}}$ is defined as the union of L^t for all $t \in S$.*

Each rule $l \rightarrow r$ in $\mathrm{L}_{\mathcal{I}}$ defines an intruder deduction relation $\rightarrow_{l \rightarrow r}$ between finite sets of terms. Given two finite sets of terms E and F we define $E \rightarrow_{l \rightarrow r} F$ if and only if there exits a substitution σ, such that $l\sigma =_{\mathcal{H}} l'$, $r\sigma =_{\mathcal{H}} r'$, $l' \subseteq E$ and $F = E \cup \{r'\}$. We denote $\rightarrow_{\mathcal{I}}$ the union of the relations $\rightarrow_{l \rightarrow r}$ for all $l \rightarrow r$ in $\mathrm{L}_{\mathcal{I}}$ and by $\rightarrow_{\mathcal{I}}^*$ the transitive closure of $\rightarrow_{\mathcal{I}}$. Note that by definition, given sets of terms E, E', F and F' such that $E =_{\mathcal{H}} E'$ and $F =_{\mathcal{H}} F'$ by definition we have $E \rightarrow_{\mathcal{I}} F$ iff $E' \rightarrow_{\mathcal{I}} F'$. We simply denote by $\rightarrow$ the relation $\rightarrow_{\mathcal{I}}$ when there is no ambiguity about $\mathcal{I}$.

A *derivation* D of length n, $n \geq 0$, is a sequence of steps of the form $E_0 \rightarrow_{\mathcal{I}}$ $E_0, t_1 \rightarrow_{\mathcal{I}} \cdots \rightarrow_{\mathcal{I}} E_n$ with finite sets of terms $E_0, \ldots E_n$, and terms $t_1, \ldots, t_n$, such that $E_i = E_{i-1} \cup \{t_i\}$ for every $i \in \{1, \ldots, n\}$. The term t_n is called the *goal* of the derivation. We define $\overline{E}^{\mathcal{I}}$ to be equal to the set of terms that can be derived from E. If there is no ambiguity on the intruder deduction system $\mathcal{I}$ we write $\overline{E}$ instead of $\overline{E}^{\mathcal{I}}$.

3.4   Simultaneous Constraint Satisfaction Problems

We now introduce the constraint systems to be solved for checking protocols. It is presented in [9] how these constraint systems permit to express the reachability of a state in a protocol execution.

Definition 4 ($\mathcal{I}$-Constraint systems). *Let $\mathcal{I} = \langle \mathcal{G}, S, \mathcal{H} \rangle$ be an intruder system. An $\mathcal{I}$-constraint system $\mathcal{C}$ is denoted $((E_i \triangleright v_i)_{i \in \{1,\ldots,n\}}, \mathcal{S})$ and is defined by a sequence of pairs $(E_i, v_i)_{i \in \{1,\ldots,n\}}$ with $v_i \in \mathcal{X}$, $E_i \subseteq \mathrm{T}(\mathcal{G}, \mathcal{X})$ for $i \in \{1,\ldots,n\}$, and $E_{i-1} \subseteq E_i$ for $i \in \{2,\ldots,n\}$, and $\mathrm{Var}(E_i) \subseteq \{v_1,\ldots,v_{i-1}\}$ and by an $\mathcal{H}$-unification system $\mathcal{S}$.*

An $\mathcal{I}$-Constraint system $\mathcal{C}$ is satisfied by a substitution σ if for all $i \in \{1,\ldots,n\}$ we have $v_i \sigma \in \overline{E_i \sigma}^{\mathcal{I}}$ and if $\sigma \models_{\mathcal{H}} \mathcal{S}$. We denote that a substitution σ satisfies a constraint system $\mathcal{C}$ by $\sigma \models_{\mathcal{I}} \mathcal{C}$.

Constraint systems are denoted by $\mathcal{C}$ and decorations thereof. Note that if a substitution σ is a solution of a constraint system $\mathcal{C}$, by definition of deduction rules and unification systems the substitution $(\sigma)\!\downarrow$ is also a solution of $\mathcal{C}$. In the context of cryptographic protocols the inclusion $E_{i-1} \subseteq E_i$ means that the knowledge of an intruder does not decrease as the protocol progresses: after receiving a message a honest agent will respond to it, this response can then be added to the knowledge of the intruder who listens to all communications. The condition on variables stems from the fact that a message sent at some step i must be built from previously received messages recorded in the variables $v_j, j < i$, and from the ground initial knowledge of the honest agents.

Our goal will be to solve the following decision problem for the intruder deduction system modelling a signature scheme having the DSKS property.

$\mathcal{I}$-Reachability Problem

> **Input:**   An $\mathcal{I}$-constraint system $\mathcal{C}$.
> **Output:** Sat iff there exists a substitution σ such that $\sigma \models_{\mathcal{I}} \mathcal{C}$.

4   Symbolic Model for Key Substitution Attacks

A digital signature scheme is defined by three algorithms: the signing algorithm, the verification algorithm and the key generation algorithm. The last algorithm generates for each user a pair of keys, one of them will be used as signing key and will be kept secret, while the other is public and will be used as a verifying key. We abstract the key generation algorithm with two functions, $\mathrm{PK}(\_)$ and $\mathrm{SK}(\_)$ denoting respectively the verification and signature keys of an agent. We assume it is not possible, given an agent's name A, to *compute* $\mathrm{PK}(A)$ or $\mathrm{SK}(A)$. The signature of a message m with signature key k is a public algorithm $\mathrm{Sig}(\_,\_)$, and the resulting signed message is denoted $\mathrm{Sig}(m, k)$. We consider signatures with appendix, where the verification algorithm $\mathrm{Ver}(\_, \_, \_)$ –which is available to everyone– takes in its input a message m, a signature s and the public verification key k. The application of the algorithm is denoted $\mathrm{Ver}(m, s, k)$, and its outcome can be 0 (s is not the signature of m with the signature key associated with the verification key k) or 1 (s is a valid signature).

In addition to these functions, we add two new functions, P'K and S'K, which are public and take as argument a signed message s and a verification key k corresponding to this signed message, and output respectively a verification and a signature key denoted P'K(s, k) and S'K(s, k). The verification of s with the verification key P'K(s, k) succeeds.

Given this informal description, the equational theory $\mathcal{H}_{DSKS}$ to which these operations abide by is presented by the following set $\mathcal{A}_{DSKS}$ of equations:

$$\mathcal{A}_{DSKS} = \begin{cases} \mathrm{Ver}(x, \mathrm{Sig}(x, \mathrm{SK}(y)), \mathrm{PK}(y)) = 1 \\ \mathrm{Ver}(x, \mathrm{Sig}(x, \mathrm{S'K}(y_1, y_2)), \mathrm{P'K}(y_1, y_2)) = 1 \\ \mathrm{Sig}(x, \mathrm{S'K}(\mathrm{PK}(y), \mathrm{Sig}(x, \mathrm{SK}(y)))) = \mathrm{Sig}(x, \mathrm{SK}(y)) \end{cases}$$

The public operations defined above are now translated into an intruder system $\mathcal{I}_{\mathrm{DSKS}} = \langle \mathcal{G}, \mathcal{L}_{DSKS}, \mathcal{H}_{DSKS} \rangle$ with:

$$\begin{cases} \mathcal{G} = \{\mathrm{Sig}, \mathrm{Ver}, \mathrm{S'K}, \mathrm{P'K}, 0, 1, \mathrm{SK}, \mathrm{PK}\} \\ \mathcal{L}_{DSKS} = \{\mathrm{Sig}(x, y), \mathrm{Ver}(x, y, z), \mathrm{S'K}(x, y), \mathrm{P'K}(x, y), 0, 1\} \end{cases}$$

Note that the presentation $\mathcal{A}_{DSKS}$ is not convergent, and thus we cannot apply results on basic narrowing as is. To this end we introduce a rewriting system $\mathcal{R}$ which is convergent and obtained by Knuth-Bendix [14] completion on $\mathcal{A}_{DSKS}$, and such that two terms have the same normal form for $\mathcal{R}$ iff they are equal modulo $\mathcal{H}_{DSKS}$.

Lemma 1. *$\mathcal{H}_{DSKS}$ is generated by the convergent rewriting system:*

$$\mathcal{R} = \begin{cases} \mathrm{Ver}(x, \mathrm{Sig}(x, \mathrm{SK}(y)), \mathrm{PK}(y)) \to 1 \\ \mathrm{Ver}(x, \mathrm{Sig}(x, \mathrm{S'K}(y_1, y_2)), \mathrm{P'K}(y_1, y_2)) \to 1 \\ \mathrm{Ver}(x, \mathrm{Sig}(x, \mathrm{SK}(y)), \mathrm{P'K}(\mathrm{PK}(y), \mathrm{Sig}(x, \mathrm{SK}(y)))) \to 1 \\ \mathrm{Sig}(x, \mathrm{S'K}(\mathrm{PK}(y), \mathrm{Sig}(x, \mathrm{SK}(y)))) \to \mathrm{Sig}(x, \mathrm{SK}(y)) \end{cases}$$

It can easily be shown, using the criterion of termination of basic narrowing on the right-hand side of rules of $\mathcal{R}$, that basic narrowing terminates when applied with the rules of $\mathcal{R}$. The main result of [13] then implies the following proposition, when applying basic narrowing with $\mathcal{R}$ non-deterministically on the two sides of an equation modulo $\mathcal{R}$ and terminates with unification modulo the empty theory.

Proposition 1. *Basic narrowing is a sound, complete and terminating procedure for finding a complete set of most general $\mathcal{H}_{DSKS}$-unifiers.*

One can actually be more precise, and we will need the following direct consequence of Hullot's unification procedure, that states that applying basic narrowing permits one to "guess" partially the normal form of a term t.

Lemma 2. *Let t be any term and σ be a normalised substitution. There exists a term t' and a substitution σ' in normal form such that $t \rightsquigarrow^*_{\mathrm{b.n.}} t'$ and $t'\sigma' = (t\sigma)\!\downarrow$.*

While this presentation by a convergent rewrite system ensures the decidability of unification modulo $\mathcal{H}_{\mathcal{DSKS}}$, we can prove (see [7]) that the unifiability problem, as well as the partial guess of a normal form, is in fact in NPTIME.

5   Saturation

5.1   Construction

The saturation of the set of deduction rules $\mathcal{L}_{\mathcal{DSKS}}$ defined modulo the equational theory $\mathcal{H}_{\mathcal{DSKS}}$ presented by the convergent rewrite system $\mathcal{R}$ is the output of the application of the saturation rules of Figure 1 starting with $\mathcal{L}_{\mathcal{DSKS}}' = \mathcal{L}_{\mathcal{DSKS}}$ until any added rule is subsumed by a rule already present in $\mathcal{L}_{\mathcal{DSKS}}'$.

Subsumption : $\quad \dfrac{l_1 \twoheadrightarrow r \in \mathcal{L} \quad l_2 \twoheadrightarrow r \in \mathcal{L}}{\mathcal{L}' \leftarrow \mathcal{L}' \setminus \{l_2 \twoheadrightarrow r\}} \; l_1 \subseteq l_2$

Closure : $\quad \dfrac{l_1 \twoheadrightarrow r_1 \in \mathcal{L}', \quad (t, l_2) \twoheadrightarrow r_2 \in \mathcal{L}'}{\mathcal{L}' \leftarrow \mathcal{L}' \cup \{(l_1, l_2 \twoheadrightarrow r_2)\sigma\}} \quad \begin{array}{l} t \notin \mathcal{X} \\ \sigma = mgu_\emptyset(r_1, t) \end{array}$

Narrow : $\quad \dfrac{l \twoheadrightarrow r \in \mathcal{L}' \quad (l, r) \rightsquigarrow_{\text{b.n.}} (l', r')}{\mathcal{L}' \leftarrow \mathcal{L}' \cup \{l' \twoheadrightarrow r'\}}$

Fig. 1. System of saturation rules

The application of the saturation rules terminates, and yields the following set of rules:

$\mathcal{L}_{\mathcal{DSKS}}' = \mathcal{L}_{\mathcal{DSKS}} \cup x, \mathrm{SK}(y) \twoheadrightarrow \mathrm{Sig}(x, \mathrm{SK}(y)) \cup x, \mathrm{S'K}(\mathrm{PK}(y), \mathrm{Sig}(x, \mathrm{SK}(y))) \twoheadrightarrow \mathrm{Sig}(x, \mathrm{SK}(y))$

We define two new *extended* intruder systems: $\mathcal{I}_{\mathrm{DSKS}}' = \langle \mathcal{G}, \mathcal{L}_{\mathcal{DSKS}}', \mathcal{H}_{DSKS} \rangle$ and $\mathcal{I}_\emptyset = \langle \mathcal{G}, \mathcal{L}_{\mathcal{DSKS}}', \emptyset \rangle$. These intruder systems do not satisfy the requirements that the left-hand side of deduction rules have to be variables. The deduction relation, the derivations and the set of reachable terms are defined as usual from ground instances of deduction rules.

5.2   Properties of a Saturated System

Let us first prove that the deduction system obtained after saturation gives exactly the same deductive power to an intruder.

Lemma 3. *For any set of normal ground terms E and any normal ground term t we have: $E \twoheadrightarrow^*_{\mathcal{I}_{\mathrm{DSKS}}} t$ if and only if $E \twoheadrightarrow^*_{\mathcal{I}_{\mathrm{DSKS}}'} t$.*

Moreover, we can prove that when considering only deductions on terms in normal form and yielding terms in normal form, it is sufficient to consider derivations modulo the empty theory (Corollary 1).

Lemma 4. *Let E (resp. t) be a set of terms (resp. a term) in normal form. We have: $E \twoheadrightarrow_{\mathcal{I}'_{DSKS}} E, t$ if and only if $E \twoheadrightarrow_{\mathcal{I}_0} E, t$.*

PROOF. See proof in [7].   □

Corollary 1. *Let E (resp. t) be a set of terms (resp. a term) in normal form. We have: $E \twoheadrightarrow^*_{\mathcal{I}'_{DSKS}} E, t$ if and only if $E \twoheadrightarrow^*_{\mathcal{I}_0} E, t$.*

Next lemma states that if a term in the left-hand side of a deduction rule of the saturated system is not a variable, then we can assume it is not the result of another saturated deduction rule.

Lemma 5. *Let E (resp. t) be a set of terms (resp. a term) in normal form. If t is in $\overline{E}^{\mathcal{I}_0}$, there exists a $\mathcal{I}_0$-derivation starting from E of goal t such that for all $s \in l \setminus \mathcal{X}$, we have $s\sigma \subseteq E$.*

6   Decidability of Reachability

The main result of this paper is the following theorem.

Theorem 1. *The $\mathcal{I}_{DSKS}$-Reachability problem is decidable.*

The rest of this paper is devoted to the presentation of an algorithm for solving $\mathcal{I}_{DSKS}$-Reachability problems and to a proof scheme of its completeness. The termination and correctness are proved in [7]. This decision procedure comprises three different steps.

6.1   First Step: Guess of a Normal Form

Step 1. Apply non-deterministically basic narrowing steps on all subterms of $\mathcal{C}$. Let $\mathcal{C}_0 = \{(E_i^0 \rhd v_i^0)_{i \in \{1,\ldots,n\}}, \mathcal{S}^0\}$ be the resulting constraint system.

Remark. Let σ be a solution of the original constraint system, with σ in normal form. This first step will non-deterministically transform each $t \in \mathrm{Sub}(\mathcal{C})$ into a term t' such that, according to Lemma 2 we will have $(t\sigma)\!\downarrow = t'\sigma'$.

6.2   Second Step: Resolution of Unification Problems

Step 2. Solve the unification system $\mathcal{S}^0$ modulo the empty theory, and apply the obtained unifier on the deduction constraints to obtain a constraint system $\mathcal{C}' = \{(E_i' \rhd t_i')_{i \in \{1,\ldots,n\}}\}$.

Remarks. We prove below that if there exists a solution to the original constraint system, then there exists a solution of $\mathcal{C}'$ for the extended intruder system $\mathcal{I}_0$. $\mathcal{C}'$ itself is not a constraint system, but an *extended* constraint system.

Lemma 6. *If σ is a substitution in normal form such that $\sigma \models_{\mathcal{I}_{DSKS}} \mathcal{C}$, there exists a $\mathcal{C}'$ at Step 2 and a substitution σ' in normal form such that $\mathcal{C} \rightsquigarrow^*_{b.n.} \mathcal{C}'$ and $\sigma' \models_{\mathcal{I}_0} \mathcal{C}'$.*

PROOF. See proof in [7].   □

Apply :
$$\frac{\mathcal{C}_\alpha, E \triangleright t, \mathcal{C}_\beta}{(\mathcal{C}_\alpha, (E \triangleright y)_{y \in l_x}, \mathcal{C}_\beta)\sigma} \quad \begin{array}{l} l_x, l_1, \ldots, l_n \twoheadrightarrow r \in \mathcal{L}_{\mathcal{DSKS}}' \text{ and } l_x \subseteq \mathcal{X}, t \notin \mathcal{X} \\ e_1, \ldots, e_n \in E \text{ and } \sigma = mgu(\{(e_i \overset{?}{=} l_i)_i, r \overset{?}{=} t\}) \end{array}$$

Unif :
$$\frac{\mathcal{C}_\alpha, E \triangleright t, \mathcal{C}_\beta}{(\mathcal{C}_\alpha, \mathcal{C}_\beta)\sigma} \quad \begin{array}{l} u, t \notin \mathcal{X} \\ u \in E, \ \sigma = mgu(u, t) \end{array}$$

Fig. 2. System of transformation rules

6.3 Third Step: Transformation in Solved Form

Step 3. To simplify the constraint system, we apply the transformation rules of Figure 2. Our goal is to transform $\mathcal{C}'$ into a constraint system such that the right-hand sides of deduction constraints (the t_i) are all variables. When this is the case, we say that the constraint system is in *solved form*. It is routine to check that a constraint system in solved form is satisfiable.

Lemma 7. *Let $\mathcal{C} = \{\mathcal{C}_\alpha, E \triangleright t, \mathcal{C}_\beta\}$ be such that $\mathcal{C}_\alpha$ is in solved form. Then, for all substitution σ, $\sigma \models \mathcal{C}$ if and only if $\sigma \models \{\mathcal{C}_\alpha, (E \setminus \mathcal{X}) \triangleright t, \mathcal{C}_\beta\}$.*

PROOF. See proof in [7]. □

It also can be proved that the lazy constraint solving procedure terminates. This lemma also helps us to prove the completeness of lazy constraint solving (stated in Lemma 9).

Lemma 8. *Let $\mathcal{C}$ be a constraint system. The application of transformation rules of the algorithm terminates.*

Lemma 9. *If $\mathcal{C}'$ is satisfied by a substitution σ', it can be transformed into a system in solved form by the rules of Figure 2.*

7 Conclusion

Besides the actual decidability result obtained in this paper, we believe that the techniques developed to obtain this result, while still at an early stage, are promising and of equal importance. Several recent work [5,2] have proposed conditions on intruder systems ensuring the decidability of reachability with respect to an active or passive intruder. In a future work we plan to research whether the given conditions imply the termination of the saturation procedure and the termination of the symbolic resolution.

References

1. Amadio, R., Lugiez, D., Vanackère, V.: On the symbolic reduction of processes with cryptographic functions. Theor. Comput. Sci. 290(1), 695–740 (2003)
2. Anantharaman, S., Narendran, P., Rusinowitch, M.: Intruders with Caps. In: Baader, F. (ed.) RTA 2007. LNCS, vol. 4533, Springer, Heidelberg (2007)

3. Armando, A., Compagna, L.: Automatic SAT-Compilation of Protocol Insecurity Problems via Reduction to Planning. In: Foundation of Computer Security & Verification Workshops, Copenhagen, Denmark (July 25-26, 2002)
4. Baek, J., Kim, K., Matsumoto, T.: On the significance of Unknown Key-Share Attacks: How to Cope With Them? In: Proc. of Symposium on Cryptography and Information Security (SCIS 2000) (January 2000)
5. Baudet, M.: Deciding Security of Protocols against Off-line Guessing Attacks. In: Proceedings of the 12th ACM Conference on Computer and Communications Security (CCS 2005), pp. 16–25. ACM Press, New York (2005)
6. Wilson, S.B., Menezes, A.: Unknown Key-Share Attacks on the Station-to-Station (STS) Protocol. In: Imai, H., Zheng, Y. (eds.) PKC 1999. LNCS, vol. 1560, pp. 154–170. Springer, Heidelberg (1999)
7. Chevalier, Y., Kourjieh, M.: Key substitution in the symbolic analysis of cryptographic protocols. Technical report, IRIT (2007)
8. Chevalier, Y., Lugiez, D., Rusinowitch, M.: Towards an Automatic Analysis of Web Services Security. In: Konev, B., Wolter, F. (eds.) Frocos 2007. LNCS (LNAI), vol. 4720, pp. 133–147. Springer, Heidelberg (2007)
9. Chevalier, Y., Rusinowitch, M.: Combining Intruder Theories. In: Caires, L., Italiano, G.F., Monteiro, L., Palamidessi, C., Yung, M. (eds.) ICALP 2005. LNCS, vol. 3580, pp. 639–651. Springer, Heidelberg (2005)
10. Chevalier, Y., Vigneron, L.: A Tool for Lazy Verification of Security Protocols. In: Proceedings of the Automated Software Engineering Conference (ASE 2001), IEEE Computer Society Press, Los Alamitos (2001)
11. Goldwasser, S., Micali, S., Rivest, R.L.: A Digital Signature Scheme Secure Against Adaptive Chosen-Message Attacks. SIAM J. Comput. 17(2), 281–308 (1988)
12. Hirose, S., Yoshida, S.: An Authenticated Diffie-Hellman Key Agreement Protocol Secure Against Active Attacks. In: Imai, H., Zheng, Y. (eds.) PKC 1998. LNCS, vol. 1431, pp. 135–148. Springer, Heidelberg (1998)
13. Hullot, J.M.: Canonical forms and unification. In: Bibel, W., Kowalski, R. (eds.) Conference on Automated Deduction, vol. 87, pp. 318–334. Springer, Heidelberg (1980)
14. Knuth, D.E., Bendix, P.B.: Simple word problems in universal algebras. In: Siekmann, J., Wrightson, G. (eds.) Automation of Reasoning 2: Classical Papers on Computational Logic 1967-1970, pp. 342–376. Springer, Heidelberg (1983)
15. Meadows, C.: The NRL protocol analyzer: an overview. Journal of Logic Programming 26(2), 113–131 (1996)
16. Menezes, A., Smart, N.P.: Security of Signature Schemes in a Multi-User Setting. Des. Codes Cryptography 33(3), 261–274 (2004)
17. Pornin, T., Stern, J.P.: Digital signatures do not guarantee exclusive ownership. In: Ioannidis, J., Keromytis, A.D., Yung, M. (eds.) ACNS 2005. LNCS, vol. 3531, pp. 138–150. Springer, Heidelberg (2005)
18. Weidenbach, C.: Towards an Automatic Analysis of Security Protocols in First-Order Logic. In: Ganzinger, H. (ed.) Automated Deduction - CADE-16. LNCS (LNAI), vol. 1632, pp. 314–328. Springer, Heidelberg (1999)

Symbolic Bisimulation for the Applied Pi Calculus*

Stéphanie Delaune[1,2,3], Steve Kremer[2], and Mark Ryan[3]

[1] LORIA, CNRS & INRIA, France
[2] LSV, ENS Cachan & CNRS & INRIA, France
[3] School of Computer Science, University of Birmingham, UK

Abstract. We propose a symbolic semantics for the finite applied pi calculus, which is a variant of the pi calculus with extensions for modelling cryptographic protocols. By treating inputs symbolically, our semantics avoids potentially infinite branching of execution trees due to inputs from the environment. Correctness is maintained by associating with each process a set of constraints on terms. We define a sound symbolic labelled bisimulation relation. This is an important step towards automation of observational equivalence for the finite applied pi calculus, e.g. for verification of anonymity or strong secrecy properties.

1 Introduction

The *applied pi calculus* [2] is a derivative of the pi calculus that is specialised for modelling cryptographic protocols. Participants in a protocol are modelled as processes, and the communication between them is modelled by means of channels, names and message passing. The main difference with the pi calculus is that the applied pi calculus allows one to manipulate *complex data*, instead of just names. These data are generated by a term algebra and equality is treated modulo an *equational theory*. For instance the equation $dec(enc(x, y), y) = x$ models the fact that encryption and decryption with the same key cancel out in the style of the Dolev-Yao model. Such complex data requires the use of a special kind of processes called *active substitutions*. As an example consider the following process and reduction step.

$$\nu a, k.out(c, enc(a, k)).P \xrightarrow{\nu x.out(c,x)} \nu a, k.(P \mid \{^{enc(a,k)}/_x\}).$$

The process outputs a secret name a which has been encrypted with the secret key k on a public channel c. The active substitution $\{^{enc(a,k)}/_x\}$ gives the environment the ability to access the term $enc(a, k)$ via the fresh variable x without revealing a or k. The applied pi calculus also generalizes the *spi calculus* [3] which only allows a fixed set of built-in primitives (symmetric and public-key encryption), while the applied pi calculus allows one to define a variety of primitives by means of an equational theory.

One of the difficulties in automating the proof of properties of systems in the applied pi calculus is the infinite number of possible behaviours of the attacker, even in

---

* This work has been partly supported by the RNTL project POSÉ, the EPSRC projects EP/E029833, *Verifying Properties in Electronic Voting Protocols* and EP/E040829/1, *Verifying anonymity and privacy properties of security protocols*, the ARA SESUR project AVOTÉ and the ARTIST2 NoE. We also thank M. Johansson and B. Victor for interesting discussions.

V. Arvind and S. Prasad (Eds.): FSTTCS 2007, LNCS 4855, pp. 133–145, 2007.

the case that the protocol process itself is finite. When the process requests an input from the environment, the attacker can give any term which can be constructed from the terms it has learned so far in the protocol, and therefore the execution tree of the process is potentially infinite-branching. To address this problem, researchers have proposed *symbolic abstractions* of processes, in which terms input from the environment are represented as symbolic variables, together with some constraints. These constraints describe the knowledge of the attacker (and therefore, the range of possible values of the symbolic variable) at the time the input was performed.

Reachability properties can be verified by deciding satisfiability of constraint systems resulting from symbolic executions of process algebras (e.g. [16,4]). Similarly, *off-line guessing attacks* coded as *static equivalence* between process states [5] can be decided using such symbolic executions, but this requires one to check the equivalence of constraint systems, rather than satisfiability. Decision procedures for both satisfiability [11] and equivalence [5] of constraint systems exist for significant families of equational theories. *Observational equivalence properties*, which can be characterized as a bisimulation, express the inability of the attacker to distinguish between two processes no matter how it interacts with them. These properties are useful for modelling anonymity and privacy properties (e.g. [12]), as well as strong secrecy. Symbolic methods have also been used for bisimulation in process algebras [14,9]. In particular, Borgström *et al.* [10] define a sound symbolic bisimulation for the spi calculus.

In this paper we propose a symbolic semantics for the applied pi calculus together with a sound symbolic bisimulation. To show that a symbolic bisimulation implies the concrete one, we generally need to prove that the symbolic semantics is both sound and complete. The semantics of the applied pi calculus is not well suited for defining such a symbolic semantics. In particular, we argue in Section 2 that defining a symbolic structural equivalence which is both sound and complete seems impossible. The absence of sound and complete symbolic structural equivalence significantly complicates the proof of our main result. We therefore split it into two parts. We define a more restricted semantics which will provide an *intermediate* representation of applied pi calculus processes. These intermediate processes are a selected (but sufficient) subset of the original processes. One may think of them as being processes in some kind of normal form. We equip these intermediate processes with a labelled bisimulation that coincides with the original one. Then we present a symbolic semantics which is both sound and complete with respect to the intermediate one and give a sound symbolic bisimulation. To keep track of the constraints on symbolic variables we associate a separate constraint system to each symbolic process. Keeping these constraint systems separate allows us to have a clean separation between the bisimulation and the constraint solving part. In particular we can directly build on existing work [5] and obtain a decision procedure for our symbolic bisimulation for a significant family of equational theories whenever the constraint system does not contain disequalities. This corresponds to the fragment of the applied pi calculus without else branches in the conditional. For this fragment, one may also notice that our symbolic semantics can be used to verify reachability properties using the constraint solving techniques from [11]. Another side-effect of the separation between the processes and the constraint system is that we forbid α-conversion on symbolic processes as we lose the scope of names in the constraint system, but allow explicit renaming when necessary (using *naming environments*). We believe that the simplicity of our intermediate calculus (especially the structural equivalence) and the absence of α-conversion is appealing in view of an implementation. Finally, one may note that as in [10,8], our technique for deciding bisimulation is incomplete (see Section 5.1). However, we argue that our technique works for many interesting cases. The intermediate semantics and proofs are omitted, but can be found in [13].

2   The Applied Pi Calculus

The applied pi calculus [2] is a language for describing processes and their interactions. We only consider the *finite* applied pi calculus which does not have process replication. Details about syntax and semantics of the original applied pi calculus may be found in [2]. We briefly recall them for the convenience of the reader.

Terms are defined as names, variables, and function symbols applied to other terms (of base type). We denote by $\mathcal{N}$ (resp. $\mathcal{X}$) the set of names (resp. variables) and distinguish the set $\mathcal{N}_{ch}$ (resp. $\mathcal{X}_{ch}$) of channel names (resp. variables) and the set $\mathcal{N}_b$ (resp. $\mathcal{X}_b$) of names (resp. variables) of base type. We define the equations which hold on terms as an equational theory E. We denote $=_E$ the equivalence relation induced by E. A typical example of an equational theory is $\mathsf{dec}(\mathsf{enc}(x, y), y) = x$.

Plain processes (P, Q, R) are built up in a similar way to processes in the pi calculus, except that messages can contain terms (rather than just names). *Extended processes* (A, B, C) add *active substitutions* $\{^M/_x\}$, and restriction on variables. An evaluation context $C[\_]$ is an extended process with a hole instead of an extended process.

As usual, names and variables have scopes, which are delimited by restrictions and by inputs. We write $fv(A)$, $bv(A)$, $fn(A)$ and $bn(A)$ for the sets of free and bound variables (resp. names). In an extended process, there is at most one substitution for each variable, and exactly one when the variable is restricted. An extended process is *closed* if all its variables are either bound or defined by an active substitution. Active substitutions allow us to map an extended process A to its *frame* $\phi(A)$ by replacing every plain process in A with 0. The domain of a frame φ, denoted by $\mathrm{dom}(\varphi)$, is the set of variables for which φ contains a substitution $\{^M/_x\}$ not under νx.

Throughout the paper we always suppose that substitutions are cycle-free. Given substitutions σ_1 and σ_2 with $\mathrm{dom}(\sigma_1) \cap \mathrm{dom}(\sigma_2) = \emptyset$, we write $\sigma_1 \cup \sigma_2$ to denote the substitution whose domain is $\mathrm{dom}(\sigma_1) \cup \mathrm{dom}(\sigma_2)$ and that is equal to σ_1 on $\mathrm{dom}(\sigma_1)$ and to σ_2 on $\mathrm{dom}(\sigma_2)$. We write $\sigma_1\sigma_2$ for the substitution σ whose domain is $\mathrm{dom}(\sigma_1)$ and such that $x\sigma = (x\sigma_1)\sigma_2$. We define $\mathrm{img}(\sigma)$ to be $\{x\sigma \mid x \in \mathrm{dom}(\sigma)\}$. We write $\sigma^\star$ to emphasize that we iterate the substitution until obtaining idempotence.

Semantics. Structural equivalence, noted $\equiv$, is the smallest equivalence relation on extended processes that is closed under α-conversion on names and variables, application of evaluation contexts, and some other standard rules such as associativity and commutativity of the parallel operator and commutativity of the bindings. In addition the following three rules are related to active substitutions and equational theories:

$$\nu x.\{^M/_x\} \equiv 0,\ \{^M/_x\} \mid A \equiv \{^M/_x\} \mid A\{^M/_x\},\ \text{and}\ \{^M/_x\} \equiv \{^N/_x\}\ \text{if}\ M =_E N$$

As mentioned in the introduction, it seems difficult to define symbolic structural equivalence ($\equiv_s$) which is sound and complete in the following (informal) sense:

- *Soundness*: $P_s \equiv_s Q_s$ implies for any valid instantiation σ, $P_s\sigma \equiv Q_s\sigma$;
- *Completeness*: $P_s\sigma \equiv Q$ implies there exists Q_s such that $P_s \equiv_s Q_s$ and $Q_s\sigma = Q$.

To see this, consider the process $P = in(c, x).in(c, y).out(c, f(x)).out(c, g(y))$ which can be reduced to $P' = out(c, f(M_1)).out(c, g(M_2))$ where M_1 and M_2 are two arbitrary terms provided by the environment. In the case that $f(M_1) =_E g(M_2)$, we have $P' \equiv \nu z.(out(c, z).out(c, z) \mid \{^{f(M_1)}/_z\})$, but this structural equivalence does not hold whenever $f(M_1) \neq_E g(M_2)$. The aim of our symbolic semantics is to avoid instantiating the variables x and y: the process P would reduce to $P'_s = out(c, f(x)).out(c, g(y))$. In this case we need to keep auxiliary information that allows us to infer that x and y may take arbitrary values. The process P'_s represents the two cases in which x and y are equal or distinct. Hence, the question of whether the symbolic structural equivalence $P'_s \equiv_s \nu z.(out(c, z).out(c, z) \mid \{^{f(x)}/_z\})$ is valid cannot be decided, as it depends on the concrete values of x and y. Therefore, our notion of symbolic structural equivalence is sound but not complete in the sense above (we will give a weaker completeness result). This seems to be an inherent problem and it propagates to internal and labelled reduction, since they are closed under structural equivalence. In this example, the *control flow* is not affected by whether $f(x) =_E g(y)$. When control flow is affected by conditions on input variables, we maintain those conditions as a set of constraints.

Internal reduction $\rightarrow$ is the smallest relation on extended processes closed under structural equivalence and application of evaluation contexts such that

COMM	$out(a, M).P \mid in(a, x).Q \rightarrow P \mid Q\{^M/_x\}$	
THEN	if $M = N$ then P else $Q \rightarrow P$	where $M =_E N$
ELSE	if $M = N$ then P else $Q \rightarrow Q$	where M, N are ground and $M \neq_E N$

Note that the presentation of the internal reduction slightly differs from the one given in [2], but it is easily shown to be equivalent.

The operational semantics is extended by a *labelled* operational semantics enabling us to reason about processes that interact with their environment. Below, a and c are channel names whereas x is a variable of base type.

IN $\quad in(a, x).P \xrightarrow{in(a,M)} P\{^M/_x\}$

SCOPE $\quad \dfrac{A \xrightarrow{\alpha} A' \quad u \text{ does not occur in } \alpha}{\nu u.A \xrightarrow{\alpha} \nu u.A'}$

OUT-CH $\quad out(a, c).P \xrightarrow{out(a,c)} P$

OPEN-CH $\quad \dfrac{A \xrightarrow{out(a,c)} A' \quad c \neq a}{\nu c.A \xrightarrow{\nu c.out(a,c)} A'}$

PAR $\quad \dfrac{bn(\alpha) \cap fn(B) = \emptyset \\ A \xrightarrow{\alpha} A' \quad bv(\alpha) \cap fv(B) = \emptyset}{A \mid B \xrightarrow{\alpha} A' \mid B}$

OUT-T $\quad out(a, M).P \xrightarrow{\nu x.out(a,x)} P \mid \{^M/_x\} \\ \qquad\qquad\qquad\qquad x \notin fv(P) \cup fv(M)$

STRUCT $\quad \dfrac{A \equiv B \quad B \xrightarrow{\alpha} B' \quad A' \equiv B'}{A \xrightarrow{\alpha} A'}$

Our rules differ slightly from those described in [2], although we prove in [13] that labelled bisimulation in our system coincides with labelled bisimulation in [2].

Equivalences. In [2], it is shown that observational equivalence coincides with labelled bisimilarity. This relation is like the usual definition of bisimilarity, except that at each step one additionally requires that the processes are statically equivalent.

Definition 1 (static equivalence ($\sim$)). *Two closed frames* φ_1, φ_2 *are statically equivalent if* $\varphi_1 \equiv \nu\tilde{n}.\sigma_1$ *and* $\varphi_2 \equiv \nu\tilde{n}.\sigma_2$ *for some names* $\tilde{n}$ *and substitutions* σ_1, σ_2 *s.t.*

(i) $\mathrm{dom}(\varphi_1) = \mathrm{dom}(\varphi_2)$,
(ii) $\forall M, N$ *such that* $(fn(M) \cup fn(N)) \cap \tilde{n} = \emptyset$, $M\sigma_1 =_{\mathsf{E}} N\sigma_1 \Leftrightarrow M\sigma_2 =_{\mathsf{E}} N\sigma_2$.

Example 1. Let $\varphi_0 = \nu k.\sigma_0$ and $\varphi_1 = \nu k.\sigma_1$ where $\sigma_0 = \{\mathrm{enc}(s_0, k)/x_1, k/x_2\}$, $\sigma_1 = \{\mathrm{enc}(s_1, k)/x_1, k/x_2\}$ and s_0, s_1 and k are names. Let E be the theory defined by the axiom $\mathrm{dec}(\mathrm{enc}(x, y), y) = x$. We have $\mathrm{dec}(x_1, x_2)\sigma_0 =_{\mathsf{E}} s_0$ whereas $\mathrm{dec}(x_1, x_2)\sigma_1 \neq_{\mathsf{E}} s_0$, thus $\varphi_0 \not\sim \varphi_1$.

Definition 2 (labelled bisimilarity ($\approx$)). Labelled bisimilarity *is the largest symmetric relation* $\mathcal{R}$ *on closed extended processes, such that* $A \mathrel{\mathcal{R}} B$ *implies*

1. $\phi(A) \sim \phi(B)$,
2. *if* $A \to A'$, *then* $B \to^* B'$ *and* $A' \mathrel{\mathcal{R}} B'$ *for some* B',
3. *if* $A \xrightarrow{\alpha} A'$ *and* $fv(\alpha) \subseteq \mathrm{dom}(A)$ *and* $bn(\alpha) \cap fn(B) = \emptyset$, *then* $B \to^* \xrightarrow{\alpha} \to^* B'$ *and* $A' \mathrel{\mathcal{R}} B'$ *for some* B'.

3   Constraint Systems

The idea of symbolic semantics is to avoid infinite branching due to inputs from the environment. This is achieved by inputting a variable rather than one of infinitely many possible terms, and maintaining *constraints* on what value the variable may take.

Definition 3 (constraint system). *A* constraint system $\mathcal{C}$ *is a set of constraints where every constraint is either*

- *a deducibility constraint of the form* $\varphi \Vdash x$ *where* φ *is a frame and* x *a variable, or*
- *a constraint of the form* $M = N$, $M \neq N$ *or* $\mathrm{gd}(M)$ *where* M, N *are terms.*

The constraint $\varphi \Vdash x$ is useful for specifying the information φ held by the environment when it supplies an input x. The constraint $\mathrm{gd}(M)$ means that M is ground. We denote by $names(\mathcal{C})$ (resp. $vars(\mathcal{C})$) for the names (resp. variables) of $\mathcal{C}$. We define $cv(\mathcal{C}) = \{x \mid \varphi \Vdash x \in \mathcal{C}\}$ to be the *constraint variables* of $\mathcal{C}$, and assume that those constraint variables do not appear in the domain of any frame in $\mathcal{C}$. The constraint systems that we consider arise while executing symbolic processes. We therefore restrict ourselves to *well-formed* constraint systems, capturing the fact that the knowledge of the environment always increases along the execution: we allow it to use more names and variables (less restrictions) or give it access to more terms (larger substitution).

More formally, $\phi_1 \stackrel{def}{=} \nu\tilde{u}_1.\sigma_1 \preceq \nu\tilde{u}_2.\sigma_2 \stackrel{def}{=} \phi_2$ if $\tilde{u}_1 \supseteq \tilde{u}_2$, and $\mathrm{dom}(\sigma_1) \subseteq \mathrm{dom}(\sigma_2)$ and $\forall y \in \mathrm{dom}(\sigma_1).\ y\sigma_1 = y\sigma_2$.

Definition 4 (well-formed constraint system). *A constraint system $\mathcal{C}$ is* well-formed *if its deducibility constraints can be written $\phi_1 \Vdash x_1, \ldots, \phi_\ell \Vdash x_\ell$ such that $\phi_1 \preceq \phi_2 \preceq \ldots \preceq \phi_n$ and $\forall i.\ 1 \leq i \leq \ell,\ \forall x \in vars(\mathrm{img}(\phi_i)) \cap cv(\mathcal{C}),\ \exists j < i.\ x = x_j$.*

The second condition corresponds to the way in which variables are bound: each time a symbolic message M (which may contain variables) is put in the frame the variables in $vars(M)$ have to have been previously instantiated. Hence, those variables have to appear on the right of a smaller deducibility constraint. Given a constraint system $\mathcal{C}$ we write $Ded(\mathcal{C}) = \{\phi_1 \Vdash x_1, \ldots, \phi_\ell \Vdash x_\ell\}$. Two well-formed constraint systems $\mathcal{C}$ and $\mathcal{C}'$ with $Ded(\mathcal{C}) = \{\phi_1 \Vdash x_1, \ldots, \phi_\ell \Vdash x_\ell\}$ and $Ded(\mathcal{C}') = \{\phi'_1 \Vdash x'_1, \ldots, \phi'_\ell \Vdash x'_\ell\}$ have *same basis* if $x_i = x'_i$ and $\mathrm{dom}(\phi_i) = \mathrm{dom}(\phi'_i)$ for $1 \leq i \leq \ell$.

Definition 5 (E-solution). *Let $\mathcal{C}$ be a well-formed constraint system such that $Ded(\mathcal{C}) = \{\phi_1 \Vdash x_1, \ldots, \phi_\ell \Vdash x_\ell\}$ where each $\phi_i = \nu\tilde{u}_i.\sigma_i$ for some $\tilde{u}_i$ and some substitution σ_i. An* E-solution *of $\mathcal{C}$ is a substitution θ whose domain is $cv(\mathcal{C})$ and such that*

- $vars(x_i\theta) \cap cv(\mathcal{C}) = \emptyset$ *and* $vars(x_i\theta) \cap (\mathrm{dom}(\phi_\ell) \smallsetminus \mathrm{dom}(\phi_i)) = \emptyset$;
- $names(x_i\theta) \cap \tilde{u}_i = \emptyset$ *and* $vars(x_i\theta) \cap \tilde{u}_i = \emptyset$;
- *for "$M = N$"* $\in \mathcal{C}$ *(resp. "$M \neq N$"* $\in \mathcal{C}$), *we have* $M(\theta\sigma_\ell)^* =_E N(\theta\sigma_\ell)^*$ *(resp. $M(\theta\sigma_\ell)^* \neq_E N(\theta\sigma_\ell)^*$);*
- *for "$\mathrm{gd}(M)$"* $\in \mathcal{C}$, *we have that the term $M(\theta\sigma_\ell)^*$ is ground.*

We denote by $Sol_E(\mathcal{C})$ the set of E-solutions of $\mathcal{C}$. An E-solution θ of $\mathcal{C}$ is closed *if $vars(x_i\theta) \subseteq \mathrm{dom}(\phi_i)$ for any $i \in \{1, \ldots, \ell\}$.*

Example 2. Let $\mathcal{C} = \{\nu k.\nu s.\{\mathrm{enc}(s,k)/y_1, k/y_2\} \Vdash x', \mathrm{gd}(c), x' = s\}$. Let E be the equational theory $\mathrm{dec}(\mathrm{enc}(x,y),y) = x$ and $\theta = \{\mathrm{dec}(y_1,y_2)/x'\}$. We have that θ is a closed E-solution of $\mathcal{C}$. Note that $\theta' = \{\mathrm{dec}(y_1,k)/x'\}$ is not an E-solution of $\mathcal{C}$.

4   Symbolic Applied Pi Calculus

Intermediate extended processes (denoted A, B, C) are given by the grammar below. They may be seen as an extended process in normal form.

$P, Q, R :=$ inter. plain process	$F, G, H := P$	inter. framed process
$\quad 0$	$\quad \{M/x\}$	
$\quad P \mid Q$	$\quad F \mid G$	
$\quad$ if $M = N$ then P else Q		
$\quad$ in$(u, x).P$	$A, B, C := F$	inter. extended processes
$\quad$ out$(u, N).P$	$\quad \nu n.A$	

A symbolic process is an intermediate extended process together with a *constraint system*. We require intermediate extended processes to be

- *name and variable distinct (nv-distinct)*: $bn(A) \cap fn(A) = bv(A) \cap fv(A) = \emptyset$ and any name and variable is bound at most once; and
- *applied*, meaning that each variable in $\mathrm{dom}(A)$ occurs only once in A.

Intuitively, in an applied process all active substitutions have been applied. For instance the extended process $\mathrm{out}(c, x) \mid \{^M/_x\}$ is not applied, as x occurs twice. A symbolic process is made up of two parts: a process and a constraint system. The nv-distinctness condition allows us to link the names and the variables in the constraint systems to those used in the process. We denote by $\psi(A)$ the substitution obtained when taking the active substitutions $\{^M/_x\}$ in A. We now define the $\downarrow$ operator which transforms an nv-distinct process into an intermediate process.

Definition 6 $(A\downarrow)$. *Given an nv-distinct extended process A, the intermediate extended process $A\downarrow$ is defined inductively as follows.*

$$0\downarrow = 0 \qquad in(u, x).P\downarrow = \nu\tilde{n}.in(u, x).P' \qquad (\nu n.A)\downarrow = \nu n.(A\downarrow)$$
$$\{^M/_x\}\downarrow = \{^M/_x\} \qquad out(u, N).P\downarrow = \nu\tilde{n}.out(u, N).P' \qquad (\nu x.A)\downarrow = \tilde{A}$$
$$\text{if } M = N \text{ then } P \text{ else } Q\downarrow = \nu\tilde{n}.\nu\tilde{m}.\text{if } M = N \text{then } P' \text{ else } Q'$$
$$(A \mid B)\downarrow = \nu\tilde{n}.\nu\tilde{m}.(A' \mid B')(\psi(A') \cup \psi(B'))^\star$$

where $P\downarrow = \nu\tilde{n}.P'$, $Q\downarrow = \nu\tilde{m}.Q'$, $A\downarrow = \nu\tilde{n}.A'$, $B\downarrow = \nu\tilde{m}.B'$, and $\tilde{A}$ is $A\downarrow$ but with the unique occurrence of $\{^M/_x\}$ replaced by 0.

For example, let $A = \nu x.(in(c, y).\nu b.out(a, x) \mid \{^{f(b)}/_x\})$. Then $A\downarrow = \nu b.in(c, y).out(a, f(b))$. Note that the processes A and $A\downarrow$ are bisimilar but not structurally equivalent. As expected, an *intermediate context* is an intermediate extended process with a hole instead of an intermediate extended process. An *intermediate evaluation context* is an intermediate context whose hole is not under a conditional, an input or an output. We also define what it means to apply an evaluation context on a constraint system. This is needed because we define the semantics in a compositional way.

Definition 7 (constraint system $C[\mathcal{C}]$). *Let $C = \nu\tilde{n}.(\_ \mid D)$ be an intermediate evaluation context and e be a constraint. We have that*

- $C[e] = e\psi(D)$ *when e is a constraint of the form $M = N$, $M \neq N$ or $\mathrm{gd}(M)$;*
- $C[\nu\tilde{v}.\sigma \Vdash x] = \nu\tilde{n}.\nu\tilde{v}.(\sigma \cup \psi(D)) \Vdash x$ *otherwise.*

Given a constraint system $\mathcal{C}$, we have that $C[\mathcal{C}] = \{C[e] \mid e \in \mathcal{C}\}$.

As we do not allow α-conversion we explicitly run intermediate extended processes in a *naming environment* $\mathsf{N} : \mathcal{N} \cup \mathcal{X} \rightarrow \{\mathsf{n}, \mathsf{f}, \mathsf{b}, \mathsf{c}\}$. Intuitively, $\mathsf{N}(u) = \mathsf{f}$ if the name or variable u occurs *free* in A, and $\mathsf{N}(u) = \mathsf{b}$ if u has been *bound* and will not be used again. $\mathsf{N}(u) = \mathsf{n}$ means u is *new* and has not been used before, either as free or bound. $\mathsf{N}(x) = \mathsf{c}$ means that the variable x is a *constraint* variable (i.e. an input from the environment subject to constraints in $\mathcal{C}$). This discipline helps us avoid name and variable conflicts. If $\mathsf{N}(u) = t$ then the naming environment $\mathsf{N}' = \mathsf{N}[u \mapsto t']$ is defined to be the same as N except that $\mathsf{N}'(u) = t'$; and $\mathsf{N}[U \mapsto t']$ is defined as $\mathsf{N}[u_1 \mapsto t', \ldots, u_n \mapsto t']$ if $U = \{u_1, \ldots, u_n\}$. If U is a set of names and variables then $\mathsf{N}(U) = \{\mathsf{N}(u) \mid u \in U\}$, and we write $N(U) = t$ if $N(U) \subseteq \{t\}$. A naming environment N is compatible with an intermediate extended process A and a constraint system C if

- $N(fn(A)) = f$ – $N(bn(A) \cup bv(A)) = b$ – $N(names(C)) \subseteq \{f, b\}$
- $N(fv(A)) \subseteq \{f, c\}$ – $N(x) = c$ iff $x \in cv(C)$ – $N(vars(C)) \subseteq \{f, c, b\}$

Definition 8 (Symbolic process). *A symbolic process is a triple* $(A \; ; \; C \; ; \; N_s)$ *where A is an intermediate extended process,* C *a constraint system and* N_s *a naming environment compatible with A and C. The symbolic process* $(A \; ; \; C \; ; \; N)$ *is* well-formed *if* C *is well-formed and if* $\phi(A) \succeq max\{\phi \mid \phi \Vdash x \in C\}$ *when* $Ded(C) \neq \emptyset$.

Given a well-formed symbolic process $(A \; ; \; C \; ; \; N)$ we define by $Sol_E(C \; ; \; N)$ the set of solutions of C which are compatible with N, i.e.

$$Sol_E(C, N) = \{\theta \mid \theta \in Sol_E(C), N(names(img(\theta)) \cup vars(img(\theta))) = f\}.$$

Example 3. Let $A = out(c, x)$, $C = \{\nu a.\nu b.\{^b/_y\} \Vdash x, \; x \neq c\}$ and N be a naming environment compatible with A and C such that $N(d) = f$. Let $\theta_1 = \{^d/_x\}$, $\theta_2 = \{^y/_x\}$. We have that $\theta_1, \theta_2 \in Sol_E(C, N)$. Hence $out(c, d)$ (resp. $out(c, b)$) is the concrete process obtained by the solution θ_1 (resp. θ_2). However, note that $out(c, a)$ is not a concretization of $(A \; ; \; C \; ; \; N)$.

4.1 Symbolic Semantics

Symbolic structural equivalence ($\equiv_s$) is the smallest equivalence relation on well-formed symbolic processes such that:

PAR-0_s $(A \; ; \; C \; ; \; N) \equiv_s (A \mid 0 \; ; \; C \; ; \; N)$
PAR-A_s $(A \mid (B \mid D) \; ; \; C \; ; \; N) \equiv_s ((A \mid B) \mid D \; ; \; C \; ; \; N)$
PAR-C_s $(A \mid B \; ; \; C \; ; \; N) \equiv_s (B \mid A \; ; \; C \; ; \; N)$
NEW-C_s $(\nu n.\nu m.A \; ; \; C \; ; \; N) \equiv_s (\nu m.\nu n.A \; ; \; C \; ; \; N)$

$$\frac{(A \; ; \; C_A \; ; \; N) \equiv_s (B \; ; \; C_B \; ; \; N)}{(C[A] \; ; \; C[C_A] \; ; \; N') \equiv_s (C[B] \; ; \; C[C_B] \; ; \; N')} \quad \begin{array}{l} \text{where } N' = N[S \mapsto b] \text{ for some set} \\ \text{of names } S \text{ such that } N(S) = f \end{array}$$

Symbolic internal reduction $\rightarrow_s$ is the smallest relation on well-formed symbolic processes closed under $\equiv_s$, application of intermediate evaluation context and such that:

COMM$_s$ $(out(u, M).P \mid in(v, x).Q \; ; \; C \; ; \; N) \rightarrow_s$
$(P \mid Q\{^M/_x\} \; ; \; C \cup \{u = v \; , \; gd(u) \; , \; gd(v)\} \; ; \; N)$
where $u, v \in \mathcal{N}_{ch} \cup (cv(C) \cap \mathcal{X}_{ch})$.

THEN$_s$ (if $M = N$ then P else $Q \; ; \; C \; ; \; N) \rightarrow_s (P \; ; \; C \cup \{M = N\} \; ; \; N)$

ELSE$_s$ (if $M = N$ then P else $Q \; ; \; C \; ; \; N) \rightarrow_s (Q \; ; \; C \cup \{M \neq N \; ; \; gd(M) \; ; \; gd(N)\} \; ; \; N)$

Symbolic labelled reduction is the smallest relation closed under symbolic structural equivalence ($\equiv_s$) and such that

$\text{IN}_s \qquad (\text{in}(u,x).P \; ; \; \mathcal{C} \; ; \; \mathsf{N}) \xrightarrow{in(u,y)}_s (P\{^y/_x\} \; ; \; \mathcal{C} \cup \{0 \Vdash y, \text{gd}(u)\} \; ; \; \mathsf{N}[y \mapsto \mathsf{c}])$
$$\text{where } u \in \mathcal{N}_{ch} \cup (\mathcal{X}_{ch} \cap cv(\mathcal{C})), \; \mathsf{N}(y) = \mathsf{n}.$$

$\text{OUT-CH}_s \quad (\text{out}(u,v).P \; ; \; \mathcal{C} \; ; \; \mathsf{N}) \xrightarrow{out(u,v)}_s (P \; ; \; \mathcal{C} \cup \{\text{gd}(u), \text{gd}(v)\} \; ; \; \mathsf{N})$
$$\text{where } u, v \in \mathcal{N}_{ch} \cup (\mathcal{X}_{ch} \cap cv(\mathcal{C})).$$

OUT-T_s

$\qquad (\text{out}(u,M).P \; ; \; \mathcal{C} \; ; \; \mathsf{N}) \xrightarrow{\nu x.out(u,x)}_s (P \mid \{^M/_x\} \; ; \; \nu x.\mathcal{C} \cup \{\text{gd}(u)\} \; ; \; \mathsf{N}[x \mapsto \mathsf{f}])$
$$\text{where } x \in \mathcal{X}_b, \; \mathsf{N}(x) = \mathsf{n}.$$

$\text{OPEN-CH}_s \quad \dfrac{(A \; ; \; \mathcal{C} \; ; \; \mathsf{N}) \xrightarrow{out(u,c)}_s (A' \; ; \; \mathcal{C}' \; ; \; \mathsf{N}') \qquad u \neq c, \; d \in \mathcal{N}_{ch}, \; \mathsf{N}(d) = \mathsf{n}}{(\nu c.A \; ; \; \nu c.\mathcal{C} \; ; \; \mathsf{N}[c \mapsto \mathsf{b}]) \xrightarrow{\nu d.out(u,d)}_s (A'\{^d/_c\} \; ; \; \nu d.(\mathcal{C}'\{^d/_c\}) \; ; \; \mathsf{N}'[c \mapsto \mathsf{b}, d \mapsto \mathsf{f}])}$

$\text{SCOPE}_s \quad \dfrac{(A \; ; \; \mathcal{C} \; ; \; \mathsf{N}) \xrightarrow{\alpha}_s (A' \; ; \; \mathcal{C}' \; ; \; \mathsf{N}') \qquad n \text{ does not occur in } \alpha}{(\nu n.A \; ; \; \nu n.\mathcal{C} \; ; \; \mathsf{N}[n \mapsto \mathsf{b}]) \xrightarrow{\alpha}_s (\nu n.A' \; ; \; \nu n.\mathcal{C}' \; ; \; \mathsf{N}[n \mapsto \mathsf{b}])}$

$\text{PAR}_s \quad \dfrac{(A \; ; \; \mathcal{C} \; ; \; \mathsf{N}) \xrightarrow{\alpha}_s (A' \; ; \; \mathcal{C}' \; ; \; \mathsf{N}')}{(A \mid B \; ; \; \mathcal{C} \mid \psi(B) \; ; \; \mathsf{N}) \xrightarrow{\alpha}_s (A' \mid B \; ; \; \mathcal{C} \mid \psi(B) \; ; \; \mathsf{N}')}$

We may note that the rules IN_s and OPEN-CH_s require "on-the-fly renaming". This will be needed in the bisimulation because we require both the left- and right-hand processes to use the same label without allowing α-conversion. When a transition is executed under a context (by the rules SCOPE_s and PAR_s) the constraint system must also be put in the context (according to Definition 7). In particular, these rules allow to add restrictions and active substitutions to the constraint $0 \Vdash y$ inserted by the rule IN_s.

Example 4. To illustrate our symbolic semantics, consider the process $(A \; ; \; \emptyset \; ; \; \mathsf{N})$ where $A = \nu k.\nu s.(\text{in}(c,x).\text{if } x = s \text{ then out}(c, ok) \mid \{^{\text{enc}(s,k)}/_{y_1}\} \mid \{^k/_{y_2}\})$ and N is a naming environment compatible with A. Let x' be a variable such that $\mathsf{N}(x') = \mathsf{n}$.

$$(A \; ; \; \emptyset \; ; \; \mathsf{N}) \xrightarrow{in(c,x')}_s (A' \; ; \; \{\nu k.\nu s.\{^{\text{enc}(s,k)}/_{y_1}, {}^k/_{y_2}\} \Vdash x', \text{gd}(c)\} \; ; \; \mathsf{N}[x' \mapsto \mathsf{c}])$$
$$\longrightarrow_s \; (\nu k.\nu s.(\text{out}(c, ok) \mid \{^{\text{enc}(s,k)}/_{y_1}\} \mid \{^k/_{y_2}\}) \; ; \; \mathcal{C} \; ; \; \mathsf{N}[x' \mapsto \mathsf{c}])$$

where $A' = \nu k.\nu s.(\text{if } x' = s \text{ then out}(c, ok) \mid \{^{\text{enc}(s,k)}/_{y_1}\} \mid \{^k/_{y_2}\})$ and $\mathcal{C}$ is the system $\{\nu k.\nu s.\{^{\text{enc}(s,k)}/_{y_1}, {}^k/_{y_2}\} \Vdash x', \text{gd}(c), x' = s\}$. Let $\theta = \{^{\text{dec}(y_1,y_2)}/_{x'}\}$. We have $\theta \in Sol_{\mathsf{E}}(\mathcal{C} \; ; \; \mathsf{N}[x' \mapsto \mathsf{c}])$ (see Example 2).

4.2 Symbolic Equivalences

We define symbolic static equivalence using a similar encoding as [5]. The tests used to distinguish two frames in the definition of static equivalence are encoded by means of two additional deduction constraints on fresh variables x, y and by the equation $x = y$.

Definition 9 (symbolic static equivalence ($\sim_s$)). *Two closed well-formed symbolic processes are statically equivalent, written* $(A_s \; ; \; \mathcal{C}_A \; ; \; \mathsf{N}) \sim_s (B_s \; ; \; \mathcal{C}_B \; ; \; \mathsf{N})$ *if for* *some variables x, y such that $N(\{x, y\}) = n$, the constraint systems C'_A, C'_B have the same basis and $Sol_E(C'_A ; N[x, y \mapsto c]) = Sol_E(C'_B ; N[x, y \mapsto c])$ where*

- $C'_A = C_A \cup \{\phi(A_s) \Vdash x \,, \phi(A_s) \Vdash y \,, x = y\}$, *and*
- $C'_B = C_B \cup \{\phi(B_s) \Vdash x \,, \phi(B_s) \Vdash y \,, x = y\}$.

Proposition 1 (soundness of $\sim_s$). *Consider two closed and well-formed symbolic processes such that $(A_s ; C_A ; N) \sim_s (B_s ; C_B ; N)$. We have that:*

1. $Sol_E(C_A ; N) = Sol_E(C_B ; N)$, *and*
2. *for all closed $\theta \in Sol_E(C_A ; N)$ we have $\phi(A_s(\theta\sigma_A)^\star) \sim \phi(B_s(\theta\sigma_B)^\star)$, where σ_A (resp. σ_B) is the substitution corresponding to the maximal frame of C_A (resp. C_B).*

Definition 10 (Symbolic labelled bisimilarity ($\approx_s$)). *Symbolic labelled bisimilarity is the largest symmetric relation $\mathcal{R}$ on closed well-formed symbolic processes with same naming environment, such that $(A_s ; C_A ; N) \mathcal{R} (B_s ; C_B ; N)$ implies*

1. $(A_s ; C_A ; N) \sim_s (B_s ; C_B ; N)$
2. *if $(A_s ; C_A ; N) \rightarrow_s (A'_s ; C'_A ; N)$ with $Sol_E(C'_A ; N) \neq \emptyset$, then there exists $(B'_s ; C'_B ; N)$ such that $(B_s ; C_B ; N) \rightarrow^*_s (B'_s ; C'_B ; N)$ and $(A'_s ; C'_A ; N) \mathcal{R} (B'_s ; C'_B ; N)$;*
3. *if $(A_s ; C_A ; N) \xrightarrow{\alpha_s}_s (A'_s ; C'_A ; N')$ with $Sol_E(C'_A ; N') \neq \emptyset$, then there exists $(B'_s ; C'_B ; N')$ such that $(B_s ; C_B ; N) \rightarrow^*_s \xrightarrow{\alpha_s}_s \rightarrow^*_s (B'_s ; C'_B ; N')$, and $(A'_s ; C'_A ; N') \mathcal{R} (B'_s ; C'_B ; N')$.*

Baudet [6] presents a (co-NP) decision procedure to check $\sim_s$ (condition 1) for constraint systems without disequality constraints and subterm convergent[1] equational theories. This includes among others the well-known Dolev-Yao theory used to model symmetric (resp. asymmetric) encryption with composed keys, signatures and pairing. Building on this existing work, we obtain a procedure to decide our symbolic bisimulation for the fragment of the finite applied pi calculus without else branches in the conditional.

Theorem 1 (Main result). *Let A and B be two closed, nv-distinct extended processes and N be a naming environment compatible with $A\downarrow$, $B\downarrow$. We have that*

$$(A\downarrow ; \emptyset ; N) \approx_s (B\downarrow ; \emptyset ; N) \text{ implies } A \approx B.$$

Note that limiting the theorem to nv-distinct processes is not a real restriction. If we want to prove that $A \approx B$, we can construct by α-conversion two nv-distinct processes A', B' such that $A' \equiv A$ and $B' \equiv B$. Showing $A' \approx B'$ implies that $A \approx B$, since $\approx$ is closed under structural equivalence.

Theorem 1 is proved by using our intermediate semantics. We define labelled bisimilarity on intermediate extended processes, and show it to coincide with labelled bisimilarity in applied pi. Soundness and completeness of the symbolic semantics is shown with respect to the intermediate semantics. This allows to obtain soundness of the symbolic bisimulation. All the details are given in [13].

---

[1] An equational theory induced by a finite set of equations $M = N$ where N is a subterm of M and such that the associated rewriting system is convergent.

5   Discussion, Related and Future Work

5.1   Sources of Incompleteness

Our techniques suffer from the same sources of incompleteness as the ones described for the spi calculus in [10]. In a symbolic bisimulation the instantiation of input variables is postponed until the point at which they are actually used, leading to a finer relation. We illustrate this point on an example, similar to one given in [10].

Example 5.   Consider the two following processes:

$$P_1 = \nu c_1.\text{in}(c_2, x).(\text{out}(c_1, b) \mid \text{in}(c_1, y) \mid \text{if } x = a \text{ then } \text{in}(c_1, z).\text{out}(c_2, a))$$
$$Q_1 = \nu c_1.\text{in}(c_2, x).(\text{out}(c_1, b) \mid \text{in}(c_1, y) \mid \text{in}(c_1, z).\text{if } x = a \text{ then } \text{out}(c_2, a))$$

We have that $P_1 \approx Q_1$ whereas $(P_1 \ ; \ \emptyset \ ; \ \mathsf{N}) \not\approx_s (Q_1 \ ; \ \emptyset \ ; \ \mathsf{N})$ for any compatible naming environment N. Depending on the value of the input, i.e. if x is equal to a or not, P_1 and Q_1 know if the test $x = a$ will succeed or not. However, on the symbolic side, the instantiation of x is postponed until the moment where x is really used, i.e. until the moment of the test itself, when it is too late to choose the right branch.

5.2   Related Work

A pioneering work has been done by Henessy and Lin [14] for value-passing CCS. However, the result which is most closely related to ours is by Borgström *et al.* [10]: they define a symbolic bisimulation for the spi calculus with the same sources of incompleteness as we have. However, our treatment of general equational theories is non trivial as illustrated by the problems implied for structural equivalence.

For many important equational theories, static equivalence has been shown to be decidable in [1]. More interestingly, some works have also been done to automate observational equivalence. The ProVerif tool [7] automates observational equivalence checking for the applied pi calculus (with process replication), but since the problem is undecidable the technique it uses is necessarily incomplete. The tool aims at proving a finer equivalence relation and relies on easily matching up the execution paths of the two processes [8]. In his thesis, Baudet [6] presents a decision procedure for a similar equivalence, called diff-equivalence, in a simplified process calculus. Examples where this equivalence relation is too fine occur when proving the observational equivalence required to show vote-privacy [15,12]. Although our symbolic bisimulation is not complete, we are able to conclude on examples where ProVerif fails. For instance, ProVerif is unable to prove that the processes $\text{out}(c, a) \mid \text{out}(c, b)$ and $\text{out}(c, b) \mid \text{out}(c, a)$ are bisimilar whereas of course we are able to deal with such examples. A more interesting example, for which our symbolic semantics plays an important role is as follows.

Example 6.   Consider the following two processes

$$P = \nu c_1.(\text{in}(c_2, x).\text{out}(c_1, x).\text{out}(c_2, a) \mid \text{in}(c_1, y).\text{out}(c_2, y))$$
$$Q = \nu c_1.(\text{in}(c_2, x).\text{out}(c_1, x).\text{out}(c_2, x) \mid \text{in}(c_1, y).\text{out}(c_2, a))$$

These two processes are labelled bisimilar and our symbolic labelled bisimilation is complete enough to prove this. In particular, let $P' = \nu c_1.(\text{out}(c_1, x').\text{out}(c_2, a) \mid \text{in}(c_1, y).\text{out}(c_2, y))$ and $Q' = \nu c_1.(\text{out}(c_1, x').\text{out}(c_2, x') \mid \text{in}(c_1, y).\text{out}(c_2, a))$. The relation $\mathcal{R}$, that witnesses the symbolic bisimulation, includes

$$(P ; \emptyset ; \mathsf{N}) \; \mathcal{R} \; (Q ; \emptyset ; \mathsf{N})$$
$$(P' ; \{\nu c_1.0 \Vdash x' , \text{gd}(c_2)\} ; \mathsf{N}') \; \mathcal{R} \; (Q' ; \{\nu c_1.0 \Vdash x' , \text{gd}(c_2)\} ; \mathsf{N}')$$
$$(\nu c_1.(\text{out}(c_2, a) \mid \text{out}(c_2, x')) ; \quad \mathcal{R} \quad (\nu c_1.(\text{out}(c_2, x') \mid \text{out}(c_2, a)) ;$$
$$\{\nu c_1.0 \Vdash x' , \text{gd}(c_2) , \text{gd}(c_1)\} ; \mathsf{N}') \quad \{\nu c_1.0 \Vdash x' , \text{gd}(c_2) , \text{gd}(c_1)\} ; \mathsf{N}')$$

The technique used in ProVerif will generally fail in the case where the two processes take different branches at some point. This is the case in Example 6: after a synchronisation (modelled by a communication on the private channel c_1) between the two parallel components of process P (resp. Q), the output action of the left component of P matches the output action of the right component of Q. This example is actually inspired by the problems we encountered when we tried to verify privacy in electronic voting protocols using ProVerif. In order to establish privacy of an electronic voting protocol (according to the definition given in [15]), we need a bisimulation relation, as the one described in this paper, which is coarse enough to allow processes to differ on their structure. We think that our symbolic bisimulation is complete enough to deal with many other interesting cases since other privacy and anonymity properties are facing the same difficulty.

5.3   Future Work

The obvious next step is to study the equivalence of solutions for constraint systems under different equational theories. Promising results have already been shown in [5] for a significant class of equational theories but for constraint systems that do not have disequalities. These results readily apply for deciding our symbolic bisimulation on the fragment without else branches in conditionals. We plan to implement an automated tool for checking observational equivalence. In particular we aim at automating proofs arising in case studies of electronic voting protocols which currently rely on hand proofs [12].

References

1. Abadi, M., Cortier, V.: Deciding knowledge in security protocols under equational theories. Theoretical Computer Science 387(1-2), 2–32 (2006)
2. Abadi, M., Fournet, C.: Mobile values, new names, and secure communication. In: Proc. 28th Symposium on Principles of Programming Languages, pp. 104–115 (2001)
3. Abadi, M., Gordon, A.D.: A calculus for cryptographic protocols: The spi calculus. In: Proc. 4th Conference on Computer and Communications Security, pp. 36–47. ACM Press, New York (1997)
4. Amadio, R., Lugiez, D., Vanackère, V.: On the symbolic reduction of processes with cryptographic functions. Theoretical Computer Science 290, 695–740 (2002)

5. Baudet, M.: Deciding security of protocols against off-line guessing attacks. In: Proc. 12th Conference on Computer and Communications Security, pp. 16–25. ACM Press, New York (2005)
6. Baudet, M.: Sécurité des protocoles cryptographiques: aspects logiques et calculatoires. Thèse de doctorat, LSV, ENS Cachan, France (January 2007)
7. Blanchet, B.: An Efficient Cryptographic Protocol Verifier Based on Prolog Rules. In: Proc. 14th Computer Security Foundations Workshop, pp. 82–96. IEEE Comp. Soc. Press, Los Alamitos (2001)
8. Blanchet, B., Abadi, M., Fournet, C.: Automated Verification of Selected Equivalences for Security Protocols. In: Proc. 20th Symposium on Logic in Computer Science, pp. 331–340. IEEE Comp. Soc. Press, Los Alamitos (2005)
9. Boreale, M., Nicola, R.D.: A symbolic semantics for the pi-calculus. Information and Computation 126(1), 34–52 (1996)
10. Borgström, J., Briais, S., Nestmann, U.: Symbolic bisimulation in the spi calculus. In: Gardner, P., Yoshida, N. (eds.) CONCUR 2004. LNCS, vol. 3170, Springer, Heidelberg (2004)
11. Delaune, S., Jacquemard, F.: A decision procedure for the verification of security protocols with explicit destructors. In: Proc. 11th ACM Conference on Computer and Communications Security (CCS 2004), pp. 278–287. ACM Press, New York (2004)
12. Delaune, S., Kremer, S., Ryan, M.D.: Coercion-resistance and receipt-freeness in electronic voting. In: Proc. 19th Computer Security Foundations Workshop, pp. 28–39. IEEE Comp. Soc. Press, Los Alamitos (2006)
13. Delaune, S., Kremer, S., Ryan, M.D.: Symbolic bisimulation for the applied pi calculus. Research Report LSV-07-14, LSV, ENS Cachan, France, pp. 47 (April 2007)
14. Hennessy, M., Lin, H.: Symbolic bisimulations. Theoretical Computer Science 138(2), 353–389 (1995)
15. Kremer, S., Ryan, M.D.: Analysis of an electronic voting protocol in the applied pi-calculus. In: Sagiv, M. (ed.) ESOP 2005. LNCS, vol. 3444, pp. 186–200. Springer, Heidelberg (2005)
16. Millen, J.K., Shmatikov, V.: Constraint solving for bounded-process cryptographic protocol analysis. In: Proc. 8th Conference on Computer and Communications Security, pp. 166–175 (2001)

Non-mitotic Sets

Christian Glaßer[1], Alan L. Selman[2,*], Stephen Travers[1,**], and Liyu Zhang[3]

[1] Julius-Maximilians-Universität Würzburg, Germany
{glasser,travers}@informatik.uni-wuerzburg.de
[2] University at Buffalo, USA
selman@cse.buffalo.edu
[3] University of Texas at Brownsville, USA
liyu.zhang@utb.edu

Abstract. We study the question of the existence of non-mitotic sets in NP. We show under various hypotheses that

- 1-tt-mitoticity and m-mitoticity differ on NP.
- T-autoreducibility and T-mitoticity differ on NP (this contrasts the situation in the recursion theoretic setting, where Ladner showed that autoreducibility and mitoticity coincide).
- 2-tt autoreducibility does not imply weak 2-tt-mitoticity.
- 1-tt-complete sets for NP are nonuniformly m-complete.

1 Introduction

A recursive set A is *T-mitotic* if there is a set $B \in P$ such that $A \equiv_T^p A \cap B \equiv_T^p A \cap \overline{B}$. Ambos-Spies [AS84] introduced this notion of mitoticity into complexity theory and he also showed how to construct recursive non-mitotic sets. Buhrman, Hoene, and Torenvliet [BHT98] showed that EXP contains non-mitotic sets. Here we investigate the question of the existence of non-mitotic sets in NP. This is a difficult question because there are no natural examples of non-mitotic sets. Natural NP-complete sets are all paddable, and for this reason are T-mitotic. Moreover, Glasser et al. [GPSZ06] proved that all NP-complete sets are m-mitotic (and therefore T-mitotic). Also, nontrivial sets belonging to the class P are T-mitotic. So any unconditional proof of the existence of non-mitotic sets in NP would prove at the same time that $P \neq NP$.

Our first result was prompted by the question of whether NP contains sets that are not m-mitotic. We prove that if $EEE \neq NEEE \cap coNEEE$, then there exists an $L \in (NP \cap coNP) - P$ that is 1-tt-mitotic but not m-mitotic. From this, it follows that under the same hypothesis, 1-tt-reducibility and m-reducibility differ on sets in NP. On the one hand, this consequence explains the need for a reasonably strong hypothesis. On the other hand, with essentially known techniques using

---

* This work was done while the author was visiting the Department of Computer Science at the University of Würzburg, Germany. Research supported in part by NSF grant CCR-0307077 and by the Alexander von Humboldt-Stiftung.
** Supported by the Konrad-Adenauer-Stiftung.

V. Arvind and S. Prasad (Eds.): FSTTCS 2007, LNCS 4855, pp. 146–157, 2007.

Table 1. Summary of our results related to NP

Assumption	Conclusion	Remark
NP ∩ coNP contains n-generic sets	$\exists A \in$ NP that is 2-tt-auto-reducible but not T-mitotic	$A \in (\text{NP} \cap \text{coNP}) - \text{P}$
EEE $\neq$ NEEE ∩ coNEEE	$\exists A \in$ NP that is 1-tt-mitotic but not m-mitotic	$A \in (\text{NP} \cap \text{coNP}) - \text{P}$
E $\neq$ NE ∩ coNE	$\exists A, B \in$ NP such that $A \leq^{\text{P}}_{1-\text{tt}} B$ but $A \not\leq^{\text{P}}_{\text{m}} B$	$A, B \in (\text{NP} \cap \text{coNP}) - \text{P}$
NP $\overset{\text{i.o.}}{\not\subseteq}$ coNP	1-tt-complete sets for NP are nonuniformly m-complete	

P-selective sets, we show that 1-tt-reducibility and m-reducibility separate within NP under the weaker hypothesis that E $\neq$ NE ∩ coNE.

This foray into questions about 1-tt-reducibility and m-reducibility provides a segue into our next result: We would like to know whether 1-tt-complete sets for NP are m-complete as well. We prove under a reasonable hypothesis that every 1-tt-complete sets for NP is complete under nonuniform m-reductions. The hypothesis states that the NP-complete set SAT does not infinitely-often belong to the class coNP.

In Glasser et al. [GPSZ06] the authors proved that every m-autoreducible set is m-mitotic. The same result follows for 1-tt-autoreducibility. In contrast, Ambos-Spies [AS84] proved that T-autoreducible does not imply T-mitotic. Also, Glasser et al. [GPSZ06] constructed a 3-tt-autoreducible set that is not weakly-T-mitotic. Hence, it is known that autoreducibility and mitoticity are not equivalent for all polynomial-time-bounded reductions between 3-tt-reducibility and Turing-reducibility. However, the question for 2-tt-reducibility has been open. Here we settle this question by showing the existence of a set in EXP that is 2-tt-autoreducible, but not weakly 2-tt-mitotic.

The last result to be proved gives evidence of non-mitotic sets in NP. We show that if NP ∩ coNP contains n-generic sets, then there exists a set $L \in$ NP ∩ coNP such that L is 2-tt-autoreducible and L is not T-mitotic. Roughly speaking, a set L is n-generic [ASFH87] if membership of x in L cannot be predicted from the initial segment $L|x$ in time 2^n, for almost all x, where $|x| = n$. This result is interesting, since under the mentioned hypothesis it shows that within NP the notions of T-autoreducibility and T-mitoticity differ. In contrast, Ladner [Lad73] showed that in the recursion theoretic setting, autoreducibility and mitoticity coincide.

2   Preliminaries

We recall basic notions. Σ denotes a finite alphabet with at least two letters, Σ^* denotes the set of all words, and $|w|$ denotes the length of a word w. A tally set is a subset of 0^*. The language accepted by a machine M is denoted by $L(M)$. $\overline{L}$ denotes the complement of a language L and $\mathrm{co}\mathcal{C}$ denotes the class of complements of languages in $\mathcal{C}$. FP denotes the class of functions computable in deterministic polynomial time.

We recall standard polynomial-time reducibilities [LLS75]. A set B *many-one-reduces* to a set C (*m-reduces* for short; in notation $B\leq_{\mathrm{m}}^{\mathrm{P}}C$) if there exists a total, polynomial-time-computable function f such that for all strings x, $x \in B \Leftrightarrow f(x) \in C$.

A set B *Turing-reduces* to a set C (*T-reduces* for short; in notation $B\leq_{\mathrm{T}}^{\mathrm{P}}C$) if there exists a deterministic polynomial-time-bounded oracle Turing machine M such that for all strings x, $x \in B \Leftrightarrow M$ with C as oracle accepts the input x.

Let $Q(M,x)$ denote the set of all queries to the oracle made by the nonadaptive oracle Turing machine M on input x.

A set B *truth-table-reduces* to a set C (*tt-reduces* for short; in notation $B\leq_{\mathrm{tt}}^{\mathrm{P}}C$) if there exists a deterministic polynomial-time-bounded oracle Turing machine M that behaves *non-adaptively* such that for all strings x, $x \in B \Leftrightarrow M$ with C as oracle accepts the input x. This means there exists a polynomial-time function g such that on input x, $g(x) = cq_1c\ldots cq_n$ where $c \notin \Sigma$ and for all $1 \leq i \leq n$, $q_i \in \Sigma^*$, and $Q(M,x) = \{q_1,\ldots,q_n\}$.

Furthermore, B 1-tt reduces to C (in notation $B\leq_{1\text{-tt}}^{\mathrm{P}}C$) if for some M, $B\leq_{\mathrm{tt}}^{\mathrm{P}}C$ via M and for all x, $|Q(M,x)| = 1$. Similarly, we define 2-tt, and so on.

If $B\leq_{\mathrm{m}}^{\mathrm{P}}C$ and $C\leq_{\mathrm{m}}^{\mathrm{P}}B$, then we say that B and C are *many-one-equivalent* (*m-equivalent* for short, in notation $B \equiv_{\mathrm{m}}^{\mathrm{P}} C$). Similarly, we define equivalence for other reducibilities. A set B is *many-one-hard* (*m-hard* for short) for a complexity class $\mathcal{C}$ if every $B \in \mathcal{C}$ m-reduces to B. If additionally $B \in \mathcal{C}$, then we say that B is *many-one-complete* (*m-complete* for short) for $\mathcal{C}$. Similarly, we define hardness and completeness for other reducibilities. We use "$\mathcal{C}$-complete" as an abbreviation for m-complete for $\mathcal{C}$.

A set B is *p-selective* [Sel79] if there exists a total function $f \in$ FP (the selector function) such that for all x and y, $f(x,y) \in \{x,y\}$ and if either of x and y belongs to B, then $f(x,y) \in B$.

Definition 1 ([AS84]). *A set A is* polynomial-time T-autoreducible *(T-auto-reducible, for short) if there exists a polynomial-time-bounded oracle Turing machine M such that $A = L(M^A)$ and for all x, M on input x never queries x. A set A is* polynomial-time m-autoreducible *(m-autoreducible, for short) if $A\leq_{\mathrm{m}}^{\mathrm{P}}A$ via a reduction function f such that for all x, $f(x) \neq x$.*

Let $\leq_{\mathrm{r}}^{\mathrm{P}}$ be a polynomial time reducibility.

Definition 2 ([AS84]). *A recursive set A is* polynomial-time r-mitotic *(r-mitotic, for short) if there exists a set $B \in$ P such that:*

$$A \equiv_{\mathrm{r}}^{\mathrm{P}} A \cap B \equiv_{\mathrm{r}}^{\mathrm{P}} A \cap \overline{B}.$$

A recursive set A is polynomial-time weakly r-mitotic *(weakly r-mitotic, for short) if there exist disjoint sets A_0 and A_1 such that $A_0 \cup A_1 = A$, and*

$$A \equiv_{\mathrm{r}}^{\mathrm{P}} A_0 \equiv_{\mathrm{r}}^{\mathrm{P}} A_1.$$

Let EEE $=$ DTIME$(2^{2^{2^{O(n)}}})$ and let NEEE $=$ NTIME$(2^{2^{2^{O(n)}}})$. A is *paddable* [BH77] if there exists $p(\cdot, \cdot)$, a polynomial-time computable, polynomial-time invertible function, such that for all a and x, $a \in A \iff p(a, x) \in A$.

3   Separation of Mitoticity Notions

Ladner, Lynch, and Selman [LLS75] and Homer [Hom90, Hom97] ask for reasonable assumptions that imply separations of polynomial-time reducibilities within NP. In this section we demonstrate that a reasonable assumption on exponential-time classes allows a separation of mitoticity notions within NP. This implies a separation of the reducibilities $\leq_m^P$ and $\leq_{1-tt}^P$ within NP. Then we show the same separation under an even weaker hypothesis. On the technical side, a key ingredient to our proof is the observation by Beigel and Feigenbaum [BF92] that very sparse sets lack certain redundancy properties.

Theorem 3. *If EEE $\neq$ NEEE $\cap$ coNEEE, then there exists an $L \in$ (NP $\cap$ coNP) $-$ P that is 1-tt-mitotic but not m-mitotic.*

The proof of this theorem can be found in the appendix.

Selman [Sel82] showed under the hypothesis E $\neq$ NE $\cap$ coNE that there exist $A, B \in$ NP $-$ P such that A tt-reduces to B but A does not positive-tt-reduce to B. The separation of mitoticity notions given in the last theorem allows us to prove a similar statement:

Corollary 4. *If EEE $\neq$ NEEE$\cap$coNEEE, then there exist $A, B \in$ (NP$\cap$coNP)$-$P such that $A{\leq}_{1-tt}^P B$, but $A \not\leq_m^P B$.*

However, a weaker assumption separates 1-tt-reducibility from m-reducibility within NP.

Theorem 5. *If E $\neq$ NE $\cap$ coNE, then there exist $A, B \in$ (NP $\cap$ coNP) $-$ P such that $A{\leq}_{1-tt}^P B$, but $A \not\leq_m^P B$.*

We now discuss that autoreducibility and weak mitoticity do not coincide for 2-tt reducibility. This completes a result by Glaßer et al. [GPSZ06] which shows that for all reducibilities between 3-tt and T, autoreducibility does not imply weak mitoticity. We present a counterexample in EXP, i.e., we construct a set $L \in$ EXP such that L is 2-tt-autoreducible but not weakly 2-tt-mitotic.

Theorem 6. *There exists $L \in$ SPARSE $\cap$ EXP such that*

- *L is 2-tt-autoreducible, but*
- *L is not weakly 2-tt-mitotic.*

The proof is based on the diagonalization proof of Theorem 4.2 in Glasser et al. [GPSZ06]. However, a straightforward adaptation does not work. The reason is that if one considers groups of three strings at certain super-exponential lengths for diagonalization, the set constructed as in the previous proof will have to be

2-tt-mitotic if we were to make it 2-tt-autoreducible. The new idea is to consider two groups of three strings at super-exponential lengths that overlap at one string. This way we can make the set 2-tt-autoreducible while not 2-tt-mitotic. The detailed construction is omitted due to space restrictions.

The full paper demonstrates that the proof technique cannot be generalized to show that there exists a set in EXP that is 2-tt-autoreducible, but not weakly T-mitotic. So this question remains open.

4   Non-mitotic Sets of Low Complexity

Buhrman, Hoene, and Torenvliet [BHT98] show that EXP contains non-m-mitotic sets. We are interested in constructing non-T-mitotic sets in NP. Recall that the existence of such sets implies that $P \neq NP$ and hence we cannot expect to prove this without a sufficiently strong hypothesis. Moreover, the same holds for the non-existence of non-m-mitotic sets in NP, since this implies $NP \neq EXP$ [BHT98].

It is known that mitoticity implies autoreducibility [AS84], hence it suffices to construct non-T-autoreducible sets in NP. Beigel and Feigenbaum [BF92] construct incoherent sets in NP under the assumption that $NEEEXP \not\subseteq BPEEEXP$. In particular, these sets are non-T-autoreducible. Moreover, Buhrman and Torenvliet [BT96] show that if $NEE \not\subseteq EE$, there are non-T-autoreducible sets in NP.

Under a slightly stronger assumption, we construct non-T-autoreducible sets in $(NP \cap coNP) - P$. We then prove that 2-tt-autoreducibility and T-mitoticity (and hence r-autoreducibility and r-mitoticity for every reduction r between 2-tt and T) do not coincide for NP. To show this, we assume that $NP \cap coNP$ contains generic sets.

Corollary 7. *If* $EEE \neq NEEE \cap coNEEE$, *then there exists* $C \in (NP \cap coNP) - P$ *such that*

- *C is not T-autoreducible and*
- *C is not T-mitotic.*

Ladner [Lad73] showed that autoreducibility and mitoticity coincide for computably enumerable sets. Under the strong assumption that $NP \cap coNP$ contains n-generic sets, we can show that the similar question in complexity theory has a negative answer.

The notion of resource-bounded genericity was defined by Ambos-Spies, Fleischhack, and Huwig [ASFH87]. We use the following equivalent definition [BM95], [PS02], where $L(x)$ denotes L's characteristic function on x.

Definition 8. *For a set* L *and a string* x *let* $L|x = \{y \in L \mid y < x\}$. *A deterministic oracle Turing machine* M *is a predictor for a set* L, *if for all* x, $M^{L|x}(x) = L(x)$. L *is a.e. unpredictable in time* $t(n)$, *if every predictor for* L *requires more than* $t(n)$ *time for all but finitely many* x.

Definition 9. *A set L is $t(n)$-generic if it is a.e. unpredictable in time $t(2^n)$.*

This is equivalent to say that for every oracle Turing machine M, if $M^{L|x}(x) = L(x)$ for all x, then the running time of M is at least $t(2^{|x|})$ for all but finitely many x.

For a given set L and two strings x and y, there are 4 possibilities for the string $L(x)L(y)$. For 1-cheatable sets L, a polynomial-time-computable function can reduce the number of possibilities to 2.

Definition 10 ([Bei87, Bei91]). *A set L is 1-cheatable if there exists a poly-nomial-time-computable function f such that $f : \Sigma^* \times \Sigma^* \longrightarrow \{0,1\}^2 \times \{0,1\}^2$ and for all x and y, the string $L(x)L(y)$ belongs to $f(x,y)$.*

Note that in this definition and in the following text we identify the pair $f(x,y) = (w_1, w_2)$ with the set $\{w_1, w_2\}$. Moreover, if $f(x,y) = (w_1, w_2)$, then $f(x,y)^R$ denotes the pair (w_1^R, w_2^R) where w^R denotes the reverse of the word w.

Theorem 11. *If $\mathrm{NP} \cap \mathrm{coNP}$ contains n-generic sets, then there exists a tally set $S \in \mathrm{NP} \cap \mathrm{coNP}$ such that*

- *S is 2-tt-autoreducible and*
- *S is not T-mitotic.*

Proof. Let $t(0) = 2$ and $t(n+1) = 2^{2^{t(n)}}$ be a tower function. Let $A' = \{0^{t(n)} \mid n \geq 0\}$, $A'' = A' \cup 0A'$, and $A''' = A' \cup 0A' \cup 00A'$. In this way, the number of primes indicates the number of words in the set with length around $t(n)$ for each n. By assumption, there exists an n-generic set $L \in \mathrm{NP} \cap \mathrm{coNP}$. Define $L'' = L \cap A''$ and observe that $L'' \in \mathrm{NP} \cap \mathrm{coNP}$.

Claim 12. *L'' is not 1-cheatable.*

Assuming that L'' is 1-cheatable we will show that L is not n-generic. Let f be a function that witnesses the 1-cheatability of L''. Without loss of generality we may assume that if $f(x,y) = (v,w)$, then $v \neq w$.

$$g(x,y) =_{\text{def}} \begin{cases} f(x,y) & : & \text{if } x < y \\ f(y,x)^R & : & \text{if } x > y \\ (00, 11) & : & \text{if } x = y \end{cases}$$

Observe that also g witnesses the 1-cheatability of L'' such that if $g(x,y) = (v,w)$, then $v \neq w$. In addition, for all x and y,

$$g(x,y) = g(y,x)^R. \tag{1}$$

We describe a predictor M for L on input x.

```
1. if x ∉ A" then accept if and only if x ∈ L
2. // here either x = 0^t(n) or x = 0^t(n)+1 for some n
```

3. if $x = 0^{t(n)}$ then let $y = 0^{t(n)+1}$ else let $y = 0^{t(n)}$
   (i.e., with y we compute the neighbor of x in A'')
4. compute $g(x,y) = (ab, cd)$ where a, b, c, and d are suitable bits
5. if $a = c$ then return a
6. if $b = d$ then accept if and only if $x \in L$
7. // here $ab = \overline{cd}$ and hence $g(x,y) = \{00, 11\}$ or $g(x,y) = \{01, 10\}$
8. if $a = b$ and $|x| > |y|$ then accept if and only if y belongs to
   the oracle $L|x$
9. if $a = b$ and $|x| \leq |y|$ then accept if and only if $x \in L$
10. // here $g(x,y) = \{01, 10\}$
11. if $|x| > |y|$ then accept if and only if y does not belong to the
    oracle $L|x$
12. accept if and only if $x \in L$

In the algorithm, the term accept if and only if $x \in L$ means that first, in deterministic time $2^{n^{O(1)}}$, we find out whether x belongs to L, and then we accept accordingly.

We observe that M is a predictor for L: In line 5, M predicts correctly, since $g(x,y) = (ab, ad)$ and therefore, $L(x) = a$. M predicts correctly in line 8, since $g(x,y) = \{00, 11\}$ implies $x \in L \Leftrightarrow y \in L$ and $|y| < |x|$ implies $y \in L|x \Leftrightarrow y \in L$. M predicts correctly in line 11, since $g(x,y) = \{01, 10\}$ implies $x \in L \Leftrightarrow y \notin L$ and again $|y| < |x|$ implies $y \in L|x \Leftrightarrow y \in L$. Hence M is a predictor for L.

If we do not take the lines 1, 6, 9, and 12 into account, then the running time of M is polynomially bounded, say by the polynomial p. Now we are going to show the following.

For all n, at least one of the following holds: $M^{L|x}(x)$ stops within $p(|x|)$ steps or $M^{L|y}(y)$ stops within $p(|y|)$ steps, where $x = 0^{t(n)}$ and $y = 0^{t(n)+1}$. $(*)$

Assume $(*)$ does not hold for a particular n, and let $x = 0^{t(n)}$ and $y = 0^{t(n)+1}$. Hence, both computations, $M^{L|x}(x)$ and $M^{L|y}(y)$ must stop in one of the lines 1, 6, 9, and 12. Since, $x, y \in A''$, these computations do not stop in line 1.

Assume $M^{L|x}(x)$ stops in line 6. In this case, $g(x,y) = (ab, cb)$. By (1), the computation $M^{L|y}(y)$ computes the value $g(y,x) = (ba, bc)$ in line 4. So $M^{L|y}(y)$ stops in line 5, which contradicts our observation that we must stop in the lines 6, 9, or 12. This shows that $M^{L|x}(x)$ does not stop in line 6. Analogously we obtain that $M^{L|y}(y)$ does not stop in line 6. So both computations must stop in line 9 or line 12.

$M^{L|y}(y)$ does not stop in line 9, since in this computation, the second condition in line 9 evaluates to false. So $M^{L|y}(y)$ stops in line 12. However, this is not possible, since $M^{L|y}(y)$ would have stopped already in line 11. This proves $(*)$.

From $(*)$ it follows that for infinitely many x, $M^{L|x}(x)$ stops within $p(|x|)$ steps. Hence L is not $(\log p(n))$-generic and in particular, not n-generic. This contradicts our assumption on L. (Note that we obtain also a contradiction if we assume L to be $t(n)$-generic such that $t(n) > c \log n$ for all $c > 0$.) This finishes the proof of Claim 12.

So far we constructed an $L'' \in \mathrm{NP} \cap \mathrm{coNP}$ such that $L'' \subseteq A''$ and L'' is not 1-cheatable. Now we define a set $L''' \subseteq A'''$ (this will be the set asserted in the theorem). For $n \geq 0$ let $x_n = 0^{t(n)}$, $y_n = 0^{t(n)+1}$, $z_n = 0^{t(n)+2}$, and $c_n = L''(x_n)L''(y_n)$. Define L''' to be the unique subset of A''' that satisfies the following conditions where $d_n = L'''(x_n)L'''(y_n)L'''(z_n)$:

1. if $c_n = 00$ then $d_n = 000$
2. if $c_n = 01$ then $d_n = 110$
3. if $c_n = 10$ then $d_n = 101$
4. if $c_n = 11$ then $d_n = 011$

Observe that L''' is a tally set in $\mathrm{NP} \cap \mathrm{coNP}$. Moreover, note that for all n, either 0 or 2 words from $\{x_n, y_n, z_n\}$ belong to L'''. This implies that L''' is 2-tt-autoreducible: If the input x is not in A''', then reject. Otherwise, determine the n such that $x \in \{x_n, y_n, z_n\}$. Ask the oracle for the two words in $\{x_n, y_n, z_n\} - \{x\}$ and output the parity of the answers.

Claim 13. L''' is not T-mitotic.

Assume L''' is T-mitotic, and let $S \in \mathrm{P}$ be a witnessing separator. Let $L''' \leq^{\mathrm{P}}_{\mathrm{T}} L''' \cap \overline{S}$ via machine M_1 and let $L''' \leq^{\mathrm{P}}_{\mathrm{T}} L''' \cap S$ via machine M_2. We will obtain a contradiction by showing that L'' is 1-cheatable. We define the witnessing function $h(x, y)$ as follows.

1. If $x = y$ then output $(00, 11)$.
2. If $|x| > |y|$ then output $h(y, x)^R$.
3. If $x \notin A''$ then output $(00, 01)$.
4. If $y \notin A''$ then output $(00, 10)$.
5. // Here $|x| < |y|$ and $x, y \in A''$.
6. If $|y| - |x| > 1$ then let $a = L''(x)$ and output $(a0, a1)$.
7. Determine n such that $x = x_n$ and $y = y_n$.
8. Distinguish the following cases.
   (a) $S \cap \{x_n, y_n, z_n\} = \emptyset$: Simulate $M_2(x_n)$, $M_2(y_n)$, and $M_2(z_n)$ where oracle queries q of length $\leq t(n-1) + 2$ are answered according to $q \in L''' \cap S$ and all other oracle queries are answered negatively. Let d_n be the concatenation of the outputs of these simulations. Let c_n be the value corresponding to d_n according to the definition of L'''. Output $(c_n, 00)$.
   (b) $\overline{S} \cap \{x_n, y_n, z_n\} = \emptyset$: Do the same as in step 8a, but use M_1 instead of M_2 and answer short queries q according to $q \in L''' \cap \overline{S}$.
   (c) $|S \cap \{x_n, y_n, z_n\}| = 1$: Without loss of generality we assume $x_n \in S$ and $y_n, z_n \notin S$. For $r \in \{\mathrm{yes}, \mathrm{no}\}$ we simulate $M_2(x_n)$, $M_2(y_n)$, and $M_2(z_n)$ where oracle queries q of length $\leq t(n-1) + 2$ are answered according to $q \in L''' \cap S$, the oracle query x_n is answered with r, and all other oracle queries q are answered negatively. Let d_r be the concatenation of the outputs of these simulations. Let c_r be the value corresponding to d_r according to the definition of L''' (if such c_r does not exist, then let $c_r = 00$). Output $(c_{\mathrm{yes}}, c_{\mathrm{no}})$.
   (d) $|\overline{S} \cap \{x_n, y_n, z_n\}| = 1$: Do the same as in step 8c, but use M_1 instead of M_2 and answer short queries q according to $q \in L''' \cap \overline{S}$.

We argue that h is computable in polynomial time. Note that if we recursively call $h(y, x)$ in step 2, then the computation of $h(y, x)$ will not call h again. So the recursion depth of the algorithm is ≤ 2. In step 6, $|x| < |y|$ and $x, y \in A''$, since $|x| = |y|$ implies that we stop in line 3 or 4. From the definition of A'' it follows that there exists an n such that $|x| \leq t(n-1) + 1$ and $|y| \geq t(n)$. So the computation of a in step 6 takes time

$$\leq 2^{|x|^{O(1)}} \leq 2^{t(n-1)^{O(1)}} \leq 2^{2^{t(n-1)}} = t(n) \leq |y|. \tag{2}$$

The n in step 7 exists, since $x, y \in A''$ and $|y| - |x| = 1$. In step 8, queries q of length $\leq t(n-1) + 2$ must be answered according to $q \in L''' \cap S$ or according to $q \in L''' \cap \overline{S}$. Similar to (2) these simulations can be done in polynomial time in $|x|$. This shows that h is computable in polynomial time.

We now argue that h witnesses that L'' is 1-cheatable, i.e., if $f(x, y) = (ab, cd)$, then $L''(x)L''(y) = ab$ or $L''(x)L''(y) = cd$. It suffices to show this for the case $|x| < |y|$. If we stop in step 3, then $x \notin L''$ and hence $L''(x)L''(y) = 00$ or $L''(x)L''(y) = 01$. Similarly, if we stop in step 4, then $y \notin L''$ and hence $L''(x)L''(y) = 00$ or $L''(x)L''(y) = 10$. If we stop in step 6, then $L''(x) = a$ and so $L''(x)L''(y) = a0$ or $L''(x)L''(y) = a1$. So it remains to argue for step 8.

Now assume the output is made in step 8a. Consider the computations $M_2^{L''' \cap S}(x_n)$, $M_2^{L''' \cap S}(y_n)$, and $M_2^{L''' \cap S}(z_n)$. Since these are polynomial-time computations, they cannot ask for words of length $\geq t(n+1) = 2^{2^{t(n)}}$. So x_n, y_n, and z_n are the only candidates for words that are of length $> t(n-1) + 2$ and that can be queried by these computations. But by assumption of case 8a, these words are not in $L''' \cap S$. Therefore, the simulations of $M_2(x_n)$, $M_2(y_n)$, and $M_2(z_n)$ in step 8a behave the same way as the computations $M_2^{L''' \cap S}(x_n)$, $M_2^{L''' \cap S}(y_n)$, and $M_2^{L''' \cap S}(z_n)$. Hence we obtain $d_n = L'''(x_n)L'''(y_n)L'''(z_n)$ and $c_n = L''(x_n)L''(y_n)$. So the output contains the string $L'''(x)L'''(y)$. Step 8b is argued similar to step 8a.

Assume the output is made in step 8c. We can reuse the argument from step 8a. The only difference is the words x_n. It can be an element of $L''' \cap S$ and it can be queried by the computations $M_2^{L''' \cap S}(x_n)$, $M_2^{L''' \cap S}(y_n)$, and $M_2^{L''' \cap S}(z_n)$. So we simulate both possibilities, the one where $x_n \in L''' \cap S$ and the one where $x_n \notin L''' \cap S$. So at least one of the strings c_{yes} and c_{no} equals $L'''(x)L'''(y)$ and so the output contains the string $L'''(x)L'''(y)$. Step 8d is argued similar to step 8c.

This shows that L'' is 1-cheatable via function h. This contradicts Claim 12 and therefore, L''' is not T-mitotic. This finishes the proof of Claim 13 and of Theorem 11. □

Corollary 14. *If NP $\cap$ coNP contains n-generic sets, then T-autoreducibility and T-mitoticity differ on NP.*

Corollary 15. *Let $t(n)$ be a function such that for all $c > 0$, $t(n) > c \log n$. If NP$\cap$coNP contains $t(n)$-generic sets, then there exists a tally set $L \in$ NP$\cap$coNP that is 2-tt-autoreducible, but not T-mitotic.*

5 Uniformly Hard Languages in NP

In this section we assume that NP contains uniformly hard languages, i.e., languages that are uniformly not contained in coNP. After discussing this assumption we show that it implies that every $\leq^{\mathrm{P}}_{1-\mathrm{tt}}$-complete set for NP is nonuniformly NP-complete.

Recall that we have separated 1-tt-reducibility from m-reducibility within NP under a reasonable assumption in Section 3. Nevertheless the main result of this section indicates that these two reducibilities are pretty similar in terms of NP-complete problems: Every $\leq^{\mathrm{P}}_{1-\mathrm{tt}}$-complete set for NP is m-complete if we allow the reducing function to use an advice of polynomial length.

Definition 16. *Let $\mathcal{C}$ and $\mathcal{D}$ be complexity classes, and let A and B be subsets of Σ^*.*

1. *$A \overset{\text{i.o.}}{=} B \overset{df}{\Longleftrightarrow}$ for infinitely many n it holds that $A \cap \Sigma^n = B \cap \Sigma^n$.*
2. *$A \overset{\text{i.o.}}{\in} \mathcal{C} \overset{df}{\Longleftrightarrow}$ there exists $C \in \mathcal{C}$ such that $A \overset{\text{i.o.}}{=} C$.*
3. *$\mathcal{C} \overset{\text{i.o.}}{\subseteq} \mathcal{D} \overset{df}{\Longleftrightarrow} C \overset{\text{i.o.}}{\in} \mathcal{D}$ for all $C \in \mathcal{C}$.*

The following proposition is easy to observe.

Proposition 17. *Let $\mathcal{C}$ and $\mathcal{D}$ be complexity classes, and let A and B be subsets of Σ^*.*

1. *$A \overset{\text{i.o.}}{=} B$ if and only if $\overline{A} \overset{\text{i.o.}}{=} \overline{B}$.*
2. *$A \overset{\text{i.o.}}{\in} \mathcal{C}$ if and only if $\overline{A} \overset{\text{i.o.}}{\in} \mathrm{co}\mathcal{C}$.*
3. *$\mathcal{C} \overset{\text{i.o.}}{\subseteq} \mathcal{D}$ if and only if $\mathrm{co}\mathcal{C} \overset{\text{i.o.}}{\subseteq} \mathrm{co}\mathcal{D}$.*

Proposition 18. *The following are equivalent:*

  (i) *coNP $\overset{\text{i.o.}}{\not\subseteq}$ NP*
  (ii) *NP $\overset{\text{i.o.}}{\not\subseteq}$ coNP*
  (iii) *There exists an $A \in$ NP such that $A \overset{\text{i.o.}}{\notin}$ coNP.*
  (iv) *There exists a paddable NP-complete A such that $A \overset{\text{i.o.}}{\notin}$ coNP.*

We define polynomial-time many-one reductions with advice. Non-uniform reductions are of interest in cryptography, where they model an adversary who is capable of long preprocessing [BV97]. They also have applications in structural complexity theory. Agrawal [Agr02] and Hitchcock and Pavan [HP06] investigate non-uniform reductions and show under reasonable hypotheses that every many-one complete set for NP is also hard for length-increasing, non-uniform reductions.

Definition 19. *$A \leq^{\mathrm{p/poly}}_{\mathrm{m}} B$ if there exists an $f \in$ FP/poly such that for all words x, $x \in A \Leftrightarrow f(x) \in B$.*

The following theorem assumes as hypothesis that NP $\overset{\text{i.o.}}{\not\subseteq}$ coNP. This hypothesis states that for sufficiently large n, there exists a tautology of size n without short proofs. We use this hypothesis to show that 1-tt-complete sets for NP are nonuniformly m-complete.

Theorem 20. *If* NP $\overset{\text{i.o.}}{\not\subseteq}$ coNP, *then every* $\leq^{\text{P}}_{1-\text{tt}}$-*complete set for* NP *is* $\leq^{\text{p/poly}}_{\text{m}}$-*complete.*

Proof. By assumption, there exists an NP-complete K such that $K \overset{\text{i.o.}}{\not\subseteq}$ coNP. Choose $g \in \text{FP}$ such that $\{(u,v) \mid u \in K \vee v \in K\} \leq^{\text{P}}_{\text{m}} K$ via g. Let A be $\leq^{\text{P}}_{1-\text{tt}}$-complete for NP. So $K \leq^{\text{P}}_{1-\text{tt}} A$, i.e., there exists a polynomial-time computable function $f : \Sigma^* \to \Sigma^* \cup \{\overline{w} \mid w \in \Sigma^*\}$ such that for all words x:

1. If $f(x) = w$ for some $w \in \Sigma^*$, then $(x \in K \Leftrightarrow w \in A)$.
2. If $f(x) = \overline{w}$ for some $w \in \Sigma^*$, then $(x \in K \Leftrightarrow w \notin A)$.

Moreover, choose $r \in \text{FP}$ such that $A \leq^{\text{P}}_{\text{m}} K$ via r. Define

$$\text{EASY} =_{\text{def}} \{u \mid \exists v, |v| = |u|, f(g(u,v)) = \overline{w} \text{ for some } w \in \Sigma^*, \text{ and } r(w) \in K\}$$

EASY belongs to NP. We see EASY $\subseteq \overline{K}$ as follows: Let $u \in$ EASY and v, w be as above. Then $r(w) \in K$ implies $w \in A$, hence $g(u,v) \notin K$, and hence $u \notin K$. From our assumption $\overline{K} \overset{\text{i.o.}}{\not\subseteq}$ NP it follows that there exists an $n_0 \geq 0$ such that

$$\forall n \geq n_0, \overline{K}^{=n} \not\subseteq \text{EASY}^{=n}.$$

So for every $n \geq n_0$ we can choose a word $w_n \in \overline{K}^{=n} - \text{EASY}$. For $n < n_0$, let $w_n = \varepsilon$. Choose fixed $z_1 \in A$ and $z_0 \notin A$. We define a reduction which witnesses $K \leq^{\text{p/poly}}_{\text{m}} A$.

$$h(v) =_{\text{def}} \begin{cases} f(g(w_{|v|}, v)) & : \text{ if } |v| \geq n_0 \text{ and } f(g(w_{|v|}, v)) \in \Sigma^* \\ z_1 & : \text{ if } |v| \geq n_0 \text{ and } f(g(w_{|v|}, v)) = \overline{w} \text{ for some } w \in \Sigma^* \\ z_1 & : \text{ if } |v| < n_0 \text{ and } v \in K \\ z_0 & : \text{ if } |v| < n_0 \text{ and } v \notin K \end{cases}$$

Observe that $h \in \text{FP/poly}$ (even FP/lin) with the advice $n \mapsto w_n$. We claim for all v,

$$v \in K \Leftrightarrow h(v) \in A. \tag{3}$$

This equivalence clearly holds for all v such that $|v| < n_0$. So assume $|v| \geq n_0$ and let $n = |v|$. If $f(g(w_n, v)) \in \Sigma^*$, then h is defined according to the first line of its definition and equivalence (3) is obtained as follows.

$$v \in K \Leftrightarrow g(w_n, v) \in K \Leftrightarrow f(g(w_n, v)) \in A$$

Otherwise, $f(g(w_n, v)) = \overline{w}$ for some $w \in \Sigma^*$. We claim that v must belong to K. If not, then $g(w_n, v) \notin K$ and hence $w \in A$ (since $K \leq^{\text{P}}_{1-\text{tt}} A$ via f). So $r(w) \in K$ which witnesses that $w_n \in$ EASY. This contradicts the choice of w_n and it follows that $v \in K$. This shows $v \in K \Leftrightarrow h(v) = z_1 \in A$ and proves equivalence (3). $\qquad \square$

References

[Agr02]   Agrawal, M.: Pseudo-random generators and structure of complete degrees. In: IEEE Conference on Computational Complexity, pp. 139–147. IEEE Computer Society Press, Los Alamitos (2002)

[AS84]   Ambos-Spies, K.: P-mitotic sets. In: Börger, E., Rödding, D., Hasenjaeger, G. (eds.) Logic and Machines: Decision Problems and Complexity. LNCS, vol. 171, pp. 1–23. Springer, Heidelberg (1984)

[ASFH87]   Ambos-Spies, K., Fleischhack, H., Huwig, H.: Diagonalizations over polynomial time computable sets. Theoretical Computer Science 51, 177–204 (1987)

[Bei87]   Beigel, R.: Query-Limited Reducibilities. PhD thesis, Stanford University (1987)

[Bei91]   Beigel, R.: Relativized counting classes: Relations among thresholds, parity, mods. Journal of Computer and System Sciences 42, 76–96 (1991)

[BF92]   Beigel, R., Feigenbaum, J.: On being incoherent without being very hard. Computational Complexity 2, 1–17 (1992)

[BH77]   Berman, L., Hartmanis, J.: On isomorphism and density of NP and other complete sets. SIAM Journal on Computing 6, 305–322 (1977)

[BHT98]   Buhrman, H., Hoene, A., Torenvliet, L.: Splittings, robustness, and structure of complete sets. SIAM Journal on Computing 27, 637–653 (1998)

[BM95]   Balcazar, J., Mayordomo, E.: A note on genericty and bi-immunity. In: Proceedings of the Tenth Annual IEEE Conference on Computational Complexity, pp. 193–196. IEEE Computer Society Press, Los Alamitos (1995)

[BT96]   Buhrman, H., Torenvliet, L.: P-selective self-reducible sets: A new characterization of P. Journal of Computer and System Sciences 53, 210–217 (1996)

[BV97]   Boneh, D., Venkatesan, R.: Rounding in lattices and its cryptographic applications. In: SODA, pp. 675–681 (1997)

[GPSZ06]   Glaßer, C., Pavan, A., Selman, A.L., Zhang, L.: Redundancy in complete sets. In: Durand, B., Thomas, W. (eds.) STACS 2006. LNCS, vol. 3884, pp. 444–454. Springer, Heidelberg (2006)

[Hom90]   Homer, S.: Structural properties of nondeterministic complete sets. In: Structure in Complexity Theory Conference, pp. 3–10 (1990)

[Hom97]   Homer, S.: Structural properties of complete problems for exponential time. In: Selman, A.L., Hemaspaandra, L.A. (eds.) Complexity Theory Retrospective II, pp. 135–153. Springer, New York (1997)

[HP06]   Hitchcock, J., Pavan, A.: Comparing reductions to NP-complete sets. Technical Report TR06-039, Electronic Colloquium on Computational Complexity (2006)

[Lad73]   Ladner, R.E.: Mitotic recursively enumerable sets. Journal of Symbolic Logic 38(2), 199–211 (1973)

[LLS75]   Ladner, R.E., Lynch, N.A., Selman, A.L.: A comparison of polynomial time reducibilities. Theoretical Computer Science 1, 103–123 (1975)

[PS02]   Pavan, A., Selman, A.L.: Separation of NP-completeness notions. SIAM Journal on Computing 31(3), 906–918 (2002)

[Sel79]   Selman, A.L.: P-selective sets, tally languages, and the behavior of polynomial-time reducibilities on NP. Mathematical Systems Theory 13, 55–65 (1979)

[Sel82]   Selman, A.L.: Reductions on NP and p-selective sets. Theoretical Computer Science 19, 287–304 (1982)

Reductions to Graph Isomorphism

Jacobo Torán

Institut für Theoretische Informatik
Universität Ulm
D-89069 Ulm, Germany
jacobo.toran@uni-ulm.de

Abstract. We show that several reducibility notions coincide when applied to the Graph Isomorphism (GI) problem. In particular we show that if a set is many-one logspace reducible to GI, then it is in fact many-one AC^0 reducible to GI. For the case of Turing reducibilities we show that for any $k \geq 0$ an NC^{k+1} reduction to GI can be transformed into an AC^k reduction to the same problem.

Keywords: Computational complexity, reducibilities, graph isomorphism.

1 Introduction

The Graph Isomorphism problem (GI) is one of the few problems in NP that is neither known to be complete for this class nor known to be solvable in polynomial time. Because of its special nature GI has been intensively studied and research on this problem has produced important results in several areas of complexity theory going beyond the GI problem itself. Examples for this are Arthur-Merlin games, interactive proof systems, descriptive complexity or quantum algorithms. The importance of the problem is such, that some authors have used the term GI-complete (see e.g. [5]) for the problems that are equivalent to GI under polynomial time reductions, as if GI were a complexity class. Often computational problems such as SAT, the set of satisfiable Boolean formulas, or the Graph Reachability problem have been identified with complexity classes. The difference here is that there in no machine model known to characterize the complexity of GI.

In this paper we study several reducibilities to GI proving gap results in the complexity of the models performing the reduction. The results we obtain basically show that the GI problem is very robust under reductions and that in some sense it behaves like a complexity class. We prove that if a set A is reducible to GI under several kinds of reducibility, then the complexity of the reduction can be reduced, and A is in fact AC^0 reducible to GI.

The motivation for studying the complexity of the reductions to GI is twofold. On the one hand, only relatively weak hardness results for GI are known. The strongest known result [11] is that GI is many-one AC^0 hard for DET, the class of problems reducible to the Determinant [4], a class included within NC^2. Several

V. Arvind and S. Prasad (Eds.): FSTTCS 2007, LNCS 4855, pp. 158–167, 2007.
© Springer-Verlag Berlin Heidelberg 2007

attempts to extend these results to other complexity classes like P, or even NC^2 or AC^1, have not been successful, even under the consideration of reductions that can use more resources than AC^0. The study of reductions to GI give some insight on why it is difficult to improve the known hardness results.

On the other hand our results help to understand the nature of several reducibility notions like for example the AC^k or NC^{k+1} reducibilities. These reducibilities are quite well understood and it is known that both notions coincide when reducing to complexity classes like the NC and AC hierarchies [12], L and NL [2], or NP [8]. We show here that they coincide also when reducing to GI[1]. This is somehow surprising since GI is not a machine based complexity class, and intuitively points to the following property of the reducibilities: If the oracle set is strong enough to encode a logarithmic space computation, then AC^k and NC^{k+1} reducibilities to this set coincide.

Our results are based on a fact that is easy to state: Imagine we have to decide whether two graphs G and H are isomorphic, but the adjacency matrices of G and H are encoded by sequences of graph pairs. The 1's and 0's in the matrix are given respectively as pairs of isomorphic and non-isomorphic graphs [2]. How hard is it to decide the isomorphism question then? We show in Lemma 2 that this problem is not harder that GI itself. This innocent looking fact has many consequences roughly implying that for several reducibilities to GI, part of the complexity of the reduction can be transferred to the isomorphism problem, thus simplifying the reduction. In Section 3 we show that sets many-one NC^1 or logarithmic space reducible to GI are in fact many-one AC^0 reducible to GI. This result can be strengthen to reductions that as strong as the hardest complexity class that can be reduced to GI. Observe that an even stronger gap result is known to hold for SAT. SAT is known to be AC^0 hard for NP (and even NC^0 hard [1]). Since every problem many-one polynomial time reducible to SAT is in NP, it is therefore also many-one AC^0 reducible to SAT. Again, the difference with our result is that we cannot build our proof on a machine based characterisation of the complexity class.

In Section 4 we study Turing reducibilities to GI. We show that the classes $\mathsf{FL}(\mathrm{GI})$ and $\mathsf{AC}^0(\mathrm{GI})$ coincide. Using this fact and adapting a result from [2] on AC and NC reductions to L to the case of GI we prove that for every $k \geq 0$, $\mathsf{AC}^k(\mathrm{GI}) = \mathsf{NC}^{k+1}(\mathrm{GI})$.

2   Preliminaries

We assume familiarity with basic notions of complexity theory such as can be found in the standard textbooks in the area.

---

[1] Ogihara [8] even shows that both reducibilities coincide when performed to a complexity class that is closed under non-deterministic conjunctive truth-table reducibility, but it is not hard to see that the closure of GI under such reducibility is NP and therefore Ogihara's result cannot be applied here.

[2] A more formal version of the statement is given in Lemma 2.

The elements of the sets we use are encoded as strings over the binary alphabet $\{0, 1\}$. A Boolean circuit is an acyclic directed graph with nodes or gates that can either be inputs $x_1, \ldots, x_n$, constants 0 or 1 or are labelled with the AND, OR or NOT functions. Some of the nodes are specified as output nodes $y_1, \ldots, y_m$. A circuit family $\{\alpha_n\}$ computes a function f in the usual way. The size of a circuit is the number of nodes it contains. The depth of a circuit in the length of its longest path from an input node to an output node. The NC and AC hierarchies contain all those functions that are computable by bounded fan-in (resp. unbounded fan-in) circuits of polynomial size and polylogarithmic depth satisfying a certain uniformity condition. Throughout this paper we consider all circuits to be DLOGTIME uniform [9,3]. Each gate i of a circuit is described by a tuple $\langle i, t, p_1, p_2, ..., p_l \rangle$ specifying the name i of the gate, its type t and the name p_j of its j-th input gate. For $k \geq 0$ we denote by NC^k (resp. AC^k) the class of functions computable by uniform bounded fan-in (resp. unbounded fan-in) circuits of polynomial size and depth $O(\log^k n)$. L and FL are the classes of set and functions computable by logarithmic space bounded Turing machines.

The known relationships among the considered function classes are:

$$AC^0 \subseteq NC^1 \subseteq FL \subseteq AC^1 \subseteq \ldots \subseteq NC^k \subseteq AC^k \subseteq NC^{k+1} \ldots$$

2.1   Reducibilities

We deal with many-one and Turing reducibilities. For a function class $\mathcal{F}$ and two sets A and B, we say that A is many-one $\mathcal{F}$ reducible to B ($A \leq_m^{\mathcal{F}} B$) if there is a total function $f \in \mathcal{F}$ such that for every $x \in \{0,1\}^*$, $x \in A \Leftrightarrow f(x) \in B$.

In order to perform Turing reductions, the NC and AC circuits can have access to oracle gates which compute the value of a functional oracle f. For AC circuits, oracle nodes have depth 1. For NC circuits, a oracle gate with m inputs contributes $\log m$ to the depth of the circuit. This is the standard way of counting the depth of oracle nodes [12]. For a complexity class of functions $\mathcal{F}$, we denote by $NC^k(\mathcal{F})$ and $AC^k(\mathcal{F})$ the class of functions computable by NC rep. AC circuits of depth $O(\log^k n)$ with oracle access to a function in $\mathcal{F}$. A Turing reduction to an oracle set A can be seen as a reduction to the characteristic function of A.

For the case of FL we will only consider here sets as oracles. $FL(A)$ is the class of functions that can be computed in logarithmic space making queries to an oracle set A. A closer description of this model is given when it is needed in the proof of Theorem 4.

2.2   Graph Isomorphism

An isomorphism between two graphs G and H is a bijection between their sets of vertices which preserves the edges. $G \cong H$ denotes that G and H are isomorphic. GI is the problem

$$GI = \{(G, H) \mid G \text{ and } H \text{ are isomorphic graphs}\}$$

A central role in some of the proofs will be played by the set of graph pairs $((G, H), (I, J))$ with exactly one of the pairs consisting of isomorphic graphs:

$$\mathrm{PGI} = \{((G, H), (I, J)) \mid G \simeq H \text{ if and only if } I \not\simeq J\}.$$

PGI will be used as a *promise problem* [10] in the sense that we will work in settings in which 2 given pairs of graphs will be known to be in PGI and the question will be to find which of the pairs are isomorphic: the first or the second[3]. It is not hard to see that GI is many-one reducible to PGI. But we need a stronger kind of reducibility:

Definition 1. *Let $\mathcal{F}$ be a class of functions. We say that a set A is strong many-one $\mathcal{F}$ reducible to PGI if there is a total function $f \in \mathcal{F}$ that for every $x \in \{0, 1\}^* \ f(x) = (G, H), (I, J) \in \mathrm{PGI}$ and $x \in A \Leftrightarrow G \cong H$.*

It is known that every set in NC^1, L, NL and in several other complexity classes is strong many-one AC^0 reducible to PGI [6,11].

In some of the proofs we will talk about graphs with colored nodes. A color is just a graph gadget or marking that forces the vertices of a color to be mapped to vertices of the same color in every possible isomorphism (see [7]).

For the proof of Lemma 2 the following result describing a parity check construction is needed. This result appears implicitly in [11].

Lemma 1. *Let $G = (V_G, E_G)$ and $H = (V_H, E_H)$ be two isomorphic graphs with n nodes. Suppose that there is an isomorphism φ between G and H mapping a sequence $U_G \ \{u_{G_0}^i, u_{G_1}^i\}_{i=1}^m$ of distinct node pairs in G to a sequence $U_H \ \{u_{H_0}^i, u_{H_1}^i\}_{i=1}^m$ of distinct node pairs in H in such a way that pairs in one of the sequences are mapped to the corresponding pairs, (i.e. for all i, $1 \le i \le m$, $\{u_{G_0}^i, u_{G_1}^i\}$ is mapped to $\{u_{H_0}^i, u_{H_1}^i\}$) Let s be the number of i, $1 \le i \le m$, such that φ maps $u_{G_0}^i$ to $u_{H_0}^i$. Then it is possible to compute in AC^0 extensions G', H' of G and H (just by adding a parity check gadget to the nodes in U_G and another one to the nodes in U_H) such that there is an isomorphism φ' from G' to H' extending φ if and only if s is even. In addition the number of nodes in the extensions G', H' is $O(n)$.*

3 Many-One Reducibility

Definition 2. *Let A be an undirected graph with n vertices. A PGI representation of A is sequence of $\binom{n}{2}$ tuples of PGI graphs (given by their adjacency matrices) $(G_{i,j}^A, H_{i,j}^A), (I_{i,j}^A, J_{i,j}^A)$, $1 \le i < j \le n$, such that for every i, j:*

$$(i, j) \in E \Rightarrow G_{i,j}^A \cong H_{i,j}^A \text{ and } I_{i,j}^A \not\cong J_{i,j}^A,$$
$$(i, j) \notin E \Rightarrow G_{i,j}^A \not\cong H_{i,j}^A \text{ and } I_{i,j}^A \cong J_{i,j}^A.$$

---

[3] In fact, in the promise problem setting this problem has been introduced by Selman [10] with the name PP-ISO.

Our results are based on the following lemma. Intuitively this result can be understood as a version of the fact $\mathsf{NP}(\mathsf{NP} \cap \mathsf{coNP}) = \mathsf{NP}$ scaled down from NP to Graph Isomorphism.

Lemma 2. *Consider two undirected graphs A and B with n vertices each, given in PGI representation. There is an AC^0 circuit that on input these representations produces the adjacency matrices of two graphs A', B' such that $A \cong B$ if and only if $A' \cong B'$.*

Proof. (sketch) The idea of the proof is to consider as a basis for A' and B' two cliques K_n^A and K_n^B with n vertices, and substitute each edge (i,j) in the K_n^A-clique by a graph gadget $E_{i,j}^A$ and every edge (k,l) in the K_n^B-clique by a gadget $E_{k,l}^B$ so that $E_{i,j}^A \cong E_{k,l}^B$ if and only if $(G_{i,j}^A \cong H_{i,j}^A$ and $G_{k,l}^B \cong H_{k,l}^B)$ or $(I_{i,j}^A \cong J_{i,j}^A$ and $I_{k,l}^B \cong J_{k,l}^B)$. In other words, $E_{i,j}^A$ and $E_{k,l}^B$ are isomorphic if and only if the edge (i,j) exists in A and the edge (k,l) exists in B or both edges do not exist. An isomorphism between A' and B' encodes then a mapping from the vertices of A to the vertices of B (the mapping restricted to the clique nodes) that guarantees that edges in A are being mapped to edges in B and non-edges are being mapped to non-edges. This is an isomorphism between A and B.

Let us define the graph gadgets. For every pair of indices $a, b, 1 \leq a < b \leq n$ consider the component $C_{a,b}^A$ containing the four graphs $G_{a,b}^A, H_{a,b}^A, I_{a,b}^A, J_{a,b}^A$ connected in a ring as in Fig. 1. There are six new vertices u^0, u^1, w, x, y and z in the component. A connection in the figure between a graph and one of the new vertices means that there is an edge in $C_{a,b}^A$ between every vertex in the graph and the new vertex.

We define also the *twisted* component $\overline{C_{a,b}^A}$ in the same way but interchanging the positions of the graphs $G_{a,b}^A$ and $H_{a,b}^A$. The components $C_{a,b}^B$ are defined in exactly the same way but using the graphs with superscript B. Observe that since we are dealing with PGI graphs, for every a, b, $C_{a,b}$ is isomorphic to $\overline{C_{a,b}}$

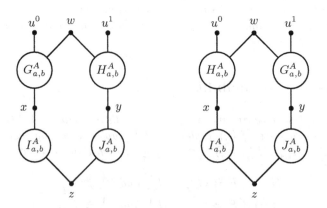

Fig. 1. The components $C_{a,b}^A$ and $\overline{C_{a,b}^A}$

(in both cases A and B). Such an isomorphism would map vertex u^0 in $C_{a,b}$ either to u^0 or to u^1 in $\overline{C_{a,b}}$ depending on whether $G_{a,b} \cong H_{a,b}$ or $I_{a,b} \cong J_{a,b}$. Exactly one of the two cases is always true.

We are now ready to define the gadgets $E_{i,j}^A$ and $E_{i,j}^B$. Consider i, j with $1 \le i < j \le n$. (For the case $i > j$, $E_{i,j}$ is equal to $E_{j,i}$ for both cases A and B). $E_{i,j}^A$ consists basically of the sequence of components

$$C_{1,2}^A, C_{1,3}^A, \ldots, \overline{C_{i,j}^A}, \ldots, C_{n-1,n}^A, C_{1,2}^B, \ldots, C_{n-1,n}^B.$$

This is the sequences of all the A components followed by all the B components but with the twisted $\overline{C_{i,j}^A}$ component. The components are connected by merging the z vertex of one component and the w vertex of the next component in the sequence. This means that the graph $E_{i,j}^A$ has just one connected component. The gadget $E_{i,j}^B$ is defined in the same way, having all the A components followed by the B components but including the twisted component $\overline{C_{i,j}^B}$ in the sequence (and having $C_{i,j}^A$ straight).

Consider now two gadgets $E_{i,j}^A$ and $E_{k,l}^B$ and let us observe that they are isomorphic. An isomorphism between both graphs must map each component in the E^A graph to the same component in the E^B graph. All components are identical except for $C_{i,j}^A$, twisted in the E^A graph and straight in the E^B graph, and $C_{k,l}^B$, straight in the E^A graph and twisted in the E^B graph. We have mentioned that every component is isomorphic to its twisted version and therefore $E_{i,j}^A$ and $E_{k,l}^B$ are always isomorphic. But the type of isomorphism can tell us whether $G_{i,j}^A \cong H_{i,j}^A$ and whether $G_{k,l}^B \cong H_{k,l}^B$. In case $G_{i,j}^A \cong H_{i,j}^A$ the vertex u^0 in $\overline{C_{i,j}^A}$ is mapped to u^0 in $C_{i,j}^A$ and otherwise this vertex is mapped to u^1. Analogously, if $G_{k,l}^B \cong H_{k,l}^B$ then vertex u^0 in $\overline{C_{k,l}^B}$ is mapped to u^0 in $C_{k,l}^B$ and otherwise this vertex is mapped to u^1. Let s be the number of u_0 vertices in $E_{i,j}^A$ being mapped to u_1 vertices in $E_{k,l}^B$. s is either

$$s = \begin{cases} 0 & \text{if } G_{i,j}^A \cong H_{i,j}^A \text{and } G_{k,l}^B \cong H_{k,l}^B \\ 1 & \text{if } G_{i,j}^A \cong H_{i,j}^A \oplus G_{k,l}^B \cong H_{k,l}^B \\ 2 & \text{if } G_{i,j}^A \ncong H_{i,j}^A \text{ and } G_{k,l}^B \ncong H_{k,l}^B \end{cases}$$

This means that the number is even if and only if the edges (i, j) in A and (k, l) in B both exist or both do not exist. Since this is the condition we need in order to allow an isomorphism between $E_{i,j}^A$ and $E_{k,l}^B$ we complete the gadgets connecting all the u^0 and u^1 vertices in the $E_{i,j}^A$ subgraphs with a parity check construction as done in Lemma 1 and doing the same thing with the u^0 and u^1 vertices in all the $E_{k,l}^B$ subgraphs. This implies that an isomorphism between gadgets $E_{i,j}^A$ and $E_{k,l}^B$ exists if an only if s is even.

Graph A' results from considering the n-clique K_n and substituting every edge (i, j) by $E_{i,j}^A$. Graph B' is obtained in the same way but substituting edge (i, j) by $E_{i,j}^B$. If every graph in the input tuples $(G_{i,j}, H_{i,j}), (I_{i,j}, J_{i,j})$ has at most m vertices, each gadget $E_{i,j}$ has $O(mn^2)$ vertices and therefore the size of A' and

B' is bounded by $O(mn^4)$ which is polynomial in the input size. Moreover the construction of A' and B' is completely local and can be performed by an AC^0 circuit.   ∎

This result can be used to move part of the complexity of a reduction to GI to the isomorphism problem itself.

Lemma 3. *Let L be a set many-one reducible to GI via a function $f : \{0,1\}^* \to \{0,1\}^*$ such that the set*

$$Bit_f = \{\langle x, i, b\rangle \mid x \in \{0,1\}^*, b \in \{0,1\} \text{ and the } i\text{-th bit of } f(x) \text{ is } b\}$$

is strongly many-one AC^0 reducible to PGI. Then L is many-one AC^0 reducible to GI.

Proof. If L is many-one reducible to GI then we can consider that for every x $f(x) \in \{0,1\}^*$ is a string representing the adjacency matrices of two graphs A and B, that are isomorphic if and only if $x \in L$. Each bit of $f(x)$ corresponds to one position in one of the adjacency matrices and it is 1 or 0 depending on whether the corresponding edge exists or not. Since the set Bit_f is strongly many-one AC^0 reducible to PGI, there is an AC^0 circuit that produces for each bit of the adjacency matrices two pairs of PGI graphs $(G, H), (I, J)$ with $G \cong H$ if the bit is 1 and $I \cong J$ if it is 0. This is exactly a PGI representation of A and B and by Lemma 2 there is an AC^0 circuit that on input this representation produces an adjacency matrix representation of two new graphs A', B' with $A \cong B$ iff $A' \cong B'$. Putting together the strong many-one reduction from Bit_f to PGI and the circuit constructing A' and B' from the PGI representation of A and B, we have an AC^0 circuit many-one reducing L to GI.   ∎

This result has several consequences.

Theorem 1. *For any set A, if A is many-one logarithmic space reducible to GI then A is many-one AC^0 reducible to GI.*

Proof. If A is many-one logarithmic space reducible to GI via a function f, then the set Bit_f belongs to L. The result follows from Lemma 3 since it is known that every set in L is strongly many-one AC^0 reducible to PGI [6,11].   ∎

Wider gaps in the complexity of the reductions to GI are possible since PGI is known to be hard for classes above L [11]. Although we do not know whether GI is hard for P, the following result relates this question to the equivalence of the closure of GI under many-one reducibilities of different strengths.

Theorem 2. *The following statements are equivalent*

  i) GI is hard for P under logspace many-one reductions.
  ii) the many-one AC^0 and polynomial time closures of GI coincide.

Proof. We show that the first statement implies the second. Let L be a set many-one reducible to GI via a polynomial time computable function f. The sets

$$\text{Bit}_f^0 = \{\langle x, i \rangle \mid x \in \{0,1\}^*, \text{and the } i\text{-th bit of } f(x) \text{ is } 0\}$$

and Bit_f^1 defined in a similar way are both in P. PGI is strongly many-one AC^0 hard for logarithmic space [11] and therefore, if GI is hard for P under logspace many-one reductions, using Corollary 1, GI would be also hard for P under AC^0 reductions. Because of this, both sets Bit_f^0 and Bit_f^1 are many-one AC^0 reducible to GI. Let h_0 and h_1 be the functions performing these reductions. Then, for every $x \in \{0,1\}^*$, $i \in \{1, \ldots, |x|\}$ and $b \in \{0,1\}$, $(h_b(\langle x, i \rangle), h_{\overline{b}}(\langle x, i \rangle))$ are two pairs of PGI graphs and define a strong many-one AC^0 reduction from the set Bit_f to PGI. Now using Lemma 3 we conclude that L is in fact many-one AC^0 reducible to GI.

For the other direction, let L be a set in P. L is trivially many-one polynomial time reducible to GI. Since we we are supposing that the many-one polynomial time and AC^0 closures of GI coincide, L is many-one AC^0 reducible to GI and therefore also reducible in logarithmic space to GI.   ∎

Observe that logarithmic space reducibility in the first statement is not really important for the proof of the result. The result would hold also for any reducibility computed by a class of functions with bit sets Bit_f strong many-one AC^0 reducible to PGI.

4   Turing Reducibility

Álvarez, Balcázar and Jenner [2] using a functional non-adaptive reduction as an intermediate step, prove the following result:

Theorem 3. *[2] For every set A and every $k \geq 0$, $\text{AC}^k(\text{FL}(A)) = \text{NC}^{k+1}(\text{FL}(A))$.*

They prove this result for the oracle function class FL but it can be observed that it relativizes to $\text{FL}(A)$ for any set A queried by the function in FL. In order to apply this result directly to GI (without the FL level) we need the following theorem:

Theorem 4. $\text{FL}(\text{GI}) = \text{AC}^0(\text{GI})$.

Proof. Let f be a function in $\text{FL}(\text{GI})$ and M be a logarithmic space bounded Turing machine computing f. A configuration of M contains a state, a position in the input tape and the contents of the work tape. Some of the configurations are query configurations. These contain states of a special kind. If M reaches a query configuration then the machine writes in the following steps a query to GI in the oracle tape and when M enters a special query state the oracle tape is deleted, one bit with the answer to the query appears in it and the computation continues. Observe that the length of the query is not affected by the logarithmic space bound of the work tape. However, the query configuration (of logarithmic size) generating the query, defines the query completely. With this configuration the query can be computed in logarithmic space. Both the number of possible query configurations and the length of $f(x)$ are polynomially bounded in the length of the input x. Consider the set

$$A = \{\langle x, K \rangle \mid K \text{ is a possible query configuration on input } x \text{ and}$$
$$\text{the query produced by this configuration belongs to GI}\}.$$

A is many-one logarithmic space reducible to GI and as a consequence of Theorem 1 also many-one AC^0 reducible to GI. Consider new machine M' that on input a string x and a set of possible query configurations and answer bits $\langle x, K_1, a_1, K_2, a_2, \ldots, K_m, a_m \rangle$ simulates M on input x and each time M enters a query configuration K, M' looks whether K is part of its input. If this is not the case then it produces some special output sequence and halts. Otherwise M' just continues its computation taking the bit next to K in its input as the answer to the corresponding query. Clearly M' is logarithmic space bounded and computes some function $g \in \mathsf{FL}$. If the set of queries is complete and the set of answers is correct then M' computes f. The set Bit_g is then in L and therefore many-one AC^0 reducible to GI [6]. We want to show that f can be computed in $\mathsf{AC}^0(\mathrm{GI})$. In order to do so we just have to put together the AC^0 circuits we already have. On input x the circuit first produces all polynomially many possible query configurations of $M(x)$. Then using the reduction from A to GI, for every such configuration the circuit produces a pair of graphs G, H and queries to the oracle set GI whether they are isomorphic. With the answers the circuit constructs a list of queries and correct answers $x, K_1, a_1, K_2, a_2, \ldots, K_m, a_m$. Finally using the AC^0 circuit reducing Bit_g to GI, for each bit of $f(x)$ a pair of graphs is constructed. A second round of queries to GI gives the value of $f(x)$ in the form of a sequence of bits as output of the circuit. The constructed circuit has constant depth, polynomial size and has two levels of queries to GI.   ∎

We can now prove the main result of this section:

Theorem 5. *For any $k \geq 0$, $\mathsf{AC}^k(\mathrm{GI}) = \mathsf{NC}^{k+1}(\mathrm{GI})$.*

Proof. The inclusion $\mathsf{AC}^k(\mathrm{GI}) \subseteq \mathsf{NC}^{k+1}(\mathrm{GI})$ is straightforward. For the other inclusion we just have to put together the previous two results. We have $\mathsf{NC}^{k+1}(\mathrm{GI}) \subseteq \mathsf{NC}^{k+1}(\mathsf{FL}(\mathrm{GI}))$ and by Theorem 3 this is equal to $\mathsf{AC}^k(\mathsf{FL}(\mathrm{GI}))$. Using Theorem 4 this class is equal to $\mathsf{AC}^k(\mathsf{AC}^0(\mathrm{GI}))$. Since every query to $\mathsf{AC}^0(\mathrm{GI})$ can be simulated by the AC^k circuit making the queries directly to GI, just by adding a constant number of levels to the circuit, we have $\mathsf{AC}^k(\mathsf{AC}^0(\mathrm{GI})) = \mathsf{AC}^k(\mathrm{GI})$.   ∎

We observe that the proofs of Theorems 4 and 5 can be extended to any complexity class in the oracle that is many one AC^0 hard for L, and for which the many-one AC^0 and logarithmic space closures coincide.

5 Conclusions and Open Problems

We have proven that several kinds of many-one and Turing reducibilities to GI coincide thus showing that the isomorphism problem is very robust and behaves in some sense as a machine based complexity class. There are several problems related to the complexity of reductions that are worth considering:

We know that GI is not hard for NP unless the polynomial time hierarchy collapses. Can one show some relation between the difficulty of showing hardness of GI for a class like P and the hardness for NP? (Something like if GI is P-hard then GI would be NP-hard.)

In this paper we have not talked about randomized reductions to GI. It has been observed in [11] that the Matching problem is randomly reducible to GI. Can also this reduction be simplified making it a deterministic reduction to GI?

We have mentioned that Lemma 2 can be considered as a version of the result $NP(NP \cap coNP) = NP$ scaled down to GI. If the input of the problem given in the lemma instead of being encoded as PGI graphs were just normal graph pairs, isomorphic when encoding a 1 and non-isomorphic when encoding a 0, we would have something like a GI version of the second level of the polynomial time hierarchy. Can one prove a collapse of this hierarchy?

Acknowledgment. The author would like to thank the anonymous referees for many helpful comments.

References

1. Agrawal, M., Allender, E., Rudich, S.: Reductions in Circuit Complexity: An Isomorphism Theorem and a Gap Theorem. JCSS 57, 17–143 (1998)
2. Álvarez, C., Balcázar, J.L., Jenner, B.: Adaptive Logspace Reducibilities and Parallel Time. Math. Systems Theory 28, 117–140 (1995)
3. Barrington, D.A.M., Immerman, N., Straubing, H.: On uniformity within NC^1. Journal of Computer and System Sciences 41, 274–306 (1990)
4. Cook, S.A.: A taxonomy of problems with fast parallel algorithms. Information and Control 64(1), 2–22 (1985)
5. Hoffmann, C.M. (ed.): Group-Theoretic Algorithms and Graph Isomorphism. LNCS, vol. 136. Springer, Heidelberg (1982)
6. Jenner, B., Köbler, J., McKenzie, P., Torán, J.: Completeness results for graph isomorphism. Journal of Computer and System Sciences 66, 549–566 (2003)
7. Köbler, J., Schöning, U., Torán, J.: Graph Isomorphism: its Structural Complexity, Birkhäuser, Boston (1992)
8. Ogihara, M.: Equivalence of NC^k and AC^{k-1} closures of NP and other classes. Information and Computation 120(1), 55–58 (1995)
9. Ruzzo, W.: On uniform circuit complexity. Journal of Computer and System Sciences 22, 365–383 (1981)
10. Selman, A.: Promise problems complete for complexity classes. Information and Computation 78, 87–98 (1988)
11. Torán, J.: On the hardness of Graph Isomorphism. SIAM Journal on Computing 33(5), 1093–1108 (2004)
12. Wilson, C.B.: Decomposing NC and AC. SIAM Journal on Computing 19(2), 384–396 (1990)

Strong Reductions and Isomorphism of Complete Sets

Ryan C. Harkins[1,*], John M. Hitchcock[1,**], and A. Pavan[2,***]

[1] Department of Computer Science, University of Wyoming
[2] Department of Computer Science, Iowa State University

Abstract. We study the structure of the polynomial-time complete sets for NP and PSPACE under strong nondeterministic polynomial-time reductions (SNP-reductions). We show the following results.

- If NP contains a p-random language, then all polynomial-time complete sets for PSPACE are SNP-isomorphic.
- If NP ∩ co-NP contains a p-random language, then all polynomial-time complete sets for NP are SNP-isomorphic.

1 Introduction

The celebrated isomorphism conjecture [13] states that all polynomial-time NP-complete sets are polynomial-time isomorphic. This conjecture can be naturally extended to other complexity classes. The isomorphism conjecture for a class $\mathcal{C}$ states that all polynomial-time complete sets for $\mathcal{C}$ are p-isomorphic. The evidence in support of this conjecture comes from the observation that for every natural complexity class, all known complete sets are polynomial-time isomorphic. The evidence to the contrary comes from the one-way functions. It has been hypothesized that if one-way functions exist, then the isomorphism conjecture is false [17].

In spite of many years of research, we do not know of a single complexity class for which the isomorphism conjecture is resolved. This naturally led to the study of several variants of the conjecture that can be obtained by varying the resource bounds of the reductions and isomorphisms. In most general terms, the conjecture for a class $\mathcal{C}$ and resource bounds r and s can be phrased as follows: "All r-complete sets for $\mathcal{C}$ are s-isomorphic."

This question has been studied extensively for resource bounds that are much smaller than polynomial-time that led to several exciting results. For example, we now know that all 1-L-complete sets for NP and PSPACE are p-isomorphic [8,7]. Allender, Balcazar, and Immerman showed that all sets that are complete under first-order projections are DLOG-uniform AC^0-isomorphic [10]. This result set the stage to investigate the structure of sets complete under AC^0-reductions. Successive papers [6,2,4] improved this result, and this line of research culminated

---

* Research supported in part by NSF grant CCF-0515313.
** Research supported in part by NSF grant CCF-0515313.
*** This research was supported in part by NSF grant 0430807.

V. Arvind and S. Prasad (Eds.): FSTTCS 2007, LNCS 4855, pp. 168–178, 2007.

with the result of Agrawal [3]. This result states that all DLOG-uniform AC^0-complete sets for many natural classes are DLOG-uniform AC^0-isomorphic. Some of these results are surveyed in [19,14,9].

As mentioned earlier, these results concern sets that are complete under weaker reductions (i.e., where r has less resources than polynomial-time computation). In this paper, we study the isomorphism conjecture for polynomial-time complete sets. In particular we consider the following question: "Are the polynomial-time complete sets for a class s-isomorphic?"

As a candidate for s, we consider strong nondeterministic polynomial-time reductions (SNP-reductions for short). These reductions were introduced by Adleman and Manders [1]. They showed that certain number-theoretic problems, which are not known to be polynomial-time NP-complete, are complete under SNP-reductions. Informally, these reductions can be thought as NP ∩ co-NP-reductions.

We show that if NP contains a p-random sequence, then all polynomial-time PSPACE-complete sets are SNP-isomorphic. This result also holds for any class that is closed under complement and union, in particular for all Δ-levels of the polynomial-time hierarchy. This hypothesis, which is equivalent to "NP does not have p-measure 0," is one of the most widely studied hypotheses in computational complexity and many plausible consequences are known to follow from it [21,22]. With a stronger hypothesis we obtain a similar consequence for the NP-complete sets. We show that if NP ∩ co-NP contains a p-random sequence, then all polynomial-time NP-complete sets are SNP-isomorphic.

We first show that if NP does not have p-measure zero, then all polynomial-time complete sets for PSPACE are also complete via one-one, length-increasing SNP-reductions. We then use the resource-bounded analogue of the Cantor-Bernstein theorem to exhibit the isomorphism [13].

Our proofs use a bound on the longest consecutive run of 0's or 1's in a p-random sequence. In classical probability theory this result is proved using the Borel-Cantelli lemma [15], but the proof does not carry over to polynomial-time randomness. Wang [24] overcame this same problem for the law of the iterated logarithm. We use his technique to prove the bound on longest runs in the polynomial-time setting.

This paper is organized as follows. Section 2 contains preliminaries on SNP-reductions and polynomial-time measure and randomness. In section 3 we present our main results. Section 4 concludes with a discussion.

2   Preliminaries

In this paper we consider both single-valued and multi-valued functions. When f is a multi-valued function, $f(x)$ is a set. Recall that if f is a total, multi-valued function, then $f(x)$ is a *nonempty* set. Unless otherwise mentioned all functions in this paper are total.

Definition 2.1. *Let f be a multi-valued function. A function g is a* single-valued refinement *of f if g is single-valued function, and for every x, $g(x) \in f(x)$.*

Definition 2.2. *Let f be a multi-valued function. We say that f is* strong non-deterministic polynomial-time computable, SNP-*computable for short, if there is a nondeterministic polynomial-time machine M such that for every x, every path of M on x outputs a member of f(x) or outputs a special symbol ⊥. At least one path of M(x) outputs a member of f(x).*

Definition 2.3. *Let f be a total, multi-valued function and A and B be two languages. We say A is* reducible to B via f *if for every x the following conditions hold:*

$$x \in A \Rightarrow f(x) \subseteq B,$$

$$x \notin A \Rightarrow f(x) \cap B = \emptyset.$$

Remark. Since we require the function f to be *total*, $f(x)$ can not be $\emptyset$ even when $x \notin A$.

Definition 2.4. *A language A is* SNP-reducible *to a language B, if there is a (possibly multi-valued) function f that reduces A to B and f is* SNP*-computable.*

Definition 2.5. *A* single-valued function f is an isomorphism *from A to B, if f is a reduction from A to B and f is a bijection.*

Recall that two languages A and B are *polynomial-time isomorphic* if there is a function f such that f reduces A to B, f^{-1} reduces B to A, both f and f^{-1} are polynomial-time computable, and f is a bijection. We can extend this definition to strong nondeterministic isomorphisms. When f is a multi-valued function $f^{-1}(y)$ is the set of all x for which $y \in f(x)$.

Definition 2.6. *Let A be B be two languages. We say that A is* strong non-deterministic isomorphic *to B,* SNP-*isomorphic for short, if there is a (possibly multi-valued) function f such that following conditions hold:*

- *A reduces to B via f.*
- *B reduces to A via f^{-1}.*
- *Both f and f^{-1} are* SNP*-computable.*
- *There is a single-valued refinement g of f that is an isomorphism from A to B.*

Observe that the definition implicitly requires f^{-1} to be a total function. We remark that there are several alternate ways to define the notion of SNP-isomorphism. We discuss these in Section 4.

2.1   Polynomial-Time Measure and Randomness

We now review the definition of polynomial-time measure [20]. The *Cantor space* **C** is the set of all infinite binary sequences. Each *language* (a subset of $\{0,1\}^*$) is identified with the element of Cantor space that is its characteristic sequence according to the standard enumeration of $\{0,1\}^*$. In this way, each complexity class (a set of languages) is viewed as a subset of Cantor space. A *martingale* is a function $d : \{0,1\}^* \to [0, \infty)$ satisfying the averaging condition

$$d(w) = \frac{d(w0) + d(w1)}{2}$$

for all $w \in \{0,1\}^*$. We say d *succeeds on* a sequence $S \in \mathbf{C}$ if

$$\limsup_{n \to \infty} d(S \restriction n) = \infty.$$

Here $S \restriction n$ is the length n prefix of S. The *success set* of d is

$$S^\infty[d] = \{ S \in \mathbf{C} \mid d \text{ succeeds on } S \}.$$

Ville [23] showed a class $X \subseteq \mathbf{C}$ has Lebesgue measure 0 if and only if there is a martingale d with $X \subseteq S^\infty[d]$. Polynomial-time measure [20] arises from putting resource bounds on the martingales. We say that $d : \{0,1\}^* \to [0, \infty)$ is *polynomial-time computable* if there is an approximation $\hat{d} : \mathbb{N} \times \{0,1\}^* \to \mathbb{Q}$ such that $|\hat{d}(r, w) - d(w)| \leq 2^{-r}$ for all $r \in \mathbb{N}, w \in \{0,1\}^*$ and $\hat{d} \in \Delta$ (with r encoded in unary and the outputs encoded in binary).

Definition 2.7. *Let $X \subseteq \mathbf{C}$.*

1. *X has p-measure 0, written $\mu_\mathrm{p}(X) = 0$, if there is a polynomial-time computable martingale d with $X \subseteq S^\infty[d]$.*
2. *X has p-measure 1, written $\mu_\mathrm{p}(X) = 1$, if $\mu_\mathrm{p}(X^c) = 0$.*

We also use the notion of resource-bounded randomness [11].

Definition 2.8. *Let L be a language.*

1. *Given a time bound $t(n)$, L is $t(n)$-random if no $O(t(n))$-time computable martingale succeeds on L.*
2. *L is p-random if for every polynomial $p(n)$, L is $p(n)$-random.*

The following result relates p-measure to p-randomness.

Lemma 2.9. *([11,18]) If C is a class that is closed under polynomial-time many-one reductions, then the following are equivalent.*

1. *C does not have p-measure 0.*
2. *C contains a p-random language.*

3   SNP Reductions and Isomorphisms

We prove our main theorem in this section. In our proof we use certain properties of p-random languages. Let R be a p-random language. Given a bit b and a finite string w, let $lr(b, w)$ denote the longest consecutive run of the bit b in w. Let $R \restriction n$ denote the first n bits of the characteristic sequence of R.

Theorem 3.1. *If R is a p-random language, then for each $b \in \{0, 1\}$,*

$$\lim_{n \to \infty} \frac{lr(b, R \upharpoonright n)}{\log n} = 1.$$

Proof of this theorem is omitted due to lack of space.

Given a string y let $r(y)$ be the rank (in lexicographic order) of y among strings of length $|y|$. Let s_r^n denote the string y such that $|y| = n$, and $r(y) = r$. Given a string y of length n let $b_y = s_{2r(y)n^2}^{n^2}$ and $e_y = s_{2(r(y)+1)n^2 - 1}^{n^2}$. The following observation follows from Lemma 2.9 and Theorem 3.1.

Observation 3.2. *Assume that* NP *does not have p-measure zero. Then there is a p-random language R in* NP *such that for every y, the interval $[b_y, e_y]$ has at least one string from R.*

We say that a multi-valued function f is length-increasing if the length of x is smaller than the length of every string from $f(x)$. We say that a multi-valued function f is one-one if for every x and y with $x \neq y$, $f(x) \cap f(y) = \emptyset$.

We first show that if NP does not have p-measure zero, PSPACE-complete sets are complete via one-one, length-increasing, SNP-reductions.

Lemma 3.3. *If* NP *does not have p-measure 0, then all* PSPACE-*complete sets are complete via one-one, length-increasing* SNP-*reductions.*

Proof. Let L be any PSPACE-complete language. Let K be the standard PSPACE-complete language that is complete via one-one, length increasing reductions. Observe that K can be decided in time 2^n. It suffices to show that K is reducible to L via a one-one, length-increasing SNP reduction. We first define an intermediate language A in PSPACE, and describe a one-one, length-increasing SNP reduction f from K to A. Then we describe a polynomial-time reduction from A to L that is one-one and length-increasing on $f(\Sigma^*)$. Combining these two reductions we obtain the desired reduction from K to L.

By our hypothesis, there is a n^4-random language R in NP.

$$A = \{\langle x, y \rangle \mid |x| = |y|^2, \text{ and } x \in R \oplus y \in K = 0\},$$

where $\oplus$ denotes the xor operation. Clearly, A is in PSPACE.

Claim. There is a one-one, length-increasing SNP reduction from K to A.

Proof. Since R is in NP, there is a polynomial-time computable function h and a polynomial $q(.)$ such that a string x is in R if and only if there is a witness w of length at most $q(|x|)$ for which $h(x, w) = 1$.

The following nondeterministic machine N is a reduction from K to A.

1. Input y, $|y| = n$.
2. Compute b_y and e_y.
3. Guess a string x_y between b_y and e_y and a possible witness w of length at most $q(n^2)$.
4. If $h(x_y, w) = 0$, then Output $\perp$ and this branch stops. If $h(x_y, w) = 1$, then Output $\langle x, y \rangle$ and stop.

Let f be the function computed by N. We first show that f is a valid reduction from K to A. Observe that N outputs a tuple $\langle x, y \rangle$ only if $x \in R$. If $x \in R$, then y belongs to K if and only if $x \in R \oplus y \in K = 0$. Thus $y \in K$ if and only if $\langle x, y \rangle \in A$. Next we claim that at least one path of N does not output $\perp$.

By Observation 3.2, at least one string from the interval $[b_y, e_y]$ belongs to R. So at least one path of N guesses such string and a valid witness of that string. The output along this path is not $\perp$.

Thus f is a total, multi-valued function that reduces K to A. For every y, every element of $f(y)$ is of the form $\langle x_y, y \rangle$, where x_y is a string of length n^2. Thus f is length-increasing. Let y and z two distinct strings. Every element of $f(y)$ is of the form $\langle ., y \rangle$ and every element of $f(z)$ is of the form $\langle ., z \rangle$. Thus $f(y) \cap f(z) = \emptyset$. Thus f is one-one.

This completes proof of Claim 3.

Since A is in PSPACE and L is PSPACE-complete, there is a polynomial-time many-one reduction g from A to L. We now show that g must be one-one and honest on $f(\Sigma^*)$. Observe that every string v in $f(\Sigma^*)$ is of the form $\langle x, y \rangle$, where $|x| = |y|^2$. We first observe that f satisfies the following stronger one-one property.

Observation 3.4. *Let* $y_1 < y_2$, $f(y_1) = \langle x_1, y_1 \rangle$, *and* $f(y_2) = \langle x_2, y_2 \rangle$. *Then* $x_1 < x_2$

Proof. Since $y_1 < y_2$, $e_{y_1} < b_{y_2}$. Thus the intervals $[b_{y_1}, e_{y_1}]$ and $[b_{y_2}, e_{y_2}]$ are disjoint. Observe that x_1 belongs to the interval $[b_{y_1}, e_{y_1}]$ and x_2 belongs to the interval $[b_{y_2}, e_{y_2}]$. Thus $x_1 < x_2$.

We first show that g must be one-one on $f(\Sigma^*)$.

Claim. For all but many strings u and v in $f(\Sigma^*)$, $g(u) \neq g(v)$.

Proof. We have to show that the following set is finite.

$$S = \{u \in f(\Sigma^*) \mid \exists v \in f(\Sigma^*), u \neq v, g(u) = g(v)\}.$$

Assume that S is infinite. Observe that a string u in $f(\Sigma^*)$ is a tuple of the form $\langle x, y \rangle$. Let $t_1(u)$ denote the first component of the tuple and $t_2(u)$ denote the second component of the tuple. Consider the following set.

$$T_1 = \{u \in f(\Sigma^*) \mid \exists v \in f(\Sigma^*), t_1(u) \neq t_1(v), t_2(u) \neq t_2(v), g(u) = g(v)\},$$

$$T_2 = S - T_1.$$

If S is infinite, then at least one of T_1 or T_2 must be infinite. We first consider the case T_1 is infinite. We will show that this contradicts the randomness of R.

Consider the following martingale d that bets on R as follows. Assume that d has capital $d(n-1)$ before it bets on any string of length n. Before betting on string of length n, d computes two tuples $\langle x_1, y_1 \rangle$, and $\langle x_2, y_2 \rangle$ such that the all of the following conditions hold.

- $|x_2| = n$, $|y_2| = \sqrt{n}$.
- $x_1 < x_2$, $|x_1| = |y_1|^2$.
- $g(\langle x_1, y_1 \rangle) = g(\langle x_2, y_2 \rangle)$.

If d can not find such tuples, then it does not bet on any string at length n. In this case $d(n) = d(n - 1)$. Suppose d finds such tuples. Since we assume that T_1 is infinite, d will find such tuples for infinitely many n. Now, d does not bet on any string up to x_2. Recall that when d is ready to bet on x_2, it has access to the partial characteristic sequence of R up to x_2. Thus d can easily determine the membership of x_1 in R. Now, d computes the membership of y_1 and y_2 in K. Since $g(\langle x_1, y_1 \rangle) = g(\langle x_2, y_2 \rangle)$,

$$(x_1 \in R \oplus y_1 \in K) = (x_2 \in R \oplus y_2 \in K)$$

Since d knows the values of $x_1 \in R$, $y_1 \in K$, and $y_2 \in K$, it can compute the value of $x_2 \in R$. Thus d bets on x_2 accordingly. This way d can double its capital. Thus we have $d(n) = 2d(n - 1)$.

Thus for every n either $d(n) = d(n-1)$ or $d(n) = 2d(n-1)$, and for infinitely many n, $d(n) = 2d(n-1)$. Thus $d(n)$ approaches infinity as n tends to ∞.

Observe that the time taken by d to search for the tuples with desired properties is bounded by 2^{4n}. In addition d needs at most $2^{\sqrt{n}}$ time to decide membership of y_1 and y_2 in K. This is because K is in DTIME(2^n) and length's of y_1 and y_2 are bounded by $\sqrt{n}$. Recall that running time of d is measured with respect to the length of the partial characteristic sequence, thus d runs in time $O(n^4)$. Thus if T_1 is infinite, then R is not n^4-random. The case where T_2 can be treated similarly.

Thus g is one-one on strings from $f(\Sigma^*)$. This completes the proof of Claim 3

Next we show that any reduction from A to L must be honest. Since the complete set L is in PSPACE, there is a constant k such that L can be decided in time 2^{n^k}.

Claim. Let g be a reduction from A to L. Let $T = \{\langle x, y \rangle \mid |x| = |y|^2\}$. For all but finitely many strings $w = \langle x, y \rangle$ from T $|g(w)| \geq |x|^{1/k}$.

Proof. Let U be the set of strings $w = \langle x, y \rangle$ from T for which $|g(w)| < |y|^{1/k}$. We show that if U is infinite, then R is not n^4-random.

Consider the following martingale d. Denote the capital that d has, before it starts to bet on strings of length n, with $d(n - 1)$. Before betting on strings of length n, the martingale cycles through all tuples $w = \langle x, y \rangle$, $n = |x| = |y|^2$, and finds a tuple w in U. If no such tuple exists, then d does not bet on any strings at length n. In this case, $d(n) = d(n - 1)$.

By our assumption, d finds such tuple at infinitely many lengths. If the martingale succeeds in finding a tuple in w, then it computes the membership of $w \in A$, by computing the membership of $g(w) \in L$. Thus d knows $x \in R \oplus y \in K$. Now, d decides the membership of y in K and finds the membership of x in R. Thus $d(n) = 2d(n - 1)$.

If U is infinite, then for infinitely many n $d(n) = 2d(n - 1)$. Thus d makes infinite amount of money on R. The time taken by d can be bounded as follows:

It takes $O(2^{2n})$ time to find a string in U. Once it finds such string, it decides the membership of w in A, by deciding the membership of $g(w)$ in L. Since $w \in U$, $|g(w)| < n^{1/k}$. Since L can be decided in 2^{n^k} time, this step takes $O(2^n)$ time. Since $|y| = \sqrt{n}$, and K is in DTIME(2^n), membership of $y \in K$ can be computed in $O(2^n)$ time. Thus the running time of the martingale, when measured with respect to the length of the characteristic sequence, is bounded by $O(n^2)$. Thus R is not n^4-random.

This completes the proof of Claim 3.

Now we will complete the proof of Lemma 3.3. By Claim 3, there is a one-one, length-increasing SNP-reduction f from K to A. By Claims 3 and 3, there is a polynomial-time reduction g from A to L that one-one is and honest on strings from $f(\Sigma^*)$. Combining the reduction f with g, we obtain a one-one, honest reduction from K to L. Since K is weakly paddable, we conclude that there is a one-one, length-increasing, SNP reduction from K to L.

Thus all PSPACE-complete sets are complete via one-one, length-increasing, SNP-reductions.

We are now ready to prove isomorphism theorem for PSPACE. We start with the following easy to prove observation.

Observation 3.5. *Let f be a length-increasing SNP-computable function. There is a nondeterministic polynomial-time machine M such that for every y that has an inverse, every path of $M(y)$ either outputs $\bot$ or outputs a member of $f^{-1}(y)$, and at least one path outputs a member of $f^{-1}(y)$. If $f^{-1}(y)$ does not exist, then every path of M outputs $\bot$.*

Theorem 3.6. *If NP does not have p-measure zero, then all polynomial-time many-one complete sets for PSPACE are SNP-isomorphic.*

Proof. Let A and B be any two PSPACE-complete sets. By Lemma 3.3, there is a one-one, length-increasing SNP-reduction f from A to B, and similarly there is a one-one, length-increasing SNP-reduction g from B to A.

Consider the following multi-valued function h: If if $g^{-1}(x)$ exists, $h(x) = f(x) \cup \{g^{-1}(x)\}$, else $h(x) = f(x)$. Observe that since g is a one-one function, $g^{-1}(x)$, if exists, is unique.

By Proposition 3.5, there is a nondeterministic machine N that computes g^{-1}. Consider the following non-deterministic machine. On input x, it guesses a bit $b \in \{0,1\}$. If $b = 0$, then it simulates the SNP-machine that computes f. If $b = 1$, the it simulates N. If $g^{-1}(x)$ exists, then the output set of this machine is exactly $f(x) \cup \{g^{-1}(x)\}$. If $g^{-1}(x)$ does not exist, then output set of this machine is $f(x)$. Thus h is SNP-computable. Observe that $h^{-1}(x) = g(x) \cup f^{-1}(x)$. Thus it follows that h^{-1} is also SNP-computable.

The value of $h(x)$ is either $f(x)$ or $f(x) \cup \{g^{-1}(x)\}$. Since f is a reduction from A to B and g is a reduction from B to A, it follows that h is a reduction from A to B, and h^{-1} is a reduction from B to A.

We now exhibit a single-valued refinement of h that is an isomorphism between A and B. Let $f_s(x)$ denote the smallest element of $f(x)$, and $g_s(x)$ denote the smallest element of $g(x)$. Observe the f_s and g_s are one-one, length increasing, single-valued functions.

Given a string x of length n, consider the following sequence.

$$S_x = g_s^{-1}(x), f_s^{-1}(g_s^{-1}(x)), g_s^{-1}(f_s^{-1}(g_s^{-1}(x))), \cdots$$

The sequence stops when either g_s^{-1} or f_s^{-1} does not exist. Since both f_s and g_s are length-increasing, f_s^{-1} and g_s^{-1} are length-decreasing. Thus the above sequence contains at most n strings.

Consider the following function e. If S_x has even number of elements then $e(x) = f_s(x)$, else $e(x) = g_s^{-1}(x)$. Clearly, e is single-valued. Consider the case S_x has odd number of elements. In this case $g^{-1}(x)$ must exist. Thus $h(x) = f(x) \cup \{g^{-1}(x)\}$. Hence, if S_x has odd number of elements, then $e(x) \in h(x)$. Observe that for every x, $f(x) \subseteq h(x)$. Thus if S_x has even number of elements, then $e(x) = f_s(x) \in h(x)$. Thus e is a single-valued refinement of h.

It remains to show that e is an isomorphism from A to B. The proof of this is exactly the same as the proof given by Berman and Hartmanis [13], so we omit the details here.

Thus A and B are SNP-isomorphic. This completes the proof of Theorem 3.6.

We observe that the isomorphism exhibited in the above proof can be computed in P^{NP}. This yields the following result.

Theorem 3.7. *If* NP *does not have p-measure zero, then all polynomial-time* PSPACE-*complete sets are* P^{NP}-*isomorphic.*

Observe that the above proof goes through for any class that is closed under $\oplus$ operation. In particular, it holds Δ_k^p levels of the polynomial-time hierarchy.

Theorem 3.8. *Assume that* NP *does not have p-measure zero. For every* $k \geq 1$, *all sets that are polynomial-time complete for* Δ_k^p *are* SNP-*isomorphic and* P^{NP}-*isomorphic.*

We next consider whether we can prove a similar result for NP-complete sets. We need a stronger hypothesis to do this.

Theorem 3.9. *If* NP$\cap$co-NP *does not have p-measure zero, then all polynomial-time complete sets for* NP *are* SNP-*isomorphic.*

For the most part, the the structure of the proof is similar to the proof of Theorem 3.6. We can first prove that all NP-complete sets are complete via one-one, length-increasing, SNP-reductions. For this we define an intermediate language A and argue that there is a one-one, length-increasing reduction from SAT to A and a one-one, length-increasing reduction from A to the desired NP-complete language. The main difference is in definition of the intermediate language A. Here we define the intermediate language A as

$$A = \{\langle x, y, z \rangle \mid |x| = |z| = |y|^2, Maj\{x \in R, y \in SAT, z \in R\} = 1\}.$$

This ensures that A is also in NP. The remainder of the proof uses similar ideas.

4 Discussion

This paper initiates the study of structure of polynomial-time complete sets under more powerful SNP reductions. The results in this paper raises several questions. We briefly discuss a few interesting questions.

As mentioned in preliminaries, there are several ways of defining the notion of SNP-isomorphism. Our current definition asks for a function h such that both h and h^{-1} are SNP-computable and some single valued-refinement of h is an isomorphism. Perhaps a more natural definition would the following: A set A is SNP-isomorphic to B if there is a (multi-valued) function h such that h reduces A to B, h^{-1} reduces B to A, both h and h^{-1} are SNP-computable, and h is bijection. A multi-valued function $h : \Sigma^* \to \Sigma^*$ is a bijection if every $y \in \Sigma^*$ has an inverse and $h(x) \cap h(y) = \emptyset$ for every x that is not equal to y. Another way of defining SNP-isomorphism is to require that h is a *single-valued* SNP-computable function.

Can we prove that PSPACE-complete sets or NP-complete sets are SNP-isomorphic using these definitions? One way to achieve this is to strengthen Lemma 3.3 to the following: If the p-measure of NP is not zero, then PSPACE-complete sets are complete via monotone, length-increasing, SNP reductions?

We note that we can obtain an affirmative answer to this question for EXP. It is known that polynomial-time EXP-complete sets are complete via one-one, length-increasing reductions [12]. A function f is monotone if $f(x) < f(y)$ whenever $x < y$. It is easy to modify Berman's proof to show that polynomial-time EXP-complete sets are complete via monotone, polynomial-time reductions. Thus we unconditionally obtain that all EXP-complete sets are single-valued SNP-isomorphic.

Ideally, we would like the resource bounds of isomorphisms and the reductions to be the same. Can we show that all SNP-complete sets for PSPACE are SNP-isomorphic? How about p-isomorphisms? Can we prove or disprove the isomorphism conjecture under the measure hypothesis?

Finally, can we show that NP-complete sets or PSPACE-complete sets are complete via one-one, length-increasing, polynomial-time computable reductions? Agrawal [5] and Hitchcock and Pavan [16] obtain some partial results.

References

1. Adleman, L., Manders, K.: Reducibility, randomness, and intractability. In: Proc. 9th ACM Symp. Theory of Computing, pp. 151–163. ACM Press, New York (1977)
2. Agrawal, A., Allender, E., Impagliazzo, R., Pitassi, T., Rudich, S.: Reducing the complexity of reductions. Computational Complexity 10, 117–138 (2001)
3. Agrawal, M.: The first-order isomorphism theorem. In: Foundations of Software Technology and Theoretical Computer Science, pp. 70–82 (2001)
4. Agrawal, M.: Towards uniform AC^0-isomorphisms. In: Proceedings of 16th IEEE Conference on Computational Complexity, pp. 13–20. IEEE Computer Society Press, Los Alamitos (2001)

5. Agrawal, M.: Pseudo-random generators and structure of complete degrees. In: 17th Annual IEEE Conference on Computational Complexity, pp. 139–145. IEEE Computer Society Press, Los Alamitos (2002)
6. Agrawal, M., Allender, E., Rudich, S.: Reductions in circuit complexity: An isomorphism theorem and a gap theorem. Journal of Computer and System Sciences 57(2), 127–143 (1998)
7. Agrawal, M., Biswas, S.: Polynomial-time isomorphism of 1-L complete sets. In: Proceedings of Structure in Complexity Theory, pp. 75–80 (1993)
8. Allender, E.: Isomorphisms and 1-L reductions. Journal of Computer and System Sciences 36, 336–350 (1988)
9. Allender, E.: Some pointed questions concerning asymptotic lower bounds, and new from the isomorphism front. In: Paun, G., Rozenberg, G., Salomaa, A. (eds.) Current Trends in Theoretical Computer Science: Entering the 21st Century, pp. 25–41. Scientific Press (2001)
10. Allender, E., Balcazar, J., Immerman, N.: A first-order isomorphism theorem. SIAM Journal on Computing 26, 557–567 (1997)
11. Ambos-Spies, K., Terwijn, S.A., Zheng, X.: Resource bounded randomness and weakly complete problems. Theoretical Computer Science 172(1–2), 195–207 (1997)
12. Berman, L.: Polynomial Reducibilities and Complete Sets. PhD thesis, Cornell University (1977)
13. Berman, L., Hartmanis, H.: On isomorphisms and density of NP and other complete sets. SIAM J. Comput. 6, 305–322 (1977)
14. Buhrman, H., Torenvliet, L.: On the structure of complete sets. In: 9th IEEE Annual Conference on Structure in Complexity Theory, pp. 118–133. IEEE Computer Society Press, Los Alamitos (1994)
15. Durrett, R.: Probability: Theory and Examples. Duxbury Press, third edition (2004)
16. Hitchcock, J., Pavan, A.: Comparing reductions to NP-complete sets. Information and Computation 205(5), 694–706 (2007)
17. Joseph, D., Young, P.: Some remarks on witness functions for nonpolynomial and noncomplete sets in NP. Theoretical Computer Science 39, 225–237 (1985)
18. Juedes, D.W., Lutz, J.H.: Weak completeness in E and E_2. Theoretical Computer Science 143(1), 149–158 (1995)
19. Kurtz, S., Mahaney, S., Royer, J.: The structure of complete degrees. In: Selman, A. (ed.) Complexity Theory Retrospective, pp. 108–146. Springer, Heidelberg (1990)
20. Lutz, J.H.: Almost everywhere high nonuniform complexity. Journal of Computer and System Sciences 44(2), 220–258 (1992)
21. Lutz, J.H.: The quantitative structure of exponential time. In: Hemaspaandra, L.A., Selman, A.L. (eds.) Complexity Theory Retrospective II, pp. 225–254. Springer, Heidelberg (1997)
22. Lutz, J.H., Mayordomo, E.: Twelve problems in resource-bounded measure. Bulletin of the European Association for Theoretical Computer Science, 68, 64–80, 1999. Also in Current Trends in Theoretical Computer Science: Entering the 21st Century, pp. 83–101, World Scientific Publishing (2001)
23. Ville, J.: Étude Critique de la Notion de Collectif. Gauthier–Villars, Paris (1939)
24. Wang, Y.: The law of the iterated logarithm for p-random sequences. In: Proceedings of the Eleventh Annual IEEE Conference on Computational Complexity, pp. 180–189. IEEE Computer Society Press, Los Alamitos (1996)

Probabilistic and Topological Semantics
for Timed Automata

Christel Baier[1], Nathalie Bertrand[1,*], Patricia Bouyer[2,3,**],
Thomas Brihaye[2], and Marcus Größer[1]

[1] Technische Universität Dresden, Germany
[2] LSV - CNRS & ENS Cachan, France
[3] Oxford University, England

Abstract. Like most models used in model-checking, timed automata
are an idealized mathematical model used for representing systems with
strong timing requirements. In such mathematical models, properties can
be violated, due to unlikely (sequences of) events. We propose two new
semantics for the satisfaction of LTL formulas, one based on probabilities, and the other one based on topology, to rule out these sequences.
We prove that the two semantics are equivalent and lead to a PSPACE-
Complete model-checking problem for LTL over finite executions.

1 Introduction

Timed automata, a model for verification. In the 90's, Alur and Dill proposed
timed automata [3] as a model for verification purposes, which takes into account real-time constraints. With this model, one can express constraints on
(possibly relative) dates of events. One of the fundamental properties of this
model is configurations in the system, many verification problems can be solved
(*e.g.* reachability and safety properties, branching-time timed temporal properties). Since then, this model has been intensively studied, and several verification
tools have been developed.

Idealization of mathematical models. Timed automata are an idealized mathematical model, in which several assumptions are implicitly made: it has infinite
precision, instantaneous events, *etc.* Several ideas have been explored to overcome the fact that these hypotheses are in practice unrealistic. The model of
implementable controllers has been proposed, where constraints and precision of
clocks are somewhat relaxed [8]. In this framework, if the model satisfies a safety
property, then, on a simple model of processor, its implementation will also satisfy this property. This implementation model has been considered in [15,7,4,6].
However, it induces a very strong notion of robustness, suitable for really critical
systems (like rockets or X-by-wire systems in cars), but maybe too strong for
less critical systems (like mobile phones or network applications).

---

* Partly supported by a Lavoisier fellowship.
** Partly supported by a Marie Curie fellowship.

V. Arvind and S. Prasad (Eds.): FSTTCS 2007, LNCS 4855, pp. 179–191, 2007.

Another robustness model has been proposed at the end of the 90's in [9] with the notion of tube acceptance: a metric is put on the set of traces of the timed automaton, and a trace is robustly accepted if and only if a tube around that trace is classically accepted. This acceptance has been further studied for language-based properties, for instance the universality problem [11]. However, this language-focused notion of acceptance is not completely satisfactory for implementability issues, because it does not take into account the structure of the automaton, and hence is not related to the most-likely behaviours of the automaton.

Using probabilities to alleviate the disadvantages of mathematical models. In their recent paper [17], Varacca and Völzer propose a probabilistic framework for finite-state systems to overcome side-effects of modelling. They use probabilities to define the notion of being fairly correct as having probability zero to fail, when every non-deterministic choice has been transformed into a 'reasonable' probabilistic choice. Moreover, in their framework, a system is fairly correct with respect to some property if and only if the set of traces satisfying that property in the system is topologically large, which somehow attests the relevance of this notion of fair correctness.

Contribution. We address both motivations, ruling out unlikely sequences of transitions (as in the approach of [17]) and ruling out unlikely events (from a time point of view, as in the implementability paradigm discussed above). In order to do so, we propose two alternative semantics for timed automata: (*i*) a *probabilistic semantics* which assigns probabilities both on delays and on discrete choices, and (*ii*) a *topological semantics*, following ideas of [9,11] but rather based on the structure of the automaton than on its accepted language. For both semantics, we can naturally address a model-checking problem for LTL: almost-sure model-checking for the probabilistic case and large model-checking for the topological case. Our results in these new frameworks are twofold. First we prove, by means of Banach-Mazur games, that the two semantics coincide: an LTL formula is almost-surely satisfied if and only if it is largely satisfied. Second we show that the almost-sure model-checking problem (and hence the large model-checking problem) for LTL specifications is PSPACE-Complete, *i.e.*, no more expensive than the classical LTL model-checking problem.

About probabilistic timed systems. Probabilities are not new in the model-checking community, and neither are timed systems. Several pieces of work even combine both. We refer to [16] for a survey on probabilistic timed systems. However, all of them were designed for modelling and analysing stochastic hybrid systems under quantitative aspects, whereas we aim at a probabilistic interpretation of non-probabilistic systems, which rule out unlikely events and yield a non-standard but still purely qualitative satisfaction relation for linear-time properties. To the best of our knowledge, we present here the first attempt to provide a probabilistic interpretation for non probabilistic timed systems in order to establish linear-time properties assuming 'fairness' on actions and delays.

Detailed proofs and complements can be found in the research report [5].

2   Timed Automata and Region Automata

In this section, we recall the classical notions of *timed automaton* and its well-known abstraction, the *region automaton* [3].

Timed Automata. Let X be a finite set of *clocks*. A *clock valuation* over X is a mapping $\nu : X \to \mathbb{R}_+$, where $\mathbb{R}_+$ is the set of nonnegative reals. We write $\mathbb{R}_+^X$ for the set of clock valuations over X. If $\nu \in \mathbb{R}_+^X$ and $\tau \in \mathbb{R}_+$, $\nu + \tau$ is the clock valuation defined by $(\nu + \tau)(x) = \nu(x) + \tau$ if $x \in X$. If $Y \subseteq X$, the valuation $[Y \leftarrow 0]\nu$ is the valuation assigning 0 to $x \in Y$ and $\nu(x)$ to $x \notin Y$. A *guard* over X is a finite conjunction of expressions of the form $x \sim c$ where $x \in X$, $c \in \mathbb{N}$, and $\sim \in \{<, \leq, =, \geq, >\}$. We denote by $\mathcal{G}(X)$ the set of guards over X. The satisfaction relation for guards over clock valuations is defined in a natural way, and we write $\nu \models g$, if ν satisfies g. We denote AP a finite set of atomic propositions.

Definition 1. *A* timed automaton *is a tuple* $\mathcal{A} = (L, X, E, \mathcal{I}, \mathcal{L})$ *such that: (i)* L *is a finite set of locations, (ii)* X *is a finite set of clocks, (iii)* $E \subseteq L \times \mathcal{G}(X) \times 2^X \times L$ *is a finite set of edges, (iv)* $\mathcal{I} : L \to \mathcal{G}(X)$ *assigns an invariant to each location, and (v)* $\mathcal{L} : L \to 2^{\mathsf{AP}}$ *is the labelling function.*

The semantics of a timed automaton $\mathcal{A}$ is given by a labelled transition system $T_{\mathcal{A}} = (S, E \cup \mathbb{R}_+, \to)$ where the set S of states is $\{s = (\ell, \nu) \in L \times \mathbb{R}_+^X \mid \nu \models \mathcal{I}(\ell)\}$, and the transition relation $\to (\subseteq S \times (E \cup \mathbb{R}_+) \times S)$ is composed of:

- *(delay transition)* $(\ell, \nu) \xrightarrow{\tau} (\ell, \nu + \tau)$ if $\tau \in \mathbb{R}_+$ and for all $0 \leq \tau' \leq \tau$, $\nu + \tau' \models \mathcal{I}(\ell)$,
- *(discrete transition)* $(\ell, \nu) \xrightarrow{e} (\ell', \nu')$ if $e = (\ell, g, Y, \ell') \in E$ is such that $\nu \models \mathcal{I}(\ell) \wedge g$, $\nu' = [Y \leftarrow 0]\nu$, and $\nu' \models \mathcal{I}(\ell')$.

A *finite run* ϱ of $\mathcal{A}$ is a finite sequence of states obtained by alternating delay and discrete transitions, *i.e.*, $\varrho = s_0 \xrightarrow{\tau_1} s_1' \xrightarrow{e_1} s_1 \xrightarrow{\tau_2} s_2' \xrightarrow{e_2} s_2 \cdots s_{n-1} \xrightarrow{\tau_n} s_n' \xrightarrow{e_n} s_n$ or more compactly $s_0 \xrightarrow{\tau_1, e_1} s_1 \xrightarrow{\tau_2, e_2} s_2 \cdots s_{n-1} \xrightarrow{\tau_n, e_n} s_n$. We write $\mathsf{Runs}(\mathcal{A}, s_0)$ for the set of finite runs of $\mathcal{A}$ from state s_0.

Given $s \in S$ and e an edge, we denote by $I(s, e) = \{\tau \in \mathbb{R}_+ \mid s \xrightarrow{\tau, e} s'\}$ and $I(s) = \bigcup_e I(s, e)$. The timed automaton $\mathcal{A}$ is said *non-blocking* whenever for every state $s \in S$, $I(s) \neq \emptyset$.

If s is a state of $\mathcal{A}$ and $(e_i)_{1 \leq i \leq n}$ is a finite sequence of edges of $\mathcal{A}$, if $\mathcal{C}$ is a convex constraint over n real-valued variables $(t_i)_{1 \leq i \leq n}$, the *(symbolic) path* starting from s, determined by $(e_i)_{1 \leq i \leq n}$, and constrained by $\mathcal{C}$, is the following set of runs:

$$\pi_{\mathcal{C}}(s, e_1 \ldots e_n) = \{\varrho = s \xrightarrow{\tau_1, e_1} s_1 \xrightarrow{\tau_2, e_2} s_2 \cdots \mid \varrho \in \mathsf{Runs}(\mathcal{A}, s) \text{ and } (\tau_i)_{1 \leq i \leq n} \models \mathcal{C} \text{ }^1\}.$$

If $\mathcal{C}$ is equivalent to 'true', we write $\pi(s, e_1 \ldots e_n)$, and say it is *unconstrained*. Occasionally, we refer to symbolic path for unconstrained symbolic path.

---

[1] We write $(\tau_i)_{1 \leq i \leq n} \models \mathcal{C}$ whenever the system $\mathcal{C}[t_i / \tau_i]$, obtained by replacing each variable t_i in $\mathcal{C}$ by the value τ_i, is true.

The Region Automaton Abstraction. The well-known region automaton construction is a finite abstraction of timed automata which can be used for verifying many properties, for instance regular untimed properties [3]. Roughly, the region automaton of $\mathcal{A}$ is the quotient of $T_{\mathcal{A}}$ by an equivalence relation over clock valuations. For lack of space, we do not redefine the region equivalence relation, and we write $R_{\mathcal{A}}$ for the set of regions of automaton $\mathcal{A}$. In this paper, we will use a slight modification of the original construction, which is still a timed automaton, but which satisfies very strong properties.

Definition 2. *Let* $\mathcal{A} = (L, X, E, \mathcal{I}, \mathcal{L})$ *be a timed automaton. The* region automaton *of* $\mathcal{A}$ *is the timed automaton* $\mathsf{R}(\mathcal{A}) = (Q, X, T, \kappa, \lambda)$ *such that:*

- $Q = L \times R_{\mathcal{A}};$ - $\kappa((\ell, r)) = \mathcal{I}(\ell)$, *and* $\lambda((\ell, r)) = \mathcal{L}(\ell)$ *for all* $(\ell, r) \in L \times R_{\mathcal{A}};$
- $T \subseteq (Q \times \mathsf{cell}(R_{\mathcal{A}}) \times E \times 2^X \times Q)$, *and* $(\ell, r) \xrightarrow{\mathsf{cell}(r''), e, Y} (\ell', r')$ *is in* T *iff there exists* $e = \ell \xrightarrow{g, Y} \ell'$ *in* E *s.t. there exist* $\nu \in r, \tau \in \mathbb{R}_+$ *with* $(\ell, \nu) \xrightarrow{\tau, e} (\ell', \nu')$, $\nu + \tau \in r''$ *and* $\nu' \in r'$ (cell(r'') *is the smallest guard containing* r'').

We recover the usual region automaton of [3] by labelling the transitions 'e' instead of '$\mathsf{cell}(r''), e, Y$', and by interpreting $\mathsf{R}(\mathcal{A})$ as a finite automaton. However, the above timed interpretation satisfies strong timed bisimulation properties that we do not detail here. To every finite path $\pi((\ell, \nu), e_1 \ldots e_n)$ in $\mathcal{A}$ corresponds a finite set of paths $\pi(((\ell, [\nu]), \nu), f_1 \ldots f_n)$ in $\mathsf{R}(\mathcal{A})$, each one corresponding to a choice in the regions that are crossed. If ϱ is a run in $\mathcal{A}$, we write $\iota(\varrho)$ for its (unique) image in $\mathsf{R}(\mathcal{A})$. Finally, note that if $\mathcal{A}$ is non-blocking, then so is $\mathsf{R}(\mathcal{A})$.

In the rest of the paper we assume timed automata are non-blocking, even though general timed automata could also be handled (but at a technical extra cost). In all examples, if a state has no outgoing transition, we implicitly add a self-loop on that state with no constraints, so that the automaton is non-blocking.

3   A Probabilistic Semantics for Timed Automata

In the literature, several models gather probabilities and timed constraints (see [16] for a survey). Here, we take the model of timed automata, and give a probabilistic interpretation to delays, so that unlikely events will happen with probability 0.

For the rest of this section, we fix a timed automaton $\mathcal{A} = (L, X, \Sigma, E, \mathcal{I}, \mathcal{L})$, which we assume is non-blocking. For every state s of $\mathcal{A}$, we assume a probability measure μ_s over $\mathbb{R}_+$ with the following requirements: (i) $\mu_s(I(s)) = \mu_s(\mathbb{R}_+) = 1;$[2] (ii) Writing λ for the Lebesgue measure, if $\lambda(I(s)) > 0$, μ_s is equivalent[3] to λ on $I(s)$; Otherwise, μ_s is equivalent on $I(s)$ to the uniform distribution over points of $I(s)$. For every state s of $\mathcal{A}$, we also assume a probability distribution p_s over edges, such that for every edge e, $p_s(e) > 0$ iff e enabled in s (*i.e.*, $s \xrightarrow{e} s'$ for some s').

---

[2] Note that this is possible, as we assume s is non-blocking, hence $I(s) \neq \emptyset$.
[3] Two measures ν and ν' are *equivalent* whenever for each measurable set A, $\nu(A) = 0 \Leftrightarrow \nu'(A) = 0$.

Remark 3. The above constraints on probability measures are rather loose and are for instance satisfied by: (i) the uniform discrete distribution over $I(s)$ if $I(s)$ is a finite set of points, (ii) the Lebesgue measure over $I(s)$, normalized to have a probability measure, if $I(s)$ is a finite set of bounded intervals, and (iii) an exponential distribution if $I(s)$ contains an unbounded interval.

3.1   Definition of a Probability Measure over Finite Paths

Definition 4. *Let $\mathcal{A}$ be a timed automaton. We define inductively the probability for an unconstrained symbolic path $\pi(s, e_1 \ldots e_n)$ to be fired (or equivalently for the sequence $e_1, \ldots, e_n$ of transitions in $\mathcal{A}$ to be fired from s) as follows:*

$$\mathbb{P}_{\mathcal{A}}(\pi(s, e_1 \ldots e_n)) = \frac{1}{2} \int_{t \in I(s, e_1)} p_{s+t}(e_1) \, \mathbb{P}_{\mathcal{A}}(\pi(s_t, e_2 \ldots e_n)) \, \mathrm{d}\mu_s(t)$$

where $s \xrightarrow{t} (s + t) \xrightarrow{e_1} s_t$. We initialize with $\mathbb{P}_{\mathcal{A}}(\pi(s)) = \frac{1}{2}$.

Using Fubini's theorem, by induction on the length of symbolic paths, we can prove that $\mathbb{P}_{\mathcal{A}}$ is well-defined. When clear from the context, we omit subscript $\mathcal{A}$.

The formula for $\mathbb{P}_{\mathcal{A}}$ can be read as follows: the probability of taking transition e_1 at time t coincides with the probability of waiting t time units and then choose e_1 among the enabled transitions, *i.e.*, $p_{s+t}(e_1)\mathrm{d}\mu_s(t)$. We need to sum up over all t's in $I(s, e_1)$ the probability of runs starting by such a move. Normalisation factor $\frac{1}{2}$ ensures that the probability of all finite runs be one.[4]

Let us illustrate the previous definition on an example.

Example 5. Consider the following timed automaton:

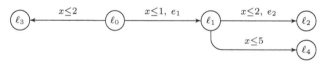

We assume a uniform distribution over delays and enabled edges in every state. Then we can compute that $\mathbb{P}(\pi((\ell_0, 0), e_1 e_2)) = \frac{1}{64}\left(1 - 3\log\left(\frac{5}{4}\right)\right)$ as $\mu_{(\ell_0, 0)} = \frac{\lambda}{2}$ (resp. $\mu_{(\ell_1, t)} = \frac{\lambda}{5-t}$) is the uniform distribution over $[0, 2]$ (resp. $[t, 5]$).

Lemma 6. *For every state s, $\mathbb{P}_{\mathcal{A}}$ is a probability measure over the set $Runs(\mathcal{A}, s)$.*

We establish that probabilities in $\mathcal{A}$ and in $\mathsf{R}(\mathcal{A})$ are closely related, provided the measures we initially assign to $\mathcal{A}$ and $\mathsf{R}(\mathcal{A})$ are similar. Hence, if $\mu^{\mathcal{A}}$ (resp. $\mu^{\mathsf{R}(\mathcal{A})}$) is the measure in $\mathcal{A}$ (resp. $\mathsf{R}(\mathcal{A})$), we assume that for every state s in $\mathcal{A}$, $\mu_s^{\mathcal{A}} = \mu_{\iota(s)}^{\mathsf{R}(\mathcal{A})}$.[5] This is possible as one can easily be convinced that $I(s) = I(\iota(s))$.

---

[4] Without this factor, for all n, the measure of runs of length n is one. This factor is not completely satisfactory as it has no 'physical' interpretation, but it is not a problem as we are only interested in qualitative properties.

[5] Note that we abuse notations and use $\iota(s)$ for $\iota(\pi(s))$.

Similarly, if $p^{\mathcal{A}}$ (resp. $p^{\mathsf{R}(\mathcal{A})}$) is the distribution over edges in $\mathcal{A}$ (resp. $\mathsf{R}(\mathcal{A})$), we assume that for every state s in $\mathcal{A}$, for every $t \in \mathbb{R}_+$ $p^{\mathcal{A}}_{s+t} = p^{\mathsf{R}(\mathcal{A})}_{\iota(s)+t}$. Under those assumptions, we have the following result.

Lemma 7. *Let $\mathcal{A}$ be a non-blocking timed automaton. Assume measures in $\mathcal{A}$ and in $\mathsf{R}(\mathcal{A})$ are related as described above. Let π be a symbolic path in $\mathcal{A}$. Then, $\iota(\pi)^6$ is a $\mathbb{P}_{\mathsf{R}(\mathcal{A})}$-measurable set of runs in $\mathsf{R}(\mathcal{A})$, and $\mathbb{P}_{\mathcal{A}}(\pi) = \mathbb{P}_{\mathsf{R}(\mathcal{A})}(\iota(\pi))$.*

3.2   Probabilistic Semantics

We consider the logic LTL [14], defined inductively as:

$$\mathsf{LTL} \ni \varphi ::= p \mid \varphi \vee \varphi \mid \varphi \wedge \varphi \mid \neg\varphi \mid \varphi \, \mathbf{U} \, \varphi$$

where $p \in \mathsf{AP}$ is an atomic proposition. We use classical shorthands like $\mathsf{tt} \stackrel{\text{def}}{=} p \vee \neg p$, $\mathsf{ff} \stackrel{\text{def}}{=} p \wedge \neg p$, $\varphi_1 \Rightarrow \varphi_2 \stackrel{\text{def}}{=} \neg\varphi_1 \vee \varphi_2$, $\mathbf{F}\,\varphi \stackrel{\text{def}}{=} \mathsf{tt} \, \mathbf{U} \, \varphi$, and $\mathbf{G}\,\varphi \stackrel{\text{def}}{=} \neg\mathbf{F}\,(\neg\varphi)$.

We interpret LTL formulas over finite runs of a timed automaton. Given a symbolic path π and an LTL formula φ, either all concretizations of π (*i.e.*, concrete runs $\varrho \in \pi$) satisfy φ, or they all do not satisfy φ. Hence, it is correct to speak of the probability $\mathbb{P}_{\mathcal{A}}\{\varrho \in \mathsf{Runs}(\mathcal{A}, s_0) \mid \varrho \models \varphi\}$, which we simply write $\mathbb{P}_{\mathcal{A}}(s_0, \varphi)$.

Let φ be an LTL formula. We say that $\mathcal{A}$ *almost-surely satisfies* φ from s_0 w.r.t. $\mathbb{P}_{\mathcal{A}}$, and we then write $\mathcal{A}, s_0 \approx_{\mathbb{P}} \varphi$, if $\mathbb{P}_{\mathcal{A}}(s_0, \varphi) = 1$.

Remark 8. Our model of timed automata has no accepting locations. This is restrictive as some formulas will be trivially wrong (for instance, eventualities). However, we can deal with accepting locations as well. Let acc be a new atomic proposition and ψ be an LTL formula characterising the accepting runs, *i.e.*, $\psi \stackrel{\text{def}}{=} \mathbf{F}\,\mathbf{G}\,\mathsf{acc}$. Instead of considering $\mathbb{P}_{\mathcal{A}}(s_0, \varphi)$ we would rather evaluate the conditional probability $\mathbb{P}_{\mathcal{A}}(s_0, \varphi \mid \psi)$. Clearly enough, verifying that $\mathbb{P}_{\mathcal{A}}(s_0, \varphi \mid \psi) = 1$ in the automaton without accepting locations corresponds to checking $\mathbb{P}_{\mathcal{A}}(s_0, \varphi) = 1$ in the automaton where accepting locations are those labelled with acc. Note that this only makes sense if $\mathbb{P}_{\mathcal{A}}(s_0, \psi) \neq 0$, however timed automata such that $\mathbb{P}_{\mathcal{A}}(s_0, \psi) = 0$ can be considered as degenerated.

Example 9. Consider the timed automaton $\mathcal{A}$ depicted below:

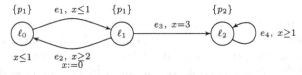

If $s_0 = (\ell_0, 0)$ is the initial state, then $\mathcal{A}, s_0 \not\models \mathbf{G}\,p_1$ but $\mathcal{A}, s_0 \approx_{\mathbb{P}} \mathbf{G}\,p_1$. Indeed, in this example, the transition e_3 will unlikely happen, because its guard $x = 3$ is much too 'small' compared with the guard $x \geq 2$ of the transition e_2.

---

^{6} Recall that, if ϱ is a run in $\mathcal{A}$, then $\iota(\varrho)$ is the image of ϱ in $\mathsf{R}(\mathcal{A})$ (see page 182).

Lemma 7 directly implies the following:

Corollary 10. *Let $\mathcal{A}$ be a non-blocking timed automaton, s a state of $\mathcal{A}$, and φ an* LTL *formula. Then,*

$$\mathcal{A}, s \models_{\mathbb{P}} \varphi \iff \mathsf{R}(\mathcal{A}), \iota(s) \models_{\mathbb{P}} \varphi.$$

4   A Topological Semantics for Timed Automata

In this section, we propose a *large* semantics for LTL over timed automata. This large semantics, based on a natural topology on timed automata, asserts that an LTL formula is *largely satisfied* if 'most of the runs' satisfy it. We use classical topological tools (including the dimension) to characterise what we mean by 'most of the runs'.

4.1   Some Topological Notions

We do not recall classical definitions in topology but refer to [12]. However, some notions are less common, we thus recall them here. The density notion is not appropriate to express a 'most of the runs' notion, because rather small sets are dense, *e.g.* the set $\mathbb{Q}$ in $\mathbb{R}$. As already pointed out in [17] the notion of *largeness*, and its complement the *meagerness* are more appropriate. Let $(A, \mathcal{T})$ be a topological space. If $B \subseteq A$, we denote by $\overset{\circ}{B}$ (resp. $\overline{B}$) the interior (resp. closure) of B. A set $B \subseteq A$ is nowhere dense if $\overset{\circ}{\overline{B}} = \emptyset$. A set is *meager* if it is a countable union of nowhere dense sets. Finally, a set is *large* if its complement is meager.

Although the notion of largeness is quite abstract, it admits a very nice characterisation in terms of a two-player game, known as *Banach-Mazur game*. A Banach-Mazur game is based on a topological space $(A, \mathcal{T})$ equipped with a family $\mathcal{B}$ of subsets of A such that: (1) $\forall B \in \mathcal{B}$, $\overset{\circ}{B} \neq \emptyset$ and (2) $\forall O \in \mathcal{T}$ s.t. $O \neq \emptyset$, $\exists B \in \mathcal{B}$, $B \subseteq O$. Given C a subset of A, players alternate their moves choosing decreasing elements in $\mathcal{B}$, and build an infinite sequence $B_1 \supseteq B_2 \supseteq B_3 \cdots$. Player 1 wins the play if $\bigcap_{i=1}^{\infty} B_i \cap C \neq \emptyset$, else Player 2 wins.

Banach-Mazur games are not always determined, even for simple topological spaces (see [13, Remark 1]). Still a natural question is to know when the players have winning strategies. The following result gives a partial answer:

Theorem 11 (Banach-Mazur [13]). *Player 2 has a winning strategy in the Banach-Mazur game with target set C if and only if C is meager.*

4.2   The Dimension of a Symbolic Path

In $\mathbb{R}^n$, open sets are among those sets of maximal dimension. Here, we are not exactly in $\mathbb{R}^n$, but each symbolic constrained path can be embedded in some $\mathbb{R}^m$.

A notion of *dimension of a symbolic path* then naturally arises. Before going to the details, let us explain through an example the intuition behind this notion.

Example 12. Let $\mathcal{A}$ be the timed automaton depicted below, let s_0 be the state $(\ell_0, 0)$ and π be the (unconstrained) symbolic path $\pi(s_0, e_1 e_2)$.

One can naturally associate a polyhedron of $(\mathbb{R}_+)^2$ with π:

$$\mathsf{Pol}(\pi) = \{(\tau_1, \tau_2) \in (\mathbb{R}_+)^2 \mid \varrho = s_0 \xrightarrow{\tau_1, e_1} s_1 \xrightarrow{\tau_2, e_2} s_2 \in \mathsf{Runs}(\mathcal{A}, s_0)\}$$
$$= \{(\tau_1, \tau_2) \in (\mathbb{R}_+)^2 \mid (0 \leq \tau_1 \leq 2) \wedge (0 \leq \tau_1 + \tau_2 \leq 5)\}$$

$\mathsf{Pol}(\pi)$ has dimension 2 in $\mathbb{R}^2$. Since it is of maximal dimension, we say the dimension of the symbolic path π is *defined*. Consider now the symbolic path $\pi' = \pi(s_0, e_1 e_3)$. The polyhedron $\mathsf{Pol}(\pi')$ associated with π' has dimension 1, and is embedded in a two-dimensional space. In that case, we say that its dimension is *undefined*.

In general, we need to be careful with singular transitions, *i.e.*, transitions which do not increase the dimension but play an important role (in the previous example, it would be the case if the edge e_1 was labelled with the guard $x = 2$; though this guard is very small, the role of edge e_1 is essential in the behaviour of the automaton).

Let $\pi_C = \pi_C(s, e_1 \ldots e_n)$ be a constrained path of a timed automaton $\mathcal{A}$. We define its associated polyhedron as follows:

$$\mathsf{Pol}(\pi_C) = \{(\tau_i)_{1 \leq i \leq n} \in (\mathbb{R}_+)^n \mid s \xrightarrow{\tau_1, e_1} s_1 \cdots \xrightarrow{\tau_n, e_n} s_n \in \pi_C(s, e_1 \ldots e_n)\}.$$

Definition 13. *Let $\mathcal{A}$ be a timed automaton, and $\pi_C = \pi_C(s, e_1 \ldots e_n)$ a constrained path. For each $0 \leq i \leq n$, we write C_i for the projection of $\mathsf{Pol}(\pi_C)$ over the variables of the i first coordinates, with the convention that C_0 is true. We say that the dimension of π_C is undefined, and we then write $\dim_\mathcal{A}(\pi_C) = \bot$, whenever there exists some index $1 \leq i \leq n$ such that*

$$\dim\left(\mathsf{Pol}\left(\pi_{C_i}(s, e_1 \ldots e_i)\right)\right) < \dim\left(\bigcup_e \mathsf{Pol}\left(\pi_{C_{i-1}}(s, e_1 \ldots e_{i-1}e)\right)\right).$$

Otherwise we say that the dimension of π_C is defined, and write $\dim_\mathcal{A}(\pi_C) = \top$.

4.3   Definition of a Topology over Finite Paths

For $\mathcal{A}$ a timed automaton, and s a state of $\mathcal{A}$, we define a *basic open set* as a constrained symbolic path $\pi_C = \pi_C(s, e_1 \ldots e_n)$ such that $\dim_\mathcal{A}(\pi_C)$ is defined, and $\mathsf{Pol}(\pi_C)$ is open in $\mathsf{Pol}(\pi)$ for the topology of $\mathbb{R}^n$ induced on $\mathsf{Pol}(\pi)$, where π stands for the (unconstrained) path $\pi(s, e_1 \ldots e_n)$.

We write $\mathcal{T}_{\mathcal{A}}$ for the topology over $\mathsf{Runs}(\mathcal{A}, s)$ induced by these basic open sets and $\mathsf{Runs}(\mathcal{A}, s)$. Note that the basic open sets $\pi_{\mathcal{C}}$ together with $\mathsf{Runs}(\mathcal{A}, s)$ form a base for $\mathcal{T}_{\mathcal{A}}$.

Example 14. Let $\mathcal{A}$ be the timed automaton of Example 9 and $s_0 = (\ell_0, 0)$ be its initial state. The basic (unconstrained) open sets of $\mathsf{Runs}(\mathcal{A}, s_0)$ are sets of the form $\pi(s_0, (e_1 e_2)^*)$ or of the form $\pi(s_0, e_1(e_2 e_1)^*)$. A (constrained) basic open set is then for instance $\pi_{\mathcal{C}}(s_0, e_1 e_2)$ with $\mathcal{C} = \{\frac{1}{3} < t_1 < \frac{1}{2}; t_1 + t_2 > 5\}$. One can be convinced that the set of paths of the form $\pi(s_0, (e_1 e_2)^* e_3 e_4^*)$ is meager.

Proposition 15. *Let $\mathcal{A}$ be a timed automaton, and s a state of $\mathcal{A}$. The topological space $(\mathsf{Runs}(\mathcal{A}, s), \mathcal{T}_{\mathcal{A}})$ is a Baire space.*[7]

Proof (Sketch). Let $\pi_{\mathcal{C}} = \pi_{\mathcal{C}}(s, e_1 \ldots e_n)$ be a non-empty basic open set. We then use Banach-Mazur games and Theorem 11 to prove that $\pi_{\mathcal{C}}$ is not meager: we prove that Player 2 has no winning strategy for the game playing with basic open sets and with $\pi_{\mathcal{C}}$ as an objective, by exhibiting a counter-strategy for Player 1.

Player 1 proceeds as follows: for the first round, she picks $\pi_1 = \pi_{\mathcal{C}}$. For the second round, Player 2 picks some $\pi_2 \subseteq \pi_1$. For the third round, Player 1 must be careful and cannot take an arbitrary open path included in π_2, because Player 1 could manage to choose the constraints so that the limit of the intersections be empty (by analogy in $\mathbb{R}$, the limit of $(0, \frac{1}{2^i})$ is the empty set). To avoid this, Player 1 can first consider a 'big' compact set F_2 within π_2 ('big' here means with a non-empty interior) — note that this is possible as the topology we consider, restricted to $\pi(s, e_1 \ldots e_n)$, can be embedded in some $\mathbb{R}^m$ through the application $\mathsf{Pol}(\cdot)$. Then, she can play with a basic open set π_3 included in F_2. The game continues like this, and Player 1 only needs to use the above-described trick at each of her rounds. The intersection of all paths that have been played then corresponds to the intersection of a chain of compact sets, hence it is non-empty, by Heine-Borel theorem.   □

We can now define a topological semantics for LTL based on the notion of largeness. Let φ be an LTL formula. We say that $\mathcal{A}$ *largely satisfies* φ from s, and we write $\mathcal{A}, s \models_{\mathcal{T}} \varphi$, if the set $\{\varrho \in \mathsf{Runs}(\mathcal{A}, s) \mid \varrho \models \varphi\}$ is topologically large. The topologies in $\mathcal{A}$ and in $\mathsf{R}(\mathcal{A})$ are equivalent in the following sense.

Lemma 16. *Let $\iota : \mathsf{Runs}(\mathcal{A}, s) \rightarrow \mathsf{Runs}(\mathsf{R}(\mathcal{A}), \iota(s))$ be the projection of finite runs ϱ in $\mathcal{A}$ onto the region automaton (see page 182). Then ι is continuous, and for every non-empty open set $\mathcal{O} \in \mathcal{T}_{\mathcal{A}}$, $\overset{\circ}{\widehat{\iota(\mathcal{O})}} \neq \emptyset$.*

Corollary 17. *Let $\mathcal{A}$ be a timed automaton, s a state of $\mathcal{A}$, and φ an LTL formula. Then,*

$$\mathcal{A}, s \models_{\mathcal{T}} \varphi \Leftrightarrow \mathsf{R}(\mathcal{A}), \iota(s) \models_{\mathcal{T}} \varphi.$$

---

[7] In modern definitions, a topological space is a Baire space if each countable union of closed sets with an empty interior has an empty interior. However, originally, a topological space is a Baire space whenever every non-empty open set is not meager. The two definitions coincide, see [12, p.295].

5   Correspondence of the Two Semantics

In this section we prove our main theorem: probabilistic and topological semantics coincide! We first relate dimension and probabilities in the region automaton.

Proposition 18. *Let* $\mathcal{A}$ *be a non-blocking timed automaton, and* π *be an unconstrained symbolic path in* $\mathsf{R}(\mathcal{A})$. *Then,* $\mathbb{P}_{\mathsf{R}(\mathcal{A})}(\pi) > 0$ *iff* $\dim_{\mathsf{R}(\mathcal{A})}(\pi) = \top$.[8]

The main result of this paper is the following theorem.

Theorem 19. *Let* $\mathcal{A}$ *be a non-blocking timed automaton,* s *a state of* $\mathcal{A}$, *and* φ *an* LTL *formula. Then,*

$$\mathcal{A}, s \models_{\mathbb{P}} \varphi \;\Leftrightarrow\; \mathcal{A}, s \models_{\mathcal{T}} \varphi.$$

Proof (Sketch). Thanks to Corollaries 10 and 17, it is equivalent to prove that $\mathsf{R}(\mathcal{A}), \iota(s) \models_{\mathcal{T}} \varphi$ iff $\mathsf{R}(\mathcal{A}), \iota(s) \models_{\mathbb{P}} \varphi$. Moreover, $\mathsf{R}(\mathcal{A}), \iota(s) \models_{\mathbb{P}} \varphi$ iff $\mathbb{P}_{\mathcal{A}}(\iota(s), \neg\varphi)$ $= 0$, thus applying Proposition 18, $\mathsf{R}(\mathcal{A}), \iota(s) \models_{\mathbb{P}} \varphi$ iff every symbolic path π in $\mathsf{R}(\mathcal{A})$ starting in $\iota(s)$ and satisfying $\neg\varphi$ has an undefined dimension. We finally prove that this last property is equivalent to $\mathsf{R}(\mathcal{A}), \iota(s) \models_{\mathcal{T}} \varphi$, *i.e.*, to the fact that $[\![\neg\varphi]\!] = \{\varrho \in \mathsf{Runs}(\mathsf{R}(\mathcal{A}), \iota(s)) \mid \varrho \not\models \varphi\}$ is topologically meager.

   For the first implication, we use Banach-Mazur games and Theorem 11 to prove that Player 2 has a winning strategy for the objective $[\![\neg\varphi]\!]$ (still playing with the basic open sets of $\mathcal{T}_{\mathsf{R}(\mathcal{A})}$). Let π_1 be the path chosen by Player 1 at the first round. This path has necesseraly defined dimension and thus, by hypothesis and Proposition 18, it satisfies φ. Whatever is played afterwards, the intersection with the objective will be empty. Hence Player 2 wins and $[\![\neg\varphi]\!]$ is meager.

   For the second implication, assume that $[\![\neg\varphi]\!]$ is meager. As the topological space $(\mathsf{Runs}(\mathsf{R}(\mathcal{A}), \iota(s)), \mathcal{T}_{\mathsf{R}(\mathcal{A})})$ is a Baire space (see Proposition 15), $\overset{\circ}{\overline{[\![\neg\varphi]\!]}} = \emptyset$. Hence, there is no path in $\mathsf{R}(\mathcal{A})$ from $\iota(s)$ with defined dimension which does not satisfy φ. $\square$

Remark 20. To handle accepting states in the previous theorem, it would be sufficient to quantify only over paths in $\mathsf{R}(\mathcal{A})$ which are accepting.

6   Decidability Issues

Theorem 21. *Over finite timed words, the almost-sure and the large* LTL *model-checking problems over non-blocking timed automata are* PSPACE-*Complete.*

Proof (Sketch). The two problems are equivalent, due to Theorem 19. The PSPACE-Hardness follows from the PSPACE-Hardness of LTL model checking over finite automata. To describe a PSPACE algorithm, we first color each edge of $\mathsf{R}(\mathcal{A})$ as follows: if e is an edge in $\mathsf{R}(\mathcal{A})$, we color it in red whenever $\mu_s(I(s, e)) = 0$

---

[8] This is in particular independent of the choice of the probability distributions over delays.

for some $s \in q$ (note that this property is independent of the choice of $s \in q$, and that it is equivalent to $\dim(I(s,e)) < \dim(I(s))$ thanks to the property of the measure μ_s, see page 182), and we color it in blue otherwise.

Lemma 22. *Let $\mathcal{A}$ be a timed automaton and $\pi = \pi(s, e_1 \ldots e_n)$ a symbolic path in $\mathsf{R}(\mathcal{A})$. Then, $\dim_{\mathsf{R}(\mathcal{A})}(\pi) = \bot$ iff at least one of the edges of π is red.*

Now, applying Proposition 18, to decide whether $\mathcal{A}, s \not\models_{\mathbb{P}} \varphi$, it is sufficient to guess a path in $\mathsf{R}(\mathcal{A})$ which has defined dimension (*i.e.*, does not contain any red edge), and does not satisfy φ. There is such a path with length at most exponential, it can thus be done in NPSPACE =PSPACE. □

7   Related Work

In this section we briefly compare our two semantics with existing works. A deeper related work section can be found in our research report [5].

The model of *real-time probabilistic processes* introduced in [1,2] seems similar to timed automata interpreted with our probabilistic semantics, but it is indeed not the case. First, such a system is composed of a number of independent processes with a single clock, which implies in particular that clocks are completely independent. Then, and this is even more important, the choice of the transition to be taken is made before choosing probabilistically a delay. As a consequence, even transitions with small firing intervals can have a high probability to be taken, even though events with much larger firing intervals are possible. This is why this model satisfies stronger properties than ours.

We now compare our topology with the one introduced in [9] and further studied in [11]. First notice that their topology is defined on finite timed words and we define our topology on the set of finite runs. In particular, as already mentioned in the introduction, their topology only depends on the language and not on the automaton, while ours does. This implies that the topologies are 'incomparable', more precisely we can find sets that are open for our topology and not for their topology, and *vice-versa*.

8   Conclusion

In this paper, we have proposed two satisfaction relations for LTL formulas over timed automata which rule out unlikely (sequences of) events. The first one is based on a probabilistic semantics of timed automata, and to the best of our knowledge, is the first attempt to provide a probabilistic interpretation for non probabilistic timed systems in order to establish linear-time properties assuming 'fairness' on actions and delays. It naturally raises (qualitative) model-checking questions, for instance whether the probability that an LTL property holds is 1 (almost-sure model-checking problem). The second one is based on the topological concept of largeness, and yields a natural large semantics for LTL. We prove that these two interpretations for LTL coincide. Moreover, we establish that LTL model checking under those non-standard semantics is not harder than ordinary LTL model-checking (PSPACE-Complete).

The method we have developed here could straightforwardly extend in various directions. All untimed properties over finite runs, whose truth is invariant by regions, can be treated that way (for instance properties expressed in the logic CTL* or in the μ-Calculus). It could also be applied to various classes of hybrid systems with a finite bisimulation quotient [10].

We are currently extending this work to the framework of infinite timed words which raises even more complex problems, and we plan to extend it further in several directions, like for properties expressed in a timed logic, or to the quantitative analysis of this model (for instance, computing the exact, or approximate, probability of satisfying a given property, *etc*), or to control problems, *etc*.

References

1. Alur, R., Courcoubetis, C., Dill, D.: Model-checking for probabilistic real-time systems. In: Leach Albert, J., Monien, B., Rodríguez-Artalejo, M. (eds.) Automata, Languages and Programming. LNCS, vol. 510, pp. 115–126. Springer, Heidelberg (1991)
2. Alur, R., Courcoubetis, C., Dill, D.: Verifying automata specifications of probabilistic real-time systems. In: Huizing, C., de Bakker, J.W., Rozenberg, G., de Roever, W.-P. (eds.) Real-Time: Theory in Practice. LNCS, vol. 600, pp. 28–44. Springer, Heidelberg (1992)
3. Alur, R., Dill, D.: A theory of timed automata. Theoretical Comp. Sci. 126(2), 183–235 (1994)
4. Alur, R., La Torre, S., Madhusudan, P.: Perturbed timed automata. In: Morari, M., Thiele, L. (eds.) HSCC 2005. LNCS, vol. 3414, pp. 70–85. Springer, Heidelberg (2005)
5. Baier, C., Bertrand, N., Bouyer, P., Brihaye, Th., Größer, M.: Probabilistic and topological semantics for timed automata. Research Report LSV–07–26, LSV, ENS de Cachan, France (2007)
6. Bouyer, P., Markey, N., Reynier, P.-A.: Robust model-checking of timed automata. In: Correa, J.R., Hevia, A., Kiwi, M. (eds.) LATIN 2006. LNCS, vol. 3887, pp. 238–249. Springer, Heidelberg (2006)
7. De Wulf, M., Doyen, L., Markey, N., Raskin, J.-F.: Robustness and implementability of timed automata. In: Lakhnech, Y., Yovine, S. (eds.) FORMATS 2004 and FTRTFT 2004. LNCS, vol. 3253, pp. 118–133. Springer, Heidelberg (2004)
8. De Wulf, M., Doyen, L., Raskin, J.-F.: Almost ASAP semantics: From timed models to timed implementations. In: Alur, R., Pappas, G.J. (eds.) HSCC 2004. LNCS, vol. 2993, pp. 296–310. Springer, Heidelberg (2004)
9. Gupta, V., Henzinger, T.A., Jagadeesan, R.: Robust timed automata. In: Maler, O. (ed.) HART 1997. LNCS, vol. 1201, pp. 331–345. Springer, Heidelberg (1997)
10. Henzinger, Th.A., Majumdar, R., Raskin, J.-F.: A classification of symbolic transition systems. ACM Transactions on Computational Logic 6(1), 1–32 (2005)
11. Henzinger, Th.A., Raskin, J.-F.: Robust undecidability of timed and hybrid systems. In: Lynch, N.A., Krogh, B.H. (eds.) HSCC 2000. LNCS, vol. 1790, pp. 145–159. Springer, Heidelberg (2000)
12. Munkres, J.R.: Topology, 2nd edn. Prentice-Hall, Englewood Cliffs (2000)

13. Oxtoby, J.C.: The Banach-Mazur game and Banach category theorem. Annals of Mathematical Studies 39, 159–163 (1957)
14. Pnueli, A.: The temporal logic of programs. In: Proc. 18th Ann. Symp. Foundations of Computer Science (FOCS 1977), pp. 46–57. IEEE Comp. Soc. Press, Los Alamitos (1977)
15. Puri, A.: Dynamical properties of timed automata. In: Ravn, A.P., Rischel, H. (eds.) FTRTFT 1998. LNCS, vol. 1486, pp. 210–227. Springer, Heidelberg (1998)
16. Sproston, J.: Model checking for probabilistic timed systems. In: Baier, C., Haverkort, B., Hermanns, H., Katoen, J.-P., Siegle, M. (eds.) Validation of Stochastic Systems. LNCS, vol. 2925, pp. 189–229. Springer, Heidelberg (2004)
17. Varacca, D., Völzer, H.: Temporal logics and model checking for fairly correct systems. In: Varacca, D. (ed.) Proc. 21st Ann. Symp. Logic in Computer Science (LICS 2006), pp. 389–398. IEEE Comp. Soc. Press, Los Alamitos (2006)

A Theory for Game Theories

Michel Hirschowitz[1], André Hirschowitz[2], and Tom Hirschowitz[3]

[1] CEA-LIST
michel.hirschowitz@cea.fr
[2] UMR 6621 CNRS-Université de Nice-Sophia-Antipolis
ah@math.unice.fr
[3] UMR 5668 CNRS-ENS Lyon-INRIA-UCBL
tom.hirschowitz@ens-lyon.fr

Abstract. Game semantics is a valuable source of fully abstract models of programming languages or proof theories based on categories of so-called games and strategies. However, there are many variants of this technique, whose interrelationships largely remain to be elucidated. This raises the question: what is a category of games and strategies?

Our central idea, taken from the first author's PhD thesis [11], is that positions and moves in a game should be morphisms in a base category: playing move m in position f consists in factoring f through m, the new position being the other factor. Accordingly, we provide a general construction which, from a selection of *legal moves* in an almost arbitrary category, produces a category of games and strategies, together with subcategories of *deterministic* and *winning* strategies.

As our running example, we instantiate our construction to obtain the standard category of Hyland-Ong games subject to the switching condition. The extension of our framework to games without the switching condition is handled in the first author's PhD thesis [11].

Keywords: Game semantics, categories.

1 Introduction

1.1 The Flavor Problem

Game semantics appeared in the early 90's [3,12] and provided convenient denotational semantics to proof theories and programming languages, including their non functional features [2,5,4,13,8,14]. However, game semantics has roughly as many variants as it has authors. Each of these game theories starts from a notion of "arrow" game (with corresponding positions and moves), yielding the natural notion of strategy. The crucial construction is then the composition of strategies, with the crucial feature that various meaningful classes of strategies (deterministic, innocent, winning) are preserved by composition.

All these compositions clearly have a common flavor (sometimes called "compose+hide"). In the present work, we propose an explanation for this common flavor. To this effect, we define, through a single construction, a huge class of game theories where the composition of strategies preserves good properties. This class contains those among existing game theories which respect the

V. Arvind and S. Prasad (Eds.): FSTTCS 2007, LNCS 4855, pp. 192–203, 2007.
© Springer-Verlag Berlin Heidelberg 2007

so-called switching condition [7]. This restriction is only due to the fact that we have chosen to present the simplest version of the construction. Indeed, the more general version [11] involves a serious amount of weak categorical material. Nevertheless, future game models relying on our framework will avoid the burden of re-proving the combinatorial lemmas leading to the category of games and strategies. We now proceed to give a more detailed overview.

1.2   Playing in a One-Way Category

In our approach, a play may take place in any *one-way* category, which we define to be a category where objects have a sign (1/0) and where morphisms cannot go from a 1-object to a 0-one. Equivalently, a one-way category is a category $\mathcal{C}$, equipped with a functor $\lambda : \mathcal{C} \rightarrow 2$, where 2 is the ordered set $0 \leq 1$.

The crucial part of our construction builds a *wild* game $W_\mathcal{C}$ from a one-way category $\mathcal{C}$. This game is wild in the sense that the two players play without any restriction (meaningful restrictions will be considered later). Let us sketch the construction of $W_\mathcal{C}$. It is a directed graph, whose vertices are the morphisms of $\mathcal{C}$. Thus we have one kind (01) of *odd* vertices and two kinds (00, 11) of *even* vertices. We think of these "states" as follows: at an odd vertex, Player has to play and reach an even vertex; at a 11-vertex, Opponent has to play "on the left-hand side" (and reach an odd vertex), while at a 00-vertex Opponent has to play "on the right-hand side" (and reach an odd vertex). This yields the following diagram of states

$$11 \underset{\mathsf{L}}{\overset{\mathsf{M}L}{\rightleftarrows}} 01 \underset{\mathsf{R}}{\overset{\mathsf{M}R}{\rightleftarrows}} 00.$$

In other words we have four kinds of edges ($\mathsf{M}L$ and $\mathsf{M}R$ for Player's moves, L and R for Opponent's) which we now describe in more detail. The rule is that only one end of the vertex (a morphism in $\mathcal{C}$) changes, and the slogan says that O composes while P decomposes, as pictured in Figure 1: an edge from f to g, consists of an odd morphism m respectively satisfying the following rule:

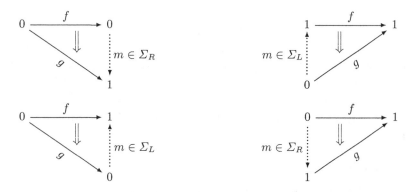

Fig. 1. The four kinds of edges in $W_\mathcal{C}$, from f to g

Kind of move	R	L	MR	ML
Rule	$g = m \circ f$	$g = f \circ m$	$f = m \circ g$	$f = g \circ m.$

Because each move changes the signs, all the m's above and in Figure 1 have sign $0 \to 1$.

The wild game we have constructed so far offers essentially the complete picture which we want to show, in particular one may define strategies and their composition. On the other hand, as far as meaning is concerned, the wild game is trivial, in the sense that players can easily neutralize each other. Indeed, for instance, assume Opponent moves from the current position f to, say, $m \circ f$ by composing with m. Then, Player may move back to f by decomposing $m \circ f$ into m and f. Thus, in the wild game, all moves are undoable. More meaningful and sufficiently general games are obtained as subgames of the wild game simply by restricting the set of odd morphisms allowed in the process of composition/decomposition. For this reason we define a *game setting* to be a one-way category equipped with two sets of odd morphisms as explained in Section 2.2. In the rest of the paper, we explain the basic theory of plays and strategies in a game setting, and we show how the theory of HO games may be recovered in terms of a game setting.

Related Work. Cockett and Seely [6] offer another categorical investigation into game semantics. The relationship between their work and ours remains unclear to us. Let us also mention a recent paper [10] which describes a categorical reconstruction of "pointer" games and *innocent* strategies from "general" games and strategies. In this sense, they reduce one sophisticated (but efficient) category of games to a much simpler one. Thus they aim at a better understanding of one (very important) category of games, and of the concept of innocence, while we aim at a better understanding of what could be a category of games, and do not consider the concept of innocence.

Organization of the Paper. In Section 2, we provide the categorical construction which, from a so-called *game setting*, constructs a double category of plays, where vertical composition is sequential composition, while horizontal composition is reminiscent of the usual composition of strategies. We then instantiate our framework in Section 3: after recalling the basics of (a standard variant of) HO games, we exhibit a game setting hidden in it, for which our construction yields the usual notion of plays and arrow arenas. In Section 4, we describe strategies in our abstract framework, as well as their composition, and we show that the obtained notion of HO strategies closely corresponds to the standard one.

2   The Abstract Framework: Building the Double Category

2.1   Game Settings

In order to restrict moves in the game sketched above, we should a priori specify four sets M_{OL}, M_{OR}, M_{PL}, M_{PR} of legal odd morphisms, one for each of the four kinds of moves in Figure 1. However, these restrictions will be compatible with the composition of strategies only if we impose $M_{OL} = M_{PR}$ and $M_{OR} = M_{PL}$. This leads to our definition: a *game setting* $G \triangleq (\mathcal{C}, \Sigma_R, \Sigma_L)$ consists of a one-way category $\mathcal{C}$ equipped with a pair of sets of odd morphisms: Σ_R is the set of *forward* moves (or *f-moves*; those going downwards in Figure 1); Σ_L is the set of *backward* moves or *b-moves*. The wild game (on $\mathcal{C}$) is obtained by taking as Σ_R and Σ_L the whole set of odd morphisms.

In a game setting G, we view objects as positions in a two-player game, actually a signed graph. Morphisms in Σ_R and Σ_L are Opponent and Player moves, respectively. On 0-labeled objects, Opponent is to play, whilst on 1-labeled ones, it's Player's turn. As illustrated in Figure 2, from some 0-labeled position p, Opponent plays by choosing an f-move $m : p \to q$ with domain p, thereby reaching the 1-labeled position q. Conversely, from such a q, Player plays by choosing a b-move $m' : r \to q$ with codomain q, thereby reaching the position r. This defines a graph whose vertices are the objects of $\mathcal{C}$, which we call the 0-*dimensional game* (0-game for short) of G and denote by $\mathcal{G}_0(G)$. We call the free category over this graph the category of 0-*plays* over G, and denote it by $\mathcal{C}_0(G)$.

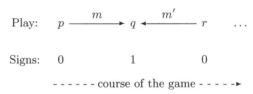

Fig. 2. Example play in the 0-game

Each 0-play v has a predecessor $\mathrm{Pred}(v)$ obtained by deleting the last move (if any).

2.2 The 1-Dimensional Game

As in standard game semantics, this yields a natural notion of arrow game, also a graph, which we call the 1-*dimensional game* (1-game for short) of G and denote by $\mathcal{G}_1(G)$. We describe the positions of this game first, then its moves, and finally we show how to equip it with signs, in a way that refines the above interpretation of signs in the 0-game. Positions (or vertices) in $\mathcal{G}_1(G)$ are morphisms in $\mathcal{C}$. Given the constraints on signs, there are just three kinds of positions: 00, 01, and 11. Then, moves from f to g in the 1-game are defined to be commutative triangles in $\mathcal{C}$, of one of the four shapes in Figure 1.

The interpretation of signs in 1-games, illustrated in Figure 3, entirely follows from the idea that in 0-games, Player lives on the left-hand side of the position, whilst Opponent lives on its right-hand side. For a 1-position, there is thus one agent M in the middle, and one agent on each side, which we call L and R in the obvious way. M plays Opponent in the domain 0-game, and Player in the

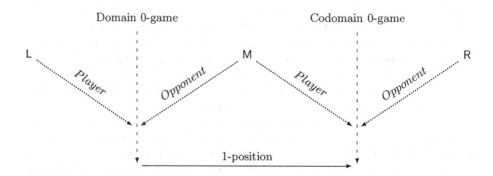

Fig. 3. All agents (L, M, R) act as Player on their rhs and as Opponent on their lhs

codomain 0-game. L plays Player in the domain 0-game, whilst R plays Opponent in the codomain 0-game. This yields the following rule for the 1-game:

Signs of the 1-position	Who's to play?
$0 \longrightarrow 0$	R
$0 \longrightarrow 1$	M
$1 \longrightarrow 1$	L .

We consider the free category over this graph $\mathcal{G}_1(G)$: we call it the category of 1-*plays* over G and denote it by $\mathcal{C}_1(G)$. Again each 1-play v has a predecessor $\mathrm{Pred}(v)$ obtained by deleting the last move (if any).

Finally, we define the (horizontal) source and target functors on 1-plays, $\mathrm{s},\mathrm{t} : \mathcal{C}_1(G) \to \mathcal{C}_0(G)$, by the obvious induction (or adjunction). We thus have a pullback category $\mathcal{C}_1(G) \,_{\mathrm{s}}\times_{\mathrm{t}} \mathcal{C}_1(G))$ of composable pairs of 1-plays.

2.3   The Double Category Associated to a Game Setting

In this section, we derive a double-categorical structure from our game setting G. For this, we will define a notion of horizontal composition of 1-plays, yielding a category whose objects are 0-plays, and whose morphisms are 1-plays. We start by defining the graph $\mathcal{G}_2(\mathcal{C})$ of *primitive interactions* as follows. As vertices, take composable pairs of morphisms in $\mathcal{C}$, and as edges from the pair $\xrightarrow{f} \xrightarrow{g}$ to the pair $\xrightarrow{f'} \xrightarrow{g'}$, take all the commutative diagrams as in Figure 4. This gives four kinds of vertices $(000, 001, 011, 111)$ according to the signs of objects, yielding the following state diagram:

$$111 \underset{M_1 L}{\overset{L}{\rightleftarrows}} 011 \underset{M_1 R}{\overset{M_2 L}{\rightleftarrows}} 001 \underset{R}{\overset{M_2 R}{\rightleftarrows}} 000.$$

For $\mathcal{G}_2(\mathcal{C})$, the intuition is that there are two players M_1 and M_2, and two opponents L and R, who interact respectively on the left-hand side with M_1 and

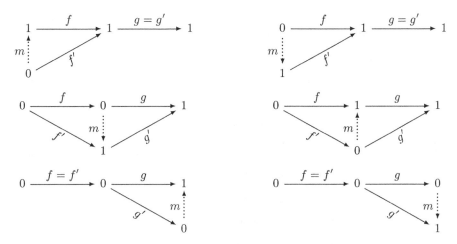

Fig. 4. The six kinds of edges in $\mathcal{G}_2(\mathcal{C})$ (each edge top-down)

on the right-hand side with M_2. Thanks to categorical composition, both players act exactly as if they were facing two opponents. For instance, M_1 interacts with L on the left-hand side, and with M_2 on the right-hand side. Because of sign rules, at most one of M_1 and M_2 may play at a given time, which prevents any conflict to arise.

Next, we let $\mathcal{C}_2(G)$ denote the free category generated by $\mathcal{G}_2(G)$, and we call its morphisms *interactions* in G. Accordingly, the edges in $\mathcal{G}_2(G)$ are *primitive interactions*. Let us also deem the primitive interactions of the middle row *internal*, and the other ones *external*. Now a key observation is that the functor

$$\mathcal{C}_2(G) \xrightarrow{\langle \pi_1, \pi_2 \rangle} \mathcal{C}_1(G) \,_s\times_t \mathcal{C}_1(G)$$

which maps a path in $\mathcal{G}_2(G)$ to its left and right borders is an isomorphism, which says altogether that interactions are determined by their projections, and that $\mathcal{C}_1(G) \,_s\times_t \mathcal{C}_1(G)$ is freely generated by the primitive interactions.

Thanks to this statement, it is enough to define our 1-horizontal composition $Y \bullet X$ on primitive interactions, which is straightforward: for an internal interaction, the 1-horizontal composition is the empty 1-play. Otherwise it is the obvious move from $g \circ f$ to $g' \circ f'$, for each external interaction as in Figure 4.

To construct our horizontal category, we finally define identity morphisms, by mimicking what is standardly called *copycat* in game semantics: let copycat be the unique functor from $\mathcal{G}_0(G)$ to $\mathcal{G}_1(G)$ such that f-moves $m : p \to p'$ and b-moves $m : p' \to p$ are respectively sent to plays

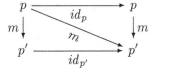

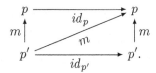

By the standard adjunction between categories and directed graphs, this defines copycat uniquely: on arbitrary plays, copycat simply piles up sequences of such elementary plays.

Proposition 1. *The horizontal composition of 1-plays is associative and unital.*

The proof of associativity relies on a freeness result concerning 3-interoctions, completely analogous to our previous freeness result concerning 2-interactions.

This all gives the data for a *double category*. A short definition is as follows: a double category is a category object in the category of categories. A more explicit, elementary definition may be found, e.g., in Melliès [15]. We've already checked all the required properties, except the *interchange law*, which makes • into a functor from the pullback $\mathcal{C}_1(G)\,_s\times_t\mathcal{C}_1(G)$ to $\mathcal{C}_1(G)$. Explicitly: $(Y_1 \bullet X_1) \circ (Y_2 \bullet X_2) = (Y_2 \circ Y_1) \bullet (X_2 \circ X_1)$. It happens to be satisfied, which entails:

Theorem 1. *For any game setting G, the categories $\mathcal{C}_0(G)$ and $\mathcal{C}_1(G)$, the domain and codomain functors $s, t : \mathcal{C}_1(G) \to \mathcal{C}_0(G)$, the horizontal composition functor $\bullet : \mathcal{C}_1(G)\,_s\times_t \mathcal{C}_1(G) \to \mathcal{C}_1(G)$, and the horizontal identity functor $I : \mathcal{C}_0(G) \to \mathcal{C}_1(G)$ form a double category.*

3   The One-Way Category Underlying Hyland-Ong Games

3.1   A Brief Review of HO-Arenas and HO-Plays

We briefly recall some definitions of HO game theory, and refer the reader to Harmer's notes [9] for details.

An *arena* A is a triple $(M_A, \lambda_A, \vdash_A)$, where M_A is a set of *moves*, λ_A gives signs to moves, i.e., is a function from M_A to $\{0, 1\}$, and $\vdash_A$ represents altogether a binary relation (justification) and a predicate (initiality) on M_A, such that:

1. if $\vdash_A m$, then $\lambda_A(m) = 0$ and for all $m' \in M_A$, $m' \not\vdash_A m$,
2. if $m \vdash_A m'$, then $\lambda_A(m) \neq \lambda_A(m')$.

Moves m such that $\vdash_A m$ are called *initial*. When $m \vdash_A m'$, we say that m *justifies* m'.

A *position* in an arena A is a pair (s, ρ), where $s = m_1 \ldots m_n$ is a sequence of moves of alternate signs in A, and ρ is a function from $\{1 \ldots n\}$ to $\{0 \ldots n-1\}$ such that for all $i \in \{1 \ldots n\}$

1. (priority condition) $\rho(i) < i$,
2. if $\rho(i) = 0$, then m_i is initial,
3. if $\rho(i) = j \neq 0$, then m_j justifies m_i.

We say that n is the length of the position. Our position p also has an *initial part* $Init_p \subset [1, \ldots, n]$ which is the set of indices i for which m_i is initial. Since positions carry their history, they also may be seen as plays, and we freely call them either way. A position of length 0 is called *initial*, and a non initial position

p of length n has a predecessor position $\text{Pred}(p)$, of length $n-1$, obtained by deleting the last move. For simplicity, we define $\text{Pred}(p) \triangleq p$ when p is initial. A set of positions is *prefix-closed* when it is closed under application of Pred.

Given a sign function λ, we write $\overline{\lambda}$ for the opposite one. Given two arenas A and B, one constructs the *arrow arena* $A \multimap B$ by taking $M_A + M_B$ as the set of moves, $[\overline{\lambda}_A, \lambda_B]$ as a sign function, the (injections of) initial moves of B as initial moves, and for the binary $\vdash_{A \multimap B}$, taking the union (up to injection) of $\vdash_A$ and $\vdash_B$, plus the pairs (m, m') with m initial in B and m' initial in A. Note that a position p in an arrow arena $A \multimap B$ determines two projections p_A and p_B which are in general not positions in A and B. Intuitively, this is because Opponent may switch sides, and, when asked a question in A, ask a question in B.

Define a position p in $A \multimap B$ to be *valid* if its two projections are again positions, respectively in A and B. Combinatorially, if n_A and n_B are the lengths of these projections, p determines a *shuffle* $p_S = [1, \ldots, n_A + n_B] \to [1, \ldots, n_B] \amalg [1, \ldots, n_A]$. We say that such a shuffle p_s satisfies the *switching condition*, or is *even* when

- if $n_A + n_B > 0$ then $p_S(1)$ is on the B-side,
- for i satisfying $1 < 2i < n_A + n_B$, $p_S(2i)$ and $p_S(2i+1)$ are on the same side.

It turns out that p is valid exactly when p_S is even. We note that p determines a restricted justification map $\text{RJ}_p : Init_{p_A} \to Init_{p_B}$. Conversely, given the projections p_A and p_B, a position p is determined by an arbitrary map $\text{RJ} : Init_{p_A} \to Init_{p_B}$ and an even shuffle compatible with RJ (with respect to the priority condition).

Strategies from A to B are defined to be non-empty, prefix-closed sets of valid positions in $A \multimap B$. One then shows that strategies compose and have identities, which yields a category of games and strategies Strat_{HO}.

3.2 The One-Way Category $\mathcal{C}_{HO}$

Let us now describe the one-way category $\mathcal{C}_{HO}$ relevant for HO games. An object $(A, (s, \rho))$ of $\mathcal{C}_{HO}$ is merely a position (s, ρ) in a game arena A, while a morphism from $p = (A, (s, \rho))$ to $q = (B, (s', \rho'))$ is a (valid) position $f = (A \multimap B, (t, \tau))$ whose projections respectively give p and q. Thus our morphisms also have predecessors. Note that f and $\text{Pred}(f)$ share one end, but in general not both.

We are especially concerned with two kinds of morphisms. Firstly, for each position $p = (A, (s, \rho))$, we have a *copycat* morphism $\text{copycat}_p : p \to p$, which is defined by induction on the length of p: the empty play on $A \multimap A$ is the copycat of the initial position on A, and for greater lengths, copycat_p is determined by the requirement that its second predecessor is the copycat of $\text{Pred}(p)$: the last two moves are determined by the given projections (p and p). Secondly, we are interested in those morphisms whose predecessor is a copycat, which we call *subcopycat* morphisms. Each subcopycat morphism is also the predecessor of a unique copycat morphism. Thus, for a non initial position p, define Sub_p to be the predecessor of copycat_p. Then, each subcopycat morphism can be written

Sub_p in a unique way. Furthermore, if p is even, then Sub_p goes from p to $\text{Pred}(p)$ while if p is odd, then Sub_p goes from $\text{Pred}(p)$ to p.

Next, we define the composition of our morphisms. Consider two consecutive arrows, i.e., valid positions f in some $A \multimap B$ and g in $B \multimap C$ with the same projection p_B on B. We denote by p_A the projection of f on A, and by p_C the projection of g on C and by n_A, n_B, n_C the corresponding lengths. We will define $h \triangleq g \circ f$ by its restricted justification map RJ_h and its even shuffle h_S. For RJ_h, we take the composition $\text{RJ}_g \circ \text{RJ}_f$. For h_S, we observe that, thanks to the switching condition, there is a unique shuffle $s : [1, \ldots, n_A + n_B + n_C] \to [1, \ldots, n_C] \amalg [1, \ldots, n_B] \amalg [1, \ldots, n_A]$ compatible with f_S and g_S. We view this shuffle as an order on $[1, \ldots, n_C] \amalg [1, \ldots, n_B] \amalg [1, \ldots, n_A]$ and take for h_S its restriction to $[1, \ldots, n_C] \amalg [1, \ldots, n_A]$.

This composition is easily seen to be associative, and it is easily checked that the identity on a position p is the copycat morphism copycat_p.

This altogether gives a category $\mathcal{C}_{HO}$, whose objects may be given a sign as follows: the sign of a position is 0 if Opponent is to play, or equivalently if its length is even, and 1 otherwise. Thus, a priori, we have four kinds of morphisms, $0 \to 0$, $0 \to 1$, $1 \to 0$, $1 \to 1$. However, we easily check that there are no morphisms of type $1 \to 0$. This is a consequence of the switching condition, and the convention that plays always start with a move by Opponent, which furthermore, in the case of arrow arenas, has to be on the right-hand side. Our category may thus be seen as a one-way category.

Remark 1 (Relaxing the switching condition). If we relax the switching condition, and allow Opponent to switch sides in an arrow game, the main new feature is that the horizontal composition of 1-plays is no more well-defined, because interactions are no more determined by their projections. As a consequence, the double category constructed above has to be replaced by some kind of weak double category, to be defined accordingly. This approach has been pursued in the first author's PhD thesis [11], where one eventually recovers a proper category when passing to strategies.

3.3   The Game Setting G_{HO}

Now we explain how HO-moves may be seen as morphisms in $\mathcal{C}_{HO}$. Playing a move in a position p in A is understood as extending p (with one move in A), yielding a new position q. To this move, we attach the morphism Sub_q. Note that Sub_q goes from p to q if p is even, and from q to p if p is odd. Hence in our view, the set of HO-moves is precisely the set of subcopycat morphisms, which we split into the set RHO of subcopycat morphisms where the length of the codomain exceeds the length of the domain by one, and the set LHO of subcopycat morphisms where the length of the domain exceeds the length of the codomain by one. Thus, standard HO plays are 0-plays starting on an initial position in the game setting $G_{HO} \triangleq (\mathcal{C}_{HO}, \text{LHO}, \text{RHO})$. (In the game setting, we also consider plays starting on non initial positions.)

Now let us see how our view fits with plays in an arrow game: consider a valid position f in the game $A \multimap B$ and its extension to a new valid position

g, through a HO-move m (in A or in B). We have four kinds of extensions corresponding to who is playing and where. A careful inspection shows that

- if O plays in B, then we have $g = m \circ f$ (in $\mathcal{C}_{HO}$),
- if O plays in A, then we have $g = f \circ m$,
- if P plays in B, then we have $f = m \circ g$,
- if P plays in A, then we have $f = g \circ m$;

which shows that, indeed, O composes the original position with her move, while P decomposes the original position with her move. Thus, standard HO arrow plays are precisely 1-plays in G_{HO} starting on an initial position.

4   An Abstract View of Strategies

In this section, we show how some standard results on strategies may be understood abstractly in a game setting $G = (\mathcal{C}, \Sigma_R, \Sigma_L)$. Recall that an object of $\mathcal{C}$ is *even* when its sign is 0 and *odd* otherwise. We say that a 1-position $f : p \to q$ is even when p and q have the same sign, and odd otherwise. We note that f is odd exactly when the middle player M is to play, and even exactly when it's L or R's turn. Let us now define strategies, writing · for concatenation.

Definition 1. *A 0-strategy (or strategy) σ on a 0-position p is a non empty, prefix-closed set of 0-plays of domain p such that, for any x in σ with even codomain q, and for any move $m : q \to r$ in $\mathcal{G}_0(G)$, $x \cdot m$ is also in σ.*

A 1-strategy (or strategy) Σ on a 1-position f is a non empty prefix-closed set of 1-plays of domain f, such that, for any X in Σ with even codomain g, and for any move $M : g \to h$ in $\mathcal{G}_1(G)$, $X \cdot M$ is also in Σ.

We use S to range over 0 or 1-strategies (or both), leaving the context to disambiguate. Given $f : p \to q$ and $g : q \to r$, we define the horizontal composition of strategies σ and σ' (respectively on f and g) to be the set of all plays on $g \circ f$ of the form $Y \bullet X$ for some (horizontally) composable $X \in \sigma$ and $Y \in \sigma'$. We easily prove that this definition is sensible:

Proposition 2. *A composition of 1-strategies is again a 1-strategy.*

Proposition 3. *The composition of 1-strategies is associative.*

The proof of the latter statement is an easy consequence of the associativity of our horizontal composition of plays.

We define the copycat strategy on an identity 1-position p as the smallest strategy containing the copycat 1-plays (as defined above) starting at p. These copycat strategies are neutral for our composition. We thus have a category $\mathrm{Strat}(G)$ whose objects are 0-positions, and morphisms are pairs of a 1-position and a strategy for it.

In the case of our running example G_{HO}, this new category fits with the "classical" one, up to the fact that we also consider non empty plays as objects in the new category.

Theorem 2. *The map sending an arena to the corresponding initial play yields a full embedding $\mathrm{Strat}_{HO} \longrightarrow \mathrm{Strat}(G_{HO})$.*

Next, we show that two crucial properties of strategies are stable under composition. A strategy is *deterministic* iff it does not contain two plays ending on an even position and sharing all their proper prefixes.

Proposition 4. *The composition of deterministic 1-strategies is again deterministic.*

A play is *final* in a strategy S when it has no extension in S. A strategy is *complete* iff its final plays all end on an even position. In other words, a complete strategy is one which never gets stuck. However, this definition is a bit loose w.r.t. potential infinite plays. Indeed, a complete strategy may contain infinite plays, and the composition of two complete strategies may not be complete. Intuitively, it may get lost in infinite internal "chattering" between M_1 and M_2. Thus, we refine the picture as follows. We deem a strategy *noetherian* iff it contains only finite plays, and *winning* iff it is noetherian and complete. This yields the following:

Proposition 5. *The composition of two winning 1-strategies is again winning.*

The previous notion of a winning strategy is not totally satisfactory. For instance, we would like copycat strategies to be winning. This somehow forces to consider some kind of non noetherian strategies. Anyway, we also wish to handle infinite plays in the spirit of Abramsky [1], but this is beyond the scope of the present work.

5   Conclusion

We have designed a notion of game theory. This is not one more category whose objects are new kinds of arenas. Rather we have shown how to build such a category from a very minimal set of data: a (one-way) category and two sets of morphisms therein. We have sketched how our composition of strategies has the desired stability properties (but we did not consider innocence). We hope that our framework will help in the design of new, helpful game semantics. We believe that it can be extended in various ways in order to encompass most of existing game semantics, and plan to explore some of these extensions in the near future.

Acknowledgements. We thank Vincent Danos for having advised the first author's PhD thesis, Pierre-Louis Curien for his constant benevolence and assistance, and Martin Hyland for encouraging us to write the present work.

References

1. Abramsky, S.: Semantics and Logics of Computation, chapter Semantics of interaction, pp. 1–31. Cambridge University Press (1997)
2. Abramsky, S., Honda, K., McCusker, G.: A fully abstract game semantics for general references. In: Proceedings of the thirteenth annual symposium on Logic In Computer Science, pp. 334–344. IEEE Computer Society Press, Los Alamitos (1998)

3. Abramsky, S., Jagadeesan, R., Malacaria, P.: Full abstraction for PCF. Information and Computation 163(2), 409–470 (2000)
4. Abramsky, S., McCusker, G.: Full abstraction for Idealized Algol with passive expressions. Theoretical Computer Science 227, 3–42 (1999)
5. Abramsky, S., Melliés, P.-A.: Concurrent games and full completeness. In: Proceedings of the fourteenth annual symposium on Logic In Computer Science, pp. 431–442. IEEE Computer Society Press, Los Alamitos (1999)
6. Cockett, R., Seely, R.: Polarized category theory, modules, and game semantics. Theory and Applications of Categories 18, 4–101 (2007)
7. Danos, V., Regnier, L.: The structure of multiplicatives. Archive for Mathematical Logic 28, 181–203 (1989)
8. Harmer, R.: Games and Full Abstraction for Nondeterministic Languages. Ph.D. thesis, Imperial College and University of London (1999)
9. Harmer, R.: Innocent game semantics, Course notes (2005)
10. Harmer, R., Hyland, M., Melliés, P.-A.: Categorical combinatorics for innocent strategies. Technical report, Paris 7 University (2007)
11. Hirschowitz, M.: Jeux abstraits et composition catégorique. Thèse de doctorat, Université Paris VII (2004)
12. Hyland, M., Ong, L.: On full abstraction for PCF. Information and Computation 163(2), 285–408 (2000)
13. Laird, J.: Full abstraction for functional languages with control. In: Proceedings of the twelfth annual symposium on Logic In Computer Science, pp. 58–67. IEEE Computer Society Press, Los Alamitos (1997)
14. Laurent, O.: Sémantique des jeux. Course notes (Paris VII) (2004)
15. Melliés, P.-A.: Double categories: a modular model of multiplicative linear logic. Mathematical Structures in Computer Science 12, 449–479 (2002)

An Incremental Bisimulation Algorithm

Diptikalyan Saha

Motorola India Research Lab, Bangalore, India
diptikalyan@motorola.com

Abstract. The notion of bisimulation has been used in various fields including Modal Logic, Set theory, Formal Verification, and XML indexing. In this paper we present the first algorithm for incremental maintenance of maximum bisimulation relation of a graph with respect to changes in the graph. Given a graph, its maximum bisimulation relation, and the changes in the graph, we determine the maximum bisimulation relation with respect to the changed graph by computing the changes in the given bisimulation relation. When the change in the graph induces small changes in the maximum bisimulation relation, our incremental algorithm is able to update the bisimulation relation on average an order of magnitude faster than the fastest available non-incremental algorithm. Preliminary experiments demonstrate the effectiveness of our algorithm. Our algorithm finds extensive use in verification where the specification changes over time, and XML indexing in database where the index structure, obtained by bisimulation on XML graph structure, needs to be maintained with respect to changes in the XML documents.

1 Introduction

The notion of bisimulation equivalence is important in many fields such as Modal Logic, Concurrency Theory, Set Theory, Formal Verification, XML Indexing, and Game Theory. Informally, a pair of automata M, M' are said to be bisimilar if for every transition in M there exists a corresponding transition in M' and vice versa. Milner and Park [15] introduced this notion in Concurrency theory for testing observational equivalence in CCS. Van Benthem [3] used it as an equivalence principal between Kripke Structures. Bisimulation in its various forms like strong or weak has also been used for checking equivalence between finite and infinite transition systems [9]. Verification systems such as the Spin [11], Concurrency Workbench of the New Century (CWB-NC) [5] and CADP [4] incorporate bisimulation checkers in their tool sets. In the area of formal verification, the notion of bisimulation has been primarily used to minimize the state space of the system's description which serves as an important factor in compositional and non-compositional model checking.

Many systems where bisimulation is used are *dynamic* in nature. For example, XML documents are indexed by its minimum bisimilar equivalent graph. As XML documents are updated in the database, their indices need to be updated too. In the area of verification, software systems undergoing verification evolve as a result of bug fixes and requirement changes. Similarly, specifications of security protocols and hardware designs required for verification are also changed over time. However, most of the verification

V. Arvind and S. Prasad (Eds.): FSTTCS 2007, LNCS 4855, pp. 204–215, 2007.

systems use their techniques as a whole on the changed input. They do not consider the changes in the input, although in many cases the changes in the specification or software have small effect to the output. In these cases, incremental algorithms are a way to efficiently recompute the output with respect to the changes in the input.

In this paper, we present an incremental bisimulation algorithm which, given a graph G, its maximum bisimulation relation P, and the changes (ΔG) in the graph, updates the old bisimulation relation to compute the maximum bisimulation relation with respect to graph ($G \cup \Delta G$). To the best of our knowledge, this is the first algorithm which incrementally recomputes the maximum bisimulation relation.

Our algorithm is based on two algorithms for finding maximum bisimulation relation of a graph, viz. Paige Tarjan's algorithm [16] (abbreviated as PTA) and its recent improvement by Dovier et. al. [6] known as fast bisimulation algorithm or FBA. PTA and FBA solve relational coarsest partition problem which is equivalent to finding maximum bisimulation relation of a graph. We assume that the initial bisimulation relation (P) is computed by FBA. After the changes to the graph G, our algorithm tries to confine the over-approximation that can occur while recomputing P.

The rest of the paper is organized as follows. We formally define the notion of bisimulation and present an overview of PTA and FBA in Section 2. We present our incremental bisimulation algorithm in Section 3. Section 4 demonstrates the effectiveness of the incremental algorithms. We compare the various strategies used by our algorithm with other incremental algorithms in Section 5. We conclude with some direction of future work in Section 6.

2 Preliminaries

In this section we formally describe the notion of bisimulation equivalence and its relation to the *relational coarsest partition problem* (abbreviated as RCPP). We also discuss an algorithm which is closest to our algorithm. Below we define the notion of bisimulation using a graph theoretic view.

Definition 1. *Given two graphs $G_1 = \langle N_1, E_1 \rangle$ and $G_2 = \langle N_2, E_2 \rangle$, a bisimulation between G_1 and G_2 is a relation $b \subseteq N_1 \times N_2$ such that:*

(1) $u_1 \, b \, u_2 \wedge \langle u_1, v_1 \rangle \in E_1 \Rightarrow \exists v_2 \in N_2(v_1 \, b \, v_2 \wedge \langle u_2, v_2 \rangle \in E_2)$
(2) $u_1 \, b \, u_2 \wedge \langle u_2, v_2 \rangle \in E_2 \Rightarrow \exists v_1 \in N_2(v_1 \, b \, v_2 \wedge \langle u_1, v_1 \rangle \in E_1)$

Given a graph G there can be many bisimulation relations between G and G. However, we are interested in the maximum bisimulation relation which is unique and always exists. Also the problem of recognizing if two graphs are bisimilar and the problem of determining the maximal bisimulation on a graph are equivalent.

The problem of our interest is that of finding minimum graph bisimilar to a given graph $G(N, E)$. This problem was studied by Kanellakis and Smolka [12] in connection with testing congruence of finite state processes in the calculus of communicating systems (CCS) [14]. They presented an algorithm requiring $O(|E|.|N|)$ time and $O(|E| + |N|)$ space. In [16] Paige and Tarjan solved the relational coarsest partition problem which is equivalent to the maximum bisimulation equivalence problem.

RCPP is described in terms of set theory. Let U be a finite set. A partition P of U is a set of pairwise disjoint subsets of U whose union is all of U. The elements of P are called its blocks. If P and Q are partitions of U, Q is a refinement of P if every block of Q is contained in a block of P. The RCPP is defined as follows: given a partition P of U and a binary relation E on U, find the coarsest partition refinement Q of P such that for each pair of blocks B_1, B_2 of Q, either $B_1 \subseteq E^{-1}B_2$ or $B_1 \cap E^{-1}B_2 = \phi$ (in this case B_1 is called stable with respect to B_2).

Given a graph $G = \langle N, E \rangle$, if Q is a partition of its nodes N, we can obtain a bisimulation relation b as u b v iff $\exists B \in Q, \{u, v\} \subseteq B$. Also given a bisimulation relation (an equivalence relation) of G, the blocks of the stable partition Q are the equivalence classes. Finding maximum bisimulation of a graph thus corresponds to the finding coarsest partition of the set of nodes in the graph with respect to its edge relation [13].

Our incremental bisimulation algorithm is based on Paige-Tarjan's algorithm and its subsequent improvement by Dovier et. al in [6]. Below we give a brief overview of the algorithms presented in [16] and [6].

Paige Tarjan's Algorithm (PTA). PTA is motivated from the algorithm presented by Hopcroft [10] for solving the problem of minimization of the number of states in a given finite automaton which is equivalent to that of determining the coarsest partition problem stable with respect to a set of functions. Hopcroft's solution is based on *negative* strategy where in each step the blocks of the partition are split if they are not stable. Following this negative strategy which is normal in greatest fixed-point computation, PTA uses a primitive refinement operation called *split* which generalizes the split operation used in Hopcroft's algorithm. For any partition Q and subset $S \subseteq U$, the $split(S, Q)$ is refinement of Q obtained by replacing each block $B \in Q$ such that $B \cap E^{-1}S \neq \phi$ and $B - E^{-1}S \neq \phi$ by the two blocks $B \cap E^{-1}S$ and $B - E^{-1}S$.

However, a straightforward use of splitting strategy where in each step union of some of the blocks of the current partition is used as splitter, yields an algorithm whose time complexity is $O(|E| \cdot |N|)$. Thus the refined algorithm exploits the idea of Hopcroft's "process of smaller half" for better way to find splitters to attain worst-case time complexity $O(|E| log(|N|))$.

Algorithm. Given an initial partition P of U, the algorithm finds a coarsest stable partition Q of P. In addition to the current partition Q, another partition X is maintained such that Q is a partition of X, and Q is stable with respect to every block of X. Initially $Q = P$, and X is the partition containing U as its single block. The algorithm consists of repeating the following steps until $Q = X$.

Step 1: Find a block $S \in X$ that is not a block of Q.
Step 2: Find a block $B \in Q$ such that $B \subseteq S$ and $|B| \leq |S|/2$. Replace S within X by the two sets B and $S - B$; replace Q by $split(S - B, split(B, Q))$.

Fast Bisimulation Algorithm. In [6] Dovier et. al. showed improvement over PTA. Their algorithm, known as FBA, reaches a linear worst case complexity for acyclic graph. They also showed the effectiveness of the algorithm for model checking packages. In the paper the authors proposed a strategy which uses positive ([17]) and negative strategies ([16]) to obtain algorithmic solution to RCPP. The algorithm has the same worst-case complexity as PTA. The initial partition is generated based on a notion of rank where *if two nodes are bisimilar, their ranks must be the same* (converse is not true). Thus using rank, the algorithm divides the graph to an over-approximate of the desired coarsest partition.

In the general case when the graph is not well-founded the ranking is done by SCC decomposition ([6]) of the graph using Kosaraju and Sharir's SCC computation algorithm [22]. To find SCCs in a graph G, the algorithm first traverses G^{-1}, the transpose of G, and gives post-order numbers to the vertices in G. Then it traverses G, starting from the vertex with the highest post-order number; this traversal builds a spanning tree for one SCC of G. Whenever the traversal ends, the algorithm begins a new traversal from the unvisited vertex with the highest post-order number, thereby building a spanning tree for another SCC. This process continues until all vertices have been visited, enumerating all SCCs of G.

For each node n, let $c(n)$ denote the SCC containing node n. The idea is to separate the graph into well-founded and non well-founded parts. The boolean flag $WFlag(u)$ denotes whether the node u is well-founded. The well-founded part $(WF(G))$ is defined as the collection of nodes in G whose transitive closure is acyclic. The other nodes in graph form the non-well-founded part of the graph. Then ranking of each node is defined below.

Definition 2. *Let $G = (N, E)$ and its SCC decomposition graph is given by $G^{scc} = (N^{scc}, E^{scc})$. The rank for each node is defined as follows:*

$r(n) = 0$ *when n is a leaf in G [Case 1]*
$r(n) = -1$ *when $c(n)$ is a leaf in G^{scc} and n is not a leaf of G [Case 2]*
$r(n) = max(\{1 + r(m) : \langle c(n), c(m) \rangle \in E^{scc}, m \in WF(G)$ *[Case 3.1]*$\}$
$\quad\quad \cup \{r(m) : \langle c(n), c(m) \rangle \in E^{scc}, m \notin WF(G)$ *[Case 3.2]*$\})$

At each stratum defined by the ranking strategy, the algorithm uses PTA or Paige-Tarjan-Bonic algorithm ([17]) to refine the stratum. Then it uses the blocks of this stratum to refine the blocks of higher ranked strata using split operation.

We now present an existing work in incremental bisimulation where an incremental algorithm for maintaining XML structural indices is presented ([25]). The initial index graph is computed using PTA applied to the data graph (XML structure). When addition/deletion of edges are done in the data graph an incremental algorithm which consist of a Split phase followed by a Merge phase is applied to update the index graph. Our incremental algorithm has similar Split and Merge phases. However, one of disadvantage of their incremental algorithm is that it does not compute the coarsest partition when the data graph is cyclic. Thus in a general sense the algorithm is not an incremental bisimulation algorithm as it does not maintain maximum bisimulation. Instead it maintains a partition called maximal bisimulation which coincides with the maximum bisimulation when the data graph is acyclic. The authors have mentioned that in case of maintaining XML structural indices, where most XML structures are acyclic, their algorithm produces the minimum index. Another drawback of their algorithm is that they do not take advantage of FBA when the graph is acyclic which is almost the case for XML data graph.

3   Incremental Bisimulation Algorithm

In this section we present our Split-Merge-Split (SMS) algorithms for incremental maintenance of relational coarsest partition. A non-incremental strategy can incorporate any changes in the graph by recomputing its coarsest partition again using the FBA [6] (from-scratch algorithm). However, such re-computation is often wasteful as small changes to the graph can potentially result into small changes to its coarsest partition. As a result, the entire coarsest partition need not be recomputed. The aim of our incremental algorithms is to identify the parts of the existing coarsest partition that need to be changed, and recompute them.

As the name suggests, the SMS algorithms have three phases, although in some cases the last split phase is not required. Let G be the initial input graph and G' be the new graph after the changes and their corresponding relational coarsest partitions are given as X and X'. Also after Split, Merge, and Split phases of the SMS algorithm, the corresponding partitions obtained be X_1, X_2, and X_3. We use small letters to denote nodes and capital letters to denote blocks, $block(u)$ to denote the block which has the node u, $\rightarrow$ to denote the edge relation among nodes, and $\Rightarrow$ is the edge relation among blocks where an $U \Rightarrow V$ iff $\exists u \rightarrow v$, $block(u) = U$, and $block(v) = V$. We use the notation $\neg U \Rightarrow V$ to denote that no block edge exists from U to V.

Our single edge addition algorithm SMS-ADD is shown in Figure 1(e). Initially the algorithm checks whether there already exists a block edge between $block(u)$ and $block(v)$ in which case the addition of $u \rightarrow v$ has no effect. The first Split phase of our algorithm is realized using the function RankedSplit (Lines 6, 66-74). The algorithm is same as the iterative split strategy of PTA, the only difference being the blocks for splits are chosen in increasing order of ranks. The partition X_1 obtained after the split phase is characterized using the following Lemma.

Lemma 1. *If two nodes are not bisimilar in G' i.e. they belong to different blocks in X', then they belong to the different blocks of X_1.*

The Merge phase performs two operations. Firstly, it incrementally recomputes the ranks and well-founded flags of the nodes. Secondly, it merges the blocks of partition X_1 to obtain the partition X_2 which is characterized using the following Lemma.

Lemma 2. *If two nodes are bisimilar in G' i.e. they belong to same block in X', then they are in the same block of X_2.*

The $r'(u)$ and $WFlag'(u)$ represent the new values of the rank and well-founded flag of node u, respectively. When an edge is added between a non well-founded node and a well-founded node (Lines 9-11), the new rank of u is given by the expression in Line 9. Any changes in the rank of the non well-founded node is propagated to the non well-founded parts of the graph by the function propagate_nwf(u) which uses Sharir's SCC decomposition algorithm starting from node u. In contrast, the function propagate_wf(u) propagates the change in rank of a well-founded node u to the well-founded parts of the graph in a bottom-up fashion (using topological order of non-updated ranks) and if necessary propagates any changes to the ranks of non-well founded nodes by calling function propagate_nwf. The details of these two functions are not provided in this paper.

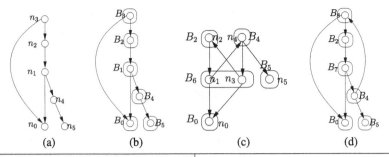

(a)   (b)   (c)   (d)

```
 1 SMS-ADD(node u, node v)
 2 if (block(u) ⇒ block(v))
 3    return;
 4 Add the edge u → v to G
 5
 6 RankedSplit(block(v))
 7
 8 if ¬WFlag(u) and WFlag(v)
 9    r'(u) = max {r(u), r(v)+1}
10    if r'(u) ≠ r(u)
11       propagate_nwf(u)
12       MergePhase(block(u),block(v))
13 else
14    if r(u) > r(v)
15       MergePhase(block(u),block(v))
16    else
17       Bu = block(u), Bv = block(v)
18       Visit blocks starting from u in
19       G⁻¹ between blocks of ranks
20       r(u) and r(v). Mark each block
21       B as visited(B). Note whether
22       it reaches Bv to form a cycle.
23       if cycle formed
24          WFlag'(u) = false
25          r'(u) = re-compute rank
26          propagate_nwf(u)
27          MergeAndSplitPhase()
28       else
29          if WFlag(u) = true
30             if WFlag(v) = true
31                r'(u) = r(v)+1
32                propagate_wf(u)
33             else
34                r'(u) = max{r(u),r(v)}
35                propagate_nwf(u)
36          else
37             r'(u) = r(v)
38             if r'(u) ≠ r(u)
39                propagate_nwf(u)
40          MergePhase(Bu,Bv)
41
42 propagate_wf(u)
43    Recompute ranks of successor
44    of u based on priority of their
45    old ranks [in bottom-up order]
46    and propagate recursively
```

```
48 MergePhase(block U, block V)
49    ∀U1,U1 ⇒ V
50       if MergeCond(U1,U)
51          rec_merge(U1,U)
52
53 rec_merge(B1, B2)
54    merge the blocks B1 and B2
55    ∀C1,C1 ⇒ B1, ∀C2,C2 ⇒ B2
56       if (MergeCond(C1,C2))
57          rec_merge(C1,C2)
58
59 MergeCond(B1,B2)
60    B1 and B2 are not mergeable
61    if label(B1) ≠ label(B2)
62    ∨ B1 = B2
63    ∨ r(B1) ≠ r(B2)
64    ∨ ∃ a causal-splitter of B1 and B2
65
66 RankedSplit(block B)
67    X=P, Q=P
68    % P is the current partition
69    split(B,Q);
70    Until Q=X
71       Perform two steps of PTA
72       with Step 1: choosing S
73       with minimum rank from X that
74       is not a block of Q
75
76 MergeAndSplitPhase()
77    % Merge phase
78    Perform DFS on G in order of
79    decreasing finishing times of
80    the last DFS.
81    During the DFS Merge the blocks
82    visited using the non-merging
83    condition as MergeCond and
84    recursively propagate merge as
85    shown in function rec_merge
86    All the blocks in traversed
87    are put in one X partition
88    % Split Phase
89    Perform PTA in X partition
90    and propagate any split using
91    RankedSplit
92
93 propagate_nwf(u)
94    Perform SCC finding algorithm from
95    node u to re-compute non
96    Well-Founded ranks
```

(e)

Fig. 1. Example 1 (a, b, c, d); (e) Incremental Addition Algorithm

Note that, the case in Lines 11-13 is the only case where only well-founded flags determine that a new SCC creation is not possible due to addition of the edge, which is also true when $r(u) > r(v)$ (Line 15). In all other cases, the algorithm performs a DFS traversal (Lines 17-22) on G^{-1} to know whether an SCC is formed due to addition of the edge. If the SCC is formed, the algorithm recomputes the rank of the node u based on well-founded flags and ranks of its predecessors using Definition 2. Otherwise, the ranks of the nodes are updated as shown in Lines 29-40. For example, if u and v are both well-founded and $r(u) \leq r(v)$, then $u \rightarrow v$ addition increases the $r(u)$ to $r(v) + 1$ (follows from Case 3.1 of Definition 2). The change is propagated using function propagate_wf(u). The other two cases follow from the Case 3.2 of Definition 2.

The aim of finding new SCC is based on two important reasons, (i) two different merge algorithms are needed based on whether a new SCC is created, and (ii) the last split phase is not required when no new SCC is formed.

When no new SCC is formed, the Merge phase (Function MergePhase) of the algorithm considers each of the predecessor blocks of $block(v)$ to merge with $block(u)$. The intuition of this merge is as follows: due to the absence of $u \rightarrow v$, a predecessor block of $block(v)$, say $U1$, which contained u got split into $V1 = U1 \cap E^{-1}\{block(v)\}$ and $block(u)$ using $block(v)$ as splitter. Thus after addition of $u \rightarrow v$, the algorithm needs to reform $U1$ by merging $V1$ and $block(u)$. Due to this merge, their predecessor blocks may also get merged. However, it is not always possible to merge two blocks B and B' as the blocks need to have the same labels and ranks (in the updated graph). Also if there exists a block C which has a predecessor block same as exactly one of blocks B and B' then blocks B and B' should not be merged (see Function MergeCond). The block C is called causal-splitter of the blocks B and B', and is formally defined below.

Definition 3 (Candidates for causal-splitter). *A block C is called a causal-splitter of block B and B', if*

- $B \Rightarrow C$ *and* $\neg B' \Rightarrow C$, *or* $B' \Rightarrow C$ *and* $\neg B \Rightarrow C$.
- C *is a block in the partition* X'.

When no new SCC is created due to the addition of the edge, the second condition of the causal-splitter trivially holds as the blocks are merged from lower ranked strata to higher ranked strata, and causal splitters are chosen from already stabled lower ranked strata. However, in general, the causal-splitter block may get affected due to the transitive effect of merging blocks B and B'. If due to the propagation of merging of B and B', C gets merged with C', then the condition of having predecessor block edge to exactly one B and B' may no longer hold. This is only possible when addition of edge creates a new SCC in the updated graph, in which case judicious selection of causal-splitters is required, a case explained in more detail with the following example.

Consider the graph in Figure 1(a) with labeling set $\{\{n_0\}, \{n_1, n_3, n_5\}, \{n_2, n_4\}\}$, initial partition in Figure 1(b), and addition of a new edge $n_4 \rightarrow n_3$. As the rank of n_4 is 1 and that of n_3 is 4, an SCC can be potentially formed because of the addition.

In the first split phase, as block B_4 only contains a single node, it is not split. The split phase ends here as no further splits are possible. The first DFS traversal of blocks from $block(u)$ in G^{-1} till the ranked stratum containing $block(v)$ (in this case blocks B_1, B_2, B_3, B_4) confirms creation of a new SCC. Next, the ranks of the nodes n_1, n_2, n_3, n_4 are updated to 1. Then the function MergeAndSplitPhase determines the new SCC in the second DFS on G. At the finish time of second DFS of each block, it is tried to merge it with other visited blocks of the SCC. For each label a list of blocks with that label is maintained where the blocks cannot be merged with each other. Firstly, B_1 is put to label-1 list. Then, B_2 is put to the label-2 list. Next, B_3 is considered for merging with B_1 as it has the same label as B_1. Note that, $B_1 \Rightarrow B_2$ and $\neg B_3 \Rightarrow B_2$, and $B_1 \Rightarrow B_4$ and $\neg B_3 \Rightarrow B_4$. But as B_2 and B_4 are marked during the first DFS visit, each of them can be potentially merged to some other visited blocks and thus can be potentially changed. For example, blocks B_2 and B_4 can be potentially merged and in that case none of them should be used as a causal-splitter. Thus B_3 and B_1 are merged to obtain a block B_6. However, as there exist blocks that can be potential causal-splitters, we are introducing over-approximation in the merge phase.

The above discussion hints at a strategy for selecting a causal splitter which preserves the second condition of causal-splitter. A block is selected as causal-splitter if it is *not visited* in the first DFS as it is not going to be affected because of the addition. This is the case when the next block B_4 is considered for merging. Although it has same label as B_2, due to the existence of the causal-splitter B_5 it is not merged with B_2. The resultant partition is shown in Figure 1(c). Although not shown in this example, the effect of merging two blocks may lead to merging of their predecessors blocks in the unvisited region of first DFS.

It can be proved that in case where an addition of an edge to a graph does not create a cycle, we do not require the last split phase of SMS algorithm. The reason is that the merging done in merge phase is not an over-approximation. In general, the merge phase can cause over-approximation of merging which is rectified in the last split phase. The PTA is run on those visited blocks and propagate the splits strata-by-strata. The final partition is shown in Figure 1(d). The below theorem expresses the correctness of the algorithm.

Theorem 1. *The partitions X_3 and X' are equal.*

Single Edge Deletion: The single edge deletion algorithm (SMS-DEL) has the similar Split, Merge, Split phases like the SMS-ADD algorithm. They differ only in the rank re-computation part and in the merging phase where after recomputing ranks if a block's rank is changed to 0, it is merged with the other block of rank 0.

Consider deletion of the edge $n_4 \rightarrow n_5$ after addition of edge $n_4 \rightarrow n_3$ in example in Figure 1(a). The first split phase is ineffective. In the merge phase, Sharir's SCC computation algorithm is performed to update any rank, and merge all the blocks in the same rank as u and reachable to u. Note that unlike in the case of addition, the blocks of nodes n_1 and n_3, n_2 and n_4 are merged as the connection to the causal-splitter block is deleted. This also serves as an example where the resultant partition of the merging phase is the final partition.

Our SMS algorithm can be adapted to multiple edge addition and deletion, subgraph addition and deletion, and update. These algorithms have the same three phases and DFS traversal where each phase and DFS traversal need to be done for *all changes* before starting processing of other phases. The main difference lies in the computation of ranks. Due to want of space we do not discuss these algorithms here.

Complexity. The complexity of the first split phase, rank re-computation, merge phase, last split phase are $O(|E_1|log(|N_1|)$, $O(|\Delta_{WF}|log(|\Delta_{WF}|) + (|E_{nwf}| + |N_{nwf}|))$, and

$O(|E'||N'|)$, and $O(|E'|log(|N'|))$ respectively. In the above expressions Δ_{WF} is the set of well-founded nodes whose ranks got changed, (N_1, E_1) and (N', E') are the subgraph of the initial graph $G = (N, E)$ whose blocks got split and merged respectively, and (N_{nwf}, E_{nwf}) is the non-well founded subgraph of G.

4   Experimental Results

We measured the performance of our algorithms by implementing those on top of the source code available from one of the author's website of [6]. The data structures used in their implementation was not changed. We ran our algorithms on benchmarks mentioned in various works for measuring effectiveness of bisimulation problems. Performance measurements were taken on a PC with 1.4Ghz Intel Core Duo processor with 512MB of physical memory running Windows XP.

We present the performance result of our insertion and deletion algorithm on the synthetic benchmarks described below. Each benchmark has different characteristics which have different effects on our algorithm. In these two benchmarks, we noted the average (over all edges) incremental deletion and insertion time as percentage of from-scratch time to be 10%. The results below will highlight the range of these timing results and reason for such distribution. We used an extra priority queue data structure apart from the data structure of FBA implementation, but it uses the memory of FBA. So our algorithm does not incur any extra memory overhead compared to FBA.

Benchmark 1. *Simple Binary Tree.* This benchmark (Benchmark 2 of [6]) consists of a binary tree with 262143 nodes and has two different labels for left and right subtree as shown in Figure 2(a) with node numbers and initial blocks. The initial FBA time is 0.3s. The height of each node gives the ranks. We added one edge and took the incremental time, and compared it with the time taken by FBA for the changed graph. We also show the time for SMS-DEL to delete the added edge. Thus SMS-DEL was not tried on Benchmark 1 but on a graph that results after an added edge to the benchmark. We provide the edges which showed the minimum and maximum time taken by SMS-ADD for three different cases based on relation of ranks and whether the added edge produces

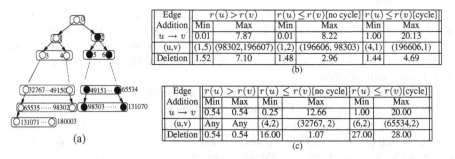

(a)

(b)

Edge	$r(u) > r(v)$		$r(u) \leq r(v)$[no cycle]		$r(u) \leq r(v)$[cycle]	
Addition	Min	Max	Min	Max	Min	Max
$u \rightarrow v$	0.01	7.87	0.01	8.22	1.00	20.13
(u,v)	(1,5)	(98302,196607)	(1,2)	(196606, 98303)	(4,1)	(196606,1)
Deletion	1.52	7.10	1.48	2.96	1.44	4.69

(c)

Edge	$r(u) > r(v)$		$r(u) \leq r(v)$[no cycle]		$r(u) \leq r(v)$[cycle]	
Addition	Min	Max	Min	Max	Min	Max
$u \rightarrow v$	0.54	0.54	0.25	12.66	1.00	20.00
(u,v)	Any	Any	(4,2)	(32767, 2)	(6,2)	(65534,2)
Deletion	0.54	0.54	16.00	1.07	27.00	28.00

Fig. 2. (a) Benchmark 1. Tree; (b) & (c) Incremental times as % or From-scratch times for Benchmark 1 and 2 respectively

a new cycle or not. The result is shown in Figure 2(b). As expected SMS-ADD takes maximum time in case the addition of edge creates cycles. Most of time in this case is attributed to the Merge phase. Note that localized addition yields lesser time than the non-local changes.

Benchmark 2. This benchmark is a downward closed tree (Test 2 of [7]) of 65535 nodes obtained by closing downward a binary tree using the rule: if $\langle m, n \rangle$ and $\langle n, p \rangle$ are edges then add a new edge $\langle n, p \rangle$ and two different labels are put to the alternate nodes in each ranked strata of the tree. The initial FBA time is 0.5s. The result for this benchmark is shown in the Figure 2(c). Note that addition of edge $\langle 65534 \rightarrow 2 \rangle$ takes 20% of from-scratch time and this time is spent on MergeCond function which checks for causal splitter which in turn is due to large number of out-degree of each node. When deletion occurs for the same edge, it takes 28% times of the from-scratch time. Deletion of edge (65534,2) will first merge the block of node 65534 with the blocks which consists of rest of even numbered nodes in rank 0. To propagate the effect of this merging the rec_merge function checks all nodes which are predecessors of the nodes in the block of rank 0. As there are large number of such edges to be considered the Merge phase takes large amount of time. This high overhead of Merge phase is attributed to the data structure selection in our implementation. If we keep block edges in our implementation then merge time is reduced; however, in that case Split phase time is increased. We use memoization technique to reduce some overhead for not having the block edges.

The above benchmark in-fact serves as an extreme case of overhead of the merge phase for single change. In most of VLTS benchmarks ([4]) the in-degree and out-degree of nodes are comparably less than this benchmark. On average the SMS algorithm took 3.94% of from-scratch time for VLTS benchmark vasy_386_1171 on 400 random deletion of edges. For 400 random insertion of edges (for each case one edge was not loaded initially and has been incrementally added), the SMS algorithm took 6.93% of from-scratch time for the same benchmark.

We note that for multiple changes in the graph which affect independent parts of the initial partition, the overhead of the merge phase can accumulate to exceed the from-scratch time. Thus it is not possible for our incremental algorithms to perform always better than the from-scratch algorithm when multiple changes are present.

5   Related Work

An important characteristic of incremental bisimulation problem is that adding or deleting an edge in the input graph can potentially result in splitting and merging of blocks in the partition. Thus incremental bisimulation problem is non-monotonic in nature. This is in contrast to the incremental algorithms in many works in view maintenance ([8]), logic programming ([18]), model checking ([23]), where the effect of addition and deletion is monotonic in nature. The problem is also different in nature to incremental functional programming ([1]) where changes can be propagated using in-place updates. Also incremental bisimulation problem cannot be reduced to incremental evaluation of logic programs with stratified negation as the nature of non-monotonism in incremental bisimulation resembles to non-stratified negation in logic programming. The only work we are aware of incremental evaluation of logic programs with non-stratified negation is in [20]. The logic program encoding ([2]) of bisimulation involves a builtin *findall* and with our earlier experience showed that the incremental algorithms do not produce great efficiency when builtins exist.

The idea of having different phases to overapproximate or underapproximate fixpoint before converging to the new fixpoint is not new. Generally in incremental least fix-point (positive strategy) computation, the first phase is a deletion phase (or negative strategy) which is used to bring the incrementally computed fix-point equal or below the final fixpoint, and second phase is used to converge to the final fixpoint ([8,18,23]). For incremental greatest fixpoint computation (negative strategy) the first phase uses the positive phase which is used to bring the current fixpoint above the final fixpoint point ([24]) in the fix-point lattice. In our case, as the from-scratch algorithm (FBA) uses split which is a negative strategy; a positive (merge) followed by a negative strategy (split) will suffice. However, we have incorporated a split phase before the merge-split phase to reduce the size of the blocks that are merged as merge operation is expensive.

We have used several strategies like labels, ranks, and causal splitter to reduce the overapproximation done in the merge phase. The ranks define regions such that blocks can only be merged within each region. The idea of regions is used in other incremental algorithms ([21]) where it is typically used to nullify effect of additions and deletions in each region before propagating the effect to other regions. The idea of finding causal-splitter which is not cyclically dependent on the blocks to be merged to restrict merge propagation is similar to the idea of primary and acyclic support used for restricting deletion propagation in incremental pointer analysis ([19]).

6   Conclusion

In this paper we presented an incremental algorithm to recompute maximum bisimulation relation. We demonstrated the effectiveness of the algorithm on several graph examples. In future we will incorporate our implementation to model checkers and XML database management system. The SMS algorithm presented here *globally* recomputes bisimulation relation. We plan to extend our solution to local bisimulation computation, and to infinite and symbolic graph structure.

Acknowledgment

We thank anonymous reviewers, Prof. Ranjit Jhala, Anu Singh, and C. Manjari for their comments to improve the quality of this paper. We are also grateful to Prof. C. R. Ramakrishnan and Dr. Subir Saha for encouraging this work.

References

1. Acar, U.A., Blelloch, G.E., Harper, R.: Adaptive functional programming. In: ACM POPL, New York, NY, USA, vol. 37, pp. 247–259. ACM Press, New York (2002)
2. Basu, S., Mukund, M., Ramakrishnan, C.R., Ramakrishnan, I.V., Verma, R.M.: Local and symbolic bisimulation using tabled constraint logic programming. In: Codognet, P. (ed.) ICLP 2001. LNCS, vol. 2237, pp. 166–180. Springer, Heidelberg (2001)

3. Benthem, J.V.: Modal Correspondence Theory. PhD thesis, University van Amsterdam (1976)
4. CADP. Caesar/aldebran developement package c1.112, Available at (2001), http://www.inrialpes.fr/vasy/cadp.html
5. CWB-NC. The concurrency workbench of new century v1.1.1, Available at (2001), http://www.cs.sunysb.edu/~cwb
6. Dovier, A., Piazza, C., Policriti, A.: An efficient algorithm for computing bisimulation equivalence. Theor. Comput. Sci. 311(1-3), 221–256 (2004)
7. Dovier, A., Piazza, C., Policriti, A., Ugel, N.: A fast bisimulation algorithm: Test, http://www.dimi.uniud.it/~piazza/bisim/web.ps
8. Gupta, A., Mumick, I.S., Subrahmanian, V.S.: Maintaining views incrementally. In: ACM SIGMOD, pp. 157–166 (1993)
9. Hennessy, M., Lin, H.: Symbolic bisimulations. Theor. Comput. Sci. 138(2), 353–389 (1995)
10. Hopcroft, J.E.: An $nlogn$ algorithm for minimizing states in a finite automaton. In: Theory of Machines and Computations, pp. 189–196. Academic Press, London (1971)
11. Hudson, S.E.: Incremental attribute evaluation: a flexible algorithm for lazy update. ACM Transaction of Programming Languages and Systems 13(3), 315–341 (1991)
12. Kanellakis, P.C., Smolka, S.A.: CCS expressions, finite state processes, and three problems of equivalence. In: PODS, pp. 228–240. ACM Press, New York (1983)
13. Kanellakis, P.C., Smolka, S.A.: CCS expressions finite state processes, and three problems of equivalence. Inf. Comput. 86(1), 43–68 (1990)
14. Milner, R.: A Calculus of Communicating Systems, Secaucus, NJ, USA. Springer, Heidelberg (1982)
15. Milner, R.: Operational and algebraic semantics of concurrent processes, 1201–1242 (1990)
16. Paige, R., Tarjan, R.E.: Three partition refinement algorithms. SIAM J. Comput. 16(6), 973–989 (1987)
17. Paige, R., Tarjan, R.E., Bonic, R.: A linear time solution to the single function coarsest partition problem. Theor. Comput. Sci. 40, 67–84 (1985)
18. Saha, D., Ramakrishnan, C.R.: Incremental evaluation of tabled logic programs. In: Palamidessi, C. (ed.) ICLP 2003. LNCS, vol. 2916, pp. 389–406. Springer, Heidelberg (2003)
19. Saha, D., Ramakrishnan, C.R.: Incremental and demand-driven points-to analysis using logic programming. In: ACM Conference on Principles and Practice of Declarative Programming, ACM Press, New York (2005)
20. Saha, D., Ramakrishnan, C.R.: Incremental evaluation of tabled prolog: Beyond pure logic programs. In: Van Hentenryck, P. (ed.) PADL 2006. LNCS, vol. 3819, pp. 215–229. Springer, Heidelberg (2005)
21. Saha, D., Ramakrishnan, C.R.: A local algorithm for incremental evaluation of logic programs. In: Etalle, S., Truszczyński, M. (eds.) ICLP 2006. LNCS, vol. 4079, pp. 56–71. Springer, Heidelberg (2006)
22. Sharir, M.: A strong connectivity algorithm and its application in data flow analysis. Computer and Mathematics with Applications 7(1), 67–72 (1981)
23. Sokolsky, O.V., Smolka, S.A.: Incremental model checking in the modal mu-calculus. In: Dill, D.L. (ed.) CAV 1994. LNCS, vol. 818, pp. 351–363. Springer, Heidelberg (1994)
24. Swamy, G.: Incremental Methods for Formal Verification and Logic Synthesis. PhD thesis, University of California at Berkeley (1996)
25. Yi, K., He, H., Stanoi, I., Yang, J.: Incremental maintenance of XML structural indexes. In: SIGMOD, pp. 491–502. ACM Press, New York (2004)

Logspace Algorithms for Computing Shortest and Longest Paths in Series-Parallel Graphs

Andreas Jakoby[*] and Till Tantau

Inst. für Theoretische Informatik, Universität zu Lübeck, Germany
{jakoby,tantau}@tcs.uni-luebeck.de

Abstract. For many types of graphs, including directed acyclic graphs, undirected graphs, tournament graphs, and graphs with bounded independence number, the shortest path problem is NL-complete. The longest path problem is even NP-complete for many types of graphs, including undirected K_5-minor-free graphs and planar graphs. In the present paper we present logspace algorithms for computing shortest and longest paths in series-parallel graphs where the edges can be directed arbitrarily. The class of series-parallel graphs that we study can be characterized alternatively as the class of K_4-minor-free graphs and also as the class of graphs of tree-width 2. It is well-known that for graphs of bounded tree-width many intractable problems can be solved efficiently, but previous work was focused on finding algorithms with low parallel or sequential *time complexity*. In contrast, our results concern the *space complexity* of shortest and longest path problems. In particular, our results imply that for directed graphs of tree-width 2 these problems are L-complete.

Keywords: Series-parallel graphs, logspace algorithms, distance problem, longest path problem, bounded tree-width, K_4-minor-free graphs.

1 Introduction

Series-parallel graphs form an extensively-studied class of graphs that has applications both in theory and in practice. Different types of series-parallel graphs have been studied in the literature; in the present paper we study their most general form, namely series-parallel graphs with an arbitrary number of terminals and with edges having arbitrary directions. There are two well-known alternative characterization, see for instance [5,13], of this class of graphs: First, it is also the class of directed graphs of tree-width at most 2. Second, it is also the class of directed graphs whose underlying undirected graph is K_4-minor-free.

For this class of graphs we study the longest and the shortest path problems. We are given an element G of the class as input together with two nodes s and t and we are asked to output a path (which may consist only of distinct nodes) of minimal or maximal length from s to t in G. For general graphs, the shortest path problem is well-known to be NL-complete, while the longest path problem is

---

[*] Part of this work was done while visiting the University of Frankfurt and the University of Freiburg, Germany.

V. Arvind and S. Prasad (Eds.): FSTTCS 2007, LNCS 4855, pp. 216–227, 2007.

Table 1. The complexity of path problems for different graph classes. In this present paper we investigate series-parallel graphs, which are the same as directed graphs of tree-width 2, and prove the results shown in bold. By "open" we mean that no nontrivial upper bounds are known.

Graph class	Reachability	Distance	Longest path	Number of paths
Digraphs of tree-width 1	L-compl.	L-compl.	L-compl.	L-compl.
Digraphs of tree-width 2	**L-compl.**	**L-compl.**	**L-compl.**	**L-compl.**
Digraphs of tree-width k, $k \geq 3$	open	open	$\in AC^1$	$\in AC^2$
Planar digraphs	$\in UL$	open	NP-compl.	#P-compl.
Tournament graphs	$\in AC^0$	NL-compl.	open	open
Undirected graphs	L-compl.	NL-compl.	NP-compl.	#P-compl.
Acyclic digraphs	NL-compl.	NL-compl.	NL-compl.	#L-compl.
Digraphs	NL-compl.	NL-compl.	NP-compl.	#P-compl.

NP-complete even for planar graphs. The different characterizations of the class of series-parallel graphs yields different insights into the complexity of the longest and shortest path problems for this particular class. Results from the theory of bounded tree-width tell us that the shortest path problem lies in the class NL and that the longest path problem lies in AC^1. Unfortunately, since it is only known that $NC^1 \subseteq L \subseteq NL \subseteq AC^1$, this does not tell us whether these problems can be solved in deterministic logspace. Results from the theory of series-parallel graphs tell us that conceptually simpler problems, like the reachability problem for directed two-terminal series-parallel graphs, lie in L.

The main result of the present paper, Theorem 5, lowers the upper bound on the complexity of shortest and longest path problems in directed graphs of tree-width 2 to L. At the same time, this result extends the previous complexity bounds on the reachability problem in directed two-terminal series-parallel graphs to the shortest and longest path problems in general multiple-terminal series-parallel graphs. Table 1 shows how these results relate to the complexity of shortest and longest path problems in other kinds of graphs. As can be seen in the table, for many types of graphs the distance problem is still NL-complete, including undirected graphs [7,23], directed acyclic graphs, tournament graphs [21], and graphs with bounded independence number [21].

Recently, it has been shown that the reachability problem is in L even for single source multiple sink planar DAGs [1]. If we restrict ourselves to planar digraphs, it is only known that the reachability problem lies in unambiguous logspace (i.e. $UL \cap co\text{-}UL$) [8].

Our formulation of the main result does not treat shortest and longest paths separately. Rather, we allow input graphs to be equipped with integer edge weights coded in unary (negative weights are indicated by a flag). We present a deterministic logspace algorithm with the following properties: On input of a directed graph with integer weights coded in unary and two nodes s and t, it either determines that the graph is not a multiple-terminal series-parallel graph or it determines that there is no path from s to t or it outputs a path from s to t of maximum total edge weight. Setting all edge weights to 1 makes a maximum-weight path a longest path and setting all edge weights to -1 makes a maximum-weight path a shortest path.

Graphs of tree-width 2. The tree-width of a graph is a measure of how close the graph is to being a tree and graphs of tree-width 1 are, indeed, trees. For a graph G of tree-width k there must exist a tree T whose nodes are labeled with so-called bags, which are just sets of up to $k + 1$ nodes of the graph G. For each edge of the graph at least one of the bags must contain both endpoints of the edge, and the set of all bags containing any given graph node must form a connected subtree of T.

Certain intractable graph problems become tractable if we restrict ourselves to graphs with small tree-width, see for instance [4,25], and the problem of constructing tree decompositions of small tree-width is a well-studied topic, see [3,6,20]. For graphs of bounded tree-width one can construct a tree decompositions of constant width in AC^1, as shown in [6], and using such a decomposition one can determine the distance and the longest path length between two nodes efficiently in parallel [10,11,17]: In detail, Chaudhuri and Zaroliagis [10,11] have presented sequential linear-time algorithms and an EREW-PRAM algorithm working in time $O(T(t, n) + \log n)$ for finding a shortest path, where $T(t, n)$ denotes the time for computing a tree-decomposition of digraphs of n nodes of tree-width t. In [6] Bodlaender and Hagerup presented an EREW-PRAM algorithm using $O(\log^2 n)$ time that generates a tree decomposition of constant width. They also show that all graph properties of a finite index can be decided by an $O(\log n \log^* n)$ time EREW-PRAM. While many problems, including Hamiltonicity and the reachability problem, are of finite index, distance and longest path problems are not. For example, the problem of deciding whether the distance between two given nodes is at most $n/2$ in a graph of size n does not have a finite index.

It is well known that parallel time complexity and space complexity are related: $NC^1 \subseteq L$ and all languages in L can be decided by an EREW-PRAM in time $O(\log n)$ with a polynomial number of processors. If we replace L by NL, we must replace EREW-PRAM by CRCW-PRAM. It is also known that $NL \subseteq LOGCFL = SAC^1$. However, it is not known whether $O(\log n)$-time-bounded EREW-PRAMs can be simulated by $O(\log n)$-space-bounded DTM.

K_4-minor-free graphs. Directed graphs of tree-width 2 can also be characterized as graphs whose underlying undirected graph does not contain the K_4 as a minor. This means we cannot obtain K_4 by forgetting the direction of the edges and then repeatedly contracting and deleting edges and deleting isolated nodes.

Defining classes of graphs by forbidden minors is a powerful tool in graph theory. For example, the undirected K_3-minor-free graphs are exactly the forests (every cycle in a graph can be contracted down to a K_3). Planar graphs can be characterized as the graphs that are both K_5- and $K_{3,3}$-minor-free. We prove results for graphs that are K_4-minor-free. A next major algorithmic step forward would be a logspace algorithm for the distance problem in graphs whose underlying undirected graph is K_5-minor-free. Such an algorithm would settle the challenging question of whether there is a logspace algorithm for the distance problem in planar graphs.

Series-parallel graphs. The third characterization of the graphs studied in this paper is the class of *mixed multiple-terminal series-parallel graphs*. More restricted versions are studied in the literature and we make use of these restricted versions in our proofs: In the proof of the main result we establish the existence of logspace algorithms for computing maximum-weight paths in more and more general forms of series-parallel graphs.

The simplest form are directed two-terminal series-parallel graphs. They are defined inductively, starting with the graph that consists of a single directed edge whose endpoints are called source terminal and sink terminal. Graphs can be composed in two ways: A serial composition fuses the sink of one graph with the source of another, a parallel composition fuses the two sources and also the two sinks of two graphs. Multiple-terminal series-parallel graphs are formed by taking a set of two-terminal series-parallel graphs and repeatedly fusing a terminal node with some node in one of the graphs.

For series-parallel graphs we can consider different possibilities for the direction of edges. For *directed* series-parallel graphs, once we choose a source and a sink terminal, the direction of all edges is also implied. Our algorithms do not only work for directed series-parallel graphs and for undirected series-parallel graphs, but also for the graphs obtained by arbitrarily redirecting the edges of a series-parallel graph. To distinguish the resulting type of graphs from directed series-parallel graphs, we will call them *mixed* series-parallel graphs.

The space complexity of problems related to series-parallel graphs has been analyzed in [19], where logspace algorithms for the recognition problem and for the reachability problem for directed two-terminal series-parallel graphs are presented. Furthermore, in the paper the problem of *decomposing* series-parallel graphs is studied. In [18], Jakoby and Liśkiewicz focus on the recognition, the reachability, and the decomposition problem for undirected series-parallel graphs and show that these problems can be solved in deterministic logspace using an SL oracle for reachability, which shows that decompositions can be computed in logspace. However, since reachability in directed graphs is NL-complete rather than SL-complete, the techniques presented in [18,19] fail for the mixed multiple-terminal series-parallel graphs that we consider in the present paper.

The time complexity of the recognition problem for series-parallel graphs has also been investigated in detail. An optimal linear-time sequential algorithm for this problem has been developed by Valdes, Tarjan, and Lawler [24] and fast parallel algorithms have been published. He and Yesha have presented an EREW-PRAM algorithm working in time $O(\log^2 n)$ while using $n + m$ processors [15]. Eppstein has reduced the time bound by constructing an algorithm that takes only $O(\log n)$ steps on the stronger CRCW-PRAM model and requires $C(m, n)$ processors [14], where $C(m, n)$ denotes the number of processors necessary to compute the connected components of a graph in logarithmic time. Finally, the

EREW-PRAM algorithm by Bodlaender and Antwerpen-de Fluiter [5] mentioned earlier also solves this problem in time $O(\log n \log^* n)$ using $O(n+m)$ operations.

2   Basic Definitions

A *graph* is a pair $G = (V, E)$ consisting of a *node set* V and an *edge set* E. A graph G is called a *directed graph* (or *digraph* for short) if $E \subseteq V \times V$ is a *set of directed edges*, G is called an *undirected graph* if $E \subseteq \{\{u, v\} \mid u, v \in V, u \neq v\}$ is a *set of undirected edges*, and G is called a *mixed graph* if $E \subseteq V \times V \cup \{\{u, v\} \mid u, v \in V, u \neq v\}$ is a *set of edges*, such that we do not have both $(u, v) \in E$ and $\{u, v\} \in E$ for any pair $u, v \in V$. A *weighted mixed graph* is a mixed graph (V, E) together with an *edge weight function* $w \colon E \to \mathbb{Z}$.

Given two nodes $u, v \in V$ of a mixed graph G, we write $u \to_G v$ if either $(u, v) \in E$ or $\{u, v\} \in E$. Given a mixed graph $G = (V, E)$, its *undirected underlying graph* $\mathrm{uug}(G)$ is obtained by replacing every directed edge by an undirected edge, that is, $\mathrm{uug}(G) = \big(V, \{\{u, v\} \mid u \to_G v, u \neq v\} \big)$.

A *path* in a graph G is a sequence $(v_0, \ldots, v_\ell)$ of *distinct* nodes such that $v_0 \to_G v_1 \to_G \cdots \to_G v_\ell$. The number ℓ is the *length* of the path. We write $v_0 \to_G^* v_\ell$ to indicate that there exists a path from v_0 to v_ℓ in G. Given a weighted mixed graph G and a path, the *weight* of the path is the sum of the weights of the edges along this path. Given two nodes $u, v \in V$ we write $\mathrm{m}_G(u, v)$ for the maximum weight of any path from u to v or $-\infty$ if there is no path between them. Note that if all weights are 1, then $\mathrm{m}_G(u, v)$ is the length of a longest path from u to v; and if all weights are -1 then $\mathrm{m}_G(u, v)$ is the negated distance from u to v. An undirected graph is *1-connected* if there is a path between any two nodes. An undirected graph is *k-connected* if we must remove at least k nodes (along with all pending edges) so that the resulting graph is no longer 1-connected.

We use the notation $\langle X \rangle$ to denote a standard binary encoding of the object X. For example, for a graph G let $\langle G \rangle$ denote the binary encoding of the adjacency matrix of G. When we code weighted mixed graphs, *the weights are always coded in unary*.

An *arithmetic tree* is a tree whose leaves are labeled with integers and whose inner nodes have two children and are labeled with functions that maps pairs of integers to integers, like addition, maximization, or multiplication. We will call such functions *binary operators*. For a set O of operators, an *O-tree* is an arithmetic tree in which only operators from O are used. For example, a $\{+, \times\}$-tree is, in essence, an arithmetic formula. Given an O-tree, we recursively assign integers to the inner nodes by applying the operator of a node to the values of the children. We call the integer assigned to an inner node its *value* and the integers assigned to the root is the *value of the tree*. Given a set O of operators, the *tree value problem* for O-trees is the problem of computing the value of O-trees. *The integers at the leaves are coded in binary or in unary; we always indicate the coding explicitly*.

2.1 Definition of Series-Parallel Graphs

We now define different types of series-parallel graphs, abbreviated s-p-graphs in the rest of the paper. We start with two-terminal s-p-graphs.

Definition 1. *We define* directed two-terminal s-p-graphs *inductively. Syntactically, they are triples* (G, a, b) *consisting of a directed graph* $G = (V, E)$, *a source terminal* $a \in V$, *and a* sink terminal $b \in V$. *The following graphs are directed two-terminal s-p-graphs:*

1. (G, a, b) *where* G *is a single directed edge from* a *to* b, *that is,* $V = \{a, b\}$ *and* $E = \{(a, b)\}$, *is a directed two-terminal s-p-graph.*
2. *Given two directed two-terminal s-p-graphs* (G_1, a, c) *and* (G_2, c, b), *their* serial composition *is a directed two-terminal s-p-graph with the terminals* a *and* b. *It is obtained by taking the disjoint union of* G_1 *and* G_2 *and identifying the two copies of the node* c.
3. *Given two directed two-terminal s-p-graphs* (G_1, a, b) *and* (G_2, a, b), *their* parallel composition *is a directed two-terminal s-p-graph, again with the terminals* a *and* b. *It is obtained by taking the disjoint union of* G_1 *and* G_2 *and identifying the two copies of* a *and also the two copies of* b.

Definition 2. *An* undirected two-terminal s-p-graph *is a triple* (G, a, b) *such that there exists a directed two-terminal s-p-graph* (G', a, b) *with* $G = \text{uug}(G')$.

Definition 3. *A* mixed two-terminal s-p-graph *is a triple* (G, a, b), *where* G *is a mixed graph, for which* $\bigl(\text{uug}(G), a, b\bigr)$ *is an undirected two-terminal s-p-graph.*

The last definition can be rephrased as follows: Mixed two-terminal s-p-graphs are obtained from directed two-terminal s-p-graphs by arbitrarily redirecting some or all of the edges.

Definition 4. *We define* undirected multiple-terminal s-p-graphs *inductively. Syntactically, they are pairs* (G, ω) *where* $\omega \subseteq V$ *is the set of* terminals. *The following graphs are undirected multiple-terminal s-p-graphs:*

1. *For every undirected two-terminal s-p-graph* (G, a, b), *the pair* $(G, \{a, b\})$ *is an undirected multiple-terminal s-p-graph.*
2. *Given two undirected multiple-terminal s-p-graphs* (G_1, ω_1) *and* (G_2, ω_2), *their* tree composition *is also an undirected multiple-terminal s-p-graph. It is obtained by taking the disjoint union of* G_1 *and* G_2 *and identifying one terminal* $f \in \omega_2$ *with an arbitrary node of* G_1. *The terminal set of the tree composition is* $\omega_1 \cup (\omega_2 - \{f\})$ *and we call* f *a* fusion node.

Definition 5. *A* mixed multiple-terminal s-p-graph *is a pair* (G, ω), *where* G *is a mixed graph and* $\bigl(\text{uug}(G), \omega\bigr)$ *is an undirected multiple-terminal s-p-graph.*

2.2 Decomposition Trees

Decomposition trees reflect the building process of series-parallel graphs. A parallel composition results in a "parallel node" in the tree, a serial composition yields a "serial node," and single edges correspond to leaves. Note that the decomposition tree of an s-p-graph is typically not unique.

Definition 6. *A* decomposition tree *of a mixed two-terminal s-p-graph* (G, a, b) *is defined as follows. Syntactically, it consists of a directed binary tree* T *("binary" meaning that inner nodes have exactly two children, a left and a right one), whose node set is the disjoint union of the three type sets* T_l, T_s, *and* T_p, *a terminal-pair information function* terminals: $T_l \cup T_s \cup T_p \rightarrow V \times V$, *and an edge information function* edge: $T_l \rightarrow E$. *The set* T_l *contains exactly the leaves of* T. *The elements of* T_s *are called* serial nodes, *the elements of* T_p *are called* parallel nodes.

Having fixed the syntax of decomposition trees, we next inductively describe which trees are decomposition trees. In all cases, terminals$(r) = (a, b)$ *must hold for the root* r *of the tree.*

1. *If* G *consists of a single edge* e *between the two nodes* a *and* b, *then* T *consists of a single node* $r \in T_l$ *and* edge$(r) = e$. *Note that the edge* e *may point from* b *to* a *for arbitrary mixed two-terminal s-p-graphs, but will always point from* a *to* b *if* (G, a, b) *is a directed two-terminal s-p-graph.*
2. *If* G *is the parallel composition of two mixed two-terminal s-p-graphs* (G_1, a, b) *and* (G_2, a, b) *and if* T_1 *and* T_2 *are their tree decompositions, respectively, then* T *consists of a root node* r *whose children are the roots of* T_1 *and* T_2 *and* $r \in T_p$.
3. *If* G *is a serial composition of two mixed two-terminal s-p-graphs* (G_1, a, c) *and* (G_2, c, b), *we do exactly the same as in the parallel case, only* $r \in T_s$.

We now extend the definition of decomposition trees to encompass multiple-terminal s-p-graphs. We then have a fourth type of nodes: "tree nodes", corresponding to *tree compositions*.

Definition 7. *Let* (G, ω) *be a mixed multiple-terminal s-p-graph. Its decomposition tree* T *is defined similarly to the decomposition tree in Definition 6, but with the following addition: There is a fourth type set* T_t, *together with the fusion information function* fusion: $T_t \rightarrow V$. *If* T_t *is not empty, its elements must form a connected component of* T *and it must contain the root. The tree* T *is defined recursively according to the same rules as in Definition 6 with the following addition:*

4. *If* G *is the tree composition of two mixed multiple-terminal s-p-graphs* (G_1, ω_1) *and* (G_2, ω_2) *and if* T_1 *and* T_2 *are their decomposition trees, respectively, then* T *consists of a root node* r *whose children are the roots of* T_1 *and* T_2. *We have* $r \in T_t$ *and* fusion(r) *is the fusion node of the tree composition.*

2.3   Facts from the Literature Used in Our Proofs

We now list facts from the literature on s-p-graphs that will be used in our proofs.

Fact 1 ([19]). *There exists a logspace machine that on input of a directed graph G decides whether G is a directed two-terminal s-p-graph and, if this is the case, outputs a decomposition tree for it.*

Fact 2 ([19]). *There exists a logspace machine that on input of a directed two-terminal s-p-graph G and two nodes s and t decides whether there is a path from s to t.*

The following fact follows from the results in [18] and the fact that L = SL, see [22].

Fact 3 ([18]). *There exists a logspace machine that on input of an undirected graph G decides whether there is a terminal set ω such that (G, ω) is an undirected multiple-terminal s-p-graph and, if this is the case, outputs a decomposition tree T for it. Furthermore, every node n of T that is not an element of T_t, but whose parent is an element of T_t, has the following property: The undirected two-terminal s-p-graph described by the subtree of T rooted at n is 2-connected.*

The following fact is a conclusion of Lemma 8 and Theorem 6 from [18].

Fact 4. *There exists a logspace machine that on the input of an undirected 2-connected two-terminal s-p-graph (G, a, b) and a node $a' \in V$ computes a node $b' \in V$ such that (G, a', b') is an undirected two-terminal s-p-graph.*

Essentially, this fact states that we can "choose" the source terminal arbitrarily. But we cannot also choose the sink terminal arbitrarily at the same time.

3   Computing Maximum-Weight Paths in Logspace

In the present section we prove the central result of the paper, Theorem 5 below. Recall that weights are given in unary.

Theorem 5. *There is a logspace algorithm whose inputs are codes of weighted mixed graphs $G = (V, E)$ together with two nodes $s, t \in V$ and whose output is one of the following:*

1. *The algorithm determines that G is not a mixed multiple-terminal s-p-graph.*
2. *The algorithm determines that there is no path from s to t in G.*
3. *The algorithm outputs a path from s to t of maximal weight.*

The first step in the proof is an algorithm for computing a maximum-weight path in a weighted directed two-terminal s-p-graph from the source to a given node. Instead of writing down an explicit algorithm, we establish a series of reductions that ends with a problem that is known to be solvable in logspace.

The second step is an algorithm for computing maximum-weight paths between the terminals in weighted mixed two-terminal s-p-graphs. The main idea is to obtain a directed version of the mixed graph and to put a heavy penalty on all edges that "point in the wrong direction." We can then use the algorithm for weighted directed two-terminal s-p-graphs.

The third step is an algorithm for computing a maximum-weight path from the source a to an arbitrary node t in weighted mixed two-terminal s-p-graphs. A recursive algorithm is used to compute the maximum weight of a path from s to t by keeping track of smaller and smaller "intervals" (which are just subgraphs) that contain t and, at the same time, keeping track of the maximum weight of paths from a to the two "endpoints" of the intervals.

The fourth and last step is to consider weighted mixed multiple-terminal s-p-graphs G.

3.1   Terminal-to-Node Paths in Directed Two-Terminal S-P-Graphs

Theorem 6. *There exists a logspace machine that on input of any weighted directed two-terminal s-p-graph (G, a, b, w) and a node t outputs a maximum-weight path from a to t.*

Recall once more that weights are coded in unary. The algorithm internally uses an oracle M_{at} and the main task is to prove that M_{at} lies in the class L. The oracle is the decision version of the path construction problem:

$$M_{at} = \{\langle G, a, b, w, t, d\rangle \mid (G, a, b, w) \text{ is a weighted directed two-terminal}$$
$$\text{s-p-graph in which there is a path from } a \text{ to } t$$
$$\text{of weight at least } d\}$$

To prove $M_{at} \in L$, we establish a line of reductions. Note that the difficulty lies in computing the maximum weight of paths, not in checking whether the input graph is, indeed, a directed two-terminal s-p-graph, see Fact 1. The first reduction reduces M_{at} to M_{ab}, which is the restricted version of M_{at} where only inputs with $t = b$ are allowed. If we consider only the subset of nodes $V' = \{v \mid v \to_G^* t\}$ of the input graph G, we can show that:

Lemma 1. *M_{at} reduces to M_{ab} via a logspace many-one reduction.*

We next reduce M_{ab} to M_{ab}^+, which is the same problem, only all weights must be positive.

Lemma 2. *M_{ab} reduces to M_{ab}^+ via a logspace many-one reduction.*

Lemma 3. *M_{ab}^+ reduces to the tree value problem for $\{+, \max\}$-trees whose leaves are labeled with positive integers coded in unary via a single-query logspace reduction.*

The last step is to reduce the tree value problem for $\{+, \max\}$-trees whose leaves are labeled with positive integers coded in unary to the tree value problem for $\{+, \times\}$-trees, which is known to lie in logspace [9,2,12,16].

Lemma 4. *The tree value problem for $\{+, \max\}$-trees whose leaves are labeled with positive integers coded in unary reduces to the tree value problem for $\{+, \times\}$-trees whose leaves are labeled with integers coded in binary via a single-query logspace reduction.*

Using M_{at} as an oracle, we can construct a maximum-weight path node by node. This proves Theorem 6.

3.2   Terminal-to-Terminal in Mixed Two-Terminal S-P-Graphs

Theorem 7. *There exists a logspace machine that on input of any weighted mixed two-terminal s-p-graph (G, a, b, w) outputs a maximum-weight path from a to b or determines that no path exists.*

To prove the theorem, we introduce the notion of *green edges*, which are edges that "point in the right direction."

Definition 8. *Let (G, a, b) be a mixed two-terminal graph and let T be a decomposition tree for it. We color the edges of G according to the following rules: Let e be an edge of G and let n be the leaf node of T with $\text{edge}(n) = e$. Then, if $e = (x, y) \in V \times V$ but $\text{terminals}(n) = (y, x)$, we color the edge red; otherwise, namely when $e = (x, y)$ and $\text{terminals}(n) = (x, y)$ or when $e = \{x, y\}$ is undirected, we color it green.*

Let (G, a, b) be a mixed two-terminal s-p-graph and let T be a decomposition tree for G. Then every path from a to b uses only green edges. The key idea in proving Theorem 7 is to turn mixed s-p-graphs into directed s-p-graphs by redirecting all red edges while assigning large negative weights to them. We can then apply the algorithm from Theorem 6 to the resulting graph.

3.3   Terminal-to-Node Paths in Mixed Two-Terminal S-P-Graphs

Theorem 8. *There exists a logspace machine that on input of any weighted mixed two-terminal s-p-graph (G, a, b, w) and a node t outputs a maximum-weight path from a to t or determines that no such path exists.*

For the proof we introduce the notion of "intervals," which contain t and which get smaller and smaller. We will keep track of the maximum weights of paths from the source to the two endpoints of the intervals.

Definition 9. *Let (G, a, b) be a mixed two-terminal s-p-graph and let T be a decomposition tree. Given a node n of T, let (G_n, a_n, b_n) denote the mixed two-terminal s-p-graph that is described by the subtree of T rooted at n. We call (G_n, a_n, b_n) the interval described by n.*

For a node n of T we write $G - G_n$ for the graph obtained from G by deleting all edges of the graph G_n and the resulting isolated nodes. The weight record for n is the tuple $\left(m_{a \to a_n}^{\neg via\ b_n}, m_{a \to a_n}^{via\ b_n}, m_{a \to b_n}^{\neg via\ a_n}, m_{a \to b_n}^{via\ a_n} \right)$ where $m_{a \to a_n}^{\neg via\ b_n}$ is the maximum weight of a path in $G - G_n$ from a to a_n that does not contain b_n, while $m_{a \to a_n}^{via\ b_n}$ is the maximum weight of a path in $G - G_n$ from a to a_n that does contain b_n. Similarly, $m_{a \to b_n}^{\neg via\ a_n}$ is the maximum weight of a path in $G - G_n$ from a to b_n that does not contain a_n, while $m_{a \to b_n}^{via\ a_n}$ is the maximum weight of a path in $G - G_n$ from a to b_n that does contain a_n.

Lemma 5. *There exists a logspace machine that on input of any weighted mixed two-terminal s-p-graph (G, a, b, w) and a node t outputs $\mathrm{m}_G(a, t)$.*

Proof (Sketch of proof). To compute $m_G(a, t)$, we generate the decomposition tree T of (G, a, b). Let r be the root of T and let n_1, ..., n_k be the path in T that leads from $n_1 = r$ to a leaf n_k where one endpoint of edge(n_k) is t. We compute for successive $i = 1, \ldots, k$ the weight records for each n_i, using only the weight record of the previous n_{i-1} as a guide. $\square$

To construct an path of maximum length we repeatedly apply the algorithm from Lemma 5 as a "guide" that tells us how we must extend the path as we descend. This proves Theorem 8.

3.4   Node-to-Node Paths in Mixed Multiple-Terminal S-P-Graphs

We first compute the tree decomposition of G. The tree decomposition allows us to identify components of G, each of which is a two-terminal s-p-graph, such that every path from s to t must go through a unique sequence of these components. Inside each component we can compute maximum-weight paths using the algorithms we obtained in the previous steps. Stringing together the paths yields the overall path. This proves Theorem 5.

4   Conclusion

In this paper we presented a logspace algorithm for computing paths of maximum weight in mixed multiple-terminal s-p-graphs. As mentioned in the introduction, little is known in comparison about the space complexity of the shortest and longest path problems for graphs with higher, but still constant tree-width. It is neither known whether one can solve the reachability problem for directed graphs of tree-width 3 in logspace nor whether the reachability problem for directed graphs of tree-width k is hard for the class NL for some constant $k \geq 3$.

   On the positive side, a closer analysis of our approach shows that one can use the algorithm to count the number of self-avoiding paths in mixed multiple-terminal s-p-graphs using a logspace algorithm. Also, the existence of an efficient algorithm for computing longest paths implies further results like an efficient algorithm for computing topological sortings. Another application is the computation of s-t-enumerations.

References

1. Allender, E., Barrington, D.A.M., Chakraborty, T., Datta, S., Roy, S.: Grid graph reachability problems. In: 21th Annual IEEE Conference on Computational Complexity (CCC), pp. 299–313 (2006)
2. Ben-Or, M., Cleve, R.: Computing algebraic formulas using a constant number of registers. SIAM J. Comput. 21, 54–58 (1992)
3. Bodlaender, H.L.: NC-algorithms for graphs with small treewidth. In: 14th International Workshop on Graph-Theoretic Concepts in Computer Science (WG), pp. 1–10.

4. Bodlaender, H.L.: Treewidth: Characterizations, applications, and computations. In: 32nd International Workshop on Graph-Theoretic Concepts in Computer Science (WG), pp. 1–14.

5. Bodlaender, H.L., de Fluiter, B.A.: Parallel algorithms for series parallel graphs and graphs with treewidth two. Algorithmica 29(4), 534–559 (2001)

6. Bodlaender, H.L., Hagerup, T.: Parallel algorithms with optimal speedup for bounded treewidth. SIAM J. Comput. 27, 1725–1746 (1998)

7. Borodin, A., Cook, S.A., Dymond, P.W., Ruzzo, W.L., Tompa, M.: Two applications of inductive counting for complementation problems. SIAM J. on Computing 18(3), 559–578 (1989)

8. Bourke, C., Tewari, R., Vinodchandran, N.V.: Directed planar reachability is in unambiguous log-space. In: 22th Annual IEEE Conference on Computational Complexity (CCC), pp. 217–221 (2007)

9. Buss, S., Cook, S., Gupta, A., Ramachandran, V.: An optimal parallel algorithm for formula evaluation. SIAM J. Comput. 21, 755–780 (1992)

10. Chaudhuri, S., Zaroliagis, C.D.: Shortest paths in digraphs of small treewidth. Part II: Optimal parallel algorithms. Theoretical Comput. Sci. 203, 205–223 (1998)

11. Chaudhuri, S., Zaroliagis, C.D.: Shortest paths in digraphs of small treewidth. Part I: Sequential algorithms. Algorithmica 27(3), 212–226 (2000)

12. Chiu, A., Davida, G., Litow, B.: Division in logspace-uniform NC^1. Theoretical Informatics and Applications 35, 259–275 (2001)

13. Duffin, R.: Topology of series-parallel networks. J. Math. Analysis and Applications 10, 303–318 (1965)

14. Eppstein, D.: Parallel recognition of series-parallel graphs. Inf. and Comp. 98, 41–55 (1992)

15. He, X., Yesha, Y.: Parallel recognition and decomposition of two terminal series parallel graphs. Inf. and Comp. 75, 15–38 (1987)

16. Hesse, W.: Division is in uniform TC^0. In: 28th International Colloquium on Automata, Languages and Programming (ICALP), pp. 104–114

17. Hohberg, W., Reischuk, R.: A framework to design algorithms for optimization problems on graphs. Technical Report ITI, Technical University Darmstadt (1990)

18. Jakoby, A., Liśkiewicz, M.: Paths problems in symmetric logarithmic space. In: 29th International Colloquium on Automata, Languages and Programming (ICALP), pp. 269–280.

19. Jakoby, A., Liśkiewicz, M., Reischuk, R.: Space efficient algorithms for series-parallel graphs. J. of Algorithms 60, 85–114 (2006)

20. Lagergren, J.: Efficient parallel algorithms for graphs of bounded tree-width. J. of Algorithms 20, 20–44 (1996)

21. Nickelsen, A., Tantau, T.: The complexity of finding paths in graphs with bounded independence number. SIAM J. Comput. 34(5), 1176–1195 (2005)

22. Reingold, O.: Undirected s-t-connectivity in log-space. In: 37th ACM Symposium on Theory of Computing (STOC), pp. 376–385 (2005)

23. Toda, S.: Counting problems computationally equivalent to computing the determinant. Technical Report CSIM 91-07, Dept. Comp. Sci. and Inform. Math., Univ. Elect.-Comm., Chofu-shi, Tokyo 182, Japan (1991)

24. Valdes, J., Tarjan, R., Lawlers, E.: The recognition of series parallel digraphs. SIAM J. Comput. 11, 298–313 (1982)

25. Wanke, E.: Bounded tree-width and LOGCFL. J. of Algorithms 16, 470–491 (1994)

Communication Lower Bounds Via the Chromatic Number*

Ravi Kumar[1] and D. Sivakumar[2]

[1] Yahoo! Research
ravikumar@yahoo-inc.com
[2] Google, Inc.
siva@google.com

Abstract. We present a new method for obtaining lower bounds on communication complexity. Our method is based on associating with a binary function f a graph G_f such that $\log \chi(G_f)$ captures $N_0(f) + N_1(f)$. Here $\chi(G)$ denotes the chromatic number of G, and $N_0(f)$ and $N_1(f)$ denote, respectively, the nondeterministic communication complexity of $\overline{f}$ and f. Thus $\log \chi(G_f)$ is a lower bound on the deterministic as well as zero-error randomized communication complexity of f. Our characterization opens the possibility of using various relaxations of the chromatic number as lower bound techniques for communication complexity. In particular, we show how various (known) lower bounds can be derived by employing the clique number, the Lovász ϑ-function, and graph entropy lower bounds on the chromatic number.

1   Introduction

Consider two computationally unbounded players Alice and Bob who wish to jointly evaluate a binary function $f(x, y)$, where Alice holds the input x and Bob holds y. The central question in communication complexity [1] is the number of bits Alice and Bob need to exchange to compute $f(x, y)$. Besides being a natural concrete computational model to study, lower bounds in communication complexity have deep connections to time-space tradeoffs, decision trees, circuit lower bounds, and pseudorandomness. For an excellent account, see the book by Kushilevitz and Nisan [2].

We develop a new and general method for proving communication complexity lower bounds for Boolean functions. Our method is based on associating a natural graph G_f for every Boolean function f such that the chromatic number of G_f precisely captures the sum (or max) of the nondeterministic and co-nondeterministic communication complexity of f. Thus, it implies a lower bound on the usual, deterministic, communication complexity of f. While lower bounding $\chi(G_f)$ could be hard in general, the fact that it is a well-studied graph-theoretic quantity opens up a whole new set of tools in the study of communication complexity; these tools include well-known relaxations of the chromatic

---

* This work was performed while the authors were at IBM Almaden.

V. Arvind and S. Prasad (Eds.): FSTTCS 2007, LNCS 4855, pp. 228–240, 2007.
© Springer-Verlag Berlin Heidelberg 2007

number such as the Lovász theta function, graph entropy, linear programming relaxations, etc.

We illustrate our method via simple examples. One of our examples shows the use of Lovász theta function — which satisfies $\chi(G_f) \geq \vartheta(\overline{G_f})$ — to lower bound $\chi(G_f)$. This connection, together with the rich properties of the Lovász theta function (such as multiplicativity), yields lower bounds in a uniform, modular way. Another of our examples illustrates the use of graph entropy to lower bound $\chi(G_f)$, and sheds new light on the information-theoretic techniques of [3,4].

En route, we also show that our method is strictly more powerful than the classical fooling set method [1,5] for communication lower bounds. In fact, we point out that any fooling set argument naturally yields a zero-error randomized communication complexity lower bounds as well. We do not know how the chromatic number method compares with another classical method in communication complexity, the rank method [6], whose relation to nondeterministic communication complexity remains open.

Related work. There are two general methods to prove deterministic communication complexity lower bounds. Both these methods crucially exploit the so-called "rectangular property" of communication protocols, that is, any correct deterministic communication protocol covers the function matrix M_f with monochromatic rectangles. The *fooling set method* [1,5] is a combinatorial method where the main idea is to exhibit a large set of input pairs such that no two of them can be in a single monochromatic rectangle; this implies that the number of monochromatic rectangles in M_f is large. The *rank method* [6] uses algebraic properties M_f; in particular, it shows that the deterministic communication complexity is lower bounded by the log of the rank (in any field) of M_f. It is also known that the rank method is strictly more powerful than the fooling set method. However, it is still a well-known open problem if the rank of M_f is a polynomial characterization of deterministic communication complexity.

For randomized communication complexity, the *discrepancy method* is a general method to show lower bounds. This method argues that every "large" rectangle has lots of 0s and 1s of the function. Hence, any protocol with low error has to use only "small" rectangles, and hence a lot of them. See [2] for a variety of applications. Recently, information-theoretic methods have been developed to show randomized lower bounds for several problems. The basic idea is to analyze the mutual information between the transcript of communication protocols and inputs, where the inputs are picked according to a suitable distribution. For applications of information-theoretic methods in communication complexity, see [7,8,9,10,4,3,11,12,13,14].

To the best of our knowledge, chromatic number has not been used in showing communication complexity lower bounds. The only exception we are aware of is in an altered model of communication complexity, where the inputs to Alice and Bob are restricted to be from some subset $S \subseteq X \times Y$ and the goal is for Bob to learn x. In this setting, the deterministic complexity for one-round protocol is exactly $\lceil \log \chi(G_S) \rceil$, where G_S is a hypergraph on vertices of X with hyperedges of the form $\{x \mid (x, y) \in S\}$. For more details, see [2, Section 4.7].

2   Communication Complexity

Let $f : \mathcal{X} \times \mathcal{Y} \to \{0,1\}$ be a binary function whose communication complexity we wish to study. Suppose Alice and Bob are two computationally unbounded players where Alice holds input $x \in \mathcal{X}$ and Bob holds input $y \in \mathcal{Y}$, and they wish to jointly evaluate $f(x,y)$ by exchanging messages on a shared blackboard (that also preserves history). A protocol Π is a set of rules that precisely describes the interactions between Alice and Bob on every possible input. (For a formal description of a communication protocol as a labeled binary tree, see, e.g., [2].) At the end of their message exchanges, a deterministic referee $R = R(\Pi)$ (who does not see x or y) examines the contents of the blackboard and announces a verdict from the set $\{0,1\}$. The protocol Π is said to be *nondeterministic* if Alice and Bob are allowed to make nondeterministic moves. The protocol Π is said to be *randomized* if Alice and Bob have their private sources of unbiased coin-tosses that they may employ during their execution of the protocol. (Again, we omit formal definitions.) When it is clear from context, we will denote by $\Pi(x,y)$ the *transcript*, or the contents of the shared blackboard when Alice and Bob execute protocol Π; if Π is randomized, then the transcript $\Pi(x,y)$ is a random variable.

A protocol Π is said to compute a function f if for all x and y, $R(\Pi(x,y)) = f(x,y)$. A nondeterministic protocol Π is said to compute a function f if for all x,y, such that $f(x,y) = 1$, there is at least one transcript τ such that $\Pi(x,y) = \tau$ and $R(\tau) = 1$, and furthermore, for all x,y such that $f(x,y) = 0$, there is no transcript τ such that $\Pi(x,y) = \tau$ and $R(\tau) = 1$. For $\delta \geq 0$, we say that Π is a δ-error protocol for f (or that Π computes f with error δ) if for all $x \in \mathcal{X}$ and $y \in \mathcal{Y}$, we have $\Pr[R(\Pi(x,y)) = f(x,y)] \geq 1 - \delta$. We say that Π is a zero-error protocol for f if for all x,y, $\Pr[R(\Pi(x,y)) = f(x,y)] = 1$. In both cases, the probability is over the coin tosses of Alice and Bob.

It is sometimes convenient to assume that every execution of a protocol Π (regardless of the inputs and of the internal coin tosses of Alice and Bob) produces transcripts of the same length. If we are given a protocol Π with error δ that has *expected* transcript length c, for any $\epsilon > 0$, we may obtain from it a protocol Π' with referee function R' that always produces transcripts of length c/ϵ, while increasing the error to at most $\delta + \epsilon$. For zero-error protocols Π, by relaxing the referee function to output a value in $\{0, 1, \text{`?'}\}$, we may obtain a new protocol Π' with referee function R' that always produces transcripts of length c/ϵ, and also satisfies, for all x,y, $\Pr[R'(\Pi'(x,y)) \in \{0,1\}] \geq 1 - \epsilon$ and $\Pr[R'(\Pi'(x,y)) = f(x,y) \mid R'(\Pi'(x,y)) \in \{0,1\}] = 1$.

Throughout the rest of this paper, we will assume this normal form, that is, all executions of a protocol produce transcripts of the same length. Furthermore, for randomized protocols, we assume that the error is a small constant (e.g., 0.01); for zero-error protocols, we assume that the probability of '?' is also a small constant.

The deterministic communication complexity of f, denoted by $cc(f)$, is the minimum, over all deterministic protocols Π that compute f, of the length of transcripts produced by Π. The nondeterministic communication complexity of f, denoted by $N_1(f)$, is the minimum, over all nondeterministic protocols Π that compute f, of the length of transcripts produced by Π. The co-nondeterministic communication complexity of f, denoted by $N_0(f)$, is the minimum, over all nondeterministic protocols Π that compute $\bar{f}$ (the complement of f), of the length of transcripts produced by Π. The zero-error communication complexity of f, denoted by $zcc(f)$, is the minimum, over all zero-error protocols Π that compute f, of the length of transcripts produced by Π. The δ-error communication complexity of f, denoted by $rcc_\delta(f)$, is the minimum, over all protocols Π that compute f with error at most δ, of the length of transcripts produced by Π.

Two natural combinatorial quantities of interest that arise in the study of communication complexity are *rectangle cover complexity* and *rectangle partition complexity*, which we explain next.

Let $f : \mathcal{X} \times \mathcal{Y} \to \{0,1\}$. A rectangle in $\mathcal{X} \times \mathcal{Y}$ is a subset $\mathcal{Z} \subseteq \mathcal{X} \times \mathcal{Y}$ such that $\mathcal{Z} = \mathcal{X}' \times \mathcal{Y}'$ for some $\mathcal{X}' \subseteq \mathcal{X}$ and $\mathcal{Y}' \subseteq \mathcal{Y}$. A rectangle $\mathcal{Z}$ is said to be monochromatic if there exists $b \in \{0,1\}$ such that for every x,y such that $(x,y) \in \mathcal{Z}$, $f(x,y) = b$; accordingly $\mathcal{Z}$ is referred to as a b-monochromatic rectangle. The 0-rectangle cover complexity of f, denoted by $C_0(f)$, is the minimum number of 0-monochromatic rectangles whose union contains every x,y such that $f(x,y) = 0$; the notion of 1-rectangle cover complexity is defined analogously. It is not hard to show (see, e.g., [2]) that $N_0(f) = \lceil \log(C_0(f)) \rceil$ and $N_1(f) = \lceil \log(C_1(f)) \rceil$. We will denote by $C(f)$ the sum of $C_0(f)$ and $C_1(f)$, and by $N(f)$ the maximum of $N_0(f)$ and $N_1(f)$. Up to tiny additive constants, we may think of $N(f)$ as equivalent to $\log(C(f))$. In the definition of $C_0(f)$ and $C_1(f)$, we (implicitly) allowed several monochromatic rectangles to contain a particular input (x,y). When this is disallowed, we obtain the notion of rectangle partition complexity. Namely, $P(f)$ will denote the minimum number of *disjoint* monochromatic (0- and 1-) rectangles whose union cover $\mathcal{X} \times \mathcal{Y}$. While it is clear that $cc(f) \geq \log(P(f))$, unlike the case of nondeterministic communication complexity, it is not known if $\log(P(f))$ captures $cc(f)$ to within constant factors [2, open problem 2.10, page 20].

Next we recall some basic facts about communication complexity; for proofs, see [2] or [4].

Lemma 1 (Fundamental Lemma of Communication Complexity). *If Π is a deterministic communication protocol for $f : \mathcal{X} \times \mathcal{Y} \to \{0,1\}$, then for any $x, x' \in \mathcal{X}$ and $y, y' \in \mathcal{Y}$ and any transcript τ, if $\Pi(x,y) = \Pi(x',y') = \tau$, then also $\Pi(x,y') = \Pi(x',y) = \tau$.*

Lemma 2 (Rectangular Property of Randomized Communication Complexity). *Let Π be a randomized communication protocol for $f : \mathcal{X} \times \mathcal{Y} \to \{0,1\}$, and let $\mathcal{T}$ denote the set of transcripts of Π. There are mappings $\pi_1 : \mathcal{T} \times \mathcal{X} \to \mathbf{R}$, $\pi_2 : \mathcal{T} \times \mathcal{Y} \to \mathbf{R}$ such that for every $x \in \mathcal{X}$, $y \in \mathcal{Y}$, and for every $\tau \in \mathcal{T}$, $\Pr[\Pi(x,y) = \tau] = \pi_1(\tau; x) \cdot \pi_2(\tau; y)$.*

We now state two lemmas that will be important in defining a graph from a function f to study its communication complexity. Note that they are stated for zero-error protocols; in particular, they apply to deterministic protocols.

Lemma 3 (X-Lemma). *Let Π be a randomized zero-error communication protocol for $f : \mathcal{X} \times \mathcal{Y} \to \{0,1\}$, let $\mathcal{T}$ denote the set of transcripts of Π, and let R denote the referee function for Π. Let inputs (x, y) and (x', y') be such that $f(x, y) \neq f(x', y')$. Then there is no transcript $\tau \in \mathcal{T}$ such that $R(\tau) \neq$ '?', $\Pr[\Pi(x, y') = \tau] > 0$ and $\Pr[\Pi(x', y) = \tau] > 0$.*

Note that the X-Lemma states that even if $f(x, y') = f(x', y)$, a zero-error protocol Π cannot place positive probability mass on the same transcript for these two inputs.

Lemma 4 (Z-Lemma). *Let Π be a randomized zero-error communication protocol for $f : \mathcal{X} \times \mathcal{Y} \to \{0,1\}$, let $\mathcal{T}$ denote the set of transcripts of Π, and let R denote the referee function for Π. Let inputs (x, y) and (x', y') be such that $f(x, y) \neq f(x, y') = f(x', y) \neq f(x', y')$. Then there is no transcript $\tau \in \mathcal{T}$ such that $R(\tau) \neq$ '?', $\Pr[\Pi(x, y') = \tau] > 0$ and $\Pr[\Pi(x', y) = \tau] > 0$.*

By symmetry, the Z-Lemma also asserts that there is no transcript τ such that $R(\tau) \neq$ '?', $\Pr[\Pi(x, y) = \tau] > 0$ and $\Pr[\Pi(x', y') = \tau] > 0$. The proof of the Z-Lemma is similar to that of the X-Lemma and is omitted.

3   A Graph-Theoretic Approach

Motivated by the X-Lemma and the Z-Lemma, we are now ready to define, for a function $f : \mathcal{X} \times \mathcal{Y} \to \{0,1\}$, a graph G_f whose chromatic number will characterize $N(f)$.

The vertex set V of G_f will be $\mathcal{X} \times \mathcal{Y}$, and the set E of the edges of G_f will be defined by the following rules:

(1) (Base edges) if $f(x, y) \neq f(x', y')$, then $((x, y), (x', y')) \in E$;
(2) (X-Rule) if $f(x, y) \neq f(x', y')$, then $((x, y'), (x', y)) \in E$;
(3) (Z-Rule) if $f(x, y) \neq f(x, y') = f(x', y) \neq f(x', y')$, then $((x, y), (x', y')) \in E$ and $((x, y'), (x', y)) \in E$.

The next fact is obvious — we state it as a lemma for future use. The main consequence of this lemma is that repeated applications of the X- and Z-Rules will not add more edges to the graph.

Lemma 5 (4-point Lemma). *For any $(x, y), (x', y')$, whether the edge $((x, y), (x', y'))$ is present in G_f depends on the value of f at at most four points — $(x, y), (x', y'), (x, y'), (x', y)$.*

A specific consequence of the 4-point lemma is that if $\mathcal{Z} \subseteq \mathcal{X} \times \mathcal{Y}$ is a monochromatic rectangle, then there is no edge between any two inputs in $\mathcal{Z}$. With this fact in hand, we now arrive at the following theorem.

Theorem 6. *For any Boolean function $f : \mathcal{X} \times \mathcal{Y} \to \{0,1\}$, $\chi(G_f) = C(f)$.*

Corollary 7. *For every $f : \mathcal{X} \times \mathcal{Y} \to \{0,1\}$, we have $N(f) = \max\{N_0(f), N_1(f)\} \geq \log \chi(G_f) - 1$.*

For zero-error communication, a direct argument implies $zcc(f) \geq \log \chi(G_f)$, saving on the additive constant 1 in Corollary 7.

4   Lower Bounds Via $\chi(G_f)$

In this section, we examine the problem of proving lower bounds on the communication complexity by lower bounding the chromatic number of G_f. A natural technique in lower bounding $\chi(G_f)$ is via the clique number $\omega(G_f)$; other techniques include the Lovász ϑ-function applied to $\overline{G_f}$. We explore these ideas now.

4.1   Fooling Sets and the Clique Number

The fooling set method is a basic technique to prove lower bounds on deterministic communication complexity. Here we note that this method also yields a lower bound on nondeterministic communication complexity.

Definition 8 (Fooling Set). *Let $f : \mathcal{X} \times \mathcal{Y} \to \{0,1\}$. Let $S \subseteq \mathcal{X} \times \mathcal{Y}$ be a collection of input pairs with the following properties: (1) all input pairs have the same value of f, that is, that exists $b \in \{0,1\}$ such that for all $(x,y) \in S$, $f(x,y) = b$; and (2) for $(x,y) \neq (x',y') \in S$, either $f(x,y') \neq b$ or $f(x',y) \neq b$.*

The following proposition is standard; see [2].

Proposition 9 (Fooling Set Bound). *If f has a fooling set of size s, then $cc(f) \geq \log s$.*

We note that if a function f has a fooling set of size s, then $\omega(G_f) \geq s$; the proof of the next proposition is easy.

Proposition 10. *If S is a fooling set for f, then for every $(x,y) \neq (x',y') \in S$, the edge $((x,y),(x',y'))$ is present in G_f; hence $\omega(G_f) \geq |S|$ and $N(f) \geq \log|S| - 1$. Also, $zcc(f) \geq \log|S|$.*

It is known (see [2, page 48, Example 4.16]) that the lower bound obtained using the fooling set method could be exponentially poorer than the true communication complexity. A candidate function f for which this gap exists is the $GF(2)$ inner product function. Later we will show that for this function, $\log\chi(G_f) = \Omega(n)$, which is the correct bound. Thus, not surprisingly, the chromatic number method is strictly more powerful than the fooling set method.

4.2   The Lovász Theta Function

For a graph H, an orthonormal labeling u is an assignment of unit vectors u_i, $i \in V(H)$, in some Euclidean space such that for all $(i,j) \notin E(H)$, u_i and u_j are orthogonal. An orthonormal labeling of H with handle c is an orthonormal labeling u of H, together with an auxiliary unit vector c in the same Euclidean space as u. Given a graph H, the *Lovász theta function of H*, denoted $\vartheta(H)$, is defined by $\vartheta(H) = \min_{(u,c)} \max_{i \in H} \frac{1}{\langle u_i, c \rangle^2}$, where the minimization is over all orthonormal labelings u with handle c [15].

The Lovász theta function is a remarkable functional on graphs with several useful properties:

— it is polynomial-time computable;

— it is sandwiched between two (NP-hard) graph quantities, that is, $\alpha(H) \leq \vartheta(H) \leq \chi(\overline{H})$, where α denotes the independence number and χ denotes the chromatic number;

— it satisfies the multiplicative property $\vartheta(H_1 \cdot H_2) = \vartheta(H_1) \cdot \vartheta(H_2)$, where $\cdot$ stands for the strong (or co-normal or conjunctive) graph product defined as follows. The vertex set of $H_1 \cdot H_2$ is $V(H_1) \times V(H_2)$, and for $(i_1, i_2) \neq (j_1, j_2)$, $((i_1, i_2), (j_1, j_2)) \in E(H_1 \cdot H_2)$ if and only if for each $t \in \{1, 2\}$, either $(i_t = j_t)$ or $(i_t, j_t) \in E(H_t)$. We denote $H \cdot H$ by H^2, and (using the associativity of $\cdot$), we denote by H^k the k-fold strong product of H with itself.

The fact that $\chi(G_f) \geq \vartheta(\overline{G_f})$ yields a natural lower bound technique for the communication complexity of f.

Corollary 11. $1 + N(f) \geq \log \chi(G_f) \geq \log \vartheta(\overline{G_f}) \geq \log \alpha(\overline{G_f}) = \log \omega(G_f)$.

We illustrate the ϑ-function method for the set intersection problem, defined formally below.

Definition 12 (The Set Intersection Problem). *In the set intersection problem, Alice is given a subset x of the n-element universe $[n]$ and Bob is given a subset y of $[n]$. (Equivalently, x and y may be thought of as strings in $\{0, 1\}^n$, representing the characteristic vectors, respectively, of x and y.) The set intersection problem, $inter(x, y)$, is defined by $inter(x, y) = 1$ if and only if $x \cap y \neq \emptyset$.*

It is known that the randomized bounded-error communication complexity of set intersection is $\Omega(n)$. We present below a lower bound for $N(f)$, based on the chromatic number approach. The fact that set intersection has a fooling set of size $\Omega(2^n)$ (the set $\{(x, [n] \backslash x) \mid x \subseteq [n]\}$) implies, via Proposition 10, that $N(inter) = \Omega(n)$. The proof below is included only to illustrate the use of the Lovász ϑ-function and its multiplicativity property in establishing communication lower bounds. We begin with the following easy fact about the ϑ function.

Proposition 13. *For graphs H' and H, if $V(H') \subseteq V(H)$ and for every pair of vertices $i, j \in V(H')$, $(i, j) \notin E(H')$ only if $(i, j) \notin E(H)$, then $\vartheta(H') \leq \vartheta(H)$. In particular, if H' is an induced subgraph of H, then $\vartheta(H') \leq \vartheta(H)$.*

Proof. Let $u = \{u_i \mid i \in V(H)\}$ be an orthonormal labeling of H that, together with handle c, achieves $\vartheta(H) = \max_{i \in V(H)} \frac{1}{\langle u_i, c \rangle^2}$. Since non-adjacency in H' implies non-adjacency in H, every orthonormal labeling of H is also an orthonormal labeling of H'; thus

$$\vartheta(H') \leq \max_{i \in V(H')} \frac{1}{\langle u_i, c \rangle^2} \leq \max_{i \in V(H)} \frac{1}{\langle u_i, c \rangle^2} = \vartheta(H). \qquad \square$$

The idea of the zcc lower bound for $f = inter$ is to pick a subgraph H of $\overline{G_f}$ such that $\vartheta(H)$, which is a lower bound on $\vartheta(\overline{G_f})$, is easier to analyze. Specifically, we will pick H that can be expressed as the strong product of a small graph with itself, that is, we will pick $H = h^n$ for some graph h. This will enable us to employ the multiplicativity of the ϑ function, and it will follow that $\vartheta(\overline{G_f}) \geq \vartheta(H) = \vartheta(h^n) = (\vartheta(h))^n$. Finally, it will be trivial to prove a lower bound larger than 1 for $\vartheta(h)$, simply by exhibiting an independent set of size at least 2.

Recall that for $f = inter$, $\mathcal{X} = \{0,1\}^n$, $\mathcal{Y} = \{0,1\}^n$, and hence the vertex set V of G_f is $\{0,1\}^n \times \{0,1\}^n$. For convenience, we will think of V as $(\{0,1\}^2)^n = \{00,01,10,11\}^n$, where each "coordinate" will contain one of Alice's input bits and one of Bob's input bits. Formally, if Alice's input is x and Bob's input is y, we will identify the vertex (x,y) with the n-tuple $(x_1y_1, x_2y_2, \ldots, x_ny_n)$.

Let h denote the 3-vertex graph on the set $\{00,01,10\}$ consisting of the edges $(00,01)$ and $(00,10)$. Define $H = h^n$, the strong n-fold product of h with itself. Precisely, for $(x,y) \neq (x',y') \in V$,

$$((x_1y_1, x_2y_2, \ldots, x_ny_n), (x_1'y_1', x_2'y_2', \ldots, x_n'y_n')) \in E(H)$$

$$\Leftrightarrow \bigwedge_{i=1}^{n} [x_iy_i = x_i'y_i' \ \vee \ (x_iy_i, x_i'y_i') \in E(h)]$$

$$\Leftrightarrow \bigwedge_{i=1}^{n} [x_iy_i = x_i'y_i' \ \vee \ \{x_iy_i, x_i'y_i'\} = \{00,01\} \ \vee \ \{x_iy_i, x_i'y_i'\} = \{00,10\}]. \quad (1)$$

The next lemma establishes that the graph $H = h^n$ occurs as an induced subgraph of $\overline{G_f}$ for $f = inter$.

Lemma 14. *The graph $H = h^n$ occurs as an induced subgraph of $\overline{G_f}$ for $f = inter$.*

Before we prove Lemma 14, note that it implies an $\Omega(n)$ lower bound on the zero-error communication complexity of $inter$. This follows since for $f = inter$,

$$\vartheta(\overline{G_f}) \geq \vartheta(H) = \vartheta(h^n) = (\vartheta(h))^n \geq (\alpha(h))^n = 2^n,$$

where the last inequality follows from the fact that the set $\{01,10\}$ is the largest independent set in h.

Proof (of Lemma 14). Let $f = inter$. Let $V' = V(H) = \{00,01,10\}^n$ denote the vertices of H; clearly $V' \subseteq V = V(\overline{G_f})$.

First we will show that every edge in H occurs in $\overline{G_f}$. Suppose $((x,y),(x',y')) \in E(H)$. We have $(x,y) \neq (x',y')$ and furthermore, from Equation (1),

$$x_iy_i = x_i'y_i' \ \vee \ \{x_iy_i, x_i'y_i'\} = \{00,01\} \vee \{x_iy_i, x_i'y_i'\} = \{00,10\}, \text{ for } i = 1, \ldots, n.$$

Specifically, for each i, we know that $(x_i \wedge y_i) = 0$ and also that $(x_i' \wedge y_i') = 0$, whence it follows that $inter(x,y) = inter(x',y') = 0$. Also, for each i, we have

$$\{x_iy_i', x_i'y_i\} \subseteq \{01,00\} \qquad \text{or} \qquad \{x_iy_i', x_i'y_i\} \subseteq \{10,00\},$$

and hence $(x_i \wedge y_i') = 0$ and $(x_i' \wedge y_i) = 0$, whence it follows that $inter(x,y') = inter(x',y) = 0$. By Lemma 5, whether the edge $((x,y),(x',y')) \in E(G_f)$ depends only the value of f at the four points $(x,y),(x',y'),(x,y')$, and (x',y), all of which are 0. Thus none of these edges is present in G_f, as required.

Next we will show that every non-edge in H is also a non-edge in $\overline{G_f}$, that is, if for some $(x, y) \neq (x', y')$, $((x, y), (x', y')) \notin E(H)$, then $((x, y), (x', y')) \in E(G_f)$. Since $((x, y), (x', y')) \notin E(H)$, it must be the case that for some i,

$$x_i y_i \neq x'_i y'_i \wedge \{x_i y_i, x'_i y'_i\} \neq \{00, 01\} \wedge \{x_i y_i, x'_i y'_i\} \neq \{00, 10\}.$$

In other words, we have $\{x_i y_i, x'_i y'_i\} = \{01, 10\}$. Wlog. let $x_i y_i = 01$ and $x'_i y'_i = 10$; then $x'_i y_i = 11$ and hence $inter(x', y) = 1$. We already know that $inter(x, y) = inter(x', y') = 0$; if $inter(x, y') = 0$, then by the X-Rule, $((x, y), (x', y')) \in E(G_f)$, and if $inter(x, y') = 1$, then by the Z-Rule, $((x, y), (x', y')) \in E(G_f)$. In either case, we have shown that $((x, y), (x', y')) \in E(G_f)$.   □

4.3   Graph Entropy

In this section, we show how one can apply ideas related to graph entropy to lower bound the chromatic number of graphs arising from communication complexity problems. Specifically, we consider the communication complexity of the inner product function, defined below.

Definition 15 (The Inner Product Problem). *In the inner product problem, Alice is given a subset x of the n-element universe $[n]$ and Bob is given a subset y of $[n]$. The inner product problem, $ip(x, y)$, is defined by $ip(x, y) = 1$ if and only if $|x \cap y|$ is odd. (Equivalently, x and y are strings in $\mathbf{Z}_2^n$, and $ip(x, y) = \langle x, y \rangle_2$, where $\langle \cdot, \cdot \rangle_2$ denotes inner product in $\mathbf{Z}_2$.)*

Theorem 16. *For $f = ip$, $\log \chi(f) = \Omega(n)$.*

The importance of the inner product function for our purposes is the fact, mentioned earlier, that the fooling set method is provably inadequate to prove an $\Omega(n)$ lower bound for this function [2]. We show that the chromatic number method achieves this lower bound, that is, for $f = ip$, $\log \chi(G_f) = \Omega(n)$. It is an intriguing open question whether $\log \vartheta(\overline{G_f}) = \Omega(n)$ for $f = ip$, and we conjecture that it is.

The notion of *graph entropy* was first defined by Körner [16] in connection with a coding problem in information theory. Since then it has found numerous applications in combinatorics as well as in theoretical computer science [17,18,19,20,21]; see [22,23,24] for excellent survey of graph entropy and related topics.

Definition 17. *Let $G = (V, E)$ be a graph, and let Q denote a probability distribution on the vertices of G. The entropy of G with respect to Q, denoted $H(G, Q)$, is defined by $H(G, Q) = \min I(U : S)$, where the minimization is over pairs of random variables (U, S) that have the following properties: the variable U takes its values in $V(G)$, S takes its values in the set of independent sets of G, their joint distribution is such that $U \in S$ occurs with probability one, and the marginal distribution of U on $V(G)$ is identical to Q.*

Surprisingly, Körner, in the same paper, also showed that this definition of graph entropy coincides with another definition. For a graph G and $Z \subseteq V(G)$, we denote by $G(Z)$ the subgraph of G induced by Z. Also, we define the *weak* (or *normal* or *disjunctive*) graph product of two graphs H_1 and H_2 as follows. The vertex set of $H_1 \times H_2$ is $V(H_1) \times V(H_2)$, and for $(i_1, i_2) \neq (j_1, j_2)$, $((i_1, i_2), (j_1, j_2)) \in E(H_1 \times H_2)$ if and only if $(i_t, j_t) \in E(H_t)$ for some $t \in \{1, 2\}$. We denote $H \times H$ by $H^{(2)}$, and (using the associativity of $\times$), we denote by $H^{(k)}$ the k-fold weak product of H with itself.

Definition 18. *For any $0 \leq \epsilon < 1$,*

$$H(G, Q) = \lim_{t \to \infty} \min_{U \subseteq V^t, Q^t(U) > 1 - \epsilon} \tfrac{1}{t} \log \chi(G^{(t)}(U)).$$

It is an easy consequence of the definitions that for any distribution Q, $H(G, Q) \leq \log \chi(G)$, and hence $H(G, Q)$ yields a lower bound on $\chi(G)$. By Definition 17, we need to lower bound $I((X, Y) : \gamma)$, where γ is an arbitrary distribution on the independent sets of G_f (for $f = ip$) such that $(X, Y) \in \gamma$.

Proof (sketch of Theorem 16). Following [4], we will pick (X, Y) according to the following distribution on the vertices of G_f. Let $S = \{00, 01\}$ and $T = \{00, 10\}$. For $i = 1, \ldots, n$, let R_i denote a random variable that is S or T with equal probability. Finally, define the r.v. (X, Y) as follows: $(X, Y) = (x, y)$, where for each i, $x_i y_i$ is chosen uniformly from the two possibilities in R_i. It is easy to see that every value (x, y) that (X, Y) takes on satisfies $ip(x, y) = 0$. Let R denote $R_1, \ldots, R_n$.

By an application of the data processing inequality similar to [4], it can be shown that $I(X, Y : \gamma) \geq I(X, Y : \gamma \mid R)$, and it suffices to lower bound the latter quantity.

For simplicity of exposition, we directly prove the following (slightly more restricted version) that applies directly to color classes of G_f rather than arbitrary distributions on independent sets.

Lemma 19. *Let γ denote a legal coloring of G_f using $\chi(G_f)$ colors. For any r.v. (X, Y) with values in $V(G_f)$ and any other random variable A, we have $\log \chi(G_f) \geq I((X, Y) : \gamma(X, Y) \mid A)$.*

The rest of the proof is analogous to a proof of [4] on the randomized communication complexity of set disjointness. We highlight the main steps.

Lemma 20. *Let γ denote a legal coloring of G_f. Then $I((X, Y) : \gamma(X, Y) \mid R) \geq \sum_{i=1}^n I(X_i Y_i : \gamma(X, Y) \mid R)$.*

The proof is identical to that of a similar lemma in [4], and is omitted.

Note that for each i, the quantity $I(X_i Y_i : \gamma(X, Y) \mid R)$ is the expectation over all values r of $R_{-i} \doteq R_1, \ldots, R_{i-1}, R_{i+1}, \ldots, R_n$, of $I(X_i Y_i : \gamma(X, Y) \mid R_{-i} = r, R_i)$. Let us denote this quantity by $\iota_{i,r,\gamma}^{ip}$. We will show that for every i and r, $\iota_{i,r,\gamma}^{ip}$ is $\Omega(1)$. Again, this is similar to an analogous statement in [4]. We will show that one can embed the graph G_{and} corresponding to the 1-bit *and* function into G_f in various ways (corresponding to various choices of $X_j Y_j$ consistent with r), and every one of them yields a legal coloring η of G_{and} by projecting the colors of the corresponding vertices of G_f. The graph G_{and} consists of four vertices $\{00, 01, 10, 11\}$ and the edges $\{(00, 11), (01, 11), (10, 11), (10, 01)\}$; the first three are base edges and the fourth one is obtained by applying the X-Rule. Consider the following distribution on the vertices of G_{and}: let ρ be a random variable with uniform distribution over $\{S, T\}$, and pick random variables U and V (as a pair) from the set ρ. Under this distribution on the vertices of G_{and}, for any random variable η with distribution over legal colorings of G_{and}, let ι_η^{and} denote $I(UV : \eta(U, V) \mid \rho)$. It is easy to see that $\iota_\eta^{and} = \Omega(1)$. The crucial remaining step is to argue that $\iota_{i,r,\gamma}^{ip} = \iota^{and}$; this is based on the following reduction, whose analysis is similar to that in [4], and hence omitted. To color the vertices of G_{and}, we proceed as follows. Fix a vertex, wlog., say 00; let C_{00} denote the sequence of colors specified by γ for all vertices of the form $(X_{-i}^{i\leftarrow 0}, Y_{-i}^{i\leftarrow 0})$ where $X_{-i} Y_{-i}$ range over all values consistent with $R_{-i} = r$, and $X_{-i}^{i\leftarrow 0}$ denotes the input with a 0 in the i-th position and agreeing with X_{-i} elsewhere. Since $ip(x, y) = 1$ precisely for the setting $x_i y_i = 11$ and $ip(x, y) = 0$ for the other three settings, the X-Lemma implies that the induced graph on any four vertices with any particular choice of $X_{-i} Y_{-i}$ consistent with $R_{-i} = r$ is precisely a copy of G_{and}, and hence any legal coloring of this sequence of vertices yields a legal coloring of G_{and}, and in particular, the sequence of colors is a coloring of G_{and} as well. $\square$

We now present an example of a function where the chromatic number of G_f gives only a weak lower bound on the deterministic communication complexity. The *andor* function is a generalization of the *inter* function: *andor* $(X_1, \ldots, X_k, Y_1, \ldots, Y_k) = \wedge_{i=1}^k inter(X_i, Y_i)$. If $k = \sqrt{n}$ and each of X_i and Y_i are of length $\sqrt{n}$, then it can be shown that $N_0(andor) = N_1(andor) = \Theta(\sqrt{n})$. However, it was shown in [13] that the randomized bounded-error (hence, deterministic) communication complexity of *andor* is $\Omega(n)$. Thus, one cannot hope to show an $\Omega(n)$ lower bound on the deterministic complexity of *andor* by studying $\chi(G_{andor})$. However it is possible to modify the arguments in Section 4.3, together with the methods in [13], to obtain an $\Omega(n)$ lower bound for *andor*, by a generalization of coloring with additional local constraints. We defer the details to the full version.

5   Conclusions and Open Problems

We have presented a novel viewpoint for communication complexity; we believe that the definition of G_f distills into a well-studied combinatorial question the complexity of computing f by a two-player communication protocol. We anticipate that the rich set of tools applicable for studying the chromatic number of graphs will be useful in proving new communication bounds. Our work raises an exciting collection of open problems, some of which we briefly mention below.

Regarding the inequality $\chi(G_f) \geq \vartheta(\overline{G_f})$, it is known [25,26] that for general graphs. that the gap between these quantities could be quite large. Specifically, there are n-vertex graphs G for which $\chi(G)$ is polynomially large in n but $\vartheta(\overline{G})$ is a constant. However, for the graphs G_f corresponding to Boolean functions f, it is not clear if such a large gap exists. The next open question is whether the chromatic number method leads to lower bounds for randomized communication complexity with error; some preliminary results are in the full version.

References

1. Yao, A.C.C.: Some complexity questions related to distributive computing. In: 11th STOC, pp. 209–213 (1979)
2. Kushilevitz, E., Nisan, N.: Communication Complexity. Cambridge University Press, Cambridge (1997)
3. Chakrabarti, A., Shi, Y., Wirth, A., Yao, A.C.C.: Informational complexity and the direct sum problem for simultaneous message complexity. In: 42nd FOCS, pp. 270–278 (2001)
4. Bar-Yossef, Z., Jayram, T.S., Kumar, R., Sivakumar, D.: An information statistics approach to communication complexity and data streams. JCSS 68(4), 702–732 (2004)
5. Lipton, R., Sedgewick, R.: Lower bounds for VLSI. In: 13th STOC, pp. 300–307 (1981)
6. Mehlhorn, K., Schmidt, E.: Las-Vegas is better than determinism in VLSI and distributed computing. In: 14th STOC, pp. 330–337 (1982)
7. Bar-Yehuda, R., Chor, B., Kushilevitz, E., Orlitsky, A.: Privacy, additional information, and communication. IEEE TOIT 39(6), 1930–1943 (1993)
8. Ablayev, F.: Lower bounds for one-way probabilistic communication complexity and their application to space complexity. TCS 157(2), 139–159 (1996)
9. Babai, L., Gál, A., Kimmel, P., Lokam, S.V.: Simultaneous messages vs. communication. Technical Report TR-96-23, University of Chicago (1996)
10. Bar-Yossef, Z., Jayram, T.S., Kumar, R., Sivakumar, D.: Information theory methods in communication complexity. In: 17th CCC, pp. 93–102 (2002)
11. Saks, M., Sun, X.: Space lower bounds for distance approximation in the data stream model. In: 34th STOC, pp. 360–369 (2002)
12. Sen, P.: Lower bounds for predecessor searching in the cell probe model. In: 18th CCC, pp. 73–83 (2003)
13. Jayram, T., Kumar, R., Sivakumar, D.: Two applications of information complexity. In: 35th STOC, pp. 673–682 (2003)
14. Jain, R., Radhakrishnan, J., Sen, P.: A direct sum theorem in communication complexity via message compression. In: Baeten, J.C.M., Lenstra, J.K., Parrow, J., Woeginger, G.J. (eds.) ICALP 2003. LNCS, vol. 2719, pp. 300–315. Springer, Heidelberg (2003)
15. Lovász, L.: On the Shannon capacity of a graph. IEEE TOIT 25(1), 1–7 (1979)
16. Körner, J.: Coding of an information source having ambiguous alphabet and the entropy of graphs. In: 6th Prague Conf. on Information Theory, pp. 411–425 (1973)
17. Fredman, M.L., Komlós, J.: New bounds for perfect hashing via information theory. SIDMA 7(4), 560–570 (1984)
18. Boppana, R.: Optimal separations between concurrent-write parallel machines. In: 21st STOC, pp. 320–326 (1989)
19. Newman, I., Wigderson, A.: Lower bounds on formula size of boolean functions using hypergraph-entropy. SIDMA 8(4), 536–542 (1995)
20. Radhakrishnan, J.: Better bounds for threshold formulas. In: 32nd FOCS, pp. 314–323 (1991)

21. Kahn, J., Kim, J.H.: Entropy and sorting. JCSS 51, 390–399 (1995)
22. Simonyi, G.: Graph entropy. In: Cook, L.L.W., Seymour, P. (eds.) Combinatorial Optimization. DIMACS Series on Discrete Math and Computer Science, vol. 20, pp. 391–441. DIMACS Press (1995)
23. Radhakrishnan, J.: Entropy and counting. In: Misra, J.C. (ed.) Computational Mathematics, Modeling, and Algorithms, Narosa Publishers, New Delhi (2003)
24. Simonyi, G.: Perfect graphs and graph entropy. an updated survey. In: Ramirez-Alfonsin, J., Reed, B. (eds.) Perfect Graphs, pp. 293–328. John Wiley and Sons, Chichester (2001)
25. Karger, D., Motwani, R., Sudan, M.: Approximate graph coloring by semidefinite programming. JACM 45(2), 246–265 (1998)
26. Szegedy, M.: A note on the Theta number of Lovász and the generalized Delsarte bound. In: 35th FOCS, pp. 36–39 (1994)

The Deduction Theorem for
Strong Propositional Proof Systems
(Extended Abstract)

Olaf Beyersdorff[*]

Institut für Informatik, Humboldt-Universität zu Berlin, Germany
beyersdo@informatik.hu-berlin.de

Abstract. This paper focuses on the deduction theorem for propositional logic. We define and investigate different deduction properties and show that the presence of these deduction properties for strong proof systems is powerful enough to characterize the existence of optimal and even polynomially bounded proof systems. We also exhibit a similar, but apparently weaker condition that implies the existence of complete disjoint NP-pairs. In particular, this yields a sufficient condition for the completeness of the canonical pair of Frege systems and provides a general framework for the search for complete NP-pairs.

1 Introduction

The classical deduction theorem for propositional logic explains how a proof of a formula ψ from an extra hypothesis φ is transformed to a proof of $\varphi \to \psi$. While this property has been analysed in detail and is known to hold for Frege systems [3,4], deduction has not been considered for stronger systems such as extensions of Frege systems, the apparent reason being that neither the extended Frege system EF nor the substitution Frege system SF satisfy the classical deduction theorem, as neither the extension nor the substitution rule is sound (in the sense that every satisfying assignment for the premises also satisfies the conclusion of these rules). We therefore relax the condition by requiring the extra hypothesis φ to be tautological. In this way we arrive at two weaker versions of the deduction property, for which we ask whether they are valid for strong proof systems with natural properties. It turns out that even these weaker versions of deduction are very powerful properties for strong proof systems as they allow the characterization of the existence of optimal and even polynomially bounded proof systems.

These characterizations are interesting as they relate two important concepts from different areas. The problem of the existence of polynomially bounded proof systems is known to be equivalent to the NP versus coNP question [7], while the question of the existence of optimal proof systems, asking for a strongest propositional proof system, is a famous and well-studied problem in proof complexity, posed by Krajíček and Pudlák [17], and with implications for a number

---

[*] Supported by DFG grant KO 1053/5-1.

of promise complexity classes (cf. [15,20]). In particular, Sadowski [20] obtained different characterizations for the existence of optimal proof systems in terms of optimal acceptors and enumerability conditions for easy subsets of TAUT. Earlier, Krajíček and Pudlák [17] established NE = coNE as a sufficient condition for the existence of optimal proof systems, while Köbler, Messner, and Torán [15] showed that optimal proof systems imply complete sets for a number of other complexity classes like NP ∩ coNP and BPP.

On the other hand, we show that weak deduction combined with suitable closure properties of the underlying proof system implies the existence of complete disjoint NP-pairs. Although disjoint NP-pairs were already introduced into complexity theory in the 80's by Grollmann and Selman [13], it was only during recent years that disjoint NP-pairs have fully come into the focus of complexity-theoretic research [18,9,10,11,12,1,2]. This interest mainly stems from the applications of disjoint NP-pairs to such different areas as cryptography [13,14] and propositional proof complexity [19,18,2].

Similarly as for other promise classes it is not known whether the class of all disjoint NP-pairs contains pairs that are complete under the appropriate reductions. This question, posed by Razborov [19], is one of the most prominent open problems in the field. On the positive side, it is known that the existence of optimal proof systems suffices to guarantee the existence of complete pairs [19]. More towards the negative, a body of sophisticated relativization results underlines the difficulty of the problem. Glaßer, Selman, and Sengupta [9] provided an oracle under which complete disjoint NP-pairs do not exist. On the other hand, in [10] they also constructed an oracle relative to which there exist complete pairs, but optimal proof systems do not exist.

Further information on the problem is provided by a number of different characterizations. Glaßer, Selman, and Sengupta [9] obtained a condition in terms of uniform enumerations of machines and also proved that the question of the existence of complete pairs receives the same answer under reductions of different strength. Additionally, the problem was characterized by provability conditions in propositional proof systems and shown to be robust under an increase of the number of components from two to arbitrary constants [1].

In this paper we exhibit several sufficient conditions for the existence of complete disjoint NP-pairs which involve properties of concrete proof systems such as Frege systems and their extensions. These results fall under a general paradigm for the search for complete NP-pairs, that asks for the existence of proof systems satisfying a weak version of the deduction theorem and moderate closure conditions. In particular, we provide two conditions that imply the completeness of the canonical pair of Frege systems and demonstrate that the existence of complete NP-pairs is tightly connected with the question whether EF is indeed more powerful than ordinary Frege systems.

The paper is organized as follows. In Sect. 2 we provide some background information on propositional proof systems and disjoint NP-pairs. In Sect. 3 we discuss various extensions of Frege systems that we investigate in Sect. 4 with respect to different versions of the deduction property. Section 5 contains the results connecting the deduction property for strong systems with the existence of complete NP-pairs. Finally, in Sect. 6 we conclude with some open problems.

2 Preliminaries

Propositional Proof Systems. Propositional proof systems were defined in a very general way by Cook and Reckhow [7] as polynomial-time functions P which have as their range the set of all tautologies. A string π with $P(\pi) = \varphi$ is called a P-proof of the tautology φ. By $P \vdash_{\leq m} \varphi$ we indicate that there is a P-proof of φ of size $\leq m$. We write $P \vdash_* \varphi_n$ if φ_n is a sequence of tautologies with polynomial-size P-proofs. A propositional proof system P is *polynomially bounded* if all tautologies have polynomial size P-proofs.

Proof systems are compared according to their strength by simulations introduced in [7] and [17]. A proof system S *simulates* a proof system P (denoted by $P \leq S$) if there exists a polynomial p such that for all tautologies φ and P-proofs π of φ there is an S-proof π' of φ with $|\pi'| \leq p(|\pi|)$. If such a proof π' can even be computed from π in polynomial time we say that S *p-simulates* P and denote this by $P \leq_p S$. If the systems P and S mutually (p-)simulate each other, they are called *(p-)equivalent*, denoted by $P \equiv_{(p)} S$. A proof system is called *optimal* if it simulates all proof systems.

In the following sections simple closure properties of propositional proof systems will play an important role. We say that a proof system P is *closed under modus ponens* if there exists a constant c such that $P \vdash_{\leq m} \varphi$ and $P \vdash_{\leq n} \varphi \to \psi$ imply $P \vdash_{\leq m+n+|\psi|+c} \psi$ for all formulas φ and ψ. Similarly, we say that P is *closed under substitutions of variables with respect to the polynomial q* if $P \vdash_{\leq m} \varphi(\bar{x})$ implies $P \vdash_{\leq q(m)} \varphi(\bar{y})$ for all formulas $\varphi(\bar{x})$ and propositional variables $\bar{y}$ that are distinct from $\bar{x}$. Not specifying the polynomial explicitly, we say that P is *closed under substitutions of variables* if there exists a polynomial q with this property. Likewise, P is *closed under substitutions by constants* if there exists a polynomial q such that $P \vdash_{\leq m} \varphi(\bar{x}, \bar{y})$ implies $P \vdash_{\leq q(m)} \varphi(\bar{a}, \bar{y})$ for all formulas $\varphi(\bar{x}, \bar{y})$ and constants $\bar{a} \in \{0,1\}^{|\bar{x}|}$.

Disjoint NP-Pairs. A pair (A, B) is called a *disjoint* NP-*pair* if $A, B \in$ NP and $A \cap B = \emptyset$. Grollmann and Selman [13] defined the following reduction between disjoint NP-pairs (A, B) and (C, D): $(A, B) \leq_p (C, D)$ if there exists a polynomial-time computable function f such that $f(A) \subseteq C$ and $f(B) \subseteq D$. A disjoint NP-pair is *complete* if every disjoint NP-pair reduces to it.

The connection between disjoint NP-pairs and propositional proof systems was established by Razborov [19], who associated a *canonical disjoint* NP-*pair* $(\mathrm{Ref}(P), \mathrm{SAT}^*)$ with a proof system P, where the first component $\mathrm{Ref}(P) = \{(\varphi, 1^m) \mid P \vdash_{\leq m} \varphi\}$ contains information about proof lengths in P and the second component $\mathrm{SAT}^* = \{(\varphi, 1^m) \mid \neg\varphi \in \mathrm{SAT}\}$ is a padded version of SAT. This canonical pair is linked to the automatizablility and the reflection property of the proof system [18]. More information on the connection between disjoint NP-pairs and propositional proof systems can be found in [18,2,11].

3   Extensions of Frege Systems

A prominent example of a class of proof systems is provided by *Frege systems* which are usual textbook proof systems based on axioms and rules. In the context of propositional proof complexity these systems were first studied by Cook and Reckhow [7] and it was proven there that all Frege systems, i.e., systems using different axiomatizations and rules, are p-equivalent.

In addition to Frege systems the *extended Frege proof system EF* can abbreviate complex formulas by propositional variables by the following *extension rule*: if q is a new propositional variable, neither occurring in the previous proof steps nor in the proven formula, then $q \equiv \varphi$ is an admissible proof step for arbitrary formulas φ not containing q. The variable q is an *extension variable*, which from now on abbreviates the formula φ. Note that $q \equiv \varphi$ is in general not tautological, and therefore q may not appear in the proven formula. This extension rule might further reduce the proof size, but it is not known whether EF is really stronger than ordinary Frege systems. Both Frege and the extended Frege system are very strong systems for which no non-trivial lower bounds to the proof size are currently known (cf. [5]).

Another way to enhance the power of Frege systems is to allow substitutions not only for axioms but also for all formulas that have been derived in Frege proofs. Augmenting Frege systems by this substitution rule leads to the *substitution Frege system SF*. The extensions EF and SF were introduced by Cook and Reckhow [7]. While it was already proven there that EF is simulated by SF, the converse simulation is considerably more involved and was shown independently by Dowd [8] and Krajíček and Pudlák [17]. For more detailed information on Frege systems and their extensions we refer to the monograph [16].

Under the notion of *Hilbert-style proof systems* we subsume all proof systems that have as proofs sequences of formulas, and formulas in such a sequence are derived from earlier formulas in the sequence by the rules available in the proof system. In particular, Frege systems and its extensions are Hilbert-style systems. Hilbert-style proof systems P can be enhanced by additional axioms in two different ways. Namely, we can form a proof system $P + \Phi$ augmenting P by a polynomial-time computable set Φ of tautologies as new axiom schemes. This means that formulas from Φ as well as substitution instances of these formulas can be freely introduced as new lines in $P + \Phi$ -proofs. In contrast to this we use the notation $P \cup \Phi$ for the proof system that extends P only by formulas from Φ but not by their substitution instances as new axioms. In our applications the set Φ will mostly be *printable*, meaning that Φ can both be decided and generated in polynomial time.

For EF there are two canonical ways how to define the extensions $EF \cup \Phi$ and $EF + \Phi$, where these two possibilities differ in the use of the extension axioms. In the first method we will allow the introduction of extension axioms $p \equiv \varphi$ only for extension variables p not occurring in Φ, whereas in the second method we can freely use extension axioms that also involve variables from Φ. For the first weaker notion we will use the notation $EF^- \cup \Phi$ and $EF^- + \Phi$, or only EF^- when we augment EF in this manner by different sets of tautologies Φ, whereas the stronger second way is indicated by the usual notation $EF \cup \Phi$, $EF + \Phi$, or simply EF. We will use the same notation $(EF + \Psi)^-$ when we use an extension $EF + \Psi$ as the base system and augment this with further axioms Φ to systems $(EF + \Psi)^- \cup \Phi$.

In principle, this gives four possible types of extensions of EF, but it is easily seen that the distinction between EF and EF^- becomes irrelevant when we augment these systems by axiom schemes Φ:

Proposition 1. *Let Φ be a polynomial-time decidable set of tautologies. Then the proof systems $EF + \Phi$ and $EF^- + \Phi$ are p-equivalent.*

These extensions of EF are particularly important as every proof system P is simulated by a proof system of the form $EF + \Phi$ where the axioms Φ provide a propositional description of the reflection principle of P, expressing a strong form of the consistency of P (cf. [16] for details).

In addition, also the systems $EF \cup \Phi$ and $EF + \Phi$ appear to be very close to each other, as also $EF \cup \Phi$ can use substitution instances of Φ in its proofs. Namely, if $\varphi(p_1, \ldots, p_n)$ is a formula from Φ and $\theta_1(\bar{q}), \ldots, \theta_n(\bar{q})$ are propositional formulas in the variables $\bar{q}$ that are disjoint from $\bar{p}$, then we can deduce $\varphi(\theta_1, \ldots, \theta_n)$ in $EF \cup \Phi$ as follows: we start with the extension axioms $p_1 \equiv \theta_1(\bar{q}), \ldots, p_n \equiv \theta_n(\bar{q})$ and use these formulas to show the equivalence $\varphi(p_1, \ldots, p_n) \equiv \varphi(\theta_1, \ldots, \theta_n)$ by induction on the formula φ. Using the original axiom $\varphi(p_1, \ldots, p_n)$ from Φ we arrive with modus ponens at the substitution instance $\varphi(\theta_1, \ldots, \theta_n)$. We leave it open, whether this idea can be extended to a full simulation of $EF + \Phi$ by $EF \cup \Phi$, but the argument shows that also the system $EF \cup \Phi$ is quite natural, as it is equivalent to the proof system $P = EF + \Phi$ where formulas from Φ use pairwise distinct variables and each P-proof may contain at most one substitution instance of each formula from Φ.

For SF the situation becomes even simpler, as there is only one sensible way to define extensions of SF. Namely, because SF can immediately generate substitution instances, we have $SF \cup \Phi \equiv_p SF + \Phi$. In total the following picture of possible extension of Frege systems emerges:

Proof system	Extensions by polynomial-time decidable axioms Φ
F	$F \cup \Phi \leq_p F + \Phi$
EF	$EF^- \cup \Phi \leq_p EF \cup \Phi \leq_p EF^- + \Phi \equiv_p EF + \Phi$
SF	$SF \cup \Phi \equiv_p SF + \Phi$

In the above table all shown simulation relations are probably strict in each line (except for $EF \cup \Phi \leq_p EF + \Phi$ as mentioned above), because the converse simulations (even for $\leq$) have unlikely consequences, as we will show in the sequel of this paper, or easily follows from known results. The next table gives an overview of these consequences, ranging in strength from the existence of complete disjoint NP-pairs to the existence of optimal proof systems.

Assumption		Consequence
$F \equiv F^- \cup \Phi$	*)	EF is optimal (cf. [16], Theorem 14.2.2)
$F \cup \Phi \equiv F + \Phi$	*)	Complete disjoint NP-pairs exist (Corollary 14)
$EF \equiv EF^- \cup \Phi$	*)	EF is optimal (cf. [16])
$EF^- \cup \Phi \equiv EF \cup \Phi$	*)	EF is optimal (Theorem 7)
$SF \equiv SF \cup \Phi$	*)	SF is optimal (cf. [16])

*) for all polynomial-time decidable sets of tautologies Φ

In contrast, we do not seem to have such indication for separating the systems in the vertical columns of the first table, as even the relation between F and $EF \equiv_p SF$ is not settled.

4   Deduction Properties for Frege Systems

The deduction theorem of propositional logic states that in a Frege system F a formula ψ is provable from a formula φ if and only if $\varphi \to \psi$ is provable in F. Because proof complexity is focusing on the length of proofs it is interesting to analyse how the proof length is changing in the deduction theorem. An F-proof of $\varphi \to \psi$ together with the axiom φ immediately yields the formula ψ with one application of modus ponens. Therefore it is only interesting to ask for the increase in proof length when constructing a proof of $\varphi \to \psi$ from an F-proof of ψ with the extra axiom φ. This was analysed in detail in [3,4].

The main application of the deduction property is to simplify proofs of complex formulas. Namely, to prove an implication $\varphi \to \psi$ it suffices to construct a proof of ψ from φ. In particular, φ can be any formula and is not necessarily a tautology. It is clear that such a deduction property is doomed to fail for strong systems like EF or SF that can immediately produce substitution instances from φ. For instance, by one application of the substitution rule we get $SF \cup \{p\} \vdash q$, whereas $p \to q$ is not even a tautology. Similarly, we get $EF \cup \{p\} \vdash q$ by introducing the extension axiom $p \equiv q$ with extension variable p as the first line of the proof, and then derive q by modus ponens. This example, however, does not work for EF^- as we have used the variable p from the extra assumption as an extension variable. In fact, such an example cannot be found as the classical deduction theorem is valid for EF^- (Theorem 3).

Aiming in particular at strong proof systems like EF we therefore restrict φ to tautologies and make the following general definition.

Definition 2 (Efficient/classical deduction property). *A Hilbert-style proof system P allows* efficient deduction *if there exists a polynomial p such that for all finite sets Φ of tautologies,*

$$P \cup \Phi \vdash_{\leq m} \psi \quad \text{implies} \quad P \vdash_{\leq p(m+m')} \left(\bigwedge_{\varphi \in \Phi} \varphi \right) \to \psi$$

where $m' = |\bigwedge_{\varphi \in \Phi} \varphi|$.

If this even holds for all finite sets Φ of propositional formulas, then we say that P has the classical deduction property.

This classical deduction property is known to hold for Frege systems (cf. [4]), but actually almost the same proof also holds for the presumably stronger system EF^-.

Theorem 3 (Deduction theorem for Frege systems). *Let Ψ be a polynomial-time decidable set of tautologies. Then every Frege system $F + \Psi$ and every extended Frege system of the form $(EF + \Psi)^-$ has the classical deduction property.*

Proof (Sketch). Let $\varphi_1, \ldots, \varphi_n$ be tautologies and let $(\theta_1, \ldots, \theta_k)$ be a proof of ψ in the system $P \cup \{\varphi_1, \ldots, \varphi_n\}$, where P is $F + \Psi$ or $(EF + \Psi)^-$. By induction on j we construct P-proofs of the implications $(\bigwedge_{i=1}^{n} \varphi_i) \rightarrow \theta_j$. This is done by distinguishing three cases on how the formula θ_j was derived: θ_j might be an axiom from $\{\varphi_1, \ldots, \varphi_n\}$ or Ψ (this case is easy), θ_j might be derived by an F-rule, or θ_j might be an application of the extension rule (if $P = (EF + \Psi)^-$).

We just make some remarks on this last case. Let θ_j be $q \equiv \theta$ with the extension variable q. Then we can also use the extension rule to get $q \equiv \theta$, and derive $(\bigwedge_{i=1}^{n} \varphi_i) \rightarrow (q \equiv \theta)$ in a proof of size $O(|\theta| + \sum_{i=1}^{n} |\varphi_i|)$. Here it is important that by the definition of $(EF + \Psi)^-$ the extension variable q does not occur in the formulas φ_i, as otherwise we would not be able to use q as an extension variable in an $EF + \Psi$-proof of $(\bigwedge_{i=1}^{n} \varphi_i) \rightarrow \theta_k$. $\qquad\square$

A still weaker form of the deduction property is given in the next definition.

Definition 4 (Weak deduction property). *A Hilbert-style proof system P allows* weak deduction *if the following condition holds. For all printable sets $\Phi \subseteq \text{TAUT}$ there exists a polynomial p such that for all finite subsets $\Phi_0 \subseteq \Phi$ we can infer from $P \cup \Phi_0 \vdash_{\leq m} \psi$ that $P \vdash_{\leq p(m+m')} (\bigwedge_{\varphi \in \Phi_0} \varphi) \rightarrow \psi$ where $m' = |\bigwedge_{\varphi \in \Phi_0} \varphi|$.*

In Definition 2 we allowed a fixed polynomial increase for the proof size in the transformation of a proof from ψ to the implication $(\bigwedge_{\varphi \in \Phi_0} \varphi) \rightarrow \psi$, whereas in the weak deduction property this polynomial might depend on the choice of the extra axioms Φ. This weakening of the deduction property allows us to show the following proposition.

Proposition 5. *Optimal Hilbert-style proof systems have the weak deduction property. Similarly, polynomially bounded Hilbert-style proof systems have the efficient deduction property.*

Proof (Idea). Let Φ be a printable set of tautologies and let π be a $P \cup \Phi$-proof of ψ. If P is optimal (or even polynomially bounded), then we can first devise polynomial-size P-proofs of the extra assumptions Φ_0 in π and thus construct a P-proof of $(\bigwedge_{\varphi \in \Phi_0} \varphi) \rightarrow \psi$. $\qquad\square$

The following theorem provides a form of a converse to the last proposition. This shows that the efficient and even the weak deduction property are very strong assumptions for natural proof systems.

Theorem 6. *Let $P \geq EF$ be a Hilbert-style proof system that fulfills the following two conditions:*

1. *P is closed under modus ponens and substitutions by constants.*
2. *For all printable sets of tautologies Φ the proof system $P \cup \Phi$ is closed under substitutions of variables.*

Then the following implications hold. If P has the weak deduction property, then P is an optimal proof system. If P even has the efficient deduction property and 2 holds for some fixed polynomial p, not depending on Φ, then P is a polynomially bounded proof system.

Proof. Let us argue for the first implication. To obtain the optimality of a proof system $P \geq EF$ that is closed under modus ponens, it suffices to show $P \vdash_* \varphi_n$ for all printable sequences of tautologies φ_n (cf. [16], Theorem 14.2.2). Let $\varphi_n(\bar{p})$ be a printable sequence in the variables $\bar{p}$, and let $\bar{q}$ be a sequence of propositional variables that is disjoint from $\bar{p}$. We consider the proof system $P' = P \cup \{\varphi_n(\bar{q}) \mid n \geq 0\}$, where the variables $\bar{p}$ from $\varphi_n(\bar{p})$ are substituted by $\bar{q}$. By assumption P' is closed under substitutions of variables and hence we have $P' \vdash_* \varphi_n(\bar{p})$. By the weak deduction property for P we get $P \vdash_* \bigwedge_{i \in I} \varphi_i(\bar{q}) \rightarrow \varphi_n(\bar{p})$ for some finite set I. Using closure under substitutions by constants we derive $P \vdash_* \bigwedge_{i \in I} \varphi_i(1, \ldots, 1) \rightarrow \varphi_n(\bar{p})$, where we have substituted all variables $\bar{q}$ in $\varphi_i(\bar{q})$ by constants 1. Because all φ_i are tautologies, the formulas $\varphi_i(1, \ldots, 1)$ are true formulas without variables and therefore admit polynomial-size P-proofs, as $P \geq EF$. Using modus ponens for P we arrive at polynomial-size P-proofs of $\varphi_n(\bar{p})$, as desired.

For the second implication we use the following characterization: a proof system P is polynomially bounded if and only if $P \vdash_{\leq p(n)} \varphi_n$ for all printable sequences of tautologies φ_n and a fixed polynomial p. In the definition of the efficient deduction property and the other closure properties we have also bounded the increase in the proof length by fixed polynomials. Hence an easy modification of the above argument yields the second implication. $\qquad\square$

Examining the situation for extensions of EF we obtain the following result.

Theorem 7. *Let Ψ be a polynomial-time decidable set of tautologies. Then the following conditions are equivalent:*

1. *$EF + \Psi$ has the weak deduction property.*
2. *$EF + \Psi$ is an optimal proof system.*
3. *For all polynomial-time decidable sets $\Phi \subset TAUT$ the systems $(EF + \Psi)^- \cup \Phi$ and $(EF + \Psi) \cup \Phi$ are equivalent.*
4. *For all polynomial-time decidable sets $\Phi \subset TAUT$ the proof system $(EF + \Psi)^- \cup \Phi$ is closed under substitutions of variables.*

In particular, the last theorem yields two seemingly unrelated characterizations for the optimality of EF, namely weak deduction for EF and closure of $EF^- \cup \Phi$ under substitutions of variables for arbitrary tautologies Φ.

Similarly, we obtain the following characterizations for the efficient deduction property of extensions of EF.

Theorem 8. *Let Ψ be a polynomial-time decidable set of tautologies. Then the following conditions are equivalent:*

1. *$EF + \Psi$ has the efficient deduction property.*
2. *$EF + \Psi$ is polynomially bounded.*
3. *There exists a polynomial p such that for all polynomial-time decidable sets $\Phi \subset TAUT$ the proof system $(EF + \Psi)^- \cup \Phi$ is closed under substitutions with respect to p.*

While one might have objections on the naturality of the above systems $(EF + \Psi) \cup \Phi$, the same results are also valid for substitution Frege systems. In particular, we obtain from Theorem 6 the following characterizations.

Corollary 9. *Let Ψ be a polynomial-time decidable set of tautologies. Then the proof system $SF + \Psi$ is optimal if and only if $SF + \Psi$ has the weak deduction property. Further, the system $SF + \Psi$ is polynomially bounded if and only if $SF + \Psi$ has the efficient deduction property.*

As we know that every proof system P is simulated by a proof system of the form $EF + \Psi$ with printable $\Psi \subset TAUT$ (for instance we can take Ψ as translations of the reflection principle of P), we can deduce the following characterization of the existence of optimal proof systems.

Corollary 10. *There exists an optimal proof system if and only if there exists a polynomial-time decidable set $\Psi \subset TAUT$ such that $EF + \Psi$ has the weak deduction property.*

Similarly, we can characterize the existence of polynomially bounded proof systems by the efficient deduction property.

Corollary 11. *There exists a polynomially bounded proof system if and only if there exists a polynomial-time decidable set $\Psi \subset TAUT$ such that $EF + \Psi$ has the efficient deduction property.*

5   Deduction Properties and Complete NP-Pairs

In this section we link the deduction property to the problem of the existence of complete disjoint NP-pairs. In this analysis properties of proof systems are transferred to properties of the corresponding canonical pairs of the systems.

Augmenting Hilbert-style proof systems P by additional axioms Φ will usually enhance the power of the proof system. The following lemma shows, however, that if P has the weak deduction property, then the canonical pair of $P \cup \Phi$ will not be more difficult than the canonical P-pair. In particular, combined with Theorem 3 the next lemma shows that the canonical pairs of F and its extensions $F \cup \Phi$ are equivalent for printable sets $\Phi \subseteq TAUT$.

Lemma 12. *Let Φ be a printable set of tautologies and let P be a proof system with the weak deduction property. Then $(\mathrm{Ref}(P \cup \Phi), \mathrm{SAT}^*) \leq_p (\mathrm{Ref}(P), \mathrm{SAT}^*)$.*

Proof (Idea). The reduction is performed by the mapping

$$(\psi, 1^m) \mapsto ((\bigwedge_{\varphi \in \Phi_m} \varphi) \to \psi, 1^{p(mq(m)+m)})$$

where $\Phi_m = \Phi \cap \Sigma^{\leq m}$ contains $\leq q(m)$ tautologies for some polynomial q, and p is the polynomial from the weak deduction property of P.   □

In the next theorem we formulate a sufficient condition for the existence of complete NP-pairs. The hypotheses in this theorem are very similar to the hypotheses in Theorem 6, which gave a sufficient condition for the existence of optimal proof systems. The decisive difference between the two theorems is that in Theorem 6 we needed closure of $P \cup \Phi$ under substitutions of variables, whereas in the following theorem closure under substitutions by constants suffices.

Theorem 13. *Let P be a Hilbert-style proof system that simulates the truth-table system and fulfills the following three conditions:*

1. *P is closed under modus ponens.*
2. *For all printable sets of tautologies Φ the proof system $P \cup \Phi$ is closed under substitutions by constants.*
3. *P has the weak deduction property.*

Then the canonical pair of P is a complete disjoint NP-pair.

Proof (Sketch). The idea of the proof is to construct suitable propositional representations of disjoint NP-pairs (A, B). Such representations for A and B can be obtained similarly as in Cook's proof of the NP-completeness of SAT [6]. We then form a proof system $P' = P \cup \Phi$ extending P, where Φ are new axioms expressing the disjointness of (A, B) with respect to the above representations. This allows to reduce (A, B) to the canonical pair of P'. As P has weak deduction, we can use Lemma 12 to reduce the canonical pair of P' to the canonical pair of P, and hence (A, B) is $\leq_p$-reducible to $(\text{Ref}(P), \text{SAT}^*)$.   □

The decisive hypotheses in Theorem 13 are assumptions 2 and 3. For Frege systems property 3 of Theorem 13 is fulfilled, but property 2 is not clear. For EF and SF, however, we have property 2, but whether property 3 holds is open. To find out whether some strong proof system fulfills both conditions 2 and 3 remains as a challenging task.

Instantiating Theorem 13 for Frege systems leads to the following corollary which asks, in principle, whether the systems $F \cup \Phi$ and $F + \Phi$ are equivalent.

Corollary 14. *Assume that for all printable sets of tautologies Φ the system $F \cup \Phi$ is closed under substitutions by constants. Then the canonical F-pair is a complete disjoint NP-pair.*

By Theorem 3 and Lemma 12 the same corollary also holds for the proof system EF^-.

Our last result shows that the existence of complete NP-pairs is tightly connected with the question whether F and EF are indeed proof systems of different strength.

Table 1. Deduction properties for different types of proof systems

Proof system P	Frege/EF^-	EF/SF
classical deduction	yes	no
efficient deduction	yes	no, unless P is optimal
weak deduction	yes	no, unless P is pol. bounded
weakest known condition for the completeness of the canonical pair of P	closure of $P \cup \Phi$ under substitutions by constants for all printable Φ	optimality of P

Corollary 15. *Assume that for all printable sequences Φ of tautologies the proof systems $F \cup \Phi$ and $EF \cup \Phi$ are equivalent. Then the canonical pair of the Frege proof system is complete for the class of all disjoint NP-pairs.*

In Table 1 we have summarized the different deduction properties and their implications for the existence of complete NP-pairs for Frege systems and their extensions.

6   Conclusion

In this paper we have brought attention to the question whether strong proof systems such as extensions of Frege systems have some kind of deduction property. On the one hand, we have shown that optimal proof systems can be characterized by the weak deduction property. On the other hand, weak deduction combined with a moderate amount of closure properties yields complete disjoint NP-pairs. It therefore seems to be interesting to investigate the following problem:

Problem 16. Are there natural strong proof systems besides Frege systems that satisfy the weak deduction property?

Given the implications above, we expect, however, that neither proving nor disproving this question will be an easy task.

It would also be interesting to know whether the condition in Corollary 14 also characterizes the completeness of the canonical Frege pair, similarly as in Corollaries 10 and 11. A more general program is to determine which consequences of the completeness of the canonical pair of some proof system P are to expect for the system P itself.

Acknowledgements. I am indebted to Emil Jeřábek, Johannes Köbler, and Pavel Pudlák for helpful suggestions on this work. I also wish to thank the anonymous referees for detailed comments on how to improve the paper.

References

1. Beyersdorff, O.: Tuples of disjoint NP-sets. Theory of Computing Systems (to appear)
2. Beyersdorff, O.: Classes of representable disjoint NP-pairs. Theoretical Computer Science 377, 93–109 (2007)
3. Bonet, M.L.: Number of symbols in Frege proofs with and without the deduction rule. In: Clote, P., Krajíček, J. (eds.) Arithmetic, Proof Theory and Computational Complexity, pp. 61–95. Oxford University Press, Oxford (1993)
4. Bonet, M.L., Buss, S.R.: The deduction rule and linear and near-linear proof simulations. The Journal of Symbolic Logic 58(2), 688–709 (1993)
5. Bonet, M.L., Buss, S.R., Pitassi, T.: Are there hard examples for Frege systems? In: Clote, P., Remmel, J. (eds.) Feasible Mathematics II, Birkhäuser, pp. 30–56 (1995)
6. Cook, S.A.: The complexity of theorem proving procedures. In: Proc. 3rd Annual ACM Symposium on Theory of Computing, pp. 151–158. ACM Press, New York (1971)
7. Cook, S.A., Reckhow, R.A.: The relative efficiency of propositional proof systems. The Journal of Symbolic Logic 44, 36–50 (1979)
8. Dowd, M.: Model-theoretic aspects of P$\neq$NP. Unpublished manuscript (1985)
9. Glaßer, C., Selman, A.L., Sengupta, S.: Reductions between disjoint NP-pairs. Information and Computation 200(2), 247–267 (2005)
10. Glaßer, C., Selman, A.L., Sengupta, S., Zhang, L.: Disjoint NP-pairs. SIAM Journal on Computing 33(6), 1369–1416 (2004)
11. Glaßer, C., Selman, A.L., Zhang, L.: Survey of disjoint NP-pairs and relations to propositional proof systems. In: Goldreich, O., Rosenberg, A.L., Selman, A.L. (eds.) Essays in Theoretical Computer Science in Memory of Shimon Even, pp. 241–253. Springer, Heidelberg (2006)
12. Glaßer, C., Selman, A.L., Zhang, L.: Canonical disjoint NP-pairs of propositional proof systems. Theoretical Computer Science 370, 60–73 (2007)
13. Grollmann, J., Selman, A.L.: Complexity measures for public-key cryptosystems. SIAM Journal on Computing 17(2), 309–335 (1988)
14. Homer, S., Selman, A.L.: Oracles for structural properties: The isomorphism problem and public-key cryptography. Journal of Computer and System Sciences 44(2), 287–301 (1992)
15. Köbler, J., Messner, J., Torán, J.: Optimal proof systems imply complete sets for promise classes. Information and Computation 184, 71–92 (2003)
16. Krajíček, J.: Bounded Arithmetic, Propositional Logic, and Complexity Theory. Encyclopedia of Mathematics and Its Applications, vol. 60. Cambridge University Press, Cambridge (1995)
17. Krajíček, J., Pudlák, P.: Propositional proof systems, the consistency of first order theories and the complexity of computations. The Journal of Symbolic Logic 54, 1079–1963 (1989)
18. Pudlák, P.: On reducibility and symmetry of disjoint NP-pairs. Theoretical Computer Science 295, 323–339 (2003)
19. Razborov, A.A.: On provably disjoint NP-pairs. Technical Report TR94-006, Electronic Colloquium on Computational Complexity (1994)
20. Sadowski, Z.: On an optimal propositional proof system and the structure of easy subsets of TAUT. Theoretical Computer Science 288(1), 181–193 (2002)

Satisfiability of Algebraic Circuits over Sets of Natural Numbers

Christian Glaßer, Christian Reitwießner,
Stephen Travers, and Matthias Waldherr

Theoretische Informatik
Julius-Maximilians-Universität Würzburg, Germany
{glasser,reitwiessner,travers}@informatik.uni-wuerzburg.de

Abstract. We investigate the complexity of *satisfiability problems* for $\{\cup, \cap, {}^-, +, \times\}$-circuits computing sets of natural numbers. These problems are a natural generalization of membership problems for expressions and circuits studied by Stockmeyer and Meyer (1973) and McKenzie and Wagner (2003).

Our work shows that satisfiability problems capture a wide range of complexity classes like NL, P, NP, PSPACE, and beyond. We show that in several cases, satisfiability problems are harder than membership problems. In particular, we prove that testing satisfiability for $\{\cap, +, \times\}$-circuits already is undecidable. In contrast to this, the satisfiability for $\{\cup, +, \times\}$-circuits is decidable in PSPACE.

1   Introduction

In complexity theory, satisfiability questions play an important role in understanding the nature of computational problems. The satisfiability test for *Boolean formulas* is the question of whether there exists an assignment of truth values *true* and *false* to the variables such that the Boolean expression evaluates to true. This was the first natural problem proven to be NP-complete [Coo71] and it is still one of the most prominent NP-complete problems today. The latter also holds for the similar problem of testing satisfiability for *boolean circuits*, where boolean expressions are described in a more succinct way.

In this paper, we investigate satisfiability questions for a more general kind of circuits, namely algebraic circuits over sets of natural numbers. The notion of algebraic circuits has its origin in *Integer Expressions* introduced by Stockmeyer and Meyer [SM73] in 1973. An integer expression is an expression built up from single natural numbers by using set operations ($^-$, $\cup$, $\cap$) and algebraic operations ($+$, $\times$). Stockmeyer and Meyer investigated the complexity of *membership problems* for such expressions, i.e., given an expression E, how difficult is it to test whether a certain natural number is a member of the set described by E? Restricting the set of allowed operations results in membership problems of different complexities.

V. Arvind and S. Prasad (Eds.): FSTTCS 2007, LNCS 4855, pp. 253–264, 2007.

Wagner [Wag84] introduced *circuits over sets of natural numbers* in 1984. The latter describe integer expressions in a more succinct way. The input gates of such a circuit are labeled with natural numbers, the inner gates compute set operations ($^{-}$, $\cup$, $\cap$) and arithmetic operations ($+$, $\times$). Wagner [Wag84], Yang [Yan00], and McKenzie and Wagner [MW03] studied the complexity of membership problems for algebraic circuits over natural numbers: Here, for a given circuit C with given numbers assigned to the input gates, one has to decide whether a given number n belongs to the set described by C. Recently, *equivalence problems* for algebraic circuits, i.e., deciding whether two given circuits compute the same set, were also studied [GHR^{+}07].

In this paper, we study generalizations of membership problems, namely *satisfiability problems* for algebraic circuits over sets of natural numbers. In contrast to membership problems, here a circuit can contain *unassigned input gates*. The question is, given a circuit C with gate labels from $\mathcal{O}$, $\mathcal{O} \subseteq \{^{-}, \cup, \cap, +, \times\}$, and given a natural number n, does there exist an assignment of natural numbers to the variable input gates such that n is contained in the set described by the circuit? We denote this problem with $\mathrm{SC}(\mathcal{O})$.

As our circuits can still contain non-variable input gates with fixed inputs, it is immediate that a satisfiability problem always is a generalization of a membership problem. Hence, solving a satisfiability problem is at least as hard as solving a membership problem.

Notice that the domain of the input variables is unbounded, hence it is not a priori clear that our satisfiability problems are decidable. Nevertheless, we can characterize the complexity of many satisfiability problems precisely by proving them to be complete for (decidable) complexity classes. In other cases however, we can formally prove the satisfiability problem to be undecidable: We show that the problem of solving diophantine equations, which was proven to be undecidable by Matiyasevich [DPR61, Mat70], can be reduced to $\mathrm{SC}(\cap, +, \times)$, the problem of testing satisfiability for $\{\cap, +, \times\}$-circuits.

Interestingly, if we start with $\mathrm{SC}(\cap, +, \times)$ and drop one of the operations $\cap$, $+$, or $\times$, then in all three cases we arrive at an NP-complete problem, namely $\mathrm{SC}(+, \times)$, $\mathrm{SC}(\cap, +)$, or $\mathrm{SC}(\cap, \times)$. The latter is of particular interest, since in contrast to most other NP-complete problems, here the membership in NP is more difficult to show than the NP-hardness. For this end, we introduce a problem that addresses the solvability of certain *systems of monom equations*. The nontrivial fact that integer programming is contained in NP allows us to show that the solvability of systems of monom equations also belongs to NP. Finally, this can be used to establish $\mathrm{SC}(\cap, \times) \in \mathrm{NP}$.

Our main open question is whether $\mathrm{SC}(^{-}, \cup, \cap, \times)$, the satisfiability problem for $\{^{-}, \cup, \cap, \times\}$-circuits, is decidable. A further open question is to find a better lower bound for the satisfiability problem for $\{\times\}$-circuits. We prove this problem to be in $\mathrm{UP} \cap \mathrm{coUP}$.

A summary of our results (Table 1) and a discussion of open problems can be found in the conclusions section.

2   Preliminaries

We fix the alphabet $\Sigma = \{0,1\}$. Σ^* is the set of words, and $|w|$ is the length of a word $w \in \Sigma^*$. $\mathbb{N}$ denotes the set of the natural numbers, $\mathbb{N}^+$ denotes the set of positive integers. We denote with L, NL, P, NP, coNP, and PSPACE the standard complexity classes whose definitions can be found in textbooks on computational complexity [Pap94].

We extend the arithmetical operations $+$ and $\cdot$ to subsets of $\mathbb{N}$: Let $M, N \subseteq \mathbb{N}$. We define the sum of M and N as $M + N \overset{df}{=} \{m + n : m \in M$ and $n \in N\}$. We define the product of M and N as $M \times N \overset{df}{=} \{m \cdot n : m \in M$ and $n \in N\}$. Unless otherwise stated, the domain of a variable is $\mathbb{N}$.

For a complexity class $\mathcal{C}$, let $\exists^p \cdot \mathcal{C}$ denote the class of languages L such that there exists a polynomial p and a $B \in \mathcal{C}$ such that for all x, $x \in L \iff \exists y \big(|y| \leq p(|x|), (x,y) \in B \big)$.

Unless stated otherwise, all hardness- and completeness-results are in terms of logspace many-one reducibility.

2.1   Satisfiability Problems for Circuits over Sets of Natural Numbers

We define the circuit model and related decision problems. A *circuit* $C=(V, E, g_C)$ is a finite, non-empty, directed, acyclic graph (V, E) with a specified node $g_C \in V$. The graph can contain multi-edges, it does not have to be connected, and $V = \{1, 2, \ldots, n\}$ for some $n \in \mathbb{N}$. Moreover, the nodes in the graph (V, E) are topologically ordered, i.e., for all $v_1, v_2 \in V$, if $v_1 < v_2$, then there is no path from v_2 to v_1. The nodes in V are also called *gates*. Nodes with indegree 0 are called *input gates* and g_C is called the *output gate*. If in a circuit there is an edge from gate u to gate v, then we say that u is a *direct predecessor* of v and v is the *direct successor* of u. If there is a path from u to v but u is not a direct predecessor of v, then u is an *indirect predecessor* of v and v is an *indirect successor* of u.

Let $\mathcal{O} \subseteq \{\cup, \cap, ^-, +, \times\}$. An $\mathcal{O}$-*circuit with unassigned input gates* $C = (V, E, g_C, \alpha)$ is a circuit (V, E, g_C) whose gates are labeled by the labeling function $\alpha : V \to \mathcal{O} \cup \mathbb{N} \cup \{\star\}$ such that the following holds: Each gate has an indegree in $\{0, 1, 2\}$, gates with indegree 0 have labels from $\mathbb{N} \cup \{\star\}$, gates with indegree 1 have label $^-$, and gates with indegree 2 have labels from $\{\cup, \cap, +, \times\}$. Input gates with a label from $\mathbb{N}$ are called *assigned* (or constant) input gates; input gates with label $\star$ are called *unassigned* (or variable) input gates.

Let $u_1 < \cdots < u_n$ be the unassigned inputs in C, and let $x_1, \ldots, x_n \in \mathbb{N}$. By assigning value x_i to the input u_i for $1 \leq i \leq n$, we obtain an $\mathcal{O}$-*circuit* $C(x_1, \ldots, x_n)$ whose input gates are all assigned. Consequently, if C has no unassigned inputs, then $C = C()$.

As all input gates of the circuit $C(x_1, \ldots, x_n)$ have some natural number assigned to it, each gate $g \in V$ computes a set $I(g) \subseteq \mathbb{N}$, inductively defined as follows:

- If g is an input gate, then $I(g) \overset{df}{=} \begin{cases} \{\alpha(g)\}, \text{ if } \alpha(g) \neq \star, \\ \{x_k\}, \quad \text{ if } g = u_k \text{ for a } k \in \{1, \ldots, n\}. \end{cases}$

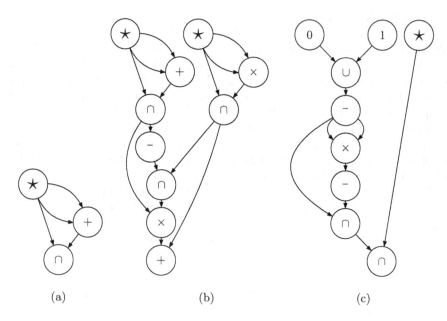

(a)   (b)   (c)

Fig. 1.

- If g has label $^-$ and direct predecessor g_1, then $I(g) \overset{df}{=} \mathbb{N} - I(g_1)$.
- If g has label $\circ \in \{\cup, \cap, +, \times\}$ and direct predecessors g_1 and g_2, then we define $I(g) \overset{df}{=} I(g_1) \circ I(g_2)$.

Define $I(C(x_1,\dots,x_n)) \overset{df}{=} I(g_C)$, the set computed by the $\mathcal{O}$-circuit $C(x_1,\dots,x_n)$. If a circuit computes a singleton, we will sometimes write $I(C(x_1,\dots,x_n)) = a$ instead of $I(C(x_1,\dots,x_n)) = \{a\}$.

Definition 1. *Let $\mathcal{O} \subseteq \{\cup, \cap, ^-, +, \times\}$. We define* membership *problems and* satisfiability *problems for circuits.*

$$\text{MC}(\mathcal{O}) \overset{df}{=} \{(C, b) \mid C \text{ is an } \mathcal{O}\text{-circuit without unassigned inputs and } b \in I(C())\}$$
$$\text{SC}(\mathcal{O}) \overset{df}{=} \{(C, b) \mid C \text{ is an } \mathcal{O}\text{-circuit with unassigned inputs } u_1 < \dots < u_n \text{ and}$$
$$\text{there exist } x_1, \dots, x_n \in \mathbb{N} \text{ such that } b \in I(C(x_1, \dots, x_n))\}$$

When an $\mathcal{O}$-circuit $C = (V, E, g_c, \alpha)$ is used as input for an algorithm, then we use a suitable encoding such that it is possible to verify in deterministic logarithmic space whether a given string encodes a valid circuit. In the following, we will therefore assume that all algorithms start with such a validation of their input strings.

2.2 Examples

Let C be the circuit in Fig. 1(a). The $\star$ indicates that the sole input gate is unassigned. Moreover, we assume that the $\cap$-gate is the output gate. If 0 is assigned to the input gate, then both the input gate and the $+$-gate compute the set $\{0\}$. Consequently, the $\cap$-gate computes $\{0\}$. For all other assignments to the input gate, the circuit computes $\emptyset$. Hence, $(C, 0) \in \mathrm{SC}(\cap, +)$ and $(C, b) \notin \mathrm{SC}(\cap, +)$ for all $b \neq 0$.

Let D be the circuit in Fig. 1(b). Depending on the assignments of the input gates, D computes either $\{1\}$ or $\emptyset$. Consequently, $(D, 1) \in \mathrm{SC}(^-, \cap, +, \times)$ and $(D, b) \notin \mathrm{SC}(^-, \cap, +, \times)$ for all $b \neq 1$. The example in Fig. 1(c) shows a circuit that generates either the empty set or any single prime.

3   Bounds That Can Be Translated from MC($\mathcal{O}$) to SC($\mathcal{O}$)

This section summarizes upper and lower bounds that can be easily obtained from known results about membership problems. Here we can directly infer the lower bounds, since satisfiability problems are generalizations of membership problems. Moreover, we show that for sets of operations $\mathcal{O} \subseteq \{\cup, \cap, ^-, +\}$ and $\mathcal{O} \subseteq \{\cup, +, \times\}$, the satisfiability problem can be expressed as a *polynomially bounded* projection of the corresponding membership problem. This allows us to easily translate several known results into upper bounds for satisfiability problems.

Proposition 1. *The following results are immediate consequences of the results by McKenzie and Wagner [MW03].*

1. $\mathrm{SC}(^-, \cup, \cap, +)$, $\mathrm{SC}(\cup, \cap, +)$, $\mathrm{SC}(\cup, \cap, \times)$, $\mathrm{SC}(^-, \cup, \cap, \times)$, $\mathrm{SC}(\cup, +, \times)$ *are $\leq_{\mathrm{m}}^{\log}$-hard for* PSPACE.
2. $\mathrm{SC}(\cup, \times)$ *is $\leq_{\mathrm{m}}^{\log}$-hard for* NP.
3. $\mathrm{SC}(\cap)$ *and* $\mathrm{SC}(\cup)$ *are $\leq_{\mathrm{m}}^{\log}$-complete for* NL.
4. $\mathrm{SC}(\times)$ *is $\leq_{\mathrm{m}}^{\log}$-hard for* NL.
5. $\mathrm{SC}(\cup, \cap)$ *is $\leq_{\mathrm{m}}^{\log}$-complete for* P.

By definition, the problem SC($\mathcal{O}$) is an unrestricted projection of MC($\mathcal{O}$). We now show that for $\mathcal{O} \subseteq \{\cup, \cap, ^-, +\}$ and $\mathcal{O} \subseteq \{\cup, +, \times\}$ this projection is polynomially bounded.

Lemma 1. *Let C be a circuit over the operations $\mathcal{O} \subseteq \{\cup, \cap, ^-, +, \times\}$ with exactly n unassigned inputs. For $b \in \mathbb{N}$, $x_1, \ldots, x_n \in \mathbb{N}$ and $c \leq b$ it holds that*

1. *if $\mathcal{O} \subseteq \{\cup, \cap, ^-, +\}$, then*
   $$c \in I(C(x_1, \ldots, x_n)) \iff c \in I(C(\min(x_1, b+1), \ldots, \min(x_n, b+1))).$$
2. *if $\mathcal{O} \subseteq \{\cup, +, \times\}$, then*
   $$c \in I(C(x_1, \ldots, x_n)) \implies c \in I(C(\min(x_1, b+1), \ldots, \min(x_n, b+1))).$$

Corollary 1. *Let C be a circuit over the operations $\mathcal{O} \subseteq \{\cup, \cap, ^-, +\}$ or $\mathcal{O} \subseteq \{\cup, +, \times\}$ with exactly n unassigned inputs and let $b \in \mathbb{N}$.*

$$(C, b) \in \mathrm{SC}(\mathcal{O}) \iff \exists x_1, \ldots, x_n \in \{0, \ldots, b+1\} \text{ s.t. } (C(x_1, \ldots, x_n), b) \in \mathrm{MC}(\mathcal{O})$$

Corollary 2. *Let* $\mathcal{O} \subseteq \{\cup, \cap, ^-, +\}$ *or* $\mathcal{O} \subseteq \{\cup, +, \times\}$ *be a set of operations and let* $\mathcal{C}$ *be a complexity class. Then it holds that* $\mathrm{MC}(\mathcal{O}) \in \mathcal{C} \implies \mathrm{SC}(\mathcal{O}) \in \exists^{\mathrm{P}} \cdot \mathcal{C}$.

Together with the results by McKenzie and Wagner [MW03] we obtain:

Corollary 3. *It holds that*

1. $\mathrm{SC}(^-, \cup, \cap, +)$, $\mathrm{SC}(\cup, \cap, +)$, *and* $\mathrm{SC}(\cup, +, \times)$ *are in* PSPACE.
2. $\mathrm{SC}(^-, \cup, \cap)$, $\mathrm{SC}(\cap, +)$, $\mathrm{SC}(\cup, \times)$, $\mathrm{SC}(\cup, +)$, $\mathrm{SC}(+)$, $\mathrm{SC}(+, \times)$ *are in* NP.

4   Satisfiability and Diophantine Equations

Circuits with gates $+$ and $\times$ can be used to compute multivariate polynomials. The presence of $\cap$ then allows us to translate the solvability of diophantine equations into the satisfiability of circuits. Hence the latter satisfiability problems are undecidable. Particularly, they are not polynomially bounded projections of their membership problems.

Lemma 2. *There exists a logspace computable function that on input of a multivariate polynomial* $p(x_1, \ldots, x_n)$ *computes a* $\{+, \times\}$-*circuit* C *with* n *unassigned inputs such that for all* $y_1, \ldots, y_n \in \mathbb{N}$, $I(C(y_1, \ldots, y_n)) = \{p(y_1, \ldots, y_n)\}$.

Theorem 1. $\mathrm{SC}(\cap, +, \times)$ *is undecidable.*

Proof. We show that the question of whether a given diophantine equation has solutions in $\mathbb{N}$ can be reduced to $\mathrm{SC}(\cap, +, \times)$. By the Davis-Putnam-Robinson-Matiyasevich theorem [DPR61, Mat70] this implies that $\mathrm{SC}(\cap, +, \times)$ is undecidable.

Let $p(x_1, \ldots, x_n) = 0$ be a diophantine equation with integer coefficients. By moving negative monoms and constants to the right-hand side, we obtain an equation $l(x_1, \ldots, x_n) = r(x_1, \ldots, x_n)$ such that all coefficients in l, and all coefficients in r are positive. According to Lemma 2, we construct circuits C_l and C_r such that $C_l(x_1, \ldots, x_n) = \{l(x_1, \ldots, x_n)\}$ and $C_r(x_1, \ldots, x_n) = \{r(x_1, \ldots, x_n)\}$. Define a new circuit by $C'(x_1, \ldots, x_n) \overset{df}{=} 0 \times (C_l(x_1, \ldots, x_n) \cap C_r(x_1, \ldots, x_n))$. Then $p(x_1, \ldots, x_n) = 0$ has a solution in $\mathbb{N}$ if and only if $(C', 0) \in \mathrm{SC}(\cap, +, \times)$. □

5   Decidable Satisfiability Problems

In this section we prove upper and lower bounds for decidable satisfiability problems for circuits. Here it turns out that the problems $\mathrm{SC}(\cap, \times)$, $\mathrm{SC}(+)$, and $\mathrm{SC}(\times)$ are particularly interesting. For $\mathrm{SC}(\cap, \times)$, proving membership in NP is nontrivial. We finally prove this with help of certain systems of monom equations and the (also nontrivial) result that integer programming belongs to NP. Moreover, we show that $\mathrm{SC}(+)$ is likely to be more difficult than $\mathrm{SC}(\times)$. While $\mathrm{SC}(+)$ is NP-hard, $\mathrm{SC}(\times)$ belongs to UP $\cap$ coUP.

5.1   Circuits with Both Arithmetic and Set Operations

The problem $SC(\cap, \times)$ has an interesting property. In contrast to most other NP-complete problems, here proving the membership in NP is more difficult than proving the hardness for NP. We start working towards a proof for $SC(\cap, \times) \in$ NP and define the following problem which asks for the solvability of *systems of monom equations*.

Name: MonEq
Instance: A list of equations of the following form.

$$x^5 z^7 = 5^9 y^3 z^2$$
$$yz^2 = 2^3 x^5$$
$$x^2 y^4 z^3 = 3^{11}$$

Question: Is this system of equations solvable over the natural numbers?

Formally, the problem MonEq is defined as follows (where we define 0^0 to be 1).

$\text{MonEq} \stackrel{df}{=} \{(A, B, C, D) \mid A = (a_{i,j}) \in \mathbb{N}^{m \times n}, B = (b_{i,j}) \in \mathbb{N}^{m \times n},$
  $C = (c_1, \ldots, c_m) \in \mathbb{N}^m, D = (d_1, \ldots, d_m) \in \mathbb{N}^m,$
  and there exist $x_1, \ldots, x_n \in \mathbb{N}$ such that
  for all $i \in [1, m]$, $\prod_{j=1}^n x_j^{a_{i,j}} = c_i^{d_i} \cdot \prod_{j=1}^n x_j^{b_{i,j}}\}$

Note that formally, this definition neither allows constant factors at the left-hand side of equations nor allows products of constant factors like $2^{91} \cdot 3^{93} \cdot 5^{97}$. However, such factors can be easily expressed by using additional variables. For example, the equation $7^3 \cdot 15^{70} \cdot x^5 y^7 = 3^7 z^3$ can be equivalently transformed into the following system.

$$a = 7^3$$
$$b = 15^{70}$$
$$abx^5 y^7 = 3^7 z^3$$

We show that systems of monom equations can be solved in nondeterministic polynomial time. Our proof transforms the original problem MonEq to a more restricted version. Then we show the latter to be in NP where we use the fact that integer programming belongs to NP.

Lemma 3. MonEq $\in$ NP.

Utilizing the fact that systems of monom equations can be solved in nondeterministic polynomial time we now show that $SC(\cap, \times)$ belongs to NP. Observe that this is nontrivial, since the smallest satisfying assignment of a $\{\cap, \times\}$-circuit can be exponentially large.

Theorem 2. $SC(\cap, \times) \in$ NP

Proof. We describe a nondeterministic polynomial-time algorithm for $SC(\cap, \times)$ on input (C, d). Without loss of generality we may assume that the nodes

$1, \ldots, m$ are the unassigned input gates and the nodes $m + 1, \ldots, m + n$ are the assigned input gates with labels $b_1, \ldots, b_n$. We recursively attach monoms of the form $x_1^7 x_2^{23} \cdots x_{m+n}^5$ to the gates of C: We attach the monom x_i to input gate i. Let i be a gate with the direct predecessors i_1 and i_2 such that the monom M_1 is attached to i_1 and M_2 is attached to i_2. If i is a $\times$-gate, then we attach the monom $M_1 \cdot M_2$ to i (where we simplify the product in the sense that multiple occurrences of variables x_j are combined). If i is a $\cap$-gate, then we attach the monom M_1 to i. In this way, we attach a monom to each gate of C. Now each $\cap$-gate i induces a monom equation $M_1 = M_2$ where M_1 and M_2 are the monoms that are attached to i's direct predecessors. These equations form a system of monom equations. Next we add the following equations to this system.

- For $i \in [1, n]$ the equation $x_{m+i} = b_i$ where b_i is the label of the assigned input gate $m + i$.
- The equation $M = d$ where M is the monom attached to the output gate.

Our algorithm accepts if and only if the obtained system of monom equations has a solution within the natural numbers. By Lemma 3, the described algorithm is a nondeterministic polynomial-time algorithm. So it remains to argue for the correctness of this algorithm.

For a monom M attached to some gate, let $M(a_1, \ldots, a_m, b_1, \ldots, b_n)$ denote the number that is obtained when M is evaluated for $x_1 = a_1$, $\ldots$, $x_m = a_m$, $x_{m+1} = b_1$, $\ldots$, $x_{m+n} = b_n$. A straightforward induction on the structure of C yields the following.

Claim. If gate g has the monom M attached, then for all $a_1, \ldots, a_m \in \mathbb{N}$, the gate g of the circuit $C(a_1, \ldots, a_m)$ either computes $\emptyset$ or computes the set $\{M(a_1, \ldots, a_m, b_1, \ldots, b_n)\}$.

We show that the algorithm accepts (C, d) if and only if $(C, d) \in \mathrm{SC}(\cap, \times)$. Assume our algorithm accepts on input (C, d). So there exist $a_1, \ldots, a_m$ such that $a_1, \ldots, a_m, b_1, \ldots, b_n$ is a solution for the constructed system of monom equations. Suppose $I(C(a_1, \ldots, a_m)) = \emptyset$. Then there exists a $\cap$-gate g with direct predecessors g_1 and g_2 such that g is connected to the output gate, $I(g_1) \neq \emptyset$, $I(g_2) \neq \emptyset$, and $I(g_1) \neq I(g_2)$. Let M, M_1, and M_2 be the monoms attached to g, g_1, and g_2 respectively. By the claim, $I(g_1) = \{M_1(a_1, \ldots, a_m, b_1, \ldots, b_n)\}$ and $I(g_2) = \{M_2(a_1, \ldots, a_m, b_1, \ldots, b_n)\}$. The equation $M_1 = M_2$ appears in our system of monom equations. Therefore it holds that $M_1(a_1, \ldots, a_m, b_1, \ldots, b_n) = M_2(a_1, \ldots, a_m, b_1, \ldots, b_n)$ and hence $I(g_1) = I(g_2)$. We have already seen that the latter is not true and so it follows that $I(C(a_1, \ldots, a_m)) \neq \emptyset$. Now let M denote the monom attached to the output gate. By the claim, $I(C(a_1, \ldots, a_m)) = \{M(a_1, \ldots, a_m, b_1, \ldots, b_n)\}$. The equation $M = d$ appears in the system of monom equations. So $I(C(a_1, \ldots, a_m)) = \{d\}$ and hence $(C, d) \in \mathrm{SC}(\cap, \times)$.

Conversely, assume now that $(C, d) \in \mathrm{SC}(\cap, \times)$, i.e., there exist $a_1, \ldots, a_m \in \mathbb{N}$ such that $I(C(a_1, \ldots, a_m)) = \{d\}$. We show that $x_1 = a_1$, $\ldots$, $x_m = a_m$, $x_{m+1} = b_1$, $\ldots$, $x_{m+n} = b_n$ is a solution for the system of monom equations that is constructed by the algorithm. The latter immediately implies that the algorithm accepts on input (C, d). In the circuit $C(a_1, \ldots, a_m)$, each $\cap$-gate g that is connected to the output gate computes a nonempty set. So if g_1 and g_2 are the predecessors of g, then $I(g) = I(g_1) = I(g_2)$. Let M, M_1, and M_2 be the monoms attached to g, g_1, and g_2 respectively. From the claim it follows that $M_1(a_1, \ldots, a_m, b_1, \ldots, b_n) = M_2(a_1, \ldots, a_m, b_1, \ldots, b_n)$. So all equations of the form $M_1 = M_2$ are satisfied. Moreover, the additional equations of the form $x_{m+i} = b_i$ are trivially satisfied by our solution. From $I(C(a_1, \ldots, a_m)) = \{d\}$ and from the claim it follows that $M(a_1, \ldots, a_m, b_1, \ldots, b_n) = d$ where M is the monom attached to C's output gate. This shows that all equations of our system are satisfied by the solution $(a_1, \ldots, a_m, b_1, \ldots, b_n)$ and it follows that the algorithm accepts. $\square$

Theorem 3. $SC(\cap, \times)$ *is* $\leq_m^{\log}$*-hard for* NP.

The next corollary shows that we can utilize the algorithm presented in Theorem 2 which evaluates $\{\cap, \times\}$-circuits also to evaluate $\{\cup, \cap, \times\}$-circuits: However, to cope with the $\cup$-gates we first have to unfold the circuit such that no inner gate has outdegree greater than 1. This can cause an exponential blow up in the size of the circuit.

Corollary 4. $SC(\cup, \cap, \times) \in$ NEXP.

5.2   Circuits with Either Arithmetic or Set Operations

We now discuss that $SC(\times)$ is easier than $SC(+)$ unless NP = coNP. More precisely, we show that $SC(\times) \in$ UP $\cap$ coUP and prove $SC(+)$ to be NP-complete. Here it is interesting to note that the same variant of the KNAPSACK-problem is used to establish both, the upper bound for $SC(\times)$ and the lower bound for $SC(+)$. The latter requires a version of KNAPSACK that allows the repeated use of weights. The upper bound for $SC(\times)$ depends on the property that KNAPSACK is *weakly* NP-complete [GJ79], i.e., the problem is easy to solve if the weights are given in unary representation. These constraints lead to the following variant of the KNAPSACK-problem which is known to be weakly NP-complete [Pap94, 9.5.33].

$$\text{KNAPSACK}' \overset{df}{=} \{(v_1, \ldots, v_n, b) \mid n \geq 0, v_1, \ldots v_n, b \in \mathbb{N} \text{ and there exist}$$
$$u_1, \ldots, u_n \in \mathbb{N} \text{ such that } \textstyle\sum_{i=1}^n u_i v_i = b\}$$

Theorem 4. $SC(+)$ *and* $SC(+, \times)$ *are* $\leq_m^{\log}$*-complete for* NP.

By $MC(\times) \in$ NL [MW03] and Corollary 2, it is immediately clear that $SC(\times) \in$ NP. We now prove the better upper bound UP$\cap$coUP by utilizing dynamic programming. More precisely, we will show that testing whether $(C, p^e) \in SC(\times)$ for a prime p and $e \geq 0$ reduces in polynomial time to solving a KNAPSACK' instance where the weights are encoded in unary. By the weak NP-completeness of KNAPSACK', the latter instance can be solved in polynomial time via dynamic programming. We obtain that an $SC(\times)$ instance can be solved in polynomial time if we know the factorization of the target number. This allows us to prove $SC(\times) \in$ UP $\cap$ coUP.

Proposition 2 ([GJ79]). KNAPSACK′ *is computable in polynomial time if the input numbers are given in unary coding.*

Theorem 5. $SC(\times) \in UP \cap coUP$.

Proof. Let C be a $\{\times\}$-circuit with unassigned inputs $u_1, \ldots, u_k$ and let $n \geq 0$. We now describe how to decide whether $(C, n) \in SC(\times)$. Recall that $MC(\times) \in NL$ [MW03], hence a circuit without unassigned inputs can be evaluated in polynomial time. If $n = 0$, we accept if and only if $I(C(0, 0, \ldots, 0)) = 0$. If $n > 0$, we compute $a \stackrel{df}{=} I(C(1, 1, \ldots, 1))$. In the case $a = 0$ we reject, since $a = 0$ implies that the circuit computes 0 regardless of the inputs. If $a \neq 0$, then no constant input that is connected to the output node can be labeled with 0. In addition, we can conclude that every number computable by the circuit is divisible by a. Consequently, if n is not divisible by a, we reject.

Let C' be the circuit obtained by replacing all labels of constant input gates in C by 1. Clearly, this transformation can be performed in polynomial time. For all $b \geq 0$ it now holds that $(C, a \cdot b) \in SC(\times) \Longleftrightarrow (C', b) \in SC(\times)$.

The following nondeterministic algorithm decides whether $(C', n') \in SC(\times)$ for $n' \stackrel{df}{=} \frac{n}{a}$:

1. `guess numbers` $m, p_1, \ldots, p_m, e_1, \ldots, e_m$ `such that` $1 \leq m \leq |n'|$,
   $2 \leq p_1 < p_2 < \cdots < p_m \leq n'$, `and for all i it holds that` $1 \leq e_i \leq |n'|$
2. `if at least one of the` p_i `is not prime then reject`
3. `if` $n' \neq p_1^{e_1} \cdots p_m^{e_m}$ `then reject`
4. `//` `here` $n' = p_1^{e_1} \cdots p_m^{e_m}$ `is the prime factorization of` n'
5. `if` $(C', p_i^{e_i}) \in SC(\times)$ `for all` $i \in [1, m]$ `then accept else reject`

Step 2 is possible in polynomial time by the algorithm by Agrawal, Kayal, and Saxena [AKS04]. We now explain that step 5 can also be carried out in polynomial time. Note that there exist $e_1, \ldots, e_k$ such that for every assignment $x_1, \ldots, x_n$ to the input gates $u_1, \ldots, u_k$, we have $I(C'(x_1, \ldots, x_k)) = x_1^{e_1} \cdots x_k^{e_k}$.

The exponents only depend on the circuit C'. Moreover, they can be computed in polynomial time: First transform C' into a +-circuit C'' as follows: Replace all ×-nodes with +-nodes. Then relabel all constant inputs with 0 instead of 1. Now observe that $I(C''(\underbrace{0, \ldots, 0}_{j-1}, 1, \underbrace{0, \ldots, 0}_{k-j})) = e_j$.

As this can be done in polynomial time, we have shown that all exponents can be computed in polynomial time.

Claim. For a prime p and $e \geq 0$, $(C', p^e) \in SC(\times)$ can be tested in polynomial time.

Proof. If a prime power p^e is computed at the output gate of C', then it follows that all input gates must have powers of p assigned to them. In this case it suffices to solve the following problem: Do there exist $y_1, \ldots, y_k$ such that $(p^{y_1})^{e_1} \cdots (p^{y_k})^{e_k} = p^e$?

We conclude that $(C', p^e) \in SC(\times) \Leftrightarrow \exists y_1, \ldots, y_k (e_1 y_1 + e_2 y_1 + \cdots + e_k y_k = e)$.

It turns out that the question of whether $(C', p^e) \in SC(\times)$ is precisely the KNAPSACK' problem. Since $e \leq \log n$, it follows that the unary coding of e is polynomial in n and hence polynomial in the input. By Proposition 2, it follows that we can check $(C, p^e) \in SC(\times)$ in polynomial time. This proves the claim. $\quad\square$

We have shown that the above algorithm runs in polynomial time. To see that the algorithm accepts if and only if $(C', n') \in SC(\times)$, observe that the following holds: $(C', n') \in SC(\times) \Leftrightarrow \forall_{1 \leq i \leq m}(C', p_i^{l_i}) \in SC(\times)$, where $n' = p_1^{l_1} \cdot \ldots \cdot p_m^{l_m}$ is the prime factorization of n'. Every number has a unique prime factorization. Therefore, there exists exactly one path on which the algorithm reaches step 5. This shows $SC(\times) \in UP$. If we exchange 'accept' and 'reject' in step 5, then we arrive at an algorithm witnessing $\overline{SC(\times)} \in UP$. This completes the proof. $\quad\square$

We now show the NP-hardness of $SC(^-, \cup, \cap)$ by reducing 3SAT to $SC(^-, \cup, \cap)$. Here we utilize the natural correspondence between $\{^-, \cup, \cap\}$ and $\{\neg, \vee, \wedge\}$.

Theorem 6. $SC(^-, \cup, \cap)$ *is* $\leq_m^{\log}$-*complete for* NP.

6 Conclusions

Table 1 summarizes our results. It shows that in most cases we can precisely characterize the complexity of the different variants of the satisfiability problem. Several open questions are apparent from it.

Table 1. Upper and lower bounds for $SC(\mathcal{O})$. All bounds are with respect to $\leq_m^{\log}$-reductions and the numbers refer to the corresponding theorems.

$\mathcal{O}$	Lower Bound		Upper Bound	
$^- \cup \cap + \times$	undecidable			
$^- \cup \cap +$	PSPACE	Pr.1	PSPACE	Co.3
$^- \cup \cap \quad \times$	PSPACE	Pr.1		
$^- \cup \cap$	NP	Th.6	NP	Co.3
$\cup \cap + \times$	undecidable			
$\cup \cap +$	PSPACE	Pr.1	PSPACE	Co.3
$\cup \cap \quad \times$	PSPACE	Pr.1	NEXP	Co.4
$\cup \cap$	P	Pr.1	P	Pr.1
$\cup \quad + \times$	PSPACE	Pr.1	PSPACE	Co.3
$\cup \quad +$	NP	Th.4	NP	Co.3
$\cup \quad \times$	NP	Pr.1	NP	Co.3
$\cup$	NL	Pr.1	NL	Pr.1
$\cap + \times$	undecidable			
$\cap +$	NP	Th.4	NP	Co.3
$\cap \quad \times$	NP	Th.3	NP	Th.2
$\cap$	NL	Pr.1	NL	Pr.1
$+ \times$	NP	Th.4	NP	Th.4
$+$	NP	Th.4	NP	Th.4
$\times$	NL	Pr.1	UP $\cap$ coUP	Th.5

Our main open question is whether $SC(^-, \cup, \cap, \times)$ is decidable. In the absence of +-gates, we cannot express general diophantine equations, which indicates the difficulty of proving undecidability. On the other hand, we do not know any decidable upper bound for this problem, since here the complementation-gates make it difficult to find a bound for the input gates. As the example in Fig. 1(c) shows, such circuits can express nontrivial statements about prime numbers. A further open question is to find a better lower bound for the satisfiability problem for $\{\times\}$-circuits. We prove this problem to be in UP∩coUP. Membership in P seems to be difficult, since $SC(\times)$ comprises the following factoring-like problem: Is the factorization of a given number n of a certain form, for instance $n = x^3 \cdot y^5 \cdot z^2$? However, proving $SC(\times)$ to be hard for factorization is still open.

References

[AKS04]   Agrawal, M., Kayal, N., Saxena, N.: Primes is in P. Annals of Mathematics 160, 781–793 (2004)

[Coo71]   Cook, S.A.: The complexity of theorem proving procedures. In: Proceedings 3rd Symposium on Theory of Computing, pp. 151–158. ACM Press, New York (1971)

[DPR61]   Davis, M., Putnam, H., Robinson, J.: The decision problem for exponential Diophantine equations. Annals of Mathematics 74(2), 425–436 (1961)

[GHR+07]   Glaßer, C., Herr, K., Reitwießner, C., Travers, S., Waldherr, M.: Equivalence problems for circuits over sets of natural numbers. In: Diekert, V., Volkov, M.V., Voronkov, A. (eds.) CSR 2007. LNCS, vol. 4649, pp. 127–138. Springer, Heidelberg (2007)

[GJ79]   Garey, M.R., Johnson, D.S.: Computers and Intractability: A Guide to the Theory of NP-Completeness. Mathematical sciences series. Freeman (1979)

[Kar72]   Karp, R.M.: Reducibility among combinatorial problems. In: Miller, R.E., Thatcher, J.W. (eds.) Complexity of Computer Computations, pp. 85–103. Plenum Press (1972)

[Mat70]   Matiyasevich, Y.V.: Enumerable sets are diophantine. Doklady Akad. Nauk SSSR 191, 279–282, 1970. Translation in Soviet Math. Doklady 11, 354–357 (1970)

[MW03]   McKenzie, P., Wagner, K.W.: The complexity of membership problems for circuits over sets of natural numbers. In: Alt, H., Habib, M. (eds.) STACS 2003. LNCS, vol. 2607, pp. 571–582. Springer, Heidelberg (2003)

[Pap94]   Papadimitriou, C.H.: Computational Complexity. Addison-Wesley, Reading, MA (1994)

[SM73]   Stockmeyer, L.J., Meyer, A.R.: Word problems requiring exponential time. In: Proceedings 5th ACM Symposium on the Theory of Computing, pp. 1–9. ACM Press, New York (1973)

[Wag84]   Wagner, K.: The complexity of problems concerning graphs with regularities. In: Chytil, M.P., Koubek, V. (eds.) Mathematical Foundations of Computer Science 1984. LNCS, vol. 176, pp. 544–552. Springer, Heidelberg (1984)

[Yan00]   Yang, K.: Integer circuit evaluation is PSPACE-complete. In: IEEE Conference on Computational Complexity, pp. 204–213 (2000)

Post Embedding Problem Is Not Primitive Recursive, with Applications to Channel Systems[*]

Pierre Chambart and Philippe Schnoebelen

LSV, ENS Cachan, CNRS
61, av. Pdt. Wilson, F-94230 Cachan, France
{chambart,phs}@lsv.ens-cachan.fr

Abstract. We introduce PEP, the Post Embedding Problem, a variant of PCP where one compares strings with the subword relation, and PEP^{reg}, a further variant where solutions are constrained and must belong to a given regular language. PEP^{reg} is decidable but not primitive recursive. This entails the decidability of reachability for unidirectional systems with one reliable and one lossy channel.

Keywords: Post correspondence problem, Lossy channel systems, Higman's Lemma.

1 Introduction

Post correspondence problem, or shortly PCP, can be stated as the question whether two morphisms $u, v : \Sigma^* \to \Gamma^*$ agree non-trivially on some input, i.e., whether $u(\sigma) = v(\sigma)$ for some non-empty $\sigma \in \Sigma^+$. This undecidable problem plays a central role in computer science because it is very often easier and more natural to prove undecidability by reduction from PCP than from, say, the halting problem for Turing machines.

In this paper we introduce PEP, a variant of PCP where one asks whether $u(\sigma)$ is a *subword* of $v(\sigma)$ for some σ. The subword relation, also called embedding, is denoted "$\sqsubseteq$": $w \sqsubseteq w' \stackrel{\text{def}}{\Leftrightarrow} w$ can be obtained from w' by erasing some letters, possibly all of them, possibly none. We also introduce PEP^{reg}, an extension of PEP where one adds the requirement that a solution σ belongs to a regular language $R \subseteq \Sigma^*$.

As far as we know, PEP and PEP^{reg} have never been considered in the literature [13,9]. This is probably because PEP is trivial (Prop. 3.1). However, and quite surprisingly, adding a regular constraint makes the problem considerably harder. In this paper we show that PEP^{reg} is decidable but that it is not primitive recursive.

Channel systems. What led us to consider PEP^{reg} are verification problems for channel systems, i.e., systems of finite-state machines that communicate asynchronously via unbounded FIFO channels. These systems are Turing-powerful in general but several restricted families or variants have decidable verification problems. For example *lossy* channel systems, where messages can be lost nondeterministically, have decidable reachability and termination problems [7,3,15]. For systems with one reliable channel (no message losses), reachability is easily decidable if the system is *unidirectional*: one

---

[*] Work supported by the Agence Nationale de la Recherche, grant ANR-06-SETIN-001.

V. Arvind and S. Prasad (Eds.): FSTTCS 2007, LNCS 4855, pp. 265–276, 2007.

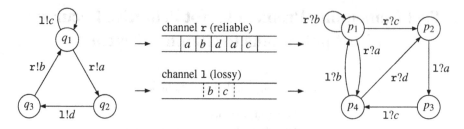

Fig. 1. A unidirectional channel system with one r eliable and one 1 ossy channel

sender sends messages to a receiver via the reliable channel, but no communication is possible in the other direction. With two (reliable) unidirectional channels between the sender and the receiver, reachability is undecidable. The open question that motivated our study is ReachUcs, i.e., reachability for channel systems with *unidirectional communication through <u>one reliable</u> and <u>one unreliable</u> channels*, as illustrated in Figure 1.

It is easy to reduce PEP and PEP^{reg} to ReachUcs. It turns out that reductions from ReachUcs to PEP^{reg} also exist. More surprisingly, we are able to reduce PEP^{reg} to ReachLcs, the reachability problem for (classical) lossy channel systems, and to reduce ReachLcs to ReachUcs. Finally, all three problems are equivalent.

Summary of our contributions

1. We introduce PEP^{reg}, a new decidable variant of the PCP problem that is based on the subword relation. A surprising fact is that the regularity constraint makes PEP^{reg} very different from PEP, and highly non-trivial.
2. We prove that PEP^{reg} is equivalent to (i.e., inter-reducible with) ReachUcs and ReachLcs, two verification problems for systems of communicating automata. This provides the decidability of ReachUcs (and a new decidability proof for ReachLcs).
3. This shows that PEP^{reg} is not primitive recursive (since ReachLcs is not either [15]).

This last point is quite interesting. In recent years, several problems coming from various areas have been shown to be not primitive recursive by reductions from ReachLcs: see, e.g., [2, 4, 6, 8, 10, 11, 12]. This is a clear indication that ReachLcs and equivalent problems occupy a specific niche that had not been identified previously. Discovering a simple and natural problem like PEP^{reg} amid this class will help extend the range of problems that can be connected to the class: PEP^{reg} can be used to simplify existing reduction proofs, and make some future proofs easier to obtain.

Outline of the paper. Section 2 recalls the necessary definitions and notations. We prove that PEP^{reg} is decidable in Section 3 and explore variants and extensions in Section 4. The reductions between PEP^{reg} and ReachLcs or ReachUcs are given in sections 5 and 6. Proofs omitted for lack of space can be found in the long version of this paper [5].

2   Notations and Definitions

Words. We write $u, v, w, t, \sigma, \rho, \alpha, \beta, \dots$ for words, i.e., finite sequences of letters such as $a, b, i, j, \dots$ from alphabets $\Sigma, \Gamma, \dots$, and denote with $u.v$, or uv, the concatenation of u

and v. The *length* of u is written $|u|$. A *morphism* from Σ^* to Γ^* is a map $h : \Sigma^* \to \Gamma^*$ that respects the monoidal structure, i.e., with $h(\varepsilon) = \varepsilon$ and $h(\sigma.\rho) = h(\sigma).h(\rho)$. A morphism h is completely defined by its image $h(1), h(2), \ldots$, on $\Sigma = \{1, 2, \ldots\}$. We often simply write $h_1, h_2, \ldots$, and h_σ, instead of $h(1), h(2), \ldots$, and $h(\sigma)$.

Quotients. Let L be a language and m a word: $m \backslash L \overset{\text{def}}{=} \{w | m.w \in L\}$ is the *(right) quotient* of L by m. When $L \subseteq \Sigma^*$, we write $\mathcal{L}(L)$ for the set $\{m \backslash L \mid m \in \Sigma^*\}$ of all quotients of L. It is well-known that if R is a regular language, then $\mathcal{L}(R)$ is finite and only contains regular languages (that still have their quotients in $\mathcal{L}(R)$). $\mathcal{L}(R)$ can be built effectively from a canonical DFA for R just by varying the initial state.

Embeddings. Given two words $u = a_1 \ldots a_n$ and $v = b_1 \ldots b_m$, we write $u \sqsubseteq v$ when u is a *subword* of v, i.e., when u can be obtained by erasing some letters (possibly none) from v. For example, $abba \sqsubseteq abracadabra$. Equivalently, $u \sqsubseteq v$ when u can be embedded in v, i.e., when there exists an order-preserving injective map $h : \{1, \ldots, n\} \to \{1, \ldots, m\}$ such that $a_i = b_{h(i)}$ for all $i = 1, \ldots, n$. It is well-known that the subword relation is a partial ordering on words, and it is a well-quasi-ordering (Higman's Lemma) when we consider words over a fixed finite alphabet. This means that any set of words has a finite number of minimal elements (minimal w.r.t. $\sqsubseteq$).

Upward-closure. A language $L \subseteq \Gamma^*$ is *upward-closed* if $u \in L$ and $u \sqsubseteq v$ imply $v \in L$. It is *downward-closed* if its complement is upward-closed. Higman's Lemma entails that upward-closed languages (hence also downward-closed languages) are regular.

Splitting words. When $u \sqsubseteq v$, we write $v[u]$ for the longest v_1 such that v is some $v_0.v_1$ with $u \sqsubseteq v_0$. Hence $v[u]$ is the longest suffix of v that can be retained if one has to remove some prefix containing u. Dually, for any u and v, we write $u\{v\}$ for the shortest u_1, such that u can be written as some $u_0.u_1$ with $u_0 \sqsubseteq v$. Hence $u\{v\}$ is the shortest suffix of u that can be obtained if one may only remove prefixes that are contained in v. Observe that $u\{v\}$ is always defined while $v[u]$ is only defined when $u \sqsubseteq v$.

When reasoning about embedding and concatenation, a natural and simple tool is the following.

Lemma 2.1 (Simple Decomposition Lemma). *If $u.w \sqsubseteq v.t$ then either $u \sqsubseteq v$ or $w \sqsubseteq t$.*

However, Lemma 2.1 only works one way. For deeper analyses, we shall need the following more powerful tool.

Lemma 2.2 (Complete Decomposition Lemma)

$$u.w \sqsubseteq v.t \text{ if and only if } \begin{cases} u \sqsubseteq v \text{ and } w \sqsubseteq v[u].t \\ \text{or } u \not\sqsubseteq v \text{ and } u\{v\}.w \sqsubseteq t. \end{cases}$$

3   PEP: Post Correspondence with Embedding

The problem we are considering is a variant of Post correspondence problem where equality is replaced by embedding, and where an additional regular constraint is imposed over the solution.

Problem PEP^reg

Instance: Two finite alphabets Σ and Γ, two morphisms $u,v: \Sigma^* \to \Gamma^*$, and a regular language $R \subseteq \Sigma^*$.

Answer: Yes if and only if there exists a $\sigma \in R$ such that $u_\sigma \sqsubseteq v_\sigma$.

In the above definition, the regular constraint applies to σ but this is inessential and our results still hold when the constraint applies to u_σ, or v_σ, or both (see Section 4).

For complexity issues, we assume that the constraint R in a PEP^reg instance is given as a nondeterministic finite-state automaton (NFA) $\mathcal{A}_R$. By a *reduction* between two decision problems, we mean a logspace many-one reduction. We say two problems are *equivalent* when they are inter-reducible.

PEP is the special case of PEP^reg where R is Σ^+, i.e., where there are no constraints over the form of a non-trivial solution. As far as we know, PEP and PEP^reg have never been considered in the literature and this is probably because PEP is trivial:

Proposition 3.1. *There is a $\sigma \in \Sigma^+$ such that $u_\sigma \sqsubseteq v_\sigma$ if and only if there is some $i \in \Sigma$ such that $u_i \sqsubseteq v_i$.*

This is a direct corollary of Lemma 2.1. A consequence is that PEP is decidable in deterministic logarithmic space.

Surprisingly, adding a regularity constraint makes the problem much harder, as will be proved later. As of now, we focus on proving the following main result.

Theorem 3.2 (Main Result). PEP^reg *is decidable.*

In the rest of this section, we assume a given PEP^reg instance made of $u,v: \Sigma^* \to \Gamma^*$ and $R \subseteq \Sigma^*$. We consider some $\mathcal{L}(R)$-indexed families of languages in Γ^*:

Definition 3.3 (Blocking family). *An $\mathcal{L}(R)$-indexed family $(A_L, B_L)_{L \in \mathcal{L}(R)}$ of languages in Γ^* is a* blocking family *if for all $L \in \mathcal{L}(R)$:*

$$\sigma \in L \text{ and } \alpha \in A_L \text{ imply } \alpha u_\sigma \not\sqsubseteq v_\sigma, \tag{B1}$$

$$\sigma \in L \text{ and } \beta \in B_L \text{ imply } u_\sigma \not\sqsubseteq \beta v_\sigma. \tag{B2}$$

The terminology "blocking" comes from the fact that the α prefix "blocks" solutions in L to $\alpha.u_\sigma \sqsubseteq v_\sigma$. For B_L, the situation is dual: adding $\beta \in B_L$ is not enough to allow solutions in L to $u_\sigma \sqsubseteq \beta.v_\sigma$.

There is a largest blocking family, called the *blocker* languages, or blocker family, $(X_L, Y_L)_{L \in \mathcal{L}(R)}$, given by:

$$X_L \stackrel{\text{def}}{=} \{\alpha \in \Gamma^* \mid \alpha u_\sigma \not\sqsubseteq v_\sigma \text{ for all } \sigma \in L\}, \tag{B3}$$

$$Y_L \stackrel{\text{def}}{=} \{\beta \in \Gamma^* \mid u_\sigma \not\sqsubseteq \beta v_\sigma \text{ for all } \sigma \in L\}. \tag{B4}$$

A blocking family provides information about the absence of solutions to several variants of our PEP^reg instance. For example, the u,v,R instance itself is positive iff $\varepsilon \notin X_R$ iff $\varepsilon \notin Y_R$.

For proving that a given family is blocking, we use a criterion called "stability".

Definition 3.4 (Stable family). *An* $L(R)$-*indexed family* $(A_L, B_L)_{L \in L(R)}$ *of languages is stable iff, for all* $L \in L(R)$:

1. $A_L \subseteq \Gamma^*$ *is upward-closed and* $B_L \subseteq \Gamma^*$ *is downward-closed,*
2. *if* $\varepsilon \in L$, *then* $\varepsilon \notin A_L \cup B_L$,
3. *for all* $i \in \Sigma$ *and* $\alpha \in A_L$:
   (a) *if* $\alpha.u_i \sqsubseteq v_i$ *then* $v_i[\alpha.u_i] \in B_{i \backslash L}$,
   (b) *if* $\alpha.u_i \not\sqsubseteq v_i$ *then* $(\alpha.u_i)\{v_i\} \in A_{i \backslash L}$,
4. *for all* $i \in \Sigma$ *and* $\beta \in B_L$:
   (a) *if* $u_i \sqsubseteq \beta.v_i$ *then* $(\beta.v_i)[u_i] \in B_{i \backslash L}$,
   (b) *if* $u_i \not\sqsubseteq \beta.v_i$ *then* $u_i\{\beta.v_i\} \in A_{i \backslash L}$.

Recall that A_L and B_L, being respectively upward- and downward-closed, must be regular languages. Observe also that $\varepsilon \in B_L$ iff $B_L \neq \varnothing$, while $\varepsilon \in A_L$ iff $A_L = \Gamma^*$.

Proposition 3.5 (Soundness). *A stable family is a blocking family.*

Proof. Assume that $(A_L, B_L)_{L \in L(R)}$ is stable. We prove that it satisfies (B1) and (B2) by induction on the length of σ.

Base case: $\sigma = \varepsilon$. Hence $u_\sigma = v_\sigma = \varepsilon$. Assuming $\alpha u_\sigma \sqsubseteq v_\sigma$ requires $\alpha = \varepsilon$ but if $\sigma \in L$, stability implies that $\varepsilon \notin A_L$. $\sigma \in L$ also implies that B_L is empty so that $u_\sigma \not\sqsubseteq \beta v_\sigma$ is vacuously true.

Inductive case: assume that σ is some $i.\rho$ with $i \in \Sigma$ and $\rho \in \Sigma^*$. Recall that $\sigma \in L$ iff $\rho \in i \backslash L$.

Let $\alpha \in A_L$. If $\alpha u_i \sqsubseteq v_i$, then $v_i[\alpha u_i] \in B_{i \backslash L}$ by stability. Hence $u_\rho \not\sqsubseteq (v_i[\alpha u_i])v_\rho$ by ind. hyp. Then $\alpha u_\sigma = \alpha u_i u_\rho \not\sqsubseteq v_i v_\rho = v_\sigma$ by Lemma 2.2. If, on the other hand, $\alpha u_i \not\sqsubseteq v_i$, then $(\alpha u_i)\{v_i\} \in A_{i \backslash L}$ by stability, hence $(\alpha u_i)\{v_i\}u_\rho \not\sqsubseteq v_\rho$ by ind. hyp., entailing $\alpha u_\sigma \not\sqsubseteq v_\sigma$ by Lemma 2.2.

For $\beta \in B_L$ the reasoning is similar. If $u_i \sqsubseteq \beta v_i$, then $(\beta v_i)[u_i] \in B_{i \backslash L}$ by stability, hence $u_\rho \not\sqsubseteq (\beta v_i)[u_i]v_\rho$ by ind. hyp., hence $u_\sigma = u_i u_\rho \not\sqsubseteq \beta v_i v_\rho = \beta v_\sigma$ by Lemma 2.2. If, on the other hand, $u_i \not\sqsubseteq \beta v_i$, then $u_i\{\beta v_i\} \in A_{i \backslash L}$ by stability, hence $u_i\{\beta v_i\}u_\rho \not\sqsubseteq v_\rho$ by ind. hyp., hence $u_\sigma \not\sqsubseteq \beta v_\sigma$. $\square$

The criterion is also sufficient:

Proposition 3.6 (Completeness). *The blocker family* $(X_L, Y_L)_{L \in L(R)}$ *is stable.*

Proof. Clearly, as defined by (B3) and (B4) and for any $L \in L(R)$, X_L is upward-closed and Y_L is downward-closed. Similarly, $\varepsilon \notin X_L$ and $\varepsilon \notin Y_L$ when $\varepsilon \in L$.

It remains to check conditions *3* and *4* for stability. We consider four cases:

3a: Assume that $\alpha u_i \sqsubseteq v_i$ for some i in Σ and some α in some X_L. If, by way of contradiction, we assume that $v_i[\alpha.u_i] \notin Y_{i \backslash L}$ then, by (B4), there is some $\rho \in i \backslash L$ such that $u_\rho \sqsubseteq v_i[\alpha.u_i]v_\rho$. Thus $\alpha u_i u_\rho \sqsubseteq v_i v_\rho$ by Lemma 2.2, i.e., $\alpha u_\sigma \sqsubseteq v_\sigma$ writing σ for $i.\rho$. But, since $\sigma \in L$, this contradicts $\alpha \in X_L$.

4a: A similar reasoning applies if we assume that $u_i \sqsubseteq \beta v_i$ for some i in Σ and some β in some Y_L while $(\beta v_i)[u_i] \notin Y_{i \backslash L}$: we derive from (B4) that $u_\rho \sqsubseteq (\beta v_i)[u_i]v_\rho$ for some $\rho \in i \backslash L$. Hence $u_i u_\rho \sqsubseteq \beta v_i v_\rho$ by Lemma 2.2, a contradiction since $i.\rho \in L$.

3b: If we assume that $\alpha u_i \not\sqsubseteq v_i$ for $\alpha \in X_L$ and $(\alpha u_i)\{v_i\} \notin X_{i\setminus L}$ then, by (B3), there is some $\rho \in i \setminus L$ s.t. $(\alpha u_i)\{v_i\} u_\rho \sqsubseteq v_\rho$. Then $\alpha u_i u_\rho \sqsubseteq v_i v_\rho$ by Lemma 2.2, a contradiction since $i.\rho \in L$.

4b: Similarly, assuming that $u_i \not\sqsubseteq \beta v_i$ while $u_i\{\beta v_i\} \notin A_{i\setminus L}$, we derive $(u_i\{\beta v_i\})u_\rho \sqsubseteq v_i v_\rho$, i.e., $u_i u_\rho \sqsubseteq \beta v_i v_\rho$, another contradiction.   □

Proposition 3.7 (Stability is decidable). *It is decidable whether an $L(R)$-indexed family $(A_L, B_L)_{L\in L(R)}$ of regular languages is a stable family.*

Proof. We can assume that the A_L and B_L are given by DFA's. Conditions *1* and *2* of stability are easy to check.

For a given $i \in \Sigma$ and $L \in L(R)$, checking condition *3a* needs only consider α's that are shorter than v_i, which is easily done.

Checking condition *3b* is trickier. One way to do it is to consider the set of all α's such that $\alpha u_i \not\sqsubseteq v_i$. This is a regular set that can be obtained effectively. Then the set of all corresponding $(\alpha u_i)\{v_i\}$ is also regular and effective (see [5]) so that we can check that it is included in $A_{i\setminus L}$.

For condition *4a*, and given some $L \in L(R)$ and some $i \in \Sigma$, the set of all β's such that $u_i \sqsubseteq \beta v_i$ is regular and effective. One can then compute the corresponding set of all $(\beta v_i)[u_i]$, again regular and effective, and check inclusion in $B_{i\setminus L}$. The complement set of all β's such that $u_i \not\sqsubseteq \beta v_i$ is also regular and effective, and one easily derives the corresponding $u_i\{\beta v_i\}$'s (a finite set of suffixes of u_i), hence checking condition *4b*.   □

Proof (of Theorem 3.2). Since PEP^{reg} is r.e., it is sufficient to prove that it is also co-r.e. For this we observe that, by Propositions 3.5 and 3.6, a PEP^{reg} instance is negative if, and only if, there exists a stable family $(A_L, B_L)_{L\in L(R)}$ satisfying $\varepsilon \in A_R$. One can effectively enumerate all families $(A_L, B_L)_{L\in L(R)}$ of regular languages and check whether they are stable (Proposition 3.7) (and have $\varepsilon \in A_R$). If the PEP^{reg} instance is negative, this procedure will eventually terminate, e.g., when it considers the blocker family.   □

Remark 3.8. Computing the blocker family for a negative PEP^{reg} instance cannot be done effectively (this is a consequence of known results on lossy channel systems). Thus when the procedure described above terminates, there is no way to know that it has encountered the largest blocking family.   □

4   Variants and Extensions

Short morphisms. PEP$^{\text{reg}}_{\leq 1}$ is PEP^{reg} with the constraint that all u_i's and v_i's have length ≤ 1, i.e., they must belong to $\Gamma \cup \{\varepsilon\}$.

Proposition 4.1. PEP^{reg} *reduces to* PEP$^{\text{reg}}_{\leq 1}$.

Proof (Sketch). Let u, v, R be a PEP^{reg} instance. For all $i \in \Sigma$, write u_i in the form $a_i^1 \dots a_i^{l_i}$ and v_i in the form $b_i^1 \dots b_i^{m_i}$. Let $k = \max\{l_i, m_i \mid i \in \Sigma\}$. One builds a PEP$^{\text{reg}}_{\leq 1}$ instance u', v', R' by letting $\Sigma' \overset{\text{def}}{=} \Sigma \times \{1, 2, \dots, k\}$, $u'(i,p) \overset{\text{def}}{=} a_i^p$ if $p \leq l_i$, and $u'(i,p) \overset{\text{def}}{=} \varepsilon$ otherwise. Similarly, $v'(i,p)$ is v_i^p, the pth letter in v_i, or ε. We now let $R' \overset{\text{def}}{=} h(R)$ where $h : \Sigma \to \Sigma'$ is the morphism defined by $h(i) = (i,1)(i,2)\dots(i,k)$. Finally u', v', R' is a PEP$^{\text{reg}}_{\leq 1}$ instance that is positive iff u, v, R is positive.   □

Constraining u_σ and v_σ. $\text{PEP}^{\text{u\_reg}}$ is like PEP^{reg} except that the constraint $R \subseteq \Gamma^*$ now applies to u_σ: a solution is some $\sigma \in \Sigma^*$ with $u_\sigma \in R$ (and $u_\sigma \sqsubseteq v_\sigma$). Similarly, $\text{PEP}^{\text{v\_reg}}$ has the constraint apply to v_σ, while $\text{PEP}^{\text{uv\_reg}}$ has two constraints, $R_1, R_2 \subseteq \Gamma^*$, that apply to, respectively and simultaneously, u_σ and v_σ.

Proposition 4.2. $\text{PEP}^{\text{uv\_reg}}$ *reduces to* PEP^{reg}.

Proof. Let u, v, R_1, R_2 be a $\text{PEP}^{\text{uv\_reg}}$ instance. Let $R \stackrel{\text{def}}{=} u^{-1}(R_1) \cap v^{-1}(R_2)$. (Recall that the image of a regular R by an inverse morphism is regular and can easily be constructed from R.) By definition $\sigma \in R$ iff $u_\sigma \in R_1$ and $v_\sigma \in R_2$. Thus the PEP^{reg} instance u, v, R is positive iff u, v, R_1, R_2 is. □

Reductions exist in the other direction, as the next two propositions show.

Proposition 4.3. PEP^{reg} *reduces to* $\text{PEP}^{\text{v\_reg}}$.

Proof (Sketch). Let u, v, R be a PEP^{reg} instance. W.l.o.g., we may assume that $\Sigma \cap \Gamma = \varnothing$. Define a $\text{PEP}^{\text{v\_reg}}$ instance u', v', R' by letting $v' : \Sigma^* \to (\Gamma \cup \Sigma)^*$ be given by $v'_i \stackrel{\text{def}}{=} i.v_i$ and keeping $u' = u$ unchanged. Let $R' \stackrel{\text{def}}{=} h^{-1}(R)$ where $h : (\Gamma \cup \Sigma)^* \to \Gamma^*$ is the erasing morphism that suppresses letters from Σ. Note that $v'_\sigma \in R'$ iff $\sigma = h(v'_\sigma) \in R$, so that u', v', R' is a positive $\text{PEP}^{\text{v\_reg}}$ instance iff u, v, R is a positive PEP^{reg} instance. □

Proposition 4.4. $\text{PEP}^{\text{reg}}_{\leq 1}$ *reduces to* $\text{PEP}^{\text{u\_reg}}$.

Proof (Sketch). Let u, v, R be a $\text{PEP}^{\text{reg}}_{\leq 1}$ instance. W.l.o.g., we assume $\Sigma = \{1, 2, \ldots, k\}$ and let $\Sigma' \stackrel{\text{def}}{=} \{0\} \cup \Sigma$ with $g : \Sigma'^* \to \Sigma^*$ the associated erasing morphism. We also assume $\Gamma \cap \Sigma' = \varnothing$ and let $\Gamma' \stackrel{\text{def}}{=} \Gamma \cup \Sigma'$, with $h : \Gamma'^* \to \Sigma^*$ as erasing morphism.

With u, v, R, we associate a $\text{PEP}^{\text{u\_reg}}$ instance u', v', R' based on Σ' and Γ', and defined by $u'_0 \stackrel{\text{def}}{=} \varepsilon$, $v'_0 \stackrel{\text{def}}{=} 1.2 \ldots k$, and, for $i \in \Sigma$, $u'_i \stackrel{\text{def}}{=} i.u_i$ and $v'_i \stackrel{\text{def}}{=} v_i$. Letting $R' = h^{-1}(R)$ ensures that $u'_\sigma \in R'$ iff $g(\sigma) \in R$. Clearly, if $u'_\sigma \sqsubseteq v'_\sigma$, then $u_{g(\sigma)} \sqsubseteq v_{g(\sigma)}$. Conversely, if $u_{\sigma'} \sqsubseteq v_{\sigma'}$, it is possible to find a $\sigma \in g^{-1}(\sigma')$ that satisfies $u'_\sigma \sqsubseteq v'_\sigma$: this is just a matter of inserting enough 0's at the appropriate places (and this is where we use the assumption that all u_i's and v_i's have length ≤ 1). □

Now, since $\text{PEP}^{\text{u\_reg}}$ and $\text{PEP}^{\text{v\_reg}}$ are special cases of $\text{PEP}^{\text{uv\_reg}}$, and since $\text{PEP}^{\text{reg}}_{\leq 1}$ is a special case of PEP^{reg}, Propositions 4.1, 4.2, 4.3 and 4.4 entail the following.

Theorem 4.5. PEP^{reg}, $\text{PEP}^{\text{reg}}_{\leq 1}$, $\text{PEP}^{\text{u\_reg}}$, $\text{PEP}^{\text{v\_reg}}$ *and* $\text{PEP}^{\text{uv\_reg}}$ *are inter-reducible.*

Context-free constraints and Presburger constraints. PEP^{cf} is the extension of PEP^{reg} where we allow the constraint R to be any context-free language (say, given in the form of a context-free grammar). PEP^{dcf} is PEP^{cf} restricted to *deterministic* context-free constraints. PEP^{Pres} is the extension where $R \subseteq \Sigma^*$ can be any language defined by a Presburger constraint over the number of occurrences of each letter from Σ (or, equivalently, the commutative image of R is a semilinear subset of the commutative monoid $\mathbb{N}^\Sigma$).

Theorem 4.6. PEP^{dcf}, PEP^{cf} *and* PEP^{Pres} *are undecidable.*

Proof. The (classic) PCP problem reduces to PEP^{dcf} or PEP^{Pres} by associating, with an instance $u, v : \Sigma^* \to \Gamma^*$, the constraint $R_{\geq} \subseteq \Sigma^+$ defined by

$$\sigma \in R_{\geq} \overset{\text{def}}{\Leftrightarrow} |u_\sigma| \geq |v_\sigma| \text{ and } \sigma \neq \varepsilon.$$

Obviously, $u_\sigma \sqsubseteq v_\sigma$ and $\sigma \in R_{\geq}$ iff $u_\sigma = v_\sigma$. Observe that $R_{\geq}$ is easily defined in the quantifier-free fragment of Presburger logic. Furthermore, since $R_{\geq}$ can be recognized by a counter machine with a single counter, it is indeed deterministic context-free. $\quad\square$

5 From PEP^{reg} to Lossy Channel Systems

We now reduce PEP^{reg} to ReachLcs, the reachability problem for lossy channel systems.

Systems composed of several finite-state components communicating via several channels (all of them lossy) can be simulated by systems with a single channel and a single component (see, e.g., [15, Section 5]). Hence we define here a lossy channel system (a LCS) as a tuple $S = (Q, \text{M}, \{\text{c}\}, \Delta)$ where $Q = \{q_1, q_2, \ldots\}$ is a finite set of *control states*, $\text{M} = \{a_1, a_2, \ldots\}$ is a finite *message alphabet*, c is the name of the single *channel*, and $\Delta = \{\delta_1, \ldots\}$ is the finite set of *transition rules*. Rules in Δ are *writing rules*, of the form $q \overset{\text{c!}u}{\longrightarrow} q'$ (where $u \in \text{M}^*$ is any sequence of messages), or *reading rules* $q \overset{\text{c?}u}{\longrightarrow} q'$. We usually omit writing "c" in rules since there is only one channel, and no possibility for confusion.

The behaviour of S is given in the form of a transition system. A *configuration* of S is a pair $\langle q, v \rangle \in Q \times \text{M}^*$ of a state and a channel contents. Transitions between configurations are obtained from the rules. Formally, $\langle q, v \rangle \to \langle q', v' \rangle$ is a valid transition iff Δ contains a reading rule of the form $q \overset{?u}{\longrightarrow} q'$ and $v = uv'$, or Δ contains a writing rule of the form $q \overset{!u}{\longrightarrow} q'$ and $v' = vu'$ for some $u' \sqsubseteq u$. The intuition behind this definition is that a reading rule consumes u from the head of the channel while a writing rule appends a (nondeterministically chosen) subsequence u' of u, and the rest of u is lost. See, e.g., [3, 15] for more details on LCS's.

Remark 5.1. This behaviour is called *write-lossy* because messages can only be lost when they are appended to the channel, but once inside c they remain there until a reading rule consumes them. This is different from, e.g., *front-lossy* semantics, where messages are lost when consumed (see [14]), or from the usual definition of LCS's, where messages can be lost at any time. These differences are completely inessential when one considers questions like reachability or termination, and authors use the definition that is technically most convenient for their purpose. In this paper, as in [1], the write-lossy semantics is the most convenient one. $\quad\square$

Remark 5.2. Below we use extended rules of the form $q \overset{!u\,?v}{\longrightarrow} q'$. These are a shorthand notation for pairs of "consecutive" rules $q \overset{!u}{\longrightarrow} s$ and $s \overset{?v}{\longrightarrow} q'$ where s is an extra intermediary state that is not used anywhere else (and that we may omit listing in Q). $\quad\square$

ReachLcs, the *reachability problem for LCS's*, is the question, given a LCS S and two states $q, q' \in Q$, whether there exists a sequence of transitions in S going from $\langle q, \varepsilon \rangle$ to $\langle q', \varepsilon \rangle$. The rest of this section proves the following theorem.

Theorem 5.3. $\mathsf{PEP}^{\mathrm{reg}}$ *reduces to* ReachLcs.

Remark 5.4. Since ReachLcs is decidable [3], Theorem 5.3 provides another proof that $\mathsf{PEP}^{\mathrm{reg}}$ is decidable. $\qquad\qquad\square$

Let u, v, R be a $\mathsf{PEP}^{\mathrm{reg}}$ instance and $\sigma \in R$ be a solution. We say σ is a *direct* solution if $u_\rho \sqsubseteq v_\rho$ for every prefix ρ of σ. An equivalent formulation is: $\sigma = i_1 \ldots i_m$ is a direct solution iff there are words $v'_1, \ldots, v'_m$ such that:

1. $v'_k \sqsubseteq v_{i_k}$ for all $k = 1, \ldots, m$,
2. $u_{i_1} \ldots u_{i_m} = v'_1 \ldots v'_m$,
3. $|u_{i_1} \ldots u_{i_k}| \leq |v'_1 \ldots v'_k|$ for all $k = 1, \ldots, m$.

A *codirect* solution is defined in a similar way, with the difference that we now require $|u_{i_1} \ldots u_{i_k}| \geq |v'_1 \ldots v'_k|$ for all $k = 1, \ldots, m$ (i.e., the u_i's are ahead of the v'_i's instead of lagging behind).

We let $\mathsf{PEP}^{\mathrm{reg}}_{\mathrm{dir}}$ and $\mathsf{PEP}^{\mathrm{reg}}_{\mathrm{codir}}$ denote the questions whether a $\mathsf{PEP}^{\mathrm{reg}}$ instance has a direct (resp. codirect) solution. Obviously, $\mathsf{PEP}^{\mathrm{reg}}_{\mathrm{dir}}$ and $\mathsf{PEP}^{\mathrm{reg}}_{\mathrm{codir}}$ are equivalent problems since an instance u, v, R has a codirect solution iff its mirror image $\widetilde{u}, \widetilde{v}, \widetilde{R}$ had a direct solution.

Proposition 5.5. $\mathsf{PEP}^{\mathrm{reg}}_{\mathrm{dir}}$ *(and* $\mathsf{PEP}^{\mathrm{reg}}_{\mathrm{codir}}$*) reduce to* ReachLcs.

Proof (Idea). Let u, v, R be a $\mathsf{PEP}^{\mathrm{reg}}_{\mathrm{dir}}$ instance. Recall that R is given via some NFA $\mathcal{A}_R = \langle Q, \Sigma, \delta, q_{\mathrm{init}}, F \rangle$. With this instance, one associates a LCS $S = \langle Q, \Gamma, \{c\}, \Delta \rangle$ with a graph structure (Q, Δ) inherited from $\mathcal{A}_R$. The difference is that an edge $r \xrightarrow{i} s$ in $\mathcal{A}_R$ gives rise to a transition rule $r \xrightarrow{!v_i \, ?u_i} s$ in S. With such rules, S can write the sequence $v'_1, v'_2, \ldots$ on c, read $u_{i_1}, u_{i_2}, \ldots$ in lock-step fashion, and finally can move from the initial configuration $\langle q_{\mathrm{init}}, \varepsilon \rangle$ to some final configuration $\langle f, \varepsilon \rangle$ with $f \in F$ iff the $\mathsf{PEP}^{\mathrm{reg}}$ instance has a direct solution. Restricting to direct solutions is what ensures that the $v'_1 \ldots v'_k$ prefix that has been written on the channel is always longer than $u_{i_1} \ldots u_{i_k}$. $\qquad\square$

If we now look at a general solution to a $\mathsf{PEP}^{\mathrm{reg}}$ instance (more precisely a $\mathsf{PEP}^{\mathrm{reg}}_{\leq 1}$ instance) it can be decomposed as a succession of alternating direct and codirect solutions to subproblems that are constrained by residuals of R.

Formally, assume u, v, R is a $\mathsf{PEP}^{\mathrm{reg}}_{\leq 1}$ instance and $\sigma = i_1 \ldots i_m$ is a solution. Then there are words $v'_1, \ldots, v'_m$ with $v'_k \sqsubseteq v_{i_k}$ for $k = 1, \ldots, m$, and such that $u_{i_1} \ldots u_{i_m} = v'_1 \ldots v'_m$. Now, for $0 \leq k \leq m$, define $d_k \stackrel{\mathrm{def}}{=} |u_{i_1} \ldots u_{i_k}| - |v'_1 \ldots v'_k|$. Then obviously $d_0 = d_m = 0$. σ is a direct solution if $d_k \leq 0$ for all k. It is codirect if $d_k \geq 0$ for all k. In general, d_k may oscillate between positive and negative values. But since all u_i's and v_i's have length ≤ 1, the difference $d_{k+1} - d_k$ is in $\{-1, 0, 1\}$. Hence d_k cannot change sign without being zero. In summary, the following holds:

Lemma 5.6. *A* $\mathsf{PEP}^{\mathrm{reg}}_{\leq 1}$ *instance* u, v, R *is positive iff there are states* $q_0, q_1, \ldots, q_{2m}$ *in* $\mathcal{A}_R$ *with* $q_0 = q_{\mathrm{init}}$, $q_{2m} \in F$, *and such that, for all* $0 \leq i < m$, u, v, R_{2i} *is a positive* $\mathsf{PEP}^{\mathrm{reg}}_{\mathrm{dir}}$

instance and u, v, R_{2i+1} is a positive $\text{PEP}^{\text{reg}}_{\text{codir}}$ instance (where R_i is the regular language recognized by $\mathcal{A}_R$ when the initial state is changed to q_i and the final states to $\{q_{i+1}\}$).

With Lemma 5.6, one may prove Theorem 5.3 by extending the construction proving Proposition 5.5. Now the LCS looks for a sequence of alternating direct and codirect solutions. In direct mode, it proceeds as earlier until some state q_{2i+1} is reached. It may then switch to codirect mode. For this, it checks that the channel is empty (see below), guesses nondeterministically q_{2i+2}, stores q_{2i+1} and q_{2i+2} in its finite memory, and now looks for a codirect solution to u, v, R_{2i+1}. This is done by working on the mirror problem $\widetilde{u}, \widetilde{v}$, and moving backward from q_{2i+2} to q_{2i+1}. When q_{2i+1} is reached (which can be checked since it has been stored when switching mode) it is possible to switch back to direct mode, starting from state q_{2i+2} (which was stored too), again after checking that the channel is empty. The emptiness checks use standard tricks, e.g., rules $q \xrightarrow{!\# ?\#} q$ that write a special symbol $\# \notin \Gamma$ and consume it immediately.

6 Reachability for Unidirectional Systems

6.1 Unidirectional Systems

ReachUcs is the reachability problem for UCS, i.e., systems of two components communicating *unidirectionally* via one reliable and one lossy channel, as illustrated in Fig. 1. A UCS has the form $S = (Q_1, Q_2, M, \{r, 1\}, \Delta_1, \Delta_2)$. The Q_1, Δ_1 pair defines the sender component, with rules of the form $q \xrightarrow{r!u} q'$ or $q \xrightarrow{1!u} q'$. The Q_2, Δ_2 pair has rules $q \xrightarrow{r?u} q'$ or $q \xrightarrow{1?u} q'$, defining the receiver component. A configuration is a tuple $\langle q_1, q_2, v_1, v_2 \rangle$ with control states q_1 and q_2 for the components, contents v_1 for channel r, and v_2 for 1.

The operational semantics is as expected. A rule $q \xrightarrow{r!u} q'$ (resp. $q \xrightarrow{1!u} q'$) from Δ_1 gives rise to all transitions $\langle q, q_2, v_1, v_2 \rangle \rightarrow \langle q', q_2, v_1 u, v_2 \rangle$ (resp. all $\langle q, q_2, v_1, v_2 \rangle \rightarrow \langle q', q_2, v_1, v_2 u' \rangle$ for $u' \sqsubseteq u$). A rule $q \xrightarrow{r?u} q'$ (resp. $q \xrightarrow{1?u} q'$) from Δ_2 gives rise to all transitions $\langle q_1, q, u v_1, v_2 \rangle \rightarrow \langle q_1, q', v_1, v_2 \rangle$ (resp. all $\langle q_1, q, v_1, u v_2 \rangle \rightarrow \langle q_1, q', v_1, v_2 \rangle$). Observe that message losses only occur when writing to channel 1.

Remark 6.1. A consequence of unidirectionality is that a run $\langle q_1, q_2, v_1, v_2 \rangle \rightarrow \cdots \rightarrow \langle q'_1, q'_2, v'_1, v'_2 \rangle$ can always be reordered so that it first uses only transitions from Δ_1 that fill the channels, followed by only transitions from Δ_2 that consume from them.   □

Theorem 6.2 [5]. ReachLcs *reduces to* ReachUcs.

6.2 From Unidirectional Systems to PEP^{reg}

We now show that PEP^{reg} is expressive enough to encode ReachUcs.

Theorem 6.3. ReachUcs *reduces to* PEP^{reg}.

Consider an ReachUcs instance that asks whether one can go from $\langle q_0, q'_0, \varepsilon, \varepsilon \rangle$ to $\langle q_f, q'_f, \varepsilon, \varepsilon \rangle$[1] in some UCS $S = (Q_1, Q_2, M, \{r, 1\}, \Delta_1, \Delta_2)$. Without loss of generality,

---

[1] For simplification purposes, this proof considers ReachUcs instances where the channels are empty in the starting and ending configurations. This is no real loss of generality since the general ReachUcs problem easily reduces to the restricted problem.

we assume that the rules in S only read or write at most one message: formally, we write M_ε for $M \cup \{\varepsilon\}$ and denote with $\alpha(\delta) \in M_\varepsilon$ (resp. $\beta(\delta) \in M_\varepsilon$) the messages that rule δ writes to, or reads from, $\mathbf{r}$ (resp. $\mathbf{1}$). Observe that whether $\alpha(\delta)$ and $\beta(\delta)$ are read or written depends on whether δ belongs to Δ_1 or Δ_2. Observe also that there is at least one ε among $\alpha(\delta)$ and $\beta(\delta)$.

Assume that the ReachUcs instance is positive and that a witness run π first uses a sequence of rules $\delta_1 \ldots \delta_m \in \Delta_1^*$, followed by a sequence $\gamma_1 \ldots \gamma_l \in \Delta_2^*$ (this special form is explained in Remark 6.1). Then π first writes $w = \alpha(\delta_1) \ldots \alpha(\delta_m)$ to $\mathbf{r}$, then reads $w' = \alpha(\gamma_1) \ldots \alpha(\gamma_l)$ from $\mathbf{r}$, and we conclude that $w = w'$. Simultaneously, it writes a subword w'' of $\beta(\delta_1) \ldots \beta(\delta_m)$ to $\mathbf{1}$, and reads it in the form $\beta(\gamma_1) \ldots \beta(\gamma_l)$.

We are now ready to express this as a $\mathsf{PEP}^{\mathrm{reg}}$ problem. Let $\Sigma \overset{\mathrm{def}}{=} \Delta_1 \cup \Delta_2$ (assuming $\Delta_1 \cap \Delta_2 = \varnothing$) and $\Gamma \overset{\mathrm{def}}{=} M$. The morphisms are given by

$$u(\delta) \overset{\mathrm{def}}{=} \begin{cases} \beta(\delta) & \text{if } \delta \in \Delta_2, \\ \varepsilon & \text{otherwise,} \end{cases} \qquad v(\delta) \overset{\mathrm{def}}{=} \begin{cases} \beta(\delta) & \text{if } \delta \in \Delta_1, \\ \varepsilon & \text{otherwise.} \end{cases}$$

Now write R_1 for the set of all sequences $\delta_1 \ldots \delta_m \in \Delta_1^*$ that form a connected path from q_0 to q_f in Q_1, and R_2 for the set of all sequences $\gamma_1 \ldots \gamma_l \in \Delta_2^*$ that form a connected path from q_0' to q_f' in Q_2. Let R_3 contains all rules $\delta \in \Delta_1 \cup \Delta_2$ with $\alpha(\delta) = \varepsilon$, and all sequences $\delta.\gamma$ in $\Delta_1 \Delta_2$ with $\alpha(\delta) = \alpha(\gamma)$. R_1 and R_2 are regular subsets of Γ^*, while R_3 is even finite.

We now let $R \overset{\mathrm{def}}{=} (R_1 \bowtie R_2) \cap R_3^*$, where $\bowtie$ denotes the shuffle of two languages (recall that this is regularity preserving). We conclude the proof of Theorem 6.3 with:

Lemma 6.4 [5]. *u, v, R is a positive $\mathsf{PEP}^{\mathrm{reg}}$ instance iff the ReachUcs instance is positive.*

By combining with Theorems 6.3 and 6.2 we obtain the equivalence (inter-reducibility) of our three problems: $\mathsf{PEP}^{\mathrm{reg}}$, ReachLcs and ReachUcs. This has two important new corollaries:

Corollary 6.5. ReachUcs *is decidable (but not primitive recursive).*

Corollary 6.6. $\mathsf{PEP}^{\mathrm{reg}}$ *is (decidable but) not primitive recursive.*

7   Concluding Remarks

We introduced $\mathsf{PEP}^{\mathrm{reg}}$, a variant of Post Correspondence Problem based on embedding (a.k.a. subword) rather than equality. Furthermore, a regular constraint can be imposed on the allowed solutions, which makes the problem non-trivial.

$\mathsf{PEP}^{\mathrm{reg}}$ was introduced while considering ReachUcs, a verification problem for channel systems where a sender may send messages to a receiver through one reliable and one lossy channel, and where no communication is allowed in the other direction.

Our main results are (1) a non-trivial proof that $\mathsf{PEP}^{\mathrm{reg}}$ is decidable, and (2) three non-trivial reductions showing that $\mathsf{PEP}^{\mathrm{reg}}$, ReachUcs and ReachLcs are equivalent. ReachLcs is the now well-known verification problem for lossy channel systems, where all channels are lossy but where no unidirectionality restriction applies. The equivalence between the three problems has two unexpected consequences: it shows that ReachUcs is decidable, and that PEP^{reg} is not primitive recursive. We also show that (3) PEP^{reg} and PEP^{reg}_{dir}, an important variant, are inter-reducible.

Beyond the applications to the theory of channel systems (our original motivation), the discovery of PEP^{reg} is interesting in its own right. Indeed, in recent years the literature has produced many hardness proofs that rely on reductions from ReachLcs. We expect that such results, existing or yet to come, are easier to prove by reducing from PEP^{reg}, or from PEP^{reg}_{dir}, than from ReachLcs.

References

1. Abdulla, P.A., Baier, C., Purushothaman Iyer, S., Jonsson, B.: Simulating perfect channels with probabilistic lossy channels. Information and Computation 197(1–2), 22–40 (2005)
2. Abdulla, P.A., Deneux, J., Ouaknine, J., Worrell, J.: Decidability and complexity results for timed automata via channel machines. In: Caires, L., Italiano, G.F., Monteiro, L., Palamidessi, C., Yung, M. (eds.) ICALP 2005. LNCS, vol. 3580, pp. 1089–1101. Springer, Heidelberg (2005)
3. Abdulla, P.A., Jonsson, B.: Verifying programs with unreliable channels. Information and Computation 127(2), 91–101 (1996)
4. Amadio, R., Meyssonnier, Ch.: On decidability of the control reachability problem in the asynchronous π-calculus. Nordic Journal of Computing 9(2), 70–101 (2002)
5. Chambard, P., Schnoebelen, Ph.: Post embedding problem is not primitive recursive, with applications to channel systems. Research Report LSV-07-28, Lab. Specification and Verification, ENS de Cachan, Cachan, France (September 2007)
6. Demri, S., Lazić, R.: LTL with the freeze quantifier and register automata. In: Proc. LICS 2006, pp. 17–26. IEEE Comp. Soc. Press, Los Alamitos (2006)
7. Finkel, A.: Decidability of the termination problem for completely specificied protocols. Distributed Computing 7(3), 129–135 (1994)
8. Gabelaia, D., Kurucz, A., Wolter, F., Zakharyaschev, M.: Non-primitive recursive decidability of products of modal logics with expanding domains. Annals of Pure and Applied Logic 142(1–3), 245–268 (2006)
9. Halava, V., Hirvensalo, M., de Wolf, R.: Marked PCP is decidable. Theoretical Computer Science 255(1–2), 193–204 (2001)
10. Konev, B., Wolter, F., Zakharyaschev, M.: Temporal logics over transitive states. In: Nieuwenhuis, R. (ed.) Automated Deduction – CADE-20. LNCS (LNAI), vol. 3632, pp. 182–203. Springer, Heidelberg (2005)
11. Lasota, S., Walukiewicz, I.: Alternating timed automata. In: Sassone, V. (ed.) FOSSACS 2005. LNCS, vol. 3441, pp. 250–265. Springer, Heidelberg (2005)
12. Ouaknine, J., Worrell, J.: On the decidability and complexity of Metric Temporal Logic over finite words. Logical Methods in Comp. Science 3(1), 1–27 (2007)
13. Ruohonen, K.: On some variants of Post's correspondence problem. Acta Informatica 4(19), 357–367 (1983)
14. Schnoebelen, P.: Bisimulation and other undecidable equivalences for lossy channel systems. In: Kobayashi, N., Pierce, B.C. (eds.) TACS 2001. LNCS, vol. 2215, pp. 385–399. Springer, Heidelberg (2001)
15. Schnoebelen, P.: Verifying lossy channel systems has nonprimitive recursive complexity. Information Processing Letters 83(5), 251–261 (2002)

Synthesis of Safe Message-Passing Systems*

Nicolas Baudru and Rémi Morin

Aix-Marseille universités — UMR 6166 — CNRS
Laboratoire d'Informatique Fondamentale de Marseille
163, avenue de Luminy, F-13288 Marseille Cedex 9, France

Abstract. We show that any regular set of basic MSCs can be implemented by a *deadlock-free* communicating finite-state machine with *local termination*: Processes stop in local dead-states independently from the contents of channels and the local states of other processes. We present a self-contained, direct, and relatively simple construction based on a new notion called context MSC.

Introduction

Message Sequence Charts (MSCs) are a popular model often used for the documentation of telecommunication protocols. They profit by a standardized visual and textual presentation and are related to other formalisms such as sequence diagrams of UML. An MSC gives a graphical description of communications between processes. It usually abstracts away from the values of variables and the actual content of messages. Such specifications are implicitly subjected to some refinement before implementation.

The class of *regular* sets of MSCs introduced in [10] is of particular interest. These languages can be described by finite automata because the number of messages within channels is bounded. Regular languages enjoy several other logical and algebraic properties and they can be model-checked with the help of specific techniques (see e.g. [1]). The theory of regular MSC languages has been extended in various directions [3,7,8,9]. In particular [3] and [7] extend to the framework of unbounded channels one of the main result from [10]: *Any regular set of MSCs can be implemented by a communicating finite-state machine (for short, a CFM) with bounded channel capacities.*

Yet, the main drawback of the CFMs built in [3,7,10] is that they possibly lead to deadlocks. In this paper we improve that result and prove that we can make sure that the CFM built from a regular set of MSCs is *deadlock-free*. As opposed to [3,7,10] the CFMs we consider satisfy two other interesting properties. First, processes stop in local final states independently from the local states of other processes, that is, we adopt a *local acceptance condition* similarly to [1,8]. Second, *final local states are dead-states*: Differently from [1,8] we require that no process can leave any final local state, that is, each process *terminates locally*. This second requirement is particularly relevant because deadlock-free CFMs with local termination are *stuck-free*: Whenever all processes stop, no unexpected message remains within the channels. This is the main difference from [1,3,7,8,10] for which the acceptance condition ensures that all channels are empty: The system relies implicitly on a global supervisor that checks emptyness of all channels and controls the termination of all processes.

---

* Supported by the ANR project SOAPDC.

V. Arvind and S. Prasad (Eds.): FSTTCS 2007, LNCS 4855, pp. 277–289, 2007.
© Springer-Verlag Berlin Heidelberg 2007

In this paper we do not assume any global supervisor. We build CFMs *with local termination* that are *deadlock-free* and such that *any accepting execution leads to empty channels*. The necessary counterpart of these strong requirements is that we build *non-deterministic* CFMs. In particular CFMs may have multiple (finitely many) initial global states: Intuitively this means that processes can synchronize in a preliminary phase in order to agree on some decisions before the system starts. Similarly to [3,7,10] and differently from [1,8] the implementation process allows to add some control information to specified messages. This refinement implements intuitively a kind of *distributed control* over the system.

A proof sketch of our result relies on the rich theory of Mazurkiewicz traces [5] and proceeds as follows. A first step due to Kuske [11] encodes the given regular set of MSCs L into a regular trace language L' over some independence alphabet that depends on the channel-bound of L. Next one applies directly a variant of Zielonka's theorem [13] which asserts that L' is accepted by a deadlock-free non-deterministic asynchronous cellular automaton Z with local termination. It remains then only to turn Z into a deadlock-free CFM with local termination that accepts L. As opposed to Kuske's encoding, *this last step is unfortunately not easy*. The main reason is that components of asynchronous cellular automata synchronize by means of shared variables whereas processes of a CFM exchange messages. In [2] we designed a rather involved method based on a bounded time-stamp protocol by Mukund, Narayan Kumar and Sohoni [12] in order to build a deadlock-free deterministic CFM from a deadlock-free deterministic asynchronous automaton. This approach can be adapted in order to preserve local termination and yield the expected deadlock-free and stuck-free CFM.

Let us now explain why we choose not to develop this proof sketch. First the technique from [2] is particularly suitable for deterministic CFMs but it is rather complicated. Since we consider here non-deterministic CFMs, we prefer to present a *simpler* construction that consists of a single technical lemma and two basic inductions. Second we believe that our *direct and self-contained approach* is more valuable than refering to the analogous result in the setting of Mazurkiewicz traces [13]. Finally there are only few known methods to build CFMs from regular languages so *our new inductive approach* may be also interesting by itself.

This paper is organized as follows. We introduce in Section 1 a straightforward and natural extension of basic MSCs called *context MSCs*: The latter are simply compositional MSCs [9] provided with a channel-state. Context MSCs come equipped with some associative product which is useful to decompose regular languages of basic MSCs into simpler components inductively in a Kleene-like manner. From an algebraic viewpoint, the composition of context MSCs forms a particular case of concurrency monoid [6] in which basic MSCs form a submonoid, that is, the product of context MSCs is a natural extension of the usual composition of basic MSCs. In Section 2 we formalize the model of CFMs with local termination together with the key notion of a deadlock. As announced above, we observe that deadlock-free CFMs with local termination are stuck-free. Section 3 presents our main technical result: We show that the iteration of some implementable and initiated set of context MSCs is implementable provided that it is valid and channel-bounded. Finally our main result (Theorem 4.1) is established by means of two elementary decomposition techniques.

1   Message Sequence Charts

Following a classical trend of concurrency theory the executions of a distributed system are regarded as labeled partial orders (called pomsets). Although our result holds for non-FIFO channels we assume in this paper that all channels are FIFO in order to simplify the presentation. Furthermore, for the same reason, the actual content of messages are abstracted from the notion of MSCs similarly to the approach adopted in [3,7,10].

In this paper, we call alphabet any non-empty set; elements of alphabets are called *actions*. A *pomset* over an alphabet Σ is a triple $t = (E, \preccurlyeq, \xi)$ where $(E, \preccurlyeq)$ is a finite partial order and ξ is a mapping from E to Σ *without autoconcurrency*: $\xi(x) = \xi(y)$ implies $x \preccurlyeq y$ or $y \preccurlyeq x$ for all $x, y \in E$. A pomset can be seen as an abstraction of an execution of a concurrent system. In this view, the elements e of E are *events* and their label $\xi(e)$ describes the basic action of the system that is performed by the event $e \in E$. Furthermore, the order $\preccurlyeq$ describes the causal dependence between events. Let $t = (E, \preccurlyeq, \xi)$ be a pomset and $x, y \in E$. Then y *covers* x (denoted $x \prec\!\!\!-\, y$) if $x \prec y$ and $x \prec z \preccurlyeq y$ implies $y = z$. An event x is minimal if $y \preccurlyeq x$ implies $y = x$.

An *order extension* of a pomset $t = (E, \preccurlyeq, \xi)$ is a pomset $t' = (E, \preccurlyeq', \xi)$ such that $\preccurlyeq \subseteq \preccurlyeq'$. A *linear extension* of t is an order extension that is linearly ordered. It corresponds to a sequential view of the concurrent execution t. Linear extensions of a pomset t over Σ can naturally be regarded as words over Σ. By $\mathrm{LE}(t) \subseteq \Sigma^*$, we denote the set of linear extensions of a pomset t over Σ.

An *ideal* of a pomset $t = (E, \preccurlyeq, \xi)$ is a downward-closed subset $H \subseteq E$: $x \in H \wedge y \preccurlyeq x \Rightarrow y \in H$. The restriction $t' = (H, \preccurlyeq \cap (H \times H), \xi \cap (H \times \Sigma))$ is called a *prefix* of t and we write $t' \leqslant t$. For all $z \in E$, we denote by $\downarrow_t z$ the ideal of events below z, i.e. $\downarrow_t z = \{y \in E \mid y \preccurlyeq z\}$. We denote by $|t|_a$ the number of events $x \in E$ such that $\xi(x) = a$.

1.1   Basic and Context Message Sequence Charts

Message sequence charts are defined in the Z.120 recommendation of the ITU-T with a formal syntax and graphical rules. They can be seen also as particular pomsets over some alphabet that we introduce first. Let $\mathcal{I}$ be a finite set of processes (also called *instances*). For any instance $i \in \mathcal{I}$, the alphabet Σ_i is the disjoint union of the set of *send actions* $\Sigma_i^! = \{i!j \mid j \in \mathcal{I} \setminus \{i\}\}$ and the set of *receive actions* $\Sigma_i^? = \{i?j \mid j \in \mathcal{I} \setminus \{i\}\}$. Observe that the alphabets Σ_i are disjoint and we let $\Sigma_{\mathcal{I}} = \bigcup_{i \in \mathcal{I}} \Sigma_i$. Given an action $a \in \Sigma_{\mathcal{I}}$, we denote by $\mathrm{Ins}(a)$ the unique instance i such that $a \in \Sigma_i$, that is the particular instance on which each occurrence of action a occurs. Finally, for any pomset $(E, \preccurlyeq, \xi)$ over $\Sigma_{\mathcal{I}}$ we denote by $\mathrm{Ins}(e)$ the instance on which the event $e \in E$ occurs: $\mathrm{Ins}(e) = \mathrm{Ins}(\xi(e))$.

A channel-state describes the number of messages in transit at some stage of an execution. Formally we let $\mathcal{K} = \{(i, j) \in \mathcal{I} \times \mathcal{I} \mid i \neq j\}$ denote the set of all channels within the instances $\mathcal{I}$. Then a channel-state is simply a mapping $\chi : \mathcal{K} \to \mathbb{N}$. The *empty channel-state* $\overline{0}$ maps each channel to 0. Let χ be a channel-state and $M = (E, \preccurlyeq, \xi)$ be a pomset over $\Sigma_{\mathcal{I}}$. We say that two events $e, f \in E$ match each other w.r.t. χ if e is a send event from i to j and f is the corresponding receive event on j: Formally, we put $e \leadsto_\chi f$ if $\xi(e) = i!j$, $\xi(f) = j?i$, and moreover $\chi(i,j) + |\downarrow_M e|_{i!j} = |\downarrow_M f|_{j?i}$.

DEFINITION 1.1. *A context MSC is a pair* (M, χ) *where* $M = (E, \preccurlyeq, \xi)$ *is a pomset over* Σ_I *and* $\chi \in \mathbb{N}^{\mathcal{K}}$ *is a channel-state such that*

M_1: $\forall e, f \in E$: $\mathrm{Ins}(e) = \mathrm{Ins}(f) \Rightarrow (e \preccurlyeq f \vee f \preccurlyeq e)$
M_2: $\forall e, f \in E$: $e \rightsquigarrow_\chi f \Rightarrow e \preccurlyeq f$
M_3: $\forall e, f \in E$: $[e {\longrightarrow\!\!\prec} f \wedge \mathrm{Ins}(e) \neq \mathrm{Ins}(f)] \Rightarrow e \rightsquigarrow_\chi f$
M_4: $\forall (i, j) \in \mathcal{K} : \chi(i, j) + |M|_{i!j} \geqslant |M|_{j?i}$

A context MSC (M, χ) is also denoted by $M@\chi$. By M_1, events occurring on the same instance are linearly ordered: Non-deterministic choice cannot be described within an MSC. Axiom M_2 formalizes that the reception of any message will occur after the corresponding send event. By M_3, causality in M consists only in the linear dependency over each instance and the ordering of pairs of corresponding send and receive events.

Let $M@\chi$ be a context MSC. Then χ is called the *domain of* $M@\chi$. The *codomain of* $M@\chi$ is the channel-state χ' such that $\chi'(i, j) = \chi(i, j) + |M|_{i!j} - |M|_{j?i}$ for all channels $(i, j) \in \mathcal{K}$. Axiom M_4 ensures that the codomain of a context MSC is a channel-state. It is clear that *the usual set of basic MSCs can be identified with the subset of context MSCs whose domain and codomain are the empty channel-state*. Observe here that context MSCs satisfy the following *consistence property*: If two context MSCs share the same domain and a common linear extension then they are identical.

1.2 Semigroup of Context Message Sequence Charts

We come now to the definition of the concatenation of two context MSCs. First we add formally a special context MSC 0 to the set of context MSCs. This additional context MSC 0 is called *non-valid* and will act as a zero: We put $x \cdot 0 = 0 \cdot x = 0$.

DEFINITION 1.2. *Let* $M_1@\chi_1 = (E_1, \preccurlyeq_1, \xi_1, \chi_1)$ *and* $M_2@\chi_2 = (E_2, \preccurlyeq_2, \xi_2, \chi_2)$ *be two valid MSCs. Let* $\rightsquigarrow$ *be the binary relation over* $E_1 \times E_2$ *such that* $e_1 \rightsquigarrow e_2$ *if* $\xi_1(e_1) = i!j$, $\xi_2(e_2) = j?i$, *and* $\chi_1(i, j) + |{\downarrow}_{M_1} e_1|_{i!j} = |M_1|_{j?i} + |{\downarrow}_{M_2} e_2|_{j?i}$.

If the codomain of $M_1@\chi_1$ *is* χ_2 *then the product* $M_1@\chi_1 \cdot M_2@\chi_2$ *is the context MSC* $(E, \preccurlyeq, \xi, \chi_1)$ *where* $E = E_1 \uplus E_2$, $\xi = \xi_1 \cup \xi_2$ *and the partial order* $\preccurlyeq$ *is the transitive closure of* $\preccurlyeq_1 \cup \preccurlyeq_2 \cup \{(e_1, e_2) \in E_1 \times E_2 \mid \mathrm{Ins}(e_1) = \mathrm{Ins}(e_2)\} \cup \rightsquigarrow$.

If the codomain of $M_1@\chi_1$ *is not* χ_2 *then* $M_1@\chi_1 \cdot M_2@\chi_2 = 0$.

This product extends the usual concatenation of basic MSCs viewed as the subset of context MSCs whose domain and codomain are the empty channel-state $\overline{0}$. The consistence property allows us to characterize this product as follows.

PROPOSITION 1.3. *Let* $M_1@\chi_1$ *and* $M_2@\chi_2$ *be two valid context MSCs such that the codomain of* $M_1@\chi_1$ *is* χ_2. *Let* u_1 *and* u_2 *be some linear extensions of* M_1 *and* M_2 *respectively. Then the product* $M_1@\chi_1 \cdot M_2@\chi_2$ *is the valid context MSC* $M@\chi_1$ *such that* $u_1.u_2 \in \mathrm{LE}(M)$.

Let cMSC denote the set of all (valid and non-valid) context MSCs. Proposition 1.3 above enables us to check easily that the product of context MSCs is associative. Thus the set of context MSCs forms a semigroup. The proof of our main result relies on a representation of MSC languages in the form of rational expressions built by means of unions ($\mathcal{L}_1 + \mathcal{L}_2$), products ($\mathcal{L}_1 \cdot \mathcal{L}_2$), and strict iterations ($\mathcal{L}^+ = \bigcup_{k \geqslant 1} \mathcal{L}^k$). We could identify formally all empty context MSCs as a single context MSC and get a concurrency monoid [4,6].

1.3   Regular Sets of MSCs

Let χ_1, χ_2 be two channel-states. A subset of valid context MSCs $\mathcal{L} \subseteq \text{cMSC} \setminus \{0\}$ is *located* at (χ_1, χ_2) if all context MSCs from $\mathcal{L}$ have domain χ_1 and codomain χ_2. Then χ_1 and χ_2 are called respectively the domain and the codomain of $\mathcal{L}$.

DEFINITION 1.4. *A located set of MSCs $\mathcal{L}$ is* regular *if the corresponding set of words* $\text{LE}(\mathcal{L}) = \bigcup_{M@\chi \in \mathcal{L}} \text{LE}(M)$ *is recognizable in the free monoid $\Sigma_\mathcal{I}^\star$. A set of context MSCs is* regular *if it is a finite union of regular located sets of context MSCs.*

In particular a subset of basic MSCs is regular in the sense of [10] if and only if it is regular according to the above definition.

For later purposes, we need to extend the usual notion of channel-bounded languages from basic MSCs to context MSCs as follows. The *channel-width* of a valid context MSC $M@\chi$ is

$$\max_{u \in \text{LE}(M)} \max_{v \leqslant u} \max_{(i,j) \in \mathcal{K}} \chi(i,j) + |v|_{i!j} - |v|_{j?i}.$$

Intuitively the channel-width of $M@\chi$ is the maximal number of messages that may be in transit within some channel at any stage of the execution of $M@\chi$. A subset of valid context MSCs $\mathcal{L}$ is *channel-bounded* by $B \in \mathbb{N}$ if each context MSC from $\mathcal{L}$ has a channel-width at most B.

Consider now a regular set of context MSCs $\mathcal{L}$ located at (χ_1, χ_2) and the minimal deterministic automaton $\mathcal{A} = (Q, \imath, F, \longrightarrow)$ over $\Sigma_\mathcal{I}$ that accepts $\text{LE}(\mathcal{L})$. All states of $\mathcal{A}$ are reachable from the initial state $\imath \in Q$ and co-reachable from the subset of final states $F \subseteq Q$. The next basic observation asserts that each state from $\mathcal{A}$ corresponds to some particular channel-state.

PROPOSITION 1.5. *There exists a mapping $\chi : Q \to \mathbb{N}^\mathcal{K}$ such that $\chi(\imath) = \chi_1$, $\chi(q) = \chi_2$ for all $q \in F$, and $q \xrightarrow{u} q'$ implies $\chi(q')(i,j) = \chi(q)(i,j) + |u|_{i!j} - |u|_{j?i}$ for all $q, q' \in Q$ and all channels $(i,j) \in \mathcal{K}$.*

It follows that any regular set of context MSCs is channel-bounded.

2   Deadlock-Free and Stuck-Free Message-Passing Systems

In this section we introduce the model of communicating finite-state machines and the related notions of deadlock, local termination, and stuck messages. The semantics of these systems is given in a natural way by means of sets of MSCs.

2.1   Communicating Finite-State Machines with Local Termination

Recall here that MSC specifications are used usually at an early stage of the design so that a refinement procedure can occur before implementation. In this paper refinement corresponds to the possibility to add some control information to messages in order to be able to build a correct implementation. To do so we use a fixed set Λ of control messages that will be added to the contents of specified messages. We denote by $i!^m j$ the action by i that sends a message with control information m to j. Its receipt by j is denoted by $j?^m i$. We put $\Sigma_i^\Lambda = \{i!^m j, i?^m j \mid j \in \mathcal{I} \setminus \{i\}, m \in \Lambda\}$ and $\Sigma_{\mathcal{I}}^\Lambda = \bigcup_{i \in \mathcal{I}} \Sigma_i^\Lambda$. A *refined channel-state* describes the sequence of control information associated with the sequence of messages in transit; it is formalized as a map $\rho : \mathcal{K} \to \Lambda^*$.

A *communicating finite-state machine (for short, a CFM)* over Λ consists of a process $\mathcal{A}_i = (Q_i, \longrightarrow_i, F_i)$ for each instance $i \in \mathcal{I}$ together with a *finite* set of initial global states $I \subseteq \left(\prod_{i \in \mathcal{I}} Q_i\right) \times (\Lambda^*)^{\mathcal{K}}$ where Q_i is a finite set of local states for process i, $\longrightarrow_i \subseteq Q_i \times \Sigma_i^\Lambda \times Q_i$ is a local transition relation for i, and $F_i \subseteq Q_i$ is a subset of final local states. All along this paper we require additionally that *all final local states are dead*: For all instances i and for all final local states $q_i \in F_i$, there is no transition $q_i \xrightarrow{a}_i q_i'$ for all $a \in \Sigma_i^\Lambda$ and all $q_i' \in Q_i$. Thus we consider only CFMs with *local termination*.

In this setting, a *global state* is a pair $s = (q, \rho)$ where $q \in \prod_{i \in \mathcal{I}} Q_i$ is a tuple of local states and $\rho : \mathcal{K} \to \Lambda^*$ is a refined channel-state. For all global states $s = (q, \rho)$ with $q = (q_i)_{i \in \mathcal{I}}$ and all $i \in \mathcal{I}$ we put $s \downarrow i = q_i$. A global state s is *final* if $s \downarrow i \in F_i$ for all $i \in \mathcal{I}$. Thus $F = \left(\prod_{i \in \mathcal{I}} F_i\right) \times (\Lambda^*)^{\mathcal{K}}$ denotes the set of all final global states.

Intuitively each process stops independently from the current contents of channels and independently from the local states of other processes. This approach is somehow more restrictive than [1,3,7,8,10] which assume that final global states are associated with the empty channel-state. On the other hand we allow multiple (finitely many) initial global states and consequently we consider in this paper *non-deterministic* CFMs.

2.2 Deadlocks and Stuck Messages

The *system of global states* associated to a communicating finite-state machine $\mathcal{S}$ is the transition system $\mathcal{A}_\mathcal{S} = (S, \longrightarrow)$ where $S = \prod_{i \in \mathcal{I}} Q_i \times (\Lambda^*)^{\mathcal{K}}$ is the set of all global states and the global transition relation $\longrightarrow \subseteq S \times \Sigma_{\mathcal{I}}^\Lambda \times S$ satisfies the two next properties for any global states $s = (q, \rho)$ and $s' = (q', \rho')$:

- for all distinct instances i and j, $s \xrightarrow{i!^m j} s'$ if
  1. $s \downarrow i \xrightarrow{i!^m j}_i s' \downarrow i$ and $s' \downarrow k = s \downarrow k$ for all $k \in \mathcal{I} \setminus \{i\}$,
  2. $\rho'(i, j) = \rho(i, j) \cdot m$ and $\rho(x) = \rho'(x)$ for all $x \in \mathcal{K} \setminus \{(i, j)\}$;
- for all distinct instances i and j, $s \xrightarrow{j?^m i} s'$ if
  1. $s \downarrow j \xrightarrow{j?^m i}_j s' \downarrow j$ and $s' \downarrow k = s \downarrow k$ for all $k \in \mathcal{I} \setminus \{j\}$,
  2. $\rho(i, j) = m \cdot \rho'(i, j)$ and $\rho(x) = \rho'(x)$ for all $x \in \mathcal{K} \setminus \{(i, j)\}$.

As usual with transition systems, for any word $u = a_1 \dots a_n$ over $\Sigma_{\mathcal{I}}^\Lambda$, we write $s \xrightarrow{u} s'$ if there are some global states $s_0, \dots, s_n \in S$ such that $s_0 = s$, $s_n = s'$ and for each $r \in [1, n]$, $s_{r-1} \xrightarrow{a_r} s_r$. For all global states $s_1, s_2 \in S$ we denote by $L(\mathcal{S}, s_1, s_2)$ the set of words u over $\Sigma_{\mathcal{I}}^\Lambda$ such that $s_1 \xrightarrow{u} s_2$. We say that a CFM $\mathcal{S}$ is *safe* if all global states reachable from I are co-reachable from F. In other words, a safe CFM has no *deadlock*.

Let $\pi : \Sigma_{\mathcal{I}}^{\Lambda} \to \Sigma_{\mathcal{I}}$ be the mapping that forgets the additional control information: $\pi(i!^m j) = i!j$ and $\pi(j?^m i) = j?i$. This mapping extends in the obvious way to a map from words over $\Sigma_{\mathcal{I}}^{\Lambda}$ to words over $\Sigma_{\mathcal{I}}$. For any refined channel-state ρ, $\pi(\rho)$ denotes the channel-state χ such that $\chi(i,j)$ is the length of $\rho(i,j)$ for all $(i,j) \in \mathcal{K}$.

Consider now a CFM $\mathcal{S}$ and two global states s_1, s_2 with respective refined channel-states ρ_1, ρ_2. For any word $u \in L(\mathcal{S}, s_1, s_2)$ there exists a unique context MSC $M@\chi$ such that $\chi = \pi(\rho_1)$ and $\pi(u)$ is a linear extension of M. Moreover $M@\chi$ has codomain $\pi(\rho_2)$. The *language of context MSCs* $\mathcal{L}(\mathcal{S})$ *accepted by* $\mathcal{S}$ consists of all valid context MSCs $M@\chi$ such that there are two global states $s = (q, \rho) \in I$ and $s' = (q', \rho') \in F$ with $\pi(\rho) = \chi$ and a word $v \in \mathrm{LE}(M)$ such that $v \in \pi(L(\mathcal{S}, s, s'))$. Noteworthy, it can be easily shown that this condition ensures that *all* linear extensions of M belong to $\pi(L(\mathcal{S}, s, s'))$. Observe also that if $\mathcal{L}(\mathcal{S})$ consists of *basic* MSCs and $\mathcal{S}$ is *safe* then all initial global states and all *reachable* final global states are associated with the empty channel-state: Thus there are no message stuck in channels when the system stops.

2.3 Implementable Languages: Two Basic Properties

We say that a language $\mathcal{L}$ of context MSCs is *implementable* if there exists a *safe* CFM that accepts $\mathcal{L}$. Clearly any finite union of implementable languages is implementable. Observe now that for any implementable *located* set $\mathcal{L}$ of context MSCs, there exists a safe CFM that accepts $\mathcal{L}$ and such that *all initial global states* $s = (q, \rho)$ *share a common refined channel-state* ρ. Now it is not difficult to check that the product of two implementable located languages is implementable if this product is valid.

LEMMA 2.1. *Let* $\mathcal{L}_1$ *and* $\mathcal{L}_2$ *be two implementable sets of context MSCs.*

1. $\mathcal{L}_1 + \mathcal{L}_2$ *is implementable.*
2. *If* $\mathcal{L}_1 \cdot \mathcal{L}_2$ *is valid, i.e.* $0 \notin \mathcal{L}_1 \cdot \mathcal{L}_2$, *then* $\mathcal{L}_1 \cdot \mathcal{L}_2$ *is implementable.*

3 Iteration of Implementable Languages

In this section we establish for the iteration operation a result analogous to Lemma 2.1. With no surprise dealing with iteration turns out to be more complicated.

Let $k \in \mathcal{I}$ be some fixed instance. A context MSC $M@\chi$ is *initiated* (by k) if M admits a least event and this event is labeled by some send action from k. A *located* set of context MSCs $\mathcal{L}$ is *initiated* (by k) if all context MSCs from $\mathcal{L}$ are initiated (by k).

THEOREM 3.1. *Let* $\mathcal{L}$ *be some initiated and implementable set of context MSCs located at some* (χ_0, χ_0). *If* $\mathcal{L}^+$ *is channel-bounded then* $\mathcal{L}^+$ *is implementable, too.*

This section is devoted to the proof of this result. We fix some initiated and implementable set of context MSCs $\mathcal{L}$ located at some (χ_0, χ_0). We assume that $\mathcal{L}^+$ is channel-bounded by B. Let $\mathcal{S}$ be a safe CFM over Λ that accepts $\mathcal{L}$. We denote by $\mathcal{A}_i$ the local process of instance i in $\mathcal{S}$. We can assume that messages initially in channels do not carry any relevant control information, that is, we assume formally that for all initial global states $s = (q, \rho)$, any global state $\tilde{s} = (q, \tilde{\rho})$ with $\pi(\tilde{\rho}) = \chi_0$ is initial, too.

3.1 Intuitive Description of the Consensus Protocol

We build from S a safe CFM S' that accepts $\mathcal{L}^+$. Control messages exchanged within S' are pairs (m, τ) where $m \in \Lambda$ is a control message from S and τ is a tag added by S'. Process k will act as a leader within S': It will make some choices along the executions and these choices will be formalized and communicated to other processes by means of these tags. The choices made by k and the tags used by S' are essentially built upon the subset I of initial global states of S. We say that an instance i is *live* in some initial global state $s \in I$ if the local state $s \downarrow i$ is not final for the local process $\mathcal{A}_i$ of S: We put $\mathrm{Live}(s) = \{i \in \mathcal{I} \mid s \downarrow i \notin F_i\}$. Since $\mathcal{L}$ is initiated, $k \in \mathrm{Live}(s)$ for all $s \in I$.

Basically each process $\mathcal{A}'_i$ of S' simulates and iterates the behaviors of $\mathcal{A}_i$: It possibly starts a new execution when it reaches a final local state of $\mathcal{A}_i$. However the global behaviors of the whole system S' must correspond also to iterations of $\mathcal{L}$: Each execution of S' has to appear as a sequence of *phases* that simulate each an execution of S. That is why all processes must follow a *consensus protocol* that determines at each step which processes should take part in the next phase and from which local states they should start. Since $\mathcal{L}$ is initiated by k, all other instances start any execution from S by receiving a first message, called the *initiating message*. The tag added to this message by S' specifies from which local state of S each instance should start a new phase.

The first role of process k is to choose on-the-fly a sequence of initial global states $s_1, ..., s_n \in I$ from S and initiate a new simulation of some execution of S from s_m as soon as it has finished the previous phase from s_{m-1}. In doing so, it moves from a final local state of $\mathcal{A}_k$ to the local state of $\mathcal{A}_k$ that corresponds to s_m and sends its first message with a tag that includes s_m. These actions are considered atomic. Instances that are not live in s_m will not take part in this phase.

The second role of process k is to choose on-the-fly a subset of processes that must terminate —that is, that will not take part in further phases. This information is necessary because each process has to know when it does not need to wait any longer for a new initiating message, that is, when it reaches a final local state of S'. The choice of terminating instances is included in the tag of messages exchanged by S' within a phase. Thus process k keeps track of the subset $\mathcal{H}$ of instances that have already terminated in previous phases. Obviously the subset $\mathcal{H} \subseteq \mathcal{I}$ grows from phase to phase. In order to avoid deadlocks, process k makes sure that the next phase can be achieved by non-terminated processes, that is, the next phase starts from some $s \in I$ with $\mathrm{Live}(s) \subseteq \mathcal{I} \setminus \mathcal{H}$. Moreover process k chooses among the live instances of s the subset of instances $\mathcal{G} \subseteq \mathrm{Live}(s)$ that will simulate their last execution of S. As a consequence the new value of $\mathcal{H}$ is $\mathcal{H} \cup \mathcal{G}$. In that way the sequence of phases $s_1, ..., s_n \in I$ is associated with an increasing sequence of dead instances $\mathcal{H}_1 \subseteq ... \subseteq \mathcal{H}_n \subseteq \mathcal{I}$. Since all processes must stop at some point, the choices by process k must lead eventually to $\mathcal{H}_n = \mathcal{I}$.

We detail now how process k chooses the sequence of initial global states $s_1, ..., s_n \in I$ together with the sequence of terminating instances $\mathcal{H}_1, ..., \mathcal{H}_n = \mathcal{I}$ starting from some set of initially dead or terminating instances $\mathcal{H}_0$. As explained above the sequence $\mathcal{H}_0, \mathcal{H}_1, ..., \mathcal{H}_n$ is increasing, $\mathcal{H}_m \setminus \mathcal{H}_{m-1} \subseteq \mathrm{Live}(s_m)$, $\mathrm{Live}(s_m) \subseteq \mathcal{I} \setminus \mathcal{H}_{m-1}$ and $\mathcal{H}_n = \mathcal{I}$. Let us consider the finite directed graph $\mathfrak{G}$ whose nodes are the subsets $\mathcal{H}$ of $\mathcal{I}$ and such that there is an edge from $\mathcal{H}$ to $\mathcal{H}'$ if there exists some initial global state $s \in I$ such that $\mathcal{H} \subseteq \mathcal{H}'$, $\mathcal{H}' \setminus \mathcal{H} \subseteq \mathrm{Live}(s)$ and $\mathrm{Live}(s) \subseteq I \setminus \mathcal{H}$. A node $\mathcal{H} \subseteq I$ is *secure* if there exists a path in $\mathfrak{G}$ from $\mathcal{H}$ to I. In particular I is secure. A pair $(s, \mathcal{H}') \in I \times 2^{I}$ is a *secure choice* for $\mathcal{H}$ if $\mathcal{H} \subseteq \mathcal{H}'$, $\mathcal{H}' \setminus \mathcal{H} \subseteq \mathrm{Live}(s)$, $\mathrm{Live}(s) \subseteq I \setminus \mathcal{H}$ and $\mathcal{H}'$ is secure. Clearly if $\mathcal{H}$ is secure and $\mathcal{H} \neq I$ then there are some secure choices $(s, \mathcal{H}')$ for $\mathcal{H}$. Before starting a new phase, process k selects arbitrarily a secure choice $(s, \mathcal{H}')$ and initiates a new phase accordingly. This new phase is associated with the extended set of dead or terminating instances $\mathcal{H}'$.

Intuitively all messages exchanged within a phase are tagged with the same information. The tag of a phase consists basically of

- the global initial state $s \in I$ so that each process $i \in I$ knows from which local state $s \downarrow i$ it should start over, and
- the subset $\mathcal{H}'$ of instances that will not take part in further phases.

However if the domain χ_0 of $\mathcal{L}$ is not empty then each process of $\mathcal{S}$ consumes a fixed sequence of messages before it receives messages sent within $\mathcal{S}$. Therefore each process $\mathcal{A}'_i$ receives first from j a fixed sequence of messages with a tag possibly different from the ongoing phase and accepts only messages with some correct tag afterwards.

Now it is crucial that two concurrent phases associated with the same tag do not interfere. For that reason process k counts the number of phases in which each instance is live modulo some constant D by means of some counter $\kappa : I \to [0, D-1]$ and adds this counter to the tag of phases. Thus tags are actually triples $(s, \mathcal{H}', \kappa)$. We take $D = |I| + B + 1$ where $|I|$ is the number of instances and $\mathcal{L}^+$ is channel-bounded by B. The proof of our technical lemma below (Lemma 3.3) explains why these counters ensure that phases with the same tag cannot interfere.

3.2 Formal Construction of $\mathcal{S}'$

We define now formally the processes $\mathcal{A}'_i$ of the CFM $\mathcal{S}'$ according to the above intuitions. Let $T = I \times 2^{I} \times [0, D-1]^{I}$ be the set of all tags. The set of messages used by $\mathcal{S}'$ is $\Lambda' = \Lambda \times T$. A local state of $\mathcal{A}'_i$ is a triple $r = (q, \tau, \chi)$ where q is a local state of $\mathcal{A}_i$, τ is a tag, and χ is a channel-state bounded by B. The latter enables each process to ensure that the appropriate number of messages from the past are received along each channel. Let i be some instance. Let $r = (q, \tau, \chi)$ and $r' = (q', \tau', \chi')$ be two local states of $\mathcal{A}'_i$ where $\tau = (s, \mathcal{H}, \kappa)$ and $\tau' = (s', \mathcal{H}', \kappa')$. We put $r \xrightarrow{a}_i r'$ in $\mathcal{A}'_i$ if one of the next conditions is satisfied:

1. Instance i is k and it initiates a new phase: $i = k$, $q \in F_i$, $i \notin \mathcal{H}$, $a = i!^{m,\tau'} j$,
   $s' \downarrow i \xrightarrow{i!^{m} j}_i q'$ in $\mathcal{A}_i$, $\chi' = \chi_0$, $(s', \mathcal{H}')$ is a secure choice for $\mathcal{H}$, $\kappa'(l) = \kappa(l) + 1$ mod D for all $l \in \mathrm{Live}(s')$, and $\kappa'(l) = \kappa(l)$ for all $l \notin \mathrm{Live}(s')$.
2. Instance i is not k and it starts a new phase: $i \neq k$, $q \in F_i$, $i \notin \mathcal{H}$, $a = i?^{m,\tau'} j$,
   $s' \downarrow i \xrightarrow{i?^{m} j}_i q'$ in $\mathcal{A}_i$, $\chi' = \chi_0$, $\chi_0(j, i) = 0$, $\mathcal{H} \subseteq \mathcal{H}'$ and $\kappa'(i) = \kappa(i) + 1 \mod D$.
3. Process i goes on the current phase and receives a message from a previous phase:
   $\tau = \tau'$, $a = i?^{n,\tau''} j$, $q \xrightarrow{i?^{m} j}_i q'$ in $\mathcal{A}_i$, $\chi(j, i) \geqslant 1$, $\chi'(j, i) = \chi(j, i) - 1$ and $\chi(x) = \chi'(x)$ for all $x \neq (j, i)$.

4. Process i goes on the current phase and receives a message with the current tag:
$\tau = \tau'$, $a = i?^{m,\tau}j$, $q \xrightarrow{i?^m j}_i q'$ in $\mathcal{A}_i$, $\chi(j,i) = 0$ and $\chi = \chi'$.
5. Process i goes on the current phase and sends a message: $\tau = \tau'$, $a = i!^{m,\tau}j$,
$q \xrightarrow{i!^m j}_i q'$ in $\mathcal{A}_i$, and $\chi = \chi'$.

A local state $r = (q,\tau,\chi)$ of $\mathcal{A}'_i$ with $\tau = (s,\mathcal{H},\kappa)$ is final if $q \in F_i$ and $i \in \mathcal{H}$, that is, if it corresponds to a final local state of $\mathcal{A}_i$ and must not take part in further phases. It is easy to check that each local final state of $\mathcal{A}'_i$ is dead.

We fix some refined channel-state ρ'_0 such that $\pi'(\rho'_0) = \chi_0$. A global state $s' = (q',\rho')$ of $\mathcal{S}'$ is initial if $\rho' = \rho'_0$ and there exists some initial global state $s_0 \in I$ of $\mathcal{S}$ and some *secure* subset of instances $\mathcal{H}_0$ such that for all $i \in \mathcal{I}$ we have $s' \downarrow i = (s_0 \downarrow i, \tau_0, \chi_0)$ where $\tau_0 = (s_0, \mathcal{H}_0, \overline{0})$.

With no surprise $\mathcal{S}'$ simulates any iteration of $\mathcal{L}$. To prove this basic fact we need to introduce some notations that relate the global states of $\mathcal{S}'$ to those of $\mathcal{S}$ in a natural way. First for any local state $r = (q_i, \tau, \chi)$ we put $\omega(r) = q_i$. Second the first projection from $\Lambda' = \Lambda \times T$ to Λ induces a mapping ω from words over Λ' to words over Λ. Then any refined channel-state ρ' over Λ' corresponds to some refined channel-state $\omega(\rho')$ such that $\omega(\rho')(i,j) = \omega(\rho'(i,j))$ for all channels $(i,j) \in \mathcal{K}$. Finally each global state $s' = (q',\rho')$ of $\mathcal{S}'$ corresponds to the global state $\omega(s') = (q,\omega(\rho'))$ of $\mathcal{S}$ where q consists of the local states $\omega(s' \downarrow i)$.

PROPOSITION 3.2. *We have $\mathcal{L}^+ \subseteq \mathcal{L}(\mathcal{S}')$.*

Proof. Let $M_0@\chi_0,..., M_n@\chi_0$ be some MSCs from $\mathcal{L}$. We show that the product $M@\chi_0 = M_0@\chi_0 \cdot ... \cdot M_n@\chi_0$ belongs to $\mathcal{L}(\mathcal{S}')$. For each $m \in [0,n]$ there are two global states s_m and s'_m of $\mathcal{S}$ and $u_m \in L(\mathcal{S}, s_m, s'_m)$ such that $s_m \in I$, $s'_m \in F$, and $\pi(u_m) \in \mathrm{LE}(M_n)$. For each $m \in [0,n]$ we denote by $\mathcal{H}_m$ the set of instances that are not live in all $s_{m+1},..., s_n$. In particular $\mathcal{H}_n = \mathcal{I}$ and for all $m \geqslant 1$ we have $\mathrm{Live}(s_m) \subseteq \mathcal{I} \setminus \mathcal{H}_{m-1}$, $\mathcal{H}_{m-1} \subseteq \mathcal{H}_m$, and $\mathcal{H}_m \setminus \mathcal{H}_{m-1} \subseteq \mathrm{Live}(s_m)$. We let s'_0 be the initial global state of $\mathcal{S}'$ that corresponds to s_0 and $\mathcal{H}_0$. By induction over $m \leqslant n$, we can check that there exists a word u that corresponds to an execution of $\mathcal{S}'$ consisting of m phases associated with the secure choices $(s_1, \mathcal{H}_1),..., (s_m, \mathcal{H}_m)$ and such that $\pi'(u) = \pi(u_0)...\pi(u_m)$. Moreover u leads $\mathcal{S}'$ from s'_0 to some global state s' such that $\omega(s')$ is a final global state of $\mathcal{S}$. In the case $m = n$, we get that $s' \downarrow i = (q_i, \tau_m, \chi_m)$ with $q_i \in F_i$ for all processes $i \in \mathcal{I}$. Recall that $\mathcal{H}_n = \mathcal{I}$. Let $i \in \mathcal{I}$ such that $i \notin \mathcal{H}_0$. Let m be the least integer such that $i \in \mathcal{H}_m$. Then $i \in \mathrm{Live}(s_m)$, i takes part in u_m, and $\tau_m = (s_m, \mathcal{H}_m, \kappa_m)$. Thus $s' \downarrow i \in F'_i$ for all $i \in \mathcal{I}$ and $M@\chi_0 \in \mathcal{L}(\mathcal{S}')$. ∎

3.3 A Technical Lemma

Let s'_0 be an initial global state of $\mathcal{S}'$ associated with $s_0 \in I$, $\mathcal{H}_0 \subseteq \mathcal{I}$ and $\tau_0 = (s_0, \mathcal{H}_0, \overline{0})$. Let s' be some global state of $\mathcal{S}'$ and u, v be two words over $\Sigma^{\Lambda'}_{\mathcal{I}}$. We say that u and v are equivalent w.r.t. s'_0 and s' if

- $u \in L(\mathcal{S}', s'_0, s')$ if and only if $v \in L(\mathcal{S}', s'_0, s')$ and
- $\pi'(u) \in \mathrm{LE}(M)$ if and only if $\pi'(v) \in \mathrm{LE}(M)$ for all context MSCs $M@\chi_0$.

We come to our key technical result. The latter formalizes that each execution of $\mathcal{S}'$ is equivalent to a series of phases that simulate possibly incomplete executions of $\mathcal{S}$.

LEMMA 3.3. *Let s' be a global state of $\mathcal{S}'$ and $u \in L(\mathcal{S}', s'_0, s')$. Let $M@\chi_0$ be the context MSC such that $\pi'(u) \in \mathrm{LE}(M)$. There exist $n \geqslant 0$, a sequence of words $u_0, ..., u_n$ over $\Sigma_{\mathcal{I}}^{\Lambda'}$, a sequence $s'_1, ..., s'_{n+1}$ of global states of $\mathcal{S}'$ with $s'_{n+1} = s'$, a sequence of tags $\tau_1, ..., \tau_n$ with $\tau_m = (s_m, \mathcal{H}_m, \kappa_m)$ for each $m \in [1, n]$, and a sequence $\bar{s}_0, ..., \bar{s}_n$ of global states of $\mathcal{S}$ such that*

- $(s_m, \mathcal{H}_m)$ *is a secure choice for $\mathcal{H}_{m-1}$ for all $m \in [1, n]$,*
- $u_0...u_n$ *is equivalent to u w.r.t. s'_0 and s',*
- $u_m \in L(\mathcal{S}', s'_m, s'_{m+1})$ *and $\pi'(u_m) \in \pi(L(\mathcal{S}, s_m, \bar{s}_m))$ for each $m \in [0, n]$,*
- *if i takes part in u_m and $m \in [0, n]$ then $s'_{m+1} \downarrow i = (\bar{s}_m \downarrow i, \tau_m, \chi)$ for some χ,*
- *if i takes part in u_m and $m \geqslant 1$ then $\omega(s'_m) \downarrow i \in F_i$,*
- *if i takes part in u_l and $i \in \mathrm{Live}(s_m)$ with $m \leqslant l$ then i takes part in u_m.*

Proof. A phase $m \in [0, n]$ is called incomplete if $\bar{s}_m \notin F$. We proceed by induction over the size of u. The base case where u is the empty word is trivial. Induction step: Assume $u = v.a$ with $a \in \Sigma_{\mathcal{I}}^{\Lambda'}$. The proof proceeds by case analysis over the five rules that define the transition relation of $\mathcal{A}'_i$. The key observation is the following. By induction hypothesis, $\pi(v)$ is a linear extension of a prefix of some MSC from $\mathcal{L}^+$. Therefore there are at most B messages pending in s'. On the other hand there are at most $|\mathcal{I}|$ instances i with $\omega(s') \downarrow i \notin F_i$. As a consequence incomplete phases in s' have distinct tags and no instance can skip any phase. ∎

COROLLARY 3.4. *We have $\mathcal{L}(\mathcal{S}') \subseteq \mathcal{L}^+$.*

Proof. We apply Lemma 3.3 with the assumption that s' is a final global state. Then $k \in \mathcal{H}_n$, $\mathcal{H}_n = \mathcal{I}$ and $\omega(s') \downarrow i \in F_i$ for all instances i. It follows that for all $i \in \mathcal{I}$ and all $m \in [0, n]$ we have $\omega(s'_{m+1}) \downarrow i \in F_i$. Furthermore i takes part in u_m whenever $i \in \mathrm{Live}(s_m)$. Therefore $\bar{s}_m$ is a *final* global state of $\mathcal{S}$ hence $\pi \circ \omega(u_m) \in \mathrm{LE}(M_m)$ for some $M_m@\chi_0$ from $\mathcal{L}$. Since $\pi'(u_m) = \pi \circ \omega(u_m)$, we get that $\pi'(u_0...u_n) \in \mathrm{LE}(M)$ with $M@\chi_0 \in \mathcal{L}^{n+1}$. It follows that $\pi'(u) \in \mathrm{LE}(M)$. Hence $\mathcal{L}(\mathcal{S}') \subseteq \mathcal{L}^+$. ∎

COROLLARY 3.5. *The CFM $\mathcal{S}'$ is safe.*

Proof. Let s'_0 be an initial global state of $\mathcal{S}'$ and s' be a global state of $\mathcal{S}'$ reachable from s'_0. Let $u \in L(\mathcal{S}', s'_0, s')$. We apply Lemma 3.3 and consider $u_0, ..., u_n$ such that $u_0...u_n$ is equivalent to u w.r.t. s'_0 and s'. The proof proceeds in two steps. We claim first that we can assume up to some completion of u that $\omega(s'_{m+1}) \downarrow i = \bar{s}_m \downarrow i$ is a final local state of $\mathcal{A}_i$ for all $m \in [0, n]$ and all $i \in \mathrm{Live}(s_m)$. This step makes use of the hypothesis that $\mathcal{S}$ is safe: Each $\omega(u_m)$ can be completed into a sequence that leads $\mathcal{S}$ from s_m to a final global state. Second we proceed similarly to the proof of Proposition 3.2 and complete u in order to reach a final global state of $\mathcal{S}'$. This step makes use of the requirement that process k chooses always secure choices so that its local value of $\mathcal{H}$ is secure after each phase. ∎

4   Elementary Decompositions of Regular Sets of MSCs

We come to the main result of this paper: *Any regular set of basic MSCs is accepted by a deadlock-free CFM with local termination.* The next statement expresses this result in the more general setting of context MSCs. Its proof follows from Lemma 2.1 and Theorem 3.1 by means of two simple inductions.

THEOREM 4.1. *All regular languages of context MSCs are implementable.*

Proof. Let $\mathcal{L}$ be a regular set of context MSCs. By Lemma 2.1 we can assume that $\mathcal{L}$ is located. We proceed by induction over the number of processes k that send messages in $\mathcal{L}$. Base case: There are no send actions in any MSC from $\mathcal{L}$. Then $\mathcal{L}$ is finite hence implementable. Induction step: We fix some instance k such that some MSCs from $\mathcal{L}$ contain some send action from k. We consider the minimal deterministic automaton $\mathcal{A} = (Q, \imath, F, \longrightarrow)$ over $\Sigma_\mathcal{I}$ that accepts $\mathrm{LE}(\mathcal{L})$. By Proposition 1.5 we can provide $\mathcal{A}$ with a canonical mapping χ which associates a channel-state $\chi(q)$ to each state $q \in Q$. For any two states $q, q' \in Q$ let $\mathcal{L}_{q,q'}$ denote the set of context MSCs $M@\chi$ such that $\chi = \chi(q)$ and $q \xrightarrow{u} q'$ for all $u \in \mathrm{LE}(M)$. Clearly $\mathcal{L}_{q,q'}$ is a regular located set of MSCs. Moreover the subset of $\mathcal{L}_{q,q'}$ that restricts to the context MSCs that are initiated by k (resp. do not contain any occurrence of any send action from k) is also regular.

Now $\mathcal{L}$ is a finite union of sets of context MSCs of the form $\mathcal{L}_k = \mathcal{L}'_k \cdot \mathcal{L}''_k$ where all $\mathcal{L}'_k$ and all $\mathcal{L}''_k$ are located and regular, no send action from some k occurs in any $\mathcal{L}'_k$, and each $\mathcal{L}''_k$ is initiated by k or consists of a single empty MSC. By induction hypothesis *we can assume that $\mathcal{L}$ is initiated by some k.* For all $q, q' \in Q$ and all $j \in \mathcal{I}$, the *round* $\mathcal{L}_{q,q',j}$ is the subset of context MSCs $M@\chi$ from $\mathcal{L}_{q,q'}$ that are initiated by k and contain a single send action from k and the latter is $k!j$. Clearly all rounds are regular. By induction hypothesis all rounds are implementable.

By Kleene's theorem, $\mathcal{L}$ can be described by some rational expression r obtained from rounds by means of union, product, and strict iteration. Since $\mathcal{L}$ is regular, it is channel-bounded and valid. It follows that any subexpression s of r describes a valid and channel-bounded set of MSCs. Moreover if s^+ is a subexpression of r then s describes a located and initiated set of context MSCs whose domain and codomain coincide. By induction over the rational expression r with the help of Lemma 2.1 and Theorem 3.1, we get immediately that $\mathcal{L}$ is implementable.   ∎

References

1. Alur, R., Etessami, K., Yannakakis, M.: Realizability and verification of MSC graphs. TCS 331, 97–114 (2005)
2. Baudru, N., Morin, R.: Safe Implementability of Regular Message Sequence Charts Specifications. In: Proc. of the ACIS 4th Int. Conf. SNDP, pp. 210–217 (2003)
3. Bollig, B., Leucker, M.: Message-passing automata are expressively equivalent to EMSO logic. TCS 358, 150–172 (2006)
4. Bracho, F., Droste, M., Kuske, D.: Representations of computations in concurrent automata by dependence orders. TCS 174, 67–96 (1997)
5. Diekert, V., Rozenberg, G.: The Book of Traces. World Scientific (1995)
6. Droste, M.: Recognizable languages in concurrency monoids. TCS 150, 77–109 (1995)

7. Genest, B., Kuske, D., Muscholl, A.: A Kleene theorem and model checking algorithms for existentially bounded communicating automata. I&C 204, 920–956 (2006)
8. Genest, B., Muscholl, A., Seidl, H., Zeitoun, M.: Infinite-State High-Level MSCs: Model-Checking and Realizability. Journal of Computer and System Sciences 72, 617–647 (2006)
9. Gunter, E.L., Muscholl, A., Peled, D.: Compositional message sequence charts. Intern. Journal on Software Tools for Technology Transfer 5(1), 78–89 (2003)
10. Henriksen, J.G., Mukund, M., Narayan Kumar, K., Sohoni, M., Thiagarajan, P.S.: A Theory of Regular MSC Languages. I&C 202, 1–38 (2005)
11. Kuske, D.: Regular sets of infinite message sequence charts. I&C 187, 80–109 (2003)
12. Mukund, M., Narayan Kumar, K., Sohoni, M.: Bounded time-stamping in message-passing systems. TCS 290, 221–239 (2003)
13. Zielonka, W.: Safe executions of recognizable trace languages by asynchronous automata. In: Meyer, A.R., Taitslin, M.A. (eds.) Logic at Botik 1989. LNCS, vol. 363, pp. 278–289. Springer, Heidelberg (1989)

Automata and Logics for Timed Message Sequence Charts

S. Akshay[1,2], Benedikt Bollig[1], and Paul Gastin[1]

[1] LSV, ENS Cachan, CNRS, France
[2] Institute of Mathematical Sciences, Chennai, India

Abstract. We provide a framework for distributed systems that impose timing constraints on their executions. We propose a timed model of communicating finite-state machines, which communicate by exchanging messages through channels and use event clocks to generate collections of timed message sequence charts (T-MSCs). As a specification language, we propose a monadic second-order logic equipped with timing predicates and interpreted over T-MSCs. We establish expressive equivalence of our automata and logic. Moreover, we prove that, for (existentially) bounded channels, emptiness and satisfiability are decidable for our automata and logic.

1 Introduction

One of the most famous connections between automata theory and classical logic, established in the early sixties by Büchi and Elgot [7], is the equivalence of finite-state machines and monadic second-order logic (MSO) over words. This study of relations between logical formalisms and automata has had many generalizations including extensions and abstractions of the definition of words themselves.

A natural extension, for instance, are timed words which are very important in the context of verification of safety critical timed systems. For this, we have automata models such as timed automata [1] and event-clock automata (ECA) [2]. The latter have implicit clocks allowing them to record or predict time lapses. This is well-suited for real-time specifications (such as bounded response time) and allows for a suitable logical characterization by a timed MSO over timed words as shown in [9].

On the other hand, in a distributed setting, we might have several agents interacting to generate a global behavior. This interaction can be specified using message sequence charts (MSCs) which generalize words and reflect the causality of events in a system execution. MSCs have been known for a long time independently, as they serve as documentation of design requirements that are referred throughout the design process and even in the final system integration and acceptance testing. MSCs are used for describing the behavior of communicating finite-state machines (CFMs) [6], which are a fundamental model for concurrent systems and communicating protocols. These CFMs have communicating channels between the constituent finite-state automata and a single MSC diagram subsumes a whole set of sequential runs of the CFM.

Our goal is to merge the timed and distributed approaches mentioned above. For this, we first consider timed MSCs (T-MSCs) which are just MSCs with time stamps at events (as in timed words). These are ideal to describe real-time system executions,

V. Arvind and S. Prasad (Eds.): FSTTCS 2007, LNCS 4855, pp. 290–302, 2007.

keeping explicitly the causal relation between events. Next, we consider MSCs with timing constraints (TC-MSCs) where we associate lower and upper bounds on the time interval between certain pairs of events. This is more suitable for a specifier and also useful to describe a (possibly infinite) family of T-MSCs in a finite way.

We introduce event clock communicating finite-state machines (EC-CFM) recognizing timed MSCs. These are CFMs equipped with implicit event clocks allowing us to record or predict time lapses as in the ECA. For the logical framework, we use a timed version of monadic second-order logic (TMSO) with additional timing predicates to specify necessary timing constraints. We interpret both EC-CFMs and TMSO over T-MSCs and prove a constructive equivalence between them, with and without bounds on channels. This is done by lifting the corresponding results from the untimed case [12,11,5] by using TC-MSCs, since they can be seen as MSCs whose labelings are extended by timing information and also as a representation of infinite sets of T-MSCs.

Further, we prove that, over "existentially bounded" channels, the emptiness checking of our automaton model and, thus, the satisfiability problem of our logic are decidable. Our approach consists of constructing a global finite timed automaton that can simulate the runs of the EC-CFM (which is a distributed machine) and so, reduce the problem to emptiness checking on a timed automaton. The hard part of the construction lies in "cleverly" maintaining the partial-order information (of the T-MSC) along the sequential runs of the global timed automaton, while using only finitely many clocks.

Related Work. Past approaches to timing in MSCs with a formal semantics and analysis have been looked at in [3,4,8,13]. While [3] and [4] only consider single MSCs or high-level MSCs, one of the first attempts to study channel automata in the timed setting goes back to Krcal and Yi [13], who provide local timed automata with the means to communicate via FIFO channels. They do not consider MSCs as a semantics of their automata but rather look at restricted channel architectures (e.g., one-channel systems) to transfer decidability of reachability problems from the untimed to the timed setting. A similar automaton model was independently introduced by Chandrasekaran and Mukund in [8], who even define its semantics in terms of timed MSCs. They propose a practical solution to a very specific matching problem using the tool UPPAAL.

Outline. We define MSCs in Section 2, together with their timed extensions. Our logic and the automaton model are introduced in Section 3. We describe the equivalence results between our automata and logic over timed MSCs in Section 4. In Section 5, it is shown that emptiness of automata is decidable for existentially bounded channels.

2   Timed Message Sequence Charts

We fix a finite set Ag of at least two *agents* or *processes*. The set of *communication actions* on process p is $Act_p = \{p!q \mid q \in Ag \setminus \{p\}\} \cup \{p?q \mid q \in Ag \setminus \{p\}\}$, where $p!q$ means that process p sends a message to process q and $p?q$ means that process p receives a message from process q. Furthermore, we let $Act = \bigcup_{p \in Ag} Act_p$.

An *Act-labeled partial order* is a triple $M = (E, \preceq, \lambda)$ where $(E, \preceq)$ is a finite partial order (elements from E are called *events*) and $\lambda : E \to Act$ is a labeling function. For $e \in E$, $\downarrow e$ denotes $\{e' \in E \mid e' \preceq e\}$. We define a message relation

$\mathrm{Msg}^M \subseteq E \times E$ matching send events with their corresponding receives, assuming a FIFO architecture on the channels. That is, $(e, e') \in \mathrm{Msg}^M$ if $\lambda(e) = p!q$ and $\lambda(e') = q?p$ for some $p, q \in Ag$, and $|{\downarrow}e \cap \lambda^{-1}(p!q)| = |{\downarrow}e' \cap \lambda^{-1}(q?p)|$.

A *message sequence chart* (MSC) is an *Act*-labeled partial order $M = (E, \preceq, \lambda)$ such that (i) for any $p \in Ag$, the restriction of $\preceq$ to process p (denoted $\preceq_p$) is a total order, (ii) the partial order $\preceq$ is the transitive closure of $\mathrm{Msg}^M \cup \bigcup_{p \in Ag} \preceq_p$, and (iii) for any distinct $p, q \in Ag$, the number of send events is equal to the number of receive events, i.e, $|\lambda^{-1}(p!q)| = |\lambda^{-1}(q?p)|$.

Fig. 1 depicts an MSC as a diagram. The events of each process are arranged along the vertical lines and messages are shown as horizontal or downward-sloping directed edges. Note that $\lambda(e_1) = p!q$, $\lambda(e_2) = q?p$, $e_1 \preceq_p e'_1$, $(e'_2, e_3) \in \mathrm{Msg}^M$ and $e_1 \preceq e_3$. The linearizations of an MSC form a word language over *Act* under λ. E.g., $(p!q)(q?p)(q!r)(p!r)(r?q)(r?p)$ is one linearization of the MSC in Fig. 1. An MSC is uniquely determined by one of its linearizations.

Fig. 1. An MSC

The first natural attempt while trying to add timing information to MSCs would be to add time stamps to the events of the MSCs. This is motivated from timed words where we have words with time stamps added at each action. This approach is quite realistic when we want to model the real-time execution of concurrent systems.

Definition 1. *A timed MSC (T-MSC) is a tuple $(E, \preceq, \lambda, t)$ where $(E, \preceq, \lambda)$ is an MSC and $t : E \to \mathbb{R}^{\geq 0}$ is a function such that if $e_1 \preceq e_2$ then $t(e_1) \leq t(e_2)$. The set of all T-MSCs is denoted $\mathbb{TMSC}$.*

A *timed linearization* of a T-MSC is a possible execution in terms of a word from $(Act \times \mathbb{R}^{\geq 0})^*$, which thus respects both the causal order and the order imposed by the time stamping. A T-MSC is shown in 2(a). Note that it has several timed linearizations as the concurrent events e_4 and f_3 occur at the same time. A possible timed linearization is $(p!q, 2)(q?p, 2.1)(p!r, 3)(r?p, 3)(p!q, 4)(q?p, 4.5)(p!r, 6)(q!r, 6)(r?q, 6)(r?p, 7)$.

Now a family of T-MSCs with the same induced MSC can be specified by timing constraints on pairs of events of the MSC. This approach is better suited to a specifier who can then decide and enforce constraints between occurrences of events. As an example consider Fig. 2(b). The label $(0, 1]$ on message from e_1 to f_1 specifies the lower bound and upper bound on the delay of message delivery. The label $[1, 5]$ from f_1 to e'_3 represents the bounds on the delay between f_1 and e'_3 and so on.

The question here is how flexible do we want this timing to be, i.e, between which pairs of events do we allow constraints. For an MSC $M = (E, \preceq, \lambda)$, one obvious set of pairs is given by Msg^M which allows us to time messages. A more flexible approach is to allow timing between the next (or previous) event of any action and an event in the MSC. For this, we define the relations $\mathrm{Next}_\sigma^M, \mathrm{Prev}_\sigma^M$ for every $\sigma \in Act$ as follows:

- $\mathrm{Next}_\sigma^M = \{(e, e') \mid \lambda(e') = \sigma, \ e \prec e', \ (e \prec e'' \wedge \lambda(e'') = \sigma) \implies e' \preceq e''\}$
- $\mathrm{Prev}_\sigma^M = \{(e, e') \mid \lambda(e') = \sigma, \ e' \prec e, \ (e'' \prec e \wedge \lambda(e'') = \sigma) \implies e'' \preceq e'\}$

E.g., in Fig. 2(b), $(e_2, e_4) \in \mathrm{Next}_{p!r}^M$, $(f_1, e'_3) \in \mathrm{Next}_{r?p}^M$, and $(e_4, e_3) \in \mathrm{Prev}_{p!q}^M$. Note that these relations are in fact partial maps and hence one can also write $f = \mathrm{Next}_\sigma^M(e)$ for $(e, f) \in \mathrm{Next}_\sigma^M$ and similarly for Prev_σ^M. In fact Msg^M can also been seen as a

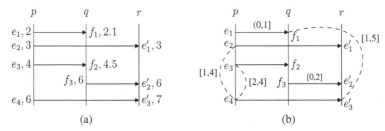

Fig. 2. A T-MSC and a TC-MSC

partial function $E \dashrightarrow E$ mapping a send event to its corresponding receive in the MSC M. Further, we remark that these relations can all be defined for a T-MSC T as well. Since they depend only on the underlying partial order, we write Msg^T, Next_σ^T, etc.

Let us denote the set of symbols $\{\mathrm{Msg}\} \cup \{\mathrm{Prev}_\sigma \mid \sigma \in Act\} \cup \{\mathrm{Next}_\sigma \mid \sigma \in Act\}$ by TC (for timing constraints). For an MSC (or T-MSC) M, we let $\mathrm{TC}^M = \bigcup_{\alpha \in \mathrm{TC}}(\alpha^M)$ be our set of allowed timing pairs. This is flexible enough to specify what we need. It also generalizes the approach of D'Souza [9] in the timed words case. Further, this is similar to the approach adopted by Alur et al. [3] to time MSCs and so we can use their analysis tool to check consistency of the timing constraints in an MSC.

To specify timing constraints we will use rational bounded intervals over the real line. These can be open or closed intervals but we require them to be nonempty and the bounds to be rational. The set of all such intervals is denoted by $\mathcal{I}$.

Definition 2. *An* MSC with timing constraints *(TC-MSC) is a tuple* $(E, \preceq, \lambda, \tau)$ *where* $M = (E, \preceq, \lambda)$ *is an MSC and* $\tau : \mathrm{TC}^M \dashrightarrow \mathcal{I}$ *is a partial function. The TC-MSC is called* maximally defined *if* τ *is a total function.*

With this definition, TC-MSCs can be considered as abstractions of T-MSCs and timed words. Let $M = (E, \preceq, \lambda, \tau)$ be a TC-MSC. A T-MSC $T = (E, \preceq, \lambda, t)$ is a *realization* of M if, for all $(e, e') \in \mathrm{dom}(\tau)$, we have $|t(e) - t(e')| \in \tau(e, e')$. Thus for instance, the T-MSC in Fig. 2(a) is a realization of the TC-MSC in Fig. 2(b).

3   Logic and Automata for Timed MSCs

Monadic Second-Order Logic. We will define several monadic second-order logics as a means to describe sets of T-MSCs. Their syntax depends on a set $\mathcal{R}$ of (binary) relation symbols, which settles the access to the partial-order relation of an MSC or T-MSC. One example is $\mathcal{R}_\preceq = \{\preceq, \mathrm{Msg}\}$ containing symbols for the partial order and the message relation. The formal syntax of our logic $\mathrm{TMSO}(\mathcal{R})$ is given by:

$$\varphi ::= P_\sigma(x) \mid x \in X \mid x = y \mid R(x, y) \mid \delta(x, \alpha(x)) \in I \mid \neg\varphi \mid \varphi \vee \varphi \mid \exists x \varphi \mid \exists X \varphi$$

where $\sigma \in Act$, $R \in \mathcal{R}$, $\alpha \in \mathrm{TC}$, $I \in \mathcal{I}$, x, y are individual (or first-order) variables, and X is a set (or second-order) variable (each from an infinite supply of variables).

Let $T = (E, \preceq, \lambda, t)$ be a T-MSC and let $\mathbb{I}$ be an *interpretation* that maps first-order variables to elements in E and second-order variables to subsets of E. Let us define when $T, \mathbb{I} \models \varphi$ for $\varphi \in \mathrm{TMSO}(\mathcal{R})$. As usual, $P_\sigma(x)$ expresses that x is labeled with σ, i.e., $\lambda(\mathbb{I}(x)) = \sigma$. The novelty is the timing predicate $\delta(x, \alpha(x)) \in I$ by which we mean that the time difference between x and $\alpha^T(x)$ is contained in I, i.e., $T, \mathbb{I} \models \delta(x, \alpha(x)) \in I$ if $\mathbb{I}(x) \in \mathrm{dom}(\alpha^T)$ and $|t(\mathbb{I}(x)) - t(\alpha^T(\mathbb{I}(x)))| \in I$. For the set $\mathcal{R}$ of binary relation symbols we will use $\mathcal{R}_\preceq = \{\preceq, \mathrm{Msg}\}$ or $\mathcal{R}_\lessdot = \{\lessdot_p \mid p \in Ag\} \cup \{\mathrm{Msg}\}$. The interpretation of $\lessdot_p$ is the immediate successor relation on process p: $\lessdot_p := \prec_p \setminus \prec_p^2$. The interpretation of Msg is indeed Msg^T. The rest of the semantics is classical for MSO logics. For sentences φ in this logic, we define $\mathcal{L}_{time}(\varphi) = \{T \in \mathrm{TMSC} \mid T \models \varphi\}$. The *existential* fragment of $\mathrm{TMSO}(\mathcal{R})$, which is denoted by $\mathrm{ETMSO}(\mathcal{R})$, comprises all formulas $\exists X_1 \ldots \exists X_n \varphi$ such that φ does not contain any set quantifier.

We will give TMSO formulas a natural semantics in terms of TC-MSCs, too. The only noteworthy difference is in the atomic predicate $\delta(x, \alpha(x)) \in I$. For a TC-MSC $M = (E, \preceq, \lambda, \tau)$, we define $M, \mathbb{I} \models \delta(x, \alpha(x)) \in I$ if $\tau(\mathbb{I}(x), \alpha^M(\mathbb{I}(x))) \subseteq I$, which implicitly implies $\mathbb{I}(x) \in \mathrm{dom}(\alpha^M)$ and $(\mathbb{I}(x), \alpha^M(\mathbb{I}(x))) \in \mathrm{dom}(\tau)$. The set of TC-MSCs that satisfy a TMSO sentence φ is denoted by $\mathcal{L}_{TC}(\varphi)$. The following implication is easy to see. Its converse holds in a restricted case, as we will see later.

Lemma 3. *Let a T-MSC T be a realization of some TC-MSC M and let φ be a TMSO formula. Then, $M \in \mathcal{L}_{TC}(\varphi)$ implies $T \in \mathcal{L}_{time}(\varphi)$.*

Event-Clock Communicating Finite-State Machines (EC-CFMs). A natural model of communication protocols are communicating finite-state machines [6], which consist of finite-state machines with message channels between any pair of them. To introduce the timed model we attach recording and predicting *clocks* (as in [2]) to these machines.

Definition 4. *An EC-CFM is a tuple $\mathcal{A} = (C, (\mathcal{A}_p)_{p \in Ag}, F)$ where C is a finite set of control messages, $\mathcal{A}_p = (Q_p, \rightarrow_p, \iota_p)$ is a finite transition system over $Act_p \times [\mathrm{TC} \dashrightarrow \mathcal{I}] \times C$ (i.e., $\iota_p \in Q_p$ is the initial state and $\rightarrow_p$ is a finite subset of $Q_p \times Act_p \times [\mathrm{TC} \dashrightarrow \mathcal{I}] \times C \times Q_p$) with $[\mathrm{TC} \dashrightarrow \mathcal{I}]$ denoting the set of partial maps from TC to $\mathcal{I}$, and $F \subseteq \prod_{p \in Ag} Q_p$ is a set of global final states.*

The input of an EC-CFM $\mathcal{A}$ is a T-MSC $T = (E, \preceq, \lambda, t)$. Consider a map $r : E \rightarrow \bigcup_{p \in Ag} Q_p$ labeling each event of process p with a state from Q_p. Define $r^- : E \rightarrow \bigcup_{p \in Ag} Q_p$ as follows: For event e in process p, if there is an event e' in process p such that $e' \lessdot_p e$, then we set $r^-(e) = r(e')$. Otherwise, we set $r^-(e) = \iota_p$. Then r is said to be a *run* of $\mathcal{A}$ on T if, for all $(e, e') \in \mathrm{Msg}^T$ with e in process p and e' in process q, there are guards $g, g' \in [\mathrm{TC} \dashrightarrow \mathcal{I}]$ and a control message $c \in C$ such that

(1) $(r^-(e), \lambda(e), g, c, r(e)) \in \rightarrow_p$ and $(r^-(e'), \lambda(e'), g', c, r(e')) \in \rightarrow_q$,
(2) for all $\alpha \in \mathrm{dom}(g)$, we have $e \in \mathrm{dom}(\alpha^T)$ and $|t(e) - t(\alpha^T(e))| \in g(\alpha)$, and
(3) for all $\alpha \in \mathrm{dom}(g')$, we have $e' \in \mathrm{dom}(\alpha^T)$ and $|t(e') - t(\alpha^T(e'))| \in g'(\alpha)$.

Let r be a run of $\mathcal{A}$ on T. We define $s_p = r(e_p)$, where e_p is the maximal event in process p. If there are no events on process p, we set $s_p = \iota_p$. Then run r is *successful* if the tuple $(s_p)_{p \in Ag}$ belongs to F. A T-MSC is *accepted* by an EC-CFM $\mathcal{A}$ if it admits a successful run. We denote by $\mathcal{L}_{time}(\mathcal{A})$ the set of T-MSCs that are accepted by $\mathcal{A}$.

As in the logic, we can give EC-CFMs a semantics in terms of TC-MSCs as well. For defining a run on TC-MSC $M = (E, \preceq, \lambda, \tau)$ we just replace condition (2) above by saying that, for all $\alpha \in \mathrm{dom}(g)$, we must have $e \in \mathrm{dom}(\alpha^M)$ and $\tau(e, \alpha^M(e)) \subseteq g(\alpha)$. We do the same for condition (3). Then, with the same notion of acceptance as above, we can denote the set of all TC-MSCs accepted by a given EC-CFM $\mathcal{A}$ as $\mathcal{L}_{TC}(\mathcal{A})$.

Lemma 5. *Let T be a realization of some TC-MSC M and let $\mathcal{A}$ be an EC-CFM. Then, $M \in \mathcal{L}_{TC}(\mathcal{A})$ implies $T \in \mathcal{L}_{time}(\mathcal{A})$.*

4   Equivalence of EC-CFMs and MSO Logic

In [5], the equivalence between EMSO formulas (with restricted signature) and CFMs over MSCs has been established. In [11], the equivalence between full MSO formulas and CFMs over MSCs has been described in the context of bounded channels. We will lift these theorems to the timed setting, using the concepts from the previous sections.

Theorem 6. *Let L be a set of T-MSCs. The following are equivalent:*

1. *There is an EC-CFM $\mathcal{A}$ such that $\mathcal{L}_{time}(\mathcal{A}) = L$.*
2. *There is $\varphi \in \mathrm{ETMSO}(\mathcal{R}_{\prec})$ such that $\mathcal{L}_{time}(\varphi) = L$.*

The construction of an ETMSO formula from an EC-CFM follows the similar constructions applied, for example, to finite and asynchronous automata. In addition, we have to cope with guards occurring on local transitions of the given EC-CFM. Assume that $g : \mathrm{TC} \dashrightarrow \mathcal{I}$ is such a guard. To ensure that the timing constraints that come along with g are satisfied we use the formula $\bigwedge_{\alpha \in \mathrm{dom}(g)} \delta(x, \alpha(x)) \in g(\alpha)$.

The rest of this section is devoted to the construction of an EC-CFM from an ETMSO formula, whose size is elementary in the size of the formula. The basic idea is to reduce this to an analogous untimed result, which has also been applied in the settings of words and traces [9,10]. For this, we establish a connection between TMSO and ordinary MSO logic without timing predicate, and between EC-CFMs and their untimed variant. Usually, these untimed formalisms are parametrized by a finite alphabet Σ to speak about structures whose labelings are provided by Σ. Hence, in our framework, we need to find a finite abstraction of the infinite set of possible time stamps. Applying this finite abstraction, we move from T-MSCs to TC-MSCs and establish the converse of Lemmas 3 and 5 in Lemmas 8 and 9, resp. This finally allows us to translate ETMSO formulas into EC-CFMs. We provide more details below.

First, we define proper interval sets. We call a set of intervals $\mathcal{S} \subseteq \mathcal{I}$ *proper* if it forms a finite partition of $\mathbb{R}^{\geq 0}$. We say that an interval set *refines* another interval set if every interval of the latter is the union of some collection of intervals of the former. For any finite interval set, we can easily obtain a proper interval set refining it.

Let $T = (E, \preceq, \lambda, t)$ be a T-MSC and $\mathcal{S}$ be a proper interval set. We introduce the TC-MSC $M_T^{\mathcal{S}} := (E, \preceq, \lambda, \tau)$ where, for any $(e, e') \in \mathrm{TC}^T$, $\tau(e, e')$ is defined to be the unique interval of $\mathcal{S}$ containing $|t(e) - t(e')|$.

Lemma 7. *Let T be a T-MSC and let $\mathcal{S}$ be a proper interval set. Then, $M_T^{\mathcal{S}}$ is the unique maximally defined TC-MSC that uses intervals from $\mathcal{S}$ and admits T as realization.*

Given a TMSO formula φ, we let $\mathrm{Int}(\varphi)$ denote the finite set of intervals I for which φ has a sub-formula of the form $\delta(x, \alpha(x)) \in I$. Similarly, for any EC-CFM $\mathcal{A}$, we have a *finite* set, denoted $\text{Int}(\mathcal{A})$, of intervals occurring in $\mathcal{A}$ as guards. Now look at any proper interval set $\mathcal{S}$ that refines $\text{Int}(\varphi)$. We can translate the TMSO formula φ to another TMSO formula $\varphi^{\mathcal{S}}$ by replacing each sub-formula of the form $\delta(x, \alpha(x)) \in I$ by the formula $\bigvee_{J \in \mathcal{S}: J \subseteq I} \delta(x, \alpha(x)) \in J$. Using Lemma 7, we can show the following Lemmas, which then enable us to prove the reverse direction of Theorem 6.

Lemma 8. *Given a T-MSC T, a TMSO formula φ, and a proper interval set $\mathcal{S}$ that refines $\text{Int}(\varphi)$, we have $T \models \varphi$ iff $M_T^{\mathcal{S}} \models \varphi$ iff $M_T^{\mathcal{S}} \models \varphi^{\mathcal{S}}$.*

Lemma 9. *Let $\mathcal{A}$ be an EC-CFM and let $\mathcal{S}$ be a proper interval set that refines $\text{Int}(\mathcal{A})$. For a T-MSC T, we have $T \in \mathcal{L}_{time}(\mathcal{A})$ iff $M_T^{\mathcal{S}} \in \mathcal{L}_{TC}(\mathcal{A})$.*

Proof (of Theorem 6, (2) $\rightarrow$ (1)). Observe that any TC-MSC can be viewed as an MSC with an additional labeling by removing the intervals from pairs of events and attaching them to the corresponding events. More precisely, a TC-MSC $M = (E, \preceq, \lambda, \tau)$ can be represented as an MSC $\overline{M} = (E, \preceq, \lambda, \gamma)$ with additional labeling $\gamma : E \rightarrow (\text{TC} \dashrightarrow \mathcal{I})$ describing the timing constraints, i.e., $\gamma(e)(\alpha) = \tau(e, \alpha^M(e))$ if $e \in \text{dom}(\alpha^M)$ and $(e, \alpha^M(e)) \in \text{dom}(\tau)$; otherwise, $\gamma(e)(\alpha)$ is undefined. This view will allow us to apply equivalences between logic and automata in the untimed case. So far, however, the additional labeling γ is over an infinite alphabet, as there are infinitely many intervals that might act as constraints. So, for any proper interval set $\mathcal{S}$, we define $\text{TCMSC}(\mathcal{S})$ as the set of TC-MSCs $M = (E, \preceq, \lambda, \tau)$ such that $\tau(e, e') \in \mathcal{S}$ for any $(e, e') \in \text{dom}(\tau)$. Note that, if $M \in \text{TCMSC}(\mathcal{S})$ and $I \in \mathcal{S}$ then $M, \mathbb{I} \models \delta(x, \alpha(x)) \in I$ iff $\tau(\mathbb{I}(x), \alpha^M(\mathbb{I}(x))) = I$ iff $\gamma(\mathbb{I}(x))(\alpha) = I$. Hence a timing predicate can be transformed into a labeling predicate: for any $\varphi \in \text{TMSO}$ such that $\text{Int}(\varphi) \subseteq \mathcal{S}$, there is an *untimed* MSO formula $\overline{\varphi}$ such that $M, \mathbb{I} \models \varphi$ iff $\overline{M}, \mathbb{I} \models \overline{\varphi}$ for all $M \in \text{TCMSC}(\mathcal{S})$. In the following, we denote by $\mathcal{L}_u(\varphi)$ the set of MSCs with additional labeling γ that satisfy an untimed MSO sentence φ. We can build an untimed $\text{MSO}(\mathcal{R}_{\prec})$ sentence $\mu_{\prec}^{\mathcal{S}}$ such that $\mathcal{L}_u(\mu_{\prec}^{\mathcal{S}})$ is the set of *maximally defined* MSCs $M = (E, \preceq, \lambda, \gamma)$ with additional labeling γ using intervals from $\mathcal{S}$, i.e., for all $e \in E$, we have $\alpha \in \text{dom}(\gamma(e))$ iff $e \in \text{dom}(\alpha^M)$ and in this case $\gamma(e)(\alpha) \in \mathcal{S}$.

Similarly, an EC-CFM $\mathcal{A}$ can be interpreted over MSCs with the additional labeling γ by replacing conditions (2) and (3) of runs by $\gamma(e) = g$ and $\gamma(e') = g'$, resp. We denote by $\mathcal{L}_u(\mathcal{A})$ the untimed MSCs with additional labeling γ that are accepted by $\mathcal{A}$. Here, for a TC-MSC $M \in \text{TCMSC}(\mathcal{S})$ and an automaton $\mathcal{A}$ with guards in $[\text{TC} \dashrightarrow \mathcal{S}]$, we have $\overline{M} \in \mathcal{L}_u(\mathcal{A})$ implies $M \in \mathcal{L}_{TC}(\mathcal{A})$. The converse does not hold in general.

Let $\varphi \in \text{ETMSO}(\mathcal{R}_{\prec})$ be the given formula and let $\mathcal{S}$ be a proper interval set that refines $\text{Int}(\varphi)$. Consider the untimed $\text{MSO}(\mathcal{R}_{\prec})$-formula $\psi = \overline{\varphi}^{\mathcal{S}} \wedge \mu_{\prec}^{\mathcal{S}}$. By [5], there is an EC-CFM $\mathcal{A}$ with guards from $[\text{TC} \dashrightarrow \mathcal{S}]$ such that $\mathcal{L}_u(\mathcal{A}) = \mathcal{L}_u(\psi)$. We will show that $\mathcal{L}_{time}(\varphi) = \mathcal{L}_{time}(\mathcal{A})$.

Let T be a T-MSC. By Lemma 8 we have $T \models \varphi$ iff $M_T^{\mathcal{S}} \models \varphi^{\mathcal{S}}$. Since $\text{Int}(\varphi^{\mathcal{S}}) \subseteq \mathcal{S}$ and $M_T^{\mathcal{S}} \in \text{TCMSC}(\mathcal{S})$ we have $M_T^{\mathcal{S}} \models \varphi^{\mathcal{S}}$ iff $\overline{M}_T^{\mathcal{S}} \models \overline{\varphi}^{\mathcal{S}}$. Now, $M_T^{\mathcal{S}}$ is maximally defined, hence we obtain $\overline{M}_T^{\mathcal{S}} \models \mu_{\prec}^{\mathcal{S}}$. Therefore, $T \in \mathcal{L}_{time}(\varphi)$ iff $\overline{M}_T^{\mathcal{S}} \in \mathcal{L}_u(\psi) = \mathcal{L}_u(\mathcal{A})$. We have seen above that this implies $M_T^{\mathcal{S}} \in \mathcal{L}_{TC}(\mathcal{A})$. We show that here the converse holds, too. If $M_T^{\mathcal{S}} \in \mathcal{L}_{TC}(\mathcal{A})$ we can build a TC-MSC $M' = (E, \preceq, \lambda, \tau')$ such that $\text{dom}(\tau') \subseteq \text{dom}(\tau)$, $\tau'(e, e') = \tau(e, e')$ for all $(e, e') \in \text{dom}(\tau')$, and

$\overline{M}' \in \mathcal{L}_u(\mathcal{A})$. Now, $\mathcal{L}_u(\mathcal{A}) \subseteq \mathcal{L}_u(\mu_{\preceq}^{\mathcal{S}})$ hence $\overline{M}'$ is maximally defined and we obtain $M' = M_T^{\mathcal{S}}$. To summarize, we have shown that $T \in \mathcal{L}_{time}(\varphi)$ iff $M_T^{\mathcal{S}} \in \mathcal{L}_{TC}(\mathcal{A})$, and we conclude with Lemma 9 that this is equivalent to $T \in \mathcal{L}_{time}(\mathcal{A})$.   □

To characterize EC-CFMs in terms of full TMSO, we need to define restrictions on the channel size. For an integer $B > 0$, a word $w \in Act^*$ is *B-bounded* if, for any $p, q \in Ag$ and any prefix u of w, the number of occurrences of $p!q$ in u exceeds that of $q?p$ by at most B. An MSC M is said to be *existentially B-bounded* ($\exists$-*B*-bounded) if it has some B-bounded linearization. A T-MSC $(E, \preceq, \lambda, t)$ is said to be *untimed-$\exists$-B-bounded* if $(E, \preceq, \lambda)$ is $\exists$-*B*-bounded. Note that, directly lifting the definition of bounds from MSCs to T-MSCs is not completely intuitive: there are untimed-$\exists$-1-bounded T-MSCs whose minimal channel capacity for a timed linearization exceeds 1.

Following the same lines as in the proof of Theorem 6 but using the equivalence result from [11], we can show the following theorem.

Theorem 10. *Let $B > 0$ and let L be a set of untimed-$\exists$-B-bounded T-MSCs. There is an EC-CFM $\mathcal{A}$ with $\mathcal{L}_{time}(\mathcal{A}) = L$ iff there is $\varphi \in \mathrm{TMSO}(\mathcal{R}_{\preceq})$ with $\mathcal{L}_{time}(\varphi) = L$. Both directions are effective.*

5   Deciding Emptiness of EC-CFMs

In this section, we investigate emptiness checking for EC-CFMs. While the problem is of course undecidable in its full generality, we give a partial solution to it.

Theorem 11. *The following problem is decidable:*

INPUT*: An EC-CFM $\mathcal{A}$ and an integer $B > 0$.*
QUESTION*: Is there $T \in \mathcal{L}_{time}(\mathcal{A})$ such that T has a B-bounded timed linearization?*

Here, a timed linearization of T is B-bounded if the channel size never exceeds B during its execution.

We fix an EC-CFM $\mathcal{A} = (C, (\mathcal{A}_p)_{p \in Ag}, F)$, with $\mathcal{A}_p = (Q_p, \rightarrow_p, \iota_p)$, and $B > 0$. From $\mathcal{A}$, we build a *(finite) timed automaton* that accepts a timed word $w \in (Act \times \mathbb{R}^{\geq 0})^*$ iff w is a B-bounded timed linearization of some T-MSC in $\mathcal{L}_{time}(\mathcal{A})$. As emptiness is decidable for finite timed automata [1], we have shown Theorem 11.

Let us first recall the basic notion of a timed automaton. For a set $\mathcal{Z}$ of *clocks*, the set Form$(\mathcal{Z})$ of *clock formulas* over $\mathcal{Z}$ is given by the grammar $\varphi ::= \mathrm{true} \mid \mathrm{false} \mid x \sim c \mid x - y \sim c \mid \neg\varphi \mid \varphi_1 \wedge \varphi_2 \mid \varphi_1 \vee \varphi_2$ where $x, y \in \mathcal{Z}$, $\sim \in \{<, \leq, >, \geq, =\}$, and c ranges over $\mathbb{R}^{\geq 0}$.

A *timed automaton (with ε-transitions)* over Σ is a tuple $\mathcal{B} = (Q, \mathcal{Z}, \delta, \iota, F)$ where Q is a set of *states*, $\mathcal{Z}$ is a set of *clocks*, $\iota \in Q$ is the *initial state*, $F \subseteq Q$ is the set of *final states*, and $\delta \subseteq Q \times (\Sigma \cup \{\varepsilon\}) \times \mathrm{Form}(\mathcal{Z}) \times 2^{\mathcal{Z}} \times Q$ is the transition relation. The definition of a run of $\mathcal{B}$ and its language $\mathcal{L}(\mathcal{B}) \subseteq (\Sigma \times \mathbb{R}^{\geq 0})^*$ are as usual.

To keep track of the clock constraints used in $\mathcal{A}$, we need to recover a partial order from a word. Firstly, the partial order of an MSC can be recovered from any of its linearizations. If w is a linearization of MSC M, then M is isomorphic to the unique MSC $(E, \preceq, \lambda)$ such that $E = \{u \in Act^* \mid u \neq \varepsilon \text{ and } w = uv \text{ for some } v\}$ (i.e.,

E is the set of nonempty prefixes of w), $\lambda(u\sigma) = \sigma$ for $u \in Act^*$ and $\sigma \in Act$, and $\preceq_p = \{(u, v) \in E \times E \mid u$ is a prefix of v and $\lambda(u), \lambda(v) \in Act_p\}$. Thus, we might consider the partial-order relation of M to be a relation over prefixes of a given linearization of M. We go further to describe deterministic finite automata (DFA) that actually run on words that are linearizations of an MSC and accept if the first and last letter of it are related under $\preceq$, Prev_σ^M, or Next_σ^M. More precisely, our finite automata will run on linearizations of MSCs with additional labelings in $\{0, \ldots, B-1\}$. We say that such an MSC $(E, \preceq, \lambda, \rho)$ (with $\rho : E \to \{0, \ldots, B-1\}$) is B-well-stamped if, for any $e \in E$, $\rho(e) = |{\downarrow}e \cap \lambda^{-1}(\lambda(e))| \mod B$.

Lemma 12. *There are DFA* $C^\lhd = (Q^\lhd, \delta^\lhd, s_0^\lhd, F^\lhd)$ *and* $C^\rhd = (Q^\rhd, \delta^\rhd, s_0^\rhd, F^\rhd)$ *over* $Act \times \{0, \ldots, B-1\}$ *with* $|Q^\lhd| = |Q^\rhd| = B^{\mathcal{O}(|Ag|^2)}$ *(for $B \geq 2$) such that, for any* $w = (\sigma, m)w'(\tau, n) \in (Act \times \{0, \ldots, B-1\})^*$ *and* $u, v \in (Act \times \{0, \ldots, B-1\})^*$, *the following holds: If uwv is a linearization of some B-well-stamped MSC M, then*

- $w \in L(C^\lhd)$ *iff* $(u(\sigma, m)w'(\tau, n), u(\sigma, m)) \in \text{Prev}_\sigma^M$ *and*
- $w \in L(C^\rhd)$ *iff* $(u(\sigma, m), u(\sigma, m)w'(\tau, n)) \in \text{Next}_\tau^M$.

From now on, we suppose $C^\lhd = (Q^\lhd, \delta^\lhd, s_0^\lhd, F^\lhd)$ and $C^\rhd = (Q^\rhd, \delta^\rhd, s_0^\rhd, F^\rhd)$ from the above lemma to be fixed. We moreover suppose that the *previous* automaton $C^\lhd$ has a unique sink state $s_{sink}^\lhd$, from which there is no final state reachable anymore.

The Timed Automaton. Let us describe a timed automaton $\mathcal{B}$ that simulates the EC-CFM $\mathcal{A}$. To simplify the presentation, we allow infinitely many clocks and infinitely many states, though on any run only finitely many states and clocks will be seen. Later, we will modify this automaton in order to get down to finitely many states and clocks.

We use $\text{Ind} = Act \times \mathbb{N}$ as (an infinite) index set. A state of the timed automaton $\mathcal{B} = (Q_\mathcal{B}, \mathcal{Z}, \delta, \iota_\mathcal{B}, F_\mathcal{B})$ will be a tuple $st = (\bar{s}, \chi, \eta, \xi^\lhd, \xi^\rhd, \gamma^\rhd, \gamma^m)$ where

- $\bar{s} = (s_p)_{p \in Ag} \in \prod_{p \in Ag} Q_p$ is a tuple of local states,
- $\chi : Ag^2 \to C^{\leq B}$ describes the contents of the channels,
- $\eta : Act \to \{0, \ldots, B-1\}$ gives the number that should be assigned to the next occurrence of an action,
- $\xi^\lhd : \text{Ind} \dashrightarrow Q^\lhd$ and $\xi^\rhd : \text{Ind} \dashrightarrow Q^\rhd$ associate with "active" indices, states in the *previous* and *next* automata as given by Lemma 12,
- $\gamma^\rhd : \text{Ind} \dashrightarrow \text{Int}(\mathcal{A})$ associates *next* constraints with active indices, and
- $\gamma^m : Ag^2 \times \{0, \ldots, B-1\} \dashrightarrow \text{Int}(\mathcal{A})$ describes the guards attached to messages.

The initial state is $\iota_\mathcal{B} = ((\iota_p)_{p \in Ag}, \chi_0, \eta_0, \xi_0^\lhd, \xi_0^\rhd, \gamma_0^\rhd, \gamma_0^m)$ where χ_0 and η_0 map any argument to the empty word and 0, resp., and the partial maps $\xi_0^\lhd, \xi_0^\rhd, \gamma_0^\rhd$, and γ_0^m are nowhere defined. We will use clocks from the (infinite) set $\mathcal{Z} = \{z_{\sigma,i}^\lhd, z_{\sigma,i}^\rhd \mid (\sigma, i) \in \text{Ind}\} \cup \{z_{p,q,i}^m \mid (p, q, i) \in Ag^2 \times \{0, \ldots, B-1\}\}$. Then, $\delta \subseteq Q_\mathcal{B} \times Act \times \text{Form}(\mathcal{Z}) \times 2^\mathcal{Z} \times Q_\mathcal{B}$ contains $((\bar{s}, \chi, \eta, \xi^\lhd, \xi^\rhd, \gamma^\rhd, \gamma^m), \tau, \varphi, R, (\bar{s}', \chi', \eta', \xi'^\lhd, \xi'^\rhd, \gamma'^\rhd, \gamma'^m))$ if there is a local transition $(s_p, \tau, g, c, s_p') \in \to_p$ on process p such that

- $s_r' = s_r$ for all $r \in Ag \setminus \{p\}$.
- if $\tau = p!q$, then $\chi'(p, q) = c \cdot \chi(p, q)$ and $\chi'(r, s) = \chi(r, s)$ for $(r, s) \neq (p, q)$.

- if $\tau = p?q$, then $\chi(q,p) = \chi'(q,p) \cdot c$ and $\chi'(r,s) = \chi(r,s)$ for $(r,s) \neq (q,p)$.
- $\eta'(\tau) = (\eta(\tau)+1) \bmod B$ and η, η' coincide on all other actions.
- The states of the *previous* automata are updated. We initialize a new copy starting on the current position in order to be able to determine which latter positions are related with the current one by Prev_τ^T. We also reset a corresponding new clock $z_{\tau,i}^\lhd$ (see below). Indeed, all existing copies of $C^\lhd$ are updated except those that would reach the $s_{sink}^\lhd$ state which are released since they will not be needed anymore.

$$\xi'^\lhd(\sigma,i) = \begin{cases} \delta^\lhd(s_0^\lhd, (\tau, \eta(\tau))) & \text{if } \sigma = \tau \ \land \ i = \min(\mathbb{N} \setminus \mathrm{dom}(\xi^\lhd(\sigma))) \\ \delta^\lhd(\xi^\lhd(\sigma,i), (\tau, \eta(\tau))) & \text{if } (\sigma,i) \in \mathrm{dom}(\xi^\lhd) \ \land \\ & \qquad \delta^\lhd(\xi^\lhd(\sigma,i), (\tau, \eta(\tau))) \neq s_{sink}^\lhd \\ \text{undefined} & \text{otherwise,} \end{cases}$$

- The states of the *next* automata are updated similarly, starting a new copy of $C^\rhd$ for each action σ such that there is a Next_σ constraint on the local transition. We also reset corresponding new clocks $z_{\sigma,i}^\rhd$ (see below).

$$\xi'^\rhd(\sigma,i) = \begin{cases} \delta^\rhd(s_0^\rhd, (\tau, \eta(\tau))) & \text{if } \mathrm{Next}_\sigma \in \mathrm{dom}(g) \ \land \ i = \min(\mathbb{N} \setminus \mathrm{dom}(\xi^\rhd(\sigma))) \\ \delta^\rhd(\xi^\rhd(\sigma,i), (\tau, \eta(\tau))) & \text{if } (\sigma,i) \in \mathrm{dom}(\xi^\rhd) \ \land \ (\sigma \neq \tau \ \lor \\ & \qquad \delta^\rhd(\xi^\rhd(\sigma,i), (\tau, \eta(\tau))) \notin F^\rhd) \\ \text{undefined} & \text{otherwise.} \end{cases}$$

- The *next* guards are updated. Each guard generating a new copy of $C^\rhd$ is recorded with the same new index. Guards that were registered before and are matched by the current action are released. All other recorded guards are kept unchanged.

$$\gamma'^\rhd(\sigma,i) = \begin{cases} g(\mathrm{Next}_\sigma) & \text{if } \mathrm{Next}_\sigma \in \mathrm{dom}(g) \ \land \ i = \min(\mathbb{N} \setminus \mathrm{dom}(\xi'^\rhd(\sigma))) \\ \text{undefined} & \text{if } \sigma = \tau \ \land \ \xi'^\rhd(\tau,i) \in F^\rhd \\ \gamma^\rhd(\sigma,i) & \text{otherwise.} \end{cases}$$

- The guards attached to message constraints are updated similarly.

$$\gamma'^m(r,s,i) = \begin{cases} g(\mathrm{Msg}) & \text{if } \mathrm{Msg} \in \mathrm{dom}(g) \ \land \ \tau = r!s \ \land \ i = \eta(\tau) \\ \text{undefined} & \text{if } \tau = s?r \ \land \ i = \eta(\tau) \\ \gamma^m(r,s,i) & \text{otherwise.} \end{cases}$$

- The guard φ makes sure that all constraints that get *matched* at the current event are satisfied. E.g., if the local transition contains a Prev_σ constraint, then we have to check $z_{\sigma,i}^\lhd \in g(\mathrm{Prev}_\sigma)$ for the (unique) i such that $\xi'^\lhd(\sigma,i) \in F^\lhd$. If there is no such i then there is no σ in the past of the current event and the Prev_σ constraint of the local transition cannot be satisfied. In this case, we set φ to false.

$$\varphi = \bigwedge_{\substack{(\sigma,i) \mid \mathrm{Prev}_\sigma \in \mathrm{dom}(g) \\ \text{and } \xi'^\lhd(\sigma,i) \in F^\lhd}} z_{\sigma,i}^\lhd \in g(\mathrm{Prev}_\sigma) \quad \land \quad \bigwedge_{\substack{\sigma \mid \mathrm{Prev}_\sigma \in \mathrm{dom}(g) \\ \text{and } \{i \mid \xi'^\lhd(\sigma,i) \in F^\lhd\} = \emptyset}} \text{false}$$

$$\land \quad \bigwedge_{\substack{i \in \mathrm{dom}(\gamma^\rhd(\tau)) \mid \\ \xi'^\rhd(\tau,i) \in F^\rhd}} z_{\tau,i}^\rhd \in \gamma^\rhd(\tau,i) \quad \land \quad \bigwedge_{\substack{(q,p,i) \in \mathrm{dom}(\gamma^m) \mid \\ \tau = p?q, \ \eta(\tau) = i}} z_{q,p,i}^m \in \gamma^m(q,p,i)$$

- All newly defined clocks have to be reset, so we set R to be the union of sets $\{z^{\triangleleft}_{\tau,i} \mid i = \min(\mathbb{N} \setminus \mathrm{dom}(\xi^{\triangleleft}(\tau)))\}$, $\{z^m_{p,q,i} \mid \tau = p!q \text{ and } i = \eta(\tau)\}$, and $\{z^{\triangleright}_{\sigma,i} \mid \mathrm{Next}_\sigma \in \mathrm{dom}(g) \text{ and } i = \min(\mathbb{N} \setminus \mathrm{dom}(\xi^{\triangleright}(\sigma)))\}$.

Finally, the set of accepting states $F_{\mathcal{B}}$ consists of all tuples $(\bar{s}, \chi, \eta, \xi^{\triangleleft}, \xi^{\triangleright}, \gamma^{\triangleright}, \gamma^m)$ in $Q_{\mathcal{B}}$ such that $\bar{s} \in F$, $\chi = \chi_0$, and the partial maps $\gamma^{\triangleright}$ and γ^m are nowhere defined. This ensures that each registered guard has been checked. Indeed, a constraint registered in $\gamma^{\triangleright}$ or γ^m is released only when it is checked with the guard φ.

One critical observation here is that, once we have specified the local transition of $\mathcal{A}$, this global transition of $\mathcal{B}$ gets determined uniquely. Thus, this step is always deterministic. Note that the above automaton $\mathcal{B}$ has no ε-transitions either.

Theorem 13. $\mathcal{B}$ *accepts precisely the B-bounded timed linearizations of* $\mathcal{L}_{time}(\mathcal{A})$.

A Finite Version of $\mathcal{B}$. To get down to a finite timed automaton that is equivalent to $\mathcal{B}$, we have to bound the number of copies of the automata $\mathcal{C}^{\triangleleft}$ and $\mathcal{C}^{\triangleright}$ that are active along a run. We can show that the number of active copies of $\mathcal{C}^{\triangleleft}$ is already bounded:

Proposition 14. *Assume that* $(\bar{s}, \chi, \eta, \xi^{\triangleleft}, \xi^{\triangleright}, \gamma^{\triangleright}, \gamma^m)$ *is a reachable state of $\mathcal{B}$. Then,* $\mathrm{dom}(\xi^{\triangleleft}) \subseteq Act \times \{0, \dots, |Q^{\triangleleft}|\}$.

We deduce that, for the *previous* constraints, we can restrict to the *finite* index set $\mathrm{Ind}^{\triangleleft} = Act \times \{0, \dots, |Q^{\triangleleft}|\}$: in a reachable state, $\xi^{\triangleleft}$ is a partial map from $\mathrm{Ind}^{\triangleleft}$ to $Q^{\triangleleft}$. This also implies that $\mathcal{B}$ uses finitely many *previous* clocks from $\{z^{\triangleleft}_{\sigma,i} \mid (\sigma, i) \in \mathrm{Ind}^{\triangleleft}\}$.

The remaining source of infinity comes from *next* constraints. The situation is not as easy as for *previous* constraints. The problem is that the number of registered Next_σ constraints, $|\mathrm{dom}(\gamma^{\triangleright})|$, may be unbounded. Assume that $(\sigma, i), (\sigma, j) \in \mathrm{dom}(\gamma^{\triangleright})$ for some $i \neq j$. Then, also $(\sigma, i), (\sigma, j) \in \mathrm{dom}(\xi^{\triangleright})$ and the clocks $z^{\triangleright}_{\sigma,i}$ and $z^{\triangleright}_{\sigma,j}$ have been reset. If we have $\xi^{\triangleright}(\sigma, i) = \xi^{\triangleright}(\sigma, j)$ then the constraints associated with i and j will be matched simultaneously. When matched, the guard on the transition of $\mathcal{B}$ will include both $z^{\triangleright}_{\sigma,i} \in \gamma^{\triangleright}(\sigma, i)$ and $z^{\triangleright}_{\sigma,j} \in \gamma^{\triangleright}(\sigma, j)$. The idea is to keep the stronger constraint and to release the other one. To determine the stronger constraint we have to deal separately with the upper parts and the lower parts of the constraints. An additional difficulty comes from the fact that the two clocks have not been reset simultaneously.

Let $x \sim c$ and $x' \sim' c'$ be two *upper*-guards which means that $\sim, \sim' \in \{<, \leq\}$. We say that $x \sim c$ is *stronger than* $x' \sim' c'$ if, when evaluated at the same instant, $x \sim c$ holds implies $x' \sim' c'$ holds as well. The stronger constraint can be determined with a diagonal guard: $x \sim c$ is stronger than $x' \sim' c'$ if either $x' - x < c' - c$ or else $x' - x \leq c' - c$ and $(\sim = <$ or $\sim' = \leq)$. The relation *stronger than* is transitive and total among upper-guards. We can define similarly *stronger than* for *lower*-guards, i.e, when $\sim, \sim' \in \{>, \geq\}$. We have $x \sim c$ stronger than $x' \sim' c'$ if either $x' - x > c' - c$ or else $x' - x \geq c' - c$ and $(\sim = >$ or $\sim' = \geq)$.

Now, we get back to our problem and show how to change $\mathcal{B}$ so that the size of $\mathrm{dom}(\xi^{\triangleright})$ in a state $st = (\bar{s}, \chi, \eta, \xi^{\triangleleft}, \xi^{\triangleright}, \gamma^{\triangleright}, \gamma^m)$ can be bounded by $|Act| \cdot (2|Q^{\triangleright}| + 1)$. Note that $\mathrm{dom}(\gamma^{\triangleright}) = \mathrm{dom}(\xi^{\triangleright})$. A transition of $\mathcal{B}$ may initiate at most $|Act|$ new copies of $\mathcal{C}^{\triangleright}$ (one for each $\sigma \in Act$ such that $\mathrm{Next}_\sigma \in \mathrm{dom}(g)$. Hence, we say that state st is *safe* if for all $\sigma \in Act$ we have $|\mathrm{dom}(\xi^{\triangleright}(\sigma))| \leq 2|Q^{\triangleright}|$. The transitions of $\mathcal{B}$ are kept in the new automaton $\mathcal{B}'$ only when they start in a safe state.

If st is not safe, then $|\{i \mid \xi^{\triangleright}(\sigma, i) = q\}| > 2$ for some $\sigma \in Act$ and $q \in Q^{\triangleright}$. In this case, we say that st is unsafe for (σ, q) and let $\text{Active}(\sigma, q) = \{i \mid \xi^{\triangleright}(\sigma, i) = q\}$.

If $\text{Active}(\sigma, q) \neq \emptyset$, let $i_u \in \text{Active}(\sigma, q)$ be such that the upper-guard defined by $z_{\sigma, i_u}^{\triangleright} \in \gamma^{\triangleright}(\sigma, i_u)$ is stronger than all upper-guards defined by $z_{\sigma, j}^{\triangleright} \in \gamma^{\triangleright}(\sigma, j)$ for $j \in \text{Active}(\sigma, q)$. Further, let $i_\ell \in \text{Active}(\sigma, q)$ be defined similarly for lower-guards.

From the definition of the relation *stronger than* we know that all constraints $z_{\sigma, j}^{\triangleright} \in \gamma^{\triangleright}(\sigma, j)$ for $j \in \text{Active}(\sigma, q)$ are subsumed by the conjunction of $z_{\sigma, i_\ell}^{\triangleright} \in \gamma^{\triangleright}(\sigma, i_\ell)$ and $z_{\sigma, i_u}^{\triangleright} \in \gamma^{\triangleright}(\sigma, i_u)$. Therefore, we can release all *next* constraints associated with (σ, j) with $j \in \text{Active}(\sigma, q) \setminus \{i_\ell, i_u\}$.

To do this, we add to $\mathcal{B}'$ an ε-transition $(\text{st}, \varphi(\sigma, q, i_\ell, i_u), \varepsilon, \emptyset, \text{st}')$. The guard should evaluate to true if i_ℓ and i_u determine stronger lower- and upper-constraints among those defined by $\text{Active}(\sigma, q)$. Since the relation *stronger than* can be expressed with diagonal constraints, we have $\varphi(\sigma, q, i_\ell, i_u) \in \text{Form}(\mathcal{Z})$. We have that, in state $\text{st}' = (\overline{s}, \chi, \eta, \xi^{\triangleleft}, \xi'^{\triangleright}, \gamma'^{\triangleright}, \gamma^m)$, only the *next* information is changed:

$$\gamma'^{\triangleright}(\tau, i) = \begin{cases} \text{undefined} & \text{if } \tau = \sigma \text{ and } i \in \text{Active}(\sigma, q) \setminus \{i_\ell, i_u\} \\ \gamma^{\triangleright}(\tau, i) & \text{otherwise} \end{cases}$$

$$\xi'^{\triangleright}(\tau, i) = \begin{cases} \text{undefined} & \text{if } \tau = \sigma \text{ and } i \in \text{Active}(\sigma, q) \setminus \{i_\ell, i_u\} \\ \xi^{\triangleright}(\tau, i) & \text{otherwise.} \end{cases}$$

Then, $\{i \mid \xi'^{\triangleright}(\sigma, i) = q\} = \{i_\ell, i_u\}$ and st' is safe for (σ, q).

We deduce that in the automaton $\mathcal{B}'$, we can restrict to the *finite* index set $\text{Ind}^{\triangleright} = Act \times \{0, \ldots, 2|Q^{\triangleright}|\}$ for the partial maps $\xi^{\triangleright}$ and $\gamma^{\triangleright}$ used for the *next* constraints. Consequently, $\mathcal{B}'$ uses finitely many *next* clocks from $\{z_{\sigma, i}^{\triangleright} \mid (\sigma, i) \in \text{Ind}^{\triangleright}\}$. The following proves Theorem 11, from which we deduce a decidability result for our logic.

Theorem 15. *The timed automaton $\mathcal{B}'$ is finite. It has $B^{\mathcal{O}(|Ag|^2)}$ many clocks (for $B \geq 2$), and we have $\mathcal{L}(\mathcal{B}') = \mathcal{L}(\mathcal{B})$.*

Corollary 16. *The following problem is decidable:*

INPUT: $\varphi \in \text{TMSO}(\mathcal{R}_{\prec})$ *and an integer $B > 0$.*
QUESTION: *Is there $T \in \mathcal{L}_{time}(\varphi)$ such that T has a B-bounded timed linearization?*

Acknowledgment. We thank Martin Leucker for motivating discussions.

References

1. Alur, R., Dill, D.L.: A theory of timed automata. TCS 126(2), 183–235 (1994)
2. Alur, R., Fix, L., Henzinger, T.A.: Event-clock automata: A determinizable class of timed automata. TCS 211(1-2), 253–273 (1999)
3. Alur, R., Holzmann, G., Peled, D.: An analyser for message sequence charts. In: Margaria, T., Steffen, B. (eds.) TACAS 1996. LNCS, vol. 1055, pp. 35–48. Springer, Heidelberg (1996)
4. Ben-Abdallah, H., Leue, S.: Timing constraints in message sequence chart specifications. In: Proc. of FORTE 1997, pp. 91–106 (1997)
5. Bollig, B., Leucker, M.: Message-passing automata are expressively equivalent to EMSO logic. TCS 358(2-3), 150–172 (2006)

6. Brand, D., Zafiropulo, P.: On communicating finite-state machines. Journal of the ACM 30(2) (1983)
7. Büchi, J.: Weak second order logic and finite automata. Z. Math. Logik, Grundlag. Math. 5, 66–72 (1960)
8. Chandrasekaran, P., Mukund, M.: Matching scenarios with timing constraints. In: Asarin, E., Bouyer, P. (eds.) FORMATS 2006. LNCS, vol. 4202, pp. 91–106. Springer, Heidelberg (2006)
9. D'Souza, D.: A logical characterisation of event clock automata. International Journal of Foundations of Computer Science 14(4), 625–640 (2003)
10. D'Souza, D., Thiagarajan, P.S.: Product interval automata: A subclass of timed automata. In: Pandu Rangan, C., Raman, V., Ramanujam, R. (eds.) Foundations of Software Technology and Theoretical Computer Science. LNCS, vol. 1738, pp. 60–71. Springer, Heidelberg (1999)
11. Genest, B., Kuske, D., Muscholl, A.: A Kleene theorem and model checking algorithms for existentially bounded communicating automata. IC 204(6), 920–956 (2006)
12. Henriksen, J.G., Mukund, M., Kumar, K.N., Sohoni, M., Thiagarajan, P.S.: A theory of regular MSC languages. IC 202(1), 1–38 (2005)
13. Krcal, P., Yi, W.: Communicating timed automata: The more synchronous, the more difficult to verify. In: Ball, T., Jones, R.B. (eds.) CAV 2006. LNCS, vol. 4144, pp. 243–257. Springer, Heidelberg (2006)

Propositional Dynamic Logic for Message-Passing Systems

Benedikt Bollig[1], Dietrich Kuske[2], and Ingmar Meinecke[2]

[1] LSV, ENS Cachan, CNRS
61, Av. du Président Wilson, F-94235 Cachan Cedex, France
bollig@lsv.ens-cachan.fr
[2] Institut für Informatik, Universität Leipzig
PF 100920, D-04009 Leipzig, Germany
{kuske,meinecke}@informatik.uni-leipzig.de

Abstract. We examine a bidirectional Propositional Dynamic Logic (PDL) for message sequence charts (MSCs) extending LTL and TLC$^-$. Every formula is translated into an equivalent communicating finite-state machine (CFM) of exponential size. This synthesis problem is solved in full generality, i.e., also for MSCs with unbounded channels. The model checking problems for CFMs and for HMSCs against PDL formulas are shown to be in PSPACE for existentially bounded MSCs. It is shown that CFMs are to weak to capture the semantics of PDL with intersection.

1 Introduction

Messages sequence charts (MSCs) are an important formalism describing the executions of message-passing systems. They are a common notation in telecommunication and defined by an ITU standard [14]. A significant task is to verify system requirements. The model checking problem asks for an algorithm that decides whether, given a formula φ of a suitable logic and a finite machine $\mathcal{A}$, every behavior of $\mathcal{A}$ satisfies φ. There exist a few such suitable temporal logics. Meenakshi and Ramanujam proposed temporal logics over Lamport diagrams (which are similar to MSCs) [17,18]. Peled [19] considered TLC$^-$ introduced in [1] for Mazurkiewicz traces. Like these logics, our logic PDL is interpreted directly over MSCs, not over linearizations; it combines elements from [18] (global next operator, past operators) and [19] (global next operator, existential interpretation of the until-operator). The ability to express properties of paths as regular expressions is also present in Henriksen and Thiagarajan's *dynamic* LTL [12,13], an extension of LTL for traces. Differently from their approach, our path expressions are not bound to speak about the events of a single process, but they can move from one process to another. Moreover, we provide past operators to judge about events that have already been executed. We call our logic PDL as it is essentially the original propositional dynamic logic as first defined by Fischer and Ladner [8] but here in the framework of MSCs.

Already for very restrictive temporal logics, the model checking problem becomes undecidable [18]. In [19,15,11,10], however, it was tackled successfully

V. Arvind and S. Prasad (Eds.): FSTTCS 2007, LNCS 4855, pp. 303–315, 2007.

for several logics by restricting to existentially B-bounded MSCs, which can be scheduled such that the channel capacity respects a given size B. As a first step, [19,15,10] translate formulas into machine models such that the semantics of the formula and the machine coincide *for existentially B-bounded MSCs* (or their linearizations). In the early stages of system design it seems more natural not to fix a channel size B but to implement the entire semantics of φ. We therefore construct, from a PDL formula φ, a communicating finite-state machine (CFM, [5]) $\mathcal{A}_\varphi$ such that $L(\varphi) = L(\mathcal{A}_\varphi)$ wrt. the class of *all* (finite and infinite) MSCs.

In the literature, one finds several techniques to construct an automaton from a temporal formula: One can use a tableau construction (cf. [7]), an incremental tableau (cf. [6]), or alternating automata [20]. Here, we use an inductive method [9]: The events of an MSC are colored by additional bits, one for each subformula of φ. Then we construct, for each such subformula γ, a CFM $\mathcal{A}_\gamma$ whose task it is to check that the bit corresponding to γ is set at precisely those nodes where γ holds. For this, the CFM $\mathcal{A}_\gamma$ reads the bits corresponding to the top-level subformulas of γ. The overall CFM is obtained by running synchronously all the CFMs arising from the subformulas.

A typical subformula in PDL is $\gamma = \langle \pi \rangle \mathit{tt}$ expressing that there is a finite path starting in the current vertex that obeys the regular expression π. The construction of a CFM for such a subformula turns out to be the most difficult part. The basic idea is to start, in the current node v, a finite automaton $\mathcal{C}$ that accepts the language of π and to ensure that $\mathcal{C}$ will eventually reach an accepting state in some event v'. To ensure that this obligation is not propagated forever, we adopt and extend the solution for sequential systems [13]: The MSC is colored nondeterministically by two colors. Then a CFM checks that, along each and every path, the color changes infinitely often (this is possible although acceptance in a CFM refers to those paths that stay in one single process, only). Then the path from v to v' is allowed to change color at most once.

Altogether, we construct, for every PDL formula φ, an equivalent CFM $\mathcal{A}_\varphi$ that is exponential in the size of φ and the number of processes. Given another CFM $\mathcal{B}$, we then build a CFM $\mathcal{A}$ from $\mathcal{A}_\varphi$ and $\mathcal{B}$ with $L(\mathcal{A}) = L(\varphi) \cap L(\mathcal{B})$. Note that up to now, no restriction on the channel capacity is imposed. Finally, we decide whether $\mathcal{A}$ accepts some existentially B-bounded MSC. Only in this decision step, the bound B is used. We also show how to model check high-level MSCs (HMSCs) against PDL formulas. Both these model checking algorithms run in space polynomial in the size of the formula and of the CFM, and in the bound B. Since the logic TLC^- of Peled is a fragment of PDL, we generalize the model checking result from [19] and provide a different algorithm.

By [4,2], existential MSO logic is expressively equivalent to CFMs, and the set of CFM-languages is not closed under complementation. Since, on the other hand, PDL does not impose any restriction on the use of negation, we obtain that PDL is a proper fragment of existential MSO although this is not obvious.

The final technical section considers an enriched logic iPDL (PDL with intersection) where a node might be described by the intersection of two different paths. This extension strengthens the expressive power of the formulas. But adapting a proof technique from colored grids [16], we show that there is an iPDL-formula φ such that no CFM accepts precisely the semantics of φ.

A full version of this paper is available [3].

2   Definitions

The communication framework used in our paper is based on sequential processes that exchange asynchronously messages over point-to-point, error-free FIFO channels. Let $\mathcal{P}$ be a finite set of process identities which we fix throughout this paper. Furthermore, let $\mathrm{Ch} = \{(p,q) \in \mathcal{P}^2 \mid p \neq q\}$ denote the set of *channels*. Processes act by either sending a message from p to q (denoted $p!q$), or by receiving a message at p from q (denoted by $p?q$). For any process $p \in \mathcal{P}$, we define a local alphabet $\Sigma_p = \{p!q, p?q \mid q \in \mathcal{P} \setminus \{p\}\}$, and we set $\Sigma = \bigcup_{p \in \mathcal{P}} \Sigma_p$.

2.1   Message Sequence Charts

Message sequence charts are special labeled partial orders. To define them, we need the following definitions: A Σ-*labeled partial order* is a triple $M = (V, \leq, \lambda)$ where $(V, \leq)$ is a partially ordered set and $\lambda : V \to \Sigma$ is a mapping. For $v \in V$ with $\lambda(v) = p\theta q$ where $\theta \in \{!, ?\}$, let $P(v) = p$ denote the process that v is located at. We define two binary relations proc and msg on V setting

- $(v, v') \in$ proc iff $P(v) = P(v')$, $v < v'$, and, for any $u \in V$ with $P(v) = P(u)$ and $v \leq u < v'$, we have $v = u$,
- $(v, v') \in$ msg iff there is a channel (p, q) with $\lambda(v) = p!q$, $\lambda(v') = q?p$, and $|\{u \mid \lambda(u) = p!q, \ u \leq v\}| = |\{u \mid \lambda(u) = q?p, \ u \leq v'\}|$.

Definition 2.1. *A* message sequence chart *or* MSC *for short is a Σ-labeled partial order $(V, \leq, \lambda)$ such that*

- $\leq = (\mathrm{proc} \cup \mathrm{msg})^*$,
- $\{u \in V \mid u \leq v\}$ *is finite for any $v \in V$,*
- $P^{-1}(p) \subseteq V$ *is linearly ordered for any $p \in \mathcal{P}$, and*
- $|\lambda^{-1}(p!q)| = |\lambda^{-1}(q?p)|$ *for any $(p, q) \in \mathrm{Ch}$.*

We refer to the elements of V as events *or* nodes.

If $(V, \leq, \lambda)$ is an MSC, then proc and msg are even partial and injective functions, so $v' = \mathrm{proc}(v)$ as well as $v = \mathrm{proc}^{-1}(v')$ are equivalent notions for $(v, v') \in$ proc; $\mathrm{msg}(v)$ and $\mathrm{msg}^{-1}(v)$ are to be understood similarly.

2.2   Propositional Dynamic Logic (PDL)

Path expressions π and *local formulas* α are defined by simultaneous induction. This induction is described by the following rules

$$\pi ::= \mathrm{proc} \mid \mathrm{msg} \mid \{\alpha\} \mid \pi; \pi \mid \pi + \pi \mid \pi^*$$
$$\alpha ::= t\!\!t \mid \sigma \mid \alpha \vee \alpha \mid \neg \alpha \mid \langle \pi \rangle \alpha \mid \langle \pi \rangle^{-1} \alpha$$

where σ ranges over the alphabet Σ.

Local formulas express properties of single nodes in MSCs. To define the semantics of local formulas, let therefore $M = (V, \leq, \lambda)$ be an MSC and v a node from M. Then we define, for $\sigma \in \Sigma$, $M, v \models \sigma$ iff $\lambda(v) = \sigma$; $M, v \models \alpha_1 \vee \alpha_2$ and $M, v \models \neg\alpha$ are defined in the obvious manner. The semantics of *forward*-path expressions $\langle\pi\rangle\,\alpha$ is given by

$$M, v \models \langle\text{proc}\rangle\,\alpha \iff \text{there exists } v' \in V \text{ with } (v, v') \in \text{proc and } M, v' \models \alpha$$
$$M, v \models \langle\text{msg}\rangle\,\alpha \iff \text{there exists } v' \in V \text{ with } (v, v') \in \text{msg and } M, v' \models \alpha$$
$$M, v \models \langle\{\alpha\}\rangle\,\beta \iff M, v \models \alpha \text{ and } M, v \models \beta$$
$$M, v \models \langle\pi_1; \pi_2\rangle\,\alpha \iff M, v \models \langle\pi_1\rangle\,\langle\pi_2\rangle\,\alpha$$
$$M, v \models \langle\pi_1 + \pi_2\rangle\,\alpha \iff M, v \models \langle\pi_1\rangle\,\alpha \text{ or } M, v \models \langle\pi_2\rangle\,\alpha$$
$$M, v \models \langle\pi^*\rangle\,\alpha \iff \text{there exists } n \geq 0 \text{ with } M, v \models (\langle\pi\rangle)^n\alpha$$

The base cases for the semantics of *backward*-path expressions $\langle\pi\rangle^{-1}\alpha$ are defined similarly by

$$M, v \models \langle\text{proc}\rangle^{-1}\alpha \iff \text{there exists } v' \in V \text{ with } (v', v) \in \text{proc and } M, v' \models \alpha$$
$$M, v \models \langle\text{msg}\rangle^{-1}\alpha \iff \text{there exists } v' \in V \text{ with } (v', v) \in \text{msg and } M, v' \models \alpha.$$

Replacing $\langle . \rangle$ with $\langle . \rangle^{-1}$ in the remaining clauses completes the definition of the semantics of local formulas.

Semantically, a local formula of the form $\langle(\{\alpha\}; (\text{proc} + \text{msg}))^*\rangle\beta$ corresponds to the until construct $\alpha\mathcal{U}\beta$ in Peled's TLC$^-$. In TLC$^-$, however, one cannot express properties such as "there is an even number of messages from p to q", which is certainly expressible in PDL.

Global formulas of PDL are positive Boolean combinations of formulas Eα and Aα where α is a local formula. Here, Eα expresses the existence of some node satisfying α while Aα says that α holds at all nodes. Because of this existential and universal quantification, the expressible global properties are closed under negation.

A local formula β is a *subformula* of a local formula α if it is a subformula of α (seen as Boolean combination of forward- and backward-path formulas), or if β is a subformula of some formula γ such that $\langle\pi\rangle\,\gamma$ or $\langle\pi\rangle^{-1}\gamma$ is a subformula of α or such that $\{\gamma\}$ appears in some path expression in α. We denote the set of subformulas of α by $\text{sub}(\alpha)$.

2.3   Communicating Finite-State Machines

This section defines CFMs [5], i.e., our model of a distributed system, together with its behavior.

Definition 2.2. *A* communicating finite-state machine *(CFM) is a tuple* $\mathcal{A} = (C, n, (\mathcal{A}_p)_{p \in \mathcal{P}}, F)$ *with* $n \geq 0$ *where*

- C is a finite set of message contents or control messages,
- $A_p = (S_p, \rightarrow_p, \iota_p)$ is a finite labeled transition system over the alphabet $\Sigma_p \times \{0,1\}^n \times C$ for any $p \in P$ with initial state $\iota_p \in S_p$,
- $F \subseteq \prod_{p \in P} S_p$ is a set of global final states.

A *run* of A on (M, c) (with $M = (V, \leq, \lambda)$ an MSC and $c : V \rightarrow \{0,1\}^n$, which can be seen as an n-tuple of mappings $V \rightarrow \{0,1\}$) is a pair of mappings $\rho : V \rightarrow \bigcup_{p \in P} S_p$ and $\mu : V \rightarrow C$ such that, for any $v \in V$,

1. $\mu(v) = \mu(\text{msg}(v))$ if $\text{msg}(v)$ is defined,
2. $(\rho(\text{proc}^{-1}(v)), \lambda(v), c(v), \mu(v), \rho(v)) \in \rightarrow_{P(v)}$ if $\text{proc}^{-1}(v)$ is defined, and
   $(\iota_p, \lambda(v), c(v), \mu(v), \rho(v)) \in \rightarrow_{P(v)}$ otherwise.

Since, even in an infinite MSC, some of the processes may execute only finitely many events, acceptance of a run will depend on the set of states appearing cofinally [2]: let $\text{cofin}_\rho(p) = \{\iota_p\}$ if $V_p = \emptyset$, and $\text{cofin}_\rho(p) = \{s \in S_p \mid \forall v \in V_p \exists v' \in V_p : v \leq v' \wedge \rho(v') = s\}$ if $V_p \neq \emptyset$, where $V_p = P^{-1}(p)$. Then the run (ρ, μ) is *accepting* if there is some $(s_p)_{p \in P} \in F$ such that $s_p \in \text{cofin}_\rho(p)$ for all $p \in P$. The *language* of A is the set $L(A)$ of all pairs (M, c) that admit an accepting run.

3 Translation of Formulas

Let α be a local formula of PDL. We will construct a "small" CFM that accepts $(M, (c_\beta)_{\beta \in \text{sub}(\alpha)})$ iff, for all positions $v \in V$ and all subformulas β of α, we have $M, v \models \beta$ iff $c_\beta(v) = 1$. This CFM will consist of several CFMs running in conjunction, one for each subformula. For instance, if $\sigma \in \Sigma$ and $\delta = \beta \vee \gamma$ are subformulas of α, then we will have sub-CFMs that check for every position v whether $c_\sigma(v) = 1$ iff $\lambda(v) = \sigma$ and $c_\delta(v) = c_\beta(v) \vee c_\gamma(v)$, resp. Similarly, for each subformula $\neg\beta$, a sub-CFM checks $c_{\neg\beta}(v) \neq c_\beta(v)$ for each position v. While the construction of these sub-CFMs is rather straightforward, more work has to be invested for subformulas of the form $\langle\pi\rangle\alpha$ and $\langle\pi\rangle^{-1}\alpha$. Since these formulas are equivalent to $\langle\pi; \{\alpha\}\rangle\, tt$ and $\langle\pi; \{\alpha\}\rangle^{-1}\, tt$, respectively, we will only deal with the latter ones.

3.1 The Backward-Path Automaton

Let π be a path expression, i.e., a regular expression over some alphabet $\Gamma = \{\text{proc}, \text{msg}, \{\alpha_1\}, \ldots, \{\alpha_n\}\}$. A word $W \in \Gamma^*$ together with a node v from an MSC M describe a path starting in that node that walks *backwards*. The letters proc and msg denote the direction of the path, the letters $\{\alpha_i\}$ denote requirements about the node currently visited, i.e., that α_i shall hold or, equivalently, that $c_i(v) = 1$ (where we write c_i instead of c_{α_i}). The existence of such a backward-path is denoted $(M, c_1, \ldots, c_n), v \models^{-1} W$.

Now let $C = (Q, \iota, \delta, G)$ be a finite automaton over Γ accepting the language of the regular expression π. Then we can naturally build a first CFM A_1 with sets of local states 2^Q such that the following are equivalent for all MSCs $M = (V, \leq, \lambda)$, all mappings $c_i : V \rightarrow \{0,1\}$, and all mappings $\rho : V \rightarrow 2^Q$:

- ρ is the state mapping of some run of $\mathcal{A}_1$ on $(M, c_1, \ldots, c_n)$
- for all $v \in V$ and $q \in Q$, we have $q \in \rho(v)$ iff there exists $W \in \Gamma^*$ with $q \xrightarrow{W}_{\mathcal{C}} G$ and $(M, c_1, \ldots, c_n), v \models^{-1} W$.

From $\mathcal{A}_1$, we obtain a CFM $\mathcal{A}_{\langle \pi \rangle^{-1} tt}$ accepting $(M, c_1, \ldots, c_n, c)$ iff $\mathcal{A}_1$ has a run on $(M, c_1, \ldots, c_n)$ such that, for all $v \in V$, we have $c(v) = 1$ iff $\iota \in \rho(v)$ (i.e., iff there exists $W \in L(\mathcal{C})$ with $(M, c_1, \ldots, c_n), v \models^{-1} W$). This construction proves

Theorem 3.1. *Let $\langle \pi \rangle^{-1} tt$ be a local formula such that π is a regular expression over the alphabet $\{\mathrm{proc}, \mathrm{msg}, \{\alpha_1\}, \ldots, \{\alpha_n\}\}$. Then there exists a CFM $\mathcal{A}_{\langle \pi \rangle^{-1} tt}$ with the following property: Let M be an MSC and let $c_i : V \to \{0, 1\}$ be the characteristic function of the set of positions satisfying α_i (for all $1 \le i \le n$). Then $(M, c_1, \ldots, c_n, c)$ is accepted by $\mathcal{A}_{\langle \pi \rangle^{-1} tt}$ iff c is the characteristic function of the set of positions satisfying $\langle \pi \rangle^{-1} tt$.*

3.2   The Forward-Path Automaton

We now turn to a similar CFM corresponding to subformulas of the form $\langle \pi \rangle tt$. We will prove the following analog to Theorem 3.1. This proof will, however, be substantially more difficult.

Theorem 3.2. *Let $\langle \pi \rangle tt$ be a local formula such that π is a regular expression over the alphabet $\Gamma = \{\mathrm{proc}, \mathrm{msg}, \{\alpha_1\}, \ldots, \{\alpha_n\}\}$. Then there exists a CFM $\mathcal{A}_{\langle \pi \rangle tt}$ with the following property: Let M be an MSC and let $c_i : V \to \{0, 1\}$ be the characteristic function of the set of positions satisfying α_i (for all $1 \le i \le n$). Then $(M, c_1, \ldots, c_n, c)$ is accepted by $\mathcal{A}_{\langle \pi \rangle tt}$ iff c is the characteristic function of the set of positions satisfying $\langle \pi \rangle tt$.*

The rest of this section is devoted to the proof of this theorem. Let $\mathcal{C} = (Q, \iota, T, G)$ be a finite automaton over Γ that accepts the language of the regular expression π.

Let $W \in \Gamma^*$, $M = (V, \le, \lambda)$ an MSC, and $v \in V$. These data describe a *forward*-path starting in v where the letters proc and msg denote the direction and the letters $\{\alpha_i\}$ requirements on the current node (i.e., that α_i shall hold). We denote the existence of such a forward path with $(M, c_1, \ldots, c_n), v \models W$.

In order to prove Theorem 3.2, it therefore suffices to construct a CFM that accepts $(M, c_1, \ldots, c_n, c)$ iff

$$\forall v \in V : c(v) = 0 \implies \forall W \in L(\mathcal{C}) : (M, c_1, \ldots, c_n), v \not\models W \quad (1)$$
$$\wedge \ \forall v \in V : c(v) = 1 \implies \exists W \in L(\mathcal{C}) : (M, c_1, \ldots, c_n), v \models W. \quad (2)$$

Since the class of languages accepted by CFMs is closed under intersection, we can handle the two implications separately (cf. Prop. 3.3 and 3.6 below).

Proposition 3.3. *There exists a CFM $\mathcal{A}_0$ that accepts $(M, c_1, \ldots, c_n, c)$ iff (1) holds.*

Proof. The basic idea is rather simple: whenever the CFM encounters a node v with $c(v) = 0$, it will start the automaton $\mathcal{C}$ (that accepts the language of the regular expression π) and check that it cannot reach an accepting state whatever path we choose starting in v. Since the CFM has to verify more than one 0 and since $\mathcal{C}$ is nondeterminsitic, the set of local states S_p equals $2^{Q \setminus G}$ with initial state $\iota_p = \emptyset$ for any $p \in \mathcal{P}$. $\square$

It remains to construct a CFM that checks (2). Again, the basic idea is simple: whenever the CFM encounters a node v with $c(v) = 1$ (i.e., a node that is supposed to satisfy $\langle \pi \rangle \textit{tt}$), it will start the automaton $\mathcal{C}$ (that accepts the language of the regular expression π) and check that it can reach an accepting state along one of the possible paths. Before, we had to prevent $\mathcal{C}$ from reaching an accepting state. This time, we have to ensure that any verification of a claim $c(v) = 1$ will eventually result in an accepting state being reached.

To explain our construction, suppose $M = (V, \leq, \lambda)$ to be an MSC and $c_1, \ldots, c_n, c : V \rightarrow \{0, 1\}$ to be mappings. In order to verify (2), any node $v \in V$ with $c(v) = 1$ forms an obligation, namely the obligation to find a word $W \in L(\mathcal{C})$ such that $(M, c_1, \ldots, c_n), v \models W$. This obligation is either satisfied immediately or propagated to the successors of v, i.e., to the nodes $\text{proc}(v)$ or $\text{msg}(v)$ (provided, they exist). Thus, every node from V obtains a set O of obligations in the form of states of the finite automaton $\mathcal{C}$. The crucial point now is to ensure that none of these obligations is propagated forever. To this aim, the set of obligations is divided into two sets O_1 and O_2. In general, the obligations from O_1 at node v are satisfied or propagated to the obligations from O_1 at the node $\text{msg}(v)$ or $\text{proc}(v)$. Similarly, obligations from O_2 are propagated to O_2; in addition, newly arising obligations (in the form of nodes v with $c(v) = 1$) are moved into O_2. The only exception from this rule is the case $O_1 = \emptyset$, i.e., all "active" obligations are satisfied. In this case, all of O_2 can be moved to O_1. Then, the run of the CFM is accepting iff, along *each* path in the MSC, the exceptional rule is applied cofinally.

The problem arising here is that the success of a run of a CFM refers to paths along a *single* process, only. Hence, infinite paths that change process infinitely often cannot be captured directly. A solution is to guess an additional 0-1-coloring c_0 such that no path can stay in one color forever, and to allow a color change only if the exceptional rule is applied.

Thus, we are left with the task to construct a CFM accepting (M, c_0) if no infinite path in M stays monochromatic eventually (it is actually sufficient to accept only such pairs, but not necessarily all, but sufficiently many). To achieve this goal, we proceed as follows.

Let M be an MSC and $c_0 : V \rightarrow \{0, 1\}$. On V, we define an equivalence relation $\sim$ whose equivalence classes are the maximal monochromatic intervals on a process line.

Let Col be the set of all pairs (M, c_0) with $c_0 : V \rightarrow \{0, 1\}$ such that the following hold

(1) if v is minimal on its process, then $c_0(v) = 1$
(2) if $(v, v') \in$ msg and $w' \leq v'$ with $P(w') = P(v')$, then there exists $(u, u') \in$ msg with $\lambda(u') = \lambda(v')$, $c_0(u) = c_0(u')$, and $u' \sim w'$
(3) any equivalence class of $\sim$ is finite.

In general, there can be messages $(u, u'') \in$ msg such that the colors of u and u'' are different, i.e., $c_0(u) \neq c_0(u'')$. Condition (2) ensures that there are also many messages (u, u') with $c_0(u) = c_0(u')$. More precisely, looking at the event w' on process q, process q will receive in the future a message from process p (at the event v'). Then the requirement is that process q receives some message from process p (a) in the $\sim$-equivalence class of w' such that (b) sending and receiving of this message have the same color.

Given the above conditions (1–3), it is almost immediate to check that Col can be accepted by some CFM:

Lemma 3.4. *There exists a CFM $\mathcal{A}_{\mathrm{Col}}$ that accepts the set* Col.

The main consequence of (1–3) is the following whose proof is elementary but not trivial:

Lemma 3.5. *Let $(M, c_0) \in$ Col and let $(v_1, v_2, \dots)$ be some infinite path in M. Then there exist infinitely many $i \in \mathbb{N}$ with $c_0(v_i) \neq c_0(v_{i+1})$.*

Proof. The crucial point is the following: Let $(v, v') \in$ msg be some message such that the numbers of mutually non-equivalent nodes on the process lines before v and v', resp., are different. Then one obtains $c_0(v) \neq c_0(v')$. □

These two lemmas and the ideas explained above prove

Proposition 3.6. *There exists a CFM $\mathcal{A}_1$ that accepts $(M, c_1, \dots, c_n, c)$ iff (2) holds.*

3.3   The Overall Construction

Theorem 3.7. *Let α be a local formula of PDL. Then one can construct a CFM $\mathcal{B}$ such that (M, c) is accepted by $\mathcal{B}$ iff $c : V \to \{0, 1\}$ is the characteristic function of the set of positions that satisfy α.*

Proof. One first constructs a CFM $\mathcal{A}$ that accepts $(M, (c_\beta)_{\beta \in \mathrm{sub}(\alpha)})$ iff

(1) $c_\sigma(v) = 1$ iff $\lambda(v) = \sigma$ for all $v \in V$ and $\sigma \in \mathrm{sub}(\alpha) \cap \Sigma$
(2) $c_{\gamma \vee \delta}(v) = \max(c_\gamma(v), c_\delta(v))$ for all $v \in V$ and $\gamma \vee \delta \in \mathrm{sub}(\alpha)$
(3) $c_{\neg \gamma}(v) \neq c_\gamma(v)$ for all $v \in V$ and $\neg \gamma \in \mathrm{sub}(\alpha)$
(4) $\mathcal{A}_{\langle \pi \rangle \gamma}$ accepts $(M, c_{\alpha_1}, \dots, c_{\alpha_n}, c_\gamma, c_{\langle \pi \rangle \gamma})$ for all formulas $\langle \pi \rangle \gamma \in \mathrm{sub}(\alpha)$ where $\alpha_1, \dots, \alpha_n$ are those local formulas for which $\{\alpha_i\}$ appears in the path expression π (cf. Theorem 3.2)
(5) $\mathcal{A}_{\langle \pi \rangle^{-1} \gamma}$ accepts $(M, c_{\alpha_1}, \dots, c_{\alpha_n}, c_\gamma, c_{\langle \pi \rangle^{-1} \gamma})$ for all $\langle \pi \rangle^{-1} \gamma \in \mathrm{sub}(\alpha)$ where $\alpha_1, \dots, \alpha_n$ are those local formulas for which $\{\alpha_i\}$ appears in the path expression π (cf. Theorem 3.1).

This can be achieved since the intersection of CFM-languages can be accepted by a CFM. The CFM $\mathcal{B}$ guesses the missing labelings c_β for $\beta \in \mathrm{sub}(\alpha) \setminus \{\alpha\}$ and simulates $\mathcal{A}$.   □

Recall that a global formula is a positive Boolean combination of formulas of the form $\mathrm{E}\alpha$ and $\mathrm{A}\alpha$ where α is a local formula. Note that the sets of pairs (M, c) with $c(v) = 1$ for at least one event (for all events, resp.) $v \in V$ can be accepted by CFMs. This, together with a careful analysis of the size of the CFMs constructed so far, leads to the following corollary:

Corollary 3.8. *Let φ be a global formula of PDL. Then one can construct a CFM $\mathcal{A}$ that accepts M iff $M \models \varphi$. The numbers of local states and of control messages of $\mathcal{A}$ belong to $2^{O((|\varphi| + |\mathcal{P}|)^2)}$.*

4   Model Checking

4.1   CFMs vs. PDL Specifications

We aim at an algorithm that decides whether, given a global formula φ and a CFM $\mathcal{A}$, every MSC from $L(\mathcal{A})$ satisfies φ. The undecidability of this problem can be shown following, e.g., the proof in [18] (the ideas from that paper can easily be transferred to our setting from Lamport diagrams and the fragment LD_0 of PDL). To gain decidability, we follow the successful approach of, e.g., [15,11,10], and restrict attention to existentially B-bounded MSCs from $L(\mathcal{A})$.

Let $M = (V, \leq, \lambda)$ be an MSC. A *linearization* of M is a linear order $\preceq \supseteq \leq$ on V of order type at most ω, which we identify with a finite or infinite word from Σ^∞.

A word $w \in \Sigma^\infty$ is B-*bounded* (where $B \in \mathbb{N}$) if, for any $(p, q) \in \mathrm{Ch}$ and any prefix u of w, $0 \leq |u|_{p!q} - |u|_{q?p} \leq B$ where $|u|_\sigma$ denotes the number of occurrences of σ in u. An MSC M is *existentially B-bounded* if it admits a B-bounded linearization.

The CFM $\mathcal{A}$ can be translated into a finite transition system that accepts precisely the B-bounded linearizations of MSCs accepted by $\mathcal{A}$. Any configuration of this transition system consists of

- the buffer contents (i.e., $|\mathrm{Ch}|$ many words over C of length at most B),
- a local state per process,
- one channel (i.e., a pair from Ch),
- a global state that is accepting in $\mathcal{A}$, and
- a counter whose value is bounded by $|\mathrm{Ch}| + |\mathcal{P}|$ in order to handle multiple Büchi-conditions.

Hence a single configuration can be stored in space $O(\log(|\mathcal{P}| + |\mathrm{Ch}|) + |\mathcal{P}| \log n + |\mathrm{Ch}| B \log |C| + \log |\mathrm{Ch}|)$ where n is the number of local states per process. This therefore also describes the space requirement for deciding whether the CFM $\mathcal{A}$ accepts at least one existentially B-bounded MSC.

Since the number of local states per process as well as that of messages of the CFM in Cor. 3.8 is exponential, we obtain the following result on the model checking of a CFM vs. a PDL specification:

Theorem 4.1. *The following is PSPACE-complete:*

Input: $B \in \mathbb{N}$ (given in unary), CFM $\mathcal{B}$, and a global formula $\varphi \in$ PDL. Question: Is there an existentially B-bounded MSC $M \in L(\mathcal{B})$ with $M \models \varphi$?

Hardness follows from PSPACE-hardness of LTL-model checking.

4.2   HMSCs vs. PDL Specifications

In [19], Peled provides a PSPACE model checking algorithm for high-level message sequence charts (HMSCs) against formulas of the logic TLC$^-$, a fragment of PDL. Now, we aim to model check an HMSC against a global formula of PDL, and, thereby, to generalize Peled's result.

Definition 4.2. *An HMSC $\mathcal{H} = (S, \rightarrow, s_0, \ell, \mathcal{M})$ is a finite, directed graph $(S, \rightarrow)$ with initial node $s_0 \in S$, $\mathcal{M}$ a finite set of finite MSCs, and a labeling function $\ell : S \rightarrow \mathcal{M}$.*

To define the semantics of an HMSC $\mathcal{H}$, one replaces the MSCs $\ell(s)$ by an arbitrary linearization and then concatenates the words along a maximal initial path in $\mathcal{H}$. Then an MSC M is accepted by $\mathcal{H}$ (i.e., belongs to $L(\mathcal{H})$) if one of its linearizations belongs to this word language $L \subseteq \Sigma^\infty$. Note that there is necessarily some $B \in \mathbb{N}$ such that all words in L are B-bounded. Furthermore, this number B can be computed from $\mathcal{H}$. Now construct, as above, from the CFM $\mathcal{A}$ from Cor. 3.8 the finite transition system that accepts all B-bounded linearizations of MSCs satisfying the global formula φ. Considering the intersection of the language of this transition system with L allows us to prove

Theorem 4.3. *The following problem is PSPACE-complete:*

Input: An HMSC $\mathcal{H}$ and a global formula $\varphi \in$ PDL. Question: Is there an MSC $M \in L(\mathcal{H})$ with $M \models \varphi$?

5   PDL with Intersection

PDL with intersection (or iPDL) allows, besides the local formulas of PDL, also local formulas $\langle \pi_1 \cap \pi_2 \rangle \alpha$ where π_1 and π_2 are path expressions and α is a local formula. The intended meaning is that there exist two paths described by π_1 and π_2, respectively, that both lead to the same node w where α holds. We show that this extends the expressive power of PDL beyond that of CFMs.

To show this result more easily, we also allow atomic propositions of the form (a, b) with $a, b \in \{0, 1\}$; they are evaluated over an MSC $M = (V, \leq, \lambda)$ together with a mapping $c : V \rightarrow \{0, 1\}^2$. Then $(M, c), v \models (a, b)$ iff $c(v) = (a, b)$. Let $\mathcal{P} = \{0, 1\}$ be the set of processes. For $m \geq 1$, we first fix an MSC $M_m = (V_m, \leq, \lambda)$ for the remaining arguments: On process 0, it executes the sequence $(0!1)^m ((0?1)(0!1))^\omega$. The sequence of events on process 1 is $(1?0) ((1?0) (1!0))^\omega$ (cf. Fig. 1). The send-events on process 0 are named in $\{0, 1, \ldots, m-1\} \times \omega$ as

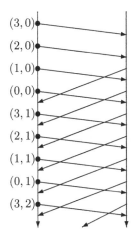

Fig. 1. MSC M_4 and the mapping f

indicated in Fig. 1. Let $\mathcal{M}$ denote the set of pairs (V_m, c) with $c : V_m \to \{0, 1\}^2$ such that $c(i, j) = 0$ iff $i = 0$.

Then one can construct a local formula α such that, for any $(M, c) \in \mathcal{M}$, we have $(M, c) \models A\alpha$ iff $c(i, j) = c(i, j + i)$ for all suitable pairs (i, j). Now suppose $\mathcal{A} = (C, 2, (\mathcal{A}_p)_{p \in \mathcal{P}}, F)$ to be a CFM that accepts all labeled MSCs $(M_m, c) \in \mathcal{M}$ satisfying $c(i, j) = c(i, j + i)$ for all suitable (i, j). Then $\mathcal{A}$ also accepts some labeled MSC $(M, c) \in \mathcal{M}$ that violates this condition. It follows:

Theorem 5.1. *There exists a local formula α of iPDL such that the set of MSCs satisfying $A\alpha$ cannot be accepted by a CFM.*

6   Open Questions

Since the semantics of every PDL formula φ is the behavior of a CFM, it is equivalent with some formula from existential monadic second-order logic [4,2]. Since PDL is closed under negation, it is a proper fragment of existential monadic second order logic. Because of quantification over paths, it cannot be captured by first-order logic. We do not know if first-order logic is captured by PDL nor do we have any precise description of its expressive power.

Since the logic iPDL, i.e., PDL with intersection, can be translated effectively into MSO, the model checking problem for CFMs and existentially B-bounded MSCs is decidable for iPDL [10]. However, the complexity of MSO model checking is non-elementary. Therefore, we would like to know if we can do any better for iPDL.

In PDL, we can express properties of the past and of the future of an event by taking either a backward- or a forward-path in the graph of the MSC. We are not allowed to speak about a zig-zag-path where e.g. a mixed use of proc and $proc^{-1}$ would be possible. It is an open question whether formulas of such a "mixed PDL" could be transformed to CFMs and what the complexity of the model checking would be.

References

1. Alur, R., Peled, D., Penczek, W.: Model-checking of causality properties. In: LICS 1995. Proceedings of the 10th Annual IEEE Symposium on Logic in Computer Science, Washington, DC, USA, pp. 90–100. IEEE Computer Society Press, Los Alamitos (1995)
2. Bollig, B., Kuske, D.: Distributed Muller automata and logics. Research Report LSV-06-11, Laboratoire Spécification et Vérification, ENS Cachan, France (2006)
3. Bollig, B., Kuske, D., Meinecke, I.: Propositional dynamic logic for message-passing systems. Research Report LSV-07-22, Laboratoire Spécification et Vérification, ENS Cachan, France (2007), http://www.lsv.ens-cachan.fr/Publis/RAPPORTS_LSV/PDF/rr-lsv-2007-22.pdf
4. Bollig, B., Leucker, M.: Message-passing automata are expressively equivalent to EMSO logic. Theoretical Computer Science 358(2-3), 150–172 (2006)
5. Brand, D., Zafiropulo, P.: On communicating finite-state machines. Journal of the ACM 30(2) (1983)
6. Clarke, E., Grumberg, O., Peled, D.: Model Checking. MIT Press, Cambridge (2000)
7. Emerson, E.A.: Temporal and modal logic. In: van Leeuwen, J. (ed.) Handbook of Theoretical Computer Science, pp. 995–1072, ch. 16, Elsevier Publ. Co., Amsterdam (1990)
8. Fischer, M.J., Ladner, R.E.: Propositional Dynamic Logic of regular programs. J. Comput. System Sci. 18(2), 194–211 (1979)
9. Gastin, P., Kuske, D.: Satisfiability and model checking for MSO-definable temporal logics are in PSPACE. In: Amadio, R.M., Lugiez, D. (eds.) CONCUR 2003. LNCS, vol. 2761, pp. 222–236. Springer, Heidelberg (2003)
10. Genest, B., Kuske, D., Muscholl, A.: A Kleene theorem and model checking algorithms for existentially bounded communicating automata. Information and Computation 204, 920–956 (2006)
11. Genest, B., Muscholl, A., Seidl, H., Zeitoun, M.: Infinite-state high-level MSCs: model-checking and realizability. In: Widmayer, P., Triguero, F., Morales, R., Hennessy, M., Eidenbenz, S., Conejo, R. (eds.) ICALP 2002. LNCS, vol. 2380, pp. 657–668. Springer, Heidelberg (2002)
12. Henriksen, J.G., Thiagarajan, P.S.: A product version of dynamic linear time temporal logic. In: Mazurkiewicz, A., Winkowski, J. (eds.) CONCUR 1997. LNCS, vol. 1243, pp. 45–58. Springer, Heidelberg (1997)
13. Henriksen, J.G., Thiagarajan, P.S.: Dynamic linear time temporal logic. Ann. Pure Appl. Logic 96(1-3), 187–207 (1999)
14. ITU-TS Recommendation Z.120: Message Sequence Chart 1996 (MSC96) (1996)
15. Madhusudan, P., Meenakshi, B.: Beyond message sequence graphs. In: Hariharan, R., Mukund, M., Vinay, V. (eds.) FST TCS 2001. LNCS, vol. 2245, pp. 256–267. Springer, Heidelberg (2001)
16. Matz, O., Thomas, W.: The monadic quantifier alternation hierarchy over graphs is infinite. In: LICS 1997, pp. 236–244. IEEE Computer Society Press, Los Alamitos (1997)

17. Meenakshi, B., Ramanujam, R.: Reasoning about message passing in finite state environments. In: Welzl, E., Montanari, U., Rolim, J.D.P. (eds.) ICALP 2000. LNCS, vol. 1853, pp. 487–498. Springer, Heidelberg (2000)

18. Meenakshi, B., Ramanujam, R.: Reasoning about layered message passing systems. Computer Languages, Systems, and Structures 30(3-4), 529–554 (2004)

19. Peled, D.: Specification and verification of message sequence charts. In: Formal Techniques for Distributed System Development, FORTE/PSTV 2000. IFIP Conference Proceedings, vol. 183, pp. 139–154. Kluwer Academic Publishers, Dordrecht (2000)

20. Vardi, M.Y.: Nontraditional applications of automata theory. In: Hagiya, M., Mitchell, J.C. (eds.) TACS 1994. LNCS, vol. 789, pp. 575–597. Springer, Heidelberg (1994)

Better Algorithms and Bounds for Directed Maximum Leaf Problems

Noga Alon[1], Fedor V. Fomin[2], Gregory Gutin[3], Michael Krivelevich[1], and Saket Saurabh[2,4]

[1] Department of Mathematics, Tel Aviv University
Tel Aviv 69978, Israel
{nogaa,krivelev}@post.tau.ac.il

[2] Department of Informatics, University of Bergen
POB 7803, 5020 Bergen, Norway
{fedor.fomin,saket}@ii.uib.no

[3] Department of Computer Science, Royal Holloway, University of London
Egham, Surrey TW20 0EX, UK
gutin@cs.rhul.ac.uk

[4] The Institute of Mathematical Sciences
Chennai-600 017, India
saket@imsc.res.in

Abstract. The DIRECTED MAXIMUM LEAF OUT-BRANCHING problem is to find an out-branching (i.e. a rooted oriented spanning tree) in a given digraph with the maximum number of leaves. In this paper, we improve known parameterized algorithms and combinatorial bounds on the number of leaves in out-branchings. We show that

- every strongly connected digraph D of order n with minimum in-degree at least 3 has an out-branching with at least $(n/4)^{1/3} - 1$ leaves;
- if a strongly connected digraph D does not contain an out-branching with k leaves, then the pathwidth of its underlying graph is $O(k \log k)$;
- it can be decided in time $2^{O(k \log^2 k)} \cdot n^{O(1)}$ whether a strongly connected digraph on n vertices has an out-branching with at least k leaves.

All improvements use properties of extremal structures obtained after applying local search and properties of some out-branching decompositions.

1 Introduction

Given a digraph D, a subdigraph T of D is an *out-tree* if T is an oriented tree with only one vertex s of in-degree zero (called *the root*) and if T is a spanning out-tree, i.e. $V(T) = V(D)$, then T is called an *out-branching* of D. The vertices of T of out-degree zero are called *leaves*. The DIRECTED MAXIMUM LEAF OUT-BRANCHING (DMLOB) problem is to find an out-branching in a given digraph with the maximum number of leaves. This problem is a natural generalization of the well studied MAXIMUM LEAF SPANNING TREE problem on connected undirected graphs [5,7,10,11,12,14,15,20,22]. Unlike its undirected

V. Arvind and S. Prasad (Eds.): FSTTCS 2007, LNCS 4855, pp. 316–327, 2007.

counterpart which has attracted a lot of attention in all algorithmic paradigms like approximation algorithms [14,20,22], parameterized algorithms [5,10,12], exact exponential time algorithms [11] and also combinatorial studies [7,15,16,19], the DIRECTED MAXIMUM LEAF OUT-BRANCHING problem has largely been neglected until recently. Apart from [2] mentioned below, the only other paper is the very recent paper [9] that describes an $O(\sqrt{\text{OPT}})$-approximation algorithms for DMLOB.

In [2] we initiated algorithmic and combinatorial study of DMLOB and obtained, as the main result of the paper, the first fixed parameter tractable algorithms for the problem on strongly connected digraphs and acyclic digraphs based on various combinatorial lemmas. In this paper we continue our investigation of DMLOB and obtain several improved parameterized algorithms for the problem as well as combinatorial results regarding the number of leaves possible in an out-branching of a digraph based on new approaches and ideas which are interesting on their own and could be useful for solving other problems on digraphs.

In parameterized algorithms, for decision problems with input size n, and a parameter k, the goal is to design an algorithm with runtime $f(k)n^{O(1)}$, where f is a function of k alone. (For DMLOB such a parameter is the number of leaves in the out-tree.) Problems having such an algorithm are said to be fixed parameter tractable (FPT). The book by Downey and Fellows [8] provides an introduction to the topic of parameterized complexity. For recent developments see the books by Flum and Grohe [13] and by Niedermeier [21].

The parameterized version of DMLOB is defined as follows: Given a digraph D and a positive integral parameter k, does there exist an out-branching with at least k leaves? We denote the parameterized versions of DMLOB by k-DMLOB. If in the above definition we do not insist on an out-branching and ask whether there exists an out-tree with at least k leaves, we get parameterized DIRECTED MAXIMUM LEAF OUT-TREE problem (denoted k-DMLOT).

In this paper we obtain the following new algorithmic and combinatorial results on k-DMLOB for strongly connected digraphs and acyclic digraphs. Before we go any further we remark that the algorithmic results presented here also hold for *all digraphs* if we consider k-DMLOT rather than k-DMLOB. However, we mainly restrict ourselves to k-DMLOB for clarity and the harder challenges it poses, and we briefly consider k-DMLOT only in the last section.

Faster Algorithm. We design a new algorithm which decides in time $2^{O(k \log^2 k)} \cdot n^{O(1)}$ whether a strongly connected digraph on n vertices has an out-branching with at least k leaves (Corollary 2). On acyclic graphs we can solve the problem even faster, in time $2^{O(k \log k)} \cdot n^{O(1)}$ (Corollary 1). These are significant improvements over running time $2^{O(k^2 \log k)} \cdot n^{O(1)}$ for both classes of digraphs obtained in [2]. The improvements do not result from a careful tuning of the algorithm from [2] but from several novel ideas. In particular, we use local search and specific tree partition arguments. While local search is a widely used technique in heuristics and approximation algorithms (see, e.g., [1]) we are not aware of its applications in parameterized complexity. We find it to be of independent interest.

Combinatorial bounds. Kleitman and West [16] and Linial and Sturtevant [19] showed that every connected undirected graph G on n vertices with minimum degree at least 3 has a spanning tree with at least $n/4+2$ leaves. In [2] we proved an analogue of this result for directed graphs: every strongly connected digraph D of order n with minimum in-degree at least 3 has an out-branching with at least $(n/2)^{1/5} - 1$ leaves. In this paper (Theorem 4), we improve this bound to $(n/4)^{1/3} - 1$. We do not know whether the last bound is tight, however we show that there are strongly connected digraphs with minimum in-degree 3 in which every out-branching has at most $O(\sqrt{n})$ leaves (Theorem 6). Another parallel between the worlds of directed and undirected graphs established in this paper (and used intensively in the algorithmic part) is the relation between the number of leaves in a maximum leaf out-branching in a digraph D and the pathwidth of its underlying graph. It is easy to check (see, e.g., [4]), that every connected undirected graph of pathwidth at least k, contains a spanning tree with at least k leaves. We show (Theorem 8) that if a strongly connected digraph D does not contain an out-branching with k leaves, then the pathwidth of its underlying graph is $O(k \log k)$.

2   Preliminaries

Let D be a digraph. By $V(D)$ and $A(D)$ we represent the vertex set and arc set of D, respectively. An *oriented graph* is a digraph with no directed 2-cycle. Given a subset $V' \subseteq V(D)$ of a digraph D, let $D[V']$ denote the digraph induced on V'. The *underlying undirected graph* $UN(D)$ of D is obtained from D by omitting all orientations of arcs and by deleting one edge from each resulting pair of parallel edges. The *connectivity components* of D are the subdigraphs of D induced by the vertices of components of $UN(D)$. A digraph D is *strongly connected* if, for every pair x, y of vertices there are directed paths from x to y and from y to x. A maximal strongly connected subdigraph of D is called a *strong component*. A vertex u of D is an *in-neighbor* (*out-neighbor*) of a vertex v if $uv \in A(D)$ ($vu \in A(D)$, respectively). The *in-degree* $d^-(v)$ (*out-degree* $d^+(v)$) of a vertex v is the number of its in-neighbors (out-neighbors).

We denote by $\ell(D)$ the maximum number of leaves in an out-tree of a digraph D and by $\ell_s(D)$ we denote the maximum possible number of leaves in an out-branching of a digraph D. When D has no out-branching, we write $\ell_s(D) = 0$. The following simple result gives necessary and sufficient conditions for a digraph to have an out-branching. This assertion allows us to check whether $\ell_s(D) > 0$ in time $O(|V(D)| + |A(D)|)$.

Proposition 1 ([3]). *A digraph D has an out-branching if and only if D has a unique strong component with no incoming arcs.*

Let $P = u_1 u_2 \ldots u_q$ be a directed path in a digraph D. An arc $u_i u_j$ of D is a *forward* (*backward*) *arc for P* if $i \leq j - 2$ ($j < i$, respectively). Every backward arc of the type $v_{i+1} v_i$ is called *double*.

For a natural number n, $[n]$ denotes the set $\{1, 2, \ldots, n\}$.

A *tree decomposition* of an (undirected) graph G is a pair (X, U) where U is a tree whose vertices we will call *nodes* and $X = (\{X_i \mid i \in V(U)\})$ is a collection of subsets of $V(G)$ such that

1. $\bigcup_{i \in V(U)} X_i = V(G)$,
2. for each edge $\{v, w\} \in E(G)$, there is an $i \in V(U)$ such that $v, w \in X_i$, and
3. for each $v \in V(G)$ the set of nodes $\{i \mid v \in X_i\}$ forms a subtree of U.

The *width* of a tree decomposition $(\{X_i \mid i \in V(U)\}, U)$ equals $\max_{i \in V(U)} \{|X_i| - 1\}$. The *treewidth* of a graph G is the minimum width over all tree decompositions of G.

If in the definitions of a tree decomposition and treewidth we restrict U to be a tree with all vertices of degree at most 2 (i.e., a path) then we have the definitions of path decomposition and pathwidth. We use the notation $tw(G)$ and $pw(G)$ to denote the treewidth and the pathwidth of a graph G.

We also need an equivalent definition of pathwidth in terms of vertex separators with respect to a linear ordering of the vertices. Let G be a graph and let $\sigma = (v_1, v_2, \ldots, v_n)$ be an ordering of $V(G)$. For $j \in [n]$ put $V_j = \{v_i : i \in [j]\}$ and denote by ∂V_j all vertices of V_j that have neighbors in $V \setminus V_j$. Setting $vs(G, \sigma) = \max_{i \in [n]} |\partial V_i|$, we define the *vertex separation* of G as

$$vs(G) = \min\{vs(G, \sigma) : \sigma \text{ is an ordering of } V(G)\}.$$

The following assertion is well-known. It follows directly from the results of Kirousis and Papadimitriou [18] on interval width of a graph, see also [17].

Proposition 2 ([17,18]). *For any graph G, $vs(G) = pw(G)$.*

3   Locally Optimal Out-Trees

Our improved parameterized algorithms are based on finding locally optimal out-branchings. Given a digraph, D and an out-branching T, we call a vertex *leaf, link* and *branch* if its out-degree in T is 0, 1 and ≥ 2 respectively. Let $S_{\geq 2}^+(T)$ be the set of branch vertices, $S_1^+(T)$ the set of link vertices and $L(T)$ the set of leaves in the tree T. Let $\mathscr{P}_2(T)$ be the set of maximal paths consisting of link vertices. By $p(v)$ we denote the *parent* of a vertex v in T; $p(v)$ is the unique in-neighbor of v. We call a pair of vertices u and v *siblings* if they do not belong to the same path from the root r in T. We start with the following well known and easy to observe facts.

Fact 1. $|S_{\geq 2}^+(T)| \leq |L(T)| - 1$.

Fact 2. $|\mathscr{P}_2(T)| \leq 2|L(T)| - 1$.

Now we define the notion of local exchange which is intensively used in our proofs.

Definition 3. ℓ-ARC EXCHANGE (ℓ-AE) OPTIMAL OUT-BRANCHING: *An out-branching T of a directed graph D with k leaves is ℓ-AE optimal if for all arc subsets $F \subseteq A(T)$ and $X \subseteq A(D) - A(T)$ of size ℓ, $(A(T) \setminus F) \cup X$ is either not an out-branching, or an out-branching with $\leq k$ leaves. In other words, T is ℓ-AE optimal if it can't be turned into an out-branching with more leaves by exchanging ℓ arcs.*

Let us remark, that for every fixed ℓ, an ℓ-AE optimal out-branching can be obtained in polynomial time. In our proofs we use only 1-AE optimal out-branchings. We need the following simple properties of 1-AE optimal out-branchings.

Lemma 1. *Let T be an 1-AE optimal out-branching rooted at r in a digraph D. Then the following holds:*

(a) *For every pair of siblings $u, v \in V(T) \setminus L$ with $d_T^+(p(v)) = 1$, there is no arc $e = (u, v) \in A(D) \setminus A(T)$;*

(b) *For every pair of vertices $u, v \notin L$, $d_T^+(p(v)) = 1$, which are on the same path from the root with $dist(r, u) < dist(r, v)$ there is no arc $e = (u, v) \in A(D) \setminus A(T)$ (here $dist(r, u)$ is the distance to u in T from the root r);*

(c) *There is no arc (v, r), $v \notin L$ such that the directed cycle formed by the (r, v)-path and the arc (v, r) contains a vertex x such that $d_T^+(p(x)) = 1$.*

4   Combinatorial Bounds

We start with a lemma that allows us to obtain lower bounds on $\ell_s(D)$.

Lemma 2. *Let D be a oriented graph of order n in which every vertex is of in-degree 2 and let D have an out-branching. If D has no out-tree with k leaves, then $n \leq 4k^3$.*

Proof. Let us assume that D has no out-tree with k leaves. Consider an out-branching T of D with $p < k$ leaves which is 1-AE optimal. Let r be the root of T.

We will bound the number n of vertices in T as follows. Every vertex of T is either a leaf, or a branch vertex, or a link vertex. By Facts 1 and 2 we already have bounds on the number of leaf and branch vertices as well as the number of maximal paths consisting of link vertices. So to get an upper bound on n in terms of k, it suffices to bound the length of each maximal path consisting of link vertices. Let us consider such a path P and let x, y be the first and last vertices of P, respectively.

The vertices of $V(T) \setminus V(P)$ can be partitioned into four classes as follows:

(a) ancestor vertices: the vertices which appear before x on the (r, x)-path of T;

(b) descendant vertices : the vertices appearing after the vertices of P on paths of T starting at r and passing through y;

(c) sink vertices: the vertices which are leaves but not descendant vertices;

(d) special vertices: none-of-the-above vertices.

Let $P' = P - x$, let z be the out-neighbor of y on T and let T_z be the subtree of T rooted at z. By Lemma 1, there are no arcs from special or ancestor vertices to the path P'. Let uv be an arc of $A(D) \setminus A(P')$ such that $v \in V(P')$. There are two possibilities for u: (i) $u \notin V(P')$, (ii) $u \in V(P')$ and uv is backward for P' (there are no forward arcs for P' since T is 1-AE optimal). Note that every vertex of type (i) is either a descendant vertex or a sink. Observe also that the backward arcs for P' form a vertex-disjoint collection of out-trees with roots at vertices that are not terminal vertices of backward arcs for P'. These roots are terminal vertices of arcs in which first vertices are descendant vertices or sinks.

We denote by $\{u_1, u_2, \ldots, u_s\}$ and $\{v_1, v_2, \ldots, v_t\}$ the sets of vertices on P' which have in-neighbors that are descendant vertices and sinks, respectively. Let the out-tree formed by backward arcs for P' rooted at $w \in \{u_1, \ldots, u_s, v_1, \ldots, v_t\}$ be denoted by $T(w)$ and let $l(w)$ denote the number of leaves in $T(w)$. Observe that the following is an out-tree rooted at z:

$$T_z \cup \{(in(u_1), u_1), \ldots, (in(u_s), u_s)\} \cup \bigcup_{i=1}^{s} T(u_i),$$

where $\{in(u_1), \ldots, in(u_s)\}$ are the in-neighbors of $\{u_1, \ldots, u_s\}$ on T_z. This out-tree has at least $\sum_{i=1}^{s} l(u_i)$ leaves and, thus, $\sum_{i=1}^{s} l(u_i) \leq k - 1$. Let us denote the subtree of T rooted at x by T_x and let $\{in(v_1), \ldots, in(v_t)\}$ be the in-neighbors of $\{v_1, \ldots, v_t\}$ on $T - V(T_x)$. Then we have following out-tree:

$$(T - V(T_x)) \cup \{(in(v_1), v_1), \ldots, (in(v_t), v_t)\} \cup \bigcup_{i=1}^{t} T(v_i)$$

with at least $\sum_{i=1}^{t} l(v_i)$ leaves. Thus, $\sum_{i=1}^{t} l(v_i) \leq k - 1$.

Consider a path $R = v_0 v_1 \ldots v_r$ formed by backward arcs. Observe that the arcs $\{v_i v_{i+1} : 0 \leq i \leq r - 1\} \cup \{v_j v_j^+ : 1 \leq j \leq r\}$ form an out-tree with r leaves, where v_j^+ is the out-neighbor of v_j on P. Thus, there is no path of backward arcs of length more than $k - 1$. Every out-tree $T(w)$, $w \in \{u_1, \ldots, u_s\}$ has $l(w)$ leaves and, thus, its arcs can be decomposed into $l(w)$ paths, each of length at most $k - 1$. Now we can bound the number of arcs in all the trees $T(w)$, $w \in \{u_1, \ldots, u_s\}$, as follows: $\sum_{i=1}^{s} l(u_i)(k - 1) \leq (k - 1)^2$. We can similarly bound the number of arcs in all the trees $T(w)$, $w \in \{v_1, \ldots, v_s\}$ by $(k - 1)^2$. Recall that the vertices of P' can be either terminal vertices of backward arcs for P' or vertices in $\{u_1, \ldots, u_s, v_1, \ldots, v_t\}$. Observe that $s + t \leq 2(k - 1)$ since $\sum_{i=1}^{s} l(u_i) \leq k - 1$ and $\sum_{i=1}^{t} l(v_i) \leq k - 1$.

Thus, the number of vertices in P is bounded from above by $1 + 2(k - 1) + 2(k - 1)^2$. Therefore,

$$n = |L(T)| + |S_{\geq 2}^+(T)| + |S_1^+(T)|$$
$$= |L(T)| + |S_{\geq 2}^+(T)| + \sum_{P \in \mathscr{P}_2(T)} |V(P)|$$
$$\leq (k - 1) + (k - 2) + (2k - 3)(2k^2 - 2k + 1)$$
$$< 4k^3.$$

Thus, we conclude that $n \leq 4k^3$. $\square$

Theorem 4. *Let D be a strongly connected digraph with n vertices.*

(a) If D is an oriented graph with minimum in-degree at least 2, then $\ell_s(D) \geq (n/4)^{1/3} - 1$.
(b) If D is a digraph with minimum in-degree at least 3, then $\ell_s(D) \geq (n/4)^{1/3} - 1$.

Proof. Since D is strongly connected, we have $\ell(D) = \ell_s(D) > 0$. Let T be an 1-AE optimal out-branching of D with maximum number of leaves. (a) Delete some arcs from $A(D) \setminus A(T)$, if needed, such that the in-degree of each vertex of D becomes 2. Now the inequality $\ell_s(D) \geq (n/4)^{1/3} - 1$ follows from Lemma 2 and the fact that $\ell(D) = \ell_s(D)$.

(b) Let P be the path formed in the proof of Lemma 2. (Note that $A(P) \subseteq A(T)$.) Delete every double arc of P, in case there are any, and delete some more arcs from $A(D) \setminus A(T)$, if needed, to ensure that the in-degree of each vertex of D becomes 2. It is not difficult to see that the proof of Lemma 2 remains valid for the new digraph D. Now the inequality $\ell_s(D) \geq (n/4)^{1/3} - 1$ follows from Lemma 2 and the fact that $\ell(D) = \ell_s(D)$. $\square$

Remark 5. *It is easy to see that Theorem 4 holds also for acyclic digraphs D with $\ell_s(D) > 0$.*

While we do not know whether the bounds of Theorem 4 are tight, we can show that no linear bounds are possible. The following result is formulated for Part (b) of Theorem 4, but a similar result holds for Part (a) as well.

Theorem 6. *For each $t \geq 6$ there is a strongly connected digraph H_t of order $n = t^2 + 1$ with minimum in-degree 3 such that $0 < \ell_s(H_t) = O(t)$.*

Proof. Let $V(H_t) = \{r\} \cup \{u_1^i, u_2^i, \ldots, u_t^i \mid i \in [t]\}$ and

$$A(H_t) = \{u_j^i u_{j+1}^i, u_{j+1}^i u_j^i \mid i \in [t], j \in \{0, 1, \ldots, t-3\}\}$$
$$\bigcup \{u_j^i u_{j-2}^i \mid i \in [t], j \in \{3, 4, \ldots, t-2\}\}$$
$$\bigcup \{u_j^i u_q^i \mid i \in [t], t-3 \leq j \neq q \leq t\},$$

where $u_0^i = r$ for every $i \in [t]$. It is easy to check that $0 < \ell_s(H_t) = O(t)$. $\square$

5   Decomposition Algorithms

By Proposition 1, an acyclic digraph D has an out-branching if and only if D possesses a single vertex of in-degree zero.

Theorem 7. *Let D be an acyclic digraph with a single vertex of in-degree zero. Then either $\ell_s(D) \geq k$ or the underlying undirected graph of D is of pathwidth at most $4k$ and we can obtain this path decomposition in polynomial time.*

Proof. Assume that $\ell_s(D) \leq k - 1$. Consider a 1-AE optimal out-branching T of D. Notice that $|L(T)| \leq k - 1$. Now remove all the leaves and branch vertices from the tree T. The remaining vertices form maximal directed paths consisting of link vertices. Delete the first vertices of all paths. As a result we obtain a collection $\mathcal{Q}$ of directed paths. Let $H = \cup_{P \in \mathcal{Q}} P$. We will show that every arc uv with $u, v \in V(H)$ is in H.

Let $P' \in \mathcal{Q}$. As in the proof of Lemma 2, we see that there are no forward arcs for P'. Since D is acyclic, there are no backward arcs for P'. Suppose uv is an arc of D such that $u \in R'$ and $v \in P'$, where R' and P' are distinct paths from $\mathcal{Q}$. As in the proof of Lemma 2, we see that u is either a sink or a descendent vertex for P' in T. Since R' contains no sinks of T, u is a descendent vertex, which is impossible as D is acyclic. Thus, we have proved that $pw(UN(H)) = 1$.

Consider a path decomposition of H of width 1. We can obtain a path decomposition of $UN(D)$ by adding all the vertices of $L(T) \cup S_{\geq 2}^+(T) \cup F(T)$, where $F(T)$ is the set of first vertices of maximal directed paths consisting of link vertices of T, to each of the bags of a path decomposition of H of width 1. Observe that the pathwidth of this decomposition is bounded from above by

$$|L(T)| + |S_{\geq 2}^+(T)| + |F(T)| + 1 \leq (k - 1) + (k - 2) + (2k - 3) + 1 \leq 4k - 5.$$

The bounds on the various sets in the inequality above follows from Facts 1 and 2. This proves the theorem. □

Corollary 1. *For acyclic digraphs, the problem k-DMLOB can solved in time* $2^{O(k \log k)} \cdot n^{O(1)}$.

Proof. The proof of Theorem 7 can be easily turned into a polynomial time algorithm to either build an out-branching of D with at least k leaves or to show that $pw(UN(D)) \leq 4k$ and provide the corresponding path decomposition. A simple dynamic programming over the path decomposition gives us an algorithm of running time $2^{O(k \log k)} \cdot n^{O(1)}$. □

The following simple lemma is well known, see, e.g., [6].

Lemma 3. *Let* $T = (V, E)$ *be an undirected tree and let* $w : V \to \mathbb{R}^+ \cup \{0\}$ *be a weight function on its vertices. There exists a vertex* $v \in T$ *such that the weight of every subtree* T' *of* $T - v$ *is at most* $w(T)/2$, *where* $w(T) = \sum_{v \in V} w(v)$.

Let D be a strongly connected digraph with $\ell_s(D) = \lambda$ and let T be an out-branching of D with λ leaves. Consider the following decomposition of T (called a β-decomposition) which will be useful in the proof of Theorem 8.

Assign weight 1 to all leaves of T and weight 0 to all non-leaves of T. By Lemma 3, T has a vertex v such that each component of $T - v$ has at most $\lambda/2 + 1$ leaves (if v is not the root and its in-neighbor v^- in T is a link vertex, then v^- becomes a new leaf). Let $T_1, T_2, \ldots, T_s$ be the components of $T - v$ and let $l_1, l_2, \ldots, l_s$ be the numbers of leaves in the components. Notice that $\lambda \leq \sum_{i=1}^s l_i \leq \lambda + 1$ (we may get a new leaf). We may assume that $l_s \leq l_{s-1} \leq$

$\cdots \le l_1 \le \lambda/2 + 1$. Let j be the first index such that $\sum_{i=1}^{j} l_i \ge \frac{\lambda}{2} + 1$. Consider two cases: (a) $l_j \le (\lambda + 2)/4$ and (b) $l_j > (\lambda + 2)/4$. In Case (a), we have

$$\frac{\lambda + 2}{2} \le \sum_{i=1}^{j} l_i \le \frac{3(\lambda + 2)}{4} \quad \text{and} \quad \frac{\lambda - 6}{4} \le \sum_{i=j+1}^{s} l_i \le \frac{\lambda}{2}.$$

In Case (b), we have $j = 2$ and

$$\frac{\lambda + 2}{4} \le l_1 \le \frac{\lambda + 2}{2} \quad \text{and} \quad \frac{\lambda - 2}{2} \le \sum_{i=2}^{s} l_i \le \frac{3\lambda + 2}{4}.$$

Let $p = j$ in Case (a) and $p = 1$ in Case (b). Add to D and T a *copy* v' of v (with the same in- and out-neighbors). Then the number of leaves in each of the out-trees

$$T' = T[\{v\} \cup (\cup_{i=1}^{p} V(T_i))] \quad \text{and} \quad T'' = T[\{v'\} \cup (\cup_{i=p+1}^{s} V(T_i))]$$

is between $\lambda(1 + o(1))/4$ and $3\lambda(1 + o(1))/4$. Observe that the vertices of T' have at most $\lambda + 1$ out-neighbors in T'' and the vertices of T'' have at most $\lambda + 1$ out-neighbors in T' (we add 1 to λ due to the fact that v 'belongs' to both T' and T'').

Similarly to deriving T' and T'' from T, we can obtain two out-trees from T' and two out-trees from T'' in which the numbers of leaves are approximately between a quarter and three quarters of the number of leaves in T' and T'', respectively. Observe that after $O(\log \lambda)$ 'dividing' steps, we will end up with $O(\lambda)$ out-trees with just one leaf, i.e., directed paths. These paths contain $O(\lambda)$ copies of vertices of D (such as v' above). After deleting the copies, we obtain a collection of $O(\lambda)$ disjoint directed paths covering $V(D)$.

Theorem 8. *Let D be a strongly connected digraph. Then either $\ell_s(D) \ge k$ or the underlying undirected graph of D is of pathwidth $O(k \log k)$.*

Proof. We may assume that $\ell_s(D) < k$. Let T be be a 1-AE optimal out-branching. Consider a β-decomposition of T. The decomposition process can be viewed as a tree $\mathcal{T}$ rooted in a node (associated with) T. The children of T in $\mathcal{T}$ are nodes (associated with) T' and T''; the leaves of $\mathcal{T}$ are the directed paths of the decomposition. The *first layer* of $\mathcal{T}$ is the node T, the *second layer* are T' and T'', the *third layer* are the children of T' and T'', etc. In what follows, we do not distinguish between a node Q of $\mathcal{T}$ and the tree associated with the node. Assume that $\mathcal{T}$ has t layers. Notice that the last layer consists of (some) leaves of $\mathcal{T}$ and that $t = O(\log k)$, which was proved above ($k \le \lambda - 1$).

Let Q be a node of $\mathcal{T}$ at layer j. We will prove that

$$pw(UN(D[V(Q)])) < 2(t - j + 2.5)k \tag{1}$$

Since $t = O(\log k)$, (1) for $j = 1$ implies that the underlying undirected graph of D is of pathwidth $O(k \log k)$.

We first prove (1) for $j = t$ when Q is a path from the decomposition. Let $W = (L(T) \cup S^+_{\geq 2}(T) \cup F(T)) \cap V(Q)$, where $F(T)$ is the set of first vertices of maximal paths of T consisting of link vertices. As in the proof of Theorem 7, it follows from Facts 1 and 2 that $|W| < 4k$. Obtain a digraph R by deleting from $D[V(Q)]$ all arcs in which at least one end-vertex is in W and which are not arcs of Q. As in the proof of Theorem 7, it follows from Lemma 1 and 1-AE optimality of T that there are no forward arcs for Q in R. Let $Q = v_1 v_2 \ldots v_q$. For every $j \in [q]$, let $V_j = \{v_i : i \in [j]\}$. If for some j the set V_j contained k vertices, say $\{v'_1, v'_2, \cdots, v'_k\}$, having in-neighbors in the set $\{v_{j+1}, v_{j+2}, \ldots, v_q\}$, then D would contain an out-tree with k leaves formed by the path $v_{j+1} v_{j+2} \ldots v_q$ together with a backward arc terminating at v'_i from a vertex on the path for each $1 \leq i \leq k$, a contradiction. Thus $vs(UN(D_2[P])) \leq k$. By Proposition 2, the pathwidth of $UN(R)$ is at most k. Let $(X_1, X_2, \ldots, X_s)$ be a path decomposition of $UN(R)$ of width at most k. Then $(X_1 \cup W, X_2 \cup W, \ldots, X_s \cup W)$ is a path decomposition of $UN(D[V(Q)])$ of width less than $k + 4k$. Thus,

$$pw(UN(D[V(Q)])) < 5k \qquad (2)$$

Now assume that we have proved (1) for $j = i$ and show it for $j = i - 1$. Let Q be a node of layer $i - 1$. If Q is a leaf of $\mathcal{T}$, we are done by (2). So, we may assume that Q has children Q' and Q'' which are nodes of layer i. In the β-decomposition of T given before this theorem, we saw that the vertices of T' have at most $\lambda + 1$ out-neighbors in T'' and the vertices of T'' have at most $\lambda + 1$ out-neighbors in T'. Similarly, we can see that (in the β-decomposition of this proof) the vertices of Q' have at most k out-neighbors in Q'' and the vertices of Q'' have at most k out-neighbors in Q' (since $k \leq \lambda - 1$). Let Y denote the set of the above-mentioned out-neighbors on Q' and Q''; $|Y| \leq 2k$. Delete from $D[V(Q') \cup V(Q'')]$ all arcs in which at least one end-vertex is in Y and which do not belong to $Q' \cup Q''$

Let G denote the obtained digraph. Observe that G is disconnected and $G[V(Q')]$ and $G[V(Q'')]$ are components of G. Thus, $pw(UN(G)) \leq b$, where

$$b = \max\{pw(UN(G[V(Q')])), pw(UN(G[V(Q'')]))\} < 2(t - i + 4.5)k \qquad (3)$$

Let $(Z_1, Z_2, \ldots, Z_r)$ be a path decomposition of G of width at most b. Then $(Z_1 \cup Y, Z_2 \cup Y, \ldots, Z_r \cup Y)$ is a path decomposition of $UN(D[V(Q') \cup V(Q'')])$ of width at most $b + 2k < 2(t - i + 2.5)k$. $\qquad \square$

Similar to the proof of Corollary 1, we obtain the following:

Corollary 2. *For a strongly connected digraph D, the problem k-DMLOB can be solved in time $2^{O(k \log^2 k)} \cdot n^{O(1)}$.*

6   Discussion and Open Problems

In this paper, we continued the algorithmic and combinatorial investigation of the DIRECTED MAXIMUM LEAF OUT-BRANCHING problem. In particular, we showed that for every strongly connected digraph D of order n and with minimum in-degree at least 3, $\ell_s(D) = \Omega(n^{1/3})$. The most interesting open combinatorial question here is whether this bound is tight. It would be even more interesting to find the maximum number r such that $\ell_s(D) = \Omega(n^r)$ for every strongly connected digraph D of order n and with minimum in-degree at least 3. It follows from our results that $\frac{1}{3} \leq r \leq \frac{1}{2}$.

We also provided an algorithm of time complexity $2^{O(k \log^2 k)} \cdot n^{O(1)}$ which solves k-DMLOB for a strongly connected digraph D. The algorithm is based on a combinatorial bound on the pathwidth of the underlying undirected graph of D. Unfortunately, this technique does not work on all digraphs. It remains an algorithmic challenge to establish the parameterized complexity of k-DMLOB on all digraphs.

Notice that $\ell(D) \geq \ell_s(D)$ for each digraph D. Let $\mathcal{L}$ be the family of digraphs D for which either $\ell_s(D) = 0$ or $\ell_s(D) = \ell(D)$. The following assertion shows that $\mathcal{L}$ includes a large number digraphs including all strongly connected digraphs and acyclic digraphs (and, also, the well-studied classes of semicomplete multipartite digraphs and quasi-transitive digraphs, see [3] for the definitions).

Proposition 3 ([2]). *Suppose that a digraph D satisfies the following property: for every pair R and Q of distinct strong components of D, if there is an arc from R to Q then each vertex of Q has an in-neighbor in R. Then $D \in \mathcal{L}$.*

Let $\mathcal{B}$ be the family of digraphs that contain out-branchings. The results of this paper proved for strongly connected digraphs can be extended to the class $\mathcal{L} \cap \mathcal{B}$ of digraphs since in the proofs we use only the following property of strongly connected digraphs D: $\ell_s(D) = \ell(D) > 0$.

For a digraph D and a vertex v, let D_v denote the subdigraph of D induced by all vertices reachable from v. Using the $2^{O(k \log^2 k)} \cdot n^{O(1)}$ algorithm for k-DMLOB on digraphs in $\mathcal{L} \cap \mathcal{B}$ and the facts that (i) $D_v \in \mathcal{L} \cap \mathcal{B}$ for each digraph D and vertex v and (ii) $\ell(D) = \max\{\ell_s(D_v) | v \in V(D)\}$ (for details, see [2]), we can obtain an $2^{O(k \log^2 k)} \cdot n^{O(1)}$ algorithm for k-DMLOT on *all* digraphs. For acyclic digraphs, the running time can be reduced to $2^{O(k \log k)} \cdot n^{O(1)}$.

Acknowledgements. Research of N. Alon and M. Krivelevich was supported in part by USA-Israeli BSF grants and by grants from the Israel Science Foundation. Research of F. Fomin was supported in part by the Norwegian Research Council. Research of G. Gutin was supported in part by EPSRC.

References

1. Aarts, E., Lenstra, J.K.: Local search in combinatorial optimization. Wiley-Interscience Series in Discrete Mathematics and Optimization. John Wiley & Sons Ltd, Chichester (1997)
2. Alon, N., Fomin, F.V., Gutin, G., Krivelevich, M., Saurabh, S.: Parameterized Algorithms for Directed Maximum Leaf Problems. In: Arge, L., Cachin, C., Jurdziński, T., Tarlecki, A. (eds.) ICALP 2007. LNCS, vol. 4596, pp. 352–362. Springer, Heidelberg (2007)

3. Bang-Jensen, J., Gutin, G.: Digraphs: Theory, Algorithms and Applications. Springer, Heidelberg (2000)
4. Bienstock, D., Robertson, N., Seymour, P.D., Thomas, R.: Quickly excluding a forest. J. Comb. Theory Series B 52, 274–283 (1991)
5. Bonsma, P.S., Brueggermann, T., Woeginger, G.J.: A faster FPT algorithm for finding spanning trees with many leaves. In: Rovan, B., Vojtáš, P. (eds.) MFCS 2003. LNCS, vol. 2747, pp. 259–268. Springer, Heidelberg (2003)
6. Chung, F.R.K.: Separator theorems and their applications. In: Paths, flows, and VLSI-layout (Bonn, 1988). Algorithms Combin, vol. 9, pp. 17–34. Springer, Berlin (1990)
7. Ding, G., Johnson, Th., Seymour, P.: Spanning trees with many leaves. Journal of Graph Theory 37, 189–197 (2001)
8. Downey, R.G., Fellows, M.R.: Parameterized Complexity. Springer, Heidelberg (1999)
9. Drescher, M., Vetta, A.: An approximation algorithm for the maximum leaf spanning arborescence problem. Manuscript (2007)
10. Estivill-Castro, V., Fellows, M.R., Langston, M.A., Rosamond, F.A.: FPT is P-Time Extremal Structure I. In: Proc. ACiD, pp. 1–41 (2005)
11. Fomin, F.V., Grandoni, F., Kratsch, D.: Solving Connected Dominating Set Faster Than 2^n. In: Arun-Kumar, S., Garg, N. (eds.) FSTTCS 2006. LNCS, vol. 4337, pp. 152–163. Springer, Heidelberg (2006)
12. Fellows, M.R., McCartin, C., Rosamond, F.A., Stege, U.: Coordinated kernels and catalytic reductions: An improved FPT algorithm for max leaf spanning tree and other problems. In: Kapoor, S., Prasad, S. (eds.) FST TCS 2000. LNCS, vol. 1974, pp. 240–251. Springer, Heidelberg (2000)
13. Flum, J., Grohe, M.: Parameterized Complexity Theory. Springer, Heidelberg (2006)
14. Galbiati, G., Morzenti, A., Maffioli, F.: On the approximability of some maximum spanning tree problems. Theoretical Computer Science 181, 107–118 (1997)
15. Griggs, J.R., Wu, M.: Spanning trees in graphs of minimum degree four or five. Discrete Mathematics 104, 167–183 (1992)
16. Kleitman, D.J., West, D.B.: Spanning trees with many leaves. SIAM Journal on Discrete Mathematics 4, 99–106 (1991)
17. Kinnersley, N.G.: The vertex separation number of a graph equals its path-width. Information Processing Letters 42, 345–350 (1992)
18. Kirousis, L.M., Papadimitriou, C.H.: Interval graphs and searching. Discrete Mathematics 55, 181–184 (1985)
19. Linial, N., Sturtevant, D.: Unpublished result (1987)
20. Lu, H.-I., Ravi, R.: Approximating maximum leaf spanning trees in almost linear time. Journal of Algorithms 29, 132–141 (1998)
21. Niedermeier, R.: Invitation to Fixed-Parameter Algorithms. Oxford University Press, Oxford (2006)
22. Solis-Oba, R.: 2-approximation algorithm for finding a spanning tree with the maximum number of leaves. In: Bilardi, G., Pietracaprina, A., Italiano, G.F., Pucci, G. (eds.) ESA 1998. LNCS, vol. 1461, pp. 441–452. Springer, Heidelberg (1998)

Faster Algorithms for All-Pairs Small Stretch Distances in Weighted Graphs

Telikepalli Kavitha

Indian Institute of Science, Bangalore, India
`kavitha@csa.iisc.ernet.in`

Abstract. Let $G = (V, E)$ be a weighted undirected graph, with non-negative edge weights. We consider the problem of efficiently computing approximate distances between all pairs of vertices in G. While many efficient algorithms are known for this problem in unweighted graphs, not many results are known for this problem in weighted graphs. Zwick [15] showed that for any fixed $\epsilon > 0$, stretch $(1+\epsilon)$ distances between all pairs of vertices in a weighted directed graph on n vertices can be computed in $\tilde{O}(n^\omega)$ time assuming that edge weights in G are not too large, where $\omega < 2.376$ is the exponent of matrix multiplication and n is the number of vertices in G. It is known that finding distances of stretch less than 2 between all pairs of vertices in G is at least as hard as Boolean matrix multiplication of two $n \times n$ matrices. It is also known that all-pairs stretch 3 distances can be computed in $\tilde{O}(n^2)$ time and all-pairs stretch $7/3$ distances can be computed in $\tilde{O}(n^{7/3})$ time. Here we consider efficient algorithms for the problem of computing all-pairs stretch $(2+\epsilon)$ distances in G, for any $0 < \epsilon < 1$.

We show that all pairs stretch $(2+\epsilon)$ distances for any fixed $\epsilon > 0$ in G can be computed in expected time $O(n^{9/4})$ assuming that edge weights in G are not too large. This algorithm uses a fast rectangular matrix multiplication subroutine. We also present a combinatorial algorithm (that is, it does not use fast matrix multiplication) with expected running time $O(n^{9/4})$ for computing all-pairs stretch $5/2$ distances in G.

1   Introduction

The all-pairs shortest paths (APSP) problem is one of the most fundamental algorithmic graph problems. Efficient algorithms for the APSP problem are very important in several applications. The complexity of the fastest known algorithm for the APSP problem in a graph with m edges, n vertices and real non-negative edge weights is $O(mn + n^2 \log \log n)$ [13]. Thus this algorithm has a running time of $\Theta(n^3)$ when $m = \Theta(n^2)$. The best upper bound currently known [5] on the worst case time complexity of this problem (in terms of n) is close to $O(n^3 / \log^2 n)$, which is marginally subcubic. An almost cubic running time is inefficient for several applications, and this has motivated faster algorithms to compute *approximate* solutions for the APSP problem.

Let $G = (V, E)$ be an undirected graph with non-negative edge weights. A path in G between $u, v \in V$ is said to be of stretch t if its length is at most

V. Arvind and S. Prasad (Eds.): FSTTCS 2007, LNCS 4855, pp. 328–339, 2007.

$t \cdot \delta(u, v)$ where $\delta(u, v)$ is the distance between u and v in G. In this paper we are interested in computing small stretch paths/distances between all pairs of vertices. Zwick [15] showed that for any $\epsilon > 0$, stretch $1 + \epsilon$ distances between all pairs of vertices in a weighted *directed* graph on n vertices can be computed in time $\tilde{O}(n^\omega/\epsilon \cdot \log(W/\epsilon))$, where $\omega < 2.376$ is the exponent of matrix multiplication and W is the largest edge weight in the graph, after the edge weights are scaled so that the smallest non-zero edge weight in the graph is 1. It is also known that finding paths of stretch *less* than 2 between all pairs of vertices in an undirected graph on n vertices is at least as hard as Boolean matrix multiplication of two $n \times n$ matrices. Given an undirected weighted graph on n vertices, computing all-pairs stretch 3 distances in $\tilde{O}(n^2)$ time and all-pairs stretch 7/3 distances in $\tilde{O}(n^{7/3})$ time is known [7] (these algorithms use only combinatorial techniques, i.e., fast matrix multiplication subroutines are not used). Researchers have been trying to explore the possible trade-off between stretch and running time for the problem of computing all-pairs stretch t distances for $t \in [2, 3)$.

1.1 Our Main Results

In this paper we consider faster algorithms for the problem of computing all-pairs stretch t distances for $2 < t < 3$ in a weighted undirected graph G on n vertices. We first present a combinatorial algorithm STRETCH$_{5/2}$ and show the following result. (For any pair of vertices u, v in G, let $\delta(u, v)$ denote the distance between u and v in G.)

Theorem 1. *Algorithm* STRETCH$_{5/2}(G)$ *runs in expected time* $O(n^{9/4})$, *where* n *is the number of vertices in the input graph* G *and constructs an* $n \times n$ *table* d *such that:* $\delta(u, v) \leq d[u, v] \leq 5/2 \cdot \delta(u, v)$.

We then augment STRETCH$_{5/2}(G)$ with a fast rectangular matrix multiplication subroutine. This yields algorithm STRETCH$_{2+\epsilon}(G)$ and we show the following result.

Theorem 2. *Given any* $\epsilon > 0$, *algorithm* STRETCH$_{2+\epsilon}(G)$ *constructs an* $n \times n$ *table* d *such that* $\delta(u, v) \leq d[u, v] \leq (2 + \epsilon)\delta(u, v)$ *in expected time* $O(n^{9/4}) + \tilde{O}(n^{2.243}(\log^2 W)/\epsilon^2)$, *where* n *is the number of vertices in the input graph* G *and* W *is the largest edge weight after scaling the edge weights so that the smallest non-zero edge weight is 1.*

Thus when all edge weights in G are polynomial in n and $\epsilon > 0$ is a constant, STRETCH$_{2+\epsilon}(G)$ computes all-pairs stretch $2 + \epsilon$ distances in expected time $O(n^{9/4})$ since $\tilde{O}(n^{2.243})$ is $o(n^{9/4})$.

Motivation. During the last 10-15 years, many new combinatorial algorithms [2,6,1,8,7,14,3,9] were designed for the all-pairs approximate shortest paths problem in order to achieve faster running times in weighted and unweighted graphs. In weighted graphs, the current fastest randomized combinatorial algorithms (from [4]) for computing all-pairs stretch t distances for $t < 3$ in G with m edges and n vertices are: computing all-pairs stretch 2 distances in expected

$\tilde{O}(m\sqrt{n} + n^2)$ time and computing all-pairs stretch 7/3 distances in expected $\tilde{O}(m^{2/3}n + n^2)$ time. These algorithms are improvements of the following deterministic algorithms: an $\tilde{O}(n^{3/2}m^{1/2})$ algorithm for stretch 2 distances and an $\tilde{O}(n^{7/3})$ algorithm for stretch 7/3 distances by Cohen and Zwick [7]. However when $m = \Theta(n^2)$, there is no improvement in the running time. There is an algorithm [4] with expected running time $\tilde{O}(n^2)$ for computing approximate (u, v) distances for all pairs (u, v), where the distance returned is at most $2\delta(u, v) +$ maximum weight of an edge on a u-v shortest path. However, note that we cannot claim that the *stretch* here is at most $3 - \epsilon$ for any fixed $\epsilon > 0$. Thus there was no $o(n^{7/3})$ algorithm known for computing all-pairs stretch $(3 - \epsilon)$ distances for any constant $\epsilon > 0$. We try to fill this gap in this paper.

Our techniques. Our algorithms construct a sequence of sets: $V = S_0 \supseteq S_1 \supseteq S_2 \supseteq S_3$. Vertices in S_i run Dijkstra's algorithm in a specific subgraph G_{i+1} of G, where the density of G_{i+1} is inversely proportional to the cardinality of S_i. Then these sets S_i *cooperate* with each other. The step where each vertex in the set S_i runs Dijkstra's algorithm in a subgraph G_{i+1} bears a lot of similarity with schemes in [7] for computing all-pairs small stretch distances. The new idea here is the cooperation between the sets S_i - this cooperation forms a crucial step of our algorithm and that is what ensures a small stretch.

In our analysis of algorithm $\mathsf{STRETCH}_{5/2}(G)$ we actually get a bound of 7/3 on the stretch in all cases, except one where we get a stretch of 5/2. The stretch in this algorithm can be improved to $2 + \epsilon$ by using a subroutine for witnessing a Boolean product matrix. This subroutine for witnessing a Boolean product matrix is implemented using fast rectangular matrix multiplication.

Related results. An active area of research in algorithms that report all-pairs small stretch distances is in designing compact data structures, to answer distance queries. Instead of storing an $n \times n$ look-up table, these algorithms use $o(n^2)$ space. More specifically, for any integer $k \geq 1$, the data structure uses $O(kn^{1+1/k})$ space and it answers any distance query with stretch $2k - 1$, in $O(k)$ time [14]. It was shown in [14] that any such data structure with stretch $t < 3$ must use $\Theta(n^2)$ space on at least one input graph. Hence, in algorithms that compute all-pairs stretch $3 - \epsilon$ distances for $\epsilon > 0$, what one seeks to optimize is the running time of the algorithm, since the space requirement is $\Theta(n^2)$.

2   Preliminaries

We will work with certain subsets S_1, S_2, S_3 of V, where $V = S_0 \supseteq S_1 \supseteq S_2 \supseteq S_3 \supseteq S_4 = \emptyset$. For each vertex $u \in V$ and for $i = 1, 2, 3$, define $\delta(u, S_i)$ as the distance between u and the vertex in S_i that is nearest to u. Let $s_i(u) \in S_i$ be the vertex in S_i that is nearest to u. That is, $\delta(u, S_i) = \delta(u, s_i(u)) \leq \delta(u, x)$ for all $x \in S_i$. In case there is more than one vertex in S_i with distance $\delta(u, S_i)$ to u, then break the tie arbitrarily to define $s_i(u)$. Note that since $S_4 = \emptyset$, we define $\delta(u, S_4) = \infty$.

Now we need to define certain neighborhoods around a vertex u.

Definition 1 (from [14]). *For any vertex u and for $i = 1, 2, 3$, define $ball_i(u)$ as:*

$$ball_i(u) = \{v \in V : \delta(u, v) < \delta(u, S_i)\}.$$

That is, $ball_i(u)$ is the set of all vertices v that are strictly closer to u than the nearest vertex in S_i is to u.

The graphs of interest to us in our algorithms are the graphs $G_i = (V, E_i)$ for $i = 1, 2, 3$, where

$$E_i = \{(u, v) \in E : v \in ball_i(u)\}.$$

Note that G_i, for $i = 1, 2, 3$, are undirected graphs. Each G_i is a subgraph of G, where each vertex $x \in V$ keeps edges to only those of its neighbors that lie in $ball_i(x)$. Note that constructing these graphs G_i is easy. In G, connect a dummy vertex s^* to all the vertices of the set S_i and assign weight zero to all these edges. Now run Dijkstra's shortest paths algorithm with source s^* in G. The distance returned between s^* and u is the distance $\delta(u, S_i)$, for any $u \in V$. The vertex $s_i(u)$ is the successor of s^* in the shortest s^*-u path in this graph. To form the edge set E_i of G_i, each u looks at its adjacency list and retains only those neighbors v where $w(u, v) < \delta(u, S_i)$, where $w(u, v)$ is the weight of the edge (u, v). We have $E_1 \subseteq E_2 \subseteq E_3 \subseteq E = E_4$.

Let us also make the following simplifying assumption in the input graph: we assume that all edge weights are positive. If the input graph had edges with weight zero, then we will contract each such edge - this will reduce the number of vertices and it is simple to see that we can easily extend the all-pairs small stretch distances table for the reduced graph to the all-pairs small stretch distances table for the entire graph. Henceforth all edge weights are positive.

The following claims, which are simple to show, are stated in the form of Proposition 1 and Proposition 2. They will be used repeatedly in the paper.

Proposition 1. *For $S_i \subseteq V$, ($i \in \{1, 2, 3\}$) the following assertions are true.*

1. *For any two vertices $u, v \in V$, if $v \in ball_i(u)$, then the subgraph $G_i = (V, E_i)$ preserves the exact distance between u and v.*
2. *For every $u \in V$, the subgraph $(V, E_i \cup E(s_i(u)))$ preserves the exact distance between u and $s_i(u)$, where $E(s_i(u))$ is the set of edges incident on $s_i(u)$.*

Proposition 2. *If the set $S_i \subseteq V$ is formed by selecting each vertex independently with probability q, then the expected size of the set E_i is $O(n/q)$.*

We now define the set $bunch_i(u)$. For any vertex $u \in V$ and $i = 1, 2, 3$, the set $bunch_i(u) \subseteq S_i$ is defined as follows: $bunch_i(u) = \{x \in S_i | \delta(u, x) < \delta(u, S_{i+1})\} \cup \{s_i(u)\}$. That is, $bunch_3(u) = S_3$ since $\delta(u, S_4) = \infty$, while $bunch_2(u)$ consists of $s_2(u)$ and all the vertices in S_2 that belong to $ball_3(u)$ and $bunch_1(u)$ consists of $s_1(u)$ and all the vertices in S_1 that belong to $ball_2(u)$. The following result about the expected size of $bunch_i(u)$ and the complexity of computing the set $bunch_i(u)$ was shown in [14].

Lemma 1. *[14] Given a graph $G = (V, E)$, let the set S_{i+1} be formed by picking each vertex of a set $S_i \subseteq V$ independently with probability q. Then*
(i) the expected size of $bunch_i(u)$ is at most $1/q$ for each u, and
(ii) the expected time to compute the sets $bunch_i(u)$, summed over all $u \in V$, is $O(m/q)$.

Another concept that we use is the notion of *overlap* of $ball_i(u)$ and $ball_i(v)$. We define this term below and Fig. 1 illustrates this.

Definition 2. *Let $u, v \in V$. For any $i = 1, 2, 3$, we say that $ball_i(u)$ and $ball_i(v)$ overlap if $\delta(u, S_i) + \delta(v, S_i) > \delta(u, v)$.*

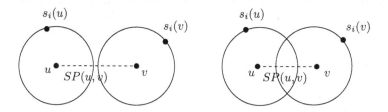

Fig. 1. In the figure on the left, $ball_i(u)$ and $ball_i(v)$ do not overlap; whereas on the right, they overlap

Constructing the sets S_1, S_2, S_3. We will use the following sampling scheme in our algorithm STRETCH$_{5/2}(G)$: let S_i, for $i = 1, 2, 3$, be obtained by sampling vertices in S_{i-1} with probability $n^{-1/4}$. Note that the expected size of S_i is $n^{1-i/4}$, it follows from Proposition 2 that the expected size of E_i is $O(n^{1+i/4})$.

3   All-Pairs Stretch 5/2 Distances

Let $G = (V, E)$ be an undirected graph with a weight function $w : E \to \mathbb{Q}^+$. Our algorithm for computing small stretch distances runs Steps 1-5 given below for 2 iterations and as the algorithm evolves, distance estimates computed till then will be stored in an $n \times n$ table d. The table d is initialized as: $d[u, u] = 0$ and $d[u, v] = w(u, v)$ for all $(u, v) \in E$. Otherwise $d[u, v] = \infty$.

A basic step that we use in our algorithm is the following: a vertex v runs Dijkstra's algorithm in a subgraph G' that is augmented with all *pairs* (v, x). That is, (v, x) need not be an edge, however pairs (v, x) with weight $d[v, x]$ for all $x \in V$ are added to the edge set of G', so that the source vertex v can use the distance estimates that it has acquired already, in order to find better paths to other vertices.

We first construct the sets $V \supseteq S_1 \supseteq S_2 \supseteq S_3$ using our sampling scheme, and build the graphs $G_i = (V, E_i)$, where $E_i = \{(u, v) \in E : v \in ball_i(u)\}$ and also construct the sets $bunch_i(u)$, for $i = 1, 2, 3$ (see Section 2 for more details).

The Algorithm STRETCH$_{5/2}(G)$

- Initialize the table d as described above.
- Each vertex $v \in S_3$ runs Dijkstra's algorithm in the entire graph G and the table d gets updated accordingly.
** Run Steps 1-5 for 2 iterations and return the table d.

1. Each vertex u runs Dijkstra's single source shortest paths algorithm in the graph $G_1 = (V, E_1)$ that is augmented with pairs (u, x) for all $x \in V$ with weight $d[u, x]$.

   (Dijkstra's algorithm will update the entries in the row corresponding to u in the table d.)

   - Each u now updates entries corresponding to the rows of all vertices s, in the table d, where $s \in bunch_1(u) \cup bunch_2(u)$. That is, if for any $y \in V$ and $s \in bunch_1(u) \cup bunch_2(u)$ we have $d[s, u] + d[u, y] < d[s, y]$, then we set $d[s, y] = d[s, u] + d[u, y]$.

2. Each vertex $s_1 \in S_1$ runs Dijkstra's algorithm in the graph $G_2 = (V, E_2)$ that is augmented with all pairs (s_1, x) with weight $d[s_1, x]$.

   - Each $s_1 \in S_1$ updates entries corresponding to the rows of all vertices in S_2 in the table d. That is, if for any $y \in V$ and $s_2 \in S_2$ we have $d[s_2, s_1] + d[s_1, y] < d[s_2, y]$, then we set $d[s_2, y] = d[s_2, s_1] + d[s_1, y]$.

3. Each vertex $s_2 \in S_2$ runs Dijkstra's algorithm in the graph $G_3 = (V, E_3)$ augmented with all pairs (s_2, x) with weight $d[s_2, x]$.

   - Each $s_2 \in S_2$ updates entries corresponding to the rows of all vertices in S_1 in the table d. That is, if for any $y \in V$ and $s_1 \in S_1$ we have $d[s_1, s_2] + d[s_2, y] < d[s_1, y]$, then we set $d[s_1, y] = d[s_1, s_2] + d[s_2, y]$.

4. For every (u, v) store in $d[u, v]$ the minimum of $d[u, v], d[u, s] + d[s, v]$, where $s \in \cup_{i=1}^{3} bunch_i(u)$.

5. Make the table d symmetric: that is, store in $d[u, v]$ the minimum of $d[u, v]$ and $d[v, u]$.

Running Time Analysis. The expected size of S_i is $n^{1-i/4}$ for $i = 1, 2, 3$ and the expected size of E_i, the set of edges in G_i, is $O(n^{1+i/4})$ (by Proposition 2). For each $i \in \{1, 2, 3\}$ the expected size of $bunch_i(u)$ for any $u \in V$ is $O(n^{1/4})$ (by Lemma 1(i)) and the time to compute all the sets $bunch_i(u)$ is $O(mn^{1/4})$ (by Lemma 1(ii)). These facts lead to the following lemma.

Lemma 2. *The expected running time of* STRETCH$_{5/2}(G)$ *is* $O(n^{9/4})$.

3.1   Correctness of the Algorithm STRETCH$_{5/2}(G)$

Lemma 3. *For each pair* $(u, v) \in V \times V$, *we have:* $\delta(u, v) \leq d[u, v] \leq 5/2 \cdot \delta(u, v)$, *where d is the table returned by the algorithm* STRETCH$_{5/2}(G)$ *and $\delta(u, v)$ is the distance between u and v in G.*

Proof. For every u, v since $d[u, v]$ is the length of some path in G between u and v, we always have $\delta(u, v) \leq d[u, v]$. The hard part of the lemma is showing the upper bound on $d[u, v]$. For any pair of vertices u and v, let $SP(u, v)$ denote a shortest path between u and v in G. Let us first show the following claim.

Claim 1. *For any $i \in \{1, 2, 3\}$, if all the edges in $SP(u, v)$ are present in $G_{i+1} = (V, E_{i+1})$ and $ball_i(u)$ and $ball_i(v)$ do not overlap, then $d[u, v] \leq 2\delta(u, v)$.*

Proof. It is given that all the edges in $SP(u, v)$ are present in E_{i+1}. So all the edges in the path[1] $s_i(u) \rightsquigarrow u \rightsquigarrow v$ obtained by concatenating $SP(s_i(u), u)$ and $SP(u, v)$ are present in $E_{i+1} \cup E(s_i(u))$ (by Proposition 1), where $E(s_i(u))$ is the set of edges incident on $s_i(u)$. Similarly, all the edges in the path $s_i(v) \rightsquigarrow v \rightsquigarrow u$ are present in $E_{i+1} \cup E(s_i(v))$. Since every vertex $x \in S_i$ performs Dijkstra in the graph G_{i+1} augmented with $E(x)$, we have $d[s_i(u), v] \leq \delta(s_i(u), u) + \delta(u, v)$ and $d[s_i(v), u] \leq \delta(s_i(v), v) + \delta(u, v)$. Also, because $ball_i(u)$ and $ball_i(v)$ do not overlap, we have $\delta(s_i(u), u) + \delta(s_i(v), v) \leq \delta(u, v)$. Combining these inequalities, we have $\min\{\delta(u, s_i(u)) + d[s_i(u), v], \ \delta(v, s_i(v)) + d[s_i(v), u]\} \leq 2\delta(u, v)$. Step 4 in our algorithm ensures that: $d[u, v] \leq \min\{\delta(u, s_i(u)) + d[s_i(u), v], \delta(v, s_i(v)) + d[s_i(v), u]\}$. Thus $d[u, v] \leq 2\delta(u, v)$. □

Claim 1 leads to the following corollary since $E_4 = E$, the edge set of G, and E obviously contains all the edges in $SP(u, v)$.

Corollary 1. *If $ball_3(u)$ and $ball_3(v)$ do not overlap, then $d[u, v] \leq 2\delta(u, v)$.*

Now let us consider the case when $ball_1(u)$ and $ball_1(v)$ overlap.

Claim 2. *If $ball_1(u)$ and $ball_1(v)$ overlap, then $d[u, v] = \delta(u, v)$.*

Proof. We are given that $ball_1(u)$ and $ball_1(v)$ overlap. So $\delta(u, v) < \delta(u, s_1(u)) + \delta(v, s_1(v))$ and we can partition the path $SP(u, v)$ as: $SP(u, v) = u \rightsquigarrow a \rightarrow b \rightsquigarrow v$, where all the vertices in $u \rightsquigarrow a$ belong to $ball_1(u)$ and all the vertices in $b \rightsquigarrow v$ belong to $ball_1(v)$. Since the graph G_1 has the edge set $\{(x, y) \in E, y \in ball_1(x)\}$, the only edge in $SP(u, v)$ that might possibly be missing in the graph G_1 is the edge (a, b) (refer Fig. 2). In the first iteration of the ** loop, in Step 1

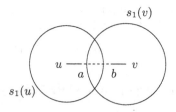

Fig. 2. $ball_1(u)$ and $ball_1(v)$ overlap

---

[1] Note that we use the symbols $x \rightsquigarrow y$ and $x \rightarrow y$ for illustrative purposes, the paths and edges here are *undirected*.

(refer Algorithm $\mathsf{STRETCH}_{5/2}(G)$), the vertex b would perform Dijkstra in G_1 augmented with the edge (a, b). Since the path $a \leadsto u$ is present in G_1, in this step, the vertex b would learn of its distance to u, i.e., $d[b, u] = \delta(u, b)$. Since the table d is made symmetric in Step 5, $d[u, b] = \delta(u, b)$ at the end of the first iteration of the ** loop.

In the second iteration of the ** loop, u would augment the "edge" (u, b) with weight $d[u, b] = \delta(u, b)$ to G_1 and since all the edges in $b \leadsto v$ are present in G_1, we have the path $u \to b \leadsto v$ in the augmented G_1. Thus u determines $d[u, v] = \delta(u, v)$. This proves the statement of Claim 2.   □

We shall assume henceforth that $ball_3(u)$ and $ball_3(v)$ overlap and $ball_1(u)$ and $ball_1(v)$ do not overlap (refer Corollary 1 and Claim 2). That leaves us with two further cases, as to whether $ball_2(u)$ and $ball_2(v)$ overlap or not. We shall call them Case 1 and Case 2.

Case 1: $ball_2(u)$ and $ball_2(v)$ do not overlap.

If all the edges in $SP(u, v)$ are present in $G_3 = (V, E_3)$, then it follows from Claim 1 that $d[u, v] \le 2\delta(u, v)$. So let us assume that some of the edges of $SP(u, v)$ are *not* present in $G_3 = (V, E_3)$.

The graph G_3 has the edge set $E_3 = \{(x, y) \in E, y \in ball_3(x)\}$. Since $ball_3(u)$ and $ball_3(v)$ overlap, the only way that some of the edges in $SP(u, v)$ are not present in E_3 is that exactly one edge in $SP(u, v)$ is missing from E_3. This edge is between the last vertex a (from the side of u) in $SP(u, v)$ that is in $ball_3(u)$ and the first vertex b in $SP(u, v)$ that is in $ball_3(v)$ (refer Fig. 3). Every other vertex and its successor in $SP(u, v)$ would either both be in $ball_3(u)$ or both be in $ball_3(v)$ and such edges have to be present in G_3.

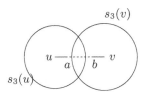

Fig. 3. $ball_3(u)$ and $ball_3(v)$ overlap but the edge (a, b) is not present in G_3

By Step 4 we know that $d[u, v]$ is at most the minimum of $\delta(u, s_3) + \delta(s_3, v)$ distances, where $s_3 \in S_3$. Hence we have the following bound on $d[u, v]$.

$$d[u, v] \le \delta(u, s_3(a)) + \delta(s_3(a), v) \tag{1}$$
$$\le \delta(u, v) + 2\delta(a, s_3(a)) \tag{2}$$
$$\le \delta(u, v) + 2w(a, b). \tag{3}$$

Inequality (3) follows from inequality (2) because the edge (a, b) is missing from $ball_3(a)$. We shall show that we also have the following inequalities.

$$d[u, v] \le \delta(u, v) + 2\delta(u, a) + 2\delta(u, s_2(u)) \quad \text{and} \tag{4}$$
$$d[u, v] \le \delta(u, v) + 2\delta(v, b) + 2\delta(v, s_2(v)). \tag{5}$$

Adding inequalities (3), (4), and (5), we get the following inequality:

$$3d[u,v] \leq 5\delta(u,v) + 2\delta(u,s_2(u)) + 2\delta(v,s_2(v))$$
$$\leq 7\delta(u,v)$$

since $\delta(u,s_2(u)) + \delta(v,s_2(v)) \leq \delta(u,v)$ because $ball_2(u)$ and $ball_2(v)$ do not overlap (by the definition of Case 1). Thus we have $d[u,v] \leq 7/3 \cdot \delta(u,v)$. So all that is left here is to prove inequalities (4) and (5).

If $s_2(u) \notin bunch_2(a)$, then we have $\delta(a,s_3(a)) \leq \delta(a,s_2(u)) \leq \delta(a,u) + \delta(u,s_2(u))$. Substituting this in inequality (2), we get inequality (4). So let us assume that $s_2(u) \in bunch_2(a)$. Then in the second iteration of the ** loop, in Step 1, the vertex a updates the entry $d[s_2(u),b]$ to at most $d[s_2(u),a] + w(a,b)$ since $s_2(u) \in bunch_2(a)$. We already have $d[s_2(u),a] \leq \delta(s_2(u),u) + \delta(u,a)$ since the path $s_2(u) \rightsquigarrow u \rightsquigarrow a$ is in the augmented G_3. Thus after Step 1 in the second iteration of the ** loop, we have $d[s_2(u),b] \leq \delta(s_2(u),a) + w(a,b)$. In Step 3, $s_2(u)$ performs Dijkstra in G_3 augmented with the "edge" $(s_2(u),b)$ with weight at most $d[s_2(u),b]$. Since all the edges of $SP(b,v)$ are in G_3, we have $d[s_2(u),v] \leq \delta(s_2(u),u) + \delta(u,v)$. Since $d[u,v] \leq \delta(u,s_2(u)) + d[s_2(u),v]$, we get $d[u,v] \leq 2\delta(u,s_2(u)) + \delta(u,v)$. This implies inequality (4). The proof of inequality (5) is analogous to the proof of inequality (4). This finishes Case 1.

Case 2: $ball_2(u)$ and $ball_2(v)$ overlap.

This case is further split into 2 cases: CASE(I), where all the edges in $SP(u,v)$ are present in $G_3 = (V,E_3)$ but not all these edges are in $G_2 = (V,E_2)$ and CASE (II), where some of the edges in $SP(u,v)$ are not present in $G_3 = (V,E_3)$. Due to lack of space, we omit the analysis of Case 2 here and refer the reader to the full version of the paper [11].

This finishes the proof of Lemma 3.   □

Lemma 3 and Lemma 2 yield Theorem 1, stated in Section 1. Note that in the proof of Lemma 3, we show a stretch of at most 7/3 in all cases, except in CASE(II) of Case 2, where we show a stretch of 5/2.

4   All-Pairs Stretch $(2 + \epsilon)$ Distances

Let $\epsilon > 0$ be any given parameter. In this section we present our algorithm STRETCH$_{2+\epsilon}(G)$ which takes as input an undirected graph $G = (V,E)$ with a weight function $w : E \rightarrow \mathbb{Q}^+$ and computes an $n \times n$ table d that stores all-pairs stretch $(2 + \epsilon)$ distances. In algorithm STRETCH$_{2+\epsilon}(G)$ we augment the algorithm STRETCH$_{5/2}$ of the previous section with some more computation so that in the new algorithm we get a stretch of at most $2 + \epsilon$. Recall that we assumed that all edge weights are positive. Let us now scale the edge weights, if necessary, so that the smallest edge weight is 1 and let W be the largest edge weight.

We will use our earlier sampling method to obtain the sets $V = S_0 \supseteq S_1 \supseteq S_2 \supseteq S_3 \supseteq S_4 = \emptyset$, except that we wish to always bound the size of S_1 by $O(n^{3/4})$ here. This bound on $|S_1|$ will be used in our running time analysis. Hence, after sampling each vertex of V independently with probability $n^{-1/4}$ to construct the set S_1, if the size of S_1 is larger than $2n^{3/4}$, then we discard this sampling and sample afresh once again. The expected number of such trials till we construct a set S_1 of size $O(n^{3/4})$ is $O(1)$. The set S_2, as earlier, is obtained by sampling vertices in S_1 with probability $n^{-1/4}$ and the set S_3 is obtained by sampling vertices in S_2 with probability $n^{-1/4}$.

The Algorithm STRETCH$_{2+\epsilon}(G)$

1. Call algorithm STRETCH$_{5/2}(G)$. An $n \times n$ table d is returned.
2. Build the sequence of matrices $M_1, M_2, \ldots, M_k$, where $k = \lceil \log_{1+\epsilon/2}(5/2 \cdot nW) \rceil$. Each M_i is a 0-1 matrix of dimension $n \times |S_1|$ which is defined as: for each $u \in V$ and $x \in S_1$

$$M_i[u, x] = 1 \text{ iff } (1 + \epsilon/2)^{i-1} \leq d[u, x] \leq (1 + \epsilon/2)^i.$$

   The value $d[u, x]$ is looked-up from the table d returned by STRETCH$_{5/2}(G)$ in Step 1.
3. For each $(i, j) \in \{1, \ldots, k\} \times \{1, \ldots, k\}$ do:
   – compute the $n \times n$ "Boolean product witness matrix" W_{ij} corresponding to the Boolean product matrix $M_i M_j^T$. That is, for each $(u, v) \in V \times V$:

$$W_{ij}[u, v] = \begin{cases} s & \text{for some } s \text{ such that } M_i[u, s] = 1 \text{ and } M_j[s, v] = 1 \\ 0 & \text{if there is no such } s. \end{cases}$$

   That is, if $M_i M_j^T[u, v] = 1$, then the entry $W_{ij}[u, v] = s$ is a *witness* for $M_i M_j^T[u, v]$ being 1.
4. For each pair $(u, v) \in V \times V$ do:
   – for each $(i, j) \in \{1, \ldots, k\} \times \{1, \ldots, k\}$ do:
     If $W_{ij}(u, v) \neq 0$ (call it x) and $d[u, x] + d[x, v] < d[u, v]$ then set $d[u, v] = d[u, x] + d[x, v]$.
5. Return the table d.

The problem of computing a Boolean product witness matrix is well-studied and [12] contains the description and analysis of such an algorithm. In the above algorithm the step whose time complexity is the most difficult to analyze is Step 3. We know that $|S_1|$ is $O(n^{3/4})$. It can be shown (see [12] for the details) that the algorithm for computing W_{ij} has expected running time $\tilde{O}(C(n))$, where $C(n)$ is the time taken to multiply an $n \times n^{3/4}$ matrix with an $n^{3/4} \times n$ matrix. Here we will use the following result.

Proposition 3 (Huang and Pan ([10] Section 8.2)). *Multiplying an $n \times n^\beta$ matrix with an $n^\beta \times n$ matrix for $0.294 \leq \beta \leq 1$ takes time $O(n^\alpha)$, where $\alpha = \frac{2(1-\beta)+(\beta-0.294)\omega}{0.706}$, and $\omega < 2.376$ is the best exponent of multiplying two $n \times n$ matrices.*

Substituting $\beta = 3/4$ in Proposition 3 yields $C(n)$ is $O(n^{2.243})$. So computing W_{ij} takes expected $\tilde{O}(n^{2.243})$ time. The entire expected running time of Step 3 is $\tilde{O}(k^2 \cdot n^{2.243})$, where $k = O(\log nW/\epsilon)$, W is the largest edge weight. It is reasonable to assume that all edge weights are polynomial in n, since we always assumed that arithmetic on these values takes unit time. Then the expected running time of this step then is $\tilde{O}(n^{2.243}/\epsilon^2)$, which is $O(n^{9/4})$ if ϵ is a constant. The call to $\mathsf{STRETCH}_{5/2}(G)$ takes expected $O(n^{9/4})$ time and thus the expected running time of the algorithm $\mathsf{STRETCH}_{2+\epsilon}(G)$ is $\tilde{O}(n^{2.243} \log W/\epsilon^2) + O(n^{9/4})$ which is $O(n^{9/4})$ when edge weights are polynomial in n and $\epsilon > 0$ is a constant.

4.1   Correctness of the Algorithm $\mathsf{STRETCH}_{2+\epsilon}(G)$

The following lemma shows the correctness of our algorithm.

Lemma 4. *For every $u, v \in V$, the estimate $d[u, v]$ computed by the algorithm $\mathsf{STRETCH}_{2+\epsilon}(G)$ satisfies: $\delta(u, v) \leq d[u, v] \leq (2 + \epsilon)\delta(u, v)$.*

Proof. Since $d[u, v]$ is always the length of some path in G between u and v, we have $\delta(u, v) \leq d[u, v]$. Now we show the harder part, that is, the upper bound claimed on $d[u, v]$. Recall from Claim 2 that if $ball_1(u)$ and $ball_1(v)$ overlap, then $d[u, v] = \delta(u, v)$. So let us assume henceforth that $ball_1(u)$ and $ball_1(v)$ do not overlap. We can show the following claim. (Due to lack of space, we omit the proof of Claim 3 here and refer the reader to [11].)

Claim 3. *If $ball_1(u)$ and $ball_1(v)$ do not overlap, then some vertex $s \in S_1$ satisfies $d[s, u] + d[s, v] \leq 2\delta(u, v)$.*

The above claim immediately shows a stretch of $2 + \epsilon$ of the distance estimate d computed. If $s = u$ or $s = v$ (which might happen if u or v is in S_1) then the above claim implies that $d[u, v] \leq 2\delta(u, v)$ which is a stretch of just 2 of the distance estimate computed. Hence let us assume that s is neither u nor v. So $1 \leq \delta(s, u) \leq nW$ which implies that $1 \leq d[s, u] \leq 5/2nW$. Since k has been chosen such that $(1 + \epsilon/2)^k \leq 5/2nW$, it follows that there exist i, j where $1 \leq i, j \leq k$ such that $(1 + \epsilon/2)^{i-1} \leq d[s, u] \leq (1 + \epsilon/2)^i$ and $(1 + \epsilon/2)^{j-1} \leq d[s, v] \leq (1 + \epsilon/2)^j$. Thus Boolean product witness matrix for $M_i M_j^T$ would compute the above witness $s \in S_1$ or some other $s' \in S_1$ which has to satisfy $(1 + \epsilon/2)^{i-1} \leq d[s', u] < (1 + \epsilon/2)^i$ and $(1 + \epsilon/2)^{j-1} \leq d[s', v] < (1 + \epsilon/2)^j$. This implies that

$$d[u, s'] + d[s', v] \leq (1 + \epsilon/2)(d[u, s] + d[s, v])$$
$$\leq (2 + \epsilon)\delta(u, v).$$

Step 4 ensures that $d[u, v] \leq d[u, s'] + d[s', v]$ which shows a stretch of at most $2 + \epsilon$ of the distance estimate computed.   □

Lemma 4 and the bound on the running time of this algorithm shown in the previous section complete the proof of Theorem 2 stated in Section 1.

5   Conclusions

In this paper we gave a combinatorial algorithm with expected running time $O(n^{9/4})$ to compute all-pairs stretch $5/2$ distances in a weighted undirected graph on n vertices. We then improved this algorithm, with the help of a subroutine for witnessing a Boolean product matrix, to compute all-pairs stretch $2 + \epsilon$ distances for any $\epsilon > 0$. The expected running time of the improved algorithm is $O(n^{9/4})$ assuming that all edge weights are polynomial in n and ϵ is a constant. An open question is to obtain faster algorithms for these problems.

Acknowledgments. I thank Surender Baswana for his helpful comments and the referees for their detailed reviews and comments.

References

1. Aingworth, D., Chekuri, C., Indyk, P., Motwani, R.: Fast estimation of diameter and shortest paths(without matrix multiplication). SIAM Journal on Computing 28, 1167–1181 (1999)
2. Awerbuch, B., Berger, B., Cowen, L., Peleg, D.: Near-linear time construction of sparse neighborhood covers. SIAM Journal on Computing 28, 263–277 (1998)
3. Baswana, S., Goyal, V., Sen, S.: All-pairs nearly 2-approximate shortest paths in $O(n^2 \operatorname{polylog} n)$ time. In: 22nd Annual Symposium on Theoretical Aspect of Computer Science, pp. 666–679 (2005)
4. Baswana, S., Kavitha, T.: Faster algorithms for approximate distance oracles and all-pairs small stretch paths. In: 47th IEEE Symposium on Foundations of Computer Science, pp. 591–602 (2006)
5. Chan, T.: More algorithms for all-pairs shortest paths in weighted graphs. In: Proceedings of 39th Annual ACM Symposium on Theory of Computing (STOC), pp. 590–598 (2007)
6. Cohen, E.: Fast algorithms for constructing t-spanners and paths with stretch t. SIAM Journal on Computing 28, 210–236 (1998)
7. Cohen, E., Zwick, U.: All-pairs small stretch paths. Journal of Algorithms 38, 335–353 (2001)
8. Dor, D., Halperin, S., Zwick, U.: All pairs almost shortest paths. Siam Journal on Computing 29, 1740–1759 (2000)
9. Elkin, M.: Computing almost shortest paths. ACM Transactions on Algorithms (TALG) 1, 282–323 (2005)
10. Huang, X., Pan, V.Y.: Fast rectangular matrix multiplication and applications. Journal of Complexity 14, 257–299 (1998)
11. K avitha, T.: Faster Algorithms for All-Pairs Small Stretch Distances in Weighted Graphs (Full version), http://drona.csa.iisc.ernet.in/~kavitha/fst07.pdf
12. Motwani, R., Raghavan, P.: Randomized Algorithms. Cambridge University Press, New York (1995)
13. Pettie, S.: A new approach to all-pairs shortest paths on real-weighted graphs. Theoretical Computer Science 312, 47–74 (2004)
14. Thorup, M., Zwick, U.: Approximate distance oracles. Journal of Association of Computing Machinery 52, 1–24 (2005)
15. Zwick, U.: All-pairs shortest paths using bridging sets and rectangular matrix multiplication. Journal of Association of Computing Machinery 49, 289–317 (2002)

Covering Graphs with Few Complete Bipartite Subgraphs

Herbert Fleischner[1], Egbert Mujuni[2,*], Daniel Paulusma[3,**],
and Stefan Szeider[3,***]

[1] Department of Computer Science, Vienna Technical University
A-1040 Vienna, Austria
fleisch@dbai.tuwien.ac.at
[2] Mathematics Department, University of Dar es Salaam
PO Box 35062, Dar es Salaam, Tanzania
emujuni@maths.udsm.ac.tz
[3] Department of Computer Science, Durham University
Durham DH1 3LE, United Kingdom
{daniel.paulusma,stefan.szeider}@durham.ac.uk

Abstract. Given a graph and an integer k, the *biclique cover problem*
asks whether the edge-set of the given graph can be covered with at
most k bicliques (complete bipartite subgraphs); the *biclique vertex-cover
problem* asks whether the vertex-set of the given graph can be covered
with at most k bicliques. Both problems are known to be NP-complete
even if the given graph is bipartite. In this paper we investigate these two
problems in the framework of parameterized complexity: do the problems
become easier if k is assumed to be small? We show that, considering
k as the parameter, the first problem is fixed-parameter tractable, while
the second one is not fixed-parameter tractable unless P = NP.

1 Introduction

The problem of covering the edges of a graph with at most k bicliques (BICLIQUE
COVER) arises in many areas such as automata and language theory, graphs compression, artificial intelligence, biology, and flow theory [1,3]. A related problem
is BICLIQUE VERTEX-COVER where it is asked to cover the vertices of a graph
with at most k bicliques. Applications of BICLIQUE VERTEX-COVER include data
mining, e-commerce, information retrieval and network analysis [11]. Both are
computationally hard problems: BICLIQUE COVER is NP-complete and remains
NP-hard for chordal bipartite graphs [15,13]. Very recently, Heydari et al. [11]
showed that BICLIQUE VERTEX-COVER is NP-complete for bipartite graphs.

In this paper we investigate the questions of whether the problems BICLIQUE
COVER and BICLIQUE VERTEX-COVER (and variants) become easier if the given

* Research supported by International Science Programme (ISP) of Sweden, un-
  der the project "The Eastern African Universities Mathematics Programme
  (EAUMP)".
** Research supported by the EPSRC, project EP/D053633/1.
*** Research supported by the EPSRC, project EP/E001394/1.

V. Arvind and S. Prasad (Eds.): FSTTCS 2007, LNCS 4855, pp. 340–351, 2007.
© Springer-Verlag Berlin Heidelberg 2007

upper bound on the number of bicliques in the cover is assumed to be small. We undertake this investigation in the framework of parameterized complexity as developed by Downey and Fellows [6]; we give some basic background of parameterized complexity in Section 2.1. As the parameter we take the upper bound k on the number of bicliques in the cover. In principle, the problems under consideration can fall into any of the following three categories.

1. For every fixed k the problem can be solved in polynomial time where the order of the polynomial is independent of k; in this case we say that the problem is *fixed-parameter tractable*.
2. For every fixed k the problem can be solved in polynomial time but the order of the polynomial grows with k.
3. For some fixed k the problem is NP-hard.

Problems that fall into the second category can be further categorized by means of the complexity classes W[1], W[2], . . . , XP (see Section 2.1).

New Results
Our results show that the problems under consideration fall into all three of the above categories, spanning a wide range of parameterized complexities.

1. *The problem* BICLIQUE COVER *is fixed-parameter tractable.*

We show this result by *kernelization*, that is, we give an algorithm that reduces an instance of BICLIQUE COVER in polynomial time into an equivalent instance where the number of vertices is bounded in terms of the parameter k.

2. For $k \leq 2$ the problem BICLIQUE VERTEX-COVER can be solved in polynomial time for bipartite graphs.

The bound $k \leq 2$ is best possible:

3. *For every fixed $k \geq 3$ the problem* BICLIQUE VERTEX-COVER *is NP-complete and remains NP-hard for bipartite graphs.*

We establish this result by a reduction from an NP-hard variant of the list-coloring problem.

In view if the NP-hardness it makes sense to study the more restricted problem b-BICLIQUE VERTEX-COVER where the bicliques in the cover are bicliques of the from $K_{r,s}$ with $\min(r,s) \leq b$. Indeed, this restriction moves the problem from the third to the second of the above categories:

4. *For every fixed $b \geq 1$ the problem b-BICLIQUE VERTEX-COVER is W[2]-complete and remains W[2]-hard for bipartite graphs.*

2 Preliminaries

2.1 Parameterized Complexity

We give some basic background on parameterized complexity; for a detailed discussion we refer the reader to other sources [6,14]. In parameterized complexity theory, we consider the problem input as consisting of two parts; that is, a pair (I, k), where I is the main part and k (usually an integer given in unary) is the parameter. We say a problem is *fixed parameter tractable* if an instance (I, k) can be solved in time $O(f(k)n^c)$, where f denotes a computable function and c denotes a constant that is independent of the parameter k. Therefore, such an algorithm may provide an efficient solution to the problem if the parameter is reasonably small. We denote by FPT the class of all fixed-parameter tractable decision problems.

Let P be a parameterized problem. A reduction to a problem *kernel* (or *kernelization*) means to replace an instance (I, k) of P with a reduced instance (I', k') of P (called *problem kernel*) such that (i) $k' \leq k$ and $|I'| \leq g(k)$ for some computable function g; (ii) the reduction from (I, k) to (I', k') is computable in polynomial time; (iii) $(I, k) \in P$ if and only if $(I', k') \in P$. It is well known that a parameterized problem is fixed-parameter tractable if and only if it is kernelizable [10,12,14].

Parameterized complexity offers a completeness theory, similar to the theory of NP-completeness, that allows the accumulation of strong theoretical evidence that a parameterized problem is not fixed-parameter tractable. This completeness theory is based on a hierarchy of complexity classes $W[1], W[2], \ldots, XP$. Each class is the equivalence class of certain parameterized satisfiability problems under fpt-reductions. An *fpt-reduction* from problem P to problem P' is an algorithm that computes for every instance (I, k) of P an instance (I', k') of P' in time $f(k)|I|^c$ such that $k' \leq g(k)$ and $(I, k) \in P$ if and only if $(I', k') \in P'$, where f, g are computable functions and c is a constant. Clearly, if P and P' are parameterized problems and if P' belongs to some complexity class W, and if there is an fpt-reduction from P to P', then P also belongs to W. The class XP consists of parameterized decision problems P such that for each instance (I, k), it can be decided in $O(f(k)|I|^{g(k)})$ time whether $(I, k) \in P$, where f, g are computable functions depending only k. That is, XP consists of parameterized decision problems which can be solved in polynomial time if the parameter is considered as a constant. The above classes form the chain FPT $\subseteq$ W[1] $\subseteq$ W[2] $\subseteq$ ... $\subseteq$ XP where all inclusions are conjectured to be proper; FPT $\neq$ XP is known [6,7].

2.2 Graphs and Covers

For graph theoretic terminology not defined in this paper, we refer the reader to standard text books [2,5]. In this paper we consider connected simple graphs $G = (V, E)$. The set of neighbors of a vertex v is denoted by $N(v)$, and we set $N(T) = \bigcup_{v \in T} N(v)$ for $T \subset V$. If $V' \subseteq V$, we denote by $G[V']$ the subgraph of G induced by V'. We write $G = ((V_1, V_2), E)$ for a bipartite graph $G = (V, E)$ having the vertex bipartition $V = V_1 \cup V_2$. A *biclique* of graph G is a complete connected bipartite subgraph of G. Note that a biclique is not necessarily vertex induced. A biclique $K = ((U_1, U_2), E)$ is *non-trivial* if it contains more than one vertex (that is, if both U_1 and U_2 are non-empty). A biclique $K = ((U_1, U_2), E)$ is a *star centered at a vertex u* if $U_1 = \{u\}$ or $U_2 = \{u\}$.

Definition 1. *Let G be a graph. A set S of subgraphs of G is a* cover *of G if every edge of G is contained in at least one of the subgraphs in S. The set S is a* vertex-cover *of G if every vertex of G is contained in at least one of the subgraphs in S. If all subgraphs in S are bicliques, then we speak of a* biclique cover *or* biclique vertex-cover, *respectively.*

We now give formal definitions of the problems we are investigating.

BICLIQUE COVER
Instance: A graph $G = (V, E)$ and a positive integer k.
Parameter: The integer k.
Question: Does G have a biclique cover of size at most k?

BICLIQUE VERTEX-COVER
Instance: A graph G and positive integer k.
Parameter: The integer k.
Question: Does G have a biclique vertex-cover of size at most k?

Remark 2. Let BICLIQUE PARTITION denote the variant of BICLIQUE VERTEX-COVER where the bicliques in the cover are required to be mutually vertex-disjoint. The (non-parameterized version) of BICLIQUE PARTITION for bipartite graphs was considered by Heydari et al. [11]. It is easy to see that one can always make the bicliques of a biclique vertex-cover disjoint without increasing the size of the cover. Hence the problems BICLIQUE VERTEX-COVER and BICLIQUE PARTITION are equivalent.

3 Biclique Covers

As mentioned in the introduction, the decision problem corresponding to BICLIQUE COVER is NP-complete even for bipartite graphs [15]. In this section we establish fixed-parameter tractability.

We start with simple reduction rules that can be easily applied to simplify an instance of the problem.

Rule 1. Given an instance (G, k) of BICLIQUE COVER and a vertex $v \in V(G)$ of degree 0, then (G, k) is a yes-instance if and only if $(G - v, k)$ is a yes-instance.

Rule 2. Given an instance (G, k) of BICLIQUE COVER and a vertex $v \in V(G)$ of degree 1. Let w be the neighbor of v. Then (G, k) is a yes-instance if and only if $(G - \{v, w\}, k - 1)$ is a yes-instance.

Rule 3. Given an instance (G, k) of BICLIQUE COVER and a pair of non-adjacent vertices u, v such that $N(u) = N(v)$, then (G, k) is a yes-instance if and only if $(G - \{v\}, k)$ is a yes-instance.

Clearly, the following is true.

Lemma 3. *Rules 1-3 are correct and can be applied in polynomial time.*

We say that an instance (G, k) of BICLIQUE COVER is *reduced* (with respect to Rules 1-3) if these rules cannot be applied.

Theorem 4 (Kernelization). *If (G, k) is a reduced yes-instance of* BICLIQUE COVER *then G has at most 2^{2k} vertices. Furthermore, if G is bipartite, then it has at most 2^{k+1} vertices.*

To establish the above theorem we need the following lemma.

Lemma 5. *Let k be a positive integer and G a complete graph on $m > 2^k$ vertices. Then every biclique cover of G has more than k elements.*

Proof. Let $\rho(G)$ denote the cardinality of a smallest biclique cover of G. We proceed by induction on k. The lemma clearly holds for $k = 1$ since in that case G contains a triangle and so $\rho(G) > 1$. Now let $k \geq 1$ and assume that the lemma is true for all $l \leq k$. Let G be a complete graph with $m > 2^{k+1}$ vertices. Let $\mathcal{S}$ be a biclique cover of G with $|\mathcal{S}| = \rho(G)$. Choose a biclique $B = ((U, V), E_B) \in \mathcal{S}$. We assume, w.l.o.g., that $|U| \geq |V|$; hence $|U| > 2^k$. Define

$$\mathcal{S}' := \mathcal{S} - \{B\},$$
$$\mathcal{S}'' := \{ B' = ((U', V'), E_{B'}) : B' \in \mathcal{S}' \wedge U \not\subseteq U' \wedge U \not\subseteq V' \},$$
$$\mathcal{S}_U := \{ B'' - V : B'' \in \mathcal{S}'' \}.$$

Since U is an independent set in B and G is complete, there must be a biclique $B' = ((U', V'), E_{B'}) \in \mathcal{S}'$ and $x, y \in U$ such that $x \in U', y \in V'$. Therefore,

$$\mathcal{S}'' \neq \emptyset, \ \mathcal{S}_U \neq \emptyset.$$

Note that $\mathcal{S}'$ covers the edges of $G[U]$ since $E(B) \cap E(G[U]) = \emptyset$. Thus, $\mathcal{S}_U$ is a biclique cover of $G[U]$. Therefore, since $G[U]$ is a complete graph and $|U| > 2^k$ we have

$$\rho(G) = |\mathcal{S}| = |\mathcal{S}'| + 1 \geq |\mathcal{S}''| + 1 = |\mathcal{S}_U| + 1 \geq \rho(G[U]) + 1 > k + 1;$$

the last inequality holding by induction. The result now follows.   □

Proof (of Theorem 4). Suppose the instance (G, k) of BICLIQUE COVER is reduced and G has a biclique cover $\{C_1, \ldots, C_l\}$ of size $l \leq k$. We will argue similarly as Gramm et al. [8]. We assign to each vertex $v \in V(G)$ a binary vector $\vec{b}_v$ of length l where the i-th component $b_{v,i} = 1$ if and only if v is contained in the biclique C_i. Since (G, k) is reduced, each vertex belongs to at least one biclique. Consider an arbitrary but fixed binary vector $\vec{b}$ of length l. Let V_b be the set of vertices of G such that $\vec{b}_u = \vec{b}$ for all $u \in V_b$. Suppose V_b contains non-adjacent distinct vertices x, y. Since $\vec{b}_x = \vec{b}_y$, it follows that x and y belong to the same bicliques. Having supposed $xy \notin E(G)$ it follows that x, y belong to the same class in the vertex bipartition of C_i whenever $b_{x,i} = b_{y,i} = 1$, which implies that $N_G(x) = N_G(y)$ since $\mathcal{C}$ covers G. Since (G, k) is reduced, we have obtained a contradiction. Thus we conclude $xy \in E(G)$ if $x, y \in V_b$ and $x \neq y$. This implies that $G[V_b]$ is a complete subgraph. Consequently, if G is bipartite, then $|V_b| \leq 2$. We claim that $|V_b| \leq 2^l$ holds in the general non-bipartite case. Suppose $|V_b| > 2^l$. Then by Lemma 5, the edges of $G[V_b]$ must be covered by at least $l + 1$ bicliques, contradicting the assumption that G has a biclique cover with l elements. Therefore, for a fixed binary vector of length l, there are at most 2^l vertices of G which are associated with this vector. Since there are 2^l binary vectors of length l, we conclude that G has at most $2^l \cdot 2^l$ vertices, and at most 2^{l+1} vertices if G is bipartite. □

The following is a direct consequence of Lemma 3 and Theorem 4.

Corollary 6. BICLIQUE COVER *is fixed-parameter tractable.*

Remark 7. As can be seen from the proof of Theorem 4, Rule 2 has no impact there (i.e., Theorem 4 remains true if we restrict the reductions to applying Rules 1 and 3 only). However, we included Rule 2 because it may be used to reduce the size of the input graph.

4 Biclique Vertex-Covers

4.1 NP-Hardness

We now proceed to show that BICLIQUE VERTEX-COVER is NP-hard for fixed $k \geq 3$, even if the given graph is bipartite. We present a polynomial-time reduction from the following problem.

LIST-COLORING
Instance: A graph $G = (V, E)$ and a mapping L that assigns to every $v \in V$ a list $L(v)$ of colors allowed for v.
Question: Is there a proper coloring c of $V(G)$ such that $c(v) \in L(v)$ for each $v \in V$?

If such a coloring c exists, then we call c an *L-coloring of G*, and we say that G is *L-colorable*. If the number of available colors $k = |\bigcup_{v \in V} L(v)|$ is fixed, then the problem is called k-LIST-COLORING. This problem is known to be NP-complete for bipartite graphs and $k \geq 3$ [9].
    Our reduction proceeds as follows. Let (G, L) be an instance of k-LIST-COLORING where $G = ((U, V), E)$ is a bipartite graph. We assume that $\bigcup_{v \in V} L(v) = \{1, 2, \ldots, k\}$. We construct a graph H as follows:

1. Let $\overline{G}$ be the bipartite complement of G; i.e., $V(\overline{G}) = V(G) = U \cup V$ and $E(\overline{G}) = \{ uv : u \in U, v \in V, uv \notin E(G) \}$.
2. For $u_i, v_i \notin V(\overline{G})$, let (u_i, v_i), $i = 1, \ldots, k$, be k disjoint copies of $K_{1,1}$.
3. Now take $\overline{G}$ and the k copies of $K_{1,1}$. For every $x \in U$ and $i \in \{1, \ldots, k\}$, if $i \in L(x)$ add an edge xv_i. For every $y \in V$ and $i \in \{1, \ldots, k\}$, if $i \in L(y)$ add an edge yu_i. Call the resulting graph H. Thus, H is a bipartite graph containing $\overline{G}$ as a proper subgraph (note that $V(H) = (U \cup \{ u_i : 1 \leq i \leq k \}) \cup (V \cup \{ v_i : 1 \leq i \leq k \}))$.

Clearly H can be constructed in polynomial time and $|V(H)| = |V(G)| + 2k$. Furthermore, the following can be established easily.

Lemma 8. *G is L-colorable if and only if $V(H)$ can be covered by k bicliques.*

For every fixed k the problem BICLIQUE VERTEX-COVER belongs to NP. Since, as mentioned above, k-LIST-COLORING is NP-complete in bipartite graphs for $k \geq 3$, the above reduction yields following result.

Theorem 9. BICLIQUE VERTEX-COVER *is NP-complete for fixed $k \geq 3$. This also holds if only bipartite graphs are considered.*

Corollary 10. BICLIQUE VERTEX-COVER *is not fixed-parameter tractable unless* P $=$ NP.

Remark 11. Theorem 9 implies that BICLIQUE VERTEX-COVER is complete for the parameterized complexity class para-NP which was introduced by Flum and Grohe [7].

4.2   Polynomial Cases

Next we study the question whether $k \geq 3$ is an optimal bound for the NP-hardness of BICLIQUE VERTEX-COVER. The case $k = 1$ is trivially solvable in polynomial time, as a graph G has a biclique vertex-cover consisting of a single biclique if and only if the complement graph $\bar{G}$ is disconnected. The case $k = 2$ is still open. However, we can establish polynomial-time results for a special graph class that includes all bipartite graphs.

For this purpose we transform BICLIQUE VERTEX-COVER for $k = 2$ into an equivalent problem involving graph homomorphisms. We need the following definitions. Let G, H be two simple graphs. A mapping $h : V(G) \to V(H)$ is a *homomorphism from G to the reflexive closure of H* if for every edge $uv \in E(G)$ we have either $h(u) = h(v)$ or $h(u)h(v) \in E(H)$. The homomorphism h is *vertex-surjective* if for each $c \in V(H)$ there is some $v \in V(G)$ with $h(v) = c$. Let C_k denote the cycle on k vertices $c_1, \ldots, c_k$ where c_i and c_j are adjacent if and only if $|i - j| \equiv 1 \pmod{k}$. We make the following observation, which is easy to see.

Observation 12. *A graph G has a biclique vertex-cover consisting of two non-trivial vertex-disjoint bicliques if and only if there is a vertex-surjective homomorphism from the complement graph $\bar{G}$ to the reflexive closure of C_4.*

A *dominating edge* of a graph G is an edge xy with $N(x) \cup N(y) = V(G)$.

Lemma 13. *We can check in polynomial time whether a given graph that has a dominating edge allows a vertex-surjective homomorphism to the reflexive closure of C_4.*

Proof. Let $F = (V, E)$ be a graph with dominating edge xy. Clearly, $\{x, y\}$ will be mapped to two different vertices of C_4 by any vertex-surjective homomorphism h from F to the reflexive closure of C_4.

Suppose such a homomorphism h exists. If h maps a vertex v to c_i, we say that v has *color* i. Then we may, w.l.o.g., assume that x has got color 1 and y has got color 2. We will show how we can check in polynomial time whether this precoloring of F can be extended to a full coloring of F that corresponds to a vertex-surjective homomorphism from F to the reflexive closure of C_4. Obviously, such a coloring uses exactly four different colors 1,2,3,4 such that neither color pair $(1,3)$ nor $(2,4)$ is used on the endvertices of an edge.

The following terminology is useful. We call a set $U \subseteq V$ *colored* if every vertex in U has received a color. In a precoloring, we denote the set of all colored neighbors of a vertex u by $N^c(u)$, and we call a colored set U j-*chromatic* if the number of different colors in U equals j.

We proceed as follows. First we guess an uncolored vertex s not adjacent to x that we assign color 3 and an uncolored vertex t not adjacent to y that we assign color 4. Note that the number of guesses is bounded by $O(|V(F)|^2)$. We apply the following rule as long as possible: if there exists an uncolored vertex u with 3-chromatic $N^c(u)$ then u can only get one possible color, which we then assign to u. Afterwards we check if there exists a vertex w with a 4-chromatic colored neighbor set. If so, then pair (s,t) was a wrong guess, because we cannot assign an appropriate color to w. We then guess another pair (s',t') that we assign color 3, 4 respectively, and so on.

Suppose that for a particular pair (s,t) we have applied the above rule as long as possible and such a vertex w (with 4-chromatic $N^c(w)$) does not exist. Since xy is a dominating edge, we can partition the uncolored vertices of F into the following sets: sets $U_{i,j}$ consisting of vertices adjacent to vertices with color i and j for $(i,j) \in \{(1,2),(1,3),(1,4),(2,3),(2,4)\}$ and sets U_i consisting of vertices *only* adjacent to color i for $i = 1,2$. Then we extend the precoloring of F by assigning color 1 to the vertices in $U_{1,2} \cup U_{1,4} \cup U_{2,4} \cup U_1 \cup U_2$ and color 2 to the vertices in $U_{1,3} \cup U_{2,3}$. This proves Lemma 13. $\square$

Theorem 1. BICLIQUE VERTEX-COVER *for fixed* $k = 2$ *can be solved in polynomial time for the class of graphs that do not contain a pair of nonadjacent vertices with a common neighbor. In particular,* BICLIQUE VERTEX-COVER *for fixed* $k = 2$ *can be solved in polynomial time for bipartite graphs.*

Proof. The first statement immediately follows from Observation 12 and Lemma 13. So, let G be a bipartite graph with bipartition classes A, B. If $N_G(a) = B$ for some $a \in A$ and $N_G(b) = A$ for some $b \in B$, then we are immediately done. Suppose G has two nonadjacent vertices $x \in A$ and $y \in B$. Then xy is a dominating edge in $\bar{G}$. Again we apply Observation 12 together with Lemma 13. $\square$

Remark 14. A homomorphism f from a graph G to a graph H is called *edge-surjective* or a *compaction* if for each $xy \in E(H)$ there is some $uv \in E(G)$ with $f(u)f(v) = xy$. The problem that asks whether there exists a compaction from a given graph to the reflexive closure of C_4 is known to be NP-complete [16].

Remark 15. Of related interest is the concept of H-*partitions* as studied by Dantas et al. [4]. Let H be a fixed graph with four vertices $h_1, \ldots, h_4$. An

H-partition of a graph $G = (V, E)$ is a partition of V into four *nonempty* sets $X_1, \ldots, X_4$ such that whenever $h_i h_j$ is an edge of H, then G contains the biclique $K = ((X_i, X_j), E_k)$. H-PARTITION denotes the problem of deciding whether a given graph admits an H-partition. Evidently, BICLIQUE VERTEX-COVER for $k = 2$ is equivalent to the problem $2K_2$-PARTITION where $2K_2$ denotes the graph on four vertices with two independent edges. $H = 2K_2$ is the only case for which the complexity of H-PARTITION is not known (cf.[4]). All other cases are known to be solvable in polynomial time.

4.3 Bounding One Side of the Bicliques

In the following we study the question of whether BICLIQUE VERTEX-COVER becomes easier when the number of vertices in one of the two classes of the vertex bipartition of bicliques is bounded. For a complete bipartite $K_{r,s}$, define $\beta(K_{r,s}) = \min\{r, s\}$. Clearly $\beta(K) = 1$ if and only if K is a star. A *b-bounded biclique* is a biclique K such that $\beta(K) \leq b$. A *b-biclique vertex-cover* of a graph G is a set of b-bounded bicliques of G such that each vertex of G is contained in one of these bicliques.

Let b be a fixed positive integer. We consider the following parameterized problem.

> b-BICLIQUE VERTEX-COVER
> *Instance:* A graph G and a positive integer k.
> *Parameter:* The integer k.
> *Question:* Does there exist a b-biclique vertex-cover S of G such that $|S| \leq k$?

It is not difficult to see that b-BICLIQUE VERTEX-COVER is in XP. The analysis of a straightforward search algorithm gives the following observation.

Observation 16. *Given a graph G with n vertices and an integer k we can check in time $O(M_{b,k} n^{bk})$ whether G has a b-biclique vertex-cover of size at most k. Here $M_{b,k}$ denotes the number of integer solutions of the equation*

$$i_1 + \ldots + i_b = k, \ 0 \leq i_j \leq k, \ j = 1, \ldots, b.$$

The following parameterized hitting set problem is W[2]-complete [6].

> HITTING SET
> *Instance:* A set $S = \{s_1, \ldots, s_n\}$, a collection $C = \{C_1, \ldots, C_m\}$, where $C_i \subseteq S$, $i = 1, \ldots, m$, and a positive integer k.
> *Parameter:* The integer k.
> *Question:* Does there exist a subset $H \subseteq S$ with $|H| \leq k$, such that $H \cap C_i \neq \emptyset$ for $i = 1, \ldots, m$?

The following result follows from the two lemmas below.

Theorem 17. *b-BICLIQUE VERTEX-COVER is W[2]-complete for every $b \geq 1$. This also holds if only bipartite graphs are considered.*

Lemma 18. *There is an fpt-reduction from HITTING SET to b-BICLIQUE VERTEX-COVER for bipartite graphs.*

Proof. Let $I = ((S, C), k)$ be an instance of HITTING SET, where $S = \{s_1, \ldots, s_n\}$ and $C = \{C_1, \ldots, C_m\}$. We transform I into an instance of b-BICLIQUE VERTEX-COVER as follows: First construct a bipartite graph $G = ((U, V), E)$ by setting $U = \{u_1, \ldots, u_n\}$, $V = \{v_1, \ldots, v_m\}$ and letting $u_i v_j \in E(G)$ if and only if $s_i \in C_j$. Now add two new vertices z and z' to G, such that z is adjacent to every u_i and z' is adjacent to z only. Finally, for each vertex v_j add bk new vertices $v_{j_1}, \ldots, v_{j_{bk}}$ and add edges such that $N(v_{j_d}) := N(v_j)$, $d = 1, \ldots, bk$. Call the resulting graph G'. Clearly, G' is bipartite. Let U', V' be the bipartition of $V(G')$, where $z \in V'$ and $z' \in U' \supset U$.

We show that (S, C) has a hitting set of size at most k if and only if G' has a b-biclique vertex-cover of size at most $k + 1$.

Let H be a hitting set of (S, C) with $|H| \leq k$. We assume, w.l.o.g., that H is minimal. Set $U^* := \{u_i : s_i \in H\}$. Clearly, $U^* \subseteq U \subset U'$. We construct recursively a star vertex-cover $\mathcal{S}$ of G' such that the centers of the stars in $\mathcal{S}$ are the elements of $U^* \cup \{z\}$, as follows. Set $U^{**} := U^*$ and $\mathcal{S} := \emptyset$. Repeat the following procedure as long as U^{**} is not empty.

- Choose a vertex $u \in U^{**}$.
- Define $K_u := N_{G'}(u) \cup \{u\}$. K_u induces a star centered at u in G'. Set $\mathcal{S} := \mathcal{S} \cup \{G'[K_u]\}$.
- Set $U^{**} := U^{**} - \{u\}$.

The final $\mathcal{S}$ is obtained by adding the star which consists of z and the elements of $U' - U^*$.

The vertices of G' have the following properties with respect to the elements of $\mathcal{S}$. (1) Every vertex $v \in V'$ belongs to a star centered at a vertex $u \in U^*$, since U^* corresponds to the hitting set H. (2) Every vertex of $u \in U^*$ belongs to the star centered at u. (3) The vertices in $U' - U^*$ belong to the star centered at z. Thus, $\mathcal{S}$ is a star cover of G' with $|\mathcal{S}| = |H| + 1 \leq k + 1$.

Conversely, suppose that G' has a b-biclique vertex-cover $\mathcal{T}$ of size at most $k + 1$. We assume, w.l.o.g., that $\mathcal{T}$ contains a star K_0 centered at the vertex z. Let $\mathcal{T}' := \mathcal{T} - \{K_0\}$. For a biclique $K = ((X', Y'), E_K) \in \mathcal{T}'$ we assume, w.l.o.g., that $X' \subseteq U'$ and $Y' \subseteq V'$. Define

$$T' := \bigcup_{K=((X',Y'),E_K)\in\mathcal{T}'} \{X' : |X'| \leq b\}.$$

We claim that $N_G(T') = V$. Suppose to the contrary that there is a vertex $v_j \in V - N_G(T')$. Consider the set $V_j = \{v_j, v_{j_1}, \ldots, v_{j_{bk}}\}$. Since $v_j \notin N_G(T')$ we have $V_j \cap N_{G'}(T') = \emptyset$ because $N_G(v_j) = N_{G'}(v_j) = N_{G'}(v_{j_d})$, $d = 1, \ldots, bk$. Thus, for each biclique $K = ((X'', Y''), E_K) \in \mathcal{T}'$ containing an element $v \in V_j$, it follows that $|X''| > b$ and $|Y''| \leq b$. Thus $|\mathcal{T}'| \geq k + 1$ since $|V_j| > bk$, a contradiction. Therefore, we obtain a set $T \subseteq U$ that corresponds to a hitting set of (S, C) of size at most k by including in T precisely one vertex in $T' \cap X'$ for each $K = ((X', Y'), E_K) \in \mathcal{T}'$.   □

Let G be a graph. A set $D \subseteq V(G)$ is a *dominating set* of G if every vertex of G is either in D or has a neighbor in D. The following parameterized problem is know to be W[2]-complete [6].

DOMINATING SET
Instance: A graph G and a positive integer k.
Parameter: The integer k.
Question: Does there exist a dominating set of G of size at most k?

Lemma 19. *There is an fpt-reduction from b-BICLIQUE VERTEX-COVER to* DOMINATING SET.

Proof. Consider an instance (G, k) of b-BICLIQUE VERTEX-COVER. For a set $S \subseteq V(G)$ let $S' \subseteq V(G)$ denote the set of common neighbors of vertices in S, i.e., $S' = \bigcap_{v \in S} N(v)$. Furthermore, let $\mathcal{S}$ denote the set of subsets $S \subseteq V(G)$ such that with $1 \leq |S| \leq b$ and $S' \neq \emptyset$.

We construct a graph $H = (V', E')$ as follows. V' consists of two new vertices z, z' and a vertex v_S for every $S \in \mathcal{S}$. E' consists of the edge zz' and all edges $v_S w$ for $w \in S \cup S' \cup \{z\}$, $S \in \mathcal{S}$. Note that H can be constructed in polynomial time as $|\mathcal{S}| = O(n^b)$ where $n = |V(G)|$.

It is easy to verify that G has a b-biclique vertex-cover of size at most k if and only if H has a dominating set of size at most $k + 1$.   □

5   Final Remarks

We have classified the parameterized complexity of the problems BICLIQUE COVER and BICLIQUE VERTEX-COVER: the former is fixed-parameter tractable, the latter is not fixed-parameter tractable unless P = NP. It would be interesting to improve our algorithm for BICLIQUE COVER. In particular, it would be interesting to improve on the 2^{2k} kernel or to show that under plausible complexity theoretic assumptions a kernelization to a kernel of size polynomial in k is not possible. Our results for the second problem, BICLIQUE VERTEX-COVER, are negative. It would be interesting to identify special graph classes for which the problem becomes fixed-parameter tractable, and to determine the complexity of BICLIQUE VERTEX-COVER for fixed $k = 2$.

Acknowledgment

The authors thank Mike Fellows for helpful discussions.

References

1. Amilhastre, J., Vilarem, M.C., Janssen, P.: Complexity of minimum biclique cover and minimum biclique decomposition for bipartite domino-free graphs. Discr. Appl. Math. 86(2-3), 125–144 (1998)
2. Chartrand, G., Lesniak, L.: Graphs & digraphs, 4th edn. Chapman & Hall/CRC, Boca Raton, FL (2005)
3. Cornaz, D., Fonlupt, J.: Chromatic characterization of biclique covers. Discrete Math. 306(5), 495–507 (2006)

4. Dantas, S., de Figueiredo, C.M., Gravier, S., Klein, S.: Finding H-partitions efficiently. RAIRO - Theoretical Informatics and Applications 39(1), 133–144 (2005)
5. Diestel, R.: Graph Theory, 2nd edn. Graduate Texts in Mathematics, vol. 173. Springer, New York (2000)
6. Downey, R.G., Fellows, M.R.: Parameterized Complexity. In: Monographs in Computer Science, Springer, Heidelberg (1999)
7. Flum, J., Grohe, M.: Parameterized Complexity Theory. In: Texts in Theoretical Computer Science. An EATCS Series, vol. XIV, Springer, Heidelberg (2006)
8. Gramm, J., Guo, J., Hüffner, F., Niedermeier, R.: Data reduction, exact, and heuristic algorithms for clique cover. In: Proc. ALENEX 2006, SIAM, pp. 86–94 (2006)
9. Gravier, S., Kobler, D., Kubiak, W.: Complexity of list coloring problems with a fixed total number of colors. Discr. Appl. Math. 117(1-3), 65–79 (2002)
10. Guo, J., Niedermeier, R.: Invitation to data reduction and problem kernelization. ACM SIGACT News 38(2), 31–45 (2007)
11. Heydari, M.H., Morales, L., Shields Jr., C.O., Sudborough, I.H.: Computing cross associations for attack graphs and other applications. In: HICSS-40 2007. 40th Hawaii International International Conference on Systems Science, Waikoloa, Big Island, HI, USA, January 3-6, 2007, p. 270 (2007)
12. Hüffner, F., Niedermeier, R., Wernicke, S.: Techniques for practical fixed-parameter algorithms. The Computer Journal (in press, 2007) doi:10.1093/comjnl/bxm040
13. Müller, H.: On edge perfectness and classes of bipartite graphs. Discrete Math. 149(1-3), 159–187 (1996)
14. Niedermeier, R.: Invitation to Fixed-Parameter Algorithms. Oxford Lecture Series in Mathematics and its Applications, Oxford University Press, Oxford (2006)
15. Orlin, J.: Contentment in graph theory: covering graphs with cliques. Nederl. Akad. Wetensch. Proc. Ser. A 80, Indag. Math. 39(5), 406–424 (1977)
16. Vikas, N.: Computational complexity of compaction to reflexive cycles. SIAM J. Comput. 32(1), 253–280 (2002/03)

Safely Composing Security Protocols*

Véronique Cortier, Jérémie Delaitre, and Stéphanie Delaune

LORIA, CNRS & INRIA, project Cassis, Nancy, France

Abstract. Security protocols are small programs that are executed in hostile environments. Many results and tools have been developed to formally analyze the security of a protocol. However even when a protocol has been proved secure, there is absolutely no guarantee if the protocol is executed in an environment where other protocols, possibly sharing some common identities and keys like public keys or long-term symmetric keys, are executed.

In this paper, we show that whenever a protocol is secure, it remains secure even in an environment where arbitrary protocols are executed, provided each encryption contains some tag identifying each protocol, like e.g. the name of the protocol.

1   Introduction

Security protocols are small programs that aim at securing communications over a public network like the Internet. Considering the increasing size of networks and their dependence on cryptographic protocols, a high level of assurance is needed in the correctness of such protocols. The design of such protocols is difficult and error-prone; many attacks have been discovered even several years after the publication of a protocol. Consequently, there has been a growing interest in applying formal methods for validating cryptographic protocols and many results have been obtained. The main advantage of the formal approach is its relative simplicity which makes it amenable to automated analysis. For example, the secrecy preservation is co-NP-complete for a bounded number of sessions [19], and decidable for an unbounded number of sessions under some additional restrictions (e.g. [2,5,20]). Many tools have also been developed to automatically verify cryptographic protocols (e.g. [4]).

However even when a protocol has been proved secure for an unbounded number of sessions, against a fully active adversary that can intercept, block and send new messages, there is absolutely no guarantee if the protocol is executed in an environment where other protocols, possibly sharing some common identities and keys like public keys or long-term symmetric keys, are executed. This is however very likely to happen since a user connected to the Internet for example, usually uses simultaneously several protocols with the same identity. The interaction with the other protocols may dramatically damage the security of a protocol. Consider for example the two following naive protocols.

---

* This work has been partly supported by the RNTL project POSÉ and the ARA SSIA Formacrypt.

V. Arvind and S. Prasad (Eds.): FSTTCS 2007, LNCS 4855, pp. 352–363, 2007.

$$P_1: \quad A \to B : \{s\}_{\text{pub}(B)} \qquad\qquad \begin{aligned} P_2: \quad & A \to B : \{N_a\}_{\text{pub}(B)} \\ & B \to A : N_a \end{aligned}$$

In protocol P_1, the agent A simply sends a secret s encrypted under B's public key. In protocol P_2, the agent sends some fresh nonce to B encrypted under B's public key. The agent B acknowledges A's message by forwarding A's nonce. While P_1 executed alone easily guarantees the secrecy of s, even against an active adversary, the secrecy of s is no more guaranteed when the protocol P_2 is executed. Indeed, an adversary may use the protocol P_2 as an oracle to decrypt any message. More realistic examples illustrating interactions between protocols can be found in e.g. [15].

The purpose of this paper is to investigate sufficient and rather tight conditions for a protocol to be safely used in an environment where other protocols may be executed as well. Our main contribution is to show that whenever a protocol is proved secure when it is executed alone, its security is not compromised by the interactions with any other protocol, provided each protocol is given an identifier (e.g. the protocol's name) that should appear in any encrypted message. Continuing our example, let us consider the two slightly modified protocols.

$$P_1': \quad A \to B : \{1, s\}_{\text{pub}(B)} \qquad\qquad \begin{aligned} P_2': \quad & A \to B : \{2, N_a\}_{\text{pub}(B)} \\ & B \to A : N_a \end{aligned}$$

Applying our result, we immediately deduce that P_1' can be safely executed together with P_2', without compromising the secrecy of s.

The idea of adding an identifier in encrypted messages is not novel. This rule is in the same spirit as those proposed in the paper of Abadi and Needham on prudent engineering practice for cryptographic protocols [1] (principle 10). The use of unique protocol identifiers is also recommended in [15,7] and has also been used in the design of fail-stop protocols [13]. However, to the best of our knowledge, it has never been proved that it is sufficient for securely executing several protocols in the same environment. Note that some other results also use tags for different purposes. For instance, Blanchet uses tags to exhibit a decidable class [5] but his tagging policy is stronger since any two encrypted subterm in a protocol have to contain different tags.

A result closely related to ours is the one of Guttman and Thayer [14]. They show that two protocols can be safely executed together without damaging interactions, as soon as the protocols are "independent". The independence hypothesis requires in particular that the set of encrypted messages that the two protocols handle should be different. As in our case, this can be ensured by giving each protocol a distinguishing value that should be included in the set of encrypted messages that the protocol handles. However, the major difference with our result is that this hypothesis has to hold on any valid *execution* of the protocol. In particular, considering again the protocol P_2', an agent should not accept a message of the form $\{2, \{1, m\}_k\}_{\text{pub}(B)}$ while he might not be able to decrypt the inside encryption and detect that it contains the wrong identifier. Another result has been recently obtained by Andova *et al.* for a broader class of composition operations and security properties [3]. In both cases, their result do not allow one to conclude when no typing hypothesis is assumed (that is, when agents are not required to check the type of each component of a message) or for protocols with cyphertext forwarding, that is, when agents have to forward unknown message components. Datta *et al.* (e.g. [12]) have also studied secure protocol composition in a more broader sense: protocols can be composed in parallel, sequentially or protocols may use other protocols as components. However, they do not provide any syntactic conditions for a protocol P to be safely executed in parallel with other protocols. For any protocol P' that might be executed in parallel, they have to prove that the two protocols P and P' satisfy each other invariants. Their approach is thus rather designed for component-based design of protocols. Our work is also related to those of Canetti *et al.* who, using a different approach, study universal composability of protocols [6]. They however require stronger security properties for their protocols to be composable.

Due to lack of space, proofs are omitted. They can be found in [10].

2   Models for Security Protocols

2.1   Syntax

Cryptographic primitives are represented by *function symbols*. More specifically, we consider the *signature* $\mathcal{F} = \{\text{enc}, \text{enca}, \text{sign}, \langle\,\rangle, \text{pub}, \text{priv}\}$ together with arities of the form $\text{ar}(f) = 2$ for the four first symbols and $\text{ar}(f) = 1$ for the two last ones. The symbol $\langle\,\rangle$ represents the pairing function. The terms $\text{enc}(m, k)$ and $\text{enca}(m, k)$ represent respectively the message m encrypted with the symmetric (resp. asymmetric) key k. The term $\text{sign}(m, k)$ represents the message m signed by the key k. The terms $\text{pub}(a)$ and $\text{priv}(a)$ represent respectively the public and private keys of an agent a. We fix an infinite set of *names* $\mathcal{N} = \{a, b \ldots\}$ among which we distinguish two particular names init and stop; and an infinite set of *variables* $\mathcal{X} = \{x, y \ldots\}$. The set of Terms is defined inductively by

$$
\begin{array}{lll}
t ::= & & \text{term} \\
& \mid\ x & \text{variable } x \\
& \mid\ a & \text{name } a \\
& \mid\ f(a) & \text{application of symbol } f \in \{\text{pub}, \text{priv}\} \text{ on a name} \\
& \mid\ f(t_1, t_2) & \text{application of symbol } f \in \{\text{enc}, \text{enca}, \text{sign}, \langle\,\rangle\}
\end{array}
$$

As usual, we write $vars(t)$ (resp. $names(t)$) for the set of variables (resp. names) occurring in t. A term is *ground* if and only if it has no variables. We write $St(t)$ for the set of *subterms* of a term t. For example, let $t = \text{enc}(\langle a, b\rangle), k)$, we have that $St(t) = \{t, \langle a, b\rangle, a, b, k\}$. This notion is extended as expected to sets of terms. *Extended names* are names or terms of the form $\text{pub}(a)$, $\text{priv}(a)$. The set of *Extended names* associated to a term t, denoted $\text{n}(t)$, is $\text{n}(t) = names(t) \cup \{\text{pub}(t), \text{priv}(t) \mid \text{pub}(t) \text{ or } \text{priv}(t) \in St(t)\}$. For example, we have that $\text{n}(\text{enc}(a, \text{pub}(b))) = \{a, b, \text{pub}(b), \text{priv}(b)\}$. Substitutions are written $\sigma = \{x_1 \mapsto t_1, \ldots, x_n \mapsto t_n\}$ with $\text{dom}(\sigma) = \{x_1, \ldots, x_n\}$. The substitution σ is *closed* if and only if all the t_i are ground. The application of a substitution σ to a term t is written $\sigma(t)$ or $t\sigma$.

$$\frac{T \vdash u \quad T \vdash v}{T \vdash \langle u, v \rangle} \qquad \frac{T \vdash u \quad T \vdash v}{T \vdash \mathrm{enc}(u, v)} \qquad \frac{T \vdash u \quad T \vdash v}{T \vdash \mathrm{enca}(u, v)} \qquad \frac{T \vdash u \quad T \vdash v}{T \vdash \mathrm{sign}(u, v)}$$

$$\frac{T \vdash \langle u, v \rangle}{T \vdash u} \qquad \frac{T \vdash \langle u, v \rangle}{T \vdash v} \qquad \frac{T \vdash \mathrm{enc}(u, v) \quad T \vdash v}{T \vdash u}$$

$$\frac{T \vdash \mathrm{enca}(u, \mathrm{pub}(v)) \quad T \vdash \mathrm{priv}(v)}{T \vdash u} \qquad \frac{T \vdash \mathrm{sign}(u, \mathrm{priv}(v))}{T \vdash u} \; \textit{(optional)} \qquad \frac{}{T \vdash u} \, u \in T$$

Fig. 1. Intruder deduction system

2.2 Intruder Capabilities

The ability of the intruder is modelled by a deduction system described in Figure 1 and corresponds to the usual Dolev-Yao rules. The first line describes the *composition* rules. The two last lines describe the *decomposition* rules and the axiom. Intuitively, these deduction rules say that an intruder can compose messages by pairing, encrypting and signing messages provided he has the corresponding keys. Conversely, it can decompose messages by projecting or decrypting provided it has the decryption keys. For signatures, the intruder is also able to *verify* whether a signature $\mathrm{sign}(m, k)$ and a message m match (provided she has the verification key), but this does not give her any new message. That is why this capability is not represented in the deduction system. We also consider an optional rule that expresses that an intruder can retrieve the whole message from its signature. This property may or may not hold depending on the signature scheme, and that is why this rule is optional. Our results hold in both cases (that is, when the deduction relation $\vdash$ is defined with or without this rule).

A term u is *deducible* from a set of terms T, denoted by $T \vdash u$ if there exists a *proof*, i.e. a tree such that the root is $T \vdash u$, the leaves are of the form $T \vdash v$ with $v \in T$ (*axiom* rule) and every intermediate node is an instance of one of the rules of the deduction system. For instance, the term $\langle k_1, k_2 \rangle$ is deducible from the set $T_1 = \{\mathrm{enc}(k_1, k_2), k_2\}$.

2.3 Protocols

We consider protocols specified in a language similar to the one of [19] allowing parties to exchange messages built from identities and randomly generated nonces using public key, symmetric encryption and digital signatures. The individual behavior of each protocol participant is defined by a *role* describing a sequence of message receptions/transmissions, and a k-party protocol is given by k such roles.

Definition 1 (Roles and protocols). *The set* Roles *of roles for protocol participants is the set of sequences of the form* $(\mathrm{rcv}_1, N_1, \mathrm{snd}_1) \cdots (\mathrm{rcv}_\ell, N_\ell, \mathrm{snd}_\ell)$

where each element, called rule, *satisfies* $(\text{rcv}_i, N_i, \text{snd}_i) \in \text{Terms} \times 2^{\mathcal{X}} \times \text{Terms}$, *and for any variable,* $x \in vars(\text{snd}_i)$ *implies* $x \in \bigcup_{1 \le j \le i} N_j \cup vars(\text{rcv}_j)$.

The length *of a role is the number of elements in its sequence. A k-party protocol is a mapping* $\Pi : [k] \to \text{Roles}$, *where* $[k] = \{1, 2, \ldots, k\}$.

The last condition ensures that each variable which appears in a sent term is either a nonce or has been introduced in a previously received message. The set of variables, names or extended names of a protocol is defined as expected, considering all the terms occurring in the role's specification.

The jth role of a protocol Π is denoted by $(\text{rcv}_1^j \xrightarrow{N_1^j} \text{snd}_1^j) \cdots (\text{rcv}_{k_j}^j \xrightarrow{N_{k_j}^j} \text{snd}_{k_j}^j)$. It specifies the messages to be sent/received by the party executing the role: at step i, the jth party expects to receive a message conformed to rcv_i^j, instantiate the variables of N_i^j with fresh names and returns the message snd_i^j. We assume the sets N_i^j to be pairwise disjoint. The special names init and stop will be used to specify that no message is expected or sent.

The *composition* of two protocols Π_1 and Π_2, denoted by $\Pi_1 \mid \Pi_2$ is simply the protocol obtained by the union of the roles of Π_1 and Π_2. If $\Pi_1 : [k_1] \to \text{Roles}$ and $\Pi_2 : [k_2] \to \text{Roles}$, then $\Pi = \Pi_1 \mid \Pi_2 : [k_1 + k_2] \to \text{Roles}$ with $\Pi(i) = \Pi_1(i)$ for any $1 \le i \le k_1$ and $\Pi(k_1 + i) = \Pi_2(i)$ for any $1 \le i \le k_2$.

Example 1. Consider the famous Needham-Schroeder protocol [18].

$$A \to B : \{N_a, A\}_{\text{pub}(B)}$$
$$B \to A : \{N_a, N_b\}_{\text{pub}(A)}$$
$$A \to B : \{N_b\}_{\text{pub}(B)}$$

The agent A sends to B his name and a fresh nonce (a randomly generated value) encrypted with the public key of B. The agent B answers by copying A's nonce and adds a fresh nonce N_B, encrypted by A's public key. The agent A acknowledges by forwarding B's nonce encrypted by B's public key. For instance, let a, b, and c be three agent names. The role $\Pi(1)$ corresponding to the first participant played by a talking to c is:

$$(\text{init} \xrightarrow{\{X\}} \text{enca}(\langle X, a \rangle, \text{pub}(c))), (\text{enca}(\langle X, x \rangle, \text{pub}(a)) \xrightarrow{\emptyset} \text{enca}(x, \text{pub}(c))).$$

The role $\Pi(2)$ corresponding to the second participant played by b with a is:

$$(\text{enca}(\langle y, a \rangle, \text{pub}(b)) \xrightarrow{\{Y\}} \text{enca}(\langle y, Y \rangle, \text{pub}(a))), (\text{enca}(Y, \text{pub}(b)) \xrightarrow{\emptyset} \text{stop}).$$

Note that, since our definition of role is not parametric, we have also to consider a role corresponding to the first participant played by a talking to b for example. If more agent identities need to be considered, then the corresponding roles should be added to the protocol. It has been shown however that two agents are sufficient (one honest and one dishonest) for proving security properties [8].

Clearly, not all protocols written using the syntax above are meaningful. In particular, some of them might not be *executable*. A precise definition of executability is not relevant for our result. We use instead a weaker hypothesis

(see Section 3). In particular, our combination result also holds for non executable protocols that satisfy our hypothesis.

2.4   Constraint Systems

Constraint systems are quite common (see e.g. [19,9,11]) in modeling security
protocols. They are used to specify secrecy preservation of security protocols
under a particular, finite scenario. We recall here their formalism and we show in
the next section that the secrecy preservation problem for an *unbounded number
of sessions* can be specified using (infinite) families of constraint systems.

Definition 2 (constraint system). *A* constraint system $\mathcal{C}$ *is either* $\perp$ *or a
finite sequence of expressions* $(T_i \Vdash u_i)_{1 \leq i \leq n}$, *called* constraints, *where each* T_i
is a non empty set of terms, called the left-*hand side of the constraint and each* u_i
is a term, called the right-*hand side of the constraint, such that:*

- $T_i \subseteq T_{i+1}$ *for every* i *such that* $1 \leq i < n$;
- *if* $x \in vars(T_i)$ *for some* i *then there exists* $j < i$ *such that* $x \in vars(u_j)$.

A solution *of* $\mathcal{C}$ *is a closed substitution* θ *such that for every* $(T \Vdash u) \in \mathcal{C}$, *we
have that* $T\theta \vdash u\theta$. *The empty constraint system is always satisfiable whereas* $\perp$
denotes an unsatisfiable system.

A constraint system $\mathcal{C}$ is usually denoted as a conjunction of constraints $\mathcal{C} =
\bigwedge_{1 \leq i \leq n}(T_i \Vdash u_i)$ with $T_i \subseteq T_{i+1}$, for all $1 \leq i < n$. The second condition in
Definition 2 says that each time a variable occurs first in some right-hand side,
it must not have occurred before in some left-hand side. The left-hand side of a
constraint system usually represents the messages sent on the network.

2.5   Secrecy

We define the general secrecy preservation problem for an unbounded number
of sessions, using infinite families of constraint systems. A role may be executed
in several sessions, using different nonces at each session. Moreover, since the
adversary may block, redirect and send new messages, all the sessions might be
interleaved in many ways. This is captured by the notion of *scenario*.

Definition 3 (scenario). *A* scenario *for a protocol* $\Pi : [k] \rightarrow$ Roles *is a sequence* sc $= (r_1, s_1) \cdots (r_n, s_n)$ *such that* $1 \leq r_i \leq k$, $s_i \in \mathbb{N}$, *the number of
identical occurrences of a pair* (r, s) *is smaller than the length of the role* r, *and
whenever* $s_i = s_j$ *then* $r_i = r_j$.

The numbers r_i and s_i represent respectively the involved role and the session
number. An occurrence of (r, s) in sc means that the role r of session s executes
its next receive-send action. The condition on the number of occurrences of a pair
ensures that such an action is indeed available. The last condition ensures that
a session number is not reused on other roles. We say that $(r, s) \in$ sc if (r, s)
is an element of the sequence sc. Let $\Pi = \Pi_1 \mid \Pi_2$ be a protocol obtained by

composition of Π_1 and Π_2 and let sc be a scenario for Π. The scenario $\mathsf{sc}|_{\Pi_1}$ is simply the sequence obtained from sc by removing any element (r, s) where r is a role of Π_2. Given a scenario, we can define a sequence of rules that corresponds to the sequence of expected and sent messages.

Definition 4. *Given a scenario* $\mathsf{sc} = (r_1, s_1) \cdots (r_n, s_n)$ *for a k-party proto-col* Π, *the sequence of rules* $(u_1, v_1) \cdots (u_n, v_n)$ *associated to* sc *is defined as follows. Let* $\Pi(j) = (\mathsf{rcv}_1^j \xrightarrow{N_1^j} \mathsf{snd}_1^j) \cdots (\mathsf{rcv}_{k_j}^j \xrightarrow{N_{k_j}^j} \mathsf{snd}_{k_j}^j)$ *for* $1 \leq j \leq k$. *Let* $p_i = \#\{(r_j, s_j) \in \mathsf{sc} \mid j \leq i, r_j = r_i\}$, *i.e. the number of previous occurrences in* sc *of the role* r_i. *We have* $p_i \leq k_{r_i}$ *and* $(u_i, v_i) = (\mathsf{rcv}_{p_i}^{r_i} \sigma_{r_i, s_i}, \mathsf{snd}_{p_i}^{r_i} \sigma_{r_i, s_i})$, *where*

- $\mathrm{dom}(\sigma_{r,s}) = \bigcup_{1 \leq i \leq k_r} (N_i^r \cup vars(\mathsf{rcv}_i^r))$, *i.e. variables occurring in* $\Pi(r)$,
- $\sigma_{r,s}(x) = n_{x,s}$ *if* $x \in \bigcup_{1 \leq i \leq k_r} N_i^r$, *where* $n_{x,s}$ *is a name.*
- $\sigma_{r,s}(x) = x_s$ *otherwise, where* x_s *is a variable.*

We assume that names (resp. variables) with different indexes are pairwise different and also different from the names (resp. variables) occurring in Π.

We say that a protocol preserves the secrecy of a data if it preserves its secrecy for any scenario. In particular, the secrecy of the data must be preserved for any possible instances of its fresh values (e.g. nonces and keys).

Definition 5 (secrecy). *A protocol* Π *preserves the secrecy of a term* m *for the initial knowledge* T_0 *if for any scenario* sc *for* Π, *for any role number* $1 \leq i \leq k$, *for any session number* $s_i \in \mathbb{N}$ *that either corresponds to role i, that is* $(i, s_i) \in \mathsf{sc}$ *or does not appear in the scenario, that is* $\forall j, (j, s_i) \notin \mathsf{sc}$, *the following constraint system is not satisfiable*

$$T_0' \Vdash u_1 \wedge \bigwedge_{1 \leq i < n} (T_0' \cup \{v_1, \ldots, v_i\} \Vdash u_{i+1}) \wedge (T_0' \cup \{v_1, \ldots, v_n\} \Vdash m\sigma_{1,s_1} \cdots \sigma_{k,s_k})$$

where $T_0' = T_0 \cup \{\mathsf{init}\}$ *and* $(u_1, v_1) \cdots (u_n, v_n)$ *is the sequence of rules associated to* sc *and* $\sigma_{r,s}$ *is the substitution defined in Definition 4.*

The initial knowledge typically contains the names and the public keys of all agents and the private keys of all dishonest agents.

Example 2. Consider again the Needham-Schroeder protocol. Let $\Pi(1)$ and $\Pi(2)$ the two roles introduced in Example 1. This protocol is well-known to be insecure w.r.t. $m = Y$ and $T_0 = \{\mathrm{priv}(c), \mathrm{pub}(c), a, b, \mathrm{pub}(a), \mathrm{pub}(b)\}$ (see [16] for a complete description of the attack). Let s_1 and s_2 be two session numbers $(s_1 \neq s_2)$ and consider $\mathsf{sc} = (1, s_1)(2, s_2)(1, s_1)(2, s_2)$. The system $\mathcal{C}$ associated to T_0, sc and $m\sigma_{1,s_1}\sigma_{2,s_2} = n_{Y,s_2}$ (according to Definition 5) is given below.

$$\mathcal{C} := \begin{cases} T_0, \mathsf{init} \Vdash \mathsf{init} \\ T_1 \stackrel{\mathrm{def}}{=} T_0, \mathsf{init}, \mathrm{enca}(\langle n_{X,s_1}, a\rangle, \mathrm{pub}(c)) \Vdash \mathrm{enca}(\langle y_{s_2}, a\rangle, \mathrm{pub}(b)) \\ T_2 \stackrel{\mathrm{def}}{=} T_1, \mathrm{enca}(\langle y_{s_2}, n_{Y,s_2}\rangle, \mathrm{pub}(a)) \Vdash \mathrm{enca}(\langle n_{X,s_1}, x_{s_1}\rangle, \mathrm{pub}(a)) \\ T_2, \mathrm{enca}(x_{s_1}, \mathrm{pub}(c)) \Vdash \mathrm{enca}(n_{Y,s_2}, \mathrm{pub}(b)) \\ T_2, \mathrm{enca}(x_{s_1}, \mathrm{pub}(c)) \Vdash n_{Y,s_2} \end{cases}$$

The substitution $\sigma = \{y_{s_2} \mapsto n_{X,s_1}, x_{s_1} \mapsto n_{Y,s_2}\}$ is a solution of $\mathcal{C}$.

3 Composition Result

3.1 Hypothesis

Even if a protocol is secure for an unbounded number of sessions, its security may collapse if the protocol is executed in an environment where other protocols sharing some common keys are executed. We have seen a first example in the introduction. To avoid a cyphertext from a protocol Π_1 to be decrypted in an another protocol Π_2, we introduce the notion of *well-tagged* protocol.

Definition 6 (well-tag, α-tag). *Let α be a term. We say that a term t is α-tagged if for every $t' \in St(t)$ of the form $t' = \mathrm{enc}(t_1, t_2)$, $t' = \mathrm{enca}(t_1, t_2)$, or $t' = \mathrm{sign}(t_1, t_2)$, we have $t_1 = \langle \alpha, t'_1 \rangle$ for some term t'_1. A term is said* well-tagged *if it is α-tagged for some term α.*

A protocol Π is α-tagged is any term occurring in the role of the protocol is α-tagged. A protocol is said well-tagged *if it is α-tagged for some term α.*

Requiring that a protocol is well-tagged can be very easily achieved in practice: it is sufficient for example to add the name of the protocol in each encrypted term. Moreover, note that (as opposite to [14]) this does not require that the agents check that nested encrypted terms are correctly tagged. For example, let Π be a protocol with one role as follows:

$$\Pi(1) = (\mathrm{enca}(\langle \alpha, x \rangle, \mathrm{pub}(a)) \to \mathrm{enca}(\langle \alpha, x \rangle, \mathrm{pub}(b))).$$

The protocol Π is α-tagged and still the message $\mathrm{enca}(\langle \alpha, \mathrm{enc}(a, k) \rangle, \mathrm{pub}(a))$ (which is not α-tagged) would be accepted by the agent playing the role.

Tagging protocols is not sufficient, indeed critical long-term keys should not be revealed in clear. Consider for example the following two well-tagged protocols

$$P_3 : \quad A \to B : \{\alpha, s\}_{k_{ab}} \qquad P_4 : \quad A \to B : k_{ab}$$

The security of protocol P_3 is again compromised by the execution of P_4. Thus we will require that long-term keys (except possibly the public ones) do not occur in plaintext in the protocol.

Definition 7 (plaintext). *The set plaintext(t) of plaintext of a term t is the set of extended names and variables, that is recursively defined as follows.*

$$
\begin{aligned}
&plaintext(u) = \{u\} && \text{if } u \text{ is a variable or a name} \\
&plaintext(f(u)) = \{f(u)\} && \text{for } f \in \{\mathrm{pub}, \mathrm{priv}\} \\
&plaintext(\langle u_1, u_2 \rangle) = plaintext(u_1) \cup plaintext(u_2) \\
&plaintext(f(u_1, u_2)) = plaintext(u_1) && \text{for } f \in \{\mathrm{enc}, \mathrm{enca}, \mathrm{sign}\}
\end{aligned}
$$

This notation is extended to set of terms and protocols as expected.

Some weird protocols may still reveal critical keys in a hidden way. Consider for example the following one role (α-tagged) protocol.

$$\Pi(1) = (\mathrm{init} \to \mathrm{enc}(\langle \alpha, a \rangle, k_{ab})), (\mathrm{enc}(\langle \alpha, a \rangle, x) \to x)$$

While the long-term key k_{ab} does not appear in plaintext, the key k_{ab} is revealed after simply one normal execution of the role. This protocol is however not realistic since an unknown value cannot be learned (and sent) if it does not appear previously in plaintext. Thus we will further require (Condition 2 of Theorem 1) that a variable occurring in plaintext in a sent message, has to previously occur in plaintext in a received message.

3.2   Composition Theorem

We show that two well-tagged protocols can be safely composed as soon as they use different tags and that critical long-term keys do not appear in plaintext.

Theorem 1. *Let Π_1 and Π_2 be two well-tagged protocols such that Π_1 is α-tagged and Π_2 is β-tagged with $\alpha \neq \beta$. Let T_0 (intuitively the initial knowledge of the intruder) be a set of extended names. Let $\mathsf{KC} = (n(\Pi_1) \cup n(\Pi_2)) \setminus T_0$ be the set of critical extended names. Let m be a term constructed from Π_1 such that m is α-tagged and $vars(m) \subseteq vars(\Pi_1)$. Moreover, we assume that*

1. *critical extended names do not appear in plaintext, that is*

$$\mathsf{KC} \cap (plaintext(\Pi_1) \cup plaintext(\Pi_2)) = \emptyset.$$

2. *for any role $(rcv_1 \overset{N_1}{\rightarrowtail} snd_1) \cdots (rcv_k \overset{N_k}{\rightarrowtail} snd_k)$ of Π_1 or Π_2, for any variable $x \in plaintext(snd_i)$, we have $x \in \bigcup_{1 \leq j \leq i} N_j \cup \{plaintext(rcv_j)\}$.*

Then Π_1 preserves the secrecy of m for the initial knowledge T_0 if and only if $\Pi_1 \mid \Pi_2$ preserves the secrecy of m for T_0.

We have seen in Section 3.1 that conditions 1 and 2 are necessary conditions. Moreover, condition 2 will be satisfied by any realistic (executable) protocol. We require that terms from Π_1 and Π_2 are tagged with distinct tags for simplicity. The key condition is actually that for any encrypted (or signed) subterm t_1 of Π_1 and for any encrypted (or signed) subterm t_2 of Π_2, the terms t_1 and t_2 cannot be unified.

Theorem 1 is proved by contradiction. Assume that $\Pi_1 \mid \Pi_2$ does not preserve the secrecy of m for T_0. It means that there exists a scenario sc for $\Pi_1 \mid \Pi_2$ such that the constraint system associated to sc, T_0 and m is satisfiable. Proposition 1 ensures that in this case, there exists a scenario sc′ for Π_1 such that the constraint system associated to sc′, T_0 and m is satisfiable, which means that Π_1 does not preserve the secrecy of m for some initial knowledge T_0, contradiction.

Proposition 1. *Let $\Pi_1 = [k_1] \rightarrow$ Roles, $\Pi_2 = [k_2] \rightarrow$ Roles, T_0 and m defined as in Theorem 1 and satisfying the conditions 1 and 2. Let $k = k_1 + k_2$ and sc be a scenario for $\Pi_1 \mid \Pi_2$. For any role number $1 \leq i \leq k$, let $s_i \in \mathbb{N}$ such that $(i, s_i) \in$ sc or $\forall j, (j, s_i) \notin$ sc. Let $\mathcal{C}$ be the constraint system associated to sc, T_0 and $m\sigma_{1,s_1} \cdots \sigma_{k,s_k}$. Let $sc' = sc|_{\Pi_1}$ and $\mathcal{C}'$ be the constraint system associated to sc′, T_0 and $m\sigma_{1,s_1} \cdots \sigma_{k_1,s_{k_1}}$. If $\mathcal{C}$ is satisfiable, then $\mathcal{C}'$ is also satisfiable.*

4   Proof of Our Combination Result

To prove our result, we first refine an existing decision procedure for solving constraint systems. Several decision procedures already exist [17,9,11,19] for solving constraint systems. Some of them [17,9,11] are based on a set of simplification rules allowing a general constraint system to be reduced to some simpler one, called *solved*, on which satisfiability can be easily decided. A constraint system is said *solved* [11] if it is different from $\perp$ and if each of its constraints is of the form $T \Vdash x$, where x is a variable. Note that the empty constraint system is solved. Solved constraint systems are particularly simple since they always have a solution. Indeed, let T_1 be the smallest (w.r.t. inclusion) left hand side of a constraint. From the definition of a constraint system we have that T_1 is non empty and has no variable. Let $t \in T_1$. Then the substitution τ defined by $x\tau = t$ for every variable x is a solution since $T \vdash x\theta$ for any constraint $T \Vdash x$ of the solved constraint system.

The *simplification rules* we consider are the following ones:

R_1 : $\mathcal{C} \wedge T \Vdash u \rightsquigarrow \mathcal{C}$ if $T \cup \{x \mid T' \Vdash x \in \mathcal{C}, T' \subsetneq T\} \vdash u$

R_2 : $\mathcal{C} \wedge T \Vdash u \rightsquigarrow_\sigma \mathcal{C}\sigma \wedge T\sigma \Vdash u\sigma$ if $\sigma = \mathrm{mgu}(t, u)$ where $t \in St(T)$, $t \neq u$, and t, u are neither variables nor pairs

R_3 : $\mathcal{C} \wedge T \Vdash u \rightsquigarrow_\sigma \mathcal{C}\sigma \wedge T\sigma \Vdash u\sigma$ if $\sigma = \mathrm{mgu}(t_1, t_2)$, $t_1, t_2 \in St(T)$, $t_1 \neq t_2$, and t_1, t_2 are neither variables nor pairs

R_4 : $\mathcal{C} \wedge T \Vdash u \rightsquigarrow \perp$ if $vars(T, u) = \emptyset$ and $T \nvdash u$

R_5 : $\mathcal{C} \wedge T \Vdash f(u, v) \rightsquigarrow \mathcal{C} \wedge T \Vdash u \wedge T \Vdash v$ for $f \in \{\langle\rangle, \mathrm{enc}, \mathrm{enca}, \mathrm{sign}\}$

All the rules are indexed by a substitution (when there is no index then the identity substitution is implicitly considered). We write $\mathcal{C} \rightsquigarrow^*_\sigma \mathcal{C}'$ if there are $\mathcal{C}_1, \ldots, \mathcal{C}_n$ such that $\mathcal{C} \rightsquigarrow_{\sigma_0} \mathcal{C}_1 \rightsquigarrow_{\sigma_1} \ldots \rightsquigarrow_{\sigma_n} \mathcal{C}'$ and $\sigma = \sigma_0\sigma_1\ldots\sigma_n$. Our rules are the same than in [11] except that we forbid unification of terms headed by $\langle\rangle$. Correction and termination are still ensured by [11] and we show that they still form a complete decision procedure. Intuitively, unification between pairs is useless since pairs can be decomposed in order to perform unification on its components. Then, it is possible to build again the pair if necessary. Note that this is not always possible for encryption since the key used to decrypt or encrypt may be unknown by the attacker. Proving that forbidding unification between pairs still leads to a complete decision procedure required in particular to introduce a new notion of minimality for tree proofs for deduction. Note that this result is of independent interest. Indeed, we provide a more efficient decision procedure for solving constraint systems, thus for deciding secrecy for a bounded number of sessions. Of course, the theoretical complexity remains the same (NP).

Theorem 2. *Let $\mathcal{C}$ be an unsolved constraint system.*

1. *(Correctness) If $\mathcal{C} \rightsquigarrow^*_\sigma \mathcal{C}'$ for some constraint system $\mathcal{C}'$ and some substitution σ and if θ is a solution of $\mathcal{C}'$ then $\sigma\theta$ is a solution of $\mathcal{C}$.*
2. *(Completeness) If θ is a solution of $\mathcal{C}$, then there exist a solved constraint system $\mathcal{C}'$ and substitutions σ, θ' such that $\theta = \sigma\theta'$, $\mathcal{C} \rightsquigarrow^*_\sigma \mathcal{C}'$ and θ' is a solution of $\mathcal{C}'$.*
3. *(Termination) There is no infinite chain $\mathcal{C} \rightsquigarrow_{\sigma_1} \mathcal{C}_1 \ldots \rightsquigarrow_{\sigma_n} \mathcal{C}_n$.*

Proposition 1 is then proved in three main steps. First, Theorem 2 serves as a key result for proving that if $\mathcal{C}$ is satisfiable, then there exists a solution θ where messages from Π_1 and Π_2 are not mixed up. This is obtained by observing that the simplification rules enable us to build θ step by step through unification of subterms of Π_1 and Π_2. Now, since unification between pairs is forbidden, the rules R_2 and R_3 only involve subterms that convey the same tag, i.e subterms issued from the same protocol. Second, conditions 1 and 2 ensure that for any solution θ of $\mathcal{C}$, the critical extended names of KC do not appear in plaintext in $\mathcal{C}\theta$. Third, thanks to the two previous steps, we prove that β-tagged terms (intuitively messages from Π_2) are not useful for deducing α-tagged terms. For this, we establish that $T \vdash u$ implies $\overline{T} \vdash \overline{u}$ where $\overline{}$ is a function that keep the terms issued from Π_1 unchanged and projects the terms issued from Π_2 on the special name init. The proof is done by induction on the proof tree witnessing $T \vdash u$. It requires in particular the introduction of a new locality lemma for deduction of ground terms. Then, we deduce that, removing from $\mathcal{C}$ all constraints inherited from Π_2 and all β-tagged terms, we obtain a satisfiable constraint $\mathcal{C}'$ that is associated to a scenario of Π_1.

5 Conclusion

In this paper, we have shown how to safely compose secure protocols by tagging encryption, focusing on secrecy properties. Whenever a protocol preserves the secrecy of some data s, it still preserves s secrecy when other tagged protocols are executed in the same environment. We plan to consider the protocol composition problem for larger classes of security properties. In particular, we believe that our result can be extended to authentication-like properties.

More broadly, we foresee composition results in a more general way. In this paper, protocols are composed in the sense that they can be executed in the same environment. We plan to develop composition results where protocols can use other protocols as sub-programs. For example, a protocol could use a secure channel, letting the implementation of the secure channel underspecified. This secure channel could be then possibly implemented by any protocol establishing session keys.

Acknowledgment. We wish to thank J. Guttman for his helpful comments on a preliminary version of this work.

References

1. Abadi, M., Needham, R.M.: Prudent engineering practice for cryptographic protocols. IEEE Trans. Software Eng. 22(1), 6–15 (1996)
2. Amadio, R., Charatonik, W.: On name generation and set-based analysis in the Dolev-Yao model. In: Brim, L., Jančar, P., Křetínský, M., Kucera, A. (eds.) CONCUR 2002. LNCS, vol. 2421, pp. 499–514. Springer, Heidelberg (2002)

3. Andova, S., Cremers, C., Steen, K.G., Mauw, S., lsnes, S.M., Radomirović, S.: Sufficient conditions for composing security protocols. Information and Computation (to appear, 2007)
4. Blanchet, B.: An efficient cryptographic protocol verifier based on Prolog rules. In: CSFW 2001. Proc. 14th Computer Security Foundations Workshop, pp. 82–96. IEEE Computer Society Press, Los Alamitos (2001)
5. Blanchet, B., Podelski, A.: Verification of cryptographic protocols: Tagging enforces termination. In: Gordon, A.D. (ed.) ETAPS 2003 and FOSSACS 2003. LNCS, vol. 2620, Springer, Heidelberg (2003)
6. Canetti, R.: Universally composable security: A new paradigm for cryptographic protocols. In: FOCS 2001. Proc. 42nd Annual Symposium on Foundations of Computer Science, Las Vegas (Nevada, USA), pp. 136–145. IEEE Computer Society Press, Los Alamitos (2001)
7. Canetti, R., Meadows, C., Syverson, P.F.: Environmental requirements for authentication protocols. In: Okada, M., Pierce, B.C., Scedrov, A., Tokuda, H., Yonezawa, A. (eds.) ISSS 2002. LNCS, vol. 2609, pp. 339–355. Springer, Heidelberg (2003)
8. Comon-Lundh, H., Cortier, V.: Security properties: two agents are sufficient. Science of Computer Programming 50(1-3), 51–71 (2004)
9. Comon-Lundh, H., Shmatikov, V.: Intruder deductions, constraint solving and insecurity decision in presence of exclusive or. In: LICS 2003. Proc. 18th Annual Symposium on Logic in Comp. Science, pp. 271–280. IEEE Computer Society Press, Los Alamitos (2003)
10. Cortier, V., Delaitre, J., Delaune, S.: Safely composing security protocols. Research Report 6234, INRIA, p. 26(2007)
11. Cortier, V., Zalinescu, E.: Deciding key cycles for security protocols. In: Hermann, M., Voronkov, A. (eds.) LPAR 2006. LNCS (LNAI), vol. 4246, pp. 317–331. Springer, Heidelberg (2006)
12. Datta, A., Derek, A., Mitchell, J.C., Roy, A.: Protocol composition logic (PCL). Electr. Notes Theor. Comput. Sci. 172, 311–358 (2007)
13. Gong, L., Syverson, P.: Fail-stop protocols: An approach to designing secure protocols. In: Proc. 5th Inter. Working Conference on Dependable Computing for Critical Applications, pp. 44–55 (1995)
14. Guttman, J.D., Thayer, F.J.: Protocol independence through disjoint encryption. In: CSFW 2000. Proc. 13th Computer Security Foundations Workshop, pp. 24–34. IEEE Computer Society Press, Los Alamitos (2000)
15. Kelsey, J., Schneier, B., Wagner, D.: Protocol interactions and the chosen protocol attack. In: Christianson, B., Lomas, M. (eds.) Security Protocols. LNCS, vol. 1361, pp. 91–104. Springer, Heidelberg (1998)
16. Lowe, G.: Breaking and fixing the Needham-Schroeder public-key protocol using FDR. In: Margaria, T., Steffen, B. (eds.) TACAS 1996. LNCS, vol. 1055, pp. 147–166. Springer, Heidelberg (1996)
17. Millen, J.K., Shmatikov, V.: Constraint solving for bounded-process cryptographic protocol analysis. In: CCS 2001. Proc. 8th ACM Conference on Computer and Communications Security, pp. 166–175. ACM Press, New York (2001)
18. Needham, R., Schroeder, M.: Using encryption for authentication in large networks of computers. Communication of the ACM 21(12), 993–999 (1978)
19. Rusinowitch, M., Turuani, M.: Protocol insecurity with finite number of sessions and composed keys is NP-complete. Theoretical Comp. Sc. 299, 451–475 (2003)
20. Seidl, H., Verma, K.N.: Flat and one-variable clauses: Complexity of verifying cryptographic protocols with single blind copying. In: Baader, F., Voronkov, A. (eds.) LPAR 2004. LNCS (LNAI), vol. 3452, Springer, Heidelberg (2005)

Computationally Sound Typing for Non-interference: The Case of Deterministic Encryption

Judicaël Courant, Cristian Ene, and Yassine Lakhnech

VERIMAG - University Joseph Fourier - CNRS - INPG
2, av. de Vignates, 38610 Gières - France
name@imag.fr

Abstract. Type systems for secure information flow aim to prevent a program from leaking information from variables that hold secret data to variables that hold public data. In this work we present a type system to address *deterministic encryption*. The intuition that encrypting a secret yields a public value, that can be stored in a public variable, is faithful for probabilistic encryption but erroneous for deterministic encryption. We prove the computational soundness of our type system in the concrete security framework.

1 Introduction

The notion of *non-interference* has been introduced in [3], with the aim of capturing unwanted information flow in programs. Non-interference assumes a separation between secret (high, private) variables and public (low) variables and requires that executing the program in two initial states that coincide on the public variables leads to final states that coincide on the public variables. In Dennings' seminal paper [2], an expression is classified H if it contains a secret variable; otherwise, it is classified L. The paper introduces two basic principles to avoid information flow: first, to prevent explicit flow, a H expression may not be assigned to a L variable; second, to prevent implicit flows, an H guarded conditional or loop may not affect L variables. Later, Volpano, Smith, and Irvine [13] casted these principles as a type system and showed that they suffice to ensure non-interference. Since this early work, information flow analysis has been extended to deal with other issues such as nontermination, concurrency, nondeterminism, and exceptions; see [9] for a survey. In many applications, however, it is desirable to allow information to flow from secret to public variables in a controlled way. This is called declassification in the literature. In a useful survey, Sabelfeld & Sands [10] classify declassification techniques according to the following dimensions: "what", "who", "where" and "when".

In this paper, we are interested in *cryptography-based declassification*, where encrypted secret data can be published without leaking information about the secrets. The non-interference setting has been extended in [12] to cope with one-way functions and in [5, 6, 11] to cope with probabilistic encryption. We consider

V. Arvind and S. Prasad (Eds.): FSTTCS 2007, LNCS 4855, pp. 364–375, 2007.

length-preserving deterministic encryption, i.e., block ciphers. These are widely used in practice (DES, AES, Idea, etc.). Non-interference type systems developed for probabilistic encryption are not applicable for deterministic encryption. To illustrate some of the subtleties of deterministic encryption, let us consider the following examples where l, l', l'' are public variables and h, h' are secret variables, νl assigns a value sampled from the uniform distribution to the variable l, $+$ is a bijective operator and $\mathsf{Enc}(k, e)$ denotes the encryption of e with the symmetric key k. We assume that the encryption function $\mathsf{Enc}(k, \cdot)$ is a pseudo-random permutation. A simple program is the following: $l := \mathsf{Enc}(k, h); l' := \mathsf{Enc}(k, h')$. The equality $\mathsf{Enc}(k, h) = \mathsf{Enc}(k, h')$ is almost never true in case of probabilistic encryption, independently whether $h = h'$. Hence, this program does not leak information in case of probabilistic encryption. This is not true in the case of deterministic encryption as we have $h = h'$ if and only if $l = l'$ at program termination. Indeed, deterministic encryption is not repetition concealing in contrast to probabilistic encryption. Consider now, the program $\nu l; l' := \mathsf{Enc}(k, l + h)$, where the value of l is randomly sampled. It does not leak information, even if the attacker is given the value of l. Yet, we have to be careful concerning how the value of l is used. Indeed, the execution of the command $l'' := \mathsf{Enc}(k, l + h')$ at the end of this program would leak information. However, the following slightly modified program : $\nu l; l' := \mathsf{Enc}(k, l + h); l'' := \mathsf{Enc}(k, l' + h')$ does not leak information. Notice that this version corresponds to a simplified block encryption, using the CBC mode: (l, l', l'') can be seen as the cipher text obtained by encrypting the secret (h, h'). Let us consider an example that shows the subtelties that may arise when deterministic encryption is used.

Example 1. In this example (inspired from [11]), '$+$" is the bitwise-xor operation over blocks of p bits; the other operations are: "$|$" the bitwise-or operation, "$\ll$" the shift-left operation and "$=$" the test for equality. Consider the following command, where h is a private variable and l, m, l_1, l_2 and l_r are public variables.

$$l := 0^p; m := 0^{p-1}1;$$
$$\textbf{while}_p\ 1\ \textbf{do} \qquad l_1 := \mathsf{Enc}(k, h|m); l_2 := \mathsf{Enc}(k, h);$$
$$\textbf{if}\ (l_1 = l_2)\ \textbf{then}\ l := l|m\ \textbf{else}\ \textbf{skip}\ \textbf{fi}\ ;$$
$$m := m \ll 1\ \textbf{od}$$

Since encryption is deterministic, this command completely leaks the value of h: it copies h into l. Consider now the following modified command.

$$l := 0^p; m := 0^{p-1}1;$$
$$\textbf{while}_p\ 1\ \textbf{do} \qquad \nu l_r; l_1 := \mathsf{Enc}(k, (h|m) + l_r); l_2 := \mathsf{Enc}(k, h + l_r);$$
$$\textbf{if}\ (l_1 = l_2)\ \textbf{then}\ l := l|m\ \textbf{else}\ \textbf{skip}\ \textbf{fi}\ ;$$
$$m := m \ll 1\ \textbf{od}$$

As the same "random l_r" is reused in the second encryption, the obtained code is insecure: it still copies h into l. However, if we re-sample l_r in the second encryption, the command becomes secure.

$l := 0^p; m := 0^{p-1}1;$
while$_p$ 1 **do** $\nu l_r; l_1 := \mathsf{Enc}(k, (h|m) + l_r); \nu l_r; l_2 := \mathsf{Enc}(k, h + l_r);$
                if $(l_1 = l_2)$ **then** $l := l|m$ **else skip fi** ;
                $m := m \ll 1$ **od**

1.1   Contributions

In this paper, we design a type system for information flow for an imperative language that includes block ciphers and show its soundness under the assumption that the encryption scheme is a pseudo-random permutation. Our soundness proof is carried in the concrete (exact) security framework that aims at providing concrete estimates about the security of the considered system.

This is to our knowledge the first time that a type system for non-interference is proven correct in the concrete security framework. One can distinguish three security proof settings: first, the symbolic setting, also called formal and Dolev-Yao, where cryptographic primitives are operators on formal expressions (terms) and security proofs are reachability or observational equivalence proofs; second, the computational setting where cryptographic primitives are algorithms and security proofs are asymptotic based on poly-time reductions; third, the concrete security setting where proofs are also by reduction but no asymptotics are involved and reductions are as efficient as possible.

1.2   Related Work

A few works on information flow study computationally sound type systems for non-interference. Peeter Laud has pioneered the area of computationally secure information flow analysis in the presence of encryption. In his first works [4, 5] the analysis was in the form of static analysis and encryption is probabilistic. In more recent work [6] co-authored with Varmo Vene, he presents a type system for information flow in presence of probabilistic encryption. Geoffrey Smith and Rafael Alpízar present in [11] a computationally sound type system for probabilistic encryption. In this work, as in ours, the generation and manipulation of keys is not considered. The main difference, however, to our work is that the above cited works assume probabilistic encryption. Volpano in [12] considers one-way functions. His definition of non-interference is, however, weaker than ours as it essentially means that a well-typed program that leaks information can be used to invert the one-way function. But this does not imply that no information about secret data is learned. Malacaria presents in [7] an information-theoretic definition of non-interference applied to imperative languages with random assignment, and gives an algorithm to approximate the information leaked in a loop. It is easy to prove that for programs that do not use encryption our definition is stronger that his definition. Extending his technique for programs that use encryption does not seem to be immediate.

1.3   Paper Structure

In section 2 we introduce some preliminaries including some terminology concerning probabilities, indistinguishability and pseudo-random permutations. In section 3, we present the syntax and semantics for an imperative language build that includes random assignment and deterministic encryption. In section 4 we introduce a type system for randomized expressions, and justify its computational soundness. In section 5, we give a type system for the language presented in section 3 and we prove its computational soundness. The soundness of the type system for this language is proved by two successive reductions: first to a language where the encryption function is interpreted as a random permutation, and then to language where there is no encryption function. Finally, we conclude, and give some possible extensions.

2   Preliminaries

A *finite probability distribution* $\mathcal{D} = (\mathcal{U}, \Pr)$ *over* $\mathcal{U}$ is a finite non-empty set $\mathcal{U}$ equipped with a function $\Pr : \mathcal{U} \to [0,1]$ such that $\sum_{u \in \mathcal{U}} \Pr[u] = 1$. $\mathsf{Distr}(\mathcal{U})$ is the set of distributions on $\mathcal{U}$. The *probability of an event* $A \subseteq \mathcal{U}$ is $\Pr[A] = \sum_{u \in A} \Pr[u]$. A property P over $\mathcal{U}$ can be seen as the event $\{x \in \mathcal{U} \mid P(x)\}$. The *uniform distribution* on $\mathcal{U}$ is such that $\Pr[u] = \frac{1}{|\mathcal{U}|}$, for any $u \in \mathcal{U}$. $[x_1 \xleftarrow{r} X_1; \ldots x_n \xleftarrow{r} X_n : e(x_1, \ldots, x_n)]$ denotes the distribution Y such that $\Pr[Y = e] = \sum_{x_1, \ldots, x_n | e(x_1, \ldots, x_n) = e} \Pr[X_1 = x_1] \ldots \Pr[X_n = x_n]$ (thus $[: u]$ is Dirac's point mass δ_u) and $\Pr[x_1 \xleftarrow{r} X_1; \ldots x_n \xleftarrow{r} X_n : P(x_1, \ldots, x_n)]$ denotes the probability of the event P over the distribution $[x_1 \xleftarrow{r} X_1; \ldots x_n \xleftarrow{r} X_n : (x_1, \ldots, x_n)]$.

Computational indistinguishability Given two distributions $\mathcal{D}$ and $\mathcal{D}'$, and an algorithm $\mathcal{A}$, we define the *advantage* of $\mathcal{A}$ in distinguishing $\mathcal{D}$ and $\mathcal{D}'$ as $\mathrm{ADV}(\mathcal{A}, \mathcal{D}, \mathcal{D}') = |\Pr[x \xleftarrow{r} \mathcal{D} : \mathcal{A}(x) = 1] - \Pr[x \xleftarrow{r} \mathcal{D}' : \mathcal{A}(x) = 1]|$ (Informally, this advantage quantifies the success of an adversary trying to guess whether some x has been drawn from $\mathcal{D}$ or from $\mathcal{D}'$ and output its guess as a boolean $0/1$.) Two distributions $\mathcal{D}$ and $\mathcal{D}'$ are (t, ϵ)-*indistinguishable*, denoted by $\mathcal{D} \sim_{(t, \epsilon)} \mathcal{D}'$, if $\mathrm{ADV}(\mathcal{A}, \mathcal{D}, \mathcal{D}') \leq \epsilon$, for any adversary $\mathcal{A}$ running in time bounded by t.

A function f from a set A to the $\mathsf{Distr}(B)$ can be canonically extended to a function $\hat{f}$ from $\mathsf{Distr}(A)$ to $\mathsf{Distr}(B)$ as follows: $\hat{f}(X) = [a \xleftarrow{r} X; b \xleftarrow{r} f(a) : b]$. We shall tacitly identify $f : A \to \mathsf{Distr}(B)$ with its canonical extension $\hat{f}$.

A block cipher is a *family of permutations* $\Pi : \mathbf{Keys}(\Pi) \times \mathcal{U} \to \mathcal{U}$, where $\mathbf{Keys}(\Pi)$ is the key space of Π, and for any $k \in Keys(\Pi)$, $\Pi(k, \cdot)$ is a permutation onto $\mathcal{U}$. We use $\mathsf{Enc}(k, \cdot)$ (resp. $\mathsf{Dec}(k, \cdot)$) instead of $\Pi(k, \cdot)$ (resp. $\Pi^{-1}(k, \cdot)$). *Pseudo-randomness.* The usual security notion for ciphers (cf.[8]), states that an adversary accessing an oracle $\mathcal{O}_b$ — either $\mathcal{O}_0$, a random permutation, or $\mathcal{O}_1$, the encryption function — has a bounded advantage to guess which one it has been given (or equivalently the value of b). Formally, consider the following experiments parameterized by b, where Perm is the set of all permutations on $\mathcal{U}$:

Experiment $\mathbf{PRP}_b(\mathcal{A})$:
$\quad k \xleftarrow{r} \mathbf{Keys}(\Pi); \mathscr{P} \xleftarrow{r} \mathsf{Perm};$
$\quad \mathcal{O}_0 = \mathscr{P}; \mathcal{O}_1 = \mathsf{Enc}(k, \cdot);$
$\quad b' \leftarrow \mathcal{A}^{\mathcal{O}_b}()$

The **PRP** advantage of $\mathcal{A}$ is defined as

$$\text{ADV}_{\Pi}^{\text{prp}}(\mathcal{A}) = |\Pr[\mathbf{PRP}_1(\mathcal{A}) = 1] - \Pr[\mathbf{PRP}_0(\mathcal{A}) = 1]|.$$

An encryption scheme Π is a (t, ϵ)-pseudo-random permutation, denoted (t, ϵ)-**PRP**, if for any adversary $\mathcal{A}$ running in time t, $\text{ADV}_{\Pi}^{\text{prp}}(\mathcal{A}) \leq \epsilon$.

3 An Imperative Language with Random Assignment and Deterministic Encryption

In this section, we present a simple while-language extended with a random assignment command and deterministic encryption. We then present in following section type systems for its underlying expressions and commands.

3.1 Expressions

We consider a signature with a sort S, a countable set of constant symbols denoted by $n, n_0, n_1, \cdots$ and two binary function symbols $+ : S \times S \rightarrow S$ and $g : S \times S \rightarrow S$. We restrict the presentation to two function symbols for simplicity. We consider an interpretation for this signature given by a structure $(\mathcal{U}, \mathcal{I}(\cdot), \mathcal{I}_+(\cdot, \cdot), \mathcal{I}_g(\cdot, \cdot))$ such that:

1. $\mathcal{U} = \{0, 1\}^p$, where p is an integer. We use $u \xleftarrow{r} \mathcal{U}$ as an alternative notation for $u \xleftarrow{r} \mathcal{D}$, where $\mathcal{D}$ is the uniform probability distribution on $\mathcal{U}$.
2. $\mathcal{I}(\cdot)$ is a deterministic algorithm that takes as input a constant symbol n and computes an element $\mathcal{I}(n)$ in $\mathcal{U}$.
3. $\mathcal{I}_+(u, v)$ is the bitwise exclusive or of u and v. (Actually, this can be generalized to any deterministic algorithm such that $[u \xleftarrow{r} \mathcal{U} : \mathcal{I}_+(u, v)]$ and $[u \xleftarrow{r} \mathcal{U} : \mathcal{I}_+(v, u)]$ coincide with the uniform distribution on $\mathcal{U}$.)
4. $\mathcal{I}_g(\cdot, \cdot)$ is a deterministic algorithm that given two elements of $\mathcal{U}$, computes an element in $\mathcal{U}$. We denote the function $\lambda(u, v) \cdot \mathcal{I}_g(u, v)$ by $\mathcal{I}(g)$.

The set **Exp** of expressions is given by the following BNF, where metavariable x ranges over a countable set **Var** of identifiers (variables):

$$e ::= x \mid n \mid e_1 + e_2 \mid g(e_1, e_2)$$

A *memory* (or state) is a mapping that associates to each variable a value in $\mathcal{U}$. The set of memories is denoted by Σ. Given a memory σ, we can associate a value $\mathcal{I}(e)\sigma \in \mathcal{U}$ to each expression e in the usual way.

3.2 Commands

The syntax of the **eWhile** language we consider is defined in Figure 1.

The loop construct is indexed with an integer number n that specifies the maximal number of permitted unfolding of the loop statement. In other words,

$c ::= x := e \mid x := \mathsf{Enc}(k, e) \mid \mathbf{skip} \mid \nu x \mid \mathbf{if}\ e\ \mathbf{then}\ c_1\ \mathbf{else}\ c_2\ \mathbf{fi}\ \mid$
$\qquad \mathbf{while}_n\ e\ \mathbf{do}\ c\ \mathbf{od}\ \mid c_1; c_2$

Fig. 1. Language syntax of eWhile

a loop statement either terminates because the loop condition becomes false or because the limit n is reached. The reason for adding this is that we are only interested in commands whose running time is bounded. The command $x := \mathsf{Enc}(k, e)$ encrypts the value of e with the key k and stores the result in x.

To a command c, we associate as meaning a function from states to distributions on states: $[\![c]\!] : \Sigma \to \mathsf{Distr}(\Sigma)$. The equations defining $[\![c]\!]$ are given in Figure 2. In the sequel, we will assume given a function $\mathbb{T}(c)$ that bounds the running time of the program c.

$$[\![x := e]\!](\sigma) = [: \sigma[\mathcal{I}(e)\sigma/x]] \qquad\qquad [\![c_1; c_2]\!] = \widehat{[\![c_2]\!]} \circ [\![c_1]\!]$$
$$[\![\nu x]\!](\sigma) = [u \xleftarrow{r} \mathcal{U}; \sigma' := \sigma[u/x] : \sigma'] \qquad [\![\mathbf{skip}]\!](\sigma) = [: \sigma]$$
$$[\![x := \mathsf{Enc}(k, e)]\!](\sigma) = [: \sigma[\mathsf{Enc}(k, \mathcal{I}(e)\sigma)/x]]$$
$$[\![\mathbf{if}\ e\ \mathbf{then}\ c_1\ \mathbf{else}\ c_2\ \mathbf{fi}\ ]\!](\sigma) = \mathbf{if}\ (\mathcal{I}(e))\sigma = 1\ \mathbf{then}\ [\![c_1]\!](\sigma)\ \mathbf{else}\ [\![c_2]\!](\sigma)\ \mathbf{fi}$$
$$[\![\mathbf{while}_n\ e\ \mathbf{do}\ c\ \mathbf{od}\ ]\!](\sigma) = \begin{cases} [\![\mathbf{if}\ e\ \mathbf{then}\ c; \mathbf{while}_{n-1}\ e\ \mathbf{do}\ c\ \mathbf{od}\ \mathbf{else}\ \mathbf{skip}\ \mathbf{fi}\ ]\!](\sigma) \\ \qquad \text{if } n > 0 \\ [: \sigma]; \text{ otherwise} \end{cases}$$

Fig. 2. Language semantics of eWhile

4   Typing Expressions

The expressions introduced so far are deterministic in the sense that the value of an expression is determined once σ is fixed. In order to reason about expressions involving random nonces, we introduce *randomized expressions* defined as follows: $re ::= e \mid \nu x \cdot re$. For $\boldsymbol{x} = (x_1, \cdots, x_n)$, we write $\nu \boldsymbol{x} \cdot e$ instead of $\nu x_1 \cdots \nu x_n \cdot e$. Consider a randomized expression re and let σ be a memory. We define $[\![re]\!] : \Sigma \to \mathsf{Distr}(\mathcal{U} \times \Sigma)$ as follows:

1. $[\![e]\!](\sigma) = [: (\mathcal{I}(e)\sigma, \sigma)]$ and
2. $[\![\nu x \cdot re]\!](\sigma) = [u \xleftarrow{r} \mathcal{U}; \sigma' := \sigma[u/x]; (v, \sigma'') \xleftarrow{r} [\![re]\!](\sigma') : (v, \sigma'')]$.

Henceforth, let $\mathbb{T}(re)$ be an upper-bound on the time needed to evaluate $[\![re]\!](\sigma)$, for any σ. Given an expression re, let $\mathsf{fvar}(re)$ denote the set of variables that occur free in re, i.e. $\mathsf{fvar}(\nu x_1 \cdots \nu x_n \cdot e) = var(e) \setminus \{x_1, \cdots, x_n\}$. In the following, we write $x \# re$ to mean $x \notin \mathsf{fvar}(re)$, and $x_1, \ldots, x_n \# re_1, \ldots, re_k$ to mean $x_i \# re_j$ for all (i, j) and $x_i \neq x_j$ for all (i, j).

4.1   Typing Expressions

The set **TypeExp** of expression types consists of pairs (τ_s, τ_r) with $\tau_s \in \{L, H\}$ and $\tau_r \in \{\top, L^r, H^r\}$. Intuitively, τ_s is the security type; while τ_r is the

$$L \sqsubseteq H \qquad\qquad H^r \sqsubseteq L^r \sqsubseteq \top \qquad\qquad \tau \sqsubseteq \tau$$

$$\frac{\tau_s \sqsubseteq \tau'_s, \ \tau_r \sqsubseteq \tau'_r}{(\tau_s, \tau_r) \sqsubseteq (\tau'_s, \tau'_r)} \qquad \frac{\tau_1 \sqsubseteq \tau_2, \ \tau_2 \sqsubseteq \tau_3}{\tau_1 \sqsubseteq \tau_3} \qquad (H, H^r) \sqsubseteq (L, L^r)$$

Subtyping rules

$$\frac{\Gamma(x) = \tau_s}{\Gamma \vdash x : (\tau_s, \top)} \ (\text{var}) \qquad\qquad \frac{\Gamma(x) = \tau_s}{\Gamma \vdash \nu x \cdot x : (\tau_s, \tau_s^r)} \ (\text{R-var})$$

$$\frac{-}{\Gamma \vdash n : (L, \top)} \ (\text{int}) \qquad\qquad \frac{\Gamma \vdash re : \tau, \ \tau \sqsubseteq \tau'}{\Gamma \vdash re : \tau'} \ (\text{Subt})$$

$$\frac{\begin{array}{c} \Gamma \vdash \nu x_1 \cdot e_1 : (\tau_s, \tau_r) \\ \Gamma \vdash \nu x_2 \cdot e_2 : (\tau_s, \tau'_r) \\ x_i \# re_j, x_j, \text{ for } i \neq j \end{array}}{\Gamma \vdash \nu x_1 \cdot \nu x_2 \cdot (e_1 + e_2) : (\tau_s, \tau_r \sqcap \tau'_r)} \ (+) \quad \frac{\begin{array}{c} \Gamma \vdash \nu x_1 \cdot e_1 : (\tau_s, \top) \\ \Gamma \vdash \nu x_2 \cdot e_2 : (\tau_s, \top) \\ x_i \# re_j, x_j, \text{ for } i \neq j \end{array}}{\Gamma \vdash \nu x_1 \cdot \nu x_2 \cdot g(e_1, e_2) : (\tau_s, \top)} \ (\text{exp})$$

Typing rules

$$\frac{\Gamma \vdash re : \tau}{\Gamma \vdash \nu x \cdot re : \tau} \ (\nu\text{-Intr}) \qquad \frac{\Gamma \vdash \nu y \cdot \nu x \cdot re : \tau}{\Gamma \vdash \nu x \cdot \nu y \cdot re : \tau} \ (\nu\text{-Comm})$$

Structural rules

Fig. 3. Typing rules for Expressions

randomness type. That is, $\top$ means that the expression can be deterministic or randomized; H^r means that it is randomized and contains a "random seed" that is secret; and L^r means that it is randomized and the "random seed" might be public. For instance, consider the expression $h_r + l$ with h_r a secret variable whose value is random and l a public variable. Then, it will be typed (H, H^r) as the random seed h_r is secret. On the other hand, $l_r + l$ will be typed (L, L^r) as it does not depend on a secret variable and the random seed is public. Why should we type these expressions differently? The reason is that the expression $(h_r + l) + h$ can be typed public (low) but the expression $(l_r + l) + h$ must be typed secret (high).

A *type environment* maps each variable in **Var** to a security type in $\{L, H\}$. Our type judgements are of the form $\Gamma \vdash e : \tau$, where $e \in$ **Exp** and $\tau \in$ **TypeExp**. We give our typing and sub-typing rules in Figure 3. A few intuition: the sub-typing rule $(H, H^r) \sqsubseteq (L, L^r)$ says that an expression that is randomized with a secret "random seed", can be downgraded (and in this case, its randomness is made public); the rule $(+)$ takes into account the good properties of $+$, if one of the arguments is randomized (and the random seed is not reused), then their sum is randomized too.

Example 2. Let Γ be a type environment such that $\Gamma(h_r) = \Gamma(h) = H$. Then, we have:

$$\frac{\Gamma(h_r) = H}{\Gamma \vdash \nu h_r \cdot h_r : (H, H^r)} \text{ (R-var)} \quad \frac{\Gamma(h) = H}{\Gamma \vdash h : (H, \top)} \text{ (var)}$$

$$\frac{\Gamma \vdash \nu h_r \cdot (h_r + h) : (H, H^r)}{\Gamma \vdash \nu h_r \cdot (h_r + h) : (L, L^r)} \text{ (Sixth subtyping rule)} \;(+)$$

Soundness of the Type System. We now undertake the endeavor to show that expressions typed (L, L^r) do not leak information. In order to rigorously define information leakage, we first introduce Γ-*equivalent distributions*.

Definition 1. *Let X be a distribution on Σ and Γ a type environment. Let $\Gamma^{-1}(L) = \{x \mid \Gamma(x) = L\}$ be the set of low variables and assume that this set is finite. We denote by $\Gamma(X)$ the distribution $[\sigma \xleftarrow{r} X : \sigma_{|\Gamma^{-1}(L)}]$. Moreover, we write $X =^\Gamma Y$, if $\Gamma(X) = \Gamma(Y)$, and $X \sim_{(t,\epsilon)}^\Gamma Y$, if $\Gamma(X) \sim_{(t,\epsilon)} \Gamma(Y)$. Similarly, for a distribution X on $\mathcal{U} \times \Sigma$, we denote by $\Gamma(X)$ the distribution $[(v,\sigma) \xleftarrow{r} X : (v, \sigma_{|\Gamma^{-1}(L)})]$.*

The following theorem expresses soundness of our type system for expressions.

Theorem 1. *Let re be an expression, Γ be a type environment and let $X, Y \in \mathsf{Distr}(\Sigma)$ arbitrary distributions.*

- *If $X =^\Gamma Y$ and $\Gamma \vdash re : (L, \top)$, then $[\![re]\!](X) =^\Gamma [\![re]\!](Y)$.*
- *If $X \sim_{(t,\epsilon)}^\Gamma Y$ and $\Gamma \vdash re : (L, \top)$, then $[\![re]\!](X) \sim_{(t - \mathbb{T}(re), \epsilon)}^\Gamma [\![re]\!](Y)$.*

5 A Type System for Commands

5.1 The Typing System

In this section, we present a computationally sound type system for the **eWhile** language of Section 3.2 . We consider programs where applications of Enc have been annotated by r, in case its argument has type (τ, τ^r), and by $\top$, in case it has type $(\tau, \top)$. Recall the following examples from Section 1:

1. $\nu \ell_r; \ell := \mathsf{Enc}^r(k, h + \ell_r); \ell' := \mathsf{Enc}^\top(k, h' + \ell_r)$,
2. $\nu \ell_r; \ell' := \mathsf{Enc}^r(k, h + \ell_r); \ell'' := \mathsf{Enc}^r(k, h' + \ell')$.

The first program is not secure since $h = h'$ iff $\ell = \ell'$. The problem here is that the same random value assigned to ℓ_r is used twice. The second program is secure since the value assigned to ℓ' after the first assignment is indistinguishable from a randomly sampled value. This is due to the properties of the encryption function that we assume to be a pseudo-random permutation. Thus, in order to have a sound type system, we need to forbid the reuse of the same sampled value in two different encryptions; and in order to have a not too restrictive type system, we need to record the variables that are assigned pseudo-random values as a result of the encryption function. This motivates the introduction of the functions $\mathcal{F}$, resp. $\mathcal{G}$, used to compute the propagation of the set of variables that should not be used inside calls of Enc annotated with $\top$, resp. that can be used as random seeds. Informally, variables in the latter set all follow the uniform distribution, and are all independent together and from all variables but the ones in the former set.

$$
\begin{aligned}
\mathcal{F}(\mathbf{skip})(F) &= F \\
\mathcal{F}(\nu x)(F) &= F \setminus \{x\} \\
\mathcal{F}(x := e)(F) &= F \setminus \{x\} \text{ if } \mathsf{fvar}(e) \cap F = \emptyset \\
\mathcal{F}(x := e)(F) &= F \cup \{x\} \text{ otherwise} \\
\mathcal{F}(x := \mathsf{Enc}^r(k, e))(F) &= F \cup \mathsf{fvar}(e) \setminus \{x\} \\
\mathcal{F}(x := \mathsf{Enc}^\top(k, e))(F) &= F \\
\mathcal{F}(c_1; c_2)(F) &= \mathcal{F}(c_2)(\mathcal{F}(c_1)(F)) \\
\mathcal{F}(\mathbf{if}\ e\ \mathbf{then}\ c_1\ \mathbf{else}\ c_2\ \mathbf{fi}\ )(F) &= \mathcal{F}(c_1)(F) \cup \mathcal{F}(c_2)(F) \\
\mathcal{F}(\mathbf{while}_n\ e\ \mathbf{do}\ c\ \mathbf{od}\ )(F) &= \mathcal{F}(c)^\infty(F) \\
\text{where } \mathcal{F}(c)^\infty(F) \text{ is defined as } &\quad \bigcap \{M \mid \mathcal{F}(c)(M) \subseteq M \text{ and } F \subseteq M\}.
\end{aligned}
$$

$$
\begin{aligned}
\mathcal{G}(\mathbf{skip})(G) &= G \\
\mathcal{G}(\nu x)(G) &= G \cup \{x\} \\
\mathcal{G}(x := e)(G) &= G \setminus (\{x\} \cup \mathsf{fvar}(e)) \\
\mathcal{G}(x := \mathsf{Enc}^r(k, e))(G) &= (G \setminus \mathsf{fvar}(e)) \cup \{x\} \\
\mathcal{G}(x := \mathsf{Enc}^\top(k, e))(G) &= G \setminus (\{x\} \cup \mathsf{fvar}(e)) \\
\mathcal{G}(c_1; c_2)(G) &= \mathcal{G}(c_2)(\mathcal{G}(c_1)(G)) \\
\mathcal{G}(\mathbf{if}\ e\ \mathbf{then}\ c_1\ \mathbf{else}\ c_2\ \mathbf{fi}\ )(G) &= \mathcal{G}(c_1)(G \setminus \mathsf{fvar}(e)) \cap \mathcal{G}(c_2)(G \setminus \mathsf{fvar}(e)) \\
\mathcal{G}(\mathbf{while}_n\ e\ \mathbf{do}\ c\ \mathbf{od}\ )(G) &= \mathcal{G}(c)^\infty(G \setminus \mathsf{fvar}(e)) \\
\text{where } \mathcal{G}(c)^\infty(G) \text{ is defined as } &\quad \bigcup \{M \mid M \subseteq \mathcal{G}(c)(M) \text{ and } M \subseteq G\}.
\end{aligned}
$$

Our type judgements have the form $\Gamma, F, G \vdash c : \tau$, where $\tau \in \{L, H\}$ is a security type. The intuitive meaning is the following: in the environment Γ, where the variables in G are assigned random values, and the variables in F are forbidden, c (detectably) affects only variables of type greater than or equal to τ; after its execution, variables in $\mathcal{G}(c)(G)$ have random values, and variables in $\mathcal{F}(c)(F)$ are forbidden. We give the typing and subtyping rules in Figure 4. Our type system ensures that encryption downgrades the security level only in case of random expressions. In other words, $\mathsf{Enc}^\top(k, h)$ has the security level H, and hence, cannot be stored into a low variable, while $\mathsf{Enc}^r(k, h + l_r)$ has security level L, because l_r is a random value that is not used elsewhere. It might appear surprising that the Rule ($\mathsf{Enc}^\top$), which does not allow downgrading, is more restrictive than Rule (Enc^r). To understand this consider the command $\nu l_r; \ell := \mathsf{Enc}^r(k, h + l_r); \ell' := \mathsf{Enc}^\top(k, l_r)$. Leaking the encryption of the low variable l_r allows to check whether $h = 0$, and hence, should be forbidden.

Example 3. This example shows that our system is able to show the security of a cipher block chaining implementation. For simplicity reasons (and because we do not consider arrays yet) we illustrate the case of encrypting two blocks.

$$
\begin{aligned}
&\nu l_0; \\
&l_1 := \mathsf{Enc}(k, l_0 + h_1); \\
&l_2 := \mathsf{Enc}(k, l_1 + h_2);
\end{aligned}
$$

$$\frac{}{\Gamma,F,G \vdash \nu x : \Gamma(x)}\ \text{nu-var} \qquad\qquad \frac{}{\Gamma,F,G \vdash \mathbf{skip} : H}\ \text{skip}$$

$$\frac{\Gamma \vdash \nu G \cdot e : (\Gamma(x), \top)}{\Gamma,F,G \vdash x := e : \Gamma(x)}\ \text{ass} \qquad\qquad \frac{\begin{array}{c}\Gamma,F,G\ \ \vdash\ \ c\ \ :\ \ \tau \\ G \subseteq G'\ \ F' \subseteq F\ \ \tau' \sqsubseteq \tau\end{array}}{\Gamma,F',G' \vdash c : \tau'}\ \text{weak}$$

$$\frac{\begin{array}{c}\Gamma \vdash \nu G \cdot e : (\Gamma(x), \top) \\ \mathsf{fvar}(\nu G \cdot e) \cap F = \emptyset\end{array}}{\Gamma,F,G \vdash x := \mathsf{Enc}^\top(k,e) : \Gamma(x)}\ \mathsf{Enc}^\top \qquad \frac{\Gamma \vdash \nu G \cdot e : (H, L^r)}{\Gamma,F,G \vdash x := \mathsf{Enc}^r(k,e) : \Gamma(x)}\ \mathsf{Enc}^r$$

$$\frac{\begin{array}{c}\Gamma,F,G \setminus \mathsf{fvar}(e) \vdash c_1 : \tau \\ \Gamma,F,G \setminus \mathsf{fvar}(e) \vdash c_2 : \tau \\ \Gamma\ \vdash\ \nu G \cdot e\ :\ (\tau, \top) \\ \mathsf{fvar}(\nu G \cdot e) \cap F = \emptyset\end{array}}{\Gamma,F,G \vdash \mathbf{if}\ e\ \mathbf{then}\ c_1\ \mathbf{else}\ c_2\ \mathbf{fi}\ : \tau}\ \text{if} \qquad \frac{\begin{array}{c}\Gamma, \mathcal{F}(c)^\infty(F), \mathcal{G}(c)^\infty(G)\ \ \vdash\ \ c\ \ :\ \ \tau \\ \Gamma\ \ \vdash\ \ \nu \mathcal{G}(c)^\infty(G)\cdot e\ \ :\ \ (\tau, \top) \\ \mathsf{fvar}(\nu \mathcal{G}(c)^\infty(G)\cdot e) \cap \mathcal{F}(c)^\infty(F) = \emptyset\end{array}}{\Gamma,F,G \vdash \mathbf{while}_n\ e\ \mathbf{do}\ c\ \mathbf{od}\ : \tau}\ \text{while}$$

$$\frac{\Gamma,F_1,G_1 \vdash c_1 : \tau \quad \Gamma, \mathcal{F}(c_1)(F_1), \mathcal{G}(c_1)(G_1) \vdash c_2 : \tau}{\Gamma,F_1,G_1 \vdash c_1;c_2 : \tau}\ \text{seq}$$

Fig. 4. Type systems for commands in **eWhile**

Let Γ be a type environment such that $\Gamma(h_0) = \Gamma(h_1) = H$ and $\Gamma(l_0) = \Gamma(l_1) = \Gamma(l_2) = L$. This program can be typed in our system as follows:

$$\frac{\Gamma,\emptyset,\emptyset \vdash \nu l_0 : L \qquad \dfrac{\dfrac{\dfrac{\dfrac{\Gamma(l_0) = L}{\Gamma \vdash \nu l_0 \cdot l_0 : (L, L^r)}\ \text{(R-var)}}{\Gamma \vdash \nu l_0 \cdot (l_0 + h_1) : (H, L^r)}\ \text{(+)}}{\Gamma, \emptyset, \{l_0\} \vdash l_1 := \mathsf{Enc}(k, l_0 + h_1) : L}\ \text{(ass)} \qquad \dfrac{\dfrac{\dfrac{\Gamma(l_1) = L}{\Gamma \vdash \nu l_1 \cdot l_1 : (L, L^r)}\ \text{(R-var)}}{\Gamma \vdash \nu l_1 \cdot (l_1 + h_2) : (H, L^r)}\ \text{(+)}}{\Gamma, \{l_0, h_1\}, \{l_1\} \vdash l_2 := \mathsf{Enc}(k, l_1 + h_2) : L}\ \text{(ass)}}{\Gamma, \emptyset, \{l_0\} \vdash l_1 := \mathsf{Enc}(k, l_0 + h_1); l_2 := \mathsf{Enc}(k, l_1 + h_2) : L}\ \text{(seq)}}{\Gamma, \emptyset, \emptyset \vdash \nu l_0; l_1 := \mathsf{Enc}(k, l_0 + h_1); l_2 := \mathsf{Enc}(k, l_1 + h_2) : L}\ \text{(seq)}$$

5.2   Soundness of the Typing System of eWhile

In this section, we state the soundness of the type system of the **eWhile** language and sketch its proof. The detailed proof is given in [1].

Let $\mathcal{T}(c)$ denote an upper bound on the number of Enc^r and $\mathsf{Enc}^\top$ calls that can be executed during any run of c. Notice that because the running time of c is bounded such a bound exists. Then, we can state the following theorem:

Theorem 2. *Let c be a program, let Γ be a type environment and let Π be an encryption scheme. Moreover, let X and Y be two distributions.*
If Π is (t', ϵ')-__PRP__, $X \sim^\Gamma_{(t,\epsilon)} Y$ and $\Gamma, \emptyset, \emptyset \vdash c : \tau$ then $[\![c]\!](X) \sim^\Gamma_{(t'',\epsilon'')} [\![c]\!](Y)$
with $t'' = \min(t - \mathbb{T}(c), t' - \mathbb{T}(c))$ and $\epsilon'' = \epsilon + 2\epsilon' + \dfrac{2\mathcal{T}(c)^2}{|\mathcal{U}|}$.

Proof (Sketch). Let **rWhile** denote the set of programs without any call to $\mathsf{Enc}(k, \cdot)$ and **pWhile** denote the set of programs where the encryption function $\mathsf{Enc}(k, \cdot)$ is interpreted as a random permutation. The main idea of the soundness proof is as follows. Consider a command c with $\Gamma, \emptyset, \emptyset \vdash c : \tau$. Then, let $[\![c]\!]^\pi$ denote its interpretation in **pWhile** and let c^r obtained from c by replacing

$x := \mathsf{Enc}^r(k, e)$ by νx and $x := \mathsf{Enc}^\top(k, e)$ by $g(e)$. Then, we can prove the following statements:

Proposition 1. *For any distribution Z, we have*

1. $[\![c]\!]^\pi(Z) \sim_{(t'-\mathbb{T}(c),\epsilon')} [\![c]\!](Z)$ *and*
2. $[\![c]\!]^\pi(Z)$ *and* $[\![c^r]\!](Z)$ *are* $\frac{\mathbb{T}(c)^2}{|\mathcal{U}|}$-*statistically close.*

We can also prove the following soundness result of our type system for **rWhile**:

Proposition 2. *Let c be a command in **rWhile**, let Γ be a type environment and let $X, Y \in \mathsf{Distr}(\Sigma)$ be arbitrary distributions.*
If $X \sim_{(t,\epsilon)}^\Gamma Y$ and $\Gamma, \emptyset, \emptyset \vdash c : \tau$ then $[\![c]\!](X) \sim_{(t-\mathbb{T}(c),\epsilon)}^\Gamma [\![c]\!](Y)$.

From Propositions 1 and 2, we obtain the theorem by transitivity.

Proof Sketch of Proposition 1. Let us consider the first item. Let $\mathcal{A}$ be an adversary trying to distinguish $[\![c]\!](Z)$ and $[\![c]\!]^\pi(Z)$. We construct an adversary $\mathcal{B}$ against the encryption scheme Π, that runs in time $t' + \mathbb{T}(c)$ and whose advantage is the same as $\mathcal{A}$'s advantage. The adversary $\mathcal{B}$ runs an experiment for $\mathcal{A}$ against $[\![c]\!](Z)$ and $[\![c]\!]^\pi(Z)$ using his oracles. First, $\mathcal{B}$ executes the command c using its encryption oracle. That is, whenever a command $x := \mathsf{Enc}(k, e)$ is to be executed in the command c, $\mathcal{B}$ computes the value of e and calls its encryption oracle. After termination of the command c in some state σ, $\mathcal{B}$ runs $\mathcal{A}$ on σ and gives the same answer as $\mathcal{A}$. Formally:

$$\textbf{Adversary } \mathcal{B}^{\mathcal{O}_b}$$
$$b \xleftarrow{r} \{0, 1\}; \quad \sigma \xleftarrow{r} [\![c]\!]^{\mathcal{O}_b}(Z); \quad \mathcal{A}(\sigma).$$

Now it is clear that $\mathrm{ADV}_\Pi^{\mathrm{prp}}(\mathcal{B}) = \mathrm{ADV}(\mathcal{A}, [\![c]\!](Z), [\![c]\!]^\pi(Z))$. Moreover, the running time of $\mathcal{B}$ is $\mathcal{A}$'s running time augmented with the time need for computing $[\![c]\!](Z)$, i.e. $\mathbb{T}(c)$. We conclude that $[\![c]\!]^\pi(Z) \sim_{(t'-\mathbb{T}(c),\epsilon')} [\![c]\!](Z)$.

Consider now the second item. Roughly speaking, the bound $\frac{\mathbb{T}(c)^2}{|\mathcal{U}|}$ corresponds to the probability of collisions between arguments of Enc^r among themselves and with with arguments of $\mathsf{Enc}^\top$; and collisions among values returned by ν. Moreover, we can then prove that c^r is a well-typed **rWhile** program. □

6   Conclusion

This extended abstract introduces a type system for an imperative language that includes deterministic encryption and random assignment. It establishes soundness of the type system under the assumption that the encryption scheme is a pseudo-random permutation. The proof is carried in the concrete security setting, thus providing concrete security estimates. Our work can be extended in several directions. First, we could consider encryption as "first class" expressions. This is not a substantial extension as any such program can be easily translated into our language and refining the type of variables to (τ_s, τ_r) as for expressions.

Second, we could consider decryption. An easy way to do this is to type the result of any decryption with H. This may not, however, be satisfactory as the so-obtained type system would be too restrictive. An other extension consists in considering generation and manipulation of keys - it is not difficult to extend the type system to deal with this, we need, however, to introduce conditions on the expressions (acyclicity) and to apply hybrid arguments; data integrity - which are in some sense dual to non-interference. Some of these extensions are considered in the full paper [1], which also contains the detailed proofs of the results presented in this extended abstract. In the full paper, we also show that our notion of non-interference implies semantic security and Laud's notion.

References

[1] Courant, J., Ene, C., Lakhnech, Y.: Computationally sound typing for non-interference: The case of deterministic encryption. Technical report, VERIMAG-University of Grenoble and CNRS (2007)

[2] Denning, D.E., Denning, P.J.: Certification of programs for secure information flow. Commun. ACM 20(7), 504–513 (1977)

[3] Goguen, J.A., Meseguer, J.: Security policies and security models. In: IEEE Symposium on Security and Privacy, pp. 11–20 (1982)

[4] Laud, P.: Semantics and program analysis of computationally secure information flow. In: Sands, D. (ed.) ESOP 2001 and ETAPS 2001. LNCS, vol. 2028, pp. 77–91. Springer, Heidelberg (2001)

[5] Laud, P.: Handling encryption in an analysis for secure information flow. In: Degano, P. (ed.) ESOP 2003 and ETAPS 2003. LNCS, vol. 2618, pp. 159–173. Springer, Heidelberg (2003)

[6] Laud, P., Vene, V.: A type system for computationally secure information flow. In: Liśkiewicz, M., Reischuk, R. (eds.) FCT 2005. LNCS, vol. 3623, pp. 365–377. Springer, Heidelberg (2005)

[7] Malacaria, P.: Assessing security threats of looping constructs. In: Hofmann, M., Felleisen, M. (eds.) POPL, ACM, New York (2007)

[8] Phan, D.H., Pointcheval, D.: About the security of ciphers (semantic security and pseudo-random permutations). In: Handschuh, H., Hasan, M.A. (eds.) SAC 2004. LNCS, vol. 3357, pp. 182–197. Springer, Heidelberg (2004)

[9] Sabelfeld, A., Myers, A.: Language-Based Information-Flow Security. IEEE Journal on Selected Areas in Comunications 21, 5–19 (2003)

[10] Sabelfeld, A., Sands, D.: Declassification: Dimensions and principles. Journal of Computer Security (2007)

[11] Smith, G., Alpzar, R.: Secure information flow with random assignment and encryption. In: FMSE, pp. 33–44 (2006)

[12] Volpano, D.M.: Secure introduction of one-way functions. In: CSFW, pp. 246–254 (2000)

[13] Volpano, D.M., Irvine, C.E., Smith, G.: A sound type system for secure flow analysis. Journal of Computer Security 4(2/3), 167–188 (1996)

Bounding Messages for Free in
Security Protocols

Myrto Arapinis and Marie Duflot

LACL - University Paris 12, France
myrto@arapinis.org, duflot@univ-paris12.fr

Abstract. The verification of security protocols has been proven to be undecidable in general. Different approaches use simplifying hypotheses in order to obtain decidability for interesting subclasses. Amongst the most common is type abstraction, *i.e.* considering only well-typed runs, therefore bounding message length. In this paper, we show how to get message boundedness "for free" under a reasonable (syntactic) assumption on protocols, which we call well-formedness. This enables us to improve existing decidability results.

1 Introduction

Security protocols are short programs that describe communication between two or more parties in order to achieve security goals such as data confidentiality, identification of a correspondent, *etc.* The protocols are executed in a hostile environment, such as the Internet, and aim at preventing a malicious agent from tampering with the messages, for instance, using encryption. However, encrypting messages is not sufficient to ensure security properties. History has shown that these protocols are extremely error-prone, and careful formal verification is needed.

Despite the apparent simplicity of such protocols, their verification is a difficult problem and has been proven undecidable in general [DLMS99, CC01]. Indeed, models we need to consider for protocols are (i) of infinite depth, and (ii) infinitly branching. The depth infinity arises from the unbounded length of traces (since an unbounded number of instances of the protocol can be involved). On the other hand, infinite branching is due to the unboundedness of message length (if no bound on the message length is set, then the intruder can input an arbitrary number of messages that must be considered). The present paper is mainly concerned with the second source of undecidability.

We introduce a syntactic condition of "well-formedness", and a strong typing system, which ensure that only well-typed runs need to be considered for security analysis. Indeed, we prove that a well-formed protocol admits an attack if and only if it admits a "well-typed" attack. This gives a bound on the size of messages that needs to be considered. Many existing results [Low99, RS03a, DLMS99, CKR+03] bound the message length, in order to obtain decidability. But while they do so in adopting a type abstraction, an *ad hoc*

V. Arvind and S. Prasad (Eds.): FSTTCS 2007, LNCS 4855, pp. 376–387, 2007.
© Springer-Verlag Berlin Heidelberg 2007

assumption according to which one can always tell the type of a given message, we provide a simple way of justifying it.

Although this question has already been addressed in [LYH04, HLS03] amongst others, and solved with tagging schemes, the syntactic criterion introduced here is significantly lighter. Moreover, the typing system we consider here is much more fine-grained. It thus refines existing results in decreasing importantly the branching that needs to be considered.

Finally, to the best of our knowledge, only very few papers [Low99,RS03a, RS03b] give decidability results with an unbounded number of sessions and nonces. Such a result is achieved in [RS03b] by means of tagging. In the last part of this paper, we show that this tagging scheme can be lightened by combining the decidability results obtained in [RS03a, Low99] under the typing abstraction, and the result presented in this paper.

2   Modelling Security Protocols

In this section, we define the trace based model used throughout the paper to define and reason about security protocols.

2.1   The Syntax

Messages exchanged are modelled as terms in the following way. We first assume several disjoint sets of atomic terms. A finite set $\mathcal{P} = \{P_1, \ldots, P_k\}$ of *principal names* standing for the different participants of the protocol. During one protocol execution, each principal P_i generates a finite set $\mathcal{K}_i = \{K_1^i, \ldots, K_{l_i}^i\}$ of short-term keys or *session keys*, as well as a finite set $\mathcal{N}_i = \{N_1^i, \ldots, N_{m_i}^i\}$ of fresh values called *nonces*. The set of session keys (*resp.* nonces) generated by all principals is denoted $\mathcal{K} = \bigcup_{1 \leq i \leq k} \mathcal{K}_i$ (*resp.* $\mathcal{N} = \bigcup_{1 \leq i \leq k} \mathcal{N}_i$). We assume a finite set $\mathcal{C} = \{c_1, \ldots, qc_n\}$ of constants. Finally, in order to model participants' beahviour, we also need to assume, for each principal P_i, a finite set $\mathcal{X}_i = \{X_1^i, \ldots, X_{p_i}^i\}$ of *variables*. Variables are used to model the fact that a principal may receive data which he cannot check (nonces generated by other principals for instance). The set of variables is then $\mathcal{X} = \bigcup_{1 \leq i \leq k} \mathcal{X}_i$.

The set of terms is defined inductively over the above sets as follows:

$$\mathcal{T} ::= \mathcal{P} \mid \text{pb}(\mathcal{P}) \mid \text{pv}(\mathcal{P}) \mid \text{sh}(\mathcal{P},\mathcal{P}) \mid \mathcal{K} \mid \mathcal{N} \mid \mathcal{C} \mid \mathcal{X} \mid \langle \mathcal{T}, \mathcal{T} \rangle \mid \{\mathcal{T}\}_{\mathcal{T}} \mid \text{sig}_{\mathcal{T}}(\mathcal{T})$$

where $\text{pb}(P)$, $\text{pv}(P)$, $\text{sh}(P, P')$ are respectively the public key, private key of principal P and shared key between principals P and P', and $\langle t_1, t_2 \rangle$, $\{t_1\}_{t_2}$, $\text{sig}_{t_1}(t_2)$ represent pairing, encryption and signature.

In what follows, we denote the set of variables of a term t by $\mathcal{V}(t)$ and the set of subterms of t by $St(t)$. These are defined as usual. The set of encrypted subterms of t is denoted by $ESt(t)$ and is defined as $ESt(t) = \{f(t_1, t_2) \mid f \in \{\{\text{-}\}_\text{-}, \text{sig}_\text{-}(\text{-})\}\}$.

In order to capture precisely what can be sent by a principal and what can be accepeted by the receiver, we split the rules commonly used to describe protocols [CJ97] into send and receive actions. We thus have a set of actions $\mathcal{D} = \mathcal{S} \cup \mathcal{R}$

where $\mathcal{S} = \{P_i!P_j : t \mid P_i, P_j \in \mathcal{P}, \ P_i \neq P_j, \ t \in \mathcal{T}\}$ is the set of *send actions* and $\mathcal{R} = \{P_i?P_j : t \mid P_i, P_j \in \mathcal{P}, \ P_i \neq P_j, \ t \in \mathcal{T}\}$ is the set of *receive actions*.

The term of an action is defined as $term(P_i!P_j : t) = term(P_i?P_j : t) = t$, and for every sequence of actions $D = d_1 \ldots d_n$, $terms(D) = \bigcup_{1 \leq i \leq n} term(d_i)$. Similarly, the set of variables of D is $\mathcal{V}(D) = \bigcup_{t \in terms(D)} \mathcal{V}(t)$, the set of sub-terms of D is $St(D) = \bigcup_{t \in terms(D)} St(t)$, and the set of encrypted subterms of D is $ESt(D) = \bigcup_{t \in terms(D)} ESt(t)$.

Finally, before giving the definition of protocols, we also need to define substitution. A *substitution* is a map θ from variables to terms. $\theta(t)$ or $t\theta$ will denote indifferently the application of substitution θ to term t. A *unifier* of two terms t and t' is a substitution θ such that $\theta(t) = \theta(t')$. The *most general unifier* of two terms t, t', $mgu(t, t')$, is a unifier θ of t and t' such that for all unifier ψ of t and t' there exists a substitution ϕ such that $\psi = \phi \circ \theta$. We will denote the fact that two terms t and t' are not unifiable by $mgu(t, t') = \perp$. The domain of a substitution θ is the set of variables actually instantiated by θ, *i.e.* $dom(\theta) = \{X \mid \theta(X) \neq X\}$.

Definition 1. *A protocol $\Pi = s_1r_1 \ldots s_lr_l$ is a sequence of send-receive actions such that, $\forall i, 1 \leq i \leq l$*

1. *$s_i \in \mathcal{S}$ and $r_i \in \mathcal{R}$*
2. *if $s_i = P!P' : t$, then $r_i = P'?P : t'$*
3. *if $X \in \mathcal{V}(term(s_i))$, then $\exists j, \ 1 \leq j < i$ such that $X \in \mathcal{V}(term(r_j))$*
4. *for every $1 \leq i \leq l$ there exists a substitution $\delta_i \neq \perp$, with*

$$\begin{cases} \delta_1 = mgu(term(s_1), term(r_1)), and \\ \delta_k = mgu(\delta_{k-1}(\ldots \delta_1(s_k)), \delta_{k-1}(\ldots \delta_1(r_k))), \ \forall 1 < k \leq l. \end{cases}$$

The composition $\delta = \delta_l \circ \cdots \circ \delta_1$ is the honest substitution for all the variables occurring in the protocol specification.

This means that a protocol is a sequence of actions, such that each send action corresponds to a matching receive action between the same two principals. Moreover, point 3 states that a variable must be received before being sent, since an agent cannot send a message it doesn't know.

A *role* of the protocol is the restriction (in the usual sense) of Π to the actions (send and receive) of one of the principals, as illustrated in the following example.

Example 1. The Needham-Schroeder protocol

$$\begin{aligned} \Pi^{NS} = \ &P_1 \ ! \ P_2 : \{P_1, N_1^1\}_{\mathrm{pb}(P_2)} \\ &P_2 \ ? \ P_1 : \{P_1, X_1^2\}_{\mathrm{pb}(P_2)} \\ &P_2 \ ! \ P_1 : \{X_1^2, N_1^2\}_{\mathrm{pb}(P_1)} \\ &P_1 \ ? \ P_2 : \{N_1^1, X_1^1\}_{\mathrm{pb}(P_1)} \\ &P_1 \ ! \ P_2 : \{X_1^1\}_{\mathrm{pb}(P_2)} \\ &P_2 \ ? \ P_1 : \{N_1^2\}_{\mathrm{pb}(P_2)} \end{aligned}$$

The protocol has two principals, hence two roles described here.

$$\Pi_1^{NS} = P_1 \; ! \; P_2 : \{P_1, N_1^1\}_{\mathrm{pb}(P_2)} \qquad \Pi_2^{NS} = P_2 \; ? \; P_1 : \{P_1, X_1^2\}_{\mathrm{pb}(P_2)}$$
$$P_1 \; ? \; P_2 : \{N_1^1, X_1^1\}_{\mathrm{pb}(P_1)} \qquad\qquad\quad P_2 \; ! \; P_1 : \{X_1^2, N_1^2\}_{\mathrm{pb}(P_1)}$$
$$P_1 \; ! \; P_2 : \{X_1^1\}_{\mathrm{pb}(P_2)} \qquad\qquad\qquad P_2 \; ? \; P_1 : \{N_1^2\}_{\mathrm{pb}(P_2)}$$

2.2   The Semantics

After having described the roles of a protocol, *i.e.* the way things should happen in an honest execution of the protocol, we will now describe how things really happen. In particular, we have to take into account the fact that a protocol can be executed several times, by different agents, and that in each case the nonces and keys generated should be different, in order to ensure freshness.

A *session* will be a partial instantiation of one of the roles of the protocol. Since we do not assume the number of sessions to be bounded, we consider an infinite set $\Sigma = \{\sigma_n \mid n \in \mathbb{N}\}$ of *session ids*. In the same vein, we consider an infinite set $\mathcal{A} = \{a_n \mid n \in \mathbb{N}\} \cup \{\epsilon\}$ of *agents* that will play the roles of the protocol, with the special agent ϵ standing for the *intruder*.

Nonces in $\mathcal{N}$ and Keys in $\mathcal{K}$ should be instantiated by different values in each session. We also need to distinguish variables from different sessions. To do so, we consider the following infinite sets, where the session id is used to distinguish two instances of the same nonce, session key and variable respectively.

$\mathfrak{K} = \{K_j^i(\sigma) \mid K_j^i \in \mathcal{K}, \; \sigma \in \Sigma\}$ of *session keys*,
$\mathfrak{N} = \{N_j^i(\sigma) \mid N_j^i \in \mathcal{N}, \; \sigma \in \Sigma\}$ of *nonces*, and
$\mathfrak{X} = \{X_j^i(\sigma) \mid X_j^i \in \mathcal{X}, \; \sigma \in \Sigma\}$ of *variables*.

We do not need to consider the intruder as a normal agent that generates keys and nonces during a session. It is provided at the beginning with a set of nonces and session keys:

$\mathfrak{N}_\epsilon = \{\mathfrak{n}_j^i \mid i,j \; s.t. \; N_j^i \in \mathcal{N}\}$, and $\mathfrak{K}_\epsilon = \{\mathfrak{k}_j^i \mid i,j \; s.t. \; K_j^i \in \mathcal{K}\}$.

Using the above defined sets, we can inductively define the set of (instantiated) terms.

$$\mathfrak{T} ::= \mathcal{A} \mid \mathrm{pb}(\mathcal{A}) \mid \mathrm{pv}(\mathcal{A}) \mid \mathrm{sh}(\mathcal{A}, \mathcal{A}) \mid \mathfrak{K} \mid \mathfrak{K}_\epsilon \mid \mathfrak{N} \mid \mathfrak{N}_\epsilon \mid \mathcal{C} \mid \mathfrak{X} \mid \langle \mathfrak{T}, \mathfrak{T} \rangle \mid \{\mathfrak{T}\}_{\mathfrak{T}} \mid \mathrm{sig}_{\mathfrak{T}}(\mathfrak{T})$$

The set $\mathfrak{M}$ of actual messages exchanged on the network is the set of ground terms, *i.e.* variable-free terms. Based on this definition of instantiated terms, we define the set $\mathfrak{D} = \mathfrak{S} \cup \mathfrak{R}$ of possible instantiations of send and reveive actions.

As said above, in a session σ, of role P_i, between participants $(b_1, \ldots, b_k) \in \mathcal{A}^k$, each nonce $N_j^i \in \mathcal{N}_i$ (*resp.* session-key $K_j^i \in \mathcal{K}_i$) must be instantiated with a fresh value $N_j^i(\sigma)$ (*resp.* session-key $K_j^i(\sigma)$), each principal name $P_j \in \mathcal{P}$ must be instantiated with agent name b_j, and each variable $X_j^i \in \mathcal{X}_i$ must be individuated in terms of the session by $X_j^i(\sigma)$. This is ensured by means of function $||\cdot||_{(\sigma, b_1, \ldots, b_k)}$ (*e.g* $||N_j^i||_{(\sigma, b_1, \ldots, b_k)} = N_j^i(\sigma)$ and $||P_j||_{(\sigma, b_1, \ldots, b_k)} = b_j$). $||\cdot||_{(\sigma, b_1, \ldots, b_k)}$ is inductively extended to terms, actions, and sequences of actions as expected.

The formal execution model is a state transition system. A global state of the system is given by (SId, q, I) where SId is a set of sessions, q is a function that describes the local state of each session in SId and $I \subseteq \mathfrak{M}$ represents the intruder's knowledge.

More precisely, $\forall \sigma \in SId$, $q(\sigma) = (i, b_1, \ldots, b_k, \theta, p)$ is the local state of session σ:

- i is the index of the role that is executed in this session,
- $(b_1, \ldots, b_k) \in \mathcal{A}^k$ are the identities of the parties that are involved in the session,
- θ is a partial instantiation of variables occuring in $||\Pi_i||_{(\sigma, b_1, \ldots, b_k)}$,
- p is the control point of the program.

Given a protocol Π, the initial state of any trace of Π is (SId_0, q_0, I_0), with $SId_0 = \emptyset$ (and thus the definition of q_0 is useless) and $I_0 = \mathcal{A} \cup \mathcal{C} \cup \mathfrak{K}_\epsilon \cup \mathfrak{N}_\epsilon \cup \{\mathbf{pb}(a) \mid a \in \mathcal{A}\} \cup \{\mathbf{sh}(a, \epsilon), \mathbf{sh}(\epsilon, a) \mid a \in \mathcal{A}\} \cup \{\mathbf{pv}(\epsilon)\}$ (the intruder knows the agent names, constants, his own session keys and nonces, every agent's public key as well as his own private key and the keys he shares with other agents).

Let $Q = (SId, q, I)$ be a global state for Π. Three types of transition $Q \xrightarrow{e} update(Q, e)$ may be allowed:

1. *Initiate a new session* for the ith role $(e = \mathbf{new}(\sigma, i, b_1, \ldots, b_k))$:
   - Event e is enabled at state Q whenever the session σ does not belong to SId, the agent b_i is not the intruder and any two agents taking part in this new session are distinct.
   - The effect of firing this transition is $update(Q, e) = (SId \cup \{\sigma\}, q', I)$ with
   $$\begin{cases} q'(\sigma') = q(\sigma'), \ \forall \sigma' \in SId \\ q'(\sigma) = (i, b_1, \ldots, b_k, \emptyset, 1). \end{cases}$$

2. *Execute next send-action of an existing session* $\sigma \in SId$ $(e = \mathbf{snd}(\sigma, p))$:
   - Event e is enabled at state Q whenever the control point of session σ is p and the next action to perform in σ is a send action.
   - The effect of firing this transition is $update(Q, e) = (SId, q', I \cup \{m\})$ with $m = \theta(||t||_{(\sigma, b_1, \ldots, b_k)})$ and
   $$\begin{cases} q'(\sigma') = q(\sigma'), \ \forall \sigma' \in SId, \ \sigma' \neq \sigma \\ (q'(\sigma) = (i, b_1, \ldots, b_k, \theta, p+1)). \end{cases}$$

3. *Execute next receive-action of an existing session* $\sigma \in SId$ $(e = \mathbf{rcv}(\sigma, p, m))$:
   - Event e is enabled at state Q whenever the control point of session σ is p and the next action to perform in σ is a receive action.
     - $m \in \mathfrak{M}$ is a message that can be computed by the intruder from I,
     - $q(\sigma) = (i, b_1, \ldots, b_k, \theta, p)$ (the control point of σ is p),
     - $\Pi_i(p) = P_i?_j : t$ (the next action is a receive),
     - $\psi \neq \bot$, where $\psi = mgu(m, \theta(||t||_{(\sigma, b_1, \ldots, b_k)}))$ (m and the expected message are unifiable).

– The effect of firing this transition is $update(Q, e) = (SId, q', I)$ with

$$\begin{cases} q'(\sigma') = q(\sigma'), \ \forall \sigma' \in SId, \ \sigma' \neq \sigma \\ q'(\sigma) = (i, b_1, \ldots, b_k, \theta \cup \psi, p + 1). \end{cases}$$

The adversary intercepts messages between honest participants and computes new messages using the deduction rule $\vdash$ defined in Fig.1. Intuitively $M \vdash m$ means that the adversary is able to compute the message m from the set of messages M. The notation m^{-1} stands for $\mathbf{pb}(a)$ if m is of the type $\mathbf{pv}(a)$, $\mathbf{pv}(a)$ if m is of the type $\mathbf{pb}(a)$, and $m^{-1} = m$ otherwise.

$$\frac{}{M \vdash m} \ m \in M$$

$$\frac{M \vdash m_1 \quad M \vdash m_2}{M \vdash \langle m_1, m_2 \rangle} \qquad\qquad \frac{M \vdash \langle m_1, m_2 \rangle}{M \vdash m_i} \ 1 \leq i \leq 2$$

$$\frac{M \vdash m_1 \quad M \vdash m_2}{M \vdash \{m_1\}_{m_2}} \qquad\qquad \frac{M \vdash \{m_1\}_{m_2} \quad M \vdash m_2^{-1}}{M \vdash m_1}$$

$$\frac{M \vdash m_1 \quad M \vdash m_2}{M \vdash \mathbf{sig}_{m_1}(m_2)} \qquad\qquad \frac{M \vdash \mathbf{sig}_{m_1}(m_2) \quad M \vdash m_1^{-1}}{M \vdash m_2}$$

Fig. 1. Deduction rules

2.3 The Secrecy Problem

Let Π be an arbitrary k-party protocol. We say that Π guarantees the secrecy of nonce $N_j^i \in \mathcal{N}$ (resp. session key $K_j^i \in \mathcal{K}$) if, in all possible executions, each honest instantiation of N_j^i (resp. K_j^i) remains unknown to the adversary. More formally,

Definition 2. We say that Π preserves secrecy of nonce $N_j^i \in \mathcal{N}$ (of session key resp. $K_j^i \in \mathcal{K}$) if for every valid trace $(SId_0, s_0, I_0) \ \rightarrow^* \ (SId_n, s_n, I_n)$ of the protocol and for every session $\sigma \in SId$ such that $q_n(\sigma)$ is of the form $(i, b_1, \ldots, b_k, \theta, p)$, $(b_1, \ \ldots, \ b_k) \in (\mathcal{A} \setminus \{\epsilon\})^k$ (i.e. k honest agents) for some θ and some p, we have $I_n \not\vdash N_j^i(\sigma)$ (resp. $I_n \not\vdash K_j^i(\sigma)$).

We say that Π admits an attack on nonce $N_j^i \in \mathcal{N}$ (resp. session key $K_j^i \in \mathcal{K}$) if Π does not preserve secrecy of N_j^i (resp K_j^i).

3 Well-Formed Protocols and Well-Typed Attacks

In this section, we state the main result of the paper. We prove that for *well-formed* protocols (*i.e.* with non unifiable subterms), for verification of the secrecy property we only need to consider well-typed runs of the protocol, *i.e* for well-formed protocols the typing abstraction, with respect to the following type system, is correct with repsect to the secrecy problem.

3.1   Types

We introduce in this section a very strong typing on messages, that will allow us to restrict significantly the set of traces to consider in order to detect an attack. For example, nonces may have different types, depending on the role that generated them, and the point of their generation in the protocol.

We first use a single type agent α for every principal name $P \in \mathcal{P}$. In particular, the intruder has the same type as any other agent.

To each session key K_j^i in $\mathcal{K}$ (resp. nonce N_j^i in $\mathcal{N}$, constant c_i in $\mathcal{C}$), we associate a different type κ_j^i (resp. ν_j^i, γ_i). The notations κ, ν and γ denote respectively the set of session key types, nonce types and constant types.

We thus obtain inductively the following type set for terms:

$$\tau ::= \alpha \mid \kappa \mid \nu \mid \gamma \mid \mathbf{pb}(\alpha) \mid \mathbf{pv}(\alpha) \mid \mathbf{sh}(\alpha,\alpha) \mid \langle \tau, \tau \rangle \mid \{\tau\}_\tau \mid \mathbf{sig}_\tau(\tau)$$

The typing rules are given in Fig.2.

$$\frac{P \in \mathcal{P}}{P : \alpha} \qquad\qquad \frac{c_i \in \mathcal{C}}{c_i : \gamma_i} \qquad\qquad \frac{K_j^i \in \mathcal{K}}{K_j^i : \kappa_j^i}$$

$$\frac{N_j^i \in \mathcal{N}}{N_j^i : \nu_j^i} \qquad\qquad \frac{P \in \mathcal{P}}{\mathbf{pb}(P) : \mathbf{pb}(\alpha)} \qquad\qquad \frac{P \in \mathcal{P}}{\mathbf{pv}(P) : \mathbf{pv}(\alpha)}$$

$$\frac{P, P' \in \mathcal{P}}{\mathbf{sh}(P,P') : \mathbf{sh}(\alpha,\alpha)} \qquad \frac{t_1 : \tau_1 \quad t_2 : \tau_2}{f(t_1, t_2) : f(\tau_1, \tau_2)} \qquad \frac{X \in \mathcal{X} \quad \delta(X) : \tau}{X : \tau}$$
$$f \in \{\langle \_, \_ \rangle, \{\_\}\_, \mathbf{sig}\_(\_)\}$$

$$\frac{t : \tau}{\|t\|_{(\sigma, b_1, \dots, b_k)} : \tau} \qquad\qquad \frac{\mathfrak{k}_j^i \in \mathfrak{K}_\epsilon}{\mathfrak{k}_j^i : \kappa_j^i} \qquad\qquad \frac{\mathfrak{n}_j^i \in \mathfrak{N}_\epsilon}{\mathfrak{n}_j^i : \nu_j^i}$$

Fig. 2. Typing rules

Definition 3. *A well-typed run is a valid trace* $(SId_0, q_0, I_0) \rightarrow^* (SId_n, q_n, I_n)$ *such that for every session id* $\sigma \in SId_n$ *with* $q_n(\sigma) = (i, b_1, \dots, b_k, \theta, p)$, *for some* $i, b_1, \dots, b_k, \theta, p$, *it is the case that* θ *preserves types, i.e. for every variable* $X \in dom(\theta)$, $X : \tau \Rightarrow \theta(X) : \tau$.

This definition states that each variable used in the specification is always instantiated (using substitution θ) by a message of the expected type. The following definition constrains unifiability between subterms of different types.

Definition 4. *A protocol* Π *(Definition 1) is said to be* well-formed *when the following condition holds:*
  $\forall t, t' \in ESt(\Pi)$, *if there exist* $(\sigma, b_1, \dots, b_k), (\sigma', b_1', \dots, b_k') \in \Sigma \times \mathcal{A}^k$ *and a substitution* θ *such that* $\theta(\|t\|_{(\sigma, b_1, \dots, b_k)}) = \theta(\|t'\|_{(\sigma', b_1', \dots, b_k')})$, *then* $\delta(t) = \delta(t')$.

This condition is often met in practice in the literature (see [CJ97]). And even when the protocol isn't well-formed, a light tagging scheme ensures well-formednes, as it is done in [BP05] in which a different label is introduced at every encryption step of the specification. We present such a tagging scheme in definition 6 when discussing the decidability results of [RS03a]. (Note that tagging is already present in protocols such as SSH.)

3.2   Considering Only Well-Typed Runs for Well-Formed Protocols

We now state the main result of this paper. Due to a lack of space we only give the main ideas of the proof here. Further details can be found in [AD07].

Theorem 1. *Let Π be a well-formed protocol. If Π admits an attack, then Π admits a well-typed attack.*

The proof is based on the fact that if a protocol admits an attack, then it admits an attack of bounded length n, which can thus be found. The proof of theorem 1 is done by induction on a procedure searching for this attack. Indeed, we show that the considered procedure from [CDD07] instantiates variables only with terms of the expected type. We will first detail this procedure and then come back to explanations concerning well-typedness of computed substitutions.

The secrecy problem for security protocols can be translated into a constraint satisfaction problem [MS01, CZ06, CDD07, RT01]. In [CDD07], it is shown that using some simplification rules, solving general constraints can be reduced to solving simpler constaint systems that are called *solved*.

Definition 5. *[CDD07] A constraint system C is a finite set of expressions $T_i \Vdash tt$ or $T_i \Vdash u_i$ where $T_i \subseteq \mathfrak{T}$, $T_i \neq \emptyset$, tt is a special symbol that represents an always deducible term, and $u_i \in \mathfrak{T}$, $1 \leq i \leq n$, such that:*

- *$T_i \subseteq T_{i+1}$, $\forall i$, $1 \leq i \leq n-1$;*
- *if $X \in \mathcal{V}(T_i)$, then $\exists j<i$ such that $T_j = \min\{T \mid T \Vdash u \in C, X \in \mathcal{V}(u)\}$ (for the inclusion relation) and $T_j \subsetneq T_i$*

$\perp$ denotes the unsatisfiable system. A constraint system is said to be solved if it is different from $\perp$ and each of its constraints are of the form $T \Vdash tt$ or $T \Vdash X$, where $X \in \mathfrak{X}$.

The left-hand side of the constraint $T \Vdash u$ is T and u is its right-hand side. The left-hand side $lhs(C)$ of the constraint system C is the maximal left-hand side of its constraints, and the right-hand side $rhs(C)$ of C is the set of messages in the right-hand side of its constraints. We consider the following sets over C defined as expected: $\mathcal{V}(C) = \mathcal{V}(lhs(C)) \cup \mathcal{V}(rhs(C))$, $terms(C) = lhs(C) \cup rhs(C)$, $St(C) = St(terms(C))$ and $ESt(C) = ESt(terms(C))$.

The simplification rules we consider are defined in Fig.3. They have been proven correct, complete and terminating in polynomial time [CDD07].

From correction, completeness and termination, it follows that the secrecy problem for a protocol Π admitting an attack can be translated into a constraint

R_1 $\quad C \wedge T \Vdash u \rightsquigarrow_\emptyset C \wedge T \Vdash tt$ $\quad\quad$ if $T \cup \{X \mid T' \Vdash X \in C, T' \subsetneq T\} \vdash u$

R_2 $\quad C \wedge T \Vdash u \rightsquigarrow_\psi C\psi \wedge T\psi \Vdash u\psi$ $\quad$ if $\psi = \mathrm{mgu}(t, u), t \in ESt(T)$
$\quad\quad\quad\quad\quad\quad\quad\quad\quad\quad\quad\quad\quad\quad\quad\quad\quad\quad\quad\quad$ $t \neq u, u$ not variable

R_3 $\quad C \wedge T \Vdash u \rightsquigarrow_\psi C\psi \wedge T\psi \Vdash u\psi$ $\quad$ if $\psi = \mathrm{mgu}(t_1, t_2), t_1, t_2 \in ESt(T)$
$\quad\quad\quad\quad\quad\quad\quad\quad\quad\quad\quad\quad\quad\quad\quad\quad\quad\quad\quad\quad$ $t_1 \neq t_2$

R_4 $\quad C \wedge T \Vdash u \rightsquigarrow_\emptyset \bot$ $\quad\quad\quad\quad\quad$ if $\mathcal{V}(T, u) = \emptyset$ and $T \nvdash u$

R_f $\quad C \wedge T \Vdash f(u, v) \rightsquigarrow_\emptyset C \wedge T \Vdash u \wedge T \Vdash v$ $\quad$ for $f \in \{\langle \_, \_ \rangle, \{\_\}\_, \mathbf{sig}\_(\_)\}$

Fig. 3. Simplification rules

system C_0 admitting a sequence of simplifications that leads to a solved constraint system C_n:

$$C_0 \rightsquigarrow_{\theta_1}^{R_{i_1}} C_1 \rightsquigarrow_{\theta_2}^{R_{i_2}} \cdots \rightsquigarrow_{\theta_n}^{R_{i_n}} C_n$$

As said before, the proof of theorem 1 is done by induction on the length n of this sequence of simplifications. We will show that C_n is well-typed (*i.e.* $\forall j$, $1 \leq j \leq n$, θ_j preserves types).

It is easy to see that rules R_1, R_4 and R_f preserve well-typedness since they do not instantiate any variable.

For rules R_2 and R_3 we show, by means of some lemmas detailed in [AD07] (again due to a lack of space), that the selected subterms t and t', such that $\psi_j = \mathrm{mgu}(t, t')$ $1 \leq j \leq n$ when $R_{i_j} \in \{R_2, R_3\}$, are of the same type, and that computing the mgu of two terms of the same type results in a well-typed substitution. This allows us to conclude that, when applying these rules, variables are instantiated only with terms of the expected type, and thus they preserve well-typedness.

The following corollary is an immediate consequence of the previous theorem and of the fact that function application (pairing, encrypting and signing) is embedded in the type of a term.

Corollary 1. *Let Π be a well-formed protocol. If Π admits an attack, and B is the length of the longest message in an honest run of the protocol, then Π admits an attack with messages of bounded length B.*

We have thus proven in this section that the encryption abstraction is correct for well-formed protocols. And that this holds for a much more fine-grained type notion than the one considered in [LYH04, HLS03], where all nonces and session keys are of the same type. This severely restricts the search space to consider for verification purposes. We now define a tagging scheme that ensures well-formedness.

Definition 6. *A tagged protocol is a protocol (Definition 1) s. t.:*

$\forall t \in ESt(\Pi), \exists c \in \mathcal{C}$ and $t_1, t_2 \in \mathfrak{T}$ s.t. $t = \{c, t_1\}_{t_2}$ or $t = \mathbf{sig}_{t_1}(c, t_2)$,
$\forall t, u, t_1, u_1, t_2, u_2 \in ESt(\Pi), \forall c \in \mathcal{C}$ s.t. $t = f(c, t_1, t_2)$ and $u = f(c, u_1, u_2)$,
$\delta(t) = \delta(u)$.

It immediately follows that such tagged protocols verify well-formedness. This tagging scheme is extremely lighter than the ones in [LYH04, HLS03] where the whole type of an encrypted subterm is used for tagging it. We have thus obtained a more refined type abstraction with a very simple tagging scheme.

4   Application to Decidability Results

As claimed in the introduction, the type assumption is often necessary in order to obtain decidability and in particular in the presence of an unbounded number of sessions and nonces. Indeed, Lowe in [Low99] as well as Ramanujam and Suresh in [RS03a] prove the decidability of a class of protocols but assume that messages are of bounded length.

In [RS03a], the authors prove decidability of the secrecy problem (for a stronger definition of secrecy than the one given in section 2) in the framework of messages of bounded length, for a class of protocols they call structured. Since structured protocols do not admit blind copies (*i.e.* do not admit variables of non-atomic type, corresponding to encrypted terms received by a participant P_i but which P_i cannot decrypt), we can slightly strengthen their definition in order to ensure well-formedness, and we claim that this does not restrict the class of protocols from a semantic point of view. Indeed, any structured protocol in the sence of [RS03a] can easily be transformed in a well-structured protocol in the sense of definition 7 (because of the absence of blind copies) without changing its purported "meaning". Hence we can combine the decidability result in [RS03a] and theorem 1.

Definition 7. *A protocol* $\Pi = s_1 r_1 \ldots s_l r_l$ *is said to be well-structured if the following conditions hold:*

- Π *doesn't have blind copies, each variable is of atomic type,*
- *keys are atomic,*
- *encrypted subterms are textually distinct, an encrypted subterm t of a protocol in the described class can be unified only with its matching send or receive* t'.

The above definition constrains unifiability of different subterms (even of the same message) whereas the one of [RS03a] only constrains unifiability of subterms of different messages.

As already argued above, the additional restriction is not severe and acceptable as it yields decidability for unbounded messages. Moreover, since two encrypted subterms of the protocol $t, t' \in ESt(\Pi)$ are unifiable *iff* the one is the send or receive message of the other, it is the case that $\delta(t) = \delta(t')$. Thus well-structured protocols as defined in definition 7 are well-formed, which permits us to conclude to the decidability of well-structured protocols in the frame of unbounded message length.

One way of ensuring well-structuredness may be by means of tags/labels. The following definition is an adaptation of definition 6 to the framework of [RS03a].

Definition 8. *A protocol* $\Pi = s_1 r_1 \ldots s_l r_l$ *is a tagged protocol if it satisfies the folowing conditions:*

- *no blind copies*,
- *keys are atomic*,
- $\forall t \in ESt(\Pi),\ \exists c \in \mathcal{C},\ \exists t_1, t_2 \in \mathfrak{T}$ such that $t = \{c, t_1\}_{t_2}$ or $t = \mathtt{sig}_{t_2}(c, t_1)$
- $\forall c, c' \in \mathcal{C}, \forall i \neq j,\ 1 \leq i, j \leq l,$ if $f(c, t_1, t_2) \in ESt(s_i)$ then $\forall f(c', u_1, u_2) \in ESt(s_j),\ c \neq c'$
- $\forall c \in \mathcal{C}, \forall i\ 1 \leq i, j \leq l,\ \forall p \in \mathbb{N}^*,$ if $term(s_i)|_p = f(c, t_1, t_2)$ then $\forall q \in \mathbb{N}^*$ s.t. $q \neq p\ \wedge\ term(s_i|_q) = f(c', u_1, u_2),\ c \neq c'$.

The third condition is similar to all definitions of tagged protocols [BP05, RS03b]. The fourth condition stipulates that each tag is used at most in one send event; and the fifth, that a tag used in a send event is used in at most one position. We have thus constrained a term to be used exactly once in the protocol. Thus any encrypted subterm is unifiable with and only with its matching send or receive action. Therefore tagged protocols are well-structured, and we can hence conclude to decidability of the secrecy problem for tagged protocols (as defined in definition 8). The secrecy problem, for the class of tagged protocols, is shown to be decidable in [RS03b], but the considered tagging scheme is heavier. Indeed, in the above definition a few bits are sufficient to tag messages, whereas in [RS03b] each encrypted subterm of the protocol is tagged with a pair (c, N) where c is a constant and N is a different nonce making the tagging scheme heavier.

5   Conclusion

The result presented in this paper is a first step towards decidability. We have proven that for a well known and wide class of protocols (that we call well-formed) the type abstraction is correct. Therefore there is no need to check for badly typed attacks, and this restricts the search space to consider in order to prove secrecy for a protocol. This was achieved in a much more economic way than in [LYH04, HLS03]. Furthermore, the type abstraction is here significantly refined and thus the search space to consider, in order to find an attack, is smaller than in [LYH04, HLS03].

In addition, we have shown how this result can improve existing decidability results. We also believe it could improve the efficiency of existing tools by restricting their search space to well-typed executions.

Our next goal is to use our theorem to get decidability for (at least a large subclass of) our well-formed protocols. The idea is that protocols at stake in existing undecidability proofs lie outside our framework. They are either not executable (*i.e.* in an honest execution, some action of the specification can never occur) or not well-formed (*i.e.* they allow, for example, to replay a message generated in a session at step m in another session at step $n < m$ without the agents noticing it). We expect that the restriction to well-formed and executable protocols will lead to a larger decidable subclass.

Acknowledgments. The authors are very grateful to Véronique Cortier, Stéphanie Delaune, Steve Kremer and S. P. Suresh for enlightening discussions while conceiving this paper.

References

[AD07]   Arapinis, M., Duflot, M.: Bounding messages for free in security protocols
           (extended version) (2007), http://www.arapinis.org/publications/
           fsttcs07ext.pdf
[BP05]   Blanchet, B., Podelski, A.: Verification of cryptographic protocols: Tagging
           enforces termination. TCS: Theoretical Computer Science 333 (2005)
[CC01]   Comon, H., Cortier, V.: Tree automata with one memory, set constraints
           and cryptographic protocols. Research Report LSV-01-13, Laboratoire
           Spécification et Vérification, ENS Cachan, France, p. 98 (2001)
[CDD07]   Cortier, V., Delaître, J., Delaune, S.: Safely composing security protocols.
           In: Arvind, V., Prasad, S. (eds.) FSTTCS 2007. LNCS, vol. 4855, Springer,
           Heidelberg (2007)
[CJ97]   Clark, J.A., Jacob, J.L.: A survey of authentication protocol literature
           (1997)
[CKR+03]   Chevalier, Y., Küsters, R., Rusinowitch, M., Turuani, M., Vigneron, L.:
           Extending the Dolev-Yao intruder for analyzing an unbounded number of
           sessions. In: Baaz, M., Makowsky, J.A. (eds.) CSL 2003. LNCS, vol. 2803,
           pp. 128–141. Springer, Heidelberg (2003)
[CZ06]   Cortier, V., Zalinescu, E.: Deciding key cycles for security protocols. In:
           Hermann, M., Voronkov, A. (eds.) LPAR 2006. LNCS (LNAI), vol. 4246,
           pp. 317–331. Springer, Heidelberg (2006)
[DLMS99]   Durgin, N., Lincoln, P., Mitchell, J., Scedrov, A.: Undecidability of
           bounded security protocols. In: Proc. Work. on Formal Methods and Se-
           curity Protocols (FMSP) (1999)
[HLS03]   Heather, J., Lowe, G., Schneider, S.: How to prevent type flaw attacks on
           security protocols. Journal of Computer Security 11(2), 217–244 (2003)
[Low99]   Lowe, G.: Towards a completeness result for model checking of security
           protocols. Journal of Computer Security 7(1) (1999)
[LYH04]   Li, Y., Yang, W., Huang, C.-W.: Preventing type flaw attacks on security
           protocols with a simplified tagging scheme. In: ISICT 2004. Proc. Int.
           symp. on Information and communication technologies, Trinity College
           Dublin, pp. 244–249 (2004)
[MS01]   Millen, J.K., Shmatikov, V.: Constraint solving for bounded-process cryp-
           tographic protocol analysis. In: Proc. 8th ACM Conf. on Computer and
           Communications Security, pp. 166–175. ACM Press, New York (2001)
[RS03a]   Ramanujam, R., Suresh, S.P.: A decidable subclass of unbounded security
           protocols. In: Proc. Work. on Issues in the Theory of Security (WITS 2003)
           (2003)
[RS03b]   Ramanujam, R., Suresh, S.P.: Tagging makes secrecy decidable with un-
           bounded nonces as well. In: Pandya, P.K., Radhakrishnan, J. (eds.) FST
           TCS 2003. LNCS, vol. 2914, Springer, Heidelberg (2003)
[RT01]   Rusinowitch, M., Turuani, M.: Protocol insecurity with finite number of
           sessions is NP-complete. In: CSFW 2001. Proc. 14th IEEE work. on Com-
           puter Security Foundations, p. 174. IEEE Computer Society Press, Los
           Alamitos (2001)

Triangulations of Line Segment Sets in the Plane

Mathieu Brévilliers, Nicolas Chevallier, and Dominique Schmitt

Laboratoire MIA, Université de Haute-Alsace
4, rue des Frères Lumière, 68093 Mulhouse Cedex, France
{Mathieu.Brevilliers,Nicolas.Chevallier,Dominique.Schmitt}@uha.fr

Abstract. Given a set S of line segments in the plane, we introduce a new family of partitions of the convex hull of S called segment triangulations of S. The set of faces of such a triangulation is a maximal set of disjoint triangles that cut S at, and only at, their vertices. Surprisingly, several properties of point set triangulations extend to segment triangulations. Thus, the number of their faces is an invariant of S. In the same way, if S is in general position, there exists a unique segment triangulation of S whose faces are inscribable in circles whose interiors do not intersect S. This triangulation, called segment Delaunay triangulation, is dual to the segment Voronoi diagram. The main result of this paper is that the local optimality which characterizes point set Delaunay triangulations [10] extends to segment Delaunay triangulations. A similar result holds for segment triangulations with same topology as the Delaunay one.

1 Introduction

The Voronoi diagram of a set S of sites in the d-dimensional Euclidean space $\mathcal{E}$ partitions $\mathcal{E}$ into regions, one per site; the region for a site s consists of all points closer to s than to any other site. In very recent years, particular attention has been paid to the study of the Voronoi diagram of a set of line segments in three dimensions [13], [18], [9], ... However, the topology of this diagram is really known only for a set of three lines [8]. The investigation for the point set Voronoi diagram has been fairly facilitated by the well understanding of its dual, the Delaunay diagram. Recall that, if no $d+1$ points of S are cospherical, the Delaunay diagram of S is the unique triangulation of S whose tetrahedra are inscribable in empty spheres, that is, spheres whose interiors do not intersect S. Among all the triangulations of S, the Delaunay diagram of S has many optimality properties, some of them extending in any dimension [15], [17]. Until now, no such properties have been given, even in the plane, for the dual of the segment Voronoi diagram which has been introduced by Chew and Kedem [5]. Surprisingly, no family of diagrams containing this dual diagram has been defined whereas many generalizations of point set triangulations have been studied: constrained triangulations [11], pseudo-triangulations [16], pre-triangulations [1], ...

In this paper, we introduce a new family of diagrams, called segment triangulations, which decompose the convex hull of a set S of points and line segments

V. Arvind and S. Prasad (Eds.): FSTTCS 2007, LNCS 4855, pp. 388–399, 2007.

in the plane. The set of faces of a segment triangulation of S is a maximal set of disjoint triangles such that the vertices of each triangle belong to three distinct sites of S and no other point of the triangle belongs to S. The edges of the segment triangulation are the (possibly two-dimensional) connected components of the convex hull of S when the sites and open faces are removed. These definitions are natural for, when S is a point set we recover the definitions of the faces and the edges of a point set triangulation. The aim of this paper is to study this new kind of triangulation in order to characterize by local properties the dual of the segment Voronoi diagram among the set of segment triangulations.

The segment triangulations are studied for their own sake in the two first sections. We show that they retain different geometrical and topological properties of point set triangulations and that they are intimately related to some generalized constrained triangulations.

In the next section, we prove that there exists one and only one segment triangulation of S whose faces are inscribable in empty circles. We show that this triangulation, called segment Delaunay triangulation, is the dual, introduced by Chew and Kedem, of the segment Voronoi diagram and can thus be constructed in $O(n \log n)$ time.

The point set Delaunay triangulation admits an important local characterization which is used to prove many of its optimality properties and enables to check in linear time whether a given triangulation is Delaunay or not. This local property states that a triangulation is Delaunay if and only if every couple of faces sharing a common edge is in Delaunay position with respect to its four defining sites [10]. The main result of the second part of the paper is that this property also characterizes the segment Delaunay triangulation among all the segment triangulations of a given set of line segments. We also give another local property that characterizes the set of segment triangulations having the same topological structure as the segment Delaunay triangulation.

2   Segment Triangulations and Constrained Triangulations

Let S be a finite set of $n \geq 2$ disjoint closed segments in the plane, which we call sites. Throughout this paper, a closed segment may possibly be reduced to a single point. We say that a circle is tangent to a site s if s meets the circle but not its interior. The sites of S are supposed to be in general position, that is, we suppose that no three segment endpoints are collinear and that no circle is tangent to four sites.

Definition 1. *A segment triangulation P of S is a partition of the convex hull $conv(S)$ of S in disjoint sites, edges and faces such that:*

(i) *Every face of P is an open triangle whose vertices belong to three distinct sites of S and whose open edges do not intersect S,*

(ii) *No face can be added without intersecting another one,*

(iii) *The edges of P are the (possibly two-dimensional) connected components of $conv(S) \setminus (F \cup S)$, where F is the set of faces of P.*

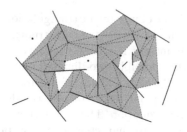

Fig. 1. A weakly constrained triangulation (dotted lines) of an S-polygon (in grey)

Such a triangulation always exists, that is, for any set S, there is a finite number of faces verifying Definition 1. Indeed, it is not difficult to see that at most two disjoint triangles can have their vertices on the same three sites (see Figure 3(a)).

There is a well-known triangulation defined on a set of points and line segments: The constrained triangulation. It is a triangulation of the set of points and segment endpoints such that every given line segment is a side of a triangle. These triangulations are mainly used to triangulate terrains with topographic constraints (mountain crests, roads, ...) or interiors of polygons. However, the triangles being mostly too irregular, so called Steiner points are added to the initial point set (see for example [3]). Steiner points added on the segments enable to split them into subsegments and to generate a better constrained triangulation. We show now that segment triangulations are intimately related to a kind of generalized Steiner triangulation that we call weakly constrained triangulation. In this triangulation (see Figure 1), a point added on a line segment does not split the segment but becomes a vertex of triangles that are on one side of the segment. Therefore, the two sides of a segment are independent. This enables, for example, to independently triangulate two slopes on both sides of a same mountain crest. We now define the weakly constrained triangulation of a restricted region.

Definition 2

(i) *Given a set S of sites, we call S-polygon (possibly with holes), any closed two-dimensional subset A of $conv(S)$, equal to the closure of its interior, such that $A \setminus S$ is connected and the boundary of A is composed of a finite number of disjoint line segments that are of the two following forms:*
    – closed and contained in S,
    – open, not intersecting S, and with their endpoints in S.
(ii) *We call weakly constrained triangulation of A (with respect to S), any partition of A in triangles whose vertices belong to S, whose interiors do not cut S, and whose open sides either do not cut S or are contained in S.*

When $A = conv(S)$, such a triangulation is also called a weakly constrained triangulation of S.

The following lemma will enable to establish the connection between segment triangulations and weakly constrained triangulations.

Lemma 1. *If A is an S-polygon that intersects at least three sites of S then every weakly constrained triangulation of A contains at least one triangle whose vertices belong to three distinct sites of S.*

Proof. Given a weakly constrained triangulation T of A, let $\Delta_T(A)$ be the (possibly empty) set of triangles of T having one side in S. We show, by induction on the number $|\Delta_T(A)|$ of triangles of $\Delta_T(A)$, that T contains at least one triangle whose vertices belong to three distinct sites of S.

Obviously, if $\Delta_T(A) = \emptyset$, the vertices of every triangle of T belong to three distinct sites. Suppose now the result true for every weakly constrained triangulation T with $|\Delta_T(A)| < k$ $(k \geq 1)$.

For every weakly constrained triangulation T of A with $|\Delta_T(A)| = k$ and for every closed triangle t of $\Delta_T(A)$, the closure $\overline{A \setminus t}$ of $A \setminus t$ intersects the same sites as A. If $A \setminus t$ is connected, $A' = \overline{A \setminus t}$ is an S-polygon. Otherwise, $A \setminus t$ has two connected components, the closure of at least one of them being an S-polygon. In the latter case, each of the S-polygons intersects the two sites to which the vertices of t belong. It follows that at least one of these S-polygons intersects at least three sites. Let A' be this S-polygon. In both cases, if T' is the restriction of T to A', $|\Delta_{T'}(A')| < |\Delta_T(A)|$. Thus, by induction hypothesis, T' contains at least one triangle whose vertices belong to three distinct sites of S. It is the same for T. □

It follows from this lemma that, in any weakly constrained triangulation of S, the set F of triangles having their vertices on three distinct sites of S is maximal. Indeed, the closure of every connected component e of $conv(S) \setminus (F \cup S)$ is either a line segment connecting two points of S or an S-polygon. In the second case, it follows from Lemma 1 that $\bar{e}$ can only intersect two sites. Therefore no triangle having its vertices on three distinct sites of S can be added without cutting $F \cup S$. Thus, the theorems:

Theorem 1. *Every weakly constrained triangulation of S is a refinement of a segment triangulation of S, that is, a segment triangulation whose edges are decomposed in triangles.*

Theorem 2. *The closure of every edge of a segment triangulation of S intersects exactly two sites of S.*

This shows that an edge of a segment triangulation P of S is really an edge in that sense that it "connects" exactly two sites of S. Its shape can also be deduced from the discussion above. The closure of an edge either is reduced to a line segment joining two points in two distinct sites of S, or is a triangle with one side and its opposite vertex in S, or is a (possibly non-convex) quadrilateral with two opposite sides in S (see Figure 2). Moreover, every edge of P contains

- either two sides of two triangles of P,
- or one side of one triangle of P and one side of $conv(S)$ that is not a site,
- or two such sides of $conv(S)$.

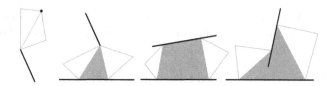

Fig. 2. Examples of edges (grey) connecting two sites in a segment triangulation

Here the edges of a segment triangulation are implicitly defined by complementarity with respect to the faces and to the sites. If we want to extend segment triangulations in d dimensions, the faces of dimension less than d have to be defined explicitly. In the plane, this could be done by defining the edges in the following way: Take a maximal set E of open disjoint line segments that do not cut S and whose endpoints belong to S (in general E is infinite). Then, it can be proved that the connected components of E are the edges of a segment triangulation of S.

3   Topological Properties of Segment Triangulations

Since every edge of a segment triangulation P of S "connects" two sites of S, we can associate an abstract graph with P such that:

- the vertices of the graph are the sites of S,
- the edges connecting two sites s and t in the graph are the edges of P whose closures intersect s and t.

Proposition 1. *The abstract graph associated with a segment triangulation P of S is planar.*

Proof. For every site s of S, let γ_s be a convex closed Jordan curve such that:

- s is inside γ_s (i.e. in the subset of the plane bounded by γ_s),
- $S \setminus s$ is outside γ_s,
- the interior of γ_s intersects only the edges of P whose closures intersect s.

Replace now every site s by a point p_s inside γ_s. For every edge e of P that intersects γ_s, replace the subset of e inside γ_s by a line segment connecting p_s to a point of e on γ_s. While doing this, the order of the edges around s remains unchanged and the reduced edges do not intersect. Once this transformation is fulfilled in every Jordan curve γ_s, replace every reduced edge by a Jordan arc included in it. Finally, we get a planar representation G of the abstract graph associated with P (see Figure 3(b)).   □

Theorem 3. *Every segment triangulation P of a set S of n sites contains $3n - n' - 3$ edges and $2n - n' - 2$ faces, where n' is the number of edges of $conv(S)$ that are not sites.*

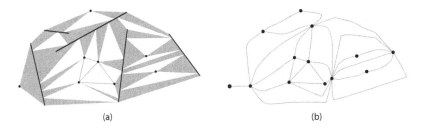

(a)   (b)

Fig. 3. A segment triangulation (a) (the sites are in black, the edges in grey, and the faces in white) and its associated graph (b)

Proof. Counting the edges and faces of P comes down to counting the edges and bounded faces of the planar representation G constructed in the proof of Proposition 1. Moreover, the unbounded face of G corresponds to the complementary of $conv(S)$. The result is then an immediate consequence of Euler's relation, of the fact that every bounded face of G has three edges, and that the edges adjacent to one (resp. no) bounded face appear once (resp. twice) while traversing the boundary of the unbounded face of G.   □

An interesting consequence of this theorem is that the size of a segment triangulation is linear with the number of sites. Moreover, it shows that the number of triangles of the triangulation is an invariant of the set of sites. This is an extension of a well-known property of the triangulations of planar point sets.

Using the planar representation G constructed in the proof of Proposition 1, we can associate a combinatorial map M with the segment triangulation P:

- the underlying graph is the abstract graph associated with the triangulation P,
- for every vertex s of M, the cyclic ordering of the edges out of s agrees with the counter-clockwise ordering of the associated Jordan arcs around s in the planar representation G.

Note that, in general, the same map M is associated with different segment triangulations of S. We say that:

Definition 3. *Two segment triangulations of S have the same topology if they have the same associated combinatorial map.*

In order to use M as a data structure to store the segment triangulation P, we only need to add the coordinates of the vertices of the triangles of P in the structure: One vertex per oriented edge. A segment triangulation of a set S of n sites can thus be stored using $O(n)$ space. Furthermore, from Theorem 1, every constrained triangulation of S is a refinement of a segment triangulation of S. There exists a sweep-line algorithm to construct a constrained triangulation in $O(n \log n)$ time [7] and this algorithm can easily be adapted to construct a segment triangulation also in $O(n \log n)$ time.

4   Segment Delaunay Triangulation and Segment Voronoi Diagram

Among the set of all segment triangulations, some are distinguished. For example, we could look for the segment triangulation whose faces have a maximal total area. Here we will be interested in the segment triangulation whose faces are inscribable in empty circles. In this section, we prove the existence and unicity of this special segment triangulation and we show that it is dual to the segment Voronoi diagram (see Figure 4). Our proof uses some properties of the segment Voronoi diagram, which can be found in [2], [4], and [14].

Let now F be the set of triangles of the plane such that the vertices of each triangle belong to three distinct sites of S and such that the interior of the circumcircle of each triangle does not intersect S.

Theorem 4

(i) The triangles of F are the faces of a segment triangulation P of S, which we call the segment Delaunay triangulation.

(ii) The combinatorial map M associated with P is dual to the segment Voronoi diagram of S.

Proof. Since the interior of the circumcircle of every triangle of F is empty, two such triangles cannot intersect. Thus, they are faces of a segment triangulation. On the one hand, the number of vertices of the Voronoi diagram $Vor(S)$ of S is known and by Theorem 3, it is the same as the number of triangles of a segment triangulation of S. On the other hand, each vertex of the Voronoi diagram corresponds to one triangle of F. Therefore, the number of triangles of F is maximal, which means that F is the set of triangles of a segment triangulation P. Furthermore, by definition of the Voronoi diagram, there is a one-to-one correspondence between the regions of $Vor(S)$ and the sites, which are, by definition, the vertices of M.

It remains to study the edges of M and of $Vor(S)$. Let a be an edge of $Vor(S)$ incident to the two Voronoi regions of s and t. Each point p in a is the center of an empty circle C_p touching the two sites s and t at the points p_s and p_t. It

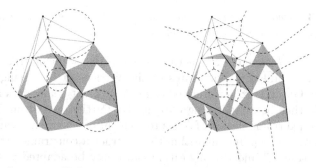

Fig. 4. A segment Delaunay triangulation and an illustration of the duality

is not difficult to prove that such an open segment $p_s p_t$ never meets a triangle of F. Thus, for each p in a, the open segment $p_s p_t$ is included in an edge of the segment triangulation P. Furthermore, the union E_a of all the open segments $p_s p_t$, $p \in a$, is a connected subset of $conv(S)$, therefore E_a is included in a single edge e of P, which is incident to s and t. The last thing to see is that for each edge e of P there is exactly one edge a of $Vor(S)$ such that $E_a \subset e$. Since the numbers of edges of P and of $Vor(S)$ are equal, it suffices to prove that for each edge e of P there is at least one edge a such that $E_a \subset e$. Now, any boundary segment of an edge e linking two sites s and t, is of the previous kind $p_s p_t$. Therefore there is an edge a of $Vor(S)$ such that $E_a \subset e$. $\square$

It is easy to see that the segment Delaunay triangulation of S defined in this theorem is equivalent to the dual of $Vor(S)$ introduced by Chew and Kedem, which they called the edge Delaunay triangulation of S [5]. Using algorithms that construct segment Voronoi diagrams, the segment Delaunay triangulation can be computed in $O(n \log n)$ time [14].

5   Legality in Segment Triangulations

An interesting property of the Delaunay triangulation of a planar point set is the legal edge property. Consider an edge of a point set triangulation and its two adjacent triangles. The edge is illegal if a vertex of one of these triangles lies inside the circumcircle of the other triangle. It is well-known that the Delaunay triangulation of a point set is the unique triangulation of this point set without illegal edge. In the following, we are going to prove a similar property for segment triangulations.

Definition 4. *An egde of a segment triangulation is legal if the circumcircles of its adjacent triangles contain no point of the sites adjacent to these triangles in their interiors.*

Theorem 5. *The segment Delaunay triangulation of S is the unique segment triangulation of S whose all edges are legal.*

Proof. Obviously, the segment Delaunay triangulation has no illegal edge. Let P be a segment triangulation which is not Delaunay and let f be a face of P whose circumcircle c_f contains a point of S in its interior d_f. We have to prove that P has an illegal edge. Let x be a point in f and p a point in d_f lying on a site. We can assume that the interior of the segment xp does not intersect S. Denote by k the number of edges crossed by the segment xp. Note that $k \geq 1$, for, by definition, p can neither be in f, nor in an edge adjacent to f. Denote e the first edge crossed by xp, g the other face adjacent to e, c_g its circumcircle, d_g the interior of c_g, ab the side of g contained in e, and u the site that contains the vertex of g that is not a vertex of e (see Figure 5). If $k = 1$, p lies on u and therefore the edge crossed by xp is illegal. Now suppose that, if xp crosses k edges then at least one of them is illegal. We have to prove that if xp crosses $(k + 1)$

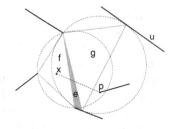

Fig. 5. Illustration of the proof of Theorem 5

edges then P has an illegal edge. If the edge e is illegal we are done. Otherwise the points a and b cannot be in the disk d_f. Moreover the point $y = ab \cap xp$ is in d_f. Therefore, the segment ab splits d_f into two parts. Denote d_1 the part containing the face f and d_2 the other part. The disk d_g must contain at least d_1 or d_2, and since e is legal it can not contain d_1. It follows that the segment yp is in d_g and crosses one edge less than xp. Using the induction hypothesis, we conclude that P has an illegal edge.   □

As remarked in section 3, different segment triangulations of S can have the same topology. Especially an infinite number of segment triangulations of S have the topology of the segment Delaunay triangulation of S. As the segment Delaunay triangulation can be easily computed when its topology is known, it is useless to store the coordinates of the vertices, which, moreover, are usually inexact. Thus it is interesting to know if a given segment triangulation of S has the topology of the segment Delaunay triangulation of S. Furthermore, suppose that a segment triangulation of S is Delaunay and that the sites of S are slightly moved. Then we can wonder if the initial topology remains the topology of the segment Delaunay triangulation of the new set S. For these reasons, we define the edge legality for maps associated with segment triangulations.

Definition 5. *Let f be a face of a segment triangulation of S. The tangency triangle of f is the triangle such that:*

 — *its vertices are on the same three sites as the vertices of f,*
 — *the interior of its circumcircle does not intersect these three sites,*
 — *if f and its tangency triangle are traversed in counter-clockwise direction, they encounter these three sites in the same order.*

Definition 6. *Let M be a map associated with a segment triangulation of S. An edge e of M is legal in the two following cases:*

 1. *e is adjacent to at most one internal triangle.*
 2. *e is adjacent to two internal triangles T_1 and T_2 and the following property holds. Denote t, r, u, v the sites such that t, r, u are incident to T_1 and r, t, v are incident to T_2 in counter-clockwise direction. Let $t_1r_1u_1$ and $r_2t_2v_2$ be the tangency triangles of T_1 and T_2 with $t_i \in t$, $r_i \in r$, $u_1 \in u$, and $v_2 \in v$. Then:*

- *The polygon $t_1t_2r_2r_1$ is either reduced to a segment or is a counter-clockwise oriented simple polygon (with three or four edges),*
- *The circumcircles' interiors of $t_1r_1u_1$ and $r_2t_2v_2$ do not intersect the sites t, r, u, v.*

Theorem 6. *Let M be a map associated with a segment triangulation P of S. Suppose that all the edges of this map are legal, then M is also the map associated with the segment Delaunay triangulation of S.*

Proof (sketch). We want to prove that the collection of tangency triangles gives rise to the segment Delaunay triangulation. Making use of previous theorem, we see that the only thing to prove is that the interiors of the tangency triangles are the faces of a segment triangulation of S.

The main idea of the proof is to use a result of Devillers et al. [6] which asserts that a representation of a combinatorial map by smooth curves in the plane is a planar graph if:

- All the circuits of the map are represented by simple closed curves,
- The ordering at each vertex s of the map is given by the geometric ordering of the curves emanating from the point representing s.

Actually, the result of Devillers et al. is stated with segments instead of smooth curves but an approximation argument leads to the same result for smooth curves.

First, for each $\varepsilon > 0$ sufficiently small, it is possible to construct a planar graph as done in Figure 6(a). All edges of this graph are smooth curves that are at a distance less than ε either from the sites or from the sides of the triangles of P. This planar graph is a representation in the plane of a new combinatorial map M' which does not depend on ε.

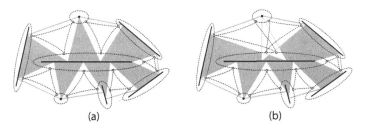

(a)   (b)

Fig. 6. (a) Planar graph deduced from P. (b) A new representation of the map M'.

Next, moving all the triangles T of P to their tangency positions T', we can define a new representation of the map M':

- The curves associated with each triangle of P moves from the initial triangle to the tangency triangle.

– The new closed curves around the sites are slightly more difficult to define. Suppose that T_1 and T_2 are two adjacent triangles of P incident to a site s. Call γ_s the "old" curve around s. There is a point p_i on γ_s associated with the vertex of T_i lying on s and there is a point p'_i on γ_s associated with the vertex of the tangency triangle T'_i lying on s. In the new representation of the map M', we take the portion of the curve γ_s going from p'_1 to p'_2 turning around s in the same direction as the portion of γ_s going from p_1 to p_2 (see Figure 6(b)).

This process ensures that the geometric ordering of the curves emanating from a vertex are the same for the old and the new representation of the map M'. Finally, thanks to the legality of all the edges, one can prove that the new representation of the circuits of M' are simple closed curves. Then, it follows by the result of Devillers et al. that the new representation of M' is a planar graph. Letting ε going to zero, we see that the tangency triangles are the faces of a segment triangulation. □

Theorem 6 enables to test whether a segment triangulation has the topology of the segment Delaunay triangulation by checking the edge legality. From Theorem 3, the number of edges is in $O(n)$ where $n = card(S)$, thus this test can be done in $O(n)$ time. Hence:

Corollary 1. *There is a linear time algorithm that checks whether a given segment triangulation has the same topology as the segment Delaunay triangulation.*

By duality this allows to check in linear time the correctness of the topology of a segment Voronoi diagram computed by a program. For more details on efficient program checkers in computational geometry see, for example, [6] and [12].

6   Conclusion

In this paper, we have notably shown that the segment Delaunay triangulation is the unique segment triangulation that is locally Delaunay in all its edges. As for point set triangulations, this should enable to prove optimality properties of the segment Delaunay triangulation and to give a flip algorithm that transforms any segment triangulation in the segment Delaunay triangulation by a sequence of local improvements. Together with this local characterization, there is a strong hint which makes us believe that a kind of flip algorithm should work with segment triangulations. Lifting a set of sites S onto the paraboloid $z = x^2 + y^2$, it is not hard to see that the triangles of the segment Delaunay triangulation are exactly the downward projection of the triangular faces of the lower convex hull of the lift of S; whereas the lift of any non-Delaunay face is above this lower convex hull, as in the case of point set triangulations. At last, we mention two possible extensions of segment triangulations. On the one hand, it is possible to define triangulations for a set S of disjoint compact convex subsets in the plane. We think that most of the results of this paper might extend to this more general setting. On the other hand, we hope that segment triangulations can be defined in higher dimensions and that it will help to better understand the topological structure of the segment Voronoi diagram in higher dimensions.

References

1. Aichholzer, O., Aurenhammer, F., Hackl, T.: Pre-triangulations and liftable complexes. In: Proc. 22th Annu. ACM Sympos. Comput. Geom., pp. 282–291 (2006)
2. Aurenhammer, F., Klein, R.: Voronoi diagrams. In: Sack, J.-R., Urrutia, J. (eds.) Handbook of Computational Geometry, Elsevier Science Publishers B.V, North-Holland, Amsterdam (1998)
3. Bern, M.W., Eppstein, D.: Mesh generation and optimal triangulation. In: Du, D.-Z., Kwang-Ming Hwang, F. (eds.) Computing in Euclidean Geometry, 2nd edn. Lecture Notes Series on Computing, vol. 4, pp. 47–123. World Scientific (1995)
4. Boissonnat, J.-D., Yvinec, M.: Géométrie algorithmique. Ediscience international, Paris (1995)
5. Chew, L.P., Kedem, K.: Placing the largest similar copy of a convex polygon among polygonal obstacles. In: Proc. 5th Annu. ACM Sympos. Comput. Geom., pp. 167–174 (1989)
6. Devillers, O., Liotta, G., Preparata, F.P., Tamassia, R.: Checking the convexity of polytopes and the planarity of subdivisions. Comput. Geom. Theory Appl. 11, 187–208 (1998)
7. Edelsbrunner, H.: Triangulations and meshes in computational geometry. Acta Numerica, 133–213 (2000)
8. Everett, H., Lazard, S., Lazard, D., Safey El Din, M.: The voronoi diagram of three lines. In: SCG 2007. Proceedings of the twenty-third annual symposium on Computational geometry, pp. 255–264. ACM Press, New York (2007)
9. Koltum, V., Sharir, M.: Three dimensional euclidean voronoi diagrams of lines with a fixed number of orientations. SIAM J. Comput. 32(3), 616–642 (2003)
10. Lawson, C.L.: Software for C^1 surface interpolation. In: Rice, J.R. (ed.) Math. Software III, pp. 161–194. Academic Press, New York (1977)
11. Lee, D.T., Lin, A.K.: Generalized Delaunay triangulation for planar graphs. Discrete Comput. Geom. 1, 201–217 (1986)
12. Mehlhorn, K., Näher, S., Schilz, T., Schirra, S., Seel, M., Seidel, R., Uhrig, C.: Checking geometric programs or verification of geometric structures. In: Proc. 12th Annu. ACM Sympos. Comput. Geom., pp. 159–165 (1996)
13. Mourrain, B., Técourt, J.-P., Teillaud, M.: On the computation of an arrangement of quadrics in 3d. Comput. Geom. Theory Appl. 30(2), 145–164 (2005)
14. Okabe, A., Boots, B., Sugihara, K.: Spatial Tessellations: Concepts and Applications of Voronoi Diagrams. John Wiley & Sons, Chichester (1992)
15. Rajan, V.T.: Optimality of the Delaunay triangulation in R^d. Discrete Comput. Geom. 12, 189–202 (1994)
16. Rote, G., Santos, F., Streinu, I.: Pseudo-triangulations - a survey. Discrete Comput. Geom. (to appear)
17. Schmitt, D., Spehner, J.-C.: Angular properties of Delaunay diagrams in any dimension. Discrete Comput. Geom. 5, 17–36 (1999)
18. Schömer, E., Wolpert, N.: An exact and efficient approach for computing a cell in an arrangement of quadrics. Comput. Geom. Theory Appl. 33(1–2), 65–97 (2006)

Reconstructing Convex Polygons and Polyhedra from Edge and Face Counts in Orthogonal Projections

(Extended Abstract)

Therese Biedl[1], Masud Hasan[2], and Alejandro López-Ortiz[1]

[1] School of Computer Science, University of Waterloo, Waterloo, Ontario, Canada N2M 3G1
{biedl,alopez-o}@uwaterloo.ca
[2] Department of Computer Science and Engineering
Bangladesh University of Engineering and Technology, Dhaka-1000, Bangladesh
masudhasan@cse.buet.ac.bd

Abstract. We study the problem of constructing convex polygons and convex polyhedra given the number of visible edges and visible faces from some orthogonal projections. In 2D, we find necessary and sufficient conditions for the existence of a feasible polygon of size N and give an algorithm to construct one, if it exists. When N is not known, we give an algorithm to find the maximum and minimum size of a feasible polygon. In 3D, when the directions span a single plane we show that a feasible polyhedron can be constructed from a feasible polygon. We also give an algorithm to construct a feasible polyhedron when the directions are covered by two planes. Finally, we show that the problem becomes NP-complete for three or more planes.

1 Introduction

Reconstructing polyhedra from projection information is an important field of research due to its applications in geometric modeling, computer vision, geometric tomography, and computer graphics. The nature of reconstruction problems and the techniques to solve them depend upon the types of information given, such as line drawings, silhouettes, and area/volume/shape of shadows, among others.

The computational geometry community has studied the problem of reconstructing convex polyhedra from triangulations of the shadow boundary. Marlin and Toussaint [15] gave an $O(n^2)$ algorithm for deciding whether such a polyhedron exists and constructing a polyhedron where possible. In another variation of this problem, where the triangulations are isomorphic to two opposite projections from the z-axis, Bereg [2] showed that the polyhedron can always be reconstructed. See [6] for a collection of similar problems on reconstruction of polyhedra.

Reconstructing polyhedra has also been studied from the point of view of applications, and various types of projection information have been considered. Among them line drawings [13,14,17,18,19,20,23,24] are possibly the most common. Line drawings may be obtained from images, from geometric drawings from the designers [20, Chapter 1], or may be freehand drawings [12,22]. The reconstruction algorithms differ for a single and multiple drawings. For multiple drawings there are two common

V. Arvind and S. Prasad (Eds.): FSTTCS 2007, LNCS 4855, pp. 400–411, 2007.

approaches based on the representation of the polyhedra to be reconstructed: constructive solid geometry and boundary representation. Both approaches are used in engineering and product design such as designing complex mechanical parts and in CAD [10,23]. It is more difficult to construct a polyhedron from a single drawing [20,23].

Reconstruction from the area and shape of projections has been considered in geometric tomography [8]. Usually convex objects are reconstructed here. A related but more application oriented field is computerized tomography, where 3D objects are reconstructed from sectioning information such as the area of a plane section of the objects. Medical CAT scanning is an important application of computerized tomography where an image of the human body is reconstructed from X-ray information [8]. The information achieved through X-rays gives the lengths, widths, volumes and shapes of different parts of an object, which are similar to area and shape of projections.

Instead of whole projections, sometimes only silhouettes are used to reconstruct polyhedra [4,5,11,16]. In volume intersection, which is a well-known technique in computer vision, the only information available is a set of silhouettes [4,5,11], sometimes even with unknown view points [4,5].

Our Results. Most reconstruction algorithms are based on fairly complex information such as triangulations, line drawings, silhouettes, and geometric measures of the projections, along with some non-geometric surface information such as shading, texture, and reflection of light. In contrast, we consider a very different and very limited type of information, which is also robust: we consider the number of visible edges for polygons and the number of visible faces for polyhedra in some orthogonal projections. Here we study reconstructing convex polygons and polyhedra from orthogonal projections only; see [9] for results on perspective projections and non-convex polygons and polyhedra.

We consider only non-degenerate orthogonal projections where the view directions are not parallel to the edges (faces) of the polygon (polyhedron). A *direction-integer pair*, or simply a *d-i pair*, $\langle d, n \rangle$ consists of a direction vector d and a positive integer n, and expresses how many edges (faces) should be seen from the direction. A *d-i set* $\mathcal{R}$ is a set of d-i pairs where no two directions are the same or opposite to each other. (We assume this because we will ultimately generate and then use the d-i pairs for all opposite directions too.) A convex polygon (polyhedron) P is *feasible* for $\mathcal{R}$ if, for each d-i pair $\langle d, n \rangle$ in $\mathcal{R}$, d is not parallel to edges (faces) of P and the number of visible edges (faces) from d is n. For a d-i set, a feasible polygon may or may not exist or it may exist for more than one possible number of edges (see Figure 1.)

In this paper, we consider the problem of given a d-i set $\mathcal{R}$ and an integer N, create a feasible polygon (or polyhedron) of size N for $\mathcal{R}$. We first give necessary and sufficient

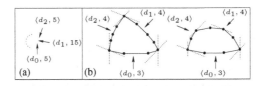

Fig. 1. (a) A d-i set with no feasible polygon. (b) Example of feasible polygons of different size.

conditions for a feasible polygon to exist, which also give an algorithm to construct the polygon, if it exists. With K directions, our algorithm runs in $O(K + N)$ time if $\mathcal{R}$ is ordered, and in $O(K \log K + N)$ time otherwise. For unknown N, the above characterization gives an $O(K + v \log v)$-time algorithm to find the maximum and minimum size of a feasible polygon where $1 \leq v < K$.

In 3D, we consider cases by the minimum number of planes that *cover* the directions, where "covering" means each direction lies in at least one plane. For one plane, 2D results are easily transferred. For two planes, we give an algorithm to construct a feasible polyhedron, whenever it exists, except for one special case. Finally, for three or more planes, we prove that testing the existence of a feasible polyhedron is NP-complete.

For space reasons, most proofs in this paper have been abbreviated or omitted and most results are covered in full detail in [9].

Impact. Our algorithm to test feasibility of reconstruction can be useful as a preliminary step in applications in which other types of information are used, in addition, for reconstruction purposes—the user can decide quickly the existence of possible resulting polyhedra before starting a rigorous reconstruction process.

Although from the applications point of view the problem of reconstructing polyhedra is more common than that of reconstructing polygons, surprisingly, the latter are themselves very rich and their solution techniques will serve as foundation for solving the former.

Preliminaries. Throughout this paper, we assume we are given a d-i set $\mathcal{R}$. Usually we also assume that the size N of the desired polygon/polyhedron is given. Clearly, we must have $N \geq 3$ or 4, respectively, and N must be strictly larger than any integer of a d-i pair. We assume this throughout.

Our problem is defined in terms of a d-i set $\mathcal{R}$, but to solve it we will use a *proper d-i set* $\mathcal{S}$ which has $2K$ d-i pairs and is derived from $\mathcal{R}$ and N as follows: For each d-i pair $\langle d, n \rangle$ in $\mathcal{R}$, $\mathcal{S}$ has both $\langle d, n \rangle$ and $\langle d', N - n \rangle$, where d' is opposite to d, and $\mathcal{S}$ has no other d-i pair. The d-i pairs $\langle d, n \rangle$ and $\langle d', N - n \rangle$ in $\mathcal{S}$ are called *opposite* to each other. Clearly a convex polygon (polyhedron) P with N edges is feasible for $\mathcal{R}$ if and only if it is feasible for $\mathcal{S}$.

In 2D, or n 3D when the directions of $\mathcal{S}$ lie in one plane, $\mathcal{S}$ is represented as $\mathcal{S} = \{\langle d_0, n_0 \rangle, \langle d_1, n_1 \rangle, \ldots, \langle d_{2K-1}, n_{2K-1} \rangle\}$, where the d-i pairs are ordered counterclockwise by directions. From now on indices of the terms related to $\mathcal{S}$ are taken modulo $2K$.

2 Reconstructing Polygons

We first study the 2D case. Let P be a feasible polygon of size N for $\mathcal{S}$ and consider the sets of visible edges of P from the directions of $\mathcal{S}$. When we move from direction d_i to d_{i+1}, there may be some edges of P that become *newly visible* and/or *newly invisible* to d_{i+1}. From n_i and n_{i+1} alone, it cannot be said exactly how many edges become newly visible or invisible to d_{i+1}. However, it is possible to lower bound these quantities. Observe that if an edge e becomes newly visible when going from d_i to d_{i+1}, then it becomes newly invisible when going from d_{i+K} to d_{i+K+1}. This implies that although the change in the visibility of each edge happens twice, the total change in the visibility for all edges can be counted by considering only their change from invisible to visible. (This use of opposite directions is the main motivation to consider the proper d-i set $\mathcal{S}$ instead of the d-i set $\mathcal{R}$.) Moreover, e is newly visible for exactly one direction of $\mathcal{S}$.

We now state the characterization formally. For each i, define $\delta_i = \mathbf{max}\{0, n_{i+1} - n_i\}$. We call δ_i the i-th view difference. There must be at least δ_i edges that become newly visible while moving from d_i to d_{i+1}. Therefore if a polygon exists, then $D := \sum_{i=0}^{2K-1} \delta_i \leq N$. Our main result here is that this necessary condition is also sufficient.

Theorem 1. Given a proper d-i set $\mathcal{S}$ and an integer N, a feasible polygon P of size N exists if and only if $D \leq N$.

Proof. The proof idea is as follows. For each view direction d_i, choose δ_i edges, if $\delta_i > 0$, such that they are newly visible for d_{i+1}. The remaining $N - D$ edges are chosen in antipodal pairs so that one becomes visible exactly when the other becomes invisible. This is possible because $N - D$ is even, and in fact, we know exactly what it is:

Lemma 1. For any i, $N - D = 2(n_i - \sum_{j=i+K}^{i-1} \delta_j)$.

To avoid constructing an unbounded polygon we have to be careful in how to chose edges. To simplify the description, we will not choose edges directly, and instead choose a *normal-point* for each edge on a circle c centered at the origin o. From these normal points, we can then reconstruct a polygon by computing the intersection of their tangent half-planes in $O(N \log N)$ time.

For any direction d_i, denote by h_i the *visible half-circle of d_i*, i.e., the (closed) half-circle of c that is visible from d_i. Clearly e is visible from d_i if and only if its normal-point is strictly within h_i. Moreover, a polygon defined by normal-points is bounded if and only if not all normal-points are within a single open half-circle.

The circular arc $\theta_i = h_{i+1} \setminus h_i$ is called the i-th d-arc ("d" for difference). Normal-points in θ_i correspond to edges that are newly visible to d_{i+1}. Normal-points will never be placed on the boundary of θ_i, and hence we will not distinguish as to whether θ_i is open or closed. Observe that θ_i and θ_{i+K} are the reflections of each other with respect to the origin and are called *opposite* to each other. (See Figure 2(a)). Since d_i and d_{i+K} are opposite directions, we have $\bigcup_{j=i-K}^{i-1} \theta_j = h_i$ for all i. (See also Figure 2(b)).

Now place δ_i arbitrary normal-points strictly within each θ_i. If $D < N$, then by Lemma 1, $N - D$ is even. Select $N - D - 2$ additional normal-points in antipodal pairs arbitrarily (but not on end-points of any θ_i). The last two normal points p_1 and p_2 are placed within two opposite d-arcs, but chosen carefully such that no half-circle contains all normal-points. Let p be one among the already selected normal-points, and place p_1 at clockwise ε (circular) distance after p. Let p' be the antipodal point of p and place p_2 at clockwise $\varepsilon/2$ distance after p'. ε is small enough so that p_1 and p_2 are within two opposite d-arcs. See Figure 2(c). Clearly no half-circle can contain all of p, p_1, and p_2.

Recall that $h_i = \bigcup_{j=i-K}^{i-1} \theta_j$. The number of normal points strictly within h_i is hence $\sum_{j=i-K}^{i-1} \delta_j + \frac{1}{2}(N - D)$, because d-arc θ_j initially gets δ_j normal points, and

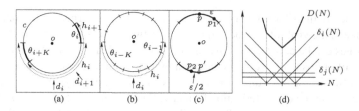

Fig. 2. (a) Visible half-circles, and d-arcs; two opposite d-arcs are in bold. (b) $h_i = \bigcup_{j=i-K}^{i-1} \theta_j$. (c) Selecting the last two normal-points when $D < N$. (d) δ_i and $D(N)$ against unknown N.

then exactly half of the additional $N - D$ points are placed within half-circle h_i. By Lemma 1 therefor h_i contains n_i normal points as desired.

All that remains to show is that no half-circle contains all normal points. This was already guaranteed if $D < N$, since the last two normal-points p_1 and p_2 were chosen carefully. If $N = D$, then each d-arc θ_i gets exactly δ_i normal-points. Any open half-circle h intersects $K - 1$ d-arcs fully, and we claim that $\delta_j > 0$ for one of them. For if not, then using $\min\{\delta_i, \delta_{i+K}\} = 0$ and adding the adjacent d-arc which achieves 0, we get K consecutive d-arcs without normal-points. Say $\sum_{j=i}^{i+K-1} \delta_i = 0$, then $n_{i+K} = \sum_{j=i}^{i+K-1} \delta_i + \frac{1}{2}(N - D) = 0 + 0 = 0$, a contradiction. □

The above proof is algorithmic, and it is straightforward how to implement it in $O(N + K)$ time if S is ordered, and in $O(N + K \log K)$ otherwise. We summarize:

Theorem 2. *Given a d-i set $\mathcal{R}$ of size K and given an integer N, a feasible polygon P with N edges can be computed, whenever it exists, in $O(N + K)$ time if $\mathcal{R}$ is ordered, or in $O(N + K \log K)$ time otherwise.*

Maximum and Minimum Polygon. Using Theorem 1, we can also find out whether there exists a feasible polygon for a given d-i set $\mathcal{R}$ if N is unknown. In fact, we find both the maximum and minimum size of a feasible polygon. Observe that if $\mathcal{R}$ contains two opposite d-i pairs, then the sum of the two integers would give the value of N. Hence, once again it is assumed that no opposite d-i pair appears in $\mathcal{R}$.

The overall idea is as follows. We compute as before a proper d-i set $S(N)$ from $\mathcal{R}$, but this time the d-i pairs of $S(N)$ will be functions of N—for each pair $\langle d, n \rangle$ in $\mathcal{R}$, the opposite pair $\langle d', N - n \rangle$ in S contains the unknown N. We call $\langle d, n \rangle$ *original* and $\langle d', N - n \rangle$ *derived*. Then we compute $\delta_i(N)$ and $D(N)$, which also become functions of N. Recall from Theorem 1 that a feasible polygon exists if and only if $D(N) \leq N$.

Analyzing cases, one can observe that the function $\delta_i(N)$ is either a constant or a V-shape with slopes ± 1 for which the tip (with $\delta_i(N) = 0$) occurs at a place well-defined in terms of n_i, n_{i+1} and whether d_i and d_{i+1} are original and derived respectively. Hence the function $D(N)$, which is the sum of these, is convex and piecewise linear. See also Figure 2(d). So $D(N) = N$ has at most two solutions, and any N between them is feasible as long as $N \geq 3$ and $N \leq \max_i\{n_i\}$. The algorithm to compute this range of N takes $O(K + v \log v)$ time, where v is the number original d-i pairs in $S(N)$ whose corresponding next d-i pairs are derived. Of course $v \in O(K)$, but v could be as small as one if all directions in $\mathcal{R}$ are spanned within a half-plane.

Theorem 3. *Given an ordered d-i set $\mathcal{R}$ of size K, the maximum and minimum size of a feasible polygon can be computed in $O(K + v \log v)$ time, where v is the number of original d-i pairs in $\mathcal{S}(N)$ whose corresponding next d-i pairs are derived. If $\mathcal{R}$ is not ordered, then the algorithm takes $O(K \log K)$ time.*

3 Reconstructing Polyhedra

Similar to 2D, in order to construct a feasible polyhedron P we will compute the proper d-i set $\mathcal{S}$ from the given d-i set $\mathcal{R}$ and instead of choosing faces directly we will choose them implicitly by choosing normal-points of the faces on the surface of an origin-centered sphere s. Then given such normal-points, we can compute a polyhedron from them by computing the intersection of their tangent half-planes in $O(N \log N)$ time [7].

A face f is visible from a direction d_i if and only if its normal-point is strictly within the *visible hemisphere* h_i of d_i. Moreover P is bounded if and only if not all normal-points intersect a single open hemisphere.

3.1 Directions Covered by a Single Plane

If all directions are in one plane, then $\mathcal{S}$ can be interpreted as an input to the 2D case. A solution to the 2D case then implies an open cylinder in 3D which can easily be converted to a solution in the 3D case. The other direction is slightly less trivial; the following theorem gives a precise proof.

Theorem 4. *Given an ordered proper d-i set $\mathcal{S}$ of size $2K$, where all the directions lie in one plane π, and given $N \geq 4$, there exists a feasible polyhedron P of size N for $\mathcal{S}$ if and only if there exists a feasible polygon p of size N for $\mathcal{S}$, interpreted as 2D directions within π. Moreover, the time required to construct P from p is $O(N \log N)$ and p from P is $O(N)$.*

Before giving the proof, we need some notations, which will be used in later sections as well. Given a proper d-i set $\mathcal{S}$ with directions in one plane and ordered counterclockwise, define the *ith d-lune* to be $\theta_i = h_{i+1} \backslash h_i$. See Figure 3(a). As in 2D, $h_i = \bigcup_{j=i-K}^{i-1} \theta_j$. All d-lunes of $\mathcal{S}$ have two common antipodal points which are called *poles* of $\mathcal{S}$.

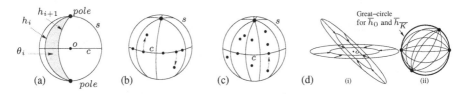

Fig. 3. (a) Visible half-sphere and d-lune. (b) P from p. (c) p from P. (d) (i) Two planes of $\mathcal{S}$ with common directions, and (ii) arrangement of the d-lunes for such $\mathcal{S}$.

Proof. Let c be the great circle of s corresponding to the plane π. Assume first that p exists. Each edge of p then corresponds to a point of c by virtue of taking its normal and computing its intersection with c. Move two of these points towards the two poles of S, respectively, but within their respective d-lunes. This still remains a solution to the d-i set, but closes up the open cylinder that would have been defined by these points otherwise. See Figure 3(b).

Now assume a polyhedron P for the 3D problem exists. Each face then corresponds to a point on the sphere s by virtue of taking the intersection of the face-normal with s. Move each of these points onto c along the great-circle through the point and the poles, using the shorter arc. See Figure 3(c). If points overlap after the movement, then move them slightly but within their respective d-lunes and keeping them on c. Now all normal-points are within a plane, and we can construct a polygon from them in $O(N)$ time.   □

3.2   Directions Covered by Two Planes

Now we consider the case when all view directions are covered by two planes $\bar{\pi}$ and $\tilde{\pi}$. The d-i set S hence gets split into $\overline{S}$ and $\widetilde{S}$, depending on which plane each direction belongs to. (One pair of opposite directions can belong to both planes.) We assume that $\overline{S}$ and $\widetilde{S}$ each are numbered counter-clowise (within their planes). This then also defines d-lunes $\bar{\theta}_i$ and $\tilde{\theta}_j$ and view differences $\bar{\delta}_i, \tilde{\delta}_i$ as before. All indices are taken modulo $\overline{K} := |\overline{S}|$ and $\widetilde{K} := |\widetilde{S}|$. We set $\overline{D} = \sum_{i=0}^{2\overline{K}-1} \bar{\delta}_i$ and $\widetilde{D} = \sum_{j=0}^{2\widetilde{K}-1} \tilde{\delta}_j$ as before.

We assume the numbering is such that $\bar{d}_0 = \tilde{d}_0$ if the two sets $\overline{S}$ and $\widetilde{S}$ have a common direction, and such that $\bar{\theta}_0$ and $\tilde{\theta}_0$ contain the poles of the other d-i set if they don't. Intersecting the two sets of lunes splits the sphere s into a grid-like structure, except near the poles if $\overline{S}$ and $\widetilde{S}$ have no direction in common. See Figure 3(d) and Figure 4(a).

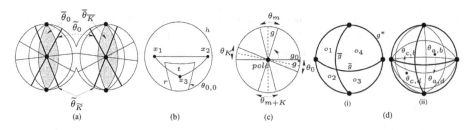

Fig. 4. (a) Arrangement of d-lunes if $\overline{S}$ and $\widetilde{S}$ have no direction in common. (b) Arranging normal points to avoid an empty half-sphere. (c) Choosing a great-circle such that d-lunes have at least two normal points. (d) (i) Splitting into octants, and (ii) shifting normal-points within octants.

Let $\theta_{a,b} = \bar{\theta}_a \cap \tilde{\theta}_b$; this is a spherical polygon called *d-polygon*, and the union of the d-polygons covers the sphere s. If $\Delta_{a,b}$ is the number of normal points assigned to $\theta_{a,b}$, then the following must hold:

- $\sum_j \Delta_{i,j} \geq \overline{\delta}_i$ for all $0 \leq i < 2\overline{K}$,
- $\sum_i \Delta_{i,j} \geq \widetilde{\delta}_j$ for all $0 \leq j < 2\widetilde{K}$,
- $\sum_{\ell=i+\overline{K}}^{i-1} \sum_j \Delta_{\ell,j} = \overline{n}_i$ for all $0 \leq i < 2\overline{K}$,
- $\sum_{\ell=j+\widetilde{K}}^{j-1} \sum_i \Delta_{i,\ell} = \widetilde{n}_j$ for all $0 \leq j < 2\widetilde{K}$,

where the unspecified sums run over all indices for which $\Delta_{a,b}$ exists, i.e., the two respective d-lunes intersect.

Satisfying these four conditions will be called the *valid assignment problem*. It is quite similar to Edmond's transportation problem, see e.g. [1], and it is not difficult to develop an algorithm to find a valid assignment if one exists. We can even add extra conditions that will be useful later:

Lemma 2. *We can find a valid assignment, if one exists, in $O(\overline{K} + \widetilde{K})$ time. Moreover, if $\max\{\overline{D}, \widetilde{D}\} < N$, then $\Delta_{0,0} > 0$ and $\Delta_{\overline{K},\widetilde{K}} > 0$.*

This yields how many normal points should be placed in each d-polygon, but not the actual locations. To find the actual location, we need to solve what we call the *valid selection problem*: Assign normal points such that no hemisphere contains all normal points. (If one hemisphere contains all normal points, then the resulting polyhedron is unbounded. If this is allowed, then the existence of a valid assignment is necessary and also sufficient for the existence of a feasible polyhedron.)

Insufficiency of a Valid Assignment. Before we study how to find a valid selection, we first show that this is a non-trivial problem, by describing an instance which has a valid assignment, but no valid selection. Consider the 2D proper d-i set $\mathcal{S}'$ of Figure 5(a). It has twelve d-i pairs and the only positive view differences are $\delta_0 = 1$, $\delta_4 = 1$, and $\delta_8 = 2$. We use $N = 4$, so $N = D$. The key property of $\mathcal{S}'$ is that this defines very thin d-lunes. We use $\mathcal{S}'$ twice, in two different planes, see Figure 5(b). There are only two possible valid assignments for the d-polygons of $\mathcal{S}$ which are shown in (c). But in either case all three positive d-polygons are strictly within a single hemisphere (shown shaded). So no valid selection exists.

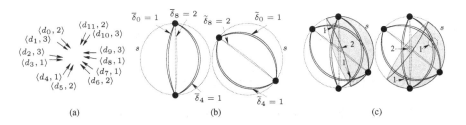

(a)   (b)   (c)

Fig. 5. Example Insufficiency of a valid assignment

Finding a Valid Selection. Despite this negative example, we can find a valid selection in two cases: (i) $\max\{\overline{D}, \widetilde{D}\} < N$ and (ii) $\overline{D} = N = \widetilde{D}$ and all directions see at least four faces. Note that neither case covers the above example.

In the first case, by Lemma 2 we can find a valid assignment where $\theta_{0,0}$ contains a normal point x_3, and $\theta_{\overline{K},\widetilde{K}}$ contains a normal point x_4. Let x_1, x_2 be two other normal points; these exist by $N \geq 4$. Without loss of generality we assume that x_1, x_2 and x_3 are all within one hemisphere; they then span a spherical triangle t, which intersects $\theta_{0,0}$. See also Figure 4(b). The antipodal triangle t' to t hence intersects $\theta_{\overline{K},\widetilde{K}}$, and we can move x_4 so that is inside $t' \cap \theta_{\overline{K},\widetilde{K}}$. This will ensure that no hemisphere contains all of x_1, x_2, x_3, x_4.

Now consider the case when $\overline{D} = N = \widetilde{D}$ and each direction sees at least four faces. This case is significantly more complicated. In fact, we are not able to find a valid selection for any given assignment, but we can find a valid selection if we are allowed to change the given assignment slightly.

We first define octants of the sphere by choosing three great circles as follows. The first one is the great circle g^* that contains the poles of $\overline{S}$ and $\widetilde{S}$. The second great-circle $\overline{g}$ is obtained by rotating a great-circle, starting at g^*, through the poles of $\overline{S}$ until the four lunes defined by g^* and $\overline{g}$ contain at least two normal points each. That this is possible is non-trivial; it requires $\overline{D} = N$ and $\overline{n}_i \geq 4$, as well as distributing normal points in d-polygons intersected by g^*. See also Figure 4(c). Similarly we find a great-circle $\widetilde{g}$ by rotating from g^* through the poles of $\widetilde{S}$ until the four lunes defined by g^* and $\widetilde{g}$ contain at least two normal points each.

Now we have eight octants defined by three great circles. A fairly straightforward proof shows that if each octant contain a normal point, then no hemisphere can be empty. However, our given valid assignment need not have a normal point in all octants. But, since the great circles were chosen such that each lune has at least two normal points, we can change the valid assignment to a different valid assignment by shifting points from octants with two normal points to empty octants. See also Figure 4(d). After doing so, we can choose arbitrary points within the d-polygons and obtain a valid selection.

None of our steps is computationally expensive, and the time complexity is dominated by the time to compute the intersection of the tangent half-planes of the computed normal points. In summary, we obtain:

Theorem 5. *Given a proper d-i set S and an integer $N \geq 4$, where the directions of S are covered by two planes. We can construct a feasible polyhedron P, if it exists, in $O(N \log N + |S|)$ time, in each of the following cases: (i) $\max\{\overline{D}, \widetilde{D}\} < N$, or (ii) $\overline{D} = N = \widetilde{D}$ and $n \geq 4$ for each d-i pair $\langle d, n \rangle$ in S.*

4   NP-Completeness for Arbitrary Directions

We will prove that the problem of finding a valid assignment, which is necessary for two or more planes, is NP-complete for three planes.

Theorem 6. *Given a proper d-i set S of size $2K$ with three planes of directions, it is NP-complete to decide the existence of a feasible polyhedron for S.*

Proof. The problem is easily seen to be in NP. Given a set of normal points for the faces of the polyhedron, we can easily test whether the right number of normal points is in each hemisphere defined by $\mathcal{S}$. Since the normal points are to be chosen somewhere within an open set, they can be chosen with polynomial size coordinates.

To prove that the problem is NP-hard, we apply a reduction from the problem of testing whether a 2-edge connected cubic planar graph G has an independent set of size k, which is proven to be NP-complete in [3]. Here, an *independent set* I of G is a set of vertices s.t. no two vertices of I are connected by an edge.

Since G is a 2-edge connected cubic planar graph, it is 3-edge colorable (by the four color theorem [21].) We draw G as follows: Place all vertices in a vertical line. Let $\mathcal{L}$ be the set of all lines of slope $i\pi/3$, $i = 0, 1, 2$ through the set of vertices. Draw each edge of color j with 3 segments: One of slope $j\pi/3$ at each end, and one of slope $(j + 1)\pi/3$ connecting them. We choose the edge lengths such that for each edge the three lines (of slope $i\pi/3$, $i = 0, 1, 2$) through the bends of the edge do not cross any other intersection point of two lines previously added to $\mathcal{L}$. This can always be done by drawing the middle segment sufficiently far out, and suitable lengths can be computed in polynomial time. Add the three new lines through bends of the edge to $\mathcal{L}$. See also Figure 6.

Now we have a (not necessarily planar) drawing of G where every edge has exactly two bends. Moreoever, we have a system of lines $\mathcal{L}$ with three slopes such that any trivalent point (a point that belongs to three lines of $\mathcal{L}$) corresponds to a vertex of G or a bend of an edge of G; no other three lines of $\mathcal{L}$ cross in one point. Since G is cubic and 3-edge-colored, one easily verifies that there are $n + m$ lines in each direction in $\mathcal{L}$, where n and m are the number of vertices and edges of G. Also $m = \frac{3}{2}n$, so $|\mathcal{L}| = \frac{15}{2}n$.

Fig. 6. Creating a set of lines from graph G (only some edges are shown); projecting lines onto a sphere, and converting lines to thin lunes

We will eventually project $\mathcal{L}$ onto the sphere, and then create a d-i set such that any solution to it can be converted to a set of points of $\mathcal{L}$ with certain properties. This will be helpful, since there is a correspondence between independent sets of G and points placed on $\mathcal{L}$ as follows:

Lemma 3. *G has an independent set of size k if and only if there exists a set $\mathcal{T}$ of $\frac{9}{2}n - 2k$ points such that each line of $\mathcal{L}$ intersects exactly one point of $\mathcal{T}$, and each point of $\mathcal{T}$ intersects either one or three (but not two) lines of $\mathcal{L}$.*

Proof. Given an independent set I of size k of G, we construct $\mathcal{T}$ as follows: (1) Add the point of every vertex in I. This adds k trivalent points. (2) For every edge (v, w) of G, at least one endpoints (say v) is not in I. Add the point of the bend adjacent to v in the drawing of (v, w). This adds $m = \frac{3}{2}n$ trivalent points. By construction no line of $\mathcal{L}$

is covered twice by the points chosen thus far. (3) For every line in $\mathcal{L}$ not covered, add one more point that intersects this line only. Since $3k + \frac{9}{2}n$ lines were already covered and $|\mathcal{L}| = \frac{15}{2}n$, this adds $3n - 3k$ points. One easily verifies the desired properties.

For the other direction, assume we are given such a point set $\mathcal{T}$, and assume it contains ℓ trivalent points. Then $|\mathcal{L}| - 3\ell = \frac{15}{2}n - 3\ell$ lines are covered by points that are on one line only, so $|\mathcal{T}| = \frac{15}{2}n - 2\ell$, which with $|\mathcal{T}| = \frac{9}{2}n - 2k$ implies $\ell = \frac{3}{2}n + k$. Let H be the graph obtained from G by subdividing each edge twice. Each of the $\ell = \frac{3}{2}n + k$ trivalent points belongs to a vertex or bend of G, hence a vertex of H, and these vertices are an independent set I' of H since every line contains only one point of $\mathcal{T}$. I' contains at most one bend per edge (v, w) of G, and if both v and w are in I', then neither bend of edge (v, w) is in I'. So by removing one vertex per edge of G we can convert I' into an independent set of size k in G.   □

Now we create an instance of our reconstuction problem from set $\mathcal{L}$ as follows. First do a stereographic projection, i.e., consider $\mathcal{L}$ as lines in an xy-plane, place a sphere s outside this plane, and map each line l of $\mathcal{L}$ to the great circle defined by the intersection of s with the plane through the center of s and l. All lines of the same slope hence get mapped to great-circles with common poles, and the three pole-sets for the three directions all lie in one xy-plane, which for ease of description we assume to be the $(z = 0)$-plane. Note that the arrangement of line appears twice on the sphere, once on each side of the $(z = 0)$-plane.

We now set up the directions of a d-i set such that each great-circle of a line gets replaced by a lune through the same poles. These lunes are thin enough such that no point is in more than 3 lunes replacing lines. We also replace the great-circle of the $(z = 0)$-plane by 12 lunes: for each pair of poles, each half-circle between them gets replaced by two adjacent thin lunes, divided at the $(z = 0)$-plane.

Finally we set up N and the integers of the d-i set such that in the half-plane above the $(z = 0)$-plane, the following holds: (1) The sum of view differences is exactly N, so the total view difference is exactly the number of normal points in any solution. (2) The lunes replacing lines all have view-difference 1. Hence any assignment of normal points will have to assign exactly one point to this line. (3) The spaces between lunes all have view-difference 0. Hence we can only place normal points at the intersection of three lunes, which correspond to trivalent points, or at the lunes replacing the $(z = 0)$-plane. (4) The total number of points in this half-plane is $\frac{3}{2}n - 2k$.

It can be shown that such a set of integers for the d-i set always exists. With this, clearly a solution to the reconstruction problem implies a set of points with properties as in Lemma 3, and hence yields an independent set of size k in G. Conversely, it is not hard to show that any set of points as in Lemma 3 can be converted to both a valid assignment and a valid selection for the d-i set; hence the reduction is complete.   □

References

1. Bazaraa, M.S., Jarvis, J.J., Sherali, H.D.: Linear Programming and Network Flows. John Wiley, Chichester (2005)
2. Bereg, S.: 3D realization of two triangulations of a convex polygon. In: 20th Eur. Work. Comp. Geom., pp. 49–52. Seville, Spain (March 2004)

3. Biedl, T., Kant, G., Kaufmann, M.: On triangulating planar graphs under the four-connectivity constraint. Algorithmica 19(4), 427–446 (1997)
4. Bottino, A., Jaulin, L., Laurentini, A.: Reconstructing 3D objects from silhouettes with unknown viewpoints: The case of planar orthographic views. In: 8th Iberoamerican Congress on Patt. Recog., pp. 153–162. Havana, Cuba (November 2003)
5. Bottino, A., Laurentini, A.: Introducing a new problem: Shape-from-silhouette when the relative positions of the viewpoints is unknown. IEEE PAMI 25(11), 1484–1493 (2003)
6. Demaine, E.D., Erickson, J.: Open problems on polytope reconstruction. Manuscript
7. Edelsbrunner, H.: Algorithms in Combinatorial Geometry. Springer, Heidelberg (1986)
8. Gardner, R.J.: Geometric Tomography. Cambridge University Press, Cambridge (1995)
9. Hasan, M.: Reconstruction and visualization of polyhedra using projections. PhD thesis, School of Computer Science, University of Waterloo, Canada (2005)
10. Hoffman, C.H.: Geometric and Solid Modelling. Morgan Kaufmann, San Francisco (1989)
11. Laurentini, A.: How many 2D silhouettes does it take to reconstruct a 3D object?. Comp. Vis. Image Unders 67(1) (1997)
12. Lipson, H., Shpitalni, M.: Optimization-based reconstruction of a 3D object from a single freehand line drawing. Computer Aided Design 28(8), 651–663 (1996)
13. Markowsky, G., Wesley, M.: Fleshing out wire frames. IBM J. Res. Dev. 24, 582–597 (1980)
14. Markowsky, G., Wesley, M.: Fleshing out projections. IBM J. Res. Dev. 25(6), 934–954 (1981)
15. Marlin, B., Toussaint, G.: Constructing convex 3-polytopes from two triangulations of a polygon. In: 14th Can. Conf. Comp. Geom., Lethbridge, Alberta, pp. 36–39 (August 2002)
16. Matusik, W., Buehler, C., Raskar, R., Gortler, S.J., McMillan, L.: Image-based visual hulls. In: SIGGRAPH 2000, pp. 369–374. New Orleans, Louisiana (July 2000)
17. Nagendra, I.V., Gujar, U.G.: 3-D objects from 2-D orthographic views– a survey. Computer and Graphics 12(1), 111–114 (1988)
18. Penna, M.: A shape from shading analysis for a single perspective image of a polyhedron. IEEE PAMI 11(6), 545–554 (1989)
19. Sugihara, K.: A necessary and sufficient condition for a picture to represent a polyhedral scene. IEEE Trans. Patt. Anal. Mach. Intell 6(5), 578–586 (1984)
20. Sugihara, K.: Machine Interpretation of Line Drawing. MIT Press, Cambridge (1986)
21. Thomas, R.: An update on four-color theorem. Notices of American Mathematical Society 45(7), 848–859 (1998)
22. Varley, P.A.C.: Automatic creation of boundary-representation models from single line drawings. PhD thesis, Dept. of Computer Science, University of Wales College of Cardiff (2003)
23. Wang, W., Grinstein, G.G.: Survey of 3d solid reconstruction from 2d projection line drawings. Computer Graphics Forum 12(2), 137–158 (1993)
24. Yan, Q.-W., Chen, C.L.P., Tang, Z.: Efficient algorithm for the reconstruction of 3d objects from orthographic projections. Computer Aided Design 26(9), 699–717 (1994)

Finding a Rectilinear Shortest Path in R^2 Using Corridor Based Staircase Structures

R. Inkulu and Sanjiv Kapoor

Department of Computer Science,
Illinois Institute of Technology, Chicago, USA
{inkuraj,kapoor}@iit.edu

Abstract. The rectilinear shortest path problem can be stated as - given a set of m non-intersecting simple polygonal obstacles in the plane, find a shortest rectilinear (L_1) path from a point s to a point t which avoids all the obstacles. The path can touch an obstacle but does not cross it. This paper presents an algorithm with time complexity $O(n + m(\lg n)^{3/2})$, which is close to the known lower bound of $\Omega(n + m \lg m)$ for finding such a path. Here, n is the number of vertices of all the obstacles together. Our algorithm is of $O(n + m(\lg m)^{3/2})$ space complexity.

1 Introduction

In this paper, we are interested in finding a 2-dimensional rectilinear (L_1) shortest path from a point s to another point t in a polygonal region P comprising m non-intersecting polygoinal obstacles with n vertices in total. This problem has numerous applications, especially in automated circuit design. In [9], deRezende, Lee and Wu present a $O(n \lg n)$ time complexity solution to the rectilinear shortest path problem when the obstacles are disjoint isothetic rectangles. In [11], Mitchell considers the case when the obstacles are rectilinear polygons and using a continuous Dijkstra's approach, obtains an $O(\frac{n(\lg n)^2}{\lg \lg n})$ algorithm. In [10] Clarkson, Kapoor, Vaidya and in [7] Mitchell study the problem where the obstacles are non-intersecting simple polygons. Two algorithms are presented in [10] : one requires $O(n \lg n)$ space and $O(n(\lg n)^2)$ time, and the other takes $O(n(\lg n)^{3/2})$ time and $O(n(\lg n)^{3/2})$ space. The algorithm presented in [7] is of $O(n \lg n)$ time and $O(n)$ space complexities.

Typically, the number of obstacles m is much smaller than the number of vertices of all the obstacles together, n. This has been used to provide efficient algorithms for finding Euclidean shortest paths on the plane among obstacles to yield a $O(n + m^2 \lg n)$ time and $O(n)$ space algorithm by Kapoor, Maheshwari and Mitchell in [4]. In this paper, we design an algorithm for computing a rectilinear shortest path in $O(n + m(\lg n)^{3/2})$ time and $O(n + m(\lg m)^{3/2})$ space. Hershberger and Suri gave $O(n \lg n)$ time and $O(n \lg n)$ space algorithm in [2] to find an Euclidean shortest path, which uses the continuous Dijkstra approach. Since the continuous Dijkstra approach ([11] and [2]) is complicated, we use a visibility graph based approach. The visibility graph method is based

V. Arvind and S. Prasad (Eds.): FSTTCS 2007, LNCS 4855, pp. 412–423, 2007.
© Springer-Verlag Berlin Heidelberg 2007

on constructing a graph whose nodes are the vertices of the obstacles and whose edges are pairs of mutually visible vertices. Welzl provides an algorithm for constructing the visibility graph with n line segments in $O(n^2)$ time [6]. Ghosh and Mount [3], and, Kapoor and Maheshwari [5] found an algorithm to construct the visibility graph of time complexity $O(n \lg n + |E|)$ (where $|E|$ is the number of edges in the graph). Applying Dijkstra's algorithm on this graph, one can determine a shortest path in $O(n \lg n + E)$. Unfortunately the visibility graph can have $\Omega(n^2)$ edges in the worst case, so any shortest path algorithm that depends on an explicit construction of the visibility graph will have a similar worst-case running-time.

We propose an algorithm that builds a restricted visibility graph and then applies Dijkstra's shortest path algorithm on this visibility graph. To construct the restricted visibility graph, our algorithm uses a partition of the polygonal region into corridors as in [1] and [4]. The construction of corridors relies on triangulating the polygonal region using the algorithm by Bar-Yehuda and Chazelle [8]. Each corridor contributes $O(1)$ vertices to the visibility graph and since there are $O(m)$ corridors this results in a reduced set of vertices in the visibility graph. However, if we construct the complete visibility graph on this reduced set of vertices the number of edges would be $O(m^2)$. To reduce the number of edges further, we generalize the staircase structure proposed in [10] to apply to the reduced vertex set and to the region partitioned into corridors. We create a set of extra vertices, termed Steiner vertices, and along with a reduced set of edges construct a restricted visibility graph G of smaller size. These Steiner vertices are chosen s.t. for every staircase structure S defined w.r.t. a point p, there exists a rectilinear path from p to any chosen vertex on S. This property facilitates the visibility graph G to contain a rectilinear shortest path from s to t.

This paper is organized as follows. Section 2 describes corridor based staircase structures and the construction of a weighted restricted visibility graph that precisely represents the staircases surrounding each point. Section 3 describes another weighted visibility graph that can be constructed efficiently and allows us to find a rectilinear shortest path. Section 4 contains conclusions.

2   Corridor Based Staircase Structures and Visibility Graph

The rectilinear shortest path problem can be stated as: Given a set of non-intersecting simple polygonal obstacles in the plane, P, find a rectilinear (L_1) shortest path from a point s to a point t which avoids all the obstacles. Here, s and t are considered as degenerate obstacles.

This problem can be solved by using a visibility graph $G = (V, E)$ where V is the set of vertices of the polygonal region and E is the set of visibility edges. Each edge in E is weighted by the rectilinear ($L1$) distance between its endpoints. However, as noted above, $|E| = O(n^2)$. In this section, we show how this problem can be solved by partitioning the polygonal region into corridors and defining a restricted visibility graph $VISTMP(V_{vistmp}, E_{vistmp})$. V_{vistmp}

will have two kinds of vertices, termed V_{ortho} and V_1. The vertices in V_{ortho} are obtained from the corridors into which the region is partitioned, and, the vertices in V_1 are obtained by horizontal and vertical projections of vertices in V_{ortho}. We justify restricting attention to these sets of vertices and an associated set of restricted visibility edges, by using the staircase structure from [10] applied to the set of corridors.

We adopt the partition of the polygonal region into corridors which is provided in [1] and [4]: Consider a triangulation of the given polygonal region P. For two triangles τ_s, τ_t in this triangulation, let $s \in \tau_s$ and $t \in \tau_t$. The points s and t are then incorporated into the triangulation by linking s to the three corners of τ_s, and, by linking t to the three corners of the triangle τ_t (we assume that $\tau_s \neq \tau_t$; otherwise, a shortest path from s to t is simply the line segment joining them). Let T denote the resulting triangulation, and let G_T denote the graph-theoretic dual of T. G_T is a planar graph having $O(n)$ nodes, $O(n)$ edges, and $m+1$ faces. Consider the recursive removal of all nodes of degree one along with its incident edges until no more degree-1 nodes can be removed from G_T. Now, G_T has $m+1$ faces and all nodes are of degree 2 and 3. Each node of degree 3 corresponds to a triangle in T termed as a *junction* of P. Removal of the junction triangles from P results in a set of simple polygons, which we refer to as the *corridors* of P.

The boundary of one such simple polygon, say C, consists of four components: (1) a polygonal chain along the boundary of an obstacle O_1, from a vertex a to a vertex b; (2) for a vertex c located on an obstacle O_2 (possibly $O_2 = O_1$), a diagonal (junction triangle edge) from b to c; (3) a polygonal chain along the boundary of O_2, from c to a vertex d; and (4) a diagonal (junction triangle edge) from d back to a. If we replace the paths from a to b and from c to d with their geodesic paths, within C, then we obtain a region, called a hourglass. The segments ad and bc are the *bounding edges of corridor* C (previously known as, *doors of C*).

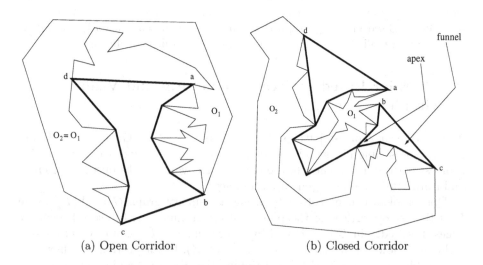

(a) Open Corridor   (b) Closed Corridor

Fig. 1. Types of Corridors

The corridors are classified by their structure into two types, *open and closed corridors*. Consider the corridor C with the boundaries $B_1 = (b, c)$ and $B_2 = (a, d)$. Suppose that there does not exist a pair of points p_1, p_2 located on B_1, B_2 respectively s.t. p_1 and p_2 are mutually visible from each other, then the corridor C is termed as a closed corridor. Otherwise, C is termed as an open corridor. A closed corridor has at most two funnels, each with an apex. (Fig 1)

To handle both the open and closed corridors uniformly, we partition each closed corridor into four convex chains and an edge (similar to the approach in [4]). The convex chains correspond to two chains incident to each of the apex points whereas the apex points of the funnels are the endpoints of the edge introduced, say e. The unique shortest path between the two apex points is precomputed and the L_1 distance along that path is the weight of the edge e. In open corridors the hourglass provides two convex chains, one from a to b and the other from c to d. There are $O(m)$ convex chains in total. The rest of the paper uses only these convex chains.

For a convex chain CC of a corridor C, note that the starting (ending) vertex of the chain, termed as an *endpoint of the corridor convex chain CC* is common to both CC and a bounding edge of C. Let p and q be points on a convex chain CC. Then the contiguous boundary along CC between p and q is known as a *section of convex chain CC*. For a corridor bounding edge e, let points $p, q \in e$. Then the line segment joining p and q is known as a *section of corridor bounding edge e*.

The set of vertices V_{ortho} is defined such that $v \in V_{ortho}$ iff either of the following is true:

(i) v is an endpoint of a corridor convex chain,
(ii) v is a vertex of some corridor convex chain CC, with the property that there exists a tangent to CC at v which is either horizontal or vertical.

Let $COOR(p)$ be the orthogonal coordinate system defined with $p \in V_{ortho}$ as the origin, horizontal x-axis and vertical y-axis. We define a set of points $\pi_i(p)$ as follows: a point $r \in \pi_i(p)$ iff $r \in V_{ortho}$ is located in the ith quadrant of $COOR(p)$. Furthermore, we define a set of points $S_i(p)$. A point q is in the set $S_i(p)$ iff (Fig 2):

- $q \in \pi_i(p)$
- there is no p' (distinct from p) s.t. p' is in $\pi_i(p)$ and q is in the ith quadrant of $COOR(p')$
- q is visible from p

We will assume that $S_i(p)$ is an ordered set with the points in $S_i(p)$ sorted by increasing x-coordinate value. It is easy to see that:

Lemma 1. *Ordering the set of points in $S_1(p)$ in increasing x-coordinates results in the same set of points being ordered in descending order w.r.t. y-coordinates (or, vice versa).*

Note that similar arguments to Lemma 1 can be given for $S_i(p)$ where $i \in \{2, 3, 4\}$.

Two points $\{p_u, p_v\} \subseteq S_i(p)$ are termed as adjacent in $S_i(p)$ if no point $p_l \in S_i(p)$ occurs in between p_u and p_v either in the x- or y-coordinate based ordering of points in the set $S_i(p)$.

Let the sequence of points in $S_i(p)$, sorted by increasing x-coordinate values, be $p_1, p_2, \ldots, p_k$. Let the horizontal ray from each point $p_j \in S_i(p)$ in increasing x direction be known as h_j. The first line/line segment that the ray h_j intersects is either a corridor convex chain, excluding its endpoints, or v_{j+1}. Let this point of intersection be h_j^p. Also, let the vertical ray from each point $p_j \in S_i(p)$ in increasing y direction be known as v_j. The first line/line segment that the ray v_j intersects is either a corridor convex chain, excluding its endpoints, or h_{j-1}. Let this point of intersection be v_j^p. Note that if the ray does not intersect any other line or line segment then the points h_j^p, v_j^p are at infinity. For any $j \in [1, k]$,

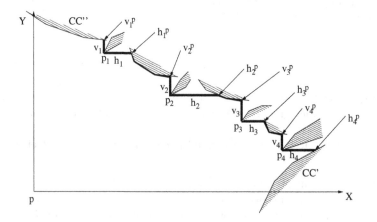

Fig. 2. Staircase structure (in bold) with $S_1(p) = \{p_1, p_2, p_3, p_4\}$

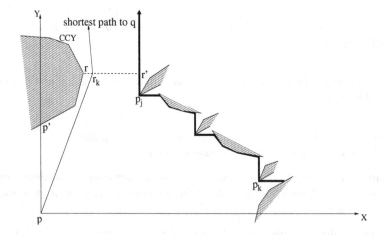

Fig. 3. Replacing a shortest path from p to q with edges in VISTMP

R_j is the contiguous sequence of sections of corridor convex chains/bounding edges joining h_j^p and v_{j+1}^p. The elements in the set $\cup_{\forall j \in \{1,2,\ldots,k\}} (v_j \cup h_j \cup R_j)$ form a contiguous sequence, termed as the $S_i(p)$-staircase (Figs. 2, 3). Note that the convex chains intersecting the coordinate axes are not defined to be part of the staircases in any quadrant. No other configuration is possible as part of the staircase structure. This is detailed in the proof of the following theorem.

Theorem 1. *Along the $S_1(p)$-staicase, any two adjacent points in $S_1(p)$ are joined by at most three geometric entities. These entities ordered in increasing x-coordinates order are : first a horizontal line segment, second a section of convex chain where each edge in that section has a negative slope, and finally a vertical line segment.*

Proof. Consider two adjacent points in $S_1(p)$, say p_j, p_{j+1}. Let h be the line segment from p_j parallel to the x-axis in increasing x-direction, and, suppose h incidents to a point h^p of a convex chain belonging to the staircase structure in the first quadrant of $COOR(p)$ or v. Also, let v be the line segment from p_{j+1} parallel to the y-axis in increasing y-direction, and, suppose v incidents to a point v^p of a convex chain belonging to the staircase structure in the first quadrant of $COOR(p)$ or h. Let REG be the region bounded by pp_j, h, sections of convex chains/corridor bounding edges between h^p and v^p along the staircase, v, $p_{j+1}p$. No convex chain can cross either of pp_j, pp_{j+1} (as both p_j and p_{j+1} are visible to p), h, v (because h^p is the chosen projection from p_j; similarly v^p from v); also, no convex chain can have an endpoint strictly in the interior of the region REG (because of the adjacency of p_j, p_{j+1} along the staircase; definition of $S_1(p)$; lemma 1). In other words, there does not exist a section of convex chain which intersects with the region REG.

First, we prove that if the point h^p is not same as the point v^p then they are incident to the same convex chain. Note that there is nothing to prove in the other case. Suppose h^p is located on a convex chain CC_k, and, v^p is located on a convex chain CC_l for $CC_k \neq CC_l$. Let $CC_k, CC_{k+1}, CC_{k+2}, \ldots, CC_{l-1}, CC_l$ be the consecutive sequence of sections of convex chains or corridor bounding edges encountered while traversing along the staircase from h^p to v^p. Let P be the set consisting of points of intersection of any two adjacent entities (where each entity can be a convex chain or a corridor bounding edge) in this sequence including h^p and v^p. Note that the vertex set V_{ortho} includes every point belonging to P. Since we have chosen p_j and p_{j+1} as adjacent points on the staircase, we obtain a contradiction if there exists at least one point in $P \cap S_1(p)$ whenever $|P| > 2$. We show below that there always exists a point in $P \cap S_1(p)$ whenever $|P| > 2$. From this we can conclude that no point joining two geometric entities (where each entity can be a convex chain or corridor bounding edge) can exist in between p_j and p_{j+1} along the staircase. In other words, at most a section of the convex chain or a section of corridor bounding edge joins h^p and v^p. However due to the staircase definition, a corridor bounding edge cannot join h^p and v^p.

Suppose $P \cap S_1(p) = \phi$ and $|P| > 2$. Let CC_j be the first convex chain along the staircase while traversing the staircase from h^p s.t. there exists a tangent pp_t to CC_j where the point p_t is located on CC_j, and, p_t is visible to p. If no such

p_t exists for any convex chain along the staircase, then the endpoint of the first convex chain along the staircase (while traversing the staircase from h^p) which is in P (as $|P| > 2$) is such a p_t. Thus at least one such CC_j always exists. Let q_b and q_e be the first and last points on CC_j (not necessarily distinct from h^p and v^p) as the staircase is traversed from h^p in increasing x-coordinates order. Let p_t be the first such possible point of tangency (satisfying the above mentioned constraints) along CC_j starting from q_e towards q_b. In [12], we prove that there exists a point r located on the section of convex chain CC_j between (including) q_b and p_t s.t. $r \in S_1(p)$ by giving an exhaustive case analysis; hence, leading to the contradiction.

Let the only possible section of convex chain between p_j and p_{j+1} along the staircase be CC. In [12], we prove that each edge of this section has a negative slope.   □

Note that similar arguments to theorem 1 can be given for $S_i(p)$ where $i \in \{2, 3, 4\}$.

We now define the weighted restricted visibility graph VISTMP($V_{vistmp} = V_{ortho} \cup V_1, E_{vistmp} = E_{orthocc} \cup E_1 \cup E_{tmp}$):

- For each $v \in V_{ortho}$, let the intersection point of a horizontal ray HL, starting at v, with the first corridor convex chain encountered while moving along HL towards the left be known as v_L whereas moving along HL towards the right be known as v_R. Further, let the intersection point of a vertical ray VL, starting at v, with the first corridor convex chain while moving along HV downwards be known as v_D whereas moving along HV upwards be known as v_U. For each point $p \in \{v_L, v_R, v_D, v_U\}$, if the rectilinear distance of p from v is finite then p is added to V_1 and the edge pv is added to E_1. The weight of the edge $e \in E_1$ is the Euclidean distance between its two endpoints.
- An edge $e = (p, q)$ belongs to $E_{orthocc}$ iff p and q are in V_{vistmp} and are adjacent along a corridor convex chain. The weight of edge e is the L_1 distance along the section of convex chain between p and q.
- An edge $e' = (p', q')$ belongs to E_{tmp} iff $q' \in S_i(p')$ for $p' \in V_{ortho}$. The weight of e' is the rectilinear distance along e'.

Theorem 2. *Let $\{p, q\} \subseteq V_{vistmp}$. Then a shortest path from p to q in VISTMP defines a shortest L_1 path from p to q that does not intersect any of the obstacles.*

Proof. Consider a shortest path P from p to q that avoids all the obstacles. We need to consider two cases:

Case (i) - The shortest path P does cross a staircase structure defined w.r.t. point p. Since convex chains on the staircase bound obstacles, the shortest path P does not intersect any of the convex chains in the staircase. Therefore, the shortest path P incidents on either a point in $S_i(p)$, or, an orthogonal line segment in the staircase. Suppose the path crosses an orthogonal segment of the staircase at p'_1. Consider replacing the path from p to p'_1 with two lines, one joining p to p_1, and, the other from p_1 to p_1'. Note that the L_1 distance along the line joining p to p_1' is same as the L_1 distance along the altered path. Let p_j, p_k be the points in $S_i(p)$ with the minimum and maximum x-coordinates when the points in $S_i(p)$ are sorted w.r.t. their x-coordinates. This new rectilinear path is always guaranteed to exist because: (i) no point of V_{ortho} exists in the region bounded by the staircase and the line segments pp_j, pp_k; (ii) neither of the convex chains intersecting the coordinates axes intersect with the interior of the altered path. The path from p_1 to q can be altered similarly without changing the length of the path. Since a shortest path from p to q does not repeat any vertex, the alteration procedure will terminate. Note that the altered path is in VISTMP because for p and every $p_l \in S_i(p)$, the edge $pp_l \in E_{vistmp}$. Therefore, the rectilinear shortest path P between p and q in the given polygonal region can be found by determining the shortest path from p to q in the graph VISTMP.

Case (ii) - The shortest path P does not cross any of the staircase structures defined w.r.t. point p. Suppose the line segment LS starting from p which is part of the shortest path P is in the first quadrant of $COOR(p)$ (other cases can be argued symmetrically). Let p_j, p_k be the points having the minimum and maximum x-coordinates among all the points in $S_1(p)$ (Fig 3). Since the shortest path P does not cross the staircase structure in $S_1(p)$, it must be the case that the x-coordinate of q is either less than the x-coordinate of p_j or greater than the x-coordinate of p_k. Consider the former case (the other case is symmetric). If no convex chain intersects y-axis in the first quadrant, then either $q \in S_1(p)$ or the interior of LS does not intersect with the first quadrant of $COOR(p)$ - leading to a contradiction. Alternatively, consider CCY, the first convex chain that intersects the y-axis while moving in increasing y-direction from p. Also, let CC' be the section of CCY in the first quadrant of $COOR(p)$. Suppose a vertex r of CC' is in V_{ortho}. Let the intersection of the horizontal line at r with the staircase in the first quadrant be r' (Fig 3). Suppose the shortest path P intersects the line segment rr'. Let this point of intersection be r_k. Also, let p' be the vertical projection of p onto CC'. Then replace the path from p to r_k with an equivalent cost path consisting of a vertical line segment pp', path from p' to r along CC', path from r to r_k. The L_1 distance along the line joining p to r_k is same as the L_1 distance along the altered path as the slopes of edges along the path from p' to r cannot be negative. Note that if the slope of any of these edges is negative, then there exists a vertex r' of CC' s.t. $r' \in S_1(p)$, causing the shortest path P to cross the staircase - hence, leading to a contradiction. The new rectilinear path is always guaranteed to exist because $pp' \in E_1$ and the edges comprising the path from p' to r along CC' are in $E_{orthocc}$. The path from r to q can be altered similarly when the y-coordinate of q is greater than r. The detailed version of this paper [12] considers several other cases to complete this proof.   □

Because of the staircase structures, the size of E_{tmp} is not quadratic and yields a better complexity in applying Dijkstra's algorithm. Let there be $O(q)$ points in $S_3(p)$, and, $O(r)$ points in $S_1(p)$. Consider the path from a point $p_k \in S_1(p)$ to $p_l \in S_3(p)$. This path can be altered to another path with L_1 distances along the lines p_k to p, and, p to p_l. Note that the altered path does not change the L_1 distance from p_k to p_l. By having an edge joining every point in $S_3(p) \cup S_1(p)$ with p, the number of visibility edges around p are reduced from $O(qr)$ to $O(q+r)$. Similar savings can be achieved among the possible edges between $S_4(p)$ and $S_2(p)$.

However, explicitly finding the staircase structures surrounding each point $p \in V_{ortho}$ can be of quadratic time complexity. To improve the efficiency, we introduce Type-II Steiner points and devise the following approach.

3   Visibility Graph with Steiner Points

In this section, we detail the construction procedure of a modified restricted weighted visibility graph $\text{VIS}(V_{vis} = V_{ortho} \cup V_1 \cup V_2, E_{vis} = E_{orthocc} \cup E_1 \cup E_2)$ where V_2 and E_2 are the additional *Steiner* vertices and edges added to the graph. The vertices $V_1 \cup V_2$ and the edges $E_1 \cup E_2$ are defined so that for any edge $e = (v_p, v_q) \in E_{tmp}$ of VISTMP, there is a path of the same L_1 length between v_p and v_q in $\text{VIS}(V_{vis}, E_{vis})$. The vertices and edges of VIS are divided into two types, Type-I $(V_{ortho} \cup V_1, E_{orthocc} \cup E_1)$ and Type-II (V_2, E_2), whose construction is described below.

3.1   Type-I Points and Edges

The Type-I points and edges are defined in section 2. These points are obtained by sweeping the obstacle space by orthogonal sweep lines. Since there are four orthogonal projections possible for a point, the algorithm sweeps a vertical sweep line from left to right and from right to left, and, a horizontal sweep line from top to bottom and from bottom to top. During a sweep, the projections onto an obstacle convex chain are generated in order. Details are presented in [12]. At the end of these four sweeps, an ordered list of the Type-I points along a convex chain are obtained. This list readily gives $E_{orthocc}$.

3.2   Type-II Points and Edges

The *TypeIIMain* procedure lists the pseudocode to obtain the Type-II Steiner points and Steiner edges. To facilitate subdividing points into strips, we maintain two lists corresponding to the sorted sequences of points in V_{vis} along the x- and y-coordinates. The points corresponding to a node in the recursion tree are obtained from the point set corresponding to its parent. The Type-II points/edges corresponding to a strip at a recursive step are obtained using these lists. All the Type-II points are found during one sweep of a vertical line, details of which are presented in [12].

Theorem 3. *Let p and q be points in V_{vis}. Then a shortest path from p to q in $\text{VIS}(V_{vis}, E_{vis})$ defines a shortest L_1 path from p to q that avoids all the obstacles.*

procedure *TypeIIMain()*
1: $V'' \leftarrow (V_{ortho} \cup V_1)$
2: TypeIISteiPoints(V'')
3: among all Steiner points V_2 with the same x-coordinate, include in E_2 edges between adjacent vertices in V_2 that are visible to each other

procedure *TypeIISteiPoints(V'')*
1: divide the points V'' into $O(|V''|/\sqrt{\lg m})$ strips parallel to the x-axis with each strip having $O(\sqrt{\lg m})$ points
2: let x_m be the median of the x-coordinates of points in V''; also, suppose the line L_m parallel to y-axis passes through x_m
3: **for** each set R consisting of all the points in a strip **do**
4:    let the point $p_t \in R$ be the one having the largest y coordinate among all the points in R s.t. the point, p'_t, obtained by projecting p_t parallel to x-axis onto L_m is visible from p_t. Then the points p'_t are added to V_2; note that if no such point p_t exists, then there is no such p'_t is introduced. Similarly, let the point $p_b \in R$ be the one having the smallest y coordinate among all the points in R s.t. the point, p'_b, obtained by projecting p_b parallel to x-axis onto L_m is visible from p_b; then the points p'_b are added to V_2; note that if no such point p_b exists, then there is no such p'_b is introduced.
5:    $R' \leftarrow R \cup \{p'_t, p'_b\}$
6: **end for**
7: for a pair of points $p, q \in R'$ we include an edge in E_2 iff the rectangle formed with p and q at the diagonal endpoints does not contain a point in V_{ortho}, and, p is visible from q
8: $V''_{tmp} \leftarrow$ points in V'' with x-coordinates less than x_m
9: TypeIISteiPoints(V''_{tmp})
10: $V''_{tmp} \leftarrow$ points in V'' with x-coordinates greater than x_m
11: TypeIISteiPoints(V''_{tmp})

Proof. To prove this, we show that if there is an edge of length l between two points in VISTMP(V, E), it is guaranteed that there exists a path of length l in the graph VIS(V_{vis}, E_{vis}) between the same two points. W.l.o.g. we consider the edges contained in the first quadrant of $COOR(p)$. For a point $p \in V$, we know that an edge $pp_i \in E$ whenever $p_i \in S_1(p)$. Suppose $p_i \in S_1(p)$ and the L_1 length of edge pp_i be l. Let R be the rectangle obtained by having p and p_i as diagonal endpoints. We need to consider the following two cases:

Case (i) - The interior of R does intersect with some corridor convex chain CC s.t. the projections from points p and p_i incident onto CC. Consider the case in which R intersects with more than one convex chain along a coordinate axis. This is not possible unless there exists a point p' distinct from p s.t. $(p' \in \pi_1(p)) \wedge (p_i \in \pi_1(p'))$. However, then the point p_i does not belong to $S_1(p)$ (due to the second constraint of $S_1(p)$ definition), a contradiction. Therefore, CC is the only corridor convex chain that intersects R along the axis. This is true for both the axes. In other words, the projections from points p and p_i are always incident to the same convex chain CC. Suppose the Type-I points due to the orthogonal projections of p and p_i onto CC be p' and p'_i respectively. Let CC'

be the section of CC from p' and p'_i. First note that no vertex of CC' belongs to V_{ortho}. Hence CC' has either only non-negative or only negative sloped edges. Suppose CC' consists of edges with non-negative slope only. Then consider the path comprising the edge $pp' \in E_1$, path from p' to p'_i comprising edges from $E_{orthocc}$, and the edge $p'_i p_i \in E_1$. The L_1 distance along this path is l. Otherwise, suppose CC' consists of edges with negative slope only. But then p_i is not visible from p as CC' cannot have an endpoint in R, therefore reaching a contradiction.

Case (ii) - The interior of R does not intersect with any corridor convex chain. Let p and p_i reside in (not necessarily distinct) strips R_k and R_l respectively. Assume that the strip R_k is located below R_l (the other case can be argued symmetrically). Then there must exist a median line, say L_m, located in between p and p_i (including p and p_i).   Let p_{kt} and p_{lb} be the top and bottom points in strips R_k and R_l respectively s.t. for two points p'_{kt}, p'_{lb} on L_m, line segments $p_{kt}p_{kt'}$ and $p_{lb}p'_{lb}$ are parallel to the x-axis with $p_{kt'}$ visible from p_{kt} and p'_{lb} visible from p_{lb} (considering either p_{kt} or p_{lb} residing on L_m itself as a degenerate case). Since $p_i \in S_1(p)$ and the rectangle R does not intersect with any convex chain, the interior of rectangle R does not contain any obstacles. Hence for p distinct from p_{kt}, as p'_{kt} is located interior to R, there exists a Type-II Steiner edge joining p and p'_{kt}. Similarly, for p_i distinct from p_{lb}, as p'_{lb} is located interior to R, there exists a Type-II Steiner edge joining p_i and p'_{lb}. Suppose there is no such p_{kt} which is distinct from p. Since no obstacle intersecs the interior of rectangle R, for a point p' on L_m with the line segment pp' parallel to the x-axis, the point p' is visible from p. Hence p' is same as p'_{kt}. Symmetric argument can be give for the case in which there is no p_{lb} distinct from p_i. Therefore, Type-II edges $pp_{kt'}$ and $p_i p_{lb'}$ always exist. Also, no convex chain can intersect L_m in between p'_{kt} and p'_{lb} as there is no obstacle strictly inside the rectangle R. Since p_{kt}, p_{lb} are chosen s.t. they are the top and bottom points in strips R_k, R_l respectively, the L_1 distance of the path consisting of Type-II edges $pp'_{kt}, p'_{kt}p'_{lb}, p'_{lb}p_i$ is of length l.   □

Theorem 4. *Computing a rectilinear shortest path from s to t is of $O(n + m(\lg n)^{3/2})$ time and $O(n + m(\lg m)^{3/2})$ space complexity.*

Proof. The number of Type-I points and edges are $O(m)$. The number of Type-II points and edges are $O(m(\lg m)^{1/2})$ and $O(m(\lg m)^{3/2})$ respectively. Hence, $|V_{vis}| = O(m(\lg m)^{1/2})$ and $|E_{vis}| = O(m(\lg m)^{3/2})$. Applying Dijkstra's algorithm takes $O(|E_{vis}| + |V_{vis}| \lg |V_{vis}|)$ i.e., $O(m(\lg m)^{3/2})$. Using the algorithm by Bar-Yehuda and Chazelle [8] the triangulation of polygonal region takes $O(n + m(\lg m)^{1+\epsilon})$, represented as $O(T)$. Finding corridors and junctions given the triangulation takes $O(n + m \lg n)$. The time involved in precomputing the rectilinear shortest distance between the apex points at all the closed corridors together takes $O(n)$ time. Computing the Type-I points and edges takes $O(m \lg n)$ time. Computing the Type-II points and edges takes $O(m(\lg m)^{3/2})$ time. Computing the point of tangencies and orthogonal tangents on all the convex chains together takes $O(m \lg n)$. Hence the overall time complexity is $O(n + m(\lg n)^{3/2})$. Only binary trees and lists are used in the algorithm. And, no data structure uses more space than the total number of Type-I/Type-II points/edges, hence the space complexity (including the input complexity). Detailed analysis is presented in [12]. □

4 Conclusion

This paper presented a $O(n + m(\lg n)^{3/2})$ time and $O(n + m(\lg m)^{3/2})$ space algorithm for finding a shortest rectilinear path from s to t through simple polygonal obstacles, where n is the number of vertices of the obstacles and m is the number of obstacles. It is of interest to find an algorithm of time complexity $O(n + m \lg m)$.

References

[1] Kapoor, S., Maheshwari, S.N.: An Efficient Algorithm for Euclidean Shortest Paths Among Polygonal Obstacles in the Plane. In: Proceedings of the ACM Symposium on Computational Geometry, pp. 172–182. ACM Press, New York (1988)

[2] Hershberger, J., Suri, S.: An Optimal Algorithm for Euclidean Shortest Paths in the Plane. SIAM Journal on Computing 28(6), 2215–2256 (1999)

[3] Ghosh, S.K., Mount, D.M.: An output-sensitive algorithm for computing visibility graphs. SIAM J. Comput. 20, 888–910 (1991)

[4] Kapoor, S., Maheshwari, S.N., Mitchell, J.S.B.: An Efficient Algorithm for Euclidean Shortest Paths Among Polygonal Obstacles in the Plane. Discrete Computational Geometry 18(4), 377–383 (1997)

[5] Kapoor, S., Maheshwari, S.N.: Efficiently constructing the visibility graph of a simple polygon with obstacles. SIAM J. Comput. 30(3), 847–871 (2000)

[6] Welzl, E.: Constructing the visibility graph for n line segments in $O(n^2)$ time. Inform. Process. Lett. 20, 167–171 (1985)

[7] Mitchell, J.S.B.: L₁ Shortest Paths Among Polygonal Obstacles in the Plane. Algorithmica 8(1), 55–88 (1992)

[8] Bar-Yehuda, R., Chazelle, B.: Triangulating disjoint Jordan chains. Int. J. Comput. Geometry Appl. 4(4), 475–481 (1994)

[9] de Rezende, P.J., Lee, D.T., Wu, Y.F.: Rectilinear Shortest Paths with Rectangular Barriers. Discrete and Computational Geometry 4, 41–53 (1989)

[10] Clarkson, K.L., Kapoor, S., Vaidya, P.M.: Rectilinear Shortest Paths through Polygonal Obstacles in O(n (lgn)3̂/2) time. Proceedings of the ACM Symposium on Computational Geometry, 251–257 (1987)

[11] Mitchell, J.S.B.: Shortest Rectilinear Paths among obstacles. Technical Report No. 739, School of OR/IE, Cornell University (1987)

[12] Shortest L_1 path in R^2 using Corridor based Staircase Structures, full manuscript, Submitted to Computational Geometry: Theory and Applications, http://www.ices.utexas.edu/~rinkulu/docs/l1sp.pdf

Compressed Dynamic Tries with Applications to LZ-Compression in Sublinear Time and Space

Jesper Jansson[1,*], Kunihiko Sadakane[1], and Wing-Kin Sung[2]

[1] Department of Computer Science and Communication Engineering,
Kyushu University, 744 Motooka, Nishi-ku, Fukuoka 819-0395, Japan
jj@tcslab.csce.kyushu-u.ac.jp, sada@csce.kyushu-u.ac.jp
[2] Department of Computer Science, National University of Singapore,
3 Science Drive 2, 117543 Singapore
Genome Institute of Singapore, 60 Biopolis Street, Genome 138672, Singapore
ksung@comp.nus.edu.sg

Abstract. The *dynamic trie* is a fundamental data structure which finds applications in many areas. This paper proposes a compressed version of the dynamic trie data structure. Our data-structure is not only space efficient, it also allows pattern searching in $o(|P|)$ time and leaf insertion/deletion in $o(\log n)$ time, where $|P|$ is the length of the pattern and n is the size of the trie. To demonstrate the usefulness of the new data structure, we apply it to the LZ-compression problem. For a string S of length s over an alphabet $\mathcal{A}$ of size σ, the previously best known algorithms for computing the Ziv-Lempel encoding (LZ78) of S either run in: (1) $O(s)$ time and $O(s \log s)$ bits working space; or (2) $O(s\sigma)$ time and $O(sH_k + s \log \sigma / \log_\sigma s)$ bits working space, where H_k is the k-order entropy of the text. No previous algorithm runs in sublinear time. Our new data structure implies a LZ-compression algorithm which runs in sublinear time and uses optimal working space. More precisely, the LZ-compression algorithm uses $O(s(\log \sigma + \log \log_\sigma s)/ \log_\sigma s)$ bits working space and runs in $O(s(\log \log s)^2/(\log_\sigma s \log \log \log s))$ worst-case time, which is sublinear when $\sigma = 2^{o(\log s \frac{\log \log \log s}{(\log \log s)^2})}$.

1 Introduction

A *trie* [7] is a rooted tree in which every edge is labeled by a symbol from an alphabet $\mathcal{A}$ in such a way that for every node u and every $a \in \mathcal{A}$, there is at most one edge from u to a child of u that is labeled by a. (From here on, we assume $\mathcal{A}$ is fixed and define $\sigma = |\mathcal{A}|$.) Each leaf ℓ in the trie represents a string obtained by concatenating the symbols on the unique path from the root to ℓ; thus, a trie can be used to store a set of strings over $\mathcal{A}$. A *dynamic* trie is a fundamental data structure allowing operations to modify it dynamically, i.e., allowing strings to be inserted or deleted from the trie. It find applications in many areas including information retrieval, natural language processing, database systems, compilers, data compression, and computer networks. As an example, in

---

* Supported by Japan Society for the Promotion of Science (JSPS).

V. Arvind and S. Prasad (Eds.): FSTTCS 2007, LNCS 4855, pp. 424–435, 2007.

computer networks, dynamic tries are used in IP routing to efficiently maintain the hierarchical organization of routing information to enable fast lookup of IP addresses [14]. In data compression, dynamic tries are used to represent the so-called LZ-trie and the Huffman coding trie which are the key data structures in the Ziv-Lempel encoding (LZ78) [20] (or its variant LZW encoding [17]) and the Huffman encoding, respectively. Furthermore, many data structures such as the suffix trie/suffix tree, the Patricia trie [11], and the associative array (hashing table) can be maintained as dynamic tries.

Without loss of generality, assume $\sigma \leq n$. A dynamic trie T of size n can be implemented using a standard tree data-structure in $O(n \log n)$ bits space such that: (1) insertion or deletion of a leaf into or from T takes $O(1)$ time; and (2) finding the longest prefix of a query pattern P in T takes $O(|P|)$ time. A number of solutions have been proposed to improve the average time and space complexities of tries [1,2,11]. However, in the worst case, those solutions still use $O(n \log n)$ bits space and pattern searching still requires $O(|P|)$ time. Employing the latest advances on compressed trees, a trie can now be maintained in $O(n \log \sigma)$ bits space under the unit-cost RAM model such that: (1) insertion or deletion of a leaf takes $O(\log n)$ time; and (2) the longest common pattern query takes $O(|P|)$ time. Note that none of the existing data structures can answer the longest common pattern query in $o(|P|)$ time.

This paper assumes a unit-cost RAM model with word size logarithmic in n, in which standard arithmetic and bitwise boolean operations on word-sized operands can be performed in constant time [9]. Also, we assume the pattern P is packed in $O(|P| \log \sigma / \log n)$ words. Under such a model, we propose a data structure which uses $O(n \log \sigma)$ bits such that: (1) insertion or deletion of a leaf takes $O((\log \log n)^2 / \log \log \log n)$ time; and (2) the longest common pattern query takes $O(\frac{|P|}{\log_\sigma n} \frac{(\log \log n)^2}{\log \log \log n})$ time. Note that when $\sigma = 2^{o(\log n \frac{\log \log \log n}{(\log \log n)^2})}$, our $O(n \log \sigma)$-bits dynamic trie data-structure can be maintained such that the longest common pattern query can be performed in $o(|P|)$ time while insertion and deletion takes $o(\log n)$ time.

In this paper we define "sublinear" as follows. We assume that the alphabet size σ is a function of n (or a constant). We say the space is sublinear if it is $o(n \log \sigma)$ because $n \log \sigma$ is the input size. We say the time is sublinear if it is $o(n \log \sigma)$. Note that no algorithm can achieve sublinear time for large alphabets such as $\log \sigma = \Omega(\log n)$ because it takes $\Omega(\frac{n \log \sigma}{\log n})$ time to read the input. We give sublinear time algorithms when $\sigma = 2^{o(\log n \frac{\log \log \log n}{(\log \log n)^2})}$.

Our improvement stems from the observation that small tries (that is, tries of size $O(\log_\sigma n)$) can be maintained very efficiently. Hence, our data structures partition the trie into many small tries and maintain them individually. With this approach, we not only store the trie using $O(n \log \sigma)$ bits, but also allow fast queries and efficient insertions and deletions.

To demonstrate the usefulness of our dynamic trie data structure, we applied it to generate the LZ78 encoding of a text. The Ziv-Lempel encoding (LZ78) [20] (or its variant LZW encoding[17]) of a text is a popular compression scheme.

Ziv and Lempel [20] showed that the LZ78 encoding scheme gives an asymptotically optimal compression ratio.

The current solutions for constructing the LZ78 encoding of a text first construct the LZ-trie and then generate the LZ78 encoding. These solutions either run in: (1) $O(s)$ time and $O(s \log s)$ bits working space [5,15]; or (2) $O(s\sigma)$ time and $O(s \log \sigma)$ bits working space [3]. None of the solutions in the literature runs in sublinear time and $O(s \log \sigma)$-bit working space. By maintaining the LZ-trie using our dynamic trie data structure, we obtain the first LZ compression algorithm which uses optimal working space and runs in sublinear time when $\sigma = 2^{o(\log s \frac{\log \log \log s}{(\log \log s)^2})}$. More precisely, we propose an algorithm which uses $O(s(\log \sigma + \log \log_\sigma s)/\log_\sigma s)$ bits working space and runs in in $O(s(\log \log s)^2/(\log_\sigma s \log \log \log s))$ worst-case time. Note that the working space is asymptotically smaller than the outputted compressed text.

The paper is organized as follows. Section 2 reviews some previously known facts about tries and LZ78 encoding. Section 3 defines the LZ78 encoding and gives some simple data structures that are useful for maintaining a LZ-trie. Sections 4 and 5 detail our dynamic trie data structure. Finally, Section 6 presents our LZ compression algorithms.

2   Previous Work

A dynamic trie data structure can be implemented naively using $O(n \log n)$ bits such that: (1) insertion and deletion of a leaf takes $O(1)$ time; and (2) the longest prefix of any query pattern P in T can be found in $O(|P|)$ time. Many practical improvements have been proposed which yield good performance (on average) for searching a pattern. Morrison [11] proposed the Patricia trie which compresses a path by merging the nodes of degree 2. This idea reduces the size of the trie. Later, Andersson and Nilsson [1] proposed the LC-trie, which reduces the depth of the trie by increasing the branching factor (level compression). This idea reduces the average running time [6].

Willard [18,19] proposed two data structures for maintaining a trie of depth $O(\log M)$ for some positive integer M: (1) the Q-fast trie [19], which uses $O(n \log M)$ bits space and searches for the pattern P in T in $O(\sqrt{\log M})$ time while inserting or deleting a leaf in $O(\sqrt{\log M})$ time; and (2) the Y-fast trie [18], which is a static trie that uses $O(n \log M)$ bits space and can report the longest prefix of any pattern P in T in $O(\log \log M)$ time.

Ziv-Lempel encoding (LZ78) is a widely used encoding scheme for compressing a text [17,20]. LZ78 also has applications in compressed indexing; Navarro [13] presented a compressed full-text self-index called *LZ-index* based on the LZ-trie whose size is proportional to the compressed text size. The LZ-index allows efficient pattern queries.

A straightforward implementation of LZ78 based on Lempel and Ziv's original definition takes $O(n^2)$ worst-case time to process a string of length n. Rodeh, Pratt, and Even [15] improved the running time to $O(n)$ using suffix trees, and

Brent [5] gave another linear time compression algorithm based on hashing. However, both algorithms use $O(n \log n)$-bits working space. This is larger than the size of the Ziv-Lempel encoding, which is $O(nH_k)$ where H_k is the k-order entropy of the text. People have recently realized the importance of space-efficient data compression algorithms [3,10]. Given a long text, we may have enough memory to store the compressed text (that is, the Ziv-Lempel encoding). However, we may be unable to construct it if the working space requirement is too large. For example, we are able to store the Ziv-Lempel encoding of the human genome in a 2GB RAM computer, but we may fail to construct the encoding due to the size of the memory. Hence, a space-efficient construction algorithm is necessary. Utilizing the solution of Arroyuelo and Navarro [3], the Ziv-Lempel encoding of a text can be constructed using $O(\sigma n)$ time and $O(nH_k + n \log \sigma / \log_\sigma n)$ bits working space.

3   Preliminaries

We first reviews simple data structures used for dynamically maintaining a set of length-$(\log_\sigma n)$ strings and a tree, respectively, in Sections 3.1 and 3.2. These data structures are the building blocks of our dynamic trie data structure, which is used to dynamically maintain a LZ-trie. Section 3.3 reviews the definitions of the LZ78 encoding and the LZ-trie.

3.1   A Data Structure for Maintaining a Set of Length-$(\log_\sigma n)$ Strings

This subsection describes a dynamic data structure for maintaining a set of k strings, each of length at most $\log_\sigma n$, over an alphabet of size σ. It needs to support three operations: (1) insertion of a length-$(\log_\sigma n)$ string, (2) deletion of a length-$(\log_\sigma n)$ string, and (3) predecessor of a string P (that is, reporting the string currently in the set which is lexicographically just smaller than P).

We make use of the *dynamic predecessor data structure* of Beame and Fich [4], whose properties are summarized in the next lemma:

Lemma 1 ([4]). *The dynamic predecessor data structure of Beame and Fich [4] can maintain a set of ℓ $O(\log n)$-bit integers using $O(\ell \log n)$ bits under insertions and deletions while supporting predecessor queries so that each insert/delete/ predecessor operation takes $O((\log \log n)^2 / (\log \log \log n))$ time.*

We immediately obtain:

Lemma 2. *Consider k strings of length at most $\log_\sigma n$ over an alphabet of size σ. We can store all strings in $O(k \log n)$ bits such that insert/delete/predecessor can be found in $O((\log \log n)^2 / \log \log \log n)$ time.*

Proof. Treat the strings as integers in the range $\{0, 1, \ldots, n - 1\}$ and apply Lemma 1.   □

3.2   Data Structures for Maintaining an Edge-Labeled Tree

This section discusses how to dynamically maintain an edge-labeled tree T. We assume the size of the tree and all labels are integers smaller than n. We support the following operations:

- $Insert(u, \kappa, v)$: Insert a leaf v as a child of u and label the edge (u, v) by κ.
- $Delete(v)$: Delete the leaf v and the edge between v and its parent (if any).
- $Child(u, \kappa)$: Return the child v of u such that the edge (u, v) is labeled by κ.

Lemma 3. *A tree T can be maintained dynamically in $O(|T| \log n)$ bits space such that $Child/Insert/Delete$ can be answered in $O((\log \log n)^2/(\log \log \log n))$ time.*

Proof. We represent T using two dynamic predecessor data structures $\mathcal{D}_1$ and $\mathcal{D}_2$, as in Lemma 1. For each edge (u, v) labeled by κ, we maintain $n^2 \cdot u + n \cdot \kappa + v$ in $\mathcal{D}_1$ and $n^2 \cdot v + n \cdot u + \kappa$ in $\mathcal{D}_2$. $\mathcal{D}_1$ and $\mathcal{D}_2$ take $O(|T| \log n)$-bit space. Since $u, v, \kappa \leq n$, there is a one-to-one mapping between (u, v, κ) and the number $w = n^2 \cdot u + n \cdot \kappa + v$ in $\mathcal{D}_1$. To be precise, $v = w \bmod n$, $u = \lfloor w/n^2 \rfloor$, $\kappa = \lfloor (w - u \cdot n^2)/n \rfloor$. Similarly for $\mathcal{D}_2$.

To insert a leaf node v, which is a child of u with edge label κ, it can be done by inserting $n^2 \cdot u + n \cdot \kappa + v$ in $\mathcal{D}_1$ and $n^2 \cdot v + n \cdot u + \kappa$ in $\mathcal{D}_2$.

To delete a leaf node v, we first query $\mathcal{D}_2$ to retrieve the integer w which is just bigger than $n^2 \cdot v$. Note that $w = n^2 \cdot v + n \cdot u + \kappa$ where u is the parent of v and κ is the label of (u, v). Then, the leaf node v can be removed by deleting $n^2 \cdot u + n \cdot \kappa + v$ from $\mathcal{D}_1$ and $n^2 \cdot v + n \cdot u + \kappa$ from $\mathcal{D}_2$.

To compute $Child(u, \kappa)$, we first retrieve the integer w which is just bigger than $n^2 \cdot u + n \cdot \kappa$ in $\mathcal{D}_1$. Then, $Child(u, \kappa)$ equals the remainder when we divide w by n.

The running time for each of the three operations is $O((\log \log n)^2/(\log \log \log n))$ time by Lemma 1.   □

3.3   LZ78 Encoding and LZ-Trie

Ziv-Lempel encoding [20], or LZ78, is a data compression scheme for strings. For a given string $S = S[1..n]$, it constructs a *phrase list* and a LZ-*trie* procedurely using the following method: First, initialize a trie T as empty, the current position $p = 1$, and the number of phrases $c = 0$. Then, parse S into phrases from left to right until $p > n$ as follows. Find the longest string, $t \in T$, that appears as a prefix of $S[p..n]$. Set $c = c + 1$. Obtain the phrase $s_c = S[p..p + |t|] = t \cdot S[p + |t|]$ and insert it into T. Then, set $p = p + |t| + 1$ and repeat the parsing for the next phrase.

The trie T generated during the above process is called the LZ-*trie* while the list of phrases $s_1, s_2, \ldots, s_c$ is called the *phrase list*. The Ziv-Lempel encoding of the given string S consists of the LZ-trie together with the phrase list for S. By [20], it holds that $\sqrt{n} \leq c \leq n/\log_\sigma n$. Also, the LZ-trie and the phrase list can be stored in $c \log c + O(c \log \sigma) = nH_k + O(n \log \sigma/\log_\sigma n)$ bits.

4   Dynamically Maintaining a Trie of Height $\log_\sigma n$

In this and the next section, we show how to maintain a trie while efficiently supporting the following operations:

- $Insert(T, u, a)$: Insert a leaf v as a child of u such that the label of (u, v) is a, where $a \in \mathcal{A}$.
- $Delete(T, u)$: Delete the leaf u and the edge between u and its parent (if any).
- $Lcp(T, P)$: Report the length ℓ such that $P[1..\ell]$ is the longest prefix which exists in T.

Here, we discuss the dynamic trie data structure for small tries. First, we consider how to maintain a trie of size $O(\log_\sigma n)$. Then, we study how to maintain a trie of height at most $\log_\sigma n$. (In the next section, we discuss how to maintain a general trie.)

4.1   Maintaining a Trie of Size $O(\log_\sigma n)$

This subsection describes how to dynamically maintain a trie T of size $O(\log_\sigma n)$.

Lemma 4. *Given a precomputed table of size $O(n^{5\epsilon})$ bits for any constant $0 < \epsilon < 0.2$, we can maintain a trie T of size $\epsilon \log_\sigma n$ using at most $3\epsilon \log n$ bits. All operations Lcp, Insert, and Delete take $O(1)$ worst case time. Also, preorder of any node can be computed in $O(1)$ time.*

Proof. The data structure has two parts. First, the topology of T is stored in $2|T| = 2\epsilon \log_\sigma n$ bits using parenthesis encoding [12,8]. Second, the edge labels of all edges are stored in preorder using $|T| \log \sigma = \epsilon \log n$ bits. Therefore the total space is at most $3\epsilon \log n$ bits.

In addition, the data structure also requires four pre-computed tables. The first table stores the value of $Lcp(R, Q)$ for any trie R of size at most $\epsilon \log_\sigma n$ and any string Q of length at most $\epsilon \log_\sigma n$. The second table stores the value of $preorder(R, Q)$, which is the preorder of any string Q in the trie R for any trie R of size at most $\epsilon \log_\sigma n$ and any string Q of length at most $\epsilon \log_\sigma n$. Since there are $O(2^{2 \cdot \epsilon \log_\sigma n} \cdot \sigma^{\epsilon \log_\sigma n} \cdot \sigma^{\epsilon \log_\sigma n}) = O(n^{4\epsilon})$ different combinations of R and Q, both tables can be stored in $O(n^{4\epsilon} \log \log_\sigma n) = O(n^{5\epsilon})$ bits space. The size of the tables for insert/delete is $O(2^{2 \cdot \epsilon \log_\sigma n} \cdot \sigma^{\epsilon \log_\sigma n} \cdot \epsilon \log_\sigma n \cdot \sigma \cdot \epsilon \log n) = O(n^{5\epsilon})$.

The four operations can be supported in $O(1)$ time as follows using a precomputed table for each operation.

- To insert/delete a node x, we update the topology and the edge label.
- $Lcp(T, P)$ can be computed by asking $O(1)$ queries. in the precomputed table.
- Preorder of any string in T can also be computed in $O(1)$ time.   □

Lemma 5. *The tables for Lcp() and preorder() can be constructed incrementally using $O(\log_\sigma n)$ time per entry. When the size of the tables is n, $Lcp(R, Q)$ and $preorder(R, Q)$ queries can be answered in $O(1)$ time for any R of size at most $0.2 \log_\sigma n$ and Q of length at most $0.2 \log_\sigma n$.*

4.2   Maintaining a Trie of Height $O(\log_\sigma n)$

This section describes how to dynamically maintain a trie of height $O(\log_\sigma n)$.

Lemma 6. *Given a precomputed table of size $O(n^{5\epsilon})$ bits for any constant $0 < \epsilon < 0.2$, we can dynamically maintain a trie T of height $\frac{\epsilon}{2} \log_\sigma n$ using $O(|T| \log \sigma)$ bits space such that all operations Lcp, Insert, and Delete take $O((\log \log n)^2 / \log \log \log n)$ time.*

Proof. Let u_i be the node in T whose preorder is i. Let $S = \{s_1, s_2, \ldots, s_{|T|}\}$ be the set of strings where s_i is the string representing the path label of u_i. Note that the s_i's are sorted in alphabetical order.

A block is defined to be a series of strings $s_i, s_{i+1}, \ldots, s_j$ where $i \leq j \leq |T|$. Note that all strings in a block can be represented as a subtrie of T. The nodes $u_i, u_{i+1}, \ldots, u_j$ are connected if we add the nodes on the path from the root to u_i. Therefore the size of the subtrie is at most $j - i + 1 + \frac{\epsilon}{2} \log_\sigma n$.

The set S can be partitioned into a set $\mathcal{B} = \{B_1, B_2, \ldots B_{|\mathcal{B}|}\}$ of non-overlapping blocks such that $B_1 \cup B_2 \cup \ldots \cup B_{|\mathcal{B}|} = S$. We also maintain the invariant that (1) every block contains at most $\frac{\epsilon}{2} \log_\sigma n$ strings and (2) at most one block has less than $\frac{\epsilon}{4} \log_\sigma n/2$ strings. Besides, for each $B_i \in \mathcal{B}$, let $s_{b(i)}$ be the smallest string in B_i.

Our dynamic data structure represents the trie T using a two-level data structure.

- **(1) Top-level:** Using the data structure in Lemma 2, we store $\{s_{b(1)}, \ldots, s_{b(|\mathcal{B}|)}\}$.
- **(2) Block-level:** For each block $B_i \in \mathcal{B}$, we can represent the strings in B_i as a trie of size $\epsilon \log_\sigma n$ and store the trie using Lemma 4.

We first show that the space required is $O(|T| \log \sigma)$ bits. Note that $|\mathcal{B}| = O(\frac{|T|}{\epsilon \log_\sigma n})$ blocks. The space required for the top-level structure is $O(\epsilon^{-1}|\mathcal{B}| \log n) = O(\epsilon^{-1}|T| \log \sigma)$ bits. Each block requires $O(\log n)$ bit space by Lemma 4. The space for the block-level structure is $O(|\mathcal{B}| \log n) = O(|T| \log \sigma)$.

The time complexity of the three operations is as follows.

- *Lcp(T, P):* Let P' be the first $\frac{\epsilon}{2} \log_\sigma n$ characters of P. To compute the longest common prefix of P in T, we first find s_i and s_{i+1} such that P' is alphabetically in between s_i and s_{i+1}; let lcp_1 be the longest common prefix of P' and s_i and lcp_2 be the longest common prefix of P' and s_{i+1}; then, $Lcp(T, P)$ equals the maximum of lcp_1 and lcp_2. To locate s_i, our strategy is to first locate the $s_{b(j)}$ which is alphabetically just smaller than or equal to P'. By Lemma 2, $s_{b(j)}$ can be found in $O((\log \log n)^2 / \log \log \log n)$ time. Then, within B_j, we locate the s_i just smaller than or equal to P'. By Lemma 4, this step takes $O(1)$ time.
- *Insert(T, u, a):* Suppose u represents a string $s \in S$. This operation is equivalent to insert a new string $s \cdot a$ after s. Let B_j be the block containing s. We first insert $s \cdot a$ into B_j using $O(1)$ time by Lemma 4. If B_j contains less than $\frac{\epsilon}{2} \log_\sigma n$ strings, then the insert operation is done. Otherwise, we need

to split B_j into two blocks each containing at least $\frac{\epsilon}{4}\log_\sigma n$ strings. The split takes $O(1)$ time since B_j is packed in $O(\log n)$ bits. Lastly, we update the top-level structure to indicate the existence of the new block, which takes $O((\log\log n)^2/\log\log\log n)$ time.

– $Delete(T, u)$: The analysis is similar to the Insert operation.   □

5 Maintaining a Trie with No Height Restrictions

This section gives a data structure to dynamically maintain a general trie T. We also show how to build an auxiliary data structure for T using $O(|T|)$ time such that the preorder of any node can be reported in $O(\log\log n)$ time.

We describe a dynamic data structure for a trie T such that insertion/deletion of a leaf takes $O((\log\log n)^2/\log\log\log n)$ time and longest common prefix of P can be computed in $O(\frac{|P|}{\log_\sigma n}\frac{(\log\log n)^2}{\log\log\log n})$ time.

Our data structure represents a general trie T by partitioning it into tries of height at most $h = \frac{\epsilon}{2}\log_\sigma n$ for some constant $0 < \epsilon < 0.2$. To formally describe the representation, we need some definitions.

Let $\delta = h/3$. For any node $u \in T$, u is denoted as a *linking node* if (1) the height of u is of multiple of δ and (2) the subtrie rooted at u has more than δ nodes.

Let LN be the set of linking nodes of T. For any $u \in LN$, let τ_u be the subtrie of T rooted at u including all descendents v of u such that there is no linking node in the path between u and v. For any non-root node $v \in T$, we denote by $p(v)$ the linking node such that $p(v)$ is the lowest ancestor of u in T.

Let T' be a tree whose vertex set is LN and whose edge set is $\{(p(u), u) \mid u \in LN \text{ and } u \text{ is not the root}\}$. The label of every edge $(p(u), u)$ in T' is the length-δ string represented by the path from $p(u)$ to u in T.

Based on the above discussion, T can be represented by storing (1) T' and (2) τ_u for all $u \in LN$. The next lemma bounds the size of LN.

Lemma 7. $|LN| \leq |T|/\delta$. Also, for any $u \in LN$, τ_u is of height smaller than 2δ.

Proof. Each $u \in LN$ has at least δ unique nodes associated to it. Hence $|T| = \sum_{u\in LN}|\tau_u| \geq |LN|\delta$. Thus, $|LN| \leq |T|/\delta$. By construction, τ_u is of height smaller than 2δ.   □

The theorem below is our main result. It states how to maintain T' and τ_u for all $u \in LN$.

Theorem 1. *We can dynamically maintain a trie T using $O(|T|\log\sigma)$ bits space such that $Lcp(T, P)$ takes $O(\frac{|P|}{\log_\sigma n}\frac{(\log\log n)^2}{\log\log\log n})$ time while insertion/deletion of a leaf takes $O((\log\log n)^2/\log\log\log n)$ time.*

Proof. We represent T' by Lemma 3 using $O(|T'|\log n) = O(\frac{|T|}{\log_\sigma n}\log n) = O(|T|\log\sigma)$ bits. For every $u \in LN$, the height of τ_u is bounded according to Lemma 7, so we can represent τ_u as in Lemma 6 using $O(|\tau_u|\log\sigma)$ bits. Since

$\sum_{u \in LN} |\tau_u| = |T|$, all τ_u's can be represented in $O(|T| \log \sigma)$ bits. Also, we maintain the lookup tables for answering queries $Lcp(R, Q)$ and $preorder(R, Q)$ for any tree R of size at most $\epsilon \log_\sigma |T|$ and any query Q of length at most $\epsilon \log_\sigma |T|$ where $0 < \epsilon < 1$.

For $Lcp(T, P)$, the longest prefix of P which exists in T can be found in two steps. First, we find the longest prefix of P in T'. It is done in $O(\frac{|P|}{\log_\sigma n} \frac{(\log \log n)^2}{\log \log \log n})$ time using the predecessor data structure in Lemma 3. Suppose u is the node in T' corresponding to the longest prefix $P[1..x]$ of P. Second, we find the longest prefix of $P[x + 1..|P|]$ in τ_u. By Lemma 6, it takes another $O(\frac{(\log \log n)^2}{\log \log n})$ time.

For insertion/deletion of a leaf node u, suppose we need to insert/delete the leaf node u in the subtrie τ_v where $v \in LN$. By Lemma 6, it takes $O(\frac{(\log \log n)^2}{\log \log \log n})$ time. Moreover, if the insertion/deletion creates/destroys a new linking node v' in τ_v, we need to do the following additional steps. (1) Insert/delete a new leaf in T' corresponding to v' (This step can be done in $O(\frac{(\log \log n)^2}{\log \log n})$ time by Lemma 3); (2) Create/delete a new subtrie $\tau_{v'}$ (Since $\tau_{v'}$ is of size smaller than $\log_\sigma n$, we can create/delete it in $O(1)$ time); and (3) Insert/delete $\tau_{v'}$ from τ_v (Since $\tau_{v'}$ is stored in $O(1)$ blocks in τ_v, we can modify those blocks in $O(\frac{(\log \log n)^2}{\log \log n})$ time). (4) For every insertion, if the size of the lookup tables $Lcp()$ and $preorder()$ is smaller than n^ϵ, we incrementally increase the size of the tables by one using Lemma 5. For every deletion, if the size of the tables is bigger than $2n^\epsilon$, we reduce the size of the tables by one using Lemma 5.   □

The following lemma states how to build an auxiliary data structure for T to answer preorder queries.

Lemma 8. *Given a trie T represented by the dynamic data structure in Theorem 1, we can generate an auxiliary data structure of size $O(|T| \log \sigma)$ bits in $O(|T|)$ time such that the preorder of a node can be computed in $O(\log \log n)$ time.*

Proof. The auxiliary data structure stores information for every linking node u (that is, $u \in T'$). First, we store the preorder of u. Then, for the corresponding subtrie τ_u, define $\mathcal{B}$ and the set $\{s_{b(1)}, s_{b(2)}, \ldots s_{b(|\mathcal{B}|)}\}$ as in Lemma 6. We store three information below.

1. By Lemma 2, using $O(|\mathcal{B}|(\log \log n)^2 / \log \log \log n)$ time, we extract all strings in $\{s_{b(1)}, s_{b(2)}, \ldots s_{b(|\mathcal{B}|)}\}$. The set $\{s_{b(1)}, s_{b(2)}, \ldots s_{b(|\mathcal{B}|)}\}$ is stored in $O(|\mathcal{B}| \log n)$ bits space using $O(|\mathcal{B}| \log \log n)$ time by the y-fast trie data structure [18]. Then, given any string P, we can report the largest i such that $s_{b(i)}$ is alphabetically smaller than or equal to P using $O(\log \log n)$ time.
2. It stores an array $V[1..|\mathcal{B}|]$ where $V[j]$ equals the preorder values of the $s_{b(i)}$. Since each preorder value can be stored in $\log n$ bits, the array V can be stored in $|\mathcal{B}| \log n = O(|T|)$ bits.
3. For each $B_i \in \mathcal{B}$, all strings in B_i are represented as a trie of size $O(\log n)$ bits using Lemma 4.

For any node $v \in T$, let u be the linking node that is the lowest ancestor of u in T. Let B be the block in τ_u which contains v and w be the node in τ_u corresponds to the smallest string in B. Note that the preorder of v equals the sum of (1) the preorder of u in T, (2) the preorder of w in τ_u, and (3) the preorder of v in B.

For (1), the preorder of u in T is stored in the auxiliary data structure. For (2), by y-fast trie, using $O(\log \log n)$ time, we can find the preorder of w in τ_u. For (3), by Lemma 4, the preorder v in B can be determined in $O(1)$ time. The lemma follows.   □

6 LZ-Compression

This section gives a two-phase algorithm to construct the LZ-compression of the input text $S[1..s]$. The first phase constructs the LZ-trie based on the trie data structure in Theorem 1. Then, it enhances the LZ-trie with an auxiliary data structure so that preorder of any node can be computed efficiently using Lemma 8. The second phase generates the phrase list. It scans the text S to output the list of preorders of the phrases. Fig. 1 describes the details of the algorithm. The lemma below states the running time of our algorithm. We assume a unit-cost RAM model with word size $\log s$, and $\sigma \leq s$.

Lemma 9. *Suppose we use the trie data structure in Theorem 1. The algorithm in Fig. 1 builds the LZ-trie T and the phrase list using $O(\frac{s}{\log_\sigma s} \frac{(\log \log s)^2}{\log \log \log s})$ time and $O(\frac{s(\log \sigma + \log \log_\sigma s)}{\log_\sigma s})$ bits working space.*

Proof. Phase 1 builds the trie T through the while-loop in Step 4 of Fig. 1. Since there are c phrases, the while-loop will execute c times and generate c phrases $s_1, s_2, \ldots, s_c$. For the i-th iteration, by Theorem 1, Step 4.1 can find s_i in $O(\frac{|s_i|}{\log_\sigma s} \frac{(\log \log s)^2}{\log \log \log s})$ time. Step 4.2 stores the length of s_i by delta-code in $1 + \lceil \log s_i \rceil + 2\lceil \log(1 + \lceil \log s_i \rceil) \rceil$ bits. Then, Step 4.3 inserts the phrase s_i into the trie T using $O((\log \log s)^2 / \log \log \log s)$ time. Finally, the LZ-trie T is enhanced with an auxiliary data structure for preorder by Lemma 8.

Since $\sum_{i=1}^{c} |s_i| = s$, the c iterations take $O(\sum_{i=1}^{c} \frac{|s_i|}{\log_\sigma s} \frac{(\log \log s)^2}{\log \log \log s})$ time, which equals $O(\frac{s}{\log_\sigma s} \frac{(\log \log s)^2}{\log \log \log s})$ time. The auxiliary data structure is constructed using $O(c) = O(\frac{s}{\log_\sigma s})$ time.

Given the trie T and the string S, Phase 2 first enhances the data structure so that preorder of any node in T can be computed in $O(\log \log s)$ time by Lemma 8. For each phrase s_i, we first obtain its length ℓ stored by delta-code. Then we search the trie for the node representing the phrase $s_i = S[p..p + \ell - 1]$. It takes $O(\frac{|s_i|}{\log_\sigma s} \frac{(\log \log s)^2}{\log \log \log s})$ time by Theorem 1. The preorder of the phrase s_i can be computed in $O(\log \log s)$ time. In total, Phase 2 takes $O(\sum_{i=1}^{c} \frac{|s_i|}{\log_\sigma s} \frac{(\log \log s)^2}{\log \log \log s})$ time, which equals $O(\frac{s}{\log_\sigma s} \frac{(\log \log s)^2}{\log \log \log s})$ time.

Algorithm   *LZcompress*
Input: A sequence $S[1..s]$.

Output: The compressed text of S.

1 Initialize T as an empty trie. /* Phase 1: Construct the trie tree T */
2 Denote empty phrase as phrase 0.
3 $p = 1$;
4 **while** $p \le n$ **do**
4.1   Find the longest phrase $t \in T$ that appears as a prefix of $S[p..s]$.
4.2   Store the length of t by delta-code.
4.3   Insert the phrase $t \cdot S[p + |t|]$ into T.
4.4 $p = p + |t| + 1$;
    endwhile
5 Enrich the trie T so that we can compute the preorder of any node in T by Lemma 8.
6 $p = 1; j = 1$ /* Phase 2: Construct the phrase list $s_1 s_2 \ldots s_c$ */
7 **while** $p \le n$ **do**
7.1   Obtain the length ℓ of the next phrase stored by delta-code.
7.2   Find the phrase $t = S[p..p + \ell - 1] \in T$.
7.3 s_j = preorder index of t in T
7.4   Output s_j.
7.5 $p = p + |t| + 1; j = j + 1$;
    endwhile
End *LZcompress*

Fig. 1. Algorithm for LZ-compression

In total, the running time is $O(\frac{s}{\log_\sigma s} \frac{(\log \log s)^2}{\log \log \log s})$ time. The working space required to store the LZ-trie is $O(c \log \sigma) = O(\frac{s \log \sigma}{\log_\sigma s})$ bits, and the space for storing lengths of the phrases is $\sum_{i=1}^c O(1 + \log s_i) = O(c \log \frac{s}{c}) = O(\frac{s \log \log_\sigma s}{\log_\sigma s})$.   □

As a final remark, the working space of the algorithm is precisely $O(c \log \sigma + c \log \log_\sigma s)$ where c is the number of phases output. Since $c \ge \sqrt{s}$, the working space must be asymptotically smaller than the output size, which is $O(c \log c + c \log \sigma)$. Note that the output size is larger than $c \log c \ge \frac{1}{2}\sqrt{s} \log s$, while the tables used in the algorithm have size $O(s^\epsilon)$ for arbitrarily small $\epsilon > 0$.

Secondly, the output codes of the algorithm in Fig. 1 are different from the original LZ78. The algorithm outputs the same codes as [16][1]. Then we can decode any substring of S of length $O(\log_\sigma s)$ in constant time. The output size of [16] is asymptotically the same as the original LZ78.

---

[1] More precisely, the output codes represents preorders of the trie. To convert it into the original LZ78, we need one more scan of S using the trie.

References

1. Andersson, A., Nilsson, S.: Improved behaviour of tries by adaptive branching. Information Processing Letters 46, 295–300 (1993)
2. Aoe, J.: An efficient digital search algorithm by using a double array structure. IEEE Transactions on Software Engineering 15(9), 1066–1077 (1989)
3. Arroyuelo, D., Navarro, G.: Space-efficient construction of LZ-index. In: Deng, X., Du, D.-Z. (eds.) ISAAC 2005. LNCS, vol. 3827, Springer, Heidelberg (2005)
4. Beame, P., Fich, F.E.: Optimal bounds for the predecessor problem. In: Proc. of the 31 st Annual ACM Symposium on the Theory of Computing (STOC 1999), pp. 295–304 (1999)
5. Brent, R.P.: A linear algorithm for data compression. Australian Computer Journal 19(2), 64–68 (1987)
6. Devroye, L., Szpankowski, W.: Probabilistic behavior of asymmetric level compressed tries. Random Structures and Algorithms 27, 185–200 (2005)
7. Fredkin, E.: Trie memory. Communications of the ACM 3, 490–500 (1960)
8. Geary, R.F., Rahman, N., Raman, R., Raman, V.: A simple optimal representation for balanced parentheses. In: Sahinalp, S.C., Muthukrishnan, S.M., Dogrusoz, U. (eds.) CPM 2004. LNCS, vol. 3109, pp. 159–172. Springer, Heidelberg (2004)
9. Hagerup, T.: Sorting and searching on the word ram. In: Proceedings of Symposium on Theory Aspects of Computer Science, pp. 366–398 (1998)
10. Hon, W.-K., Lam, T.-W., Sadakane, K., Sung, W.-K.: Constructing compressed suffix arrays with large alphabets. In: Ibaraki, T., Katoh, N., Ono, H. (eds.) ISAAC 2003. LNCS, vol. 2906, Springer, Heidelberg (2003)
11. Morrison, D.R.: PATRICIA - Practical Algorithm To Retrieve Information Coded In Alphanumeric. Journal of the ACM 15(4), 514–534 (1968)
12. Munro, J.I., Raman, V.: Succinct representation of balanced parentheses and static trees. SIAM Journal on Computing 31(3), 762–776 (2001)
13. Navarro, G.: Indexing text using the Ziv-Lempel trie. Journal of Discrete Algorithmcs (JDA) 2(1), 87–114 (2004)
14. Nilsson, S., Karlsson, G.: IP-address lookup using lc-tries. Journal on Selected Areas in Communications IEEE 17(6), 1083–1092 (1999)
15. Rodeh, M., Pratt, V.R., Even, S.: Linear algorithm for data compression via string matching. Journal of ACM 28(1), 16–24 (1981)
16. Sadakane, K., Grossi, R.: Squeezing Succinct Data Structures into Entropy Bounds. In: Proc. ACM-SIAM SODA, pp. 1230–1239. ACM Press, New York (2006)
17. Welch, T.A.: A technique for high-performance data compression. IEEE Computer, 8–19 (1984)
18. Willard, D.E.: Log-logarithmic worst case range queries are possible in space $\theta(n)$. Information Processing Letters 17, 81–84 (1983)
19. Willard, D.E.: New trie data structures which support very fast search operations. Journal of Computer and System Sciences 28, 379–394 (1984)
20. Ziv, J., Lempel, A.: Compression of individual sequences via variable-rate coding. IEEE Transactions on Information Theory IT-24(5), 530–536 (1978)

Stochastic Müller Games are PSPACE-Complete*

Krishnendu Chatterjee

EECS, University of California, Berkeley, USA
c_krish@eecs.berkeley.edu

Abstract. The theory of graph games with ω-regular winning conditions is the foundation for modeling and synthesizing reactive processes. In the case of stochastic reactive processes, the corresponding stochastic graph games have three players, two of them (System and Environment) behaving adversarially, and the third (Uncertainty) behaving probabilistically. We consider two problems for stochastic graph games: the *qualitative* problem asks for the set of states from which a player can win with probability 1 (*almost-sure winning*); and the *quantitative* problem asks for the maximal probability of winning (*optimal winning*) from each state. We consider ω-regular winning conditions formalized as Müller winning conditions. We show that both the qualitative and quantitative problem for stochastic Müller games are PSPACE-complete. We also consider two well-known sub-classes of Müller objectives, namely, upward-closed and union-closed objectives, and show that both the qualitative and quantitative problem for these sub-classes are coNP-complete.

1 Introduction

A stochastic graph game [6] is played on a directed graph with three kinds of states: player-1, player-2, and probabilistic states. At player-1 states, player 1 chooses a successor state; at player-2 states, player 2 chooses a successor state; and at probabilistic states, a successor state is chosen according to a given probability distribution. The result of playing the game forever is an infinite path through the graph. If there are no probabilistic states, we refer to the game as a *2-player graph game*; otherwise, as a $2\frac{1}{2}$-*player graph game*. There has been a long history of using 2-player graph games for modeling and synthesizing reactive processes [1,18]: a reactive system and its environment represent the two players, whose states and transitions are specified by the states and edges of a game graph. Consequently, $2\frac{1}{2}$-player graph games provide the theoretical foundation for modeling and synthesizing processes that are reactive and stochastic.

For the modeling and synthesis (or "control") of reactive processes, one traditionally considers ω-regular winning conditions, which naturally express the temporal specifications and fairness assumptions of transition systems [15]. In

* This research was supported in part by the the AFOSR MURI grant F49620-00-1-0327, and the NSF grant CCR-0225610.

V. Arvind and S. Prasad (Eds.): FSTTCS 2007, LNCS 4855, pp. 436–448, 2007.

this work we study the complexity of $2\frac{1}{2}$-player graph games with respect to a canonical form of ω-regular winning conditions; namely *Müller* conditions [19].

In the case of 2-player graph games, where no randomization is involved, a fundamental determinacy result of Gurevich and Harrington [12] based on LAR (*latest appearance record*) construction ensures that, given an ω-regular winning condition, at each state, either player 1 has a finite-memory strategy to ensure that the condition holds, or player 2 has a finite-memory strategy to ensure that the condition does not hold. Thus, the problem of solving 2-player graph games consists in finding the set of *winning states*, from which player 1 can ensure that the condition holds. The elegant algorithm of Zielonka [20] uses the LAR construction to compute winning sets in 2-player graph games with Müller conditions. In [10] the authors present an insightful analysis of Zielonka's algorithm to present optimal memory bounds for winning strategies in 2-player graph games with Müller conditions. From the analysis of [20] a PSPACE algorithm can be obtained to compute winning sets in 2-player games with Müller objectives. The result of [14] proves a matching lower bound and thus deciding the winner in 2-player Müller games is PSPACE-complete.

In the case of $2\frac{1}{2}$-player graph games, where randomization is present in the transition structure, the notion of winning needs to be clarified. Player 1 is said to *win surely* if she has a strategy that guarantees to achieve the winning condition against all player-2 strategies. While this is the classical notion of winning in the 2-player case, it is less meaningful in the presence of probabilistic states, because it makes all probabilistic choices adversarial (it treats them analogously to player-2 choices). To adequately treat probabilistic choice, we consider the *probability* with which player 1 can ensure that the winning condition is met. We thus define two solution problems for $2\frac{1}{2}$-player graph games: the *qualitative* problem asks for the set of states from which player 1 can ensure winning with probability 1; the *quantitative* problem asks for the maximal probability with which player 1 can ensure winning from each state (this probability is called the *value* of the game at a state). The previous best known algorithm for $2\frac{1}{2}$-player Müller games is obtained by an exponential reduction of Müller objectives to parity objectives [19], and then applying the algorithms for $2\frac{1}{2}$-player parity games [5,4]. This approach yields an EXPTIME bound for qualitative analysis and 2EXPTIME bound for quantitative analysis. An exponential bound on the memory for optimal strategies in $2\frac{1}{2}$-player Müller games is known from [2]; and it follows from [13] that in general optimal strategies require memory of exponential size (even for randomized strategies). Simply fixing optimal strategies for both players yields an exponential size Markov chain, and then a naive analysis on the precision of values provides an upper bound of exponentially many bits to express the values. Thus naive approaches fail to provide PSPACE algorithms for $2\frac{1}{2}$-player Müller games. In this work we present PSPACE algorithms for both qualitative and quantitative problem for $2\frac{1}{2}$-player Müller games. We now state the basic idea of our proof.

1. First we present a PSPACE algorithm for qualitative analysis; the algorithm is a generalization of the algorithm of [20].

2. By a detailed analysis of the structure of optimal strategies, we relate the value of a $2\frac{1}{2}$-player Müller game with the probability of reaching a set of states in a Markov chain that is linear in the size of the $2\frac{1}{2}$-player game. Thus we obtain a bound on the precision of values that can be expressed with polynomially many bits in the size of the game. The bound on precision and the algorithm for qualitative analysis is used to obtain a NPSPACE algorithm for quantitative analysis.

Thus we obtain the PSPACE algorithms, and the result of [14] provides a matching lower bound to prove PSPACE-completeness for both the problems. We also consider two well-known sub-classes of Müller objectives, namely, union-closed and upward-closed objectives. We show that both the qualitative and quantitative problem is coNP-complete for these sub-classes. Our main contribution is the coNP-upper bound, and the lower bound follows from the results of [14].

2   Definitions

We consider several classes of turn-based games, namely, two-player turn-based probabilistic games ($2\frac{1}{2}$-player games), two-player turn-based deterministic games (2-player games), and Markov decision processes ($1\frac{1}{2}$-player games).

Notation. For a finite set A, a *probability distribution* on A is a function $\delta\colon A \to [0,1]$ such that $\sum_{a\in A} \delta(a) = 1$. We denote the set of probability distributions on A by $\mathcal{D}(A)$. Given a distribution $\delta \in \mathcal{D}(A)$, we denote by $\mathrm{Supp}(\delta) = \{x \in A \mid \delta(x) > 0\}$ the *support* of δ.

Game graphs. A *turn-based probabilistic game graph* ($2\frac{1}{2}$-*player game graph*) $G = ((S,E),(S_1,S_2,S_\bigcirc),\delta)$ consists of a directed graph (S,E), a partition $(S_1, S_2, S_\bigcirc)$ of the finite set S of states, and a probabilistic transition function $\delta\colon S_\bigcirc \to \mathcal{D}(S)$, where $\mathcal{D}(S)$ denotes the set of probability distributions over the state space S. The states in S_1 are the *player-1 states*, where player 1 decides the successor state; the states in S_2 are the *player-2 states*, where player 2 decides the successor state; and the states in $S_\bigcirc$ are the *probabilistic states*, where the successor state is chosen according to the probabilistic transition function δ. We assume that for $s \in S_\bigcirc$ and $t \in S$, we have $(s,t) \in E$ iff $\delta(s)(t) > 0$, and we often write $\delta(s,t)$ for $\delta(s)(t)$. For technical convenience we assume that every state in the graph (S,E) has at least one outgoing edge. For a state $s \in S$, we write $E(s)$ to denote the set $\{t \in S \mid (s,t) \in E\}$ of possible successors.

A set $U \subseteq S$ of states is called δ-*closed* if for every probabilistic state $u \in U \cap S_\bigcirc$, if $(u,t) \in E$, then $t \in U$. The set U is called δ-*live* if for every nonprobabilistic state $s \in U \cap (S_1 \cup S_2)$, there is a state $t \in U$ such that $(s,t) \in E$. A δ-closed and δ-live subset U of S induces a *subgame graph* of G, indicated by $G \upharpoonright U$.

The *turn-based deterministic game graphs* (*2-player game graphs*) are the special case of the $2\frac{1}{2}$-player game graphs with $S_\bigcirc = \emptyset$. The *Markov decision processes* ($1\frac{1}{2}$-*player game graphs*) are the special case of the $2\frac{1}{2}$-player game graphs with $S_1 = \emptyset$ or $S_2 = \emptyset$. We refer to the MDPs with $S_2 = \emptyset$ as *player-1 MDPs*, and to the MDPs with $S_1 = \emptyset$ as *player-2 MDPs*. Markov chains are the special case of $2\frac{1}{2}$-player game graphs such that $S_1 = \emptyset$ and $S_2 = \emptyset$, i.e., it consists of probabilistic states only.

Plays and Strategies. An infinite path, or *play*, of the game graph G is an infinite sequence $\omega = \langle s_0, s_1, s_2, \ldots \rangle$ of states such that $(s_k, s_{k+1}) \in E$ for all $k \in \mathbb{N}$. We write Ω for the set of all plays, and for a state $s \in S$, we write $\Omega_s \subseteq \Omega$ for the set of plays that start from the state s.

A *strategy* for player 1 is a function $\sigma: S^* \cdot S_1 \to \mathcal{D}(S)$ that assigns a probability distribution to all finite sequences $\boldsymbol{w} \in S^* \cdot S_1$ of states ending in a player-1 state (the sequence represents a prefix of a play). Player 1 follows the strategy σ if in each player-1 move, given that the current history of the game is $\boldsymbol{w} \in S^* \cdot S_1$, she chooses the next state according to the probability distribution $\sigma(\boldsymbol{w})$. A strategy must prescribe only available moves, i.e., for all $\boldsymbol{w} \in S^*$, and $s \in S_1$ we have $\mathrm{Supp}(\sigma(\boldsymbol{w} \cdot s)) \subseteq E(s)$. The strategies for player 2 are defined analogously. We denote by Σ and Π the set of all strategies for player 1 and player 2, respectively.

Once a starting state $s \in S$ and strategies $\sigma \in \Sigma$ and $\pi \in \Pi$ for the two players are fixed, the outcome of the game is a random walk $\omega_s^{\sigma,\pi}$ for which the probabilities of events are uniquely defined, where an *event* $\mathcal{A} \subseteq \Omega$ is a measurable set of paths. Given strategies σ for player 1 and π for player 2, a play $\omega = \langle s_0, s_1, s_2, \ldots \rangle$ is *feasible* if for every $k \in \mathbb{N}$ the following three conditions hold: (1) if $s_k \in S_\bigcirc$, then $(s_k, s_{k+1}) \in E$; (2) if $s_k \in S_1$, then $\sigma(s_0, s_1, \ldots, s_k)(s_{k+1}) > 0$; and (3) if $s_k \in S_2$ then $\pi(s_0, s_1, \ldots, s_k)(s_{k+1}) > 0$. Given two strategies $\sigma \in \Sigma$ and $\pi \in \Pi$, and a state $s \in S$, we denote by $\mathrm{Outcome}(s, \sigma, \pi) \subseteq \Omega_s$ the set of feasible plays that start from s given strategies σ and π. For a state $s \in S$ and an event $\mathcal{A} \subseteq \Omega$, we write $\mathrm{Pr}_s^{\sigma,\pi}(\mathcal{A})$ for the probability that a path belongs to $\mathcal{A}$ if the game starts from the state s and the players follow the strategies σ and π, respectively. In the context of player-1 MDPs we often omit the argument π, because Π is a singleton set.

Objectives. An *objective* for a player consists of an ω-regular set of *winning plays* $\Phi \subseteq \Omega$ [19]. We study zero-sum games, where the objectives of the two players are complementary; that is, if the objective of one player is Φ, then the objective of the other player is $\overline{\Phi} = \Omega \setminus \Phi$. We consider ω-regular objectives specified as Müller objectives. For a play $\omega = \langle s_0, s_1, s_2, \ldots \rangle$, let $\mathrm{Inf}(\omega)$ be the set $\{ s \in S \mid s = s_k \text{ for infinitely many } k \geq 0 \}$ of states that appear infinitely often in ω. We use colors to define objectives as in [10]. A $2\frac{1}{2}$-player game $(G, C, \chi, \mathcal{F} \subseteq \mathcal{P}(C))$ consists of a $2\frac{1}{2}$-player game graph G, a finite set C of colors, a partial function $\chi : S \rightharpoonup C$ that assigns colors to some states, and a winning condition specified by a subset $\mathcal{F}$ of the power set $\mathcal{P}(C)$ of colors. The winning condition defines subset $\Phi \subseteq \Omega$ of winning plays, defined as follows: $\mathrm{Müller}(\mathcal{F}) = \{ \omega \in \Omega \mid \chi(\mathrm{Inf}(\omega)) \in \mathcal{F} \}$, that is the set of paths ω such that the colors appearing infinitely often in ω is in $\mathcal{F}$.

Sure, Almost-Sure, Positive Winning and Optimality. Given a player-1 objective Φ, a strategy $\sigma \in \Sigma$ is *sure winning* for player 1 from a state $s \in S$ if for every strategy $\pi \in \Pi$ for player 2, we have $\mathrm{Outcome}(s, \sigma, \pi) \subseteq \Phi$. A strategy σ is *almost-sure winning* for player 1 from the state s for the objective Φ if for every player-2 strategy π, we have $\mathrm{Pr}_s^{\sigma,\pi}(\Phi) = 1$. A strategy σ is *positive winning* for player 1 from the state s for the objective Φ if for every player-2 strategy π, we have $\mathrm{Pr}_s^{\sigma,\pi}(\Phi) > 0$. The sure, almost-sure and positive winning strategies for player 2 are defined analogously. Given an objective Φ, the *sure winning set* $\langle\!\langle 1 \rangle\!\rangle_{sure}(\Phi)$ for player 1 is the set of states from which player 1 has a sure winning strategy. Similarly, the *almost-sure winning set* $\langle\!\langle 1 \rangle\!\rangle_{almost}(\Phi)$ and the *positive winning set* $\langle\!\langle 1 \rangle\!\rangle_{pos}(\Phi)$ for player 1 is the set of states from which player 1 has an almost-sure winning and a positive winning strategy, respectively. The sure winning set $\langle\!\langle 2 \rangle\!\rangle_{sure}(\Omega \setminus \Phi)$, the almost-sure winning set $\langle\!\langle 2 \rangle\!\rangle_{almost}(\Omega \setminus \Phi)$ and the positive winning set $\langle\!\langle 2 \rangle\!\rangle_{pos}(\Omega \setminus \Phi)$ for player 2 are defined analogously. It follows from the definitions that for all $2\frac{1}{2}$-player game graphs and all objectives Φ, we have $\langle\!\langle 1 \rangle\!\rangle_{sure}(\Phi) \subseteq \langle\!\langle 1 \rangle\!\rangle_{almost}(\Phi) \subseteq \langle\!\langle 1 \rangle\!\rangle_{pos}(\Phi)$. Computing sure, almost-sure and positive winning sets and strategies is referred to as the *qualitative* analysis of $2\frac{1}{2}$-player games.

Given ω-regular objectives $\Phi \subseteq \Omega$ for player 1 and $\Omega \setminus \Phi$ for player 2, we define the *value* functions $\langle\!\langle 1 \rangle\!\rangle_{val}$ and $\langle\!\langle 2 \rangle\!\rangle_{val}$ for the players 1 and 2, respectively, as the following functions from the state space S to the interval $[0,1]$ of reals: for all states $s \in S$, let $\langle\!\langle 1 \rangle\!\rangle_{val}(\Phi)(s) = \sup_{\sigma \in \Sigma} \inf_{\pi \in \Pi} \mathrm{Pr}_s^{\sigma,\pi}(\Phi)$ and $\langle\!\langle 2 \rangle\!\rangle_{val}(\Omega \setminus \Phi)(s) = \sup_{\pi \in \Pi} \inf_{\sigma \in \Sigma} \mathrm{Pr}_s^{\sigma,\pi}(\Omega \setminus \Phi)$. In other words, the value $\langle\!\langle 1 \rangle\!\rangle_{val}(\Phi)(s)$ gives the maximal probability with which player 1 can achieve her objective Φ from state s, and analogously for player 2. The strategies that achieve the value are called *optimal*: a strategy σ for player 1 is *optimal* from the state s for the objective Φ if $\langle\!\langle 1 \rangle\!\rangle_{val}(\Phi)(s) = \inf_{\pi \in \Pi} \mathrm{Pr}_s^{\sigma,\pi}(\Phi)$. The optimal strategies for player 2 are defined analogously. Computing values and optimal strategies is referred to as the *quantitative* analysis of $2\frac{1}{2}$-player games.

Determinacy. For sure winning, the $1\frac{1}{2}$-player and $2\frac{1}{2}$-player games coincide with 2-player (deterministic) games where the random player is interpreted as an adversary, i.e., as player 2. Theorem 1 states the classical determinacy and complexity result for 2-player games with Müller objectives. Theorem 2 states the quantitative determinacy for $2\frac{1}{2}$-player games with Müller objectives.

Theorem 1 (Qualitative determinacy). *The following assertions hold.*

1. *([16]). For all 2-player game graphs and Müller objectives Φ, the sure winning sets $\langle\!\langle 1 \rangle\!\rangle_{sure}(\Phi)$ and $\langle\!\langle 2 \rangle\!\rangle_{sure}(\Omega \setminus \Phi) = \emptyset$ form a partition of S.*
2. *([14]). The problem of deciding whether a state s is a sure winning state, i.e., $s \in \langle\!\langle 1 \rangle\!\rangle_{sure}(\Phi)$, is PSPACE-complete for 2-player game graphs with Müller objectives.*

Theorem 2 (Quantitative determinacy [17]). *For all $2\frac{1}{2}$-player game graphs, for all Müller objectives Φ, and all states s, we have $\langle\!\langle 1 \rangle\!\rangle_{val}(\Phi)(s) + \langle\!\langle 2 \rangle\!\rangle_{val}(\Omega \setminus \Phi)(s) = 1$.*

3   The Complexity of Stochastic Müller Games

In this section we show that both the qualitative and quantitative problem for stochastic Müller games can be decided in PSPACE, and from the lower bound for the special case of 2-player games we obtain the completeness result. Due to space limitations we omit the details of qualitative analysis (proofs are available in [3]); other proofs omitted for lack of space are also available in [3].

Theorem 3 (Qualitative complexity). *Given a $2\frac{1}{2}$-player game graph G, a Müller objective Φ, and a state s, it is PSPACE-complete to decide whether $s \in \langle\!\langle 1 \rangle\!\rangle_{almost}(\Phi)$.*

We now study the complexity of quantitative analysis of stochastic Müller games. We start with a few definitions.

Definition 1 (Value classes). *Given a Müller objective Φ, for every real $r \in [0,1]$ the* value class *with value r is $\mathrm{VC}(\Phi, r) = \{\, s \in S \mid \langle\!\langle 1 \rangle\!\rangle_{val}(\Phi)(s) = r \,\}$ is the set of states with value r for player 1. For $r \in [0,1]$ we denote by $\mathrm{VC}(\Phi, > r) = \bigcup_{q > r} \mathrm{VC}(\Phi, q)$ the value classes greater than r and by $\mathrm{VC}(\Phi, < r) = \bigcup_{q < r} \mathrm{VC}(\Phi, q)$ the value classes smaller than r.* ∎

Definition 2 (Boundary probabilistic states). *Given a set U of states, a state $s \in U \cap S_{\bigcirc}$ is a* boundary probabilistic state *for U if $E(s) \cap (S \setminus U) \neq \emptyset$, i.e., the probabilistic state has an edge out of the set U. We denote by $\mathsf{Bnd}(U)$ the set of boundary probabilistic states for U. For a value class $\mathrm{VC}(\Phi, r)$ we denote by $\mathsf{Bnd}(\Phi, r)$ the set of boundary probabilistic states of value class r.* ∎

Observation. For all Müller objectives Φ, for a state $s \in \mathsf{Bnd}(\Phi, r)$ we have $E(s) \cap \mathrm{VC}(\Phi, > r) \neq \emptyset$ and $E(s) \cap \mathrm{VC}(\Phi, < r) \neq \emptyset$, i.e., the boundary probabilistic states have edges to higher and lower value classes. For all Müller objectives Φ we have $\mathsf{Bnd}(\Phi, 1) = \emptyset$ and $\mathsf{Bnd}(\Phi, 0) = \emptyset$.

Reduction of a Value Class. Given a set U of states, such that U is δ-live, let $\mathsf{Bnd}(U)$ be the set boundary probabilistic states for U. We denote by $G_{\mathsf{Bnd}(U)}$ the subgame $G \upharpoonright U$ where every state in $\mathsf{Bnd}(U)$ is converted to an absorbing state (state with a self-loop). Since U is δ-live, we have $G_{\mathsf{Bnd}(U)}$ is a subgame. Given a value class $\mathrm{VC}(\Phi, r)$, let $\mathsf{Bnd}(\Phi, r)$ be the set of boundary probabilistic states in $\mathrm{VC}(\Phi, r)$. We denote by $G_{\mathsf{Bnd}(\Phi,r)}$ the subgame where every boundary probabilistic state in $\mathsf{Bnd}(\Phi, r)$ is converted to an absorbing state. We denote by $G_{\Phi,r} = G_{\mathsf{Bnd}(\Phi,r)} \upharpoonright \mathrm{VC}(\Phi, r)$: this is a subgame since every value class is δ-live, and δ-closed as all states in $\mathsf{Bnd}(\Phi, r)$ are converted to absorbing states. We now state two lemmas proved in [2].

Lemma 1 (Almost-sure reduction[2]). *Let G be a $2\frac{1}{2}$-player game graph and $\mathcal{F} \subseteq \mathcal{P}(C)$ be a Müller winning condition. Let $\Phi = M\ddot{u}ller(\mathcal{F})$. For $0 < r < 1$, the following assertions hold.*

1. *Player 1 wins almost-surely for objective $\Phi \cup Reach(\mathsf{Bnd}(\Phi, r))$ from all states in $G_{\Phi,r}$, i.e., $\langle\!\langle 1 \rangle\!\rangle_{almost}(\Phi \cup Reach(\mathsf{Bnd}(\Phi, r))) = \mathrm{VC}(\Phi, r)$ in $G_{\Phi,r}$.*
2. *Player 2 wins almost-surely for objective $\overline{\Phi} \cup Reach(\mathsf{Bnd}(\Phi, r))$ from all states in $G_{\Phi,r}$, i.e., $\langle\!\langle 2 \rangle\!\rangle_{almost}(\overline{\Phi} \cup Reach(\mathsf{Bnd}(\Phi, r))) = \mathrm{VC}(\Phi, r)$ in $G_{\Phi,r}$.*

Lemma 2 (Almost-sure to optimality[2]). *Let G be a $2\frac{1}{2}$-player game graph and $\mathcal{F} \subseteq \mathcal{P}(C)$ be a Müller winning condition. Let $\Phi = Müller(\mathcal{F})$. Let σ be a strategy such that (a) σ is an almost-sure winning strategy from the almost-sure winning states ($\langle\langle 1 \rangle\rangle_{almost}(\Phi)$ in G); and (b) σ is an almost-sure winning strategy for objective $\Phi \cup Reach(\mathsf{Bnd}(\Phi, r))$ in the game $G_{\Phi,r}$, for all $0 < r < 1$. Then σ is an optimal strategy.*

Lemma 3. *For all $2\frac{1}{2}$-player game graphs, for all Müller objectives Φ, there exist optimal strategies σ and π for player 1 and player 2 such that the following assertions hold:*

1. *for all $r \in (0,1)$, for all $s \in VC(\Phi, r)$ we have $\Pr_s^{\sigma,\pi}(Reach(\mathsf{Bnd}(\Phi, r))) = 1$;*
2. *for all $s \in S$ we have (a) $\Pr_s^{\sigma,\pi}(Reach(W_1 \cup W_2)) = 1$; (b) $\Pr_s^{\sigma,\pi}(Reach(W_1)) = \langle\langle 1 \rangle\rangle_{val}(\Phi)(s)$; and (c) $\Pr_s^{\sigma,\pi}(Reach(W_2)) = \langle\langle 2 \rangle\rangle_{val}(\overline{\Phi})(s)$; where $W_1 = \langle\langle 1 \rangle\rangle_{almost}(\Phi)$ and $W_2 = \langle\langle 2 \rangle\rangle_{almost}(\overline{\Phi})$.*

Proof. Consider an optimal strategy σ that satisfies the conditions of Lemma 2, and a strategy π that satisfies analogous conditions for player 2. Such strategies exist by Lemma 1. For all $r \in (0,1)$, the strategy σ is almost-sure winning for the objective $\Phi \cup Reach(\mathsf{Bnd}(\Phi, r))$ and the strategy π is almost-sure winning for the objective $\overline{\Phi} \cup Reach(\mathsf{Bnd}(\Phi, r))$, in the game $G_{\Phi,r}$. Thus we obtain that for all $r \in (0,1)$, for all $s \in VC(\Phi, r)$ we have (a) $\Pr_s^{\sigma,\pi}(\Phi \cup Reach(\mathsf{Bnd}(\Phi, r))) = 1$; and (b) $\Pr_s^{\sigma,\pi}(\overline{\Phi} \cup Reach(\mathsf{Bnd}(\Phi, r))) = 1$. It follows that for all $r \in (0,1)$, for all $s \in VC(\Phi, r)$ we have $\Pr_s^{\sigma,\pi}(Reach(\mathsf{Bnd}(\Phi, r))) = 1$. From the above condition it easily follows that for all $s \in S$ we have $\Pr_s^{\sigma,\pi}(Reach(W_1 \cup W_2)) = 1$. Since σ and π are optimal strategies, all the requirements of the second condition are fulfilled. Thus the strategies σ and π are witness strategies to prove the result. ∎

Characterizing Values for $2\frac{1}{2}$-Player Müller Games. We now relate the values of $2\frac{1}{2}$-player game graphs with Müller objectives with the values of a Markov chain, on the same state space, with reachability objectives. Once the relationship is established we obtain bound on preciseness of the values. We use Lemma 3 to present two transformations to Markov chains.

Markov Chain Transformation. Given a $2\frac{1}{2}$-player game graph G with a Müller objective Φ, let $W_1 = \langle\langle 1 \rangle\rangle_{almost}(\Phi)$ and $W_2 = \langle\langle 2 \rangle\rangle_{almost}(\overline{\Phi})$ be the set of almost-sure winning states for the players. Let σ and π be optimal strategies for the players (obtained from Lemma 3) such that

1. for all $r \in (0,1)$, for all $s \in VC(\Phi, r)$ we have $\Pr_s^{\sigma,\pi}(Reach(\mathsf{Bnd}(\Phi, r))) = 1$;
2. for all $s \in S$ we have (a) $\Pr_s^{\sigma,\pi}(Reach(W_1 \cup W_2)) = 1$; (b) $\Pr_s^{\sigma,\pi}(Reach(W_1)) = \langle\langle 1 \rangle\rangle_{val}(\Phi)(s)$; and (c) $\Pr_s^{\sigma,\pi}(Reach(W_2)) = \langle\langle 2 \rangle\rangle_{val}(\overline{\Phi})(s)$.

We first consider a Markov chain that mimics the stochastic process under σ and π. The Markov chain $\widetilde{G} = (S, \widetilde{\delta}) = \mathsf{MC}_1(G, \Phi)$ with the transition function $\widetilde{\delta}$ is defined as follows:

1. for $s \in W_1 \cup W_2$ we have $\widetilde{\delta}(s)(s) = 1$;
2. for $r \in (0,1)$ and $s \in \mathsf{VC}(\Phi, r) \setminus \mathsf{Bnd}(\Phi, r)$ we have $\widetilde{\delta}(s)(t) = \mathrm{Pr}_s^{\sigma,\pi}(\mathrm{Reach}(\{t\}))$, for $t \in \mathsf{Bnd}(\Phi, r)$ (since for all $s \in \mathsf{VC}(\Phi, r)$ we have $\mathrm{Pr}_s^{\sigma,\pi}(\mathrm{Reach}(\mathsf{Bnd}(\Phi, r)))$ $= 1$, the transition function $\widetilde{\delta}$ at s is a probability distribution);
3. for $r \in (0,1)$ and $s \in \mathsf{Bnd}(\Phi, r)$ we have $\widetilde{\delta}(s)(t) = \delta(s)(t)$, for $t \in S$.

The Markov chain $\widetilde{G}$ mimics the stochastic process under σ and π and yields the following lemma.

Lemma 4. *For all $2\frac{1}{2}$-player game graphs G and all Müller objectives Φ, consider the Markov chain $\widetilde{G} = \mathsf{MC}_1(G, \Phi)$. Then for all $s \in S$ we have $\langle\!\langle 1 \rangle\!\rangle_{val}(\Phi)(s) = \mathrm{Pr}_s(\mathrm{Reach}(W_1))$, that is, the value for Φ in G is equal to the probability to reach W_1 in the Markov chain $\widetilde{G}$.*

Second Transformation. We now transform the Markov chain $\widetilde{G}$ to another Markov chain $\widehat{G}$. We start with the observation that for $r \in (0,1)$, for all states $s, t \in \mathsf{Bnd}(\Phi, r)$ in the Markov chain $\widetilde{G}$ we have $\mathrm{Pr}_s(\mathrm{Reach}(W_1)) = \mathrm{Pr}_t(\mathrm{Reach}(W_1)) = r$. Moreover, for $r \in (0,1)$, every state $s \in \mathsf{Bnd}(\Phi, r)$ has edges to higher and lower value classes. Hence for a state $s \in \mathsf{VC}(\Phi, r) \setminus \mathsf{Bnd}(\Phi, r)$ if we chose a state $t_r \in \mathsf{Bnd}(\Phi, r)$ and make the transition probability from s to t_r to 1, the probability to reach W_1 does not change. This motivates the following transformation: given a $2\frac{1}{2}$-player game graph $G = ((S, E), (S_1, S_2, S_\bigcirc), \delta)$ with a Müller objective Φ, let $W_1 = \langle\!\langle 1 \rangle\!\rangle_{almost}(\Phi)$ and $W_2 = \langle\!\langle 2 \rangle\!\rangle_{almost}(\overline{\Phi})$ be the set of almost-sure winning states for the players. The Markov chain $\widehat{G} = (S, \widehat{\delta}) = \mathsf{MC}_2(G, \Phi)$ with the transition function $\widehat{\delta}$ is defined as follows:

1. for $s \in W_1 \cup W_2$ we have $\widehat{\delta}(s)(s) = 1$;
2. for $r \in (0,1)$ and $s \in \mathsf{VC}(\Phi, r) \setminus \mathsf{Bnd}(\Phi, r)$, pick $t \in \mathsf{Bnd}(\Phi, r)$ and $\widehat{\delta}(s)(t) = 1$;
3. for $r \in (0,1)$ and $s \in \mathsf{Bnd}(\Phi, r)$ we have $\widehat{\delta}(s)(t) = \delta(s)(t)$, for $t \in S$.

Observe that for $\delta_{>0} = \{\, \delta(s)(t) \mid s \in S_\bigcirc, \ t \in S, \ \delta(s)(t) > 0 \,\}$ and $\widehat{\delta}_{>0} = \{\widehat{\delta}(s)(t) \mid s \in S, \ t \in S, \ \widehat{\delta}(s)(t) > 0\}$, we have $\widehat{\delta}_{>0} \subseteq \delta_{>0} \cup \{1\}$, i.e., the transition probabilities in $\widehat{G}$ are subset of transition probabilities in G. The following lemma is immediate from Lemma 4 and the equivalence of the probabilities to reach W_1 in $\widetilde{G}$ and $\widehat{G}$. Lemma 6 follows from Lemma 5 and the results of [7,21]. Lemma 7 presents the basic ingredients of the algorithm for the quantitative analysis of $2\frac{1}{2}$-player Müller games.

Lemma 5. *For all $2\frac{1}{2}$-player game graphs G and all Müller objectives Φ, consider the Markov chain $\widehat{G} = \mathsf{MC}_2(G, \Phi)$. Then for all $s \in S$ we have $\langle\!\langle 1 \rangle\!\rangle_{val}(\Phi)(s) = \mathrm{Pr}_s(\mathrm{Reach}(W_1))$, that is, the value for Φ in G is equal to the probability to reach W_1 in the Markov chain $\widehat{G}$.*

Lemma 6. *For all $2\frac{1}{2}$-player game graphs $G = ((S, E), (S_1, S_2, S_\bigcirc), \delta)$ and all Müller objectives Φ, for all states $s \in S \setminus (W_1 \cup W_2)$ we have $\langle\!\langle 1 \rangle\!\rangle_{val}(\Phi)(s) = \dfrac{p}{q}$*

where p, q are integers with $0 < p < q \leq \delta_u^{4 \cdot |E|}$, where $\delta_u = \max\{ q \mid \delta(s)(t) = \frac{p}{q} \text{ for } p, q \in \mathbb{N}, \ s \in S_\bigcirc \text{ and } \delta(s)(t) > 0 \}$; and W_1 and W_2 are the almost-sure winning states for player 1 and player 2, respectively.

Lemma 7. *Let $G = ((S, E), (S_1, S_2, S_\bigcirc), \delta)$ be a $2\frac{1}{2}$-player game with a Müller objective Φ. Let $\mathcal{P} = (V_0, V_1, \ldots, V_k)$ be a partition of the state space S, and let $r_0 > r_1 > r_2 > \ldots > r_k$ be k-real values such that the following conditions hold:*

1. *$V_0 = \langle\!\langle 1 \rangle\!\rangle_{almost}(\Phi)$ and $V_k = \langle\!\langle 2 \rangle\!\rangle_{almost}(\overline{\Phi})$;*
2. *$r_0 = 1$ and $r_k = 0$;*
3. *for all $1 \leq i \leq k - 1$ we have $\mathsf{Bnd}(V_i) \neq \emptyset$ and V_i is δ-live;*
4. *for all $1 \leq i \leq k - 1$ and all $s \in S_2 \cap V_i$ we have $E(s) \subseteq \bigcup_{j \leq i} V_j$;*
5. *for all $1 \leq i \leq k-1$ we have $V_i = \langle\!\langle 1 \rangle\!\rangle_{almost}(\Phi \cup Reach(\mathsf{Bnd}(\overline{V_i})))$ in $G_{\mathsf{Bnd}(V_i)}$;*
6. *let $x_s = r_i$, for $s \in V_i$, and for all $s \in S_\bigcirc$, let x_s satisfy $x_s = \sum_{t \in E(s)} x_t \cdot \delta(s)(t)$.*

Then we have $\langle\!\langle 1 \rangle\!\rangle_{val}(\Phi)(s) \geq x_s$ for all $s \in S$.

Algorithm for Quantitative Analysis. We now present a PSPACE algorithm for quantitative analysis for $2\frac{1}{2}$-player games with Müller objectives Müller($\mathcal{F}$). A PSPACE lower bound is already known for the qualitative analysis of 2-player games with Müller objectives [14]. To obtain an upper bound we present a NPSPACE algorithm. The algorithm is based on Lemma 7. Given a $2\frac{1}{2}$-player game $G = ((S, E), (S_1, S_2, S_\bigcirc), \delta)$ with a Müller objective Φ, a state s and a rational number r, the following assertion hold: if $\langle\!\langle 1 \rangle\!\rangle_{val}(\Phi)(s) \geq r$, then there exists a partition $\mathcal{P} = (V_0, V_1, V_2, \ldots, V_k)$ of S and rational values $r_0 > r_1 > r_2 > \ldots > r_k$, such that $r_i = \frac{p_i}{q_i}$ with $p_i, q_i \leq \delta_u^{4 \cdot |E|}$, such that conditions of Lemma 7 are satisfied, and $s \in V_i$ with $r_i \geq r$. The witness $\mathcal{P}$ is the value class partition and the rational values represent the values of the value classes. From the above observation we obtain the algorithm for quantitative analysis as follows: given a $2\frac{1}{2}$-player game graph $G = ((S, E), (S_1, S_2, S_\bigcirc), \delta)$ with a Müller objective Φ, a state s and a rational r, to verify that $\langle\!\langle 1 \rangle\!\rangle_{val}(\Phi)(s) \geq r$, the algorithm guesses a partition $\mathcal{P} = (V_0, V_1, V_2, \ldots, V_k)$ of S and rational values $r_0 > r_1 > r_2 > \ldots > r_k$, such that $r_i = \frac{p_i}{q_i}$ with $p_i, q_i \leq \delta_u^{4 \cdot |E|}$, and then verifies that all the conditions of Lemma 7 are satisfied, and $s \in V_i$ with $r_i \geq r$. Observe that since the guesses of the rational values can be made with $O(|G| \cdot |S| \cdot |E|)$ bits, the guess is polynomial in size of the game. The condition 1 and the condition 5 of Lemma 7 can be verified in PSPACE by the PSPACE qualitative algorithms (see Theorem 3), and all the other conditions can be checked in polynomial time. Since NPSPACE=PSPACE we obtain a PSPACE upper bound for quantitative analysis of $2\frac{1}{2}$-player games with Müller objectives. The result improves the previous 2EXPTIME algorithm (obtained by an exponential reduction of Müller objectives to parity objectives [19] and applying algorithms of quantitative analysis for parity objectives [4]) for the quantitative analysis for $2\frac{1}{2}$-player games with Müller objectives.

Theorem 4 (Quantitative complexity). *Given a $2^{1}/_{2}$-player game graph G, a Müller objective Φ, a state s, and a rational r in binary, it is PSPACE-complete to decide if $\langle\langle 1 \rangle\rangle_{val}(\Phi)(s) \geq r$.*

4   Union-Closed and Upward-Closed Objectives

We now consider two special classes of Müller objectives: namely, union-closed and upward-closed objectives. We will show the quantitative analysis of both these classes of objectives in $2^{1}/_{2}$-player games under succinct representation is co-NP-complete. We first present these conditions.

1. *Union-closed and basis conditions.* A Müller winning condition $\mathcal{F} \subseteq \mathcal{P}(C)$ is *union-closed* if for all $I, J \in \mathcal{F}$ we have $I \cup J \in \mathcal{F}$. A *basis* condition $\mathcal{B} \subseteq \mathcal{P}(C)$, given as a set $\mathcal{B}$ specifies the winning condition $\mathcal{F} = \{ I \subseteq C \mid \exists B_1, B_2, \ldots, B_k \in \mathcal{B}. \bigcup_{1 \leq i \leq k} B_i = I \}$. A Müller winning condition $\mathcal{F}$ can be specified as a basis condition only if $\mathcal{F}$ is union-closed.

2. *Upward-closed and superset conditions.* A Müller winning condition $\mathcal{F} \subseteq \mathcal{P}(C)$ is *upward-closed* if for all $I \in \mathcal{F}$ and $I \subseteq J \subseteq C$ we have $J \in \mathcal{F}$. A *superset* condition $\mathcal{U} \subseteq \mathcal{P}(C)$, specifies the winning condition $\mathcal{F} = \{ I \subseteq C \mid J \subseteq I \text{ for some } J \in \mathcal{U} \}$. A Müller winning condition $\mathcal{F}$ can be specified as a superset condition only if $\mathcal{F}$ is upward-closed. Any upward-closed condition is also union-closed.

The results of [14] showed that the basis and superset conditions are more succinct ways to represent union-closed and upward-closed conditions, respectively, than the explicit representation. The following proposition was also shown in [14] (see [14] for the formal description of the notion of succinctness and translability). Proposition 2 follows from the results of [2].

Proposition 1 ([14]). *A superset condition is polynomially translatable to an equivalent basis condition.*

Proposition 2. *For all union-closed winning conditions $\mathcal{F}$ we have pure memoryless optimal strategies exist for objective Müller$(\overline{\mathcal{F}})$ for all $2^{1}/_{2}$-player game graphs, where a pure memoryless strategy uniquely chooses a successor at every state independent of the history of the play.*

Complexity of Basis and Superset Conditions. The results of [14] established that deciding the winner in 2-player games (that is qualitative analysis for 2-player game graphs) with union-closed and upward-closed conditions specified as basis and superset conditions is coNP-complete. The lower bound for the special case of 2-player games, yields a coNP lower bound for the quantitative analysis of $2^{1}/_{2}$-player games with union-closed and upward-closed conditions specified as basis and superset conditions. We will prove a matching upper bound. We prove the upper bound for basis conditions, and by Proposition 1 the result also follows for superset conditions.

The Upper Bound for Basis Games. We present a coNP upper bound for the quantitative analysis for basis games. Given a $2^{1}/_{2}$-player game graph and a

Müller objective $\Phi = \text{Müller}(\mathcal{F})$, where $\mathcal{F}$ is union-closed and specified as a basis condition defined by $\mathcal{B}$, let s be a state and r be a rational given in binary. We show that the problem whether $\langle\!\langle 1 \rangle\!\rangle_{val}(\Phi)(s) \geq r$ can be decided in coNP. We present a polynomial witness and polynomial time verification procedure when the answer to the problem is "NO". Since $\mathcal{F}$ is union-closed, it follows from Proposition 2 that pure memoryless optimal strategy π exists for player 2. The pure memoryless optimal strategy is the polynomial witness to the problem, and once π is fixed we obtain a $1\frac{1}{2}$-player game graph G_π. To present a polynomial time verification procedure we present a polynomial time algorithm to compute values in an MDP (or $1\frac{1}{2}$-player games) with basis condition $\mathcal{B}$. We develop some facts on *end components* [8,9] that will be useful for analysis of MDPs.

Definition 3 (End component). *A set $U \subseteq S$ of states is an* end component *if U is δ-closed and the subgame graph $G \restriction U$ is strongly connected.*   ∎

Lemma 8. [8,9] *For all states $s \in S$ and strategies $\sigma \in \Sigma$, we have $\Pr_s^\sigma(\text{Müller}(\mathcal{E})) = 1$, where $\mathcal{E}$ is the set of all end components of G.*

Given a Müller condition $\mathcal{F}$, let $\mathcal{U} = \mathcal{E} \cap \{ F \subseteq S \mid \chi^{-1}(F) \in \mathcal{F} \}$ be the set of end components that are Müller sets. These are the *winning* end components. Let $T_{end} = \bigcup_{U \in \mathcal{U}} U$ be their union. Lemma 9 follows from Lemma 8.

Lemma 9. *For all $1\frac{1}{2}$-player games and for all Müller objectives Müller$(\mathcal{F})$ we have $\langle\!\langle 1 \rangle\!\rangle_{val}(\text{Müller}(\mathcal{F})) = \langle\!\langle 1 \rangle\!\rangle_{val}(\text{Reach}(T_{end}))$.*

Maximal End Components. An end component $U \subseteq S$ is *maximal* in $V \subseteq S$ if $U \subseteq V$, and if there is no end component U' with $U \subset U' \subseteq V$. Given a set $V \subseteq S$, we denote by $\text{MaxEC}(V)$ the set consisting in all maximal end components U such that $U \subseteq V$.

Polynomial Time Algorithm for MDPs with Basis Condition. Given an $1\frac{1}{2}$-player game graph G, let $\mathcal{E}$ be the set of end components. Consider a basis condition $\mathcal{B} = \{ B_1, B_2, \ldots, B_k \} \subseteq \mathcal{P}(C)$, and let $\mathcal{F}$ be the union-closed condition generated from $\mathcal{B}$. The set of winning end-components are $\mathcal{U} = \mathcal{E} \cap \{ F \subseteq S \mid \chi^{-1}(F) \in \mathcal{F} \}$, and let $T_{end} = \bigcup_{U \in \mathcal{U}} U$. It follows from above that the value function in G can be computed by computing the maximal probability to reach T_{end}. Once the set T_{end} is computed, the value function for reachability objective in $1\frac{1}{2}$-player game graphs can be computed in polynomial time by linear-programming [11]. To complete the proof we present a polynomial time algorithm to compute T_{end}.

Computing Winning End Components. The algorithm is as follows. Let $\mathcal{B}$ be the basis for the winning condition and G be the $1\frac{1}{2}$-player game graph. Initialize $\mathcal{B}_0 = \mathcal{B}$ and repeat the following:

1. let $X_i = \bigcup_{B \in \mathcal{B}_i} \chi^{-1}(B)$;
2. partition the set X_i into maximal end components $\text{MaxEC}(X_i)$;
3. remove an element B of $\mathcal{B}_i$ such that $\chi^{-1}(B)$ is not wholly contained in a maximal end component to obtain $\mathcal{B}_{i+1}$;

until $\mathcal{B}_i = \mathcal{B}_{i-1}$. When $\mathcal{B}_i = \mathcal{B}_{i-1}$, let $X = X_i$, and every maximal end component of X is an union of basis elements (all Y in X are members of basis elements, i.e., $\chi^{-1}(Y) \in \mathcal{B}$, and an basis element not contained in any maximal end component of X is removed in step 3). Moreover, any maximal end component of G which is an union of basis elements is a subset of an maximal end component of X, since the algorithm preserves such sets. Hence we have $X = T_{end}$. The algorithm requires $|\mathcal{B}|$ iterations and each iteration requires the decomposition of an $1\frac{1}{2}$-player game graph into the set of maximal end components, which can be achieved in $O(|S| \cdot |E|)$ time [9]. Hence the algorithm works in $O(|\mathcal{B}| \cdot |S| \cdot |E|)$ time. This completes the proof and yields the following result.

Theorem 5. *Given a $2\frac{1}{2}$-player game graph and a Müller objective $\Phi = Müller(\mathcal{F})$, where $\mathcal{F}$ is an union-closed condition specified as a basis condition defined by $\mathcal{B}$ or $\mathcal{F}$ is an upward-closed condition specified as a superset condition $\mathcal{U}$, a state s and a rational r given in binary, it is coNP-complete to decide whether $\langle\!\langle 1 \rangle\!\rangle_{val}(\Phi)(s) \geq r$.*

References

1. Büchi, J.R., Landweber, L.H.: Solving sequential conditions by finite-state strategies. Transactions of the AMS 138, 295–311 (1969)
2. Chatterjee, K.: Optimal strategy synthesis for stochastic Müller games. In: Seidl, H. (ed.) FoSSaCS 2007. LNCS, vol. 4423, pp. 138–152. Springer, Heidelberg (2007)
3. Chatterjee, K.: The complexity of stochastic Müller games. Technical Report, UC Berkeley, UCB/EECS-2007-110 (2007)
4. Chatterjee, K., Henzinger, T.A.: Strategy improvement and randomized subexponential algorithms for stochastic parity games. In: Durand, B., Thomas, W. (eds.) STACS 2006. LNCS, vol. 3884, pp. 512–523. Springer, Heidelberg (2006)
5. Chatterjee, K., Jurdziński, M., Henzinger, T.A.: Simple stochastic parity games. In: Baaz, M., Makowsky, J.A. (eds.) CSL 2003. LNCS, vol. 2803, pp. 100–113. Springer, Heidelberg (2003)
6. Condon, A.: The complexity of stochastic games. Information and Computation 96(2), 203–224 (1992)
7. Condon, A.: On algorithms for simple stochastic games. In: Advances in Computational Complexity Theory. American Mathematical Society, vol. 13, pp. 51–73 (1993)
8. Courcoubetis, C., Yannakakis, M.: Markov decision processes and regular events. In: Paterson, M.S. (ed.) Automata, Languages and Programming. LNCS, vol. 443, pp. 336–349. Springer, Heidelberg (1990)
9. de Alfaro, L.: Formal Verification of Probabilistic Systems. PhD thesis, Stanford University (1997)
10. Dziembowski, S., Jurdzinski, M., Walukiewicz, I.: How much memory is needed to win infinite games? In: LICS 1997, pp. 99–110. IEEE Computer Society Press, Los Alamitos (1997)
11. Filar, J., Vrieze, K.: Competitive Markov Decision Processes. Springer, Heidelberg (1997)
12. Gurevich, Y., Harrington, L.: Trees, automata, and games. In: STOC 1982, pp. 60–65. ACM Press, New York (1982)

13. Horn, F.: Dicing on the Streett. In: IPL (2007)
14. Hunter, P., Dawar, A.: Complexity bounds for regular games. In: Jedrzejowicz, J., Szepietowski, A. (eds.) MFCS 2005. LNCS, vol. 3618, pp. 495–506. Springer, Heidelberg (2005)
15. Manna, Z., Pnueli, A.: The Temporal Logic of Reactive and Concurrent Systems: Specification. Springer, Heidelberg (1992)
16. Martin, D.A.: Borel determinacy. Annals of Mathematics 102(2), 363–371 (1975)
17. Martin, D.A.: The determinacy of Blackwell games. The Journal of Symbolic Logic 63(4), 1565–1581 (1998)
18. Ramadge, P.J., Wonham, W.M.: Supervisory control of a class of discrete-event processes. SIAM Journal of Control and Optimization 25(1), 206–230 (1987)
19. Thomas, W.: Languages, automata, and logic. In: Handbook of Formal Languages, vol. 3, ch. 7, pp. 389–455. Springer, Heidelberg (1997)
20. Zielonka, W.: Infinite games on finitely coloured graphs with applications to automata on infinite trees. TCS 200(1-2), 135–183 (1998)
21. Zwick, U., Paterson, M.S.: The complexity of mean payoff games on graphs. TCS 158, 343–359 (1996)

Solving Parity Games in Big Steps[*]

Sven Schewe

Universität des Saarlandes, 66123 Saarbrücken, Germany

Abstract. This paper proposes a new algorithm that improves the complexity bound for solving parity games. Our approach combines McNaughton's iterated fixed point algorithm with a preprocessing step, which is called prior to every recursive call. The preprocessing uses ranking functions similar to Jurdziński's, but with a restricted codomain, to determine all winning regions smaller than a predefined parameter. The combination of the preprocessing step with the recursive call guarantees that McNaughton's algorithm proceeds in big steps, whose size is bounded from below by the chosen parameter. Higher parameters result in smaller call trees, but to the cost of an expensive preprocessing step. An optimal parameter balances the cost of the recursive call and the preprocessing step, resulting in an improvement of the known upper bound for solving parity games from approximately $O(m\,n^{\frac{1}{2}c})$ to $O(m\,n^{\frac{1}{3}c})$.

1 Introduction

Parity games have many applications in model checking [1,2,3,4,5,6] and synthesis [5,1,7,8,9,10]. In particular, modal and alternating-time μ-calculus model checking [5,4], synthesis [10,9] and satisfiability checking [5,1,7,8] for reactive systems, module checking [6], and ATL* model checking [3,4] can be reduced to solving parity games. This relevance of parity games led to a series of different approaches to solving them [11,12,13,14,15,16,17,18,19,20,21,22,23,24,25].

The complexity of solving parity games is still an open problem. All current deterministic algorithms have complexity bounds which are (at least) exponential in the number of colors [11,12,15,16,17,19,25] ($n^{O(c)}$), or in the squareroot of the number of game positions [13,24,25] ($n^{O(\sqrt{n})}$). Practical considerations suggest to assume that the number of colors is small compared to the number of positions. Indeed, all listed applications but μ-calculus model checking are guaranteed to result in parity games where the number of states is exponential in the number of colors. In μ-calculus model checking, the size of the game is determined by the product of the transition system under consideration (which is usually large), and the size of the formula (which is usually small). The number of colors is determined by the alternation depth of the specification, which, in turn, is usually small compared to the specification itself. Algorithms that are exponential only in the number of colors are thus considered the most attractive.

---

[*] This work was partly supported by the German Research Foundation (DFG) as part of the Transregional Collaborative Research Center "Automatic Verification and Analysis of Complex Systems" (SFB/TR 14 AVACS).

V. Arvind and S. Prasad (Eds.): FSTTCS 2007, LNCS 4855, pp. 449–460, 2007.

The first representatives of algorithms in the complexity class $n^{O(c)}$ follow the iterated fixed point structure induced by the parity condition [11,12,17]. The iterated fixed point construction leads to a time complexity of $O(m\,n^{c-1})$ for parity games with m edges, c colors, and n game positions. The upper complexity bound for solving parity games was first reduced by Browne et al. [16] to $O(mn^{\lceil 0.5c\rceil+1})$, and slightly further by Jurdziński [19] to $O(cm\,(\frac{n}{\lceil 0.5c\rceil})^{\lfloor 0.5c\rfloor})$.

The weakness of recursive algorithms that follow the iterated fixed point structure [11,12,17] is the potentially incremental update achieved by each recursive call. Recently, a big-step approach [24] has been proposed to reduce the complexity of McNaughton's algorithm for games with a high number of colors ($c \in \omega(\sqrt{n})$) to the bound $n^{O(\sqrt{n})}$ known from randomized algorithms [13,25].

We discuss a different big-step approach that improves the complexity for the relevant lower end of the spectrum of colors, resulting in the complexity $O\big(m\,(\frac{\kappa n}{c})^{\gamma(c)}\big)$ for solving parity games, where κ is a small constant and $\gamma(c) = \frac{c}{3} + \frac{1}{2} - \frac{1}{3c} - \frac{1}{\lceil\frac{c}{2}\rceil\lfloor\frac{c}{2}\rfloor}$ if c is even, and $\gamma(c) = \frac{c}{3} + \frac{1}{2} - \frac{1}{\lceil\frac{c}{2}\rceil\lfloor\frac{c}{2}\rfloor}$ if c is odd.

To guarantee big update steps, we use an algorithm which is inspired by Jurdziński's [19] approach for solving parity games. His approach is adapted by restricting the codomain of the used ranking function. The resulting algorithm is exploited in a preprocessing step for finding winning regions bounded by the size of a parameter. Compared to [24], this results in a significant cut in the cost for finding small winning regions, since the running time for the preprocessing algorithm is polynomial in the parameter, and exponential only in the number of colors ($O((\binom{\pi+\lceil 0.5c\rceil}{\pi})))$. Using a parameter of approximately $\sqrt[3]{c\,n^2}$ results in the improved $O\big(m\,(\frac{\kappa n}{c})^{\gamma(c)}\big)$ complexity bound for solving parity games.

2   Preliminaries

2.1   Parity Games

A parity game $\mathcal{P} = (V_{even}, V_{odd}, E, \alpha)$ consists of a finite directed game graph $\mathcal{D} = (V_{even} \uplus V_{odd}, E)$ without sinks, whose vertices are partitioned into two sets V_{even} and V_{odd}, called the game positions of player *even* and *odd*, respectively, and an evaluation function $\alpha : V_{even} \uplus V_{odd} \to \mathbb{N}$ that maps each game position v to an integer value $\alpha(v)$, called the color of v. For technical reasons we additionally require that the minimal color is 0, and use games with highest color d and games with $c = d + 1$ colors as synonyms. We use $V = V_{even} \uplus V_{odd}$ for the game positions, and extend the common intersection and subtraction operations on digraphs to parity games. ($\mathcal{P} \cap F$ and $\mathcal{P} \smallsetminus F$ thus denote the parity games resulting by restricting the game graph $\mathcal{D}$ of $\mathcal{P}$ to $\mathcal{D} \cap F$ and $\mathcal{D} \smallsetminus F$, respectively.)

Plays. Intuitively, a game is played by placing a pebble on a vertex $v \in V_{even} \uplus V_{odd}$ of $\mathcal{D}$. Whenever the pebble is on a position $v \in V_{even}$, player *even* chooses an edge $e = (v, v') \in E$ originating in v, and moves the pebble to v'. Symmetricly, if the pebble is on a position $v \in V_{odd}$, player *odd* chooses an edge $e = (v, v') \in E$

originating in v, and moves the pebble to v'. In this way, they successively construct an infinite *play* $\pi = v_0 v_1 v_2 v_3 \ldots \in (V_{even} \uplus V_{odd})^\omega$.

A play is evaluated by the highest color that occurs infinitely often. Player *even* (*odd*) wins a play $\pi = v_0 v_1 v_2 v_3 \ldots$ if the highest color occurring infinitely often in the sequence $\alpha(\pi) = \alpha(v_0)\alpha(v_1)\alpha(v_2)\alpha(v_3)\ldots$ is even (odd).

Strategies. Let $\mathcal{D} = (V_{even} \uplus V_{odd}, E)$ be a finite game graph with positions $V = V_{even} \uplus V_{odd}$. A *strategy* for player *even* is a function $f : V^* V_{even} \to V$ which maps each finite history of a play that ends in a position $v \in V_{even}$ to a successor v' of v. (That is, there is an edge $(v, v') \in E$ from v to v'.) A play is *f-conform* if every decision of player *even* in the play is in accordance with f. A strategy is called *memoryless* if it only depends on the current position. A memoryless strategy for *even* can be viewed as a function $f : V_{even} \to V$ such that $(v, f(v)) \in E$ for all $v \in V_{even}$. For a memoryless strategy f of player *even*, we denote with $\mathcal{D}_f = (V_{even} \uplus V_{odd}, E_f)$ the game graph obtained from $\mathcal{D}$ by deleting all transitions from states in V_{even} that are not in accordance with f. (That is, $\mathcal{D}_f$ is a directed graph where all positions owned by player *even* have outdegree 1.) The analogous definitions are made for player *odd*.

A strategy f of player *even* (*odd*) is called *v-winning* if all f-conform plays that start in v are winning for player *even* (*odd*). A position $v \in V$ is *v-winning* for player *even* (*odd*) if *even* (*odd*) has a v-winning strategy. We call the sets of v-winning positions for player *even* (*odd*) the *winning region* of *even* (*odd*). Parity games are memoryless determined:

Theorem 1. *[11] For every parity game $\mathcal{P}$, the game positions are partitioned into a winning region W_{even} of player* even *and a winning region W_{odd} of player* odd. *Moreover, player* even *and* odd *have memoryless strategies that are v-winning for all positions in their respective winning region.*

Dominions and Attractors. We call a subset $D \subseteq W_\sigma$ of a winning region a *dominion* of player $\sigma \in \{even, odd\}$, if player σ has a memoryless strategy f that is v-winning for all $v \in D$, such that D is not left in any f-conform play ($E_f \cap D \times V \smallsetminus D = \emptyset$). The *$\sigma$-attractor* $A \subseteq V$ of a set $F \subseteq V$ of game positions is the set of those game positions, from which player σ has a memoryless strategy to force the pebble into a position in F. The σ-attractor A of a set F can be defined as the least fixed point of sets that contain F, and that contain a game position v of player σ ($\overline{\sigma}$) if they contain some successor (all successors) of v. (For convenience, we use $\overline{odd}$ and $\overline{even}$ for *even* and *odd*, respectively.)

Constructing this least fixed point is obviously linear in the number of edges of the parity game, and we can fix a memoryless strategy (the attractor strategy) for player σ to reach F in finitely many steps during this construction.

Lemma 1. *For a given parity game $\mathcal{P} = (V_{even}, V_{odd}, E, \alpha)$, and a set F of game positions, we can compute the σ-attractor A of F and a memoryless strategy for σ on $A \smallsetminus F$ to reach F in finitely many steps in time $O(m)$.* $\square$

For a given dominion D for player σ in a parity game $\mathcal{P}$, we can reduce solving $\mathcal{P}$ to computing the σ-attractor A of D, and solving $\mathcal{P} \smallsetminus A$.

Lemma 2. *[24] Let $\mathcal{P}$ be a parity game, D a dominion of player $\sigma \in \{even, odd\}$ for $\mathcal{P}$ with σ-attractor A. Then the winning region (and strategy) of player $\bar{\sigma}$ in $\mathcal{P}$ is her winning region (and strategy) in the subgame $\mathcal{P} \smallsetminus A$. The winning strategy of player σ can be composed by her winning strategy on $\mathcal{P} \smallsetminus A$, her attractor strategy (on $A \smallsetminus D$), and her winning strategy on her dominion (in $\mathcal{P} \cap D$).*

2.2   A Ranking Function Based Approach to Solving Parity Games

So far, Jurdziński's algorithm [19] for solving parity games has been the technique with the best complexity bound. His algorithm draws from the comparably small codomain of the used ranking function (the progress measure).

The method for computing small dominions discussed in Section 3 adopts his techniques by restricting the codomain of the ranking function, sacrificing completeness. Some of the theorems stated in this subsection are thus slightly more general than the theorems in [19], but they are arranged such that the proofs provided in [19] can be applied without changes.

For a parity game $\mathcal{P} = (V_{even}, V_{odd}, E, \alpha)$ with maximal color d, a σ-*progress measure* is, for $\sigma \in \{even, odd\}$, a function $\rho : V_{even} \uplus V_{odd} \rightarrow \mathcal{M}^\sigma$ whose codomain $\mathcal{M}^\sigma \subseteq \{f : \{0, \ldots, d\} \rightarrow \mathbb{N} \mid f(c) = 0$ if c is σ, and $f(c) \leq |\alpha^{-1}(c)|$ otherwise$\} \cup \{\top\}$ contains a maximal element $\top$ and a set of functions from $\{0, \ldots, d\}$ to the integers. The codomain $\mathcal{M}^\sigma$ satisfies the requirements that every σ ($\in \{even, odd\}$) integer $\leq d$ is mapped to 0, while all other integers c are mapped to a value bounded by the number $|\alpha^{-1}(c)|$ of c-colored game positions. (Jurdziński uses the maximal codomain $\mathcal{M}^\sigma_\infty$ defined by replacing containment with equality.) For simplicity, we require downward closedness: if $\mathcal{M}^\sigma$ contains a function $f \in \mathcal{M}^\sigma$, then every function f' which is pointwise smaller than f ($f'(c) \leq f(c) \forall c \leq d$) is also contained in $\mathcal{M}^\sigma$.

For each color $c \leq d$, we define a relation $\rhd_c \subseteq \mathcal{M}^\sigma \times \mathcal{M}^\sigma$. $\rhd_c$ is the smallest relation that contains $\{\top\} \times \mathcal{M}^\sigma$ and a pair of functions $(f, f') \in \rhd_c$ if there is a color $c' \geq c$ such that $f(c') > f'(c')$, and $f(c'') = f'(c'')$ holds true for all colors $c'' > c'$, or if c is σ and $f(c') = f'(c')$ holds true for all $c' \geq c$. That is, $\rhd_c$ is defined by using the lexicographic order, ignoring all colors smaller than c. f needs to be greater than f' by this order, and strictly greater if c is $\bar{\sigma}$. $\rhd_0$ defines an order $\succeq$ on $\mathcal{M}^\sigma$ (the lexicographic order). From this order, we infer the preorder $\sqsupseteq$ on progress measures, which requires that $\succeq$ is satisfied pointwise ($\rho \sqsupseteq \rho' \Leftrightarrow \forall v \in V. \rho(v) \succeq \rho'(v)$). We call a σ progress measure ρ *valid* iff every position $v \in V_\sigma$ has some successor $v' \in V$ with $\rho(v) \rhd_{\alpha(v)} \rho(v')$, and if, for every position $v \in V_{\bar{\sigma}}$ and every successors $v' \in V$ of v, $\rho(v) \rhd_{\alpha(v)} \rho(v')$ holds true.

Let, for a σ progress measure ρ, $\|\rho\| = V \smallsetminus \rho^{-1}(\top)$ denote the game positions that are not mapped to the maximal element $\top$ of $\mathcal{M}^\sigma$. A valid σ progress measure ρ serves as a witness for a winning strategy for player σ on $\|\rho\|$: If we fix a memoryless strategy f for player σ that satisfies $\rho(v) \rhd_{\alpha(v)} \rho(f(v))$ for all $v \in V_\sigma$, then every cycle $v_1 v_2 \ldots v_l = v_1$ with maximal color $c_{max} = \alpha(v_1)$ that is reachable in an f-conform play satisfies $\rho(v_1) \rhd_{\alpha(v_1)} \rho(v_2) \rhd_{\alpha(v_2)} \ldots \rhd_{\alpha(v_{l-1})} \rho(v_l)$. If c_{max} is not σ, this can be relaxed to $\rho(v_1) \rhd_{c_{max}} \rho(v_2) \rhd_{c_{max}-1} \rho(v_3) \rhd_{c_{max}-1} \ldots \rhd_{c_{max}-1} \rho(v_l)$, which is only satisfied if $\rho(v_i) = \top$ holds for all $i = 1, \ldots, l$.

Theorem 2. *[19] Let $\mathcal{P} = (V_{even}, V_{odd}, E, \alpha)$ be a parity game with valid σ progress measure ρ. Then player σ wins on $\|\rho\|$ with any memoryless winning strategy that maps a position $v \in \|\rho\| \cap V_\sigma$ to a position v' with $\rho(v) \rhd_{\alpha(v)} \rho(v')$.*

Such a successor must exist, since the progress measure is valid. The $\sqsupseteq$-*least* valid σ progress measure is well defined and can be computed efficiently.

Theorem 3. *[19] The $\sqsupseteq$-least valid σ progress measure ρ_μ exists and can, for a parity game with m edges and c colors, be computed in time $O(c\,m\,|\mathcal{M}^\sigma|)$.*

When using the maximal codomain $\mathcal{M}^\sigma_\infty$, which contains the function ρ that assigns each $\overline{\sigma}$ value c to $\rho(c) = |\alpha^{-1}(c)|$, for the progress measures, the $\sqsupseteq$-least valid σ progress measure ρ_μ determines the complete winning region of player σ.

Theorem 4. *[19] For a parity game $\mathcal{P} = (V_{even}, V_{odd}, E, \alpha)$, and for the codomain $\mathcal{M}^\sigma_\infty$ for the progress measures, $\|\rho_\mu\|$ coincides with the winning region W_σ of player σ for the $\sqsupseteq$-least valid σ progress measure ρ_μ.*

For parity games with c colors, the size $|\mathcal{M}^\sigma_\infty|$ of the maximal codomain can be estimated by $(\frac{n}{\lfloor 0.5c \rfloor})^{\lfloor 0.5c \rfloor} + 1$ if σ is even, and by $(\frac{n}{\lceil 0.5c \rceil})^{\lceil 0.5c \rceil} + 1$ if σ is odd.

Corollary 1. *[19] Parity games with three colors can be solved and a winning strategy for the player who wins on the highest color constructed in time $O(m\,n)$.*

3   Computing Small Dominions

Computing small dominions efficiently is an essential step in the algorithm introduced in Section 4. In this section, we show that we can efficiently compute a dominion of either player, which is guaranteed to contain all dominions with size bounded by a parameter π. To compute such a dominion, we draw from the efficient computation of the $\sqsupseteq$-least valid σ progress measure (Theorem 3).

Instead of using Jurdziński's codomain $\mathcal{M}^\sigma_\infty$, we use the smaller codomain $\mathcal{M}^\sigma_\pi$ for the progress measures, which contains only those functions f that satisfy $\sum_{c=0}^{d} f(c) \leq \pi$ for some parameter $\pi \in \mathbb{N}$. (d denotes the highest color of the parity game). The size of $\mathcal{M}^\sigma_\pi$ can be estimated by $|\mathcal{M}^\sigma_\pi| \leq \binom{\pi + \lceil 0.5(d+1) \rceil}{\pi} + 1$.

Using $\mathcal{M}^\sigma_\pi$ instead of $\mathcal{M}^\sigma_\infty$, $\|\rho_\mu\|$ contains all dominions of player σ of size $\leq \pi + 1$ (where ρ_μ denotes the $\sqsupseteq$-least valid σ progress measures).

Theorem 5. *Let $\mathcal{P} = (V_{even}, V_{odd}, E, \alpha)$ be a parity game, and let $D \subseteq V$ be a dominion of player $\sigma \in \{even, odd\}$ of size $|D| \leq \pi + 1$. Then there is a valid σ progress measure $\rho : V \to \mathcal{M}^\sigma_\pi$ with $F = \|\rho\|$.*

Proof. Let $\mathcal{P}' = \mathcal{P} \cap D$ be the restriction of $\mathcal{P}$ to D. To solve $\mathcal{P}'$, we can use the maximal codomain $\mathcal{M}^{\sigma\,\prime}_\infty$. Since D is a dominion of player σ for $\mathcal{P}$, she has a winning strategy f on the complete subgame $\mathcal{P}'$, and the $\sqsupseteq'$-least progress measure ρ'_μ for this codomain satisfies $\|\rho'_\mu\| = D$ by Theorem 4. Since D has size $|D| \leq \pi + 1$, it contains at most π postions with $\overline{\sigma}$ color (at least one position needs to have σ color), and thus ρ'_μ is in $\mathcal{M}^{\sigma\,\prime}_\pi$ (and $\mathcal{M}^{\sigma\,\prime}_\pi = \mathcal{M}^{\sigma\,\prime}_\infty$ holds true).

Since D is a dominion of player σ for $\mathcal{P}$, all positions in $V_{\overline{\sigma}} \cap D$ have only successors in D, and we can extend ρ'_{μ} to a valid σ progress measue ρ for $\mathcal{P}$ by setting $\rho(v) = \rho'_{\mu}(v)$ for all $v \in D$, and $\rho(v) = \top$ otherwise. ρ is by construction a valid σ progress measure in $\mathcal{M}^{\sigma}_{\pi}$ that satisfies $\|\rho\| = D$. □

By Theorem 3, we can compute the $\sqsupseteq$-least valid σ progress measure ρ_{μ} in time $O(cm\,|\mathcal{M}^{\sigma}_{\pi}|)$, and by Theorem 2, we can construct a winning strategy for player σ on $\|\rho_{\mu}\|$ within the same complexity bound.

Corollary 2. *For a given parity game $\mathcal{P}$ with c colors and m edges, we can construct a forced winning region F for player σ that contains all forced winning regions F' of size $|F'| \leq \pi + 1$ in time $O\big(cm\,(\frac{\pi + \lceil 0.5c\rceil}{\pi})\big)$. A winning strategy for player σ on F can be constructed within the same complexity bound.* □

4   Solving Parity Games in Big Steps

The algorithm proposed in this paper accelerates McNaughton's iterated fixed point approach for solving parity games [11,12,17] by using the approximation technique discussed in the previous section to restrict the size of the call tree.

McNaughton's Algorithm. McNaughton's algorithm, as depicted below in Procedure *McNaughton*, takes a parity game $\mathcal{P} = (V_{even}, V_{odd}, E, \alpha)$ as input and returns the ordered pair (W_{even}, W_{odd}) of winning regions for both players.

> <u>Procedure</u> *McNaughton*($\mathcal{P}$):
>
> 1. set d to the highest color occurring in $\mathcal{P}$
> 2. <u>if</u> $d = 0$ <u>then</u> <u>return</u> $(V, \emptyset)$
> 3. set $(\sigma, \overline{\sigma})$ to (*even*,*odd*) if d is even, and to (*odd*,*even*) otherwise
> 4. set $W_{\overline{\sigma}}$ to $\emptyset$
> 5. <u>repeat</u>
>   (a) set $\mathcal{P}'$ to $\mathcal{P} \setminus \sigma$-*Attractor*$(\alpha^{-1}(d), \mathcal{P})$
>   (b) set (W'_{even}, W'_{odd}) to *McNaughton*($\mathcal{P}'$)
>   (c) <u>if</u> $W'_{\overline{\sigma}} = \emptyset$ <u>then</u>
>   i. set W_{σ} to $V \setminus W_{\overline{\sigma}}$
>   ii. <u>return</u> (W_{even}, W_{odd})
>   (d) set $W_{\overline{\sigma}}$ to $W_{\overline{\sigma}} \cup \overline{\sigma}$-*Attractor*$(W'_{\overline{\sigma}}, \mathcal{P})$
>   (e) set $\mathcal{P}$ to $\mathcal{P} \setminus \overline{\sigma}$-*Attractor*$(W'_{\overline{\sigma}}, \mathcal{P})$

Evaluating one-color games is trivial, and Procedure *McNaughton* returns the winning regions for this case without further computations (line 2, this case servers as induction basis for the correctness prove).

Procedure *McNaughton* computes in every recursive call (line 5b) a *dominion* of player $\overline{\sigma}$ for $\mathcal{P}$: Player $\overline{\sigma}$ has (by induction hypothesis) a winning strategy f for $W_{\overline{\sigma}}$ in $\mathcal{P}'$ and no f-conform strategy starting in the statespace V' of $\mathcal{P}'$ can leave V' in $\mathcal{P}$, since V' is the complement of a σ-attractor (line 5a). Solving $\mathcal{P}$ can thus be reduced to constructing the $\overline{\sigma}$-attractor $A_{\overline{\sigma}}$ of $W_{\overline{\sigma}}$ (line 5d), and solving $\mathcal{P} \setminus A_{\overline{\sigma}}$ (line 5e).

If the recursive call (line $5b$) provides the result that player σ wins from every position in $\mathcal{P}'$, she wins from every position in $\mathcal{P}$ (following her winning strategy for $\mathcal{P}'$ in V' and an attractor strategy to d-colored positions (line $5a$) otherwise), and Procedure *McNaughton* terminates (lines $5c - 5cii$).

Proceeding in Big Steps. As observed by Jurdziński, Paterson and Zwick [24], McNaughton's algorithm can be adopted by computing any dominion of player $\overline{\sigma}$ (instead of the particular dominion returned by the recursive call). In [24], this observation is exploited by performing a brute-force search for dominions of size $\sqrt{n}$ (where $n = |\mathcal{P}|$ denotes the number of game positions), and performing a recursive call only if no such dominion exists. The cost for each brute-force search is $n^{\sqrt{n}}$, which coincides with the upper bound on the size of the call tree, improving the complexity bound for the theoretical case of parity games with a high number of colors – $c \in \omega(\sqrt{n})$ – to $O(n^{\sqrt{n}})$.

Brute-force search, however, is too expensive, and does not improve the complexity bound for the common case that the number of colors is small. We therefore propose to use the efficient approximation technique introduced in Section 3 instead. As a further difference, we propose to perform a recursive call after each

Procedure *Winning-Regions*$(\mathcal{P})$:

1. set d to the highest color occurring in $\mathcal{P}$
2. if $d = 0$ then return $(V, \emptyset)$ – one color $\Rightarrow$ use McNaughton's [11,12,17] algorithm
3. set $(\sigma, \overline{\sigma})$ to $(even, odd)$ if d is even, and to $(odd, even)$ otherwise
4. set n to the size $|V|$ of $\mathcal{P}$
5. if $d = 2$ then   – three colors $\Rightarrow$ use Jurdziński's [19] algorithm
    (a) set W_{even} to *Approximate*$(\mathcal{P}, n, even)$ – c.f. Corollary 1
    (b) return $(W_{even}, V \setminus W_{even})$
6. set $W_{\overline{\sigma}}$ to $\emptyset$
7. repeat
    (a) if $d > 2$ then   – two colors $\Rightarrow$ use McNaughton's [11,12,17] algorithm
        i. set $W'_{\overline{\sigma}}$ to $\overline{\sigma}$-*Attractor*$(Approximate(\mathcal{P}, \pi(n, d+1), \overline{\sigma}), \mathcal{P})$ – c.f. Corollary 2
        ii. set $W_{\overline{\sigma}}$ to $W_{\overline{\sigma}} \cup W'_{\overline{\sigma}}$
        iii. set $\mathcal{P}$ to $\mathcal{P} \setminus W'_{\overline{\sigma}}$
    (b) set $\mathcal{P}'$ to $\mathcal{P} \setminus \sigma$-*Attractor*$(\alpha^{-1}(d), \mathcal{P})$
    (c) set (W'_{even}, W'_{odd}) to *Winning-Regions*$(\mathcal{P}')$
    (d) if $W'_{\overline{\sigma}} = \emptyset$ then
        i. set W_σ to $V \setminus W_{\overline{\sigma}}$
        ii. return (W_{even}, W_{odd})
    (e) set $W_{\overline{\sigma}}$ to $W_{\overline{\sigma}} \cup \overline{\sigma}$-*Attractor*$(W'_{\overline{\sigma}}, \mathcal{P})$
    (f) set $\mathcal{P}$ to $\mathcal{P} \setminus \overline{\sigma}$-*Attractor*$(W'_{\overline{\sigma}}, \mathcal{P})$

Fig. 1. Procedure *Winning-Regions*$(\mathcal{P})$ returns the ordered pair (W_{even}, W_{odd}) of winning regions for player *even* and *odd*, respectively. V and α denote the game positions and the coloring function of the parity game $\mathcal{P}$. *Approximate*$(\mathcal{P}, \pi, \sigma)$ computes a dominion for player σ, which contains all dominions of player σ of size less than or equal to $\pi + 1$ (c.f. Corollary 2). σ-*Attractor*$(F, \mathcal{P})$ computes the respective σ-attractor of a set F of game positions in a game parity $\mathcal{P}$ (c.f. Lemma 1).

approximation step, resulting in the guarantee that the progress (that is, the set of evaluated positions) in each iteration step exceeds the size defined by the chosen parameter. The resulting algorithm is depicted in Figure 1.

The set $W'_{\bar{\sigma}}$ computed in line 7ai is the $\bar{\sigma}$-attractor of the dominion of player $\bar{\sigma}$ in $\mathcal{P}$ computed by the approximation procedure (c.f. Corollary 2) introduced in Section 3, and thus itself a dominion of player $\bar{\sigma}$. The set $W''_{\bar{\sigma}}$ computed in the recursive call (line 7c) is a dominion of player $\bar{\sigma}$ in $\mathcal{P} \setminus W'_{\bar{\sigma}}$, and thus $D = W'_{\bar{\sigma}} \cup W''_{\bar{\sigma}}$ is a dominion in $\mathcal{P}$. If the size of D does not exceed the chosen parameter by at least two, D must be contained in the dominion computed in $Approximate(\mathcal{P}, \pi(n, d + 1), \bar{\sigma})$, and $W''_{\bar{\sigma}}$ is empty. In this case, the procedure terminates (line 7d), otherwise, we obtain a progress of at least $\pi(n, d + 1) + 2$.

While bigger parameters slow down the approximation procedure (c.f. Corollary 2), they thus restrict the size of the call tree. The best results are obtained if the parameter is chosen such that the cost of calling the approximation procedure (line 7ai) and the cost of the recursive call (line 7c) are approximately equivalent. If c is of reasonable size (that is, in $O(\sqrt{n})$), this is the case if we set the parameter approximately to $\sqrt[3]{cn^2}$. (The function β defined below for the proof of the complexity quickly converges to $\frac{2}{3}$.)

Starting point for the complexity estimation is the case of three colors, where we use Jurdziński's algorithm [19] (Corollary 1). (Skipping lines $5 - 5b$ moves the induction basis further down, resulting in the complexity of $O(mn^{1.5})$ for the case of three colors. The optimization obtained by using [19] for three-color games accounts for the $- \frac{1}{\lceil 0.5c \rceil \lceil 0.5c \rceil}$ part of the function γ introduced below.)

For fixed numbers of colors, the resulting complexities evolve as follows:

number of colors	3	4	5	6	7	8	$\cdots$
approximation complexity	-	$O(mn)$	$O(mn^{1\frac{1}{2}})$	$O(mn^2)$	$O(mn^{2\frac{1}{3}})$	$O(mn^{2\frac{3}{4}})$	$\cdots$
chosen parameter $\pi_c(n)$	-	$\sqrt{n}$	$\sqrt{n}$	$\sqrt[3]{n^2}$	$\sqrt[12]{n^7}$	$\sqrt[16]{n^{11}}$	$\cdots$
number of iterations $\frac{n}{\pi_c(n)}$	-	$\sqrt{n}$	$\sqrt{n}$	$\sqrt[3]{n}$	$\sqrt[12]{n^5}$	$\sqrt[16]{n^5}$	$\cdots$
solving complexity	$O(mn)$	$O(mn^{1\frac{1}{2}})$	$O(mn^2)$	$O(mn^{2\frac{1}{3}})$	$O(mn^{2\frac{3}{4}})$	$O(mn^{3\frac{1}{16}})$	$\cdots$

The approximation complexity for $c + 1$ colors is chosen to coincide with the complexity of solving a game with c colors. (Its complexity thus coincides with the complexity of each iteration of the repeat loop). The parameter $\pi_c(n)$ is chosen to result in this complexity, and the number of iterations is $i_c(n) = \frac{n}{\pi_c(n)}$, results from this choice. Finally, the resulting complexity for solving games with $c + 1$ colors is $i_c(n)$ times the complexity for solving parity games with c colors.

Correctness. In this paragraph, we demonstrate that Procedure *Winning-Regions* computes the winning regions correctly.

Theorem 6. *For a given parity game* $\mathcal{P}$, *Procedure* Winning-Regions *computes the complete winning regions of both players.*

Proof. We prove the claim by induction. Let d denote the highest color of $\mathcal{P}$.

Induction Basis ($d = 0$, $d = 2$): For $d = 0$, the highest color on every path is obviously 0, and every strategy for player *even* is winning. For $d = 2$, the algorithm follows Jurdziński's [19] algorithm (c.f. Theorem 4 and Corollary 1).

<u>Induction Step</u> $(d \mapsto d+1)$: Let $\mathcal{P}$ be a parity game with highest color $d+1$.

The call of the Procedure *Approximate* in line 7*ai* provides a (possibly empty) dominion D for player $\overline{\sigma}$ (Theorem 5). The $\overline{\sigma}$-attractor of this set is then added to the winning region of $\overline{\sigma}$ (line 7*aii*), and subtracted from $\mathcal{P}$, which is safe by Lemma 2.

In line 7*b*, the σ-attractor A of the set of states with color $d+1$ is subtracted from $\mathcal{P}$, and the resulting parity game $\mathcal{P}' = \mathcal{P} \setminus A$ is solved by recursively calling the Procedure *Winning-Regions* (line 7*c*). Since the highest color of $\mathcal{P}'$ is $\leq d$, the resulting winning regions are correct by induction hypothesis. $W_{\overline{\sigma}}''$ is a dominion of player $\overline{\sigma}$ in $\mathcal{P}'$, and, due to the σ-attractor construction, also in $\mathcal{P}$. If $W_{\overline{\sigma}}''$ is non-empty, then the $\overline{\sigma}$-attractor of this set is added to the winning region of $\overline{\sigma}$ (line 7*e*), and subtracted from $\mathcal{P}$ (line 7*f*), which is safe by Lemma 2.

Since the size of $\mathcal{P}$ is strictly reduced in every iteration of the loop, the set $W_{\overline{\sigma}}''$ returned after the recursive call in line 7*c* is eventually empty, and the procedure terminates. When $W_{\overline{\sigma}}''$ is empty, player σ wins from all positions in (the remaining) parity game $\mathcal{P}$ by following a memoryless strategy that agrees on every position in $\mathcal{P}'$ with a memoryless winning strategy f on $\mathcal{P}'$, makes an arbitrary (but fixed) choice for positions with color $d+1$, and follows an attractor strategy (from the σ-attractor construction of line 7*b*) on the remaining positions. An f-conform play either eventually stays in $\mathcal{P}'$, in which case it is winning for player σ by induction hypothesis, or always eventually visits a position with color $d+1$, in which case $d+1$ is the highest color that occurs infinitely many times. Since $d+1$ is σ, player σ wins in this case, too.   □

Complexity. While the correctness of the algorithm is independent of the chosen parameter, its complexity crucially depends on this choice. We will choose the parameter such that the complexity for the recursive call (line 7*c*) coincides with the complexity of computing the approximation (line 7*ai*).

First, we show that the Procedure *Winning-Regions* proceeds in big steps.

Lemma 3. *For every parameter $\pi(n,c)$, the main loop of the algorithm is iterated at most $\lfloor \frac{n}{\pi(n,c)+2} \rfloor + 1$ times.*

Proof. The $\overline{\sigma}$-attractor $W_{\overline{\sigma}}'$ of the computed approximation D (line 7*ai*) and the winning region $W_{\overline{\sigma}}''$ of $\overline{\sigma}$ are dominions for $\overline{\sigma}$ on $\mathcal{P}$ and $\mathcal{P} \setminus W_{\overline{\sigma}}'$, respectively. Thus, their union $U = W_{\overline{\sigma}}' \cup W_{\overline{\sigma}}''$ is a dominion on $\mathcal{P}$. If the size of U does not exceed $\pi+1$, than U is contained in D by Corollary 2. In this case, $W_{\overline{\sigma}}''$ is empty, and the loop terminates. Otherwise, a superset of U is subtracted from P during the iteration (line 7*aiii* and 7*f*), which can happen at most $\lfloor \frac{n}{\pi(n,c)+2} \rfloor$ times.   □

Building on this lemma, it is simple to define the parameter π such that the requirement of equal complexities is satisfied: We fix the function γ such that $\gamma(c) = \frac{c}{3} + \frac{1}{2} - \frac{1}{\lceil 0.5c \rceil \lfloor 0.5c \rfloor}$ if c is odd, and $\gamma(c) = \frac{c}{3} + \frac{1}{2} - \frac{1}{3c} - \frac{1}{\lceil 0.5c \rceil \lfloor 0.5c \rfloor}$ if c is even, and $\beta(c) = \frac{\gamma(c-1)}{\lceil 0.5c \rceil}$. Finally, we choose $\pi(n,c)$ to be the smallest natural number that satisfies $\frac{n}{\pi(n,c)+2} < \frac{n^{1-\beta(c)}}{2\sqrt[3]{c}} - 1$ $(\pi(n,c) \approx 2\sqrt[3]{c}n^{\beta(c)})$.

Theorem 7. *Solving a parity game $\mathcal{P}$ with $c > 2$ colors, m edges, and n game positions can be performed in time $O\big(m\big(\frac{\kappa n}{c}\big)^{\gamma(c)}\big)$. ($\kappa$ is a small constant.)*

Proof. First we estimate the running time of the procedure without the recursive calls. To estimate the running time of the approximation algorithm $(\pi(n,c) + \lceil 0.5c \rceil)^{\lceil 0.5c \rceil}$ can be estimated by $\kappa_1(\kappa_2\pi(n,c))^{\lceil 0.5c \rceil}$, and the running time of each iteration step (plus the part before the loop (lines $1 - 6$) and minus the recursive call) can be estimated by $\frac{\kappa_3\, m}{\sqrt[3]{(c-1)!}}(\kappa_4\, n)^{\gamma(c-1)}$. ($\kappa_1$, κ_2, κ_3 and κ_4 are suitable constants.) We show by induction that the overall running time of the procedure can be estimated by $\frac{\kappa_3\, m}{\sqrt[3]{c!}}(\kappa_4\, n)^{\gamma(c)}$.

<u>Induction Basis</u> $(c \le 3)$: For parity games with one or two and with three colors, we use the algorithms of McNaughton and Jurdziński, respectively, resulting in the complexities $O(n)$, $O(m\, n)$ and $O(m\, n) = O(m\, n^{\gamma(3)})$, respectively.

<u>Induction Step</u> $(c \mapsto c + 1)$: By induction hypothesis, the cost of every recursive call can (as well as the remaining cost of each iteration step) be estimated by $\frac{\kappa_3\, m}{\sqrt[3]{(c-1)!}}(\kappa_4\, n)^{\gamma(c-1)}$. Since Lemma 3 implies that the loop is iterated at most $\lfloor \frac{n^{1-\beta(c)}}{2\sqrt[3]{c}} \rfloor$ times, the claim follows immediately $(\gamma(c) = \gamma(c-1) + 1 - \beta(c))$. $\square$

If we impose the restriction that c is not linear in $\sqrt{n}$, that is, if we assume that $c \in o(\sqrt{n})$, this coarse estimation already suffices to show that we can choose any value higher than 1, $2\sqrt{2e}$, and $(2e)^{1.5}$ for κ_2, κ_4, and κ, respectively.

Strategies. If we want to construct the winning strategies of one or both players, the complexity is left unchanged in most cases. The only exception is the construction of winning strategies for player *odd* in three-color games.

Theorem 8. *The algorithm can be extended to compute the winning strategies for both players. The winning strategy for player* odd *on her complete winning region in s parity game with three colors can be constructed in time $O(m\, n^{1.5})$. In all other cases, constructing the winning strategies does not increase the complexity of the algorithm.*

Proof. Extending the procedure to return winning strategies for both players on their respective winning regions only comprises fixing an arbitrary strategy for player *odd* in the trivial case of single-color games (line 2), computing winning strategies for both players for three-color games (line 5a), computing winning strategies for player $\overline{\sigma}$ in the approximation procedure in line 7ai, computing the attractor strategies in lines 7ai, 7b, and 7e, and fixing arbitrary strategies for d-colored positions prior to returning the winning regions in line 7aiii. By the Corollaries 1 and 2, and by Lemma 1, all these extension with the exception of constructing the winning strategy of player *odd* for games with three colors (line 5a) can be made without changing the complexity.

Computing the winning strategy of player *odd* immediately would increase the complexity of the algorithm. For these three-color games, we therefore *postpone* computing the strategies of player *odd* till after solving the complete game by pushing the respective three-color game (or rather its intersection with the winning region of player *odd*) on a solve-me-later stack. While postponing the construction of the strategies for player *odd* in these subgames, we compute a partial strategy for player *odd* that can be completed to a winning strategy on her complete winning region by filling in winning strategies for these subgames.

Completing the strategies *after* solving the complete game is cheaper, because solving most of the three-color games becomes obsolete: If the recursive call (line 7c) returns a non-empty set $W''_{\bar{\sigma}}$, then the set W''_{σ} is discarded, and it is safe to delete all those games from the top of the solve-me-later stack that refer to W''_{σ}.

As a result, we only need to solve the subgames remaining on the stack after the parity game $\mathcal{P}$ has been solved to complete the winning strategies. Since the sum of the sizes of these games is bounded by the size of the complete game $\mathcal{P}$, this step can be performed in time $O(m\,n^{1.5})$ (using the just established complexity bound for solving games with four colors) if $\mathcal{P}$ has n game positions and m edges, independent of the number of colors of $\mathcal{P}$.   □

5   Conclusions

We proposed a novel approach to solving parity games, which reduces the complexity bound for solving parity games from $O\big(c\,m\,(\frac{n}{\lceil 0.5c\rceil})^{\lfloor 0.5\,c\rfloor}\big)$ [19] to $O\big(m\,\big(\frac{\kappa\,n}{c}\big)^{\gamma(c)}\big)$ for $\gamma(c) = \frac{c}{3}+\frac{1}{2}-\frac{1}{3c}-\frac{1}{\lceil\frac{c}{2}\rceil\lfloor\frac{c}{2}\rfloor}$ if c is even, and $\gamma(c) = \frac{c}{3}+\frac{1}{2}-\frac{1}{\lceil\frac{c}{2}\rceil\lfloor\frac{c}{2}\rfloor}$ if c is odd. (κ is a small constant that can be fixed to approximately $(2e)^{1.5}$).

This reduces the exponential factor from $\lfloor\frac{c}{2}\rfloor$ to less than $\frac{c}{3}+\frac{1}{2}$. It is, after the reduction from $c-1$ [11,12,17] to $\lceil\frac{c}{2}\rceil+1$ by Browne et al. [16], the second improvement that reduces the exponential growth with the number of colors.

Besides solving parity games, we are often interested in winning strategies for the players, since they serve as witnesses and counter examples in model checking, and as models in synthesis. When constructing these strategies, the improvement in the complexity of the discussed approach is even higher. Constructing winning strategies for both players increase the complexity of the proposed algorithm only for parity games with three colors, where the complexity increases slightly from $O(m\,n)$ to $O(m\,n^{1.5})$. The best previously known bound for constructing winning strategies [19] has been $O\big(c\,m\,(\frac{n}{\lceil 0.5c\rceil})^{\lceil 0.5\,c\rceil}\big)$.

The suggested approach thus provides a significantly improved complexity bound for solving parity games with more than 2, and up to $o(\sqrt{n})$ colors.

References

1. Kozen, D.: Results on the propositional μ-calculus. Theor. Comput. Sci. 27, 333–354 (1983)
2. Emerson, E.A., Jutla, C.S., Sistla, A.P.: On model-checking for fragments of μ-calculus. In: CAV, pp. 385–396 (1993)
3. de Alfaro, L., Henzinger, T.A., Majumdar, R.: From verification to control: Dynamic programs for omega-regular objectives. In: Proc. LICS, June 2001, pp. 279–290. IEEE Computer Society Press, Los Alamitos (2001)
4. Alur, R., Henzinger, T.A., Kupferman, O.: Alternating-time temporal logic. Journal of the ACM 49(5), 672–713 (2002)

5. Wilke, T.: Alternating tree automata, parity games, and modal μ-calculus. Bull. Soc. Math. Belg. 8(2) (2001)
6. Kupferman, O., Vardi, M.Y.: Module checking revisited. In: Grumberg, O. (ed.) CAV 1997. LNCS, vol. 1254, pp. 36–47. Springer, Heidelberg (1997)
7. Vardi, M.Y.: Reasoning about the past with two-way automata. In: Larsen, K.G., Skyum, S., Winskel, G. (eds.) ICALP 1998. LNCS, vol. 1443, pp. 628–641. Springer, Heidelberg (1998)
8. Schewe, S., Finkbeiner, B.: The alternating-time μ-calculus and automata over concurrent game structures. In: Ésik, Z. (ed.) CSL 2006. LNCS, vol. 4207, pp. 591–605. Springer, Heidelberg (2006)
9. Piterman, N.: From nondeterministic Büchi and Streett automata to deterministic parity automata. In: Proc. LICS, pp. 255–264. IEEE Computer Society Press, Los Alamitos (2006)
10. Schewe, S., FinkbUeiner, B.: Synthesis of asynchronous systems. In: LOPSTR 2006, pp. 127–142. Springer, Heidelberg (2006)
11. McNaughton, R.: Infinite games played on finite graphs. Ann. Pure Appl. Logic 65(2), 149–184 (1993)
12. Emerson, E.A., Lei, C.: Efcient model checking in fragments of the propositional μ-calculus. In: Proc. LICS, pp. 267–278. IEEE Computer Society Press, Los Alamitos (1986)
13. Ludwig, W.: A subexponential randomized algorithm for the simple stochastic game problem. Inf. Comput. 117(1), 151–155 (1995)
14. Puri, A.: Theory of hybrid systems and discrete event systems. PhD thesis, Computer Science Department, University of California, Berkeley (1995)
15. Zwick, U., Paterson, M.S.: The complexity of mean payoff games on graphs. Theoretical Computer Science 158(1–2), 343–359 (1996)
16. Browne, A., Clarke, E.M., Jha, S., Long, D.E., Marrero, W.: An improved algorithm for the evaluation of fixpoint expressions. Theoretical Computer Science 178(1–2), 237–255 (1997)
17. Zielonka, W.: Infinite games on finitely coloured graphs with applications to automata on infinite trees. Theor. Comput. Sci. 200(1-2), 135–183 (1998)
18. Jurdziński, M.: Deciding the winner in parity games is in UP ∩ co-UP. Information Processing Letters 68(3), 119–124 (1998)
19. Jurdziński, M.: Small progress measures for solving parity games. In: Reichel, H., Tison, S. (eds.) STACS 2000. LNCS, vol. 1770, pp. 290–301. Springer, Heidelberg (2000)
20. Vöge, J., Jurdziński, M.: A discrete strategy improvement algorithm for solving parity games. In: Emerson, E.A., Sistla, A.P. (eds.) CAV 2000. LNCS, vol. 1855, pp. 202–215. Springer, Heidelberg (2000)
21. Obdržálek, J.: Fast mu-calculus model checking when tree-width is bounded. In: Hunt Jr., W.A., Somenzi, F. (eds.) CAV 2003. LNCS, vol. 2725, pp. 80–92. Springer, Heidelberg (2003)
22. Lange, M.: Solving parity games by a reduction to SAT. In: Majumdar, R., Jurdziski, M. (eds.) Proc. Int. Workshop on Games in Design and Verification (2005)
23. Berwanger, D., Dawar, A., Hunter, P., Kreutzer, S.: Dag-width and parity games. In: Durand, B., Thomas, W. (eds.) STACS 2006. LNCS, vol. 3884, pp. 436–524. Springer, Heidelberg (2006)
24. Jurdziński, M., Paterson, M., Zwick, U.: A deterministic subexponential algorithm for solving parity games. In: Proc. SODA, ACM/SIAM, pp. 117–123 (2006)
25. Björklund, H., Vorobyov, S.: A combinatorial strongly subexponential strategy improvement algorithm for mean payoff games. Discrete Appl. Math. 155(2), 210–229 (2007)

Efficient and Expressive Tree Filters

Michael Benedikt[1] and Alan Jeffrey[2]

[1] Computing Laboratory, Oxford University
[2] Bell Labs, Alcatel-Lucent

Abstract. We investigate streaming evaluation of filters on XML documents, evaluated both at the root node and at an arbitrary node. Motivated by applications in protocol processing, we are interested in algorithms that make one pass over the input, using space that is independent of the data and polynomial in the filter. We deal with a logic equivalent to the XPath language, and also an extension with an Until operator. We introduce restricted sublanguages based on looking only at "reversed" axes, and show that these allow polynomial space streaming implementations. We further show that these fragments are expressively complete. Our results make use of techniques developed for the study of Linear Temporal Logic, applied to XML filtering.

1 Introduction

The eXtensible Markup Language (XML) is a common standard for data exchange on the Web. In a common scenario an application is required to manipulate an incoming XML document online, processing it as a stream of tags, using limited memory. This can occur in XML-based subscription services: an application registers for one or more XML feeds, and filters from within these the XML data that is of interest. A very different sort of application is in monitoring XML-based protocols; here the goal is to determine of the data as a whole (that is, the protocol message) whether it should be forwarded for further processing. What both scenarios have in common is the need for a flexible filtering description mechanism and a stream processor that can enforce these filter descriptions.

In terms of the description mechanism, the typical assumption is that filtering will be specified in some variant of the XPath language [25]. In this work we will look at *filters* defined in several languages:

- HML, a logic equivalent in expressiveness to *Navigational XPath* – the fragment of XPath in which only the tag structure of the document is utilized, ignoring the attribute and PCDATA content.
- +HML, a fragment of HML which is equivalent in expressiveness to Positive XPath, the subset of Navigational XPath without negation.
- $\mathcal{X}_{until}$, an extension of HML equivalent in expressiveness to Marx's [17,18] Conditional XPath, given by adding strong until to Navigational XPath.

V. Arvind and S. Prasad (Eds.): FSTTCS 2007, LNCS 4855, pp. 461–472, 2007.
© Springer-Verlag Berlin Heidelberg 2007

Filters select a subset of the nodes in an XML document, for example, the Positive XPath filters:

$$F_1 = [\text{child::}A] \quad F_2 = [\text{preceding-sibling::}A] \quad F_3 = [\text{following-sibling::}A]$$

select all nodes that have an A element as a child, left- or right-sibling.

In the context of streaming, we must consider what it means to evaluate a filter. We will consider both *root semantics* and *nodeset semantics*. In root semantics, the stream processor takes in a streamed XML document and at the close of the stream returns true or false, depending on whether or not the filter holds at the root. For example, on the stream given as:

$$S_1 = \langle B \rangle \langle C \rangle \langle /C \rangle \langle A \rangle \langle /A \rangle \langle D \rangle \langle /D \rangle \langle /B \rangle$$

the processor should return true for F_1 and false for F_2 and F_3.

In the case of a query returning a set of nodes, we will consider the *begin-tag marking problem* that produces an output stream marking the begin tags of the selected nodes. For example, the output for F_1, F_2, F_3 on input S_1 is:

$$F_1 : \langle B^* \rangle \langle C \rangle \langle /C \rangle \langle A \rangle \langle /A \rangle \langle D \rangle \langle /D \rangle \langle /B \rangle$$
$$F_2 : \langle B \rangle \langle C \rangle \langle /C \rangle \langle A \rangle \langle /A \rangle \langle D^* \rangle \langle /D \rangle \langle /B \rangle$$
$$F_3 : \langle B \rangle \langle C^* \rangle \langle /C \rangle \langle A \rangle \langle /A \rangle \langle D \rangle \langle /D \rangle \langle /B \rangle$$

We will also consider the corresponding *end-tag marking problem*, with output:

$$F_1 : \langle B \rangle \langle C \rangle \langle /C \rangle \langle A \rangle \langle /A \rangle \langle D \rangle \langle /D \rangle \langle /B^* \rangle$$
$$F_2 : \langle B \rangle \langle C \rangle \langle /C \rangle \langle A \rangle \langle /A \rangle \langle D \rangle \langle /D^* \rangle \langle /B \rangle$$
$$F_3 : \langle B \rangle \langle C \rangle \langle /C^* \rangle \langle A \rangle \langle /A \rangle \langle D \rangle \langle /D \rangle \langle /B \rangle$$

Moreover, we are interested in *zero-lookahead* algorithms for the marking problem, that generate one token of output upon reading each token of input. Note that there is no zero-lookahead algorithm for begin-tag marking of F_1 or F_3:

$$F_1 : \langle B^? \rangle \langle C \rangle \langle /C \rangle \cdots$$
$$F_3 : \langle B \rangle \langle C^? \rangle \langle /C \rangle \cdots$$

and no zero-lookahead algorithm for end-tag marking of F_3:

$$F_3 : \langle B \rangle \langle C \rangle \langle /C^? \rangle \cdots$$

We shall call filters for which zero-lookahead begin-tag or end-tag markings exist *begin-tag determined* or *end-tag determined*. From a begin-tag marking algorithm, it is trivial to produce an algorithm to output the selected nodeset in constant additional space, as no buffering is required. From an end-tag marking algorithm, the space required for buffering is proportional to the size of the largest node to be output – in many applications this will be significantly smaller than the whole input document.

There has been a significant amount of work on these problems within the database community. The most common approach has been to compile expressions into machines that use an *unbounded amount of memory* to keep track of state. They may, for example, compile an expression into a deterministic push-down automaton (DPDA)[1]. The use of unbounded memory results from the fact that the set of streams that satisfy a given Navigational XPath expression, even at a fixed node, is not necessarily regular [24].

In this work we are interested in algorithms that can be done in *space and per-token time that is bounded independently of the input tree, and depending only polynomially on the expression and alphabet.* By the results above, the requirement that the space be independent of the input already requires some restriction on target trees. One key observation is that many applications that require stream-processing are concerned with content that is "data-oriented" [8]; in particular, it is common that the input data is un-nested, in the sense that an element does not occur nested inside another element with the same tag. We will restrict our attention to un-nested documents; equivalently, we assume that our trees satisfy a "non-recursive DTD" – one in which the dependency relation between tags is acyclic.

We will show that over un-nested trees $\mathcal{X}_{until}$ filters can be compiled into bounded-space machines under the root semantics, but that the bound may be exponential in the size of the formula. We will present a subset of the $\mathcal{X}_{until}$ filters that can be implemented in space usage polynomial in the formula and alphabet. We will also show that this subset is *expressively complete* for $\mathcal{X}_{until}$ over un-nested trees. We will get similar results for +HML, and for determined filters under nodeset semantics.

Our approach for getting space usage polynomial in the formula and alphabet will be to compile filters into polynomial-sized *finite state transducer networks.* This is a refinement of the approach of Olteanu [21] and Peng and Chawathe [22], where XPath expressions are compiled into a *pushdown transducer network* – consisting of pushdown automata that can output signals to other automata. A more detailed discussion of related work can be found in Section 5.

In summary, our contributions are:

- For the root semantics over un-nested trees, we identify fragments of +HML and $\mathcal{X}_{until}$ that are expressively complete, and have streaming implementations using time and space polynomial in the formula and alphabet.
- For the nodeset semantics over un-nested trees, we identify fragments of +HML and $\mathcal{X}_{until}$ that can express all begin-tag (resp. end-tag) determined queries, and have streaming begin-tag (resp. end-tag) marking implementations using both time and space polynomial in the formula and alphabet.

These results are proved for +HML and $\mathcal{X}_{until}$, but are applicable to Positive XPath and Conditional XPath.

Organization. Section 2 gives preliminaries and definitions. Sections 3 and 4 investigate streaming algorithms for boolean and nodeset queries respectively. All proofs are in the full paper [5].

---

[1] For simple subsets of XPath, these DPDAs can be represented using a finite state machine [12,1,7]. However, a stack is still needed at runtime to store the path from the root to the current node being processed.

2 Notation

2.1 Trees

XML documents consist of ordered labeled trees with additional data attached at nodes, either as attributes or as leaf content ('PCDATA'). In this work we will be considering filtering specifications that only deal with the ordered tree structure, so we can use a simple data model of an ordered tree:

Definition 1 (Ordered tree). *An ordered tree T with labels Σ is a finite set N together with a function $\lambda \in N \to \Sigma$ and two partial orders $\xrightarrow{\text{down}^*}$, $\xrightarrow{\text{right}^*} \subseteq (N \times N)$ such that:*

- $\xrightarrow{\text{right}}$, $\xrightarrow{\text{left}}$ *and* $\xrightarrow{\text{up}}$ *are partial functions* $N \to N$,
- $\xrightarrow{\text{down}} = (\xrightarrow{\text{down}} \xrightarrow{\text{right}^*}) = (\xrightarrow{\text{down}} \xrightarrow{\text{left}^*})$, *and*
- $(\xrightarrow{\text{up}^*} \xrightarrow{\text{down}^*}) = (N \times N)$,

where we write (for $\pi \in \{\text{left}, \text{right}, \text{up}, \text{down}\}$):

- $\xrightarrow{\text{up}}$ *for* $\xrightarrow{\text{down}^{-1}}$ *and* $\xrightarrow{\text{left}}$ *for* $\xrightarrow{\text{right}^{-1}}$,
- $n \xrightarrow{\pi^+} m$ *whenever* $n \xrightarrow{\pi^*} m$ *and* $n \neq m$, *and*
- $n \xrightarrow{\pi} m$ *whenever* $n \xrightarrow{\pi^+} m$ *but not* $n \xrightarrow{\pi^+} \xrightarrow{\pi^+} m$.

Note that any ordered tree has a root node n_0.

In many applications that require stream processing, the underlying documents do not have repeated instances of a tag within any downward path. This is the case, for example, of XML documents validated against a non-recursive DTD. *Most of the results of this paper will hold only for these "un-nested trees".*

Definition 2 (Un-nested tree). *An ordered tree is un-nested whenever $n \xrightarrow{\text{down}^+} m$ implies $\lambda(n) \neq \lambda(m)$.*

Stream processing will deal with the standard serialization of XML documents, as a sequence of begin and end tags:

Definition 3 (Streamed tree). *Define the alphabet of a streamed tree with labels Σ as:*

$$\text{Tags}(\Sigma) = \{\langle A \rangle, \langle /A \rangle \mid A \in \Sigma\}$$

For any ordered tree T with node labels Σ, define $\text{stream}(T) \in (\text{Tags}(\Sigma))^*$ as $\text{stream}(n_0)$, given by:

$$\text{stream}(n) = \langle A \rangle \, \text{stream}(n_1) \dots \text{stream}(n_k) \, \langle /A \rangle$$

where $\forall i \leq k . n \xrightarrow{\text{down}} n_i$ and $\xleftarrow{\text{left}}{} n_1 \xrightarrow{\text{right}} \dots \xrightarrow{\text{right}} n_k \xrightarrow{\text{right}}{}$ and $\lambda(n) = A$.

2.2   Filtering Specifications

In this paper, we will consider specifications for nodeset queries using Marx's [17] $\mathcal{X}_{until}$ logic, which is a modal logic with a strong until operation. It extends Linear Time Temporal Logic (LTL, [9]) by allowing more than one partial order (LTL considers only one order of time). By restricting uses of until, we recover Hennessy-Milner Logic (HML) [14] as a special case.

Definition 4 ($\mathcal{X}_{until}$, HML and +HML). *Let $\mathcal{X}_{until}$ over labels Σ be defined:*

$$\phi, \psi, \chi ::= A \mid \top \mid \bot \mid \neg\phi \mid \phi \wedge \psi \mid \phi \vee \psi \mid \pi(\phi, \psi)$$

where π ranges over $\{\mathsf{left}, \mathsf{right}, \mathsf{up}, \mathsf{down}\}$, and A ranges over Σ. The satisfaction relation for $\mathcal{X}_{until}$ is defined with the usual logical operations, together with:

- $T, n \vDash A$ *whenever* $\lambda(n) = A$, *and*
- $T, n \vDash \pi(\phi, \psi)$ *whenever there exists an ℓ such that $n \xrightarrow{\pi^+} \ell$ and $T, \ell \vDash \phi$ and for all m such that $n \xrightarrow{\pi^+} m \xrightarrow{\pi^+} \ell$ it holds that $T, m \vDash \psi$.*

We will write $\langle\pi\rangle\phi$ for $\pi(\phi, \bot)$ and $\langle\pi^+\rangle\phi$ for $\pi(\phi, \top)$. Let HML be the fragment of $\mathcal{X}_{until}$ where all modalities are of the form $\langle\pi\rangle\phi$ or $\langle\pi^+\rangle\phi$. Let +HML be the negation-free fragment of HML.

Marx [18] has shown that Conditional XPath filters (an extension of Navigational XPath with until) are equal in expressive power to $\mathcal{X}_{until}$ formulae, and that these both are equal in expressive power to first-order logic over the axis relations. Navigational XPath filters [4] are equal in expressive power to HML formulae. Positive XPath filters (negation-free Navigational XPath filters) are equal in expressive power to +HML formulae. An easy extension of Benedikt *et al.*'s argument [4] shows that +HML has the same expressive power as positive existential first-order logic over the axis relations.

We will now proceed to show results about fragments of $\mathcal{X}_{until}$, knowing that they can be applied to the appropriate fragment of Conditional XPath.

2.3   The Streaming Problem

A logical formula ϕ (in, for example, $\mathcal{X}_{until}$) defines several streaming problems.

The *root filtering problem* is to determine, given T, whether or not ϕ holds at the root. Gottlob and Koch [11] have shown that this can be done in time linear in the combined sizes of ϕ and T, if one allows the tree T to be stored in memory. In contrast, we want an algorithm that has limited access to T.

A *root stream processor* is a Turing machine TM with one input tape and one working tape, such that TM can only move forward on its input tape. Such a TM is a *root streaming implementation* of ϕ if TM accepts on input stream(T) iff T satisfies ϕ at the root. The *runtime space usage* of such a TM on an input s is the number of workspace tape elements used. The *total space usage* is the runtime space usage plus the size of the TM. The *per-token time usage* of such a TM on an input s is the number of steps taken, divided by $|s|$.

In Section 3, we will show that every formula has a root streaming implementation with total space and per-token time that is independent of the tree. Implementations which use polynomial total space and per-token time do not exist for every formula, but we will find a fragment of $\mathcal{X}_{\text{until}}$ which does support polynomial implementation, and moreover with no loss of expressive power.

We now turn to nodeset queries given by filters – that is to filters not restricted to the root node. In main-memory processing, the entire set of subtrees of nodes satisfying the filter would be returned. In a streaming setting, we may be interested in an output stream that includes indicators of which nodes are in the solution nodeset. We will consider adding these indicators to either the begin tags or to the end tags.

Definition 5 (Streamed document tree with selected begin tags). *For any ordered tree T with node labels Σ, and any formula ϕ, define $\text{bstream}(T, \phi) \in (\text{Tags}(\Sigma) \times 2)^*$ as $\text{bstream}(n_0, \phi)$, given by:*

$$\text{bstream}(n, \phi) = (\langle A \rangle, b) \, \text{bstream}(n_1, \phi) \ldots \text{bstream}(n_k, \phi) \, (\langle /A \rangle, \bot)$$

where $\forall i \leq k \, . \, n \xrightarrow{\text{down}} n_i$ and $\xleftarrow{\text{left}} n_1 \xrightarrow{\text{right}} \cdots \xrightarrow{\text{right}} n_k \xrightarrow{\text{right}}$ and $\lambda(n) = A$ and $T, n \vDash \phi \leftrightarrow b$ (where $2 = \{\top, \bot\}$, the boolean constants).

The *begin-tag filtering problem* is, given as input ϕ and $\text{stream}(T)$, to output $\text{bstream}(T, \phi)$. We can similarly define the *end-tag filtering problem*, defining the stream $\text{estream}(T, \phi)$ analogously to bstream above, but with booleans annotating end-tags.

A *nodeset stream processor* is a Turing machine TM with one read-only input tape, one working tape, and one write-only output tape such that TM can only move forward on its input tape, and only add symbols to the end of its output tape. Such a processor has *zero-lookahead* if it produces exactly one output symbol whenever it moves its head on the input tape. Such a processor TM is a *begin-tag streaming implementation* of ϕ if TM outputs $\text{bstream}(T, \phi)$. We can similarly talk about an *end-tag streaming implementation*. The notions of space and per-token time efficiency in a processor are as before.

In Section 4, we will show that not every formula has a begin-tag or end-tag streaming implementation with total space and per-token time that is independent of the tree. Again, we will find a fragment of $\mathcal{X}_{\text{until}}$ which does admit efficient implementations, with no loss of expressive power.

3   Filtering of Boolean Queries

We first show that every formula has a root streaming implementation with total space and per-token time independent of the input tree.

Proposition 1. *For every $\mathcal{X}_{\text{until}}$ formula ϕ over labels Σ there is a number k and a root streaming implementation $TM_{\phi, \Sigma}$ over un-nested ordered trees with labels Σ using at most k total space and per-token time.*

Even for simple queries, we may not be able to get space-efficient implementations. Consider the formulae ϕ_n over labels $\{A, B, C, T_1, F_1, \ldots, T_n, F_n\}$ defined:

$$\phi_n = \langle \mathsf{down} \rangle (A \wedge \psi_1 \wedge \cdots \wedge \psi_n)$$
$$\psi_i = (\langle \mathsf{down} \rangle T_i \wedge \langle \mathsf{right}^+ \rangle (B \wedge \langle \mathsf{down} \rangle T_i))$$
$$\vee (\langle \mathsf{down} \rangle F_i \wedge \langle \mathsf{right}^+ \rangle (B \wedge \langle \mathsf{down} \rangle F_i))$$

evaluated over trees with streaming representations of the form:

$$\langle C \rangle \langle A \rangle s_1 \langle /A \rangle \cdots \langle A \rangle s_k \langle /A \rangle \langle B \rangle s \langle /B \rangle \langle /C \rangle$$
$$\text{where } s, s_1, \ldots, s_k \in \{\langle T_1/ \rangle, \langle F_1/ \rangle\} \times \cdots \times \{\langle T_n/ \rangle, \langle F_n/ \rangle\}$$

It is clear that such a tree satisfies ϕ_n precisely when $s \in \{s_1, \ldots, s_k\}$, and there are 2^{2^n} such sets, and so there is no polynomial space implementation of +HML:

Proposition 2. *There is no subexponential F such that every +HML formula ϕ over labels Σ has a root streaming implementation $TM_{\phi,\Sigma}$ over un-nested ordered trees with labels Σ using at most $F(|\phi|, |\Sigma|)$ total space.*

We must thus look for a sublanguage of $\mathcal{X}_{\mathrm{until}}$ that has efficient implementations.

The notion of a subformula of a formula is as usual. A top-level subformula is one which does not occur inside a subformula of the form $\pi(\phi, \psi)$.

Definition 6 (Backward $\mathcal{X}_{\mathrm{until}}$). *Backward $\mathcal{X}_{\mathrm{until}}$ is the fragment of $\mathcal{X}_{\mathrm{until}}$ in which:*

- *all occurrences of* up *are of the form* $\mathsf{up}(\phi, \psi)$, *where ϕ and ψ have no top-level occurrences of* down, *and*
- *all occurrences of* right *are of the form* $\mathsf{down}(\phi \wedge \neg \langle \mathsf{right} \rangle \top, \psi)$.

Note that the restriction on right disallows examples such as those used in the proof of Proposition 2, and that the restriction on up bans the similar formula where $\langle \mathsf{right}^+ \rangle$ is replaced by $\langle \mathsf{up} \rangle \langle \mathsf{down} \rangle$. Also note that we cannot completely ban right, as there is no right-free backward equivalent of $\langle \mathsf{down} \rangle (A \wedge \neg \langle \mathsf{right} \rangle \top)$ ("my last child is an A"). Our first main result is:

Theorem 1. *There is a polynomial P such that every backward $\mathcal{X}_{\mathrm{until}}$ formula ϕ over labels Σ has a root streaming implementation $TM_{\phi,\Sigma}$ over un-nested ordered trees with labels Σ using at most $P(|\phi|, |\Sigma|)$ total space and per-token time. Furthermore, one can produce $TM_{\phi,\Sigma}$ from ϕ and Σ in polynomial time.*

The construction of $TM_{\phi,\Sigma}$ is given by building an appropriate *synchronous transducer network*, an acyclic collection of synchronous transducers [6] where the output of one transducer is allowed as input to another. Transducers whose input-output relation is a function are called *sequential*, and networks built from sequential transducers generate deterministic automata, so can be executed in polynomial space and per-token time.

The construction makes use of *named* $\mathcal{X}_{\mathrm{until}}$ formulae, which require every modality to specify the label of one of the nodes involved (for down and up, the parent node is named, and for left and right, the parent of the context node is).

Definition 7 (Named $\mathcal{X}_{until}$). *Named $\mathcal{X}_{until}$ is the fragment of $\mathcal{X}_{until}$ in which:*

- *all occurrences of* down *are of the form* $A \wedge$ down(ϕ, ψ)*, where* $A \in \Sigma$
- *all occurrences of* up *are of the form* up$(A \wedge \phi, \psi)$*,*
- *all occurrences of* left *are of the form* $\langle$up$\rangle A \wedge$ left(ϕ, ψ)*, and*
- *all occurrences of* right *are of the form* $\langle$up$\rangle A \wedge$ right(ϕ, ψ)*.*

Theorem 2. *Every $\mathcal{X}_{until}$ formula ϕ over labels Σ has an implementation $TN_{\phi,\Sigma}$ as a network of $O(|\phi| \times |\Sigma|)$ synchronous transducers, each of which has $O(|\Sigma|)$ states. If ϕ is in named $\mathcal{X}_{until}$, then $TN_{\phi,\Sigma}$ contains $O(|\phi|)$ transducers. If ϕ is in backward $\mathcal{X}_{until}$, then $TN_{\phi,\Sigma}$ is sequential. Furthermore, $TN_{\phi,\Sigma}$ can be constructed in polynomial time.*

What do we give up from staying within backward $\mathcal{X}_{until}$? The next result shows that, in terms of expressiveness over un-nested trees, we lose nothing, and in fact we can be even more restrictive, and only require downward formulae:

Definition 8 (Downward $\mathcal{X}_{until}$). *Downward $\mathcal{X}_{until}$ is the fragment of $\mathcal{X}_{until}$ in which:*

- *there are no occurrences of* up*, and*
- *there are no top-level occurrences of* left *or* right*.*

Theorem 3. *Every $\mathcal{X}_{until}$ formula ϕ has a backward downward $\mathcal{X}_{until}$ formula ψ which agrees with ϕ on the root node of any un-nested ordered tree.*

The proof makes use of an analog of Marx's variant [17] of Gabbay's Separation Theorem [10] for ordered trees, showing that $\mathcal{X}_{until}$ formulas can be rewritten into "strict backward", "strict forward", and "backward downward" formulae. For formulae evaluated at the root node, we can then eliminate the strict backward and forward components. A similar completeness result holds within positive HML, but without any restriction on nesting:

Theorem 4. *For every +HML formula ϕ there is a backward downward +HML formula ψ which agrees with ϕ on the root node of any ordered tree.*

This result is proven using a simpler argument, a variant of that used in [20] and Theorem 5.1 of [4]. We translate +HML queries to logical formulas, and then show that these formulas can be normalized to be of a special form. This normal form is a variant of the "tree pattern queries" of [4]. Given a normalized formula, we can apply root-equivalence, end-equivalence, or begin-equivalence to the normalized formula, arriving at a logical formula in which all the bound variables are restricted to lie in a certain relation to the free variable. Finally, we translate the syntactic restrictions back into +HML, where they produce a formula that is backward and downward. It is interesting that the analogous completeness result does not hold for HML (or for Navigational XPath).

Theorem 5. *The HML filter $\langle$down$\rangle(B \wedge \neg\langle$right$^+\rangle)A)$ is not equivalent to any filter in backward HML.*

The proof uses trees T and T' parameterized by a bound K:

$$\text{stream}(T) = \langle R \rangle (\langle A/\rangle \langle C/\rangle^{K-1} \langle B/\rangle \langle C/\rangle^{K-1})^K \langle A/\rangle \langle C/\rangle^{K-1} \langle /R \rangle$$
$$\text{stream}(T') = \langle R \rangle (\langle A/\rangle \langle C/\rangle^{K-1} \langle B/\rangle \langle C/\rangle^{K-1})^K \langle /R \rangle$$

Clearly the formula $\langle \text{down} \rangle (B \wedge \neg \langle \text{right}^+ \rangle A)$ is false at the root of T and true at the root of T'. Using a bisimulation argument, we can show that no backward formula with size bounded by K can distinguish T from T'.

4   Filtering of Nodeset Queries

We now turn to nodeset queries, and begin with a negative result. Even without requiring zero-lookahead, it is not always possible to implement filters (for example $\langle \text{right}^+ \rangle A$) in space independent of the tree.

Proposition 3. *There is a +HML formula ϕ over labels Σ such that for no k is there a begin-tag or end-tag streaming implementation TM that uses at most k total space over un-nested ordered trees with labels Σ.*

We shall call the formulae which have zero-lookahead end-tag streaming implementations "end-tag determined", and similarly for "begin-tag determined".

Definition 9 (Determined formulae). *For any tree T with node $n \in T$, the subtrees $\text{btree}(T, n)$ and $\text{etree}(T, n)$ are such that:*

$$n' \in \text{btree}(T, n) \quad \text{whenever} \quad n \xrightarrow{\text{up}^*} n' \text{ or } n \xrightarrow{\text{up}^*} \xrightarrow{\text{left}^+} \xrightarrow{\text{down}^*} n' \text{ in } T$$

$$n' \in \text{etree}(T, n) \quad \text{whenever} \quad n' \in \text{btree}(T, n) \text{ or } n \xrightarrow{\text{down}^*} n' \text{ in } T$$

A formula ϕ is end-tag determined whenever, for all $n \in T$ and $n' \in T'$ with $\text{etree}(T, n)$ isomorphic to $\text{etree}(T', n')$, we have $T, n \vDash \phi$ precisely when $T', n' \vDash \phi$. The begin-tag determined formulae are defined similarly.

It is easy to see that a filter has a zero-lookahead end-tag (resp. begin-tag) streaming implementation precisely when it is end-tag (resp. begin-tag) determined. It is also easy to see that backward $\mathcal{X}_{\text{until}}$ formulae are end-tag determined, since they only look at the nodes in the end-tag preceding subtree of the input node, and that *strict backward* $\mathcal{X}_{\text{until}}$ formulae are begin-tag determined:

Definition 10 (Strict backward $\mathcal{X}_{\text{until}}$). *A formula is in strict backward $\mathcal{X}_{\text{until}}$ if it is in backward $\mathcal{X}_{\text{until}}$ and has no top-level occurrences of down.*

Our transducer network results show that backward (resp. strict backward) $\mathcal{X}_{\text{until}}$ formulae have efficient end-tag (resp. begin-tag) streaming implementations:

Theorem 6. *There is a polynomial P such that every backward (resp. strict backward) $\mathcal{X}_{\text{until}}$ formula ϕ over labels Σ has an end-tag (resp. begin-tag) streaming implementation $TM_{\phi, \Sigma}$ over un-nested ordered trees with labels Σ using at most $P(|\phi|, |\Sigma|)$ total space and per-token time. Furthermore, one can produce $TM_{\phi, \Sigma}$ from ϕ and Σ in polynomial time.*

The notion of begin-tagged and end-tagged determined turns out to be decidable: convert a formula into a deterministic automaton with no sink states, then check whether any state has transitions on both marked and unmarked variants of the same tag. However, checking that a formula is determined cannot be done efficiently; it can be shown, by reduction to the satisfiability problem for XPath [3], that the problem is PSPACE-hard. We now show that working within backward $\mathcal{X}_{\text{until}}$ does not restrict our ability to express determined queries, and in fact we can be even more restrictive, requiring only *oscillation-free* formulae:

Definition 11 (Oscillation-free $\mathcal{X}_{\text{until}}$). *Oscillation-free $\mathcal{X}_{\text{until}}$ is the fragment of $\mathcal{X}_{\text{until}}$ in which all occurrences of* down *contain no occurrences of* up.

Theorem 7. *Every end-tag (resp. begin-tag) determined $\mathcal{X}_{\text{until}}$ formula ϕ has a backward (resp. strict backward) oscillation-free $\mathcal{X}_{\text{until}}$ formula ψ which agrees with ϕ on any node of any un-nested ordered tree.*

The proof is similar to that of Theorem 3. For positive HML, we can again get a stronger completeness result:

Theorem 8. *Every end-tag (resp. begin-tag) determined +HML formula ϕ has an backward (resp. strict backward) oscillation-free +HML formula ψ which agrees with ϕ on any node of any ordered tree.*

This result also uses a rewriting argument, analogous to those of Benedikt et al. [4] or Olteanu [20]. The analogous completeness results do not hold for HML (for example, it is not true that end-tag determined HML formulas can be rewritten into backward HML) – the argument is along the lines of Theorem 5.

5   Related Work

Much of the preceding work deals with XPath *expressions* rather than filters; expressions are functions that take a node and return a nodeset: for example descendant::A returns all A-tagged descendants of a given node. It is known from Marx [19] that the expressiveness of Navigational XPath filters is the same as that of Navigational XPath expressions evaluated at the root node. This distinction between filters and expressions is what accounts for the emphasis on reverse axes in our work, versus forward axes in the work of Olteanu [20].

As mentioned above, work on XPath filtering generally assumes that documents may have nested tags, and thus looks for streaming models that require an unbounded stack. Bar-Yossef et al. [2] and Grohe et al. [13] prove lower-bounds on the memory usage in streaming algorithms; for example Grohe et al. show that any streaming algorithm for XPath on general XML documents requires space at least proportional to the tree depth.

In contrast, there has been work on constant-space evaluation of constraints expressed by DTDs and XML Schemas. Segoufin and Vianu [24] investigate which DTDs can be validated in constant space on streams, and observes that a DTD can be validated in constant space if all trees that satisfy it are un-nested.

Begin-tag and end-tag determined XPath filters have not previously been investigated, although they have been studied in the context of XML Schemas by Martens et al. [16] and Madhusadan et al. [15].

The two main components of our work: transducer networks and rewriting, both appear in the work of Olteanu. His use of rewriting [20] is to eliminate reverse axes within an XPath-like language over general trees. Our Theorem 4 is thus a variant of his result, and in Theorem 3 we show that this phenomena extends to the much richer language $\mathcal{X}_{\text{until}}$, provided that we restrict to un-nested trees. Our Theorem 5 shows that this elimination cannot be done within full Navigational XPath, even over un-nested trees. Although this appears to contradict Corollary 5.2 of [20], the term "XPath" in that corollary is used to refer to a language LGQ, which is closer in expressiveness to Positive XPath rather than XPath. Our use of transducer networks extends Olteanu's work in [21], which works over general XML documents, and hence the networks are DPDAs rather than DFAs. The networks are used for the forward fragment of positive XPath. Our results show that the construction extends to the much more expressive language $\mathcal{X}_{\text{until}}$, and that it provides a finite state transducer network when restricted to un-nested trees.

Our rewriting of $\mathcal{X}_{\text{until}}$ filters makes use of a separation result very similar to Theorem 8 of Marx [17]. Marx's result is over general trees, and does not separate filters that look "to the left and up" from those that look "to the right and up" – such a separation is needed for our result on un-nested trees, but does not hold in general. Unfortunately, an error has been found in the proof of Theorem 8 in [17] – Lemma 10 of that paper includes a distributivity property $(\mathsf{down}(\phi, \psi \wedge \chi) = \mathsf{down}(\phi, \psi) \wedge \mathsf{down}(\phi, \chi))$ which is only true when $\xrightarrow{\text{down}}$ is deterministic. As a result, his induction (in an un-numbered "final step" at the end of Section 4) fails. Semantic separation has been shown, using Marx's expressive completeness result for Conditional XPath [18]. But this proof does not imply syntactic separation for $\mathcal{X}_{\text{until}}$.

Our completeness results for boolean queries can be seen as extensions to the ordered tree setting of the well-known fact that LTL with only future operators has the same expressiveness as LTL with both past and future, if one considers only the initial node of a string. Transducer networks have been utilized several times in the verification literature (e.g. Pnueli and Zaks [23]), but their use in conjunction with reverse-direction fragments is, to our knowledge, new.

References

1. Altinel, M., Franklin, M.: Efficient filtering of XML documents for selective dissemination of information. In: Proc. 26th International Conference on Very Large Data Bases (VLDB), pp. 53–64 (2000)
2. Bar-Yossef, Z., Fontoura, M., Josifovski, V.: On the memory requirements of XPath evaluation over XML streams. In: Proc. 23rd ACM SIGACT-SIGMOD-SIGART Symposium on Principles of Database Systems (PODS), pp. 177–188. ACM Press, New York (2004)
3. Benedikt, M., Fan, W., Geerts, F.: XPath satisfiability in the presence of DTDs. In: Proc. 24th ACM SIGACT-SIGMOD-SIGART Symposium on Principles of Database Systems (PODS), ACM Press, New York (2005)
4. Benedikt, M., Fan, W., Kuper, G.: Structural properties of XPath fragments. Theoretical Computer Science 336(1), 3–31 (2005)

5. Benedikt, M., Jeffrey, A.S.A.: Efficient and expressive tree filters. Full version available from the authors web pages (2007)
6. Besterel, J., Perrin, D.: Algorithms on words. In: Lothaire, M. (ed.) Applied Combinatorics on Words, ch. 1, Cambridge University Press, Cambridge (2005)
7. Chan, C.Y., Felber, P., Garofalakis, M.N., Rastogi, R.: Efficient filtering of XML documents with XPath expressions. In: Proc. 18th IEEE International Conference on Data Engineering (ICDE), IEEE Computer Society Press, Los Alamitos (2002)
8. Choi, B.: What are real DTDs like. In: Proc. Fifth International Workshop on the Web and Databases (WebDB) (2002)
9. Clarke, E.M., Grumberg, O., Peled, D.: Model Checking. MIT Press, Cambridge (2000)
10. Gabbay, D.: Expressive functional completeness in tense logic. In: Mönnich, U. (ed.) Aspects of Philosophical Logic, pp. 67–89 (1981)
11. Gottlob, G., Koch, C.: Monadic datalog and the expressive power of web information extraction languages. Journal of the ACM 51(1), 74–113 (2004)
12. Green, T.J., Miklau, G., Onizuka, M., Suciu, D.: Processing XML streams with deterministic automata. In: Calvanese, D., Lenzerini, M., Motwani, R. (eds.) ICDT 2003. LNCS, vol. 2572, Springer, Heidelberg (2002)
13. Grohe, M., Koch, C., Schweikardt, N.: Tight lower bounds for query processing on streaming and external memory data. In: Caires, L., Italiano, G.F., Monteiro, L., Palamidessi, C., Yung, M. (eds.) ICALP 2005. LNCS, vol. 3580, Springer, Heidelberg (2005)
14. Hennessy, M., Milner, R.: Algebraic laws for nondeterminism and concurrency. Journal of the ACM 32, 137–161 (1985)
15. Kumar, V., Madhusadan, P., Viswanathan, M.: Visibly pushdown automata for streaming XML. In: WWW (2007)
16. Martens, W., Neven, F., Schwentick, T.: Which XML schemas admit 1-pass preorder traversal. In: Eiter, T., Libkin, L. (eds.) ICDT 2005. LNCS, vol. 3363, Springer, Heidelberg (2004)
17. Marx, M.: Conditional XPath, the first order complete XPath dialect. In: Proc. 23rd ACM SIGACT-SIGMOD-SIGART Symposium on Principles of Database Systems (PODS), pp. 13–22. ACM Press, New York (2004)
18. Marx, M.: Conditional XPath. ACM Transactions on Database Systems, 929–959 (2005)
19. Marx, M.: First order paths in ordered trees. In: Eiter, T., Libkin, L. (eds.) ICDT 2005. LNCS, vol. 3363, Springer, Heidelberg (2004)
20. Olteanu, D.: Forward node-selecting queries over trees. ACM TODS (2007)
21. Olteanu, D.: Streamed and progressive evaluation of XPath. IEEE Transactions on Knowledge and Data Engineering 19(7) (July 2007)
22. Peng, F., Chawathe, S.: XPath queries on streaming data. In: Proc. 2003 ACM SIGMOD International Conference on Management of Data (SIGMOD), ACM Press, New York (2003)
23. Pnueli, A., Zaks, A.: PSL model checking and runtime verification via testers. In: Misra, J., Nipkow, T., Sekerinski, E. (eds.) FM 2006. LNCS, vol. 4085, Springer, Heidelberg (2006)
24. Segoufin, L., Vianu, V.: Validating streaming XML documents. In: Proc. 21st ACM SIGACT-SIGMOD-SIGART Symposium on Principles of Database Systems (PODS), ACM Press, New York (2002)
25. World Wide Web Consortium. XML path language (XPath) 2.0: W3C recommendation, http://www.w3.org/TR/xpath20/2007

Markov Decision Processes with Multiple Long-Run Average Objectives*

Krishnendu Chatterjee

UC Berkeley
c_krish@eecs.berkeley.edu

Abstract. We consider Markov decision processes (MDPs) with multiple long-run average objectives. Such MDPs occur in design problems where one wishes to simultaneously optimize several criteria, for example, latency and power. The possible trade-offs between the different objectives are characterized by the Pareto curve. We show that every Pareto optimal point can be ε-approximated by a memoryless strategy, for all $\varepsilon > 0$. In contrast to the single-objective case, the memoryless strategy may require randomization. We show that the Pareto curve can be approximated (a) in polynomial time in the size of the MDP for irreducible MDPs; and (b) in polynomial space in the size of the MDP for all MDPs. Additionally, we study the problem if a given value vector is realizable by any strategy, and show that it can be decided in polynomial time for irreducible MDPs and in NP for all MDPs. These results provide algorithms for design exploration in MDP models with multiple long-run average objectives.

1 Introduction

Markov decision processes (MDPs) are standard models for dynamic systems that exhibit both probabilistic and nondeterministic behaviors [11,5]. An MDP models a dynamic system that evolves through stages. In each stage, a controller chooses one of several actions (the nondeterministic choices), and the system stochastically evolves to a new state based on the current state and the chosen action. In addition, one associates a cost or reward with each transition, and the central question is to find a strategy of choosing the actions that optimizes the rewards obtained over the run of the system. The two classical ways of combing the rewards over the run of system are as follows: (a) the discounted sum of the rewards and (b) the long-run average of the rewards. In many modeling domains, however, there is no unique objective to be optimized, but multiple, potentially dependent and conflicting objectives. For example, in designing a computer system, one is interested not only in maximizing performance but also in minimizing power. Similarly, in an inventory management system, one wishes to optimize several potentially dependent costs for maintaining each kind of product, and in AI planning, one wishes to find a plan that optimizes several distinct goals. These motivate the study of MDPs with multiple objectives.

---

* This research was supported by the NSF grants CCR-0225610 and CCR-0234690.

V. Arvind and S. Prasad (Eds.): FSTTCS 2007, LNCS 4855, pp. 473–484, 2007.

We study MDPs with multiple long-run average objectives, an extension of the MDP model where there are several reward functions [7,13]. In MDPs with multiple objectives, we are interested not in a single solution that is simultaneously optimal in all objectives (which may not exist), but in a notion of "trade-offs" called the *Pareto curve*. Informally, the Pareto curve consists of the set of realizable value profiles (or dually, the strategies that realize them) that are not dominated (in every dimension) by any other value profile. Pareto optimality has been studied in co-operative game theory [9] and in multi-criterion optimization and decision making in both economics and engineering [8,14,12]. Finding *some* Pareto optimal point can be reduced to optimizing a single objective: optimize a convex combination of objectives using a set of positive weights; the optimal strategy must be Pareto optimal as well (the "weighted factor method") [7]. In design space exploration, however, we want to find not one, but *all* Pareto optimal points in order to better understand the trade-offs in the design. Unfortunately, even with just two rewards, the Pareto curve may have infinitely many points, and also contain irrational payoffs. Many previous works has focused on constructing a sampling of the Pareto curve, either by choosing a variety of weights in the weighted factor method, or by imposing a lexicographic ordering on the objectives and sequentially optimizing each objective according to the order [4,5]. Unfortunately, this does not provide any guarantee about the quality of the solutions obtained.

The study of the *approximate* version of the problem, the ε-approximate Pareto curve [10] for MDPs with multiple objectives is recent: the problem was studied for discounted sum objectives in [2] and for qualitative ω-regular objectives in [3]. Informally, the ε-approximate Pareto curve for $\varepsilon > 0$ contains a set of strategies (or dually, their payoff values) such that there is no other strategy whose value dominates the values in the Pareto curve by a factor of $1 + \varepsilon$.

Our Results. In this work we study the complexity of approximating the Pareto curve for MDPs with multiple long-run average objectives. For a long-run average objective, given an infinite sequence $\langle v_0, v_1, v_2, \ldots \rangle$ of finite reward values the payoff is $\liminf_{T \to \infty} \frac{1}{T} \sum_{t=0}^{T-1} v_t$. We summarize our results below.

1. We show that for all $\varepsilon > 0$, the value vector of a Pareto-optimal strategy can be ε-approximated by a memoryless strategy. In the case of single objective the definition of long-run average objective can be also alternatively defined as lim sup instead of lim inf, and the optimal values coincide. In contrast, in the case of multiple objectives we show that if the long-run average objectives are defined as lim sup, then the Pareto-optimal strategies cannot be ε-approximated by memoryless strategies.
2. We show that an approximate Pareto curve can be computed in polynomial time for *irreducible* MDPs [5]; and in polynomial space for general MDPs. The algorithms are obtained by reduction to multi-objective linear-programming and applying the results of [10].
3. We also study the related *realizability* decision problem: given a profile of values, is there a Pareto-optimal strategy that dominates it? We show that the realizability problem can be decided in polynomial time for irreducible MDPs and in NP for general MDPs.

Our work is closely related to the works of [2,3]. In [2] MDPs with multiple discounted reward objectives was studied. It was shown that memoryless strategies suffices for Pareto optimal strategies, and polynomial time algorithm was given to approximate the Pareto curve by reduction to multi-objective linear-programming and using the results of [10]. In [3] MDPs with multiple qualitative ω-regular objectives was studied. It was shown that the Pareto curve can be approximated in polynomial time: the algorithm first reduces the problem to MDPs with multiple reachability objectives, and then MDPs with multiple reachability objectives can be solved by multi-objective linear-programming. In our case we have the undiscounted setting as well as quantitative objectives and there are new obstacles in the proofs. For example, the notion of "discounted frequencies" used in [2] need not be well defined in the undiscounted setting. Our proof technique uses the results of [2] and a celebrated result Hardy-Littlewood to obtain the result on sufficiency of memoryless strategies for Pareto optimal strategies. Also our reduction to multi-objective linear-programming is more involved: we require several multi-objective linear-programs in the general case, it uses techniques of [3] for transient states and approaches similar to [2] for recurrent states.

2   MDPs with Multiple Long-Run Average Objectives

We denote the set of probability distributions on a set U by $\mathcal{D}(U)$.

Markov Decision Processes (MDPs). A Markov decision process (MDP) $G = (S, A, p)$ consists of a finite, non-empty set S of states and a finite, non-empty set A of actions; and a probabilistic transition function $p : S \times A \to \mathcal{D}(S)$, that given a state $s \in S$ and an action $a \in A$ gives the probability $p(s, a)(t)$ of the next state t. We denote by $\text{Dest}(s, a) = \text{Supp}(p(s, a))$ the set of possible successors of s when the action a is chosen. Given an MDP G we define the set of edges $E = \{ (s, t) \mid \exists a \in A.\ t \in \text{Dest}(s, a) \}$ and use $E(s) = \{ t \mid (s, t) \in E \}$ for the set of possible successors of s in G.

Plays and Strategies. A *play* of G is an infinite sequence $\langle s_0, s_1, \ldots \rangle$ of states such that for all $i \geq 0$, $(s_i, s_{i+1}) \in E$. A strategy σ is a recipe that specifies how to extend a play. Formally, a strategy σ is a function $\sigma : S^+ \to \mathcal{D}(A)$ that, given a finite and non-empty sequence of states representing the history of the play so far, chooses a probability distribution over the set A of actions. In general, a strategy depends on the history and uses randomization. A strategy that depends only on the current state is a *memoryless or stationary* strategy, and can be represented as a function $\sigma : S \to \mathcal{D}(A)$. A strategy that does not use randomization is a *pure* strategy, i.e., for all histories $\langle s_0, s_1, \ldots, s_k \rangle$ there exists $a \in A$ such that $\sigma(\langle s_0, s_1, \ldots, s_k \rangle)(a) = 1$. A *pure memoryless* strategy is both pure and memoryless and can be represented as a function $\sigma : S \to A$. We denote by Σ, Σ^M, Σ^P and Σ^{PM} the set of all strategies, all memoryless strategies, all pure strategies and all pure memoryless strategies, respectively.

Outcomes. Given a strategy σ and an initial state s, we denote by $\text{Outcome}(s, \sigma)$ the set of possible plays that start from s, given strategy σ, i.e.,

Outcome$(s, \sigma) = \{ \langle s_0, s_1, \ldots, s_k, \ldots \rangle \mid \forall k \geq 0. \exists a_k \in A. \sigma(\langle s_0, s_1, \ldots, s_k \rangle)(a_k) >$ $0;$ and $s_{k+1} \in \text{Dest}(s_k, a_k) \}$. Once the initial state and a strategy is chosen, the MDP is reduced to a stochastic process. We denote by X_i and θ_i random variables for the i-th state and the i-th chosen action in this stochastic process. An event is a measurable subset of Outcome(s, σ), and the probabilities of the events are uniquely defined. Given a strategy σ, an initial state s, and an event $\mathcal{A}$, we denote by $\Pr_s^\sigma(\mathcal{A})$ the probability that a path belongs to $\mathcal{A}$, when the MDP starts in state s and the strategy σ is used. For a measurable function f that maps paths to reals, we write $\mathbb{E}_s^\sigma[f]$ for the expected value of f when the MDP starts in state s and the strategy σ is used.

Rewards and Objectives. Let $r : S \times A \to \mathbb{R}$ be a reward function that associates with every state and action a real-valued reward. For a reward function r the *inf-long-run* average value is defined as follows: for a strategy σ and an initial state s we have $Val_{inf}^\sigma(r, s) = \liminf_{T \to \infty} \frac{1}{T} \sum_{t=0}^{T-1} \mathbb{E}_s^\sigma[r(X_t, \theta_t)]$. We will also consider the *sup-long-run* average value that is defined as follows: for a strategy σ and an initial state s we have $Val_{sup}^\sigma(r, s) = \limsup_{T \to \infty} \frac{1}{T} \sum_{t=0}^{T-1} \mathbb{E}_s^\sigma[r(X_t, \theta_t)]$.

We consider MDPs with k-different reward functions $r_1, r_2, \ldots, r_k$. Given an initial state s, a strategy σ, the inf-long-run average value vector at s for σ, for $\boldsymbol{r} = \langle r_1, r_2, \ldots, r_k \rangle$ is defined as $Val_{inf}^\sigma(\boldsymbol{r}, s) = \langle Val_{inf}^\sigma(r_1, s), Val_{inf}^\sigma(r_2, s), \ldots,$ $Val_{inf}^\sigma(r_k, s) \rangle$. The notation for sup-long-run average objectives is similar.

Comparison operators on vectors are interpreted in a point-wise fashion, i.e., given two real-valued vectors $\boldsymbol{v}_1 = \langle v_1^1, v_1^2, \ldots, v_1^k \rangle$ and $\boldsymbol{v}_2 = \langle v_2^1, v_2^2, \ldots, v_2^k \rangle$, and $\bowtie \in \{ <, \leq, = \}$ we write $\boldsymbol{v}_1 \bowtie \boldsymbol{v}_2$ if and only if for all $1 \leq i \leq k$ we have $v_1^i \bowtie v_2^i$. We write $\boldsymbol{v}_1 \neq \boldsymbol{v}_2$ to denote that vector $\boldsymbol{v}_1$ is not equal to $\boldsymbol{v}_2$, i.e., it is not the case that $\boldsymbol{v}_1 = \boldsymbol{v}_2$.

Pareto-Optimal Strategies. Given an MDP G and reward functions $r_1, r_2, \ldots, r_k$, a strategy σ is a *Pareto-optimal* strategy [9] for inf-long-run average objective from a state s, if there is no $\sigma' \in \Sigma$ such that $Val_{inf}^\sigma(\boldsymbol{r}, s) \leq$ $Val_{inf}^{\sigma'}(\boldsymbol{r}, s)$, and $Val_{inf}^\sigma(\boldsymbol{r}, s) \neq Val_{inf}^{\sigma'}(\boldsymbol{r}, s)$, i.e., there is no strategy σ' such that for all $1 \leq j \leq k$, we have $Val_{inf}^\sigma(r_j, s) \leq Val_{inf}^{\sigma'}(r_j, s)$ and exists $1 \leq j \leq k$, with $Val_{inf}^\sigma(r_j, s) < Val_{inf}^{\sigma'}(r_j, s)$. The definition for sup-long-run average objectives is similar. In case $k = 1$, the class of Pareto-optimal strategies are called optimal strategies.

Sufficiency of Strategies. Given reward functions $r_1, r_2, \ldots, r_k$, a family $\Sigma^{\mathcal{C}}$ of strategies suffices for ε-Pareto optimality for inf-long-run average objectives if for all $\varepsilon > 0$, for every Pareto-optimal strategy $\sigma \in \Sigma$, there is a strategy $\sigma_c \in \Sigma^{\mathcal{C}}$ such that for all $j = 1, 2, \ldots, k$ and all $s \in S$ we have $Val_{inf}^\sigma(r_j, s) \leq$ $Val_{inf}^{\sigma_c}(r_j, s) + \varepsilon$. The notion of sufficiency for Pareto optimality is obtained if the above inequality is satisfied for $\varepsilon = 0$. The definition is similar for sup-long-run average objectives.

Theorem 1 (Strategies for optimality [5]). *In MDPs with one reward function r_1, the family Σ^{PM} of pure memoryless strategies suffices for optimality for inf-long-run average and sup-long-run average objectives, i.e., there exists* *a pure memoryless strategy $\sigma^* \in \Sigma^{PM}$, such that for all strategies $\sigma \in \Sigma$, the following conditions hold: (a) $Val_{inf}^{\sigma}(r_1, s) \leq Val_{inf}^{\sigma^*}(r_1, s)$; (b) $Val_{sup}^{\sigma}(r_1, s) \leq Val_{sup}^{\sigma^*}(r_1, s)$; and (c) $Val_{inf}^{\sigma^*}(r_1, s) = Val_{sup}^{\sigma^*}(r_1, s)$.*

3   Memoryless Strategies Suffice for Pareto Optimality

In this section we study the properties of the family of strategies that suffices for Pareto optimality. It can be shown that ε-Pareto optimal strategies, for $\varepsilon > 0$, require randomization for both sup-long-run average and inf-long-run average objectives; and for sup-long-run average objectives the family of memoryless strategies does not suffice for ε-Pareto optimality (see [1] for details). We present the main result of this section that shows the family of memoryless strategies suffices for ε-Pareto optimality for inf-long-run average objectives.

Markov Chains. A *Markov chain* $G = (S, p)$ consists of a finite set S of states, and a stochastic transition matrix p, i.e., $p(s, t) \geq 0$ denotes the transition probability from s to t, and for all $s \in S$ we have $\sum_{t \in S} p(s, t) = 1$. Given an MDP $G = (S, A, p)$ and a memoryless strategy $\sigma \in \Sigma^M$ we obtain a Markov chain $G_\sigma = (S, p_\sigma)$ obtained as follows: $p_\sigma(s, t) = \sum_{a \in A} p(s, a)(t) \cdot \sigma(s)(a)$. From Theorem 1 it follows that the values for inf-long-run average and sup-long-run average objectives coincide for Markov chains.

Corollary 1. *For all MDPs G, for all reward functions r_1, for all memoryless strategies $\sigma \in \Sigma^M$, and for all $s \in S$, we have $Val_{inf}^{\sigma}(r_1, s) = Val_{sup}^{\sigma}(r_1, s)$.*

We now state a result of Hardy-Littlewood (see Appendix H of [5] for proof).

Lemma 1 (Hardy-Littlewood result). *Let $\{d_t\}_{t=0}^{\infty}$ be an arbitrary sequence of bounded real-numbers. Then the following assertions hold:*

$$\liminf_{T \to \infty} \frac{1}{T} \sum_{t=0}^{T-1} d_t \leq \liminf_{\beta \to 1^-} (1 - \beta) \cdot \sum_{t=0}^{\infty} \beta^t \cdot d_t$$

$$\leq \limsup_{\beta \to 1^-} (1 - \beta) \cdot \sum_{t=0}^{\infty} \beta^t \cdot d_t \leq \limsup_{T \to \infty} \frac{1}{T} \sum_{t=0}^{T-1} d_t.$$

Lemma 2. *Let $G = (S, A, p)$ be an MDP with k reward functions $r_1, r_2, \ldots, r_k$. For all $\varepsilon > 0$, for all $s \in S$, for all $\sigma \in \Sigma$, there exists a memoryless strategy $\overline{\sigma} \in \Sigma^M$ such that for all $i = 1, 2, \ldots, k$, we have $Val_{inf}^{\sigma}(r_i, s) \leq Val_{inf}^{\overline{\sigma}}(r_i, s) + \varepsilon$.*

Proof. Given a strategy σ and an initial state s, for $j = 1, 2, \ldots, k$ define a sequence $\{d_t^j\}_{t=0}^{\infty}$ as follows: $d_t^j = \mathbb{E}_s^{\sigma}[r_j(X_t, \theta_t)]$; i.e., d_t^j is the expected reward of the t-th stage for the reward function r_j. The sequence $\{d_t^j\}_{t=0}^{\infty}$ is bounded as follows: $\min_{s \in S, a \in A} r_j(s, a) \leq d_t^j \leq \max_{s \in S, a \in A} r_j(s, a)$, for all $t \geq 0$ and for all $j = 1, 2, \ldots, k$. By Lemma 1 we obtain that for all $\varepsilon > 0$, there exists $0 < \beta < 1$ such that for all $j = 1, 2, \ldots, k$ we have $\liminf_{T \to \infty} \frac{1}{T} \sum_{t=0}^{T-1} d_t^j \leq (1 - \beta) \cdot \sum_{t=0}^{\infty} \beta^t \cdot d_t^j + \varepsilon$; i.e., in other words, for all $j = 1, 2, \ldots, k$ we have

$Val^{\sigma}_{inf}(r_j, s) \leq \mathbb{E}^{\sigma}_s[\sum_{t=0}^{\infty}(1-\beta)\cdot\beta^t\cdot r_j(X_t, \theta_t)] + \varepsilon$. By Theorem 2 of [2] for every strategy σ, there is a memoryless strategy $\overline{\sigma} \in \Sigma^M$ such that for all $j = 1, 2, \ldots, k$ we have $\mathbb{E}^{\sigma}_s[\sum_{t=0}^{\infty}(1-\beta)\cdot\beta^t\cdot r_j(X_t, \theta_t)] = \mathbb{E}^{\overline{\sigma}}_s[\sum_{t=0}^{\infty}(1-\beta)\cdot\beta^t\cdot r_j(X_t, \theta_t)]$. Consider a memoryless strategy $\overline{\sigma}$ that satisfies the above equalities for $j = 1, 2, \ldots, k$. For $j = 1, 2, \ldots, k$ define a sequence $\{\overline{d}^j_t\}_{t=0}^{\infty}$ as follows: $\overline{d}^j_t = \mathbb{E}^{\overline{\sigma}}_s[r_j(X_t, \theta_t)]$. Again the sequence $\{\overline{d}^j_t\}_{t=0}^{\infty}$ is bounded as follows: $\min_{s \in S, a \in A} r_j(s, a) \leq \overline{d}^j_t \leq \max_{s \in S, a \in A} r_j(s, a)$, for all $t \geq 0$ and for all $j = 1, 2, \ldots, k$. By Lemma 1 for all $j = 1, 2, \ldots, k$ we obtain that $(1-\beta)\cdot\sum_{t=0}^{\infty}\beta^t\cdot\overline{d}^j_t \leq \limsup_{T\to\infty}\frac{1}{T}\sum_{t=0}^{T-1}\overline{d}^j_t$; i.e., for all $j = 1, 2, \ldots, k$ we have $\mathbb{E}^{\overline{\sigma}}_s[\sum_{t=0}^{\infty}(1-\beta)\cdot\beta^t\cdot r_j(X_t, \theta_t)] \leq Val^{\overline{\sigma}}_{sup}(r_j, s)$. Since $\overline{\sigma}$ is a memoryless strategy, by Corollary 1 we obtain that for all $j = 1, 2, \ldots, k$ we have $Val^{\overline{\sigma}}_{sup}(r_j, s) = Val^{\overline{\sigma}}_{inf}(r_j, s)$. Hence it follows that for all $j = 1, 2, \ldots, k$ we have $Val^{\sigma}_{inf}(r_j, s) \leq Val^{\overline{\sigma}}_{inf}(r_j, s) + \varepsilon$. The desired result follows. ■

Theorem 2. *The family of Σ^M of memoryless strategies suffices for ε-Pareto optimality for inf-long-run average objectives.*

4   Approximating the Pareto Curve

Pareto Curve. Let G be an MDP with reward functions $\boldsymbol{r} = \langle r_1, \ldots, r_k \rangle$. The *Pareto curve* $P^{inf}(G, s, \boldsymbol{r})$ of the MDP G at state s with respect to inf-long-run average objectives is the set of all k-vector of values such that for each $\boldsymbol{v} \in P^{inf}(G, s, \boldsymbol{r})$, there is a Pareto-optimal strategy σ such that $Val^{\sigma}_{inf}(\boldsymbol{r}, s) = \boldsymbol{v}$. We are interested not only in the values, but also the Pareto-optimal strategies. We often blur the distinction and refer to the Pareto curve $P^{inf}(G, s, \boldsymbol{r})$ as a set of strategies which achieve the Pareto-optimal values (if there is more than one strategy that achieves the same value vector, $P^{inf}(G, s, \boldsymbol{r})$ contains at least one of them). For an MDP G, and $\varepsilon > 0$, an ε-approximate Pareto curve, denoted $P^{inf}_{\varepsilon}(G, s, \boldsymbol{r})$, is a set of strategies σ such that there is no other strategy σ' such that for all $\sigma \in P^{inf}_{\varepsilon}(G, s, \boldsymbol{r})$, we have $Val^{\sigma'}_{inf}(r_i, s) \geq (1 + \varepsilon)Val^{\sigma}_{inf}(r_i, s)$, for all rewards r_i. That is, the ε-approximate Pareto curve contains strategies such that any Pareto-optimal strategy is "almost" dominated by some strategy in $P^{inf}_{\varepsilon}(G, s, \boldsymbol{r})$.

Multi-objective Linear Programming and Pareto Curve. A multi-objective linear program L consists of a set k of objective functions $o_1, o_2, \ldots, o_k$, where $o_i(x) = c_i^T \cdot x$, for a vector c_i and a vector x of variables; and a set of linear constraints specified as $A \cdot x \geq b$, for a matrix A and a vector b. A valuation of x is feasible if it satisfies the set of linear constraints. A feasible solution x is a Pareto-optimal point if there is no other feasible solution x' such that $(o_1(x), o_2(x), \ldots, o_k(x)) \leq (o_1(x'), o_2(x'), \ldots, o_k(x'))$ and $(o_1(x), o_2(x), \ldots, o_k(x)) \neq (o_1(x'), o_2(x'), \ldots, o_k(x'))$. Given a multi-objective linear program L, the Pareto curve for L consists of the k-vector of values such that for each $\boldsymbol{v} \in P(L)$ there is a Pareto-optimal point x such that $\boldsymbol{v} = (o_1(x), o_2(x), \ldots, o_k(x))$. The definition of ε-approximate Pareto curve $P_{\varepsilon}(L)$ for L is similar to the definitions of the curves as defined above. The following theorem is a direct consequence of the corresponding theorems in [10].

Theorem 3 ([10]). *Given a multi-objective linear program L with k-objective functions, the following assertions hold:*

1. *For all $\varepsilon > 0$, there exists an approximate Pareto curve $P_\varepsilon(L)$ consisting of a number of feasible solution that is polynomial in $|L|$ and $\frac{1}{\varepsilon}$, but exponential in the number of objective functions.*
2. *For all $\varepsilon > 0$, there is an algorithm to construct $P_\varepsilon(L)$ in time polynomial in $|L|$ and $\frac{1}{\varepsilon}$ and exponential in the number of objective functions.*

4.1   Irreducible MDPs

In this subsection we consider a special class of MDPs, namely, *irreducible* MDPs[1] and present algorithm to approximate the Pareto curve by reduction to multi-objective linear-programming.

Irreducible MDPs. An MDP G is *irreducible* if for every pure memoryless strategy $\sigma \in \Sigma^{PM}$ the Markov chain G_σ is completely ergodic (or irreducible), i.e., the graph of G_σ is a strongly connected component. Observe that if G is an irreducible MDP, then for all memoryless strategy $\sigma \in \Sigma^M$, the Markov chain G_σ is completely ergodic.

Long-Run Frequency. Let $G = (S, A, p)$ be an irreducible MDP, and $\sigma \in \Sigma^M$ be a memoryless strategy. Let $q(s, \sigma)(u) = \lim_{T \to \infty} \frac{1}{T} \cdot \sum_{t=0}^{T-1} \mathbb{E}_s^\sigma [\mathbf{1}_{X_t = u}]$, where $\mathbf{1}_{X_t = u}$ is the indicator function denoting if the t-th state is u, denote the "long-run average frequency" of state u, and let $x_{ua} = q(s, \sigma)(u) \cdot \sigma(u)(a)$ be the "long-run average frequency" of the state action pair (u, a). It follows from the results of [5] (see section 2.4) that $q(s, \sigma)(u)$ exists and is positive for all states $u \in S$, and x_{ua} satisfies the following set of linear-constraints: let $\delta(u, u')$ be the Kronecker delta, and we have the following constraints

$$(i) \sum_{u \in S} \sum_{a \in A} \big(\delta(u, u') - p(u, a)(u')\big) \cdot x_{ua} = 0; \qquad u' \in S;$$

$$(ii) \sum_{u \in S} \sum_{a \in A} x_{ua} = 1; \qquad (iii)\ x_{ua} \geq 0; \qquad a \in A, u \in S.$$

We denote the above set of constraints by $C_{\mathrm{irr}}(G)$.

Multi-objective Linear-Program. Let G be an irreducible MDP with k reward functions $r_1, r_2, \ldots, r_k$. We consider the following multi-objective linear-program over the variables x_{ua} for $u \in S$ and $a \in A$. The k-objectives are as follows: $\max \sum_{u \in S} \sum_{a \in A} r_j(u, a) \cdot x_{ua}$; for $j = 1, 2, \ldots, k$; and the set of linear-constraints are specified as $C_{\mathrm{irr}}(G)$. We denote the above multi-objective linear-program as $L_{\mathrm{irr}}(G, \boldsymbol{r})$.

Lemma 3. *Let G be an irreducible MDP, with k reward functions $r_1, r_2, \ldots, r_k$. Let $\boldsymbol{v} \in \mathbb{R}^k$ be a vector of real-values. The following statements are equivalent.*

---

[1] See section 2.4 of [5] for irreducible MDPs with a single reward function.

1. *There is a memoryless strategy $\sigma \in \Sigma^M$ such that $\wedge_{j=1}^{k}\left(Val_{inf}^{\sigma}(r_j, s) \geq v_j\right)$.*
2. *There is a feasible solution x_{ua} for multi-objective linear-program $L_{irr}(G, \boldsymbol{r})$ such that $\wedge_{j=1}^{k}\left(\sum_{u \in S} \sum_{a \in A} r_j(u, a) \cdot x_{ua} \geq v_j\right)$.*

Proof

1. [(1). $\Rightarrow$ (2).] Given a memoryless strategy σ, let $x_{ua} = \sigma(u)(a) \cdot \lim_{T \to \infty} \frac{1}{T} \cdot \sum_{t=0}^{T-1} \mathbb{E}_s^{\sigma}[\mathbf{1}_{X_t=u}]$. Then x_{ua} is a feasible solution to $L_{irr}(G, \boldsymbol{r})$. Moreover, the value for the inf-long-run average objective can be expressed as follows: $Val_{inf}^{\sigma}(r_j, s) = \sum_{u \in S} \sum_{a \in A} \sigma(u)(a) \cdot r_j(u, a) \cdot \lim_{T \to \infty} \frac{1}{T} \cdot \sum_{t=0}^{T-1} \mathbb{E}_s^{\sigma}[\mathbf{1}_{X_t=u}]$. The desired result follows.
2. [(2). $\Rightarrow$ (1).] Let x_{ua} be a feasible solution to $L_{irr}(G, \boldsymbol{r})$. Consider the memoryless strategy σ defined as follows: $\sigma(u)(a) = \frac{x_{ua}}{\sum_{a' \in A} x_{ua'}}$. Given the memoryless strategy σ, it follows from Lemma 2.4.2 and Theorem 2.4.3 of [5] that $x_{ua} = \sigma(u)(a) \cdot \lim_{T \to \infty} \frac{1}{T} \cdot \sum_{t=0}^{T-1} \mathbb{E}_s^{\sigma}[\mathbf{1}_{X_t=u}]$. The desired result follows. ∎

It follows from Lemma 3 that the Pareto curve $P(L_{irr}(G, \boldsymbol{r}))$ characterizes the set of memoryless Pareto-optimal points for the MDP with k inf-long-run average objectives. Since memoryless strategies suffices of ε-Pareto optimality for inf-long-run average objectives (Theorem 2), the following result follows from Theorem 3.

Theorem 4. *Given an irreducible MDP G with k reward functions $\boldsymbol{r}$, for all $\varepsilon > 0$, there is an algorithm to construct a $P_{\varepsilon}^{inf}(G, s, \boldsymbol{r})$ in time polynomial in $|G|$ and $\frac{1}{\varepsilon}$ and exponential in the number of reward functions.*

4.2   General MDPs

In the case of general MDPs, if we fix a memoryless strategy $\sigma \in \Sigma^M$, then in the resulting Markov chain G_σ, in general, we have both recurrent states and transient states. For recurrent states the "long-run-average frequency" is positive and for transient states the "long-run-average frequency" is zero. For the transient states the strategy determines the probabilities to reach the various closed connected set of recurrent states. We will obtain several multi-objective linear-programs to approximate the Pareto curve: the set of constraints for recurrent states will be obtained similar to the one of $C_{irr}(G)$, and the set of constraints for the transient states will be obtained from the results of [3] on multi-objective reachability objectives. We first define a partition of the set Σ^M of memoryless strategies.

Partition of Strategies. Given an MDP $G = (S, A, p)$, consider the following set of functions: $\mathcal{F} = \{ f : S \to 2^A \setminus \emptyset \}$. The set $\mathcal{F}$ is finite, since $|\mathcal{F}| \leq 2^{|A| \cdot |S|}$. Given $f \in \mathcal{F}$ we denote by $\Sigma^M \upharpoonright f = \{ \sigma \in \Sigma^M \mid f(s) = \text{Supp}(\sigma(s)), \forall s \in S \}$ the set of memoryless strategies σ such that support of $\sigma(s)$ is $f(s)$ for all states $s \in S$.

Multi-objective Linear Program for $f \in \mathcal{F}$. Let G be an MDP with reward functions $r_1, r_2, \ldots, r_k$. Let $f \in \mathcal{F}$, and we will present a multi-objective linear-program for memoryless strategies in $\Sigma^M \upharpoonright f$. We first observe that for all $\sigma_1, \sigma_2 \in \Sigma^M \upharpoonright f$, the underlying graph structures of the Markov chains G_{σ_1} and G_{σ_2} are the same, i.e., the recurrent set of states and transient set of states in G_{σ_1} and G_{σ_2} are the same. Hence the computation of the recurrent states and transient states for all strategies in $\Sigma^M \restriction f$ can be achieved by computing it for an arbitrary strategy in $\Sigma^M \restriction f$. Given G, the reward functions, an initial state s, and $f \in \mathcal{F}$, the multi-objective linear program is obtained by applying the following steps.

1. Consider the memoryless strategy $\overline{\sigma} \in \Sigma^M \restriction f$ that plays at u all actions in $f(u)$ uniformly at random, for all $u \in S$. Let U be the reachable subset of states in $G_{\overline{\sigma}}$ from s, and let $\mathcal{R} = \{ R_1, R_2, \ldots, R_l \}$ be the set of closed connected recurrent set of states in $G_{\overline{\sigma}}$, i.e., R_i is a bottom strongly connected component in the graph of $G_{\overline{\sigma}}$. The set U and $\mathcal{R}$ can be computed in linear-time. Let $R = \bigcup_{i=1}^{l} R_i$, and the set $U \setminus R$ consists of transient states.

2. If $s \in R$, then consider R_i such that $s \in R_i$. In the present case, consider the multi-objective linear-program of subsection 4.1 with the additional constraint that $x_{ua} > 0$, for all $u \in R_i$ and $a \in f(u)$, and $x_{ua} = 0$ for all $u \in R_i$ and $a \notin f(u)$. The Pareto curve of the above multi-objective linear-program coincides with the Pareto curve for memoryless strategies in $\Sigma^M \restriction f$. The proof essentially mimics the proof of Lemma 3 restricted to the set R_i.

3. We now consider the case when $s \in U \setminus R$. In this case we will have three kinds of variables: (a) variables x_{ua} for $u \in R$ and $a \in A$; (b) variables y_{ua} for $u \in U \setminus R$ and $a \in A$ (c) variables y_u for $u \in R$. Intuitively, the variables x_{ua} will denote the "long-run average frequency" of the state action pair x_{ua}, and the variables y_{ua} and y_u will play the same role as the variables of the multi-objective linear-program of [3] for reachability objectives (see Fig 3 of [3]). We now specify the multi-objective linear-program

$$\textbf{Objectives } (j = 1, 2, \ldots, k): \qquad \max \sum_{u \in S} \sum_{a \in A} r_j(u, a) \cdot x_{ua};$$

Subject to

(i) $\displaystyle\sum_{u \in R_i} \sum_{a \in A} \left(\delta(u, u') - p(u, a)(u') \right) \cdot x_{ua} = 0; \qquad u' \in R_i;$

(ii) $\displaystyle\sum_{u \in R} \sum_{a \in A} x_{ua} = 1;$ (iii) $x_{ua} \geq 0; \qquad a \in A, u \in R;$

(iv) $x_{ua} > 0; \qquad a \in f(u), u \in R;$ (v) $x_{ua} = 0; \qquad a \notin f(u), u \in R;$

(vi) $\displaystyle\sum_{a \in A} y_{ua} - \sum_{u' \in U} \sum_{a' \in A} p(u', a')(u) \cdot y_{u'a'} = \alpha(u); \qquad u \in U \setminus R;$

(vii) $\displaystyle y_u - \sum_{u' \in U \setminus R} \sum_{a' \in A} p(u', a')(u) \cdot y_{u'a'} = 0; \qquad u \in R;$

(viii) $y_{ua} \geq 0; \qquad u \in U \setminus R, a \in A;$ (ix) $y_u \geq 0; \qquad u \in R;$

(x) $y_{ua} > 0; \qquad u \in U \setminus R, a \in f(u);$ (xi) $y_{ua} = 0; \qquad u \in U \setminus R, a \notin f(u);$

(xii) $\displaystyle\sum_{u \in R_i} \sum_{a \in A} x_{ua} = \sum_{u \in R_i} y_u; \qquad i = 1, 2, \ldots, l;$

where $\alpha(u) = 1$ if $u = s$ and 0 otherwise. We refer the above set of constraints as $C_{\text{gen}}(G, r, f)$ and the above multi-objective linear-program as $L_{\text{gen}}(G, r, f)$. We now explain the role of each constraint: the constraints $(i) - (iii)$ coincides with constraints $C_{\text{irr}}(G)$ for the subset R_i, and the additional constraints $(iv) - (v)$ are required to ensure that we have witness strategies such that they belong to $\Sigma^M \upharpoonright f$. The constraints $(vi) - (ix)$ are essentially the constraints of the multi-objective linear-program for reachability objectives defined in Fig 3 of [3]. The additional constraints $(x) - (xi)$ are again required to ensure that witness strategies satisfy that they belong to $\Sigma^M \upharpoonright f$. Intuitively, for $u \in R_i$, the variables y_u stands for the probability to hit u before hitting any other state in R_i. The last constraint specify that the sum total of "long-run average frequency" in a closed connected recurrent set R_i coincides with the probability to reach R_i. We remark that the above constraints can be simplified; e.g., the (iv) and (v) implies (iii), but we present the set constraints in a way such that it can be understood that what new constraints are introduced.

Lemma 4. *Let $G = (S, A, p)$ be an MDP, with k reward functions $r_1, r_2, \ldots, r_k$. Let $\boldsymbol{v} \in \mathbb{R}^k$ be a vector of real-values. The following statements are equivalent.*

1. *There is a memoryless strategy $\sigma \in \Sigma^M \upharpoonright f$ such that $\wedge_{j=1}^{k} \left(Val_{inf}^{\sigma}(r_j, s) \geq v_j \right)$.*
2. *There is a feasible solution for the multi-objective linear-program $L_{gen}(G, \boldsymbol{r}, f)$ such that $\wedge_{j=1}^{k} \left(\sum_{u \in S} \sum_{a \in A} r_j(u, a) \cdot x_{ua} \geq v_j \right)$.*

Proof. The case when the starting s is a member of the set R of recurrent states, the result follows from Lemma 3. We consider the case when $s \in U \setminus R$. We prove both the directions as follows.

1. $[(1). \Rightarrow (2).]$ Let $\sigma \in \Sigma^M \upharpoonright f$ be a memoryless strategy. We now construct a feasible solution for $L_{gen}(G, \boldsymbol{r}, f)$. For $u \in R$, let $x'_{ua} = \sigma(u)(a) \cdot \lim_{T \to \infty} \frac{1}{T} \cdot \sum_{t=0}^{T-1} \mathbb{E}_s^{\sigma}[\mathbf{1}_{X_t=u}]$. Consider a square matrix P^{σ} of size $|U \setminus R| \times |U \setminus R|$, defined as follows: $P_{u,u'}^{\sigma} = \sum_{a \in A} \sigma(u)(a) \cdot p(u, a)(u')$, i.e., P^{σ} is the one-step transition matrix under p and σ. For all $u \in U \setminus R$, let $y'_{ua} = \sigma(u)(a) \cdot \sum_{n=0}^{\infty} (P^{\sigma})_{s,u}^n$. In other words, y'_{ua} denotes "the expected number of times of visiting u and upon doing so choosing action a, given the strategy σ and starting state s". Since states in $U \setminus R$ are transient states, the values y'_{ua} are finite (see Lemma 1 of [3]). For $u \in R$, let $y'_u = \sum_{u' \in U \setminus R} \sum_{a' \in A} p(u', a')(u) \cdot y'_{u'a'}$, i.e., y'_u is the "expected number of times that we will transition into state u for the first time". It follows from arguments similar to Lemma 3 and the results in [3] that above solution is feasible solution to the linear-program $L_{gen}(G, \boldsymbol{r}, f)$. Moreover, $\sum_{u \in R_i} y'_u = \Pr_s^{\sigma}(\Diamond R_i)$, for all R_i, where $\Diamond R_i$ denotes the event of reaching R_i. It follows that for all $j = 1, 2, \ldots, k$ we have $Val_{inf}^{\sigma}(r_j, s) = \sum_{u \in R} \sum_{a \in A} r_j(u, a) \cdot x'_{ua}$. The desired result follows.
2. $[(2). \Rightarrow (1).]$ Given a feasible solution to $L_{gen}(G, \boldsymbol{r}, f)$ we construct a memoryless strategy $\sigma \in \Sigma^M \upharpoonright f$ as follows:

$$\sigma(u)(a) = \begin{cases} \frac{x_{ua}}{\sum_{a' \in A} x_{ua'}} & u \in R; \\ \frac{y_{ua}}{\sum_{a' \in A} y_{ua'}} & u \in U \setminus R; \end{cases}$$

Observe the constraints $(iv) - (v)$ and $(x) - (xi)$ ensure that the strategy $\sigma \in \Sigma^M \upharpoonright f$. The strategy constructed satisfies the following equalities: for all R_i we have $\Pr_s^{\sigma}(\Diamond R_i) = \sum_{u \in R_i} y_u$ (this follows from Lemma 2 of [3]);

and for all $u \in R_i$ we have $x_{ua} = \sigma(u)(a) \cdot \lim_{T \to \infty} \frac{1}{T} \cdot \sum_{t=0}^{T-1} \mathbb{E}_s^\sigma[\mathbf{1}_{X_t=u}]$. The above equality follows from arguments similar to Lemma 3. The desired result follows. ∎

Theorem 5. *Given an MDP G with k reward functions $\mathbf{r}$, for all $\varepsilon > 0$, there is an algorithm to construct a $P_\varepsilon^{\mathrm{inf}}(G, s, \mathbf{r})$ in (a) time polynomial in $\frac{1}{\varepsilon}$, and exponential in $|G|$ and the number of reward functions; (b) using space polynomial in $\frac{1}{\varepsilon}$ and $|G|$, and exponential in the number of reward functions.*

Proof. It follows from Lemma 4 that the Pareto curve $P(L_{\mathsf{gen}}(G, \mathbf{r}, f))$ characterizes the set of memoryless Pareto-optimal points for the MDP with k inf-long-run average objectives for all memoryless strategies in $\Sigma^M \restriction f$. We can generate all $f \in \mathcal{F}$ in space polynomial in $|G|$ and time exponential in $|G|$. Since memoryless strategies suffices of ε-Pareto optimality for inf-long-run average objectives (Theorem 2), the desired result follows from Theorem 3. ∎

4.3 Realizability

In this section we study the realizability problem for multi-objective MDPs: the *realizability problem* asks, given a multi-objective MDP G with rewards $r_1, \ldots, r_k$ (collectively, $\mathbf{r}$) and a state s of G, and a value profile $\mathbf{w} = (w_1, \ldots w_k)$ of k rational values, whether there exists a strategy σ such that $Val_{inf}^\sigma(\mathbf{r}, s) \geq \mathbf{w}$. Observe that such a strategy exists if and only if there is a Pareto-optimal strategy σ' such that $Val_{inf}^{\sigma'}(\mathbf{r}, s) \geq \mathbf{w}$. Also observe that it follows from Theorem 2 that if a value profile $\mathbf{w}$ is realizable, then it is realizable within ε by a memoryless strategy, for all $\varepsilon > 0$. Hence we study the *memoryless realizability* problem that asks, given a multi-objective MDP G with rewards $r_1, \ldots, r_k$ (collectively, $\mathbf{r}$) and a state s of G, and a value profile $\mathbf{w} = (w_1, \ldots w_k)$ of k rational values, whether there exists a memoryless strategy σ such that $Val_{inf}^\sigma(\mathbf{r}, s) \geq \mathbf{w}$. The realizability problem arises when certain target behaviors are required, and one wishes to check if they can be attained on the model.

Theorem 6. *The memoryless realizability problem for multi-objective MDPs with inf-long-run average objectives can be (a) decided in polynomial time for irreducible MDPs; (b) decided in NP for MDPs.*

Proof. The result is obtained as follows.

1. For an irreducible MDP G with k reward functions $r_1, r_2, \ldots, r_k$, the answer to the memoryless realizability problem is "Yes" iff the following set of linear constraints has a solution. The set of constraints consists of the constraints $C_{\mathsf{irr}}(G)$ along with the constraints $\wedge_{j=1}^k \left(\sum_{s \in S} \sum_{a \in A} r_j(s, a) \cdot x_{ua} \geq w_j \right)$. Hence we obtain a polynomial time algorithm for the memoryless realizability problem.
2. For an MDP G with k reward functions $r_1, r_2, \ldots, r_k$, the answer to the memoryless realizability problem is "Yes" iff there exists $f \in \mathcal{F}$ such that the following set of linear constraints has a solution. The set of constraints consists of the constraints $C_{\mathsf{gen}}(G, \mathbf{r}, f)$ along with the constraints

$\wedge_{j=1}^{k} \left(\sum_{s \in S} \sum_{a \in A} r_j(s,a) \cdot x_{ua} \geq w_j \right)$. Hence given the guess f, we have a polynomial time algorithm for verification. Hence the result follows.   ∎

Concluding Remarks. In this work we studied MDPs with multiple long-run average objectives: we proved ε-Pareto optimality of memoryless strategies for inf-long-run average objectives, and presented algorithms to approximate the Pareto-curve and decide realizability for MDPs with multiple inf-long-run average objectives. The problem of approximating the Pareto curve and deciding the realizability problem for sup-long-run average objectives remain open. The other interesting open problems are as follows: (a) whether memoryless strategies suffices for Pareto optimality, rather than ε-Pareto optimality, for inf-long-run average objectives; (b) whether the problem of approximating the Pareto curve and deciding the realizability problem for general MDPs with inf-long-run average objectives can be solved in polynomial time.

References

1. Chatterjee, K.: Markov decision processes with multiple long-run average objectives. Technical Report, UC Berkeley, UCB/EECS-2007-105 (2007)
2. Chatterjee, K., Majumdar, R., Henzinger, T.A.: Markov decision processes with multiple objectives. In: Durand, B., Thomas, W. (eds.) STACS 2006. LNCS, vol. 3884, pp. 325–336. Springer, Heidelberg (2006)
3. Etessami, K., Kwiatkowska, M., Vardi, M.Y., Yannakakis, M.: Multi-objective model checking of Markov decision processes. In: Grumberg, O., Huth, M. (eds.) TACAS 2007. LNCS, vol. 4424, Springer, Heidelberg (2007)
4. Etzioni, O., Hanks, S., Jiang, T., Karp, R.M., Madari, O., Waarts, O.: Efficient information gathering on the internet. In: FOCS 1996, pp. 234–243. IEEE Computer Society Press, Los Alamitos (1996)
5. Filar, J., Vrieze, K.: Competitive Markov Decision Processes. Springer, Heidelberg (1997)
6. Garey, M.R., Johnson, D.S.: Computers and Intractability. W.H. Freeman, New York (1979)
7. Hartley, R.: Finite discounted, vector Markov decision processes. Technical report, Department of Decision Theory, Manchester University (1979)
8. Koski, J.: Multicriteria truss optimization. In: Multicriteria Optimization in Engineering and in the Sciences (1988)
9. Owen, G.: Game Theory. Academic Press, London (1995)
10. Papadimitriou, C.H., Yannakakis, M.: On the approximability of trade-offs and optimal access of web sources. In: FOCS 2000, pp. 86–92. IEEE Computer Society Press, Los Alamitos (2000)
11. Puterman, M.L.: Markov Decision Processes. John Wiley and Sons, Chichester (1994)
12. Szymanek, R., Catthoor, F., Kuchcinski, K.: Time-energy design space exploration for multi-layer memory architectures. In: DATE 04, IEEE Computer Society Press, Los Alamitos (2004)
13. White, D.J.: Multi-objective infinite-horizon discounted Markov decision processes. Journal of Mathematical Analysis and Applications 89(2), 639–647 (1982)
14. Yang, P., Catthoor, F.: Pareto-optimization based run time task scheduling for embedded systems. In: CODES-ISSS 2003, pp. 120–125. ACM Press, New York (2003)

A Formal Investigation of `Diff3`

Sanjeev Khanna[1], Keshav Kunal[2], and Benjamin C. Pierce[1]

[1] University of Pennsylvania
[2] Yahoo

Abstract. The `diff3` algorithm is widely considered the gold standard
for merging uncoordinated changes to list-structured data such as text files.
Surprisingly, its fundamental properties have never been studied in depth.

We offer a simple, abstract presentation of the `diff3` algorithm and
investigate its behavior. Despite abundant anecdotal evidence that people find `diff3`'s behavior intuitive and predictable in practice, characterizing its good properties turns out to be rather delicate: a number of
seemingly natural intuitions are incorrect in general. Our main result is
a careful analysis of the intuition that edits to "well-separated" regions
of the same document are guaranteed never to conflict.

1 Introduction

Users often want to edit a local copy of a replicated data structure, postponing
the moment when their changes become visible to others until sometime later—
when a set of changes has been finished and tested, when an offline laptop
is reconnected to the network, etc. In general, when multiple users can edit
at the same time, this reconciliation process requires a tool—a *synchronizer*—
that can propagate non-conflicting changes between different copies of the data,
while recognizing and flagging conflicts. Source code management systems, long-
distance collaborative editing environments, and file synchronizers are examples.

Operation-based synchronizers work by keeping track of the complete sequences of operations that have been applied to each replica and, during reconciliation, attempting to synthesize a single unified view of the data structure's edit
history. By contrast, a *state-based* synchronizer sees only the current versions of
the replicas to be reconciled, together with an *archive* of the last state they had
in common (perhaps saved away at the end of the last synchronization).

A crucial problem faced by a state-based synchronizer is how to *align* the information in the current replicas and the archive, so that it can tell where changes have
been made. This can be accomplished in a variety of ways, depending on the nature of the data being synchronized. Where the data is rigidly structured or where
keys are available (e.g., in personal information management applications such as
address books), the proper alignment is generally clear. For more flexibly structured data, such as semistructured databases, file systems, and text documents, it
is less clear how to reliably choose alignments that users consider natural. The issue is particularly vexing for pure textual (or, more generally, *list-structured*) data,
which offers no predetermined points of reference for alignment—the structures are
presented to the synchronizer as flat sequences of uninterpreted atoms (characters,

V. Arvind and S. Prasad (Eds.): FSTTCS 2007, LNCS 4855, pp. 485–496, 2007.

words, or lines of text)—and for which common edits include arbitrary insertions, deletions, and rearrangements of existing material.

The best known tool for synchronization of textual data is diff3. Developed by Randy Smith in 1988 [1] and popularized in revision control systems such as CVS and Subversion, diff3 and its relatives are relied on by millions of users for a huge range of collaborative tasks. The basic ideas of diff3 also appear in numerous hybrid tools for synchronizing semi-structured data in formats like XML, such as Lindholm's 3DM [2], the work of Chawathe *et al.* [3], and FCDP [4].

Given its popularity, it is surprising that the fundamental properties of the diff3 algorithm have never been explored. The published descriptions of its behavior (the GNU difftools manual [5] and comments in the source code) are helpful but rather low-level and operational, and we have been unable to find in the literature any rigorous analysis of the properties that users might want or expect from diff3 and the circumstances under which they hold.

Our first contribution is to put the diff3 algorithm itself on a more rigorous footing by offering a concise description of its behavior (§2-§3). Our model here is diff [6,7,8]—the two-way comparison algorithm used as a subroutine by diff3—which has not one but two elegant specifications: it can be viewed as computing either a longest common subsequence of its two inputs or a minimum-length edit script for turning one into the other by single-element insertions and deletions. Our specification of diff3 is not quite this concise, but nearly. We give a compact reference implementation in half a page of pseudo-code.

Our second and main contribution is an analysis of diff3's properties (§4). Most importantly, we examine the common intuition that, if the changes to the replicas are *local* to distinct and "well separated" regions, then diff3 will always be able to merge them without conflicts. We show that the most obvious formulations of this intuition are, in fact, wrong, but identify a common and easily checked separation condition under which the property does hold. We also formalize intuitive notions of *idempotence* (the results of synchronization are "fully synchronized" except where edits conflict), *stability* (similar inputs lead to similar outputs), and the guarantee of *near-complete success* when the inputs have been changed in similar ways (even if these changes are large compared to the archive version), and show that none of these properties hold in general.

We cite only closely related work. Broader surveys of the literature on synchronization algorithms for other kinds of data and algorithms founded on different assumptions (such as operation-based techniques) can be found in [9,10].

2   Warmup

Let us begin with a small example illustrating the basic operation of diff3. Figure 1(a) shows the initial configuration: O is the archive—the last common version—and A and B are the current versions that have diverged from O. (Whoever edited A has swapped $4,5$ and $2,3$, while 3 has gotten moved after 5 in B.) The first thing diff3 does is to call the two-way comparison tool diff to find *maximum matchings* (or longest common subsequences) between O and A

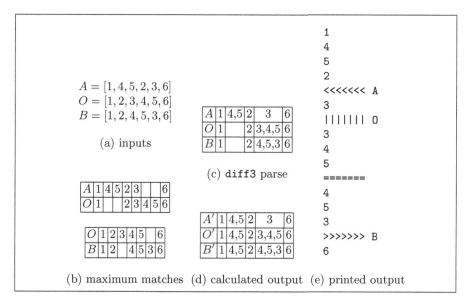

Fig. 1. Warmup Example

and between O and B, as shown in Figure 1(b). It then takes the regions where O differs from either A or B and coalesces the ones that overlap, leading to the alternating sequence of *stable* (all replicas equal) and *unstable* (one or both replicas changed) *chunks* shown in Figure 1(c).[1] Finally, it examines what has changed in each chunk and decides what changes can be propagated, as shown in Figure 1(d)—here, the second chunk is changed only in A (by inserting $4, 5$), so this change can be propagated to B, but the fourth chunk has changes in both A and B, so nothing can be propagated.

At this point, the actual `diff3` tool is finished: it simply walks over the chunks and, depending on what flags are provided on the command line, outputs something appropriate for each chunk. For example, Figure 1(e) shows the output from invoking `diff3 -m A O B`, where the `-m` flag requests a merged version of the files. For non-conflicting chunks, a single version is printed; for conflicts, the whole chunk.

Our analysis is a tiny bit more refined: We consider `diff3` as having *three* outputs—the new versions of A, O, and B with all non-conflicting changes in A reflected in B' and O' and all non-conflicting changes in B reflected in A' and O'. At the same time, we calculate a new archive O' that reflects all the changes that were successfully propagated, keeping the state from O in conflicting regions. (This extra refinement is just for purposes of analysis. In principle, it could also be useful in practice: after a partially successful synchronization, the current replicas are left in a partially updated but usable state, in contrast with tools like CVS based on the actual `diff3`, where conflicts cause the current replicas to

---

[1] The `diff3` manual [11] uses the term *hunks* for what we are calling unstable chunks; stable chunks are not named explicitly.

be polluted with information about conflicting chunks. However, we will see in
§4.2 that re-running `diff3` after a partially conflicting run can have unexpected
consequences.)

3   The `Diff3` Algorithm

We assume given some set of *atoms* $\mathcal{A}$. (In practice, these might be lines of text,
as in GNU `diff3`, or they could be words, characters, etc.) We write $\mathcal{A}^*$ for the
set of lists with elements drawn from $\mathcal{A}$ and use variables J, K, L, O, A, B,
and C to stand for elements of $\mathcal{A}^*$. If L is a list and $k \in \{1, \ldots, |L|\}$, then $L[k]$
denotes the kth element of L. A *span* in a list L is a pair of indices $[i..j]$ with
$1 \leq i, j \leq |L|$. We write $L[i..j]$ for the list of elements of L in locations i through
j; if $j < i$, this is the empty list. The *length* of a span $[i..j]$ is $j - i + 1$ if $i \leq j$
and 0 if $i > j$.

A *configuration* is a triple $(A, O, B) \in \mathcal{A}^* \times \mathcal{A}^* \times \mathcal{A}^*$. We usually write
configurations in the more suggestive notation $(A \leftarrow O \rightarrow B)$ to emphasize that
O is the archive from which A and B have been derived.

A *synchronizer* is a function that takes as input a configuration $(A \leftarrow O \rightarrow B)$
and yields another configuration $(A' \leftarrow O' \rightarrow B')$. We say that $(A \leftarrow O \rightarrow B) \Rightarrow$
$(A' \leftarrow O' \rightarrow B')$ is a *run* of the synchronizer. A run $(A \leftarrow O \rightarrow B) \Rightarrow (C \leftarrow$
$C \rightarrow C)$, where the three components of the output configuration are identical,
is said to be *conflict free*. We write $(A \leftarrow O \rightarrow B) \Rightarrow C$ in this case.

The first step of `diff3` is to call a two-way comparison subroutine on (O, A)
and (O, B) to compute a non-crossing matching M_A between the indices of O
and A—that is, a boolean function on pairs of indices from O and A such that if
$M_A[i, j] = \textit{true}$ then (a) $O[i] = A[j]$, (b) $M_A[i', j] = \textit{false}$ and $M_A[i, j'] = \textit{false}$
whenever $i' \neq i$ and $j' \neq j$, and (c) $M_A[i', j'] = \textit{false}$ whenever either $i' < i$
and $j' > j$ or $i' > i$ and $j' < j$—and a non-crossing matching M_B between the
indices of O and B. We treat this algorithm as a black box, simply assuming (a)
that it is deterministic, and (b) that it always yields *maximum* matchings. For
the counterexamples in the next section, we have verified that the matchings we
use correspond to the ones actually chosen by GNU `diff3`.

A *chunk* (from A, O, and B) is a triple $H = ([a_i..a_j], [o_i..o_j], [b_i..b_j])$ of a
span in A, a span in O, and a span in B such that at least one of the three is
non-empty. The *size* of a chunk is the sum of the lengths of all three spans. Write
$A[H]$ for $A[a_i..a_j] \in \mathcal{A}^*$, and similarly $O[H] = O[o_i..o_j]$ and $B[H] = B[b_i..b_j]$.

A *stable chunk* is a chunk in which all three spans have the same length and
corresponding indices are matched in all three—i.e., a chunk $([a..a + k - 1], [o..o +$
$k - 1], [b..b + k - 1])$ for some $k > 0$, with $M_A[o + i, a + i] = M_B[o + i, b + i] = \textit{true}$
for each $0 \leq i < k$. That is, a stable chunk corresponds to a span in O that is
matched in both M_A and M_B. An *unstable chunk* is one that is not stable. An
unstable chunk H is classified as follows:

H is *changed in A*   if $O[H] = B[H] \neq A[H]$
H is *changed in B*   if $O[H] = A[H] \neq B[H]$
H is *falsely conflicting*   if $O[H] \neq A[H] = B[H]$
H is *(truly) conflicting*   if $O[H] \neq A[H] \neq B[H] \neq O[H]$

---

1. Initialize $\ell_O = \ell_A = \ell_B = 0$.
2. Find the least positive integer i such that either $M_A[\ell_O + i, \ell_A + i] = false$ or $M_B[\ell_O + i, \ell_B + i] = false$. If i does not exist, then skip to step 3 to output a final stable chunk.

   (a) If $i = 1$, then find the least integer $o > \ell_O$ such that there exist indices a, b with $M_A[o, a] = M_B[o, b] = true$. If o does not exist, then skip to step 3 to output a final unstable chunk. Otherwise, output the (unstable) chunk

   $$C = ([\ell_A + 1 .. a - 1], [\ell_O + 1 .. o - 1], [\ell_B + 1 .. b - 1]).$$

   Set $\ell_O = o - 1$, $\ell_A = a - 1$, and $\ell_B = b - 1$, and repeat step 2.

   (b) If $i > 1$, output the (stable) chunk

   $$C = ([\ell_A + 1 .. \ell_A + i - 1], [\ell_O + 1 .. \ell_O + i - 1], [\ell_B + 1 .. \ell_B + i - 1]).$$

   Set $\ell_O = \ell_O + i - 1$, $\ell_A = \ell_A + i - 1$, and $\ell_B = \ell_B + i - 1$, and repeat step 2.

3. If $(\ell_O < |O|$ or $\ell_A < |A|$ or $\ell_B < |B|)$, output a final chunk

   $$C = ([\ell_A + 1 .. |A|], [\ell_O + 1 .. |O|], [\ell_B + 1 .. |B|]).$$

Fig. 2. The `Diff3` Algorithm

A chunk is called *conflicting* if it is either falsely or truly conflicting; a *non-conflicting* chunk is thus either stable or else changed only in A or B. Given a chunk H, we define the *output* of H to be the following triple of lists:

$$out(H) \;\; = \;\; \begin{cases} (A[H], O[H], B[H]) & \text{if } H \text{ is stable or conflicting} \\ (A[H], A[H], A[H]) & \text{if } H \text{ is changed in } A \\ (B[H], B[H], B[H]) & \text{if } H \text{ is changed in } B \end{cases}$$

A `diff3` *parse* of A, O, and B with respect to the matchings M_A and M_B is a sequence of stable and unstable chunks such that, (I) whenever $M_A[o, a] = M_B[o, b] = true$, the indices a, o, and b appear together in some stable chunk, and (II) each stable chunk is as large as possible. Observe that, under these conditions, the given matchings M_A and M_B uniquely determine the division of the inputs into an alternating sequence of stable and unstable chunks. Figure 2 gives a concrete algorithm for computing these chunks from the matchings.

Lemma 3.1. For any matchings M_A between A and O and and M_B between B and O, the algorithm in Figure 2 outputs a `diff3` parse.

Proof. For (I), observe that the beginning of each unstable chunk, identified in step 2(a), is an index $\ell_O + 1$ in O such that $M_A[\ell_O + 1, \ell_A + 1] = false$ or $M_B[\ell_O + 1, \ell_B + 1] = false$. The chunk then spans the elements $O[\ell_O + 1], ..., O[o - 1]$ in O, where $o > \ell_O$ is the least index such that (i) there exist a, b with $M_A[o, a] = M_B[o, b] = true$, or (ii) $O[o - 1]$ is the last element in O. Thus an unstable chunk can not contain an element in O that is matched in both M_A and M_B.

Now suppose property (II) is violated in some parse output by the algorithm. Consider the first stable chunk C that violates the maximality condition. The chunk (if any) that precedes C must be an unstable chunk or else C is not the first stable chunk to violate the maximality property. By (I), we know that no elements in the unstable chunk preceding C (if any) could have been included in C. Also, if C is output in step 2(b), it terminates at $A[\ell_A + i - 1]$, $O[\ell_O + i - 1]$, and $B[\ell_B + i - 1]$ where i satisfies the condition that either $M_A[\ell_O + i, \ell_A + i] = false$ or $M_B[\ell_O + i, \ell_B + i] = false$. Clearly, no more elements could be included in C. Similarly, if C is output in step 3, then none of A, O, or B can contain any elements that follow C. Thus C must be maximal—a contradiction.   □

Finally, if $P = [H_1, \ldots, H_n]$ is a parse—a sequence of chunks—then the *output* of P is obtained by concatenating the outputs for each chunk,

$$out(P) \quad = \quad (concat([A_1..A_n]), \; concat([O_1..O_n]), \; concat([B_1..B_n])),$$

where $out(H_i) = (A_i, O_i, B_i)$ for each $1 \le i \le n$.

4   Properties of Diff3

We now explore a number of intuitive properties that one might expect a synchronization algorithm such as diff3 to possess... and encounter some surprises.

4.1   Locality

Users of version control systems such as CVS can often be heard saying things like "I'll change this section of the file and you change that one and we'll sync up when we're done," in perfect confidence that this synchronization will be unproblematic. Indeed, perhaps the most important property that users of diff3 expect in practice is that, if A and B have been changed only in "non-overlapping ways," then synchronization will produce a unique, conflict-free result.

To investigate this intuition, let us focus on the case where A makes changes only at one end of the file while B makes changes only at the other end of the file. Define a *tiling* τ for a list O to be a partition of O into three lists O_1, O_2, and O_3 such that $O = O_1 O_2 O_3$. A configuration $(A \leftarrow O \rightarrow B)$ is τ-*respecting* if O_1 and O_3 are each modified in at most one of A and B and O_2 is modified in neither. If only one of O_1 or O_3 gets modified at all or if both O_1 and O_3 are modified in the same list, the result will obviously be conflict free. The interesting case is when both A and B make changes.

Next, we need to formalize the intuitive condition of the edited regions being "well separated." Two possible ways of doing this come immediately to mind:

- require that the edited regions be separated by a *large* untouched region—
  i.e., that O_2 be longer than any of A_1, O_1, O_3, or B_3; or
- require that the separating region be *different* from anything appearing anywhere else—i.e., that the string O_2 not occur in O_1, A_1, O_3, or B_3.

A	$1, 2, (1, 2)^{n-1}$	$1, 2, 1, 2$
O	$(1, 2)^n$	$1, 2$
B	$(1, 2)^n$	3
	stable	conflict

Fig. 3. Counter-example for locality

Most users of `diff3` would probably guess (as we did) that either of these conditions is enough to guarantee a conflict-free synchronization. As the following example shows, this guess is wrong on both counts.

Let $O_1 = \emptyset, O_2 = (1, 2)^n$, and $O_3 = 1, 2$, for some positive integer n. In replica A, the O_1 component is modified to $A_1 = 1, 2$ while in the replica B, the O_3 component is modified to $B_3 = 3$. Consider the maximum matching M_A for pair (O, A) where the $1, 2$ term in A_1 is matched to the first $1, 2$ term in O_2 component of O. Then the $(1, 2)^{n-1}$ prefix in the O_2 component in A is matched to the $(1, 2)^{n-1}$ suffix in the O_2 component of O. Finally, the last $(1, 2)$ term in the O_2 component of A is matched to the O_3 component of O. For the pair (O, B), the only maximum matching is one where their O_2 components are matched. As shown in Fig. 3, we have a ("true") conflict in this run. Note that the conflict is independent of the value of the parameter n and that it occurs even when the stable region O_2 is arbitrarily large.

At this point, one might begin to wonder whether, despite all the anecdotal evidence to the contrary, `diff3` might not be safe to use under *any* set of conditions that can be concisely characterized. Fortunately, this is too pessimistic. We can get the property we want by strengthening the second intuition.

Call a τ-respecting configuration $(A \leftarrow O \rightarrow B)$ *safe* if the O_2 component contains an element x that occurs exactly once in each of O, A, and B. Notice that there are no constraints on the length of O_2: it may contain just x.

Theorem 4.1.1. Every safe τ-respecting configuration $(A \leftarrow O \rightarrow B)$ leads to a unique conflict-free synchronization.

Such configurations are common in practice: for example, if the structures being synchronized are replicas of a source code file, it is reasonable to expect that O_2 will contain some completely unique line, such as a procedure header or a distinctive comment. The theorem can thus be viewed as justifying the common belief in `diff3`'s locality. Its proof rests on a technical property.

Lemma 4.1.2. Suppose we are given a configuration $(A \leftarrow O \rightarrow B)$, a matching M_A between O and A, and a matching M_B between O and B. If there exists an element z that occurs uniquely in each of A, O, B and if both M_A and M_B match the element z, then z must be contained in a stable chunk in the `diff3` parse that results from M_A and M_B.

Proof. Let α_O, α_A, and α_B respectively denote the locations of the element z in O, A, and B. We prove the property by iteratively considering the chunks that are output by the `diff3` algorithm until the point that element z appears in some output chunk for the first time. Let ℓ_O, ℓ_A, and ℓ_B (see Figure 2) be the indices denoting the locations of the last elements in O, A, and B that were processed by the algorithm. By assumption, $\ell_O < \alpha_O, \ell_A < \alpha_A$, and $\ell_B < \alpha_B$.

If the next chunk being output is an unstable chunk as in step 2(a), then the chunk ends just before the least offset in O at which there exists an element matched in both M_A and M_B. Clearly, the updated indices ℓ_O, ℓ_A, and ℓ_B must again satisfy the property $\ell_O < \alpha_O, \ell_A < \alpha_A$, and $\ell_B < \alpha_B$ since $M_A[\alpha_O, \alpha_A] = M_B[\alpha_O, \alpha_B] = true$. On the other hand, if the next chunk being output is a stable chunk as in step 2(b), then the chunk ends just before the least offset at which there exists an element in O that is not matched in at least one of M_A or M_B. If the updated indices still satisfy $\ell_O < \alpha_O, \ell_A < \alpha_A$, and $\ell_B < \alpha_B$, then we continue with the iterative process, maintaining the invariant. Otherwise, the element z must appear in this stable chunk, establishing the desired property.

Proof of 4.1.1. Assume wlog that O_1 is modified to A_1 in A (i.e., $A = A_1 O_2 O_3$) and that O_3 is modified to B_3 in B (i.e., $B = O_1 O_2 B_3$). Consider any maximum matching M_A between O and A. We claim that the element x must be matched in M_A. Suppose not. Let ℓ denote the number of elements that are matched by M_A between the A_1 component of A and O_1 component of O. Since the element x is not matched in M_A, the total number of elements matched by M_A is bounded by $\ell + (|O_2| + |O_3| - 1)$. Now consider the matching M'_A that agrees with M_A in the matching of elements between A_1 and O_1 and also completely matches the O_2 and O_3 components of A and O. Then the total number of elements matched by M'_A is $\ell + (|O_2| + |O_3|)$, contradicting the assumption that M_A is a maximum matching. Thus x must be matched in M_A. Moreover, since A and O are identical after x, M_A must match all elements in A after x to all elements in O after x, in order to be a maximum matching. Similarly, M_B must match all the elements up to x in B to all the elements up to x in O.

By Lemma 4.1.2, x must be contained in a stable chunk in `diff3`'s output. To complete the proof, consider any *unstable* chunk H output by the algorithm. Since the unique element x is contained in a stable chunk, either all elements in the A, O, and B components of chunk H precede x or they all follow x. In the former case, H must only be "changed in A," since M_B matches all elements up to x in B to all elements up to x in O. Similarly, in the latter case, H must be "changed in B." Thus, every unstable chunk is conflict free.

Finally, to see that the resulting output is unique, note that, in every parse, all the chunks above x are either stable or changed in A and those below x are stable or changed in B. Thus, in the output, the elements up to x will be taken from A while the elements following x will come from B.   □

This well-separation condition is quite delicate, and we have found it difficult to generalize. For example, one might guess that it can be extended to situations where each user has made edits in multiple regions of the list, provided that these regions are separated by unique elements and no region is edited in both A and B. More precisely, let us say that a *generalized tiling* τ is a partition of O in

A	1	2	4		6		8
O	1	2,3	4	5,5,5	6	7	8
B	1		4	5,5,5	6	2,3,4	8
	stable	conflict	stable	changed in A	stable	conflict	stable

A	1		2		4	6	8
O	1		2	3	4	6, 7	8
B	1	4,6	2	3	4		8
	stable	changed in B	stable	changed in A	stable	conflict	stable

Fig. 4. Counter-example to idempotence

to $2k+1$ non-empty pieces for some positive integer $k \geq 1$, say, $O_1, O_2, ..., O_{2k+1}$. We now say a configuration $(A \leftarrow O \rightarrow B)$ is τ-*respecting* if each piece O_{2i+1} for $0 \leq i \leq k$ is modified in at most one of A and B, while each piece O_{2i} for $0 \leq i \leq k$ is modified in neither. A τ-respecting configuration $(A \leftarrow O \rightarrow B)$ is said to be *safe* if each O_{2i} component contains an element x_{2i} that occurs exactly once in each of O, A, and B.

But this generalization no longer ensures a conflict-free synchronization. For example, consider the extension even to $k = 2$; so $O = O_1 O_2 O_3 O_4 O_5$. Furthermore, assume that for any $1 \leq i < j \leq 5$, O_i and O_j are disjoint, that is, they do not share any elements. Let $A = A_1 O_2 O_3 O_4 A_5$, and let $B = O_1 O_2 B_3 O_4 O_5$. Also, let $A_1 = O_5$, and $A_5 = B_3 = \emptyset$. Now if $|O_5| > |O|/2$, then the unique maximum matching M_A between A and O matches the A_1 component in A to O_5 in O. On the other hand, consider the maximum matching M_B between B and O that matches them in all components except B_3 to O_3. It is easy to see that the first `diff3` chunk will be a conflict.

4.2 Idempotence

In the rest of this section, we consider some other intuitive properties that users might expect of `diff3` and show that, in fact, it possesses none of them.

To begin, let us take the intuition that every run of a synchronizer should "do as much as possible" and reach a stable state: synchronizing again immediately should propagate no further changes. This can be stated formally as follows:

Property 4.2.1. A synchronization algorithm is *idempotent* if $(A \leftarrow O \rightarrow B) \Rightarrow (A' \leftarrow O' \rightarrow B')$ implies $(A' \leftarrow O' \rightarrow B') \Rightarrow (A' \leftarrow O' \rightarrow B')$.

Fact 4.2.2. `Diff3` is *not* idempotent.

Counterexample. Consider the run in the top part of Figure 4, where

$$([1, 2, 4, 6, 8] \leftarrow [1, 2, 3, 4, 5, 5, 5, 6, 7, 8] \rightarrow [1, 4, 5, 5, 5, 6, 2, 3, 4, 8])$$
$$\Rightarrow ([1, 2, 4, 6, 8] \leftarrow [1, 2, 3, 4, 6, 7, 8] \rightarrow [1, 4, 6, 2, 3, 4, 8]).$$

The output configuration can take another step, shown in the bottom part of Figure 4, leading to

$$([1,2,4,6,8] \leftarrow [1,2,3,4,6,7,8] \rightarrow [1,4,6,2,3,4,8])$$
$$\Rightarrow ([1,4,6,2,4,6,8] \leftarrow [1,4,6,2,4,6,7,8] \rightarrow [1,4,6,2,4,8]).$$

Note that `diff3` has no choice in either case: each of the input configurations has just one pair of maximum matchings. (Ensuring this is the role of the blocks of repeated 5s in the first configuration.) □

4.3   Near Success on Similar Replicas

The `diff3` algorithm begins by comparing O, separately, with A and with B; it never compares A and B directly. Nevertheless, it seems reasonable to expect that, even if A and B are very different from O, we should still be able to synchronize successfully, as long as A and B themselves are similar. Unfortunately, this intuition is misleading.

For any pair of replicas A, B, let $m(A, B)$ denote the length of a largest common subsequence for A and B. Let ϵ be some function mapping natural numbers to reals between 0 and 1. A pair of replicas A, B is said to be ϵ-*close* if $m(A, B) \geq (1 - \epsilon(n))n$, where $n = \max\{|A|, |B|\}$. We can now formally define stability properties involving the notion of "similarity."

Property 4.3.1. A synchronization algorithm guarantees *near success on similar replicas* if there exists a universal constant $c > 0$ such that, for any ϵ-close pair (A, B), if $(A \leftarrow O \rightarrow B) \Rightarrow (A' \leftarrow O' \rightarrow B')$, then A' and B' are $(c\epsilon)$-close.

Fact 4.3.2. `Diff3` does *not* guarantee near success on similar replicas.

Counterexample. Consider the input configuration

$$(A \leftarrow O \rightarrow B) = \begin{pmatrix} [1, \frac{n}{2}+1, \ldots, n-1, 2, \ldots, \frac{n}{2}, n] \\ \uparrow \\ [1, \ldots, n] \\ \downarrow \\ [1, 2, \frac{n}{2}+1, \ldots, n-1, 3, \ldots, \frac{n}{2}, n] \end{pmatrix}$$

(generalizing the one we saw in Section 2). Note that the pair (A, B) is $\frac{1}{n}$-close, as their largest common subsequence is of length $n - 1$. The unique maximum common subsequence of O and A is $[1, 2, \ldots, n/2, n]$; between O and B it is $[1, 2, n/2 + 1, \ldots, n - 1, n]$. This leads to three stable `diff3` chunks and two unstable chunks, as shown in Figure 5. Though the second of these is conflicting, the first is updated only in A; the output of this chunk thus propagates $[n/2 + 1, \ldots, n - 1]$ to O and B , yielding the complete output

$$(A' \leftarrow O' \rightarrow B') = \begin{pmatrix} [1, \frac{n}{2}+1, \ldots, n-1, 2, \ldots, \frac{n}{2}, n] \\ \uparrow \\ [1, \frac{n}{2}+1, \ldots, n-1, 2, \ldots, n] \\ \downarrow \\ [1, \frac{n}{2}+1, \ldots, n-1, 2, \frac{n}{2}+1, \ldots, n-1, 3, \ldots, \frac{n}{2}, n] \end{pmatrix}.$$

A	1	$\frac{n}{2}+1, \ldots, n-1$	2	$3, \ldots, \frac{n}{2}$	n
O	1		2	$3, \ldots, n-1$	n
B	1		2	$\frac{n}{2}+1, \ldots, n-1, 3, \ldots, \frac{n}{2}$	n
	stable	changed in A	stable	conflict	stable

Fig. 5. Counter-example to several properties

In the final reconciled state, A' and B' are only about $\frac{1}{3}$-close ($m(A', B') = n$, while $\max\{|A'|, |B'|\}$ is about $\frac{3n}{2}$), and so no constant c exists such that they are $\frac{c}{n}$-close for every positive n.   □

4.4 Stability

Another intuitively reasonable property is that any two runs whose inputs are similar should have similar outputs.

Property 4.4.1. A synchronization algorithm is *stable* if there exists a universal constant $c > 0$ such that, for any three pairs (O_1, O_2), (A_1, A_2), and (B_1, B_2), such that each pair is ϵ-close, if $(A_1 \leftarrow O_1 \rightarrow B_1) \Rightarrow (A_1' \leftarrow O_1' \rightarrow B_1')$ and $(A_2 \leftarrow O_2 \rightarrow B_2) \Rightarrow (A_2' \leftarrow O_2' \rightarrow B_2')$, then each pair of replicas (O_1', O_2'), (A_1', A_2'), and (B_1', B_2') is $c\epsilon$-close.

Fact 4.4.2. `Diff3` is *not* stable, even for non-conflicting runs.

Counterexample. Consider the runs

$$([X, Y, X] \leftarrow [X, Y, 0, Y, X] \rightarrow [Y, X, 0, Y]) \Rightarrow [Y, X, 0]$$
$$([X, Y, X] \leftarrow [X, Y, 0, Y, X] \rightarrow [0, Y, X, Y]) \Rightarrow [0, X, Y],$$

where $X = [1, \ldots, \frac{n}{2}]$ and $Y = [\frac{n}{2}+1, \ldots, n]$. It is easy to see that the corresponding pairs in the two input configurations are all $\frac{2}{3n}$-close while the output is only about $\frac{1}{2}$-close.   □

5 Future Work

Our formalization suggests a number of interesting variations on `diff3`. For example, instead of asking for separate matchings of (O, A) and (O, B) could we try to compute a maximum *joint* matching of (A, O, B)? (Note that having maximum matchings for (O, A) and (O, B) does not imply having a maximum matching of (A, O, B). For instance, if $O = [1, 2, 3, 4, 5, 6]$, $B = [4, 5, 1, 2, 3]$, and $A = [4, 5, 6, 1, 2]$, the unique maximum matchings for the pairs leads to an empty match for the triple though clearly one can choose either $[1, 2]$ or $[4, 5]$ as the matching elements.) Alternatively, the choice of two-way matchings could be biased by their effect on the output, especially when deciding between two similar choices, since there are instances when a choosing a different maximum match or even a slightly sub-optimal matching can lead to better results.

Acknowledgments

We gratefully acknowledge stimulating discussions about list synchronization with James Leifer and Catuscia Palamidessi. Nate Foster helped us understand some of the intricacies of diff3's behavior. This research has been supported by the National Science Foundation under grants 0113226, *Principles and Practice of Synchronization*, and 0429836, *Harmony: The Art of Reconciliation.*

References

1. Smith, R.: GNU diff3, Version 2.8.1, April 2002; distributed with GNU diffutils package (1988)
2. Lindholm, T.: A three-way merge for xml documents. In: DocEng 2004: Proceedings of the 2004 ACM symposium on Document engineering, pp. 1–10. ACM Press, New York (2004)
3. Chawathe, S.S., Rajamaran, A., Garcia-Molina, H., Widom, J.: Change detection in hierarchically structured information. ACM SIGMOD Record 25(2), 493–504 (1996)
4. Lanham, M., Kang, A., Hammer, J., Helal, A., Wilson, J.: Format-independent change detection and propagation in support of mobile computing. In: Brazilian Symposium on Databases (SBBD), Gramado, Brazil, pp. 27–41 (October 2002)
5. MacKenzie, D., Eggert, P., Stallman, R.: Comparing and Merging Files with GNU diff and patch. Network Theory Ltd. Printed version of GNU manual (2003)
6. Miller, W., Myers, E.W.: A file comparison program. Softw., Pract. Exper. 15(11), 1025–1040 (1985)
7. Myers, E.W.: An o(nd) difference algorithm and its variations. Algorithmica 1(2), 251–266 (1986)
8. Ukkonen, E.: Algorithms for approximate string matching. Information and Control 64(1-3), 100–118 (1985)
9. Foster, J.N., Greenwald, M.B., Kirkegaard, C., Pierce, B.C., Schmitt, A.: Exploiting schemas in data synchronization. Journal of Computer and System Sciences (2007) To appear. Extended abstract in Database Programming Languages (DBPL) (2005)
10. Mens, T.: A state-of-the-art survey on software merging. IEEE Trans. Software Eng. 28(5), 449–462 (2002)
11. Stallman, R., et al.: Comparing and merging files, Manual for GNU diffutils (2002), available at www.gnu.org

Probabilistic Analysis of the Degree Bounded Minimum Spanning Tree Problem

Anand Srivastav and Sören Werth

Institut für Informatik
Christian-Albrechts-Universität zu Kiel
Christian-Albrechts-Platz 4, 24098 Kiel, Germany
{asr,swe}@informatik.uni-kiel.de

Abstract. In the b-degree constrained Euclidean minimum spanning tree problem (bMST) we are given n points in $[0, 1]^d$ and a degree constraint $b \geq 2$. The aim is to find a minimum weight spanning tree in which each vertex has degree at most b. In this paper we analyze the probabilistic version of the problem and prove in affirmative the conjecture of Yukich stated in 1998 on the asymptotics of the problem for uniformly (and also some non-uniformly) distributed points in $[0, 1]^d$: the optimal length $L_{bMST}(X_1, \ldots, X_n)$ of a b-degree constrained minimal spanning tree on $X_1, \ldots, X_n$ given by iid random variables with values in $[0, 1]^d$ satisfies

$$\lim_{n \to \infty} \frac{L_{bMST}(X_1, \ldots, X_n)}{n^{(d-1)/d}} = \alpha(L_{bMST}, d) \int_{[0,1]^d} f(x)^{(d-1)/d} dx \text{ c.c.,}$$

where $\alpha(L_{bMST}, d)$ is a positive constant, f is the density of the absolutely continuous part of the law of X_1 and c.c. stands for complete convergence. In the case $b = 2$, the b-degree constrained MST has the same asymptotic behavior as the TSP, and we have $\alpha(L_{bMST}, d) = \alpha(L_{TSP}, d)$. We also show concentration of L_{bMST} around its mean and around $\alpha(L_{bMST}, d)n^{(d-1)/d}$. The result of this paper may spur further investigation of probabilistic spanning tree problems with degree constraints.

1 Introduction

The bMST-Problem: Complexity and Approximation. In the b-degree constrained Euclidean minimum spanning tree problem (bMST) we are given a set $\mathcal{P}$ of n points in $[0, 1]^d$, and a degree bound $b \geq 2$. The aim is to find a minimum spanning tree in which the degree of each vertex is at most b (the length or weight of an edge is given by its Euclidean length). The total length of such a bMST is denoted by $L_{bMST}(\mathcal{P})$.

This is a generalization of the path version of the Euclidean TSP. Furthermore it is the most basic problem of a family of well-studied problems about finding degree constrained structures. A nice survey on this topic is given by Raghavachari [12]. Concerning complexity, since the case $b = 2$ is equivalent to the path version of the traveling salesman problem, it is NP-hard. For $b = 3$ Papadimitriou and Vazirani [11] showed that the problem remains NP-hard even

V. Arvind and S. Prasad (Eds.): FSTTCS 2007, LNCS 4855, pp. 497–507, 2007.
© Springer-Verlag Berlin Heidelberg 2007

in the Euclidean plane. They conjectured that the problem is NP-hard also for $b = 4$, but this question is still open. For $b = 5$ the problem in the Euclidean plane is solvable in polynomial time [9].

Considering approximation algorithms, Arora and Chang [2] developed a quasi-polynomial time approximation scheme for the problem using Arora's divide-and-conquer technique for the Euclidean TSP [1]. The best polynomial approximation algorithms are due to Chan [5], who proved a 1.40 approximation for $b = 3$ resp. a 1.14 approximation for $b = 4$ in $\mathbb{R}^2$ and a 1.63 approximation for $b = 3$ in $\mathbb{R}^d$.

Probabilistic Analysis. The probabilistic analysis of Euclidean combinatorial optimizations problems has its roots in the celebrated theorem of Bearwood, Halton and Hammersley [4]. In 1959 they proved that for n independently and identically distributed random variables $X_1, \ldots, X_n$ in $[0, 1]^d$, $d \geq 2$, the optimal TSP tour length $L_{TSP}(X_1, \ldots, X_n)$ is asymptotically $n^{(d-1)/d}$, more precisely there is a constant $\alpha(L_{TSP}, d) > 0$ such that

$$\lim_{n \to \infty} L_{TSP}(X_1, \ldots, X_n)/n^{(d-1)/d} = \alpha(L_{TSP}, d) \int_{[0,1]^d} f(x)^{(d-1)/d} dx$$

almost surely, where f is the density of the absolutely continuous part of the law of X_1.

Note that for a uniform distribution we have $f = 1$, thus also the integral over f is 1. In the general case those non-uniform distributions of X_1 (thus of any X_i as we have iid random variables) are addressed where f is the density function of the absolutely continuous probability measure appearing in the decomposition of the distribution into an absolutely continuous and a singular probability measure (for exact definitions and the decomposition theorem we refer to [15, 17]).

This is the description of the above used phrase from the literature, that "f is the absolutely continuous part of the law of X_1". We will use this notion henceforth.

Papadimitriou [10] in 1978 modified the proof and showed a similar result for the minimum matching problem in two dimensions. This was the first general approach where some conditions for Euclidean optimization problems were defined so that all problems satisfying these conditions have the same asymptotic behavior. In 1981 Steele [15] also presented a general approach and showed that a large class of problems has the same $n^{(d-1)/d}$ asymptotics as the TSP. Twelve years later, in 1993, Rhee [14] brought isoperimetric inequalities into play and showed that Steele's results hold in the sense of complete convergence, which is stronger than almost sure convergence. In 1994 Redmond and Yukich [13] extended Steele's and Rhee's results to an even broader class of problems.

The work of Beardwood, Halton and Hammersley [4] motivated a large body of research on the probabilistic analysis of Euclidean optimization problems as minimum spanning tree, minimum perfect matching, etc. Today, there is a good understanding of the general structure that underlies the asymptotic behavior of these problems. An overview on the history and main developments in this area is given in the books of Yukich [19] and Steele [16]. Recent applications to Euclidean multidepot vehicle routing problems were given by the authors in FSTTCS 2005 and will appear in [3].

However, it was not possible to determine the asymptotics of the probabilistic bMST-Problem. Yukich [19] in 1998 conjectured that the asymptotics of the bMST-problem for n uniformly (and also non-uniformly) distributed points in $[0,1]^d$ is governed by $n^{(d-1)/d}$. We settle this conjecture by showing that the asymptotic behavior of the length functional of the b-degree constrained MST problem can be analyzed with the help of its boundary modification:

Theorem 1. *Let $\mathcal{P} = \{X_1, \ldots, X_n\}$ be a set of points in $[0,1]^d$ given by iid random variables and let f be the density of the absolutely continuous part in the law of X_1. The optimal length $L_{bMST}(\mathcal{P})$ of a b-degree constrained minimum spanning tree on $\mathcal{P}$ satisfies*

$$\lim_{n \to \infty} \frac{L_{bMST}(\mathcal{P})}{n^{(d-1)/d}} = \alpha(L_{bMST}, d) \int_{[0,1]^d} f(x)^{(d-1)/d} dx \ \ c.c.,$$

where $\alpha(L_{bMST}, d)$ is a positive constant. In the case $b = 2$, the b-degree constrained MST has the same asymptotics as the Euclidean TSP, and $\alpha(L_{bMST}, d) = \alpha(L_{TSP}, d)$.

The main idea and work in the proof is the invention of an approximation of the length functional of the bMST-problem and its combinatorial analysis so that a limit theorem of Redmond and Yukich [13] resp. a concentration inequality of Rhee [14] can be invoked.

2   Facts on Subadditive Euclidean Functionals

We recall the notion of complete convergence of random variables. First of all, one can show that complete convergence implies almost surely convergence. Considering a Euclidean functional F on points given by random variables $X_1, \ldots, X_n$, the main benefit of complete convergence is that it yields convergence results for two different random problem models that differ in the transition from $F(X_1, \ldots, X_n)$ to $F(X_1, \ldots, X_n, X_{n+1})$. In the *incrementing problem model* an additional sample point is given by X_{n+1} in order to get $F(X_1, \ldots, X_n, X_{n+1})$, while in the *independent problem model* a completely new sample of $n+1$ points is used. The important point is that almost sure convergence results for the independent model imply almost sure convergence for the incrementing model, but the converse is generally true only for complete convergence. Weide [18] was the first to distinguish the models in the probabilistic analysis of algorithms.

We give a short overview of the theory of subadditive and superadditive Euclidean functionals. First, we list some general properties of a length function F that is defined for a Euclidean optimization problem in $\mathbb{R}^d$. Let $F : \mathcal{S} \to \mathbb{R}^+$ be a function, where $\mathcal{S}$ is the set of finite subsets of $\mathbb{R}^d$. Let $\mathcal{R}$ be the set of d-dimensional rectangles. F has the *translation invariance* property if for all $y \in \mathbb{R}^d$ and all finite subsets $\mathcal{P} \subset \mathbb{R}^d$,

$$F(\mathcal{P}) = F(\mathcal{P} + y) ,$$

the *homogeneity* property, if for all $\alpha > 0$ and all finite subsets $\mathcal{P} \subset \mathbb{R}^d$,

$$F(\alpha\mathcal{P}) = \alpha F(\mathcal{P}) \ ,$$

and the *normalization* property, if $F(\emptyset) = 0$. F is called a *Euclidean functional* if it has the above three properties.

F is called *subadditive* if for all rectangles $R \subset \mathbb{R}^d$, all finite subsets $\mathcal{P} \subset R$ and all partitions of R into subrectangles R_1 and R_2,

$$F(\mathcal{P}) \leq F(\mathcal{P} \cap R_1) + F(\mathcal{P} \cap R_2) + C_d \cdot \text{diam}(R) \ ,$$

where the constant C_d may depend on d and $\text{diam}(R)$ denotes the diameter of R.

Rhee [14] showed the following growth bound for a subadditive Euclidean functional.

Lemma 1 (see [14]). *Let F be a subadditive Euclidean functional. There exists a constant $C > 0$ such that for all rectangles $R \subseteq [0,1]^d$ and all finite point sets $\mathcal{P} \subset R$, we have*

$$F(\mathcal{P}) \leq C|\mathcal{P}|^{(d-1)/d} \ .$$

Normally, the subadditivity is used to express the global graph length as a sum of local components. This can also be done via superadditivity. A functional F is called *superadditive*, if for all rectangles $R \subset \mathbb{R}^d$, all finite subsets $\mathcal{P} \subset R$ and all partitions of R into subrectangles R_1 and R_2

$$F(\mathcal{P}) \geq F(\mathcal{P} \cap R_1) + F(\mathcal{P} \cap R_2) \ .$$

Another strong property of Euclidean functionals is smoothness. A Euclidean functional F is *smooth* if there is a constant $C > 0$ (which may depend on d) such that for all finite sets $\mathcal{P}_1, \mathcal{P}_2 \subset \mathbb{R}^d$

$$|F(\mathcal{P}_1 \cup \mathcal{P}_2) - F(\mathcal{P}_1)| \leq C(|\mathcal{P}_2|)^{(d-1)/d} \ .$$

So the smoothness describes the variation of F when points are added and deleted.

Often the functional under consideration does not have properties required in the probabilistic analysis, for example smoothness or additivity. This fact motivated Redmond and Yukich to introduce the so called boundary functional. Properly defined it has properties required in the probabilistic analysis. This approach of course only works if the boundary functional is a good approximation of the given functional. In the next section we will give the definition of the boundary functional for the bMST problem.

Two Euclidean functionals F and F^* are called *pointwise close* if for all finite $\mathcal{P} \subset [0,1]^d$

$$|F(\mathcal{P}) - F^*(\mathcal{P})| = o(|\mathcal{P}|^{(d-1)/d}) \ .$$

Redmond and Yukich call a smooth subadditive functional that is pointwise close to its superadditive boundary functional *quasiadditive*. We state the limit theorem by Redmond and Yukich, which will be used later.

Theorem 2 (see [13]). *Let $X_1, \ldots, X_n$ be independent identically distributed random variables with values in $[0,1]^d$, $d \geq 2$, and let $F(X_1, \ldots, X_n)$ be a quasi-additive smooth Euclidean functional, then*

$$\lim_{n \to \infty} F(X_1, \ldots, X_n)/n^{(d-1)/d} = \alpha(F) \int f(x)^{(d-1)/d} dx \quad c.c.,$$

where f is the absolutely continuous part of the law of X_1.

Rhee proved a strong concentration inequality which can be used to derive complete convergence. It shows that, except for a small set with polynomially small probability, smooth Euclidean functionals are close to their means. By the inequality it is sufficient to determine the asymptotics of the mean in order to show complete convergence of the functional. This simplified the probabilistic analysis of many problems.

Theorem 3 (see [14]). *Let $U_1, \ldots, U_n$ be independent uniformly distributed random variables with values in $[0,1]^d$, $d \geq 2$, and let $F(U_1, \ldots, U_n)$ be a smooth Euclidean functional. Then there are positive constants C, C', C'' such that for all $t > 0$:*

$$\mathbb{P}\left[\,|F(U_1, \ldots, U_n) - \mathbb{E}\left[F(U_1, \ldots, U_n)\right]| > t\right]$$

$$\leq C \exp\left(-\frac{1}{C''n}\left(\frac{t}{C'}\right)^{2d/(d-1)}\right).$$

3   The Boundary bMST Functional

In this section we analyze the properties of the b-degree constrained MST, particularly with regard to the conditions in Theorem 2, where the functional L_{bMST} will take the role of F. After that we will introduce the boundary modification of L_{bMST}, which will help to prove the main result (Theorem 1).

Lemma 2. *L_{bMST} is a subadditive and smooth Euclidean functional.*

Proof. It is obvious that L_{bMST} has the translation invariance, homogeneity and normalization properties, and it is also easy to see that the functional is subadditive: consider a finite set $\mathcal{P}$, a d-dimensional rectangle R with diameter $\text{diam}(R)$, a partition of R into two rectangles $R = R_1 \cup R_2$ and let $bMST_1$ and $bMST_2$ be optimal b-degree constrained minimal spanning trees in R_1 respectively R_2. Each tree contains two leaves, vertices with degree 1, and the trees are merged into a single tree by connecting two leaves. The length of the used edge is at most $\text{diam}(R)$. So we have

$$L_{bMST}(\mathcal{P} \cap R) \leq L_{bMST}(\mathcal{P} \cap R_1) + L_{bMST}(\mathcal{P} \cap R_2) + \text{diam}(R) \ .$$

In the second part of the proof we show that the functional is smooth:

$$|L_{bMST}(\mathcal{P}_1 \cup \mathcal{P}_2) - L_{bMST}(\mathcal{P}_1)| \leq C|\mathcal{P}_2|^{(d-1)/d} \ ,$$

for some positive constant C. We begin with a bMST on $\mathcal{P}_1$ and add a bMST on $\mathcal{P}_2$. Each of the graphs contains at least two leaves, we connect the graphs by a single edge between two leaves of length at most $\sqrt{d}$. The resulting graph is a feasible b-degree constrained MST on $\mathcal{P}_1 \cup \mathcal{P}_2$. By Lemma 1 the total edge length of the added bMST on $\mathcal{P}_2$ is at most $C|\mathcal{P}_2|^{(d-1)/d}$ for some constant $C > 0$, since the bMST is a subadditive Euclidean functional. Thus,

$$L_{bMST}(\mathcal{P}_1 \cup \mathcal{P}_2) \leq L_{bMST}(\mathcal{P}_1) + C|\mathcal{P}_2|^{(d-1)/d} .$$

Now we start with a bMST on $\mathcal{P}_1 \cup \mathcal{P}_2$ and construct a bMST on $\mathcal{P}_1$. All points of $\mathcal{P}_2$ and edges incident with these points are deleted. The deletion generates at most $b|\mathcal{P}_2|$ connected components, and each component is a tree. We choose a leaf of each tree and add a TSP tour through these leaves to the graph. An edge of the TSP tour has to be deleted to construct a feasible bMST on $\mathcal{P}_1 \cup \mathcal{P}_2$. The total length of the added TSP tour is bounded by $C|\mathcal{P}_2|^{(d-1)/d}$ by Lemma 1. We have

$$L_{bMST}(\mathcal{P}_1) \leq L_{bMST}(\mathcal{P}_1 \cup \mathcal{P}_2) + C|\mathcal{P}_2|^{(d-1)/d} ,$$

hence, the functional is smooth.   □

We proceed to the definition of the boundary graph resp. functional. In a boundary bMST graph we have either bMSTs that are all connected to the boundary or a single bMST without a connection to the boundary, see Figure 1 and 2. Here is the formal definition of the boundary functional of the b-degree constrained MST: For all rectangles $R \subset \mathbb{R}^d$, finite point sets $\mathcal{P} \subset R$ and points a on the boundary of R let $L'_{bMST}(\mathcal{P}, a)$ denote the length of the minimal b-degree constrained spanning tree on $\mathcal{P} \cup \{a\}$. The *boundary bMST functional* L^B_{bMST} is defined by

$$L^B_{bMST}(\mathcal{P}) := \min \left\{ L_{bMST}(\mathcal{P}), \ \inf \left\{ \sum_i L'_{bMST}(\mathcal{P}_i, a_i) \right\} \right\} ,$$

where the infimum ranges over all sequences $(a_i)_{i \geq 1}$ of points on the boundary of R and all partitions $(\mathcal{P}_i)_{i \geq 1}$ of $\mathcal{P}$.

We show that the boundary bMST functional is a good approximation of the bMST functional:

Lemma 3. *The b-degree constrained MST functional and its boundary functional are pointwise close:*

$$|L_{bMST}(\mathcal{P}) - L^B_{bMST}(\mathcal{P})| \leq C|\mathcal{P}|^{(d-2)/(d-1)} ,$$

where C is a positive constant.

Proof. Since $L^B_{bMST}(\mathcal{P}) \leq L_{bMST}(\mathcal{P})$, we only have to show that

$$L_{bMST}(\mathcal{P}) \leq L^B_{bMST}(\mathcal{P}) + C|\mathcal{P}|^{(d-2)/(d-1)} ,$$

for some constant $C > 0$. We start with a graph associated to $L^B_{bMST}(\mathcal{P})$ and modify it into a feasible b-degree constrained MST by adding edges of total

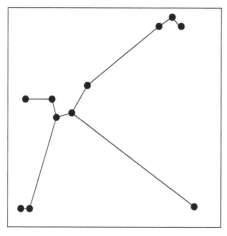
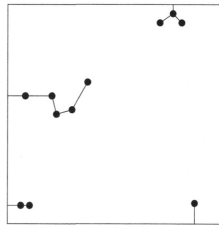

Fig. 1. A 3-degree constrained MST

Fig. 2. A boundary 3-degree constrained MST

length at most $C|\mathcal{P}|^{\frac{d-2}{d-1}}$: let $\mathcal{B}$ denote the set of points where the graph meets the boundary of $[0,1]^d$. Note that the vertices in $\mathcal{B}$ have degree 1. We add to the graph a TSP tour through $\mathcal{B}$ with edges lying on the boundary of $[0,1]^d$ and delete an arbitrary edge in order to construct a b-degree constrained MST (note $b \geq 3$). Since the boundary of $[0,1]^d$ has dimension $d-1$ and the TSP functional is a subadditive Euclidean functional, the total length of the added MST is at most $C|\mathcal{B}|^{(d-2)/(d-1)}$ by Lemma 1 and C being the constant appearing there. Due to the fact that $|\mathcal{B}| \leq |\mathcal{P}|$, we have

$$L_{bMST}(\mathcal{P}) \leq L_{bMST}^B(\mathcal{P}) + C|\mathcal{P}|^{(d-2)/(d-1)}$$

and the claim follows. □

The next lemma shows that the boundary bMST functional has the properties required by Theorem 2.

Lemma 4. *The boundary functional L_{bMST}^B of the b-degree constrained MST is a superadditive and smooth Euclidean functional.*

Proof. It is easy to verify that L_{bMST}^B has the translation invariance, homogeneity and normalization properties. Furthermore the functional is superadditive: consider a finite set $\mathcal{P}$, a d-dimensional rectangle R with a partition into two rectangles $R = R_1 \cup R_2$ and let $bMST^B$ be an optimal boundary b-degree constrained minimal spanning tree in R. The restrictions of $bMST^B$ to R_1 and R_2 define boundary b-degree constrained minimal spanning trees in R_1 respectively R_2, in case that the restrictions contain paths that start and end at the boundary one has to remove an arbitrary edge in the path. The restrictions are at least as large as $L_{bMST}^B(\mathcal{P} \cap R_1)$ respectively $L_{bMST}^B(\mathcal{P} \cap R_2)$. Thus,

$$L_{bMST}^B(\mathcal{P} \cap R) \geq L_{bMST}^B(\mathcal{P} \cap R_1) + L_{bMST}^B(\mathcal{P} \cap R_2) .$$

It remains to show that the functional is smooth:

$$|L_{bMST}^B(\mathcal{P}_1 \cup \mathcal{P}_2) - L_{bMST}^B(\mathcal{P}_1)| \leq C|\mathcal{P}_2|^{(d-1)/d} \ ,$$

where $C > 0$ is a constant. We start with a graph associated to $L_{bMST}^B(\mathcal{P}_1 \cup \mathcal{P}_2)$ and delete all points of $\mathcal{P}_2$ and all edges incident with these points. The resulting graph consists of at most $b|\mathcal{P}_2|$ connected components that are not connected to the boundary. These components are trees, so each of them contains vertices with degree 1. Choose a vertex with degree 1 in every component and add a TSP tour through these vertices (note that we are considering $b \geq 3$). Then we delete an arbitrary edge in the tour and choose a vertex with degree 1 in the component and connect it to the boundary in order to construct a feasible boundary $bMST$ on $\mathcal{P}_1$. The total length of all added edges is at most $C|\mathcal{P}_2|^{(d-1)/d}$, since the TSP functional is a subadditive Euclidean functional, by Lemma 1 and the constant C appearing there. Thus,

$$L_{bMST}^B(\mathcal{P}_1) \leq L_{bMST}^B(\mathcal{P}_1 \cup \mathcal{P}_2) + C|\mathcal{P}_2|^{(d-1)/d} \ .$$

To show $L_{bMST}^B(\mathcal{P}_1 \cup \mathcal{P}_2) \leq L_{bMST}^B(\mathcal{P}_1) + C|\mathcal{P}_2|^{(d-1)/d}$, we begin with a graph associated to $L_{bMST}^B(\mathcal{P}_1)$ and add a $bMST$ on $\mathcal{P}_2$ to the graph. A leaf of the $bMST$ on $\mathcal{P}_2$ and a leaf of the boundary $bMST$ on $\mathcal{P}_1$ are connected by an edge of length at most $\sqrt{d}$ in order to construct a feasible boundary $bMST$ on $\mathcal{P}_1 \cup \mathcal{P}_2$. Since the $bMST$ functional is a subadditive Euclidean functional, we have by Lemma 1 that $L_{bMST}(\mathcal{P}_2) \leq C|\mathcal{P}_2|^{(d-1)/d}$. Thus,

$$L_{bMST}^B(\mathcal{P}_1 \cup \mathcal{P}_2) \leq L_{bMST}^B(\mathcal{P}_1) + C|\mathcal{P}_2|^{(d-1)/d} \ ,$$

and all in all the assumption follows:

$$|L_{bMST}^B(\mathcal{P}_1 \cup \mathcal{P}_2) - L_{bMST}^B(\mathcal{P}_1)| \leq C|\mathcal{P}_2|^{(d-1)/d} \ . \qquad \square$$

4   Proof of Theorem 1 and Concentration

Proof of Theorem 1: By the Lemmata 2, 3 and 4 the $bMST$ functional is a smooth and subadditive Euclidean functional which is close to its smooth and superadditive Euclidean boundary functional. We can thus apply Theorem 2 and this yields Theorem 1. $\qquad \square$

In the following we consider points that are given by iid random variables with uniform distribution. Remond and Yukich [13] have shown that boundary functionals are an ideal tool to provide rates of convergence of Euclidean functionals. The subadditive structure of a functional is not enough to prove rates of convergence, one gets only one-sided estimates. With the help of the boundary functional, the functional can be made superadditive and one can extract rates of convergence. The idea of modifying functionals to get a superadditive structure was known before the work of Redmond and Yukich, see e.g. Hammersley [7], but they provide a general and simple approach. The formulation of the following lemma is from McGivney and Yukich [8]:

Lemma 5 (see [8]). *Let $U_1, \ldots, U_n$ be iid uniform random variables on $[0,1]^d$, $d \geq 3$. Suppose that L is a smooth, subadditive Euclidean functional, L^B is a smooth, superadditive Euclidean functional and*

$$|\,\mathbb{E}\,L[(U_1, \ldots, U_n)] - \mathbb{E}[L^B(U_1, \ldots, U_n)]| \leq \beta(n) \ ,$$

where $\beta(n)$ denotes a function of n. Then there is a positive constant C such that

$$|\,\mathbb{E}\,L[(U_1, \ldots, U_n)] - \alpha(L, d)n^{(d-1)/d}| \leq \max\{\beta(n), Cn^{(d-1)/2d}\} \ .$$

With the help of this lemma we can show:

Lemma 6. *Let $\mathcal{P} = \{U_1, \ldots, U_n\}$ be a set of points in $[0,1]^d$ given by independent uniformly distributed random variables. The mean of the bMST functional satisfies*

$$|\mathbb{E}[L_{bMST}(U_1, \ldots, U_n)] - \alpha(L_{bMST}, d)n^{(d-1)/d}| \leq Cn^{(d-2)/(d-1)} \ .$$

where C is a positive constant.

Proof. By Lemma 3 we have

$$|L_{bMST}(\mathcal{P}) - L^B_{bMST}(\mathcal{P})| \leq Cn^{(d-2)/(d-1)} \ ,$$

and with Jensen's inequality

$$|\mathbb{E}[L_{bMST}(\mathcal{P})] - \mathbb{E}[L^B_{bMST}(\mathcal{P})]| \leq Cn^{(d-2)/(d-1)} \ .$$

So by Lemma 5 we obtain

$$|\mathbb{E}[L_{bMST}(U_1, \ldots, U_n)] - \alpha(L_{bMST}, d)n^{(d-1)/d}| \leq Cn^{(d-2)/(d-1)} \ . \qquad \square$$

We are now able to prove concentration.

Theorem 4. *Let $\mathcal{P} = \{U_1, \ldots, U_n\}$ be a set of points in $[0,1]^d$ given by independent uniformly distributed random variables.*

(i) There are constants positive C, C', C'' such that for all $t > 0$:

$$\mathbb{P}\left[|L_{bMST}(U_1, \ldots, U_n) - \mathbb{E}\left[L_{bMST}(U_1, \ldots, U_n)\right]| > t\right]$$
$$\leq Ce^{-\frac{(t/C')^{2d/(d-1)}}{C''n}} \ .$$

(ii) Let $\delta = \frac{d^2 - 2d - 1}{d^2 - 2d + 1}$. Let C be the constant in Lemma 6. There are positive constants c_1 and $c = c(d)$ such that

$$\mathbb{P}\left[|L_{bMST}(U_1, \ldots, U_n) - \alpha(L_{bMST})n^{(d-1)/d}| > (1 + C)n^{(d-2)/(d-1)}\right]$$
$$\leq c_1 e^{-c(d)n^\delta} \ .$$

Proof

(i) By Lemma 2, L_{bMST} satisfies the assumption of Theorem 3 and we are done.

(ii) The assertion follows using the triangle inequality, Lemma 6 and part (i).

$$\square$$

5   Conclusion

We have proved the conjectured asymptotics for the probabilistic version of the d-dimensional Euclidean degree bounded minimum spanning tree problem along with a concentration result. In future work this work might be useful to fix the asymptotics for other degree constrained spanning tree problems, like orthogonal networks, which were recently studied (STACS 2007, [6]). Such special problems are interesting in the context of network analysis, but perhaps may show a different asymptotic behavior than $n^{(d-1)/d}$ due to their special structure.

References

[1] Arora, S.: Polynomial time approximation schemes for Euclidean TSP and other geometric problems. Journal of the ACM 45(5), 754–782 (1998)

[2] Arora, S., Chang, K.: Approximation schemes for degree-restricted MST and red-blue separation problems. Algorithmica 40(3), 189–210 (2004)

[3] Baltz, A., Dubhashi, D., Srivastav, A., Tansini, L., Werth, S.: Probabilistic analysis of a multidepot vehicle routing problem. In: Ramanujam, R., Sen, S. (eds.) FSTTCS 2005. LNCS, vol. 3821, Springer, Heidelberg (2005), and in Random Structures and Algorithms, 30(1-2), 206–225 (2007)

[4] Beardwood, J., Halton, J.H., Hammersley, J.M.: The shortest path through many points. Proceedings of the Cambridge Philosophical Society 55, 299–327 (1959)

[5] Chan, T.M.: Euclidean bounded-degree spanning tree ratios. In: Proceedings of the 19th ACM Symposium on Computational Geometry, pp. 11–19. ACM Press, New York (2003)

[6] Dumitrescu, A., Tóth, C.D.: Light orthogonal networks with constant geometric dilation. In: Thomas, W., Weil, P. (eds.) STACS 2007. LNCS, vol. 4393, pp. 175–187. Springer, Heidelberg (2007)

[7] Hammersley, J.M.: Postulates for subadditive processes. Annals of Probability 2, 652–680 (1974)

[8] McGivney, K., Yukich, J.E.: Asymptotics for geometric location problems over random samples. Advances in Applied Probability 31, 632–642 (1999)

[9] Monma, C., Suri, S.: Transitions in geometric minimum spanning trees. Discrete & Computational Geometry 8(3), 265–293 (1992)

[10] Papadimitriou, C.H.: The probabilistic analysis of matching heuristics. In: Proceedings of the 15th Allerton Conference on Communication, Control and Computing, pp. 368–378 (1978)

[11] Papadimitriou, C.H., Vazirani, U.V.: On two geometric problems related to the travelling salesman problem. Journal of Algorithms 5(2), 231–246 (1984)

[12] Raghavachari, B.: Algorithms for finding low degree structures. In: Hochbaum, D. (ed.) Approximation algorithms, pp. 266–295. PWS Publishers Inc. (1996)

[13] Redmond, C., Yukich, J.E.: Limit theorems and rates of convergence for Euclidean functionals. Annals of Applied Probability 4(4), 1057–1073 (1994)

[14] Rhee, W.T.: A matching problem and subadditive Euclidean functionals. Annals of Applied Probability 3(3), 794–801 (1993)

[15] Steele, J.M.: Subadditive Euclidean functionals and non-linear growth in geometric probability. Annals of Probability 9, 365–376 (1981)

[16] Steele, J.M.: Probability theory and combinatorial optimization. In: CBMS-NSF Regional Conference Series in Applied Mathematics, Society for Industrial and Applied Mathematics (SIAM), Philadelphia, PA, vol. 69 (1997)

[17] Strassen, V.: The existence of probability measures with given marginals. Annals of Mathematical Statistics 36, 423–439 (1965)

[18] Weide, B.: Statistical methods in algorithm design and analysis, Ph.D. thesis, Computer Science Department, Carnegie Mellon University (1978)

[19] Yukich, J.E.: Probability theory of classical Euclidean optimization problems. Lecture Notes in Mathematics, vol. 1675. Springer, Heidelberg (1998)

Undirected Graphs of Entanglement 2

Walid Belkhir and Luigi Santocanale

Laboratoire d'Informatique Fondamentale de Marseille
Université de Provence

Abstract. Entanglement is a complexity measure of directed graphs that origins in fixed point theory. This measure has shown its use in designing efficient algorithms to verify logical properties of transition systems. We are interested in the problem of deciding whether a graph has entanglement at most k. As this measure is defined by means of games, game theoretic ideas naturally lead to design polynomial algorithms that, for fixed k, decide the problem. Known characterizations of directed graphs of entanglement at most 1 lead, for $k = 1$, to design even faster algorithms. In this paper we give two distinct characterizations of *undirected* graphs of entanglement at most 2. With these characterizations at hand, we present a linear time algorithm to decide whether an undirected graph has this property.

1   Introduction

Entanglement is a complexity measure of finite directed graphs introduced in [1,2] as a tool to analyze the descriptive complexity of the Propositional Modal μ-calculus. Roughly speaking, its purpose is to quantify to what extent cycles are intertwined in a directed graph. Its game theoretic definition – by means of robbers and cops – makes it reasonable to consider entanglement a generalization of the tree-width of undirected graphs [3] to another kind of graphs, a role shared with other complexity measures appeared in the literature [4,5,6,7].

A peculiar aspect of entanglement, and also our motivation for studying it among the other measures, is its direct filiation from fixed point theory. Its first occurrence takes place within the investigation of the variable hierarchy [8,9] of the Propositional Modal μ-Calculus [10]. The latter, hereby noted $\mathbb{L}_\mu$, is nowadays a well known and appreciated logic, capable to express many computational properties of transition systems while allowing their verification in some feasible way. As a μ-calculus [11] $\mathbb{L}_\mu$ increases the expressive power of Hennessy-Milner logic, i.e. multimodal logic $\mathbb{K}$, by adding to it least and greatest fixed point operators that bind monadic variables. Showing that there are μ-formulas ϕ_n that are semantically equivalent to no formula with less than n bound variables is the variable hierarchy problem for a μ-calculus. Such a hierarchy is also meaningful in the simpler setting of iteration theories [12].

The relationship between entanglement and the number of bound variables in a μ-term might be too technical to be elucidated here. Let us say, however, that entanglement roughly is a syntactic analogous of the variable hierarchy, the

V. Arvind and S. Prasad (Eds.): FSTTCS 2007, LNCS 4855, pp. 508–519, 2007.
© Springer-Verlag Berlin Heidelberg 2007

latter being defined only w.r.t. a given semantics. To argue in this direction, the relevant fact is Proposition 14 of [1], stating that the entanglement of a directed graph is the minimal feedback of its finite unravellings.

A second important topic in fixed point theory is the model checking problem for $\mathbb{L}_\mu$. The main achievement of [1] states that parity games whose underlying graphs have bounded entanglement can be solved in polynomial time. This is a relevant result for the matter of verification, since model checking $\mathbb{L}_\mu$ is reducible in linear time to the problem of deciding the winner of a parity game. Berwanger's result calls for the problem of *deciding whether a graph has entanglement at most k*, a problem which we address in this paper. When settled, we can try to exploit the main result of [1], for example by designing algorithms to model check $\mathbb{L}_\mu$ that may perform well in practice. We shall argue that, for fixed k, deciding whether a graph has entanglement at most k is a problem in the class P. The algorithms solving these problems can be combined to show that deciding the entanglement of a graph is in the class EXPTIME. We have no reasons to believe that the problem is in NP. Let us mention on the way that a problem that we indirectly address is that of solving parity games on undirected graphs. These games can be solved in linear time if Eva's and Adam's moves alternate. Yet, the complexity of the problem is not known if consecutive moves of the same player are allowed.

In this paper we show that deciding whether an undirected graph G belongs to $\mathcal{U}_2$, the class of undirected graphs of entanglement at most 2, can be solved in time $O(|V_G|)$. We shall present an algorithm that crucially depends on two characterizations of the class $\mathcal{U}_2$. One of them proceeds by forbidden subgraphs: an undirected graph belongs to $\mathcal{U}_2$ if and only if it does not contain (i) a simple cycle of length strictly greater than 4, (ii) a length 3 simple cycle whose vertices have all degree 3, (iii) a length 4 simple cycle with two adjacent vertices of degree 3. A second characterization constructs the class $\mathcal{U}_2$ from a class of atomic graphs, called the *molecules*, and an operation, the *legal collapse*, that glues together two graphs along a prescribed pair of vertices.

The two characterizations may be appreciated on their own, independently of the algorithm they give rise. Entanglement is an intrinsically dynamic concept, due to its game theoretic definition. As such it is not an easy object of study, while the two characterizations prepare it for future investigations with standard mathematical tools. They also suggest that entanglement is a quite robust notion, henceforth worth being studied independently of its fix-point theoretic background. As a matter of fact, some of the properties we shall encounter have already been under focus: the combinatorial characterization exhibits surprising analogies with the class of House-Hole-Domino free graphs, see [13,14], a sort of generalization of graphs admitting a perfect elimination ordering. These graphs arise as the result of looking for wider notions of ordering for graphs that still ensure nice computational properties. On the other hand, the algebraic characterization recalls the well known fact that graphs of fixed arbitrary tree-width may be constructed by means of an algebra of pushouts and relabelings [15]. The algebra of legal collapses suggests that, for entanglement, it might be possible to develop an analogous generic algebraic framework. It also points to standard graph theoretic ideas, such as n-connectiveness, as the proper tools by which to analyze entanglement.

Clearly, a work that still need to be carried out is to look for some useful characterization of *directed* graphs of entanglement at most k. At present, characterizations are known only for $k \leq 1$ [1, Proposition 3]. We believe that the results presented here suggest useful directions to achieve this goal. In particular, a suggestive path is to generalize the algebra of molecules and legal collapses to an undirected setting. This path might be a feasible one considering that many scientists have recently developed ideas and methods to lift some algebraic framework from an undirected to a directed setting. W.r.t. the algebra of entanglement, a source of ideas might be the recent development of directed homotopy theory from concurrency [16].

2   Entanglement Games

The entanglement of a finite digraph G, denoted $\mathcal{E}(G)$, was defined in [1] by means of some games $\mathcal{E}(G,k)$, $k = 0, \ldots, |V_G|$. The game $\mathcal{E}(G,k)$ is played on the graph G by Thief against Cops, a team of k cops. The rules are as follows. Initially all the cops are placed outside the graph, Thief selects and occupies an initial vertex of G. After Thief's move, Cops may do nothing, may place a cop from outside the graph onto the vertex currently occupied by Thief, may move a cop already on the graph to the current vertex. In turn Thief must choose an edge outgoing from the current vertex whose target is not already occupied by some cop and move there. If no such edge exists, then Thief is caught and Cops win. Thief wins if he is never caught. The entanglement of G is the least $k \in N$ such that k cops have a strategy to catch the thief on G. It will be useful to formalize these notions.

Definition 1. *The entanglement game $\mathcal{E}(G,k)$ of a digraph G is defined by:*

- *Its positions are of the form (v, C, P), where $v \in V_G$, $C \subseteq V_G$ and $|C| \leq k$, $P \in \{Cops, Thief\}$.*
- *Initially Thief chooses $v_0 \in V$ and moves to $(v_0, \emptyset, Cops)$.*
- *Cops can move from $(v, C, Cops)$ to $(v, C', Thief)$ where C' can be*
  1. *C : Cops skip,*
  2. *$C \cup \{v\}$: Cops add a new Cop on the current position,*
  3. *$(C \setminus \{x\}) \cup \{v\}$: Cops move a placed Cop to the current position.*
- *Thief can move from $(v, C, Thief)$ to $(v', C, Cops)$ if $(v, v') \in E_G$ and $v' \notin C$.*

Every finite play is a win for Cops, and every infinite play is a win for Thief. We let

$$\mathcal{E}(G) = \min\{\, k \mid Cops \ have \ a \ winning \ strategy \ in \ \mathcal{E}(G,k)\,\}.$$

It is not difficult to argue that there exist polynomial time algorithms that, for fixed $k \geq 0$ decide on input G whether $\mathcal{E}(G) \leq k$. Such an algorithm constructs the game $\mathcal{E}(G, k)$ whose size is polynomial in $|V_G|$ and $|E_G|$, since k is fixed. Since the game $\mathcal{E}(G, k)$ is clopen, i.e. it is a parity game of depth 1, it is well known [17] that such game can be solved in linear time w.r.t. the size of the graph underlying $\mathcal{E}(G, k)$.

In [1] the authors proved that $\mathcal{E}(G) = 0$ if and only if it is G is acyclic, and that $\mathcal{E}(G) \leq 1$ if and only if each strongly connected component of G has a vertex whose removal makes the component acyclic. Using these results it was argued that deciding whether a graph has entanglement at most 1 is a problem in NLOGSPACE.

While wondering for a characterization of graphs of entanglement at most 2, we observed that such a question has a clear answer for *undirected* graphs. To deal with this kind of graphs, we recall that an undirected edge $\{u, v\}$ is just a pair (u, v), (v, u) of directed edges. We can use the results of [1] to give characterizations of undirected graphs of entanglement at most 1. To this goal, for $n \geq 0$ define the n-star of center x_0, noted $\varsigma_{x_0}^n$, to be the undirected graph (V, E) where $V = \{x_0, a_1, ..., a_n\}$ and $E = \{\{x_0, a_1\}, ..., \{x_0, a_n\}\}$. More generally, say that a graph is a star if it is isomorphic to some $\varsigma_{x_0}^n$. Then we can easily deduce:

Proposition 2. *If G is an undirected graph, then $\mathcal{E}(G) = 0$ if and only if $E_G = \emptyset$, and $\mathcal{E}(G) \leq 1$ if and only if G is a disjoint union of stars.*

To end this section we state a Lemma that later will be used often. We remark that its scope does not restrict to undirected graphs.

Lemma 3. *If H is a subgraph of G then $\mathcal{E}(H) \leq \mathcal{E}(G)$.*

As a matter of fact, Thief can choose an initial vertex from H and then he can restrict his moves to edges of H. In this way he can simulate a winning strategy from $\mathcal{E}(H, k)$ to a winning strategy in $\mathcal{E}(G, k)$.

3   Molecules, Collapses, and the Class ζ_2

In this section we introduce a class of graphs and prove that the graphs in this class have entanglement at most 2. It will be the goal of the next sections to prove that these are all the graphs of entanglement at most 2.

Definition 4. *A molecule $\theta_{a,b}^{\varepsilon,n}$, where $\varepsilon \in \{0, 1\}$ and $n \geq 0$, is the undirected graph (V, E) with $V = \{a, b, c_1, ..., c_n\}$ and*

$$
E = \begin{cases} \{\{a, c_1\}, ..., \{a, c_n\}, \{b, c_1\}, ..., \{b, c_n\}\}, & \varepsilon = 0, \\ \{\{a, b\}, \{a, c_1\}, ..., \{a, c_n\}, \{b, c_1\}, ..., \{b, c_n\}\}, & \varepsilon = 1. \end{cases}
$$

The glue points *of a molecule $\theta_{a,b}^{\varepsilon,n}$ are a, b. Its* dead points *are $c_1, ..., c_n$.*

It is not difficult to prove that molecules have entanglement at most 2.

Definition 5. *Let G_1 and G_2 be two undirected graphs with $V_{G_1} \cap V_{G_2} = \emptyset$, let $a_1 \in V_{G_1}$ and $a_2 \in V_{G_2}$. The* collapse *of G_1 and G_2 on vertices a_1 and a_2, denoted $G_1 \bigoplus_{a_1, a_2}^z G_2$, is the graph G defined as follows:*

$$V_G = (V_{G_1} \setminus \{a_1\}) \cup (V_{G_2} \setminus \{a_2\}) \cup \{z\}, \quad \text{where } z \notin V_{G_1} \cup V_{G_2},$$
$$E_G = \{\{x_1, y_1\} \in E_{G_1} \mid a_1 \notin \{x_1, y_1\}\} \cup \{\{x_2, y_2\} \in E_{G_2} \mid a_2 \notin \{x_2, y_2\}\}$$
$$\cup \{\{x, z\} \mid \{x, a_1\} \in E_{G_1} \text{ or } \{x, a_2\} \in E_{G_2}\}.$$

We remark that $\bigoplus$ is a coproduct in the category of pointed undirected graphs and, for this reason, this operation is commutative and associative up to isomorphism. The graph η, whose set of vertices is a singleton, is a neutral element. As we have observed, a molecule is an undirected graph coming with a distinguished set of vertices, its glue points. Let us call a pair (G, Gl) with $Gl \subseteq V_G$ a *glue graph*. For glue graphs we can define what it means that a collapse is legal.

Definition 6. *If G_1, G_2 are glue graphs, then we say that $G_1 \bigoplus_{a,b}^z G_2$ is a legal collapse if $a \in Gl_{G_1}$ and $b \in Gl_{G_2}$. We shall then use the notation $G_1 \overline{\bigoplus}_{a,b}^z G_2$ and define*

$$Gl_{G_1 \overline{\bigoplus}_{a,b}^z G_2} = (Gl_{G_1} \setminus \{a\}) \cup (Gl_{G_2} \setminus \{b\}) \cup \{z\},$$

so that $G_1 \overline{\bigoplus}_{a,b}^z G_2$ is a glue graph.

Observe that the graph η can be made into a unit for the legal collapse by letting $Gl_\eta = V_\eta$. Even if the operation $\overline{\bigoplus}$ is well defined only after the choice of the two glue points that are going to be collapsed, it should be clear what it means that a family of glue graphs is closed under legal collapses.

Definition 7. *We let ζ_2 be the least class of glue graphs containing the molecules, the unit η, and closed under legal collapses and graph isomorphisms.*

We need to make precise some notation and terminology. Firstly we shall abuse of notation and write

$$G = H \overline{\bigoplus}_v K$$

to mean that there exist subgraphs H, K of G such that $v \in Gl_G \cap V_H \cap V_K$ and G is isomorphic to the legal collapse $H \overline{\bigoplus}_{v,v}^z K$. Notice that if H and K are distinct from η, then v is an articulation point of G. Second, we shall say that a graph G belongs to ζ_2 to mean that there exists a subset $Gl \subseteq V_G$ such that the glue graph (G, Gl) belongs to ζ_2. We can now state the main result of this section.

Proposition 8. *If G belongs to the class ζ_2, then $\mathcal{E}(G) \leq 2$.*

Proof. Observe that, given a molecule $\theta_{a,b}^{\varepsilon,n}$ occurring in an algebraic expression for G, we can rearrange the summands of the algebraic expression to write

$$G = L \overline{\bigoplus}_a \theta_{a,b}^{\varepsilon,n} \overline{\bigoplus}_b R \tag{1}$$

where $L, R \in \zeta_2$. A Cops winning strategy in the game $\mathcal{E}(G, 2)$ is summarized as follows. If Thief occupies some vertex of the molecule $\theta_{a,b}^{\varepsilon,n}$, Cops will place its two cops on a and b, in some order. By doing that, Cops will force Thief to move (i) on the left component L, in which case Cops can reuse the cop on b on L, (ii) on the molecule $\theta_{a,b}^{\varepsilon,n}$, in which case Thief will be caught in a dead point of the molecule, (iii) on the right component R, in which case Cops can reuse the cop on a on R.

Cops can recursively use the same strategy in $\mathcal{E}(L,2)$ and $\mathcal{E}(R,2)$. The recursion terminates as soon as in the expression (1) for G we have $L = R = \eta$. □

The reader will have noticed similarities between the strategy proposed here and the strategy needed in [1] to argue that undirected trees have entanglement at most 2. As a matter of fact, graphs in ζ_2 have an underlying tree structure. For a glue graph G, define the derived graph ∂G as follows: its vertices are the glue points of G, and $\{a,b\} \in E_{\partial G}$ if either $\{a,b\} \in E_G$ or there exists $x \in V_G \setminus Gl_G$ such that $\{a,x\},\{x,b\} \in E_G$. The following Proposition is not difficult to prove.

Proposition 9. *A glue graph G is in ζ_2 if and only if ∂G is a forest, and each $x \in V_G \setminus Gl_G$ has exactly two neighbors, which moreover are glue points.*

4   Combinatorial Properties

The goal of this section is to setup the tools for the characterization Theorem 16. We deduce some combinatorial properties of undirected graphs of entanglement at most 2. To this goal, let us say that a simple cycle is long it its length is strictly greater than 4, and say otherwise that it is short. Also, let us call a simple cycle of length 3 (resp. 4) a triangle (resp. square).

Proposition 10. *An undirected graph G such that $\mathcal{E}(G) \leq 2$ satisfies the following conditions:*

- *a simple Cycle of G is Short,* (CS)
- *a triangle of G has at least one vertex of degree 2,* (No-3C)
- *a square of G cannot have two adjacent vertices*

of degree strictly greater than 2. (No-AC)

Condition (No-3C) forbids as subgraphs of G the graphs arising from the scheme on the left of figure 1. These are made up of a triangle and 3 distinct Collapses, with vertices x, y, z that might not be distinct. Condition (No-AC) forbids the scheme on the right of figure 1, made up of a square and two Adjacent Collapses, with vertices x, y that might not be distinct. Let us remark that graphs satisfying (CS), (No-3C), and (No-AC) are House-Hole-Domino free, in the sense of [14]. With respect to HDD-free graphs, the requirement is here stronger since for example long cycles are forbidden as subgraphs, not just as induced subgraphs.

We shall see with Theorem 16 that these properties completely characterize the class of undirected graphs of entanglement at most 2. Proposition 10 is an immediate consequence of Lemma 3 and of the following Lemmas 11, 12, 13.

Let P_0 be the empty graph and, for $n \geq 1$, let P_n be the path with n vertices and $n-1$ edges: $V_{P_n} = \{0,...,n-1\}$ and $\{i,j\} \in E_{P_n}$ iff $|i-j| = 1$. For $n \geq 3$, let C_n be the cycle with n vertices and edges: $V_{C_n} = \{0,...,n-1\}$ and $\{i,j\} \in E_{C_n}$ iff $|i-j| \equiv 1 \mod n$.

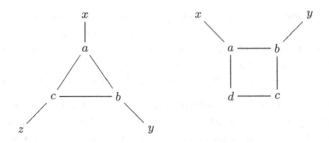

Fig. 1. The graphs $3C$ and AC

Lemma 11. *If $n \geq 5$ then $\mathcal{E}(C_n) \geq 3$.*

Proof. To describe a winning strategy for Thief in the game $\mathcal{E}(C_n, 2)$ consider that the removal of one or two vertices from C_n transforms such graph into a disjoint union $P_i + P_j$ with $i + j \geq n - 2 \geq 3$: notice in particular that $i \geq 2$ or $j \geq 2$. In a position of the form $(v, C, Thief)$ with $v \in C$, Thief moves to a component P_i with $i \geq 2$. From a position of the form $(v, C, Thief)$ with $v \notin C$, v in some component P_i, and $i \geq 2$, Thief moves to some other vertex in the same component. This strategy can be iterated infinitely often, showing that Thief will never be caught.   □

Lemma 12. *Let $3C$ be a graph on the left of figure 1. We have $\mathcal{E}(3C) \geq 3$.*

Proof. A winning strategy for Thief in the game $\mathcal{E}(3C, 2)$ is as follows. By moving on a, b, c, Thief can force Cops to put two cops there, say for example on a and b. Thief can then escape to c and iterate moves on the edge $\{c, z\}$ to force Cops to move one cop on one end of this edge. From a position of the form $(c, C, Thief)$ with $c \in C$, Thief moves to a free vertex among a, b. From a position of the form $(z, C, Thief)$ with $c \notin C$ Thief moves to c and forces again Cops to occupy two vertices among a, b, c. Up to a renaming of vertices, such a strategy can be iterated infinitely often, showing that Thief will never be caught.

Observe that the proof does not depend on x, y, z being distinct.   □

Lemma 13. *Let AC be a graph on the right of figure 1. We have $\mathcal{E}(AC) \geq 3$.*

Proof. By moving on a, b, c, d, Thief can force Cops to put two cops either on a, c or on b, d: let us say a, c. Thief can then escape to b and iterate moves on the edge $\{b, y\}$ to force Cops to move one cop on one end of this edge. From a position of the form $(b, C, Thief)$ with $b \in C$, Thief moves to a free vertex among a, c. From a position of the form $(y, C, Thief)$ with $b \notin C$ Thief moves to b and forces again Cops to occupy either a, c or b, d. Up to a renaming of vertices, such a strategy can be iterated infinitely often, showing that Thief will never be caught. Again, we observe that the strategy does not depend on x, y being distinct.   □

We end this section by pointing out that $\mathcal{E}(C_n) = \mathcal{E}(3C) = \mathcal{E}(AC) = 3$ $(n \geq 5)$.

5   Characterization of Entanglement at Most 2

In this section we accomplish the characterization of the class of undirected graphs of entanglement at most 2: we prove that this class coincides with ζ_2.

The following Lemma is the key observation by which the induction works in the proof of Proposition 15. It is worth, before stating it, to recall the difference between $\bigoplus$, the collapse of two ordinary undirected graphs, and $\overline{\bigoplus}$, the legal collapse of two glue graphs.

Lemma 14. *Let G be an undirected graph satisfying* (No-3C) *and* (No-AC). *If $G = \theta_{v,b}^{\varepsilon,n} \bigoplus_b H$ and $H \in \zeta_2$, then there is a subset $Gl' \subseteq V_G$ such that (H, Gl') is a glue graph in ζ_2, $b \in Gl'$, and moreover G is the result of the legal collapse $G = \theta_{v,b}^{\varepsilon,n} \overline{\bigoplus}_b (H, Gl')$. Consequently, $G \in \zeta_2$, with v a glue point of G.*

The proof of the Lemma doesn't present difficulties and therefore it is omitted.

Proposition 15. *If G is an undirected graph satisfying* (CS), (No-3C), *and* (No-AC), *then $G \in \zeta_2$.*

Proof. The proof is by induction on $|V_G|$. Clearly the Proposition holds if $|V_G| = 1$, in which case $G = \eta \in \zeta_2$. Let us suppose the Proposition holds for all graphs H such that $|V_H| < |V_G|$.

If all the vertices in G have degree less than or equal to 2, then G is a disjoint union of paths and cycles of length at most 4. Clearly such a graph belongs to ζ_2. Otherwise, let v_0 be a vertex such that $\deg_G(v_0) \geq 3$ and consider the connected components G_ℓ, $\ell = 1, \ldots, h$, of the graph $G \setminus \{ v_0 \}$. Let $G_\ell^{v_0}$ be the subgraph of G induced by $V_{G_\ell} \cup \{ v_0 \}$. We shall show that this graph is of the form

$$G_\ell^{v_0} = \theta_{v_0, v_1}^{\varepsilon, m} \bigoplus_{v_1} H \,, \tag{2}$$

for some $\varepsilon \in \{ 0, 1 \}$, $m \geq 0$, and a graph $H \in \zeta_2$.

Clearly, if G_ℓ is already a connected component of G, then $G_\ell \in \zeta_2$ by the inductive hypothesis. We can pick any $v_1 \in V_{G_\ell}$ and argue that formula (2) holds with $m = \varepsilon = 0$, $H = G_\ell$.

Otherwise, let $\mathcal{N}_\ell = \{ a_1, \ldots, a_n \}$, $n \geq 1$, be the set of vertices of $G_\ell^{v_0}$ at distance 1 from v_0. We claim that either the subgraph of G_ℓ induced by $\mathcal{N}_\ell$, noted $\mathcal{N}_{G_\ell}$, is a star or there exists a unique $v_1 \in G_\ell$ at distance 1 from $\mathcal{N}_\ell$, and moreover the subgraph of G_ℓ induced by $\mathcal{N}_\ell \cup \{ v_1 \}$ is a star. In both cases, a vertex of such a star which is not the center has degree 2 in G.

(i) If $E_{\mathcal{N}_{G_\ell}} \neq \emptyset$, then $\mathcal{N}_{G_\ell}$ is a star. Let us suppose that $\{ a_1, a_2 \} \in E_{G_\ell}$. Since G_ℓ is connected, if $a_k \in \mathcal{N}_\ell \setminus \{ a_1, a_2 \}$ then there exists a path from a_k to both a_1 and a_2. Condition (CS) implies that either $\{ a_1, a_k \} \in E_{G_\ell}$, or $\{ a_k, a_2 \} \in E_{G_\ell}$. If $x_0 \in V_{G_\ell} \setminus \{ a_2 \}$ then there cannot be a simple path $a_k \ldots x_0 \ldots a_1$ otherwise $v_0 a_k \ldots x_0 \ldots a_1 a_2 v_0$ is a long cycle. Therefore, a simple path from a_k to a_1 is of the form $a_k a_1$ or $a_k a_2 a_1$. By condition (No-3C) it is not the case that $\{ a_k, a_1 \}, \{ a_k, a_2 \} \in E_{G_\ell}$, otherwise $\{ v_0, a_1, a_2, a_k \}$ is a clique of cardinality 4. Finally, if $\{ a_k, a_1 \} \in E_{G_\ell}$ and $a_l \in \mathcal{N}_\ell \setminus \{ a_1, a_2, a_k \}$, then $\{ a_l, a_1 \} \in E_{G_\ell}$ as well, by condition (CS), otherwise $v_0 a_k a_1 a_2 a_l v_0$ is a long cycle. Therefore, if $|\mathcal{N}_\ell| > 2$, then $\mathcal{N}_{G_\ell}$ is a star with a prescribed center, which we can assume to be a_1. Since $\deg_G(v_0) \geq 3$, by condition (No-3C) only a_1 among vertices in $\mathcal{N}_\ell$ may have degree greater than 2. Otherwise $|\mathcal{N}_\ell| = 2$ and again at most one among a_i, $i = 1, 2$, has $\deg_G(a_i) > 2$. Again, we can assume that $\deg_G(a_2) = 2$. We deduce that the subgraph of $G_\ell^{v_0}$ induced by $\{v_0\} \cup \mathcal{N}_\ell$ is of the form $\theta_{v_0,a_1}^{1,n-1}$.

(ii) If $E_{\mathcal{N}_{G_\ell}} = \emptyset$, then we distinguish two cases. If $|\mathcal{N}_\ell| = 1$, then the subgraph of $G_\ell^{v_0}$ induced by $\{v_0\} \cup \mathcal{N}_\ell$ is $\theta_{v_0,a_1}^{1,0}$. Otherwise, if $|\mathcal{N}_\ell| \geq 2$, between any two distinct vertices in $\mathcal{N}_\ell$ there must exist a path in G_ℓ, since G_ℓ is connected. By condition (CS), if $a_i \ldots x_{i,j} \ldots a_j$ is a simple path from a_i to a_j with $x_{i,j} \in V_{G_\ell} \setminus \mathcal{N}_\ell$, then $\{a_i, x_{i,j}\}, \{a_j, x_{i,j}\} \in E_{G_\ell}$. Also (CS) implies that, for fixed i, $x_{i,k} = x_{i,j}$ if $k \neq j$, otherwise $v_0 a_k x_{i,k} a_i x_{i,j} a_j v_0$ is a long cycle. We can also assume that $x_{i,j} = x_{j,i}$, and therefore $x_{i,j} = x_{i,k} = x_{l,k}$ whenever $i \neq j$ and $l \neq k$. Thus we can write $x_{i,j} = v_1$ for a unique v_1 at distance 2 from v_0. Since $|\mathcal{N}_\ell| \geq 2$ and $\deg_G(v_0) \geq 3$, condition (No-AC) implies that $\deg_G(a_i) = 2$ for $i = 1, \ldots, n$. We have shown that in this case the subgraph of $G_\ell^{v_0}$ induced by $\mathcal{N}_\ell \cup \{v_0, v_1\}$ is a molecule $\theta_{v_0,v_1}^{0,n}$, with $n \geq 2$.

Until now we have shown that (2) holds with H a graph of entanglement at most 2. Since for such a graph $|V_H| < |V_G|$, the induction hypothesis implies $H \in \zeta_2$. Lemma 14 in turn implies that $G_\ell^{v_0} \in \zeta_2$, with v_0 a glue point of $G_\ell^{v_0}$. Finally we can use

$$ G = G_1^{v_0} \overline{\bigoplus}_{v_0} G_2^{v_0} \overline{\bigoplus}_{v_0} \cdots \overline{\bigoplus}_{v_0} G_h^{v_0}, $$

to deduce that $G \in \zeta_2$. $\square$

We can now state our main achievement.

Theorem 16. *For a finite undirected graph G, the following are equivalent:*

1. *G has entanglement at most 2,*
2. *G satisfies conditions (CS), (No-3C), (No-AC),*
3. *G belongs to the class ζ_2.*

As a matter of fact, we have shown in the previous section that 1 implies 2, in this section that 2 implies 3, and in section 3 that 3 implies 1.

6   A Linear Time Algorithm

In this section we present a linear time algorithm that decides whether a connected undirected graph G has entanglement at most 2. The generalization to disconnected graphs does not present difficulties. We would like to thank the anonymous referee for pointing to us the ideas and tools needed to transform the algebraic characterization of Section 3 into a linear time algorithm.

Let us recall that, for $G = (V, E)$ and $v \in V$, v is an *articulation point* of G iff there exist distinct $v_0, v_1 \in V \setminus \{v\}$ such that every path from v_0 to v_1 visits v. Equivalently, v is an *articulation point* iff the subgraph of G induced by $V \setminus \{v\}$ is disconnected. The graph G is *biconnected* if it does not contain articulation points. A subset of vertices $V' \subseteq V$ is biconnected iff the subgraph induced by V' is biconnected. A *biconnected component* of G is biconnected subset $C \subseteq V$ such that if $C \subseteq V'$ and V' is biconnected then $C = V'$. The *superstructure* of G is the graph F_G defined as follows. Its set of vertices is the disjoint union $V_{F_G} = \mathcal{A}(G) \uplus \mathcal{C}(G)$, where

$$\mathcal{A}(G) = \{\, a \in V \mid a \text{ is an articulation point of G} \,\},$$
$$\mathcal{C}(G) = \{\, C \subseteq V \mid C \text{ is a biconnected component of } G \,\},$$

and its set of edges is of the form

$$E_{F_G} = \{\, \{a, C\} \mid a \in \mathcal{A}(G), C \in \mathcal{C}(G), \text{ and } a \in C \,\}.$$

It is well known that F_G is a tree whenever G is connected and that Depth-First-Search techniques may be used to compute the superstructure F_G in time $O(|V| + |E|)$, see [18, §23-2]. Observe also that this implies that $\sum_{C \in \mathcal{C}(G)} |C| = O(|V| + |E|)$. This relation that may also be derived considering that biconnecetd components do not share common edges, so that $|V_{F_G}| = O(|V| + |E|)$ and $|E_{F_G}| = O(|V| + |E|)$ since F_G is a tree. We have therefore

$$\sum_{C \in \mathcal{C}(G)} |C| = |V \setminus \mathcal{A}(G)| + \sum_{a \in \mathcal{A}(G)} |\{\, C \in \mathcal{C}(G) \mid a \in C \,\}|$$
$$= |V \setminus \mathcal{A}(G)| + |E_{F_G}| = O(|V| + |E|).$$

The algorithm ENTANGLEMENT-TWO relies on the following considerations. If a graph G belongs to the class ζ_2, then it has an algebraic expression explaining how to construct it using molecules as building blocks and legal collapses as operations. We can assume that in this expression the molecule $\theta_{a,b}^{0,1}$ does not appear, since each such occurrence may be replaced by the collapse $\theta_{a,x}^{1,0} \overline{\bigoplus}_x \theta_{x,b}^{1,0}$. W.r.t. this normalized expression, if G is connected then its articulation points are exactly those glue points v of G that appears in the algebraic expression as subscripts of some legal collapse $\overline{\bigoplus}_v$; the molecules are the biconnected components of G.

The algorithm computes the articulation points and the biconnected components of G – that is, its superstructure – and afterwards it checks that each biconnected component together with its articulation points is a molecule.

```
1  ENTANGLEMENT–TWO( G )
2  // Input a connected undirected graph G, accept if G ∈ ζ₂
3  if |E| ≥ 3|V| then reject
4  foreach v ∈ V do deg(v) := |vE|
5  let  F_G = (A(G) ⊎ C(G), E_FG) be the superstructure of G
6  foreach C ∈ C(G)
7      if not IS–MOLECULE(C, { a ∈ A(G) | a ∈ C }) then reject
8  accept
```

For a biconnected component together with a set of candidate glue points to be a molecule we need of course these candidates to be at most 2. Also, every vertex whose degree in G is not 2 is a candidate glue point. Improving on these observations we arrive at the following characterization.

Lemma 17. *Let $G = (V, E)$ be a biconnected graph and $D \subseteq V$ be such that $\{ v \in V \mid \deg(v) \neq 2 \} \subseteq D$. Then G is isomorphic to a molecule $\theta_{a,b}^{\epsilon,n}$, with D isomorphically sent to a subset of $\{ a, b \}$, if and only if either (i) $|D| = 2$ and $\{ x, d \} \in E$ for each $x \in V \setminus D$ and $d \in D$ or (ii) $|D| < 2$ and $|V| \in \{ 3, 4 \}$.*

Therefore the recognition algorithm for a molecule is as follows.

```
1   IS–MOLECULE( C, A )
2   if  |A| > 2 then return false
3   let  D = { x ∈ C | deg(x) ≠ 2 } ∪ A
4   if  |D| > 2 then return false
5   if  |D| < 2 then
6       if  |C| ∈ { 3, 4 } then return true
7       else return false
8   foreach  x ∈ C \ D
9       if  D ⊄ xE then return false
10  return true
```

Let us now argue about time resources of this algorithm.

Fact. *Algorithm ENTANGLEMENT-TWO(G) runs in time $O(|V_G|)$.*

It is clear that the function IS-MOLECULE runs in time $O(|C|)$, so that the loop (lines 7-8) of ENTANGLEMENT-TWO runs in time $O(\sum_{C \in \mathcal{C}(G)} |C|) = O(|V| + |E|)$. Therefore the algorithm requires time $O(|V| + |E|)$.

The following Lemma, whose proof depends on considering a tree with back edges arising from a Depth-First-Search on the graph, elucidates the role of the 3rd line of the algorithm.

Lemma 18. *If a graph (V, E) does not contain a simple cycle C_n with $n \geq k$, then it has at most $(k - 2)|V| - 1$ undirected edges.*

Line 3 ensures $|E_G| = O(|V_G|)$ and that the algorithm runs in time $O(|V_G|)$.

Acknowledgement. We thank the anonymous referees for their useful comments, and for suggesting how to obtain the algorithm presented in Section 6 out of the algebraic framework introduced in Section 3.

References

1. Berwanger, D., Grädel, E.: Entanglement—a measure for the complexity of directed graphs with applications to logic and games. In: Baader, F., Voronkov, A. (eds.) LPAR 2004. LNCS (LNAI), vol. 3452, pp. 209–223. Springer, Heidelberg (2005)
2. Berwanger, D.: Games and Logical Expressiveness. PhD thesis, RWTH Aachen (2005)
3. Seymour, P.D., Thomas, R.: Graph searching and a min-max theorem for tree-width. J. Combin. Theory Ser. B 58(1), 22–33 (1993)
4. Gottlob, G., Leone, N., Scarcello, F.: Hypertree decompositions: A survey. In: Sgall, J., Pultr, A., Kolman, P. (eds.) MFCS 2001. LNCS, vol. 2136, pp. 37–57. Springer, Heidelberg (2001)

5. Johnson, T., Robertson, N., Seymour, P.D., Thomas, R.: Directed tree-width. J. Combin. Theory Ser. B 82(1), 138–154 (2001)

6. Safari, M.A.: d-width: a more natural measure for directed tree width. In: Jedrzejowicz, J., Szepietowski, A. (eds.) MFCS 2005. LNCS, vol. 3618, pp. 745–756. Springer, Heidelberg (2005)

7. Berwanger, D., Dawar, A., Hunter, P., Kreutzer, S.: Dag-width and parity games. In: Durand, B., Thomas, W. (eds.) STACS 2006. LNCS, vol. 3884, pp. 524–536. Springer, Heidelberg (2006)

8. Berwanger, D., Grädel, E., Lenzi, G.: On the variable hierarchy of the modal mu-calculus. In: Bradfield, J.C. (ed.) CSL 2002 and EACSL 2002. LNCS, vol. 2471, pp. 352–366. Springer, Heidelberg (2002)

9. Berwanger, D., Lenzi, G.: The variable hierarchy of the μ-calculus is strict. In: Diekert, V., Durand, B. (eds.) STACS 2005. LNCS, vol. 3404, pp. 97–109. Springer, Heidelberg (2005)

10. Kozen, D.: Results on the propositional μ-calculus. Theoret. Comput. Sci. 27(3), 333–354 (1983)

11. Arnold, A., Niwiński, D.: Rudiments of μ-calculus. Studies in Logic and the Foundations of Mathematics, vol. 146. North-Holland Publishing Co, Amsterdam (2001)

12. Bloom, S.L., Ésik, Z.: Iteration theories. Springer, Berlin (1993)

13. Jamison, B., Olariu, S.: On the semi-perfect elimination. Adv. in Appl. Math. 9(3), 364–376 (1988)

14. Chepoi, V., Dragan, F.: Finding a central vertex in an HHD-free graph. Discrete Appl. Math. 131(1), 93–111 (2003)

15. Courcelle, B.: Graph rewriting: an algebraic and logic approach. In: Handbook of theoretical computer science, vol. B, pp. 193–242. Elsevier, Amsterdam (1990)

16. Goubault, E., Raußen, M.: Dihomotopy as a tool in state space analysis. In: Rajsbaum, S. (ed.) LATIN 2002. LNCS, vol. 2286, pp. 16–37. Springer, Heidelberg (2002)

17. Jurdzinski, M.: Small progress measures for solving parity games. In: Reichel, H., Tison, S. (eds.) STACS 2000. LNCS, vol. 1770, pp. 290–301. Springer, Heidelberg (2000)

18. Cormen, T.H., Leiserson, C.E., Rivest, R.L.: Introduction to Algorithms. The MIT Electrical Engineering and Computer Science Series. MIT Press, Cambridge (1990)

Acceleration in Convex Data-Flow Analysis

Jérôme Leroux and Grégoire Sutre

LaBRI, Université de Bordeaux, CNRS
Domaine Universitaire, 351, cours de la Libération, 33405 Talence, France
{leroux,sutre}@labri.fr

Abstract. In abstract interpretation-based data-flow analysis, widening operators are usually used in order to speed up the iterative computation of the minimum fix-point solution (MFP). However, the use of widenings may lead to loss of precision in the analysis. Acceleration is an alternative to widening that has mainly been developed for symbolic verification of infinite-state systems. Intuitively, acceleration consists in computing the exact effect of some control-flow cycle in order to speed up reachability analysis. This paper investigates acceleration in convex data-flow analysis of systems with real-valued variables where guards are convex polyhedra and assignments are translations. In particular, we present a simple and algorithmically efficient characterization of MFP-acceleration for cycles with a unique initial location. We also show that the MFP-solution is a computable algebraic polyhedron for systems with two variables.

1 Introduction

Formal verification of safety properties on a system is usually based on the automatic (or manual) generation of *invariants* of the system. Invariants are over-approximations of the set of all reachable configurations in the system. This over-approximation must be precise enough in order to determine which safety properties are satisfied by the system. Data-flow analysis, and in particular abstract interpretation [CC77], provides a powerful framework to develop analysis for computing such invariants.

For systems with numerical variables, *linear relation analysis* aims at computing invariants expressing linear relationships between variables [Kar76, CH78, Min01, SSM04, BHRZ05]. The desired invariant corresponds to the minimum fix-point (MFP) solution of the system's approximate semantics in some numerical domain, and it may be computed by Kleene fix-point iteration. However, the computation may diverge and *widening/narrowing operators* [CC77, CC92] are often used in order to enforce convergence at the expense of precision. This may lead to invariants that are too coarse to prove the desired safety properties on the system to be verified.

Acceleration is an alternative to widening that has mainly been developed for symbolic verification of infinite-state systems [BW94, CJ98, FIS03, FL02, BIL06]. Intuitively, acceleration consists in computing the exact effect of some control-flow cycle in order to speed up Kleene fix-point computations in reachability analysis. Accelerated symbolic model checkers such as LASH, TREX, and FAST successfully implement this approach. While being more precise than widening, acceleration is also more computationally expensive.

V. Arvind and S. Prasad (Eds.): FSTTCS 2007, LNCS 4855, pp. 520–531, 2007.

Our contribution. We aim at developing methods that speed up the iterative computation of the MFP-solution, *without any loss of precision*. We focus on a class of systems with real-valued variables, the so-called *guarded translation systems (GTSs)*. This class intuitively represents programs where conditions are closed convex sets and transformations are restricted to translations. We investigate acceleration of data-flow analysis for this class in the complete lattice of closed convex subsets of $\mathbb{R}^n$. To discuss computability issues, we devote particular attention to the class of rational polyhedral GTSs, where conditions are rational polyhedra and translation vectors are rational.

Recast in our setting, the (exact) acceleration techniques mentioned above consist in computing the merge over all path (MOP) solution along some (simple) cycle, which we call *MOP-acceleration*. We show that the MOP-acceleration of any cycle is an effectively computable rational polyhedron for rational polyhedral GTSs. However MOP-acceleration is not in general sufficient to guarantee termination of the Kleene fix-point iteration, even for cyclic GTSs. We therefore investigate *MFP-acceleration*, which basically amounts to computing the MFP-solution of the system restricted to a given cycle. In other words, MFP-acceleration directly gives the MFP-solution for cyclic GTSs.

We obtain a surprisingly simple expression of the MFP-acceleration for cycles with a unique initial location. For rational polyhedral GTSs, this characterization shows that the MFP-acceleration is an effectively computable rational polyhedron for these cycles. This result cannot be extended to arbitrary cycles, as we give a 3-dim (i.e. three real-valued variables) cyclic example where the MFP-solution is not a polyhedron. We then focus on 2-dim GTSs and we prove that the MFP-solution is an effectively computable algebraic polyhedron (i.e. with algebraic coefficients) for general rational polyhedral 2-dim GTSs. Even for cyclic GTSs in this class, the polyhedral MFP-solution can be non-rational.

Related work. Karr introduced in [Kar76] an algorithm for computing the exact MFP-solution in the lattice of linear equalities. In [CH78], Cousot and Halbwachs framed linear relation analysis as an abstract interpretation and provided the first widening operator over the lattice of rational polyhedra. This approach only provides an over-approximation of the MFP-solution. Many refinements of this original widening operator have since been studied [BHRZ05] to limit the loss of precision. Recently Gonnord and Halbwachs [GH06] introduced the notion of abstract-acceleration as a complement to widening for linear relation analysis. We show that while maintaining the same computational complexity, our MFP-acceleration is "better" than abstract-acceleration in the sense that MFP-acceleration enforces convergence of the Kleene fix-point iteration strictly more often than abstract-acceleration. On another hand [GH06] also investigates acceleration of multiple loops and the combination of translations and resets.

Outline. The rest of the paper is organized as follows. Section 2 recalls some background material on lattices and convex sets. We introduce guarded translation systems in section 3, along with MOP-acceleration and MFP-acceleration for these systems. We present in sections 4 and 5 our results on MOP-acceleration and MFP-acceleration for guarded translation systems. Section 6 is devoted to the MFP-solution of general guarded translation systems in dimension not greater than 2. Due to space limitations, most proofs are only sketched in this paper. A long version of the paper with detailed proofs can be obtained from the authors.

2 The Complete Lattice of Closed Convex Sets

2.1 Numbers, Lattices and Languages

The paper follows the ISO 31-11 international standard for mathematical notation. We respectively denote by $\mathbb{Z}$, $\mathbb{Q}$ and $\mathbb{R}$ the usual sets of integers, rationals and real numbers. Recall that a (real) *algebraic number* is any real number that is the root of some non-zero polynomial with rational coefficients. We write $\mathbb{A}$ the set of all (real) algebraic numbers. It is well-known from Tarski's theorem that *real arithmetic*, the first-order theory $\langle \mathbb{R}, +, \cdot \rangle$ of reals with addition and multiplication, admits quantifier elimination and hence is decidable. It follows that any real number x is algebraic iff $\{x\}$ is definable in real arithmetic. We denote by $\mathbb{N}, \mathbb{Q}_+, \mathbb{A}_+, \mathbb{R}_+$ the restrictions of $\mathbb{Z}, \mathbb{Q}, \mathbb{A}, \mathbb{R}$ to the non-negatives.

Recall that a *complete lattice* is any partially ordered set $(L, \sqsubseteq)$ such that every subset $X \subseteq L$ has a *least upper bound* $\bigsqcup X$ and a *greatest lower bound* $\bigsqcap X$. The *supremum* $\bigsqcup L$ and the *infimum* $\bigsqcap L$ are respectively denoted by $\top$ and $\bot$. A function $f \in L \to L$ is *monotonic* if $f(x) \sqsubseteq f(y)$ for all $x \sqsubseteq y$ in L. It is well-known from Knaster-Tarski's theorem that any monotonic function $f \in L \to L$ has a *least fix-point* given by $\bigsqcap \{x \in L \mid f(x) \sqsubseteq x\}$. For any monotonic function $f \in L \to L$, we define the monotonic function f^* in $L \to L$ by $f^*(x) = \bigsqcap \{y \in L \mid (x \sqcup f(y)) \sqsubseteq y\}$. In other words $f^*(x)$ is the least post-fix-point of f greater than x. Observe that $f^*(x) = x \sqcup f(f^*(x))$ for every $x \in L$.

For any complete lattice $(L, \sqsubseteq)$ and any set S, we also denote by $\sqsubseteq$ the partial order on $S \to L$ defined as the point-wise extension of $\sqsubseteq$, i.e. $f \sqsubseteq g$ iff $f(s) \sqsubseteq g(s)$ for all $s \in S$. The partially ordered set $(S \to L, \sqsubseteq)$ is also a complete lattice, with lub $\bigsqcup$ and glb $\bigsqcap$ satisfying $(\bigsqcup F)(s) = \bigsqcup \{f(s) \mid f \in F\}$ and $(\bigsqcap F)(s) = \bigsqcap \{f(s) \mid f \in F\}$ for any subset $F \subseteq S \to L$.

For any set S, we write $\mathbb{P}(S)$ for the set of subsets of S. The partially ordered set $(\mathbb{P}(S), \subseteq)$ is a complete lattice, with lub $\bigcup$ and glb $\bigcap$. The *identity* function over any set S is written $\mathbb{1}_S$, and shortly $\mathbb{1}$ when the set S is clear from the context.

Let Σ be a (potentially infinite) a set of *letters*. We write Σ^* for the set of all (finite) *sequences* $l_1 \cdots l_k$ over Σ, and ε denotes the *empty* sequence. Given any two sequences w and w', we denote by $w \cdot w'$ (shortly written $w\,w'$) their *concatenation*. A subset of Σ^* is called a *language*.

2.2 Closed Convex Sets and Polyhedra

We assume a fixed positive integer n called the *dimension*. The components of a *vector* $x \in \mathbb{R}^n$ are denoted by $x = (x_1, \ldots, x_n)$. Operations on vectors are extended to subsets of $\mathbb{R}^n$ in the obvious way, e.g. $S + S' = \{x + x' \mid x \in S, x' \in S'\}$ for any $S, S' \subseteq \mathbb{R}^n$. When there is no ambiguity, the singleton $\{x\}$ is shortly written x to unclutter notation, e.g. we write $x + S$ instead of $\{x\} + S$. Recall that the *maximum norm* $\|\cdot\|_\infty$ on $\mathbb{R}^n$ is defined by $\|x\|_\infty = \max\{|x_1|, \ldots, |x_n|\}$. A subset S of $\mathbb{R}^n$ is called *bounded* if $\{\|x\|_\infty \mid x \in S\} \subseteq [0, b]$ for some $b \in \mathbb{R}$. The *(topological) closure*, *interior* and *boundary* of a subset S of $\mathbb{R}^n$ are respectively denoted by $\mathrm{clo}(S)$, $\mathrm{int}(S)$ and $\mathrm{bd}\,(S)$.

We now recall some notions about *convex* subsets of $\mathbb{R}^n$ (see [Sch86] for details). Recall that this class of subsets of $\mathbb{R}^n$ is closed under arbitrary intersection. The *convex hull* of any subset $S \subseteq \mathbb{R}^n$, written conv(S), is the smallest (w.r.t. inclusion) convex set that contains S. Note that conv(S) is closed when S is finite, but this is not true in general. We devote particular attention in the sequel to closed convex subsets of $\mathbb{R}^n$. This class of subsets of $\mathbb{R}^n$ is also closed under arbitrary intersection. The *closed convex hull* of any subset $S \subseteq \mathbb{R}^n$, written cloconv(S), is the smallest (w.r.t. inclusion) closed convex set that contains S. Remark that cloconv$(S) = $ clo(conv(S)). For any vector $d \in \mathbb{R}^n$, we define $\uparrow d$ to be the convex set $\uparrow d = \{\lambda d \mid \lambda \in \mathbb{R}_+\}$. The *recession cone* 0^+S of any subset S of $\mathbb{R}^n$ is the set of all vectors $d \in \mathbb{R}^n$ such that $S + \uparrow d \subseteq S$. Note that $0 \in 0^+S$. If C is a closed convex subset of $\mathbb{R}^n$ then 0^+C is also closed and convex. If moreover C is non-empty then for any $d \in \mathbb{R}^n$, we have $d \in 0^+C$ iff there exists $x \in C$ such that $x + \uparrow d \subseteq C$.

Let us fix $\mathbb{F} \in \{\mathbb{Q}, \mathbb{A}, \mathbb{R}\}$. A subset S of $\mathbb{R}^n$ is called an $\mathbb{F}$-*half-space* if there exists $\alpha \in \mathbb{F}^n \setminus \{0\}$ and $c \in \mathbb{F}$ such that $S = \{x \in \mathbb{R}^n \mid \alpha_1 x_1 + \cdots + \alpha_n x_n \leq c\}$. An $\mathbb{F}$-*polyhedron* is any finite intersection of $\mathbb{F}$-half-spaces. In the sequel, $\mathbb{Q}$-polyhedrality (resp. $\mathbb{A}$-polyhedrality, $\mathbb{R}$-polyhedrality) is also called *rational polyhedrality* (resp. *algebraic polyhedrality, real polyhedrality*). Moreover, $\mathbb{R}$-polyhedra and a $\mathbb{R}$-half-spaces are shortly called *polyhedra* and *half-spaces*. Remark that any subset of $\mathbb{R}^n$ is $\mathbb{A}$-polyhedral iff it is both polyhedral and definable in $\langle \mathbb{R}, +, \cdot \rangle$.

The class of closed convex subsets of $\mathbb{R}^n$ is written $\mathcal{C}_n$. We denote by $\sqsubseteq$ the inclusion partial order on $\mathcal{C}_n$. Observe that $(\mathcal{C}_n, \sqsubseteq)$ is a complete lattice, with lub $\bigsqcup$ and glb $\bigsqcap$ satisfying $\bigsqcup X = $ cloconv$(\bigcup X)$ and $\bigsqcap X = \bigcap X$ for any subset $X \subseteq \mathcal{C}_n$.

3   Convex Acceleration for Guarded Translation Systems

We now define the class of guarded translation systems, for which we investigate the computability of data-flow solutions in the complete lattice $(\mathcal{C}_n, \sqsubseteq)$. This class intuitively represents programs with real-valued variables, where conditions are closed convex sets and transformations are restricted to translations.

An n-dim *action* is any pair (G, d) where $G \in \mathcal{C}_n$ is called the *guard* and $d \in \mathbb{R}^n$ is called the *displacement*. We write $\mathcal{A}_n = \mathcal{C}_n \times \mathbb{R}^n$ the set of all n-dim actions. A *trace* is any finite sequence $a_1 \cdots a_k \in \mathcal{A}_n^*$. The *data-flow semantics* $[\![a]\!]$ of any n-dim action $a = (G, d)$ is the monotonic function in $\mathcal{C}_n \to \mathcal{C}_n$ defined by $[\![a]\!](C) = (G \cap C) + d$.

An n-dim *guarded translation system* (GTS) is any pair $\mathcal{S} = (\mathcal{X}, T)$ where $\mathcal{X}$ is a finite set of *variables* and $T \subseteq \mathcal{X} \times \mathcal{A}_n \times \mathcal{X}$ is a finite set of *transitions*. A transition $t = (X, a, X')$ is also written $X \xrightarrow{a} X'$ or $X' := a(X)$, and we say that a (resp. X, X') is the *action* (resp. *input variable, output variable*) of t. A *path* in $\mathcal{S}$ is any finite sequence $t_1 \cdots t_k \in T^*$ such that the output variable of t_i is equal to the input variable of t_{i+1} for every $1 \leq i < k$. We say that a path π is a *path from X to X'* if either (1) $\pi = \varepsilon$ and $X = X'$, or (2) $\pi = t_1 \cdots t_k$ and X, X' respectively are the input variable of t_1 and the output variable of t_k. Any path with no repeated variable is called a *simple path*. A *cycle* is any non-empty path from some variable X to X. Any cycle of the form $t \cdot \pi$ where t is a transition and π is a simple path is called a *simple cycle*. A *valuation* is any function ρ in $\mathcal{X} \to \mathcal{C}_n$. An n-dim *initialized guarded translation system* (IGTS) is any triple $\mathcal{S} = (\mathcal{X}, T, \rho_0)$ where $(\mathcal{X}, T)$ is an n-dim GTS and $\rho_0 \in \mathcal{X} \to \mathcal{C}_n$ is an *initial valuation*.

Intuitively, a transition $X \xrightarrow{a} X'$ assigns variable X' to $a(X)$ and does not change the other variables. Formally, the *data-flow semantics* $[\![t]\!]$ of any transition $t = X \xrightarrow{a} X'$ is the monotonic function in $(\mathcal{X} \to \mathcal{C}_n) \to (\mathcal{X} \to \mathcal{C}_n)$ defined by $[\![t]\!](\rho)(X') = [\![a]\!](\rho(X))$ and $[\![t]\!](\rho)(Y) = \rho(Y)$ for all $Y \neq X'$. The data-flow semantics $[\![\cdot]\!]$ is extended to sequences w in $\mathcal{A}_n^* \cup T^*$ in the obvious way: $[\![\varepsilon]\!] = \mathbb{1}$ and $[\![l \cdot w]\!] = [\![w]\!] \circ [\![l]\!]$. We also extend the data-flow semantics to languages L in $\mathbb{P}(\mathcal{A}_n^*) \cup \mathbb{P}(T^*)$ by $[\![L]\!] = \bigsqcup_{w \in L} [\![w]\!]$.

For computability reasons, we extend $\mathbb{F}$-polyhedrality, where $\mathbb{F} \in \{\mathbb{Q}, \mathbb{A}, \mathbb{R}\}$, to actions, valuations and guarded translation systems. An n-dim action $(G, \mathbf{d})$ is called $\mathbb{F}$-*polyhedral* if G is $\mathbb{F}$-polyhedral and $\mathbf{d} \in \mathbb{F}^n$. An n-dim GTS $(\mathcal{X}, T)$ is called $\mathbb{F}$-*polyhedral* if the action of every transition $t \in T$ is $\mathbb{F}$-polyhedral. A valuation ρ in $\mathcal{X} \to \mathcal{C}_n$ is called $\mathbb{F}$-*polyhedral* if $\rho(X)$ is $\mathbb{F}$-polyhedral for every $X \in \mathcal{X}$. An n-dim IGTS $(\mathcal{X}, T, \rho_0)$ is called $\mathbb{F}$-*polyhedral* if $(\mathcal{X}, T)$ and ρ_0 are $\mathbb{F}$-polyhedral.

Example 3.1. Consider the C-style source code given on the left-hand side below and assume that the initial values of variables z_1 and z_2 satisfy $z_1 = 1$ and $-1 \leq z_2 \leq 1$. The corresponding IGTS $\mathcal{E}$ is depicted graphically on the right-hand side below.

```
1    while (z₁ ≥ 0 ∧ z₂ ≥ 0) {
2        z₁ = z₁ − 1;
3        z₂ = z₂ + 1;
4    }
```

Formally, the set of variables of $\mathcal{E}$ is $\{X_1, X_2, X_3, X_4\}$, representing the values of variables z_1 and z_2 at program points 1, 2, 3 and 4. Its initial valuation is $\{X_1 \mapsto \{1\} \times [-1, 1], X_2 \mapsto \bot, X_3 \mapsto \bot, X_4 \mapsto \bot\}$, and its set of transitions is $\{t_1, t_2, t_3, t_4\}$, with:

$$t_1 = X_1 \xrightarrow{a_1} X_2, \; a_1 = (\mathbb{R}_+^2, \mathbf{0}) \qquad t_2 = X_2 \xrightarrow{a_2} X_3, \; a_2 = (\mathbb{R}^2, (-1, 0))$$
$$t_4 = X_4 \xrightarrow{a_4} X_1, \; a_4 = (\mathbb{R}^2, \mathbf{0}) \qquad t_3 = X_3 \xrightarrow{a_3} X_4, \; a_3 = (\mathbb{R}^2, (0, 1)) \qquad \square$$

Given any n-dim IGTS $\mathcal{S} = (\mathcal{X}, T, \rho_0)$, the *merge over all paths solution (MOP-solution)* of $\mathcal{S}$, written $\Pi_\mathcal{S}$, and the *minimum fix-point solution (MFP-solution)* of $\mathcal{S}$, written $\Lambda_\mathcal{S}$, are the valuations defined as follows:

$$\Pi_\mathcal{S} = \bigsqcup \{[\![\pi]\!](\rho_0) \mid \pi \in T^* \text{ is a path}\}$$
$$\Lambda_\mathcal{S} = \bigsqcap \{\rho \in \mathcal{X} \to \mathcal{C}_n \mid \rho_0 \sqsubseteq \rho \text{ and } [\![t]\!](\rho) \sqsubseteq \rho \text{ for all } t \in T\}$$

Remark that for any sequence $\pi \in T^*$ and variable $X \in \mathcal{X}$, there exists a path π' such that $[\![\pi]\!](\rho_0)(X) = [\![\pi']\!](\rho_0)(X)$. Recall also that $[\![T]\!]^*(\rho)$ denotes the least post-fix-point of $[\![T]\!]$ greater than ρ. Therefore it follows from the above definitions that $\Pi_\mathcal{S} = [\![T^*]\!](\rho_0)$ and $\Lambda_\mathcal{S} = [\![T]\!]^*(\rho_0)$.

Example 3.2. Consider the IGTS $\mathcal{E}' = (\{X\}, \{X \xrightarrow{a} X\}, \{X \mapsto C_0\})$ with $a = (\mathbb{R}_+^2, (-1, 1))$ and $C_0 = \{1\} \times [-1, 1]$. Intuitively $\mathcal{E}'$ corresponds to a compact version of the IGTS $\mathcal{E}$ from Example 3.1, where the cycle is shortened into a single "self-loop" transition. The convex sets C_0, $[\![a]\!](C_0)$ and $[\![aa]\!](C_0)$ are depicted below (respectively in black, blue and red). Since $[\![aaa]\!](C_0)$ is empty, we get that $[\![a^*]\!](C_0) = C_0 \sqcup [\![a]\!](C_0) \sqcup [\![aa]\!](C_0)$. The characterization of $[\![a]\!]^*(C_0)$ is more complex ; the key point here is to show that the set $\{0\} \times [0,2]$ is necessarily contained $[\![a]\!]^*(C_0)$. The sets $[\![a^*]\!](C_0)$ and $[\![a]\!]^*(C_0)$ are also depicted below.

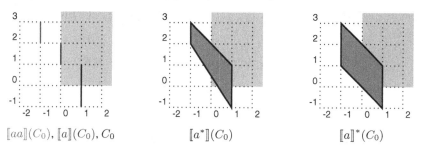

$[\![aa]\!](C_0), [\![a]\!](C_0), C_0$ $[\![a^*]\!](C_0)$ $[\![a]\!]^*(C_0)$

The MOP-solution $\Pi_{\mathcal{E}'}$ and the MFP-solution $\Lambda_{\mathcal{E}'}$ of the IGTS $\mathcal{E}'$ are the valuations $\Pi_{\mathcal{E}'} = \{X \mapsto [\![a^*]\!](C_0)\}$ and $\Lambda_{\mathcal{E}'} = \{X \mapsto [\![a]\!]^*(C_0)\}$.   □

Recall that our objective is to speed up, using acceleration-based techniques, the computation of the MFP-solution for initialized guarded translation systems. Recast in our setting, exact acceleration [BW94, CJ98, FIS03, FL02, BIL06] intuitively consists in computing the exact effect $\bigcup_{k \in \mathbb{N}} [\![(a_1 \cdots a_k)^k]\!](C_0)$ of some cycle $X \xrightarrow{a_1} X_1 \cdots X_{k-1} \xrightarrow{a_k} X$, starting with some $C_0 \in \mathcal{C}_n$ in X. Thus we may want define acceleration as the closed convex hull of this expression. However it would be even more desirable to compute the larger set $[\![(a_1 \cdots a_k)]\!]^*(C_0)$ since it is contained in the MFP-solution. We thus come to the following definition. Given any trace σ in $\mathcal{A}_n^*$, the function $[\![\sigma^*]\!]$ (resp. $[\![\sigma]\!]^*$) is called the *MOP-acceleration of σ* (resp. the *MFP-acceleration of σ*).

As will be apparent in section 5, trace-based acceleration is not in general sufficient to guarantee termination of the Kleene fix-point iteration, even for "cyclic" IGTS. The reason is that trace-based acceleration distinguishes a variable X (the "input variable" of the cycle to be accelerated) and abstracts away all other variables in the "current" valuation ρ of the fix-point iteration. Hence we also introduce acceleration of cycles, where we intuitively consider the MOP-solution or MFP-solution of the system restricted to this cycle. Formally, given any simple cycle π in T^*, the *MOP-acceleration of π* (resp. the *MFP-acceleration of π*) is the function $[\![U^*]\!]$ (resp. $[\![U]\!]^*$) where U is the set of transitions that occur in π. Note that these accelerations may be extended to arbitrary cycles through the notion of unfoldings [LS07].

The rest of the paper is devoted to the characterization and computation of these accelerations: section 4 focuses on acceleration for traces and section 5 investigates acceleration for simple cycles.

4   Acceleration for Traces

We focus in this section on MOP-acceleration and MFP-acceleration for traces. Remark that for any $\sigma = a_1 \cdots a_k \in \mathcal{A}_n^*$, with $a_i = (G_i, \boldsymbol{d_i})$, we have $[\![\sigma]\!] = [\![a_\sigma]\!]$ where

$a_\sigma = (G_\sigma, d_\sigma)$ is defined by $d_\sigma = \sum_{i=1}^k d_i$ and $G_\sigma = \bigcap_{i=1}^k \left(G_i - \sum_{j=1}^{i-1} d_j\right)$. It follows that $\llbracket \sigma^* \rrbracket = \llbracket a_\sigma^* \rrbracket$ and $\llbracket \sigma \rrbracket^* = \llbracket a_\sigma \rrbracket^*$. Therefore we will w.l.o.g. restrict our attention to MOP-acceleration and MFP-acceleration for single actions.

Consider an n-dim action $a = (G, d)$ and a closed convex set $C_0 \in \mathcal{C}_n$. Recall that $\llbracket a^* \rrbracket(C_0) = \bigsqcup_{k \in \mathbb{N}} \llbracket a^k \rrbracket(C_0)$. Observe that for every $k \in \mathbb{N}$ we have $\llbracket a^k \rrbracket(C_0) = (G_k \cap C_0) + k\,d$ where $G_k = \bigcap_{i=0}^{k-1}(G - i\,d)$. By convexity of G we deduce that $G_k = G \cap (G - (k-1)\,d)$ for every $k \geq 1$. Hence we have:

$$\llbracket a^* \rrbracket(C_0) \quad = \quad C_0 \sqcup (\mathrm{cloconv}\,(G \cap ((G \cap C_0) + \mathbb{N}\,d)) + d)$$

The main difficulty here lies in the computation of $\mathrm{cloconv}\,(G \cap ((G \cap C_0) + \mathbb{N}\,d))$.

We introduce the class of poly-based semilinear sets and show that this class is closed under sum, union and intersection. We call *poly-based linear* any subset of $\mathbb{R}^n$ of the form $B + \sum_{p \in P} \mathbb{N}\,p$ where B is a bounded polyhedron and P is a finite subset of $\mathbb{Z}^n$. A *poly-based semilinear* set is any finite union of poly-based linear sets. Note that poly-based semilinearity generalizes standard (integer) semilinearity [GS66] in that for any subset Z of $\mathbb{Z}^n$, Z is semilinear iff Z is poly-based semilinear.

Lemma 4.1. *Every polyhedron is a poly-based linear set. Poly-based semilinear sets are closed under sum, union and intersection.*

We obtain from Lemma 4.1 that $\llbracket a^* \rrbracket(C_0) = C_0 \sqcup (\mathrm{cloconv}\,(S) + d)$ for some poly-based semilinear set S. Since $\mathrm{cloconv}\left(\sum_{p \in P} \mathbb{N}\,p\right) = \sum_{p \in P} \uparrow p$ for any subset P of $\mathbb{R}^n$, we get that $\mathrm{cloconv}\,(S)$ is a polyhedron and hence we come to the following proposition.

Proposition 4.2. *For any n-dim action $a = (G, d)$ and closed convex set $C_0 \in \mathcal{C}_n$, if G and C_0 are polyhedra then $\llbracket a^* \rrbracket(C_0)$ is a polyhedron.*

Remark that the proof of Proposition 4.2 is constructive (since the proof of Lemma 4.1 is constructive). It follows that for each $\mathbb{F} \in \{\mathbb{Q}, \mathbb{A}\}$, the set $\llbracket a^* \rrbracket(C_0)$ is an effectively computable $\mathbb{F}$-polyhedron when a and C_0 are $\mathbb{F}$-polyhedral. The following proposition gives a simple expression of the MOP-acceleration for bounded closed convex sets.

Proposition 4.3. *For any n-dim action $a = (G, d)$ and closed convex set $C_0 \in \mathcal{C}_n$, if $G \cap C_0$ is bounded then we have:*

- *if $G \cap C_0 \neq \emptyset$ and $d \in 0^+ G$ then $\llbracket a^* \rrbracket(C_0) = C_0 + \uparrow d$, and*
- *otherwise $\llbracket a^k \rrbracket(C_0) = \emptyset$ for some $k \in \mathbb{N}$, and $\llbracket a^* \rrbracket(C_0) = \bigsqcup_{i=0}^{k-1} \llbracket a^i \rrbracket(C_0)$.*

Our next result gives a surprisingly simple expression of the MFP-acceleration for arbitrary n-dim actions.

Proposition 4.4. *For any n-dim action $a = (G, d)$ and closed convex set $C_0 \in \mathcal{C}_n$, we have:*

$$\llbracket a \rrbracket^*(C_0) \quad = \quad \begin{cases} C_0 & \text{if } G \cap C_0 = \emptyset \\ C_0 \sqcup ((G \cap (C_0 + \uparrow d)) + d) & \text{otherwise} \end{cases}$$

It follows from Proposition 4.4 that $[\![a]\!]^*(C_0)$ is a polyhedron when G and C_0 are polyhedra. If moreover a and C_0 are $\mathbb{F}$-polyhedral, with $\mathbb{F} \in \{\mathbb{Q}, \mathbb{A}\}$, then $[\![a]\!]^*(C_0)$ is an effectively computable $\mathbb{F}$-polyhedron.

We now compare our MFP-acceleration approach with *abstract loop acceleration* introduced in [GH06] as a complement to widening for linear relation analysis. Let us recast the definition of [GH06] in our setting. The *abstract-acceleration* $[\![a]\!]^{\otimes}$ of any n-dim action $a = (G, d)$ is the monotonic function in $\mathcal{C}_n \to \mathcal{C}_n$ defined by $[\![a]\!]^{\otimes}(C_0) = C_0 \sqcup \text{cloconv}(\{x \in \mathbb{R}^n \mid \exists x_0 \in G \cap C_0, x \in (x_0 + \uparrow d) \cap (G + d)\})$. Observe that $[\![a]\!]^{\otimes}(C_0) = C_0 \sqcup ((G \cap C_0) + \uparrow d) \cap (G + d)$. Hence we obtain the following relationships between MOP-acceleration, MFP-acceleration and abstract-acceleration:

$$[\![a^*]\!](C_0) \sqsubseteq [\![a]\!]^{\otimes}(C_0) = C_0 \sqcup [\![a]\!]^*(C_0 \cap G) \sqsubseteq [\![a]\!]^*(C_0)$$

Note in particular that $[\![a]\!]^{\otimes}(C_0) = [\![a]\!]^*(C_0)$ when $C_0 \subseteq G$. It turns out that abstract-acceleration is not sufficient to guarantee termination of the Kleene fix-point iteration even for guarded translation systems consisting in a single "self-loop" transition.

Consider our running example, the IGTS given in Example 3.2, and recall that $C_0 = \{1\} \times [-1, 1]$. The sequence $(C_k)_{k \in \mathbb{N}}$ defined by $C_{k+1} = [\![a]\!]^{\otimes}(C_k)$ corresponds, for this example, to the abstract-accelerated Kleene fix-point iteration suggested in [GH06]. An induction on k shows that for every $k \geq 1$, the set C_k is the convex hull of $\{(1, -1), (1, 1), (-1, 3), (-1, y_k)\}$ where $y_k = 1 + \frac{1}{2^k - 1}$. The first sets C_0, C_1, C_2 and C_3 of the iteration are depicted on the right (darker sets corresponds to smaller indices). It follows that the sequence $(C_k)_{k \in \mathbb{N}}$ is (strictly) increasing and hence this accelerated Kleene fix-point iteration does not terminate. Note that the situation would not be better with MOP-acceleration. However as already noted in Example 3.2, MFP-acceleration of a directly produces the MFP-solution. Hence the MFP-accelerated Kleene

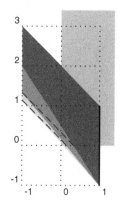

fix-point iteration would reach the fix-point after just one iteration. Notice that MFP-acceleration and abstract-acceleration have the same computational complexity.

5 Acceleration for Cycles

We investigate the computation of the MOP-acceleration (resp. the MFP-acceleration) of a simple cycle. Following our definitions, this problem reduces to the computation of the MOP-solution (resp. the MFP-solution) of an IGTS that contains all its transitions into a unique (up to permutations) simple cycle $\pi = X_1 \xrightarrow{a_1} \cdots X_k \xrightarrow{a_k} X_1$, called *cyclic*. We only consider the MFP-solution computation in the sequel since the following equality shows that the MOP-solution of a cyclic IGTS reduces to the computation of the MOP-acceleration of the trace $\sigma = a_1 \ldots a_k$:

$$\Pi_\mathcal{S}(X_1) = \bigsqcup_{i=1}^{k} [\![\sigma^*]\!] \circ [\![a_{i+1} \ldots a_k]\!] (\rho_0(X_i))$$

We first explain why the previous reduction cannot be extended to the MFP-solution. Naturally, when the initial valuation ρ_0 satisfies $\rho_0(X) = \bot$ for all but one variable X_i, the following equality shows that the MFP-solution reduces to the MFP-acceleration of traces (values of Λ_8 in $X_2, \ldots, X_k$ are obtained by circular permutations):

$$\Lambda_8(X_1) = [\![\sigma]\!]^* \circ [\![a_{i+1} \ldots a_k]\!](\rho_0(X_i))$$

However, this case is not sufficient since we want to apply MFP-acceleration at any point during an iterative computation of MFP-solutions. The 2-dim cyclic rational polyhedral IGTS $\mathcal{E}_2$ formally defined below shows that the MFP-solution Λ_8 cannot be reduced to MFP-acceleration of traces for a general initial valuation ρ_0. In fact, we prove in the sequel that the MFP-solution of $\mathcal{E}_2$ is $\mathbb{A}$-polyhedral but not $\mathbb{Q}$-polyhedral. Since MFP-accelerations of traces only produce $\mathbb{Q}$-polyhedral valuations we deduce that the MFP-solution cannot be obtained using MFP-acceleration of traces.

Example 5.1. Consider the cyclic 2-dim IGTS $\mathcal{E}_2$ depicted graphically on the left-hand side below.

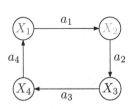
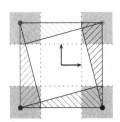
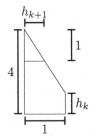

Formally the initial valuation ρ_0 of $\mathcal{E}_2$ is $\{X_1 \mapsto \{(-2,2)\}, X_2 \mapsto \{(2,2)\}, X_3 \mapsto \{(2,-2)\}, X_4 \mapsto \{(-2,-2)\}\}$, and its actions $a_1 = (G_1, \mathbf{0}), a_2 = (G_2, \mathbf{0}), a_3 = (G_3, \mathbf{0}), a_4 = (G_4, \mathbf{0})$ are defined by $G_1 = \,]-\infty, -1] \times [1, +\infty[, G_2 = [1, +\infty[\times [1, +\infty[, G_3 = [1, +\infty[\times \,]-\infty, -1]$ and $G_4 = \,]-\infty, -1] \times \,]-\infty, -1]$.   □

The MFP-solution of the IGTS $\mathcal{E}_2$ can be obtained by first proving that the Kleene iteration $(\mathbb{1} \sqcup [\![T]\!])^{k+2}(\rho_0)$ is equal to the valuation $\Lambda_{\mathcal{E}_2, h_k}$ (The values of $\Lambda_{\mathcal{E}_2, h}$ in X_1, X_2, X_3, X_4 are graphically pictured in red, green, black and blue in the center of the previous figure) where $\Lambda_{\mathcal{E}_2, h}$ is the following valuation parameterized by a real number h and where $(h_k)_{k \geq 0}$ is the sequence of rational numbers defined by $h_0 = 0$ and $h_{k+1} = \frac{1}{4-h_k}$ (this last equality can be geometrically obtained from the right-hand side picture of the previous figure).

$$\Lambda_{\mathcal{E}_2, h}(X_1) = \text{conv}(\{ \ (-2,2) \ , (-2,-2), (-1,-2), (-1,-2+h) \})$$
$$\Lambda_{\mathcal{E}_2, h}(X_2) = \text{conv}(\{ \ (2,2) \ , (-2,2) \ , (-2,1) \ , (-2+h,1) \})$$
$$\Lambda_{\mathcal{E}_2, h}(X_3) = \text{conv}(\{ \ (2,-2) \ , \ (2,2) \ , \ (1,2) \ , \ (1,2-h) \})$$
$$\Lambda_{\mathcal{E}_2, h}(X_4) = \text{conv}(\{ (-2,-2), \ (2,-2) \ , \ (2,-1) \ , \ (2-h,-1) \})$$

Lemma 5.2. *We have* $(\mathbb{1} \sqcup [\![T]\!])(\Lambda_{\mathcal{E}_2, h}) = \Lambda_{\mathcal{E}_2, \frac{1}{4-h}}$ *for any* $0 \leq h \leq 2 - \sqrt{3}$.

As $\Lambda_{\mathcal{E}_2, 0} = (\mathbb{1} \sqcup [\![T]\!])^2(\rho_0)$ we deduce that $\Lambda_{\mathcal{E}_2, h_k} = (\mathbb{1} \sqcup [\![T]\!])^{k+2}(\rho_0)$ for any $k \geq 0$ from the previous lemma 5.2.

Lemma 5.3. *The sequence* $(h_k)_{k \geq 0}$ *converges to the algebraic number* $2 - \sqrt{3}$.

Since $\Lambda_{\mathcal{E}_2, h_k} \sqsubseteq \Lambda_{\mathcal{E}_2}$, we deduce from lemma 5.3 that $\Lambda_{\mathcal{E}_2, 2-\sqrt{3}} \sqsubseteq \Lambda_{\mathcal{E}_2}$. Observe that lemma 5.2 proves that $\Lambda_{\mathcal{E}_2, 2-\sqrt{3}}$ is a post-fix-point. Thus $\Lambda_{\mathcal{E}_2, 2-\sqrt{3}}$ is the MFP-solution. Note that this valuation is $\mathbb{A}$-polyhedral but not $\mathbb{Q}$-polyhedral. We will actually show in the next section that the MFP-solution of any 2-dim $\mathbb{A}$-polyhedral IGTS (not necessarily cyclic) is $\mathbb{A}$-polyhedral.

Now we provide an example of 3-dim cyclic $\mathbb{Q}$-polyhedral IGTS $\mathcal{E}_3$ corresponding to a slightly modified version of $\mathcal{E}_2$ that exhibits a non-polyhedral MFP-solution.

Example 5.4. Consider the cyclic 3-dim IGTS $\mathcal{E}_3$ formally defined as $\mathcal{E}_2$ except for (a) its initial valuation ρ_0 equal to $\{X_1 \mapsto (-1, 1, 0) + \uparrow e_3, \ X_2 \mapsto (1, 1, 0) + \uparrow e_3, \ X_3 \mapsto (1, -1, 0) + \uparrow e_3, \ X_4 \mapsto (-1, -1, 0) + \uparrow e_3\}$ where $e_3 = (0, 0, 1)$, and (b) its actions a_1, a_2, a_3, a_4 defined as follows ($\mathbb{R}_-$ is the set of non-positive real numbers $-\mathbb{R}_+$):

$$a_1 = (\ \mathbb{R}_- \times \mathbb{R}_+ \times \mathbb{R}, \ e_3\ ) \qquad a_2 = (\ \mathbb{R}_+ \times \mathbb{R}_+ \times \mathbb{R}, \ e_3\ )$$
$$a_4 = (\ \mathbb{R}_- \times \mathbb{R}_- \times \mathbb{R}, \ e_3\ ) \qquad a_3 = (\ \mathbb{R}_+ \times \mathbb{R}_- \times \mathbb{R}, \ e_3\ ) \qquad \square$$

Let us denote by $\Lambda_{\mathcal{E}_3, k}$ for any $k \in \{2, \ldots, +\infty\}$ the following valuation where $h_i = \frac{1}{i}$ for $i \geq 1$, $(z_i)_{i \geq 1}$ is defined by the initial value $z_1 = \frac{3}{2}$ and the induction $z_{i+1} = 1 + z_i \cdot \frac{i}{i+1}$, and $e_3 = (0, 0, 1)$.

$$\Lambda_{\mathcal{E}_3, k}(X_1) = \text{conv}(\{\ (-1, 1, 0)\ , (-1, -1, 1)\} \cup \{(0, -h_i, z_i) \mid 1 \leq i < k\}) + \uparrow e_3$$
$$\Lambda_{\mathcal{E}_3, k}(X_2) = \text{conv}(\{\ (1, 1, 0)\ , \ (-1, 1, 1)\} \cup \{(-h_i, 0, z_i) \mid 1 \leq i < k\}) + \uparrow e_3$$
$$\Lambda_{\mathcal{E}_3, k}(X_3) = \text{conv}(\{\ (1, -1, 0)\ , \ (1, 1, 1)\ \} \cup \{\ (0, h_i, z_i)\ \mid 1 \leq i < k\}) + \uparrow e_3$$
$$\Lambda_{\mathcal{E}_3, k}(X_4) = \text{conv}(\{(-1, -1, 0), \ (1, -1, 1)\ \} \cup \{\ (h_i, 0, z_i)\ \mid 1 \leq i < k\}) + \uparrow e_3$$

Lemma 5.5. *Values of* $\Lambda_{\mathcal{E}_3, +\infty}$ *in* X_1, X_2, X_3, X_4 *are closed convex sets but they are not polyhedral.*

Since $(\mathbb{1} \sqcup [\![T]\!])^2 (\rho_0) = \Lambda_{\mathcal{E}_3, 2}$, the following lemma 5.6 proves that $(\mathbb{1} \sqcup [\![T]\!])^k (\rho_0) = \Lambda_{\mathcal{E}_3, k}$ for any $k \in \{2, \ldots, +\infty\}$.

Lemma 5.6. *We have* $(\mathbb{1} \sqcup [\![T]\!])(\Lambda_{\mathcal{E}_3, k}) = \Lambda_{\mathcal{E}_3, k+1}$ *for any* $k \in \{2, \ldots, +\infty\}$.

We deduce that $\Lambda_{\mathcal{E}_3, +\infty}$ is the MFP-solution of $\mathcal{E}_3$.

Theorem 5.7. *There exists a 3-dim cyclic rational polyhedral IGTS with a MFP-solution that is not polyhedral.*

6 MFP-Solution in Dimension ≤ 2

We have proved in the previous section that the MFP-solution of a 2-dim cyclic rational polyhedral IGTS may be not rational. In this section the MFP-solution of any 2-dim $\mathbb{F}$-polyhedral IGTS (not necessary cyclic) is proved $\mathbb{F}$-polyhedral for any $\mathbb{F} \in \{\mathbb{A}, \mathbb{R}\}$.

Remark 6.1. In [SW05, LS07] the 1-dim case is fully studied.

Let us first consider any n-dim action $a = (G, d)$, a set $S \subseteq \mathbb{R}^n$ and observe that the inclusion cloconv $((G \cap S) + d) \sqsubseteq (G \cap \text{cloconv}(S)) + d$ is strict in general. Nevertheless, the following lemma provides a sufficient condition to obtain the equality. Recall that bd (G) is the *boundary* of G.

Lemma 6.2. *We have* cloconv $((G \cap S) + d) = (G \cap \text{cloconv}(S)) + d$ *for any n-dim action $a = (G, d)$ and for any set $S \subseteq \mathbb{R}^n$ such that* bd $(G) \cap \text{cloconv}(S) \subseteq S$.

Let $\mathcal{S} = (\mathcal{X}, T, \rho_0)$ be any n-dim polyhedral IGTS and let $\Lambda_{\mathcal{S}}$ be the following valuation:

$$\Lambda_{\mathcal{S}}(X) = \rho_0(X) \sqcup \bigsqcup \{\text{bd}(G) \cap \Lambda_{\mathcal{S}}(X) \mid X \xrightarrow{a=(G,d)} X'\}$$

Observe that $\Lambda_{\mathcal{S}}$ is an intermediate valuation $\rho_0 \sqsubseteq \Lambda_{\mathcal{S}} \sqsubseteq \Lambda_{\mathcal{S}}$. Let us denote by L_{X,X_0} (resp. $L_{X_0,X}^E$) the set of traces σ that label some path (resp. simple path) $X_0 \xrightarrow{\sigma} X$. Let $\Lambda_{\mathcal{S}}'$ be the valuation defined by $\Lambda_{\mathcal{S}}'(X) = \text{cloconv}(S(X))$ where $S(X)$ is the following set:

$$S(X) = \bigcup \{[\![\sigma]\!](\Lambda_{\mathcal{S}}(X_0)) \mid X_0 \in \mathcal{X}, \ \sigma \in L_{X_0,X}\}$$

Observe that $S(X)$ satisfies lemma 6.2, we deduce that $\Lambda_{\mathcal{S}}'$ is a post-fix-point, i.e. $[\![T]\!](\Lambda_{\mathcal{S}}') \sqsubseteq \Lambda_{\mathcal{S}}'$. Moreover, as $\Lambda_{\mathcal{S}}' \sqsubseteq \Lambda_{\mathcal{S}}$ we get the equality $\Lambda_{\mathcal{S}}' = \Lambda_{\mathcal{S}}$.

Lemma 6.3. *We have the following equality:*

$$\Lambda_{\mathcal{S}}(X) = \bigsqcup \{[\![\sigma]\!](\Lambda_{\mathcal{S}}(X_0)) \mid X_0 \in \mathcal{X}, \ \sigma \in L_{X_0,X}^E\} + 0^+ \Lambda_{\mathcal{S}}(X)$$

We now focus on dimension 2 and assume that $\mathcal{S}$ is a 2-dim polyhedral IGTS. As 2-dim closed convex cones are polyhedral we deduce that $0^+ \Lambda_{\mathcal{S}}(X)$ is polyhedral for any variable X. Moreover, since a polyhedron is a finite (eventually empty) intersection of half-spaces, by adding some new extra variables to the IGTS, we may assume without loss of generality that all guards are either half-spaces or the whole set $\mathbb{R}^2$. Note that the boundary of an half-space $\{x \in \mathbb{R}^n \mid \alpha_1.x_1 + \alpha_2.x_2 \leq c\}$ is the line $\{x \in \mathbb{R}^n \mid \alpha_1.x_1 + \alpha_2.x_2 = c\}$, and the boundary of $\mathbb{R}^2$ is the empty-set. Thus bd $(G) \cap \Lambda_{\mathcal{S}}(X)$ is polyhedral for any guard G and any variable X. We deduce that $\Lambda_{\mathcal{S}}$ is polyhedral.

Theorem 6.4. *The MFP-solution of any 2-dim polyhedral IGTS is polyhedral.*

Finally, assume that the 2-dim IGTS $\mathcal{S}$ is a $\mathbb{A}$-polyhedral and observe that for any variable $X \in \mathcal{X}$ and for any transition $X \xrightarrow{a} X'$ with $a = (G, d)$, there exists:

- three vectors $d_1, d_2, d_3 \in \mathbb{R}^2$ such that $0^+ \Lambda_{\mathcal{S}}(X) = \uparrow d_1 + \uparrow d_2 + \uparrow d_3$.
- two half-spaces H_1, H_2 such that bd $(G) \cap \Lambda_{\mathcal{S}}(X) = \text{bd}(G) \cap H_1 \cap H_2$.

Since any vector (resp. any half-space) can be defined with 2 reals (resp. 3 reals), we may constructively deduce from lemma 6.3 a formula in $\text{FO}(\mathbb{R}, +, *, \leq)$ defining $\Lambda_{\mathcal{S}}$.

Theorem 6.5. *The MFP-solution of any 2-dim $\mathbb{A}$-polyhedral IGTS is effectively $\mathbb{A}$-polyhedral.*

References

[BHRZ05]   Bagnara, R., Hill, P.M., Ricci, E., Zaffanella, E.: Precise widening operators for convex polyhedra. Science of Computer Programming 58(1–2), 28–56 (2005)

[BIL06]   Bozga, M., Iosif, R., Lakhnech, Y.: Flat parametric counter automata. In: Bugliesi, M., Preneel, B., Sassone, V., Wegener, I. (eds.) ICALP 2006. LNCS, vol. 4052, pp. 577–588. Springer, Heidelberg (2006)

[BW94]   Boigelot, B., Wolper, P.: Symbolic verification with periodic sets. In: Dill, D.L. (ed.) CAV 1994. LNCS, vol. 818, pp. 55–67. Springer, Heidelberg (1994)

[CC77]   Cousot, P., Cousot, R.: Abstract interpretation: A unified lattice model for static analysis of programs by construction or approximation of fixpoints. In: Proc. 4th ACM Symp. Principles of Programming Languages, pp. 238–252. ACM Press, New York (1977)

[CC92]   Cousot, P., Cousot, R.: Comparing the Galois connection and widening/narrowing approaches to abstract interpretation. In: Bruynooghe, M., Wirsing, M. (eds.) PLILP 1992. LNCS, vol. 631, pp. 269–295. Springer, Heidelberg (1992)

[CH78]   Cousot, P., Halbwachs, N.: Automatic discovery of linear restraints among variables of a program. In: Proc. 5th ACM Symp. Principles of Programming Languages, pp. 84–96. ACM Press, New York (1978)

[CJ98]   Comon, H., Jurski, Y.: Multiple counters automata, safety analysis and Presburger arithmetic. In: Vardi, M.Y. (ed.) CAV 1998. LNCS, vol. 1427, pp. 268–279. Springer, Heidelberg (1998)

[FIS03]   Finkel, A., Iyer, S.P., Sutre, G.: Well-abstracted transition systems: Application to FIFO automata. Information and Computation 181(1), 1–31 (2003)

[FL02]   Finkel, A., Leroux, J.: How to compose Presburger-accelerations: Applications to broadcast protocols. In: Agrawal, M., Seth, A.K. (eds.) FSTTCS 2002. LNCS, vol. 2556, pp. 145–156. Springer, Heidelberg (2002)

[GH06]   Gonnord, L., Halbwachs, N.: Combining widening and acceleration in linear relation analysis. In: Yi, K. (ed.) SAS 2006. LNCS, vol. 4134, pp. 144–160. Springer, Heidelberg (2006)

[GS66]   Ginsburg, S., Spanier, E.H.: Semigroups, Presburger formulas and languages. Pacific J. Math. 16(2), 285–296 (1966)

[Kar76]   Karr, M.: Affine relationship among variables of a program. Acta Informatica 6, 133–141 (1976)

[LS07]   Leroux, J., Sutre, G.: Accelerated data-flow analysis. In: Riis Nielson, H., Filé, G. (eds.) SAS 2007. LNCS, vol. 4634, pp. 184–199. Springer, Heidelberg (2007)

[Min01]   Miné, A.: A new numerical abstract domain based on difference-bound matrices. In: Danvy, O., Filinski, A. (eds.) PADO 2001. LNCS, vol. 2053, pp. 155–172. Springer, Heidelberg (2001)

[Sch86]   Schrijver, A.: Theory of Linear and Integer Programming. Wiley, Chichester (1986)

[SSM04]   Sankaranarayanan, S., Sipma, H.B., Manna, Z.: Constraint-based linear-relations analysis. In: Giacobazzi, R. (ed.) SAS 2004. LNCS, vol. 3148, pp. 53–68. Springer, Heidelberg (2004)

[SW05]   Su, Z., Wagner, D.: A class of polynomially solvable range constraints for interval analysis without widenings. Theoretical Computer Science 345(1), 122–138 (2005)

Model Checking Almost All Paths Can Be Less Expensive Than Checking All Paths

Matthias Schmalz[1], Hagen Völzer[2], and Daniele Varacca[3],*

[1] ETH Zürich, Switzerland
Matthias.Schmalz@inf.ethz.ch
[2] IBM Zurich Research Laboratory, Switzerland
hvo@zurich.ibm.com
[3] PPS - CNRS & Univ. Paris 7, France
varacca@pps.jussieu.fr

Abstract. We compare the complexities of the following two model checking problems: checking whether a linear-time formula is satisfied by all paths (which we call *universal* model checking) and checking whether a formula is satisfied by almost all paths (which we call *fair* model checking here). For many interesting classes of linear-time formulas, both problems have the same complexity: for instance, they are PSPACE-complete for LTL.

In this paper, we show that fair model checking can have lower complexity than universal model checking, viz., we prove that fair model checking for $L(F^\infty)$ can be done in time linear in the size of the formula and of the system, while it is known that universal model checking for $L(F^\infty)$ is co-NP-complete. $L(F^\infty)$ denotes the class of LTL formulas in which F^∞ is the only temporal operator. We also present other new results on the complexity of fair and universal model checking. In particular, we prove that fair model checking for RLTL is co-NP-complete.

1 Introduction

A reactive system satisfies a specification expressed by a formula of linear-time temporal logic if *all* its executions satisfy the formula. In this case, we say that a system is *universally correct*, and the problem of verifying universal correctness is called *universal model checking*.

Sometimes a system does not satisfy a specification, but only because of a "small" set of executions that do not satisfy the formula. From a measure-theoretic point of view, "small" means having probability 0. From a topological point of view, it means being a *meager* set. The topological point of view corresponds to the notion of *fairness* [15], i.e., a set of executions Y of a system is meager if and only if there exists some fairness assumption F for the system such that each execution in Y is unfair w. r. t. F.

Varacca and Völzer [12] have shown that, for LTL formulas and finite-state systems, the two notions of smallness coincide. More importantly, they coincide

---

* Most of the work was done while the first two authors were affiliated with the University of Lübeck, Germany.

V. Arvind and S. Prasad (Eds.): FSTTCS 2007, LNCS 4855, pp. 532–543, 2007.
© Springer-Verlag Berlin Heidelberg 2007

independently of the probability measure chosen (provided it belongs to a very general class of measures).

If the set of executions that do not satisfy the specification is small, we say that the system is *almost correct* or *fairly correct*. The problem of verifying fair correctness is called *fair model checking* in this paper.[1] As indicated above, fair model checking is — for finite systems and LTL specifications — equivalent to *qualitative probabilistic model checking* (i.e., checking a specification for probability 1) (cf. [12]). Fair model checking is an interesting alternative to universal model checking even for non-probabilistic systems that are desired to be universally correct for the following reasons:

- The difference between the two notions of correctness is small; most errors (i.e. violations of the specification) found by universal checking are also found by fair checking. In particular, both notions of correctness coincide for *safety* properties (cf. [12]).
- In fair model checking, there is no need to specify any fairness assumption on the system. (Additional fairness assumptions do not change fair correctness [12].)

It is known that universal and fair model checking for LTL have the same complexity: both are PSPACE-complete and can be solved in time linear in the system and exponential in the formula [10,6,13,3]. In this paper, we compare the complexities of universal and fair model checking for subclasses of LTL. Studying subclasses helps to understand the scope of the PSPACE-completeness results and also helps to develop optimised algorithms for frequently used formulas.

It is known that also for some sub- and superclasses of LTL, universal and fair model checking have the same complexity, e.g. LTL+past [10,6,3], Büchi automata [11,14,13,3] and Street constraints [1,12]. We show that this remains true for some additional subclasses. In particular, fair and universal model checking for $L(\mathrm{F})$ (also known as RLTL: the class of LTL formulas built using only the temporal operator F) are both co-NP-complete.

However, as the main result of the paper, we show that fair (and hence qualitative probabilistic) model checking can be easier than universal model checking. We prove that fair model checking for $L(\mathrm{F}^\infty)$ (LTL restricted to F^∞, where F^∞ is short for $\mathrm{G\,F}$) can be done in time linear in the size of the formula (and linear in the size of the system), whereas universal model checking for $L(\mathrm{F}^\infty)$ is co-NP-complete.

To this end, we define and characterise an interesting subclass of $L(\mathrm{F}^\infty)$, called *Muller formulas*, which already separates the two model checking problems with respect to their complexity. The satisfaction of a Muller formula in an execution depends only on the set of states which are visited infinitely often in that execution. Finally, we clarify the scope of our results by looking at some simple subclasses of RLTL.

Missing proofs can be found in the technical report [8].

---

[1] Note that in this paper fair model checking is *not* the problem of checking whether a system is correct under some fixed fairness assumption. Instead, it is the problem of checking whether there *exists* some fairness assumption for a system such that the system is correct under this fairness assumption.

2   Preliminaries

2.1   Systems and Temporal Properties

Let Q be a finite set of *states*. The sets Q^*, Q^+ and Q^ω contain all finite, non-empty finite, and infinite sequences over Q, respectively. Finite sequences are called *path fragments (over Q)* and denoted by α, β, and infinite ones are called *paths (over Q)* and denoted by x, y. The i-th element of a path (or path fragment) x is denoted x_i. We have $x = x_0 x_1 \ldots$ A set $Y \subseteq Q^\omega$ is called a *(linear-time temporal) property (over Q)* or a *specification*. If Q is clear from the context, we write Y^c for the complement of Y in Q^ω.

Throughout the entire paper, we fix a nonempty set AP of *atomic propositions*. A *system* $\Sigma = (Q, q_0, \rightarrow, v)$ consists of a finite set of states $Q \subseteq AP$, an initial state $q_0 \in Q$, a *state relation* $\rightarrow \subseteq Q \times Q$, and a *valuation function* $v : Q \rightarrow 2^{AP}$ such that $q \in v(q)$, for each $q \in Q$. The technical assumption $Q \subseteq AP$ allows us later to use states as part of temporal formulas. We require that for each $p \in Q$ there be a $q \in Q$ such that $p \rightarrow q$. A *path of* Σ is a path x over Q such that $x_0 = q_0$ and $x_i \rightarrow x_{i+1}$ ($i \in \mathbb{N}$). Finite prefixes of paths of Σ are called *path fragments of* Σ.

A set $K \subseteq Q$ is a *strongly connected component of* Σ (s. c. c. for short) if it is a strongly connected component of the directed graph $(Q, \rightarrow)$. A *bottom strongly connected component of* Σ *(b. s. c. c.)* K is an s. c. c. with no outgoing edges, i.e., there is no edge $(p, q) \in \rightarrow$ such that $p \in K$ and $q \notin K$.

The *size* of a system $\Sigma = (Q, q_0, \rightarrow, v)$ is defined as $|\Sigma| := |Q| + | \rightarrow |$.

2.2   Temporal Logic

In this paper, we consider several languages of linear-time temporal logic. The most expressive one is LTL+past [4], which is defined by the following syntax rules, where ξ ranges over atomic propositions and Φ over *path formulas*:

$$\Phi := \xi \mid \neg \Phi \mid \Phi \vee \Phi \mid X \Phi \mid \Phi U \Phi \mid X^- \Phi \mid \Phi U^- \Phi$$

Additional operators such as *true, false*, $\wedge$, $\Rightarrow$, F, G, etc. are defined as abbreviations as usual [4]. We will also make use of the operator F^∞, defined as abbreviation for G F, and G^∞ the abbreviation for F G. Non-boolean operators are called *temporal* operators. If Φ does not contain a temporal operator, it is called a *state formula*. By $L(op_1, \ldots, op_n)$ we denote the set of LTL+past formulas that contain only the temporal operators $op_1, \ldots, op_n$. $L(X, U)$ is known as LTL, $L(F)$ as RLTL. Note that $L(F) \subseteq L(X, U)$ because F can be expressed by U. Likewise, formulas in $L(F)$ can also contain G, F^∞ and G^∞.

Satisfaction $x \vDash \Phi$, $x, i \vDash \Phi$ is defined as usual [4]. By $Sat(\Phi)$ we denote the set of all paths of the underlying system that satisfy Φ. The *size* $|\Phi|$ of a formula Φ is given by the number of its temporal and boolean operators.

2.3   Universal and Fair Correctness

A system is *universally* correct w. r. t. *a specification* Y iff each path of the system belongs to Y. It is *universally* correct w. r. t. *a formula* Φ iff each path of the system satisfies Φ. Fair correctness can be defined equivalently in language-theoretic, game-theoretic, topological, or probability-theoretic terms [12]. In particular, the system underlying a finite-state Markov chain is *fairly correct* w. r. t. a specification given by a formula Φ if and only if $Sat(\Phi)$ has measure 1. This property is independent of the precise probabilities in the Markov chain, and fair correctness can in fact be defined without probability. We give the game-theoretic definition here because that will be the most useful in the sequel.

Let $\Sigma = (Q, q_0, \rightarrow, v)$ be a system and Y a property. The *Banach-Mazur game* $G(\Sigma, Y)$ is played by the two players Alter and Ego, and the state of a play is a path fragment of Σ. Alter moves first by choosing a path fragment α_0 of Σ. The players alternately move, and the player of the i-th move ($i \in \mathbb{N}$) extends the path fragment by a finite, nonempty sequence α_i, yielding the path fragment $\alpha_0 \ldots \alpha_i$ of Σ. The play goes on forever, converging to a path x of Σ. Ego wins if $x \in Y$, otherwise Alter wins. A *strategy* is a mapping $f : Q^* \rightarrow Q^+$ such that, for each path fragment α of Σ, $\alpha f(\alpha)$ is a path fragment of Σ. A strategy f is *winning* for player $P \in \{\text{Alter}, \text{Ego}\}$ if, for each strategy g of the other player, P wins the play that results from P playing f and the other player playing g. It is well-known that if Y is given by an LTL-formula, then $G(\Sigma, Y)$ is *determinate* (cf. [2]), i.e., either Ego or Alter has a winning strategy.

The system Σ is *fairly* correct w. r. t. Y iff Ego has a winning strategy in $G(\Sigma, Y)$. For convenience, we say that Σ is *fairly* correct w. r. t. Φ iff Ego has a winning strategy in $G(\Sigma, Sat(\Phi))$. *Universal model checking*, denoted by $\text{UMC}(L)$, is the problem of deciding whether a given system is universally correct, and *fair model checking*, denoted by $\text{FMC}(L)$, is the problem of deciding whether a given system is fairly correct w. r. t. a specification. In both cases, the specification is given by a formula drawn from the language L.

3   Comparing Universal and Fair Model Checking

3.1   Known Results

It is known that both universal and fair model checking of LTL are PSPACE-complete [10,13,3]. Both problems can be solved in time linear in the system and exponential in the formula [6,3]. The same holds for the language LTL+past. For universal model checking, this was shown by Sistla and Clarke [10,9,6], and for fair model checking, this was claimed by Courcoubetis and Yannakakis [3], but no proof was published. A formal original proof is given in Schmalz' thesis [7].

These results can also be transferred to branching-time logics, where the model checking problems for CTL and a fair version of CTL (as well as for CTL* and a fair version of CTL*) have the same complexities (cf. [12]). Finally, fair and universal model checking for specifications given by a Büchi automaton are both PSPACE-complete [13,3,11,14].

3.2   RLTL

Sistla and Clarke [10] have shown that universal model checking for RLTL is co-NP-complete. In this section, we show that this is also the case for the fair model checking problem for RLTL. Indeed, fair satisfaction of an RLTL formula can be expressed by another RLTL formula. In this way, fair model checking for RLTL can be reduced to universal model checking for RLTL. To this end, we need the notion of a *complete property*.

Definition 1. *Let L be a sublanguage of LTL+past and Σ a system that is fairly correct w. r. t. a property Y. We say that Y is L-complete w.r.t. Σ iff $Y \subseteq Sat(\Phi)$ for each $\Phi \in L$ such that Σ is fairly correct w. r. t. Φ.*

If Y is L-complete, then we have that Σ is fairly correct w. r. t. Φ iff $Y \subseteq Sat(\Phi)$, provided that $\Phi \in L$ (cf. [12]). This yields an alternative way of proving and disproving fair correctness.

We will use the fact that *state fairness* is complete for RLTL and expressible in RLTL. Let x be a path and p, q states of a system $\Sigma = (Q, q_0, \rightarrow, v)$. We say that q is *enabled* at p iff $p \rightarrow q$; moreover, q is *enabled at some position i* of x iff q is enabled at x_i. We say that q is *taken* at position i of x iff $x_i = q$. The path x is *state fair* w. r. t. Σ iff each state q of Σ that is enabled at infinitely many positions of x is also taken at infinitely many positions of x. The set of all state fair paths of Σ is denoted by SF_Σ.

It is easy to show that Σ is fairly correct w. r. t. SF_Σ. A winning strategy for Ego consists in first going to a b. s. c. c., and then, at each subsequent turn, taking each state of that b. s. c. c. at least once.

Theorem 2. *Let Σ be a finite system. Then, SF_Σ is $L(\mathrm{F})$-complete w. r. t. Σ.*

The intuitive meaning of Theorem 2 is the following: whenever we want to prove that Σ is fairly correct w. r. t. a formula $\Phi \in L(\mathrm{F})$, this can be accomplished by showing that each state fair path of Σ satisfies Φ. Theorem 2 was observed already by Zuck et al. [16], who also gave a proof sketch. In [8], we give a detailed alternative proof.

State fairness can easily be expressed by the following formula of $L(\mathrm{F})$:

$$\Psi(\Sigma) := \bigwedge_{q \in Q} (\mathrm{F}^\infty\, enabled(q) \Rightarrow \mathrm{F}^\infty\, q),$$

where, for each $q \in Q$, $enabled(q)$ is an atomic proposition that holds exactly at these states of Σ at which q is enabled. As F^∞ is a shorthand for $\mathrm{G\,F}$, and G can be defined in terms of F, $\Psi(\Sigma) \in L(\mathrm{F})$.

We are now ready to prove the main result of this section.

Theorem 3. *The problem $\mathrm{FMC}(L(\mathrm{F}))$ is co-NP-complete.*

Proof. Hardness is a consequence of Theorem 10 stated below or can be shown similar as in the universal case (cf. [10]).

We prove co-NP membership of $\text{FMC}(L(\text{F}))$ by a reduction from $\text{FMC}(L(\text{F}))$ to $\text{UMC}(L(\text{F}))$. Given a system Σ and a formula $\Phi \in L(\text{F})$, the reduction maps (Φ, Σ) to $(\hat{\Phi}, \Sigma)$, where $\hat{\Phi} := (\Psi(\Sigma) \Rightarrow \Phi) \in L(\text{F})$. By Theorem 2, Σ is fairly correct w.r.t. Φ iff Σ is universally correct w.r.t. $\hat{\Phi}$.

We remark here that also $\text{FMC}(L(\text{X}))$ and $\text{UMC}(L(\text{X}))$ are co-NP-complete. See [9] for the universal case. In the fair case, the assertion follows from the fact that Σ is correct w.r.t. Φ iff Σ is fairly correct w.r.t. Φ, provided that $\Phi \in L(\text{X})$.

4   Fair Model Checking Can Be Less Expensive Than Universal Model Checking

In this section, we show that for $L(\text{F}^\infty)$ the complexities of fair and universal model checking differ. It is known that universal model checking for $L(\text{F}^\infty)$ formulas is co-NP-complete [5]. We show that fair model checking can be done in linear time in the size of the formula and the system. For this, we first introduce a natural subclass of $L(\text{F}^\infty)$ for which the two complexities already differ.

4.1   Muller Formulas

A *Muller formula* is an LTL formula where F^∞ is the only temporal operator and where every variable is in the scope of some temporal operator:

Definition 4. *The language $L^+(\text{F}^\infty)$ of* Muller formulas *is the smallest set of LTL formulas that satisfies the following two conditions M1 and M2:*

M1: *If $\Psi \in L(\text{F}^\infty)$, then $\text{F}^\infty \Psi \in L^+(\text{F}^\infty)$.*
M2: *If $\Psi, \Phi \in L^+(\text{F}^\infty)$, then $\Psi \vee \Phi, \neg\Psi \in L^+(\text{F}^\infty)$.*

The key property of Muller formulas is that their validity in a path x only depends on the set $inf(x)$, i.e., the set of states that occur infinitely often in x.

Definition 5. *Let $\Sigma = (Q, q_0, \rightarrow, v)$ be a system. A property Y over Q is a* Muller property *iff for all paths x, y over Q with $inf(x) = inf(y)$ we have $x \in Y$ iff $y \in Y$.*

Theorem 6. *Let Σ be a system. Then, for each $\Phi \in L^+(\text{F}^\infty)$, $Sat(\Phi)$ is a Muller property.*

It is easy to see that each Muller property can be expressed by a Muller formula (cf. [7]).

4.2   Fair Model Checking of Muller Formulas

In this subsection, we show that fair model checking of Muller formulas can be done in linear time w.r.t. the formula. We are going to present an algorithm for $\text{FMC}(L^+(\text{F}^\infty))$ based on the fact that, for systems Σ that consist of only one

s. c. c. and formulas $\Phi \in L(\mathrm{F}^\infty)$, we have that Σ is either fairly correct w. r. t. Φ or w. r. t. $\neg\Phi$.

We are given a system Σ and a Muller formula Φ. Without loss of generality, we assume that Σ has no *isolated states*, i.e., each state of Σ is eventually taken by some path of Σ. First, the algorithm computes the b. s. c. c.s of Σ. Then, for each subformula Υ of Φ, the algorithm partitions each b. s. c. c. K of Σ into K_Υ and $K_{\neg\Upsilon} := K \setminus K_\Upsilon$ as follows. (The meaning of K_Υ is that whenever a state fair path of Σ takes a state of K_Υ, Υ is satisfied at the same position.)

1. If Υ is a state formula, then exactly these states of K that satisfy Υ belong to K_Υ.
2. If $\Upsilon = \Theta \vee \Psi$, then $K_\Upsilon := K_\Theta \cup K_\Psi$.
3. If $\Upsilon = \neg\Theta$, then $K_\Upsilon := K_{\neg\Theta}$.
4. If $\Upsilon = \mathrm{F}^\infty \Theta$, then $K_\Upsilon := K$ if $K_\Theta \neq \varnothing$; otherwise, $K_\Upsilon := \varnothing$.

The algorithm accepts its input iff $K = K_\Phi$ for each b. s. c. c. K of Σ.

Proposition 7. *The above algorithm is correct, i.e., the algorithm always terminates, and accepts if and only if Σ is fairly correct w. r. t. Φ.*

Proof. The algorithm obviously terminates. It can be shown by induction over the structure of Υ that the following applies:

1. We have $q \in K_\Upsilon$ iff $SF_\Sigma \subseteq Sat(\mathrm{G}(q \Rightarrow \Upsilon))$.
2. We have $q \in K_{\neg\Upsilon}$ iff $SF_\Sigma \subseteq Sat(\mathrm{G}(q \Rightarrow \neg\Upsilon))$.

Suppose the algorithm accepts Σ and Φ. As Σ is fairly correct w. r. t. SF_Σ, it suffices to show that $SF_\Sigma \subseteq Sat(\Phi)$. Let $x \in SF_\Sigma$. It can be shown that there is a b. s. c. c. K of Σ and a position $i \in \mathbb{N}$ such that $x_i \in K$. Therefore $x_i \in K_\Phi$. With claim 1, $x \vDash \mathrm{G}(x_i \Rightarrow \Phi)$. Hence, $x, i \vDash \Phi$. With Theorem 6, $x \vDash \Phi$.

Now, suppose the algorithm rejects Σ and Φ. Because of Theorem 2, it suffices to show that $SF_\Sigma \not\subseteq Sat(\Phi)$. Let $x \in SF_\Sigma$ such that, for some $i \in \mathbb{N}$, $x_i \in K_{\neg\Phi}$, where K is a b. s. c. c. of Σ with $K \neq K_\Phi$. With claim 2, $x \vDash \mathrm{G}(x_i \Rightarrow \neg\Phi)$. Hence, $x, i \vDash \neg\Phi$. With Theorem 6, $x \nvDash \Phi$.

The computation of the b. s. c. c.s of Σ can be done in $O(|\Sigma|)$ steps. For a given subformula Υ of Φ, also the partition of the b. s. c. c.s K into K_Υ and $K_{\neg\Upsilon}$ can be accomplished in $O(|\Sigma|)$. As Φ has $O(|\Phi|)$ subformulas, the total running time of the algorithm is in $O(|\Sigma||\Phi|)$. We have thus shown the following:

Theorem 8. *The problem* $\mathrm{FMC}(L^+(\mathrm{F}^\infty))$ *can be solved in* $O(|\Sigma||\Phi|)$, *where* Σ *is the input system and* Φ *the input formula.*

4.3   Fair Model Checking of $L(\mathrm{F}^\infty)$

Theorem 8 can be extended from $L^+(\mathrm{F}^\infty)$ to $L(\mathrm{F}^\infty)$.

Theorem 9. *The problem* $\mathrm{FMC}(L(\mathrm{F}^\infty))$ *can be solved in* $O(|\Sigma||\Phi|)$, *where* Σ *is the input system and* Φ *the input formula.*

Proof. The algorithm translates Φ to a formula Φ' by applying the following rules as often as possible:

1. Replace each atomic proposition, which is not in the scope of a temporal operator, by its truth value (*true* or *false*) at the initial state of Σ.
2. Replace *true* $\vee \Psi$ by *true*.
3. Replace *false* $\vee \Psi$ by Ψ.
4. Replace $\neg true$ by *false*.
5. Replace $\neg false$ by *true*.

It is straightforward to show that, for each path x of Σ, $x \vDash \Phi$ iff $x \vDash \Phi'$. Recall that the only difference between $L(\mathrm{F}^\infty)$ and $L^+(\mathrm{F}^\infty)$ is that in $L^+(\mathrm{F}^\infty)$ each atomic proposition is in the scope of a temporal operator. Therefore, it is not too difficult to see that Φ' is a Muller formula.

After this translation, the algorithm applies Theorem 8. As the translation can be done in $O(|\Phi|)$, the total running time belongs to $O(|\Sigma||\Phi|)$.

5   Canonical Subclasses of RLTL

In this section, we shed more light on the above results by studying the complexity of some simple subclasses of RLTL. The formulas in these subclasses are 'flat', i.e., there is no nesting of temporal operators.

5.1   Conjunctive Formulas

We start by observing that top-level conjunctions are easily dealt with: in order to check $\Phi \wedge \Psi$, it is sufficient to check Φ and Ψ in isolation. This is trivial for universal model checking, but is also easily verified for fair model checking: a system is fairly correct w.r.t. $\Phi \wedge \Psi$ iff it is fairly correct w.r.t. Φ and w.r.t. Ψ (cf. for instance [15]).

Thus, if $\{\Psi_1, \ldots, \Psi_n\}$ is a set of formulas whose length is bounded by some constant k, then $\Phi = \bigwedge_{i=1}^n \Psi_i$ can be checked in time $O(|\Sigma| \cdot n \cdot 2^k)$. This implies, for example, that *Street formulas*, i.e., formulas of the form $\bigwedge_{i=1}^n (\mathrm{F}^\infty \psi_i \vee \mathrm{G}^\infty \xi_i)$ with ψ_i, ξ_i state formulas, can be checked in linear time (i.e. $O(|\Sigma||\Phi|)$).

5.2   Disjunctive Formulas of RLTL

Disjunctions are more interesting. In particular, we show that co-NP-hardness of fair and universal model checking of RLTL is implied by the fact that fair and universal model checking for formulas of the form $\bigvee_{i=1}^n (\mathrm{F} \, \psi_i \wedge \mathrm{F} \, \xi_i)$ is already co-NP-hard.

Theorem 10

1. *Fair and universal model checking a formula* $\Phi = \bigvee_{i=1}^n (\mathrm{F} \, \psi_i \wedge \mathrm{F} \, \xi_i)$ *and a system* Σ *are co-NP hard.*

2. *Fair and universal model checking a formula $\Phi = \bigvee_{i=1}^{n}(G\,\psi_i \wedge G\,\xi_i)$ and a system Σ can be done in linear time.*
3. *Fair and universal model checking a formula $\Phi = \bigvee_{i=1}^{n} F\,\psi_i$ and a system Σ can be done in linear time.*
4. *Fair and universal model checking a formula $\Phi = \bigvee_{i=1}^{n} G\,\psi_i$ and a system Σ can be done in linear time.*

Here ψ_i and ξ_i are state formulas $(1 \le i \le n)$.

Proof. For 1, we define a reduction from the complement of $3-\mathrm{SAT}$ to both fair and universal model checking of formulas $\Phi = \bigvee_{i=1}^{n}(F\,\psi_i \wedge F\,\xi_i)$. Let $\phi = \bigwedge_{i=1}^{m}\psi_i$ be a 3-CNF formula, where $\psi_i = \xi_{i,1} \vee \xi_{i,2} \vee \xi_{i,3}$ and $\xi_{i,j} \in \{\zeta_1, \ldots, \zeta_n, \overline{\zeta_1}, \ldots, \overline{\zeta_n}\}$ $(1 \le i \le m, 1 \le j \le 3)$. Then the reduction maps ϕ to the formula $\Phi :=$ $\bigvee_{k=1}^{n}(F\,\zeta_k \wedge F\,\overline{\zeta_k})$ and the system $\Sigma = (Q, q_0, \rightarrow, v)$ with the following properties:

- $Q = \{q_0, \ldots, q_m\} \cup \{p_{i,j} \mid 1 \le i \le m, 1 \le j \le 3\}$,
- $\rightarrow$ is the smallest relation such that, for $0 \le i < m, 1 \le j \le 3$,
  - $q_i \rightarrow p_{i+1,j}$,
  - $p_{i+1,j} \rightarrow q_{i+1}$,
  - $q_m \rightarrow q_m$.
- $v(q_i) = \{q_i\} \ (0 \le i \le m)$,
- $v(p_{i,j}) = \{\xi_{i,j}, p_{i,j}\} \ (1 \le i \le m)$.

First, we prove that ϕ is satisfiable iff Σ is not universally correct w.r.t. Φ. Suppose that ϕ is satisfiable. Then there are $j_1, \ldots, j_m \in \{1, 2, 3\}$ such that, for each $i \in \{1, \ldots, m\}$, $\xi_{i,j_i} = \zeta_k$ implies that, for each $i' \in \{1, \ldots, m\}$, $\xi_{i',j_{i'}} \ne \overline{\zeta_k}$. Intuitively, ξ_{i,j_i} is the satisfying literal of the i-th clause. We define $x :=$ $q_0 p_{1,j_1} q_1 p_{2,j_2} \cdots q_{m-1} p_{m,j_m} q_m q_m q_m \cdots$ Then x is a path of Σ violating Φ; thus, Σ is not universally correct w.r.t. Φ.

The opposite direction can be shown with similar arguments. For the case of fair model checking, note that Σ is universally correct w.r.t. an arbitrary specification iff it is fairly correct w.r.t. that specification. So the reduction is also valid for fair model checking. Clearly, the reduction can be computed in polynomial time; part 1 of the assertion follows.

For 4, we assume, without loss of generality, that Σ has no isolated states. In the case of universal model checking, we propose the following algorithm:

1. Compute the s.c.c. graph of Σ and a topological ordering of the s.c.c.s.
2. Travel through the s.c.c.s in topological order, and compute for each s.c.c. K of Σ:

$$valid(K) = \{i \in \{1, \ldots, n\} \mid \forall q \in K : q \vDash \psi_i\} \cap \bigcap_{K': K' \rightarrow K} valid(K').$$

Given s.c.c.s K_1, K_2 of Σ, $K_1 \rightarrow K_2$ means that there are $p \in K_1, q \in K_2$ such that $p \rightarrow q$.
3. The input is accepted iff there is no s.c.c. K of Σ with $valid(K) = \varnothing$.

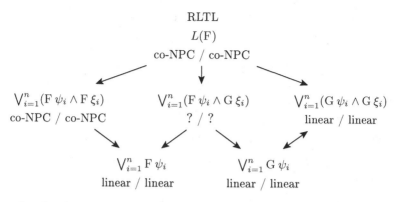

Fig. 1. Results for subclasses of $L(\mathrm{F})$ showing the complexity of universal model checking/fair model checking

By induction over the number of s. c. c.s the algorithm has already processed, it can be shown that $i \in valid(K)$ iff each path fragment α of Σ that ends in a state of K at each position satisfies ψ_i. From this, the correctness of the algorithm can be derived:

Let x be a path of Σ with $x \not\models \Phi$. Choose j such that each of the ψ_i is violated at at least one position of $x_0 x_1 \ldots x_j$. Let K be the s. c. c. of Σ such that $x_j \in K$. Then, for each $i \in \{1, \ldots, n\}$, we have $i \notin valid(K)$, because $x_0 x_1 \ldots x_j$ does not satisfy ψ_i at each position. Thus, $valid(K) = \varnothing$.

On the other hand, suppose that $valid(K) = \varnothing$ for some s. c. c. K of Σ. Then there is a path fragment α of Σ such that, for each $i \in \{1, \ldots, n\}$, ψ_i is violated at some position of α. Thus, α can be extended to a path of Σ that violates the specification $Sat(\Phi)$.

In the case of fair model checking, the same algorithm can be applied, because Σ is universally correct w. r. t. Φ iff Σ is fairly correct w. r. t. Φ.

Part 2 of the assertion can be derived from 4, as we have $Sat(\mathrm{G}\, \psi_i \wedge \mathrm{G}\, \xi_i) = Sat(\mathrm{G}(\psi_i \wedge \xi_i))$ for $1 \leq i \leq n$.

For 3, observe that $Sat(\bigvee_{i=1}^{n} \mathrm{F}\, \psi_i) = Sat(\mathrm{F} \bigvee_{i=1}^{n} \psi_i)$. So the problems of 3 can be reduced to the related model checking problems for a formula of the form $\mathrm{F}\, \zeta$, where $\zeta \in AP$. The latter can be solved in linear time (cf. [6,3]), as the formula has bounded size.

Figure 1 summarises the results for the disjunctive formulas of $L(\mathrm{F})$. An arrow denotes containment, where we also allow trivial translations, e.g., $\mathrm{G}\, \psi_i$ can be written as $\mathrm{G}\, \psi_i \wedge \mathrm{G}\, true$ and $\mathrm{G}\, \psi_i \wedge \mathrm{G}\, \xi_i$ can be written as $\mathrm{G}(\psi_i \wedge \xi_i)$. The complexities of fair and universal model checking of formulas of the form $\bigvee_{i=1}^{n}(\mathrm{F}\, \psi_i \wedge \mathrm{G}\, \xi_i)$ remain open.

5.3   Disjunctive Formulas of $L(\mathrm{F}^{\infty})$

The dual of a Streett formula, called a *Rabin formula*, is a formula of the form $\bigvee_{i=1}^{n}(\mathrm{F}^{\infty}\, \psi_i \wedge \mathrm{G}^{\infty}\, \xi_i)$. Universal model checking of Rabin formulas can be done

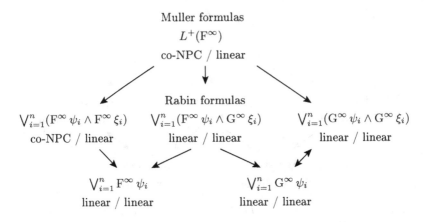

Fig. 2. Results for subclasses of $L^+(F^\infty)$ showing the complexity of universal model checking/fair model checking

in linear time, whereas the proof of co-NP-hardness of $L(F^\infty)$ uses only formulas of the form $\bigvee_{i=1}^n (F^\infty \psi_i \wedge F^\infty \xi_i)$ (cf. [5]). We thus have:

Theorem 11

1. *Universal model checking a formula* $\Phi = \bigvee_{i=1}^n (F^\infty \psi_i \wedge F^\infty \xi_i)$ *and a system* Σ *is co-NP hard.*
2. *Fair model checking a formula* $\Phi = \bigvee_{i=1}^n (F^\infty \psi_i \wedge G^\infty \xi_i)$ *and a system* Σ *can be done in linear time.*

In particular universal model checking for formulas of the form $\bigvee_{i=1}^n F^\infty \psi_i$ or $\bigvee_{i=1}^n G^\infty \psi_i$ can be done in linear time.

Figure 2 summarises the results for subclasses of $L^+(F^\infty)$.

6   Conclusion

We have shown that for formulas in $L(F^\infty)$ fair model checking can be done more efficiently than universal model checking. We are not aware of any natural sublanguage of LTL for which universal model checking can be done more efficiently than fair model checking. This adds another argument in favour of fair model checking as an interesting alternative or complement to universal model checking, as mentioned in the introduction.

Studying model checking for sublanguages can help to optimise algorithms, as the more general algorithms may not perform optimally for the sublanguage. In fact, the algorithm of Courcoubetis and Yannakakis [3] for fair model checking of LTL can perform exponentially worse on $L(F^\infty)$ than our algorithm (see [7]). Moreover, our algorithm for Muller formulas can be integrated with the algorithm of Courcoubetis and Yannakakis [3], which allows us to detect Muller formulas as subformulas of the input LTL formula (or any intermediate formula produced by the algorithm), solve the fair model checking problem for these Muller formulas in linear time and use the result for checking the input formula. The presentation of this integration is beyond the scope of this paper, but it is available in Schmalz' thesis [7]. There it is also shown that, with this optimisation, the algorithm never performs worse but can perform exponentially better than the original.

References

1. Alur, R., Henzinger, T.A.: Local liveness for compositional modeling of fair reactive systems. In: Wolper, P. (ed.) CAV 1995. LNCS, vol. 939, pp. 166–179. Springer, Heidelberg (1995)
2. Berwanger, D., Grädel, E., Kreutzer, S.: Once upon a time in the west - determinacy, definability, and complexity of path games. In: Vardi, M.Y., Voronkov, A. (eds.) LPAR 2003. LNCS, vol. 2850, pp. 229–243. Springer, Heidelberg (2003)
3. Courcoubetis, C., Yannakakis, M.: The complexity of probabilistic verification. J. ACM 42(4), 857–907 (1995)
4. Emerson, E.A.: Temporal and modal logic. Handbook of Theoretical Computer Science B(16), 995–1072 (1990)
5. Emerson, E.A., Lei, C.-L.: Modalities for model checking: Branching time logic strikes back. Sci. Comput. Program. 8(3), 275–306 (1987)
6. Lichtenstein, O., Pnueli, A.: Checking that finite state concurrent programs satisfy their linear specification. In: POPL, pp. 97–107. ACM Press, New York (1985)
7. Schmalz, M.: Extensions of an algorithm for generalised fair model checking. Diploma Thesis, Technical Report B 07-01, University of Lübeck, Germany (2007), www.tcs.uni-luebeck.de/Forschung/B0701.pdf
8. Schmalz, M., Völzer, H., Varacca, D.: Model checking almost all paths can be less expensive than checking all paths. Technical Report 573, ETH Zürich, Switzerland (2007), www.inf.ethz.ch/research/disstechreps/techreports
9. Schnoebelen, P.: The complexity of temporal logic model checking. In: AiML, pp. 393–436. King's College Publications (2002)
10. Sistla, A.P., Clarke, E.M.: The complexity of propositional linear temporal logics. J. ACM 32(3), 733–749 (1985)
11. Sistla, A.P., Vardi, M.Y., Wolper, P.: The complementation problem for Büchi automata with applications to temporal logic. In: Brauer, W. (ed.) Automata, Languages and Programming. LNCS, vol. 194, pp. 465–474. Springer, Heidelberg (1985)
12. Varacca, D., Völzer, H.: Temporal logics and model checking for fairly correct systems. In: LICS, pp. 389–398. IEEE Computer Society Press, Los Alamitos (2006)
13. Vardi, M.Y.: Automatic verification of probabilistic concurrent finite-state programs. In: FOCS, pp. 327–338. IEEE Computer Society Press, Los Alamitos (1985)
14. Vardi, M.Y., Wolper, P.: An automata-theoretic approach to automatic program verification. In: LICS, pp. 332–344. IEEE Computer Society Press, Los Alamitos (1986)
15. Völzer, H., Varacca, D., Kindler, E.: Defining fairness. In: Abadi, M., de Alfaro, L. (eds.) CONCUR 2005. LNCS, vol. 3653, pp. 458–472. Springer, Heidelberg (2005)
16. Zuck, L.D., Pnueli, A., Kesten, Y.: Automatic verification of probabilistic free choice. In: Cortesi, A. (ed.) VMCAI 2002. LNCS, vol. 2294, pp. 208–224. Springer, Heidelberg (2002)

Closures and Modules Within Linear Logic Concurrent Constraint Programming

Rémy Haemmerlé, François Fages, and Sylvain Soliman

INRIA Paris-Rocquencourt – France
FirstName.LastName@inria.fr

Abstract. There are two somewhat contradictory ways of looking at modules in a given programming language. On the one hand, module systems are largely independent of the particulars of programming languages. On the other hand, the module constructs may interfere with the programming constructs, and may be redundant with the other scope mechanisms of a specific programming language, such as closures for instance. There is therefore a need to unify the programming concepts that are similar, and retain a minimum number of essential constructs to avoid arbitrary programming choices. In this paper, we realize this aim in the framework of linear logic concurrent constraint programming (LCC) languages. We first show how declarations and closures can be internalized as agents in a variant of LCC for which we provide precise operational and logical semantics in linear logic. Then, we show how a complete module system can be represented within LCC, and prove for it a general code protection property. Finally we study the instanciation of this scheme to the implementation of a safe module system for constraint logic programs, and conclude on the generality of this approach to programming languages with logical variables.

1 Introduction

Module systems are an essential feature of programming languages as they facilitate the re-use of existing code and the development of general purpose libraries. There are however two contradictory ways of looking at a module system. On the one hand, a module system is essentially independent of the particulars of a given programming language. "Modular" module systems have thus been designed and indeed adapted to different programming languages, see e.g. [15]. On the other hand, module constructs often interfere with the programming constructs and may be redundant with other scope mechanisms supported by a given programming language, such as closures for instance. There is therefore a need to unify the programming concepts that are similar in order to retain a minimum number of essential constructs and avoid arbitrary programming choices. In this paper, we realize this aim in the framework of linear logic concurrent constraint (LCC) programming languages.

The class of concurrent constraint (CC) programming languages was introduced in [18] as an elegant merge of constraint logic programming (CLP) and

V. Arvind and S. Prasad (Eds.): FSTTCS 2007, LNCS 4855, pp. 544–556, 2007.

concurrent logic programming. In the CC paradigm, CLP goals become concurrent agents communicating through a common store of constraints, each agent being able to post constraints to the store, and to synchronize by asking whether a guard constraint is entailed by the store. Research on the logical semantics of CC languages [6] led to a simple solution in Girard's Linear Logic [8]. Through a straightforward translation of CC agents into intuitionistic LL (ILL) formulas, CC operational transitions indeed correspond to deductions in ILL, and completeness theorems hold for the observation of successes as well as accessible stores [6].

Moreover, the soundness and completeness theorems still hold when considering constraint systems based on Linear Logic instead of classical logic, that constitutes the LCC framework. From a programming point of view, ILL constraint systems are a refinement of classical constraint systems allowing for the non-monotonic evolution of the constraint store, as advocated in [2], through the consumption of Linear Logic tokens by linear implication [6]. In LCC, constraint programming and imperative programming features are thus reconciled in a unified framework, and LCC has been proposed in [9] as a kernel language for developing constraint programming libraries in a modular fashion.

In this paper, we focus on a closure mechanism and a module system that can be naturally internalized in LCC. We first show in Sect. 2, that the linear tokens and the bang operator of LL can be used to internalize CC declarations and procedure calls as respectively constraint posting and constraint asking in LCC. A quite general notion of closure can then be encoded as a banged agent with an environment. The case of an empty environment corresponds to the usual CC declarations. Then in Sect. 3, we develop a complete module system for LCC via a simple syntactical convention for encapsulating procedure declarations and calls. This restriction allows us to prove a general property of code protection by showing that the implementation hiding follows from the usual scope mechanism for variables. This module system is then illustrated in Sect. 4, by its instantiation to constraint logic programming (CLP) languages, and by its relationship to the module system proposed in [10]. Its implementation is discussed there along the lines of its semantics in LCC, and is illustrated with examples of code hiding, closure programming and module parameterization in CLP. Finally, we conclude on the generality of this approach for programming languages with logical variables.

Related Work

Concerning CC languages, the implementation of modules has not been much discussed up to now, being considered as an orthogonal issue. For instance, the MOZART-OZ language [17,4] contains an *ad-hoc* module system allowing for separate compilation, but presented as an extra logical feature separated from the other programming constructs.

Concerning programming languages developed in Linear Logic using the Logic Programming paradigm, like for instance LO [1], Lolli [13] or Lygon [12], it is worth noticing that persistent asks (which could be represented as implications under a ! in most of these languages) have not been considered, nor the direct encoding of dynamic clause assertions. On the other hand, the banged ask appears in the recent work of [16] on the expressiveness of linearity and persistence in process calculi for security. In LCC, we shall use the full power provided by both persistent and non persistent inputs and outputs.

The internalization of declarations as agents proposed in this paper also goes somehow in the opposite direction to that of definition-based logics, as described for instance in [11]. Here, we represent definitions are represented by banged agents as first-class citizens. This makes it possible to represent closures just by definitions sharing variables with other agents.

2   Declarations as Agents

In this paper, a set of variables is denoted by x, y, z... while a sequence of variables is denoted by $\boldsymbol{x}$, $\boldsymbol{y}$... The set of free variables occurring in a formula A is denoted by $\mathcal{V}(A)$, $A[\boldsymbol{x}\backslash\boldsymbol{t}]$ denotes the formula A in which the free occurrences of variables $\boldsymbol{x}$ have been replaced by terms $\boldsymbol{t}$ (with the usual renaming of bound variables, avoiding variable clashes).

In this section, we give a presentation of LCC languages where the usual CC declarations are replaced by banged ask agents, called *persistent asks*. This construct actually generalizes usual declarations to closures with the environment represented by the free variables in the persistent asks. Before that, we recall the definition of linear logic constraint systems as given in [6].

2.1   Linear Logic Constraint Systems

LCC languages essentially extend CC languages by considering constraint systems based on Girard's Linear Logic [8] instead of classical logic [6]. From a programming point of view, this extension introduces state change and imperative features in constraint languages by allowing a non-monotonic evolution of the store of constraints [2].

Let $\mathcal{T}$ be the set of terms (noted t, s, ...) formed from a set V of variables and a set Σ_F of function symbols. An *atomic constraint* is a formula built from V, Σ_F and a set Σ_C of relation symbols. The *constraint language* is the least set containing all atomic constraints, closed by multiplicative conjunction ($\otimes$) existential quantification ($\exists$) and exponentiation (!).

Definition 1 (LL Constraint System). *A* linear constraint system *is a pair* $(\mathcal{C}, \Vdash_C)$ *where* $\mathcal{C}$ *is a constraint language containing* $\mathbf{1}$ *the neutral element of the multiplicative conjunction and* $\Vdash_C$ *is a subset of* $\mathcal{C} \times \mathcal{C}$ *which defines the non-logical axioms of the system. The entailment relation* $\vdash_C$ *is the least subset of* $\mathcal{C}^* \times \mathcal{C}$ *containing* $\Vdash_C$ *and closed by the rules of ILL for* $\mathbf{1}$, $\top$, !, $\exists$ *and* $\otimes$.

In this setting, classical constraints are written under a bang !, while linear logic constraints without bang can be consumed by linear implication. In practice, the non classical constraints will be restricted to *linear tokens* which have no axiom, except the general axiom of equality : $l(x) \otimes !(x = y) \vdash l(y)$.

The vocabulary of predicate symbols Σ_C is thus partitioned into two sets Σ_D, Σ_L, where Σ_D contains the *classical constraints* with at least *true* (**1**), *false* (**0**) and $=$, and Σ_L contains the *linear token predicates*. The constraint languages built from Σ_D and Σ_L are noted $\mathcal{D}$ and $\mathcal{L}$ respectively.

Example 1. A typical LL constraint system is that of a combination of classical constraints, such as Herbrand terms, with linear tokens like $value(x, v)$ that can be added added to and deleted from the store to encode imperative variables and assignment. In the following, linear tokens will also be used to represent procedure calls, by tokens consumed by the procedure definition at the time of its execution.

As no classical constraint but **0** can entail a linear token, we have:

Proposition 1. *Let $c \in \mathcal{D}$ and $l \in \mathcal{L}$. If $c \vdash l \otimes \top$ then $c \vdash \mathbf{0}$.*

The set of free variables occurring in the linear tokens of some constraint c is denoted by $\mathcal{V}_l(c)$. Formally, $\mathcal{V}_l(l(t)) = \mathcal{V}(t)$ if $l \in \Sigma_L$, and $\mathcal{V}_l(l(t)) = \emptyset$ if $l \in \Sigma_D$, and this is extended to non-atomic constraints as usual.

2.2   Syntax and Operational Semantics of LCC Agents

Given an LL constraint system $(\mathcal{C}, \Vdash_{\mathcal{C}})$, the syntax of $LCC(\mathcal{C}, \Vdash_{\mathcal{C}})$ agents is defined by the following grammar : $A ::= A \| A \mid \exists x.A \mid c \mid \forall \boldsymbol{x}(c \to A) \mid \forall \boldsymbol{x}(c \Rightarrow A)$ where c stands for any constraint in $\mathcal{C}$ and $\boldsymbol{x} \subset \mathcal{V}_l(c)$. As usual $\|$ stands for parallel composition, the $\exists$ operator hides variables in an agent, and the *tell* agent, written as a constraint, adds that constraint to the store. Two forms of ask agents are considered here : $\forall \boldsymbol{x}(c \to A)$ for the usual ask, and $\forall \boldsymbol{x}(c \Rightarrow A)$ for the persistent ask that will serve to represent procedure definitions. In both cases we impose $\boldsymbol{x} \subset \mathcal{V}_l(c)$. This restriction limits the binding of variables by pattern matching to the variables occurring in linear tokens, and prevents the possible enumeration of all variables by ask agents.

The choice operator is defined here as an abbreviation as in the classical encoding of the non-deterministic choice in CLP with two clauses with the same head : $A + B = \exists x(choice(x) \| (choice(x) \Rightarrow A) \| (choice(x) \Rightarrow B))$.

The operational semantics of LCC with persistent ask is defined similarly to [6] with an equivalence and a transition relation defined over configurations. A *configuration* is a tuple $\langle X; c; \Gamma \rangle$ where X is a set of variables, Γ a multiset of agents and c a constraint, called *store*. $\equiv$ is the least equivalence satisfying the following rule of *parallel composition:* $\langle X; c; A \| B, \Gamma \rangle \equiv \langle X; c; A, B, \Gamma \rangle$.

The transition relation $\longrightarrow$ is the least relation satisfying the following rules modulo $\equiv$ (its transitive and reflexive closure is denoted by $\overset{*}{\longrightarrow}$):

Hiding
$$\frac{z \notin X \cup \mathcal{V}(c, \Gamma)}{\langle X; c; \exists z.A, \Gamma \rangle \longrightarrow \langle X \cup \{z\}; c; A, \Gamma \rangle}$$

Tell
$$\langle X; c; \boldsymbol{d}, \Gamma \rangle \longrightarrow \langle X; c \otimes d; \Gamma \rangle$$

Ask
$$\frac{c \vdash_C \exists Y.(d[z \backslash s] \otimes e) \qquad Y \cap (X \cup \mathcal{V}(A, \Gamma)) = \emptyset}{\langle X; c; \forall z(\boldsymbol{d} \rightarrow \boldsymbol{A}), \Gamma \rangle \longrightarrow \langle X \cup Y; e; \boldsymbol{A}[z \backslash s], \Gamma \rangle}$$

Persistent ask
$$\frac{c \vdash_C \exists Y.(d[z \backslash s] \otimes e) \qquad Y \cap (X \cup \mathcal{V}(A, \Gamma)) = \emptyset}{\langle X; c; \forall z(\boldsymbol{d} \Rightarrow \boldsymbol{A}), \Gamma \rangle \longrightarrow \langle X \cup Y; e; \boldsymbol{A}[z \backslash s], \forall z(\boldsymbol{d} \Rightarrow \boldsymbol{A}), \Gamma \rangle}$$

Definition 2 (Observables). *Let A be an LCC($\mathcal{C}$) agent. We say that a constraint $d \in \mathcal{C}$ is an* accessible constraint *for A if there exists a derivation of the form $\langle \emptyset; \boldsymbol{1}; A \rangle \xrightarrow{\ *\ } \langle X; c; \Gamma \rangle$ such that $\exists X.c \vdash_C d \otimes \top$. Similarly, d is a* success *for A, if in addition Γ is a multiset of persistent asks , $\exists X.c \vdash_C d$, and $\langle X; c; \Gamma \rangle \not\longrightarrow$.*

Definition 3 (Operational Semantics)

- $\mathcal{O}^{const}(A)$ *is the set of accessible constraints for the agent A.*
- $\mathcal{O}^{\mathcal{D}const}(A) = \mathcal{O}^{const}(A) \cap \mathcal{D}$ *is the set of accessible $\mathcal{D}$-constraints for A.*
- $\mathcal{O}^{succ}(A)$ *is the set of successes for the agent A.*
- $\mathcal{O}^{\mathcal{D}succ}(A) = \mathcal{O}^{succ}(A) \cap \mathcal{D}$ *is the set of $\mathcal{D}$-successes for the agent A.*

Example 2. In LCC, the scope mechanism of variables and the persistent ask make it possible to encode *closures*. For instance, the agent $\forall x(apply(c, x) \Rightarrow min(x, minint) \otimes max(x, maxint))$ waits for a token of application of a closure c to a variable x to add new constraints on x. From a functional perspective, C is equivalent to $(\lambda X.min(X, minint) \otimes max(X, maxint))$, and the agent $apply(C, X)$ to $C.X$. This schema for closures makes it possible to define iterators on data structures such as `forall` on lists, passing the closure as an argument as follows (the frist two lines define the iterator and the last one uses it):

$\forall C.forall(C, []) \Rightarrow true \ ||$
$\forall H, T, C.forall(C, [H|T]) \Rightarrow apply(C, H) \otimes forall(C, T) \ ||$
$\exists C.(\forall X(apply(C, X) \Rightarrow min(X, minint) \otimes max(X, maxint)) \ || \ forall(C, L))$

Example 3. Rewriting rules with constraints such as in the CHR [7] can be easily encoded in LCC. For instance, the three following CHR rules for defining the ordering constraint =< assuming the built-in equality constraint =:

```
X=<Y <=> X=Y|true.     X=<Y,Y=<X <=> X=Y.     X=<Y,Y=<Z ==> X=<Z.
```

can be represented by the following LCC agent (Note that as in the naive semantics of CHR, the last rule does not terminate):

$\forall X, Y((X =< Y \otimes X = Y) \Rightarrow \boldsymbol{1}) \ ||$
$\forall X, Y((X =< Y \otimes Y =< X) \Rightarrow X = Y) \ ||$
$\forall X, Y, Z((X =< Y \otimes Y =< Z) \Rightarrow (X =< Y \otimes Y =< Z \otimes X =< Z))$

This example illustrates the mixing in ask guards of linear tokens =< with the classical (built-in) constraint =.

2.3 Logical Semantics of LCC Agents

In this section, we show how the logical semantics of LCC in ILL [6] extends to persistent asks. The translation of LCC agents into ILL is straightforward:

$$c^\dagger = c \qquad (\exists x.c)^\dagger = \exists x.c^\dagger \qquad (A \parallel B)^\dagger = A^\dagger \otimes B^\dagger$$
$$(\forall \boldsymbol{x}(c \to A))^\dagger = \forall \boldsymbol{x}(c \multimap A^\dagger) \qquad (\forall \boldsymbol{x}(c \Rightarrow A))^\dagger = !\forall \boldsymbol{x}(c^\dagger \multimap A^\dagger)$$

This translation extends to a multiset of agents Γ by $\{A_1, \ldots, A_n\}^\dagger = A_1^\dagger \otimes \cdots \otimes A_n\dagger$, and $\emptyset^\dagger = \mathbf{1}$. The translation of a configuration $\langle X; c; \Gamma \rangle$ is the formula $\langle X; c; \Gamma \rangle \dagger = \exists X.(c \otimes \Gamma)$. As in [6], we get:

Theorem 1 (Soundness). *Let $\langle X; c; \Gamma \rangle$ and $\langle Y; d; \Delta \rangle$ be two configurations. If $\langle X; c; \Gamma \rangle \xrightarrow{*} \langle Y; d; \Delta \rangle$ then $\langle X; c; \Gamma \rangle^\dagger \vdash_C \langle Y; d; \Delta \rangle^\dagger$.*

Theorem 2 (Completeness). *For any LCC agent A, $\mathcal{O}^{const}(A) = \{c \in \mathcal{C} \mid A^\dagger \vdash_C c \otimes \top\}$, $\mathcal{O}^{\mathcal{D}const}(A) = \{d \in \mathcal{D} \mid A^\dagger \vdash_C d \otimes \top\}$.*

Because LCC declarations are represented here with persistent asks using the bang operator, the logical characterization of successes requires persistent asks to have a linear token in their guard:

Definition 4 ($\mathcal{L}$-persistent). *Let $\mathcal{C}$ be a constraint system partitioned into classical constraints $\mathcal{D}$ and linear tokens $\mathcal{L}$. An agent is $\mathcal{L}$-persistent if the guards in its persistent asks all contain tokens in $\mathcal{L}$.*

Theorem 3 (Completeness on $\mathcal{D}$-successes). *For any $\mathcal{L}$-persistent LCC($\mathcal{C}$) agent A for which $\mathbf{0}$ is not an accessible constraint we have $\mathcal{O}^{\mathcal{D}succ}(A) = \{d \in \mathcal{D} \mid A^\dagger \vdash_C d\}$.*

3 Modules as Agents

3.1 Syntactical Conventions

The declaration and closure mechanism provided by the persistent ask in LCC can be used to build a complete module system within LCC. In this approach, a module is named by a variable and the scope of module declarations thus depends on the scope of these variables. It is worth noting that for the issue of separate compilation not considered here, modules should also be named by constants making them visible by separate modules. That will be used in the next section.

We use the syntactical convention $x\{A\}$ to denote the agent A in module x. Similarly, telling a token constraint l of module x is denoted by $x : l$, while classical constraints are not localized. With these conventions, the syntax of modular LCC (MLCC) agents is the following: $A ::= x\{A\} \mid x : l \mid d \mid A \parallel A \mid \exists x.A \mid \forall \boldsymbol{x}(c \to A) \mid \forall \boldsymbol{x}(c \Rightarrow A)$ where l stands for a linear token constraint, d stands for a classical constraint and c stands for an arbitrary constraint.

Now, MLCC agents are translated into LCC agents over a modified constraint system, noted $\dot{\mathcal{C}}$, in which an extra argument is added to every linear token. The resulting LCC agents enjoy some sort of code protection as shown in next section.

Definition 5 (Translation in LCC). *For any variable x referencing a module, the translation ()^x of MLCC(C) agents to LCC($\dot{C}$) agents is defined recursively by:*

$$d(t)^x = d(t) \quad l(t)^x = \dot{l}(x,t) \quad (c \otimes c')^x = c^x \otimes c'^x \quad (\exists \boldsymbol{y}.c)^x = \exists \boldsymbol{y}.c^x$$
$$(\exists \boldsymbol{y}.A)^x = \exists \boldsymbol{y}.A^x \quad (y\{A\})^x = A^y \quad (y{:}l)^x = l^y \quad (A \parallel B)^x = A^x \parallel B^x$$
$$(!c)^x = !c^x \quad (\forall \boldsymbol{y}(c \to A))^x = \forall \boldsymbol{y}(c^x \to A^x) \quad (\forall \boldsymbol{y}(c \Rightarrow A))^x = \forall \boldsymbol{y}(c^x \Rightarrow A^x)$$

where $\boldsymbol{y} \cap \mathcal{V}(x) = \emptyset$, $d \in \Sigma_D$, $l \in \Sigma_L$, $c \in \mathcal{C}$ and $c' \in \mathcal{C}$.

   An LCC($\dot{C}$) agent A is modular *if it is the translation of an MLCC(C) agent i.e. there exists an MLCC(C) agent B and a variable x such that $A = B^x$. An LCC($\dot{C}$) configuration is* modular *if all its agents are modular.*

Example 4. With these conventions, a module for lists can be defined with internal anonymous modules for hiding the implementation of predicates, such as the *reverse* predicate with a ternary implementation using an accumulator:

$$List\{\exists I. (\ \forall X, Y.reverse(X,Y) \Rightarrow I : reverse(X,[],Y) \parallel$$
$$I \{ \ \forall X, Y.reverse([],X,Y) \Rightarrow !(X{=}Y) \parallel$$
$$\forall X, Y, Z, T.reverse([X|Y], Z, T) \Rightarrow reverse(Y, [X|Z], T).)\}\}$$

For the sake of readability, in the following section, constraints of $\dot{C}$ and agents of LCC($\dot{C}$) will be denoted respectively by $\dot{c}, \dot{d}, \dot{e}\ldots$ and by $\dot{A}, \dot{B} \ldots$, whereas constraints of $\mathcal{C}$ and agents of MLCC($\mathcal{C}$) will be denoted respectively by $c, d, e \ldots$ and by $A, B \ldots$. Moreover, note that if κ is a modular configuration and $\kappa \overset{*}{\longrightarrow} \kappa'$ then κ' is modular.

3.2   Code Protection

MLCC programs enjoy a general property of code protection provided that the constraint system does not allow to make arbitrary variables equal. This is enforced by assuming that $\{x, y\} \subset \mathcal{V}(c)$ whenever $c \Vdash_\mathcal{C} x{=}y \otimes \top$ for any distinct variables x and y.

Definition 6. *Let $\langle X; \dot{c}; \Delta, \dot{B}, \dot{l} \rangle$ be a modular configuration. The transitions from $\dot{B}$ are* independent *from the linear tell agent $\dot{l}$ if for any derivation that first reduces tell $\dot{l}$ then B, i.e. of the form:*

$$\langle X; \dot{c}; \Delta, \dot{B}, \dot{l} \rangle \longrightarrow \langle X; \dot{c} \otimes \dot{l}; \Delta, \dot{B} \rangle \longrightarrow \langle Y; \dot{d}'; \Delta, \dot{B}' \rangle$$

there exists a derivation that first reduces B then l of the form:

$$\langle X; \dot{c}; \Delta, \dot{B}, \dot{l} \rangle \longrightarrow \langle Y'; \dot{e}; \Delta, \dot{B}', \dot{l} \rangle \longrightarrow \langle Y; \dot{c}' \otimes \dot{l}; \Delta, \dot{B}' \rangle \qquad \text{with } \dot{c}' \otimes \dot{l} \dashv\vdash_{\dot{c}} \dot{d}'.$$

Definition 7 (Code Protection). *An agent $\dot{A}$ is* protected *in a modular agent $C[\dot{A}]$ if the transitions from $\dot{B}$ are independent from $\dot{l}$ in any configuration $\langle X; \dot{c}; \Delta, \dot{B}, \dot{l} \rangle$ such that $\langle \emptyset; 1; C[\dot{A}], \Gamma \rangle \overset{*}{\longrightarrow} \langle X; \dot{c}; \Delta, \dot{B}, \dot{l} \rangle$, $\dot{B}$ derives from $\dot{A}$ and $\dot{l}$ derives from Γ.*

Theorem 4. *Let A and B be two MLCC(C) agents. If A has no inner module and y is used in A and B only in modular tells of the form $y{:}l$ with $y \notin \mathcal{V}(l)$, then $(A)^y$ is protected in $(\exists y.(y\{A\} \parallel B))^x$ for any variable x.*

The proof of this theorem relies on general properties on the scope of variables, and on technical properties of constraint decomposability and variable accessibility. The intuition behind decomposability is that linear tokens can be separated from the rest of the constraint without making it logically weaker.

Definition 8 (Decomposable constraint). *A constraint is in* separated form *if it is of the form $d \otimes \dot{l}_1 \otimes \cdots \otimes \dot{l}_k$ where d is a classical constraint and the $\dot{l}_i$'s are atomic linear token constraints. A constraint is in* decomposed form *if it is of the form $\exists Y.\dot{d}$ where $\dot{d}$ is in separated form. A constraint is* decomposable *(resp.* separable*) if it is equivalent to a decomposed (resp. separated) form.*

Lemma 1. *Let Γ be a multiset of consistent constraints in decomposed form, $\dot{c} \in \dot{\mathcal{C}}$ a constraint, and Y a set of variables. If $\Gamma \vdash_{\dot{c}} \exists Y.(\dot{c} \otimes \top)$ then $\dot{c}$ is decomposable.*

Proposition 2. *Let $\langle X; \dot{c}; \Gamma \rangle \xrightarrow{*} \langle Y; \dot{d}; \Delta \rangle$ be a derivation between two modular configurations. If $\dot{c}$ is consistent and decomposable then $\dot{d}$ is decomposable.*

Let $\dot{c} \in \dot{\mathcal{C}}$ be a separable constraint and X a set of variables. We define the set of variables *accessible by unification* in $\dot{c}$ from X as:

$$\mathcal{A}^u_{\dot{c}}(X) = X \cup \{x \in \mathcal{V}(\dot{c}) | \ d \in \mathcal{D}, \ y \in \mathcal{V}(d), \ \mathcal{V}(\dot{c}) \cap \mathcal{V}(d) \subset X,$$
$$\dot{c} \otimes d \vdash_{\dot{c}} x = y \otimes \top \text{ and } \Gamma, d \nvdash_{\dot{c}} \mathbf{0}\}.$$

The set of variables *accessible by substitution* in $\dot{c}$ from X is:

$$\mathcal{A}^s_{\dot{c}}(X) = X \cup \{x \in \mathcal{V}(t) \mid \dot{l} \in \Sigma m \quad y \in X \quad \dot{c} \vdash_{\dot{c}} \dot{l}(y,t) \otimes \top \quad \dot{c} \nvdash_{\dot{c}} \mathbf{0}\}$$

The set of *directly accessible* variables in $\dot{c}$ from X is $\mathcal{A}^1_{\dot{c}}(X) = \mathcal{A}^s_{\dot{c}}(X) \cup \mathcal{A}^u_{\dot{c}}(X)$.

Proposition 3. *For any consistent separable constraint $\dot{c}$, $\mathcal{A}^1_{\dot{c}}$ is extensive, monotone and bound.*

This proposition allows us to define the set of *accessible* variables in $\dot{c}$ from X, noted $\mathcal{A}_{\dot{c}}(X)$, as the least fix point of $\mathcal{A}^1_{\dot{c}}$ containing X. The set of *accessible* variables in a decomposable constraint $\dot{d}$ is $\mathcal{A}_{\dot{c}}(X) \backslash Y$ where Y is a set of variables and $\dot{c}$ is a separable constraint such that $\dot{d} \vdash_{\dot{c}} \exists Y.\dot{c}$ and without loss of generality $Y \cap X = \emptyset$.

Lemma 2. *Let $\dot{c}$ and $\dot{d}$ be two consistent decomposable constraints of $\dot{\mathcal{C}}$ and X an arbitrary set of variables. If $\dot{c} \vdash_{\dot{c}} \dot{d} \otimes \top$ then $\mathcal{A}_{\dot{c}}(X) \supset \mathcal{A}_{\dot{d}}(X)$.*

Proposition 4. *Let $\langle X; \dot{c}; \Gamma, \Delta \rangle \xrightarrow{*} \langle Y; \dot{d}; \Gamma', \Delta' \rangle$ be a derivation between two consistent configurations such that Γ' be the reduced of Γ, and $\dot{c}$ is decomposable. If $x \in \mathcal{V}(X, \Delta)$ and $x \notin \mathcal{A}_{\dot{c}}(\mathcal{V}(\Gamma))$ then $x \notin \mathcal{A}_{\dot{d}}(\mathcal{V}(\Gamma'))$.*

4 Implementation as a Module System for CLP

The MLCC scheme presented above instantiates into a powerful module system for Constraint Logic Programming languages, called mCLP. This module system is an extension including dynamic modules of the module system proposed for CLP in [10]. It is provided here with a logical semantics in linear logic, and with an implementation with closures in the line of its semantics in LCC. A prototype implementation of mCLP is available for download at `http://contraintes.inria.fr/~haemmerl/pub/mclp.tgz`.

4.1   mCLP Syntactical Conventions

We shall adopt for mCLP a pragmatic syntax close to that of classical CLP systems. The `typewriter` font is used for programs, where, as in classical Prolog programs, the identifiers beginning with a capital letter represent variables. The syntax defined by the following grammar distinguishes declarations from goals as usual:

$$G ::= \texttt{module(T, E)\{D\}} \mid \texttt{T} : \texttt{p(S}_1, \ldots, \texttt{S}_n\texttt{)} \mid \texttt{p(S}_1, \ldots, \texttt{S}_n\texttt{)} \mid \texttt{c(S}_1, \ldots, \texttt{S}_n\texttt{)} \mid \texttt{G, G} \mid \texttt{G; G}$$
$$D ::= \texttt{p(S}_1, \ldots, \texttt{S}_n\texttt{)} : -\texttt{G.D} \mid \texttt{p(S}_1, \ldots, \texttt{S}_n\texttt{).D} \mid : -\texttt{G.D} \mid \epsilon$$

where T is a term, E a list of variables, $\texttt{S}_1, \ldots, \texttt{S}_n$ a sequence of terms, c a constraint of $\mathcal{C}$ and p a predicate construct using the alphabet Σ_L.

An mCLP declaration is either a clause, a fact or a goal of the form `:- G.` executed at the initialization of the module. Besides the usual conjunction, disjunction and constraint posting goals, the goal `module(T, E){D}` denotes the *instantiation* of a module T with the *implementation* D and the *environment* E. This environment is simply a list of *global variables* whose scope is the entire module clauses. If T is a free variable, the resulting module is *anonymous*, whereas if T is an atom (or a compound term), it is a *named* module, as proved useful for separate compilation. The goal $\texttt{T:p(S}_1, \ldots, \texttt{S}_n\texttt{)}$ denotes the *external call* of the predicate p/n defined in the module T, which is distinguished from the *local call*, noted $\texttt{p(S}_1, \ldots, \texttt{S}_n\texttt{)}$, of the predicate p/n defined in the current module.

4.2   Interpretation and Compilation

Classical clauses are interpreted by *persistent asks* waiting for the linear token that represents the procedure call. The module environment provides a new feature allowing for global variables in a module. Formally, the interpretation of mCLP goals and declaration in MLCC is defined by $[\![G]\!]^{\texttt{T}}$ and $[\![D]\!]^{\texttt{T}}_{\texttt{E}}$ where T is the current module and E the current environment:

$$\begin{array}{lll} [\![\texttt{G}_1, \texttt{G}_2]\!]^{\texttt{T}} = [\![\texttt{G}_1]\!]^{\texttt{T}} \parallel [\![\texttt{G}_2]\!]^{\texttt{T}} & [\![\texttt{P}]\!]^{\texttt{T}} = \texttt{T:P} & [\![\texttt{S:P}]\!]^{\texttt{T}} = \texttt{S:P} \\ [\![\texttt{G}_1; \texttt{G}_2]\!]^{\texttt{T}} = [\![\texttt{G}_1]\!]^{\texttt{T}} + [\![\texttt{G}_2]\!]^{\texttt{T}} & [\![\texttt{C}]\!]^{\texttt{T}} = \texttt{T:(!C)} & [\![\texttt{module(S, E)\{D\}}]\!]^{\texttt{T}} = \texttt{S}\{[\![\texttt{D}]\!]^{\texttt{S}}_{\texttt{E}}\} \\ [\![:- \texttt{G.D}]\!]^{\texttt{T}}_{\texttt{E}} = \exists \overline{\texttt{Y}} [\![\texttt{G}]\!]^{\texttt{S}} \parallel [\![\texttt{D}]\!]^{\texttt{T}}_{\texttt{E}} & [\![\texttt{p(t).D}]\!]^{\texttt{T}}_{\texttt{E}} = \forall \texttt{X}(\texttt{p(X)} \Rightarrow \exists \overline{\texttt{Y}} [\![\texttt{X=t}]\!]^{\texttt{S}}) \parallel [\![\texttt{D}]\!]^{\texttt{T}}_{\texttt{E}} \\ \multicolumn{3}{c}{[\![\texttt{p(t)} :- \texttt{G.D}]\!]^{\texttt{T}}_{\texttt{E}} = \forall \texttt{X}(\texttt{p(X)} \Rightarrow \exists \overline{\texttt{Y}} [\![\texttt{X = t, G}]\!]^{\texttt{S}}) \parallel [\![\texttt{D}]\!]^{\texttt{T}}_{\texttt{E}}} \end{array}$$

where X is a set of fresh variables and $\overline{\texttt{Y}} = \mathcal{V}(\texttt{t, G}) \setminus \texttt{E}$.

Let $\Vdash_{\mathcal{C}^\circ}$ be the translation of the constraint system $\mathcal{C}$ into linear logic (using for example the well know Girard's translation classical logical into LL [8]). The constraint system $(\mathcal{CP}, \Vdash_{\mathcal{CP}})$ corresponding to this translation is defined such that $\Vdash_{\mathcal{CP}}$ is the smallest set respecting the following conditions (1) if $(\mathtt{C} \Vdash_{\mathcal{C}\circ} \mathtt{C})$ then $(\mathtt{C} \Vdash_{\mathcal{CP}} \mathtt{C})$ and (2) for any predicate symbol $\mathtt{p}$ $(\mathtt{p(X)}, \mathtt{X=Y} \Vdash_{\mathcal{CP}} \mathtt{p(Y)})$.

Notice that all the $[\![A]\!]_{\mathrm{E}}^{\mathrm{T}}$ are $\mathcal{L}$-persistent (see Def. 4), therefore all results of previous Section can be applied to mCLP programs.

In addition to a first order logical semantics, this translation provides a way to compile mCLP using classical Prolog compilation techniques. Typically a module is referenced by a special variable to which module environment and module procedures are attached as attributes [14]. A mCLP predicate is then implemented by a Prolog predicate with an extra-argument, inherit from logical semantics of persistent (c.f. Def. 5) storing the current module variable.

4.3   Global Variables

Module environments introduce *global* variables, i.e. variables shared among the different clauses of the module. This construct can be used for instance to avoid passing an argument to numerous module predicates. However, these variables are still usual, backtrackable, logic variables.

The following code illustrates the use of a global variable `Depth` to implement a Prolog meta-interpreter with a fair search strategy proceeding by iterative deepening [19]. The predicate *clause* looks for clause definitions [5]; the predicate `for(I, Begin, End)` produces a choice point where I will be assigned any of the integer values between `Begin` and `End` (see for instance [3]).

Example 5. (Iterative Deepening):

```
:-module(iter_deep, [Depth]){
    solve(G):- for(Depth,1,1000), iter_deep(G,0).
    iter_deep(_,I) :- I >= Depth, !, fail.
    iter_deep(((A,B)),I) :- !, iter_deep(A,I), iter_deep(B,I).
    iter_deep(A,_) :- clause((A:-true)), !.
    iter_deep(A,I) :- clause((A:-B)), J is I+1, iter_deep(B,J).    }.
```

4.4   Code Hiding

As above, one can use an environment to make a variable *global* to a module, but this time, this variable will be used to keep an anonymous inside module hidden from the outside. Since the *name* of the inside module is this variable, only accessible to the clauses inside the module definition, the corresponding implementation is protected from the clauses outside the external module.

This is illustrated in the following program that provides the `sort` predicate and hides the implementation `quicksort` predicate.

Example 6. (Quicksort):

```
:- module(sort, [Impl]){
    sort(Lst,SrtdLst):- Impl:quicksort(Lst,SrtdLst).
```

```
:- module(Impl,[]){
    quicksort([],[]).
    quicksort([X|Tl],Srtd) :- split(X,Tl,Smll,Bg),
        quicksort(Smll,SrtdSmll), quicksort(Bg,SrtdBg),
        list:append(SrtdSmll,[X|SrtdBg],Srtd).
    split(X,[],[],[]).
    split(X,[Y|Tl],[Y|Smll],Bg) :- X<Y,!,split(X,Tail,Small,Big).
    split(X,[Y|Tl],Smll,[Y|Bg]) :- split(X,Tl,Smll,Bg).    }. }.
```

The code protection property 3.2 ensures that no call to the `quicksort` predicate is possible outside the `sort` predicate. The execution of the following goal prints on screen the sorted list `[2/7,1/2,2/3,1,4/3,5]`.

```
? L=[1, 2/3, 5, 4/3, 1/2, 2/7], sort:sort(L, L1), print(L1), nl.
```

4.5   Closures

The classical notion of *closure* can be recovered through the definition of modules with a predicate `apply/1` waiting for the argument to apply the persistant ask (corresponding to the clauses of `apply/1`).

This makes it possible to define iterators on data structures such as `forall` on lists, passing the closure as an argument as follows:

Example 7. :
```
:- module(iterator,  []){
        forall([], _).
        forall([H|T],  C) :- C:apply(H), forall(T, C).  }.
```

The usual `domain/3` (or `fd_domain/3`) built-in predicate of finite domain constraint solvers, can be implemented using the list iterator on its arguments:

```
fd_domain(Vars,Min,Max):-module(Cl,[Min,Max]){apply(X):-Min=<X,X=<Max.},
    (list(Vars)->iterator:forall(Vars, Cl) ; var(Vars)->Cl:apply(Vars)).
```

4.6   Module Parameterization

Parameterized modules greatly enhance the programmer capabilities to re-use code by making its module implementation depend on other modules. Combining the idea of using the environment to parameterize a closure, and the code hiding features demonstrated above, one can obtain a module with a hidden implementation, parameterized from outside. The following example shows how to parameterize the previous *sort* module by creating a `generic_sort/2` predicate that dynamically creates a sorting module (its first argument) using the comparison predicate given as second argument.

Example 8. (Parameterized quicksort):

```
:- module(sort,  []){
    generic_sort(Sort,Order):- module(Sort,[Order, Impl]){
        sort(List,SortedList):-Impl:qsort(List,SortedList).
```

```
:-module(Impl, [Order]){
    qsort([],[]).
    qsort([X|T],Srtd):-split(X,T,Smll Bg),qsort(Smll,SrtdSmll),
        qsort(Bg,SrtdBg),list:append(SrtdSmll,[X|SrtdBg],Srtd).
    split(X,[],[],[]).
    split(X,[Y|T],[Y|Smll],Bg):-Order:(X >= Y),!,
        split(X,T,Smll, Bg).
    split(X,[Y|T],Smll,[Y|Bg]):-split(X,T,Smll,Bg).  }. }.}.
```

Let math be a module defining the ordering predicate >= over numbers, and term a module defining the ordering predicate @>= over terms. The execution of the following goal prints the lists [2/7,1/2,2/3,1,4/3,5] and [1,5,1/2,2/3, 2/7,4/3] which shows the parameterized use of the module sort.

```
?- L=[1, 2/3, 5, 4/3, 1/2, 2/7],
    sort:factory(Sort1, math), Sort1:sort(L, L1), print(L1), nl,
    module(OrderLex, []) X >= Y:- term:(X @>= Y) ,
    sort:factory(Sort2, OrderLex), Sort2:sort(L, L2) print(L2), nl.
```

5   Conclusion

We have shown that a powerful module system for linear concurrent constraint programming (LCC) languages can be internalized into LCC, by representing declarations by persistent asks, referencing modules by variables and thus benefiting from implementation hiding through the usual hiding operator for variables. We have presented the operational semantics of MLCC programs, showing a code protection property, and proving the equivalence with the logical semantics in linear logic for the observation of stores and successes.

These results have been illustrated with an instantiation of the MLCC scheme to constraint logic programs, leading to a simple yet powerful module system similar to the one proposed in [10], supporting code hiding, closures and module parameterization, and provided here with a simple logical semantics in linear logic. Another interesting use is the boostrapping of a complete implementation of LCC that is currently under development [9].

We believe that this approach to internalizing a module system within a programming language is of a quite general scope for programming languages with logical variables, as well as its implementation with a closure mechanism.

References

1. Andreoli, J.-M., Pareschi, R.: Linear objects: Logical processes with built-in inheritance. New Generation Computing 9, 445–473 (1991)
2. Best, E., de Boer, F.S., Palamidessi, C.: Concurrent constraint programming with information removal. In: Proceedings of Coordination. LNCS, Springer, Heidelberg (1997)
3. Diaz, D.: GNU Prolog user's manual (1999–2003)

4. Duchier, D., Kornstaedt, L., Schulte, C., Smolka, G.: A higher-order module discipline with separate compilation, dynamic linking, and pickling. draft (1998)
5. Ed-Dbali, P.D.A., Cervoni, L.: Prolog: The Standard. Springer, Heidelberg (1996)
6. Fages, F., Ruet, P., Soliman, S.: Linear concurrent constraint programming: operational and phase semantics. Infor. and Comput. 165(1), 14–41 (2001)
7. Frühwirth, T.: Theory and practice of constraint handling rules. Journal of Logic Programming 37(1-3), 95–138 (1998)
8. Girard, J.-Y.: Linear logic. Theoretical Computer Science 50(1) (1987)
9. Haemmerlé, R.: SiLCC is linear concurrent constraint programming (doctoral consortium). In: Gabbrielli, M., Gupta, G. (eds.) ICLP 2005. LNCS, vol. 3668, pp. 448–449. Springer, Heidelberg (2005)
10. Haemmerlé, R., Fages, F.: Modules for Prolog revisited. In: Etalle, S., Truszczyński, M. (eds.) ICLP 2006. LNCS, vol. 4079, pp. 41–55. Springer, Heidelberg (2006)
11. Hallnäs, L.: A proof-theoretic approach to logic programming. ii. programs as definitions. Journal of Logic and Computation 1(5), 635–660 (1991)
12. Harland, J., Pym, D.J., Winikoff, M.: Programming in lygon: An overview. In: Proceedings of the Fifth International Conference on Algebraic Methodology and Software Technology, Munich, pp. 391–405 (July 1996)
13. Hodas, J.S., Miller, D.: Logic programming in a fragment of intuitionistic linear logic. Information and Computation 110(2), 327–365 (1994)
14. Holzbaur, C.: Metastructures vs. attributed variables in the context of extensible unification. TR-92-23, Österreichisches Forschungsinstitut für AI, Wien (1992)
15. Leroy, X.: A modular module system. J. of Func. Prog. 10(3), 269–303 (2000)
16. Palamidessi, C., Saraswat, V.A., Valencia, F.D., Victor, B.: On the expressiveness of linearity vs persistence in the asychronous pi-calculus. In: Proc. of the 21th Annual IEEE Symposium on Logic In Computer Science, pp. 59–68. IEEE Computer Society Press, Los Alamitos (2006)
17. Roy, P.V., et al.: Logic programming in the context of multiparadigm programming: the Oz experience. TPLP 3(6), 715–763 (2003)
18. Saraswat, V.A.: Concurrent constraint programming. ACM Doctoral Dissertation Awards. MIT Press, Cambridge (1993)
19. Stickel, M.E.: A prolog technology theorem prover: implementation by an extended prolog compiler. Journal of Automated Reasoning 44, 353–380 (1988)

Author Index

Lecture Notes in Computer Science

Sublibrary 1: Theoretical Computer Science and General Issues

For information about Vols. 1– 4501
please contact your bookseller or Springer